May 27-30, 2018
Amsterdam, Netherlands

I0027518

Association for Computing Machinery

Advancing Computing as a Science & Profession

WebSci'18

Proceedings of the 10th ACM Conference on
Web Science

Sponsored by:
ACM SIGWEB

Supported by:
Web Science Trust, Vrije Universiteit Amsterdam, Network Institute, Elsevier, Web Alliance for Regreening in Africa, SIKS, IOS Press, 2CoolMonkeys, TVE The Value Engineers, W3C

**Association for
Computing Machinery**

Advancing Computing as a Science & Profession

The Association for Computing Machinery
2 Penn Plaza, Suite 701
New York, New York 10121-0701

ISBN: 978-1-4503-5563-6 (Digital)

ISBN: 978-1-4503-6167-5 (Print)

Additional copies may be ordered prepaid from:

ACM Order Department
PO Box 30777
New York, NY 10087-0777, USA

Phone: 1-800-342-6626 (USA and Canada)
+1-212-626-0500 (Global)
Fax: +1-212-944-1318
E-mail: acmhelp@acm.org
Hours of Operation: 8:30 am – 4:30 pm ET

WebSci'18 Chairs' Welcome

It is our great pleasure to welcome you to the *10th ACM Conference on Web Science, Amsterdam, 27-30 May 2018.*

This year's edition of the WebSci conference (WebSci'18) celebrates the ten year anniversary of the unique conference series where a multitude of disciplines converge in a creative and critical dialogue with the aim of understanding the Web and its impacts.

The WebSci conference brings together researchers from multiple disciplines, like computer science, sociology, economics, information science, anthropology and psychology. Web Science is the emergent study of the people and technologies, applications, processes and practices that shape and are shaped by the World Wide Web. Web Science aims to draw together theories, methods and findings from across academic disciplines, and to collaborate with industry, business, government and civil society, to develop our knowledge and understanding of the Web: the largest socio-technical network in human history.

This year we were very pleased to receive 113 submissions for the regular research track. Given the high quality of submissions, it has been a hard job to decide which of the contributions to select for the conference. We are grateful for the support of the Program Committee which consisted of 10 senior members and 35 regular members. All PC members worked hard, based on which we could select an interesting, varied, exciting program comprising 30 long and 15 short papers.

The final program for the main track will include sessions touching different, interesting, timely topics, as one can judge from their titles:

- Digging Into Social Networks
- Flow, Information and News
- New Perspectives on Web Science
- Methods and Practice
- The Reality of Social Media
- Location, Geography & Fragmentation
- Networks, Collaboration and Participation
- Controversy and Culture
- Finding Information Now and Then
- Methods and Navigation
- and a special session with the Best of Web Science 2018

We thank all the authors who have contributed to Web Science, as well as the PC members and reviewers for their commitment, patience, and hard work.

The program also includes the ACM Turing Award Lecture by Sir Tim Berners-Lee. Sir Tim Berners-Lee, the inventor of the World Wide Web and the recipient of the 2016 ACM A.M. Turing Award, popularly known as the Nobel Prize for Informatics, will deliver his Turing Lecture as a keynote at our WebSci'18 Conference.

A second keynote is given by Prof. Dr. John Domingue, Director of the Knowledge Media Institute, The Open University, UK, and President of STI International, Vienna, Austria, on The Future of Semantics on the Web.

We are confident that participants will be able to appreciate the high quality of all the contributions that have been selected and enjoy the very special keynotes.

Hans Akkermans
General Chair
Vrije Universiteit Amsterdam, the Netherlands

Victor de Boer
Proceedings Chair
Vrije Universiteit Amsterdam, the Netherlands

Geert-Jan Houben
Program Chair
TU Delft, the Netherlands

Matthew S. Weber
Program Chair
Rutgers University, New Jersey, USA

Table of Contents

Session: New Perspectives on Web Science

Session: Methods and Practice

Session: The Reality of Social Media

Session: Location, Geography and Fragmentation

Session: Networks, Collaboration and Participation

Session: Controversy and Culture

Session: Finding Information Now and Then

Session: Methods and Navigation

Author Index

WebSci'18 Conference Organization

General Chair: Hans Akkermans *(Vrije Universiteit Amsterdam, The Netherlands)*

General Co-Chairs Kathy Fontaine *(Rensselaer Polytechnic Institute, USA)*
Ivar Vermeulen *(Vrije Universiteit Amsterdam, The Netherlands)*

Program Chairs: Geert-Jan Houben *(TU Delft, The Netherlands)*
Matthew S. Weber *(Rutgers University, New Jersey, USA)*

WebSci'18 Event Chairs: Paolo Boldi *(Università degli Studi di Milano, Italy)*
Anna Bon *(Vrije Universiteit Amsterdam, The Netherlands)*
Susan Halford *(University of Southampton, UK)*
Katharina Kinder-Kurlanda, *(GESIS – Leibniz Institute for the Social Sciences, Germany)*

WebSci Interdisciplinary PhD Symposium Chairs: Pete Burnap *(Cardiff University, UK)*
Leslie Carr *(Web Science Institute, University of Southampton, UK)*
Mark Weal *(Web Science Institute, University of Southampton, UK)*

ACM Proceedings Chair: Victor de Boer *(Vrije Universiteit Amsterdam, The Netherlands)*

WebSci'18 Events Proceedings Chair: Jaap Gordijn *(TVE The Value Engineers, The Netherlands)*

Poster Chairs: Pete Burnap *(Cardiff University, UK)*
Leslie Carr *(Web Science Institute, University of Southampton, UK)*
Mark Weal *(Web Science Institute, University of Southampton, UK)*

Sponsorship & Student Grants Chair: Carlos Pedrinaci *(Roche, UK)*

Communication and PR Chair: Wendelien Tuijp *(Vrije Universiteit Amsterdam, The Netherlands)*

Nonlocal Organization Chair: Susan Davies *(Web Science Trust, University of Southampton, UK)*

Local Organization Committee: Hans Akkermans
Melein Ankersmit
Anna Bon
Bert Haans
Mojca Lovrencak
Wendelien Tuijp
Caroline Waij
Lydeke Waardenburg

Program Committee: Hans Akkermans *(Vrije Universiteit Amsterdam)*

Virgilio Almeida *(UFMG)*

Lora Aroyo *(Vrije Universiteit Amsterdam)*

Ricardo Baeza-Yates *(Yahoo Labs)*

Elena Cabrio *(Université Côte d'Azur, CNRS, Inria, I3S, France)*

Carlos Castillo *(Universitat Pompeu Fabra)*

Michele Catasta *(Stanford University)*

Oscar Corcho *(Universidad Politécnica de Madrid)*

Victor de Boer *(Vrije Universiteit Amsterdam)*

Ying Ding *(Indiana University Bloomington)*

Alessandro Epasto *(Google)*

Catherine Faron Zucker *(Université Nice Sophia Antipolis)*

Miriam Fernandez *(Knowledge Media Institute)*

Aldo Gangemi *(Università di Bologna & CNR-ISTC)*

Susan Halford *(University of Southampton)*

Harry Halpin *(World Wide Web Consortium)*

Geert-Jan Houben *(Delft University of Technology)*

Krzysztof Janowicz *(University of California, Santa Barbara)*

Young Ji Kim *(University of California Santa Barbara)*

Katharina Kinder-Kurlanda *(GESIS Leibniz Institute for the Social Sciences)*

Lorraine Kisselburgh *(Purdue University)*

Martin Klein *(Los Alamos National Laboratory)*

Gertraud Koch *(University of Hamburg)*

Juhi Kulshrestha *(MPI-SWS)*

Elisabeth Lex *(Graz University of Technology)*

Athanasios Mazarakis *(Kiel University / ZBW)*

Wagner Meira Jr. *(UFMG)*

Stasa Milojevic *(Indiana University Bloomington)*

Pascal Molli *(University of Nantes - LS2N)*

Mirco Musolesi *(University College London)*

Wolfgang Nejdl *(L3S and University of Hannover)*

Alexandra Olteanu *(IBM)*

Nicola Perra *(University of Greenwich)*

Isabella Peters *(ZBW)*

Alessandro Provetti *(Birkbeck, University of London)*

Hemant Purohit *(George Mason University)*

Cornelius Puschmann *(Alexander von Humboldt Institute for Internet and Society)*

Luca Rossi *(IT University of Copenhagen)*

Giancarlo Ruffo *(Universita' di Torino)*

Program Committee (continued):   Harald Sack *(FIZ Karlsruhe, Leibniz Institute for Information Infrastructure*
               & KIT Karlsruhe)

        Salvatore Scellato *(Google)*

        Patrick C. Shih *(Indiana University Bloomington)*

        Steffen Staab *(Institut WeST, University Koblenz-Landau and WAIS,*
               University of Southampton)

        Thanassis Tiropanis *(University of Southampton)*

        Christoph Trattner *(University of Bergen)*

        Matthew Weber *(Rutgers University)*

        Ingmar Weber *(Qatar Computing Research Institute)*

        Katrin Weller *(GESIS - Leibniz Institute for the Social Sciences)*

        Sergej Zerr *(L3S Research Center)*

WebSci'18 Sponsors & Supporters

Sponsors:

Supporters:

IOS
Press

2COOLMONKEYS

TVE
THE VALUE ENGINEERS

W3C®

Understanding the Roots of Radicalisation on Twitter

Miriam Fernandez
Open University, UK
miriam.fernandez@open.ac.uk

Moizzah Asif
Open University, UK
moizzah.asif@open.ac.uk

Harith Alani
Open University, UK
h.alani@open.ac.uk

ABSTRACT

In an increasingly digital world, identifying signs of online extremism sits at the top of the priority list for counter-extremist agencies.[1] Researchers and governments are investing in the creation of advanced information technologies to identify and counter extremism through intelligent large-scale analysis of online data. However, to the best of our knowledge, these technologies are neither based on, nor do they take advantage of, the existing theories and studies of radicalisation. In this paper we propose a computational approach for detecting and predicting the radicalisation influence a user is exposed to, grounded on the notion of 'roots of radicalisation' from social science models. This approach has been applied to analyse and compare the radicalisation level of 112 pro-ISIS vs.112 "general" Twitter users. Our results show the effectiveness of our proposed algorithms in detecting and predicting radicalisation influence, obtaining up to 0.9 F-1 measure for detection and between 0.7 and 0.8 precision for prediction. While this is an initial attempt towards the effective combination of social and computational perspectives, more work is needed to bridge these disciplines, and to build on their strengths to target the problem of online radicalisation.

KEYWORDS

Online Radicalisation, Radicalisation Influence, Counter-terrorism

ACM Reference Format:
Miriam Fernandez, Moizzah Asif, and Harith Alani. 2018. Understanding the Roots of Radicalisation on Twitter. In *WebSci '18: 10th ACM Conference on Web Science, May 27–30, 2018, Amsterdam, Netherlands.* ACM, New York, NY, USA, 10 pages. https://doi.org/10.1145/3201064.3201082

1 INTRODUCTION

Traditionally, the process of radicalisation took place through physical interaction in social environments, such as in places of worship, prisons, and meeting venues. However, in recent years this process has migrated to the virtual environment of the Internet, where many terrorist organisations are now using social media to promote their ideology and propaganda, and to recruit individuals to their cause. With the spread of social media and encrypted communications, not only radicalisation but also operational planning can easily occur entirely online.[2] Recruitment conversations often start with open social media sites (e.g., Twitter, Facebook, Tumblr, Ask.fm, Instagram, YouTube, etc.) and then move onto private messages with target individuals.

A well known example is the so-called Islamic State (IS), which is arguably one of the leading organisations in the use of social media for sharing their propaganda, for raising funds, and for radicalising and recruiting individuals around the globe. According to a 2015 U.S government report,[3] this organisation succeeded in recruiting more than 25,000 foreign fighters in Syria and Iraq, including 4,500 from Europe and North America. In a desperate attempt to disrupt and disconnect such radicalisation channels, some governments, organisations, and social media platforms continuously search and disable social media accounts that are found to be associated with such terrorist groups. For example, in response to the Paris attacks in November 2015, the hacker community Anonymous took down more than 20,000 Twitter accounts that were allegedly linked to ISIS. However, the method they deployed to categorise such accounts was too imperfect, evidenced by their inclusion in the blockage the social media accounts of the U.S president Barack Obama, the White House, the BBC, the New York Times, and many other anti IS accounts.[4]

Parallel to the development of these systems and methods, multiple models have emerged from psychology and social sciences that aim to investigate what are the **factors** that drive people to get radicalised [25] (e.g., failed integration, poverty, discrimination), their different **roots** [31][9] (micro-level, or individual level, meso-level, or group/community level, and macro-level, or global level, the influence of government and society at home and abroad), and how the radicalisation process happens and evolves, i.e., what are its different **stages** [33] (e.g., pre-radicalisation, self-identification, indoctrination, Jihadisation).

It is however difficult to understand how the radicalisation process tends to kickstart and evolve online, especially when the amount of traffic generated in social media is so vast. Manual analysis is impractical and thus automatic techniques need to be used. We need to look at online radicalisation as a process, and to leverage closer the knowledge of theoretical models of radicalisation to design more effective technological solutions to tracking online radicalisation. To bridge this gap, our work investigates two main research questions:

- *How can we translate the different aspects of social theories of radicalisation into computational methods to enable the automatic identification of radicalised behaviour?* This work proposes an approach based on Natural Language Processing

---

[1]http://www.voxpol.eu/identifying-radical-content-online/

[2]https://www.foreignaffairs.com/articles/western-europe/2016-07-26/myth-lone-wolf-terrorism
[3]https://homeland.house.gov/wp-content/uploads/2015/09/TaskForceFinalReport.pdf
[4]http://www.bbc.co.uk/newsbeat/article/34919781/anonymous-anti-islamic-state-list%2Dfeatures-obama-and-bbc-news

(NLP) and Collaborative Filtering (CF), that automatically captures the different roots of radicalisation (micro, meso and macro) [31] for each user and represents them as keyword-based vector descriptions.

- *How the incorporation of theoretical perspectives into computational approaches can help us to develop effective radicalisation detection and prediction approaches?* Based on our proposed keyword-based representation, we propose an approach to automatically detect and predict the level of radicalisation influence a user is subjected to. Note that our aim is not to determine whether someone is being radicalised or not, but to provide a risk level for each user based on the individual, social and global influences to which she is exposed to in social media. To assess this risk, we take into account the social media history of a user (in this case, the Twitter time-lines - up to a maximum of 3,200 posts per user, which is the limit imposed by Twitter in their API)

By investigating these research questions, we provide the following contributions:

- A summary and analysis of a wide range of theories and models of radicalisation, including their different roots, factors and stages involved in the process.
- The translation of the different roots of radicalisation (micro-individual-, meso-social- and macro-global-) into computational elements to study their impact on the radicalisation process of different users.
- The development of an approach that automatically assigns each user a risk of radicalisation based on the the individual, social and global influences to which she is exposed to in social media

The following sections are structured as follows. Section 2 describes a compendium of different theories and models of radicalisation, as well as the different automatic approaches that have been proposed so far in the literature to detect radicalisation online. Section 3 shows our proposed approach to automatically identify the individual, meso and macro level influence of online content on each user, as well as our approach to automatically compute a score of radicalisation for each user based on these influences. Section 4 discusses our evaluation of this model. An in-depth discussion of our findings is reported in Section 5, while Section 6 concludes.

2 STATE OF THE ART

Understanding the mechanisms that govern the process of radicalisation, and online radicalisation in particular, has been the topic of investigation in the domain of social sciences and psychology [25][31], in computing technology [5], and in policing [33].

In this section, we first take a look at theoretical studies to get insights into the different models that have been proposed to describe the radicalisation process, its roots, influencing factors and stages. We then focus on those works that have addressed the problem from a computational perspective. As a result of the analysis of these theories and the observation of how previous computational approaches have targeted the problem, we propose an integrated approach that can be used to capture how the different roots influence the process of online radicalisation and to detect the level of radicalisation influence each user is undergoing.

2.1 Models of Radicalisation

Different models have been proposed in the literature that aim to capture the process of radicalisation [18].[5]

In 2003 Borum [8] proposed a four-staged radicalisation model. The first stage, **context**, begins by identifying some event or condition as being "not right"; poverty, unemployment, government-imposed restrictions, etc. People in the first stage display a propensity of being radicalised. The second stage, **comparison**, is formed when such event or condition is framed as unjust in comparison to others. In the third stage, **attribution**, the injustice is blamed on a target policy, person or nation. Second and third stages are understood as the process of indoctrination. Finally, in the fourth stage, **reaction**, the responsible party is vilified, often demonised, to facilitate justification for aggression. This last stage falls under extremism. When discussing the motives leading to these stages, Borum highlights the importance of the information the user is exposed to; her values and her life experiences. In a most recent publication he stresses the need of investigating the role that the different roots micro (individual) -meso (group) and macro (global) play in understanding the etiology of radicalisation.[9]

Moghaddam proposed in 2005 the stair-case model of radicalisation [25]. This model describes a similar progression to the model proposed by Borum [8]. The initial step, **perceived deprivation**, starts with feelings of discontent and perceived adversity, which people seek to alleviate. When those attempts are unsuccessful, they become frustrated, **perceived options to unfair treatment**, leading to feelings of aggression, **displacement of aggression**, which are displaced on to some perceived causal agent (who is then regarded as an enemy). With increasing anger directed towards the enemy, some come to sympathise with the violent, extremist ideology of the terrorist groups that act against them; **moral engagement**. Some of those sympathisers eventually join an extremist group, organisation or movement that advocates for, and perhaps engages in, terrorist violence; **legitimacy of the terrorist organisation**. At the top or final level among those who have joined are those who overcome any barriers to action and actually commit a terrorist attack; **the terrorist act**. The validity of this linear stepwise model has been criticised, suggesting that multiple mechanisms/factors could combine in different ways to produce terrorism [23].

In 2007 the New York Police Department (NYPD) published their own model of radicalisation [33], focused on Jihadi-Salafi ideology and "the west". This model is composed of four distinct phases. **Pre-radicalisation**; most individuals at this stage have lived "ordinary" lives and have little, if any criminal history. In a second stage, **self-identification**, individuals, influenced by both, internal and external factors, (loosing a job, alienation and discrimination, death in the close family, etc.) begin to explore Salafi Islam. In the third phase, **indoctrination**, individuals progressively intensify their beliefs and conclude that circumstances exist where action is required to support the cause. In the final phase, **jihadisation**, individuals accept their individual duty to participate in violent jihad and self-designate themselves as holy warriors. The model also highlights the influence of the individual, group, and global

---
[5]http://wanainstitute.org/sites/default/files/publications/Publication_UnderstandingRadicalisation_SecondEditionJuly2017.pdf

roots of radicalisation in this process. In particular they highlight "group-think" as one of the most powerful catalysts for leading an individual and/or group to commit a terrorist attack. The model states that all individuals that begin the radicalisation process do not necessarily pass through all the stages and that many do abandon the process at different points. Although the model is sequential, individuals do not always follow a perfectly linear progression, and individuals who do pass through this entire process are likely to be involved in the planning or implementation of a terrorist attack.

McCauley and Moskalenko proposed another model in 2008 [24]. This model also highlights the importance of the different roots of radicalisation. Individuals are radicalised by personal grievances (micro), group grievances (meso) and by global factors like mass-media (macro). Based on these roots the model defines twelve mechanisms of radicalisation. Mechanisms associated with individual factors include **personal victimisation** and **political grievance**. Mechanisms associated with group factors include joining a radical group, either via step-by step self-persuasion -**the slippery slope**- or via personal connections with people who are already radicalised (friends, loved ones, family members) -**the power of love**-. They also include **extremity shift in like-minded individuals** or group polarisation, where like-minded individuals join under discussion groups and feed each other with more and more extreme views; **extreme cohesion under isolation and threat**, which generally occurs in small combat groups where members can trust only one another; **competition for the same base of support**, where a subgroup gain status by proposing/conducting more radical actions in support of a cause; **competition with state power**, where violent government reactions against civil disobedience create sympathy for the victims of state repression; and **within group competition**, where competition within the group provokes the group to fission in radical subgroups. Macro mechanisms include **Jujitsu politics**, where displays of patriotism or nationalism create cohesion within the minority/discriminated group, **hate**, where mass conflicts become more extreme and **martyrdom** where individuals giving their life for the cause obtain the status of heroes, giving some people a life purpose.

In 2014, Kruglanski and colleagues [21] presented a new model or radicalisation, and de-radicalisation, based on the notion that the quest for personal significance constitutes a major motivational force that may push individuals towards violent extremism. This model is composed by three key components. The **motivational component** or the quest for personal significance, represents the goal to which one may be committed. The **ideological component** identifies the means of violence as appropriate for this goal's pursuit. **The social component**, or the process of networking and group dynamics through which the individual comes to share in the violence-justifying ideology. This model highlights the need of defining radicalisation as a process with different degrees.

More recently (2015), Hafez and Mullins [17] have focused on Islamic extremism in the West. In their model they highlight four factors that come together to produce violent radicalisation. **Grievances** include economic marginalisation and cultural alienation, deeply held sense of victimisation, or strong disagreements regarding the foreign policies of states. **Networks** refer to preexisting friendship ties between ordinary individuals and radicals that lead to the diffusion of extreme beliefs. **Ideologies** refer to master narratives

about the world and one's place in it. **Enabling environments and support structures** encompass physical and virtual settings such as the Internet, social media, prisons, or foreign terrorist training camps that provide ideological and material aid for radicalising individuals. While some of these factors are very similar to the ones highlighted in previous models, the authors propose a puzzle metaphor, i.e., a nonlinear, evolutionary approach to radicalisation, rejecting the idea of a sequential process of steps, as proposed by previous models [8][25].

As we can see in all these models, radicalisation often starts with individuals who are frustrated with their lives, society or their governments and their policies. These individuals meet other like-minded people, and start being influenced by information, ideas and events that ultimately can result in terrorism. However, the radicalisation process does not unfold in the same way for all people. The mechanism will vary even among those who may be exposed to the same factors and conditions. Radicalisation occurs through a **process**, typically either through gradual escalation, or as a series of discrete actions or decisions [9]. What all these models highlight are the different roots that influence the radicalisation process of a user:

- **Micro or Individual roots**: The micro roots of radicalisation relate to factors self-affecting the individual. Perceptions of deprivation, perceived procedural injustice, and symbolic and realistic threat can motivate individuals to seek out extreme organisations [34]

- **Meso or group/community roots**: Individuals find support for their ideas and a relationship within a group or community. Some individuals are attracted to a group due to the perceived legitimacy of this group, others via love connections (friends, loved ones or family members who are already part of the group). Groups often use comparison with other groups to show injustice which often creates us-versus-them thinking. Besides the group identity and social interaction, individuals can also be attracted to radicalisation through the use of radical rhetoric by the group

- **Macro or global roots**: Macro roots include the influence of government and society at home and abroad. Typical examples are the effect of globalisation and modernisation as well as foreign policy of some (Western) countries. While globalisation can threaten the group identity it can also expand the radical group by feeding the us-versus-them thinking.

As we can see from our literature analysis, there is a clear association between the three roots of radicalisation (micro, meso and macro) and the various factors and stages identified in the models or frameworks of radicalisation. While those roots originally developed from off-line interactions (e.g., attending mosques to discuss radical views) they are now rapidly developing online. Edwards and colleagues [14, 36] investigated internet radicalisation in Europe by speaking with convicted terrorists. Among the salient findings of their work they highlighted that: (i) the internet increases opportunities for self-radicalisation (micro), (ii) the internet allows radicalisation to occur without physical contact by replacing in-person meetings by in-person communication, and by enabling connection with like-minded individuals from across the world 24/7 (meso) and (iii) the internet creates more opportunities to become radicalised by providing access to information and propaganda, as well as by acting as echo-chamber for extremist believes (macro).

2.2 Computational approaches

Researchers from the areas of counter-terrorism and cyber-security have begun to examine the radicalisation phenomenon and to understand the social media presence and actions of extremist organisations [1]. In this section we summarise some of these computational approaches developed towards the **analysis**, **detection** and **prediction** of radicalisation. A summary of these approaches, their goals, the data they used, their key conclusions, and whether they make use of previous knowledge of social science models (see Section 2.1) is reported in Table 1

Among the works developed towards **analysing** the online radicalisation phenomenon we can highlight the works of Klausen [19], Carter [11], Chatfield [12], Vergani [35] and Rowe [28].

Klausen [19] studied the role of social media, and particularly Twitter, in the jihadists' operational strategy in Syria and Iraq. During 2014, they collected information on 59 Twitter accounts of Western-origin fighters known to be in Syria, and their networks (followers and followees), leading to a total of 29,000 studied accounts. The 59 original accounts were manually identified by the research team. They used known network metrics, like degree-centrality, number of followers or number of tweets, to identify the most influential users. The authors also conducted a manual analysis of the top recent posts of influential individuals to determine the key topics of conversation (religious instruction, reporting battle and interpersonal communication), as well as the content of pictures and videos. The study highlights the direction of the communication flow, from the terrorist accounts, to the fighters based in the insurgent zones, to the followers in the west, and the prominence of female members acting as propagandist.

Carter [11], collected during 12 months information from 190 social media accounts of Western and European foreign fighters affiliated with Jabhat al-Nusrah and ISIS. These accounts were manually identified and comprise both, Facebook and Twitter accounts. The paper aimed to examine how foreign fighters receive information and who inspires them. The analysis looked at the most popular Facebook pages by "likes", or the most popular Twitter accounts by "follows", as well as the numbers of comments and shares of different posts. The paper also looked at the word clouds of different profiles ,revealing terms like (islamic, Allah, fight, Mujahideen, ISIS, etc.) The paper reveals the existence of spiritual authorities who foreign fighters go to for inspiration and guidance.

Chatfield [12] investigated how ISIS members/supporters used Twitter to radicalise and recruit other users. For this purpose they study 3,039 tweets from one account of a known ISIS "information disseminator". Two annotators categorised those posts manually as: propaganda (information), radicalisation (believes in support of a intergroup conflict and violence), terrorist recruitment (enticing others to join in fighting the jihad war) and other. Examples of these tweets and their content is provided as a result of this exercise. The analysis also studies the frequency and times of posting, indicating him as highly active user, as well as the network of users mentioned in the tweets, which were manually categorised as: international media, regional Arabic media, IS sympathisers and IS fighters.

Vergani [35] investigated the evolution of the ISIS's language by analysing the text contained in the first 11 issues of Dabiq; the official ISIS internet magazine in English. To conduct their analysis they made use of the Linguistic Inquiry and and Word Count (LIWC) text analysis program. Their analysis highlights: (i) the use of expressions related to achievement, affiliation and power, (ii) a focus on emotional language, which is considered to be effective in mobilising individuals, (ii) frequent mentions of death, female, and religion, which are related to the ISIS ideology and the recruitment of women to the cause and (iv) the use of internet jargon ("btw", "lol", etc.), which may be more effective in establishing a communication with the youngest generations of potential recruits.

While [11, 12, 19] studied the social media behaviour of users once radicalised, Rowe and Saif [28] studied the social media actions and interactions of Europe-based Twitter users before, during, and after they exhibited pro-ISIS behaviour. Starting from 512 radicalised Twitter accounts, manually identified in the work of O'Callagan [26], they collected their followers, filtered those based in Europe and determined whether those followers were radicalised based on two hypothesis: (i) use of pro-ISIS terminology, a lexicon was generated to test this hypothesis, and (ii) content shared from pro-ISIS accounts. Their filtering process lead to the study of 727 pro-ISIS Twitter accounts and their complete timelines. The study concluded that prior to being activated/radicalised users go through a period of significant increase in adopting innovations (i.e., communicating with new users and adopting new terms). They also highlight that social homophily has a strong bearing on the diffusion process of pro-ISIS terminology through Twitter.

Bermingham and colleagues [7] looked at the user profiles and comments of a YouTube video group which purpose was "the conversion of infidels" with the aim of assessing whether users were being radicalised by the group and how this was reflected in comments and interactions. They collected a total of 135,000 comments posted by 700 members and 13,000 group contributors. They performed term frequency to observe the top-terms used in the group as well as sentiment analysis over a subset of comments filtered by a list of keywords of interest (Islam, Israel, Palestine, etc.). They also used centrality measures to identify influencers. They observed that the group was mostly devoted to religious discussion (not radicalisation) and that female users show more extreme and less tolerant views.

Regarding **detection** we can highlight the works of Berger [5, 6], Agarwal [2], Ashcroft [3] and Saif [29].

In 2013 Berger and Strathearn [5] developed an approach to detect individuals more prone to extremism (in this case white supremacy) among those with interest in violent ideologies. Their approach started by collecting the social networks of twelve known extremists on Twitter (3,542 accounts were collected using this process and a maximum of 200 tweets per account was analysed) and measuring three dimensions for each user: (i) their influence (number of times their content was retweeted), (ii) exposure (number of times they retweeted other's content) and (iii) interactivity (by looking for keywords in tweets like DM -Direct Message- or email). They concluded that high scores of influence and exposure showed a strong correlation to engagement with the extremist ideology.

Table 1: Computational approaches towards the analysis (A), detection (D) and prediction (P) of radicalisation. SMM refers to the use of Social Science Models

Work	Goal	Data	Conclusions	SSM
Klausen [19] A	Study Influence in the jihadists' operational strategy in Syria and Iraq	59 pro-ISIS **Twitter** accounts (manually assessed) and their networks (29,000 accounts)	Communication flow, from the terrorist accounts, to the fighters based in the insurgent zones, to the followers in the west. Prominence of female members acting as propagandist	no
Carter [11] A	Examine how foreign fighters receive information and who inspires them	190 pro-ISIS **Twitter** and **Facebook** accounts (manually assessed)	existence of spiritual authorities who foreign fighters look to for inspiration and guidance	no
Chatfield [12] A	Investigate how ISIS members/supporters used Twitter to radicalise and recruit other users	3,039 tweets from one account of a known ISIS "information disseminator" (**Twitter**)	Posts about propaganda, radicalisation and terrorist recruitment mentioning international media, regional Arabic media, IS sympathisers and IS fighters	no
Vergani [35] A	Investigated the evolution of the ISIS's language	first 11 issues of **Dabiq**, the official ISIS's internet magazine	Use expressions related to achievement, affiliation and power. Emotional language. Mentions of death female and religion and use of internet jargon	no
Rowe [28] A	Study Europe-based Twitter users before, during, and after they exhibited pro-ISIS behaviour to better understand the radicalisation process	727 pro-ISIS **Twitter** accounts. Categorised as pro-ISIS base on the use of radicalised terminology and sharing from radicalised accounts	Prior to being activated/radicalised users go through a period of significant increase in adopting innovations (i.e. communicating with new users and adopting new terms). Social homophily has a strong bearing on the diffusion process of pro-ISIS terminology.	no
Bermingham [7] A	Explore the use of sentiment and network analysis to determine whether a YouTube group was used as radicalisation channel	135,000 comments and 13,700 user profiles. **YouTube** group manually assessed	The group was mostly devoted to religious discussion (not radicalisation). Female users show more extreme and less tolerant views	no
Berger [5] D	Identify individuals prone to extremism from the followers of extremist accounts	3,542 **Twitter** accounts (followers of 12 known pro-ISIS accounts)	High scores of influence an exposure showed a strong correlation to engagement with the extremist ideology (manual evaluation)	no
Saif [29] D	Create classifiers able to automatically identify pro-ISIS users in social media.	1,132 **Twitter** users (566 pro-ISIS, 556 anti-ISIS). Annotation based on the terminology used and the sharing from known radicalised accounts	Classifiers trained on semantic features outperform those trained from lexical, sentiment, topic and network features	no
Berger [6] D	Create a demographic snapshot of ISIS supporters on Twitter and outline a methodology for detecting pro-ISIS accounts	20,000 pro-ISIS **Twitter** accounts (7574 manually annotated to test classification)	The authors concluded that pro-ISIS supporters could be identified from their profiles descriptions: with terms such as succession, linger, Islamic State, Caliphate State or In Iraq all being prominent	no
Agarwal [2] D	Automatic identification of hate and extremism promoting tweets	10,486 hate and terrorism-related **Twitter** posts (extracted based on hashtags) + 1M random tweets annotated by students for validation	Presence of religious, war related terms, offensive words and negative emotions are strong indicators of a tweet to be hate promoting	no
Ashcroft [3] D	Automatically detect messages released by jihadist groups on Twitter	2,000 pro-ISIS **Twitter** posts (containing pro-ISIS terminology and extracted from the accounts 6,729 ISIS sympathisers), 2,000 anti-ISIS tweets(extracted from manually assessed anti-ISIS accounts), 2000 random tweets. Numbers of pro and anti-ISIS tweets are not reported but estimated based on the experiments	Fridays are a key date to spread radical tweets. Automatic detection is viable but can never replace human analysts. It should be seen as a complementary way to detect radical content.	no
Lara-Cabrera [22] D	Translate a set of indicators found in social science models into a set of computational features	17K **Twitter** posts from pro-ISIS users provided by Kaggle[6]. 76K tweets from pro-ISIS users provided by Anonymous[7]. 173K tweets randomly selected	The proposed metrics (mainly based on keywords) show promising results. More refined metrics can be proposed to map social science indicators	yes
Ferrara [16] **P**	Propose a computational framework for detection and prediction of extremism in social media	Over 3M **Twitter** posts generated by over 25 thousand extremist accounts (manually identified, reported, and suspended by Twitter [15]). 29M posts from the followers of these accounts	The ratio of retweets to tweets, the average number of hashtags adopted, the sheer number of tweets and the average number of retweets generated by each user, systematically rank very high in terms of predictive power	no

Manual analysis of the top 200 accounts was used for evaluating the proposed scoring.

In 2015 Berger and Morgan [6] aimed to create a demographic snapshot of ISIS supporters on Titter and outline a methodology for detecting pro-ISIS accounts. Starting from a set of 454 seed accounts (identified by previous research [5] and recursively obtaining followers of those accounts and filtering them based on availability of the account, robot identification, etc., they obtained a final list of 20,000 pro-ISIS accounts to analyse. They estimated that at least 46,000 pro-ISIS accounts were active (as Dec 2014). They created classifiers from a subset of 6,000 accounts that were manually annotated as ISIS supporters or non-supporters. The authors concluded that pro-ISIS supporters could be identified from their profile descriptions: with terms such as succession, linger, Islamic State, Caliphate State or In Iraq all being prominent. When testing this classifier with 1,574 manually annotated accounts they obtained 94% of classification accuracy. However, profile information is only available for around 70% of accounts.

In 2015 Agarwal [2] aimed to investigate techniques to automatically identify hate and extremism promoting tweets. Starting from 2 crawls of Twitter data[8] they used a semi-supervised learning approach based on a list of hashtags (#Terrorism, #Islamophobia, #Extremist) to filter those tweets related to hate and extremism. The training dataset has 10,486 tweets. They used random sampling to generate the validation dataset (1M tweets). Tweets were in english and manually annotated by four students. The created and validated two different classifiers (KNN and SVM) based on the generated datasets to classify a tweet as hate promoting or unknown. By creating and validating these classifiers they concluded that the presence of religious, war related terms, offensive words and negative emotions are strong indicators of a tweet to be hate promoting.

In 2015 Ashcroft [3] aimed to automatically detect messages released by jihadist groups on Twitter. They collected tweets from 6729 Jihadist sympathisers . Two additional datasets, one of 2,000 randomly selected tweets, and one of tweets from accounts manually annotated as anti-ISIS, were collected for validation. Numbers of tweets for the pro and anti-ISIS datasets are not reported, but based on the provided experiments we estimate they should be around 2,000 each. SVM, Naive Bayes and Adaboost classifiers were trained with this data using stylometric, time and sentiment features. Authors conclude that Fridays are a key date to spread radical tweets. Automatic detection is viable but can never replace human analysts. It should be seen as a complementary way to detect radical content.

In 2017 Saif [29] proposed a semantic graph-based approach to identify pro vs. anti-ISIS social media accounts. The authors developed multiple classifiers and showed that, their proposed classifier, trained for semantic features, outperformed those trained from lexical, sentiment, topic and network features by 7.8% on average F1-measure. Evaluation was done on a dataset 1,132 Twitter users (with their timelines). 566 pro-ISIS accounts, obtained from [28] and 566 anti-ISIS users, whose stance was determined by the use of anti-ISIS rhetoric.

In 2017 Lara-Cabrera [22] translated a set of indicators found in social science theories of radicalisation (feelings of frustration, introversion, perception of discrimination, etc.) into a set of computational features (mostly sets of keywords) that they could automatically extract from the data. They asses the appearance of these indicators in: (i) a set of 17K tweets from pro-ISIS users provided by Kaggle[9], a set of 76K tweets from pro-ISIS users provided by Anonymous[10] and a set of 173K tweets randomly selected by opening the Twitter stream. The authors conclude that, while the proposed metrics show promising results, these metrics are mainly based on keywords. More refined metrics can therefore be proposed to map social science indicators.

Regarding the works on **prediction** we can highlight a recent work of Ferrara [16]. In this work the authors propose a computational framework for detection and prediction of extremism in social media. For this purpose they use a dataset of over 3M tweets generated by over 25 thousand extremist accounts, who have been manually identified, reported, and suspended by Twitter [15], and a dataset of 29M posts from the followers of these users. Random forest and logistic regression are used for classification and prediction based on user metadata and activity features, time features, and features based on network statistics. Two types of predictions are made: (i) whether the follower will adopt extremist content (retweet from a known pro-ISIS account) and (ii) whether the follower will interact (reply) with a known pro-ISIS account. The authors conclude that the ratio of retweets to tweets, the average number of hashtags adopted, the sheer number of tweets and the average number of retweets generated by each user, systematically rank very high in terms of predictive power.

In this section we provided some examples of the types of computational methods that have been developed to analyse, detect and predict radicalisation. An exhaustive list of works and classification is provided in the following article by Correa [13]. Various aspects however can be highlighted from this survey.

- Except the work of Lara-Cabrera [22] we have found no other computational works grounded on social science theories or models.
- Radicalisation detection is generally considered as a binary problem rather than as a process with different degrees or levels, where classifiers are generated to distinguish pro- vs. anti- ISIS stances.
- Approaches tend to categorise users based on a few pieces of their generated content (few comments, their most recent posts, etc.) but few works consider the complete history of the user (i.e., their entire timelines) when detecting radicalisation
- While most of the identified approaches focus on the analysis and detection of radicalisation, to the best of our knowledge, only the work of [16] is focused on predicting radicalisation

We will provide a step forward with respect to previous works by introducing an approach that integrates the knowledge of social science models into a computational method to identify the risk of radicalisation for a user. Rather than treating the problem as a binary classification, our approach will provide a score that symbolises the

---

[8]https://wiki.illinois.edu/wiki/display/forward/SoftwareDatasets

[9]https://www.kaggle.com/fifthtribe/how-isis-uses-twitter
[10]https://pastebin.com/u/CyberRog

influence of radicalisation to which a user is exposed to, based on the micro, meso and macro roots. As opposed to previous works, our approach uses the complete timelines of users when measuring this score, considering radicalisation as a long-term process. In addition to the detection of the influence or radicalisation in an individual, our approach also aims to predict the potential future level of radicalisation influence by employing CF techniques.

3 DETECTING AND PREDICTING RADICALISATION INFLUENCE

In Section 2, we highlighted how the theoretical models point at different roots of the radicalisation process (micro, meso and macro) [31]. Our first task has therefore been to model these roots in terms of social media content. Once acquired an understanding on how these three different roots can be identified and represented, we develop an approach to automatically assess the influence of each of these roots on a user to determine up to which level she is undergoing a radicalisation process.

3.1 Modelling Roots of Radicalisation

When a user participates in a social media platform, she can perform two main actions in terms of posting: (i) creating and posting new content and (ii) sharing content posted by someone within her network. In our work we assume that the micro (individual) root is captured by all the posts that the user has created. Similarly, the meso (or social) influence is captured by all the post that the user has shared. We are aware that a user is exposed to more information than the one that she shares. However, when a user is sharing a piece of content, it is a strong indicator that that piece of content has somehow influenced the user who is making it part of her own ideas and believes. Within the posts that a user creates or shares from her network we can also find links (URLs) to external sites (YouTube videos, news sites, blogs, etc.). These sites capture the macro (global) level of influence over an individual.

Given a user u, her complete timeline in a given social media platform P_u, her subset of original posts $P_{uo} \subset P_u$, her subset of shared posts $P_{ur} \subset P_u$, and the set of URLs (links) contained in her posts L_u, we define the different roots of influence over a user as:

- $\vec{Micro}_u = (p_1, p_2, ... p_n), p_i \in P_{uo}$
- $\vec{Meso}_u = (p_1, p_2, ... p_m), p_j \in P_{ur}$
- $\vec{Macro}_u = (l_1, l_2, ... l_o), l_k \in L_u$

Vectors of posts representing the micro and meso influences over a user are then broken into smaller units, in this case n-grams (unigrams, bigrams and trigrams). For that purpose we parse the posts to remove all URLs as well as numeric and punctuation symbols. We also remove all stopwords based on the Ranks NL List.[11] As in [30], we also remove all those infrequent n-grams that appear only once in the corpus. Giving the set of n-grams obtained after preprocessing all the post, W_p, we define the micro and meso vectors of the user u as:

- $V\vec{micro}_u = (w_1, w_2, ... w_n), w_i \in P_{uo}$ and $w_i \in W_p$
- $V\vec{meso}_u = (w_1, w_2, ... w_m), w_j \in P_{ur}$ and $w_i \in W_p$

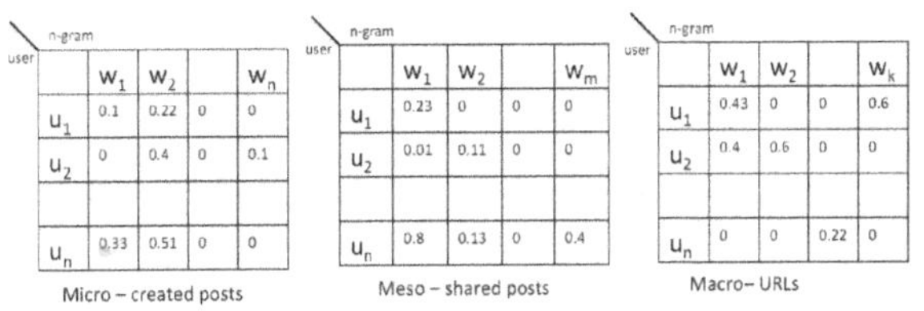

Figure 1: Vector representation of roots of radicalisation

The value of each n-gram in the micro vector of the user u is computed as the frequency of the n-gram in the posts created by the user, normalised by the number of posts created by the user, $val(w_i) = freq(w_i)/|P_{uo}|$.

The value of each n-gram in the meso vector of the user u is computed as the frequency of the n-gram in the posts shared by the user, P_{ur}, normalised by the number posts shared by the user, $val(w_j) = freq(w_j)/|P_{ur}|$

In the case of the macro influence, we perform automatic data scrapping over the URLs included in $\vec{Macro}_u$ by automatically parsing the HTML and extracting the title and description of the websites. For YouTube videos we also include their titles and descriptions. Giving the set of n-grams obtained after preprocessing all the links W_l we define the macro vector of the user u as:

- $V\vec{macro}_u = (w_1, w_2, ... w_o), w_k \in L_u$ and $w_k \in W_l$

The value of each word in the macro vector of the user u is computed as the frequency of the n-gram in all the URL entries shared by the user L_u, normalised by the number of URLs $val(w_k) = frequ(w_k)/|L_u|$

Please note that, while we include the macro vector in our model, it has not been possible for us to compute a complete representation of this vector for all users in our experiments (Section 4). 63% of the URLs we collected to generate the macro vectors point to tweets, YouTube videos, and other websites that are now closed. Therefore, while we keep the **macro vector** in our model for completeness, we have **discarded it from our analysis**. We will therefore use only the micro and meso vector representations to determine the level of radicalisation influence over the user.

3.2 Detecting Radicalisation Influence

To measure the influence of each individual root on the radicalisation process of an individual we based our idea on previous approaches [6, 22, 28, 35], who have shown that language is a key descriptor of radicalised behaviour. Our hypothesis is that, if any of the previous extracted vectors contains radicalised terminology, that means that there is a certain influence over a user.

Note that, at not point we aim to claim that the user is radicalised, but we aim to estimate the level of radicalisation influence (individual, social, and global) a user is undergoing.

Compiling Radicalisation Terminology. The use of radicalised terminology has been extensively studied in the state of the art from both, computational and social science approaches. Lexicons have been developed by experts, and have also been created from ISIS generated material, such as the Dabiq [12] and Inspire [13] magazines.

---

[11]https://www.ranks.nl/stopwords/

[12]https://en.wikipedia.org/wiki/Dabiq_(magazine)
[13]https://en.wikipedia.org/wiki/Inspire_(magazine)

Term	Translation and definition	Variants
1. Abu Mus'ab az-Zarqawi	ISIS's spiritual founder & a former leader of al-Qaeda in Iraq	Abu Musab az-Zarqawi
2. Al-'Adu al-qarib العدو القريب	The near enemy - In the perception of jihaids these are local Muslim governments	Al-Adu al-qarib
3. Al-'Adu al-bai'd العدو البعيد	The far enemy - - In the perception of jihaids these are Western governments	Al-Adu al-baid

Figure 2: ICT Radicalisation Glossary

In this work we have collected, integrated and extended existing lexicons with the aim of providing a wider set of terms and expressions representing radicalisation terminology. The integrated lexicons are summarised below:

- ICT Glossary: created by experts of the International Institute for Counter Terrorism,[14] this glossary contains a total of 100 terms or expressions with their variants in both, English and Arabic. A screenshot with some of these expressions and their variants is displayed in Figure 2
- Saffron Experts: created by experts of the Romanian Intelligence Service as part of their participation in the Saffron EU project.[15] This lexicon contains 22 terms and expressions with their variants, only in English.
- Saffron Dabiq Magazines: this lexicon has been also generated by the Saffron EU project by compiling the list of most common terms from 27 editions of the Dabiq and Inspire Magazines. These magazines are generated by ISIS and constitute a key medium to spread their propaganda. This lexicon is composed by 257 English terms, no variants included.
- Rowe and Saif: this lexicon was generated by [28] and it is composed of 7 English terms, no variances included.

To merge these lexicons we consider as one unique lexical entry the term and their variances. We first incorporate syntactic variances of each term, particularly: (i) lowercase (e.g., Al-'Adu al-bai'd → al-'adu al-bai'd), (ii) removal of apostrophes (e.g., → Al-Adu al-baid), (iii) removal of hyphens (e.g., → Al 'Adu al bai'd) and (iv) removal of diacritics (e.g., Amīrul-Mu'minīn → Amir al-Mu'minin). If two lexicons contain a lexical entry with at least one term in common, we merge these entries in one unique one in the final lexicon. The final lexicon contains 305 entries, including 556 terms, expressions and variances.

Computing Influence. To compute the radicalisation influence of the different roots over the user u we compute the cosine similarity between the micro and meso vectors and the generated lexicon $\vec{L}$. As explained in Section 3.1, we have not been able to compute the macro vectors due to lots of URLs being now closed. We however add here the computation of macro influence for completeness.

$$MicroInfluence(u) = sim(\vec{Vmicro_u}, \vec{L}) = \frac{\vec{Vmicro_u} \bullet \vec{L}}{|\vec{Vmicro_u}| \times |\vec{L}|}$$

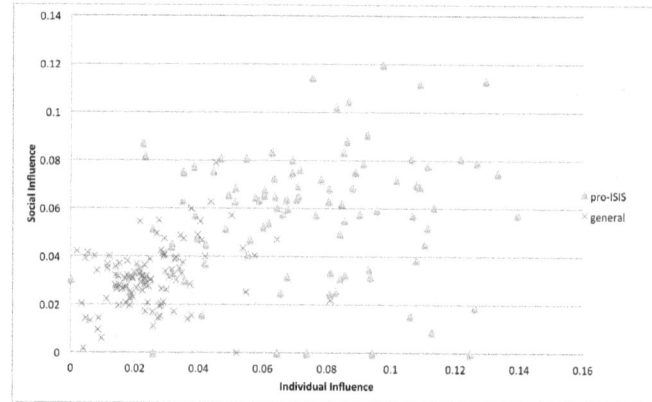

Figure 3: Individual and Social Influence

$$MesoInfluence(u) = sim(\vec{Vmeso_u}, \vec{L}) = \frac{\vec{Vmeso_u} \bullet \vec{L}}{|\vec{Vmeso_u}| \times |\vec{L}|}$$

$$MacroInfluence(u) = sim(\vec{Vmacro_u}, \vec{L}) = \frac{\vec{Vmacro_u} \bullet \vec{L}}{|\vec{Vmacro_u}| \times |\vec{L}|}$$

3.3 Predicting Radicalisation Influence

Collaborative Filtering (CF) strategies make automatic predictions (filter) about the interests of a user by collecting preference information from many users (collaborating)[32]. This approach usually consists of two steps: 1) look for users that have a similar rating pattern to that of the active user (the user for whom the prediction is done), and 2) use the ratings of users found in step 1 to compute the predictions for the active user. In our model, items are n-grams (terms and expressions used by the users) and ratings are the values of those n-grams (computed based on their frequency) in the posts created and shared by the users. The Purpose of using CF strategies is to predict the future micro, meso and macro influences for a user.

4 EVALUATION

4.1 Evaluation Set Up

We use two publicly available datasets to study radicalisation, from Kaggle datascience community. The first dataset contains 17,350 tweets from 112 distinct pro-ISIS accounts.[16] Based on a three-month period study, users were identified using a set of keywords, such as Dawla, Amaq, Wilayat, etc., and filtered based on their use of images (ISIS flags, images of radical leaders like al-Baghdadi, Anwar Awlaki) and on their network of followers/followers.[17]

The second dataset was created as a counterpoise of the previous dataset. It contains 122K tweets from 95,725 distinct users collected on two separate days 7/4/2016 and 7/11/2016. Tweets were collected based on the following keywords (isis, isil, daesh, islamicstate, raqqa, Mosul, 'islamic state').[18] Many of these accounts have now been blocked. To ensure that this dataset contains only users that are **not pro-ISIS** (they could be anti-ISIS or neutral), we randomly selected 112 of them that are still active today. We have collected the timelines of 112 of these users (197,743 tweets in total). To

---

[14]https://www.ict.org.il
[15]http://www.saffron-project.eu/

[16]https://www.kaggle.com/fifthtribe/how-isis-uses-twitter
[17]http://blog.kaggle.com/2016/06/03/dataset-spotlight-how-isis-uses-twitter/
[18]https://www.kaggle.com/activegalaxy/isis-related-tweets

Table 2: Classification results

Classifier	P	R	F1	P	R	F1	avgF1
J48	0.862	0.853	0.857	0.870	0.879	0.874	0.866
N Bayes	0.904	0.895	0.899	0.907	0.916	0.912	**0.906**
Log R	0.901	0.863	0.882	0.883	0.916	0.899	0.891

Table 3: Prediction results for micro and meso vectors

CF algorithim	P	R	MAE
pro-ISIS micro	0.792	0.655	0.068
pro-ISIS meso	0.686	0.711	0.082
neutral micro	0.86	0.66	0.11
neutral meso	0.872	0.51	0.15

verify that these accounts are not pro-ISIS, we randomly selected and manually checked 40 of these accounts, using two annotators (authors), who agreed (inter annotator agreement of 1.0 - Cohen's Kappa) that these accounts do not show signs of support to ISIS.

Micro and meso influence vectors have been computed for each of the 224 users based on their tweets and retweets. Regarding the macro influence vector 5,160 URLs were extracted for the first dataset and 176,877 for the second one. When collecting information for those URLs as described in Section 3.1, we discovered that 63% of those URLs are now closed. These URLs point mainly to other tweets. We have therefore discarded the global influence from the rest of our analysis, since this signal is now incomplete for many of the users in our dataset.

4.2 Results

Figure 3 displays for all users: on the X axis the score of individual influence ($MicroInfluence(u)$, similarity of the micro vector and the lexicon) and on the Y axis the level of social influence ($MesoInfluence(u)$, similarity of the meso vector and the lexicon). We can observe two distinct clusters differentiating the group of pro-ISIS vs. general users. As expected, individual and social influences of radicalisation are both higher for pro-ISIS users. Although we do not aim to determine radicalisation stances, we created multiple classifiers to observe how the computed individual (micro) and social (meso) influence could help differentiating users in both datasets when used as features for classification. Results of this classification, using 10-fold cross validation, are reported in Table 2. All classifiers obtained more than 86% precision, with the best classifier obtaining an F1 value of 90.6%. The high accuracy is mainly due to the difference in content posted by the pro-ISIS and by the neutral accounts.

To evaluate our prediction model we split the timelines of each user into two sets, the first 80% of the post are used training and the newest 20% for testing. We use 80% of the data to create the micro and meso vectors for all users (see Figure 1). These matrices are then used to predict preferences (with regard to terms and expressions) for a user by considering the preference information (micro and meso vectors, for many users). The training data is therefore composed of a list of user, item, rating, where the items are the terms and expressions used by the user and the ratings are their values, $val(w_i)$, computed based on frequencies (Section 3).

To perform our experiments we used the librec library,[19] and tested multiple recommender algorithms and configurations for our problem.[20] Best results were obtained with the asdvpp recommender [20]. As we can see in Table 3, precision is higher for the neutral user group, while recall is higher for the pro-ISIS group. Our hypothesis is that the time window of prediction may be a key influencing factor, since data for the non pro-ISIS group spans a

longer time period. A key priority is to consider a more fine-grained definition of time in our future work (see Section 5). The Mean Absolute Error (MAE) value is low in all cases. A low value of MAE indicates the effectiveness of the models, since it assess the mean of the absolute differences between the ratings and the predicted values. While there is ample room for improvement, these results demonstrate the possibility of predicting the radicalisation influence, both individual and social, affecting a user by considering information for many users.

5 DISCUSSION

Detection of online radicalisation is faced by multiple challenges. From an accuracy perspective, the majority of the "ground truth" datasets used in previous work lack solid verification. Many such datasets (e.g., [2, 3, 28]) were collected using sets of keywords, where users whose tweets contain those words would be regarded as in the "radicalised" set. However, we continue to observe that many who use radicalisation terminology in their tweets are simply reporting current events (e.g., *"Islamic State hacks Swedish radio station"*, or sharing harmless religious rhetoric (e.g., *"If you want to talk to Allah, pray. If you want Allah to talk to you, read the Qur'an"*, or even countering extremism (*"armed jihad is for defence of muslim nation. Not for establishment of khilafah."*).

There remains a great need for a *gold standard* dataset of accounts to be used for training our detection models. Such a dataset should be manually verified by experts, to ensure that cases such as the above would not be regarded as in the positive set. Currently, we are working with law enforcement agencies and experts to be able to obtain such gold standards. One source of manually identified radical accounts is Ctrl-sec,[21] which uses volunteers to report the existence of ISIS propaganda in social media. Their initiative claims to be the one responsible of closing more than 200,000 Twitter accounts in three years. While these are key mechanisms to fight online radicalisation, the fact that accounts are rapidly closed once identified as radical means that data cannot be further collected and analysed to train automated methods.

From a policing perspective, radicalisation is not a crime. Radicals from all religions and ideologies can freely express their beliefs and practice their freedom-of-speech. However, adopting or preaching for violent-radicalisation is a criminal offence. Nevertheless, none of the related works we encountered made this distinction. In future work we will add violence detection to our methods (e.g., [4]).

We have proposed an approach to measure and predict radicalisation influence using a keyword-based representations of the roots of radicalisation and on a combined lexicon of radical terminology. However, as in the case of generating reliable gold standards, the use of a bag of words approach can be enhanced to consider other factors (such as the semantics of the language, or social network

---

[19]https://www.librec.net
[20]https://www.librec.net/dokuwiki/doku.php?id=AlgorithmList

[21]https://twitter.com/CtrlSec

structures) for a more complete representation. For example, when computing the meso vector (or social influence) we are not currently considering further interactions, such as 'likes', 'replies' or even 'direct messages'. Hence, the social influence could actually be higher than the one reported in our work. While we took these aspects into consideration when designing the approach, this information is not always available for all social networks, and mostly not available in the existing datasets, hence we have discarded these elements for this first version of our model. Similarly, the fact that many of the URLs shared in those posts are no longer available have made us taken the decision of discarding the macro influence out of our analysis.

To perform our predictions we have split the user timeliness into 80-20. However, radicalisation is indeed a process, and therefore, a more fine-grained temporal analysis can and should be considered for prediction. As part of our future work we aim to explore temporal models in recommender systems [10], as well as the use of language models [27] for radicalisation prediction.

To conclude, it is important to highlight that, while in this work we have integrated the knowledge of social science models by considering the 'roots of radicalisation', we have not yet taken into account the different identified stages and factors (Section 1). There is ample room for investigation, since all these elements could be designed and modelled computationally in a variety of ways, which opens a novel and exciting interdisciplinary line of research.

6 CONCLUSIONS

Creating intelligent technologies to automatically identify online radicalisation is a key priority of counter-extremist agencies. However, little effort has been devoted to integrate the knowledge of existing theories of radicalisation in the development of these technologies. In this paper we propose a computational approach for detecting and predicting the radicalisation influence a user is exposed to, grounded on the concept of 'roots of radicalisation', identified in social science models. While our approach constitutes a first step to bridge these disciples, a stronger collaboration is needed to effectively target the problem online radicalisation.

Acknowledgments. Trivalent, H2020, grant agreement 740934.

REFERENCES

[1] Swati Agarwal and Ashish Sureka. 2015. Applying social media intelligence for predicting and identifying on-line radicalization and civil unrest oriented threats. *arXiv preprint arXiv:1511.06858* (2015).
[2] Swati Agarwal and Ashish Sureka. 2015. Using knn and svm based one-class classifier for detecting online radicalization on twitter. In *International Conference on Distributed Computing and Internet Technology*. Springer, 431–442.
[3] Michael Ashcroft, Ali Fisher, Lisa Kaati, Enghin Omer, and Nico Prucha. 2015. Detecting jihadist messages on twitter. In *Intelligence and Security Informatics Conference (EISIC), 2015 European*. IEEE, 161–164.
[4] Amparo Elizabeth Cano Basave, Yulan He, Kang Liu, and Jun Zhao. 2013. A weakly supervised Bayesian model for violence detection in social media. In *Int. Joint Conf. Natural Language Processing*. Nagoya, Japan.
[5] JM Berger and Bill Strathearn. 2013. Who Matters Online: Measuring influence, evaluating content and countering violent extremism in online social networks. *International Centre for the Study of Radicalisation and Political Violence* (2013).
[6] Jonathon M Berger and Jonathon Morgan. 2015. The ISIS Twitter Census: Defining and describing the population of ISIS supporters on Twitter. *The Brookings Project on US Relations with the Islamic World* 3, 20 (2015), 4–1.
[7] Adam Bermingham, Maura Conway, Lisa McInerney, Neil O'Hare, and Alan F Smeaton. 2009. Combining social network analysis and sentiment analysis to explore the potential for online radicalisation. In *Int. Conf. Advances in Social Network Analysis and Mining (ASONAM'09)*.
[8] Randy Borum. 2003. Understanding the terrorist mind-set. *FBI L. Enforcement Bull.* 72 (2003), 7.
[9] Randy Borum. 2016. The Etiology of Radicalization. *The Handbook of the Criminology of Terrorism* (2016), 17.
[10] Pedro G Campos Soto et al. 2011. *Temporal models in recommender systems: an exploratory study on different evaluation dimensions*. Master's thesis.
[11] Joseph A Carter, Shiraz Maher, and Peter R Neumann. 2014. # Greenbirds: Measuring Importance and Influence in Syrian Foreign Fighter Networks. (2014).
[12] Akemi Takeoka Chatfield, Christopher G Reddick, and Uuf Brajawidagda. 2015. Tweeting propaganda, radicalization and recruitment: Islamic state supporters multi-sided twitter networks. In *Proceedings of the 16th Annual International Conference on Digital Government Research*. ACM, 239–249.
[13] Denzil Correa and Ashish Sureka. 2013. Solutions to detect and analyze online radicalization: a survey. *arXiv preprint arXiv:1301.4916* (2013).
[14] Charlie Edwards and Luke Gribbon. 2013. Pathways to violent extremism in the digital era. *The RUSI Journal* 158, 5 (2013), 40–47.
[15] Emilio Ferrara. 2017. Contagion dynamics of extremist propaganda in social networks. *Information Sciences* 418 (2017), 1–12.
[16] Emilio Ferrara, Wen-Qiang Wang, Onur Varol, Alessandro Flammini, and Aram Galstyan. 2016. Predicting online extremism, content adopters, and interaction reciprocity. In *International conference on social informatics*. Springer, 22–39.
[17] Mohammed Hafez and Creighton Mullins. 2015. The radicalization puzzle: A theoretical synthesis of empirical approaches to homegrown extremism. *Studies in Conflict & Terrorism* (2015).
[18] Michael King and Donald M Taylor. 2011. The radicalization of homegrown jihadists: A review of theoretical models and social psychological evidence. *Terrorism and Political Violence* 23, 4 (2011), 602–622.
[19] Jytte Klausen. 2015. Tweeting the Jihad: Social media networks of Western foreign fighters in Syria and Iraq. *Studies in Conflict & Terrorism* 38, 1 (2015).
[20] Yehuda Koren. 2008. Factorization meets the neighborhood: a multifaceted collaborative filtering model. In *Proceedings of the 14th ACM SIGKDD international conference on Knowledge discovery and data mining*. ACM, 426–434.
[21] Arie W Kruglanski, Michele J Gelfand, Jocelyn J Bélanger, Anna Sheveland, Malkanthi Hetiarachchi, and Rohan Gunaratna. 2014. The psychology of radicalization and deradicalization: How significance quest impacts violent extremism. *Political Psychology* 35, S1 (2014), 69–93.
[22] Raúl Lara-Cabrera, Antonio Gonzalez-Pardo, and David Camacho. 2017. Statistical analysis of risk assessment factors and metrics to evaluate radicalisation in Twitter. *Future Generation Computer Systems* (2017).
[23] Ragnhild B Lygre, Jarle Eid, Gerry Larsson, and Magnus Ranstorp. 2011. Terrorism as a process: A critical review of Moghaddam's "Staircase to Terrorism". *Scandinavian journal of psychology* 52, 6 (2011), 609–616.
[24] Clark McCauley and Sophia Moskalenko. 2008. Mechanisms of political radicalization: Pathways toward terrorism. *Terrorism and political violence* 20, 3 (2008).
[25] Fathali M Moghaddam. 2005. The staircase to terrorism: A psychological exploration. *American Psychologist* 60, 2 (2005), 161.
[26] Derek O'Callaghan, Nico Prucha, Derek Greene, Maura Conway, Joe Carthy, and Pádraig Cunningham. 2014. Online social media in the Syria conflict: Encompassing the extremes and the in-betweens. In *Int. Conf. Advances in Social Networks Analysis and Mining (ASONAM)*. Beijing, China.
[27] Jay M Ponte and W Bruce Croft. 1998. A language modeling approach to information retrieval. In *Proceedings of the 21st annual international ACM SIGIR conference on Research and development in information retrieval*. ACM, 275–281.
[28] Matthew Rowe and Hassan Saif. 2016. Mining Pro-ISIS Radicalisation Signals from Social Media Users.. In *Int. Conf. Weblogs and Social Media (ICWSM)*. Cologne, Germany.
[29] Hassan Saif, Thomas Dickinson, Leon Kastler, Miriam Fernandez, and Harith Alani. 2017. A semantic graph-based approach for radicalisation detection on social media. In *European Semantic Web Conference*. Springer, 571–587.
[30] Hassan Saif, Miriam Fernández, Yulan He, and Harith Alani. 2014. On stopwords, filtering and data sparsity for sentiment analysis of twitter. (2014).
[31] Alex P Schmid. 2013. Radicalisation, de-radicalisation, counter-radicalisation: A conceptual discussion and literature review. *ICCT Research Paper* 97 (2013), 22.
[32] Yue Shi, Martha Larson, and Alan Hanjalic. 2014. Collaborative filtering beyond the user-item matrix: A survey of the state of the art and future challenges. *ACM Computing Surveys (CSUR)* 47, 1 (2014), 3.
[33] Mitchell D Silber, Arvin Bhatt, and Senior Intelligence Analysts. 2007. *Radicalization in the West: The homegrown threat*. Police Department New York.
[34] Jaap van der Veen. 2016. Predicting susceptibility to radicalization: An empirical exploration of psychological needs and perceptions of deprivation, injustice, and group threat. (2016).
[35] Matteo Vergani and Ana-Maria Bliuc. 2015. The evolution of the ISIS' language: a quantitative analysis of the language of the first year of Dabiq magazine. *Sicurezza, Terrorismo e Società= Security, Terrorism and Society* 2, 2 (2015), 7–20.
[36] Ines Von Behr. 2013. Radicalisation in the digital era: The use of the Internet in 15 cases of terrorism and extremism. (2013).

Collective Attention towards Scientists and Research Topics

Claudia Wagner
GESIS - Leibniz Institute for the Social Sciences and U. of
Koblenz-Landau
Cologne/Koblenz, Germany
claudia.wagner@gesis.org

Olga Zagovora
GESIS - Leibniz Institute for the Social Sciences
Cologne, Germany
olga.zagovora@gesis.org

Tatiana Sennikova
U. of Koblenz-Landau
Koblenz, Germany
tsennikova@uni-koblenz.de

Fariba Karimi
GESIS - Leibniz Institute for the Social Sciences
Cologne, Germany
fariba.karimi@gesis.org

ABSTRACT

Emergent patterns of collective attention towards scientists and their research may function as a proxy for scientific impact which traditionally is assessed via committees that award prizes to scientists. Therefore it is crucial to understand the relationships between scientific impact and online demand and supply for information about scientists and their work. In this paper, we compare the temporal pattern of information supply (article creations) and information demand (article views) on Wikipedia for two groups of scientists: scientists who received one of the most prestigious awards in their field and influential scientists from the same field who did not receive an award.

Our research highlights that awards function as external shocks which increase supply and demand for information about scientists, but hardly affect information supply and demand for their research topics. Further, we find interesting differences in the temporal ordering of information supply between the two groups: (i) award-winners have a higher probability that interest in them precedes interest in their work; (ii) for award winners interest in articles about them and their work is temporally more clustered than for non-awarded scientists.

KEYWORDS

altmetrics; social-media-metrics; online attention; science of science; Wikipedia

ACM Reference Format:
Claudia Wagner, Olga Zagovora, Tatiana Sennikova, and Fariba Karimi. 2018. Collective Attention towards Scientists and Research Topics. In *WebSci '18: 10th ACM Conference on Web Science, May 27–30, 2018, Amsterdam, Netherlands.* ACM, New York, NY, USA, 5 pages. https://doi.org/10.1145/3201064.3201097

1 INTRODUCTION

The temporal dynamics of online information supply and demand [5] for research topics and scientists may reveal information about their

impact. For example, if a scientist innovates a new research topic, the interest of the general public in the topic will be most likely connected with the interest in the scientists (or the other way around). Therefore the interest will be temporally clustered. If interest in the scientist increases, the topic will probably also gain interest or vice versa. Conversely, if a scientist's works on a research topic had attracted attention from the general public long before anyone was interested in the scientist, then the interest in the research topic was not driven by the scientist since the temporal order is a necessary (but not a sufficient) condition for causality.

In this work, we compare the temporal patterns of information supply (article creations) and information demand (article views) on Wikipedia for two groups of scientists: scientists who received one of the most prestigious awards in their field and influential scientists that work in the same field but did not receive an award.

Our research highlights that awards function as external shocks which increase information supply and demand about scientists, but hardly affect the demand and supply for information about research topics. Though 95% of articles about scientists have been created before they received an award, information supply is impacted by awards since we find a discontinuity in the growth patterns during the time of the award. After the award, articles about award-winners start to grow much faster than those of non-awarded scientists, while the growth pattern is identical for both groups before that day.

Further, we find interesting differences in the temporal ordering of information supply about scientists and their research topics within the two groups: for award winners information supply about scientists and their research topics is temporally more clustered than for non-award winners. That means for award-winners articles about their research topics are created around the same time as the article about the scientist, while for non-award winners larger time-lags are observed. Award-winners also have a higher probability that interest in them precedes interest in their work, while for non-awarded scientists, 90% (for award-winners only 73%) of the articles about their research topics have been created before the article about the scientist was created. It is not surprising that for both groups the majority of topics were described on Wikipedia before the articles about the scientist was created, since "normal science" is cumulative [9]. That means most scientists work on research topics that have attracted attention in the past. But for award-winners we find more exceptions; 27% of their research

WebSci'18, May 27-30, 2018, Amsterdam, Netherlands

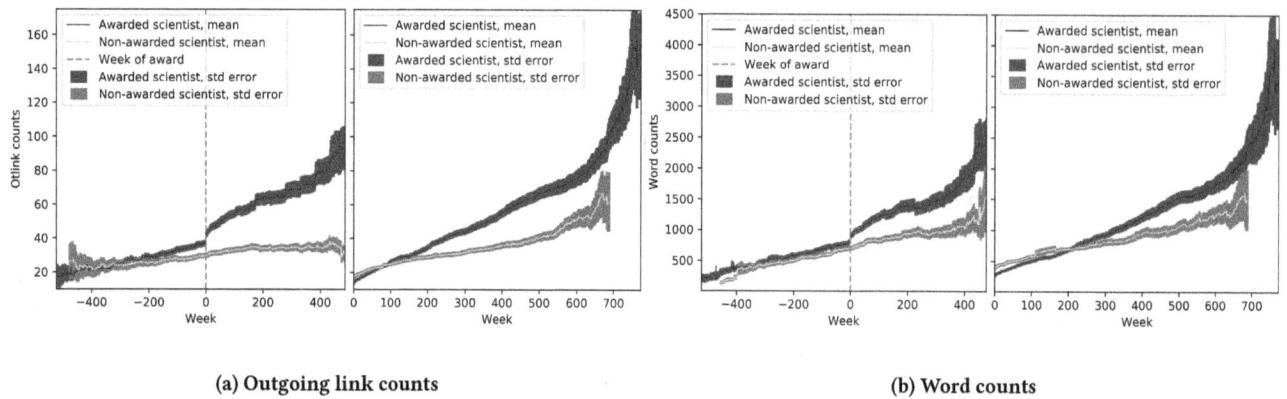

(a) Outgoing link counts

(b) Word counts

Figure 1: Cumulative growth of articles on Wikipedia: article length is measured via outgoing links in subfigure (1a) and via word counts in subfigure (1b). The zero point refers either to the week when the scientist was awarded (dashed red line) or the week when the article about the scientist was created (in plots without dashed red line). For the non-awarded scientists we picked a random week out of the range during which awards happened (i.e. between 2008-03-27 and 2015-10-12) as placebo points. One can see a discontinuity in the growth of outlinks and words that is related with the award.

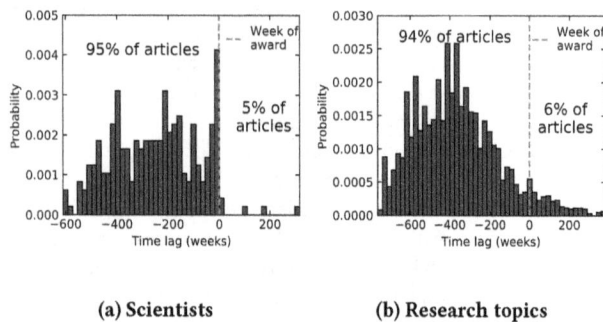

(a) Scientists

(b) Research topics

Figure 2: Time lag between the award and the creation date for articles about awarded scientist in subfigure (2a) and for their research topics in subfigure (2b). The zero point on the x-axis refers to the week of the award. Most articles about awarded scientists and their research topics have been created before they received the award.

topics become of interest to the general public after the scientists attracted attention on Wikipedia. One potential explanation is that award winners may innovate new topics or work on relatively new topics. Examples of Wikipedia articles about research topics that were created after the article of the scientists, provide anecdotal evidence for this explanation: Bayesian Networks after Judea Pearl, Public key cryptography after Whitfield Diffie and Martin Hellman, and Tablet PC after Charles P. Thacker.

To our best knowledge, this is the first study that investigates the impact of scientific awards on the production and consumption of information on Wikipedia. We hope that this work is relevant for the Altmetrics community since it sheds light on the temporal dynamics of supply and demand for information about scientists and their research topics online.

2 DATA AND METHODS

We use Wikipedia article creation dates, edits and views as a proxy for online attention. All data were collected in August 2016. Our code, stopwords list, and datasets are available online[1]. Both datasets of awarded and non-awarded scientist contain the same number of academics from different fields: 57 Physicists, 18 Mathematicians, 18 Computer Scientists, 50 Chemists, 58 Medicine and Physiology researchers, 9 Biologists, and 54 Economists. All together, there are 262 unique researchers in each dataset.

Awarded scientists: This dataset focuses on scientists from the aforementioned fields whose work was honoured through some of the most prestigious academic prizes. We consider the awards between 2008 and 2015, since the Wikipedia page view statistics are not available for earlier years. Within this time frame, we compile a list of winners of the following prizes and awards: Nobel Prize (77 winners), Abel Prize (10), Fields Medal (8), Turing Award (10), IEEE Medal of Honor (8), and International Prize for Biology (9). We also include 163 Thomson Reuters Citation Laureates[2] (23 of whom also received the Nobel Prize), which are selected for outstanding contributions based on the citation impact of their published research. We manually map these winners to the corresponding Wikipedia articles in the English edition, and record their scientific field, gender, award year, and the date when the Wikipedia article was created. The final sample consists of 262 awarded scientists and is available online[3].

Non-awarded Scientists: For a fair comparison, we select a sample of influential, highly cited scientists who worked at the same time, in the same scientific fields as the award winners, using the Thomson Reuters database of Highly Cited Scientists[1]. We use all records between 2001 and 2015 and remove scientists who have

---

[1]https://github.com/tsennikova/scientists-analysis (accessed Apr. 11, 2018) and https://github.com/gesiscss/scientists-analysis-wikipedia (accessed Apr. 11, 2018)
[2]http://stateofinnovation.thomsonreuters.com/hall-of-citation-laureates (accessed Jul. 28, 2016)
[3]https://github.com/tsennikova/scientists-analysis/blob/master/data/seed/seed_creation_date.json (accessed Apr. 11, 2018)

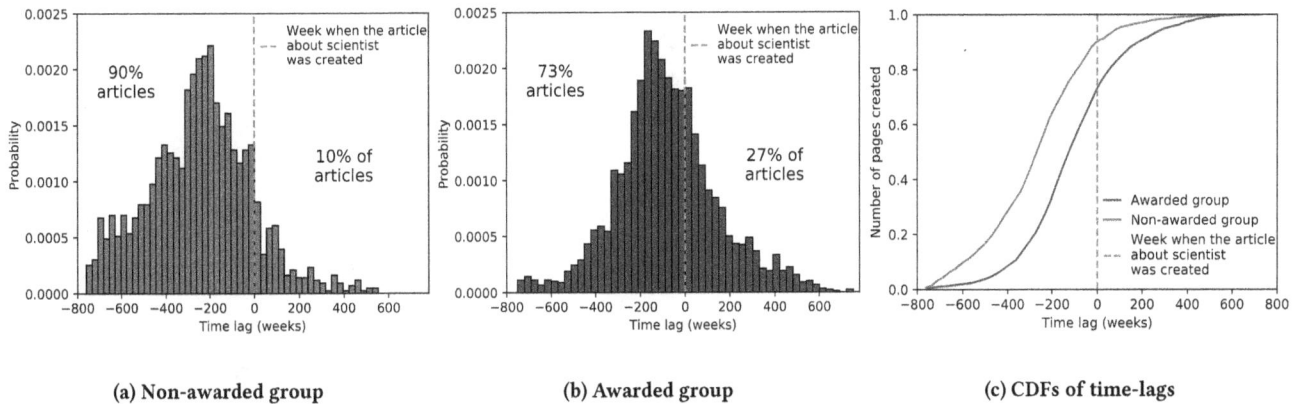

(a) Non-awarded group   (b) Awarded group   (c) CDFs of time-lags

Figure 3: Time-lags between creation dates of Wikipedia articles about scientists and their research topics. The zero point on the x-axis corresponds to the week when the article about the scientist was created. Subfigure (3a) shows that the time-lag is negative for 90% of all articles about research topics of non-awarded scientists. This suggests that most articles about research topics have been created before the articles about the non-awarded scientists. For awarded-scientists we see a similar pattern in (3b), but the fraction of articles about research topics that are created after the article about the scientist was created is higher (25%) for awarded scientists than for non-awarded scientists (10%). Subfigure (3c) shows that articles about research topics of non-awarded scientists are created earlier than those of awarded scientists relative to the creation date of articles about scientists.

received an award. Finally, we draw a random stratified sample of 262 academics with the same distribution across scientific fields as in the awarded dataset. We also map these researchers to articles in the English Wikipedia and add information about their scientific field and the date when the Wikipedia article was created (available online[4]).

Scientific Topics: For all researcher in our sample we analyze their Wikipedia article and construct a list of scientific topics related to the scientist. For that, we extract all outgoing links from the articles about scientists in the English Wikipedia. Each of these articles has a category section (found at the bottom of the page) which displays a subject area of the article, and helps readers to navigate through related concepts. We use this concept list and a manually created set of stop words (available online[5]) to remove articles that are related with a scientists but are not related to research areas (e.g. locations, institutions). We evaluate our filtering approach by comparing the algorithmic assessment with a manual assessment for 10 randomly selected articles about scientists and all outgoing links from these articles. The evaluation results show that our filtering method is very effective: the overall accuracy is 0.96, precision is 0.93, and recall is 0.9. Overall, we construct a list of 1,911 topics[6] that are related to awarded scientists and 1,070 topics[7] that are related to non-awarded scientists.

Wikipedia page views: We collect daily page views of all articles about scientists and their research topics. We use page view statistics from the project Wiki Trends[2], which itself is based on the Wikimedia data dumps[3]. Wiki Trends data provides aggregated number of daily visits to Wikipedia articles and all redirects to them, collected from the English edition. In order to eliminate influences of daily and seasonal fluctuations of article views, we normalize the data as follows:

$$\bar{V}_{i,d} = \frac{V_{i,d} * max(M)}{M_d}. \tag{1}$$

where $V_{i,d}$ refers to the number of visits to an article i on day d, M_d is the number of Wikipedia Main Page views for the same day, and $max(M)$ is the maximum number of Wikpedia Main Page views. We collect page views that happened between 01.01.2008 and 01.05.2016.

3 RESULTS

Information supply: First we explore how collective attention on Wikipedia is affected by external events such as awards, looking at the temporal order of article creations and edits on Wikipedia. Figure 1 shows that articles for awarded and non-awarded scientists grow similarly before the award. But the award creates a discontinuity since articles of awarded scientists start to grow faster than those of their non-awarded colleagues; more hyperlinks and more words are added. This suggests that the award triggers additional information supply, though most articles about awarded scientists and their research topics are created before they receive the award (see Figure 2).

But what came first: the interest in the scientist or the interest in her research? To address this question, we examine the time lag between the article creation about scientists and the scientific topics associated with them. We compare the differences in weeks between the creation dates. The time lag is positive if the topic

---

[4]https://github.com/tsennikova/scientists-analysis/blob/master/data/baseline/baseline_creation_date.json (accessed Apr. 11, 2018)

[5]https://github.com/tsennikova/scientists-analysis/blob/master/data/neighbors/stop_list.txt (accessed Apr. 11, 2018)

[6]https://github.com/tsennikova/scientists-analysis/blob/master/data/neighbors/seed_neighbors_list_clean_en.json (accessed Apr. 11, 2018)

[7]https://github.com/tsennikova/scientists-analysis/blob/master/data/neighbors/baseline_neighbors_list_clean_en.json (accessed Apr. 11, 2018)

(a) View counts for scientists

(b) View counts for research topics

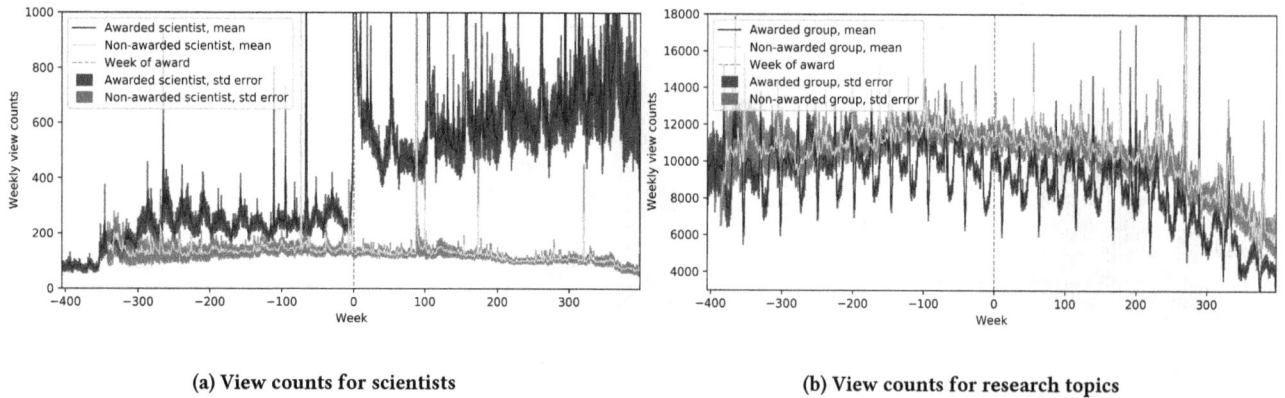

Figure 4: Weekly view counts for articles about scientists and research topics. The zero point refers to the week when the scientists was awarded (dashed red line). For the non-awarded scientists we picked a random week out of the range during which awards happened (i.e. between 2008-03-27 and 2015-10-12) as placebo points. One can see that the information demand on scientists is clearly impacted by the award, however the interest in research topics associated with the scientists seems to be unaffected.

article was created after the article about the scientist, and it is negative otherwise. Figure 3 shows the probability density function of time lags for both groups of scientists. The zero point on the x-axis refers to the week when the article about the scientist was created. One can see that for both groups most articles about research topics that are associated with a scientist are created before the article about the scientist is created. That means, information supply for research topics usually precedes information supply for scientists. This is not surprising since "normal science" is cumulative [9] and most scientists work on research topics that have attracted attention in the past. But award-winners have a higher probability that interest in them precedes interest in their work. For award winners 27% of articles about research topics related to the scientist have been created after the article about the scientist was created, while for non-award winners only 10% of the articles have been created after the article about the scientist was created. One potential explanation for this difference is that award winners are more likely to innovate new topics or work on relatively new topics and therefore articles about these topics have not yet been created.

Figure 3 also shows that the dispersion of the time-lag distribution for award winners is lower which means that the temporal distances between the creation dates of articles about award-winners and their research topics vary less than for non-award winners. This suggests that interest in scientists and their research topics is more interrelated for award-winners than for non-award winners.

Information demand: So far we have seen that awards impact the production of new information on Wikipedia. Articles about scientists grow faster after they receive an award. However, it remains unclear how the consumption of information is affected by the award. Is the demand for information about scientists and their research topics increasing after they win an award? And how long-lasting is this effect?

Figure 4 shows that the information demand for scientists is impacted by the award, since we see a clear discontinuity in the

view counts for articles about scientists who won an award. For non-awarded scientists we pick a random day out of the range during which awards happened (i.e. between 2008-03-27 and 2015-10-12) as placebo points to compute a baseline. The baseline indicates how much change we would expect to see by chance. The discontinuity which we see in Figure 4 clearly goes beyond what we would expect by chance. Also the increased information demand seems to remain rather stable over time. Even 300 weeks after the award, we see that the information demand for awarded scientists is on average higher than those for non-awarded scientists. Interestingly, we see that the information demand for articles about research topics associated with the award-winners seems to be unaffected by the award (cf. Figure 4b).

4 RELATED WORK

Quantifying and predicting scientific success is a topic of high interest for the academic community [4, 6, 11, 14]. While it is clear that online attention to scientists does not always coincide with their academic rigor [12], more research is needed to understand the reasons of such inconsistencies, and the meaning behind them.

Work on collective attention has mainly focused on the consumption of information [8, 15–17] and has shown information consumption correlates with real-world events, such as the spread of influenza [7], box office returns [10] and scientific performance [13].

Only recently researchers started exploring the interplay between information production and consumption. In [5] the authors show that the production of new information on Wikipedia is associated with significant shifts of collective attention measured via article views. That means, in many cases, demand for information precedes its supply. However, unexpected events may lead to almost instantaneously article creations which are followed by a short period of high information demand. A scientific award can be an expected or an unexpected event. Therefore, it is unclear if new articles about scientists will be created on Wikipedia directly after the award, even if no changes in information demand are observed before the award. Our work shows that in most cases articles about scientist and research topics precede the award. However, we see that awards boost the demand for information about scientists and that the increased demand lasts over the next few years.

5 DISCUSSION

How does an award impact information supply and consumption online? If awards would be totally unexpected and hit scientists randomly, they would lead to almost instantaneous article creations which would be followed by a short increase in information demand [5]. Our work shows a different pattern and suggests that awards are probably not so unexpected and have long term effects. 95% of the articles about scientists are created before they receive an award, but information supply is impacted by awards since articles about award-winners grow faster than those of non-awarded scientists. Also information supply is impacted by the award since we find a discontinuity in the view counts in the week when the prize was awarded. Interestingly the increased information demand is rather stable over time. Even five years after the award, we see that the information demand for awarded scientists is on average higher than the demand for non-awarded scientists.

The discontinuity which we see during the week when the prizes are awarded suggests that awards may have a causal effect on information production and consumption. However, to establish a hard causal link future research is necessary since other factors that correlate with awards may exist and confound our analysis.

We also find interesting differences between the two groups of scientists when looking at the information production side. For award-winners articles about them and their research topics are temporally more clustered than for non-award winners. Award-winners also have a higher probability that interest in them precedes interest in their work. One potential explanation is that award winners are more connected with their research topic since they may innovate new topics or work on relatively new topics. Examples of topic articles that were created after the article of the scientist provide anecdotal evidence for this explanation: Bayesian Networks after Judea Pearl, Public key cryptography after Whitfield Diffie and Martin Hellman, and Tablet PC after Charles P. Thacker. However, further research is necessary to explore the different types of relationships between scientists and their research topics that will lead to the creation of a hyperlink on Wikipedia.

6 CONCLUSIONS

The goal of this work was to understand the impact of awards on the production and consumption of information about scientists and their research topics on Wikipedia.

Our work shows that (i) scientists who win a prestigious prize attract more attention afterwards (i.e., information supply and demand increases but only for articles about scientists); (ii) information supply for award winners and their research topics is temporally more clustered than for non-award winners; and (iii) information supply for award winners is more likely to precede information supply for their research topics compared to non-award winner.

For future work it would be interesting to extend this group level analysis with an individual level analysis and further investigate the different types of relationships between scientists and their research topics that may lead to a hyperlink on Wikipedia. We also collected gender information about scientists and plan to compare the information supply and demand for female and male award-winners and influential scientists that did not receive an award in future work.

7 ACKNOWLEDGMENTS

This work is part of the DFG-funded research project *metrics (project number: 314727790). Further information on the project can be found at https://metrics-project.net.

REFERENCES

[1] 2016. Thomson Reuters database of Highly Cited Scientists. http://hcr.stateofinnovation.thomsonreuters.com/page/archives. Accessed: 2016-06-28.
[2] 2016. Wiki Trends Project. http://www.wikipediatrends.com/. Accessed: 2016-06-28.
[3] 2016. Wikimedia Data Dumps. https://dumps.wikimedia.org/. Accessed: 2016-06-28.
[4] Judit Bar-Ilan, Stefanie Haustein, Isabella Peters, Jason Priem, Hadas Shema, and Jens Terliesner. 2012. Beyond citations: Scholars' visibility on the social Web. (2012). http://arxiv.org/abs/1205.5611 17th International Conference on Science and Technology Indicators, Montreal, Canada, 5-8 Sept. 2012.
[5] Giovanni Luca Ciampaglia, Alessandro Flammini, and Filippo Menczer. 2015. The production of information in the attention economy. *Scientific Reports* 5 (2015), 9452. https://doi.org/10.1038/srep09452
[6] Santo Fortunato, Carl T. Bergstrom, Katy Börner, James A. Evans, Dirk Helbing, Staša Milojević, Alexander M. Petersen, Filippo Radicchi, Roberta Sinatra, Brian Uzzi, Alessandro Vespignani, Ludo Waltman, Dashun Wang, and Albert-László Barabási. 2018. Science of science. *Science* 359, 6379 (March 2018), eaao0185. https://doi.org/10.1126/science.aao0185
[7] Jeremy Ginsberg, Matthew H. Mohebbi, Rajan S. Patel, Lynnette Brammer, Mark S. Smolinski, and Larry Brilliant. 2009. Detecting influenza epidemics using search engine query data. *Nature* 457, 7232 (Feb. 2009), 1012–1014. https://doi.org/10.1038/nature07634
[8] Nathan Oken Hodas and Kristina Lerman. 2012. How Visibility and Divided Attention Constrain Social Contagion. In *Proceedings of the 2012 ASE/IEEE International Conference on Social Computing and 2012 ASE/IEEE International Conference on Privacy, Security, Risk and Trust (SOCIALCOM-PASSAT '12)*. IEEE Computer Society, Washington, DC, USA, 249–257. https://doi.org/10.1109/SocialCom-PASSAT.2012.129
[9] Thomas S. Kuhn. 2012. *The Structure of Scientific Revolutions: 50th Anniversary Edition.* University of Chicago Press, Chicago 60637.
[10] Márton Mestyán, Taha Yasseri, and János Kertész. 2013. Early Prediction of Movie Box Office Success Based on Wikipedia Activity Big Data. *PLOS ONE* 8, 8 (Aug. 2013), e71226. https://doi.org/10.1371/journal.pone.0071226
[11] Orion Penner, Raj K. Pan, Alexander M. Petersen, Kimmo Kaski, and Santo Fortunato. 2013. On the Predictability of Future Impact in Science. *Scientific Reports* 3 (Oct. 2013), 3052. https://doi.org/10.1038/srep03052
[12] Anna Samoilenko and Taha Yasseri. 2014. The distorted mirror of Wikipedia: a quantitative analysis of Wikipedia coverage of academics. *EPJ Data Science* 3, 1 (Dec. 2014), 1. https://doi.org/10.1140/epjds20
[13] Hua-Wei Shen and Albert-László Barabási. 2014. Collective credit allocation in science. *Proceedings of the National Academy of Sciences* 111, 34 (2014), 12325–12330. https://doi.org/10.1073/pnas.1401992111
[14] Roberta Sinatra, Dashun Wang, Pierre Deville, Chaoming Song, and Albert-László Barabási. 2016. Quantifying the evolution of individual scientific impact. *Science* 354, 6312 (2016). https://doi.org/10.1126/science.aaf5239
[15] Mike Thelwall, Kayvan Kousha, Katrin Weller, and Cornelius Puschmann. 2012. *Chapter 9 Assessing the Impact of Online Academic Videos.* Emerald Group Publishing Limited, Chapter 9, 195–213. https://doi.org/10.1108/S1876-0562(2012)0000005011
[16] Lilian Weng, Alessandro Flammini, Alessandro Vespignani, and Filippo Menczer. 2012. Competition among memes in a world with limited attention. *Scientific Reports* 2 (March 2012), 335. https://doi.org/10.1038/srep00335
[17] Fang Wu and Bernardo A. Huberman. 2007. Novelty and collective attention. *Proceedings of the National Academy of Sciences* 104, 45 (Nov. 2007), 17599–17601. https://doi.org/10.1073/pnas.0704916104

Fake News vs Satire: A Dataset and Analysis

Jennifer Golbeck, Matthew Mauriello, Brooke Auxier, Keval H Bhanushali, Christopher Bonk,
Mohamed Amine Bouzaghrane, Cody Buntain, Riya Chanduka, Paul Cheakalos,
Jeannine B. Everett, Waleed Falak, Carl Gieringer, Jack Graney, Kelly M. Hoffman, Lindsay Huth,
Zhenye Ma, Mayanka Jha, Misbah Khan, Varsha Kori, Elo Lewis, George Mirano,
William T. Mohn IV, Sean Mussenden, Tammie M. Nelson, Sean Mcwillie, Akshat Pant,
Priya Shetye, Rusha Shrestha, Alexandra Steinheimer, Aditya Subramanian, Gina Visnansky
University of Maryland
jgolbeck@umd.edu

ABSTRACT

Fake news has become a major societal issue and a technical challenge for social media companies to identify. This content is difficult to identify because the term "fake news" covers intentionally false, deceptive stories as well as factual errors, satire, and sometimes, stories that a person just does not like. Addressing the problem requires clear definitions and examples. In this work, we present a dataset of fake news and satire stories that are hand coded, verified, and, in the case of fake news, include rebutting stories. We also include a thematic content analysis of the articles, identifying major themes that include hyperbolic support or condemnation of a figure, conspiracy theories, racist themes, and discrediting of reliable sources. In addition to releasing this dataset for research use, we analyze it and show results based on language that are promising for classification purposes. Overall, our contribution of a dataset and initial analysis are designed to support future work by fake news researchers.

KEYWORDS

fake news, datasets, classification

ACM Reference Format:
Jennifer Golbeck, Matthew Mauriello, Brooke Auxier, Keval H Bhanushali, Christopher Bonk, Mohamed Amine Bouzaghrane, Cody Buntain, Riya Chanduka, Paul Cheakalos, Jeannine B. Everett, Waleed Falak, Carl Gieringer, Jack Graney, Kelly M. Hoffman, Lindsay Huth, Zhenye Ma, Mayanka Jha, Misbah Khan, Varsha Kori, Elo Lewis, George Mirano, William T. Mohn IV, Sean Mussenden, Tammie M. Nelson, Sean Mcwillie, Akshat Pant, Priya Shetye, Rusha Shrestha, Alexandra Steinheimer, Aditya Subramanian, Gina Visnansky. 2018. Fake News vs Satire: A Dataset and Analysis. In *Proceedings of 10th ACM Conference on Web Science (WebSci'18)*. ACM, New York, NY, USA, Article 4, 5 pages. https://doi.org/10.1145/3201064.3201100

1 INTRODUCTION

"Fake news" was never a technical term, but in the last year, it has both flared up as an important challenge to social and technical

Pope Francis Shocks World, Endorses Donald Trump for President, Releases Statement

TOPICS: Pope Francis Endorses Donald Trump

Figure 1: Fake news.

systems and been co-opted as a political weapon against anything (true or false) with which a person might disagree. Identifying fake news can be a challenge because many information items are called "fake news" and share some of its characteristics. Satire, for example, presents stories as news that are factually incorrect, but the intent is not to deceive but rather to call out, ridicule, or expose behavior that is shameful, corrupt, or otherwise "bad". Legitimate news stories may occasionally have factual errors, but these are not fake news because they are not intentionally deceptive. And, of course, the term is now used in some circles as an attack on legitimate, factually correct stories when people in power simply dislike what they have to say.

If actual fake news is to be combatted at web-scale, we must be able to develop mechanisms to automatically classify and differentiate it from satire and legitimate news. To that end, we have built a hand coded dataset of fake news and satirical articles with the full text of 283 fake news stories and 203 satirical stories chosen from a diverse set of sources. Every article focuses on American politics and was posted between January 2016 and October 2017, minimizing the possibility that the topic of the article will influence the classification. Each fake news article is paired with a rebutting article from a reliable source that rebuts the fake source.

We were motivated both by the desire to contribute a useful dataset to the research community and to answer the following research questions: RQ1: Are there differences in the language of fake news and satirical articles on the same topic such that a word-based classification approach can be successful?

RQ2: Are there substantial thematic differences between fake news and satirical articles on the same topic?

Initial experiments show there is a relatively strong signal here that can be used for classification, with our Naive Bayes-based approach achieving 79.1% with a ROC AUC of 0.880 when differentiating fake news from satire. We also qualitatively analyzed the themes that appeared in these articles. We show that there are both similarities and differences in how these appear in fake news and satire, and we show that we can accurately detect the presence of some themes with a simple word-vector approach.

2 RELATED WORK

We are interested in *truly* fake news in this study - not stories people don't like, stories that have unintentional errors, or satire. We define the term as follows:

> Fake news is information, presented as a news story that is factually incorrect and designed to deceive the consumer into believing it is true.

Our definition builds on the work and analysis of others who have attempted to define this term in recent years, including the following.

Fallis [4] examines the ways people have defined disinformation (as opposed to misinformation). His conclusion is that "disinformation is misleading information that has the function of misleading." More specifically about fake news, researchers in [11] look at the uses of the term. They found six broad meanings of the term "fake news": news satire, news parody, fabrication, manipulation (e.g. photos), advertising (e.g. ads portrayed as legitimate journalism), and propaganda. They identified two common themes: intent and the appropriation of "the look and feel of real news."

In [10], Rubin breaks fake news into three categories: Serious fabrications, large scale hoaxes, and and humorous fakes. They don't explain why they chose these categories instead of some other classification. However, they do go into depth about what each category would contain and how to distinguish them from each other. They also stress the lack of a corpus to do such research, and emphasize 9 guidelines for building such a corpus: "Availability of both truthful and deceptive instances", "Digital textual format accessibility", "Verifiability of ground truth", "Homogeneity in lengths", "Homogeneity in writing matter", "Predefined timeframe", "The manner of news delivery", "Language and culture", and "pragmatic concerns".

The impact of fake news has become increasingly an important issue, due to its potential to impact important events. For example, [1] examined how fake news articles are shared on social media; their analysis suggests that the average American adult saw on the order of one or perhaps several fake news stories in the months around the election and (through a large scale survey) they found that consumers of fake news were more likely to believe stories that favor their preferred candidate or ideology.

In [9], the authors examine the impact of cognitive ability on the durability of opinions based on fake news reports. Four hundred respondents answered an online questionnaire, using a test-control design to see how their impressions and evaluations of an individual (test condition) changed after being told the information they received was incorrect. They found that individuals with lower cognitive ability adjusted their assessments after being told the information they were given was incorrect, but not nearly to the same extent as those with higher cognitive ability. Those with higher cognitive ability, when told they received false information, adjust their assessments in line with those who had never seen the false information to begin with. This was true regardless of other psychographic measures like right-wing authoritarianism and need for closure. This study suggests that for those with lower cognitive capability, the bias created by fake news, while mitigated by learning the initial information was incorrect, still lingers.

Pew Research Center conducted a survey of 1002 U.S. adults to understand attitudes about fake news, its social impact, and individual perception of susceptibility to fake news reports [2]. A majority of Americans believe that fake news is creating confusion about basic facts. This is true across demographic groups, with a correlation between income and the level of concern and across political affiliations. Still, they feel confident that that can tell what is fake when they encounter it, and show some level of discernment between what is patently false versus what is partially false. Seeing fake news more frequently increases the likelihood an individual believes it, creates confusion, and decreases the likelihood that one can tell the difference. Whether this is due to the accuracy of their perception that they can tell the difference, or their predilection to see news as fake is unknown, as the data is self-reported. Twenty three percent acknowledge sharing fake news, with 14% doing so knowingly.

Using the GDELT Global Knowledge graph, which monitors and classifies news stories, the researchers in [12] examined the topics covered by different media groups (such as fake news websites, fact-checking websites, and news media websites) from 2014 to 2016. By tracking the topics discussed across time by these three groups, the researchers were able to determine which groups of media were setting the agenda on different topics. They found that fake news coverage set the agenda for the topic of international relations all three years, and for two years the issues of economy and religion. Overall, fake news was responsive to the agenda set by partisan media on the topics of economy, education, environment, international relations, religion, taxes, and unemployment, indicated an "intricately entwined" relationship between fake news and partisan media. However, in 2016, the data indicates that partisan media became much more responsive to the agendas set by fake news. The authors suggest that future research should look at the flow from fake news to partisan media to all online media.

Researchers in [8] describe several studies investigating the relationships between believing fake news, Cognitive Reflection Test (CRT) scores, tendency to "over claim" (e.g., claim to recognize the name of a fictional historical figure), scores on the authors "bullshit receptivity task" (e.g. rating the profundity of meaningless jargon), and motivated reasoning. They conclude that "people fall for fake news because they fail to think; not because they think in a motivated or identity-protective way."

Our work address several recent calls to action regarding Fake News and the spread of misinformation online (e.g. [6]) by creating a datasets that can be used to (i) analyze and detect fake news and (ii) be used in replication studies.

2.1 Detecting and Classifying Fake News

Looking at how fake news can spread in social media - and what to do about it - [7] describes a potential automated policy for determining when to have a human intervene and check a story being shared (to be used by Facebook/Twitter). They found that automated agents, attempting to pass on only good news and to fact check when appropriate, can actually amplify fake news and lend credibility to it. Their simulations offer insights into when fake news should be addressed and investigated by social media platforms.

In [13], Wang introduced a human-labeled and fact-checked dataset of over 12,000 instances of fake news, in contexts such as political debate, TV ads, Facebook posts, tweets, interview, news release, etc. Each instance was labeled for truthfulness, subject, context/venue, speaker, state, party, and prior history. Additionally, Wang used this new dataset to evaluate three popular learning-based methods for fake news detection, logistic regression, support vector machines, long short-term memory networks (Hochreiter and Schmidhuber, 1997), and a convolutional neural network model (Kim, 2014). Wang goes on to show that a neural network architecture that integrates text and meta-data was more accurate at identifying fake news than the text-only convolutional neural networks baseline.

[3] goes into detail about assessment methods from two approaches: linguistic cues and network analysis. The latter involves information we dont have in our dataset, namely incoming and outgoing links to the article and relevant topics which can be used to create a network. They break the former problem down into data representation and analysis. Their review suggests that the bag of words approach may be useful in tandem with other representations, but not individually. Instead, they suggest a parse tree, as well as using attribute:descriptor pairs to compare with other articles. They also theorize that using a Rhetorical Structure Theory (RST) analytic framework as the distance measure for clustering or other types of algorithms. Finally, they suggest using sentiment as a classifier, as there are often negative emotional undertones in deceptive writing.

The dataset we present in this work contains 283 fake news articles and 203 satirical stories. All articles are focused on American politics, were posted between January 2016 and October 2017, and are in English. The dataset contains the title, a link, and the full text of each article. For fake news stories, a rebutting article is also provided that disproves the premise of the original story.

Below, we describe the process of collecting and labeling stories and the characteristics of the data.

2.2 Collection and Annotation

We established several guidelines at the beginning of this project to guide the collection of fake news and satirical stories:

- A definition of Fake News - "Fake News" has many definitions, but we chose to use "Fake news is information, presented as a news story that is factually incorrect and designed to deceive the consumer into believing it is true." This eliminates legitimate news that may have a factual inaccuracy, satire, and opinion pieces from the scope of our definition.

- American Politics - While fake news is certainly not limited to American politics, we restricted our dataset to that domain to ensure a consistency of topics among all articles. This minimizes the chance that topical differences between fake and satirical stories could affect a classifier.

- Recent articles, posted after January 2016 - The logic here echoes that above; we wanted to ensure that the topics discussed in the articles were similar.

- Diverse sources - There are many fake news and satire websites online and each has hundreds, if not thousands, of articles. It can be tempting to build a large dataset from a few of these sources. However, we wanted to create a highly diverse set with articles from many different sources. Thus, we restricted our dataset to have **no more than five articles from a single website**. Again, this minimizes any chance that a classifier could pick up on the language or style of a certain site when building a model.

- No Borderline Cases - There is a spectrum from fake to satirical news, and this is a fact that we found was exploited by fake news sites. Many fake news websites include disclaimers at the bottom of their pages that they are "satire", but there is nothing satirical about their articles; they simply use this as an "out" from the accusation that they are fake. While working on the borderlines between satire and fake news will be interesting, there is a more pressing challenge to simply differentiate the most obvious cases of each. Thus, we decided our dataset would eliminate any articles that researchers believed fell in a grey area. The fake news stories are all factually incorrect and deceptive. The satirical stores are quite obviously satirical.

Researchers began by identifying fake news and satirical websites. While our goal was not to create a list of sites, this process served our purpose of creating a diverse set of sources. By enumerating websites first, researchers could take responsibility for all the articles taken from an existing site and work would not be duplicated. Each researcher did just that, claiming several fake news or satire sites and providing no more than five articles from each to the dataset. For each article, the researcher provided a text file with the full text and, if the story was a fake news story, they provided a link to a well-researched, factual article that rebutted the fake news story. That may be an article from a fact checking site that specifically debunks a story, or a piece of information that disproves a claim. For example, one fake news story claimed that Twitter banned Donald Trump from the platform. A link to Donald Trump's very active Twitter account proved that this story was false.

When the initial data collection was complete, each article was then reviewed by another researcher. They checked it against all the criteria listed above. Articles that could not be rebutted, that were off topic or out of the time frame, or that were borderline cases were eliminated from the dataset. Inter-rater agreement given by Cohen's kappa was 0.686 with an accuracy of 84.3%.

3 CLASSIFICATION

With a labeled dataset in hand, we could now address RQ1: Are there differences in the language of fake news and satirical articles on the same topic such that a word-based classification approach can be successful?

Table 1: Detailed accuracy measurements for classification of Fake News vs. Satire.

	TP Rate	FP Rate	Precision	Recall	F-Measure	MCC	ROC Area	PRC Area	Class
	0.811	0.236	0.828	0.811	0.819	0.572	0.880	0.907	Fake
	0.764	0.189	0.742	0.764	0.752	0.572	0.880	0.847	Satire
Weighted Avg.	0.791	0.217	0.792	0.791	0.791	0.572	0.880	0.882	

Table 2: Distribution of theme pairs

Pair	C-H	H-S	C-S	H-R	D-H	C-R	C-D	F-H	C-F	R-S	H-P	F-R	D-S	F-S	D-R	C-P	D-P
Overall	19.50%	6.40%	4.10%	7.00%	2.90%	1.90%	1.20%	1.20%	1.40%	1.20%	1.20%	1.00%	0.40%	0.40%	0.40%	0.40%	0.20%
Satire	9.40%	3.40%	0.00%	7.40%	1.50%	1.50%	0.00%	0.50%	1.50%	1.50%	2.00%	1.50%	0.00%	0.00%	0.50%	1.00%	0.50%
Fake	26.90%	8.50%	7.10%	6.70%	3.90%	2.10%	2.10%	1.80%	1.40%	1.10%	0.70%	0.70%	0.70%	0.70%	0.40%	0.00%	0.00%

Our goal with this research question was not to do a deep linguistic analysis of the types of articles, but rather to understand if the basic word usage patterns differed substantially enough that it would allow for relatively accurate classification. With no additional analysis, we built a model to classify an article based only on the language it used. Each article was represented as a word vector with a class of Fake or Satire. We used Weka [5] to train a model using the Naive Bayes Multinomial algorithm and tested with 10-fold cross validation. We achieved accuracy of 79.1% with a ROC AUC of 0.880. Detailed accuracy measurements are shown in table 1. This high-performing model suggests strong differences in the type of language used between the fake news and satire in our dataset.

4 THEMES OF FAKE NEWS VS. SATIRE

After collecting the data, we explored the themes of our articles more deeply. Unlike [10] which looks at the mechanism for sharing fake news, we look at the types of content that are shared. Using a grounded theory open coding approach, our team developed a code book with major themes that appeared across the dataset. We settled on seven codes:

- H - Hyperbolic position against one person or group (e.g. Trump, Clinton, Obama, Islam, refugees)
  Example headline: "Obama Signs Executive Order Banning The Pledge of Allegiance In Schools Nationwide"
- F - Hyperbolic position in favor of one person or group (e.g. Trump, Clinton, Obama, Islam, refugees)
  BECAUSE TRUMP WON THE PRESIDENCY, FORD SHIFTS TRUCK PRODUCTION FROM MEXICO TO OHIO!
- D - Discredit a normally credible source
  MIT Researchers: Global Warming Data Is Complete Bunk
- S - Sensationalist crimes and violence
  George Zimmerman Found DEAD Just Hours After Bragging About Killing Trayvon Martin
- R - Racist messaging
  Trump Has Fired Muslim Sharia Judge Arrested And Charged
- P - Paranormal theories (e.g. Aliens, Flat Earth)
  Donald Trump Says The Earth Is Flat
- C - Conspiracy theories
  Hillary Clinton Busted in the Middle of Huge Pedophilia Ring Cover Up At State Department

Researchers could also leave an article unlabeled if none of the codes applied.

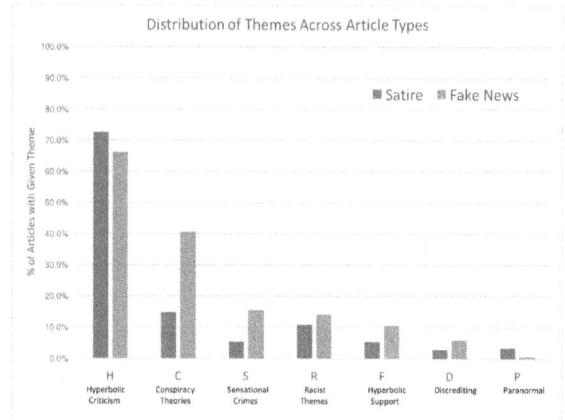

Figure 2: Distribution of themes across article types

Once the code book was finalized and researchers had trained on a subset of articles, they labeled each article with the appropriate codes. Articles could be labeled with multiple codes.

Overall, we found that hyperbolic criticism of a person - usually Trump, Obama, or Clinton - was the most common theme, appearing in more than 2/3rds of articles. Conspiracy theories were also common, appearing in almost 30%. While we were able to identify a common practice of attempting to discredit normally credible sources or the use of paranormal theories (e.g. aliens), these were relatively uncommon, both appearing in less than 5% of articles.

We then compared the distribution of themes within each article type to see if there were major differences in how the themes appeared in fake news vs. satire. Figure 2 shows a side-by-side comparison. The themes followed a generally similar distribution in each article type. However, conspiracy theories were notably more common in fake news stories than in satire. Descriptions of sensationalist crimes were also more common in fake news. Paranormal themes, though uncommon overall, were more apparent in satire than in fake news.

As noted above, articles could have more than one theme, and many did. Overall, 213 articles (43.8%) had multiple themes. This was much more common in fake news ($N = 157, 55.5\%$) than in satire ($N = 56, 27.6\%$). By far the most common pair of themes to appear together were Conspiracy Theories and Hyperbolic Criticism of a person. Examples of these topics include articles about President Obama's birth certificate, the accusation that "illegal aliens" cast 3 million votes in the last election, and that the murder of DNC

Table 3: Accuracy and ROC AUC for Classifying the Themes of Articles

Theme	Accuracy	ROC AUC
H	56.3%	0.583
C	80.1%	0.754
S	89.3%	0.750
R	89.8%	0.669
F	92.4%	0.610
D	96.3%	0.433
P	98.7%	0.672

staffer Seth Rich was orchestrated by George Soros (it was not). This combination appeared on 19.5% of all articles, 26.9% of fake news articles, and 9.4% of satire. It was the most common pairing for both types of article. Among satire articles, the only two other combination that appears on more than 10 articles was Hyperbolic criticism and racist themes. This pair occurred in 7.4% of satirical articles and 6.7% of fake news. Fake news also had popular pairings of Sensationalist Crimes appearing with Hyperbolic Criticism (8.5% of articles) and with Conspiracy Theories (7.1% of articles). Table 2 shows the full data for these theme pair distributions.

4.1 Themes and Classification

4.1.1 Using Themes To Distinguish Fake News from Satire. Our bag of words approach to classification described above was successful, but we wanted to see if including the themes of an article alongside the word vector would improve classification. To do this, we duplicated our word vector dataset and included the themes. We compared the results with this data to those achieved without the themes and found no significant difference in the accuracy or AUC. This suggests that the themes are not providing any real differentiating information that was not already detectable in the word vector itself. We hypothesize if we used these in a classifier that also considered real news, the themes may be more useful.

4.1.2 Detecting Themes from Language. Because some of these themes, which would be uncharacteristic of *real* news, are common in fake news and satire, we investigated if we could automatically determine whether an article contained a particular theme based on the words in the article. Using the same word vector as before, we built a model for each theme separately using only the word vector features.

As shown in table 3, we achieve high accuracy and medium or strong effects for many of the themes. While this is just a preliminary evaluation, it indicates that building useful theme classifiers may be possible and that, in turn, may be useful for understanding and detecting articles that are not "real" news.

5 DISCUSSION

The dataset we have created here, including full text of the articles, labels indicating their type (fake news or satire) and themes, and debunking articles for all fake news is available at https://github.com/jgolbeck/fakenews.git. We hope this dataset will be of use to the community of researchers studying fake news from a variety of perspectives.

Our initial thematic analysis offers insight that may be useful for both automated and qualitative analysis of fake news. Specifically, the fact that Hyperbolic Criticism and Conspiracy Theories are so common in fake news may mean that the presence of these themes may be useful for automatically detecting fake stories. Our preliminary results show that some of these themes can be detected quite accurately, and we believe this is an interesting space for future work.

One concern that arose in our initial discussions and that drove this work is the potential to conflate fake news and satire. Both are untrue stories with differences in intent. And while we found thematic similarities between the two, we also showed that a simple word vector classifier can strongly distinguish between the two. Again, there is much future work to be done here, but the good results we achieved on this dataset suggest that fake news detectors should also be able to tell the difference.

6 CONCLUSIONS

In this paper, we built a dataset of Fake News stories and Satire to serve as a contribution to the Fake News research community. The publicly available dataset includes full text of articles, links to the original stories, rebutting articles for fake news, and thematic codes. We included satirical articles because they, like fake news, are untrue, but vary in their *intention* and we showed preliminary results that indicate it is possible to automatically distinguish between the two types.

We hope this dataset is useful to the research community and that these preliminary results spark future work on understanding the nature of fake news and ways of fighting it.

REFERENCES

[1] Hunt Allcott and Matthew Gentzkow. 2017. *Social media and fake news in the 2016 election.* Technical Report. National Bureau of Economic Research.
[2] Michael Barthel, Amy Mitchell, and Jesse Holcomb. 2016. Many Americans believe fake news is sowing confusion. *Pew Research Center* 15 (2016).
[3] Niall J Conroy, Victoria L Rubin, and Yimin Chen. 2015. Automatic deception detection: Methods for finding fake news. *Proceedings of the Association for Information Science and Technology* 52, 1 (2015), 1–4.
[4] Don Fallis. 2014. A Functional Analysis of Disinformation. *iConference 2014 Proceedings* (2014).
[5] Mark Hall, Eibe Frank, Geoffrey Holmes, Bernhard Pfahringer, Peter Reutemann, and Ian H Witten. 2009. The WEKA data mining software: an update. *ACM SIGKDD explorations newsletter* 11, 1 (2009), 10–18.
[6] Nicco Mele, David Lazer, Matthew Baum, Nir Grinberg, Lisa Friedland, Kenneth Joseph, Will Hobbs, and Carolina Mattsson. 2017. Combating Fake News: An Agenda for Research and Action. (2017).
[7] Yiangos Papanastasiou. 2017. Fake news propagation and detection: A sequential model. (2017).
[8] Gordon Pennycook and David G Rand. 2017. Who falls for fake news? The roles of analytic thinking, motivated reasoning, political ideology, and bullshit receptivity. (2017).
[9] Arne et al. Roets. 2017. Fake news: Incorrect, but hard to correct. The role of cognitive ability on the impact of false information on social impressions. *Intelligence* 65 (2017), 107–110.
[10] Victoria L Rubin, Yimin Chen, and Niall J Conroy. 2015. Deception detection for news: three types of fakes. *Proceedings of the Association for Information Science and Technology* 52, 1 (2015), 1–4.
[11] Edson C Tandoc Jr, Zheng Wei Lim, and Richard Ling. 2017. Defining Fake News A typology of scholarly definitions. *Digital Journalism* (2017), 1–17.
[12] Chris J Vargo, Lei Guo, and Michelle A Amazeen. 2017. The agenda-setting power of fake news: A big data analysis of the online media landscape from 2014 to 2016. *new media & society* (2017), 1461444817712086.
[13] William Yang Wang. 2017. " Liar, Liar Pants on Fire": A New Benchmark Dataset for Fake News Detection. *arXiv preprint arXiv:1705.00648* (2017).

Third Party Tracking in the Mobile Ecosystem

Reuben Binns, Ulrik Lyngs, Max Van Kleek, Jun Zhao, Timothy Libert*, Nigel Shadbolt
Department of Computer Science, University of Oxford
*Reuters Institute for the Study of Journalism, University of Oxford
Oxford
reuben.binns|ulrik.lyngs|max.van.kleek|jun.zhao|nigel.shadbolt@cs.ox.ac.uk
timothy.libert@politics.ox.ac.uk

ABSTRACT

Third party tracking allows companies to identify users and track their behaviour across multiple digital services. This paper presents an empirical study of the prevalence of third-party trackers on 959,000 apps from the US and UK Google Play stores. We find that most apps contain third party tracking, and the distribution of trackers is long-tailed with several highly dominant trackers accounting for a large portion of the coverage. The extent of tracking also differs between categories of apps; in particular, news apps and apps targeted at children appear to be amongst the worst in terms of the number of third party trackers associated with them. Third party tracking is also revealed to be a highly trans-national phenomenon, with many trackers operating in jurisdictions outside the EU. Based on these findings, we draw out some significant legal compliance challenges facing the tracking industry.

CCS CONCEPTS

• **Security and privacy → Economics of security and privacy**; *Software reverse engineering*; • **Applied computing → Law**; • **Networks** → *Mobile and wireless security*;

KEYWORDS

privacy, tracking, behavioural advertising, mobile, android, static analysis, data protection

ACM Reference Format:
Reuben Binns, Ulrik Lyngs, Max Van Kleek, Jun Zhao, Timothy Libert, Nigel Shadbolt. 2018. Third Party Tracking in the Mobile Ecosystem. In *WebSci '18: 10th ACM Conference on Web Science, May 27–30, 2018, Amsterdam, Netherlands*. ACM, New York, NY, USA, 9 pages. https://doi.org/10.1145/3201064.3201089

1 INTRODUCTION

Billions of people use smartphones every day, generating vast amounts of data about themselves. Much of the functionality afforded by these devices comes in the form of applications which derive revenue from monetising user data and displaying behaviourally targeted advertising. Firms with the ability to collect such data have become a significant part of the digital economy [3], with the online advertising industry earning $59.6 billion per year in the U.S. alone [20].

This business model is primarily enabled through 'third-party' trackers [27], which track users via 'first-party' mobile applications, whose developers embed their technology into application source code. Such networks link activity across multiple apps to a single user, and also link to their activities on other devices or mediums like the web. This enables construction of detailed profiles about individuals, which could include inferences about shopping habits, socio-economic class or likely political opinions. These profiles can then be used for a variety of purposes, from targeted advertising to credit scoring and targeted political campaign messages.

This paper aims to provide a high-level empirical overview of the extent of third party tracking on the mobile ecosystem. In particular, we aim to answer the following:

(1) How are third party trackers distributed across apps on the Google Play Store?[1]
(2) Which companies ultimately own these tracking technologies, and in which jurisdictions are they based?
(3) Do different trackers prevail amongst different genres of apps?

Our motivation is to shed light on the status quo, in order that future efforts to address and mitigate third party tracking can be more informed and targeted.

2 BACKGROUND

We begin by introducing previous work on tracker detection methods, and on large-scale field studies of tracking on the web and mobile. Then, to motivate some of the present analysis, we provide an overview of existing approaches to addressing mobile tracking, including end-user controls, OS provider rules, and legal regulation. The shortcomings of the first two approaches have driven a renewed focus on the latter; by surveying the existing state of mobile tracking, we aim to provide insights into the extent to which current tracking activities may be affected by certain key data protection regulations.

2.1 Detecting third party tracking at scale in the wild

The third party tracking ecosystem has been studied on both the web and mobile using a variety of methods. Large scale web tracking studies detect third-party trackers by inspecting network traffic associated with a website. Some approaches use crowd-sourcing

---

[1]We did not study the Apple iOS App Store because there are no equivalently scalable iOS app collection and analysis methods

(e.g. [36, 39]) while others use automated web crawlers (e.g. [15, 23, 32, 39]. In all cases, a small number of dominant trackers are observed.

Several studies of third-party tracking have also been conducted on mobile platforms [10, 36], using both dynamic and static detection methods. Dynamic methods, as in web-based tracking studies, involve inspecting network traffic from the browser / device and identifying any third party destinations that relate to tracking. One common approach has been OS-level instrumentation, such as those of TaintDroid [14], and AppTrace [29]. An alternative to low-level OS instrumentation is to analyse all communications traffic transmitted by an app whilst it is in use [31]. Other methods involve unpacking an application's source code (on Android systems, this comes as an Android Application Package (APK)) and detecting use of third-party tracking libraries [5, 8, 13, 24].

Other aspects of tracking have been studied, including the variety of techniques that are used, from cookies [6, 15, 16] to fingerprinting [2]. A more recent field study by Yu et al. provided a finer-grained view into tracker behaviour, by classifying data being transmitted to trackers as either 'safe' or 'unsafe' [39]. Another factor is the permissions requested by an app, which constrain the kinds of data a third party can obtain; longitudinal research has found that Android apps request additional privacy-risking permissions on average every three months [34].

The crossover between the mobile and web tracking ecosystem has also attracted attention in recent research. Various comparisons have shown that web and mobile tracking are different, both in terms of the companies that operate on each environment [36], and the specific kinds of personal information that are shared by web and mobile versions of the same service [22]. In previous work comparing 5,000 apps and 5,000 websites, it was found that while certain companies dominate both environments, the overlap between top trackers is only partial, even for web and mobile versions of the same service [9].

2.2 Existing approaches to addressing risks of tracking

There are three main approaches for addressing the risks of tracking; end-user privacy controls, industry self-regulation, and traditional legal regulation.

2.2.1 End-user privacy controls.
Tracking exists on both the web and on mobile apps, but web browsers have traditionally enabled end-users to control tracking via default browser settings or through third party plugins. By contrast, no major smartphone platform OS currently gives end-users the ability to block or otherwise control third party tracking by apps (although tracker blocking is available on mobile web browsers). The privacy settings are primarily focused on app-by-app permissions, or permissions regarding certain data types (e.g. location, contacts, etc.). While various changes have been introduced like run-time permissions, and advertising identifier controls [28], these do not address the distinction between first party apps and third party trackers. More recently, awareness-raising tools have been proposed which do reveal the presence of third-parties. They make use of techniques including reverse-engineering of app source code and network traffic analysis [5, 8, 13, 14, 18, 29, 40], allowing identification of personal data

flows from apps to first and third parties. These tools have been used to map data flows and display them to end-users [7, 11, 33, 37]. Such focus on third-party data collection, rather than app-level permissions, may be a more meaningful way to enact privacy choices. However, until such controls are enabled by the OS providers, third party tracking via apps remains largely invisible to end-users. This is in contrast to the web, where millions of users make use of tracker protection tools such as uBlock Origin or Ghostery.

2.2.2 Self-regulation by platforms.
In response to the development and proliferation of trackers, and the lack of wide-scale deployment of effective end-user tracker controls, various efforts have been made by mobile OS platform developers to address the risks. Mobile application developers are required to follow the rules of the app market providers in order for their apps to be listed [4]. Since few consumers use multiple app stores on a single smartphone, these platforms are in a stronger position to impose industry self-regulation than browser vendors, because they have the ability to effectively kick an application off the platform entirely.

Industry-led self-regulatory initiatives have thus far attempted to strike a balance between protecting users from malicious behaviour and creating a relatively permissive environment. With respect to smartphone operating systems, Apple and Google have the power to exert varying degrees of control over the behaviour of apps appearing in their default app stores. Thus far, both of their respective developer agreements permit third-party tracking, although certain user-protective practices are required, such as collecting a replaceable advertising identifier (IDFA / AAID) rather than the permanent device identifier.

More stringent action against third party tracking may also have been held back by vested interests of the OS providers. Both Google and Apple have historically had a stake in the digital advertising industry. Google own several tracker companies such as DoubleClick and others. Apple used to take a cut of advertising revenue from ad network trackers in iPhone apps, through the iADs program, but this scheme ended in 2016.

2.2.3 Legal regulation.
These self-regulatory efforts, such as they are, sit alongside a variety of specific legal regulations with varying levels of enforcement in different countries around the world. Perhaps the most stringent and far-sighted of these is the data protection legal regime in Europe. With updated rules incoming this year in the form of the European Union's General Data Protection Regulation, new enforcement powers including the issuing of larger fines and scope for indefinitely suspending processing may substantially curtail the activities of third party trackers.

For instance, the specific identities and purposes of third party trackers will have to be made transparent to the data subject (i.e. the user of the app); and special safeguards must be applied in the case of children. While profiling of children is not outright prohibited by the GDPR, the Article 29 Working Party (the EU body responsible for providing guidance on data protection), advise that organisations should 'refrain from profiling them for marketing purposes'.

Regarding transfer of data across borders, while existing requirements are not fundamentally different under the GDPR, transnational data transfer is likely to receive additional scrutiny in light of the introduction of stronger enforcement powers. Under the existing regime, personal data is permitted to flow from one jurisdiction to another, subject to compliance with certain conditions. The least onerous condition is if the recipient organisation is based in a country whose existing data protection regime has been assessed by the European Commission and deemed 'adequate'. Otherwise, special arrangements such as standard contractual clauses and binding agreements between organisations in both jurisdictions may be necessary in order to make cross-jurisdictional data flows legitimate. Similar data flow agreements exist between other countries. In some cases these are reciprocal (such as between the EU and Andorra), while others are not (e.g., the Russian privacy regulator allows personal data to flow from Russia to EU countries[2], but the reverse is not true).

Such cross-border rules and data 'trade blocs' have consequences for the legal basis for third party tracking when tracking companies, app developers, app stores and end-users are located in different jurisdictions. While the transfer of data from people residing in the EU to countries whose data protection regime is deemed inadequate could be legitimate in principle, more onerous conditions would need to be met. As such, any efforts to assess the legality of current practices must consider the extent to which tracking occurs across borders.

3 DATA COLLECTION & METHODOLOGY

3.1 Play Store Indexing and App Discovery

The first step was to identify available apps. We programmatically identified popular search terms in the Play Store by autocompleting all character strings of up to a length of five, and then issued each search term to get a list of apps, ranked by popularity [17]. The identified apps were then downloaded using the gplaycli [25], a command line tool for interacting with the Play Store.

3.1.1 Static analysis method. An Android Package Kit (APK) is an Android file format that contains all resources needed by an app to run on a device. Upon download, each APK was unpacked and decoded using APKTool [35] to obtain the app's assets, in particular its icon, bytecode (in the DEX format) and metadata (in XML format). Finally, permission requests were parsed from the XML and hosts were found in the bytecode using a simple regex[3].

3.1.2 Mapping hostnames to known tracker companies. While this static analysis process effectively identified references to hosts in the APKs, it did not provide a means of mapping them to companies, let alone selecting only those companies who are in fact engaged in tracking. A large number of the hostnames found in the static code analysis refer to a wide range of benign external resources which are not necessarily engaged in tracking. In order to isolate only those engaged in tracking, we combined two lists of trackers derived from previous research. One list is compiled by the Web X-Ray project [23]. It maps third party web tracking domains to companies that own them, as well as parent-subsidiary

relationships. The second list is compiled from previous research by the authors of the present paper [9, 38], which also maps domains to companies, and companies to their owners, but incorporates mobile app-centric trackers which are missing from web-oriented tracker lists. An example of domain-company ownership in the resulting aggregated list is shown in Figure 1, and parent-subsidiary relationship in Figure 2.

Host names in the tracker lists were shortened to 2-level domains using the python library tldextract[4] (e.g. for 'subdomain.example.com', the domain name 'example' and top-level domain suffix '.com' were kept and any subdomains were omitted). Tracker hosts were then matched to hosts identified in app bytecode with a regular expression which excluded matches that was followed by a dot or an alphabetic character (matching 'google.com' to 'google.com/somepath' but not 'google.com.domain' or 'google.coming').

3.2 Data analysis

Most of the data analysis was conducted in R, using RStudio[5].

4 RESULTS

4.1 Numbers of tracker hosts in apps

The distribution of number of tracker hosts per app was highly right-skewed (see Figure 3). Gini inequality coefficient was 0.44. Across all analyzed apps (n = 959,426), the median number of tracker hosts included in the bytecode of an app was 10. 90.4% of apps included at least one, and 17.9% more than twenty.

4.2 Numbers of distinct tracker companies behind hosts

The distribution of number of distinct tracker companies (at the lowest subsidiary level) behind the hosts in an app was similarly right-skewed (see Figure 4). The median number of companies was 5, 90.4% of apps included hosts associated with at least one company, and 17.4% with more than ten companies.

There were 13 apps for which our analysis identified 30 or more different tracking companies referred to via hosts in the bytecode. In some cases, these high numbers can be explained by the particular function of the app; for instance, some of these apps integrate multiple different services into one app (e.g. 'Social Networks All in One'); in such cases, any tracking domains associated with those integrated services will be identified by our method. For others, mostly gaming apps, the high numbers of trackers serve no obvious function other than the usual kinds of behaviourally targeted advertising and analytics.

Rather than simply counting number of companies, we can query the proportion of apps containing hosts associated with specific companies. As illustrated in Figure 2, however, many companies have been acquired by larger parent or holding companies, such as Alphabet. The result of grouping by 'root parent' the percentages of apps which include hosts associated with specific companies is shown in Table 1.

---

[2]https://www.huntonprivacyblog.com/2017/08/16/russian-privacy-regulator-\adds-countries-list-nations-sufficient-privacy-protections/

[3]We note that this method has the inherent problem that we cannot confirm if bytecode relating to or referencing such hosts is ever called. More sophisticated static analysis methods might better distinguish but this is left for future work. The regex used to identify hosts in the bytecode is available on osf.io/4nu9e

[4]https://github.com/john-kurkowski/tldextract

[5]Analysis scripts plus data are available via the Open Science Framework at osf.io/4nu9e. For access to the full data set, contact the authors.

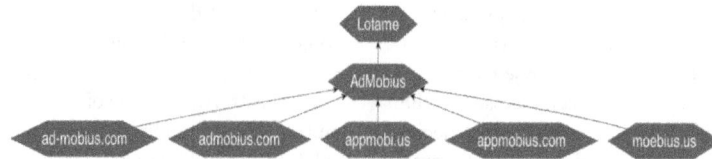

Figure 1: Example of domain-company ownership. The domain Admobi.us is owned by the company *AdMobius*, which is owned by the parent company *Lotame*.

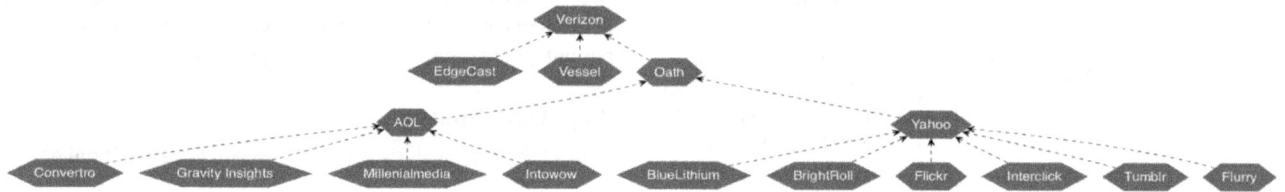

Figure 2: Example of parent-subsidiary company ownership (domains omitted). *Flurry* is owned by *Yahoo*, which is owned by *Oath*, which is owned by *Verizon* (the 'root parent').

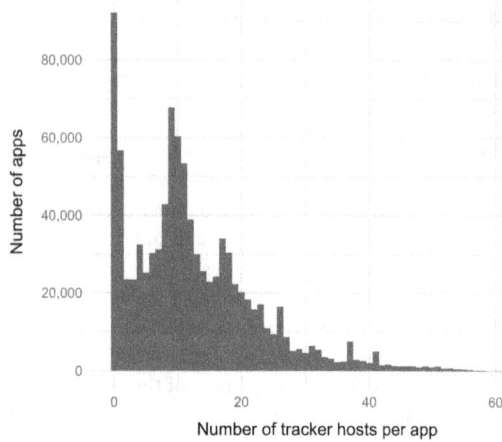

Median	Q1	Q3	>20 hosts	No hosts
10	5	18	17.9%	9.6%

Figure 3: Histogram and descriptive statistics for number of tracker hosts per app (free apps on the Google Play store).

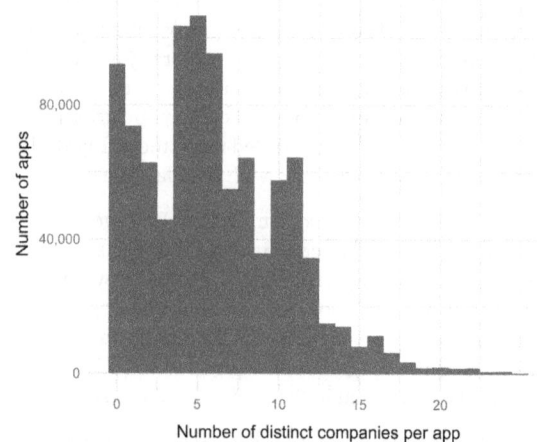

Median	Q1	Q3	>10 companies	No companies
5	3	9	17.4%	9.6%

Figure 4: Number of distinct tracker companies behind hosts in apps (free apps on the Google Play store).

4.3 Company prevalence by genre

The Google Play store metadata divides apps into 49 different genres (no less than 17 of these are subcategories of games, e.g. 'Casino Games' and 'Adventure Games'). To provide a high-level analysis, we grouped these genres into 8 more succinct 'super genres'

(by e.g. clustering all game genres, plus the genres 'Comics', 'Entertainment', 'Sports' and 'Video Players' into a single 'Games & Entertainment' category[6]). In addition, given concern of in particular tracking of children[1], we created a super genre consisting of

---

[6]See osf.io/4nu9e for details of this grouping.

Root parent	% apps	Subsidiary	% apps	Country
Alphabet	88.44	Google	87.57	US
		Google APIs	67.51	US
		DoubleClick	60.85	US
		Google Analytics	39.42	US
		Google Tag Manager	33.88	US
		Adsense	30.12	US
		Firebase	19.20	US
		Admob	14.67	US
		YouTube	9.51	US
		Blogger	0.46	US
Facebook	42.55	Facebook	42.54	US
		Liverail	1.03	US
		Lifestreet	<0.01	US
Twitter	33.88	Twitter	30.94	US
		Crashlytics	5.10	US
		Mopub	2.51	US
Verizon	26.27	Yahoo	20.82	US
		Flurry	6.28	US
		Flickr	1.37	US
		Tumblr	1.22	US
		Millennialmedia	0.71	US
		Verizon	0.11	US
		AOL	0.06	US
		Intowow	<0.01	US
		One By AOL	<0.01	US
		Brightroll	<0.01	US
		Gravity Insights	<0.01	US
Microsoft	22.19	Microsoft	22.11	US
		Bing	0.12	US
LinkedIn	20.62	LinkedIn	20.62	US
Amazon	17.91	Amazon Web Services	11.57	US
		Amazon	7.72	US
		Amazon Marketing Services	1.73	US
		Alexa	<0.01	US
Unitytechnologies	5.78	Unitytechnologies	5.78	US
Chartboost	5.45	Chartboost	5.45	US
Applovin	3.95	Applovin	3.95	US
Cloudflare	3.85	Cloudflare	3.85	US
Opera	3.20	Adcolony	3.12	US
		Admarvel	0.09	US

Table 1: The most prevalent root parent tracking companies and their subsidiaries (full list available on osf.io/4nu9e).

Genre	K	$\sum K$
Productivity & Tools	0.14	5.5
Games & Entertainment	0.13	5.41
Health & Lifestyle	0.1	5.5
Communication & Social	0.09	5.29
Art & Photography	0.09	5.12
Family	0.04	4.33
News	0.03	4.5
Education	0.03	5.42
Music	0.02	5.24

Table 2: K distances between tracker rankings for each genre compared to all apps (K), and sum of pairwise distances between each genre and every other genre ($\sum K$).

apps included in one of the Google Play store's 'family' categories.[7] For each super genre, we reran the company analysis, which revealed some important differences between the nature of tracking by genre.

First, there are differences in the number of distinct tracking companies associated with apps from different genres. Figure 5 shows the number of apps in each super genre, and descriptive statistics of number of distinct tracker companies associated with apps within each. *News* and *Family* apps have the highest median number of tracker companies associated with them, and over 20% of apps in the *News*, *Family*, and *Games & Entertainment* super genres are linked to more than ten tracker companies. Meanwhile, the lowest median number of trackers are found within *Productivity & Tools*, *Education*, *Communication & Social*, and *Health & Lifestyle* apps, and over 10% of *Productivity & Tools*, *Education* and *Communication & Social* apps have no trackers at all.

Second, there are differences in which particular trackers are associated with apps from each super genre. By comparing rankings for each, we can see the extent to which different trackers dominate each super genre. In addition to comparing the difference in rankings for any given tracker, we use an overall distance metric, the Kendall tau distance, in order to measure the extent to which rankings differ between super genres [21].

The Kendall Tau distance may be defined as:

$$K(\tau_1, \tau_2) = \sum_{\{i,j\} \in P} \bar{K}_{i,j}(\tau_1, \tau_2)$$

where:

(1) "P" is the set of unordered pairs of distinct elements in τ_1 and τ_2
(2) $\bar{K}_{i,j}(\tau_1, \tau_2) = 0$ if "i" and "j" are in the same order in τ_1 and τ_2
(3) $\bar{K}_{i,j}(\tau_1, \tau_2) = 1$ if "i" and "j" are in the opposite order in τ_1 and τ_2.

In this context, "P" is the set of unordered pairs of trackers (e.g. 'DoubleClick' and 'AdChina'), in one genre ranking τ_1 (e.g. 'Games')

---

[7] All apps on the Google Play store have an ordinary genre classification, but some apps are in classified into one of the Play store's family genres.

Super genre	# apps	Med.	Q1	Q3	>10	None
News	26281	7	4	11	29.9%	6.5%
Family	8930	7	4	11	28.3%	7.2%
Games & Entertainment	291952	6	4	10	24.5%	7.3%
Art & Photography	27593	6	4	10	16.8%	3.6%
Music	65099	6	4	8	13.5%	4.1%
Health & Lifestyle	163837	5	3	8	15.4%	9.0%
Communication & Social	39637	5	2	8	16.2%	13.4%
Education	79730	5	2	8	13.3%	11.9%
Productivity & Tools	265297	5	2	8	11.9%	13.5%

(a)

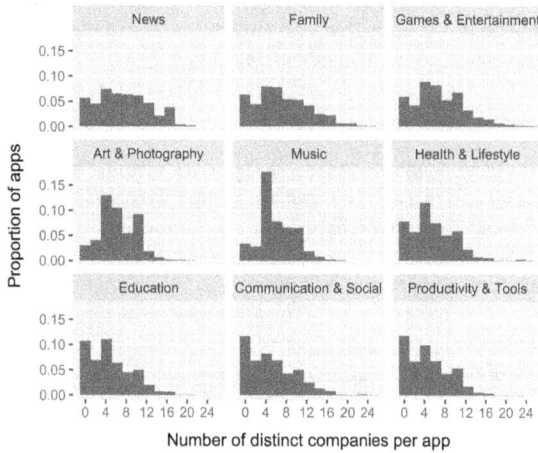

Figure 5: Descriptive statistics (a) and histograms (b) of number of distinct tracker companies behind hosts referenced in apps, grouped by super genre.

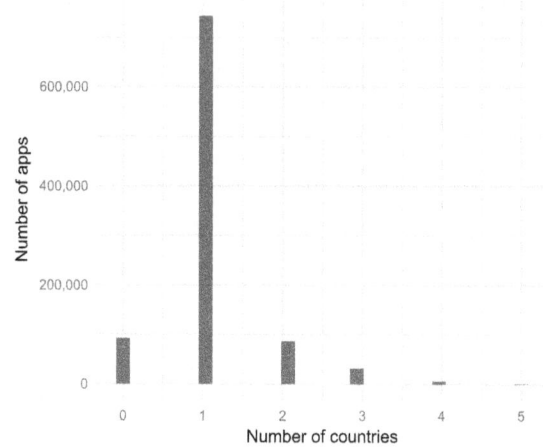

Figure 6: **Number of distinct countries in which tracker companies behind hosts in an app (free apps on the Google Play store) are based.**

Country	# apps present	% apps
U.S.	865369	90.2%
China	48451	5.1%
Norway	30674	3.2%
Russia	24889	2.6%
Germany	24773	2.6%
Singapore	19323	2.0%
UK	14451	1.5%
Austria	4754	0.5%
South Korea	3366	0.4%
Japan	1801	0.2%

Table 3: **Apps including at least one tracker associated with a subsidiary or root parent within a given country.**

and another genre ranking τ_2 (e.g. 'News'). K is based on the number of discordant pairs between τ_1 and τ_2, where a higher K indicates greater distance.

We find that the Productivity & Tools and Games & Entertainment categories exhibit the biggest differences in ranking of trackers compared to the overall ranking of trackers across the whole Play Store, while the ranking of trackers in the Music category is the closest to the overall ranking (see Table 2).

In addition to calculating the distance between the rankings of each genre and the rankings for the entire Play Store, we also calculated the distances between each distinct pair of genres and summed them to get an idea of the overall distance of a single genre from every other genre. When considering the distance in tracker rankings from the tracker rankings of all other categories, Productivity & Tools and Health & Lifestyle appear to be the biggest outliers; the top 20 trackers in the former include companies not present in the top 20 for all apps, like Mapbox (rank #64 across all apps) as well as Chinese companies Alibaba and Baidu.

4.4   Country differences

We also analysed the prevalence of countries in which the tracker companies are based (including both subsidiary and root parent level; see Table 3). Just over 90% of all apps contained at least one tracker owned by a company based in the United States. China, Norway, Russia, Germany, Singapore, and the United Kingdom were the next most common destinations. The median number of unique countries associated with the companies referred to in an app was 1 (see Figure 6).

We also calculated the country prevalence figures on a genre-by-genre basis. While the US remained the most prevalent in every case, (between 86-96%), the prevalence rankings for other countries differed by super genre. For instance, UK-based trackers were the second-most prevalent in 'Art & Photography', despite being only 7th overall.

5 DISCUSSION

We begin by discussing the limitations of our data collection methods. Next we consider some differences between tracking on websites and on mobile apps, and finally we draw out implications for the regulatory approaches outlined in section 2.2.3.

5.1 Limitations of data collection methods

There are several limitations to our tracker detection methods. First, it is incomplete; our knowledge base of tracker domain to company mappings is limited to those trackers which have been discovered in the course of previous research (namely [9, 23, 38]). While these lists were compiled in a systematic way, focusing on the most prevalent tracking domains, including the entire long tail of less prevalent domains might change the results reported. The inclusion and exclusion criteria for what constitutes a 'tracker' are also open to debate; the list compiled in prior works, and relied on here, defines a third-party tracker as 'an entity that collects data about users from first-party websites and / or apps, in order to link such data together to build a profile about the user', but the definition and its application are debateable.[8] Another issue is that without dynamic network traffic analysis of all apps, including successful man-in-the-middle proxying and ability to interpret the data payloads, we cannot confirm precisely what data is sent to each tracker. Finally, different trackers serve different purposes; some facilitate targeted advertising, while others are used for analytics. Without further fine-grained distinctions between such purposes, the figures presented here do not represent the full nuance and variety of third party tracking and its impacts.

5.2 Web vs. Mobile

Previous large-scale studies of tracking have largely focused on the web. The distribution model of the web allows measurement of tracking to scale in a way that the model for smartphone app distribution does not; web services are delivered in a standardised way through a browser which can easily be automated. As a result, large-scale web tracking studies typically include millions of sites. By contrast, the largest smartphone app tracking study to our knowledge at the time of writing is derived from network traffic detected by the Lumen app, which includes the data flows of 14,599 apps installed on Lumen user's devices [30]. While such crowd-sourced methods have many advantages in terms of the granularity of the data flows and ecological validity, at best they scale to tens of thousands of apps. By contrast, our method is scalable to hundreds of thousands of apps (indeed, our dataset of apps is close to a million).

5.3 Implications for tracker regulation

While the distribution of trackers across apps is of general interest from a privacy and data protection regulation perspective, we focus here on several particular regulatory implications arising from our findings.

5.3.1 Cross-jurisdictional data flow. As explained in Section 2.2.3, the rules regarding transfers of data outside the EU under the

GDPR are similar to the previous regime (under the Data Protection Directive), but with some new details as well as larger associated fines. In so far as these developments result in more investigation and enforcement by authorities, the impact will be different for companies depending on their jurisdiction. There will be no impact on those based in the EU, such as Germany (the fifth-most prevalent country in which trackers are based), who benefit from rules permitting the free flow of data within the Union. Some third countries such as Canada also benefit from being on the EU Commission's list of legal regimes that are deemed "adequate' and therefore data transfers to trackers in those jurisdictions are legitimate without further measures in place.

However, amongst the top-10 most prevalent countries there are several which lie outside the E.U. and are not deemed adequate, such as China, Russia, Singapore, South Korea and Japan. In order for transfers to these countries to be legitimate, additional safeguards must be in place as explained in Section 2.2.3. We cannot determine whether such arrangements have been put in place by the identified companies based in non-approved jurisdictions, but our figures give an indication of the volume of companies to whom these more onerous rules apply. While the percentages of apps which include trackers from such jurisdictions are small compared to the US—China (5.1%), Russia (2.6%), Singapore (2%) versus US (90%)—they are still significant, numbering in the tens of thousands.

5.3.2 Profiling. The GDPR uses the term 'profiling' to describe any fully or partly automated processing of personal data with the objective of evaluating personal aspects of a natural person (Article 4(4)). Many of the tracking companies included in our knowledge base engage in data processing activity that would likely constitute 'profiling' under this definition. For instance, the purpose of many of the most common trackers is behaviourally targeted advertising, whereby individuals are evaluated along demographic and behavioural dimensions to determine their propensity to respond to certain marketing messages. Profiling is prohibited if it has 'legal or significant' effects on the data subject. While the definition of 'significant effects' is not entirely clear, the Article 29 Working Party has advised that even profiling for marketing purposes could potentially give rise to significant effects, including if it is: intrusive; targets vulnerable, minority groups, or those in financial difficulty; involves differential pricing; or deprives certain groups of opportunities.[9] Trackers which enable such activities without consent of the data subject could therefore be in breach of Article 22 (unless such profiling is necessary for entering or performing a contract, or it is authorised by another member state law). Many of the most prevalent trackers observed in our study have the capacity to be used in such ways, and evidence of such practices is beginning to emerge. For instance, DoubleClick (present on 60% of apps analysed) has been shown to target adverts for higher-paid jobs to men at a higher rate than to women [12]; while web-based price discrimination has also been documented by numerous studies in recent years [19, 26].

5.3.3 Rights and obligations regarding children. Like the old Directive, the GDPR defines certain additional rights and obligations

---

[8]The principles behind the criteria used here are discussed in the aforementioned prior works

[9]Article 29 Working Party: Guidelines on Automated individual decision-making and Profiling for the purposes of Regulation 2016/679 http://ec.europa.eu/newsroom/article29/item-detail.cfm?item_id=612053

regarding processing the personal data of children (defined as anyone under the age of 16, and for certain additional protections, 13). If a tracker is relying on consent as a legitimating ground for processing, then such consent would not be valid from a child under 13; instead a parent or guardian would need to consent. Furthermore, as discussed above, Recital 38 states that special protections should be in place if children's data are being processed for marketing and user profiling. This description would likely cover many of the trackers which are embedded in apps from the Family and Games & Entertainment genre categories, which are clearly targeted at children. Problematically, apps from these two genres are especially exposed to third party tracking, with the average app including hosts associated with 7 distinct tracker companies for Family apps, and 6 for Games & Entertainment apps (only News apps are more exposed). Given the relatively higher level of protection set in the law regarding profiling children for marketing, it seems that tracking is most rampant in the very context in which regulators are most concerned to constrain it.

6 CONCLUSION

We believe that by undertaking analysis of the distribution of tracking technology on close to 1 million smartphone apps, we gain insight into the breadth and scale of this highly important phenomenon. Unlike previous studies whose coverage of apps numbers in the tens of thousands, and may be skewed towards the app choices of the users from whom data is gathered, our study is a systematic analysis of apps on the Play Store.

Our genre-by-genre analysis suggests that there are differences in the behaviour and distribution of trackers depending on the functionality or purpose the app provides. News and Games apps appear amongst the worst in terms of the number of tracker companies associated with them. Tracking is also a substantially trans-national phenomenon; around 100,000 apps we analysed send data to trackers located in more than one jurisdiction.

These findings suggests that there are challenges ahead both for regulators aiming to enforce the law, and for companies who intend to comply with it. Full audits of mobile app stores such as this could help regulators identify areas to focus on. Previous privacy enforcement 'sweeps'[10] have focused on the most popular apps, and their terms of service and privacy policies. But the analysis here suggests that apps may not necessarily be the most efficient point of analysis; rather, identifying and investigating the most prevalent trackers might be a better target. Some of the practices likely to be involved - such as allowing profiling of children without attempting to obtain parental consent - may be downright unlawful. It remains to be seen how and if regulators will attempt to detect and prevent behavioural targeting that has 'significant effects' on data subjects.

The governance of these activities is complex, involving many stakeholders, including: users, smartphone operating system developers, equipment manufacturers, alternative app market operators, app developers, and tracking companies (who also operate multisided markets with advertisers and therefore have the ability to impose constraints on what ads can be served). Effective regulation will require collaboration between regulators and these myriad other actors.

ACKNOWLEDGMENTS

All authors are supported under *SOCIAM: The Theory and Practice of Social Machines*, funded by the UK Engineering and Physical Sciences Research Council (EPSRC) under grant number EP/J017728/2 and comprises the University of Oxford, the University of Southampton, and the University of Edinburgh. Reuben Binns and Max Van Kleek are also supported by *ReTiPS: Repectful Things in Private Spaces*, a project funded through the PETRAS IoT Hub Strategic Fund, which, in turn, was funded by the EPSRC under grant number N02334X/1. Timothy Libert is also supported by the Google Digital News Project at the Reuters Institute for the Study of Journalism. Jun Zhao is also supported by KOALA (http://SOCIAM.org/project/koala): Kids Online Anonymity & Lifelong Autonomy, funded by EPSRC Impact Acceleration Account Award, under the grant number of EP/R511742/1.

REFERENCES

[1] 2010. EU kids online. *Zeitschrift für Psychologie - Journal of Psychology* 217, 4 (2010), 236–239. https://doi.org/10.1027/0044-3409.217.4.233

[2] Gunes Acar, Marc Juarez, Nick Nikiforakis, Claudia Diaz, Seda Gürses, Frank Piessens, and Bart Preneel. 2013. FPDetective: dusting the web for fingerprinters. In *Proc. of ACM SIGSAC conference on Computer & communications security*. ACM, 1129–1140.

[3] Alessandro Acquisti, Curtis R Taylor, and Liad Wagman. 2016. The economics of privacy. *Journal of Economic Literature* 52, 2 (2016).

[4] Jonathan Anderson, Joseph Bonneau, and Frank Stajano. 2010. Inglorious Installers: Security in the Application Marketplace.. In *WEIS*. Citeseer.

[5] Steven Arzt, Siegfried Rasthofer, Christian Fritz, Eric Bodden, Alexandre Bartel, Jacques Klein, Yves Le Traon, Damien Octeau, and Patrick McDaniel. 2014. Flowdroid: Precise context, flow, field, object-sensitive and lifecycle-aware taint analysis for android apps. *ACM SIGPLAN Notices* 49, 6 (2014), 259–269.

[6] Arslan Aziz and Rahul Telang. 2015. *What is a Cookie Worth?* Technical Report. Technical Report.

[7] Rebecca Balebako, Jaeyeon Jung, Wei Lu, Lorrie Faith Cranor, and Carolyn Nguyen. 2013. Little brothers watching you: Raising awareness of data leaks on smartphones. In *Proceedings of the Symposium on Usable Privacy and Security*. ACM, 12.

[8] Leonid Batyuk, Markus Herpich, Seyit Ahmet Camtepe, Karsten Raddatz, Aubrey-Derrick Schmidt, and Sahin Albayrak. 2011. Using static analysis for automatic assessment and mitigation of unwanted and malicious activities within Android applications. In *Malicious and Unwanted Software (MALWARE), 2011 6th International Conference on*. IEEE, 66–72.

[9] Reuben Binns, Jun Zhao, Max Van Kleek, and Nigel Shadbolt. 2018. Measuring third party tracker power across web and mobile. *arXiv preprint arXiv:1802.02507* (2018).

[10] Theodore Book and Dan S Wallach. 2015. An empirical study of mobile ad targeting. *arXiv preprint arXiv:1502.06577* (2015).

[11] Saksham Chitkara, Nishad Gothoskar, Suhas Harish, Jason I Hong, and Yuvraj Agarwal. 2017. Does this App Really Need My Location?: Context-Aware Privacy Management for Smartphones. *Proceedings of the ACM on Interactive, Mobile, Wearable and Ubiquitous Technologies* 1, 3 (2017), 42.

[12] Amit Datta, Michael Carl Tschantz, and Anupam Datta. 2015. Automated experiments on ad privacy settings. *Proceedings on Privacy Enhancing Technologies* 2015, 1 (2015), 92–112.

[13] Manuel Egele, Christopher Kruegel, Engin Kirda, and Giovanni Vigna. 2011. PiOS: Detecting Privacy Leaks in iOS Applications.. In *NDSS*. 177–183.

[14] William Enck, Peter Gilbert, Seungyeop Han, Vasant Tendulkar, Byung-Gon Chun, Landon P Cox, Jaeyeon Jung, Patrick McDaniel, and Anmol N Sheth. 2014. TaintDroid: an information-flow tracking system for realtime privacy monitoring on smartphones. *ACM Transactions on Computer Systems (TOCS)* 32, 2 (2014), 5.

[15] Steven Englehardt and Arvind Narayanan. 2016. Online tracking: A 1-million-site measurement and analysis. In *Proceedings of ACM Computer and Communications Security 2016*.

[16] Steven Englehardt, Dillon Reisman, Christian Eubank, Peter Zimmerman, Jonathan Mayer, Arvind Narayanan, and Edward W Felten. 2015. Cookies that give you away: The surveillance implications of web tracking. In *Proc. of the 24th International Conference on World Wide Web*. ACM, 289–299.

---

[10]See https://www.privacyenforcement.net/node/906

[17] Google. 2017. Search using Autocomplete. (2017). https://support.google.com/websearch/answer/106230?co=GENIE.Platform%3DAndroid&hl=en-GB

[18] Michael I Gordon, Deokhwan Kim, Jeff H Perkins, Limei Gilham, Nguyen Nguyen, and Martin C Rinard. 2015. Information Flow Analysis of Android Applications in DroidSafe.. In *NDSS*.

[19] Aniko Hannak, Gary Soeller, David Lazer, Alan Mislove, and Christo Wilson. 2014. Measuring price discrimination and steering on e-commerce web sites. In *Proceedings of the 2014 conference on internet measurement conference*. ACM, 305–318.

[20] IAB. 2016. IAB Internet Advertising Revenue Report 2015. (2016).

[21] Maurice G Kendall. 1938. A new measure of rank correlation. *Biometrika* 30, 1/2 (1938), 81–93.

[22] Christophe Leung, Jingjing Ren, David Choffnes, and Christo Wilson. 2016. Should You Use the App for That? Comparing the Privacy Implications of App-and Web-based Online Services. In *Proc. of the 16th ACM Internet Measurement Conference*. To appear.

[23] Timothy Libert. 2015. Exposing the Invisible Web: An Analysis of Third-Party HTTP Requests on 1 Million Websites. *International Journal of Communication* 9 (2015), 18.

[24] Jialiu Lin, Bin Liu, Norman Sadeh, and Jason I. Hong. 2014. Modeling Users' Mobile App Privacy Preferences: Restoring Usability in a Sea of Permission Settings. In *Symposium On Usable Privacy and Security (SOUPS 2014)*. USENIX Association, Menlo Park, CA, 199–212. https://www.usenix.org/conference/soups2014/proceedings/presentation/lin

[25] Matlink. 2017. Google Play Downloader via Command Line. Website. (2017). https://github.com/matlink/gplaycli

[26] Jakub Mikians, László Gyarmati, Vijay Erramilli, and Nikolaos Laoutaris. 2012. Detecting price and search discrimination on the internet. In *Proceedings of the 11th ACM Workshop on Hot Topics in Networks*. acm, 79–84.

[27] Rodrigo Montes, Wilfried Sand-Zantman, and Tommaso M Valletti. 2015. The value of personal information in markets with endogenous privacy. (2015).

[28] Mohammad Nauman, Sohail Khan, and Xinwen Zhang. 2010. Apex: extending android permission model and enforcement with user-defined runtime constraints. In *Proceedings of the 5th ACM symposium on information, computer and communications security*. ACM, 328–332.

[29] Lingzhi Qiu, Zixiong Zhang, Ziyi Shen, and Guozi Sun. 2015. AppTrace: Dynamic trace on Android devices. In *2015 IEEE International Conference on Communications*. IEEE, 7145–7150.

[30] Abbas Razaghpanah, Rishab Nithyanand, Narseo Vallina-Rodriguez, Srikanth Sundaresan, Mark Allman, Christian Kreibich, and Phillipa Gill. 2018. Apps, Trackers, Privacy, and Regulators: A Global Study of the Mobile Tracking Ecosystem. (2018).

[31] Jingjing Ren, Ashwin Rao, Martina Lindorfer, Arnaud Legout, and David Choffnes. 2016. Demo: ReCon: Revealing and Controlling PII Leaks in Mobile Network Traffic. In *Proceedings of the International Conference on Mobile Systems, Applications, and Services Companion (MobiSys '16 Companion)*. 117–117.

[32] Franziska Roesner, Tadayoshi Kohno, and David Wetherall. 2012. Detecting and defending against third-party tracking on the web. In *Proc. of the 9th USENIX conference on Networked Systems Design and Implementation*. USENIX Association, 12–12.

[33] Gaurav Srivastava, Saksham Chitkara, Kevin Ku, Swarup Kumar Sahoo, Matt Fredrikson, Jason Hong, and Yuvraj Agarwal. 2017. PrivacyProxy: Leveraging Crowdsourcing and In Situ Traffic Analysis to Detect and Mitigate Information Leakage. *arXiv preprint arXiv:1708.06384* (2017).

[34] V. F. Taylor and I. Martinovic. 2017. To Update or Not to Update: Insights From a Two-Year Study of Android App Evolution. In *ACM Asia Conference on Computer and Communications Security (ASIACCS'17)*. https://doi.org/10

[35] Connor Tumbleson. 2017. Apktool - A tool for reverse engineering 3rd party closed binary Android apps. (2017). https://ibotpeaches.github.io/Apktool/

[36] Narseo Vallina-Rodriguez, Srikanth Sundaresan, Abbas Razaghpanah, Rishab Nithyanand, Mark Allman, Christian Kreibich, and Phillipa Gill. 2016. Tracking the Trackers: Towards Understanding the Mobile Advertising and Tracking Ecosystem. *arXiv preprint arXiv:1609.07190* (2016).

[37] Max Van Kleek, Ilaria Liccardi, Reuben Binns, Jun Zhao, Daniel J Weitzner, and Nigel Shadbolt. 2017. Better the devil you know: Exposing the data sharing practices of smartphone apps. In *Proceedings of the 2017 CHI Conference on Human Factors in Computing Systems*. ACM, 5208–5220.

[38] Max Van Kleek, Ilaria Liccardi, Reuben Binns, Jun Zhao, Daniel J. Weitzner, and Nigel Shadbolt. 2017. Better the Devil You Know: Exposing the Data Sharing Practices of Smartphone Apps. In *Proceedings of the 2017 CHI Conference on Human Factors in Computing Systems (CHI '17)*. ACM, New York, NY, USA, 5208–5220. https://doi.org/10.1145/3025453.3025556

[39] Zhonghao Yu, Sam Macbeth, Konark Modi, and Josep M Pujol. 2016. Tracking the Trackers. In *Proceedings of the 25th International Conference on World Wide Web*. International World Wide Web Conferences Steering Committee, 121–132.

[40] Jinyan Zang, Krysta Dummit, James Graves, Paul Lisker, and Latanya Sweeney. 2015. Who knows what about me? A survey of behind the scenes personal data sharing to third parties by mobile apps. *Proceeding of Technology Science* (2015).

A Quality Type-aware Annotated Corpus and Lexicon for Harassment Research

Mohammadreza Rezvan
Kno.e.sis Center
Dayton, Ohio, USA
rezvan@knoesis.org

Saeedeh Shekarpour
University of Dayton
Dayton, Ohio, USA
sshekarpour1@udayton.edu

Lakshika Balasuriya
Kno.e.sis Center
Dayton, USA, Ohio
lakshika@knoesis.org

Krishnaprasad Thirunarayan
Kno.e.sis Center
Dayton, Ohio, USA
tkprasad@knoesis.org

Valerie L. Shalin
Kno.e.sis Center
Dayton, Ohio, USA
valerie@knoesis.org

Amit Sheth
Kno.e.sis Center
Dayton, Ohio, USA
amit@knoesis.org

ABSTRACT

A quality annotated corpus is essential to research. Despite the recent focus of the Web science community on cyberbullying research, the community lacks standard benchmarks. This paper provides both a quality annotated corpus and an offensive words lexicon capturing different types of harassment content: (i) sexual, (ii) racial, (iii) appearance-related, (iv) intellectual, and (v) political[1]. We first crawled data from Twitter using this content-tailored offensive lexicon. As mere presence of an offensive word is not a reliable indicator of harassment, human judges annotated tweets for the presence of harassment. Our corpus consists of 25,000 annotated tweets for the five types of harassment content and is available on the Git repository[2].

CCS CONCEPTS

• **Applied computing** → **Annotation**; *Document analysis*; Document management and text processing; • **Social and professional topics** → *Hate speech*; *User characteristics*;

KEYWORDS

Annotated corpus, context, sexual, racial, political, appearance-related, intellectual, cyberbullying, harassment, offensive Lexicon, profane word.

ACM Reference Format:
Mohammadreza Rezvan, Saeedeh Shekarpour, Lakshika Balasuriya, Krishnaprasad Thirunarayan, Valerie L. Shalin, and Amit Sheth. 2018. A Quality Type-aware Annotated Corpus and Lexicon for Harassment Research. In *WebSci '18: 10th ACM Conference on Web Science, May 27–30, 2018, Amsterdam, Netherlands*. ACM, New York, NY, USA, 4 pages. https://doi.org/10.1145/3201064.3201103

1 INTRODUCTION

Social media is being used extensively by people from various age-groups (e.g., 80+% usage for young adults (18-49) and 45+% usage for old adults (50+)[3]). Despite the communication advantages, participants may experience insult, humiliation, bullying, and harassing comments from strangers, colleagues or anonymous users. One-in-five, around 18% are affected[4]), posing numerous challenges to social engagement and trust, resulting in emotional distress, privacy concerns and threats to physical safety. All instances of harassment necessarily reflect a combination of sender intentionality and recipient experience. Our focus here is on the sender, whose messages are intended to harass. We study harassment[7] in five content areas: (i) sexual, (ii) racial, (iii) appearance-related, (iv) intellectual, and (v) political. Below, we briefly describe each type.

- **Sexual harassment** concerns sexuality and often targets females. The harasser might refer to a victim's sex organs with slang or describe sexual relations with slang. However, slang itself is not sufficient to indicate sexual harassment[5][6].
- **Racial harassment** targets race and ethnicity characteristics of a victim such as color, country, culture, faith, and religion[7].
- **Appearance-related harassment** is related to body appearance apart from sexuality. All dimensions of appearance are candidates, for example, hair style or looks. Fat shaming [1] and body shaming are critical sub-types.
- **Intellectual harassment** concerns intellectual power or the merits of individual opinion. Sub-types include level of formal education and grammar. Victims may in fact be intellectually gifted[8].

---

[1]Disclaimer: This paper is concerned with violent online harassment. To describe the subject at an adequate level of realism, examples of our collected tweets involve violent, threatening, vulgar and hateful speech language in the context of racial, sexual, political, appearance and intellectual harassment. While these examples are shared to portray the reality, the readers are alerted in advance and may wish to avoid reading this material if it could cause discomfort and disagreement.

[2]https://github.com/Mrezvan94/Harassment-Corpus

---

[3]Observed statistics on January 8, 2018, from Pew research at http://www.pewinternet.org/fact-sheet/social-media/.
[4]http://www.pewinternet.org/2017/07/11/online-harassment-2017/
[5]https://www.joshuafriedmanesq.com/sexual-harassment.html
[6]https://www.eeoc.gov/laws/types/sexual_harassment.cfm
[7]https://www.joshuafriedmanesq.com/racial-slurs-and-racial-harassment.html
[8]http://www.corrections.com/news/article/26649-ranking-bully-types-the-points-system

- **Political harassment** relates to political views[9], regarding issues under governmental influence such as global warming, the opiod epidemic, immigration or gun control. Typical targets are politicians and politically active individuals[10].

The absence of a quality, annotated corpus of online harassment impedes comparative research on harassment detection. Our work [7] pioneers the content-specific study of cyberbullying. We publish here (i) our annotated content-specific lexicon and (ii) our content-specific annotated corpus validated by inter-rater reliability statistics. This paper is organized as follows: Section 2 reviews the related work. Section 3 explains the process for developing the five content-specific lexicons. In Section 4, we present the strategies for collecting and annotating our corpus. Section 5 provides examples of harassing as well as non-harassing tweets. We close with concluding remarks and our future plans.

2 RELATED WORK

Cyberbullying refers to the use of abusive language in social media or online interactions. While the majority of the prior research focuses on methods for detecting cyberbullying, there is no standard benchmark to evaluate and compare the performance of the existing approaches. The publicly available Golbeck corpus [3] contains 25,000 unique tweets with the binary annotation labels (i.e., harassing H or non-harassing N). There, authors use harassment hashtags such as #whitegenocide, #fuckniggers, #WhitePower, and #WhiteLivesMatter as crawling seeds. Human judges annotate the tweets using the binary labeling scheme.

Another harassment related dataset [8] focuses on racism and sexism. This dataset was collected during two months when the authors manually identified related hateful terms targeting groups based on aspects such as, ethnicity, sexual orientation, gender, and religion. Another corpus [2] distinguished between cyberbullying and cyber-aggression. Collection occurred from June 2016 till August 2016 with snowball sampling. This dataset contains 9,484 tweets from 1,303 users. Crowdsourcing workers labeled tweets according to four categories: 1) bullying, 2) aggressive, 3) spam, and 4) normal.

With respect to the methods for detecting harassment, [4] predicts cyberbullying incidents in Instagram. They extract features from text content, and the neighboring network along with temporal attributes to feed the predictive model. Another approach employed in [9] detects harassment features using content, sentiment, and context. These contextual features extracted from discussion and conversation improve the accuracy of harassment detection. Extending the context focus, [6] applies machine learning for detecting harassers and victims in a given cyberbullying incident. Their method considers social connections and infers which participants tend to bully and which participants are victimized. Their model is based on the connectivity of the users (network), the user interactions and the language of the active users.

Category	Count	Example
Sexual	453	assfuck, ball licker, finger fucker, Anal Annie, ass blaster
Appearance-related	15	assface, dickface, fatass, fuckface, shitface
Intellectual	34	assbag, asshat, assshit, dickbrain, dumbbitch
Racial	168	assnigger, beaner, Bigger, mulatto, mosshead
Political	23	Cockmuncher, towelhead, dickwad, propaganda, demon
Generic	44	arsehole, cockknoker, dick, fucker, sextoy

Table 1: Lexicon Statistics and Examples.

3 COMPILING AN OFFENSIVE WORDS LEXICON

The identification of cyberbullying typically begins with a lexicon of potentially profane or offensive words. We created a lexicon (compiled from online resources[11] [12] [13] [14] [15]) containing offensive (i.e., profane) words covering five different types of harassment content. The resulting compiled lexicon includes six categories: (i) sexual, (ii) racial, (iii) appearance-related, (iv) intellectual, (v) political, and (vi) a generic category that contains profane words not exclusively attributed to the five specific types of harassment. A native English speaker conducted this categorization. Table 1 represents the statistics and examples of offensive words in each category.

4 CORPUS DEVELOPMENT AND ANNOTATION

We employ Twitter as the social media data source because of its growing public footprint[16]. Although the size of a tweet is restricted to 140 characters, once we consider a more extensive aggregation of tweets on a specific topic, mining approaches reveal valuable insights. We utilized the first five categories of our lexicon as seed terms for collecting tweets from Twitter between December 18th, 2016 to January 10th 2017. Requiring the presence of at least one lexicon item, we collected 10,000 tweets for each contextual type for a total of 50,000 tweets. As shown in Table 2, nearly half of these tweets were annotated. However, the mere presence of a lexicon item in a tweet does not assure that the tweet is harassing because the individuals might utilize these words with a different intention, e.g., in a friendly manner or as a quote. Therefore, human judges annotated the corpus to discriminate harassing tweets from non-harassing tweets. Three native English speaking annotators determined whether or not a given tweet is harassing with respect to the type of harassment content and assigned one of three labels "yes", "no", and "other". The last label indicates that the given tweet either does not belong to the current context or cannot be decided. Finally, we can conclude 75,000 annotation work had been done totally.

---

[9]http://www.brighthub.com/office/career-planning/articles/89787.aspx
[10]https://www.performanceicreate.com/political-discrimination-harassment/

[11]http://www.bannedwordlist.com/lists.
[12] https://www.cs.cmu.edu/~biglou/resources.
[13]http://www.noswearing.com/dictionary.
[14]http://www.rsdb.org/races#iranians.
[15]http://www.macmillandictionary.com/us/thesaurus-category/american/offensive-words-for-people-according-to-nationality\-or-ethnicity.
[16]Twitter reports 313 million monthly active users that generate over 500 million tweets per day https://about.twitter.com/company.

Contextual Type	Annotated Tweets	no. ✓	no. ✗
Sexual	3855	230	3619
Racial	4976	701	4275
Appearance-related	4828	678	4150
Intellectual	4867	811	4056
Political	5663	699	4964
Combined	24189	3119	21070

Table 2: Annotation statistics of our categorized corpus.

Agreement Rate. Although the annotators employed three labels, i.e., *"yes"*, *"no"*, and *"other"*, the eventual corpus excluded all of the tweets that did not have a consensus label of *"yes"* and *"no"*. In other words, the corpus only contains tweets that receive at least two *"yes"* or two *"no"* labels. Cohen's kappa coefficient [5] measures the quality of our annotation by category in Table 3. The appearance-related context shows the highest agreement rate whereas the political and sexual contexts have the lowest indicating that these contents are more challenging to judge (ambiguity is higher).

Content Type	Agreement Rate
Sexual	0.70
Racial	0.84
Appearance-related	1.00
Intellectual	0.80
Political	0.69

Table 3: Agreement rate.

Comparison to Golbeck Corpus. The public state-of-the-art harassment-related corpus is Golbeck corpus [3] that only provides generic annotation, i.e., (i) harassing and (ii) non-harassing. This corpus contains 20,428 **non-redundant** annotated tweets of which only 5,277 are labeled as harassing. As we require a content-sensitive corpus, we created our own corpus. In the following, we present the principles and strategies employed in collecting, categorizing, annotating and preparing our corpus. We also categorized the Golbeck corpus according to our lexicon. It can be observed in Table 4 that more than 75% of harassing tweets are racial. This statistic confirms Golbeck's observation. While this may be an accurate reflection of the base rate, our view is that different harassment content may have different consequence. An imbalanced corpus at the foundation of our research effort could result in misses of particular import to teenage mental health, concerning sexuality, appearance and intellect.

Contextual Type	#of Tweets
Sexual	380
Racial	4148
Appearance-related	145
Intellectual	381
Political	163
Non Harassing	41
Total	5277

Table 4: Statistics of Golbeck corpus after our annotation w.r.t. contextual type.

5　SAMPLES FROM OUR CORPUS

Below we provide some examples from our corpus, by content area. For each content area, we first show examples annotated as harassing with respect to the content in question. Then we show examples with similar content which are not annotated as harassing with respect to the content in question.

Sexual Harassing.
- @user: and you don't gotta pay none of ya bills baby ima do all that just don't fuck another nigga or ima shoot you
- to the dumbass bitch who tried opening my front door at 4 am nigga i'll kill you if i hear you again bro. i ain't a (URL)

Sexual non-harassing.
- make up is a form of art. i do not want to be a girl with real boobs or a vagina. i may want to do drag but two very different things.
- hot lesbian gets a pussy pounding with toy.
- three awesome teen babes licking each other pussies in absolute lesbian sex.

Appearance-related Harassing.
- @user @user we started killing you because our backs couldn't handle the weight of your fatass anymore.
- @user @user you dat skank postn pix of my girl sab- so show ya fuckin ugly greasy mug ya getto bitch

Appearance-related Non-harassing.
- think it's funny when girls finish a tweet with babes like they're talking down to them when really they're the same level of skank.
- competition time follow me & amp; retweet & amp; you can win a petite spaffnoshing oaty camel toe blotter out of my bin.
- @user: @user most insulting thing a skank can do to a woman who is worth having is mock her to a woman who isn't.É

Intellectual Harassing.
- @user what a complete disgrace of human u r.real cool wish death. no surprise from a washed up fucktard re- ally__
- shoutout to dumb asses who go around clicking like or rt all the hot chicks posts no matter how stupid the shit it be.

Intellectual non-harassing.
- maybe this isn't sadness maybe this is just being a fuck- head __
- @user oh no i'm so sorry to hear that another one of your family members is a shithead
- @user is doing so well and his finally feeling happy we know his been lonely and we know how tired he is ? why can't our asses be happy.

Racial Harassing.
- @user shut the fuck up chink frog nigger.
- @user go back off private you chink.
- @user @user @user shut up you stupid paki.

Racial Non-harassing.
- @user do you know which exactly are the reasons for the police to release the paki? was it only cause of the 1 day period?!

- rt @user: coming up on gmb odious man-child @user interviews racist pathological lying asshat @user.
- @user 90% of paki names are islamic hence they are not in urdu. while urdu itself is a mixture/copy of other languages even in urdu

Political Harassing.

- # thanksdonald for getting rid off that asshat who has been president for 8 yrsb.
- @user how are u a jr high dickwad and president. a true leader doesn't taunt citizens who don't support him. pathetic. sad!
- @user: you're passive aggressive petty fuckbag who values a murderer fascist like putting over our own president. you're o*f*.

Political non-harassing.

- @user yep and that's how the democrats do it. you know they pretend to know what their doing but really couldn't tell their asses.
- @user: liberals still continue to develop conspiracy theories in order to blame everyone else for having their asses hande *f*.
- @user those 4 trump supporters we're bad asses to jump 20 black lives. i call bs.

6 CONCLUSION AND FUTURE WORK

In this paper, we discussed the creation of a quality tweet corpus related to harassment and annotated that with respect to the five types of harassment content (i) sexual, (ii) racial, (iii) appearance-related, (iv) intellectual, and (v) political. This is the first corpus that takes content type into account. Furthermore, we have also developed a lexicon of content-specific offensive words along with a generic category of offensive words. We are making this dataset available to encourage comparative analysis of harassment detection algorithms. In future, we plan to employ this corpus for advancing our research on studying harasser and victim language.

7 ACKNOWLEDGEMENT

Thilini Wijesiriwardene assisted in the preparation of the corpus. We acknowledge support from the National Science Foundation (NSF) award CNS 1513721: Context-Aware Harassment Detection on Social Media. Any opinions, findings, and conclusions, recommendations expressed in this material are those of the author(s) and do not necessarily reflect the views of the NSF.

REFERENCES

[1] Sofia Berne, Ann Frisén, and Johanna Kling. 2014. Appearance-related cyberbullying: A qualitative investigation of characteristics, content, reasons, and effects. *Body image* 11, 4 (2014), 527–533.
[2] Despoina Chatzakou, Nicolas Kourtellis, Jeremy Blackburn, Emiliano De Cristofaro, Gianluca Stringhini, and Athena Vakali. 2017. Mean Birds: Detecting Aggression and Bullying on Twitter. *CoRR* abs/1702.06877 (2017). arXiv:1702.06877 http://arxiv.org/abs/1702.06877
[3] Jennifer Golbeck, Zahra Ashktorab, Rashad O Banjo, Alexandra Berlinger, Siddharth Bhagwan, Cody Buntain, Paul Cheakalos, Alicia A Geller, Quint Gergory, Rajesh Kumar Gnanasekaran, et al. 2017. A Large Labeled Corpus for Online Harassment Research. In *Proceedings of the 2017 ACM on Web Science Conference.* ACM, 229–233.
[4] Homa Hosseinmardi, Rahat Ibn Rafiq, Richard Han, Qin Lv, and Shivakant Mishra. 2016. Prediction of cyberbullying incidents in a media-based social network. In *Advances in Social Networks Analysis and Mining (ASONAM), 2016 IEEE/ACM International Conference on.* IEEE, 186–192.
[5] Mary L McHugh. 2012. Interrater reliability: the kappa statistic. *Biochemia medica: Biochemia medica* 22, 3 (2012), 276–282.
[6] Elaheh Raisi and Bert Huang. 2017. Cyberbullying detection with weakly supervised machine learning. In *Proceedings of the IEEE/ACM International Conference on Social Networks Analysis and Mining.*
[7] Mohammadreza Rezvan, Saeedeh Shekarpour, Thirunarayan Krishnaprasad, Valerie Shalin, and Amit Sheth. 2018. Analyzing and Learning Language for Harassment in Different Contexts. In *Submitted to THE 12TH INTERNATIONAL AAAI CONFERENCE ON WEB AND SOCIAL MEDIA (ICWSM-18).*
[8] Zeerak Waseem and Dirk Hovy. 2016. Hateful symbols or hateful people? predictive features for hate speech detection on twitter. In *Proceedings of the NAACL student research workshop.* 88–93.
[9] Dawei Yin, Zhenzhen Xue, Liangjie Hong, Brian D Davison, April Kontostathis, and Lynne Edwards. 2009. Detection of harassment on web 2.0. *Proceedings of the Content Analysis in the WEB* 2 (2009), 1–7.

Uncovering the Nucleus of Social Networks

Braulio Dumba, Zhi-Li Zhang
University of Minnesota, Twin Cities, MN, USA
braulio,zhzhang@cs.umn.edu

ABSTRACT

Many social network studies have focused on identifying communities through clustering or partitioning a large social network into smaller parts. While community structure is important in social network analysis, relatively little attention has been paid to the problem of "core structure" analysis in many social networks. Intuitively, one may expect that many social networks possess some sort of a "core" which holds various parts of the network (or constituent "communities") together. We believe that it is just as important to uncover and extract the "core" structure – referred to as the "nucleus" in this paper – of a social network as to identify its community structure. In this paper, we propose a scalable and effective procedure to uncover the "nucleus" of social networks by building upon and generalizing ideas from the existing k-shell decomposition approach. We employ our approach to uncover the nucleus in several example communication, collaboration, interaction, location-based and online social networks. Our methodology is very scalable and can also be applied to massive networks (hundreds million nodes and billion edges).

CCS CONCEPTS

• **Information systems** → **Social networks**; • **Human-centered computing** → *Social network analysis*; • **Theory of computation** → Shortest paths;

KEYWORDS

Social Network; K-Shell Decomposition; Network Core

ACM Reference Format:
Braulio Dumba, Zhi-Li Zhang. 2018. Uncovering the Nucleus of Social Networks. In *WebSci '18: 10th ACM Conference on Web Science, May 27–30, 2018, Amsterdam, Netherlands.* ACM, New York, NY, USA, 10 pages. https://doi.org/10.1145/3201064.3201075

1 INTRODUCTION

Networks are often abstractly modelled as a graph where vertices represent entities and edges capture the relations (e.g., connections) or interactions between them. In the context of (online) social networks, community identification has received a lot of attention. A community is often considered to be a subset of vertices that are densely connected internally but sparsely connected to the rest

of the network [9, 30, 35–37]. The majority of studies on identifying communities structures in social networks have relied on clustering techniques, namely, by partitioning the underlying network/social graph into *disjoint* (sometimes *overlapping*) communities. For example, Newman proposes a measure of betweenness – modularity [36, 37] – for identifying disjoint communities in a social network. Andersen et al [9] design a local graph partitioning algorithm to indentify community structures. This algorithm is based on personalized PageRank vectors. Ahn et al [6] introduce a novel perspective for discovering hierarchical community structures by categorizing links only. To obtain an optimal partition and to find communities at multiple levels, an information-theoretic framework is proposed by the authors in [38, 40]. Several studies use link and content information for uncovering meaningful communities in networks [22, 50].

Although existing studies of community structure have been very successful, most have not considered the existence of "core structure" in many networks. Intuitively, one expects that many social networks possess some sort of "core" as part of their meso-scale structure, which holds various parts of the network (or constituent "communities") together. We believe that it is just as important to uncover and extract the "core" structure – referred to as the "nucleus" – of a social network as identify its community structure [39, 49]: unlike "ordinary" constituent communities, the "core" structure plays a crucial role in the formation and evolution of a social network, to which other (constituent) "communities" are attached. Chung and Lu [18] show that power-law random graphs almost surely contain a core "subgraph" when the exponent β in the power-law degree distribution is such that $\beta \in (2, 3)$. This theoretical result suggests that many real-world social networks likely posess some sort of cohesive core structure.

One of the most popular notion of network core is given by the *k-shell decomposition* method [15]. This classical graph decomposition technique decomposes a network into hierarchically ordered layers from the periphery to the core. This method has also be extended to weighted graphs [24, 48] and dynamic networks [32]. The k-shell decomposition method has often been used as a visualization tool for studying the core structure of massive complex networks such as the Internet [15]. In addition, it has been used to identify influential spreaders in a network [23, 28].

When applying the standard k-shell decomposition to uncover the core of several example social networks (see § 2), we find that the resulting "innermost" structure is unlikely to represent the "core" of these networks. For example, this "innermost" structure may contain the maximum clique of a network but which lies rather at its periphery, or it is simply a single vertex in a dense graph. This appears to the effect of the (iterative) degree-based pruning process of k-shell decomposition, where despite at some point we reach the vicinity of the core, the k-shell decomposition continues further, which then destroys the "core" structure of the network (see § 3 for more illustration). This raises the following important question: *When should we stop the k-shell decomposition pruning process in order to preserve the core graph G_C of a network?*

In an attempt to address this question, we develop an effective procedure to uncover the *nucleus* structure of a social network by building upon and generalizing ideas from the existing k-shell decomposition [15] approach, as follows. Firstly, we propose a new metric, the *dependence value*, that measures the location importance of a node in a network. Intuitively, the dependence of node v captures the number of nodes recursively dependent of v that have been removed in earlier steps of the k-shell decomposition method. Secondly, we derive a new measure called *nucleon-index* (NI) that captures the extend to which a subgraph is a densely intra-connected and topological central core. This index can be used with a wide variety of functions to transition between core and peripheral nodes (e.g., dependence value, closeness [41] and betweenness [41] centralities, etc). Using these metrics, we therefore modify the standard k-shell decomposition method to stop the process earlier, in order to extract a meaningful "core" for social networks (see § 4). For a Facebook [4, 29] friendship network composed of 63,731 nodes and 817,035 edges, this process yields a dense "core" subgraph G_C with approximately 285 nodes and 9,616 edges. Given a dense core subgraph G_C, we investigate the importance of this substructure for the network by analysing the following metrics (see § 5): i) the distance between a node v to the core subgraph G_C; ii) the ratio of the distance between nodes u and v to their respective distance to G_C and iii) lastly, the impact of removing G_C in the structure of the network G ($G_C \subset G$).

We discuss implications and related work in § 6 and § 7. Section 8 concludes the paper. We summarize the major contributions of our paper as follows:

- We propose two *new* metrics: i) the *dependence value*, that measures the location importance of a node in the network; ii) the *nucleon-index* (NI) that captures the extend to which a subgraph is a densely intra-connected and topological central core . Using these metrics, we therefore modify the standard k-shell decomposition method to stop the process earlier, in order to extract a meaningful "core" for social networks.
- We apply our approach to uncover the core structure in example communication, collaboration, interaction, location-based and online social networks. Our methodology is very scalable and can also be applied to uncover the core structure of massive networks (hundreds million nodes and billion edges).

2 DATASETS

This section presents a summary of the datasets that we use for our analysis:

Autonomous systems graph: This dataset is an undirected graph of the AS peering information inferred from Oregon route-views between March 31 and May 26, 2001 [2], and its main features are summarized on Table 1.

Social networks graphs: This dataset is a collection of 9 undirected graphs of communication, collaboration, interaction, location-based and online social networks [1–5, 11, 25, 29, 46](see Table 1 for a summary of the main features):

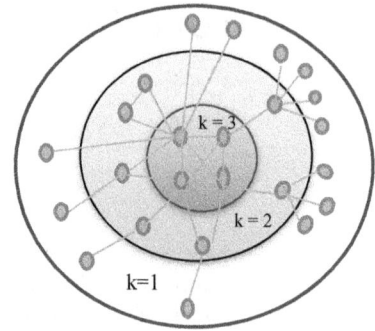

Figure 1: A schematic representation of a network under k-shell decomposition: the network can be viewed as the union of shell 1 up to $k_{max} = 3$ (network core).

Table 1: Main characteristics of the social networks and AS graphs: d - node degree; % LCC - percentage size of the largest connected component of the original network

ID	# nodes	# edges	max(d)	% LCC
arenas-jazz	198	2,742	100	1.00
dnc-corecipient	906	20,858	368	0.94
arenas-pgp	10,680	24,316	205	1.00
Oregon-1	11,174	23,409	2,389	1.00
ca-HepPh	12,008	118,521	491	0.93
ca-AstroPh	18,722	198,110	504	0.95
ca-CondMat	23,133	93,497	280	0.92
email-Enron	36,692	183,831	1,383	0.92
loc-brightkite	58,228	214,078	1,134	0.97
Facebook	63,731	817,035	1,098	0.99

- *ca-AstroPh, ca-HepPh, ca-CondMat*: collaboration networks between authors for papers submitted to Astro Physics, High Energy Physics (Phenomenology category) and Condense Matter Physics – a graph contains an undirected edge (i, j), if author i co-authored a paper with author j.
- *arenas-jazz*: collaboration network between jazz musicians – the graph contains an undirected edge (i, j), if two musicians have played together in a band.
- *email-Enron*: email communication network – the graph contains an undirected edge (i, j), if address i sent at least one email to address j.
- *arenas-pgp*: interaction network of users of the Pretty Good Privacy (PGP) algorithm.
- *dnc-corecipient*: online contact network for people having received the same email in the 2016 Democratic National Committee email leak – the graph contains an undirected edge (i, j), if two persons received the same email.
- *Facebook*: an undirected subgraph of the friendship network for the users in Facebook.
- *loc-brightkite*: an undirected graph for the friendship network for the users from loc-brightkite location-based online social network.

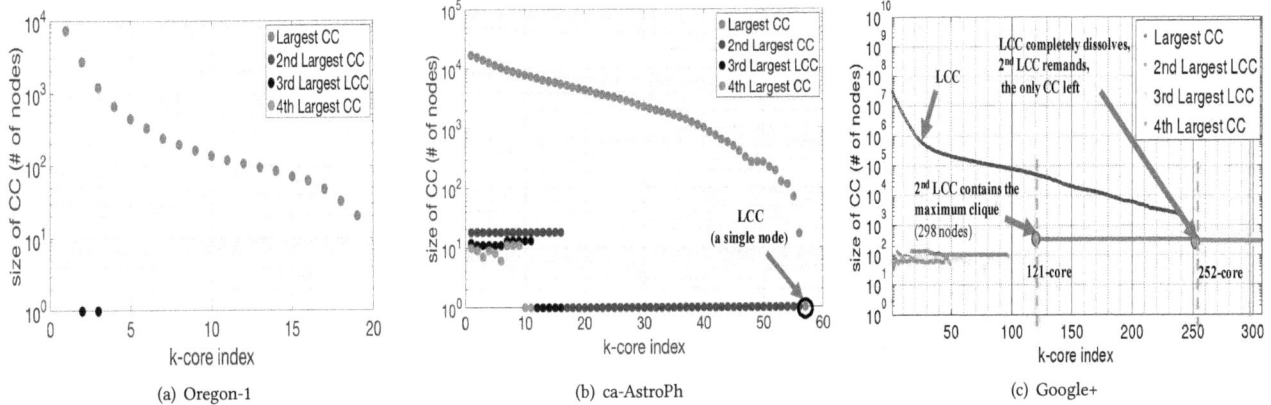

Figure 2: The size of the largest as well as those of the 2nd, 3rd and 4th largest connected components in the k-core subgraphs

3 K-SHELL NETWORK CORE

K-shell decomposition [15] is one of the most popular and scalable method to investigate and visualize the core-periphery structure in complex networks. This method assigns to each node an integer representing its coreness location according to successive layers or shells in the network. It works as follows: a) first, remove all nodes in the network with degree 1 (and their respective edges) – these nodes are assigned to the 1-shell; b) more generally, at step $k = 2, \ldots$, remove all nodes in the remaining network with degree k or less (and their respective edges) – these nodes are assigned to the k-shell; and c) the process stops when all nodes are removed at the last step. Small values of k define the periphery of the network and the *innermost network core* corresponds to the highest shell index (k_{max}) – see Fig. 1. (Note that this is distinct from k-core decomposition[1] defined in the literature [7, 8]).

In the k-shell decomposition process, at each step k, the remaining subgraph is referred to as "k-core" (C_k). The k-core subgraph is the union of all shells with indices larger or equal to k or it is the maximal induced subgraph $C_k \subseteq G$ such that if $v \in C_k$, then node v must have at least $k + 1$ neighbors that belong to C_{k-1} and $deg^k(v) > 0$ (we use $deg(v)$ to denote the degree of v in the network and $deg^k(v)$ to denote the degree of v in C_k). Similarly, k-shell (S_k) can be defined as the subgraph induced by the set of nodes with $d^{k-1}(v) \leq k$ and if $v \in S_k \rightarrow deg^k(v) = 0$.

Clearly, for a node to belong to the k-core (thus $shell(v) \geq k$), it must have at least degree k, i.e., $deg(v) \geq k$. However, $deg(v) \geq k$ is not sufficient to guarantee it to belong to the k-core. For example, a node v with only neighbors of degree 1 (i.e., v is the root of a star structure) belongs to the 2-shell, i.e., $shell(v) = 2$, no matter how high its degree is. On the other hand, it is easy to see that if a node v is part of a clique of k nodes, then $shell(v) \geq k$. However, a node v does not need to be part of a k-clique to have $shell(v) \geq k$. Consider a tree T of n nodes (the sparsest graph with n nodes). We can in fact provide a complete characterization of nodes in T to have $shell(v) \geq k$ in a recursive manner: for v to have $shell(v) \geq k$, it must have at least k-neighbors u's with $shell(u) \geq k - 1$ – this

characterization also applies to a general graph. We see that in the case of a tree, nodes with higher k-shell indices must lie more at the "core" (i.e., the increasingly "denser" part) of the tree. For a general graph, however, a node with a high k-shell index may not lie at the "core" of the graph: it can be part of a large clique that is "isolated" on a periphery of a massive graph. In such a case, the large clique will break off from the "core" of the network (e.g., as represented by the largest connected component remaining in the k-core) in the early stage of the k-shell decomposition process.

This method has been successfully used as a visualization tool for studying and uncovering the core structure of networks such as the Internet AS graph [15]. We apply it to the *Oregon-1* AS dataset. Fig. 2(a) shows the size of the largest as well as those of the 2nd, 3rd and 4th largest connected components in the k-core graph. We observe that the largest connected component decreases smoothly as k varies from 1 to 20. At $k_{max} = 20$, we are left with a very dense core subgraph composed of 20 nodes and 164 edges – the network nucleus. This result shows that for the AS graph, nodes with the highest k-shell indices indeed lie at the "core" (i.e., the increasingly "denser" part) of the graph. However, our experiments reveal that applying the k-shell decomposition for other types of graphs, especially social graphs, may not yield the same results. There are two possible reasons:

First, for some graphs the k_{max}-shell seems to contain some "residual" portions of the nucleus of a graph or simply a singleton node. For example, Fig. 2(b) shows the k-core graph for the 4 largest connected components in the *ca-AstroPh* dataset. We see that at k_{max}=57, we are left with just a single node in the k-core graph, which is unlikely to be the complete inner-core of the graph.

Second, in other graphs the k_{max}-shell does not appear to lie at the "core" of the graph: it could be part of a large community structure (e.g. a maximum clique) that is "isolated" on a periphery of a graph. To illustrate this, we apply the k-shell decomposition method to a *Google+* reciprocal network[2] obtained from a previous

---

[1]Which simply removes all nodes with degree less than k in a graph.

[2]A network composed with only bi-directional edges, extracted from a directed social graph. A reciprocal network can be viewed as the stable "skeleton" network of a directed social network that holds it together and encodes its main topological characteristics [20]. For more on the reciprocal network of Google+ the reader is referred to [19, 20].

study [19, 20] - it consists of more than 40 million nodes and ≈ 400 million edges. Figure 2(c) shows the size of the largest as well as those of the 2nd, 3rd and 4th largest connected components in the k-core, as k varies from 1 to 308. We note that at step $k = 121$, a small subgraph containing the maximum clique (of size 290) breaks off from the largest connected component which desolves after $k = 253$, whereas this subgraph containing the maximum clique persists after $k = 252$ and becomes the largest component; at $k_{max} = 308$, we are left with this maximum clique plus 10 additional nodes that are connected to the maximum clique. Closer inspection of the nodes in the maximum clique reveals that its users belong to a single institution in Taiwan, forming a close-knit community where each user follows everyone else – which is unlikely to be the network core of Google+.

From these results, we see that directly applying the standard k-shell decomposition to some graphs (especially, social networks) produces an "innermost" structure that does not represent "core" of these networks. This is due to the fact that at a certain k-index, we reach the vicinity of the core; but going far beyond this index would destroy the core structure of the network.

4 NODE DEPENCENCE VALUES AND NETWORK CORE

In order to extract a meaningful "core" for a general graph $G = (V, E)$ (e.g., social networks), we therefore modify the standard k-shell decomposition method to stop the process earlier. To achieve this, we propose a new metric that provides important information about the structural function of each node in the graph (we label it as "dependence" value) at each k-step. Then, we present a new measure called *nucleon-index* (NI) that captures the extend to which a subgraph is a densely intra-connected and topological central core – it can be used with a wide variety of functions to transition between core and peripheral nodes (e.g., dependence value, closeness and betweenness centralities, etc).

4.1 Node Depencence Values

The *dependence* value of node v at step k is defined as follows: for $v \in V$, $dep^0(v, \beta) = 0$ and for $k = 1, \ldots, c(v)$,

$$dep^k(v, \beta) := dep^{k-1}(v, \beta) + \delta^k(v) + \beta \times \Sigma_{u \in N^k(v)}[dep^{k-1}(u, \beta)]$$

(1)

where β is a control parameter, $0 \leq \beta \leq 1$; $N^k(v)$ is the set of neighbors of node v that are removed at step k, and $\delta^k(v) = |N^k(v)|$. The dependency of node v is recursively defined by measuring the number of nodes u (the h-hop neighbors of v, $h = 1, ..., k$) that are removed in earlier steps up to $k = c(v)$ –the *coreness* of node v (and for $k \geq c(v)$, by convention, we define $dep^k(v, \beta) = dep^{c(v)}(v, \beta)$).

Intuitively, $dep^k(v, \beta)$ captures the number of nodes recursively dependent on v that have been removed in earlier steps up to k. With $\beta = 0$, we note that $dep^k(v, \beta)$ captures the number of v's neighbors removed at each step up to k, and for $k \geq c(v)$, $dep^k(v, \beta) = \sum_k \delta^k(v) = deg(v)$, the degree of node v. With $\beta > 0$, $dep^k(v, \beta)$ captures not simply the dependence of its neighbors, but that of its neighbors' neighbors, and so forth. However, the number of nodes u removed at each step up to k does not influence the

Table 2: *Arenas − jazz*: **peak nucleon-indices (NI) and their respective k_C-indices (set SK) and β values**

β	max(NI)	k_C
0.0	0.011019	26
0.1	0.006561	25
0.2	0.006125	24
0.3	0.006841	24
0.4	0.007256	24
0.5	0.007500	24
0.6	0.007818	25
0.7	0.008545	25
0.8	0.009222	25
0.9	0.009849	25
1.0	0.010433	25

dependence value of the node v uniformly. Their contribution is weighted by the parameter β in eq.(1). The parameter β quantifies the contribution of node u to the total dependence value of node v. More precisely, at the kth-step, we multiply the number of h-step removed neighbors of v by β^{h-1} (see the proof in the appendix). Thus, the further a node u is to node v, the less it will contribute to the total dependence value of node v. Hence, a node v having more nodes u with high dependence values in its vicinity will also have a high dependence value, creating the *dependency propagation* effect. Therefore, we posit that the network core should contain only nodes with very high dependence because the $dep^k(v, \beta)$ values of any $v \in V$ grows as k increases (more nodes are removed as we move from the periphery of the graph to its core). In the next section, we use the dependence value of node v as a measure of its coreness.

4.2 Nucleon Index and Network Nucleus

To derive a meaningful "core" structure in social networks, we postulate that the *nucleus* of a network $G(V, E)$ is an induced subgraph G_C having the following properties:

(1) Subgraph $G_C(V_C, E_C)$ is *connected* and composed of a collection of nodes in G with *dense* aggregate centralities by some measure.

(2) The set V_C is fundamental for the *structural properties* of the network, e.g., in terms of connecting nodes via short paths through the network.

(3) G_C is the minimal subgraph with these properties.

To find a subgraph G_C with the above properties, we consider an appropriately defined "decomposition" process (e.g., the k-shell decomposition) which yields a (filtration) sequence of (sub)graphs $\{G_k\}$'s of G: $G_0 := G \supset G_1 \supset \cdots \supset G_K = \emptyset$. Given a node centrality measure $\theta(i)$, $i \in V$, we define the *nucleon-index* (NI) to capture the extent to which a subgraph constitutes a "densely connected", topological central core in this sequence:

$$NI(G_k, \theta(i)) := \frac{V_k}{V_{k-1}} \times \frac{E_k}{V_k \times (V_k - 1)} \times \{\frac{1}{V_k} \times \sum_{i \in G_k} \theta(i)\} \quad (2)$$

where by abuse of notation, we use E_k to denote the number of edges between nodes in G_k and V_k the number of nodes in G_k (and $|V_K| = 0$). The second term in eq.(2) measure the density of G_k and the last term the average centrality of G_k. Ideally, if G_k

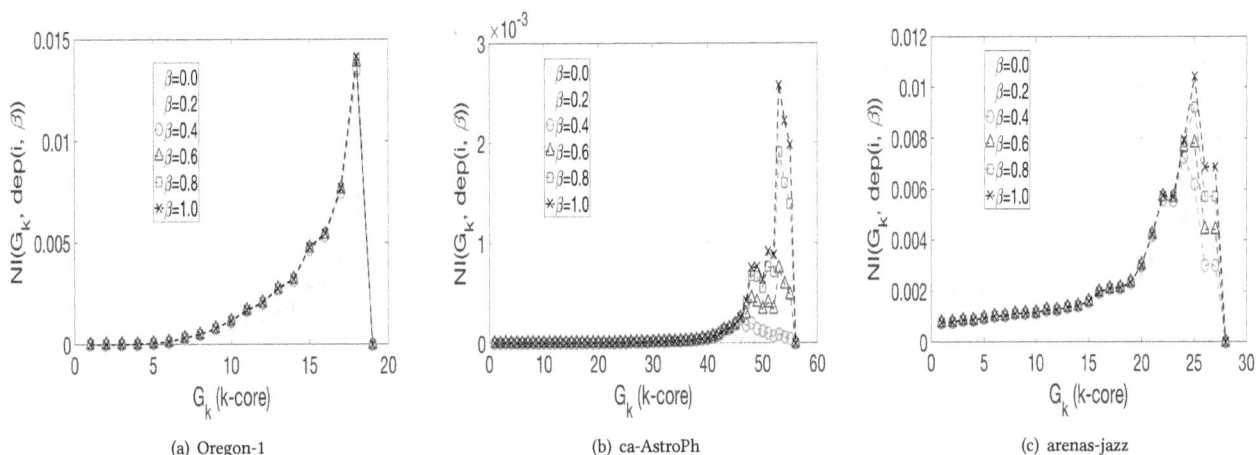

(a) Oregon-1   (b) ca-AstroPh   (c) arenas-jazz

Figure 3: Variation of the nucleon-index per k-core index for several β parameters in the dependence computation

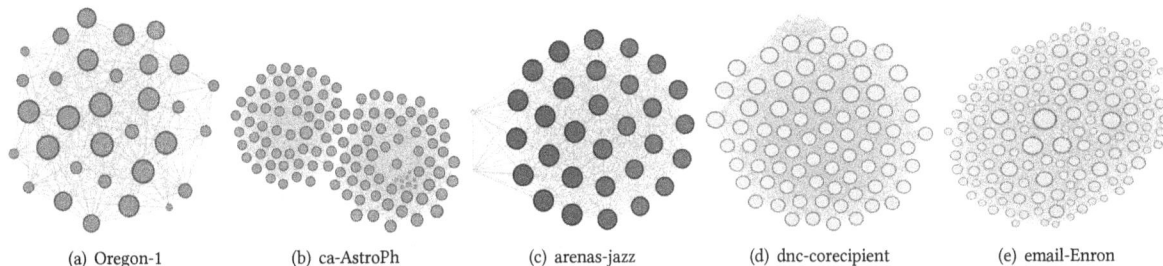

(a) Oregon-1   (b) ca-AstroPh   (c) arenas-jazz   (d) dnc-corecipient   (e) email-Enron

Figure 4: Visualization of the core subgraphs: the size of a node is proportional to its degree

is a "dense core" of G, the product of these two terms should be large. The first term controls the rate of changes in size from G_k to G_{k+1}: intuitively, if G_k is the "nucleus" of G, going from G_{k-1} to G_k should not drastically change its size; but going from G_k to G_{k+1} amounts to breaking G_k apart, yielding a collection of small connected components. In other words, V_{k+1} would fall off quickly, as G_{k+1} is a small connected subgraph or an empty graph. Hence, G_k with the largest NI represents the *nucleus* of G (as produced by the decomposition process).

Considering the node dependence value as a centrality measure, we define $\theta(i)$ as follows:

$$\theta(i) := \frac{dep^{c(i)}(i,\beta)}{\sum_{j \in G} dep^{c(j)}(j,\beta)}. \qquad (3)$$

Using $\theta(i)$ defined above and applying the nucleon-index to the k-shell decomposition procedure, we develop the following *stop rule* for core extraction.

Stopping rule for core extraction: For any graph G with a dense core structure, we should stop the k-shell decomposition method at the induced subgraph of the k_C-core with maximal nucleon-index. Thus, we seek a k_C-index that maximizes the nucleon-index (NI).

Figure 3 plots the nucleon-indices per k-core (C_k) for Oregon-1, ca-AstroPh and arenas-jazz networks. To select the optimal β parameter for eq. (1), we use the following criteria: let's assume

that SK is the set of the k-indices corresponding to the maximum nucleon-indices, as β varies in the interval [0, 1] and k increases from 1 up to k_{max}. Then, we select any β associated with the k-index which appears most often in the set SK. For example, Table 2 shows the set SK for arenas-jazz. We select a β corresponding to the mode k_C-index value of 25 (i.e., $\beta = 0.1$; $\beta = 0.6$; $\beta = 1.0$).

Table 3 shows the (k_{max}, β, k_C) indices for our social network and Internet AS datasets and Fig. 4 provides a visualization of our extracted core subgraphs (G_C) for several example networks[3]. The smallest subgraph has 32 nodes and 362 edges (Oregon-1), whereas the largest one has 239 nodes and 28,441 edges (ca-HepPh). We will further investigate the structure of these core subgraphs (network nuclei) in the remaining sections.

4.3 Other Centralities and Nucleus

Nodes are more likely to be part of a network's core if they have high centrality score and if they are connected to other core nodes. Equation (2) can be used with a wide variety of $\theta(i)$ functions to transition between core and peripheral nodes. Thus, it allows one to use different ways to compute the nucleon-index (NI) and measure core quality. Here, we compute the nucleon-index using some of the most common centrality metrics: closeness centrality (c_c) [41,

---

[3]We omit the others plots here due to space constraint.

Table 3: maximum k-shell index (k_{max}); β parameter; k-index to stop the shells pruning process (k_C); number of nodes and edges in the core subgraph N(G_C) and E(G_C)

Network	k_{max}	β	k_C	$N(G_C)$	$E(G_C)$
arenas-jazz	29	0.6	25	32	466
dnc-corecipient	75	0.5	67	87	3,118
arenas-pgp	33	0.5	31	38	658
Oregon-1	20	0.5	18	32	362
ca-HepPh	238	0.5	99	239	28,441
ca-AstroPh	57	0.6	53	126	3,378
ca-CondMat	51	0.5	37	37	382
email-Enron	51	0.5	48	150	4,395
loc-brightkite	58	0.5	56	66	1,893
Facebook	64	0.5	61	285	9,616

Table 4: k-index to stop the shells pruning process (k_C) for several centralities: c_c - closeness centrality; b_c - betweenness centrality; e_c - eigenvector centrality; dep - dependence

	k_C			
Network	$\theta(i) = c_c$	$\theta(i) = b_c$	$\theta(i) = e_c$	$\theta(i) = dep$
arenas-jazz	26	25	26	25
dnc-corecipient	68	65	68	67
arenas-pgp	31	30	31	31
Oregon-1	18	18	18	18
ca-HepPh	99	99	99	99
ca-AstroPh	53	53	53	53
ca-CondMat	42	37	37	37
email-Enron	48	48	48	48
loc-brightkite	55	48	56	56
Facebook	60	60	60	61

42, 45], betweenness centrality (b_c) [14, 41, 45] and eigenvalue centrality (e_c) [12, 34, 41, 45] – we compare the obtained k_C-indices with the values computed in the previous section.

The closeness centrality measures how central a node is in terms of its distance (shortest path) from all other nodes [41], while the betweenness centrality for a node measures the number of shortest paths that pass through that node [41]. The eigenvalue centrality computes the centrality for a node based on the centrality of its neighbors. It is based on the notion that a node should be viewed as important if it is linked to other important nodes, where a node importance (or centrality score) corresponds to the largest eigenvector of the adjacency matrix [41]. Table 4 shows the k_C-indices for the different centrality measures and Fig. 5 plots the nucleon-indices versus k-core indices of several example networks[4]. In general, we observe that all the centralities give consistent k_C-indices or core structures for our datasets. In particular, we observe that our dependence metric, $dep(i, \beta)$, derives similar core structure when compared to the other metrics. From the consistency of the results given by the studied centrality metrics, we can infer that our social networks (see § 2) truly have a core structure.

Table 5: Comparing classical k-shell decomposition (KS), Nucleon Index (NI) + k-shell decomposition (KS) and Rich-Club network core (G_C) in real-world networks : N - number of nodes; E - number of edges; D - diameter; P - path length; ρ - density

method	dataset	N	E	D	P	ρ
Classical KS	Oregon-1	20	164	2.0	1.14	0.86
	ca-AstroPh	17	136	1.0	1.00	1.00
	email-Enron	36	472	2.0	1.25	0.75
NI + KS	Oregon-1	32	363	2.0	1.27	0.73
	ca-AstroPh	126	3,378	3.0	1.87	0.43
	email-Enron	150	4,395	3.0	1.61	0.39
Rich-Club	Oregon-1	37	314	3.0	1.57	0.47
	ca-AstroPh	82	994	3.0	1.80	0.30
	email-Enron	106	1,660	4.0	1.77	0.30

All the centrality metrics discussed here are designed to measure notions of node importance in a network. Nevertheless, they have different computational complexity and require different network information. For example, the closeness and eigenvalue centralities need the full network information and have a high complexity of $O(V^3)$. The betweenness centrality has a lower complexity of $O(VE)$ [14]. Our approach to calculate the $dep(v, \beta)$ score for node v is dependent on the k-shell decomposition method and degree computation which have a complexity of $O(V + E)$. Then, given that the degree and coreness of each node are known, our procedure has a complexity of $O(E)$. For a large sparse social network with $O(n)$ edges, this yields a linear time algorithm. Therefore, our methodology is highly scalable and can be applied to massive networks (hundreds million nodes and billion edges).

We compare our methodology to extract core subgraphs to the classical k-shell decomposition [15] and rich club [31, 51] methods. Table 5 provides statistics for the structure of the derived core subgraphs (G_C) for three of our networks (i.e., *Oregon-1*, *ca-AstroPh* and *email-Enron*) – we omit the others networks here due to space constraint. In general, for our dataset, we observe that the classical k-shell decomposition method (KS) is bias toward small and highly dense core subgraphs, G_C^{KS}, (i.e., a clique) which may not represent the "network core" (see § 3). In contrast, our modified k-shell decomposition method ($NI + KS$) generates larger core subgraphs than KS. In fact, our core subgraphs are supersets of the cores extracted using KS: $G_C^{NI+KS} \supset G_C^{KS}$. When compared to rich-club, we see that for some networks our modified k-shell decomposition method ($NI + KS$) generates core subgraphs of similar size (e.g., *Oregon-1*). However, our core subgraphs have more compact structure: small diameter, small path length and high density. For other networks, our methodology generates larger and denser core subgraphs than the rich-club method (e.g., *email-Enron*). This can be explained due to the fact that the rich-club is bias toward nodes with higher degree[5]. Differently, our definition of core is more general, and it allows low-degree nodes to belong to the core, as long as, they are important components in the structure of the network.

---

[4]We omit the others plots here due to space constraint.

[5]Rich-club is a group of high-degree nodes in a network that preferentially connect to one another. This structure might be the core subgraph for power law networks

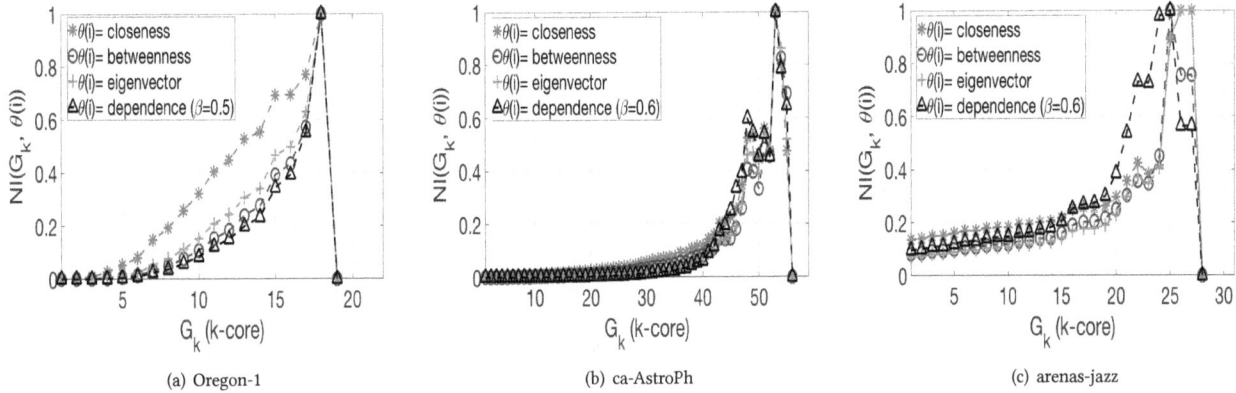

(a) Oregon-1

(b) ca-AstroPh

(c) arenas-jazz

Figure 5: Variation of the nucleon-index (NI) per k-core index for several centrality metrics: the value of NI is normalized; the k-index to stop the shells pruning process (k_C) corresponds to the max(NI)

Table 6: Summary of path length (P) and diameter (D) characteristics: $\delta(u, G_C)$ - shortest path from node u to the core subgraph G_C

Network	P	D	$Avg(\delta(u, G_C))$
arenas-jazz	2.21	6	1.27
dnc-corecipient	2.27	8	1.63
arenas-pgp	7.65	24	4.27
Oregon-1	3.62	10	1.54
ca-HepPh	4.67	13	2.38
ca-AstroPh	4.17	14	2.24
ca-CondMat	5.35	14	3.25
email-Enron	4.03	13	1.74
loc-brightkite	4.92	18	3.41
Facebook	4.31	15	2.42

Table 7: Ratio of the distance between nodes u and v to their respective distance to the core subgraph G_C: $R(u, v)$

Network	k	$Avg(R(u, v))$
arenas-jazz	70	0.96
dnc-corecipient	700	0.90
arenas-pgp	8,000	0.89
Oregon-1	8,000	1.21
ca-HepPh	8,000	1.03
ca-AstroPh	8,000	0.96
ca-CondMat	20,000	0.84
email-Enron	20,000	1.21
loc-brightkite	20,000	0.73
Facebook	20,000	0.92

5 ANALYSIS OF THE NETWORK CORE STRUCTURE

Given the dense structures of our core subgraphs, illustrated in Figure 4, we now investigate the importance of this substructure for the network. To achieve this, we define and analyse the following metrics:

Core Path Length: To understand how much the network core contributes towards the small path lengths, we measure how many hops there are between any user to the core subgraph: $\delta(u, G_C) = min_{y \in G_C}\{d(u, y)\}; G_C \subset G$. Figure 6 presents the core path length and network path length distributions for *Oregon-1, ca-AstroPh* and *arenas-jazz*[6], whereas Table 6 shows the average values and the diameter for all the networks. From these results, we can see that most users are approximately 4 hops away from a random user and at most 2 hops away from the core (G_C), which implies that our core subgraphs are important structure for the connectivity of the nodes in the network.

Core Centrality: We now investigate the importance of the core subgraph for communication and information diffusion in the network. To achieve this, we use the following procedure: first, we randomly sample k unique pairs of nodes (u, v). Then, we measure, $R(u, v)$, the ratio of the distance between nodes u and v to their respective distance to the core subgraph, as expressed in eq.(4), where $d(u, v)$ represents the shortest path between u and v, and $d(u, G_C)$ or $d(v, G_C)$ represents the shortest path between u or v to the core subgraph G_C.

Table 7 shows the average $R(u, v)$ for $k = 70, k = 700, k = 8,000$ and $k = 20,000$ respectively. We observe that the avg($R(u, v)$) is very close to the optimal value of 1.0, which implies that our core subgraph G_C contains the nodes with the highest *betweeness* in the network and they act as "bridges" for the connectivity between the other nodes in the network.

$$R(u, v) = \frac{d(u, v)}{d(u, G_C) + d(v, G_C)} \quad (4)$$

Core Removal: Lastly, we investigate the impact of removing the core subgraph G_C in the structure of the studied networks. We observe that all the neworks described in § 2 have a giant connected component (GCC) contaning more than 90% of all the nodes and more than 85% of all edges in the network. After the core removal,

---

[6]We obtain similar results for the other datasets. We omit the plots here due to space constraint.

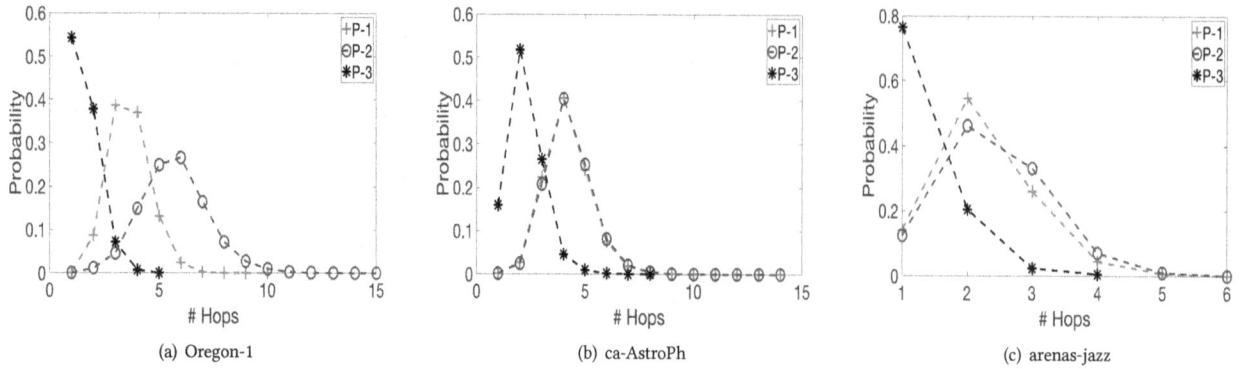

(a) Oregon-1

(b) ca-AstroPh

(c) arenas-jazz

Figure 6: Path length distribuitions: P-1: distance between nodes in the original network; P-2: distance between nodes in the original network, after core removal; P-3: nodes distance to the core subgraph G_C

we see that, for some networks (i.e., arenas-jazz, dnc-corecipient, Oregon-1 and email-Enron), at least 20% of the nodes break away from GCC, forming many isolated components of smaller sizes. Table 8 shows the number of these new connected components per network as well as the ratio of the size of the GCC after and before call removal in terms of the number of nodes and edges. From these results, we deduce that removing G_C significantly affects the connectivity and density for some of the networks.

Figure 6 shows the path length distribuition after we remove the core from our networks. We observe that the average path length increases after the core removal for most of the networks. For example, ca-AstroPh, email-Enron and Oregon-1 have average path length of 4.17, 4.03 and 3.62 before core removal, and 4.25, 4.49 and 5.72 after core removal. This result provides further evidence that the core subgraph G_C is an important structure for reachability, communication and information diffusion in these networks. Next, we discuss the implications of our results.

Table 8: Basic stats of the giant (largest) connected components (GCC) after core removal: c_n - number of connected components; n_j and n_i - number of nodes in GCC before and after core removal; e_j and e_i - number of edges in GCC before and after core removal

Network	# c_n	n_i/n_j	e_i/e_j
arenas-jazz	2	0.833	0.612
dnc-corecipient	104	0.757	0.404
arenas-pgp	26	0.993	0.940
Oregon-1	3,183	0.688	0.503
ca-HepPh	73	0.967	0.645
ca-AstroPh	12	0.946	0.929
ca-CondMat	2	0.997	0.978
email-Enron	3,350	0.800	0.711
loc-brightkite	65	0.972	0.957
Facebook	66	0.994	0.930

6 DISCUSSION

Using examples from communication networks as well as collaboration, location-based, interaction, and online social networks, we have demonstrated that our method can effectively uncover and extract the nucleus of these networks. In this section, we discuss the limitations and implications of our method and results.

First, our proposed methodology to uncover the nucleus of networks can also be applied to weighted and directed networks by using a variation of the k-shell decomposition method: Garas et al. [24] presented a weighted k-shell decomposition method and Batagelj et al. [10] generalized the k-shell decomposition to directed networks. Our method can be applied with these generalized algorithms because our dependence and nucleon-index metrics are independent to the k-shell decomposition method. Once the k-shells are provided by decomposing the network into k-layers, the dependence and nucleon-index values can be computed.

Second, the "coreness" centrality or k-shell index has been argued to be a better measure than node degree for identifying influential spreaders in a network [23, 28]. However, our results show that using k-shell indices as a predictor of spreading influence of a node can be misleading. This is due to the fact that for a node to have a high k-shell index, it just needs to be a part of a very strong structure (e.g., a clique). This structure, however, may be isolated and lie at the edge or periphery of the network, instead of its core (see § 3). Our analysis shows that the dependency value of a node, $dep^k(i)$, provides important information about the structure function of each node in the graph. Thus, we believe that by using a node dependency value along with its k-shell index (dep^k, k), we can better predict the spreading influence of a node than simply using its k-shell index. We will investigate this in the future.

Third, unveiling the core structure of social networks may have implications in the design of algorithms for information flow, and in development of techniques for analysing the vulnerability or robustness of networks. In addition, analysis of the core structure of social networks can help us uncover and understand possible organizing principles shaping the observed network topological structure and network formation.

7 RELATED WORK

In contrast to the wealth of attention given to community structure analysis in the literature, there are comparatively few methods for extracting and analyzing the core structure of a network. Some studies simply define the network "core" as the maximal clique composed of the highest degree nodes in a network [44], while other studies focus instead on some notion of connectivity information (e.g. betweeness, closeness, etc.) to find the core and periphery of a network [16, 17, 27, 33, 43].

One of the most popular quantitative methods to investigate core-periphery structure was proposed by Borgatti and Everett in 1999 [13]. Based on this study, several methods for identifying the core-periphery of a network have been proposed [16, 17, 27]. These algorithms attempt to determine which nodes are part of a densely-connected core and which are part of a sparsely connected periphery by solving some complex optimization problem. Consequently, most of these methods are computationally expensive and do not scalable to large networks.

The authors in [47] used the notion of α-β community to extract the "core" of a graph. An α-β community is a connected subgraph C with each vertex in C connected to at least β vertices of C and each vertex outside of C connected to at most α vertices of C ($\alpha < \beta$). They extract the network core structure by taking the intersection of α-β communities of different size k. A core thus corresponds to one or multiple dense regions of the graph. As a result, the proposed heuristics in [47] may return multiple dense regions ("cores") for a given network. In addition, this algorithm does not guarantee to terminate within a reasonable amount of running time.

8 CONCLUSION

In this paper, we have advanced and developed an effective procedure to extract the *core* structure of social networks. First, we introduce a new metric – the node "dependence value" – that measures the location importance of a node in a network. Second, we define a new measure called *nucleon-index* that captures the extend to which a subgraph is a densely intra-connected and topological central core. Then, using these metrics, we proposed a modified version of the k-shell decomposition method by identifying the k_C-index where we should stop pruning the network in order to preserve its core structure. For our social network datasets, we found that they contain very dense core subgraphs G_C. The smallest core has 32 nodes and 362 edges (Oregon-1), whereas the largest one has 239 nodes and 28,441 edges (ca-HepPh). Finally, given a dense core subgraph G_C, we investigate the importance of this substructure for the network by analysing the following metrics: i) the distance between a node v to the core subgraph G_C; ii) the ratio of the distance between nodes u and v to their respective distance to G_C and iii) lastly, the impact of removing G_C in the structure of the network G ($G_C \subset G$).

As part of ongoing and future work, we will provide a more in-depth analysis of the dense core subgraph G_C of social networks. We also plan to apply our method to a massive Google+ dataset [19, 20, 26] (with more than 170 million nodes and $\approx$ 3 billion edges), a massive Twitter dataset [21] (with more than 500 million nodes and $\approx$ 23 billion edges) and other social networks.

ACKNOWLEDGMENTS

This research was supported in part by DoD ARO MURI Award W911NF-12-1-0385, DTRA grant HDTRA1- 14-1-0040, NSF grant CNS-1411636, CNS-1618339 and CNS-1617729.

9 APPENDIX

Beta Parameter Selection: We now establish that the contribution of the h-step removed neighbors of node i is attenuated by β^{h-1}:

Given that $dep^0(i) = 0$ and $dep^1(i) = \delta^1(i)$, we can write an expression for $dep^2(i)$ as following:

$$dep^2(i) = dep^1(i) + \delta^2(i) + \beta \times \Sigma_{j \in N^2(i)} dep^1(j)$$
$$= \delta^1(i) + \delta^2(i) + \beta \times \Sigma_{j \in N^2(i)} \delta^1(j) \quad (5)$$

Let us assume that node i has $c(i) = 4$, then $dep^4(i)$ is computed as following:

$$dep^4(i) = dep^3(i) + \delta^4(i) + \beta \Sigma_{j \in N^4(i)} [dep^3(j)] \quad (6)$$

Expanding eq. (6) yields:

$$dep^4(i) = dep^3(i) + \delta^4(i) + \beta \Sigma_{j \in N^4(i)} [dep^2(j) + \delta^3(j) + \beta \Sigma_{j' \in N^3(j)} dep^2(j')]$$

Substituting eq. (5) yields:

$$dep^4(i) := dep^3(i) + \delta^4(i) + \beta \Sigma_j [M^3(j) + \beta \delta^2(j) \rho^1(j'^*) + \beta \Sigma_{j'} [M^2(j') + \beta \delta^2(j') \rho^1(j'')]]$$

where $M^k(i) = \Sigma_k \delta^k(i)$ and $\delta^k(i) = \rho^k(i), \forall i \in V$.

Further simplify $dep^4(i)$ yields:

$$dep^4(i) := dep^3(i) + \delta^4(i) + \Sigma_j [\beta M^3(j) + \beta^2 \delta^2(j) \rho^1(j'^*) + \Sigma_{j'} [\beta^2 M^2(j') + \beta^3 \delta^2(j') \rho^1(j'')]]$$

We can rewrite the above expressions as:

$$dep^4(i) := dep^3(i) + \beta^0 A + \Sigma_j [\beta B + \beta^2 C + \Sigma_{j'} [\beta^2 D + \beta^3 E]] \quad (7)$$

where:

- $A = \delta^4(i)$: 1-step neighbors of i removed at $k = 4$
- $B = M^3(j)$: 2-step neighbors of i removed at $k = 1, 2, 3$
- $C = \delta^2(j) \rho^1(j'^*)$: 3-step neighbors of i removed at $k = 1$
- $D = M^2(j')$: 3-step neighbors of i removed at $k = 1, 2$
- $E = \delta^2(j') \rho^1(j'')$: 4-step neighbors of i removed at $k = 1$

By generalizing eq. (7) ($k = 5, ..., n$), we observe that at every k-index, the number of h-step removed neighbors of i is multiplied by β^{h-1}. This concludes our proof. As stated before, the parameter β quantifies the contribution of node j to the total dependence value of node i. Thus, by varying β, we are impacting the contribution of any node j to the total dependence value of node i by the same proportion.

REFERENCES

[1] [n. d.]. Pretty Good Privacy network dataset – KONECT.
[2] [n. d.]. Stanford Large Network Dataset Collection. https://snap.stanford.edu/data/.
[3] 2016. DNC emails co-recipients network dataset – KONECT. http://konect.uni-koblenz.de/networks/dnc-corecipient.
[4] 2016. Facebook friendships network dataset – KONECT. http://konect.uni-koblenz.de/networks/facebook-wosn-links
[5] 2016. Jazz musicians network dataset – KONECT. http://konect.uni-koblenz.de/networks/arenas-jazz.
[6] Yong-Yeol Ahn, James P Bagrow, and Sune Lehmann. 2010. Link communities reveal multiscale complexity in networks. Nature 466, 7307 (2010), 761–764.
[7] José Ignacio Alvarez-Hamelin, Luca Dall'Asta, Alain Barrat, and Alessandro Vespignani. 2005. K-core decomposition of internet graphs: hierarchies, self-similarity and measurement biases. arXiv preprint cs/0511007 (2005).
[8] J Ignacio Alvarez-Hamelin, Luca Dall'Asta, Alain Barrat, and Alessandro Vespignani. 2006. Large scale networks fingerprinting and visualization using the k-core decomposition. In Advances in neural information processing systems. 41–50.
[9] Reid Andersen, Fan Chung, and Kevin Lang. 2006. Local graph partitioning using pagerank vectors. In Foundations of Computer Science, 2006. FOCS'06. 47th Annual IEEE Symposium on. IEEE, 475–486.
[10] Vladimir Batagelj and Matjaž Zaveršnik. 2002. Generalized cores. arXiv preprint cs/0202039 (2002).
[11] MariÃ¡n BoguÃ±Ã¡, Romualdo Pastor-Satorras, Albert DÃaz-Guilera, and Alex Arenas. 2004. Models of Social Networks based on Social Distance Attachment. Phys. Rev. E 70, 5 (2004), 056122.
[12] Phillip Bonacich. 1987. Power and centrality: A family of measures. American journal of sociology 92, 5 (1987), 1170–1182.
[13] Stephen P Borgatti and Martin G Everett. 2000. Models of core/periphery structures. Social networks 21, 4 (2000), 375–395.
[14] Ulrik Brandes. 2001. A faster algorithm for betweenness centrality. Journal of mathematical sociology 25, 2 (2001), 163–177.
[15] Shai Carmi, Shlomo Havlin, Scott Kirkpatrick, Yuval Shavitt, and Eran Shir. 2007. A model of Internet topology using k-shell decomposition. Proceedings of the National Academy of Sciences 104, 27 (2007), 11150–11154.
[16] Marcio Rosa Da Silva, Hongwu Ma, and An-Ping Zeng. 2008. Centrality, network capacity, and modularity as parameters to analyze the core-periphery structure in metabolic networks. Proc. IEEE 96, 8 (2008), 1411–1420.
[17] Fabio Della Rossa, Fabio Dercole, and Carlo Piccardi. 2013. Profiling core-periphery network structure by random walkers. Scientific reports 3 (2013), 1467.
[18] Patrick Doreian. 1985. Structural equivalence in a psychology journal network. Journal of the American Society for Information Science 36, 6 (1985), 411–417.
[19] Braulio Dumba, Golshan Golnari, and Zhi-Li Zhang. 2016. Analysis of a Reciprocal Network Using Google+: Structural Properties and Evolution. In International Conference on Computational Social Networks. Springer, 14–26.
[20] Braulio Dumba and Zhi-Li Zhang. 2016. Unfolding the Core Structure of the Reciprocal Graph of a Massive Online Social Network. In International Conference on Combinatorial Optimization and Applications. Springer, 763–771.
[21] Maksym Gabielkov, Ashwin Rao, and Arnaud Legout. 2014. Studying social networks at scale: macroscopic anatomy of the twitter social graph. In ACM SIGMETRICS Performance Evaluation Review, Vol. 42. ACM, 277–288.
[22] Jing Gao, Feng Liang, Wei Fan, Chi Wang, Yizhou Sun, and Jiawei Han. 2010. On community outliers and their efficient detection in information networks. In Proceedings of the 16th ACM SIGKDD international conference on Knowledge discovery and data mining. ACM, 813–822.
[23] Antonios Garas, Panos Argyrakis, Céline Rozenblat, Marco Tomassini, and Shlomo Havlin. 2010. Worldwide spreading of economic crisis. New journal of Physics 12, 11 (2010), 113043.
[24] Antonios Garas, Frank Schweitzer, and Shlomo Havlin. 2012. A k-shell decomposition method for weighted networks. New Journal of Physics 14, 8 (2012), 083030.
[25] Pablo M. Gleiser and Leon Danon. 2003. Community Structure in Jazz. Advances in Complex Systems 6, 4 (2003), 565–573.
[26] Roberto Gonzalez, Ruben Cuevas, Reza Motamedi, Reza Rejaie, and Angel Cuevas. 2013. Google+ or google-?: dissecting the evolution of the new osn in its first year. In Proceedings of the 22nd international conference on World Wide Web. ACM, 483–494.
[27] Petter Holme. 2005. Core-periphery organization of complex networks. Physical Review E 72, 4 (2005), 046111.
[28] Maksim Kitsak, Lazaros K Gallos, Shlomo Havlin, Fredrik Liljeros, Lev Muchnik, H Eugene Stanley, and Hernán A Makse. 2010. Identification of influential spreaders in complex networks. Nature physics 6, 11 (2010), 888–893.
[29] JÃ©rÃ´me Kunegis. 2013. KONECT – The Koblenz Network Collection. In Proc. Int. Conf. on World Wide Web Companion. 1343–1350. http://userpages.uni-koblenz.de/~kunegis/paper/kunegis-koblenz-network-collection.pdf

[30] Jure Leskovec, Kevin J Lang, Anirban Dasgupta, and Michael W Mahoney. 2008. Statistical properties of community structure in large social and information networks. In Proceedings of the 17th international conference on World Wide Web. ACM, 695–704.
[31] Julian J McAuley, Luciano da Fontoura Costa, and Tibério S Caetano. 2007. Rich-club phenomenon across complex network hierarchies. Applied Physics Letters 91, 8 (2007), 084103.
[32] Daniele Miorandi and Francesco De Pellegrini. 2010. K-shell decomposition for dynamic complex networks. In Modeling and Optimization in Mobile, Ad Hoc and Wireless Networks (WiOpt), 2010 Proceedings of the 8th International Symposium on. IEEE, 488–496.
[33] Alan Mislove, Massimiliano Marcon, Krishna P Gummadi, Peter Druschel, and Bobby Bhattacharjee. 2007. Measurement and analysis of online social networks. In Proceedings of the 7th ACM SIGCOMM conference on Internet measurement. ACM, 29–42.
[34] Mark Newman. 2010. Networks: an introduction. Oxford university press.
[35] Mark EJ Newman. 2004. Detecting community structure in networks. The European Physical Journal B-Condensed Matter and Complex Systems 38, 2 (2004), 321–330.
[36] Mark EJ Newman. 2004. Fast algorithm for detecting community structure in networks. Physical review E 69, 6 (2004), 066133.
[37] Mark EJ Newman. 2006. Finding community structure in networks using the eigenvectors of matrices. Physical review E 74, 3 (2006), 036104.
[38] Spiros Papadimitriou, Jimeng Sun, Christos Faloutsos, and S Yu Philip. 2008. Hierarchical, parameter-free community discovery. In Joint European Conference on Machine Learning and Knowledge Discovery in Databases. Springer, 170–187.
[39] M Puck Rombach, Mason A Porter, James H Fowler, and Peter J Mucha. 2014. Core-periphery structure in networks. SIAM Journal on Applied mathematics 74, 1 (2014), 167–190.
[40] Martin Rosvall and Carl T Bergstrom. 2007. An information-theoretic framework for resolving community structure in complex networks. Proceedings of the National Academy of Sciences 104, 18 (2007), 7327–7331.
[41] Diego F Rueda, Eusebi Calle, and Jose L Marzo. 2017. Robustness comparison of 15 real telecommunication networks: Structural and centrality measurements. Journal of Network and Systems Management 25, 2 (2017), 269–289.
[42] Gert Sabidussi. 1966. The centrality index of a graph. Psychometrika 31, 4 (1966), 581–603.
[43] Murray Shanahan and Mark Wildie. 2012. Knotty-centrality: finding the connective core of a complex network. PLoS One 7, 5 (2012), e36579.
[44] Georgos Siganos, Sudhir Leslie Tauro, and Michalis Faloutsos. 2006. Jellyfish: A conceptual model for the as internet topology. Journal of Communications and Networks 8, 3 (2006), 339–350.
[45] Lei Tang and Huan Liu. 2010. Community detection and mining in social media. Synthesis lectures on data mining and knowledge discovery 2, 1 (2010), 1–137.
[46] Bimal Viswanath, Alan Mislove, Meeyoung Cha, and Krishna P. Gummadi. 2009. On the Evolution of User Interaction in Facebook. In Proc. Workshop on Online Social Networks. 37–42.
[47] Liaoruo Wang, John Hopcroft, Jing He, Hongyu Liang, and Supasorn Suwajanakorn. 2013. Extracting the core structure of social networks using (α, β)-communities. Internet Mathematics 9, 1 (2013), 58–81.
[48] Bo Wei, Jie Liu, Daijun Wei, Cai Gao, and Yong Deng. 2015. Weighted k-shell decomposition for complex networks based on potential edge weights. Physica A: Statistical Mechanics and its Applications 420 (2015), 277–283.
[49] Jaewon Yang and Jure Leskovec. 2012. Structure and overlaps of communities in networks. arXiv preprint arXiv:1205.6228 (2012).
[50] Tianbao Yang, Rong Jin, Yun Chi, and Shenghuo Zhu. 2009. Combining link and content for community detection: a discriminative approach. In Proceedings of the 15th ACM SIGKDD international conference on Knowledge discovery and data mining. ACM, 927–936.
[51] Shi Zhou and Raúl J Mondragón. 2004. The rich-club phenomenon in the Internet topology. IEEE Communications Letters 8, 3 (2004), 180–182.

Viewpoint Discovery and Understanding in Social Networks

Mainul Quraishi
L3S Research Center,
Leibniz University of Hannover
Hannover, Germany
quraishimainul@gmail.com

Pavlos Fafalios
L3S Research Center,
Leibniz University of Hannover
Hannover, Germany
fafalios@L3S.de

Eelco Herder
Radboud University
Nijmegen, the Netherlands
eelcoherder@acm.org

ABSTRACT

The Web has evolved to a dominant platform where everyone has the opportunity to express their opinions, to interact with other users, and to debate on emerging events happening around the world. On the one hand, this has enabled the presence of different viewpoints and opinions about a – usually controversial – topic (like Brexit), but at the same time, it has led to phenomena like media bias, echo chambers and filter bubbles, where users are exposed to only one point of view on the same topic. Therefore, there is the need for methods that are able to *detect* and *explain* the different viewpoints. In this paper, we propose a graph partitioning method that exploits social interactions to enable the discovery of different communities (representing different viewpoints) discussing about a controversial topic in a social network like Twitter. To explain the discovered viewpoints, we describe a method, called *Iterative Rank Difference* (IRD), which allows detecting descriptive terms that characterize the different viewpoints as well as understanding how a specific term is related to a viewpoint (by detecting other related descriptive terms). The results of an experimental evaluation showed that our approach outperforms state-of-the-art methods on viewpoint discovery, while a qualitative analysis of the proposed IRD method on three different controversial topics showed that IRD provides comprehensive and deep representations of the different viewpoints.

CCS CONCEPTS

• **Information systems** → **Clustering and classification**;

KEYWORDS

Viewpoint discovery; Viewpoint understanding; Social networks

ACM Reference Format:
Mainul Quraishi, Pavlos Fafalios, and Eelco Herder. 2018. Viewpoint Discovery and Understanding in Social Networks. In *WebSci'18: 10th ACM Conference on Web Science, May 27–30, 2018, Amsterdam, Netherlands.* ACM, New York, NY, USA, Article 4, 10 pages. https://doi.org/10.1145/3201064.3201076

1 INTRODUCTION

Social Media has now emerged as the dominant platform to discuss and comment on breaking news and noteworthy events that are happening around the world. On Twitter, for example, every second around 6,000 tweets are posted, which corresponds to over 350,000 tweets per minute, 500 million tweets per day and around 200 billion tweets per year[1].

Although such networking services facilitate the expression of diverse opinions and viewpoints about particular topics, it has led to the widespread observation of phenomena such as *media bias* and the so-called *echo chamber* effect, where users are increasingly exposed to conforming opinions.

Different viewpoints and bias have been observed in tweets from regular newspaper publishers, and previous research has shown that based on these tweets it is possible to position these publishers with respect to their stance on economic and personal issues [15]. Similarly, it has been shown that there is bias in the selection of which parts of ongoing events are reported and in which depth they are covered [44], arguably due to differences in national or regional interests, differences in political or societal orientation, and other factors.

It has been also shown that individuals generally read publications that are ideologically quite similar and are usually exposed to only one side of the political spectrum [17]. Due to these self-selected echo chambers and the observation that users with similar interests and opinions are more likely to be friends on social media (the so-called *homophily effect*) [1], polarized discussions of user groups with sometimes very different viewpoints are very common on social media.

As a large part of the population is nowadays exposed to biased, filtered or fake news, and actively participates in discussions with like-minded, there are real social costs and effects, as observed in the 2016 US election [3]. In order to understand ongoing political or societal debates, or to analyze and interpret the course of historical events retrospectively, there is the need for methods that are able to detect the different viewpoints pertaining a topic and to understand what they are about.

In a nutshell, this paper makes the following contributions:

- We propose the use of a popular graph partitioning method that exploits social interactions to cluster the users of a social network based on their viewpoint on a controversial topic. Contrary to existing works that follow a similar approach, the proposed method can be applied in cases with unknown number of viewpoints and also enables the detection of noisy groups of users that do not represent clear viewpoints.

---

[1]http://www.internetlivestats.com/twitter-statistics/ (April 4, 2018)

- To obtain a deeper understanding of a viewpoint, we introduce a method, called *Iterative Rank Difference (IRD)*, which is based on the iterative use of an automatic term recognition algorithm. The proposed method can automatically identify descriptive terms that characterize the different viewpoints and also allows understanding how one or more specific terms are related to a viewpoint.
- We present evaluation results which showcase that: i) the proposed viewpoint discovery method outperforms existing state-of-the-art topic models, ii) IRD provides comprehensive descriptions of the different viewpoints as well as of the terms that characterize them.

The remainder of this paper is organized as follows: Section 2 reports related works and the difference of our approach. Section 3 models the problems of *viewpoint discovery* and *viewpoint understanding*. Section 4 details the proposed *viewpoint discovery* method. Section 5 describes the proposed *viewpoint understanding* method. Section 6 presents evaluation results. Finally, Section 7 concludes the paper and discusses interesting directions for future research.

2 RELATED WORK

Given a controversial topic, for example an issue like *climate change* or an entity like *Donald Trump*, viewpoint discovery aims to find the different viewpoints expressed about the topic in a set of documents or in a social network. This task can be considered a sub-task of Opinion Mining, which aims to analyze opinionated documents and to infer properties such as subjectivity or polarity[2]. Discovering the different viewpoints usually involves (or is performed in parallel with) two other tasks: i) grouping the corresponding documents or users based on their viewpoints; ii) finding descriptive terms that characterize the viewpoints.

Viewpoint discovery has been applied to both documents and social media data. Below, we report works for both types of data sources.

2.1 Viewpoint Discovery in Documents

Paul and Girju [32] introduced a model, called Topic-Aspect Model (TAM), that jointly considers topics and aspects (where aspects can be interpreted as viewpoints in our case). TAM decomposes each document into a mix of topics that are characterized by a multinomial distribution over words and also exploits a second mix of aspects that affect the topics. To describe the viewpoints pertaining to a topic, [33] proposed a contrastive viewpoint summarization framework which is based on TAM and is able to find phrases that best reflect the different viewpoints.

Thonet et al [42] proposed the Viewpoint and Opinion Discovery Unification Model (VODUM), an unsupervised topic model based on LDA [6] that leverages parts of speech to jointly discover viewpoints, topics, and opinions in a text (helping to discriminate between topic and opinion words).

Al Khatib et al [2] studied the slightly different problem on how to automatically detect the differences in viewpoints between two articles in Wikipedia, where one article describes the subject matter in a more positive or negative way than the other. A statistical

classifier is trained to predict the viewpoint score of a document, which reflects how positive or negative the viewpoint is.

Another interesting work studied the prediction and analysis of the ideological stance of legislators [29]. The proposed topic model integrates regression techniques to estimate real-valued ideal points and can also extract and provide a vocabulary that characterizes the ideological discourse.

2.2 Viewpoint Discovery in Social Media

Given a controversial topic as well as the texts and interactions from the users discussing it on a social network, Thonet et al [43] propose an unsupervised topic model, called Social Network Viewpoint Discovery Model (SNVDM), which jointly identifies subtopics, viewpoints and the discourse pertaining to the different subtopics and viewpoints. To infer the viewpoints, SNVDM exploits the *homophily* phenomenon (the tendency of individuals to associate and bond with similar others) and relies on the social interactions among the users. Moreover, to account for the sparsity of social networks and the weak connections between users, the authors extend SNVDM into the SNVDM-GPU model which leverages the Generalized Pólya Urn (GPU) scheme [24].

Under the same assumption that social networks are homophilic, Barberá [5] proposes a Bayesian Spatial Following model that groups Twitter users along a common ideological dimension based on who they follow.

Ren et al [39] describe a dynamic modeling strategy to infer contrastive opinions in a given stream of multilingual social texts by jointly modeling topics, entities and sentiment labels. However, contrast is based only on sentiment (positive, negative, neutral), not on viewpoints, and thus this approach actually models and infers sentiment polarity and partisanship.

Joshi et al [20] present a topic model, called Political Issue Extraction (PIE), that estimates word-specific distributions denoting political issues and positions from an unlabeled dataset of tweets. The model uses affiliation information of political users as well as Twitter timelines of both political and non-political users. In the same context, [12] investigated how social media shape the networked public sphere and facilitate communication between communities with different political orientations. The authors showed that mentions and retweets, the two major mechanisms for public political interaction on Twitter, induce distinct network topologies: the retweet network is highly polarized, while the mention network is not.

Sachan et al [40] study the different yet related problem of detecting communities on Twitter. The proposed topic model, called Social Network Latent Dirichlet Allocation (SN-LDA), combines both text and social interactions. However, such methods focus on discovering topical communities (for instance, users discussing about football) and not different viewpoints expressed on a common controversial topic. A similar community detection technique was combined with topic modeling to characterize opinions about human papillomavirus vaccines (HPV) on Twitter [41]. Papadopoulos et al. [31] provide a comprehensive literature review of community detection approaches applied in social media.

There are also works that have applied traditional machine learning (supervised) classifiers to automatically identify the political

---

[2]The survey in [30] provides a general review on Opinion Mining and Sentiment Analysis.

affiliation and viewpoint of social media users, such as Naive Bayes [16], Support Vector Machine [11], Decision Trees [34] or Neural Networks [38]. However, although such models usually achieve high precision, they need training examples which may be very difficult to obtain.

Another related line of research has applied topic models for viewpoint discovery in forums [36, 37]. These works exploit the threaded nature of forum posts which though is not the case in social networks like Twitter where threaded interactions are scarce.

Finally, there is a number of works that tackle the related problem of *controversy detection*. This task focuses on distinguishing whether a topic of online discussion is controversial or not. Works in this field handle the problem from different perspectives, e.g., by analyzing news articles [10, 25], by exploiting the social media [18, 35], or by focusing on Wikipedia pages [8, 14]. As regards social media, controversy detection has been studied on Twitter using both supervised [35] and unsupervised [18] methods. Popescu and Pennacchiotti [35] proposed and evaluated three regression machine learning models for identifying controversial events in Twitter. The models make use of a variety of features, including linguistic, structural, sentiment and news-based ones. On the other hand, Garimella et al. [18] developed a framework to identify controversy without prior domain-specific knowledge about the topics in question. The framework builds a conversation graph about a topic, partitions the graph to identify potential sides of the controversy, and measures the amount of controversy by analyzing characteristics of the graph.

2.3 Our approach

Compared to the existing works, in this paper we also exploit social interactions (like [43] and [12]) and build an interaction graph where nodes correspond to users and edges to endorsements among the users. To detect the different viewpoints, actually the groups of users that represent the viewpoints, we make use of a popular multi-level graph partitioning algorithm, inspired by the work in [18] which applies the same algorithm for the problem of controversy detection and quantification. However, contrary to this work, we propose the use of the quality metric *conductance* for deciding on the clusters that hold different viewpoints. In this way, our method can be also applied in cases of unknown number of viewpoints as well as for the identification of noisy groups of users that do not represent a clear viewpoint.

With respect to the problem of *viewpoint understanding*, in order to provide a deep understanding of a viewpoint, we propose the iterative use of an automatic term recognition algorithm that is based on *rank difference* [23]. To our knowledge, this kind of algorithms has not been previously applied to a similar problem.

3 PROBLEM MODELING

In our context, a *controversial topic* is a subject of public interest discussed in a social networking service where its users can post texts and also interact with each other. A controversial topic can be a specific event (e.g., *US Election 2016*), a general issue (e.g., *abortion* or *gun control*), or even an entity (e.g., *Donald Trump* or *Palestine*).

For a controversial topic t, let P be the set of all texts (posts) related to t, posted in a social networking service by a set of users

U, in a specific time period. We can gather these texts by querying the social network using specific keywords that describe the topic. Let also W be the vocabulary of P, i.e., all terms/words that exist in the texts of P. Now, let I be the set of *endorsement* interactions among the users (e.g., likes or retweets) where each such interaction is associated with a post in P and two users in U (i.e., the interactions are related to the topic). For a post $p \in P$ and two users $u_1, u_2 \in U$, we can represent an interaction $I_i \in I$ as a triple of the form $\langle u_1, p, u_2 \rangle$, where the user u_1 is the initiator (or sender) of the interaction, user u_2 is the receiver, and p is the mean (or channel) of interaction (e.g., u_1 likes the text p posted by u_2).

We now model the problems of *viewpoint discovery* and *viewpoint understanding* as follows:

- *Viewpoint discovery*: compute a set of k user groups $G = \{G_1, \ldots, G_k\}$, where each group $G_i \subset U$ corresponds to a different viewpoint.
- *Viewpoint understanding*: for each group $G_i \in G$, compute a set of top-n descriptive terms $W_i \subset W$ that characterize the viewpoint. In addition, for a descriptive term $w \in W_i$, compute a new set of descriptive terms $W_i' \subset W$ that characterize w in the context of the viewpoint G_i.

4 VIEWPOINT DISCOVERY

Similar to [18] and [12], we build an *interaction graph* $\mathcal{G}(U, I)$, where nodes correspond to users and edges correspond to endorsements among the users. In our case, an edge connecting two users is undirected and exists if there is a sufficient number of interactions that involve them. In our case studies and experiments we draw an edge when there are at least 2 endorsements between the two users (similar to [18]). This number seems to be sufficient for indicating a common viewpoint on a topic, while it also reduces the noise in the considered data.

Below, we first discuss how we decided on the clustering method to use in our problem (Section 4.1), and then describe the method we propose for detecting the clusters that hold different viewpoints (Section 4.2).

4.1 Choosing the proper clustering method

We need a clustering method which can ensure sparse connections among the different clusters. The intuition for this requirement is the following: the absence of an edge between two users does not imply different viewpoints, however users with different viewpoints will probably not endorse each other. Thus, contrary to classic community detection algorithms, ensuring dense connections within the same cluster is not a requirement for our problem. In addition, since the network can be quite large, containing thousands or even millions of users, we should avoid approaches that require pairwise node comparisons.

We studied the applicability of different network clustering algorithms:

- Node similarity
- The Louvain method (community detection)
- Multi-Level Graph Partitioning (MLGP)

Node similarity algorithms aim to find nodes that are topologically similar, i.e., they share many of the same neighbors. Various similarity measures can be used, like cosine similarity, Pearson coefficient, or the Euclidean distance [27]. However, similarity is measured between each pair of nodes, which makes their computation very time consuming for networks with large number of nodes.

The goal of community detection algorithms is the detection of the dense portions of the network. There is a plethora of algorithms for this kind of problem, like hierarchical clustering and modularity maximization. We tried one of the most popular modularity maximization algorithms called the Louvaine Method [7]. Modularity is a measure designed to measure the strength of division of a network into modules (groups or communities), where networks with high modularity have two main characteristics: i) dense connections between the nodes within modules, and ii) sparse connections between nodes in different modules [28]. This means that, if there is no edge connecting two nodes in the same cluster, modularity get decreases as a penalty, for ensuring that the detected clusters are very dense. However, as we have already discussed, sparsity is common in large social networks: no edges between two users does not imply different viewpoints.

The goal of Multi-Level Graph Partitioning (MLGP) algorithms is the detection of partitions with a minimum "cut", i.e., a minimum number of edges connecting different clusters. In such a method, the network is divided into a predetermined number of parts, chosen such that the cut is minimized. This approach is suitable in our case because it ensures sparse connections between nodes in different clusters. To avoid getting partitions of very different sizes (e.g., one partition containing only one node, and one containing all the other nodes), the size of the partitions need to be also taken into consideration. This can be done by computing the degree of the nodes that are inside each cluster. This normalized measure can be then used as the optimization criterion for finding the best solution. To find the optimal solution, we exploited a *multi-level graph partitioning* algorithm (of the METIS software package [22]) which falls under the type of heuristic algorithms.

4.2 Detecting the viewpoints

4.2.1 Choosing the right quality metric. We now need a quality metric for deciding on the clusters that hold different viewpoints. We experimented with the following measures [4]:

- Modularity
- Silhouette index
- Coverage
- Performance
- Conductance

As we have already explained (cf. Section 4.1), *modularity* should be avoided for sparse graphs, since it gives high scores to clusters with sparse internal connections. The *Silhouette index* considers the similarity and dissimilarity between the nodes which in our case can be measured by their shortest path. However, this requires finding the shortest path for all pairs of nodes, which is impractical for very large sparse graphs. The *coverage* of a clustering is given as the fraction of the weight of all intra-cluster edges with respect to the total weight of all edges in the whole graph. Higher values of coverage means that there are more edges inside the clusters than edges linking different clusters, which translates to a better clustering. However, this measure does not consider the size of a

cluster, which makes it unsuitable for our case, since it can give high scores to a clustering having a large number of very small clusters. *Performance* counts the number of internal edges in a cluster along with the edges that don't exist between the cluster's nodes and other nodes in the graph. Higher values indicate that a cluster is both internally dense and externally sparse. Similar to *modularity*, this measure is not suitable for large sparse graphs [4].

Finally, the *conductance* of a cut is the ratio between the size of the cut and the minimum cluster volume [21]. The volume of a cluster is the total number (or the sum of the weights) of the edges with at least one endpoint in the cluster. Specifically, the conductance of a cluster of users $G_i \in G$ can be computed as follows:

$$conductance(G_i) = \frac{\sum_{u \in G_i} \sum_{v \notin G_i} weight(u, v)}{minimum(volume(G_i), volume(\overline{G_i}))} \quad (1)$$

where $\overline{G_i} = U \setminus G_i$ and:

$$volume(G_i) = \sum_{u \in G_i} \sum_{v \in U} weight(u, v) \quad (2)$$

In simple words, the formula computes the percentage of edges starting from nodes within the cluster that point to nodes outside the cluster. Since conductance considers both the cut size and the volume of the clusters, this measure is suitable in our problem: a large cluster having a small cut (small number of edges pointing to nodes outside the cluster) will get a low conductance score, making it a good candidate for representing a concrete viewpoint.

4.2.2 Deciding on the clusters that hold different viewpoints. To find the clusters that hold different viewpoints, we inspect the conductance of the clusters for different graph partitioning approaches (values of k). If a cluster has a large conductance value, this means that the cluster has a strong connection with one or more of the other clusters and thus does not hold a different and clear viewpoint. In general, large conductance values is an indication of poor clustering. Hence, an ideal partitioning provides clusters with very low conductance values. In this case, the network exhibits a highly segregated structure, with limited connectivity among the different clusters, meaning that each cluster represents a different viewpoint.

Figure 1 depicts the conductance values for different graph partitioning scenarios for the controversial topic *2014 Scottish Independence Referendum*, using the dataset provided in [9] which contains only supporters of "yes" and "no" (more in Section 6). We notice that for $k = 2$, the two clusters have very low conductance value. Notice that, since the considered graph is undirected, the clusters have always the same conductance value for $k = 2$ (same number of edges connecting the two clusters, same minimum volume of the two clusters). For $k = 3$, there are two clusters with much bigger (compared to $k = 2$) conductance value, while the third cluster has a very large value meaning that this cluster has a strong connection with one or both of the other two clusters. Thus, we should partition the graph using $k = 2$ and select both clusters as representing different viewpoints.

The conductance plot can also indicate cases where a bigger value of k should be selected even if not all k clusters represent viewpoints, because then we can filter out noisy data (i.e., users with no clear viewpoint). This can result in a better selection of the groups of users that hold different viewpoints. For instance, Figure

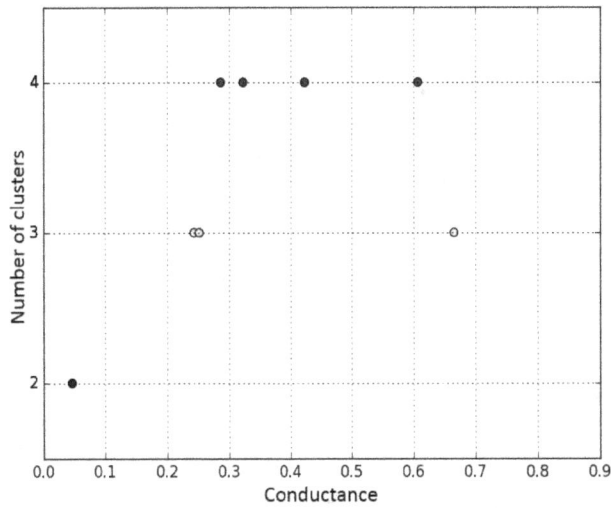

Figure 1: Conductance values for different number of clusters (value of k), for the topic "2014 Scottish Independence Referendum".

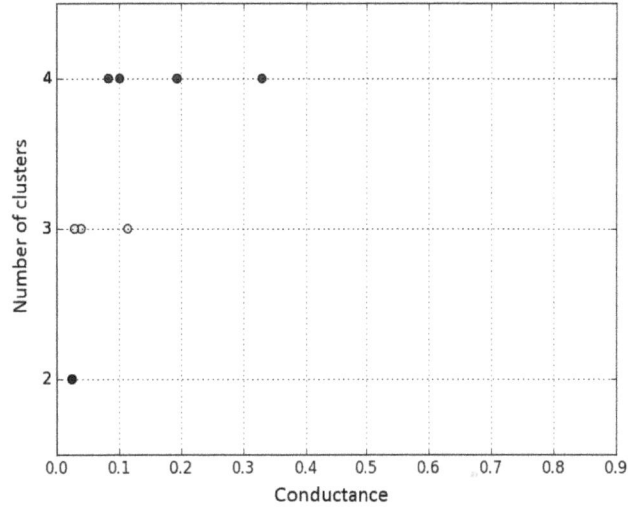

Figure 2: Conductance values for different number of clusters (value of k), for the topic "2016 US Presidential Election".

2 depicts the conductance plot for the topic *2016 US Presidential Election* (using a manually created dataset, more in Section 6). Here we should better decide to partition the graph using $k = 3$ because two of the clusters have very low conductance values (similar to the case of $k = 2$) while the third one has a much larger value. Thus, in this case we can consider as viewpoints only the two clusters with the small conductance values and ignore the third cluster. To validate this, Figure 3 shows the network clustering for $k = 2$ (left) and $k = 3$ (right) using a force-directed layout algorithm [19], where colors correspond to different viewpoints detected by our method. We notice that, for $k = 2$ there are two large well-concentrated clusters that correspond to two different viewpoints, but also several other very small clusters assigned to these two viewpoints. These small clusters is an indication of "noisy" groups of users with no clear viewpoint. For $k = 3$ we notice that there are again two large well-concentrated clusters corresponding to two different viewpoints, while the third viewpoint (in green color) is very scattered and consists of several very small clusters.

Figure 4 shows another example where three clusters are selected as representing different viewpoints. The plot corresponds to the topic *2016 Brexit referendum* (more about the dataset in Section 6). We notice that using $k = 4$ for graph partitioning, three clusters have low conductance values (below 0.1). Since the fourth cluster has a much larger value, we can consider it as noisy and ignore it. As we will see in Section 6, one cluster corresponds to supporters of Brexit, one to supporters of Bremain, and the third to the neutral viewpoint where users generally discuss the consequences of Brexit and its relation to other topics.

A simple algorithm for deciding both the number of clusters for partitioning the graph (value of k) and the number of clusters that hold different viewpoints is the following: We start by applying the proposed MLGP clustering method for $k = 2$ and inspecting the conductance value of the two clusters (which should be the same). If it is large (above a threshold δ, e.g., $\delta = 0.10$), it means that the topic

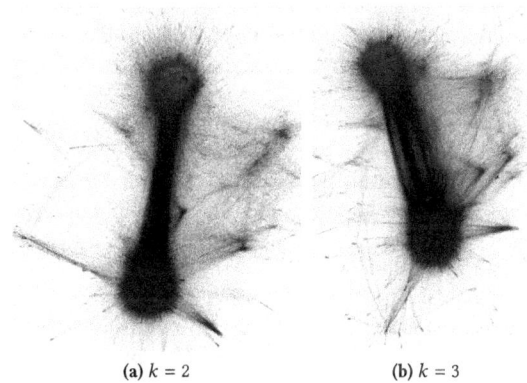

(a) $k = 2$　　　　　　　(b) $k = 3$

Figure 3: Force-directed network visualization of the topic "2016 US Presidential Election" for different number of clusters (value of k). Colors correspond to different viewpoints detected by the proposed MLGP method.

is probably not controversial or has not induced much discussion on the underlying social network, or the gathered tweets/retweets used for building the graph are not a good representation of the topic. On the contrary, if the value is below the threshold, then they are both selected as candidate clusters representing different viewpoints. Then we partition the graph using $k = 3$. If the conductance value of all three clusters is very low, this means that all clusters should be selected since they all hold a different viewpoint. If only two of the clusters have low conductance value (below the threshold), then we should better select $k = 3$ and ignore the third "noisy" cluster. We continue in a similar way for larger values of k until we get the maximum number of clusters below the threshold for the larger value of k.

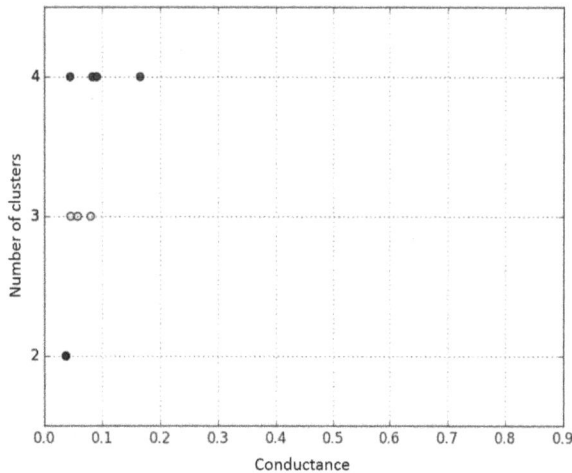

Figure 4: Conductance values for different number of clusters (value of k), for the topic "2016 Brexit Referendum".

5 VIEWPOINT UNDERSTANDING

To understand a viewpoint, we propose the iterative use of a simple rank difference method introduced in [23]. We call the proposed method *Iterative Rank Difference*, for short IRD.

First, we try to answer the question: *what is a viewpoint about?* Given a group of users $G_i \in G$ representing a specific viewpoint, we analyze the texts P_i posted by the users of G_i and derive a list of top-n descriptive terms $W_i = \{w_1, \ldots w_n\}$ that characterize the viewpoint. Then, to obtain a deeper understanding of a specific viewpoint, we try to answer the question: *what is a term about?* This allows understanding why a term appears in the list of a viewpoint's top descriptive terms. For example, as regards the *US 2016 presidential election*, we may want to understand why the hashtag *#trumpleaks* appears in the top descriptive terms of the *"against Donald Trump"* viewpoint. Given a term $w \in W_i$, we answer this question by computing a set of other descriptive terms $W_i' = \{w_1', \ldots, w_n'\}$ that characterize t in the context of G_i.

5.1 Rank Difference

The rank difference algorithm tries to distinguish the important terms of a specific corpus and filter out terms that do not characterize the corpus [23]. The algorithm operates over two ranked lists of terms: one that has been extracted from the "subject corpus" (corpus of interest related to a subject for which we want to find the descriptive terms), and one extracted from a "contrasting corpus" (a general corpus or corpus representing a different subject). Both lists are ranked according to the same criterion, e.g., the frequency of the terms in the corresponding corpus. Rank Difference identifies those terms with the largest difference in ranking between both corpora, in other words those terms that are most specific for the subject corpus. The algorithm also considers the size of the lists in order to make the term ranks in the two corpora fairly comparable.

Formally, given the two ranked lists of terms W_s and W_c (one for the *subject* corpus and one for the *contrasting* corpus), the score of a term w is computed as the difference in rank between the two

corpora:

$$score(w) = \frac{rank(w, W_c)}{|W_c|} - \frac{rank(w, W_s)}{|W_s|} \qquad (3)$$

where $rank(w, W_x) \in [-1, 1]$ is the rank (position) of w in the corresponding list. A term receives a high score if its position in the subject corpus is high and its position in the contrasting corpus is low (notice that the highest position in a list has rank 1). The higher the score of a term, the more important this term is for the subject corpus. By contrast, the lower the score of a term, the more important this term is for the contrasting corpus. If a term is in the same rank in the two lists and the lists have the same size, then its score is zero meaning that this term is not important, neither for the subject corpus nor for the contrasting corpus.

Although normalization by the size of the lists makes the term ranks in the two corpora comparable, considering very large lists can affect the performance of this algorithm, e.g., by overemphasizing the importance of some terms with a low ranking criterion (e.g., frequency). For instance, if the top-100 terms of a list have a high frequency (e.g., $> 1,000$) but there is a long tail of noisy terms with very low frequency (e.g., 10,000 terms with frequency < 10), we should consider to cut the list in position 100.

5.2 First iteration: *What is a viewpoint about?*

To answer this question, we analyze the texts posted by all users in U and create two lists of terms:

- W_s (*subject* list): Top-n terms that occur in texts posted by the group of users G_i representing the query viewpoint.
- W_c (*contrasting* list): Top-n terms that occur in texts posted by all other groups of users representing the other viewpoints.

In both lists, the term frequency (number of occurrences in the texts) is used as the ranking criterion. Then, we run the rank difference algorithm in these two lists and get the list of descriptive terms W_i that characterize G_i.

5.3 Next iterations: *What is a term about?*

In the next iterations, we want to understand why one or more terms appear in the top-n descriptive terms of a specific viewpoint. Given a term $w \in W_i$ that characterizes a viewpoint G_i, we run the rank difference algorithm on the following two lists:

- W_s (*subject* list): Top-n terms in texts mentioning w, posted by all users in G_i.
- W_c (*contrasting* list): Top-n terms in texts <u>not</u> mentioning w, posted by all users in G_i.

The term frequency is used again as the ranking criterion in both lists.

6 EVALUATION

6.1 Effectiveness of Viewpoint Discovery

We evaluated the effectiveness of the proposed viewpoint discovery method using the two Twitter datasets introduced in [9][3]. The first dataset (*Indyref*) contains tweets about the 2014 Scottish Independence Referendum, where there are two main viewpoints: *Yes*

---

[3]http://dx.doi.org/10.6084/m9.figshare.1430449

Table 1: Effectiveness of viewpoint discovery.

Method	Indyref		Midterms	
	Purity	NMI	Purity	NMI
SNVDM-GPU	0.969	0.800	0.964	0.778
MLGP	**0.988**	**0.908**	**0.983**	**0.876**

(meaning support to Scottish independence), and *No* (meaning opposition to Scottish independence). The second dataset (*Midterms*) contains tweets about the 2014 U.S. Midterm Election. Here again, there are two main viewpoints: *Democratic party supporters* and *Republican party supporters*. Details about the creation of the datasets and the ground truth can be found in [9]. Notice here that the ground truth for both datasets contains only users that belong to one of the two viewpoints, which however is not realistic. In a real setting, one has to collect a set of tweets and retweets related to a topic using some search terms, hashtags and/or user accounts, and then create a retweet graph which contains a very diverse and noisy set of users, many of who may not belong to a specific viewpoint. This makes the viewpoint discovery task much harder. However, since we are not aware of any other ground truth dataset that can be used for our problem (discovery of user-level viewpoints in a social network), we evaluate our approach using the aforementioned two datasets.[4]

We compare the proposed multi-level graph partitioning method (MLGP) with the best (for each dataset) unsupervised topic model proposed in [43], which outperforms previous works on the same problem using the same datasets. In order to have comparable results, we also discarded all the tweets with no interactions (replies or retweets) from the users in the dataset. We used *Purity* and *Normalized Mutual Information (NMI)* as the evaluation metrics. Purity measures the proportion of users who are assigned to the correct ground truth class, while NMI is based on mutual information and entropy [13].

Table 1 shows the results. The proposed MLGP method outperforms the best setting of the state-of-the-art topic model (SNVDM-GPU) in terms of both purity and NMI on both datasets. Figure 5 shows the conductance plots of the two datasets. We notice that, for $k = 2$ the produced clusters have very low conductance values of around 0.04 in both datasets, while for $k = 3$ the values are highly increased, especially on the *Indyref* dataset.

6.2 Qualitative Analysis of Viewpoint Understanding

We used the proposed *Iterative Rank Difference (IRD)* method to try to understand the viewpoints of the following controversial topics:

- **Indyref**: 2014 Scottish Independence Referendum
- **USElection**: 2016 US Presidential Election
- **Brexit**: 2016 Brexit referendum

For *Indyref*, we used the existing collection of tweets provided in [23] (Footnote 3), and we partitioned the graph using $k = 2$. For *USElection* and *Brexit*, we crawled topic-related tweets and

retweets using the Twitter *Advanced Search* service and the retweet API. Tables 2 and 3 show the hashtags and user accounts used for collecting the tweets related to these two topics. For the *USElection*, we used $k = 3$ for graph partitioning and selected the two clusters with the lowest conductance values as those representing different viewpoints, while for *Brexit* we used $k = 4$ and selected three clusters (this selection is based on the method described in Section 4). For creating the *subject* (W_s) and *contrasting* (W_c) lists of top-n terms required by IRD, we preprocessed the texts of the tweets, removed user mentions, stopwords, punctuations, 1- and 2-char words, and URLs, and lemmatized the remaining terms. Moreover, we used $n = 200$ to cut the subject and contrasting lists in all cases except the 2nd iteration of the Indyref topic where we used $n = 50$ (for Indyref the data is less and the term frequencies smaller compared to the other two topics).

Table 2: Hashtags and user accounts used for collecting the tweets related to *USElection*.

#USElection, #USElection2016, #trump, #MakeAmericaGreatAgain, @DaysOfTrump, #TrumpLeaks, #obamacare, #obama, #realDonaldTrump, #trump2016, #nevertrump, #Clinton, #Hillary, #hillaryClinton, #USElection, #BARACKOBAMA, #gop, #Republican, #ObamaFarewell, #OurFirstStand, #MAGA, #fakenews, @realdonaldtrump, @hfa @GOP, @BarackObama, @HillaryClinton, @TheDemocrats

Table 3: Hashtags used for collecting the tweets related to *Brexit*.

#brexit, #notoeu, #betteroffout, #britainout, #leaveeu, #beleave, #loveeuropeleaveeu, #yestoeu, #betteroffin, #votein, #bremain, #strongerin, #leadnotleave, #voteremain, #stopbrexit

6.2.1 What is a viewpoint about. In the first iteration, our objective is to understand what each viewpoint represents. For each topic, Tables 4-6 show the top descriptive terms of the corresponding viewpoints, as derived by the proposed method.

Regarding *Indyref*, we notice that the first viewpoint (Viewpoint 1) clearly represents the supporters of "Yes", including terms like the hashtags *#voteyes*, *#yes*, and the words *independent* and *national*. The second viewpoint (Viewpoint 2) clearly represents the supporters of "No" containing many related terms like *#nothanks*, *#bettertogether*, *#labourno*, and *#voteno*. Moreover, *currency* seems to be an important topic for this viewpoint.

In the *USElection* topic, the first viewpoint (Viewpoint 1) represents the supporters of Hillary Clinton (or the opponents of Donald Trump), while the second (Viewpoint 2) the supporters of Donald Trump. We notice that the supporters of Hillary Clinton used hashtags like *#nevertrump*, *#theresistance*, *#imwithher*, and *#trumpleaks* to oppose to Donald Trump, while Trump's supporters use hashtags like *#trump2016*, *#trumptrain*, *#draintheswamp*, *#makeamericagreatagain*, and *#fakenews*.

For *Brexit*, we see that the first viewpoint (Viewpoint 1) represents Brexit supporters (*#go*, *#leave*, *free*, *control*, *#leaveeu*), the second (Viewpoint 2) characterizes Bremain supporters (*#votein*,

---

[4]The SemEval 2016 Task 6 (Detecting Stance in Tweets) [26] focuses on tweet-level stance detection.

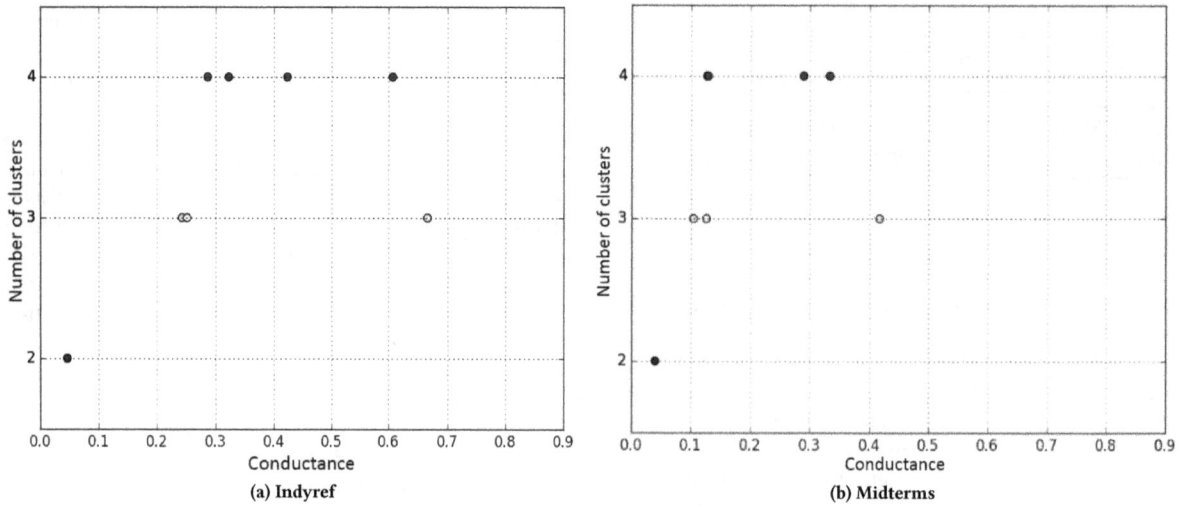

Figure 5: Conductance values for different number of clusters (value of *k*), for the topics *Indyref* (a) and *Midterm* (b).

Table 4: Top descriptive terms of viewpoints about the *2014 Scottish Independence Referendum*.

Viewpoint 1	Viewpoint 2
#voteyes, #yes, westminster, meeting, independent, #scotland, murphy, event, national, folk	#nothanks, #bettertogether, currency, #labourno, #scotdecides, speech, alex, #voteno, part, seperation

Table 5: Top descriptive terms of viewpoints about the *2016 US Presidential Election*.

Viewpoint 1	Viewpoint 2
#nevertrump, #theresistance, #obamafarewell, #imwithher, #resist, #trumps, gop, tweet, #gop, #trumpleaks, tax, #notmypresident, putin	#tcot, #trump2016, #pjnet, #trumptrain, #draintheswamp, video, #makeamericagreatagain, #fakenews, breaking, god, #realdonaldtrump, usa, fbi

#stopbrexit) and their worry about the National Health Service (*#nhs, cost*), while the third (Viewpoint 3) reflects a more neutral viewpoint about the general consequences of Brexit (*#stocks, #healthinnovations, #banking, #pharma, global*) and its relation to other topics (*#maga, #cdnpoli, #trumptrain*), probably discussed by users of non-English languages (*#ue, unido, reino, londres*). We also notice that Viewpoint 2 (Bremain supporters) contains the terms *#theresamay* and *johnson* which characterize Brexit (Theresa May and Boris Johnson belong to the Conservative Party which supported Brexit). This is not surprising since users supporting a specific viewpoint may use terms and hashtags that characterize another viewpoint for criticizing it.

Table 6: Top descriptive terms of viewpoints about the *2016 Brexit referendum*.

Viewpoint 1	Viewpoint 2	Viewpoint 3
democracy, #nexit, try, #go, #referendumm, #leave, #britain, free, control, #leaveeu	#tory, tory, johnson, #theresamay, boris, #votein, #stopbrexit, #nhs, cost, nhs	#ue, unido, reino, #maga, #stocks, #cdnpoli, europa, londres, #americafirst, royaumeuni, #trumptrain, #healthinnovations, #banking, #pharma

6.2.2 What is a term about? In the next iterations, our objective is to find more information about specific terms that characterize a viewpoint. This can help to obtain a deeper understanding of the viewpoint and its related context.

In the *Indyref* topic, Table 7 shows the top-5 descriptive terms of *murphy* and *#voteyes* (Viewpoint 1). Regarding *murphy*, we notice that the list provides context information about Jim Murphy: Jim Murphy was the *leader* of the Scottish *Labour* Party during the referendum, suggested that Labour could offer more *tax* and welfare powers for Scotland, while he is also believed to have supported the Iraq *war*. As regards *#voteyes*, we notice that the list does not provide much information. The reason is that there is also the hashtag *#yes* which semantically is the same with *#voteyes*. Both hashtags were interchangeably used by Twitter users to indicate their support to Scottish Independence, meaning that there are almost no tweets containing both hashtags. Thus, by creating the *subject* list W_s without considering the similar hashtag *#yes*, we indirectly consider this term as belonging to the *contrasting* corpus. Table 8 shows the top-5 descriptive terms when considering both hashtags in the *subject* corpus. Now we notice that the list contains terms that characterize the support to "Yes": an *independent Scotland* will give *power* and *future* to the *country*. Studying methods for the

Table 7: Top-5 descriptive terms of *murphy* and *#voteyes* (Viewpoint 1 of *Indyref*).

murphy	#voteyes
leader, war, tax, labour, really	#scotland, future, #sexysocialism, #yesscot, #midlothiansaysyes

Table 8: Top-5 descriptive terms of both *#voteyes* and *#yes* (Viewpoint 1 of *Indyref*).

{#voteyes, #yes}
scotland, independent, power, future, country

Table 9: Top-5 descriptive terms of *#trumpleaks* (Viewpoint 1) and *fbi* (Viewpoint 2) of *USElection*.

#trumpleaks	fbi
#trumprussia, #impeachtrump, #dworkinreport, #amjoy, #muslimban	investigation, comey, reopen, director, case

identification of identical terms is beyond the scope of this paper but an interesting direction for future research.

Regarding the *USElection* topic, Table 9 shows the top-5 descriptive terms of *#trumpleaks* (Viewpoint 1) and *fbi* (Viewpoint 2). For *#trumpleaks* we see that this term is related to a report authored by Scott Dworkin (*#dworkinreport*) which shows that Donald Trump has incorporated many registered businesses in Russia (*#trumprussia*), while the opponents of Donald Trump ask Congress to investigate whether sufficient grounds exist for his impeachment (*#impeachtrump*). As regards *fbi*, we notice that this term is related to the *reopening* of an *investigation/case* as well as to *James Comey* who served as the seventh *director* of FBI during the US election. Indeed, James Comey reopened an FBI investigation into Hillary Clinton's use of private email server while she was secretary of State.

Finally, in the *Brexit* topic, Table 10 shows the top-5 descriptive terms of *#nexit* (Viewpoint 1), *control* (Viewpoint 1), *{boris, johnson}* (Viewpoint 2), and *banking* (Viewpoint 3). We notice that the top descriptive terms of *#nexit* (which is the hashtag used for the hypothetical Dutch withdrawal from the European Union) is related to similar hashtags used for other countries (France, Italy, Denmark, Sweden) as well as *#euistheproblem*, meaning that the supporters of Brexit contravene European Union. As regards *control*, it is clear that the supporters of Brexit believe that UK must take back the total control of the country as well as of its borders. Regarding *{boris, johnson}* (Viewpoint 2) we get general information about Boris Johnson who is member of the Conservative Party in the United Kingdom (*conservative*). Boris Johnson has been Secretary of State for Foreign and Commonwealth Affairs since 2016 (*#foreignsecretary*) and the Member of Parliament (MP) for Uxbridge and South Ruislip since 2015 (*#mp*). We also see the term *biscuit* which is related to his visit to a biscuit factory during his "Vote Leave" campaign. Finally, the top descriptive terms about *banking* (Viewpoint 3) relate this viewpoint to the effect of Brexit to UK

Table 10: Top-5 descriptive terms of *#nexit* (Viewpoint 1), *control* (Viewpoint 1), *{boris, johnson}* (Viewpoint 2), and *banking* (Viewpoint 3) of *Brexit*.

#nexit	control	{boris, johnson}	banking
#frexit, #italexit, #dexit, #swexit, #euistheproblem	#takecontrol, border, uncontrolled, #betterofout, #takebackcontrol	conservative, biscuit, #foreignsecratery, #mp, #borisjohnson	#stocks, #healthinnovations, #pharma, decrease, index

stocks (*#stocks, decrease, index*) and the pharma industry (*#healthinnovations, #pharma*).

7 CONCLUSION

We have proposed to combine a popular graph partitioning algorithm with a clustering quality metric for the problem of viewpoint discovery in social networks. A distinctive characteristic of the proposed method is that it does not require the number of viewpoints to be given as input. This makes our approach applicable also for cases with an unknown number of viewpoints, while it can also detect noisy groups of users that do not represent clear viewpoints. Evaluation results on publicly available ground truth datasets showed that our approach outperforms state-of-the-art topic models on the same problem.

To understand what a viewpoint is about, we proposed the iterative use of a simple rank difference algorithm. The introduced *Iterative Rank Difference* (IRD) method can automatically identify descriptive terms that characterize a viewpoint, allowing also to understand how a specific term is related to a viewpoint. Case studies on three different controversial topics showed that IRD can provide comprehensive representations of viewpoints and terms.

Regarding future research, we plan to study approaches for the *timeline summarisation* of topics and viewpoints that will allow understanding how a controversial topic evolves over time and with respect to the involved entities, events and subtopics. Another interesting direction is the *semantic representation* of topics and viewpoints which will enable the construction of queryable knowledge graphs about controversial topics.

ACKNOWLEDGMENTS

The work was partially funded by the European Commission for the ERC Advanced Grant ALEXANDRIA (No. 339233).

REFERENCES

[1] Luca Maria Aiello, Alain Barrat, Rossano Schifanella, Ciro Cattuto, Benjamin Markines, and Filippo Menczer. 2012. Friendship Prediction and Homophily in Social Media. *ACM Trans. Web* 6, 2, Article 9 (2012), 9:1–9:33 pages.
[2] Khalid Al Khatib, Hinrich Schütze, and Cathleen Kantner. 2012. Automatic Detection of Point of View Differences in Wikipedia.. In *COLING*. 33–50.
[3] Hunt Allcott and Matthew Gentzkow. 2017. Social media and fake news in the 2016 election. *Journal of Economic Perspectives* 31, 2 (2017), 211–36.
[4] Hélio Almeida, Dorgival Guedes, Wagner Meira, and Mohammed J Zaki. 2011. Is there a best quality metric for graph clusters?. In *Joint European Conference on Machine Learning and Knowledge Discovery in Databases*. Springer, 44–59.
[5] Pablo Barberá. 2014. Birds of the same feather tweet together: Bayesian ideal point estimation using Twitter data. *Political Analysis* 23, 1 (2014), 76–91.

[6] David M Blei, Andrew Y Ng, and Michael I Jordan. 2003. Latent dirichlet allocation. *Journal of machine Learning research* 3, Jan (2003), 993–1022.
[7] Vincent D Blondel, Jean-Loup Guillaume, Renaud Lambiotte, and Etienne Lefebvre. 2008. Fast unfolding of communities in large networks. *Journal of statistical mechanics: theory and experiment* 2008, 10 (2008), P10008.
[8] Erik Borra, Esther Weltevrede, Paolo Ciuccarelli, Andreas Kaltenbrunner, David Laniado, Giovanni Magni, Michele Mauri, Richard Rogers, and Tommaso Venturini. 2015. Societal controversies in Wikipedia articles. In *Proceedings of the 33rd annual ACM conference on human factors in computing systems*. ACM, 193–196.
[9] Igor Brigadir, Derek Greene, and Pádraig Cunningham. 2015. Analyzing discourse communities with distributional semantic models. In *Proceedings of the ACM Web Science Conference*. ACM, 27.
[10] Yoonjung Choi, Yuchul Jung, and Sung-Hyon Myaeng. 2010. Identifying controversial issues and their sub-topics in news articles. *Intelligence and Security Informatics* (2010), 140–153.
[11] Raviv Cohen and Derek Ruths. 2013. Classifying political orientation on Twitter: It's not easy!. In *ICWSM*.
[12] Michael Conover, Jacob Ratkiewicz, Matthew R Francisco, Bruno Gonçalves, Filippo Menczer, and Alessandro Flammini. 2011. Political polarization on twitter. *ICWSM* 133 (2011), 89–96.
[13] Leon Danon, Albert Diaz-Guilera, Jordi Duch, and Alex Arenas. 2005. Comparing community structure identification. *Journal of Statistical Mechanics: Theory and Experiment* 2005, 09 (2005), P09008.
[14] Shiri Dori-Hacohen and James Allan. 2015. Automated controversy detection on the web. In *European Conference on Information Retrieval*. Springer, 423–434.
[15] Erick Elejalde, Leo Ferres, and Eelco Herder. 2017. The Nature of Real and Perceived Bias in Chilean Media. In *Proceedings of the 28th ACM Conference on Hypertext and Social Media*. 95–104.
[16] Anjie Fang, Iadh Ounis, Philip Habel, Craig Macdonald, and Nut Limsopatham. 2015. Topic-centric classification of twitter user's political orientation. In *Proceedings of the 38th International ACM SIGIR Conference on Research and Development in Information Retrieval*. ACM, 791–794.
[17] Seth Flaxman, Sharad Goel, and Justin M Rao. 2016. Filter bubbles, echo chambers, and online news consumption. *Public Opinion Quarterly* 80, S1 (2016), 298–320.
[18] Kiran Garimella, Gianmarco De Francisci Morales, Aristides Gionis, and Michael Mathioudakis. 2016. Quantifying controversy in social media. In *Proceedings of the Ninth ACM International Conference on Web Search and Data Mining*. ACM, 33–42.
[19] Mathieu Jacomy, Tommaso Venturini, Sebastien Heymann, and Mathieu Bastian. 2014. ForceAtlas2, a continuous graph layout algorithm for handy network visualization designed for the Gephi software. *PloS one* 9, 6 (2014), e98679.
[20] Aditya Joshi, Pushpak Bhattacharyya, and Mark James Carman. 2016. Political Issue Extraction Model: A Novel Hierarchical Topic Model That Uses Tweets By Political And Non-Political Authors.. In *WASSA@ NAACL-HLT*. 82–90.
[21] Ravi Kannan, Santosh Vempala, and Adrian Vetta. 2004. On clusterings: Good, bad and spectral. *Journal of the ACM (JACM)* 51, 3 (2004), 497–515.
[22] George Karypis and Vipin Kumar. 1995. METIS–unstructured graph partitioning and sparse matrix ordering system, version 2.0. (1995).
[23] Chunyu Kit and Xiaoyue Liu. 2008. Measuring mono-word termhood by rank difference via corpus comparison. *Terminology. International Journal of Theoretical and Applied Issues in Specialized Communication* 14, 2 (2008), 204–229.
[24] Hosam Mahmoud. 2008. *Pólya urn models*. CRC press.
[25] Yelena Mejova, Amy X Zhang, Nicholas Diakopoulos, and Carlos Castillo. 2014. Controversy and sentiment in online news. *Computation and Journalism Symposium* (2014).
[26] Saif Mohammad, Svetlana Kiritchenko, Parinaz Sobhani, Xiaodan Zhu, and Colin Cherry. 2016. Semeval-2016 task 6: Detecting stance in tweets. In *Proceedings of the 10th International Workshop on Semantic Evaluation (SemEval-2016)*. 31–41.
[27] Mark Newman. 2010. *Networks: an introduction*. Oxford university press.
[28] Mark EJ Newman. 2004. Analysis of weighted networks. *Physical review E* 70, 5 (2004), 056131.
[29] Viet-An Nguyen, Jordan Boyd-Graber, Philip Resnik, and Kristina Miler. 2015. Tea Party in the House: A Hierarchical Ideal Point Topic Model and Its Application to Republican Legislators in the 112th Congress. In *Association for Computational Linguistics*.
[30] Bo Pang, Lillian Lee, et al. 2008. Opinion mining and sentiment analysis. *Foundations and Trends® in Information Retrieval* 2, 1–2 (2008), 1–135.
[31] Symeon Papadopoulos, Yiannis Kompatsiaris, Athena Vakali, and Ploutarchos Spyridonos. 2012. Community detection in social media. *Data Mining and Knowledge Discovery* 24, 3 (2012), 515–554.
[32] Michael Paul and Roxana Girju. 2010. A two-dimensional topic-aspect model for discovering multi-faceted topics. *Urbana* 51, 61801 (2010), 36.
[33] Michael J Paul, ChengXiang Zhai, and Roxana Girju. 2010. Summarizing contrastive viewpoints in opinionated text. In *Proceedings of the 2010 Conference on Empirical Methods in Natural Language Processing*. Association for Computational Linguistics, 66–76.
[34] Marco Pennacchiotti and Ana-Maria Popescu. 2011. Democrats, republicans and starbucks afficionados: user classification in twitter. In *Proceedings of the 17th ACM SIGKDD international conference on Knowledge discovery and data mining*. ACM, 430–438.
[35] Ana-Maria Popescu and Marco Pennacchiotti. 2010. Detecting controversial events from twitter. In *Proceedings of the 19th ACM international conference on Information and knowledge management*. ACM, 1873–1876.
[36] Minghui Qiu and Jing Jiang. 2013. A Latent Variable Model for Viewpoint Discovery from Threaded Forum Posts. In *Proceedings of NAACL-HLT*. 1031–1040.
[37] Minghui Qiu, Liu Yang, and Jing Jiang. 2013. Modeling interaction features for debate side clustering. In *Proceedings of the 22nd ACM international conference on Information & Knowledge Management*. ACM, 873–878.
[38] Adithya Rao and Nemanja Spasojevic. 2016. Actionable and Political Text Classification using Word Embeddings and LSTM. *CoRR* (2016).
[39] Zhaochun Ren, Oana Inel, Lora Aroyo, and Maarten de Rijke. 2016. Time-aware multi-viewpoint summarization of multilingual social text streams. In *Proceedings of the 25th ACM International on Conference on Information and Knowledge Management*. ACM, 387–396.
[40] Mrinmaya Sachan, Avinava Dubey, Shashank Srivastava, Eric P Xing, and Eduard Hovy. 2014. Spatial compactness meets topical consistency: jointly modeling links and content for community detection. In *Proceedings of the 7th ACM international conference on Web search and data mining*. ACM, 503–512.
[41] Didi Surian, Dat Quoc Nguyen, Georgina Kennedy, Mark Johnson, Enrico Coiera, and Adam G Dunn. 2016. Characterizing Twitter discussions about HPV vaccines using topic modeling and community detection. *Journal of medical Internet research* 18, 8 (2016).
[42] Thibaut Thonet, Guillaume Cabanac, Mohand Boughanem, and Karen Pinel-Sauvagnat. 2016. VODUM: a topic model unifying viewpoint, topic and opinion discovery. In *European Conference on Information Retrieval*. Springer, 533–545.
[43] Thibaut Thonet, Guillaume Cabanac, Mohand Boughanem, and Karen Pinel-Sauvagnat. 2017. Users Are Known by the Company They Keep: Topic Models for Viewpoint Discovery in Social Networks. In *CIKM*.
[44] Giang Binh Tran and Eelco Herder. 2015. Detecting Filter Bubbles in Ongoing News Stories.. In *UMAP 2015 Extended Proceedings*.

Guidelines for Online Network Crawling: A Study of Data Collection Approaches and Network Properties

Katchaguy Areekijseree, Ricky Laishram and Sucheta Soundarajan

Department of Electrical Engineering and Computer Science, Syracuse University

Syracuse, NY

{kareekij,rlaishra,susounda}@syr.edu

ABSTRACT

Over the past two decades, online social networks have attracted a great deal of attention from researchers. However, before one can gain insight into the properties or structure of a network, one must first collect appropriate data. Data collection poses several challenges, such as API or bandwidth limits, which require the data collector to carefully consider which queries to make. Many online network crawling methods have been proposed, but it is not always clear which method should be used for a given network. In this paper, we perform a detailed, hypothesis-driven analysis of several online crawling algorithms, ranging from classical crawling methods to modern, state-of-the-art algorithms, with respect to the task of collecting as much data (nodes or edges) as possible given a fixed query budget. We show that the performance of these methods depends strongly on the network structure. We identify three relevant network characteristics: community separation, average community size, and average node degree. We present experiments on both real and synthetic networks, and provide guidelines to researchers regarding selection of an appropriate sampling method.

KEYWORDS

Experiments; Online Sampling Algorithm; Network Crawling; Network Sampling; Complex Networks.

ACM Reference Format:

Katchaguy Areekijseree, Ricky Laishram and Sucheta Soundarajan. 2018. Guidelines for Online Network Crawling: A Study of Data Collection Approaches and Network Properties. In *WebSci '18: 10th ACM Conference on Web Science, May 27–30, 2018, Amsterdam, Netherlands*. ACM, New York, NY, USA, 10 pages. https://doi.org/10.1145/3201064.3201066

1 INTRODUCTION

The study of complex networks has become a critical aspect of research in a wide range of fields. Often, network data is collected from online sources, including online social networking sites (OSNs) such as Facebook or Twitter. Such sites may provide APIs, which are a convenient channel for accessing data. However, the data collection process can require a significant amount of time. Thus, when collecting data, efficiency is extremely important. In this paper, we

consider the problem of **network sampling through crawling**, or **online sampling**, in which the only way to obtain more information about the network is to query observed nodes for their neighbors, and thus expand the observed network. In this paper, we use *network sampling* and *network crawling* interchangeably.

In network crawling, there are a number of important goals, such as finding samples that are unbiased with respect to some property, locating 'important' nodes, or finding a sample that preserves information flow patterns. In this work, however, we focus on the efficiency of the crawling algorithm itself (i.e., How quickly nodes and edges can be discovered through the crawling process). Our first considered goal is maximizing the total number of nodes observed, which we refer to as the *node coverage* goal. Second goal is maximizing number of edges observed, which we refer to as the *edge coverage* goal. These two goals have been closely tied to other application-specific crawling goals, including crawling for census-type applications (i.e., collecting node or edge attribute information) [10] and crawling to preserve community structure [15].

While network crawling is a critically important step in a network analysis tasks, it is often difficult for users to select a crawling technique. The literature contains a large number of crawling algorithms, and it is rarely clear which method is best to use for a given network. Existing work in the literature has typically attempted to determine which crawling method is the 'best'. In this paper, rather than arguing for usage of one single crawling algorithm, our goal is to investigate the relationship between network structure and crawler performance. More specifically, we investigate those network structural properties that govern the ability of a crawler being able to move between 'regions' of a graph, and demonstrate that these features have a strong effect on the performance of various crawling methods.

However, the knowledge of how structural properties affect the performance of a crawler might not be immediately helpful, because one does not know ahead of time what the properties of network are! To address this, we consider broad categories of networks, and show that for networks in the same category (which exhibit similar structural properties), the crawling methods tend to have similar performance relative to one another. Based on these properties, we provide general guidelines on selecting a crawling method for a particular network type.

Our work has several novel contributions:

(1) To the best of our knowledge, this is the first work to systematically examine the effect that network structural properties have on the performance of network crawling methods.

(2) We provide an extensive, scientific analysis of the relationship between network structural properties and the performance of popular crawling algorithms. Unlike existing

works on sampling algorithms, which typically perform a high-level comparison of crawling methods, our goal is to understand the relationship between network structure and crawler performance.

(3) We provide a framework for classifying network crawling algorithms, based on how their performance changes as network structure changes, and categorize networks according to their structural properties.

The rest of this paper is organized as follows. In the following Section 2, we give an overview of the existing works in this area. In Section 3, we discuss the problem, preliminaries, details of the network crawling methods and the network structural properties of interest. We describe our experiments and discuss about the results in Section 4. We present conclusion in Section 5 and future works in 6.

2 RELATED WORK

Work on network sampling can be separated into two main scenarios: *down-sampling* and *sampling through crawling*. When down-sampling, one possesses the complete network dataset, and wishes to scale it down to some desired size (perhaps because the entire dataset is too large to fit into the memory or would take too long to analyze). The good sample network will maintain the relevant properties and characteristics of the original network.

In the crawling scenario, one starts with *no information* about the network other than the knowledge of a single node. One can obtain addition information by iteratively performing queries on observed nodes (e.g., through an API) to collect the information about the unobserved network. In this way, the observed sample is expanded from the single initially observed node. While both of these problems are often broadly referred to as 'sampling', they require intrinsically different approaches. In this work, we consider algorithms that are used in the *crawling scenario*.

Due to the vast amount of literature in this area, we cannot provide a complete discussion of the field. For a more comprehensive discussion, we refer the reader to the excellent survey in [2].

Algorithms for Network Crawling: Network crawling has been used extensively to collect data from the Internet and other large networks like the WWW and online social network platforms. One of the largest online social network studies is presented by Mislove, et al. They study four online social network sites (Orkut, Youtube, Live Journal and Flickr) and collect the data by using a BFS crawler [16]. A similar study on other online social networking sites, such as CyWorld and MySpace, is presented by Ahn, et al. in [3]. However, the sampled networks produced by a BFS crawler contains bias. Kurant, et al. suggest a solution for correcting the bias from a BFS crawler [9]. Similarly, Gjoka, et al. propose another approach baseed on Metropolis-Hastings-based Random Walk for crawling an unbiased sample and use it for collecting Facebook network [7].

There has also been a great deal of interest on network crawling for specific applications. Salehi, et al. introduce PageRank-Sampling [18] to preserve community structure. Avrachenkov, et al. present a greedy crawling method, called Maximum Observed Degree (MOD), for maximizing number of nodes in the sample in [4] by querying the node with the highest observed degree in each

step. A similar approach is used by the OPIC algorithm, which considers PageRank as a measurement of importance [1]. Results show that both MOD and OPIC significantly outperform other methods.

Analysis of Sampling Algorithms: There has also been a significant amount of work comparing the performance of sampling algorithms. In [12], Leskovec and Faloutsos study the characteristics of different down-sampling methods and attempt to find out the best method that produces the smallest bias for all the defined network properties, arguing that Random Walk is the best at preserving network properties. Similarly, Kurant, et al. analyze BFS crawler [8]. The experiment results show that the crawler is biased towards high degree nodes.

Ye, et al. present a large-scale empirical study that compares crawling methods on the basis of performance, sensitivity, and bias, on the tasks of node and edge coverage [19]. Ahmed, et al. provide a detailed framework for classifying sampling algorithms and examine the performance of various algorithms at the task of preserving graph statistics [2]. While these works perform an important evaluation of existing algorithms, they typically conduct a high-level comparison of sampling methods.

In contrast, the purpose of our work is to perform a detailed analysis of *the effects of network structure on the performance of crawling algorithms*, rather than evaluating the performance of algorithms, we seek to answer *how* and *why* algorithms succeed or fail. Thus, we can give some insights and guildlines on how to pick an appropriate method when data collection need to be performed.

Community Structure: We draw heavily from the literature on community structure in networks. To characterize the strength of communities in networks, we use the popular modularity metric and the corresponding Louvain method for optimizing modularity [5]. Mixing between communities is an important part of our analysis: for example, Leskovec, et al. suggest that communities are well defined and distinct if they are small, but that large communities tends to mix with one another [13].

Our work differs from existing work in important ways: (1) We present a comprehensive analysis of sampling algorithms for the *crawling scenario* (in contrast to most existing work, which is for down-sampling). (2) Our primary goal is not to determine which existing algorithms are best, but rather to gain insight into the interplay between network structure and crawler performance, and thus understand *why* certain algorithms perform better or worse. (3) We provide guidelines for selecting the appropriate sampling approach if the network category is known.

3 NETWORK SAMPLING THROUGH DATA CRAWLING

Suppose that we are collecting data from an online social network through its API, and we only have 24 hours to collect data. The process starts with one known user account. As our first step, we must query that user, and the server responds with a list of neighbors. Then, one of these returned users is selected for the next query, and so on. This process is repeated until 24 hours have passed. The problem is to decide which node to select for each query such that the total number of nodes or edges observed is maximized.

3.1 Problem Definition

Let $G = (V, E)$ be a static unobserved, undirected network. We are given a starting node $n_s \in V$ and a total query budget b. To collect data, we may perform a query on an previously-observed node. In this work, we assume that in response to a query, we receive all neighbors of the queried node. In each step, the crawler queries an observed-but-not-queried node (i.e., a node that was observed as a neighbor of a previously-queried node, but has itself not yet been queried). This process is repeated until b queries have been made. The output is a sample graph $S = (V', E')$, where $V' \subseteq V$ and $E' \subseteq E$, containing all nodes and edges observed. Table 1 shows the notation used in the paper.

Table 1: Notations and Definitions.

Notation	Definition
n_s	A seed node from which the crawler begins.
V_o'	The set of nodes that have been observed but not queried ('*open*' nodes).
V_c'	The set of nodes that have been observed and queried ('*closed*' nodes).
V'	The set of all observed nodes, $V' = V_o' \cup V_c'$.
E'	The set of all observed edges.
d_v	The degree (number of neighbors) of node v.

We consider two different sampling goals:

Goal 1: Node Coverage - Collect a sample graph $S = (V', E')$, where $V' \subseteq V$ and $E' \subseteq E$ so that the number of nodes in V' is maximized.

Goal 2: Edge Coverage - Collect a sample graph $S = (V', E')$, where $V' \subseteq V$ and $E' \subseteq E$ so that the number of edges in E' is maximized.

We selected these goals because they are closely related to many other application-specific goals: for example, the community-based sampling techniques in [15] use the node coverage goal to identify a sample that captures the community structure of the network. The authors in [14] also use this goal to identify a set of most influential nodes across several centrality measures. We do not discount the importance of crawling for other applications (such as obtaining unbiased samples), but these are fundamentally different problems.

Note that a sampling algorithm that is successful with respect to one of these goals may not be successful with respect to the other. For example, suppose an open node (i.e., a node that has been observed through other nodes but not yet queried) has many unobserved edges adjacent to it, but these edges lead to other open nodes. Querying this node would lead to a large increase in the number of observed edges, but not the number of observed nodes.

3.2 Online Crawling Methods

In our study, we compare nine popular crawling methods. As mentioned in the previous section, the crawler expands the sample by selecting for query a node that had been previously observed. The details of each algorithm are as follows:

Random Crawling (Rand): In each iteration, the crawler randomly selects a node from V_o' for the next query.

Random Walk (RW): In each iteration, the crawler transitions to a random neighbor of the node that was just queried. Nodes can be visited multiple times but crawler only performs a new query on node $v \in V_o'$ if it had not been previously queried. The results of Random Walk came out on top in [12].

Breadth-First Search (BFS): The crawler selects the node that has been in the list of unqueried nodes the longest (i.e., First-In, First-Out). BFS is widely used for network sampling because of its simplicity. In addition, the obtained network gives a complete view (all nodes and edges) of a particular area in the graph, which may be useful for network analysis. An example of one of the largest network analysis using BFS is presented in [16].

Snowball Sampling (SB): The crawler acts similarly to BFS, except that when a node is queried, only p fraction of its neighbors are added to the queue for future queries. Here, we set p to 0.5. Experimental results in [3] show that this approach is capable of discovering hub nodes (i.e., nodes with high degree), which helps the crawler in expanding to unexplored areas in the graph.

Depth-first Search (DFS): The crawler acts similarly to BFS, except that a node is selected in LIFO fashion (i.e., Last-In, First-Out).

Maximum Observed Degree (MOD): This is a greedy algorithm based on the intuition that a node with high observed degree likely has high unobserved degree. For each query, the crawler selects an open node with the highest observed degree [4]. Experimental results in [4] demonstrated that MOD substantially outperforms other algorithms at the node coverage task.

Maximum Observed PageRank (PR): The crawler acts similarly to MOD. The PageRank score of every observed node is calculated when new nodes (or new edges) are added to the sample graph. The node with the highest observed PageRank score is selected for the next query. As argued in [18], this algorithm can capture the community structure of the network.

Online Page Importance Computation (OPIC): This is an online algorithm that aims to calculate the nodes importance score without recalculating from the whole sample. The algorithm only updates the scores of the most recently queried node and its neighbors. Initially, each observed node is given an equal amount of *"cash"*. In each step, the crawler selects the node with the most cash and its cash is distributed evenly to its neighbors. Results in [1] show that OPIC can compute the importance of nodes as in standard methods, but it is faster.

Volatile Multi-armed Bandit (VMAB): VMAB is a reinforcement learning algorithm that balances *exploration* and *exploitation*. This approach is used for finding target nodes on a network in [6]. The UCB1 algorithm is used for selecting an arm. Each arm represents a set of unqueried nodes with equivalent structural properties (we use 'common neighbors', as described [6], for the implementation in our experiment). In [6], VMAB modifies UCB1 to handle non-stationary bandits, because arms can appear, disappear or merge (because nodes are added to the sample which affect the change of structural properties). In each iteration, the crawler selects the arm that maximizes $\bar{W}_i + C_p \cdot \sqrt{\frac{2 \cdot \ln(n - z_i)}{T_i(n)}}$ and randomly picks a node from this arm to query.

3.3 The Effects of Network Structure on Algorithm Performance

The purpose of our study is to examine the effects of network structural properties on the relative performance of network crawlers. It is known that crawler performance may vary substantially by network [19]. This variance must be due to differences in structural properties of the underlying networks: but what are those properties, and how do they affect the comparative performance of crawling methods?

3.3.1 Structural Properties of Interest. Our hypothesis is that *the performance of crawling methods is mostly affected by the ease with which a crawler can move between regions of the graph.* If it is difficult to move between regions of the graph, and the crawler gets stuck in one general area, then it will eventually start seeing the same nodes and edges over and over again. We thus consider three structural features:[1]

Community Separation: We consider a community to be a subgraph with high internal density and relatively few edges to the rest of the graph. To determine how well-separated communities are, we use modularity Q, as defined by Newman [17], which is defined as follows:

$$Q = \frac{1}{2m} \sum_{vm} \left[A_{vw} - \frac{d_v d_w}{2m} \right] \delta(c_v, c_w),$$

where A, m and d_i are the adjacency matrix, total edges, and degree of node i, respectively. $\delta(c_v, c_w)$ is a delta function which returns one when node v and w are in the same community. Otherwise, it returns zero. The higher the modularity, the better the separation between communities, and so a crawler is more likely to get trapped in a region. We find communities using the Louvain method [5].

Average Degree: If the average node degree is high relative to community size, then a node is more likely to have neighbors outside of its own community, making it easier for a crawler to move between regions. It is defined as

$$d_{avg} = \frac{\sum_{v \in V} d_v}{m}.$$

Average Community Size: As described above, community size is relevant in conjunction with average degree.

$$CS_{avg} = \frac{\sum_{c_i \in C} |c_i|}{|C|},$$

where C is a set of communities, c_i is the set of nodes in community i and $|\cdot|$ refers to a cardinality of a set.

3.3.2 Properties of Real Networks. As we will see, the properties described above have a large effect on crawler performance: but if one begins without any knowledge of the network, how can one take advantage of our results to select an algorithm? As it is well-known, networks of the same type tend to have similar structural properties. For example, social networks tend to have more near-cliques than citation networks, which are more likely to have many long chain-like structures. Unfortunately, while it is not possible for a single algorithm to be the best on every network, we are able to produce general guidelines for selecting a crawling algorithm

---

[1]We explored other structural properties, such as clustering coefficient, but these three emerged as having the greatest effect on crawler performance.

for a particular type of network. These results are presented in sections 4.1.2 and 4.2.

4 EXPERIMENTAL STUDIES

We first perform a series of controlled experiments on synthetic networks, in which we methodically modify structural properties of the network and observe the effect of these variations on the performance of the crawling algorithms. We then validate our observations with real world networks. Using these results, we group the crawling algorithms into three distinct classes. We additionally group the network datasets into categories based on domain. Within each category of network, crawling algorithms show consistent performance, allowing a user to select the method that is best for a particular category.

4.1 Effects of Network Properties

As mentioned in the earlier section, we consider three network structural properties: the community separation , the average degree, and the average community size.

4.1.1 Synthetic networks. We use the LFR network model [11] to generate synthetic networks. This model is usually used as a benchmark networks for evaluating different community detection algorithms. The model allows us to control average node degree, community size, and community mixing. We set each network to have 5000 nodes and a maximum node degree of 300. We vary the community mixing parameter μ (the fraction of edges crossing between communities, ranging from 0 to 1), average node degree, and community size.

Note that community mixing μ and modularity Q are inversely related, meaning that networks with high community mixing will have low modularity. Here, we consider values of μ from 0.1 to 0.9, average degrees from 15 to 200, and average community sizes from 100 to 2500. Higher values of μ indicate fuzzier community borders.

For each set of parameters, we generate 10 networks. We generate multiple graphs with same parameters instead of running multiple experiments on a single generated graph, because we want to reduce the error or bias that might come from the generated graphs. We consider budgets of up to 1000 queries, representing sampling up to 20% of the nodes in the network.

Based on our experimental results, we are able to categorize the nine crawling algorithms into three groups (G1 - G3). The algorithms in each groups are as follows:

G1: **Node Importance-based algorithms:** Maximum observed degree, OPIC and Maximum observed PageRank

G2: **Random Walk**

G3: **Graph Traversal-based algorithms:** BFS, DFS, SB, Random, and VMAB

A summary of how structural properties affect each group is shown in Table 2. We plot results for methods from each group in Figures 2-4. For brevity, we show only results for the best method in each group: MOD, Random Walk and BFS. Results are as follows:

Node Coverage: Figure 2 depicts results for the node coverage task as average degree and average community size are varied, with community mixing fixed at 0.1 (i.e., few connections between

Table 2: Categorization and summary of the performances of sampling algorithms.

Coverage	Property	G1: Node Importance-Based	G2: Random Walk	G3: Graph Traversal-Based
Node	Community Separation	Excellent performance when community overlap is high (i.e. low Q or high μ).	Stable	Stable
Node	Average community size	Strong performance when communities are large if μ is low. Community size does not matter if μ is high.	Stable	Stable
Node	Average degree	Strong performance when average degree is extremely low (<10) even if μ is low. Otherwise, stable	Stable	Performance improvement when average degree increases.
Edge	Community Separation	Excellent performance when community overlap is high (i.e. low Q or high μ).	Stable	Stable
Edge	Average community size	Strong performance when communities are large if μ is low. Community size does not matter if μ is high.	Stable	Stable
Edge	Average degree	Strong performance when d_{avg} is low (<10) even if μ is low. Otherwise, performance drops when d_{avg} increases.	Performance drops when d_{avg} increases.	Stable
Best Method in Group		MOD	RW	BFS

communities). Plots further to the right have larger average community sizes (CS_{avg} ranges from 100 to 2500), and plots higher on the y-axis have higher average degrees (d_{avg} ranging from 7 to 100). Within each plot, the x-axis shows the fraction of nodes queried, and the y-axis shows the fraction of nodes observed in the sample. Figure 1 illustrates the results when community mixing is varied, and average degree and average community size are fixed at 15 and 300, respectively. Figure 3 shows results when average degree is varied, when average community size is fixed at 300 and community mixing at 0.6. For brevity, we cannot show results for all parameter settings, but the depicted results are representative of the full set of results. We make several important observations from this set of plots:

G1 - Node Importance-based methods: These methods greedily pick a node with high centrality (degree or PageRank), and tend to behave similarly. This is not surprising, as there is a high correlation between the various centrality measures. The performances of methods in G1 significantly improve as the size of the community is increased. If community mixing is low (fewer connections between communities), and communities are small, G1 methods perform poorly, as they tend to get 'stuck' in a region: if there are few connections between communities, these methods have difficulty transitioning to new communities. They thus exhibit diminishing marginal returns: while no method will query the same node multiple times, they tend to query nodes with similar neighborhoods, resulting in redundant information. One interesting observation is that when the average degree is extremely low (last row on Figure 2), G1 methods perform worse than both G2 and G3 methods for low query budgets, but the performance rapidly increases and

outperforms the other methods when budget increases. We observed the same behavior for every generated network with the same parameter setting that has average degree less than 10.

As illustrated in Figure 1, G1 methods perform better when μ increases. We can see similar results as shown in Figure 3. When community mixing is high (there are many connections between communities), G1 methods are consistently the best, as a node outside of the crawler's current community may have a high observed degree, so the crawler can escape easily.

G2 - Random Walk: As we can clearly see from Figure 2 and 3, the Random Walk crawler is a very stable algorithm. Its performance seems to be unaffected by all considered properties. Since

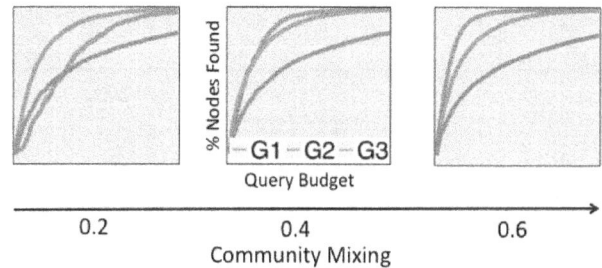

Figure 1: (Node coverage) Results on synthetic networks with different values of community mixing μ when average degree is fixed at 15 and average community size is fixed at 300. For the individual plots, the x-axes show query budgets (0% to 20% of total nodes). The y-axes show the percent of node observed (0% to 100%). G1 methods improve as μ increases, while other methods are stable.

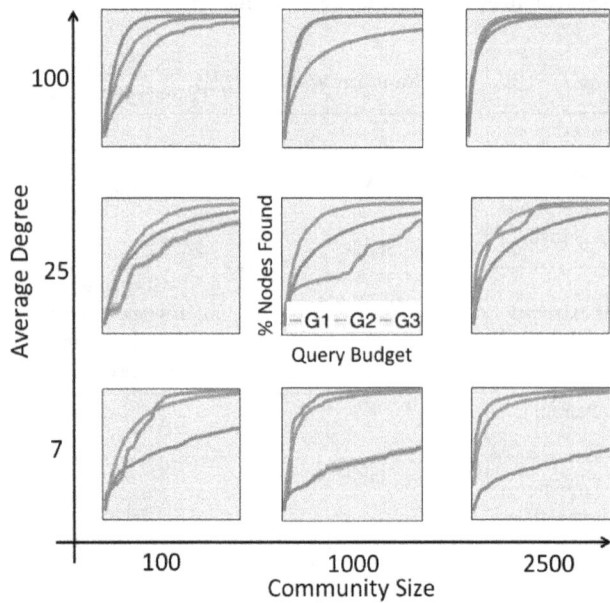

Figure 2: (Node coverage) Results on synthetic networks with different values of d_{avg} and CS_{avg} when community mixing μ is fixed at 0.1. Plots to the right (along x-axis) have higher average community sizes, while plots near the top (along y-axis) have higher average degree. For the individual plots, the x-axes show query budgets ranging from 0% to 20% of total nodes in the network. The y-axes show the node coverage (measured in % of total nodes observed), ranging from 0% to 100%. The performance of the G2 random walk method is stable. G1 methods improve when CS_{avg} increases, while G3 methods improve when d_{avg} increases.

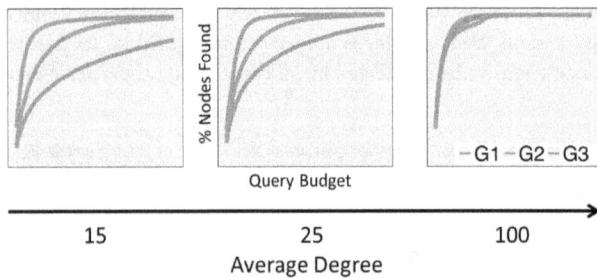

Figure 3: (Node coverage) Results on synthetic networks with different values of average degree, when community mixing fixed at 0.6 and community size is 300. For the individual plots, the x-axes show query budgets (0% to 20% of total nodes). The y-axes show the percent of node observed (0% to 100%). G1 outperforms the others methods. The performance of G3 methods improve as average degree and average community size increases.

the Random Walk crawler selects next node randomly from the last queried node's neighbors, the crawler can escape from the current

region easily, while leaves some partial region unobserved. However, the crawler has a freedom to move back and forth, partially explored region, and them discover more nodes of this region in later steps.

G3 - Graph Traversal-based methods: These methods are not meaningfully affected by community size. These methods expand the frontier of the sample uniformly, and so can easily move between graph regions. However, the choice of next queried node depends on when that node was put into the query queue. It is likely that nodes with small and medium degree will be queried and the number of new nodes added to sample will be low. The performance of these methods improves as the average degree increases (moving up the y-axis in Figure 3), because they can quickly reach and escape the boundaries of a community. For large average degree, these methods outperform Random Walk sampling. Note that, VMAB is put into this group because of its performance. VMAB often performs poorly at the task of node coverage because new arms appear frequently, resulting in nearly random query choices.

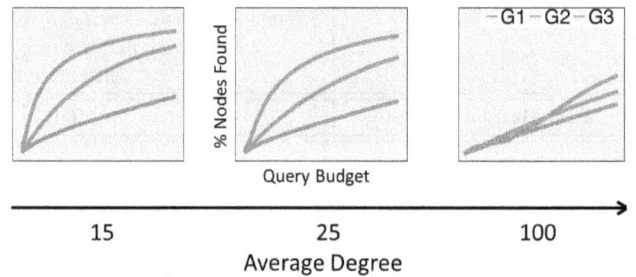

Figure 4: (Edge coverage) Results on synthetic networks with different values of average degree, when community mixing fixed at 0.6 and community size is 1000. For the individual plots, the x-axes show query budgets (0% to 20% of total nodes). The y-axes show the percent of edge observed (0% to 100%). The performance of G3 are stable, while G1 and G2 show a decrease in performance.

Edge Coverage Task: Figure 5 is interpreted similarly to Figure 2, showing how the performances of G1 - G3 change as average degree and community sizes vary, with fixed low community mixing (μ = 0.1). When varying μ, performance is similar to the node coverage task, as shown in Figure 1, and due to space constraints, we do not include it. As before, these limited results are representative of the full set of results. The key observations are as follows:

G1 - Node Importance-based methods: These methods are the best algorithms if 1) community mixing μ is high or 2) communities are large, even if community mixing μ is low (along the x-axis in Figure 5, the performance increases). As in the node coverage task, having fuzzy borders between communities leads to improved performance by G1 methods. However, if communities are very large, then even if a G1 method gets 'stuck' in a single community, it is still able to discover many edges (here, 'large' is measured with respect to the sample budget). G1 methods also show the best performance when average degree is extremely low. However, the performance degrades when average degree increases as shown in Figure 4.

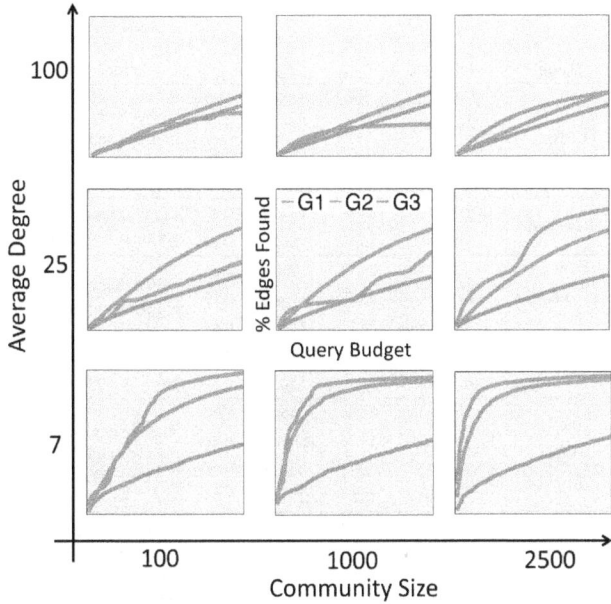

Figure 5: (Edge coverage) Results on synthetic networks with different values of d_{avg} and CS_{avg} when community mixing μ is fixed at 0.1. Plots to the right have higher average community sizes, while plots near the top have higher average degree. For the individual plots, the x-axes show query budgets ranging from 0% to 20% of total nodes in the network. The y-axes show the edge coverage (measured in % of total edges observed), ranging from 0% to 100%. The G3 methods are stable throughout. The G2 method is not affected by average community size, but decreases as average degree increases. G1 algorithms improve as community size increases, but worsen as average degree increases.

G2 - Random Walk: The performance seems to be very stable when community size increases regardless of whether community mixing μ is high or low.

G3 - Graph Traversal-based methods: These methods are stable as parameters vary, but these methods generally perform worse than Random Walk and methods in G1.

4.1.2 Real-World Networks: The previous experiments demonstrate that a major factor in the performance of each method is the ability to transition between different regions of the graph. Here, we test to see whether this conclusion holds on real graphs.

We perform three sets of controlled experiments. In each set, we locate two pairs of networks (Pair 'A' and 'B'), each containing networks that are similar with respect to two of the three structural features, but are very different with respect to the third. For example, *Wiki-Vote* and *Twitter* networks have average degree around 30 and average community size around 1100, but differ in modularity (0.42 vs. 0.81). Statistics for the selected network pairs are listed in Table 3 (with the feature being varied shown in bold).[2] In order to find

---

[2]Network datasets from http://networkrepository.com.

Table 3: Network statistics of realworld networks used in the controlled experiments.

Test Prop.	Pair	Network	d_{avg}	CS_{svg}	Q
Q	A	Wiki-Vote	28.51	1,177.67	**0.42**
		Twitter	33.01	1,129.25	**0.81**
	B	Brightkite	7.51	274.10	**0.68**
		MathSciNet	4.93	594.09	**0.80**
CS_{avg}	A	Shipsec1	24.36	**4,117.50**	0.89
		Shipsec5	24.61	**5,252.15**	0.90
	B	Github	7.25	**83.68**	0.43
		P2P-gnutella	4.73	**1,276.76**	0.50
d_{avg}	A	P2P-gnutella	**4.73**	1,276.76	0.50
		Bingham	**72.57**	1,250.13	0.45
	B	Amazon	**2.74**	272.44	0.99
		UK-2005	**181.19**	157.13	1.00

communities, we use the modularity Q of communities found by the *Louvain method* [5] and use it as a proxy for community mixing. As mentioned in the previous section, modularity and community mixing are inversely related ($\Uparrow Q \approx \Downarrow \mu$). Because networks are of different sizes and structures, rather than setting a fixed number of queries, we set the query budget to be 5% of the number of nodes. We perform 10 trials for each network and sampling method.

For each pair of networks, we refer to one of the networks as the *'High'-valued network (H)* and another as the *'Low'-valued network (L)*. These designations are relative to the other network in the pair (e.g., the network with higher test value is labeled 'H').

Because Random Walk is the most stable method (i.e., shows consistent performance regardless of the structural properties we consider), we use it as a reference point. We show the number of nodes or edges discovered by each sampling method as a *percentage improvement above (or below)* the number of nodes and edges discovered by Random Walk. Results are shown in Table 4. Each cell contains $\begin{bmatrix} x \\ y \end{bmatrix}$, where x is the percentage improvement of the algorithm performs on the 'Low'-valued network and y is the percentage improvement of the algorithm performs on the 'High'-valued network compare to Random Walk performance. An arrow indicates how the performance changes when the value of test properties changes from Low to High value. A symbol '$\Uparrow$' represents the performance improves when the test property increases and '$\Downarrow$' shows the performance degrades when test property increases.

First, we consider pairs with similar average degree and average community size, but different values of modularity Q (0.42 vs. 0.81, and 0.68 vs. 0.8). As expected, G1 methods perform extremely well when modularity is low in pair A ($\Downarrow$ indicates the G1 performance drops when modularity increases) for both node coverage and edge coverage tasks. On the other hand, G1 methods perform very well on both networks in pair B, because both networks have extremely low average degree ($d_{avg} < 10$). The performance of G3 methods are worse than Random walk, as we expected.

Table 4: Experimental results of the controlled experiments. An arrow indicates how the performance changes when test property changes from Low to High (⇑: improve, ⇓: degrade). In $\begin{bmatrix} x \\ y \end{bmatrix}$, x and y indicate the percentage improvement of Low- and High- valued networks, respectively ('+': outperform RW, '-': underperform RW).

Test Prop.	Pair	Node Coverage		Edge Coverage	
		% Imprv. G1 vs. RW	% Imprv. G3 vs. RW	% Imprv. G1 vs. RW	% Imprv. G3 vs. RW
Q	A	⇓ $\begin{bmatrix} 7.62\% \\ -5.24\% \end{bmatrix}$	⇑ $\begin{bmatrix} -22.44\% \\ -13.97\% \end{bmatrix}$	⇓ $\begin{bmatrix} 21.12\% \\ -2.90\% \end{bmatrix}$	⇑ $\begin{bmatrix} -58.13\% \\ -49.33\% \end{bmatrix}$
	B	⇑ $\begin{bmatrix} 12.47\% \\ 19.81\% \end{bmatrix}$	⇑ $\begin{bmatrix} -28.27\% \\ -17.64\% \end{bmatrix}$	⇑ $\begin{bmatrix} 31.85\% \\ 53.49\% \end{bmatrix}$	⇑ $\begin{bmatrix} -47.22\% \\ -23.10\% \end{bmatrix}$
CS_{avg}	A	⇑ $\begin{bmatrix} -71.52\% \\ -70.32\% \end{bmatrix}$	⇓ $\begin{bmatrix} -20.53\% \\ -27.68\% \end{bmatrix}$	⇑ $\begin{bmatrix} -19.65\% \\ -10.48\% \end{bmatrix}$	⇓ $\begin{bmatrix} -5.34\% \\ -6.38\% \end{bmatrix}$
	B	⇑ $\begin{bmatrix} 10.14\% \\ 15.67\% \end{bmatrix}$	⇑ $\begin{bmatrix} -35.21\% \\ -15.18\% \end{bmatrix}$	⇑ $\begin{bmatrix} 20.01\% \\ 34.68\% \end{bmatrix}$	⇑ $\begin{bmatrix} -58.44\% \\ -19.39\% \end{bmatrix}$
d_{avg}	A	⇓ $\begin{bmatrix} 10.14\% \\ -14.38\% \end{bmatrix}$	⇑ $\begin{bmatrix} -15.18\% \\ -0.87\% \end{bmatrix}$	⇓ $\begin{bmatrix} 34.68\% \\ -3.19\% \end{bmatrix}$	⇓ $\begin{bmatrix} -19.39\% \\ -27.72\% \end{bmatrix}$
	B	⇑ $\begin{bmatrix} -0.40\% \\ 6.25\% \end{bmatrix}$	⇑ $\begin{bmatrix} 2.09\% \\ 334.34\% \end{bmatrix}$	⇓ $\begin{bmatrix} -0.48\% \\ -1.42\% \end{bmatrix}$	⇑ $\begin{bmatrix} 1.53\% \\ 82.61\% \end{bmatrix}$

Table 5: Categories of the realworld networks and their structural characteristics.

Type	Network	d_{avg}	CS_{avg}	Q	Properties
Collab.	Citeseer	7.16	988.35	0.90	Low degree, medium-sized and clear communities
	Dblp-2010	6.33	739.91	0.86	
	Dblp-2012	6.62	1248.35	0.82	
	MathSciNet	4.93	594.09	0.80	
Recmnd.	Amazon	2.74	272.44	0.99	Low degree, small and clear communities
	Github	7.25	83.68	0.43	
FB	OR	25.77	1074.44	0.63	High degree, large and clear communities
	Penn94	65.59	2186.11	0.49	
	Wosn-friends	25.77	856.65	0.63	
Tech.	P2P-gnutella	4.73	1276.76	0.50	Low degree, large and clear communities
	RL-caida	6.37	856.12	0.86	
Web.	Arabic-2005	21.36	115.86	1.00	High degree, medium-sized and fuzzy communities
	Italycnr-2000	17.36	1134.34	0.91	
	Sk-2005	5.51	338.22	0.99	
	Uk-2005	181.19	157.13	1.00	
OSNs.	Slashdot	10.24	173.87	0.36	High degree, small-to-medium-sized and fuzzy communities
	Themarker	29.87	458.90	0.31	
	BlogCatalog	47.15	1455.48	0.32	
Scientific	PKUSTK13	68.73	3,514.56	0.88	High degree, large and clear communities
	PWTK	51.89	4,635.81	0.93	
	Shipsec1	24.36	4,117.50	0.89	
	Shipsec5	24.61	5,252.15	0.90	

Next, we consider networks with similar modularity and average degree, but different average community sizes (4118 vs. 5252 and 84 vs. 1277). Our earlier experiment predicted that G1 methods will perform better on networks with larger community sizes. As expected, G1 performance improves for networks with larger communities for both pairs.

Finally, we consider networks with similar modularity and average community size, but different average degrees (5 vs. 73 and 3 vs. 181). As predicted, G3 methods perform better on networks with higher average degree in both pairs. However, we see less consistent results for edge coverage. Overall, the experiments on real networks bear out our results on synthetic networks.

4.2 Network Types

In a real application, the network properties are not known until the sample is generated: so how can one select an appropriate crawling method? Here, we analyze how well the algorithms perform by network type (web, collaboration, technology, scientific, Facebook, recommendation and other OSNs)[3]. The statistics of all networks are listed in Table 5. Again, we set the maximum query budget to be 5 percent of total nodes and perform 10 trials for each method. We depict the mean and standard deviation of the percentage of nodes and edges found in Table 6.

We make the following observations:

(1) G1 or G2 methods are almost always the best, regardless of network type or coverage task.

(2) On collaboration, technological, recommendation, web and online social networks, G1 methods perform the best, while

on Facebook and scientific networks, the G2 method is the best.

(3) Methods in G3 seem not to be a good choice when considering these two goals on all types of network.

As suggested by Newman in [17], a modularity $Q \geq 0.3$ indicates a good community structure. As we can see, OSNs have the lowest modularity as compared to others. This indicates that the communities are fuzzy and overlapping. Since these are social networks, people can be part of several groups in real life (group of friends, family, co-workers, etc.). So, consistent with our earlier results, G1 methods performs the best on networks in this category.

Other networks typically have higher values of modularity Q (ranging between 0.4 and 0.9), and the determining factor of which method is best thus depends on average community size and average degree. The ratio between average degree and average community size of collaboration, technology is around 200, while this ratio on recommendation and web networks is about 35. This ratio indicates how large the community is compared to average degree. The average degrees of these four types of networks are quite low, between 2 and 15. As we expected from the previous experiment, G1 methods perform very well in this case. In contrast, on average, Facebook and scientific computing networks have communities only 12 and 80 times larger than their average degrees, which range from 15 to 70. Method in G2 performs the best.

In view of our earlier experiments, we see that in the networks with communities that are small relative to average degree, G1 methods quickly see all of a community, and then have trouble escaping (because of the strong community structure). However, when communities are large relative to average degree, both G1

---

[3]Network datasets from http://networkrepository.com.

Table 6: Summary of the network characteristics and performance of algorithms. Algorithms tend to perform similarly on networks in the same category.

Type	Network	Node coverage			Edge coverage		
		G1	G2	G3	G1	G2	G3
Collaboration: Low d_{avg}, Medium CS_{avg}, High Q	Citeseer	**25.66±2.94**	25.15±0.55	21.01±0.23	**20.48±1.68**	19.49±0.42	15.1±0.52
	Dblp-2010	**32.59±0.12**	26.53±0.37	18.22±0.16	**29.16±0.08**	19.53±0.39	12.72±0.29
	Dblp-2012	**38.33±0.04**	31.74±0.28	26.21±0.11	**33.47±0.03**	22.39±0.36	17.09±0.07
	MathSciNet	**36.14±0.09**	30.17±0.26	24.85±0.13	**36.27±0.06**	23.63±0.3	18.17±0.09
Recommendation: Low d_{avg}, Low CS_{avg}, High Q	Amazon	**5.71±0.16**	5.73±0.06	5.85±0.18	**5.60±0.06**	**5.61±0.08**	5.50±0.17
	Github	**53.59±0.02**	46.33±0.24	30.02±0.08	**72.57±0.02**	60.47±0.29	25.13±0.18
Facebook: High d_{avg}, High CS_{avg}, High Q	OR	38.99±2.50	**55.94±0.68**	51.00±0.22	**31.05±3.69**	27.37±0.57	16.2±0.17
	Penn94	75.30±1.05	**82.52±0.34**	80.07±0.24	**24.04±1.74**	19.47±0.41	12.39±0.13
	Wosn-friends	38.20±3.05	**55.80±0.49**	50.93±0.19	**30.92±3.12**	27.85±0.7	16.46±0.17
Technology: Low d_{avg}, High CS_{avg}, High Q	P2P-gnutella	**36.02±0.11**	32.71±0.17	27.74±0.22	**26.96±0.08**	20.02±0.1	16.13±0.17
	RL-caida	**28.86±0.12**	27.71±0.47	26.62±0.10	**39.57±0.18**	30.21±0.85	20.26±0.11
Web: High d_{avg}, Medium CS_{avg}, Low Q	Arabic-2005	**9.47±2.49**	6.47±0.72	9.54±1.48	**6.97±0.94**	5.40±1.28	6.75±0.95
	Italycnr-2000	8.52±2.25	**15.66±6.37**	13.65±2.84	14.9±3.83	**24.59±12.51**	11.93±2.89
	Sk-2005	**10.33±0.87**	6.41±1.04	8.21±0.65	**9.69±0.51**	6.21±0.96	8.03±1.02
OSNs: High d_{avg}, Low-to-medium CS_{avg}, Low Q	Slashdot	**70.68±0.01**	61.23±0.25	36.81±0.75	**75.85±0.01**	57.74±0.24	21.84±0.56
	BlogCatalog	**90.38±0.02**	90.38±0.37	90.38±0.49	**90.51±0.01**	82.28±0.32	18.81±0.26
	Themarker	**89.48±0.01**	86.04±0.2	47.40±0.12	**82.28±0.01**	67.4±0.25	19.72±0.12
Scientific: High d_{avg}, High CS_{avg}, High Q	PKUSTK13	7.40±0.51	**43.94±9.74**	33.78±1.51	5.68±0.17	**10.58±0.61**	9.41±0.22
	PWTK	5.61±0.12	**20.08±2.68**	15.45±0.74	5.27±0.05	**8.13±0.21**	7.99±0.10
	Shipsec1	7.81±0.44	**27.47±1.43**	21.77±0.52	7.80±0.89	**9.71±0.54**	9.17±0.35
	Shipsec5	8.17±0.81	**27.85±2.46**	20.02±0.91	8.75±0.50	**9.79±0.52**	9.15±0.44

and G2 methods tend to stay in the same community for much longer, and G1 methods perform the best.

All in all, the G1 and G2 methods are the best, depending on structural properties. G1 methods expand the sampled network by quickly filling out the unobserved nodes (or edges) in a particular region before moving out of the region. However, these methods are obstructed by sharp community borders. In contrast, the G2 method Random Walk has the freedom to move around, and so the crawler observes parts of many communities before it fills out individual regions. Because of this, a Random Walk takes longer to fully explore regions, but reaches more of the network.

5 CONCLUSION

Data collection is the first process of any network analysis task. However, the literature contains a vast selection of network sampling algorithms, and so it is often difficult for users to select a single method that works well for their data, as sampling methods that work well on one network may not work well on a different network. In this paper, we performed a large-scale, comprehensive study to understand how the structural features of networks affect the performance of sampling methods. We identified three network properties of interest: community separation, community size, and average degree. We performed a large set of controlled experiments on synthetic and real graphs, and considered two sampling

goals: *node* and *edge* coverage. We considered nine important sampling methods, ranging from well-understood, classical methods like Random Walk and BFS to modern, cutting-edge algorithms. We performed experiments on real and synthetic networks, and demonstrated that the performance of the sampling methods is highly dependent on the network structure, and in particular, whether the sampling method is able to transition between different regions of the graph. As a result of our experiments, we categorized the nine crawling methods into three groups: Node Importance-based, Random Walk-based and Graph Traversal-based approaches.

We observed that Random Walk and Node Importance-based algorithms performed well, depending on the network structure. In particular, on networks with clear and sharp community structure, the Node Importance-based algorithms tend to get 'stuck' in a region of a graph, while the Random Walk method is able to transition between regions. However, when boundaries between communities are fuzzier, or the communities overlap, the Node Importance-based methods demonstrate excellent performance.

Finally, we showed how a user can select an appropriate crawling method based on the network type: in particular, the Random Walk method is suitable for crawling Facebook and scientific computing networks, but for collaboration, recommendation, technological, web and other online social networks, Node Importance-based methods are best.

6 FUTURE WORK

As part of our future research, we plan to investigate different types of query responses. In this work, we assumed that all neighbors are returns for each query. However, in certain settings, this assumption may not hold, and the crawler may need multiple queries to obtain all of a node's neighbors. For example, an online social network API may divide a node's neighbors into *pages*, where each page contains k records and only one page is returned at a time. Also, we want to expand our findings and give the insight on directed networks. It is not clear that our results will generalize to such a setting, and we plan to investigate it further.

7 ACKNOWLEDGEMENTS

The authors would like to thank Jeremy Wendt of Sandia National Laboratories for thoughtful comments and conversations.

REFERENCES

[1] Serge Abiteboul, Mihai Preda, and Gregory Cobena. 2003. Adaptive on-line page importance computation. In *Proceedings of the 12th international conference on World Wide Web*.
[2] Nesreen K. Ahmed, Jennifer Neville, and Ramana Kompella. 2014. Network Sampling: From Static to Streaming Graphs. *ACM Transactions on Knowledge Discovery from Data (TKDD)* 8, 2 (2014).
[3] Yong-Yeol Ahn, Seungyeop Han, Haewoon Kwak, Sue Moon, and Hawoong Jeong. 2007. Analysis of topological characteristics of huge online social networking services. In *International conference on WWW*.
[4] Konstantin Avrachenkov, Prithwish Basu, Giovanni Neglia, Bruno Ribeiro, and Don Towsley. 2014. Pay few, influence most: Online myopic network covering. In *Computer Communications Workshops*.
[5] Vincent D Blondel, Jean-Loup Guillaume, Renaud Lambiotte, and Etienne Lefebvre. 2008. Fast unfolding of communities in large networks. *Journal of statistical mechanics: theory and experiment* (2008).
[6] Zahy Bnaya, Rami Puzis, Roni Stern, and Ariel Felner. 2013. Bandit algorithms for social network queries. In *2013 International Conference on Social Computing*. IEEE, 148–153.
[7] Minas Gjoka, Maciej Kurant, Carter T Butts, and Athina Markopoulou. 2009. Unbiased sampling of facebook. *preprint arXiv* 906 (2009).
[8] Maciej Kurant, Athina Markopoulou, and Patrick Thiran. 2010. On the bias of BFS (breadth first search). In *Teletraffic Congress (ITC), 2010 22nd International*. IEEE, 1–8.
[9] Maciej Kurant, Athina Markopoulou, and Patrick Thiran. 2011. Towards unbiased BFS sampling. *IEEE Journal on Selected Areas in Communications* 29, 9 (2011), 1799–1809.
[10] Haewoon Kwak, Changhyun Lee, Hosung Park, and Sue Moon. 2010. What is Twitter, a social network or a news media?. In *19th international conference on World wide web*.
[11] Andrea Lancichinetti, Santo Fortunato, and Filippo Radicchi. 2008. Benchmark graphs for testing community detection algorithms. *Physical review E* 78, 4 (2008), 046110.
[12] Jure Leskovec and Christos Faloutsos. 2006. Sampling from large graphs. In *Proceedings of the 12th ACM SIGKDD international conference on Knowledge discovery and data mining*. ACM, 631–636.
[13] Jure Leskovec, Kevin J Lang, Anirban Dasgupta, and Michael W Mahoney. 2009. Community structure in large networks: Natural cluster sizes and the absence of large well-defined clusters. *Internet Mathematics* 6, 1 (2009), 29–123.
[14] Arun S Maiya and Tanya Y Berger-Wolf. 2010. Online sampling of high centrality individuals in social networks. In *Pacific-Asia Conference on Knowledge Discovery and Data Mining*. Springer, 91–98.
[15] Arun S Maiya and Tanya Y Berger-Wolf. 2010. Sampling community structure. In *Proceedings of the 19th international conference on World wide web*. ACM, 701–710.
[16] Alan Mislove, Massimiliano Marcon, Krishna P Gummadi, Peter Druschel, and Bobby Bhattacharjee. 2007. Measurement and analysis of online social networks. In *7th ACM SIGCOMM conference on Internet measurement*. ACM, 29–42.
[17] Mark EJ Newman. 2004. Fast algorithm for detecting community structure in networks. *Physical review E* 69, 6 (2004), 066133.
[18] Mostafa Salehi, Hamid R Rabiee, and Arezo Rajabi. 2012. Sampling from complex networks with high community structures. *Chaos* 22, 2 (2012).
[19] Shaozhi Ye, Juan Lang, and Felix Wu. 2010. Crawling online social graphs. In *12th International Asia-Pacific Web Conference*.

Under the Shadow of Sunshine: Characterizing Spam Campaigns Abusing Phone Numbers Across Online Social Networks

Srishti Gupta
IIIT-Delhi
srishtig@iiitd.ac.in

Dhruv Kuchhal
MAIT, GGSIPU
dhruvkuchhal96@gmail.com

Payas Gupta
Pindrop
pgupta@pindrop.com

Mustaque Ahamad
Georgia Institute of Technology
mustaq@cc.gatech.edu

Manish Gupta
Microsoft, India
gmanish@microsoft.com

Ponnurangam Kumaraguru
IIIT-Delhi
pk@iiitd.ac.in

ABSTRACT

Cybercriminals abuse Online Social Networks (OSNs) to lure victims into a variety of spam. Among different spam types, a less explored area is OSN abuse that leverages the telephony channel to defraud users. Phone numbers are advertized via OSNs, and users are tricked into calling these numbers. To expand the reach of such scam / spam campaigns, phone numbers are advertised across multiple platforms like Facebook, Twitter, GooglePlus, Flickr, and YouTube. In this paper, we present the first data-driven characterization of cross-platform campaigns that use multiple OSN platforms to reach their victims and use phone numbers for monetization.

We collect ~23M posts containing ~1.8M unique phone numbers from Twitter, Facebook, GooglePlus, Youtube, and Flickr over a period of six months. Clustering these posts helps us identify 202 campaigns operating across the globe with Indonesia, United States, India, and United Arab Emirates being the most prominent originators. We find that even though Indonesian campaigns generate highest volume (~3.2M posts), only 1.6% of the accounts propagating Indonesian campaigns have been suspended so far. By examining campaigns running across multiple OSNs, we discover that Twitter detects and suspends ~93% more accounts than Facebook. Therefore, sharing intelligence about abuse-related user accounts across OSNs can aid in spam detection. According to our dataset, around ~35K victims and ~$8.8M could have been saved if intelligence was shared across the OSNs. By analyzing phone number based spam campaigns running on OSNs, we highlight the unexplored variety of phone-based attacks surfacing on OSNs.

CCS CONCEPTS

• Information systems; • Security and privacy → Human and societal aspects of security and privacy;

ACM Reference Format:
Srishti Gupta, Dhruv Kuchhal, Payas Gupta, Mustaque Ahamad, Manish Gupta, and Ponnurangam Kumaraguru. 2018. Under the Shadow of Sunshine: Characterizing Spam Campaigns Abusing Phone Numbers Across Online Social Networks. In WebSci '18: 10th ACM Conference on Web Science, May 27–30, 2018, Amsterdam, Netherlands. ACM, New York, NY, USA, 10 pages. https://doi.org/10.1145/3201064.3201065

1 INTRODUCTION

The increasing popularity of Online Social Networks (OSNs) has attracted a cadre of criminals who craft large-scale phishing and spam campaigns targeted against OSN users. Traditionally, spammers have been driving traffic to their websites by luring users to click on URLs in their posts on OSNs [11, 13, 33]. A significant fraction of OSN spam research has looked at solutions driven by URL blacklists [11, 32], manual classification [5], and honeypots [20, 31]. Since defence mechanisms against malicious / spam URLs have already matured, cybercriminals are looking for other ways to engage with users. Telephony has become a cost-effective medium for such engagement, and phone numbers are now being used to drive call traffic to spammer operated resources (e.g., call centers, Over-The-Top messaging applications like WhatsApp).

In this paper, we explore a data-driven approach to understand OSN abuse that makes use of phone numbers as action tokens in the realization / monetization phase of spam campaigns. Telephony has turned out to be an effective tool for spammers because Internet crime reports suggest that people fell victim to phone scams leading to a loss of $7.4B in 2015 for Americans alone [1]. Specifically, in the phone-based abuse of OSNs, spammers advertise phone numbers under their control via OSN posts and lure OSN users into calling these numbers. Since spammers use phone calls to trap victims, it is safe to assume that spammers would provide real phone numbers under their control. In addition, advertising phone numbers reduce spammers' overhead of finding the set of potential victims who can be targeted via the phone. Over phone conversations, they try convincing the victims that their services are genuine, and deceive them into making payments [25]. To maximize their reach and impact, we observe that spammers disseminate similar content across multiple OSNs.

While URLs help spammers attract victims to websites that host malicious content, phone numbers provide more leverage to spammers. Due to the inherent trust associated with the telephony medium and the impact of human touch over phone calls, spammers using phone numbers stand a better chance of convincing and hence are likely to make more impact. Besides, they can use fewer phone numbers as compared to URLs; a large number

---

[1]https://blog.truecaller.com/2017/04/19/truecaller-us-spam-report-2017/

of URLs are required to evade filtering mechanisms incorporated by OSNs. [2] Moreover, the monetization and advertising channel in phone-based campaigns i.e., (Phone) and (Web) respectively is different as compared to a single channel (Web) used in URL-based campaigns. Hence, phone-based spam requires correlation of abuse information across channels which makes it harder for OSN service providers to build effective solutions. Since the modus operandi in URL-based and phone-based spam campaigns is different, leaving phone-based spams unexplored can limit OSN service providers' ability to defend their users from spam. While extensive solutions have been built to educate users about URL-based spam [19], limited education is available for phone-based attacks. This is evident from several well publicized and long running Tech Support spam campaigns (since 2008) that use phone numbers to lure victims leading to huge financial losses in the past, as reported by the Federal Bureau of Investigation [26]. Although detecting and avoiding OSN abuse using phone numbers is so critical now, to the best of our knowledge, this space is largely unexplored.

In this paper, we address this gap by taking the *first* step in *identifying* and *characterizing* spam campaigns that abuse phone numbers across multiple OSNs. Studying phone-based spam across multiple OSNs provides a new perspective and helps in understanding how spammers work in coordination to increase their impact. From 22M posts collected from Twitter, Facebook, GooglePlus, YouTube, and Flickr, we identify 202 campaigns running across different countries, leveraging 806 unique abusive phone numbers. Studying these campaigns, we make the following key observations:

(1) We find that the cross-platform phone based spam campaigns originate from more than 16 countries, but most of them come from Indonesia, United States of America (USA), India, and United Arab Emirates (UAE). These campaigns are supported less number of phone numbers as compared to URLs, perhaps due to (a) the high cost of acquiring a phone number, and (b) weak defense mechanisms against phone - based spam. Victims that fall prey to these campaigns are offered banned filmography, personal products and a variety of other services; but the services are not delivered even after successful payment.

(2) As reported in earlier research [12], we also find evidence that suggests spammers collude to maximize their reach either by creating multiple accounts or promoting other spammers' content. To evade suspension strategies of each OSN, spammers keep the volume per account low. Our results show that accounts are suspended after being active for 33 days (on average); while literature suggests that spammers involved in URL-based spam campaigns, on the other hand, could survive only for three days after their first post [33]. In addition, 68.7% of spammer accounts are never suspended. Again, this suggests a crucial need to build effective solutions to combat phone-based spam.

(3) Our analysis also suggests that OSN service providers should work together in the fight against phone-based spam campaigns. By examining phone numbers involved in campaigns across OSNs, we find that although all OSNs are consistently

being abused, Twitter is the most preferred OSN for propagating a phone campaign. By analyzing spammers' multiple identities across OSNs, we find that Twitter is able to suspend 93.3% more accounts than Facebook. Thus, *cross-platform intelligence* can be useful in preventing the onset and reducing the lifetime of a campaign on a particular network with good accuracy. We estimate that cross-platform intelligence can help protect 35,407 victims across OSNs, resulting in potential savings of $8.8M.

Altogether, our results shed light on phone-based spam campaigns where spammers are using one channel (OSN) to spread their content, and the other channel (voice / SMS / message via phone) to convince their victims to fall prey to their campaigns. Given that no timely and effective filters exist on either channel to combat such spam, there is an imperative need to build one.

2 RELATED WORK

Spam is a growing problem for OSNs, and several researchers have looked at different ways to combat it. In this section, we present prior research in detecting spam campaigns on OSNs.

Handling non-phone based spam: There has been a large body of work that reports the existence of spam on multiple OSNs like YouTube [5], Twitter [13], and Facebook [11]. Thomas et al. studied the characteristics of suspended accounts on Twitter [33]. With an in-depth analysis of several spam campaigns, they reported that 77% spam accounts suspended by Twitter were taken down on the day of their first tweet. Apart from this, there has been work done to differentiate a spammer from a non-spammer [2, 4, 21, 34, 36]. Lumezanu et al. studied the spread of URL campaigns on email and Twitter and found that spam domains receive better coverage when they appear both on Twitter and email [22]. In addition to characterizing URL-based spam, methods have been proposed for detecting [8, 20, 35] and preventing [10, 29] such campaigns. While a lot of work has been done on characterizing and detecting URL-based spam campaigns, campaigns abusing phone numbers have been largely ignored.

Handling phone based spam: A large fraction of phone spam includes robocalling and spoofing, wherein spammers call the victims and trick them into giving personal or financial information [3]. Studies have shown that, in spam activities, phone numbers are more stable over time than email, and hence can be more helpful in identifying spammers [9, 18]. Christin et al. analyzed a type of scam targeting Japanese users, threatening to reveal the users' browsing history, in case they do not give them money [7]. In studies mentioned above, the authors relied on publicly available datasets to perform their analyses. In contrast, we develop an infrastructure to collect millions of posts from OSNs, cluster them into campaigns, and conduct our analyses. Researchers have investigated phone number abuse by analyzing cross-application features in Over-The-Top applications [17], cross-channel SMS abuse [30], characterizing spam campaigns on Twitter [15], and by characterizing honeypot numbers [3, 14, 16, 24]. Recently, Miramirkhani et al. studied the Tech Support campaign that abuse phone numbers, from the perspective of domains that were used to host malicious content [25]. The authors also interacted with spammers to understand their

---

[2]https://support.twitter.com/articles/90491

[3]https://www.consumer.ftc.gov/articles/0076-phone-scams

social engineering tactics. While they focused on URLs and domains abused by spammers, we study the cross-platform spread of phone-based spam campaigns across OSNs, along with strategies adopted by spammers for sustainability and visibility. Besides, we highlight how cross-platform intelligence about spam accounts can be shared across OSNs to aid in spam detection.

3 DATASET

In this section, we discuss our methodology for collecting phone numbers, posts and other metadata; which we use later to find campaigns on OSNs. These campaigns are then tagged as benign or spam. Figure 1 shows the architecture of our data collection subsystem that is used to collect phone numbers across multiple OSNs. We picked Twitter as the starting point to find phone numbers, as it provides easier access to large amounts of data as compared to other online social networks [27]. We set up a framework to collect a stream of tweets containing phone numbers. Some of the keywords used in data collection and regular expressions used to extract phone number from a text are listed in the Appendix 9.1. For each unique phone number received every day, a query was made to other OSNs viz. Facebook, [4] GooglePlus, Flickr, and YouTube, and for every search, we stored the following details: user details (user ID, screen name, number of followers and friends), post details (time of publication, text, URL, number of retweets, likes, shares, and reactions), and whether the ID were suspended. The data collection ran over a period of six months, between April 25, 2016 and October 26, 2016. Our system collected 22,690,601 posts containing 1,845,150 unique phone numbers, posted by 3,365,017 unique user accounts on five different OSNs. After removing noise (i.e., the posts which do not contain a phone number), the filtered set was used for finding campaigns.

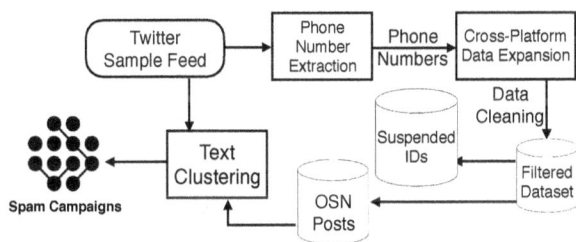

Figure 1: System Architecture for Data Collection across Multiple OSNs.

We acknowledge that our dataset may contain two kinds of bias: (1) Only 1% sample of all public tweets is available from the Twitter Streaming API; it can underestimate the spam campaigns observed on Twitter. (2) Since we treat Twitter as the starting point, we may miss some campaigns which are popular on other social networks, but not on Twitter. However, Twitter provides best access to user posts, justifying our choice.

Campaigns: A *campaign* is defined as a collection of posts made by a set of users sharing similar text and phone numbers. To make

sure that we do not tag any benign campaign as spam, we filtered out the phone numbers used by even one Twitter verified account. Every phone number, say *ph1*, is represented by a set of frequent unigram tokens which occur around the phone number. All posts that contain at-least 33% tokens from the representative token set are put together in a cluster; indicating posts related to the phone number. Different phone numbers, say *ph1* and *ph2*, are put together in the same cluster if the average Jaccard coefficient between the corresponding set of posts is greater than 0.7. We calculated different values of Jaccard coefficient and average silhouette scores to measure quality of clusters [1], and found 0.7 as knee point for corresponding value of silhouette score as 0.8. All users that post about any phone number in the clustered set are put together. A cluster thus formed is marked as a campaign. Using this method, we found 22,390 campaigns in the dataset, collectively amounting to ~10.9M posts.

Spam Campaigns: We flag a campaign as *spam* if it meets the following criteria: (a) phone number involved in the campaign is present in the United States Federal Trade Commission's Do Not Call (DNC) dataset [6], or (b) even if one OSN account involved in the campaign is suspended. Further, to be able to characterize the spam campaigns in detail, we focused only on campaigns with at least 5000 posts. With this, we identified 6,171 out of 22,390 campaigns as spam. From this set of campaigns, we did a manual inspection to verify if the campaign is indeed spam. This results in a working dataset of *202 campaigns comprising of ~4.9M posts*. During manual inspection, we also assigned topics to the 202 campaigns, where multiple campaigns could be assigned the same topic. For instance, a campaign selling shoes and other selling jackets would be assigned the topic – "Product Marketing".

4 CHARACTERIZING SPAM CAMPAIGNS

In this section, we focus on the following research questions. Where do spam campaigns originate from? Do spammers use automation when posting phone numbers or answering "phone calls"? What does a spammer OSN account suspension depend on? What is the typical modus operandi of the spammers?

4.1 Where does Phone-based Spam Originate?

It is important to know from which countries does the spam originate; it can be used in developing anti-spam filtering solution. We assume that the country associated with a phone number is the source country. For the analysis, we need to extract the country of the spam phone number. This is done either by identifying (a) the language of the post containing the spam phone number via the 'lang' field in the tweet object, or (b) by the country code using Google's phone number library. [7] These two methods helped in identifying countries for 127 campaigns. For rest of the campaigns, we called up the top two frequently occurring phone numbers in the campaign using Tropo [8], a VoIP software that can be used to make spoofed calls. We recorded all the calls and used Google's Speech API [9] to detect language and country of the campaign. We could

---

[4]Collecting data from Facebook was challenging. In April 2015, Facebook deprecated their post-search API end-point [5], so we used an Android mobile OAuth token to search content using the Graph API [17].

[6]https://www.ftc.gov/site-information/open-government/data-sets/do-not-call-data
[7]https://github.com/googlei18n/libphonenumber
[8]https://www.tropo.com/
[9]https://cloud.google.com/speech/

identify origin country for 26 more campaigns; for the remaining 49, the country is unknown. Table 1 presents topic distribution across various campaigns originating from different countries along with the average number of posts being made in each campaign. While majority of the spam was similar to advanced-fee scam [10], where spammers trick victims to make payments in advance, there were certain different type of campaigns observed in the dataset as well: Hacking (Tech Support) and Alternating Beliefs (Love Guru). In the *LoveGuru* campaign, astrologers promise victims to fix their love and marriage related problems. In the *Tech Support* campaign, spammers pose as technical support representatives or claim to be associated with big technological companies (like Amazon, Google, Microsoft, Quebec, Norton, Yahoo, Mcafee, Dell, HP, Apple, Adobe, TrendMicro, and Comcast) and offer technical support fixes.

Top four source countries selected by the volume of campaigns viz. Indonesia, United States of America (USA), India, and United Arab Emirates (UAE) show interesting characteristics. From Table 1, we observe that there is a good overlap of campaign categories across countries, while some countries have specific categories of campaigns running. Among all the campaign categories, volume generated by Indonesian campaigns is significantly higher than any other country.

4.2 Do Spammers use Automation?

While investigating further, we found that 99.3% pairs of consecutive posts related to the same campaign appeared on Twitter in less than 10 minutes. Given that a major fraction of content appeared within a few minutes, it is likely that content generation is automated. To ascertain this, we looked at the information of the client (provided by the Twitter API) used by spammers to interact with the Twitter API or their web portal. We found that most of the content was generated using 'twittbot.net', a popular bot service, known to be used by spammers [33]. Apart from the bot service, several other clients like RoundTeam (0.25%), IFFTT (0.03%), Buffer (0.017%), and Botize (0.016%), were used for Twitter. Besides, we found that volume per phone number was also high in Indonesian campaigns; 80% phone numbers had more than 1000 posts. One would assume that volume per phone number would be low since there are humans at the other end to service the requests. However, by processing the text in the posts created in this campaign, we found that spammers requested users to communicate via SMS or WhatsApp (~ 71% posts). This explains why spammers would be able to handle the load of interacting with victims. There are many other advantages of using these messaging services – spammers can further send phishing messages to victims, communicate with them unmonitored, and potentially use automated bots to reply to SMSs or Whatsapp messages.

4.3 What Factors Govern Spammers' Suspension?

As expected, we find that the visibility (number of likes, shares, and retweets) of a post is positively correlated with the number of posts (Pearson correlation coefficient = 0.97). While this may sound intuitive, the number of accounts that were suspended within a campaign were not positively correlated with the number of posts.

10

Table 1: Distribution of Campaigns across Topics and Source Countries. (#C denotes the number of campaigns).

Country	Campaign Topics	#C	#Posts
Argentina	Party Reservations	1	39,476
	Pornography	1	30,751
Chile	Delivering Goods	1	6,691
Columbia	Hotel Booking	1	18,228
	Pornography	1	5,324
Ghana	Alternating Beliefs (Marriage, Anxiety)	2	12,825
Guatemala	Product Marketing	1	8,821
India	Hotel Booking	1	10,986
	Alternating Beliefs (Marriage, Anxiety)	1	15,128
	Hacking(Tech Support)	1	43,552
Indonesia	Hotel Booking	1	8,291
	Product Marketing	75	2,689,616
	Pornography	4	164,382
	Alternating Beliefs (Marriage, Anxiety))	7	101,799
	Purchasing Followers	15	406,713
	Finance, Real Estate	3	23,700
	Selling Adult Products	5	48,109
	Uncategorized	3	29,043
Kuwait	Charity (Donation)	1	46,494
Mexico	Pornography	1	8,204
Nigeria	Alternating Beliefs (Marriage, Anxiety)	1	29,226
Pakistan	Finance, Real Estate	1	16,058
Spain	Charity (Donation)	1	14,311
UAE	Escorts	5	69,263
USA	Party Reservations	8	172,090
	Product Marketing	1	22,804
	Pornography	1	19,653
	Alternating Beliefs (Marriage, Anxiety)	1	12,936
	Escorts	1	9,652
UK	Escorts	1	9,268
	Charity (Donation)	2	17,184
Venezuela	Hotel Booking	1	6,813
	Free Games, Downloads	1	9,028
Unknown	Party Reservations	10	323,565
	Hotel Booking	2	11,334
	Product Marketing	10	108,634
	Free Games, Books, Downloads	1	8,834
	Pornography	17	211,714
	Alternating Beliefs (Marriage, Anxiety)	5	48,093
	Finance, Loans, Real Estate	2	34,226
	Charity (donation)	2	29,740
	Uncategorized	2	10,266

We noticed that even though the volume generated by Indonesian campaigns was 98.2% higher than Indian campaigns, the fraction of users suspended in Indian campaigns was 85.6% higher. Further, we observed that the account suspension is dependent on the nature of campaigns; campaigns providing escort services or technical support services had more accounts suspended.

Surprisingly, for similar escort service campaign running in two different countries, USA and UAE, there was a significant difference in the number of accounts suspended. Before concluding that the country plays a major role in account suspension, we performed detailed analysis as follows.

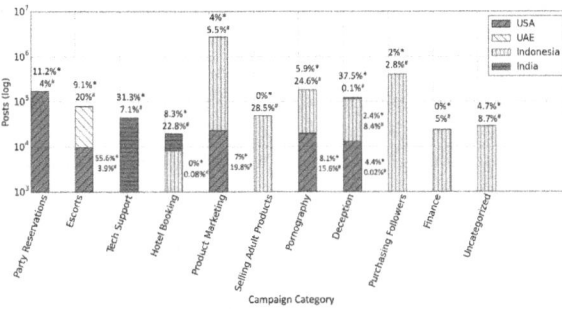

Figure 2: Comparison of campaigns running in the top 4 countries – Indonesia, USA, India, and UAE across different campaign categories. While visibility that a post receives is positively correlated with volume, account suspension in a campaign is not. Escort service and Tech Support campaigns had largest percentage of suspended accounts. The number of users suspended is represented by * and # denotes the fraction of posts getting visibility.

The number of posts generated by escort campaign running in the USA (9,652) was lower than that running in UAE (69,263), but 55.6% user accounts were suspended in the USA in comparison to only 9.1% accounts suspended in UAE. We looked at several reasons which could potentially lead to account suspension – volume generated per user or URLs used in the posts. We noticed that volume per user was higher for UAE users (Figure 3(a)), number of URLs shared in UAE campaign was higher, and words used in both the campaigns had a good overlap. Also, from Figure 3(b), we observed that inter-arrival time between two consecutive posts made by all the users in the USA (41s on an average) is lesser than that of posts made in the UAE campaign (392s on an average).

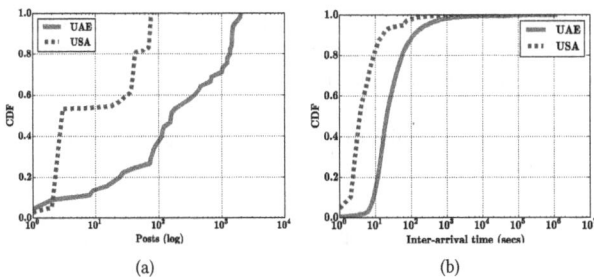

(a)   (b)

Figure 3: Comparing Escort service campaign in USA vs. UAE. Even though volume generated per USA account is lower than UAE accounts (a), inter-arrival time between two consecutive posts in the USA is lesser which could be a potential reason for suspension of accounts (b).

4.4 What is the Spammers' Modus Operandi?

To ascertain the attack methodology the victims faced, we performed an experiment after receiving our institute's Institutional Review Board (IRB) approval. Pretending to be a potential victim,

we called up phone numbers mentioned in campaigns selling adult (Viagra) pills in USA and UAE. In Indonesia, we interacted with spammers selling herbal products, and in India with those promoting tech support and astrology services (providing solutions to marriage and love problems). To avoid time zone conflict, we called the spammers in their local time of the day. Overall, we made 41 calls to different phone numbers from Indonesia, India, USA and UAE. Apart from Indonesia, campaigns from other countries had an IVR deployed, before reaching a spammer. We posit this can help in load balancing between limited human resources on the spammers' end. Due to language limitation in Indonesia, spammers preferred chatting over platforms like WhatsApp, where they were extremely responsive.

The campaigns in USA and UAE were not limited by any delivery location; they had a usual delivery time of 2–4 weeks. These campaigns were operating solely over the phone and had no option of visiting an online portal to make the transaction. The attackers confidently asked for the credit card details over the phone even though banks advise otherwise. Spammers from Indonesia told that they would start delivery only after receiving the payment, which was to be done via bank transfer. During the interactions, spammers were persuasive in selling products by claiming their products to be the best as compared to similar products in the market. Tech support campaigns in India were providing service to users remotely over the Internet and charged over call once the issue was 'fixed'. The catch was that the spammers pretended that there was a problem with the victims' computer and then tried to convince the victim to pay them to fix it, as reported in several complaints [11]. Another astrology based spam campaign running in India tricked by promising to fix users' marriage and love related problems within 48 hours [12]. We called 4 numbers in different Indian states. Interestingly, all the spammers had a similar way of dealing with the problem, where they asked to send personal details over WhatsApp.

It is evident that spammers running campaigns in different countries deploy similar mechanisms to let the victim reach them (posts on social media), to set up the product / service delivery operation (product delivery post payment and service delivery prior to payment), and model of payment (details transfer via phone, WhatsApp, verbal). It is the product delivery operation that creates deliberate confusion for a victim; intuitively, the delivery mechanism is similar for benign campaigns. Spammers leverage the advantage of similar delivery mechanisms, offer fake promises and later do not deliver.

5 CHARACTERIZING CROSS-PLATFORM SPAM CAMPAIGNS

In this section, we aim to answer the following research questions. Are spam campaigns run in a cross-OSN manner? How does the content cross-pollinate across OSNs? How do spammers maximize visibility? To what extent OSNs are able to detect phone based spam? Can existing intelligence on URL based spam be trivially adapted to handle the growing phone based spam problem? Can cross-platform intelligence help?

[11] https://800notes.com/Phone.aspx/1-800-549-5301/2
[12] https://www.complaintboard.in/complaints-reviews/
vashikaran-fake-vashikaran-fraud-cheater-money-taker-l149781.html

5.1 Do Phone-based Spam Campaigns run in a Cross-OSN Manner?

We observed that spam campaigns do not limit themselves to one OSN and are rather present on multiple networks. The distribution of posts across platforms in top 3 spam campaigns: Loveguru (from Alternating Beliefs category), Tech Support, and Indonesian Herbal Product (from Product Marketing category) is shown in Table 2. Even though Twitter has the largest fraction (possibly thanks to the first data source bias in our data collection method), all OSNs are abused to carry out spam campaigns.

Table 2: Top Cross-Platform Spam Campaigns

Campaign	TW	FB	G+	YT	FL
Tech Support	28,984	2,151	7,830	2,850	1,737
LoveGuru	6,934	1,418	4,257	101	63
Indonesia Herbal Product	1,443,619	9,238	21	46	336

Due to lack of space, in this section, we focus on studying in detail the Tech Support campaign. The details for other campaigns are available at *http://bit.ly/phcamp-dash*. Tech support scams have been around for a long period [13],incurring financial losses of $2.2M to victims in 2016 alone, as reported by the US Federal Bureau of Investigation (FBI) [26]. Earlier, attackers used to call victims offering to fix their computer or PC. Now, attackers have changed their strategy; instead of calling victims, attackers float their phone numbers on OSNs and ask users to call them in case they need any technical assistance related to their computers. Once the victim calls the phone number, the attacker asks for remote access to their machine to diagnose the problem. The attacker fudges the expected problems with victim's machine and convinces her to get it fixed. The reason this campaign is identified as spam, is because attackers deceive in believing that there exists some problem with their PC and charge money in return. Previous work has focused on the methods used by attackers to convince the victim and to make money [25]. In this paper, we are interested in looking at the cross-platform behavior of such tech support scam campaigns.

Over the course of six months of data collection, we got a total of 43,552 posts spread across all the five OSNs propagating to the extent of 41 phone numbers. The complete dataset description for tech support campaigns is shown in Table 3.

Table 3: Statistics for Tech Support Campaign

Features	TW	FB	G+	YT	FL
Total Posts	28,984	2,151	7,830	2,850	1,737
Posts with URLs	25,245	1,391	5,714	227	1,503
Distinct Phone Numbers	41	33	37	39	20
Distinct User IDs	748	289	360	433	79
Distinct Posts	16,142	1,797	6,570	2,050	1,449
Distinct URLs	68	951	3,189	80	293

As phone numbers are one of the primary tokens used by spammers, we examined carrier information tied to each number to identify what kind of phone numbers spammers use viz. landline, mobile, VoIP, or toll-free). We derived this information from several

[13]https://blog.malwarebytes.com/tech-support-scams/

online services like Twilio (mobile carrier information) [14], Truecaller (spam score assigned to the phone number) [15], and HLR lookups (current active location of the phone number). [16] We found that all the phone numbers used in the Tech Support campaign were toll-free numbers. Using a toll-free number offers several advantages to a spammer: (1) increased credibility: it does not incur a cost to the person calling, hence people perceive it to be legitimate, (2) it provides international presence: spammers can be reached from any part of the world. Further, we found that spammers used services like ATL, Bandwidth, and, Wiltel Communications to obtain these toll-free numbers and that a majority of them were registered between 2014 and 2016.

5.2 How does Content Cross-pollinate?

Now, we answer the following question: *Is a particular OSN preferred to start the spread of a campaign? Is there a specific pattern in the way spam propagates on different OSNs?*

Figure 4(a) shows the temporal pattern of content across OSNs. Note that our data collection was done over a period of six months while a campaign may have existed before and / or after this period. Hence, while the longest detected active time for a campaign in our dataset is 186 days, the actual time may be greater. A majority

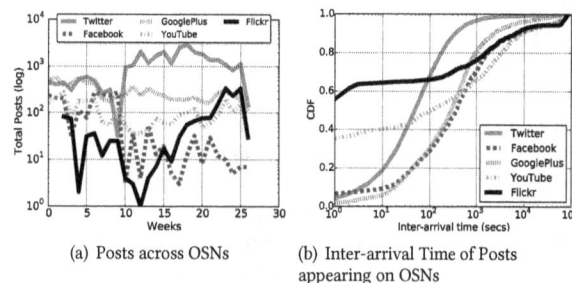

(a) Posts across OSNs

(b) Inter-arrival Time of Posts appearing on OSNs

Figure 4: Temporal properties of Tech Support Campaign across OSNs – all OSNs are abused to spread the campaign but volume is maximum on Twitter. Inter-arrival time between two consecutive posts is minimum for Twitter. Spammers began to heavily abuse Flickr towards the end of our data collection.

of these posts are densely packed into a small number of short time bursts, while the entire campaign spans a much longer period. Though the volume of content is significantly higher on Twitter, all OSNs are consistently being abused for propagation. Inter-arrival time, i.e., the average time between two successive posts is observed to be least on Twitter (308s), as shown in Figure 4(b). It is interesting to note that a few campaigns on Flickr have an inter-arrival time between two posts close to 1s, even though the average inter-arrival time is highest on Flickr. As Figure 4(a) shows, the volume on Flickr increased during the last few weeks of our data collection period. We divided the inter-arrival time into two time windows; first 15 weeks, and last 11 weeks. We observed that the average

[14]https://www.twilio.com/
[15]http://truecaller.com/
[16]https://www.hlr-lookups.com/

inter-arrival time in latter time window dropped from 9786s to 2543s which means spammers had started heavily abusing Flickr to spread the Tech Support campaign. It is hard to ascertain the motivation of the spammers in sending high volume content on Twitter, but, we speculate one of the reasons could be the public nature of the Twitter platform, as compared to closed OSNs like Facebook. For all the phone numbers, we analyzed the appearance of phone numbers on different OSNs, and the order in which they appear, as reported in Table 4. For each network that is picked

Table 4: Distribution of phone numbers according to their first appearance amongst OSNs. Flickr is never chosen as a starting point and there is no particular sequence in which spam propagates across OSNs.

Starting OSN	#Cases	Most common sequence
Twitter (TW)	12	TW → G+ → YT
GooglePlus (G+)	10	G+ → TW → YT → FB → FL
Facebook (FB)	6	FB → G+ → TW → YT
YouTube (YT)	13	YT → G+ → TW → FB

as the starting point, we identified the most common sequence in which phone numbers appeared subsequently on other OSNs. We found that Flickr was *never* chosen as the starting OSN to initiate the spread of a phone number. Further, we noticed that the posts originating from YouTube took the maximum time to reach a different OSN with an average inter-OSN time of 5 hours.

To summarize, we observed that all OSNs were abused to spread the Tech Support campaign, and no particular OSN was preferred to drive the campaign. In addition, there was no particular sequence in which spam propagated across OSNs.

5.3 How do Spammers Maximize Visibility?

We observed various strategies adopted by spammers to increase the dissemination of their posts. In this section, we discuss those strategies and their effectiveness.

The *Visibility* of a post is defined as the action performed by the user (consumer of the post) in terms of liking or sharing the post, which accounts for traction a particular post received. For each network, we define the value of visibility as follows: number of likes and reshares on Facebook, +1s and reshares on GooglePlus, number of likes and retweets on Twitter, and video like count on YouTube. We did not consider Flickr in our analysis since Flickr API gives only the view count of the image posted on the platform. A user only viewing an image cannot be assumed to be a victim of the campaign. To calculate visibility in all scenarios, we collected the *likes / retweets, plus-oners / reshares,* and *likes* from Twitter, GooglePlus, and Facebook respectively using their APIs. Apart from calculating values for each visibility attribute, we also collected properties of the user accounts involved, i.e., the IDs of user accounts involved in retweeting / liking / resharing the content. Due to rate limiting constraints on each of the APIs, we could not fetch visibility information daily. We collected this data six months after our data collection period, as posts take time to reach their audience. Due to this, (1) we might have missed information of tweets posted by suspended accounts, and (2) our total visibility values represent a lower bound.

To increase the visibility of content, we observed that the spammers use the following tricks: 67% of posts contained hashtags (for marketing [6], gaining followers [23]), 82.7% of posts contained URLs (for increased engagement with potential victims), 12.1% of posts contained short URLs (for obfuscating the destination of a URL and getting user engagement analytics), and 72% of posts contained photos (as visual content gathers more attention). We also noticed collusion between accounts and cross-referenced posts to increase the visibility of the campaign.

Cross-referenced posts: We call a post cross-referenced if it was posted to OSN X, but contains a URL redirecting to OSN Y. For instance, a Twitter post containing a link 'fb.me/xxxx' which would redirect to a different OSN, Facebook. Spammers either direct victims to existing posts or to another profile which is propagating the same campaign on a different OSN. In the Tech Support campaign, we observed that 3.2% of Facebook posts redirected to YouTube, and 1.78% of posts redirected from GooglePlus to YouTube.

Collusion between accounts: In the Tech Support campaign, we observed traces of collusion, i.e., spammers involved in a particular campaign, *like / share* each other's posts on OSNs or like their content to increase reachability. Collusion helps in cascading information to other followers in the network.

We calculated the visibility received by all the posts after removing likes / reshares / retweets by the colluders (i.e., accounts spreading the campaign already present in the dataset). We noticed that the posts containing the above-mentioned attributes (hashtags, URLs, short URLs, photos, cross-referencing, and collusion) garnered around ten times more visibility than posts not containing them. Around 10% of the posts saw traces of collusion, contributing to 20% of the total visibility. Maximum visibility (22.1% of total visibility) was observed for posts containing hashtags. In addition, we observed that a major chunk of visibility came from GooglePlus, followed by Facebook. This shows that the audience targeted influences the visibility garnered by a particular campaign, as GooglePlus is known to be consumed mostly by IT professionals [17].

5.4 To what Extent OSNs Suspend User Accounts?

To aid in the propagation of a campaign, spammers manage multiple accounts to, garner a wider audience, withstand account suspension, and in general increase the volume. Individual spammer accounts can either use automated techniques to aggressively post about a campaign or use hand-crafted messages. In this section, we examine the behavior of user accounts behind the Tech Support campaign. Spammers want to operate accounts in a stealth mode, which requires individual accounts to post few posts. It costs effort to get followers to a spam account, and the number of 'influential' accounts owned by a spammer is limited. Thus, the spammer tends to repeatedly use accounts to post content keeping volume low per account (Figure 5(b)), while creating new accounts once in a while (Figure 5(a)).

Long-lived user accounts: During our data collection, we found that 68.7% (1,305) of the accounts were *never* suspended or taken down on any of the five OSNs. This is in stark contrast to the URL based campaigns [33], where the authors observed that 92% of

---

[17] https://insight.globalwebindex.net/chart-of-the-day-who-is-most-likely-to-use-google

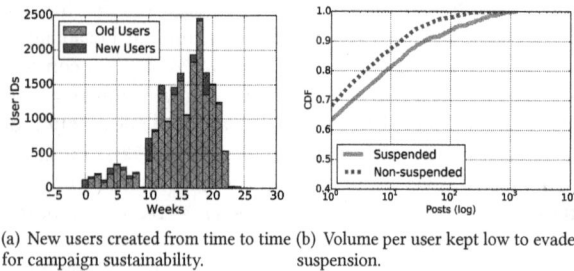

(a) New users created from time to time for campaign sustainability.

(b) Volume per user kept low to evade suspension.

Figure 5: New user accounts created from time to time and volume per ID kept low, to avoid suspension in the Tech Support Campaign.

the user accounts were suspended within three days of their first tweet. To take into account delays in the OSNs' account suspension algorithm, we queried all the accounts six months after the data collection to determine which accounts were deleted / suspended. This process consists of a bulk query to each OSN's API with the profile ID of the account. [18] For each of these accounts, we looked at the time stamp of the first and last post within our dataset, after which we assumed that the account was suspended immediately. Out of the accounts which were suspended, around 35% of the accounts were suspended within a day of their first post; the longest lasting account was active for 158 days, before finally getting suspended. On an average, accounts got suspended after being active for 33 days. This is in clear contrast to users getting suspended within three days for URL based spam campaigns, and thus, focused efforts are needed to strengthen defense from evolving phone-based spam campaigns.

5.5 Is Existing Intelligence based on URLs Useful to Handle Phone-based Spam?

Apart from creating accounts to propagate content, and using phone numbers to interact with victims, spammers also need a distinct set of URLs to advertise. In this section, we look at the domains, subdomains and URL shorteners used by spammers. Of all the posts, we had 4,581 unique URLs and 594 distinct domains. Of all the URLs, 12.1% were shortened using bit.ly; 3% of them received over 69,917 clicks (data collected from bit.ly API), showing that the campaign was fairly successful.

Given the prevalence of spam on OSNs, we examined the effectiveness of existing blacklists to detect malicious domains. Specifically, we used Google safe browsing [19] and Web of Trust (WOT) [20] to see if they were effective in flagging domains as malicious. Web of Trust categorizes the domains into several reputation buckets along with the confidence to assign a category. Please note that one domain may be listed in multiple categories. We marked a domain as malicious if the domain appeared in any of the following

---

[18] If the account is deleted / suspended, (a) Twitter redirects to http://twitter.com/ suspended, and returns error 404, (b) Youtube returns 'user not found', (c) Facebook returns error 403 in case the account is suspended, (d) GooglePlus throws a 'not found' error, (e) Flickr responds with a 'user not found' error.
[19] https://developers.google.com/safe-browsing/v4/lookup-api
[20] https://www.myWOT.com/wiki/API

categories – negative (malware, phishing, scam, potentially illegal), questionable (adult content). We checked the URLs and domains even after six months of data collection since blacklists may be slow in updating response to new spam sites. We marked a URL malicious if it was listed as malicious either by Google safe browsing or WOT. We checked these domains against the blacklists, finding that 10% of the domains were blacklisted by WOT, none by Google safe browsing. Overall, we found that existing URL infrastructure was ineffective to blacklist URLs used in phone-based spam campaigns.

5.6 Can Cross-Platform Intelligence be used?

Given that existing URL infrastructure is ineffective, we study if cross-platform intelligence across OSNs can be used. To this end, we look at the spam user profiles across OSNs to figure out which OSN is most effective in building the intelligence.

Homogeneous identity across OSNs: Simply analyzing users' previous posts might not be sufficient, as users can switch between multiple identities, making it hard for OSN service providers to detect and block them. Moreover, spammers may appear legitimate based on the small number of posts made by a single identity. The challenge remains in analyzing the aggregate behavior of multiple identities. To understand how user activity is correlated across OSNs, we pose the question: *do users have a unique identity on a particular OSN or do they share identities across OSNs? Within the same network, can we find the same users sharing multiple identities?*

To answer this, we looked at user identities across different OSNs in *aggregate* (multiple identities of the same user across different OSNs) and *individual* (multiple identities of the same user on a single OSN) forms. If the *same* user has multiple identities, sharing similar name or username, it is said to exhibit a homogeneous identity. To define user identity in a particular campaign, we used two textual features: *name* and *username* [28]. Since networks like YouTube and Google Plus do not provide the username, we restrict matching to identities sharing the same name. We used Levenshtein distance to find similarity in usernames. $LD(s_i, s_j)$ is the Levenshtein edit distance between usernames s_i and s_j. Here, $LD(s_i, s_j) = 1$ means the strings are identical, while $LD(s_i, s_j) = 0$ means they are completely different. After manual verification by comparing profile images across OSNs, we found users having LD >= 0.7 are homogeneous identities. We found four cases where multiple user identities were found for the same user within the same network, and in 65 instances, multiple user identities were present for the same user in more than two networks. Specifically, we found 51 users sharing multiple identities across two different OSNs, and 10 users sharing multiple identities across 3 OSNs. We noticed that these accounts shared same phone numbers across OSNs; some accounts post more phone numbers that are part of tech support campaign.

We found that the total number of posts made by these accounts was highest on GooglePlus (2696), followed by Twitter (1776), Facebook (577), Flickr (387), and YouTube (323). Out of all the homogeneous identities, the following are the percentages of accounts suspended on each OSN – Twitter (60%), YouTube (48%), GooglePlus (32%) Flickr (33%), and Facebook (4%). Our data is insufficient to determine whether account suspension is due to dissemination of content across OSNs or other unobserved spammers' properties.

Notwithstanding, the association between user identities across OSNs, strengthens the fact that sharing information about spammer accounts across OSNs could help OSNs to detect spammers accurately.

Reducing financial loss and victimization: The actual number of users that are impacted depends on how many victims called spammers and bought the products advertised by campaigns. Since it is hard to get this data, we provide a rough estimate of the number of victims falling for campaigns identified in our dataset. We find reputation of spammers in terms of their followers count on Twitter, friends / page likes on Facebook, circle count on GooglePlus, and subscriber count on Youtube. As these users have subscribed to spammers to get more content, they are likely to fall for the spam. Some of the users would be the ones who aren't aware of the campaign being spam, while some followers / friends could be spammers themselves who have followed other spammers' accounts. We again collected this data after 6 months of our data collection and recorded 637,573 followers on Twitter, 21,053 friends on Facebook, 11,538 followers on GooglePlus, and 2,816 likes on YouTube amounting to a total of 670,164 users. Please note that this number is a lower bound, as we were not able to retrieve statistics for suspended / deleted accounts. Assume that we transfer knowledge from Twitter to other OSNs and prevent the onset of campaigns on other OSNs, we analyzed how much money and victims could be saved. Looking only at the friends, followers, and likers on Facebook, GooglePlus, and YouTube respectively, we could save 35,407 (21,053 + 11,538 + 2,816) unique victims and $8.8M (35,407 * $290.9) by transferring intelligence across OSNs. We used the average cost of the Tech Support Spam to be $290.9 per victim, as reported by Miramirkhani et al. [25].

6 DISCUSSION

In this section, we provide a synthesis of our evaluations and propose some recommendations to OSN service providers.

How spammers can be choked? Phone numbers are a stable resource for spam since spammers need to provide their real phone numbers so that victims can reach out to them. A solution built around phone numbers, therefore, would be more reliable in bringing down spammers. As a countermeasure, there are two potential mechanisms – a) phone blacklist and b) suspension of OSN accounts. A *phone blacklist* should be created, similar to URL blacklists, to check if a phone number is involved in a spam / scam campaign. Blacklisting a phone number would break the connecting link between victims and spammers, thus bringing down the spammers' monetization infrastructure. However, it is difficult to create one, because there are little identifiable features associated with a phone number as there are with URLs like landing page, some special characters, domain typo-squatting, etc. Therefore, user suspension which can be collected from OSNs can come to rescue. From this research we established that the link between a phone number and the spammer account is crucial. Thus, one can focus on removing malicious users from user communities sharing the same phone number. In this network of user accounts, some users would already be suspended by OSNs. The labels can be recursively propagated to other unknown nodes from the known suspended nodes using several graph-based algorithms like Page Rank. Bringing down

the spammers propagating phone numbers would disintegrate the entire campaign.

There exist some services, like Truecaller [21] and FTC's do-not-call complaint dataset [22], which collect information about phone numbers that spammers use to call victims (*incoming spam communication*). In this work, however, we demonstrated that spammers advertise their phone numbers across OSNs, so that victims would call them instead (*outgoing spam communication*). We found the overlap between our collected phone numbers (associated with potential spam campaigns) with the FTC (0.001%) and Truecaller (0.4%) databases to be minimal. It is, therefore, imperative that solutions also be built on outgoing spam communication.

Measuring Impact using Honeypots. In this work, we focused on using friends and followers of the user as a metric to measure the impact; it might not capture the actual victims who fell for those campaigns. As an alternative approach, one can simulate a campaign; changing the phone number (say to phone number X) and keeping the text intact. There are certain services like Twilio [23] that aid in making calls over the Internet, which can be used to record the number of calls being made to phone number X. Spammer networks are dense; to ensure that these simulated campaigns are visible to a large OSN population, one can use Facebook Ads [24] or Twitter Ads [25] for campaign promotion as advertisements. We believe this is a potential way to measure the impact of campaigns.

7 CONCLUSION

With the convergence of telephony and the Internet, the phone channel has become an attractive target for spammers to exploit and monetize spam conducted over the Internet. This paper presents the first large-scale study of cross-platform spam campaigns that abuse phone numbers. We collect ~23 million posts containing ~1.8 million unique phone numbers from Twitter, Facebook, GooglePlus, Youtube, and Flickr over a period of six months. We identified 202 campaigns running from all over the world with Indonesia, United States, India, and the United Arab Emirates being the highest contributors. We showed that even though Indonesian campaigns generated ~3.2 million posts, only 1.6% have been suspended so far. However, the number of accounts suspended in a campaign is not correlated with volume. Campaigns providing escort services and technical support solutions had more account suspensions. After interacting with spammers, we observed that they adopt tactics similar to legitimate services, to convince victims. By examining campaigns running across OSNs, we showed that Twitter could suspend ~93% more accounts spreading spam as compared to Facebook. Therefore, sharing intelligence about spam user accounts across OSNs can aid in spam detection; ~35K victims and $8.8M could be saved based on exploratory analysis of our data. We acknowledge that our validations on some possible explanations proposed in this work may be not rigorous, due to difficulties in thoroughly obtaining spammers' motivations. However, we believe that our first-of-its-kind analysis of these phenomena still provides great

---

[21] https://www.truecaller.com/
[22] https://www.ftc.gov/site-information/open-government/data-sets/do-not-call-data
[23] https://www.twilio.com/
[24] https://www.facebook.com/about/ads
[25] https://business.twitter.com/en/twitter-ads.html

value and opens new doors to understand the phone-based spammer ecosystem across OSNs better.

8 ACKNOWLEDGMENT

Mustaque Ahamad's participation in this research was supported in part by US National Science Foundation (NSF) grant no. CNS-1514035. We would like to thank members of Precog, IIIT-Delhi for their valuable feedback; special thanks to Paridhi Jain.

REFERENCES

[1] Hélio Almeida, Dorgival Guedes, Wagner Meira, and Mohammed J Zaki. 2011. Is there a best quality metric for graph clusters?. In *Joint European Conference on Machine Learning and Knowledge Discovery in Databases*. Springer, 44–59.
[2] Amit A Amleshwaram, Narasimha Reddy, Sandeep Yadav, Guofei Gu, and Chao Yang. 2013. Cats: Characterizing automation of twitter spammers. In *Communication Systems and Networks (COMSNETS), 2013 Fifth International Conference on*. IEEE, 1–10.
[3] Marco Balduzzi, Payas Gupta, Lion Gu, Debin Gao, and Mustaque Ahamad. 2016. MobiPot: Understanding Mobile Telephony Threats with Honeycards. In *Proceedings of the 11th ACM SIGSAC Symposium on Information, Computer and Communications Security (ASIA CCS '16)*. ACM, New York, NY, USA.
[4] Fabricio Benevenuto, Gabriel Magno, Tiago Rodrigues, and Virgilio Almeida. 2010. Detecting spammers on twitter. In *Collaboration, electronic messaging, anti-abuse and spam conference (CEAS)*, Vol. 6. 12.
[5] Fabrício Benevenuto, Tiago Rodrigues, Virgílio Almeida, Jussara Almeida, and Marcos Gonçalves. 2009. Detecting spammers and content promoters in online video social networks. In *Proceedings of the 32nd international ACM SIGIR conference on Research and development in information retrieval*. ACM, 620–627.
[6] Juan Miguel Carrascosa, Roberto González, Rubén Cuevas, and Arturo Azcorra. 2013. Are trending topics useful for marketing?. *Proc. COSN* (2013).
[7] Nicolas Christin, Sally S Yanagihara, and Keisuke Kamataki. 2010. Dissecting one click frauds. In *Proceedings of the 17th ACM conference on Computer and communications security*. ACM, 15–26.
[8] Zi Chu, Indra Widjaja, and Haining Wang. 2012. Detecting social spam campaigns on twitter. In *International Conference on Applied Cryptography and Network Security*. Springer, 455–472.
[9] Andrei Costin, Jelena Isacenkova, Marco Balduzzi, Aurélien Francillon, and Davide Balzarotti. 2013. The role of phone numbers in understanding cyber-crime schemes. In *Privacy, Security and Trust (PST), 2013 Eleventh Annual International Conference on*. IEEE, 213–220.
[10] Michalis Faloutsos. 2013. Detecting malware with graph-based methods: traffic classification, botnets, and facebook scams. In *Proceedings of the 22nd International Conference on World Wide Web*. ACM, 495–496.
[11] Hongyu Gao, Jun Hu, Christo Wilson, Zhichun Li, Yan Chen, and Ben Y Zhao. 2010. Detecting and characterizing social spam campaigns. In *Proceedings of the 10th ACM SIGCOMM conference on Internet measurement*. ACM, 35–47.
[12] Saptarshi Ghosh, Bimal Viswanath, Farshad Kooti, Naveen Kumar Sharma, Gautam Korlam, Fabricio Benevenuto, Niloy Ganguly, and Krishna Phani Gummadi. 2012. Understanding and combating link farming in the twitter social network. In *Proceedings of the 21st international conference on World Wide Web*. ACM, 61–70.
[13] Chris Grier, Kurt Thomas, Vern Paxson, and Michael Zhang. 2010. @ spam: the underground on 140 characters or less. In *Proceedings of the 17th ACM conference on Computer and communications security*. ACM, 27–37.
[14] Payas Gupta, Mustaque Ahamad, Jonathan Curtis, Vijay Balasubramaniyan, and Alex Bobotek. 2014. *M3AAWG Telephony Honeypots: Benefits and Deployment Options*. Technical Report.
[15] Payas Gupta, Roberto Perdisci, and Mustaque Ahamad. 2018. Towards Measuring the Role of Phone Numbers in Twitter-Advertised Spam. In *Proceedings of the 13th ACM on Asia Conference on Computer and Communications Security (ASIA CCS '18)*. ACM, New York, NY, USA, 12. https://doi.org/10.1145/3196494.3196516
[16] Payas Gupta, Bharath Srinivasan, Vijay Balasubramaniyan, and Mustaque Ahamad. 2015. Phoneypot: Data-driven Understanding of Telephony Threats.. In *NDSS*.
[17] Srishti Gupta, Payas Gupta, Mustaque Ahamad, and Ponnurangam Kumaraguru. 2016. Exploiting Phone Numbers and Cross-Application Features in Targeted Mobile Attacks. In *Proceedings of the 6th Workshop on Security and Privacy in Smartphones and Mobile Devices*. ACM, 73–82.
[18] Jelena Isacenkova, Olivier Thonnard, Andrei Costin, Aurélien Francillon, and David Balzarotti. 2014. Inside the scam jungle: A closer look at 419 scam email operations. *EURASIP Journal on Information Security* 2014, 1 (2014), 4.
[19] Ponnurangam Kumaraguru, Lorrie Faith Cranor, and Laura Mather. 2009. Anti-phishing landing page: Turning a 404 into a teachable moment for end users. *Conference on Email and Anti-Spam* (2009). http://precog.iiitd.edu.in/Publications_files/APWGLandingPage-Turning404intoEducation.pdf

[20] Kyumin Lee, James Caverlee, and Steve Webb. 2010. Uncovering social spammers: social honeypots+ machine learning. In *Proceedings of the 33rd international ACM SIGIR conference on Research and development in information retrieval*. ACM, 435–442.
[21] Kyumin Lee, Brian David Eoff, and James Caverlee. 2011. Seven Months with the Devils: A Long-Term Study of Content Polluters on Twitter.. In *ICWSM*.
[22] Cristian Lumezanu and Nick Feamster. 2012. Observing common spam in Twitter and email. In *Proceedings of the 2012 ACM conference on Internet measurement conference*. ACM, 461–466.
[23] Eva García Martín, Niklas Lavesson, and Mina Doroud. 2016. Hashtags and followers. *Social Network Analysis and Mining* 6, 1 (2016), 1–15.
[24] Aude Marzuoli, Hassan A Kingravi, David Dewey, and Robert Pienta. 2016. Uncovering the Landscape of Fraud and Spam in the Telephony Channel. In *Machine Learning and Applications (ICMLA), 2016 15th IEEE International Conference on*. IEEE, 853–858.
[25] Najmeh Miramirkhani, Oleksii Starov, and Nick Nikiforakis. 2017. Dial One for Scam: A Large-Scale Analysis of Technical Support Scams. In *Proceedings of the 24th Network and Distributed System Security Symposium (NDSS)*.
[26] Federal Bureau of Investigation. 2016. TECH SUPPORT SCAM - Federal Bureau of Investigation. https://www.ic3.gov/media/2016/160602.aspx. (June 2016).
[27] Miles Osborne and Mark Dredze. 2014. Facebook, Twitter and Google Plus for breaking news: Is there a winner?. In *ICWSM*.
[28] Raphael Ottoni, Diego B Las Casas, Joao Paulo Pesce, Wagner Meira Jr, Christo Wilson, Alan Mislove, and Virgílio AF Almeida. 2014. Of Pins and Tweets: Investigating How Users Behave Across Image-and Text-Based Social Networks.. In *ICWSM*.
[29] Md Sazzadur Rahman, Ting-Kai Huang, Harsha V Madhyastha, and Michalis Faloutsos. 2012. Frappe: detecting malicious facebook applications. In *Proceedings of the 8th international conference on Emerging networking experiments and technologies*. ACM, 313–324.
[30] Bharat Srinivasan, Payas Gupta, Manos Antonakakis, and Mustaque Ahamad. 2016. Understanding Cross-Channel Abuse with SMS-Spam Support Infrastructure Attribution. In *European Symposium on Research in Computer Security*. Springer, 3–26.
[31] Gianluca Stringhini, Christopher Kruegel, and Giovanni Vigna. 2010. Detecting spammers on social networks. In *Proceedings of the 26th Annual Computer Security Applications Conference*. ACM, 1–9.
[32] Kurt Thomas, Chris Grier, Justin Ma, Vern Paxson, and Dawn Song. 2011. Design and evaluation of a real-time url spam filtering service. In *2011 IEEE Symposium on Security and Privacy*. IEEE, 447–462.
[33] Kurt Thomas, Chris Grier, Dawn Song, and Vern Paxson. 2011. Suspended accounts in retrospect: an analysis of twitter spam. In *Proceedings of the 2011 ACM SIGCOMM conference on Internet measurement conference*. ACM, 243–258.
[34] Alex Hai Wang. 2010. Don't follow me: Spam detection in twitter. In *Security and Cryptography (SECRYPT), Proceedings of the 2010 International Conference on*. IEEE, 1–10.
[35] Steve Webb, James Caverlee, and Calton Pu. 2008. Social Honeypots: Making Friends With A Spammer Near You.. In *CEAS*.
[36] Sarita Yardi, Daniel Romero, Grant Schoenebeck, et al. 2009. Detecting spam in a twitter network. *First Monday* 15, 1 (2009).

9 APPENDIX

9.1 Regular Expressions for Data Collection

We used a curated list of 400 keywords like call, SMS, WhatsApp, ring, contact, dial, reach etc to filter relevant tweets from Twitter's Streaming API. While extracting phone numbers from the tweets, we encountered variations in representation of phone numbers, for instance the number 1-888-551-2881 can be represented as 1(888)551-2881, 1(888) 551-2881, 1.888.551.2881, or 1 888 551 2881 where all variations were being counted as different phone numbers. We filtered out this noise by post-processing the data, where a couple of regular expressions were used to obtain a valid phone number from the text obtained from each post are listed below:

```
1. ('(?<= )\d{6}-\d{3}(?= )|
(?<=\[)\d{6}-\d{3}(?=\])|(?<=\()\d{6}-\d{3}(?=\))')
2. (' (\d[\d ]{5,13}\d{2}) ')
3. ('\$ *\d+[\.]*\d+|\d+[\.]*\d+\$')
4. ('^\d+\s|\s\d+\s|\s\d+$')
```

Wisdom in Sum of Parts: Multi-Platform Activity Prediction in Social Collaborative Sites

Roy Ka-Wei Lee
Living Analytics Research Centre
Singapore Management University
roylee.2013@smu.edu.sg

David Lo
Singapore Management University
davidlo@smu.edu.sg

ABSTRACT

In this paper, we proposed a novel framework which uses user interests inferred from activities (a.k.a., *activity interests*) in multiple social collaborative platforms to predict users' platform activities. Included in the framework are two prediction approaches: (i) *direct platform activity prediction*, which predicts a user's activities in a platform using his or her activity interests from the same platform (e.g., predict if a user answers a given Stack Overflow question using the user's interests inferred from his or her prior *answer* and *favorite* activities in Stack Overflow), and (ii) *cross-platform activity prediction*, which predicts a user's activities in a platform using his or her activity interests from another platform (e.g., predict if a user answers a given Stack Overflow question using the user's interests inferred from his or her *fork* and *watch* activities in GitHub). To evaluate our proposed method, we conduct prediction experiments on two widely used social collaborative platforms in the software development community: GitHub and Stack Overflow. Our experiments show that combining both *direct* and *cross* platform activity prediction approaches yield the best accuracies for predicting user activities in GitHub (AUC=0.75) and Stack Overflow (AUC=0.89).

KEYWORDS

Social Collaborative Platforms; Prediction; Stack Overflow; GitHub

ACM Reference Format:
Roy Ka-Wei Lee and David Lo. 2018. Wisdom in Sum of Parts: Multi-Platform Activity Prediction in Social Collaborative Sites. In *WebSci'18: 10th ACM Conference on Web Science, May 27-30, 2018, Amsterdam, Netherlands*. ACM, New York, NY, USA, 10 pages. https://doi.org/10.1145/3201064.3201067

1 INTRODUCTION

Software developers are increasingly adopting social collaborative platforms for software development. *GitHub* and *Stack Overflow* are two of such popular platforms. GitHub is a collaborative software development platform that allows code sharing and version control. Users can participate in various activities in GitHub, for example, users may *fork* (i.e., create a copy of) repositories of other users or *watch* the activities of repositories of interest. Stack Overflow is a

technical question-and-answer community-based website where users post and answer questions relating to software development.

As these social collaborative platforms gain popularity, many research studies have proposed recommender systems to improve the usability of these platforms. For example, there are work which predict and recommend relevant Stack Overflow questions and answers to aid users in software development [7, 32, 34]. While for GitHub, researchers have proposed methods to predict which software repositories are more relevant to a target user [9, 11, 43]. Nevertheless, many of these studies only consider the users' behaviours and interests in a single platform when predicting and recommending user platform activities.

There have been few existing inter-platform studies on GitHub and Stack Overflow. Vasilescu et al. [29] studied how users' involvement in Stack Overflow impacted their productivity in GitHub. Badashian et al. [2] did an empirical study on the correlation between different types of user activities in GitHub and Stack Overflow. In a more recent study by Lee and Lo [15], the researchers found that users who have accounts on both GitHub and Stack Overflow do share similar interests across the two platforms. For example, a user who commits to Java-related repositories in GitHub, is likely to also answer Java-related questions in Stack Overflow. In this paper, we aim to extend the study in [15], and propose a multi-platform activity prediction method, which predicts a user's activities in a platform using the user's interests inferred from his or her activities in multiple platforms.

Figure 1 illustrates an example for activity prediction in a multi-platform setting. Consider user u, who has accounts on both GitHub and Stack Overflow. If we adopt a *direct platform activity prediction* approach, i.e., predicts a user's activities in a platform using his or her activity interests from the same platform, we could predict that u is likely to answer or *favorite*[1] question X in Stack Overflow as u has previously answered a *LSTM* related question. However, if we adopt a *cross-platform activity prediction* approach, i.e., predicts a user's activities in a platform using his or her activity interests from another platform, we could predict that u is also likely to answer or favorite a *SVM* related question Y as u has previously *watched*[2] a *SVM* related repository B in GitHub.

The social collaborative nature of these platforms could also be exploited for activity prediction. According to Lee and Lo [15], users who participated in the same GitHub repositories and Stack Overflow questions tend to share common interests. Therefore, we also explore the possibility to expand a user's interests to include the interests of users whom he or she had co-participated activities with. Referencing to the same example in Figure 1, user v co-forked

---

[1]Bookmark a question in Stack Overflow
[2]Subscribe and receive updates on a repository in GitHub

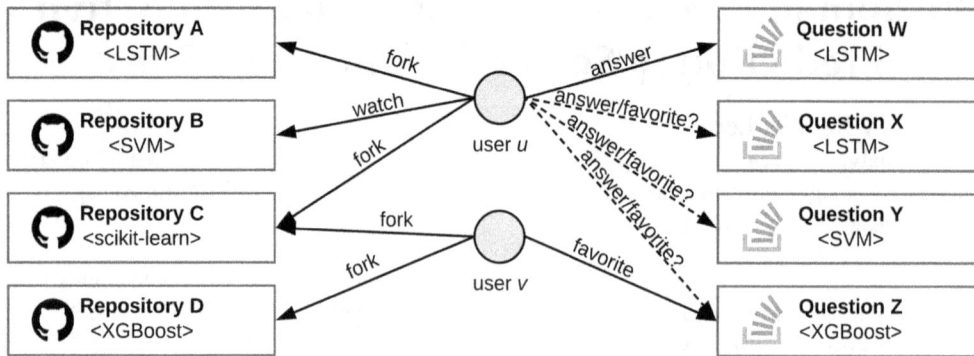

Figure 1: Example of Activity Prediction in Multi-Platform Setting

the same *scikit-learn* related repository as *u* and forked another *XGBoost* related repository. Although *u* did not participate in any *XGBoost* related repositories and questions, we can "expand" *u*'s interests to include *XGBoost* as it is an interest of user *v*. Finally, we could predict that *u* is likely to also answer or favorite a *XGBoost* related question. This expansion of interests could be particularly useful when a user has participated in very few activities on either platform. Note that the example also work for predicting GitHub activities using user's activities in Stack Overflow.

There are a number of benefits for using user interests from multi-platforms for activity prediction. Firstly, it enables prediction and recommendation of user activities in social collaborative platforms even when past activity history of a user is minimal or unavailable, i.e, cold-start problem [23]. For example, if we learn from a user's activities in GitHub that she is interested in *Python* and *text mining* techniques, we would predict that she will likely participate in *Python* and *text mining* related Stack Overflow questions even when she has just newly joined Stack Overflow and has not participated in any questions. Second, it could cover the *blind spots* of activity recommender systems which use only data from a single platform. For example, if a user has forked *Android* related repositories in GitHub, recommender systems which are built on user's past activity in GitHub will likely to recommend the user more *Android* related repositories. However, the same user may have also participated in some *iOS* related questions in Stack Overflow, and such observations can be used to make relevant GitHub activity recommendations to the user.

Contributions. This work improves the state-of-the-art of inter-platform studies on multiple social collaborative platforms. Key contributions of this work include: Firstly, we proposed a novel framework which enables predicting users' activities using interests inferred from their activities in multiple social collaborative platforms. Secondly, we evaluate our method using large real-world datasets from Stack Overflow and GitHub. The results from our prediction experiments show that our proposed method is able to predict users' activities in GitHub and Stack Overflow with good accuracy, achieving an AUC score of up to 0.75 and 0.89 respectively.

Paper outline. The rest of the paper is organized as follows. Section 2 introduces the social collaborative platform activity prediction problem and describe our proposed the multi-platform prediction framework. Section 3 describe the data extraction process and the two real-world datasets, Stack Overflow and GitHub, that we used in our prediction experiments. Section 4 presents our experiments to predict user activities in the two social collaborative platforms using our proposed framework. Threat to validity of our study are discussed in Section 5. Section 6 reviews the literature related to our study. Finally, we summarize and conclude our work in Section 7.

2 PROPOSED METHOD

In this section, we first present our proposed multi-platform activity prediction framework. We then define the prediction problem and describe the features used in our proposed prediction method.

2.1 Multi-Platform Prediction Framework

Figure 2 shows the framework that we adopt for multi-platform activity prediction. We begin with data extraction from two social collaborative platforms: Stack Overflow and GitHub. There are three sub-processes in data extraction: (i) matching of users Stack Overflow and GitHub accounts, (ii) extracting the users' platform activities, and (iii) inferring users' interests from their activities. The details of these sub-processes will be covered in Section 3. Next, we construct the Stack Overflow and GitHub user features which we will use in our prediction.

Our framework also incorporates two approaches to predict users' platform activities, namely: *direct* and *cross* platform activity prediction. We define *direct platform activity prediction* as predicting a user's platform activity using features from the same platform. For example, we predict if a given user will answer a given Stack Overflow question using the user's Stack Overflow features. Conversely, we define *cross-platform activity prediction* as predicting a platform activity to a user using features from a different platform. For example, we predict if a given user will answer a given Stack Overflow question using the user's GitHub features. The performance of both prediction approaches will be evaluated on four prediction tasks, which will be described in Section 4.

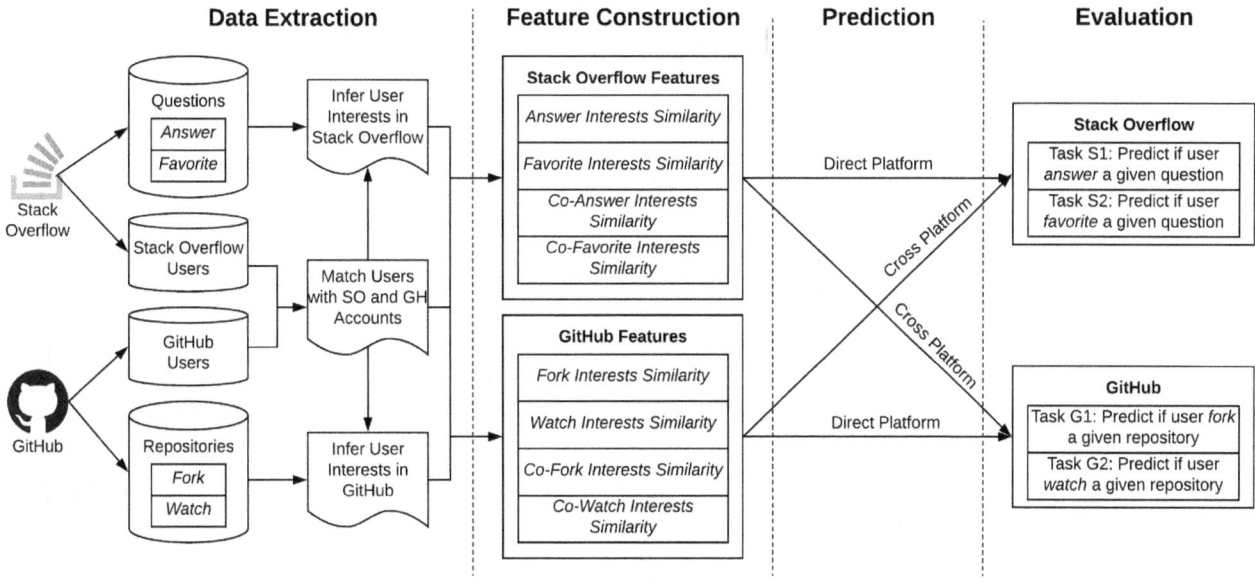

Figure 2: Cross-Platform Activity Prediction Framework

2.2 Problem Statement

Given a pair of query user and item (i.e., question or repository), (u, k), we aim to predict if u will perform an activity (e.g. answer, favorite, fork or watch) on k. There are various ways to measure the likelihood of u performing an activity on k. For example, we could consider the similarity between k's description and u's interests inferred from different activities, or the similarity between k's description and the inferred interests of the user who co-participate activities with u. In our proposed framework, we propose two types of user features, namely:*user activity interest similarity features* and *user co-activity interest similarity features*. The notations used throughout this paper are summarized in Table 1.

We denote the estimated interests of a user given a repository r that he or she forked and watched in GitHub as $I(r)$. Similarly, we denote the estimated interests of a user given a question q that he or she answered and favorited in Stack Overflow as $I(q)$. Since the estimated interests given a repository or a question is the same for all users participated in it, we also refer to $I(r)$ and $I(q)$ as the interests in r and q. For simplicity, we also refer to them as r's interests and q's interests respectively.

2.3 User Activity Interest Similarity Features

This set of features measures the similarity between a query item k and a query user u's *fork, watch, answer* and *favorite* activity interests in GitHub and Stack Overflow. The intuition behind this set of features comes from the empirical study from Lee and Lo [15], where they found that users in GitHub and Stack Overflow shared similarities between their interests in different types of activities and across the two platforms. Suppose that we want to predict if a user would fork a given repository in GitHub, we would measure the similarity between the given repository's interests and the developer's interests for the different activity types. Intuitively,

Table 1: List of notations used

Symbol	Description
u	Query user
k	Query item
v	User who co-participated activities with user u
r	Repository
q	Question
$I(r)$	Interests of repository r
$I(q)$	Interests of question q
$I(k)$	Interests of query item k
$u.RF$	Set of repositories forked by user u
$u.RW$	Set of repositories watched by user u
$u.QA$	Set of questions answered by user u
$u.QF$	Set of questions favorited by user u
$Co^{Fork}(u)$	Set of users who co-forked at least one repository with user u
$Co^{Watch}(u)$	Set of users who co-watched at least one repository with user u
$Co^{Ans}(u)$	Set of users who co-answered at least one question with user u
$Co^{Fav}(u)$	Set of users who co-favorited at least one question with user u

the higher the similarity scores, the more likely the user would fork the given repositories. Equation 1 captures the above intuition and measures similarity between k and u's fork activity interests (i.e., $Sim_{Fork}(u, k)$), by dividing $\{r \in u.RF | I(r) \in I(k)\}$, which is the number of u's forked repositories that shared common interests with the item interests of k, by the total number of repositories forked by u (i.e.,$u.RF$).

Example. Referencing to the earlier example in Figure 1, we could predict if user u will answer question X by computing the similarity between question X and u's fork activity interests. In this example, the common interests between u and question X will be *LSTM*. The number of u's forked repositories that shared common interests with question X (i.e., $\{r \in u.RF|I(r) \in I(k))\}$) will then be 1 (i.e., Repository A), while the total number of repositories forked by u is 2 (i.e., Repository A and B). Thus, $Sim_{Fork}(u,k) = \frac{1}{2} = 0.5$.

$$Sim_{Fork}(u,k) = \frac{|\{r \in u.RF|I(r) \in I(k))\}|}{|u.RF|} \quad (1)$$

$$Sim_{Watch}(u,k) = \frac{|\{r \in u.RW|I(r) \in I(k)\}|}{|u.RW|} \quad (2)$$

$$Sim_{Ans}(u,k) = \frac{|\{q \in u.QA|I(q) \in I(k)\}|}{|u.QA|} \quad (3)$$

$$Sim_{Fav}(u,k) = \frac{|\{q \in u.QF|I(q) \in I(k)\}|}{|u.QF|} \quad (4)$$

We compute the similarities between k and u's watch, answer and favorite activities interests in similar ways as shown in Equation 2, 3 and 4 respectively.

2.4 User Co-Activity Interest Similarity Features

This set of features measures the similarity between a query item k and the activity interests of other users v who have co-participated in an activity with a query user u. The intuition behind this set of features also comes from the empirical study from Lee and Lo [15], where they found that users share similar interests with other users who they co-participated an activity (even minimally) in a social collaborative platform. Suppose that we want to predict if a user would fork a given repository in GitHub, we would measure the similarity between the given repository's interests and the interests of other users who had co-forked repositories with the user in GitHub. Intuitively, we would also expect that the higher the similarity score, the more likely the user would answer the given question. Equation 5 captures the above intuition and measures the average similarity between k and fork activity interests of all users v, who had co-forked at least one question with u (i.e., $Co^{Fork}(u)$).

As users also share common interests across different activities and platforms, we would expect that considering other users who had co-participated in other types of platform activities with the target user can also potentially help to predict if the target user would participate in a given platform activity. For instance, we are potentially able to predict if a user would fork a given repository by measuring the similarity between the given repository's interest and the interests of other users who have co-participated with the user in *watch*, *answer* and *favorite* activities.

Example. Referencing to the example in Figure 1, we could predict if user u will favorite question Z by computing the similarity between question Z and the fork activity interests of other users who have co-fork a repository with user u. Assuming that user u only has 1 other user, v, who co-fork repositories with him or her, the common interests between v and question Z will be *XGBoost*. The number of v's forked repositories that shared common interests with question Z (i.e., $\{r \in v.RF|I(r) \in I(k))\}$) will then be 1 (i.e.,

Repository C), while the total number of repositories forked by v is 2 (i.e., Repository C and D). Finally, $Sim_{CoFork}(u,k) = \frac{\frac{1}{2}}{1} = 0.5$.

$$Sim_{CoFork}(u,k) = \frac{\left[\sum_{v \in Co^{Fork}(u)} \frac{|\{r \in v.RF|I(r) \in I(k)\}|}{|v.RF|}\right]}{|Co^{Fork}(u)|} \quad (5)$$

$$Sim_{CoWatch}(u,k) = \frac{\left[\sum_{v \in Co^{Watch}(u)} \frac{|\{r \in v.RW|I(r) \in I(k)\}|}{|v.RW|}\right]}{|Co^{Watch}(u)|} \quad (6)$$

$$Sim_{CoAns}(u,k) = \frac{\left[\sum_{v \in Co^{Ans}(u)} \frac{|\{q \in v.QA|I(q) \in I(k)\}|}{|v.QA|}\right]}{|Co^{Ans}(u)|} \quad (7)$$

$$Sim_{CoFav}(u,k) = \frac{\left[\sum_{v \in Co^{Fav}(u)} \frac{|\{q \in v.QF|I(q) \in I(k)\}|}{|v.QF|}\right]}{|Co^{Fav}(u)|} \quad (8)$$

We compute the similarities between k and activity interests of other users v who have co-watched, co-answered and co-favorited with a target user u in similar ways as shown in Equation 6, 7 and 8 respectively.

3 DATA EXTRACTION & EXAMINATION

In this section, we first introduce the two large real-world datasets that we use in our activity prediction experiments. Next, we discuss the user accounts linkage process to retrieve users who are active in multiple social collaborative sites, and a summary of the users' activities retrieved. We then discuss the heuristic used to infer user interests from their participated activities. Finally, we empirically examine the similarity between the GitHub repositories and Stack Overflow questions participated by users on both social collaborative sites.

3.1 Datasets

There are two main datasets used in our study. For the GitHub dataset, we use the MongoDB database dump released on March 2015 [8]. The dataset contains GitHub activities from October 2013 to March 2015 of about 2.5 million users. Specifically, we are interested in the *fork* and *watch* repositories activities of the GitHub users. For Stack Overflow, we use the XML dataset released on March 2015[3]. This dataset contains information of estimated 1 million Stack Overflow users and their activities from October 2013 to March 2015. We are particularly interested in the *answer* and *favorite* activities of the Stack Overflow users.

3.2 User Account Linkage

As this study intends to investigate user interests across GitHub and Stack Overflow, we need to identify users who were using both platforms. For this work, we used the dataset provided by Badashian et al. [2], where they utilized GitHub users' email addresses and Stack Overflow users' email MD5 hashes to find the intersection between the two datasets. We also filter out users who do not have

---

[3]https://archive.org/details/stackexchange

at least 1 activity on both platforms between October 2013 and March 2015. In total, we identify 92,427 users, which forms our *base users* set. After the base users have been identified, we extract their GitHub and Stack Overflow activities from the datasets. In total, we have extracted 416,171 *fork*, 2,168,871 *watch*, 766,315 *answer* and 427,093 *favorite* activities from the base users.

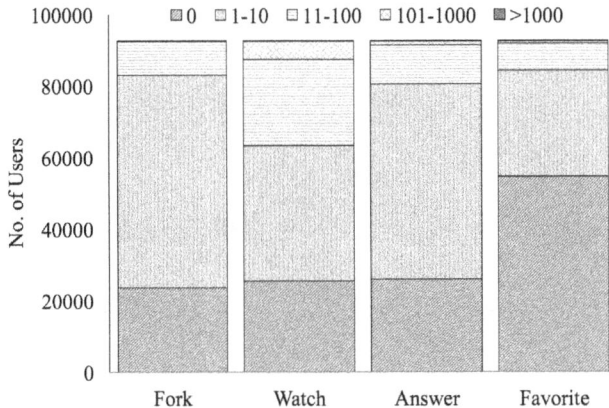

Figure 3: Base users' Stack Overflow and GitHub Activity Distributions

Figure 3 shows the distributions of base users' activities in GitHub and Stack Overflow. Most of the base users forked 1-10 repositories (64% of the base users), answered 1-10 questions (54% of the base users). There are also quite a number of developers who watched 11-100 repositories (26% of the base users). We also observe that more than half of base users have at least answered 1 questions (71%) and a substantial number of base users also answered 11-100 questions (12%).Interestingly, the high contribution of answers to questions in Stack Overflow could also suggest that the many of these active developers in our study were experts in their domain or areas of interest. Lastly, we also notice that there are developers (albeit very few in number) who were extremely active in GitHub and Stack Overflow; they forked, watched, committed, pull-requested more than 1000 repositories, or asked, answered and favorited more than 1000 questions.

3.3 Inferring User Interests

Next, we infer user interests by observing repositories and questions that users participated in GitHub and Stack Overflow. We use the following heuristics to infer user interests:

(1) To infer user interests in Stack Overflow, we use the descriptive tags of the questions that they answered and favorited. For example, consider a question related to mobile programming for Android smartphones which contain the following set of descriptive tags: {*Java, Android*}. If a user answered, or favorited that question, we infer that his interests include *Java* and *Android*.

(2) In the time period covered in our dataset, GitHub does not allow users to tag repositories but it allows users to describe their repositories. These descriptions often contain important keywords that can shed light on user interests. To infer

user interests from the repositories that a user had participated, we first collect all descriptive tags that appear in our Stack Overflow dataset. In total, 39,837 unique descriptive tags are collected. Next, we perform keyword matching between the collected Stack Overflow tags and a GitHub repository description. We consider the matched keywords as the inferred interests. We choose to use Stack Overflow tags to ensure that developer interests across the two platforms can be mapped to the same vocabulary.

3.4 Similarity between GitHub repositories and Stack Overflow Questions

In [15], Lee and Lo had empirically studied the similarity between user activity interests in GitHub and Stack Overflow. We extend their study by examining the descriptive tags of GitHub repositories and Stack Overflow questions participated by the base users. The objective is to investigate what are the popular descriptive tags used by the users on two sites and if there are overlaps among the popular descriptive tags.

Table 2: Top 10 most used descriptive tags in Stack Overflow and GitHub

Rank	Stack Overflow		GitHub	
	Tag	% Questions	Tag	% Repositories
1	javascript	3.758	javascript	8.163
2	java	3.104	ruby	2.698
3	python	2.760	python	2.604
4	c	1.940	c	2.163
5	php	1.884	java	1.928
6	android	1.787	objective-c	1.731
7	jquery	1.577	php	1.330
8	ios	1.459	go	1.275
9	ruby	1.031	css	1.236
10	css	0.963	shell	0.884

Table 2 shows the top 10 most used descriptive tags and the percentages of Stack Overflow questions and GitHub repositories containing these tags. We observe quite a significant number of overlap in the top 10 descriptive tags between the two social collaborative sites (known as *overlapped tags*); i.e., *javascript, java, python, c, php, ruby* and *css*. This suggests that generally, the base users participated in questions and repositories of similar domain and nature in Stack Overflow and GitHub. Another interesting observation is the proportions of questions and repositories with the top 10 descriptive tags; the overlapped tags are used in similar proportions of Stack Overflow questions and GitHub repositories, with the exception of *javascript*, which seems to be more popular in GitHub (i.e., ~8% of repositories) than Stack Overflow (i.e., ~3% of questions).

We further investigate the usage of these descriptive tags in the different Stack Overflow and GitHub user activities. Figure 4 shows the activity bar charts for the most used descriptive tags. For example, ~7% of the repositories watched by the base users contained the descriptive tag *javascript*, while only ~3% of the questions answered by the base users contained the same tag. We observe that for a

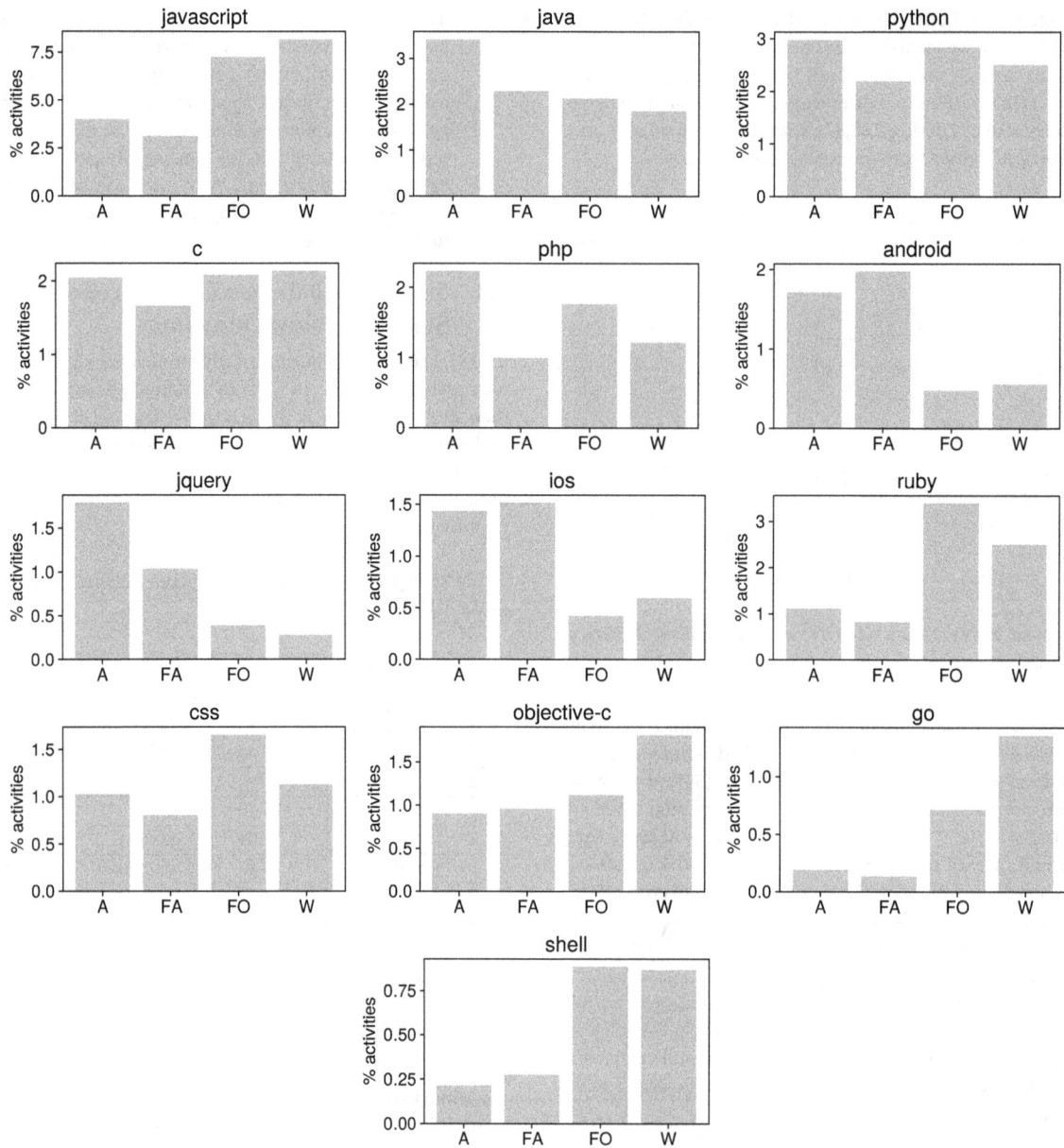

Figure 4: Bar chats of percentages of activities that use the different descriptive tags. Note that "A", "FA", "FO" and "W" denote *answer, favorite, fork* **and** *watch* **activities respectively.**

given descriptive tag, the proportion of activities involving the tag is not uniform even within the same social collaborative site. For example, the base users answered more Stack Overflow questions on *php* than favoriting them. Conversely, for *android* related questions, the base users favorited these question more than answering them. This unevenness in activity proportions is also observed to be greater for activities involving non-overlaps descriptive tags. For example, the base users fork and watch significantly more *shell* related repositories than answering and favoriting t*shell* related questions. This suggests that although the users do participate in

questions and repositories of similar domains, the activity preferences involving the similar domains varies. Thus, it would be more natural to learn the user interests at the activity level instead of aggregating the interests at the platform level.

4 EXPERIMENTS

In this section, we describe the supervised prediction experiments conducted to evaluate our proposed method. Specifically, we consider the following activity prediction tasks:

- *Answer Prediction.* Given a Stack Overflow *user-question* pair, predict if the user will answer the question
- *Favorite Prediction.* Given a Stack Overflow *user-question*, predict if the user will favorite the question
- *Fork Prediction.* Given a GitHub *user-repository*, predict if the user will fork the repository
- *Watch Prediction.* Given a GitHub *user-repository*, predict if the user will watch the repository

4.1 Experiment Setup

Data Selection. For *answer prediction* task, we retrieve all the Stack Overflow questions that the base users have answered and define a positive instance as a *user-question* pair where a base user had answered the particular question in Stack Overflow. For negative instances, we randomly assign a Stack Overflow question to the base users and check that the randomly assigned pair does not exist in the positive instance set. For the training datasets used in *answer prediction task*, we randomly generated 5,000 negative instances and randomly selected 5,000 positive instances from the questions answered by users between October 2013 and June 2014 (9 months). The same approach was used to generate the positive and negative instances for test sets using the questions answered by the users between July 2014 and March 2015 (9 months). Similar approach was used to generate the *user-question* and *user-repository* pairs for positive and negative instances used in *favorite, fork* and *watch prediction* tasks.

Note that we have repeated the prediction experiments for five runs, and the random selection of train and tests set are repeated for each of the runs. Also, although we know the true labels of the *user-question* and *user-repository* pairs, we do not take the labels into consideration when deriving the values of our proposed features, i.e., we assume that we do not know the labels of the pairs.

Feature Configuration. To compare the performance of *direct* and *cross* platform activity prediction approaches, we use Support Vector Machine (SVM) with linear kernel and apply the following feature sets on all prediction tasks:

- **SO_Act**: This set of features includes the *Answer* (Eqn. 3) and *Favorite* (Eqn. 4) *Interests Similarity* scores for a given user-question or user-repository pair.
- **SO_CoAct**: This set of features includes the *Co-Answer* (Eqn. 7) and *Co-Favorite* (Eqn. 8) *Interests Similarity* scores for a given user-question or user-repository pair.
- **GH_Act**: This set of features includes the *Fork* (Eqn. 1) and *Watch* (Eqn. 2) *Interests Similarity* scores for a given user-question or user-repository pair.
- **GH_CoAct**: This set of features includes the *Co-Fork* (Eqn. 5) and *Co-Watch* (Eqn. 6) *Interests Similarity* scores for a given user-question or user-repository pair.
- **ALL**: This set of features is the union of all features.

4.2 Prediction Results

We measure the prediction accuracy for each feature configuration by computing the average area under the ROC curve (AUC) over a set of positive and negative examples drawn from the test set for each of the five runs. The results for the four prediction tasks are shown in Figure 5. We observe that feature configuration **ALL**

performed the best in all prediction tasks, achieving an AUC of 0.89, 0.77, 0.75 and 0.67 for *answer, favorite, fork* and *watch* prediction tasks respectively.

Performance of cross-platform prediction approach. Although the *cross-platform prediction approach* did not outperform the *direct platform prediction approach* in user activity prediction, they still yield good accuracy. For example, when predicting user's *answer* and *favorite* activities in Stack Overflow, the GitHub *user activity interests similarity* features (i.e., **GH_Act**) has AUC of 0.71 and 0.64 respectively, and when predicting user's *fork* and *watch* activities in GitHub, the Stack Overflow *user activity interests similarity* features (i.e., **SO_Act**) has AUC of 0.65 and 0.58 respectively. The AUC for predicting user's answer activities in Stack Overflow using *user activity interests similarity* features (i.e., **GH_Act**) is observed to be slightly higher than the prediction for other activities. A possible explanation for this could be the difference between the nature of user activities; answering a question in Stack Overflow would require that a user possesses a particular domain expertise, whereas other activities such as watching a GitHub repository or favoriting a Stack Overflow question depend on the user's interests. As such, we observe higher AUC score for *predicting answer activity* task as the users' expertise are usually more specialized and less diverse than their interests.

More interestingly, using *cross-platform prediction approach* with *user co-activity interests similarity* features (i.e., **GH_CoAct** and **SO_CoAct**), have also yielded reasonable prediction accuracies. For example, when predicting user's answer activities in Stack Overflow, **GH_CoAct** has yielded an AUC of 0.62. This suggests that even with no information about a user's past activities in the Stack Overflow and only minimal information such as the user's co-activities in GitHub, we are still able to reasonably predict user's activity in Stack Overflow. Similar observations are made when predicting user activities in GitHub using user's co-activities in Stack Overflow.

4.3 Discussion

The results of the four prediction tasks offer us some insights in performing recommendations in social collaborative platforms.

Solving cold-starts. The reasonably good accuracies of cross-platform prediction approach also demonstrate its potential to solve the cold-start problem; i.e., predicting and recommending a user's activities without knowing the users' past activity history on the platform. For example, when predicting user's answer activities in Stack Overflow, we are able to achieve AUC as high as 0.71 without using any Stack Overflow features (i.e, using GitHub features **GH_Act** only). Similar observations were made for fork, watch and favorite activities.

We further conduct a small case study to retrieve and review fork predictions of users who did not have any past fork activities. For example, we successfully predicted that user *U420338* would forked repository *R12172473* in GitHub even when this was the first repository forked by the user (i.e., no past user fork activity). Examining into details, we found that *R12172473* has description tags ⟨*svg, javascript*⟩, and among the 95 questions *U420338* had answered in Stack Overflow, 83 contain the tags ⟨*javascript*⟩ or ⟨*svg*⟩ or both. By analyzing *U420338*'s Stack Overflow activities,

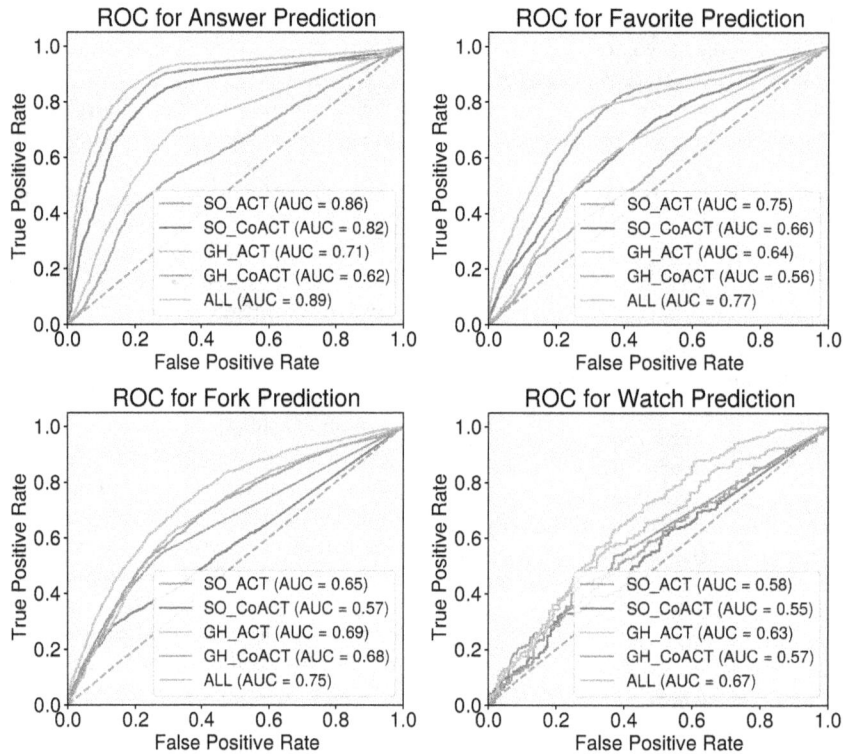

Figure 5: ROCs for Four Prediction Tasks

our approach can identify his interests, which ultimately help in predicting the user's GitHub activities.

Heterogeneous behaviors in cross-platform. There are existing research work on recommendations in cross-platform setting. For example, Yan et al.[38] addressed the cold-start friend recommendation problem by combining random walk with Flickr platform features to recommend friends on Twitter. Lee and Lim [13] performed similar cross-platform friendship recommendation in Instagram and Twitter using friendship maintenance features derived from users' friendship behaviours in multiple social platforms. In a more recent study, Lee et al [14] proposed a probabilistic model to predict which social media platform would a user publish a given post.

However, most of these cross-platform recommendation studies only focus on recommending homogeneous behaviours (e.g. connecting users, publishing post, etc) in online social platforms. In our study, we handled recommendation of heterogeneous behaviors (e.g. user *fork* and *watch* repositories in GitHub) in a cross-platform setting. Although our prediction experiments are conducted on social collaborative platforms, the cross-platform activity prediction framework can also be applied to other online social platforms. For example, we can predict if a user will *like*, *comment* or *retweet* a post in Twitter by learning the same user's heterogeneous behaviors in Facebook.

5 THREATS TO VALIDITY

Threats to Internal Validity. Threats to internal validity often refer to experimenter biases. In this study, most of our processes are automated. The positive and negative instances in our training and testing datasets were also randomly selected and generated. when estimating the developer interests on GitHub, we matched the keywords in repositories' descriptions to the tags collected from Stack Overflow questions. There could be cases where the words from a repository's descriptions did not match any of the collected tags, and thus we are not able to infer the interest of the developer using that repository. In the future, we plan to mitigate this by labelling the repositories using a tag recommendation approach [27, 28, 33, 35, 36].

Threats to External Validity. Threats to external validity refer to the generalizability of our findings. We have used large datasets from GitHub and Stack Overflow for our analysis and experiments. Our study findings are based on 92,427 developers, which is close to 10% of the Stack Overflow users who are active during the studied period, the interests of these users were derived using the data from the whole GitHub and Stack Overflow datasets (2.5 million and 1 million active users respectively). The current studied users were also obtained from the dataset provided in previous research by Badashian et al. [2]. Both Vasilescu et al. [29] and Badashian et al. [2] had utilized GitHub users' email address and Stack Overflow users' email MD5 hashes to find the intersection between the two platform datasets. However, this existing method is no longer valid as Stack Overflow no longer make the email hash of their user available [26], thus motivating new methods to match users in two social collaborative platforms. As part of our future work, we will explore new user matching methods such as matching users by their username to generate a large dataset of cross-platform users.

Threats to Construct Validity. Threats to construct refer to the appropriateness of metrics used. In this work, we use precision, recall and F1-measure to evaluate the results of our prediction experiments. These metrics were commonly used for other prediction experiments, e.g., [5, 12, 16, 17].

6 RELATED WORK

In this section, we review three groups of existing research work related to our research. The first group discuss the studies on user interests in social collaborative platforms, in particularly, GitHub and Stack Overflow. The second group focuses on studies on prediction and recommendation in GitHub and Stack Overflow. The last group reviews the inter-platform studies on users in the two platforms.

The user interests in social collaborative platforms have been a widely studied research area. There were research work that focused on analyzing topics asked by the user in Stack Overflow [3, 4, 22, 40, 44]. Barua et al. [4] conducted an extensive empirical study to mine the topics discussed by users in Stack Overflow. Bajaj et al. [3] performed a similar study specific to web development while Rosen and Shihab [22] performed a similar study specific to mobile application development. Similarly, there were also work on analyzing programming languages used by users in GitHub and their relationships to GitHub contributions [18, 20, 24, 30]. Our work extends this group of research by comparing user interests in the two social collaborative platforms.

Prediction and recommendation in social collaborative platforms have been widely studied. These work can be further categorized into two groups: (i) finding experts to perform a certain platform tasks or activities [1, 6, 10, 19, 21, 31, 37, 39, 41, 42] and (ii) recommending content or activities to users in the platforms [7, 9, 11, 32, 34, 43]. For work in group (i), there were work which proposed methods to find experts to answer questions in Stack Overflow [6, 21, 31, 37, 39], while for GitHub, experts are predicted if they will review *pull-requests* and code for repositories [19, 41, 42]. For work in group (ii), Wang et al.[34] conducted a study in Stack Overflow to recommend questions and answers concerning API issues to users. de Souza et al. [7] conducted an experiment to recommend Stack Overflow question-answer pairs relevant to selected software programming problems. Zhang et al. [43] predict and recommend relevant repositories to users based on the users' past activities (e.g. fork, watch, etc) in the platform. In a more recent work, Jiang et al. [11] proposed to use user programming language preferences and one-class collaborative filtering to improve prediction of which GitHub repositories are relevant to a user. Our study adds on to the state-of-the-art in group (ii) by proposing a novel method that use *multiple* platform data to predict platform activities

There have been few existing inter-platform studies on GitHub and Stack Overflow. Vasilescu et al. performed a study on developers' involvement and productivity in Stack Overflow and GitHub [29]. They found that users who are more active on GitHub (in terms of GitHub commits), tend to ask and answer more questions on Stack Overflow. Badashian et al. [2] did an empirical study on the correlation between different types of activities in the two platforms. Silvestri et at. [25] proposed a user linkage model to link users' Stack Overflow, GitHub and Twitter accounts. More recently, Lee and Lo [15] did an extensive study on users' interests across GitHub and Stack Overflow. In that study, the researchers found that users who have accounts with GitHub and Stack Overflow do exhibit similar interests observed from their activities in the two social collaborative platforms. Our work builds upon insights reported in [15] by proposing a prediction method based on user interests across and within social collaborative platforms.

7 CONCLUSION AND FUTURE WORK

In this paper, we propose a novel framework which predicts users activities in multiple social collaborative platforms. We conducted experiments on large real-world datasets which contain activities of 92,427 users who are active in GitHub and Stack Overflow. Our proposed methods achieved good accuracy in predicting various user activities (up to an AUC score of 0.89).

Our experiments have shown that user activities in Stack Overflow can be predicted with reasonable accuracy using the same user's interests inferred from his or her activities in GitHub. The same observation was made when predicting a user's activities in GitHub using his or her interests inferred from his or her activities in Stack Overflow. The reasonable accuracies yield by cross-platform prediction approach demonstrates its potential in solving the cold-start problem in user activity prediction and recommendation in social collaborative platforms.

For future work, we intend to consider more advanced techniques (e.g., topic models or deep learning models) to derive and measure user interests similarity across multiple platforms. We will also consider platforms aside from Stack Overflow and GitHub (e.g. Quora).

ACKNOWLEDGMENTS

This research is supported by the Living Analytics Research Centre (LARC), a research centre set up in Singapore Management University (SMU) with Carnegie Mellon University (CMU) that focuses on behavioural and social network analytics in the fields of Urban and Community Liveability, Personalised Urban Mobility, Jobs and Skills Intelligence, as well as Smart Consumption and Healthy Lifestyle.

REFERENCES

[1] Mohammad Y. Allaho and Wang-Chien Lee. 2014. Increasing the Responsiveness of Recommended Expert Collaborators for Online Open Projects. In *CIKM*.
[2] Ali Sajedi Badashian, Afsaneh Esteki, Ameneh Gholipour, Abram Hindle, and Eleni Stroulia. 2014. Involvement, contribution and influence in GitHub and stack overflow. In *CSSE*.
[3] Kartik Bajaj, Karthik Pattabiraman, and Ali Mesbah. 2014. Mining Questions Asked by Web Developers. In *MSR*.
[4] Anton Barua, Stephen W. Thomas, and Ahmed E. Hassan. 2014. What Are Developers Talking About? An Analysis of Topics and Trends in Stack Overflow. *Empirical Software Engineering* 19, 3 (2014).
[5] Gerardo Canfora, Andrea De Lucia, Massimiliano Di Penta, Rocco Oliveto, Annibale Panichella, and Sebastiano Panichella. 2013. Multi-objective cross-project defect prediction. In *ICST*.
[6] Morakot Choetkiertikul, Daniel Avery, Hoa Khanh Dam, Truyen Tran, and Aditya Ghose. 2015. Who Will Answer My Question on Stack Overflow?. In *ASWEC*.

[7] Lucas B. L. de Souza, Eduardo C. Campos, and Marcelo de A. Maia. 2014. Ranking Crowd Knowledge to Assist Software Development. In *ICPC*.

[8] Georgios Gousios. 2013. The GHTorrent dataset and tool suite. In *MSR*.

[9] Mohamed Guendouz, Abdelmalek Amine, and Reda Mohamed Hamou. 2015. Recommending relevant GitHub repositories: a collaborative-filtering approach. *on Networking and Advanced Systems* (2015).

[10] Chaoran Huang, Lina Yao, Xianzhi Wang, Boualem Benatallah, and Quan Z Sheng. 2017. Expert as a Service: Software Expert Recommendation via Knowledge Domain Embeddings in Stack Overflow. In *ICWS*.

[11] Jyun-Yu Jiang, Pu-Jen Cheng, and Wei Wang. 2017. Open Source Repository Recommendation in Social Coding. In *SIGIR*.

[12] Sunghun Kim, E James Whitehead, and Yi Zhang. 2008. Classifying software changes: Clean or buggy? *Software Engineering, IEEE Transactions on* 34, 2 (2008), 181–196.

[13] Ka-Wei Roy Lee and Ee-Peng Lim. 2016. Friendship maintenance and prediction in multiple social networks. In *Proceedings of the 27th ACM Conference on Hypertext and Social Media*. ACM, 83–92.

[14] Roy Ka-Wei Lee, Tuan-Anh Hoang, and Ee-Peng Lim. 2017. On Analyzing User Topic-Specific Platform Preferences Across Multiple Social Media Sites. In *Proceedings of the 26th International Conference on World Wide Web*. International World Wide Web Conferences Steering Committee, 1351–1359.

[15] Roy Ka-Wei Lee and David Lo. 2017. GitHub and Stack Overflow: Analyzing Developer Interests Across Multiple Social Collaborative Platforms. In *SOCINFO*.

[16] Jaechang Nam, Sinno Jialin Pan, and Sunghun Kim. 2013. Transfer defect learning. In *ICSE*.

[17] Foyzur Rahman, Daryl Posnett, and Premkumar Devanbu. 2012. Recalling the imprecision of cross-project defect prediction. In *FSE*.

[18] Mohammad Masudur Rahman and Chanchal K. Roy. 2014. An Insight into the Pull Requests of GitHub. In *MSR*.

[19] Mohammad Masudur Rahman, Chanchal K Roy, and Jason A Collins. 2016. CoR-ReCT: code reviewer recommendation in GitHub based on cross-project and technology experience. In *ICSE*.

[20] Baishakhi Ray, Daryl Posnett, Vladimir Filkov, and Premkumar Devanbu. 2014. A Large Scale Study of Programming Languages and Code Quality in Github. In *FSE*.

[21] Fatemeh Riahi, Zainab Zolaktaf, Mahdi Shafiei, and Evangelos Milios. 2012. Finding Expert Users in Community Question Answering. In *WWW*.

[22] Christoffer Rosen and Emad Shihab. 2015. What are mobile developers asking about? A large scale study using stack overflow. *Empirical Software Engineering* (2015).

[23] Andrew I Schein, Alexandrin Popescul, Lyle H Ungar, and David M Pennock. 2002. Methods and metrics for cold-start recommendations. In *SIGIR*.

[24] Jyoti Sheoran, Kelly Blincoe, Eirini Kalliamvakou, Daniela Damian, and Jordan Ell. 2014. Understanding "Watchers" on GitHub. In *MSR*.

[25] Giuseppe Silvestri, Jie Yang, Alessandro Bozzon, and Andrea Tagarelli. 2015. Linking Accounts across Social Networks: the Case of StackOverflow, Github and Twitter.. In *KDWeb*.

[26] StackExchange. 2014. Where did EmailHash go? (2014). http://meta.stackexchange.com/questions/221027/where-did-emailhash-gom

[27] Clayton Stanley and Michael D Byrne. 2013. Predicting tags for stackoverflow posts. In *ICCM*.

[28] Santiago Vargas-Baldrich, Mario Linares-Vasquez, and Denys Poshyvanyk. 2015. Automated Tagging of Software Projects Using Bytecode and Dependencies (N). In *ASE*.

[29] Bogdan Vasilescu, Vladimir Filkov, and Alexander Serebrenik. 2013. StackOverflow and GitHub: associations between software development and crowdsourced knowledge. In *SocialCom*.

[30] Bogdan Vasilescu, Yue Yu, Huaimin Wang, Premkumar Devanbu, and Vladimir Filkov. 2015. Quality and Productivity Outcomes Relating to Continuous Integration in GitHub. In *FSE*.

[31] Jian Wang, Jiqing Sun, Hongfei Lin, Hualei Dong, and Shaowu Zhang. 2017. Convolutional neural networks for expert recommendation in community question answering. *Science China Information Sciences* 60, 11 (2017).

[32] Lin Wang, Bin Wu, Juan Yang, and Shuang Peng. 2016. Personalized recommendation for new questions in community question answering. In *ASONAM*.

[33] S. Wang, D. Lo, B. Vasilescu, and A. Serebrenik. 2014. EnTagRec: An Enhanced Tag Recommendation System for Software Information Sites. In *ICSME*.

[34] Wei Wang, Haroon Malik, and Michael W. Godfrey. 2015. Recommending Posts Concerning API Issues in Developer Q&sA Sites. In *MSR*.

[35] Xin Xia, David Lo, Xinyu Wang, and Bo Zhou. 2013. Tag recommendation in software information sites. In *MSR*.

[36] Bowen Xu, Deheng Ye, Zhenchang Xing, Xin Xia, Guibin Chen, and Shanping Li. 2016. Predicting Semantically Linkable Knowledge in Developer Online Forums via Convolutional Neural Network. In *ASE*.

[37] Congfu Xu, Xin Wang, and Yunhui Guo. 2016. Collaborative Expert Recommendation for Community-Based Question Answering. In *ECML-KDD*.

[38] Ming Yan, Jitao Sang, Tao Mei, and Changsheng Xu. 2013. Friend transfer: Cold-start friend recommendation with cross-platform transfer learning of social knowledge. In *2013 IEEE International Conference on Multimedia and Expo (ICME)*. IEEE, 1–6.

[39] Liu Yang, Minghui Qiu, Swapna Gottipati, Feida Zhu, Jing Jiang, Huiping Sun, and Zhong Chen. 2013. CQArank: Jointly Model Topics and Expertise in Community Question Answering. In *CIKM*.

[40] Xin-Li Yang, David Lo, Xin Xia, Zhi-Yuan Wan, and Jian-Ling Sun. 2016. What Security Questions Do Developers Ask? A Large-Scale Study of Stack Overflow Posts. *Journal of Computer Science and Technology* 31, 5 (2016).

[41] Yue Yu, Huaimin Wang, Gang Yin, and Charles X Ling. 2014. Reviewer recommender of pull-requests in GitHub. In *ICSME*.

[42] Yue Yu, Huaimin Wang, Gang Yin, and Tao Wang. 2016. Reviewer recommendation for pull-requests in GitHub: What can we learn from code review and bug assignment? *Information and Software Technology* 74 (2016).

[43] Lingxiao Zhang, Yanzhen Zou, Bing Xie, and Zixiao Zhu. 2014. Recommending relevant projects via user behaviour: an exploratory study on github. In *CrowdSoft*.

[44] Jie Zou, Ling Xu, Weikang Guo, Meng Yan, Dan Yang, and Xiaohong Zhang. 2015. Which Non-functional Requirements Do Developers Focus On? An Empirical Study on Stack Overflow Using Topic Analysis. In *MSR*.

On Identifying Anomalies in Tor Usage with Applications in Detecting Internet Censorship

Joss Wright
University of Oxford
Oxford, United Kingdom
joss.wright@oii.ox.ac.uk

Alexander Darer
University of Oxford
Oxford, United Kingdom
alexander.darer@linacre.ox.ac.uk

Oliver Farnan
University of Oxford
Oxford, United Kingdom
oliver.farnan@balliol.ox.ac.uk

ABSTRACT

We develop a means to detect ongoing per-country anomalies in the daily usage metrics of the Tor anonymous communication network, and demonstrate the applicability of this technique to identifying likely periods of internet censorship and related events. The presented approach identifies contiguous anomalous periods, rather than daily spikes or drops, and allows anomalies to be ranked according to deviation from expected behaviour.

The developed method is implemented as a running tool, with outputs published daily by mailing list. This list highlights per-country anomalous Tor usage, and produces a daily ranking of countries according to the level of detected anomalous behaviour. This list has been active since August 2016, and is in use by a number of individuals, academics, and NGOs as an early warning system for potential censorship events.

We focus on Tor, however the presented approach is more generally applicable to usage data of other services, both individually and in combination. We demonstrate that combining multiple data sources allows more specific identification of likely Tor blocking events. We demonstrate the our approach in comparison to existing anomaly detection tools, and against both known historical internet censorship events and synthetic datasets. Finally, we detail a number of significant recent anomalous events and behaviours identified by our tool.

CCS CONCEPTS

• **Networks** → **Network measurement**; • **Social and professional topics** → **Technology and censorship**; • **Security and privacy** → *Pseudonymity, anonymity and untraceability*;

KEYWORDS

information controls, censorship, filtering, anomaly detection

ACM Reference Format:
Joss Wright, Alexander Darer, and Oliver Farnan. 2018. On Identifying Anomalies in Tor Usage with Applications in Detecting Internet Censorship. In *WebSci '18: 10th ACM Conference on Web Science, May 27–30, 2018,* Amsterdam, Netherlands. ACM, New York, NY, USA, 10 pages. https://doi.org/10.1145/3201064.3201093

1 INTRODUCTION

Nation states, and others, increasingly employ internet filtering as a means of controlling access to information, and as a tool to limit social and political organisation. Given the central role that the internet plays in communications for a large proportion of the global population, understanding the application and development of filtering technologies, and the effects of these methods on individuals and society, is of great importance. Whilst analyses of known filtering regimes allow us to identify tools, techniques, and limitations of filtering approaches, we consider that discovering internet filtering behaviour in less-studied regions is of great importance.

Much existing research into internet filtering has focused either on observing practices of states already known engage in filtering, or in the development of censorship circumvention tools. Whilst multilateral studies of censorship have been conducted, most notably the seminal work of Deibert et al. [11], these approaches have typically amalgamated manual country-specific investigations. In the case of Deibert et al., countries were hand-ranked according to a number of broad criteria for internet freedom, based on network measurements as well as media reporting and expert interviews.

The work presented here provides a means to alert researchers and activists to developing events that may otherwise have been missed by focusing on patterns of circumvention tool usage around the world. As an initial step our tool currently reports new anomalies and a current ranking of most anomalous countries to a mailing list on a daily basis. The `<infolabe-anomalies>` mailing list has been running publicly since August 2016, has subscribers from academia and civil society organisations, and has provided the first known detection of a number of significant ongoing Tor-related blocking events that we detail in §7.

1.1 Contributions

This work presents a theoretical contribution to network anomaly detection, a practical contribution in the form of an implemented tool for detecting anomalous events in Tor usage data, a resource in the form of a public dataset of detected anomalies in historical Tor traffic, and a practical analysis demonstrating the detection of real-world events: we identify known, previously unreported, and newly-detected filtering-related events.

We make the following practical contributions:

- An open tool to detect and highlight anomalies in per-country usage of the Tor network;

- a continually-updated daily ranking of the most anomalous countries in terms of their usage of Tor.

These are built on our key methodological contribution:

- An approach for detecting and quantifying anomalous periods of per-country Tor usage incorporating multiple usage measurements.

We validate the effectiveness of our approach in detecting both a range of artificial anomalies, and known reported filtering events against the Tor network. We also demonstrate our approach's improved detection accuracy compared to the existing Tor metrics anomaly detector, as well showing its additional capabilities in terms of identifying anomalous periods and ranking anomalies by strength.

1.2 Problem and Approach

When an entity, such as a state or ISP, chooses to filter or block certain types of information, the resulting patterns of traffic reflect the intervention in the form of statistical anomalies. In a global system, in which many entities may be interfering with traffic or publicising their attempts to do so, it is desirable to identify *localised* anomalies and to gain an understanding of their nature.

To detect anomlies, we model each country's Tor usage *relative* to the behaviour of other countries, not as an individual time series. A given country's usage pattern is judged as anomalous if it deviates from its previous behaviour *relative to other countries*.

The usage patterns of a tool such as Tor, explicitly developed and publicised as a means for bypassing network censorship, are affected by a range of factors such as filtering, social and political unrest, unrelated network outages, and media reporting [4]. The work presented here therefore identifies *statistical anomalies* in Tor usage metrics, but we highlight that such anomalies serve as an indicator, not a proof, of censorship or interference.

In later sections we make use of both standard Tor traffic and blocking-resistant *bridge node* traffic to identify direct blocking of Tor. Combining anomalies across metrics allows identification of declines in normal usage combined with rises in blocking-resistant bridge usage. This corresponds to users being unable to access Tor normally, and so switching to blocking resistant approaches. As we demonstrate in §7, this provides a targeted identification of filtering-related anomalies.

We extend a line of research initially proposed by Jackson and Mudholkar [18] for application in industrial process control, and later employed by Lakhina et al. [22] to detect network-wide traffic anomalies from per-link data in high-performance networks. Our approach differs from that of [22] in a number of ways. Firstly, we do not assume that the underlying set of time series are stationary, but instead allow for series to evolve over time. Secondly, we account for *seasonality* in time series. Most importantly, however, we identify *per-country* anomalies rather than global. Finally, we dynamically adapt our anomaly thresholds for each series to account for long-term evolution of the data.

We directly apply our tool to analysis of Tor usage anomalies, and report on its demonstrated utility for detecting anomalies of practical concern to activists and NGOs working to support censorship circumvention and freedom of expression. A number of

such actors subscribe to our public mailing list, and have used our detection results to identify newly-emerging filtering behaviours.

2 EXISTING WORK

Internet filtering has received attention from various fields. Technical research has focused on mechanisms of censorship and the development of circumvention approaches. The social sciences have investigated motivations of censors, and their legal, economic, and societal effects.

2.1 Technical Analysis

Arguably the most well-known national-level filtering system is that of China, commonly known as the Great Firewall. One of the earliest significant studies of this system was presented by Clayton et al.[5], who isolated one mechanism by which connections were interrupted if particular keywords were identified in traffic. The mechanism discovered by Clayton et al. resulted in TCP RST packets being sent from an intermediary router to both source and destination of a connection if a filtering criterion was met. The authors further demonstrated that if the two endpoints of the connection ignored the TCP RST, the connection could successfully continue.

In more recent work, it has become apparent that the Chinese approach to filtering is both complex and evolving. In two recent papers, a group of anonymous researchers have explored manipulation, or poisoning, of DNS records that pass through China [2, 3]. This work has identified DNS manipulation as one of the most prevalent forms of filtering in China. Similarly, Wright [37] demonstrated that DNS censorship had different effects between different regions within China, with significant variation in the nature of the DNS poisoning seen across the country. Similarly, Farnan et al. [14] showed that the approach taken to DNS poisoning in China resulted in pollution of both network requests and DNS servers themselves.

Crandall et al.[7] make use of *latent semantic analysis* to derive, from known terms blocked in HTTP traffic going into China, semantically related keywords that might also be blocked. These derived keywords can then be verified by the simple process of attempting to make HTTP connections into China containing the suspect words. This approach aims to produce a continually-updated list of blocked terms that could be used to maintain an understanding of those terms most offensive to the filtering authorities. Similarly, Darer et al. [9, 10] have used keyword- and crawling-based approaches to discover previously unindentified blocked domains.

2.2 Global Studies

Perhaps the most comprehensive study to date of global filtering practices is given by Deibert et al. [11]. In this work the authors carried out a range of remote and in-country analyses over a number of years, incorporating both technical measurements and interviews with local experts. The resulting research presented a series of snapshots of individual countries, with both an overview of the social, political, and technical landscape, and censorship practices rated on a simple scale in various categories of content: political, social, conflict and security, and internet tools.

Some forms of filtering act not at the network layer, but on application level or social filtering. King et al. [21] studied manual censorship practices in Chinese long-form blogging, and demonstrated that the Chinese censorship authorities were chiefly concerned with preventing calls to *collective action* whilst allowing significant levels of government criticism.

2.3 Anomaly Detection

The Tor project maintain a censorship flagging tool, as described by Danezis[8]. This tool uses a particle-filtering approach to model the ratio of daily connections for each country in a seven-day time period. If a country's ratio of current to past users increases or decreases significantly more than the average of the fifty largest Tor-using countries, then an anomaly is flagged. These reported anomalies are available at the Tor Project's metrics portal [29]. We evaluate our approach's accuracy against that of Danezis in §6.

A related approach was used by Lakhina et al. [22] to identify *network-wide* anomalies in high-speed networks. This work assumed that long-term network usage was stable, and made use of data gathered from a restricted set of link-level observation points to detect network-wide anomalies. Our approach relaxes both of these assumptions, neither of which hold for the Tor metrics data. These extensions are discussed in greater detail in §4.1.2.

Several other works have extended or expanded aspects of [22], notably [34], [39], and [16]. These largely focus, however, on using a small number of network observation points to infer network-wide anomalies, and as such typically begin from relatively low-dimensional data. Our approach inverts this concept by detecting per-observation anomalies across a dataset with several hundred dimensions, representing individual countries' usage, in order to highlight states displaying anomalous behaviour.

3 CONCEPTS

In this section we discuss the fundamental techniques underlying our approach, and discuss their application to the dataset we use in the rest of this work.

3.1 Tor

Tor [12] is an approach to anonymous web-browsing that offers realistic compromises between latency, usability, and the strength of the anonymity properties that it provides. The most visible end-user aspect of Tor is the Tor Browser Bundle, which provides a web-browser that both uses the Tor network for transport, and is tailored to reduce identifiability of end users.

Managed by the Tor Project, Tor has developed into a global network of volunteer-run relays that forward traffic on behalf of other users. The network makes use of an *onion routing* approach that build encrypted circuits between relays, preventing most realistic adversaries from linking Tor users to particular streams of traffic exiting the network.

The most sigificant aspect of the Tor network for the present work is that, by its nature, users' traffic is relayed via third parties. As such, and in addition to its anonymity properties, Tor provides a means to bypass many forms of internet filtering. Censorship circumvention is a core aspect of the Tor Project's goals, and significant ongoing research work[26, 33, 36] is aimed at ensuring

that Tor is resilient against attacks and continues to offer means to evade national-level filters.

While the extent and popularity of Tor's use in regions that experience significant levels of filtering, such as China, is open to debate [32], Tor is known to have been blocked actively by a number of states, including China and Iran, that object to its use to bypass local internet restrictions and to act anonymously. Significantly, Tor is also arguably the highest-profile censorship circumvention tool at the international level and has received significant media coverage, making it one of the tools of choice for internet activists.

3.1.1 Tor Metrics Data. Tor's role as a high-profile censorship circumvention network make it a useful indicator of global filtering practices. To support analysis of the tool, the Tor project provide estimated daily per-country usage statistics, gathered by counting the number of client requests to central *directory authorities* on a daily basis.

It is assumed that each client, on average, will make ten requests per day, and as such the aggregate user statistics are divided by ten to provide a final estimate of usage. This data is averaged across each 24-hour period to provide the average number of concurrently connected Tor clients for that day[30]. Whilst the number of distinct clients per day cannot be estimated with any accuracy, the methodology of the Tor metrics portal provides a sufficiently stable estimate.

From these estimates we obtain a set of 251 time series representing individual countries according to the GeoIP database used by Tor. These time series comprise daily observations ranging from the beginning of September 2011 to the time of writing. From these, we remove those countries whose Tor usage never rises above 100 users to discount countries whose variance is too high to allow meaningful anomaly detection.

In later sections, we combine normal usage trends in Tor with censorship-resistant *bridge node* usage to identify correlated anomalies. This is discussed in further detail in §4.4.

3.2 Principal Component Analysis

Principal component analysis was developed by Pearson[27] as a means to produce tractable low-dimensional approximations of high-dimensional datasets. The original set of variables, which may display correlations, are transformed to a set of linearly uncorrelated variables know as *principal components*.

When data displays a high degree of correlation between variables then a small number of the most significant principal components may be sufficient to describe the original data to a high degree of accuracy. In many practical scenarios, high dimensional data can be described using only two or three of the most significant principal components. See [19] for a detailed treatment of principal component analysis and the various choices and compromises to be made when applying the technique.

The practical result of this is that our results are not influenced by countries with large usage numbers; the principal component analysis considers variance, not magnitude, in calculating the contribution of each country to the model.

4 APPROACH

The basic operation of our approach are described here, and are given as pseudocode in Algorithm 1.

```
1  PCATagAnomaly
      input  : usage ← Set of per-country time series
      output : anomalies ← Set of per-country anomaly time
               series
2     (Clean data; remove seasonality)
3     medians ← {median residual errors for each country}
4     mads ← {median absolute deviations (MADs) of
               residual errors for each country}
5     foreach day in usage do
6        pc ← calculate principal components over all
               countries' usage[(day-179):day]
7        foreach country do
8           recons ← reconstruct day value for country
                    using pc[1 : 12]
9           obsv ← observed value for final day for country
10          err ← abs( obsv - recons ).
11          medians_country ← update median using err
12          mads_country ← update MADs using
                         medians_country and err
13          if abs(err) > abs( mads_country × 2.5 ) then
14              | anomalies_{country×day} ← 1
15          end
16          else
17              | anomalies_{country×day} ← 0
18          end
19       end
20    end
```

Algorithm 1: Basic anomaly tagging algorithm. (Anomaly magnitudes omitted for brevity.)

4.1 Overview

Starting from Tor's per-country usage data, we initially remove all countries whose usage never rises above 100 users, to avoid the unacceptably high variance in such data. We then apply the STL algorithm to identify and remove any seasonality – in our case weekly trends – in individual countries.

For each 180-day period in the dataset we apply a principal component analysis over the usage time series for all countries, resulting in a set of components for that time window. Taking the true observed usage for each country for the final day of each window, we calculate the *approximated* value from the first 12 principal components. This provides the expected value for each country based on previous behaviour[1].

For each country we calculate the difference between the true value and the reconstructed value, providing a *residual error* that was not captured by the restricted set of principal components.

We maintain a rolling calculation of both the median observed residual error and the median absolute deviation of the errors for each country. We mark a day as anomalous if the observed residual error falls outside of 2.5 median absolute deviations from the median.

We now detail the individual steps listed above, and justify our choices of parameters.

4.1.1 Removal of Seasonality. Per-country Tor usage data, as with much network usage data, exhibits significant *seasonality*, typically on a weekly basis, reflecting changes between usage on weekdays and at weekends. This continual cyclical change in usage can reduce the accuracy of principal component analysis due to varying levels of seasonality exhibited by different countries.

We employ the *Seasonal and Trend Decomposition using Loess* (STL) method of Cleveland et al. [6] to remove the seasonal component of each series, leaving the trend component and the residual noise as inputs to our anomaly detector. In later sections, however, we show the original data with seasonality restored.

4.1.2 Rolling Analysis. Principal component analysis does not account for ordering in observations, and as such cannot account for evolution of a dataset according to trends or seasonablity. To account for developing patterns, therefore, we perform a rolling principal component analysis over smaller time windows within the series. For the purposes of our experiments, we make use of a 180-day window as a balance between sufficient data for useful principal component analysis, given the number of dimension in the data, against the evolution of the daily Tor metrics. See Ringberg et al. [31] for a discussion of the sensitivity of PCA to such factors.

4.1.3 Selection of Components. For PCA, the full set of principal components allows reconstruction of the full data set. As fewer components are selected, less variance in the original dataset is captured. A common approach to selecting an appropriate number of components for modelling is to make use of *Kaiser's criterion* [20] to select only those principal components with eigenvalue greater than 1, representing those components that provide more information than a single average component. Based on this heuristic, our experimental results suggest twelve principal components as broadly optimal across the dataset.

With appropriately calculated principal components, we can reconstruct an approximate value for each day's Tor usage based on previous behaviour. We highlight that at no point do we *predict* forecasted values for usage in future days. In each case, we reconstruct a day's usage based on principal components in order to compare against the true observed value, and thus to calculate deviance from prior behaviour relative to other countries.

4.2 Calculation of Residuals

After reconstructing data from principal components, the result is a set of *residuals* that express variances in the observed data not captured by the current principal component model. A sufficiently large-scale residual represents behaviour that deviates significantly from previous patterns, and is thus of interest.

---

[1]Using the full set of principal components at this stage would result in a perfect reconstruction of the original observed values.

4.3 Identifying Anomalies through Residuals

The residual errors calculated during the reconstruction accounts for variance in the dataset that is not expressed by the chosen principle components in the approximate model.

- Positive residuals represent drops in expected Tor usage for a country.
- Negative residuals represent increases in expected Tor usage for a country.
- Magnitude of residuals expresses how much a country varies from its previous behaviour relative to other countries.

A key advantage of identifying anomalies from residual errors rather than raw usage numbers is that it incorporates the expected *trend* of the data. This identifies anomalous periods even when no visible shift in usage is seen: a flat usage trend where the expectation is a rise or fall is correctly identified as anomalous by our approach. This capacity to identify anomalies in apparently typical usage is an important and unusual aspect of our technique, taking advantage of the relative patterns of usage between countries.

A second advantage of this approach is that each day can be judged as anomalous or not based on a model of behaviour relative to other countries. As such, in contrast to many other anomaly detection approaches, we identify *periods* of anomalous behaviour in which a country may be experiencing ongoing elevated or reduced usage. Other approaches typically flag an individual day as a significant spike or drop, but cannot identify ongoing periods as anomalous. This capability greatly aids our ability to study time-bounded changes in Tor usage.

4.4 Combining Features to Identify Targeted Filtering

It is fundamental to the broader goals of this work that usage anomalies in appropriately selected traffic, and in particular from circumvention tools, can be indicative of the imposition or relaxation of filtering. At the same time, it is clear that other types of event, both technical and sociopolitical, can lead to shifting patterns of usage in these tools.

We aim to identify two forms of event: firstly, direct blocking of the Tor network; secondly, changing characteristics of Tor usage in response to exogenous factors. The censorship of a major international website, such as YouTube, has the potential to drive a noticeable number of users to Tor, and as such Tor becomes a useful *proxy variable* [35] for a broader class of filtering behaviour. We discuss this in relation to specific events in §7.

For the first of these classes of event, we detect likely candidates by carrying out anomaly detection on multiple metrics and combining outputs to highlight periods in which anomalies were detected in more than one series. The most useful of these for our purposes is to combine negative trends in standard Tor usage with positive trends in blocking-resistant bridge node usage, reflecting users unable to access Tor normally switching to the tool's blocking-resistant mode.

As such we can identify days in which both standard and blocking-resistant time series were anomalous. Even without refinements, such as allowing time lags between anomalies in each series, this approach already highlight a number of significant cases, which are illustrated in §7.

4.5 Expected Error and Anomalous Threshold

A key element in the approach presented in this work is to determine an appropriate threshold for events to be considered anomalous. The size of this threshold value is inherently linked to the expected error in the technique. We here discuss and justify our approach to calculating this threshold, making use of *robust statistics*[17] to minimise false detection rates.

A naïve anomalous threshold can be defined as a proportion of the usage for that day. If the reconstructed value deviates by more than some percentage of the observed value, an anomaly is detected.

This approach is problematic. Critically, different countries may be modelled more or less accurately than others. As such, countries that are typically modelled poorly would produce a high proportion of anomalous periods.

As such, we calculate an ongoing threshold based on the characteristics of each country. By tracking the expected residual value for each country an expected anomalous threshold can be determined based on typical observed errors.

The standard approach of basing this threshold on the mean and standard deviations are, however, not *robust* against outliers in the dataset due to their assumption that errors are Gaussian. We therefore calculate thresholds based on the *median absolute deviation about the median* (MAD) to define the expected error in normal usage [24].

The median is robust against outliers in the dataset; a small number of extreme events do not significantly alter its value. Similarly, by taking the median of the absolute deviations about the median as a measure of the statistical dispersion in the dataset, we avoid anomalies from overly affecting the remaining data points.

As a default, we consider events as anomalous if they fall outside of 2.5 median absolute deviations[2] from the rolling median value. See [24] for a discussion of the robustness of the median and MAD against outliers, and a justification of a 2.5 median absolute deviation threshold.

4.6 Ranking of Countries

The size of the residual error from the principal componenet analysis provides a convenient metric by which to rank countries according to the level of anomalous behaviour that they exhibit in a given time period. We make use of the size of the median absolute deviation about the median to rank countries, as shown in Figure 1.

We now proceed to discuss the application of our technique, and the validation of the approach.

In §6 we evaluate our approach against synthetically injected anomalies in the data to analyse the effectiveness of our detection methods as the magnitude and severity of the anomalies vary. We also compare our detection mechanism against the small number of verified reported blocking events against the Tor network.

Finally, in §7 we conduct a series of analyses of the Tor metrics data to identify anomalous countries and specific periods of anomalous behaviour.

---

[2]Corresponding to roughly one expected false positive every 80 days. See §6 for an experimental analysis of false positives in our approach.

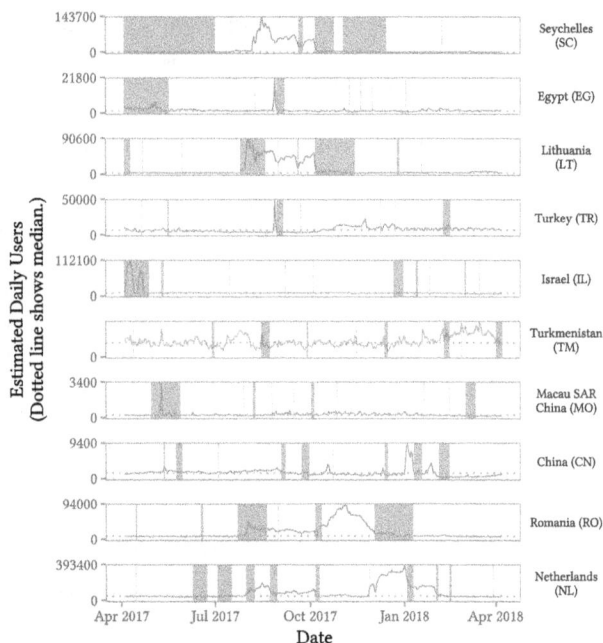

Figure 1: Ten most anomalous countries according to median absolute deviation of residuals over the previous year. Grey areas highlight detected anomalous periods.

5 ETHICS

Conducting research into network filtering presents a number of ethical issues [38]. The most significant of these is that approaches to investigating network filtering may require direct access to filtered networks. In practice this often involves the participation of in-country experts to conduct local network tests.

Due to the uncertain legal, or quasi-legal, status of violating or investigating state-level network filters, it is generally impossible to quantify the risks to research participants in carrying out network tests. The classic models of informed consent used in many other fields of research can be difficult to apply for a number of reasons, the most important of which is the lack of meaningful informed consent afforded by automated testing on behalf of users, and the legal uncertainty surrounding attempted access to filtered resources on a test subject's network connection.

We therefore assert that, where possible, research into network filtering should make use of passive measurements and existing available data sources. The work in this paper is a deliberate attempt to maximise the effectiveness of such a passive approach.

6 VALIDATION

In this section, we judge the efficacy of our method in terms of its ability to detect anomalies, in a variety of circumstances, as well as its false classification rate.

A significant dificulty in validating unsupervised machine learning systems is that it is largely impossible to obtain comprehensive ground truth for internet filtering events, nor are there publicly-available exhaustive lists of filtering events. Indeed, the work here was motivated partially in an attempt to allow a more exhaustive

tracking of such events. Filtering is, by and large, an opaque process that is rarely announced. Even when states do choose to filter connections openly, the details of that filtering are not typically made public.

As observed in [15], this is an inherent problem in *unsupervised* anomaly detection algorithms. In the the following sections we address this lack by injecting artificial anomalies into a synthetic dataset and comparing this to the Tor Project's existing anomaly detection approach, as well as evaluating our method against an existing list of known filtering events.

In the following, we examine both false positive and false negative rates in evaluating detection rates of anomalous behaviour. A false positive in this context is a period in which there is no genuinely anomalous activity, but anomalous activity is reported. A false negative is a period in which there is anomalous activity but is is not detected.

6.1 Evaluation in Synthetic Data

To test our approach, and to create a fair comparison against the existing deployed tool from the Tor Project, we inject artificial anomalies into synthetic data generated according to underlying features of real-world Tor usage.

An alternative test for false negatives is to compare the results from our approach with an external list of known censorship events. This allows us to test whether periods exist in which we did not detect anomalous behaviour during a period where external sources believe an event occurred. We take this approach in §6.5.

6.2 Generating Synthetic Data

To evaluate our approach against an approximation of real-world data, we use the underlying features of genuine observed Tor data to generate a synthetic set of time series.

To do so, we select a year-long period of Tor data in which no major global events can be observed. This was to avoid an unfair basis for comparison between our approach and that of the Danezis. As such, we selected the year running from the 1st January 2014 to the 31st December 2014.

To remove, as far as possible, genuine anomalies from this dataset we first decompose the series into trend, seasonal, and residual components through use of the STL algorithm [6]. This allowed us to preserve seasonal properties of the data separately from the underlying trend. We emphasise that, whilst STL is also used in our anomaly detection approach, the application of it here preserves, rather than removes, the underlying features of the data and thus is not unfairly biasing the synthetic dataset towards our approach.

The underlying trend data is then smoothed using a 28-day rolling median average. Due to the robust nature of the median against small outliers, this approach preserves broad-scale trends in the data whilst removing, as far as possible, small-scale deviations. Without an objective labelled set of anomalies we cannot guarantee that no anomalies were preserved in the final dataset, but a visual inspection did not reveal any significant causes for concern.

We then calculate, for each country, the mean and the standard deviation of the residual errors after the trend and seasonal components have been removed. This gives a base set of parameters from which to generate random noise to be added to each series.

To create the final synthetic dataset, we recombine the smoothed underlying trend data with the seasonal component and add randomised noise. As it is impossible to characterise the "true" noise process without having labelled anomalies we conservatively add Gaussian noise drawn according to the observed mean and standard deviation. This provides a "clean" dataset without anomalies, based on real-world patterns of behaviour.

6.3   Injecting Anomalies

As with the underlying data, we generate anomalies based on properties observed in real-world data. The strength of the injected anomalies is based on the average daily users for each country, and magnified upwards or downwards gradually to create the anomaly.

To create an anomaly, the number of users in each set was increased or decreased by 0–100%. Anomalies are added to the data gradually, ranging over periods from one to four weeks. These parameters were selected based on observation of known anomalies and visual inspection of the original dataset.

In total, for the year of synthetic data, we injected a total of 250 anomalies across all countries, randomly drawn from the space of possible parameters.

This synthetic, labelled dataset provides the basis both for objective evaluation of the effectiveness of our technique, and as an unbiased means of comparison between our approach and that of [8]. We now evaluate the effectiveness of these two approaches.

6.4   Comparison of Tools

An evaluation of false positive and false negative rates in detecting anomalous periods allows both an objective judgement on the effectiveness of our approach, and a comparison against the existing tool used by the Tor Project [8]. To carry out this comparison, we formatted the clean synthetic dataset appropriately for each tool and compared the detected anomaly series from each to the injected set of anomalies.

One problematic element of such a comparison is in the nature of event reporting from each tool. As mentioned, our approach reports day-by-day anomalies based on principal component modelling. By comparison, [8] bases its detection on significant spikes and dips on a day-by-day basis. As such, it is far less likely that Tor Project's existing tool will report anomalous periods, but will instead detect only the points at at which an anomaly starts and ends. This should hypothetically result in a much higher detection accuracy rate for our tool on a day-by-day comparison: an anomaly that lasts for ten days will typically only produce two anomalously flagged days in the Tor Project's detection scheme, whereas it may result in ten days for our tool as each day in the anomalous period may be identified. By contrast, however, our tool's approach leaves us open to a potentially higher false negative rate when a period is falsely judged to be anomalous.

We highlight again, however, that this period-based rather than event-based approach is one of the key strengths of our improved approach – we report entire periods as anomalous rather than simply identifying point anomalies.

As such, to compare, we perform a simple analysis: the output of each tool is evaluated according to the ground truth in the labelled synthetic dataset. Days correctly identified as anomalous contribute

	Tor Metrics	Principal Component
True Positives	8.57%	20.08%
True Negatives	92.75%	94.25%
False Positives	7.25%	5.75%
False Negatives	91.43%	79.92%
Total Days Flagged	2962	2820
Minimal Detection Total[1]	88	139

Total anomalous days across entire set was 4214.
[1] Anomalies during which at least one day was identified.

Table 1: Comparison between Tor Metrics and Principal Component approach on synthetic data.

to the *true positive* rate, whilst days marked as anomalous that are not in the synthetic data contribute to the *false positive* rate. Similarly, if a day is anomalous in the synthetic data and missed by our tool, it contributes to the *false negative* rate, whilst days correctly identified as not anomalous contribute to the *true negative* rate. These values are reported in Table 1.

Our principal component-based approach significantly outperforms the currently deployed Tor Metrics detector both in marking genuine anomalies and in avoiding marking non-anomalous days incorrectly.

The overall detection rate of our approach is over twice that of the alternative, at 20% of all genuinely anomalous days being identified. This figure is somewhat misleadingly low, however, as this includes many correctly-identified anomalous *periods* for which, however, some individual days were not themselves considered anomalous.

These results suggest that in realistic data generated from observed real-world trends, the proposed principal component analysis-based approach significantly outperforms the existing deployed tool.

6.4.1   Ranking. We have attempted, as far as possible, to undertake a fair comparison of the quantitatively comparable elements of these two approaches, despite significant differences in their output. In addition, however, our approach offers a number of advantages for analysis. The most significant of these is the ability to rank countries according to the strength of the anomalies they have demonstrated over time in terms of deviation from expected behaviour. The `infolabe-anomalies` mailing list reports daily the top-ranking anomalous countries for the previous day, week, and month in addition to a list of all countries anomalous for that day.

It is worth highlighting that whilst realtime detection is of great interest to the commmunity, the ability to study historical anomalies in the Tor metrics dataset is also of significant value.

6.5   Detection of Known Events

Having calculated anomalous statistics over a synthetic data set, we now aim to validate our approach by comparing anomalies detected in real data against countries and periods in which internet restrictions are known to have been applied, or in which significant events were occurring that may have influenced usage of circumvention tools.

Date	Country	Description of Event
2012-10-18	Iran	TLS key exchange DPI.[1]
2012-12-16	Syria	DPI on TLS renegotiation.
2013-01-30	Japan	Bridge blocked.
2013-03-09	Iran	SSL handshake filtered.
2013-03-26	China	Probing obfs2 bridges.
2014-03-28	Turkey	Tor website blocked.
2014-07-29	Iran	Block directory authorities.
2015-02-01	China	Obfs4 bridges blocked.

[1] See §6.5 for a discussion of this particular anomaly.

Table 2: Complete list of reported, and detected, Tor blocking events.

For this purpose we use [1], a list of reported and verified filtering events against the Tor network dating from 2008 to 2015. This list includes a brief description of each reported event, the dates when the event was first reported, and how the blocking was resolved.

The list of events used in this evaluation[1] was compiled through bug reports, talks, examination of blog postings, and the use of machine learning on blog postings to identify reports of censorship automatically. As such, the exact timing of the events is somewhat fuzzy; a blocking event against Tor could have occurred some time before bug reports and blog postings were filed.

In addition, [1] is unfortunately brief, reflecting a significant lack of data available concerning this topic. As discussed, a motivation for this work is to provide a baseline of reliable indicators to allow for potentially censorship-related anomalies to be identified and investigated more thoroughly.

The Tor Project's metrics data does not cover the full time range of the events listed in [1]. For those events that do fall within the available data, we analyse here whether these would be detected by our approach.

As shown in Table 2, only eight reported events coincide with the available published metrics data. Of these, our approach successfully classifies all events as anomalous[3]. In all cases except the Iranian DPI filtering on TLS that occurred in 2012, our anomalies coincide with the reported event from [1]. In the case of Iran in 2012, we detect an anomalous period beginning two weeks *before* the reported event, corresponding to an immediate sharp fall in Tor usage, followed by a longer period of slow decline over the following month.

6.6 Recent Events

We have, in the course of investigating Tor metrics data with the tool detailed in this work, discovered and reported a number of significant Tor usage anomalies in countries including Ukraine, Israel, Bangladesh, UAE, and Turkmenistan. In some of these cases anomalies are due to filtering behaviour, such as Bangladesh's blocking of Facebook and chat applications in November 2015. In other cases the anomalies are due to external factors such as Ukraine's blocking of the popular Russian social networking site VKontakte in

---

[3]Two events corresponded to direct blocking of Tor bridge nodes, and these were identified as anomalous in the bridge usage statistics. All other anomalies were detected in normal Tor usage.

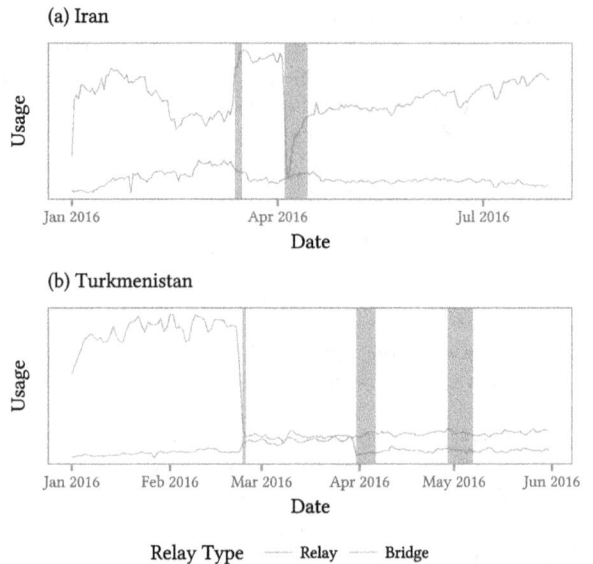

(a) Iran

(b) Turkmenistan

Relay Type —— Relay —— Bridge

Figure 2: Combined relay and bridge Tor usage anomalies.

May 2017 [25] that led to a large spike in circumvention tool usage. Numerous other events have been detected, but space limitations prevent significant discussion of individual cases.

7 EXAMPLE RESULTS

Due to space constraints, we will not discuss specific cases in detail. This section shows a number of example outputs that highlight detected anomalies. As far as possible, we have extended the range of time shown in each plot to highlight that detected anomalies are not a frequent occurrence.

7.1 Most Anomalous Countries

Figure 1 illustrates the ten most anomalous countries according to their median absolute deviation from the median in the past year. Shaded regions denote periods of anomalous usage, according to our tool.

7.2 Combined Tor Metric Anomalies

Figure 2 highlights example combined anomalies that demonstrate periods in which Tor usage via normal relays and access via bridge nodes experienced simultaneous but opposing anomalies.

Over the period included in the available Tor metrics data, which covers late 2011 until the time of writing, our technique identified 485 anomalous periods in which both Tor usage and bridge usage were jointly anomalous, across 102 countries out of the total 251 for which Tor assigns usage statistics. This number is somewhat inflated due to the fact that a number of these anomalous periods are separated only by a small number of days and are likely the result of the same event.

Of these countries, Georgia had the highest number of combined detected anomalies, with 16 anomalous periods identified since 2011. The median number of anomalous periods over the set of all 102 countries that showed any anomalous behaviour was four.

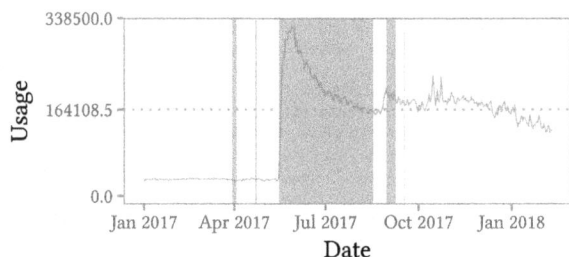

Figure 3: Anomalous usage following Ukraine's ban on major Russian network services.

It is possible that this number may increase if the combination of anomalous periods is made more flexible, as discussed in §4.4, however this demonstrates that events that exceed the threshold for combined anomalies are relatively rare.

7.3 Ukraine Russian Service Ban

In early May 2017 the Ukrainian government blocked a number of major Russian online services, used by a significant number of Ukrainian citizens, including social network sites VKontakte and Odnoklassniki, mail provider mail.ru, and Yandex, a major search engine[25]. Figure 3 shows a strong surge in Tor usage in the immediate aftermath of this, causing Ukraine to rise to the top of the daily anomaly rankings on the <name-redacted> mailing list. This example represents a significant anomaly in Tor usage related to blocking of standard internet services beyond Tor, and is in direct comparison to the Turkmenistan example of Figure 2 that highlights blocking of the Tor network itself.

8 DISCUSSION

The validation and results of §6 and §7 demonstrate that our approach is practically useful for identifying both Tor blocking and, more generally, for identifying periods of anomalous Tor usage. The highlighted anomalies detected by our approach are strong indicators of regions of likely interest to the internet filtering research and activist communities, and in particular in the combination of normal Tor and bridge node usage.

More directly, the experimental validation in the previous section demonstrates that our approach does detect a significant number of anomalies with varying magnitudes and durations.

9 FUTURE WORK

A main aspect of future work, for which these techniques were developed, will be to perform analysis on historical filtering behaviour and to maintain an ongoing watch for new potential filtering events. By combination with datasets such as Google's Global Database of Events, Language, and Tone (GDELT) [23], and through collaboration with researchers and activists, the authors hope to develop and maintain a contextualised time series of per-country filtering events for the benefit of future researchers.

Whilst the work presented here has focused on the application of our technique to Tor metrics data, the method is more generally applicable. Applying the techniques presented here to other data sources is the most obvious direct extension to this work. We have made preliminary analyses based on data from Psiphon, CAIDA, Measurement Lab [13], and the Wikimedia Foundation, as well as evaluating data from the OONI Project [28] for its applicability in detecting filtering. Other data sources, such as social media, are also likely candidates for analysis.

Given the results of combining multiple Tor metrics, an interesting line of enquiry would be to investigate the speed with which users respond to filtering of Tor by adopting bridge nodes, and to understand the proportion of users that make this change. As more data sources are combined, further analysis of filtering's effects in different countries and under different conditions becomes possible.

10 CONCLUSIONS

We have developed a principal component analysis-based multivariate anomaly detection system to detect anomalous periods in per-country usage statistics of Tor metrics data. Our approach allows detection of per-country anomalies in time series that are non-stationary and that demonstrate significant seasonality. Our approach discounts global trends and even large-scale global events by considering individual countries' usage patterns as relative to that of others.

We have demonstrated the application of this tool to data from the Tor Project's metrics portal, showing that it provides a means to indicate potential censorship-related events, and others, at the global level. We have further shown that combining multiple metrics to identify jointly-anomalous periods can greatly improve the usefulness of the detected anomalies for identifying periods of direct blocking of Tor.

This work presents a generally applicable tool for detecting a broad class of internet filtering events on a global scale, without the need to focus on individual countries, and that dynamically adapts to changing patterns of usage. Countries exhibiting anomalous behaviour are automatically identified, and can be subjected to further, more targeted, investigation.

We have validated our approach both by evaluating detection rates of injected anomalies in a synthetically-generated time series, and demonstrated that our detection rates are significantly higher than those used in the existing anomaly detector used by the Tor project. Additionally, our tool provides useful ranking of anomalies according to strength, as well as highlighting anomalous periods rather than single-day events.

We have further evaluated our tool by successfully comparing detected anomalous periods with an external list of known Tor blocking events. This evaluation successfully identified each reported blocking event, supporting the tool's practical effectiveness in detecting real-world anomalies.

Using our approach, we have demonstrated that combining anomalies detected in multiple metrics can be an effective means to identify more targeted forms of anomaly that indicate filtering behaviour. Our initial combination of opposite-signed normal Tor usage and bridge node usage anomalies is a key step, but there are other behaviours that could be of specific interest; there is also significant potential for further combination with metrics from other tools and data sources.

Beyond the technique itself, the analyses presented in this work have identified several states that are known to engage in active filtering, but have also highlighted patterns of anomalous behaviour in several states that have not received significant attention from the internet censorship research community. Conducting more detailed investigations of these countries is a promising focus for future research.

Our anomaly detection tool is running actively on a nightly basis, with results output to a dedicated anomaly mailing list. This list has an audience amongst NGOs and research projects working in the field of investigating filtering and circumventing censorship, and has seen active use in detecting emerging real-world filtering events.

In addition to the underlying technique and tool developed to detect anomalous periods of behaviour, we have suggested, and provided initial evidence, that the use of the Tor metrics data, amongst other sources, is of use not only as an indicator of its own usage patterns, but as a practical proxy variable for a much wider class of political and social events. This presents significant potential for researchers, policy makers, and activists investigating global freedom of expression.

11 ACKNOWLEDGEMENTS

This work was supported by The Alan Turing Institute under the EPSRC grant EP/N51012. Joss Wright is partially funded by the Alan Turing Institute as a Turing Fellow under Turing Award Number TU/B/000044.

REFERENCES

[1] Sadia Afroz and David Fifield. [n. d.]. Timeline of Tor Censorship. www1.icsi. berkeley.edu/~sadia/tor_timeline.pdf. ([n. d.]). Accessed 25th February, 2018.
[2] Anonymous. 2012. The Collateral Damage of Internet Censorship by DNS Injection. *SIGCOMM Comput. Commun. Rev.* 42, 3 (June 2012), 21–27. https://doi.org/10.1145/2317307.2317311
[3] Anonymous. 2014. Towards a Comprehensive Picture of the Great Firewall's DNS Censorship. In *4th USENIX Workshop on Free and Open Communications on the Internet (FOCI 14)*. USENIX Association, San Diego, CA. https://www.usenix.org/conference/foci14/workshop-program/presentation/anonymous
[4] Yana Breindl and Joss Wright. 2012. Internet Filtering in Liberal Democracies. In *Presented as part of the 2nd USENIX Workshop on Free and Open Communications on the Internet*. USENIX, Bellevue, WA. https://www.usenix.org/system/files/conference/foci12/breindl2012foci.pdf
[5] Richard Clayton, Steven J. Murdoch, and Robert N. M. Watson. 2006. Ignoring the Great Firewall of China. In *Proceedings of the 6th International Conference on Privacy Enhancing Technologies (PET'06)*. Springer-Verlag, Berlin, Heidelberg, 20–35. https://doi.org/10.1007/11957454_2
[6] R. B. Cleveland, W. S. Cleveland, J. E. McRae, and I. Terpenning. 1990. STL: A Seasonal-Trend Decomposition Procedure Based on Loess. *Journal of Official Statistics* 6 (1990), 3–73.
[7] Jedidiah R. Crandall, Daniel Zinn, Michael Byrd, Earl Barr, and Rich East. 2007. ConceptDoppler: A Weather Tracker for Internet Censorship. Computer and Communications Security. http://www.cs.unm.edu/~
[8] George Danezis. 2011. *An anomaly-based censorship-detection system for Tor*. Technical Report. The Tor Project. https://research.torproject.org/techreports/detector-2011-09-09.pdf
[9] Alexander Darer, Oliver Farnan, and Joss Wright. 2017. FilteredWeb: A Framework for the Automated Search-Based Discovery of Blocked URLs. In *Network Traffic Measurement and Analysis*. IFIP. http://tma.ifip.org/wordpress/wp-content/uploads/2017/06/tma2017_paper32.pdf
[10] A. Darer, O. Farnan, and J. Wright. 2018. Automated Discovery of Internet Censorship by Web Crawling. *ArXiv e-prints* (April 2018). arXiv:cs.CY/1804.03056
[11] Ronald Deibert. 2007. *Access Denied: The Practice and Policy of Global Internet Filtering (Information Revolution and Global Politics Series)* (1 ed.). MIT Press. http://www.worldcat.org/isbn/0262541963
[12] Roger Dingledine, Nick Mathewson, and Paul Syverson. 2004. Tor: The Second-Generation Onion Router. In *IN PROCEEDINGS OF THE 13 TH USENIX SECURITY SYMPOSIUM*.
[13] Constantine Dovrolis, P. Krishna Gummadi, Aleksandar Kuzmanovic, and Sascha D. Meinrath. 2010. Measurement lab: overview and an invitation to the research community. *Computer Communication Review* 40, 3 (2010), 53–56. https://doi.org/10.1145/1823844.1823853
[14] Oliver Farnan, Alexander Darer, and Joss Wright. 2016. Poisoning the Well: Exploring the Great Firewall's Poisoned DNS Responses. In *Proceedings of the 2016 ACM on Workshop on Privacy in the Electronic Society*. ACM, 95–98.
[15] Nicolas Goix. 2016. How to Evaluate the Quality of Unsupervised Anomaly Detection Algorithms? (2016). arXiv:arXiv:1607.01152
[16] Ling Huang, Xuanlong Nguyen, Minos Garofalakis, and Joseph M. Hellerstein. 2007. Communication-efficient online detection of network-wide anomalies. In *In IEEE Conference on Computer Communications (INFOCOM)*. IEEE, 134–142.
[17] P.J. Huber. 2004. *Robust Statistics*. Wiley. https://books.google.co.uk/books?id=e62RhdqIdMkC
[18] J. E. Jackson and G. S. Mudholkar. 1979. Control Procedures for Residuals Associated with Principal Component Analysis. *Technometrics* 21, 3 (1979), 341–349.
[19] I. T. Jolliffe. 2002. *Principal component analysis*. Springer, New York. http://link.springer.com/book/10.1007%2Fb98835
[20] Henry F. Kaiser. 1960. The Application of Electronic Computers to Factor Analysis. *Educational and Psychological Measurement* 20 (1960), 141–151. Issue 1. https://doi.org/10.1177/001316446002000116
[21] Gary King, Jennifer Pan, and Margaret E. Roberts. 2013. How Censorship in China Allows Government Criticism but Silences Collective Expression. *American Political Science Review* 107 (2013), 1–18.
[22] Anukool Lakhina, Mark Crovella, and Christophe Diot. 2004. Diagnosing Network-Wide Traffic Anomalies. In *Proceedings of ACM SIGCOMM 2004*. 219–230. http://www.cs.bu.edu/faculty/crovella/paper-archive/sigc04-network-wide-anomalies.pdf
[23] Kalev Leetaru and Philip A. Schrodt. 2013. GDELT: Global data on events, location, and tone. *ISA Annual Convention* (2013).
[24] Christophe Leys, Christophe Ley, Olivier Klein, Philippe Bernard, and Laurent Licata. 2013. Detecting outliers: Do not use standard deviation around the mean, use absolute deviation around the median. *Journal of Experimental Social Psychology* 49, 4 (2013), 764 – 766. https://doi.org/10.1016/j.jesp.2013.03.013
[25] Alec Luhn. 2017. Ukraine blocks popular social networks as part of sanctions on Russia. (May 2017). https://www.theguardian.com/world/2017/may/16/ukraine-blocks-popular-russian-websites-kremlin-role-war
[26] Hooman Mohajeri Moghaddam, Baiyu Li, Mohammad Derakhshani, and Ian Goldberg. 2012. SkypeMorph: Protocol Obfuscation for Tor Bridges. In *Proceedings of the 19th ACM conference on Computer and Communications Security (CCS 2012)*.
[27] Karl Pearson. 1901. On lines and planes of closest fit to systems of points in space. *Philos. Mag.* 2, 6 (1901), 559–572.
[28] The OONI Project. [n. d.]. The Open Observatory of Network Interference. https://ooni.torproject.org/. ([n. d.]). Accessed 25th February, 2018.
[29] The Tor Project. [n. d.]. Tor Metrics Portal. https://metrics.torproject.org/. ([n. d.]). Accessed 25th February, 2018.
[30] The Tor Project. [n. d.]. Tor Metrics: Questions and answers about user statistics. https://gitweb.torproject.org/metrics-web.git/tree/doc/users-q-and-a.txt. ([n. d.]). Accessed 25th February, 2018.
[31] Haakon Ringberg, Augustin Soule, Jennifer Rexford, and Christophe Diot. 2007. Sensitivity of PCA for traffic anomaly detection. In *SIGMETRICS '07: Proceedings of the 2007 ACM SIGMETRICS international conference on Measurement and modeling of computer systems*. ACM Press, New York, NY, USA, 109–120. https://doi.org/10.1145/1254882.1254895
[32] David Robinson, Harlan Yu, and Anne An. 2013. *Collateral Freedom: A Snapshot of Chinese Users Circumventing Censorship*. Technical Report.
[33] Fatemeh Shirazi, Claudia Diaz, and Joss Wright. 2015. Towards Measuring Resilience in Anonymous Communication Networks. In *Proceedings of the 14th ACM Workshop on Privacy in the Electronic Society (WPES '15)*. ACM, New York, NY, USA, 95–99. https://doi.org/10.1145/2808138.2808152
[34] Augustin Soule, Kavé Salamatian, and Nina Taft. 2005. Combining filtering and statistical methods for anomaly detection. In *In Proceedings of IMC*.
[35] Graham Upton and Ian Cook. 2002. *Oxford dictionary of statistics*. Oxford university press Oxford, UK.
[36] Zachary Weinberg, Jeffrey Wang, Vinod Yegneswaran, Linda Briesemeister, Steven Cheung, Frank Wang, and Dan Boneh. 2012. StegoTorus: A Camouflage Proxy for the Tor Anonymity System. In *Proceedings of the 19th ACM conference on Computer and Communications Security (CCS 2012)*.
[37] Joss Wright. 2014. Regional variation in Chinese internet filtering. *Information, Communication & Society* 17, 1 (2014), 121–141. https://doi.org/10.1080/1369118X.2013.853818 arXiv:http://dx.doi.org/10.1080/1369118X.2013.853818
[38] Joss Wright, Tulio de Souza, and Ian Brown. 2011. Fine-Grained Censorship Mapping: Information Sources, Legality and Ethics. In *Free and Open Communications on the Internet*. USENIX, San Francisco, CA, USA. http://static.usenix.org/event/foci11/tech/final_files/Wright.pdf
[39] Yin Zhang, Zihui Ge, Albert Greenberg, and Matthew Roughan. 2005. Network anomography. In *In IMC*.

Web Access Literacy Scale to Evaluate How Critically Users Can Browse and Search for Web Information

Yusuke Yamamoto
Shizuoka University
Hamamatsu, Shizuoka, Japan
yusuke_yamamoto@acm.org

Takehiro Yamamoto
Kyoto University
Kyoto, Japan
tyamamot@dl.kuis.kyoto-u.ac.jp

Hiroaki Ohshima
University of Hyogo
Kobe, Hyogo, Japan
ohshima@ai.hyogo-u.ac.jp

Hiroshi Kawakami
Kyoto University
Kyoto, Japan
kawakami@design.kyoto-u.ac.jp

ABSTRACT

We propose a web access literacy scale to assess user ability to scrutinize web information and gather accurate information using information access systems, such as web search engines.

We conducted an online study with participants recruited through a crowdsourcing service. Analysis of the questionnaire responses confirmed that the proposed web access literacy scale is reliable and valid. We also noted the following pointers: (1) Web users may not pay significant attention to web page authors and their expertise when judging information credibility. (2) Users may have weaknesses relative to the use of web search engines and tolerance for cognitive bias that appears in credibility assessment of web information.

The results of this study are expected to contribute to the design of information access systems or educational classes to encourage users to reflect on and improve their web access literacy relative to critical information seeking.

CCS CONCEPTS

• **Human-centered computing** → **User studies**; • **Information systems** → *Web searching and information discovery*; • **Applied computing** → *Education*;

KEYWORDS

Literacy; web information credibility; psychological scale; human factors

ACM Reference Format:
Yusuke Yamamoto, Takehiro Yamamoto, Hiroaki Ohshima, and Hiroshi Kawakami. 2018. Web Access Literacy Scale to Evaluate How Critically Users Can Browse and Search for Web Information. In *WebSci '18: 10th ACM Conference on Web Science, May 27–30, 2018, Amsterdam, Netherlands*. ACM, New York, NY, USA, 10 pages. https://doi.org/10.1145/3201064.3201072

1 INTRODUCTION

In today's world, people are increasingly relying on the World Wide Web (web) for information; however, much of the information available on the web is not credible. For example, Sillence et al. reported that more than half of the medical information on the web has not been authorized by medical experts [22]. In addition, the dissemination of "fake news", i.e., deliberate misinformation, propaganda, and hoaxes, on social networks is now becoming a social problem. Nevertheless, several studies have found that people frequently do not consider the source or the accuracy of the information they find on the web [17, 18]. Therefore, creating information access environments and methods that help people obtain accurate information and thereby make effective decisions is important.

Information retrieval researchers have proposed various approaches to evaluate web information credibility, such as algorithms that analyze credibility [4, 21], evidence search systems [10], disputed information suggestion systems [5, 25], and systems that visualize credibility-related scores [26]. In addition, to motivate users to apply credibility assessment when considering web information, researchers have discussed search systems that focus on the priming effect, which refers to a stimulus that activates a mental concept and infuences subsequent behaviors [27]. However, such systems are only effective if users understand how to use them. In addition, the effectiveness of such systems and their performance relative to credibility judgment rely on user abilities and skills [27]. Thus, both improving such abilities and skills in users and developing systems that support information credibility judgments is important.

Generally, improving user abilities requires metrics to assess competencies, as well as understanding each user's strengths and weaknesses. In this paper, we propose a *web access literacy scale*, a questionnaire-based method to evaluate web access literacy. We define *web access literacy* as the ability to examine web information critically and collect accurate information using information access systems, such as search engines.

The proposed web access literacy scale focuses on information seeking and evaluation processes. Thus, web access literacy is related to information literacy, which is the ability to identify information needs, find the required information efficiently, evaluate the information critically, and use it [1].

Several library science studies have proposed educational methods to develop information literacy. However, only few methods have been proposed for measuring information literacy, particularly user abilities pertaining to information seeking and evaluation. Nevertheless, some researchers have proposed indicators to measure information literacy; however, these indicators are quite generic (e.g., "an information literate student articulates and applies initial criteria to evaluate the information and its sources" [1]). Therefore, it is difficult for users to use these indicators to improve their ability to evaluate web information critically in order to obtain accurate information.

In addition to information literacy, critical thinking is related to web access literacy. Critical thinking is defined as rational and reflective thinking to determine what to believe and do [6]. Previous studies have shown that critical thinking plays a key role in determining whether information is correct [9, 16]. Several methods to assess critical thinking ability have been developed [7]; however, such methods can only measure some aspects of web access literacy, such as logical thinking skills and the tendency to be critical. In addition, other aspects should be considered when evaluating web access literacy, such as understanding the characteristics of web information and familiarity with search engines.

In this paper, we discuss the following elements of web access literacy:

- Strategies to verify information credibility
- Tolerance for cognitive biases in credibility judgments
- Skill level in using web search engines
- Critical thinking attitudes

We developed a questionnaire-based scale to assess the above-mentioned elements and web access literacy. In addition, we used a crowdsourcing service to recruit participants. To evaluate the proposed literacy scale, we analyzed correlations between literacy and relevant external references, such as educational background, previous experience with information literacy classes, and trust in web information. In addition, we reveal user weaknesses relative to careful information seeking.

2 CONCEPT OF WEB ACCESS LITERACY

2.1 Elements of Web Access Literacy

We define *web access literacy* as the ability to examine web information critically and collect correct information using information access systems, such as search engines. Here, *critical* examination involves the ability to consider evidence logically and consider whether the individual's opinions are correct for better decision making and problem solving.

In this paper, we discuss the elements of the literacy from two perspectives, i.e., *the search process* and *the evaluation process*. A previous study on information literacy reported that the search process requires the ability to identify issues, develop a search plan, and collect information [1]. Typically, such abilities are required to use web search engines effectively. Harvey and White reported that, to collect web information efficiently, users should be able to construct effective queries and use search engine options [8, 23]. Therefore, we focus on the skills required to use web search engines effectively as one element of web access literacy.

In the information evaluation process, the ability to examine information critically is essential to avoid misinformation. Metzger et al. pointed out that critical thinking is important when searching for information from resources that are known to contain incorrect information [16]. Several researchers have stated that critical thinking requires cognitive skills, such as logical thinking and inference skills, and attitudes to evaluate information critically in order to draw a conclusion reflectively (hereafter, this is referred to as critical thinking attitude). Kusumi et al. suggested that effective critical thinking constitutes a logical approach, inquisitiveness, objectivity, and reliance on evidence [9]. When developing the proposed web access literacy scale, we considered critical thinking attitude relative to these four elements.

Understanding methods to evaluate web information critically is also important. Even if people possess excellent critical thinking abilities and know how to use web search engines effectively, if they do not know how to evaluate web information, they will be not able to assess it efficiently and effectively. Guidelines to help university students obtain credible information from the web have been published [11, 14]. Such guidelines suggest checking author information and the publication date, as well as comparing the obtained information to information from other sources. To develop the proposed web access literacy scale, we also considered strategies to evaluate web information credibility.

In addition, we considered tolerance for biases when assessing the credibility of web information. To evaluate information effectively, web users should understand the concept of cognitive bias, i.e., deviation from rational judgments due to personal preferences or beliefs [24]. Previous studies have identified the following cognitive biases noted during web search/browsing:

- Position bias: people often prefer to click higher ranked web search results [28],
- Readability bias: web search results that are more readable are clicked more frequently [3],
- Aesthetic bias: people trust visually-pleasing web pages more than they trust poorly designed web pages [12].

Thus, when developing the proposed web access literacy scale, we also considered tolerance of such cognitive biases relative to the critical evaluation of information.

2.2 Verification of Web Access Literacy

We expect that people with web access literacy can identify suspicious information more efficently in order to make more precise decisions than those without such literacy. Thus, we propose hypothesis 1.

H1 The level of web access literacy predicts task performance when candidates choose the most probable answer after using web search engines.

Health literacy scales that measure the ability to use web-based health information effectively have been developed [19]; thus, we consider health literacy a specific type of web access literacy. Therefore, we propose hypothesis 2.

H2 Web access literacy is positively correlated with health literacy.

Moreover, we expect that, given experience with critical information seeking, people with web access literacy are aware that significant amounts of misinformation can be found on the web. Consequently, their trust in web information may be low. Thus, we propose hypothesis 3.

H3 Web access literacy is negatively correlated with trust in web information.

Several studies have reported that learning and research activities in universities enhance critical thinking [20]. while suggesting that such activities also contribute to improving web access literacy related to critical thinking. Similarly, we expect that, if people have taken classes or attended seminars on information literacy, they may have acquired evaluation strategies related to information credibility and cognitive biases, which would improve their web access literacy. Thus, we propose hypotheses 4 and 5.

H4 Web access literacy is positively correlated with education.
H5 Experience with information literacy courses predicts the level of web access literacy.

3 METHOD

This section describes an online study performed to develop the proposed web access literacy scale and to test the above hypotheses. The online study was conducted between February 9 and 13, 2018. We asked participants to perform search tasks and answer a questionnaire. Note that we used Laners.jp[1], a Japanese crowdsourcing service, to recruit participants. This study was conducted in Japanese.

3.1 Participants

We recruited 683 participants through Lancers.jp for the online study. We excluded 149 participants from analysis because they did not complete all tasks or work seriously[2]. As a result, we used data from 534 participants in total (male: 215; female: 313; N/A: 6). Each participant received approximately $2.50 for their time.

3.2 Procedure

Each participant was required to register prior to conducting the online study. Then, the participants were asked to view the website related to the study. After they visited the website, we explained the study and introduced its procedure. Then, we asked the participants to complete the provided search tasks and questionnaire. At first, the participants completed the search tasks. After the search tasks, the participants answered the questionnaire. Note that the study was conducted anonymously. The study took approximately 20-30 minutes to finish.

3.3 Search Tasks

To analyze the relationship between web access literacy and practical ability to search the web for accurate information, we prepared web search tasks to find answers to medical questions. For the search tasks, we picked five medical symptoms for which various suspicious treatments can be found on the web. We provided

three answer possibilities for treating or improving each symptom. Then, the participants were asked to select a single answer; they were allowed to use a web search engine of their choice. The prepared medical symptoms and answer candidates are listed below (the underlined answer candidates are the correct ones).

- High blood pressure (cacao, eucommia, and euglena)
- Diabetes (honey, cinnamon, and sunchoke)
- Constipation (plantago psyllium, prune, and lotus leaf)
- High cholesterol (barley, onion, and spirulina)
- Brittle-bone disease (soy bean, flaxseed oil, and dolomite)

We confirmed that the reliability/unreliability of each medical treatment has been studied by the Ministry of Health, Labour and Welfare, Japan.

At the beginning of each search task, we presented the following description to introduce the task.

Imagine that you are suffering from high blood pressure. Someone told you that one of the following three items could improve your medical condition. Please choose the most reliable item using a web search engine. Then, select the answer while providing evidential web pages. For this search task, please use the web search engine that you usually use. If you have not used web search engines, please use the Google search engine.

3.4 Questionnaire tasks

Table 1 lists the questionnaire items used in this study. Each question ID in the table gives the order in which the question corresponding to the ID was asked in the questionnaire task. As shown in the table, the questionnaire comprised the following.

(1) Eight question sets related to web access literacy
(2) Three question sets related to external relevant criteria
(3) Demographic questions
(4) Two types of malicious participant filter questions[3].

For the questions about tolerance for cognitive biases in web information credibility judgment, we asked participants about their tendencies of assessing credibility based on criteria or heuristics that are irrelevant to correctness when web searching/browsing. Some example questions are as follows:

- Do you trust information on well-designed web pages?
- Do you trust content on web pages that look technical or specialized?
- Do you trust information on easy-to-understand web pages?

The participants answered these questions using a five-point Likert scale (1: never trust; 5: completely trust).

For questions about search/browsing strategies to verify web information credibility, we asked about the frequencies of verification actions that were considered effective. A few example questions are given as follows:

- How often do you check if the content on web pages is updated?

---

[1]Lancers.jp: https://www.lancers.jp/
[2]The questionnaire contained questions to filter malicious participants, such as "Have you never told a lie?" and "Choose the same word as a word displayed below."

[3]Due to space limitations, all question items are available at https://github.com/hontolab/web-access-literacy.

Table 1: Questionnaire items

Category	Question ID	Content	Count
Web access literacy	19-29	Tolerance for biases in web information credibility judgment	11
	30-41	Browsing strategies to verify web information credibility	12
	42-49	Search strategies to verify web information credibility	8
	50-54	Web search engine utilization skills	5
	56-68	Critical thinking attitude: logical approach	13
	69-78	Critical thinking attitude: inquisitiveness	10
	79-85	Critical thinking attitude: objectivity	7
	86-88	Critical thinking attitude: reliance on evidence	3
External relevant criteria	1-18	Trust in various web information	18
	90-97	Health literacy	8
	98	Experience through attending information literacy classes	1
Demographic	100	Sex	1
	101	Academic background	1
	102	Age	1
Malicious participant filter	99	Have you never told a lie?	1
	55,89	Choose the same word as the word displayed below	2

- How often do you check for the author of the content on web pages?
- How often do you compare multiple web pages when browsing a topic?

These questions were prepared by referencing guidelines in the information literacy and library science fields [11, 14, 15]. The participants answered these questions using a five-point Likert scale (1: never; 5: every time).

For questions about web search engine utilization skills, we asked the participants about the frequencies at which they use web search engine options.

- How often do you use double-quotation operators for a phrase query search?
- How often do you use NOT operators to narrow down web search results?
- How often do you use a publication date filter to obtain the latest web search results?

The participants answered these questions using a five-point Likert scale (1: never use; 5: frequently use).

To examine the four types of critical thinking attitudes, we used 33 questions from the critical thinking attitude scale developed by Kusumi et al.[9]. For questions about logical approaches, we asked 13 questions. Some example questions are given as follows:

- Are you good at thinking about complicated problems in an organized way?
- Are you good at summarizing ideas?

For questions about inquisitiveness, we asked 10 questions, such as follows:

- Do you want to learn a lot by communicating with various types of people?
- Do you want to continue learning new things over your lifetime?

We asked seven questions about objectivity, such as follows.

- Do you always try to make fair judgments?
- Do you always try to adopt an objective attitude when deciding something?

We asked three questions about reliance on evidence.

- Do you stick to the existence of concrete evidence when drawing a conclusion?
- Do you pursue as many facts and as much evidence as possible when making a decision?

For these questions, the participants answered using a five-point Likert scale (1: strongly disagree; 5: strongly agree).

For demographic variables, participants reported their sex, age, and educational background. For educational background, the participants chose from the following options: junior high school, high school, technical college, two-year college, university, and graduate school. Note that participants were permitted to not answer the demographics questions.

To evaluate the criterion-related validity of web access literacy, we asked participants whether they had taken any information literacy classes till date[4]. For this question, the participants responded with a yes or no. Furthermore, we prepared 18 questions about trust in web information. Example questions are given as follows.

- Two questions about general trust in web information (e.g., How much credible information do you think exists on the web?)
- Nine questions about web trust according to different sources (e.g., To what extent do you trust information on Wikipedia?)

[4]In Japan, the Ministry of Education, Culture sports, Science and Technology (MEXT) revised curriculum guidelines for high schools in 2013, and learning information literacy has been compulsory in high schools since then.

- Seven questions about web trust according to content type (e.g., To what extent do you trust news information on the web?)

The participants answered these questions using a five-point Likert scale (1: never trust; 5: completely trust).

In addition to the above two question sets, we asked about the health literacy scale (the eHealth literacy scale: eHEALs) with reference to Norman's study [19]. The eHEALs questionnaire comprised eight questions, such as follows:

- Do you know what health resources are available on the Internet?
- Do you know where to find helpful health resources on the Internet?
- Do you have the skills to evaluate the health resources you find on the Internet?

The participants answered these questions using a five-point Likert scale (1: strongly disagree; 5: strongly agree).

4 RESULTS

We obtained and analyzed response data from 534 participants. The various results are discussed in the following subsections.

4.1 Factor analysis

We conducted a factor analysis of 70 items from the web access literacy scale (maximum likelihood extraction with promax rotation). The number of factors was determined to be seven by the bayesian information criterion (BIC). We considered items with factor loading exceeding 0.4 as meaningful. The analytical results are shown in Table 2.

We interpreted that factor 1 represented logical approaches because items such as "I am good at thinking about complicated problems in an organized way" had high factor loadings. We interpreted that factor 2 represented content-based verification strategies for information credibility because items such as "I try to check other web pages or information resources to verify content credibility" had high factor loadings. We interpreted that factor 3 represented inquisitiveness because items such as "I want to learn a lot by communicating various types of people" had high factor loadings. We interpreted that factor 4 represented tolerance for cognitive biases in information credibility judgment because items such as "I trust information on easy-to-understand web pages" had high factor loadings. We interpreted that factor 5 represented objectivity because items such as "I try to adopt an objective attitude when deciding something" had high factor loadings. We interpreted that factor 6 represented skill level in using web search engines because items such as "I use double-quotation operators for phrase query searches" had high factor loadings. We interpreted that factor 7 represented author-based verification strategies for information credibility because items such as "I try to verify the author's qualifications or credentials on web pages" had high factor loadings.

The Cronbach α coefficient was 0.88 for the "logical approach" factor, 0.87 for the "content-based verification strategy" factor, 0.88 for the "inquisitiveness" factor, 0.81 for the "tolerance for cognitive biases in credibility judgment" factor, 0.83 for the "objectivity" factor, 0.80 for the "skill level in using web search engines"

factor, and 0.76 for the "author-based verification strategy" factor. Through these α coefficient analyses, we confirmed that the items of each factor had internal consistency. In addition, most of the constructed factors and their interpretation were roughly equal to the elements of web access literacy we considered before conducting the online study, although the "reliance on evidence" element disappeared. Therefore, we think that the constructed factors demonstrated factor validity. From these results, we defined each constructed factor as a sub-scale of the web access literacy scale. Furthermore, we calculated web access literacy scores by averaging the item scores of each sub-scale.

4.2 Relationship between web access literacy scale and external criteria

Table 3 shows the score statistics for the web access literacy scale and its sub-scales. As shown, for the content-based verification strategy (3.62), logical approach (3.24), inquisitiveness (3.83), and objectivity (3.62) factors, the participants had positive responses (>3) on average. On the other hand, on average, the participants had negative responses (<3) for the author-based verification strategy (2.81), skill level in using web search engines (1.95), and tolerance for cognitive biases in credibility judgment (2.89) factors. This suggests that the participants had weaknesses relative to author-based verification strategy, skill level in using web search engines, tolerance for cognitive biases in information credibility judgment compared to other factors.

Figure 1 illustrates the correlation between the sub-scale scores. As can be seen, the content-based verification strategy factor is correlated with the author-based verification strategy factor ($r = 0.54$). Furthermore, there were correlations between the logical approach (L), inquisitiveness (I), and objectivity (O) factors, which contribute to critical thinking attitudes (L-I: 0.43; I-O: 0.45; O-L: 0.52).

Search task performance. To answer H1, we examined the correlation between the web access literacy score and the participant performance in critical web search tasks. First, we calculated the average precision of each participant for the tasks (mean: 0.412; standard deviation (SD): 0.209). Then, we analyzed the correlation between the average precisions and web access literacy scores; however, we did not confirm a correlation between them ($r = 0.04$, $p = 3.59e$-2). Thus, H1 was not supported.

Health literacy. To answer H2, we examined the correlation between eHEALs scores and web access literacy scale scores. The eHEALs scores were measured by averaging the scores for answers to questions 90-97 (mean: 2.92, SD: 0.662). A Pearson correlation analysis showed a weak correlation between the two literacy scores ($r = 0.32$, $p = 2.10e$-14< .001). The validity coefficient was 0.36. These results suggest that participants with a high web access literacy score were likely to have a high health literacy score. Thus, H2 was partially supported.

Trust in web information. To answer H3, we analyzed the correlation between trust in web information and the level of web access literacy. For this analysis, we calculated the average score of each participant for answers to questions 1-18 (mean: 3.32; SD: 0.452).

Table 2: Factor analysis results of the web access literacy scale (promax rotation; N = 534). Items with an asterisk are reverse code scale items.

Item	M	SD	Factor 1	Factor 2	Factor 3	Factor 4	Factor 5	Factor 6	Factor 7
Factor 1: Logical approach (α = .88)									
I am good at thinking about complicated problems in an organized way	3.25	0.96	.835	-.041	-.036	-.031	-.097	.024	.028
I am good at summarizing ideas	3.27	1.02	.754	-.067	.047	-.011	-.073	-.034	.046
I set a roadmap when thinking about something	3.70	0.91	.705	.036	-.065	.025	.024	-.124	.045
I am good at making constructive proposals	3.18	0.94	.700	-.187	-.001	.015	.034	-.012	.152
I am good at explaining so that anyone can understand me	2.92	0.98	.685	-.188	.035	-.047	-.021	.103	.157
I am confident about my ability to think precisely	3.25	0.89	.679	.023	-.012	-.076	-.025	-.035	.045
I get confused whenever thinking about complicated problems (*)	3.74	0.92	.620	.125	.056	-.051	-.034	-.016	-.184
I can maintain concentration while working on a problem	2.72	1.04	.600	-.095	-.037	.089	-.054	.078	-.031
I can continue to challenge tough problems	3.26	0.99	.508	.073	.204	-.017	-.094	-.006	-.010
I am easily distracted (*)	2.84	1.09	.484	-.077	-.122	.051	.109	-.035	-.113
I can look into a problem carefully	3.70	0.87	.480	.212	.044	-.011	.058	-.025	-.097
My colleagues often ask me to make judgments because I am fair	3.04	0.95	.415	-.062	.094	-.064	.206	.056	.100
Factor 2: Content-based verification strategy for information credibility (α = .87)									
I try to spend as much time as possible on web searches	3.54	0.87	-.002	.804	.049	-.023	-.105	.011	-.175
I try to modify search queries to examine web page content more intricately	3.90	0.84	-.114	.741	.004	-.017	-.024	-.014	-.041
I try to compare multiple web pages	4.17	0.76	-.079	.741	.024	-.004	-.040	-.013	-.078
I try to issue multiple search queries to collect information in a broad perspective	3.85	0.86	-.069	.720	.067	-.027	.008	.001	-.128
I try to check other web pages or information resources to verify content credibility	3.73	0.93	-.012	.687	-.084	-.018	-.039	-.079	.160
I try to check similar or the same information on other web pages	3.54	0.90	-.042	.684	-.067	-.081	-.011	-.100	.143
I try to check to see that the information is complete and comprehensive	3.21	0.91	-.038	.492	.028	.024	-.014	.006	.263
I try to browse web pages in lower- and higher-ranked web search results	3.12	0.93	-.072	.490	-.021	.109	.016	.088	.066
I try to obtain evidence to verify the information on web pages	3.36	0.96	.017	.488	-.035	.071	-.046	-.011	.355
I try evaluating whether views represented on web pages are facts or opinions	3.79	0.98	.023	.428	-.002	.069	.086	-.147	.320
Factor 3: Inquisitiveness (α = .88)									
I want to learn a lot by communicating with various types of people	3.84	1.02	-.052	-.027	.785	-.105	.003	-.018	.083
I want to learn various cultures	3.90	1.04	-.040	-.010	.724	.006	-.002	-.030	.055
I want to continue learning new things over my lifetime	4.07	0.94	.136	.027	.703	.048	-.052	-.058	.021
I want to learn as much as possible even if I am unsure if the information will be useful	3.81	1.05	.029	.029	.666	.087	.033	-.038	-.034
I am interested in people with opinions that differ from mine	3.76	1.00	-.089	-.082	.658	.013	.176	.060	.029
I like to challenge new things	3.67	1.07	.182	.051	.635	-.051	-.104	-.042	-.031
I want to learn more about any topic	3.62	1.05	.038	-.001	.615	.067	-.064	.092	-.053
I like to discuss with those who have opinions that differ from mine	3.44	1.11	-.053	-.113	.576	-.009	.178	.074	.074
Learning how foreigners think is useful	4.13	0.88	-.097	-.001	.570	-.083	.087	.000	.052
I try to ask about what I do not understand	4.01	0.93	.085	.169	.432	-.026	-.134	-.126	.098
Factor 4: Tolerance for biases in information credibility judgment (α = .81)									
I trust information that is shared by many users or liked on social networking websites (*)	3.04	0.88	-.049	.063	-.071	.718	.067	-.104	.056
I trust information that my friends share on social networking websites (*)	2.96	0.85	.010	.034	-.071	.695	.071	-.148	.004
I trust information that my followers share on social networking websites (*)	3.35	0.85	.026	.082	-.025	.608	.041	-.171	.022
I trust information on easy-to-understand web pages (*)	2.51	0.71	.084	-.073	.016	.543	-.085	.036	.046
I trust posts that someone indicates are the best answers on Q/A sites (*)	2.80	0.93	-.016	.017	.020	.511	-.028	-.006	.043
I trust information on web pages with titles such as "the 20 best XXs" (*)	3.24	1.00	-.075	-.002	-.019	.507	.037	.084	.092
I trust information on web pages with a high rank on search engines (*)	2.66	0.81	-.068	.048	.002	.499	.014	.095	.068
I trust products or services with good reputations, on average, on review sites (*)	2.68	0.95	.071	-.118	-.027	.481	-.009	.068	-.003
I trust information on well-designed web pages (*)	2.77	0.68	.052	-.072	-.002	.474	-.027	.041	.038
Factor 5: Objectivity (α = .83)									
I try to adopt an objective attitude when deciding something	3.81	0.87	.041	-.107	.051	-.070	.710	.053	.040
I try to make fair judgments	3.64	0.90	.022	-.054	.068	-.072	.691	-.010	-.048
I try to think from multiple viewpoints	3.75	0.88	.005	.007	.170	.020	.653	.019	.030
I try to reflect if I have unconscious biased opinions	3.72	0.93	-.139	.030	.189	-.054	.599	.084	.030
I stick to my position when thinking about something (*)	3.60	0.93	.197	-.044	-.044	.058	.544	-.114	-.030
I have difficulty being neutral when discussing my opinions with others (*)	2.91	0.98	.011	-.015	-.165	.043	.541	.035	-.129
I try to listen to those with different opinions	3.91	0.87	-.012	-.005	.229	-.036	.530	-.060	-.015
Factor 6: Skill level in using web search engines (α = .80)									
I use double-quotation operators for phrase query searches	1.80	0.99	.050	-.082	-.004	.011	.024	.767	-.084
I use the NOT operator to exclude web pages containing specific keywords	1.80	0.93	-.007	.046	-.060	.112	.062	.735	-.112
I use a search tool to filter web pages updated within a specific time frame	1.76	0.93	-.084	-.047	.027	.011	.063	.720	.009
I use a search tool to filter web search results by specific domains or sites	1.61	0.80	-.016	-.092	-.029	.029	-.033	.679	.112
I check web page domains before clicking web search results	2.25	1.08	.028	-.040	-.023	-.026	-.013	.485	.213
I use a publication date filter to obtain new web pages	2.50	1.09	-.063	.094	.068	-.002	-.038	.449	.101
Factor 7: Author-based verification strategy for information credibility (α = .76)									
I try to verify the author's qualifications or credentials on web pages	2.63	1.03	.023	-.050	.088	.010	-.114	-.019	.714
I try to identify the author of the web page	2.97	1.09	.036	.057	.020	.071	-.120	-.049	.703
I try to look for a stamp of approval or recommendation from third parties on web pages	2.72	1.00	-.090	.021	.035	-.030	.093	.067	.573
I try to check if contact information is provided for the author	2.64	1.01	-.012	.180	-.001	.015	-.097	.087	.441
I try to consider the author's goals/objectives in posting information on the web	3.07	1.10	.129	.114	-.072	.132	.072	-.016	.431
Sum of squared factor loadings			5.68	5.64	5.04	4.13	3.30	2.27	2.19
Contribution ratio			0.20	0.20	0.18	0.15	0.12	0.08	0.08

Table 3: Score statistics of web access literacy scale and its sub-scales. Numbers in parentheses are the number of items in each scale. Each score ranges from 1 to 5.

Scale	Mean	SD
Content-based verification strategy (10)	3.62	0.39
Author-based verification strategy (5)	2.81	0.75
Skill level in using web search engines (6)	1.95	0.69
Tolerance for biases in web information credibility judgment (9)	2.89	0.54
Logical approach (12)	3.24	0.64
Inquisitiveness (10)	3.83	0.71
Objectivity (7)	3.62	0.64
Web access literacy (59)	3.23	0.39

Table 4: Effects of independent variables on trust in web information (adjusted R^2 = 0.45, $F(7, 521)$ = 61.9, p = 2.2e-16) (***: significance level at 0.001, **: at 0.01, and *: at 0.05)

Variables	β coefficient	t-value	p-value
Content-based verification strategy	.007	0.03	0.81
Author-based verification strategy	-.055	-2.21	*
Tolerance for biases in credibility judgment	-.539	-19.4	***
Skill level in using web search engines	-0.02	-0.88	0.38
Logical approach	.066	2.33	*
Inquisitiveness	.015	0.60	0.55
Objectivity	-0.03	-1.10	0.27

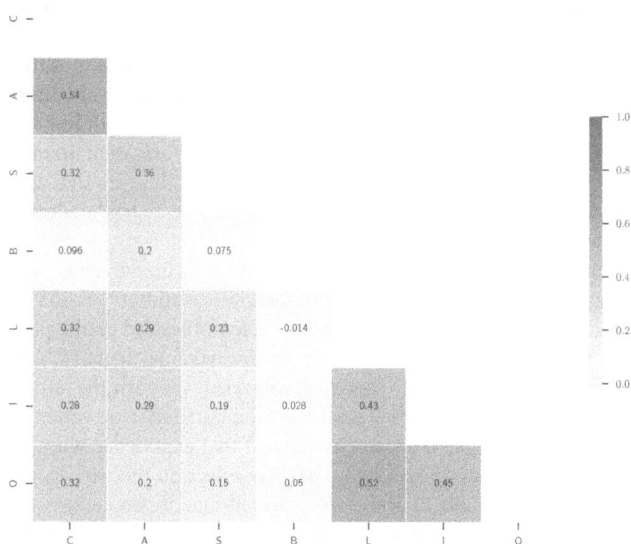

Figure 1: Correlation between sub-scales of the web access literacy Scale (C: content-based verification strategy; A: author-based verification strategy; S: skill level in using web search engines; B: bias tolerance; L: logical approach; I: inquisitiveness; O: objectivity)

A Pearson correlation analysis showed a weak negative correlation between trust in web information and the web access literacy score ($r = -0.20, p < .001$). Here, the validity coefficient was -0.23. These results suggest that participants with a high web access literacy score were likely to not trust web information.

We performed a multiple regression analysis to examine the relationship between trust in web information and the sub-scales of web access literacy. Table 4 shows the results of the regression analysis, where the dependent variable was the average score of answers to questions 1-18 (trust in web information) and the independent variables were the web access literacy sub-scale scores. As

can be seen, the adjusted R^2 was 0.45, which is considered a moderate value. We also observed statistical significance for author-based verification strategy, tolerance for cognitive biases in credibility judgment, and logical approach. In particular, the β coefficient's abstract value relative to tolerance for biases in credibility judgment was much greater than those of the other sub-scales ($\beta = -0.539$). These results suggest that participants with high scores relative to tolerance for cognitive biases in web information credibility judgment were not likely to trust web information.

In conclusion, we think that the results of the correlation and multiple regression analyses partially supported H3.

Learning activity. To answer H4 and H5, we examined the relationships among web access literacy, educational background, and experience with information literacy classes. For this analysis, we focused on 529 participants who provided details about their educational background (five participants provided no answer). We then classified the participants who graduated from or currently belong to universities or graduate schools into a *university-educated* group. The other participants were classified into a *not university-educated* group. Finally, we examined their web access literacy scores.

Figure 2 shows the mean web access literacy scores according to educational background and experience with information literacy classes. According to the figure, on average, *university-educated* participants who have experience with information literacy classes obtained higher web access literacy scores than participants without the same experience (87 participants with experience: 3.32; 210 participants without experience: 3.19). We observed the same trend in the *not university-educated* group (34 participants with experience: 3.41; 198 participants without experience: 3.19).

We employed a two-way ANOVA with educational background and experience with information literacy classes as factors. The results revealed that experience with information literacy classes affected the web access literacy scores ($F(1, 525)$ = 8.82, $p < 0.01$). On the other hand, against our expectation, participants did not exhibit statistical differences due to their educational background ($F(1, 525)$ = 7.7e-5, p = 0.993). In addition, we did not find statistical significance relative to the interaction between educational background and experience with information literacy classes ($F(1, 525)$ = 1.07, p = 0.301). From these results, we can say

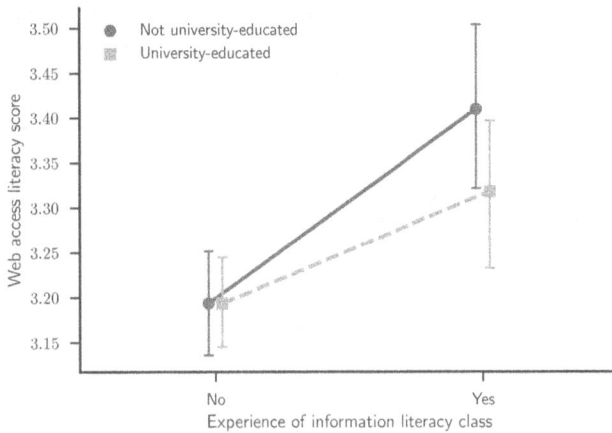

Figure 2: Web access literacy scores according to educational background and experience with information literacy classes

that at least experience with information literacy classes had positive impact on the web access literacy scores. In other words, relative to experiences with information literacy classes, H5 was supported, while H4 was not supported relative to educational background.

For a more detailed analysis, we examined the score differences related to the web access literacy sub-scales caused by experience with information literacy classes. Table 5 shows seven of the sub-scale scores of participants with/without experience with information literacy classes on average. As can be seen, the mean scores of the following sub-scales for participants with experience were significantly greater than those of participants without experience: content-based verification strategy (3.74 vs. 3.58), author-based verification strategy (2.95 vs. 2.76), skill level in using web search engines (2.12 vs. 1.90), logical approach (3.35 vs. 3.21), and objectivity (3.71 vs. 3.59). On the other hand, experience with information literacy classes did not affect tolerance for biases relative to credibility assessment and objectivity. Although we observed statistical significances relative to these sub-scales, the mean scores for the author-based verification strategy and skill level in using web search engines were not high, even for participants having experience with information literacy classes (<3).

5 DISCUSSION

5.1 Reliability and validity

We constructed the web access literacy scale and evaluated its reliability and validity in an online study with participants obtained using a crowdsourcing service. Through factor analysis, we observed that the web access literacy scale comprised the following seven sub-scales (Table 2).

- Content-based verification strategy for web information
- Author-based verification strategy for web information
- Skill level in using web search engines
- Tolerance for cognitive biases in web information credibility judgment

- Logical approach
- Inquisitiveness
- Objectivity

As shown in Table 2, the Cronbach's α coefficient values for all of the sub-scales exceeded 0.7. Therefore, we consider that the web access literacy scale has no problem relative to reliability.

Prior to conducting the online study, we expected that the searching/browsing strategies for web information credibility judgment elements would be contained in the web access literacy scale. However, the results of the factor analysis showed that the items of the two strategy elements were classified into other new concepts, i.e., content-based and author-based verification strategies. In addition, the *reliance on evidence* element disappeared in the extracted sub-scales. On the other hand, we observed the other five web access literacy elements in the extracted sub-scales. Therefore, we consider that the construct validity of web access literacy was moderately confirmed.

In the criterion-validity analyses, we observed a weak positive correlation between the web access literacy scores and health literacy scale scores ($r = 0.32$ in Section 4.2). Note that health literacy is considered a specialized type of web access information literacy for medical topics. Therefore, the existence of this positive correlation indicates that the web access literacy scale has moderate criterion validity.

Furthermore, we observed that the web access literacy score was negatively correlated with trust in web information ($r = -0.20$). Prior to conducting the online study, we hypothesized that, if people have web access literacy, they do not have particularly high trust in web information. Therefore, this result supports the notion that the web access literacy scale has moderate criterion validity.

Similarly, the ANOVA results showed that experience with information literacy classes had a positive effect on the web access literacy score (Table 5). Here, we expected that, if people have attended information literacy classes, their web access literacy could be high. Therefore, the ANOVA results also support the notion that the web access literacy scale has criterion validity.

On the other hand, the ANOVA results did not support a correlation between the level of web access literacy and educational background, although we had expected that learning activity in higher education would enhance the essential knowledge and skills for critical web searching/browsing. One possible interpretation is that we should focus on the actual learning activity rather than educational background. For example, some university-educated participants may have experience in research projects where survey and logical thinking skills can be trained, while others may not have had such experiences at their university. When we focused on experience with information literacy classes, the results of the online study indicated that such experience had a significant effect on the web access literacy score.

Furthermore, against our expectation, the online study revealed that there was no correlation between task performance relative to searching for correct answers and the web access literacy score. A possible cause for this result is task design and the method used to evaluate the literacy. In the online study, we expected that if the participants had web access literacy, their task answer accuracy

Table 5: Mean sub-scale scores according to experience with information literacy class. Numbers in parentheses are standard deviations (***: significance level at 0.001, **: at 0.01, *: at 0.05, and ·: at 0.1).

| Sub-scale | Experienced in taking literacy classes | | |
	Yes (123 participants)	No (411 participants)	p-value
Content-based verification strategy	3.74 (0.56)	3.58 (0.62)	**
Author-based verification strategy	2.95 (0.73)	2.76 (0.75)	**
Skill level in using web search engines	2.12 (0.74)	1.90 (0.67)	**
Tolerance for cognitive biases in web information credibility judgment	2.86 (0.56)	2.90 (0.53)	0.54
Logical approach	3.35 (0.54)	3.21 (0.66)	*
Inquisitiveness	4.03 (0.69)	3.78 (0.70)	***
Objectivity	3.71 (0.65)	3.59 (0.63)	·
Web access literacy	3.34 (0.37)	3.19 (0.40)	***

rate would be high. However, some participants may have provided incorrect answers, even if they had web access literacy and scrutinized web pages in the task process (and vice versa). Therefore, we consider that using search task performance is not appropriate to evaluate web access literacy. First, it can be quite difficult to predict critical web search/browsing performance using a questionnaire-based web access literacy scale because the scale relies on user's metacognition of their knowledge, skills, and attitudes relative to critical web search/browsing. In other words, web access literacy does not always predict the real ability to use knowledge, skills, and attitudes. Therefore, we must also analyze user behavior data to understand how and how frequently users verify information credibility during web search/browsing by developing a method to directly predict the critical web information seeking performance.

5.2 Implications for web access literacy development

By analyzing the web access literacy scores of the 534 participants, we found that the participants had weaknesses in the following factors: author-based verification strategy (2.81), skill level in using web search engines (1.95), and tolerance for cognitive biases in web information credibility judgment (2.89) (Table 3). Interestingly, although most participants reported that they frequently attempt to verify web information credibility based on web page content (3.62), they reported that they did not consider web page authors. This finding is critical because even non-experts can publish information on the web. In addition, we found that most participants did not use advanced web search engine options effectively, even though such options are helpful to obtain current web information and collect evidence for credibility judgment.

Figure 2 and Table 5 suggest that information literacy classes can contribute to improved web access literacy, particularly relative to content-based verification strategy (3.58→3.74), author-based verification strategy (2.76→2.95), skill level in using web search engines (1.90→2.12), logical approach (3.21→3.35), and objectivity (3.59→3.71). On the other hand, as shown in Table 5, we observed that experience with information literacy classes had no significant effect on tolerance for cognitive biases in web information credibility judgment. Bias tolerance in information credibility

judgment is very important for rational and critical judgment relative to web information credibility. As explained in Section 2, researchers have observed that web users have various cognitive biases during web search/browsing, such as position and readability biases. On the other hand, Table 4 suggests that people with bias tolerance may pay attention to web information credibility. The above findings suggest that it is necessary to improve the design of classes related to information literacy to overcome weaknesses in web access literacy, including author-verification strategies and bias tolerance in credibility judgment. We think that the web access literacy scale designed in this study can be used to benchmark and improve information literacy education.

In addition, we must develop methods and applications that general users can use to reflect on and develop web access literacy skills outside of educational institutions. One possible application is a system that enables users to reflect on their behavior when using information systems. For example, Malacria et al. proposed *Skillometers*, which visualizes usage of shortcut keys for comparison with expert usage [13]. Furthermore, Bateman et al. proposed *SearchDashboard*, a search user interface that summarizes user search histories. They indicated that SearchDashboard can help users modify their search behavior to improve search performance [2]. In the future, we plan to develop a browser extension to visualize user behavior tendencies in order to encourage people to improve deficiencies relative to critical web information seeking.

6 CONCLUSION

In this paper, we have proposed a web access literacy scale to assess a user's ability to scrutinize web information and gather correct information from the web using information access systems, such as web search engines. To evaluate the proposed literacy scale, we conducted an online study with participants obtained using a crowdsourcing service. Through factor analysis, we confirmed that the proposed web access literacy scale comprises the following sub-scales:

- Content-based verification strategy for web information
- Author-based verification strategy for web information
- Skill level in using web search engines

- Tolerance for cognitive biases in web information credibility judgment
- Logical approach
- Inquisitiveness
- Objectivity

The analytical results indicate that the web access literacy scale and its sub-scales demonstrate both reliability and validity.

From the statistics of the web access literacy scale, we observed that web users may not pay significant attention to web page authors and their expertise when judging information credibility. Furthermore, we found that users may have weaknesses relative to the use of web search engines and tolerance for cognitive biases that appear when assessing credibility of web information. In the future, we plan to develop a browser extension to enable web users to visualize and reflect on their strengths and weaknesses relative to web information credibility judgment.

Abundant misinformation exists on the web, and many people use the web as an essential information resource; thus, it is possible that they will be unknowingly misled by incorrect information. We believe that the results of our study will support the design of systems or educational classes to encourage users to reflect on and improve their web access literacy to achieve improved critical information seeking skills.

ACKNOWLEDGMENTS

The work was supported in part by the Grants-in-Aid for Scientific Research (17K17832, 16H01756, 16K16156, 15H01718, 16H02906, 25240050) from the MEXT of Japan.

REFERENCES

[1] American Library Association and Association for College and Research Libraries. 2000. *Information Literacy Competency Standards for Higher Education*. Technical Report.
[2] Scott Bateman, Jaime Teevan, and Ryen W White. 2012. The Search Dashboard: How Reflection and Comparison Impact Search Behavior. In *Proceedings of the 30th ACM International Conference on Human Factors in Computing Systems (CHI 2012)*. ACM, 1785-1794.
[3] Charles L A Clarke, Eugene Agichtein, Susan Dumais, and Ryen W White. 2007. The Influence of Caption Features on Clickthrough Patterns in Web Search. In *Proceedings of the 30th ACM SIGIR International Conference (SIGIR 2007)*. ACM, 135-142.
[4] Xin Luna Dong, Evgeniy Gabrilovich, Kevin Murphy, Van Dang, Wilko Horn, Camillo Lugaresi, Shaohua Sun, and Wei Zhang. 2015. Knowledge-based trust: estimating the trustworthiness of web sources. In *Proceedings of the VLDB Endowment (VLDB 2015)*. ACM.
[5] Rob Ennals, Beth Trushkowsky, and John Mark Agosta. 2010. Highlighting disputed claims on the web. In *Proceedings of the 19th International World Wide Web Conference (WWW 2010)*. ACM, 341-350.
[6] Robert H. Ennis. 1987. A taxonomy of critical thinking dispositions and abilities. In *Series of books in psychology. Teaching thinking skills: Theory and practice*, J. B. Baron and R. J. Sternberg (Eds.). W H Freeman/Times Books/ Henry Holt & Co, New York, 9-26.
[7] Peter A Facione, Carol A Sanchez, Noreen C Facione, and Joanne Gainen. 1995. The disposition toward critical thinking. *The Journal of General Education* (1995), 1-25.
[8] Morgan Harvey, Claudia Hauff, and David Elsweiler. 2015. Learning by Example: Training Users with High-quality Query Suggestions. In *Proceedings of the 38th ACM International ACM SIGIR Conference (SIGIR 2015)*. ACM, 133-142.
[9] Takashi Kusumi, Rumi Hirayama, and Yoshihisa Kashima. 2017. Risk Perception and Risk Talk: The Case of the Fukushima Daiichi Nuclear Radiation Risk. *Risk Analysis* 37, 12 (2017), 2305-2320.
[10] Chee Wee Leong and Silviu Cucerzan. 2012. Supporting Factual Statements with Evidence from the Web. In *Proceedings of the 21st ACM International Conference on Information and Knowledge Management (CIKM 2012)*. ACM, 1153-1162.
[11] UC Berkeley Library. 2014. Evaluating resources. http://guides.lib.berkeley.edu/evaluating-resources
[12] Gitte Lindgaard, Cathy Dudek, Devjani Sen, Livia Sumegi, and Patrick Noonan. 2011. An Exploration of Relations between Visual Appeal, Trustworthiness and Perceived Usability of Homepages. *ACM Transactions on Computer-Human Interaction (TOCHI)* 18, 1 (2011), 1-30.
[13] Sylvain Malacria, Joey Scarr, Andy Cockburn, Carl Gutwin, and Tovi Grossman. 2013. Skillometers: Reflective Widgets that Motivate and Help Users to Improve Performance. In *Proceedings of the 26th annual ACM symposium on User interface software and technology (UIST 2013)*. ACM, 321-330.
[14] Marc Meola. 2004. Chucking the Checklist: A Contextual Approach to Teaching Undergraduates Web-Site Evaluation. *portal: Libraries and the Academy* 4, 3 (2004), 331-344.
[15] Miriam J Metzger, Andrew J Flanagin, Alex Markov, Rebekah Grossman, and Monica Bulger. 2015. Believing the Unbelievable: Understanding Young People's Information Literacy Beliefs and Practices in the United States. *Journal of Children and Media* 9, 3 (2015), 325-348.
[16] Miriam J Metzger, Andrew J Flanagin, and Lara Zwarun. 2003. College student Web use, perceptions of information credibility, and verification behavior. *Computers & Education* 41, 3 (2003), 271-290.
[17] Meredith Ringel Morris, Jaime Teevan, and Katrina Panovich. 2010. What Do People Ask Their Social Networks, and Why?: A Survey Study of Status Message Q&A Behavior. In *Proceedings of the 28th ACM International Conference on Human Factors in Computing Systems (CHI 2010)*. ACM, 1739-1748.
[18] Satoshi Nakamura, Shinji Konishi, Adam Jatowt, Hiroaki Ohshima, Hiroyuki Kondo, Taro Tezuka, Satoshi Oyama, and Katsumi Tanaka. 2007. Trustworthiness Analysis of Web Search Results. In *Proceedings of the 11th European conference on Research and Advanced Technology for Digital Libraries (ECDL 2007)*. 38-49.
[19] Cameron D Norman and Harvey A Skinner. 2006. eHEALS: The eHealth Literacy Scale. *Journal of Medical Internet Research* 8, 4 (2006), e27-10.
[20] Ernest T. Pascarella. 1989. The development of critical thinking: Does college make a difference? *Journal of College Student Development* 30, 1 (1989), 19-26.
[21] Jeff Pasternack and Dan Roth. 2013. Latent credibility analysis. In *Proceedings of the 22nd International World Wide Web Conference (WWW 2013)*. ACM, 1009-1020.
[22] Elizabeth Sillence, Pam Briggs, Lesley Fishwick, and Peter Harris. 2004. Trust and Mistrust of Online Health Sites. In *Proceedings of the 22nd ACM International Conference on on Human Factors in Computing Systems (CHI 2004)*. ACM, 663-670.
[23] Ryen W White, Susan T Dumais, and Jaime Teevan. 2009. Characterizing the Influence of Domain Expertise on Web Search Behavior. In *Proceedings of the 2nd ACM International Conference on Web Search and Data Mining (WSDM 2009)*. ACM, 132-141.
[24] Ryen W White and Eric Horvitz. 2015. Belief Dynamics and Biases in Web Search. *ACM Transactions on Information Systems* 33, 4 (2015), 1-46.
[25] Yusuke Yamamoto and Satoshi Shimada. 2016. Can Disputed Topic Suggestion Enhance User Consideration of Information Credibility in Web Search?. In *Proceedings of the 27th ACM Conference on Hypertext and Social Media (HT 2016)*. ACM, 169-177.
[26] Yusuke Yamamoto and Katsumi Tanaka. 2011. Enhancing Credibility Judgment of Web Search Results. In *Proceedings of the 29th ACM Conference on Human Factors in Computing Systems (CHI 2011)*. ACM, 1235-1244.
[27] Yusuke Yamamoto and Takehiro Yamamoto. 2018. Query Priming for Promoting Critical Thinking in Web Search. In *Proceedings of the 3rd ACM SIGIR Conference on Human Information Interaction and Retrieval (CHIIR 2018) (to appear)*. ACM, 1-10.
[28] Yisong Yue, Rajan Patel, and Hein Roehrig. 2010. Beyond Position Bias: Examining Result Attractiveness as a Source of Presentation Bias in Clickthrough Data. In *Proceedings of the 19th International World Wide Web Conference (WWW 2010)*. 1011-1018.

Investigating the Effects of Google's Search Engine Result Page in Evaluating the Credibility of Online News Sources

Emma Lurie
Computer Science Department
Wellesley College
emma.lurie@wellesley.edu

Eni Mustafaraj
Computer Science Department
Wellesley College
eni.mustafaraj@wellesley.edu

ABSTRACT

Recent research has suggested that young users are not particularly skilled in assessing the credibility of online content. A follow-up study comparing students to fact checkers noticed that students spend too much time on the page itself, while fact checkers performed "lateral reading", searching other sources. We have taken this line of research one step further and designed a study in which participants were instructed to do lateral reading for credibility assessment by inspecting Google's search engine result page (SERP) of unfamiliar news sources. In this paper, we summarize findings from interviews with 30 participants. A component of the SERP noticed regularly by the participants is the so-called Knowledge Panel, which provides contextual information about the news source being searched. While this is expected, there are other parts of the SERP that participants use to assess the credibility of the source, for example, the freshness of top stories, the panel of recent tweets, or a verified Twitter account. Given the importance attached to the presence of the Knowledge Panel, we discuss how variability in its content affected participants' opinions. Additionally, we perform data collection of the SERP page for a large number of online news sources and compare them. Our results indicate that there are widespread inconsistencies in the coverage and quality of information included in Knowledge Panels.

CCS CONCEPTS

• Information systems → Web search engines; *Search interfaces*; • Human-centered computing → *Empirical studies in HCI*;

KEYWORDS

Google; search; news sources; credibility; user studies

ACM Reference Format:
Emma Lurie and Eni Mustafaraj. 2018. Investigating the Effects of Google's Search Engine Result Page in Evaluating the Credibility of Online News Sources. In *Proceedings of 10th ACM Conference on Web Science (WebSci '18)*. ACM, New York, NY, USA, 10 pages. https://doi.org/10.1145/3201064.3201095

1 INTRODUCTION

Researchers have been sounding the alarm for years that being born in the Internet age doesn't make one better at assessing content

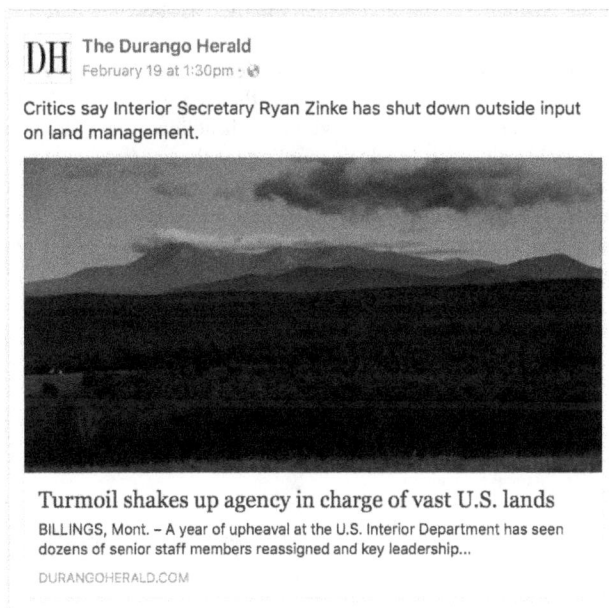

Figure 1: Screenshot of a Facebook news story card, the common way to display news in a user's News Feed. Such a card contains tidbits of the content as well as the name and URL of the source.

encountered online [4]. "Digital natives" are mostly a myth, as task-based studies have demonstrated [18, 19]. The 2016 large-scale study by the Stanford History Education Group (SHEG), which assessed 7804 middle school to college-aged participants on their ability to judge online information, discovered troubling results [9]. Students couldn't distinguish real news articles from promoted content, information by biased think tanks from peer reviewed research publications, and were deceived by domain endings such as .org. The authors of the SHEG study followed up with another study [32], in which they compared how fact-checkers and students approach the task of evaluating the credibility of an unknown online source. They observed that students spent most of the time on the website of the source, accessing different pages and trying to reason about its credibility. Meanwhile, fact checkers engaged in what the researchers call "lateral reading," leaving the site to google the organization, its associated members, and to gather information from other sources.

How effective is "lateral reading" for users who are not trained in fact-checking? Given the public calls for teaching media literacy [5], it's important to investigate the value of different proposed approaches. To answer the question of the effectiveness of googling as a literacy skill, we conducted a user study with 30 participants (age 18-22), in which they performed "lateral reading" to assess the credibility of three U.S.-based online news sources that were **unfamiliar** to them: *The Durango Herald*, *The Tennessean*, and *The Christian Times*. The scenario we imagined and shared with the participants is the following: most users encounter news stories in their social media feeds such as Facebook and Twitter in the form of "story cards", which contain a title, some text from the article, an image, the name of the website and the URL, as shown in Figure 1. Many of the fake news sites that were successful in spreading misinformation during the 2016 U.S. Election took advantage of Facebook's news cards feature, to make their stories look legitimate [14]. Thus, encountering cards with news headlines from unknown sources is a situation in which googling for the source is a logical step and is what literacy experts suggest [6]. Accordingly, we asked our study participants to google the three above-mentioned news sources and recorded how they used the Google search engine page result (SERP) to reason about the credibility of each website.

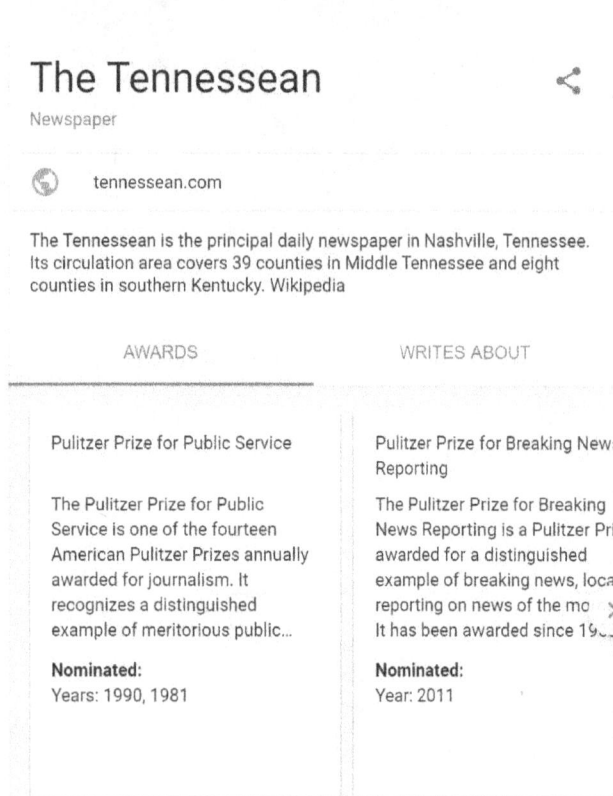

The Tennessean

Newspaper

tennessean.com

The Tennessean is the principal daily newspaper in Nashville, Tennessee. Its circulation area covers 39 counties in Middle Tennessee and eight counties in southern Kentucky. Wikipedia

AWARDS	WRITES ABOUT
Pulitzer Prize for Public Service	Pulitzer Prize for Breaking News Reporting
The Pulitzer Prize for Public Service is one of the fourteen American Pulitzer Prizes annually awarded for journalism. It recognizes a distinguished example of meritorious public...	The Pulitzer Prize for Breaking News Reporting is a Pulitzer Pri awarded for a distinguished example of breaking news, loca reporting on news of the mo It has been awarded since 19...
Nominated: Years: 1990, 1981	**Nominated:** Year: 2011

Figure 2: Partial screenshot of Google's SERP for The Tennessean. This box is known as a Knowledge Panel. In addition to a snippet retrieved from the Wikipedia page, it also contains two tabs titled "Awards" and "Writes About". Not all Knowledge Panels of newspapers contain these two tabs. This feature was announced on Nov 7, 2017 [33].

Our major findings from this study are the following:

(1) Participants find Knowledge Panels valuable in assessing credibility, especially when they contain the "Awards" tab. (Please refer to the Knowledge Panel displayed in Figure 2. We discuss Knowledge Panels later in the paper).

(2) Knowledge Panels are insufficient to make definitive credibility assessments, and sometimes generate more confusion.

(3) "Top Stories" and social media feeds provide meaningful signals for participants to incorporate into their assessment.

Given the importance that participants attributed to Knowledge Panels, we undertook a quantitative study of three different datasets of online news sources to investigate what information the SERP contains for each news source. We performed the data collection twice and compared the results. A major finding is that while in the January 2018 dataset the Knowledge Panel for some online sources contained a tab on "reviewed claims", presenting information from fact-checkers (see Figure 3), in February 2018, Knowledge Panels no longer contained "reviewed claims". This disappearance of useful information is worthy of notice and discussion. There is speculation in the media that Google bowed to political pressure[1] and removed the information from the Knowledge Panel.

To the best of our knowledge, this is the first research paper that studies how users perform on lateral reading tasks through Google, as well as the first paper that focuses on the role of Knowledge Panels for evaluating the credibility of an online news source.

The rest of the paper is organized as follows: we provide an overview of online credibility research in the past years, focusing on how young people evaluate sources. We describe in detail elements of the Google SERP for a news source, to show what information is available to users when they google for a source. Our user study is then explained in detail, with a discussion of both its findings and limitations. We report the results of the SERP data collection for three datasets of online news sources on two different dates and highlight the differences. Finally, we conclude with a discussion of Google's role in news literacy efforts, and the role that the research community can play in monitoring the quality of SERP information.

2 RELATED RESEARCH

Credibility is not an easy concept to pinpoint and it is studied in many research communities. The most recent literature survey on credibility in information systems [16], which extends previous work [13], identifies trustworthiness, expertise, quality, and reliability as its ingredients. In this section, we confine our review on credibility on the web, as well as on the inherent trust that users put on search engines like Google.

2.1 Credibility on the Web

Early research in communication studies defined credibility as the believability of a piece of information based on its content and source [22], and treated it as dependent on perceived expertise and trustworthiness [11]. Many studies emphasized that evaluating credibility on the Web is most successful when examining the following five criteria: accuracy, authority, objectivity, currency, and coverage [26]. These criteria are often part of checklists that are given to students by research librarians, who always advise

---

[1]https://www.poynter.org/news/blame-bugs-not-partisanship-google-wrongly-appending-fact-check-daily-caller

2.2 Search Engine Result Page

The Search Engine Result Page (SERP) has been studied by both academics and Internet marketers. In 2005, Internet marketing firm Enquiro coined the term "Google Golden Triangle" after noticing in an eye-tracking study that users' eyes naturally focus on the upper left of the SERP and travel in a small area down and around the SERP forming a triangle that only extends to a few search results [21]. However, as more heterogeneous SERPs began to emerge with the inclusion of images, videos, and the Knowledge Graph content on SERP, a 2014 study found that the "Golden Triangle" no longer existed, users now examine the SERP more vertically due to (1) mobile device scrolling habits and (2) top organic results are no longer always found in the upper left-hand corner due to the added elements on the SERP [8, 25].

Another line of research has illustrated that college students trust Google's ranking of SERP results [20] and are willing to click on the first couple of results, even when more relevant links were ranked towards the bottom of the SERP [27]. Such studies have been repeated with younger children, indicating that age is a factor in SERP behavior [17]. As more rich media snippets and Knowledge Graph information is found on the SERP, [24] explored the relationship between fewer results on the SERP and an increased attention to the higher ranked organic results. [30] explores the connection between high-quality Google SERPs and Wikipedia content.

Given the recency of Knowledge Panels, there is no current research that has assessed its effects on user behavior, something we are trying to partially address in this study.

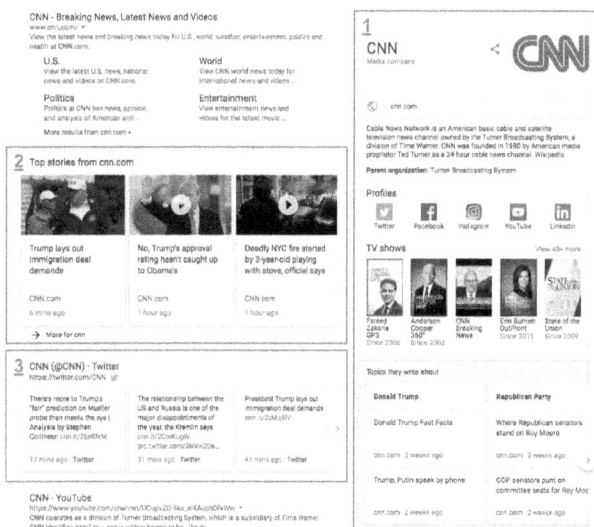

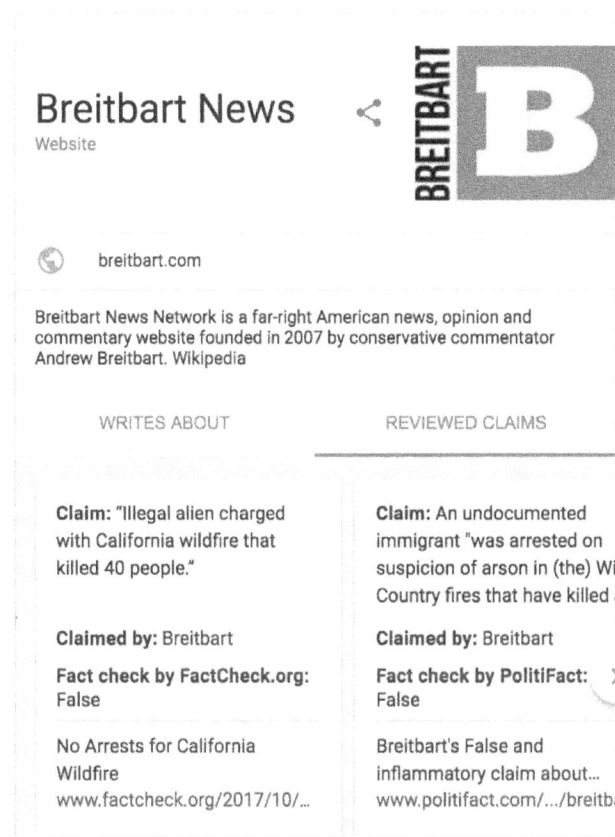

Figure 3: January 2018 screenshot for the Knowledge Panel for Breitbart.com, showing the "reviewed claims" section that contains fact-checked claims. As of February 2018, the "reviewed claims" section is not part of the panel anymore.

skepticism in dealing with sources. Current media literacy efforts have evolved from the "checklist" to "lateral reading", i.e. googling claims or stories to verify information [7, 32].

Especially in the 2000s, the public perception of the Internet was that of a source as credible as television, radio, and magazines, and Internet users reported rarely verifying what they read on the Web [11, 31]. Users are even less likely to perform time intensive source verification techniques, which are often the more deterministic measures of credibility [26]. Given this known user aversion to verification work, communication researchers such as [26] have proposed several tools such as credibility seals [12] or rating systems [28] to assist users in evaluating credibility.

When over 2,500 users were asked to describe the features they actually used to determine website credibility, almost half mentioned "site presentation" as a key factor [12]. In general, users seem to have a *positive evaluation bias*, thinking that sites are more credible than they actually are [1]. However, with expert suggestions on the credibility of Web sources at their disposal, users are able to make better decisions [1]. This idea of added context improving decision-making motivated our interest in investigating Knowledge Panels closely.

Figure 4: A screenshot of the Google search page results for CNN. It contains (1) the Knowledge Panel, (2) a section on top stories; and (3) a section of recent tweets. The panel "Topics they write about" contains stories from "2 weeks ago", indicating that topics are not "discovered" on the fly.

3 SERP: AN ANATOMY

Searching information on Google reveals the complex and increasingly intertwined behavior of three different actors:

(1) **Google's algorithms**, which, depending on the query, can display additional information on the SERP, e.g., Knowledge Panels which can be populated in different ways, top stories, tweets, direct answers, etc. (see Figure 4 for an example of some of these components);

(2) **users**, whose informational needs are revealed in the panel of "searches related to query phrase" (see Figure 5) commonly located at the bottom of a search page; or in a panel titled "People also ask" (see Figure 6), which occasionally appears either at the top or middle of a search results page.

(3) **online publishers**, whose links to relevant content appear in the search results. Such publishers include Wikipedia, content from which is displayed in the Knowledge Panels, as well as other publishers who are savvy in creating lists, tables, or answering common questions, often by using known search engine optimization techniques.

While for a long time the Google search page operated as a transactional "middleman": receiving a request (a query phrase) and displaying a list of organic results ranked from 1 to 10 (with ads on the side), things changed in 2012 with the introduction of the Knowledge Graph [29]. The Knowledge Graph pulls factual information about things in the real world from databases such as Wikipedia, Freebase, CIA World Factbook, etc., and shows them in separate panels in different parts of the SERP. Often, a user doesn't need to click on any of the links of a SERP, because these featured panels contain the answer to their query. Google regards the purpose of the SERP as both answering a query and a way of discovering other related things, therefore, the number of featured panels (also known as snippets) has increased over time [15]. We will discuss in the following two of the most prominent and sometimes controversial panels: the Knowledge Panel and the direct answer panel.

3.1 Knowledge Panels

Examples of the Knowledge Panel are shown in three figures. Figure 2 displays the panel for *The Tennessean*, Figure 3 shows the panel for *Breitbart News*, and the screenshot in Figure 4 contains the panel for *CNN*. These panels are different, with the CNN panel providing more information, including pictures of its TV anchors, and links to its social web presence. All three panels contain a section on "Writes About" which is populated with links of stories grouped in topics, though our figures only reveal the topics for CNN, for example, "Donald Trump", "Republican Party", etc. For several newspapers, such as *NY Times*, *Washington Post*, and other, the Knowledge Panel contains a tab dedicated to "Awards", which we also see in Figure 2 for *The Tennessean*. The existence of the "Awards" tab can be considered as a way to signal their authority in the field of journalism. For a two-month period, November 2017-January 2018, the Knowledge Panel also contained a tab on "Reviewed Claims." This tab included claims published by the source and reviewed by third-party fact-checkers such as Snopes or Politifact with a verdict of being found "True" or "False" (or something in between). An example can be seen in Figure 3.

Figure 5: A screenshot from a Google search page. At the bottom of most search result pages is a section titled "searches related to query phrase", in this particular case, the query is "best rated newspapers". This portion provides insights into users' informational needs.

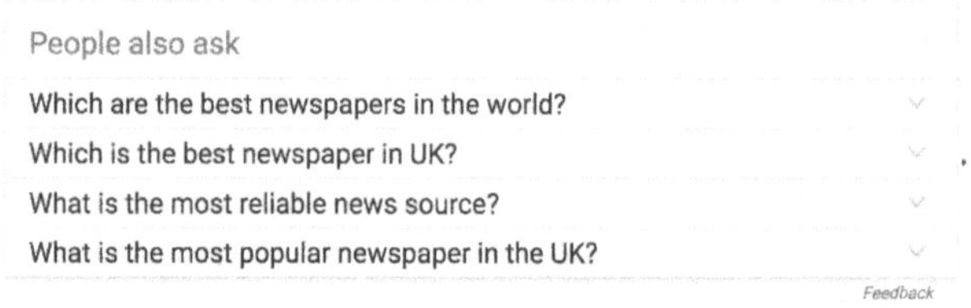

Figure 6: A screenshot from a Google search page. Some result pages contain a panel titled "People also ask" that shows full questions asked by users in relation to the query. One can click on the down arrow on the right side and read the answer directly in the panel, without visiting the page.

3.2 Direct Answer

One of the featured snippets that has gained prominence in the past years is the so-called "direct answer", or "position zero" (because it is shown above the ranked results), see Figure 7 for an example. An annual study from the market research company Stone Temple, which collected the content of search page results for 1.4 million queries, found out that currently, 30% of queries contain a "direct answer", and the rate of direct answers is continuing to rise [10]. However, the practice of answering queries in this way has drawn criticism in the media [23], because it is prone to manipulation. One of the examples included in [23] displayed a featured snippet from a conspiracy website that claimed that President Obama is planning a communist coup d'etat before the 2016 election. The snippet was shown as direct answer to the query: "is Obama planning a coup."

In addition to potentially propagating misinformation, direct answer results can also be exploited by content creators who use search engine optimization techniques to bias Google search algorithms into considering their page as highly relevant. See Figure 7, for an example of a featured snippet that fails at providing a substantive answer to the question of newspaper quality, providing instead an answer about newspaper circulation. Although direct answers are not shown when looking up entities such as news websites, as an important part of SERP they need attention from researchers, something we plan to pursue in our future research.

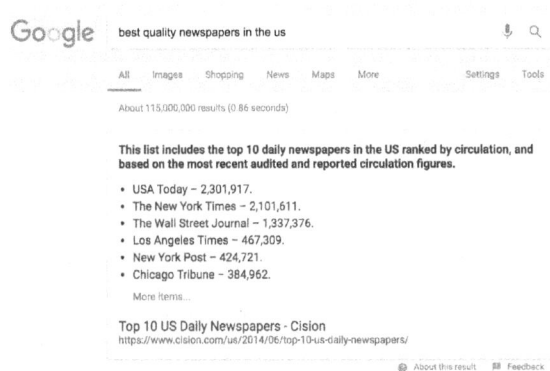

Figure 7: An example of a "direct answer", a featured snippet that is shown above the ranked search results. Notice that the content is from 2014 (the date in the URL of the article), although the query was performed on Jan 3, 2018.

4 USER STUDY: EVALUATING CREDIBILITY THROUGH SERP

Given that users might often encounter a news story from an unfamiliar website in their news feed, how would googling for the source help them believe or reject the story? More specifically, how would the composition and content displayed on the Google's SERP affect their decision making process for assessing the credibility of the source?

We designed a user study with in-person interviews and a think-aloud protocol to observe how users behave when asked to google unfamiliar news sources. Given that the one of the goals of lateral reading is to receive contextual information, we chose sources are not familiar to most people, but have a Knowledge Panel on their SERP. They are:

(1) **The Durango Herald** - a local newspaper in southwestern Colorado. The Knowledge Panel for this SERP has a detailed Wikipedia snippet that includes the date the newspaper was established as well as the region the paper primarily serves. *The Durango Herald's* Knowledge Panel also includes a "Topics they write about" section. A "Top Stories" and Twitter feed are also featured on The *Durango Herald's* SERP.

(2) **The Tennessean** - the principal daily newspaper in the Nashville, Tennessee region. The Knowledge Panel contains an "Awards" tab featuring three Pulitzer Prize nominations, as well as a "Writes About" tab. There is also a Wikipedia snippet, although it is noticeably less descriptive than the *Durango Herald's* Wikipedia excerpt. While there is a "Top Stories" on the SERP, there is no featured Twitter feed, although the newspaper has its Twitter account.

(3) **The Christian Times** - an online newspaper that is part of the Christian Media Corporation (CMC Group) that owns a number of Christian-issues focused online and print papers. The Christian Times does not have a Wikipedia page, however, Google still shows a Knowledge Panel for it from an unknown source, see Figure 8. It is worth noting here that Google is wrong about the parent company that owns

the Christian Times. Further complicating the matters is the conflation of search results with the ones belonging to the former fake news site "Christian Times Newspaper." As a result, Snopes, Media Bias/Fact Check, and a CBS News' "Fake News Sites to Watch Out For" article are all featured on the SERP. While The Christian Times has a self-professed religious bias, it is not the fake news site that SERP indicates. This is a clear case in which a fake news site used a very similar name to a real source's website to receive legitimacy, and now that the fake news website is defunct, its footprints on the Web are inherited by the legitimate website, damaging its reputation.

Screenshots of all SERPs mentioned in the paper can be found online[2].

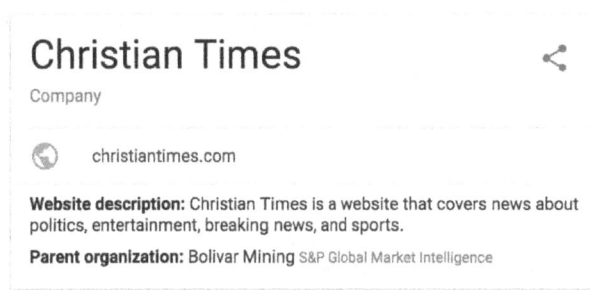

Figure 8: Excerpt from the Knowledge Panel for *The Christian Times*. The website description is generated automatically, and the Parent Organization information is wrong. Google doesn't provide the source for these pieces of information. Screenshot was captured on February 24, 2018. As of April 11, 2018, there is no longer a website description.

4.1 User Study Methodology

This study obtained IRB approval from our institution. Participation was voluntary, unpaid, and subjects signed a consent form before starting the interview. The following procedure was applied:

(1) Participants were asked to evaluate their ability to assess the trustworthiness of sources, describe their process for evaluating unknown online stories, and explain the factors that they believe to be important when assessing online content.

(2) Participants were asked to query Google on a desktop for the three online sources in a randomized order. After only viewing the SERP, they were asked to evaluate the credibility of each source. Participants were then asked what information they found compelling when determining credibility, or if they were unsure about the credibility of the source, what information was needed to make an accurate determination.

(3) Participants were then invited to visit the homepage of the site and any other pages on the SERP they wished to explore. They were then asked how their evaluation of the site's credibility changed.

---

[2]http://cs.wellesley.edu/~credlab/websci18/

(4) Finally, participants were asked which parts of the SERP were most useful when determining credibility and what they thought would improve the SERP.

4.2 Existing Techniques for Evaluating Credibility

At the beginning of the survey, participants were asked (1) how to test the reliability of an unknown website and (2) the most important factors to think about when determining the trustworthiness of a website. The most common response (53%) described a "lateral reading" approach that verifies claims based on similarly reported stories (typically through a Google search). Some participants (30%) also expressed a desire to only visit known, reputable sources to avoid all ambiguity. The most frequently mentioned techniques to determine the trustworthiness of an unknown news site were: the authors reputation and qualifications (30%), the domain ending of the site (.com, .org, .edu, etc.) (27%), and presentation of the page (23%) (site layout and spelling errors).

4.3 Credibility Signals Identified by Participants

By coding participants' responses using the qualitative data analysis software Atlas.ti, trends in participants responses emerged. In this section, we have highlighted the four most compelling: Knowledge Panels, organic results, the Top Stories panel, and social media-related results.

4.3.1 Knowledge Panel. When presented with the SERP of each of the sources, participants initially glanced at the Knowledge Panel. However, the information on the Knowledge Panel was often insufficient to make a credibility determination. According to participants, the most persuasive element when assessing the credibility of a source was the "Awards" tab (53%). The Wikipedia snippet was the most often-referenced piece of the Knowledge Panel (66%). Participants discussed the information in the Wikipedia description, especially the establishment date of *the Durango Herald* (33%) and the regional location of the local papers (23%). The "Awards" panel only appeared in one of the three Knowledge Panels, and was talked about in 60% of interviews, but the "Topics they write about" section appears on all three Knowledge Panels, but only a fraction of participants (20%) referenced it. Even fewer (10%) found it useful.

Beneath the title of a source on the Knowledge Panel, there is a label describing the entity. For *the Durango Herald* and *the Tennessean* the label is "newspaper," but for *the Christian Times* the label is "company" (see Figure 8). Some participants (20%) commented on this discrepancy as a reason why *the Christian Times* is not credible.

4.3.2 Organic Results. Even while acknowledging the value of the "Awards" section of the Knowledge Panel of *the Tennessean*, 93% of participants still assessed other parts of the SERP before making a credibility evaluation. All participants surveyed at least the first two results on the SERP for at least one of the three sites. On the *Durango Herald* and *the Tennessean's* SERP, the first result was the website itself. For the *Christian Times*, the website was the second result[3], decreasing its credibility for some participants (20%).

---

[3]This ranking was true for the time period of the study. It might change in the future.

All participants identified the *Christian Times* as not credible. On the SERP, the first result, a Snopes archive link, did not contain the term "fake news," but the first sentence of the snippet was "Maryland Lawmaker's Aide Fired for Creating Fake News Site." Nine participants discussed "fake news" being mentioned in the first result as a factor in believing the Christian Times as not credible. While this is 30% of our sample, we expected this number to be higher given that typically users do not look further than the first three results [21]. In our experiment, participants kept scrolling, identifying links further on the SERP that explicitly called into question the credibility of the *Christian Times*, such as "Christiantimes.com - Fake news sites to watch out for," "How Christian Times Traded Its Good Name-Twice," and "Christian Times Newspaper - Media Bias/Fact Check." 13 participants did not reference the Snopes result specifically, but either mentioned generally that results on the SERP indicate *the Christian Times* as unreliable or referenced other specific fact-checking links lower on the SERP.

Additionally, some participants were impressed by the sitelinks (30%), the links under a Google result that enhance page navigation) of the *Durango Herald* and the *Tennessean.*

4.3.3 Top Stories. The "Top Stories" panel on the *Durango Herald* and the *Tennessean's* SERP was persuasive to 53% of the participants. They referred to the "Top Stories" feed as a resource that provided recently published headlines and the publishing dates of the stories. Participants used the headlines as a signal to determine the scope of the source, for example, the *Durango Herald* primarily publishes information about southwestern Colorado, as well as the perceived bias of the source. Some participants also commented that they were more willing to trust sources that had published more recently and with greater frequency (33%), but other participants (17%) were also concerned that they either had not previously heard of the source or believed that papers covering local issues are less reliable. However, when offering a rationale for the credibility of a source based on the "Top Stories", participants were more likely to reference the source's frequency of publication than the headlines' biases.

4.3.4 Social Media. Participants were also interested in the social media pages of the news sources (53%). *The Durango Herald's* Twitter feed was featured on the SERP and the Facebook pages for *the Tennessean* and an imitator site of *the Christian Times* (Christian Times Magazine) displayed ratings on the SERP. Participants were interested in seeing if sources were Twitter verified, and one participant became skeptical of the *Durango Herald* because of its only three-star Facebook rating visible on the Facebook result's rich snippet. Two other participants mentioned the social media rating of the news sources in the rich snippet. For one participant, the absence of a featured Twitter feed was a factor in labeling the *Christian Times* as unreliable.

4.4 Discussion of Results

Our experiments revealed several interesting results. In this section, we have chosen to discuss Knowledge Panels, "Top Stories", organic search results, SERP layout, and the limitations of domain knowledge. We also discuss the differences in claimed participant credibility evaluation behavior and actual behavior.

Table 1: Results of the credibility assessment of *the Durango Herald*, *Tennessean*, and *Christian Times* based on their SERP, following step (2) in the study procedure.

Online source	Is credible?	Is not credible?
Durango Herald	21	9
The Tennessean	23	7
Christian Times	0	30

4.4.1 Knowledge Panel and "Top Stories". A revealing result that requires future inquiry is that participants did not know how to evaluate the credibility of the content on the Knowledge Panel itself. While not all of them mentioned this concern, some participants believed that the news source curated its own Knowledge Panel, while others speculated that Wikipedia produced the Knowledge Panels. No participant explicitly mentioned that Google had developed the Knowledge Panel, but for some it was possibly inferred. The Knowledge Panel is only useful as a signal if participants value the information it provides.

However, participants reacted positively to the contextual information, most notably the Wikipedia description and "Awards" tab. A surprise was how poorly the "Topics They Write About" section performed. The think-aloud protocol makes it difficult to know why participants did not think about a given topic, but one participant remarked that she was dubious of the credibility of the "Topics they write about" panel because the stories in that section are over a month old. Comparing the stale articles to the content on the "Top Stories" panel which contains current news stories, seems to be a plausible answer to why the "Topics they write about" section was not valued more, but further research is required.

4.4.2 Organic Search Results and the Christian Times. The search results themselves are important to participants for assessing the credibility of the source. Beyond the content on the page, the ranking of the news source itself on the SERP was very valuable, too.

The *Christian Times* was the second result on the SERP, providing a negative signal of the perceived credibility of the source. Even when participants did not know that the first result, Snopes, was a fact-checking organization, they still were dubious of the authority of a source that was ranked second for its own name. Additionally, the bold and explicit title from a CBSNews article proclaiming "christiantimes.com - Fake news sites to watch out for" was a big hit with the participants. The irony is that `christiantimes.com` has never been a fake news site. While the current website is clearly not a fake news site, a thorough evaluation of the Wayback Machine page archives revealed that the website never looked the way the CBSNews article [4] claimed. The other articles on the SERP were referring to the far-right conspiracy site `christiantimesnewspaper.com`, active during the 2016 U.S. presidential election.

This is not an isolated example of SERP results from legitimate sources and their sound-alike fakes being combined on the same SERP. Searches for the now defunct fake news site the *Boston Tribune* produce a Knowledge Panel for the reputable *Boston Herald*.

---

[4]https://web.archive.org/web/20180412003913/https://www.cbsnews.com/pictures/dont-get-fooled-by-these-fake-news-sites/12/

4.4.3 Effects of SERP Layout. Another notable result of our study is the role that the layout of the SERP itself (what blocks it contains and how they are organized) plays in the assessment of credibility. As discussed in the related research section, previous research has identified the importance of a site's layout [12] or has commented on how non-HTML link content changes the behavior of users on SERP [8]. However, no studies have investigated how the site layout of the Google SERP itself changes perceptions of credibility. Observations from our study appear to suggest that enhanced social media presence on the SERP improves the perceived credibility of sources. Therefore, further research is needed to explore the link between a strong social media presence and perceived credibility for news sources on SERP. This makes the errors of Google on generating the SERP for a news source even more costly. The *Tennessean* newspaper has a Twitter account, (@Tennessean), but the Twitter feed is not shown when one searches for "the tennessean". The inconsistency of the SERP content for slightly differing query phrases might have a big impact on decisions that users make about the credibility of sources.

4.4.4 Challenges of Domain Knowledge. 23% of participants evaluated a news source that was nominated for multiple Pulitzer Prizes as not credible (see Table 1). What made the award-winning Tennessean an unreliable site for some users? Of the 7 incorrect classifications, 4 directly involved a distrust of local journalism. This is an important example of the limits of lateral reading for users with limited knowledge of journalism. Regardless of the information Google could place on the SERP, people can make incorrect credibility assessments, because they lack domain knowledge to make sense of the provided information. Concretely, we suspect these participants were not aware that a Pulitzer Prize rewards high-quality journalism.

Similarly, even though the first result for *the Christian Times* was a Snopes article fact-checking the *Christian Times Newspaper*, most participants were unfamiliar with Snopes (90%). So, even though the Google algorithm has helpfully prioritized the fact-checker as the first result, the value of this algorithmic decision is lost on most participants who are unfamiliar with Snopes.

Both the Pulitzer Prize and Snopes examples illustrate that adding context does not empirically increase the ability of web users to accurately access sources.

4.4.5 Contrasting Claimed and Actual Credibility Evaluation Techniques. While the focus of our study is the behavior of web users when performing a lateral reading task, an additional finding is that there is a gap between the claimed and actual behavior of participants with regards to which credibility signals they find important. The top five most frequent responses from the pre-task survey were: "lateral reading" techniques (i.e. see what other sources are reporting the story), only search within reputable sites, find journalist credentials, glance at the end domain name, and examine the page layout. These findings are generally in line with other user studies discussed in the related research section.

In this study, we set participants up to perform lateral reading strategies by instructing them to google the news sources, thereby encouraging the behavior. For example, many participants (67%) commented on what the other search results on the page said about *the Christian Times*.

The second most frequently "claimed" strategy, only using reputable sites, was not possible for this experiment with unfamiliar news sources. However, the language that participants used to describe these reputable sources, included terms such as "trustworthy", "reliable", and "objective" indicating that participants had a solid understanding of the definition of credibility.

Investigating the author or journalist's credentials (30%) was the next most common response; however, when participants were permitted to examine the site itself, only two (7%) commented on the journalists or suggested that Knowledge Panels include journalist information. No participants commented on the fact that all three sources were ".com" sites. Using end domain suffixes to test the credibility of news sources is ineffective, and observed behavior of participants illustrates that it is not actually attempted. The importance of site layout of the SERP has already been discussed, but participants were referring to the actual website layout in this exercise. This finding is replicated in our study with 80% of participants mentioning page layout when viewing one of the three sites' home pages.

While the gap in self-reported and observed behavior is not unique to this experiment, it does prompt the question: how do people select which elements of the SERP they value most? How does the SERP that Google serves to participants alter what they think is a valuable credibility signal? These questions should be explored further in future studies.

4.5 Limitations of the Study

Several factors limit the power of this study. The first one is that this was a study with a sample of convenience: 30 undergraduate students of ages 18-22, who skewed heavily female. Because of their education level, these students are most likely more familiar with more recent web literacy approaches than the general public. A bigger sample with more diversity in demographic traits needs to be interviewed.

Our interviews lasted between 10-20 minutes providing several minutes for participants to examine the credibility of news sources. Users typically do not spend 3-5 minutes on the SERP evaluating the credibility of sources. As a result of the lack of a time constraint, participants were frequently observed scrolling through the entire SERP, a practice that [21, 25] indicate is not typical online behavior.

The ever changing nature of the SERP also created challenges, since our study was conducted over a six-day period. Originally, the prompt for *the Tennessean* was to search "tennessean", but on day five, it was discovered that the Knowledge Panel belonging to the newspaper had disappeared for that query, so that one participant was not able to use the Knowledge Panel to make a credibility assessment. In subsequent interviews, the query "*the* tennessean" produced the expected Knowledge Panel on the SERP.

The Christian Times was selected because its Knowledge Panel did not contain the word fake news, but the other results on the SERP claimed that it was a "fake news" site (due to a mix-up with a similarly named fake news website). However, nine participants (30%) explained that because the source name contained the word "Christian", they were less likely to deem the site as credible. When pressed what about the word "Christian" makes the site unreliable,

they clarified that Christian didn't mean unreliable, but at the very least meant biased.

Finally, it is important to mention that the interviewers never defined credibility for the participants. In fact, we used the terms credibility, reliability, and trustworthy interchangeably. When prompted by the study participants about the definition of credibility, interviewers responded with the "story card" scenario described earlier. While the presence of the *Christian Times* website led to interesting discoveries about the inaccuracy of the SERP, as well as participants' prior biases, in future studies we will make sure to choose sources that force participants to do more thinking of what is important to them given the contextual information on the SERP.

5 ANALYSIS OF KNOWLEDGE PANELS

Although the participants in the study were not sure about the provenance of information in the Knowledge Panel, they nevertheless valued the contextual information that it provided about the sources. Given this interest, Google's decision to provide Knowledge Panels that summarize information about an entity in one place seems very helpful. But how consistent and how accurate is the information shown in a Knowledge Panel? We set out to test this for a large number of news sources. Concretely, we tested three different datasets:

(1) The top 100 news sources from the Amazon Web Service Alexa Top Sites, which lists the highest-performing websites globally according to the Alexa Traffic Rank algorithm (AlexaRank). The AlexaRank of a site is calculated from the site traffic over the past three months and is a measure of how many pages a user visits on that site. The "news" category that was used for this analysis features sites such as CNN and The New York Times, as well as news aggregators such as Reddit and Google News.
(2) The USNPL (United States Newspaper List)[5], which is a database of US-based local newspapers, TV, and radio stations broken down by state (n = 7269). We chose to use this list instead of each state's Wikipedia list of newspapers, because we found the USNPL list to be more evenly distributed state-to-state and equally, if not more, complete.
(3) A Buzzfeed News list of highly partisan news sites (n = 677) [6] that includes sites such as MSNBC as well as classic examples of fake news such as 100percentfedup.com. Many of these sites are of low-authority, the kind of sources users would need support to learn more about.

Through an automatic script, we searched the names of the sources on Google Search, for example, "fox news", and recorded whether the Knowledge Panel existed or not. For the first two datasets we checked whether the panel title corresponded to the site name, to avoid spurious results. This was not possible for the third dataset, for which we used the provided domain names, for example "yesimright", instead of the site name "Yes I'm Right".

Table 2 indicates that the majority of popular sites have the Knowledge Panel, but roughly a third of sources for the two other datasets do. This is problematic. Users are already familiar with

---

[5] http://www.usnpl.com
[6] https://github.com/BuzzFeedNews/2017-08-partisan-sites-and-facebook-pages/tree/master/data

Table 2: The occurrence and composition of Knowledge Panels in the three datasets on January 3, 2018.

	Knowledge Panel	Writes About	Reviewed Claims
{1} Alexa (n= 100)	96 (96%)	63 (63%)	3 (3%)
{2} USNPL (n= 7269)	2702 (37%)	698 (10%)	1 (0%)
{3} BuzzFeed (n= 677)	230 (34%)	114 (17%)	145 (21%)

Table 3: The occurrence and composition of Knowledge Panels in the three datasets on February 24, 2018.

	Knowledge Panel	Writes About	Reviewed Claims
{1} Alexa (n= 100)	96 (96%)	63 (63%)	0 (0%)
{2} USNPL (n= 7269)	2784 (38%)	1120 (15%)	0 (0%)
{3} BuzzFeed (n =677)	239 (36%)	128 (19%)	0 (0%)

popular sites. It is the least known ones, such as local newspapers or online sources pretending to be legitimate local or national sources, about which users want to learn more.

For the sources that have a Knowledge Panel, their information comes usually from Wikipedia. While some established partisan and "fake news" sites have full Wikipedia pages, many of the sites that we anticipate users should be googling to evaluate their credibility do not rise to the level of notability warranted for a Wikipedia page. Google has recognized the need to still provide supplemental information about these sites and has developed an alternate format (see Figure 9) that replaces the Wikipedia snippet with a a summary of the topics from the "Writes about" section. Based on our observations, it appears that the "Writes About" section is periodically created from topic models [2] of articles the site has published. For the websites of the datasets {1} and {2} we see no examples of this alternative format for describing a website.

We were also curious whether different panels of the search results page co-occur. Concretely, did the presence of a "Top Stories" panel (see Figure 4) increase the likelihood for the existence of a Knowledge Panel? Of the 2835 pages from {2} that have a "Top Stories Panel ", 1307 do not have a Knowledge Panel. Here lies an opportunity for improvement on Google's part: if a source is already recognized as a content publisher in the "Top Stories" panel, there should be an accompanying Knowledge Panel providing context for the source. Table 3 summarizes the data for the repeat data collection in February 2018.

5.1 SERP from January 2018 to February 2018

Google's search algorithm is incredibly dynamic with 500-600 changes being implemented annually [7]. As discussed in the introduction, the most meaningful change from January to February was the removal of the "Reviewed claims" section. While we do not have results from our user study emphasizing the importance of this section for credibility assessment, based on users desire for explicit fact-checks in organic results, it is likely that the "Reviewed Claims" would be perceived as valuable.

---
[7] moz.com/google-algorithm-change

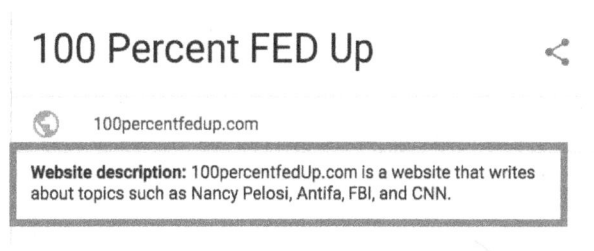

Figure 9: A website description without a Wikipedia citation. This website is part of the Buzzfeed dataset of partisan or fake news websites. The Website description portion is generated automatically by an algorithm. As of April 2018, this description isn't available anymore.

For all three datasets, Knowledge Panel numbers stayed relatively constant. The one notable change was the expansion of the "Writes About" section. In the USNPL dataset, there were only 82 Knowledge Panels added between January and February, but 422 "Writes About" sections added. This increase indicates that Google is actively expanding its "Writes about" section. This is an interesting observation given that many of the participants in our study preferred the "Top Stories" panel.

5.2 Wikipedia's Role

Our analysis reveals that in the majority of cases, the information in the Knowledge Panel is lifted directly from the Wikipedia page. For media companies, such as Fox News, CNN, ABC, the Knowledge Panel also contains information that Google algorithms are inserting from other sources: links to social media presence, or list of anchors and flagship programs. Because the information is coming directly from Wikipedia, this increases the pressure on Wikipedia to both maintain accuracy of information, as well as increase the coverage.

Since less than half of all news sites have Knowledge Panels, we were particularly interested in what separated the sites that have Knowledge Panels from the ones that did not. The best predictor of a knowledge panel was the presence of a Wikipedia page for that site. There are only 373 sites in dataset 2 that have a Knowledge Panel but not a Wikipedia page.

However, not all Wikipedia pages are created equal. An examination of 1043 Wikipedia pages for U.S. newspapers from all 50 states shows several inconsistencies in the infobox panel. We found 79 unique fields for the infobox, fields such as editor, format, owner, etc., but frequently, only a few of these contain information. There is much to be done to provide more information in Wikipedia too.

6 DISCUSSION AND FUTURE WORK

In our digital age, news lives on the web, so the credibility of news sources and their claims should be verified through the web. Often, the first stop in such a verification process is performing "lateral reading" through Google. "I've taken to generally Googling things just to try to get a concept of it."—said one of the participants in a recent study about news consumption [3]. What users look for and what they find when searching on Google influences their decision making and their news literacy. Google's SERP has become an arena where algorithms, humans, and publishers with good or not-so-good intentions meet and try to influence one another. While most approaches for news literacy focus on the responsibility of the users to evaluate sources, one cannot discount that online platforms, such as Google, which users already trust, play a crucial role in supporting decision making when it comes to deciding which source to trust and why. In our study, the distorted SERP for *the Christian Times* led all participants to label it a not credible source. How could other actors influence and support news literacy efforts? Here are some ideas to consider:

Wikipedia editors could contribute pages for all recognized news sources (e.g., the USNPL database) while also taking care of being consistent in what information they provide. They should also be alert to possible manipulation. It is to be expected that as Knowledge Panels become more prominent, there will be efforts to modify existing pages with incorrect information or to create pages for non-existing sources.

Researchers could build new algorithms to automatically monitor the quality of search results about news and media related queries and point out to Google what is doing wrong. Similarly to how the computer security research community is always watching out for possible failures and weak points in various hardware and software systems, we should treat the information ecosystem enabled by Google Search as something that requires constant monitoring. Researchers in the Web Science community may be well-suited to take the lead on this task.

Educators and literacy organizations could write meaningful web content that provides background and domain knowledge about what makes news sources credible. For example: explain the value of local journalism and its long tradition, the value of recognition by a third party such as a Pulitzer Prize, but also how easy it is to fake Facebook ratings or have a Twitter feed that is constantly tweeting (signals that our participants used to assign credibility).

One thing is clear: we all have a lot of work to do. In the near future, we plan (1) to perform similar experiments on a more representative sample and (2) to examine the credibility signals on mobile devices rather than desktops. The long-term goal of our research is to model how users reason about the credibility of online sources.

REFERENCES

[1] Katarzyna Abramczuk, Michał Kakol, and Adam Wierzbicki. 2016. How to Support the Lay Users Evaluations of Medical Information on the Web?. In *International Conference on Human Interface and the Management of Information*. Springer, 3-13.

[2] David M Blei. 2012. Probabilistic topic models. *Commun. ACM* 55, 4 (2012), 77-84.

[3] Pablo Boczkowski. 12/2017. The Rise of Skeptical Reading. *NiemanLab Predictions for Journalism 2018* (12/2017). http://www.niemanlab.org/2017/12/the-rise-of-skeptical-reading/

[4] Danah Boyd. 2014. *It's complicated: The social lives of networked teens*. Yale University Press.

[5] Monica Bulger and Patrick Davison. 2018. The Promises, Challenges, and Futures of Media Literacy. (2018).

[6] Mike Caulfield. 07/03/2017. How to Find Out If a "Local" Newspaper Site Is Fake (Using a New-ish Google Feature). *Hapgood: A personal blog* (07/03/2017). https://hapgood.us/2017/07/03/how-to-find-out-if-a-local-newspaper-site-is-fake-using-a-new-ish-google-feature/

[7] Mike Caulfield. 2017. *Web Literacy for Student Fact-checkers*. https://webliteracy.pressbooks.com/

[8] Danqi Chen, Weizhu Chen, Haixun Wang, Zheng Chen, and Qiang Yang. 2012. Beyond Ten Blue Links: Enabling User Click Modeling in Federated Web Search.

In *Proceedings of the Fifth ACM International Conference on Web Search and Data Mining (WSDM '12)*. ACM, New York, NY, USA, 463-472. https://doi.org/10.1145/2124295.2124351

[9] Brooke Donald. 2016-11-22. Stanford researchers find students have trouble judging the credibility of information online. https://ed.stanford.edu/news/stanford-researchers-find-students-have-trouble-judging-credibility-information-online (2016-11-22).

[10] Eric Enge. 05/24/2017. Featured Snippets: New Insights, New Opportunities. *Stone Temple Company Blog* (05/24/2017). https://www.stonetemple.com/featured-snippets-new-Insights-new-opportunities/

[11] Andrew J Flanagin and Miriam J Metzger. 2000. Perceptions of Internet information credibility. *Journalism & Mass Communication Quarterly* 77, 3 (2000), 515-540.

[12] BJ Fogg, Cathy Soohoo, David R Danielson, Leslie Marable, Julianne Stanford, and Ellen R Tauber. 2003. How do users evaluate the credibility of Web sites?: a study with over 2,500 participants. In *Proceedings of the 2003 conference on Designing for user experiences*. ACM, 1-15.

[13] BJ Fogg and Hsiang Tseng. 1999. The elements of computer credibility. In *Proceedings of the SIGCHI conference on Human Factors in Computing Systems*. ACM, 80-87.

[14] Sarah Frier. 12/17/2017. He Got Rich by Sparking the Fake News Boom. Then Facebook Broke His Business. *Bloomberg* (12/17/2017). https://www.bloomberg.com/news/articles/2017-12-12/business-takes-a-hit-when-fake-news-baron-tries-to-play-it-straight

[15] Michael Galvez. 12/05/2017. Improving Search and discovery on Google. *Google Blog* (12/05/2017). https://blog.google/products/search/improving-search-and-discovery-google/

[16] Alexandru L. Ginsca, Adrian Popescu, and Mihai Lupu. 2015. Credibility in Information Retrieval. *Foundations and TrendsÃĆÃ́ô in Information Retrieval* 9, 5 (2015), 355-475. https://doi.org/10.1561/1500000046

[17] Jacek Gwizdka and Dania Bilal. 2017. Analysis of Children's Queries and Click Behavior on Ranked Results and Their Thought Processes in Google Search. In *Proceedings of the 2017 Conference on Conference Human Information Interaction and Retrieval (CHIIR '17)*. ACM, New York, NY, USA, 377-380. https://doi.org/10.1145/3020165.3022157

[18] Eszter Hargittai. 2003. The digital divide and what to do about it. *New Economy Handbook* (2003), 821-839.

[19] Eszter Hargittai. 2010. Digital na(t)ives? Variation in internet skills and uses among members of the "net generation". *Sociological inquiry* 80, 1 (2010), 92-113.

[20] Eszter Hargittai, Lindsay Fullerton, Ericka Menchen-Trevino, and Kristin Yates Thomas. 2010. Trust online: Young adults' evaluation of web content. *International journal of communication* 4 (2010), 27.

[21] Gord Hotchkiss and Steve Alston. 2005. *Eye tracking study: An in depth look at interactions with Google using eye tracking methodology*. Enquiro Search Solutions Incorporated.

[22] Carl I Hovland, Irving L Janis, and Harold H Kelley. 1953. Communication and persuasion; psychological studies of opinion change. (1953).

[23] Adrianne Jeffries. 03/05/2017. Google's Featured Snippets are Worse than Fake News. *The Outline* (03/05/2017). https://theoutline.com/post/1192/google-s-featured-snippets-are-worse-than-fake-news

[24] Diane Kelly and Leif Azzopardi. 2015. How many results per page?: A Study of SERP Size, Search Behavior and User Experience. In *SIGIR*.

[25] R Maynes and I Everdell. 2014. The evolution of Google search results pages and their effects on user behaviour. *USA: Mediative* (2014).

[26] Miriam J Metzger. 2007. Making sense of credibility on the Web: Models for evaluating online information and recommendations for future research. *Journal of the Association for Information Science and Technology* 58, 13 (2007), 2078-2091.

[27] Bing Pan, Helene Hembrooke, Thorsten Joachims, Lori Lorigo, Geri Gay, and Laura Granka. 2007. In google we trust: UsersâĂŹ decisions on rank, position, and relevance. *Journal of computer-mediated communication* 12, 3 (2007), 801-823.

[28] Joshua J Seidman. 2006. The mysterious maze of the World Wide Web: How can we guide consumers to high-quality health information on the Internet. *Internet and health care: Theory, research and practice* (2006), 195-212.

[29] Amit Singhal. 05/16/2012. Introducing the Knowledge Graph: things, not strings. *Google Official Blog* (05/16/2012). https://googleblog.blogspot.com/2012/05/introducing-knowledge-graph-things-not.html

[30] Nicholas Vincent, Isaac Johnson, and Brent Hecht. 2018. Examining Wikipedia With a Broader Lens: Quantifying the Value of Wikipedia's Relationships with Other Large-Scale Online Communities. (2018).

[31] Stanley Wilder. 2005. Information literacy makes all the wrong assumptions. *The Chronicle Review* 51, 18 (2005).

[32] Sam Wineburg and Sarah McGrew. 2017. Lateral Reading: Reading Less and Learning More When Evaluating Digital Information. *Stanford History Education Group Working Paper No. 2017-A1* (2017). https://ssrn.com/abstract=3048994

[33] Ranna Zhou. 11/07/2017. Learn more about publishers on Google. *Google Blog* (11/07/2017). https://www.blog.google/products/search/learn-more-about-publishers-google/

Observing Burstiness in Wikipedia Articles during New Disease Outbreaks

Reham Al Tamime
Web Science Institute
University of Southampton
Southampton, UK
rat1g15@soton.ac.uk

Richard Giordano
Faculty of Health Sciences
University of Southampton
Southampton, UK
r.giordano@soton.ac.uk

Wendy Hall
Web Science Institute
University of Southampton
Southampton, UK
wh@soton.ac.uk

ABSTRACT

Wikipedia can be conceptualized as an open sociotechnical environment that supports communities of humans and bots that update and contest information in Wikipedia articles. This environment affords a view to community or domain interactions and reactions to salient topics, such as disease outbreaks. But do reactions to different topics vary, and how can we measure them? One widely-used approach when answering these questions is to delineate levels of burstiness—communication flows characterized by repeated bursts instead of a continuous stream—in the construction of a Wikipedia article. A literature review, however, reveals that current burstiness approaches do not fully support efforts to compare Wikipedia community reactions to different articles. Through an empirical analysis of the construction of Wikipedia health-related articles, we both extend and refine burstiness as an analytical technique to understand the community dynamics underlying the construction of Wikipedia articles. We define a method by which we can categorize burstiness as high medium and low. Our empirical results suggest a proposed a model of burstiness.

CCS CONCEPTS

• **Human-centered computing** → **Collaborative and social computing**; *Collaborative and social computing systems and tools*; Wikipedia.

KEYWORDS

Burstiness; human-machine network; online community; peer production; collective behavior; Wikipedia.

WebSci '18, May 27–30, 2018, Amsterdam, Netherlands
© 2018 Copyright is held by the owner/author(s).
ACM ISBN 978-1-4503-5563-6/18/05.
https://doi.org/10.1145/3201064.3201080

1 INTRODUCTION

Burstiness is a sudden increase in *something*, especially for a short period; [6] it refers intermittent high or low frequencies of events. Many activities exhibit some of form of burstiness, such as sending emails [3], market trading [37], watching movies [46], listening to music [17], playing games [14], network traffic [34], and natural events such as earthquakes [44] and neuronal firing [15]. Burstiness has also been widely defined as a sudden surge of the frequency of a single term or phrase in a text stream. The concept has been used to describe unusual surges of online activities or interactions [45]. In addition, the concept has been used as a sociological method to predict the emergence of new fields and trends in research by looking at the occurrence of common terms throughout a body of knowledge, such as the full text of a journal [30].

This paper focuses on periods of high activity in a stream, and can be used to detect behavior that is correlated with a particular event. In the context of the Wikipedia editing stream, bursts of editing activity across a set of Wikipedia articles could be related to some external (or internal) social phenomenon or trigger, such as a controversial topic, the injection of biased information, or some form of vandalism [39]. The trigger we have identified for the purposes of this paper is news of an outbreak of a new disease.

A disease outbreak is the occurrence of cases of disease in excess of what would normally be expected in a defined community, geographical area or season. An outbreak may occur in a restricted geographical area, or may extend over several countries. It may last for a few days or weeks, or for several years [36]. Outbreaks of formerly unknown diseases, such as the 1976 Legionnaires Disease Outbreak in Philadelphia [2] often represent uncertain knowledge to both specialists and the general public because of limited knowledge of the disease etiology. Outbreaks of new or formerly unknown diseases still remain a great challenge even for some of the world's most capable and well-resourced health systems [5].

Wikipedia has become the most prominent source of online health information for the general public compared to other online health information providers, such as MedlinePlus or NHS Direct [27]. Although research has been conducted on page views to health-related articles [38] [12], there is but a modest set of research that focuses on how contributors to Wikipedia react during new disease outbreaks.

Various methodological approaches have been used to study and understand contributors' reactions in Wikipedia. Burstiness—time-delimited periods of high editorial activity—is one measure that has been used to reveal and study these reactions. Previous work has touched on developing methods to detect and measure burstiness, such as burstiness of text streams [21], burstiness of Twitter posts [16], and burstiness on Wikipedia both in general [39], and in particular Wikipedia articles [20] [40]. There is only limited research that focuses on comparing burstiness across articles on Wikipedia. Therefore, our research questions are, *How do we compare burstiness across Wikipedia articles? How do we categorize burstiness?* This paper has two goals: To measure burstiness across topically-related Wikipedia articles (in this case articles related to new disease outbreaks); and, to categorize different types of burstiness. The paper also describes a model of burstiness and suggests that measuring and classifying burstiness of a Wikipedia article can be an important element in establishing the provenance of the article. This, in turn, can influence the level of confidence a reader may have in the article.

2 LITERATURE REVIEW

Different approaches have been developed to detect and measure burstiness. Search engines rely on frequency-based measures to capture the burstiness of each term in the underlying collection. These measures work by recording the frequency of an individual term in each document, typically normalized by a global frequency measure [25]. Other measures have been developed to consider the moment in time that burstiness occurs by identifying temporal bursts. A temporal burst is typically identified by determining: (a) an interval on the timeline that specifies the timeframe during which the unusually high frequency was observed; and, (b) a score that indicates the burst's strength (i.e. the extent of the deviation from the object's usual frequency) [26]. Different techniques have been proposed to detect temporal burstiness such as by computing the moving average of the time series of terms or phrases. Specifically, bursts are the points that have a value higher than a specific standard deviation above the mean [24]. Additionally, parameter-free methods have been investigated to detect temporal burstiness. The parameter-free approach does not require estimating parameters or using any weighting schemes to find burstiness. However, this approach relies on a probabilistic model that uses the time series alone to identify bursty terms and group them into bursty events [11]. Along the same lines, Lappas et al. [25] developed a parameter-free technique to identify the maximum burstiness intervals for a given term. This technique is based on discrepancy theory which is used to describe the deviation of a situation from the expected behavioral baseline. Kleinberg [21] developed a two-state automation model to identify temporal burstiness. The algorithm works by modelling bursts efficiently and avoids identifying a large number of short spurious bursts or fragmenting long bursts into many smaller bursts. This algorithm is based on the hidden Markov model that assigns different burstiness states depending on the frequency levels of an individual term. State transitions (bursts) correspond to points in time, around which the frequency of a term changes significantly. Given a frequency sequence of a term, dynamic programming is used to fit the most possible state sequence that is likely to have generated the frequency sequence [42] [25]. Researchers have also studied the relaxation distribution after the burst of activities in order to allow for the classification of collective human dynamics [4]. Other approaches have been extended to take into consideration the context of the burstiness. For example, a language modelling approach has been applied to not only detect burstiness, but also to explain the background and the details of events around bursts [45].

Research in subgraph burstiness in social networks quantify burstiness using two models. The first model detects burstiness by treating each user as an independent unit—users share information due to genuine interest and not due to influence by neighbors who actively share or produce related content. The second model detects burstiness by treating each user as a dependent unit by taking into account the effect of neighbors' influence [8].

There are models to connect bursty terms to real-world events, such as detecting bursty terms in Twitter data streams that correspond with events such as natural disasters and health alerts. For example, Guzman and Poblete [16] built a model that computes keyword frequencies, normalizes them by relevance, and compares them in adjacent time windows. The model also ranks bursty terms according to their relative frequency. The model takes into consideration that the occurrence of bursty words is not constant during the day. Therefore, the model creates independence between the frequency values and the hour of the day. Moreover, the model can identify stop words by finding the relative standard deviation rate since stop words tend to have higher standard deviation than non-stop words. The model also ranks bursty terms according to their relative frequency, which is computed by finding the probability of occurrence of a non-stop word term in a window. Lu at al. [32] identified real-world events by determining the basic frequency of words in a microblogging site, taking into account the dynamic information of online social networks. They constructed a model that detects burstiness if the frequency of keywords related to an emerging event increases suddenly during a specific current time interval but remains constant across multiple time intervals. For example, in order to improve situational awareness during disaster-related events, Lee at al. [28] developed a term-weighting scheme for multiple text streams that assesses the term's burstiness by ascertaining skewness (bursty terms have thicker tail distribution), consistency (bursty terms occurrence across different channels), periodicity (bursty terms are less likely to be periodic), and variation (reducing the possibility of identifying bursty terms if they are bursty only in a specific channel). Lappas et al. [26] identified burstiness by taking into account both spatial and temporal burstiness of terms.

In the context of Wikipedia, Tinati et al. [40] developed an information cascade model that uses a string-matching function for the text associated with each revision entry. The function applies a regular expression to identify noun phrases within text across different articles, and links articles based on a pattern match. Then, the model identifies burstiness related to different types of information and investigates several properties related to burstiness. For example, edit-war bursts last much longer than other bursts related to breaking news events and involve a small set of articles.

Burstiness is usually measured based on spikes of edits. For example, Keegan et al. [20] selected the Tōhoku catastrophe article to examine how the Wikipedia community responds to unexpected events and emergencies. The study identified several dynamic features of collaboration during unexpected events which include change in the number of revisions and unique editors of articles related to these events. Previous research examined specific Wikipedia articles to measure the spike of editing activities to understand a specific community's reactions.

Our research builds on Tinati's definition [39] that burstiness in Wikipedia is a period of high activity in a stream by applying a comparative approach that not only measures, but also compares burstiness across a set of Wikipedia articles. This approach delineates the community's reactions to different types of articles. Also, this approach reveals *relative* burstiness instead of *absolute* burstiness. This distinction is useful when considering a topic that involves a group of different articles, and when studying burstiness as a surge in two variables—the number of revisions per day and unique editors of articles per day.

3 MEASURING BURSTINESS

3.1 Candidate disease outbreaks

We now demonstrate a method to measure burstiness on Wikipedia articles. The topic of interest here is new disease outbreaks that occurred in the past ten years. The study population includes 52 Wikipedia articles on the Zika virus, Ebola, swine influenza, avian influenza (H7N9) and Middle East Respiratory Syndrome (MERS). Their editing histories were harvested from the Wikipedia API, covering all revisions from 2001 until 2016. Each revision includes an ID, username, timestamp, and comment on the change made. Usernames include bots and anonymous users, as marked by 'anon' in the entry.

Articles related to new disease outbreaks are of interest for two reasons. First, they often represent diseases where there is relatively little known about the disease, and therefore the magnitude of the public health threat posed by them is not immediately known. Second, at the time of the outbreak, there was relatively little known either about the etiology of each disease, or the conditions by which the disease would spread, as well as the scope of their spread. It is self-evident that the relative lack of certainty about the etiology and transmission of a communicable life-threatening disease at once aroused the interest of the press and increased public concern and anxiety. Anxiety and disease outbreaks are often both coupled and socially contagious [18].

Table 1: Number of news articles in twelve-month period from start of outbreak.

Disease Outbreak	Frequency
MERS	1762
H7N9	13481
ZIKA	50939
EBOLA	290375
SWINE FLU	294829

Source: Nexis search results of newspapers, newswires, press releases, web-based publications, industry trade press, news transcripts, blogs, newsletters.

The public mostly relied either on press reports or World Health Organization updates. The World Health Organization had declared the Zika virus, Ebola and swine influenza as a Public Health Emergency of International Concern (PHEIC), and the Zika virus, Ebola and the Swine Influenza received particularly wide press coverage. Table 1 depicts that the news coverage of topics to these disease outbreaks.

3.2 Fitting bursts to the ARIMA model.

The ARIMA model was developed by Box and Jenkins in 1970 [1]. This model can detect outliers in a time series data which helps to find surge in the number of revisions and the number of unique editors over time. Incorporating the daily number of unique editors—excluding bots—into the model helps to distinguish between the spike of edits that occurs as a result of one or two users editing the article and the spike that is the result of a collective action of many editors interested to edit the article.

The model combines the autoregressive model (AR) and the moving average model (MA) with non-seasonal differences added to the model. The model can be written as:

$$Y_t = c + \phi_i y_{t-1} + \phi_i y_{t-p} + \ldots + \theta_i e_{t-1} + \theta_i e_{t-q} + e_t$$

where ϕ is a parameter for the model, *and Y is differenced d* times and *c* is a constant. The ARIMA model has been applied elsewhere to examine Wikipedia page views bursts over time. It has achieved a total accuracy of 98% [43]. To test the ARIMA model on our dataset, we chose the Zika Virus article as a sample, and two annotators manually labeled the daily data as bursts or not with inter-annotator agreement Fleiss Kappa score of 0.83. We fit the autoregressive an integrated moving average (ARIMA) model to (1) the number of revisions, and (2) the number of unique editors time series data. Most of the daily data has been labeled correctly by the ARIMA model with a total accuracy of 93%.

We then applied this model to all of the selected disease outbreaks. Figures 1-5 display the results of the burstiness over time in both Wikipedia and news reports concerning new disease outbreaks. These five articles were selected because they received the highest number of edits, and we therefore considered them to be the main articles of each disease outbreak. Also, the subplots depict the daily number of news articles for each disease as retrieved from NEXIS. These subplots cover news from the start of the outbreak until one year after the outbreak.

The results show that articles related to MERS and H7N9 have experienced less burstiness than articles related to Zika, Ebola and Swine Influenza. Burstiness occurred in the latter articles after the World Health Organization (WHO) declared the epidemics as public health emergencies of international concern (PHEIC).

We were then interested in discovering whether or not there was a correlation between the number of news articles that appeared during the outbreaks and the number of revisions and the number of unique editors. Table 2 and Table 3 examine the relationships between the number of news articles and the number of revisions and the number of unique editors. A Pearson correlation test was applied to data from the start of the outbreak until one year after the outbreak. Tables 2 and 3 suggest that there is a positive and moderate relationship between the increase in news coverage and the increase in editing activities in Wikipedia during disease outbreaks.

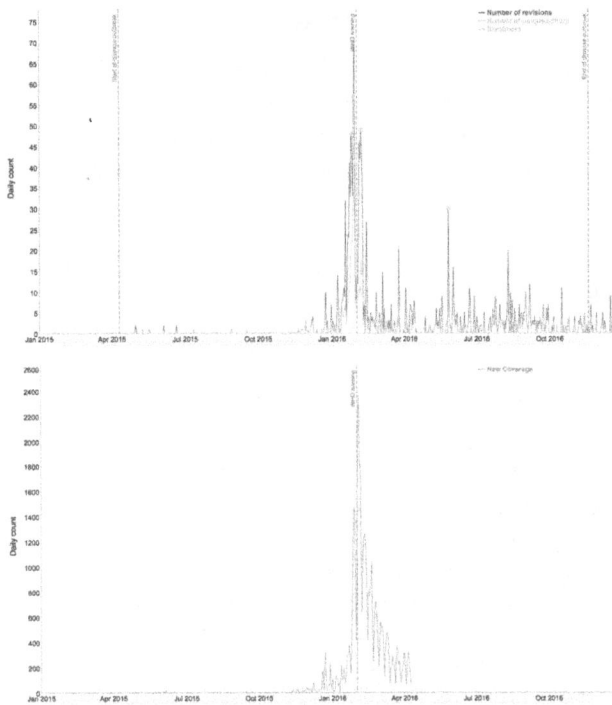

Figure 1:
Top Plot, Zika virus Wikipedia articles;
Bottom Plot, Corresponding news coverage.

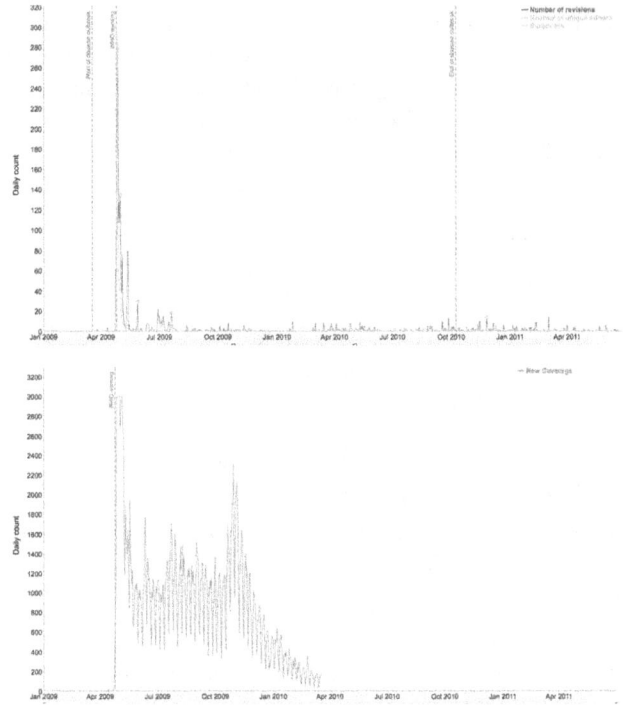

Figure 3:
Top plot, Swine influenza Wikipedia article;
Bottom plot, Corresponding news coverage

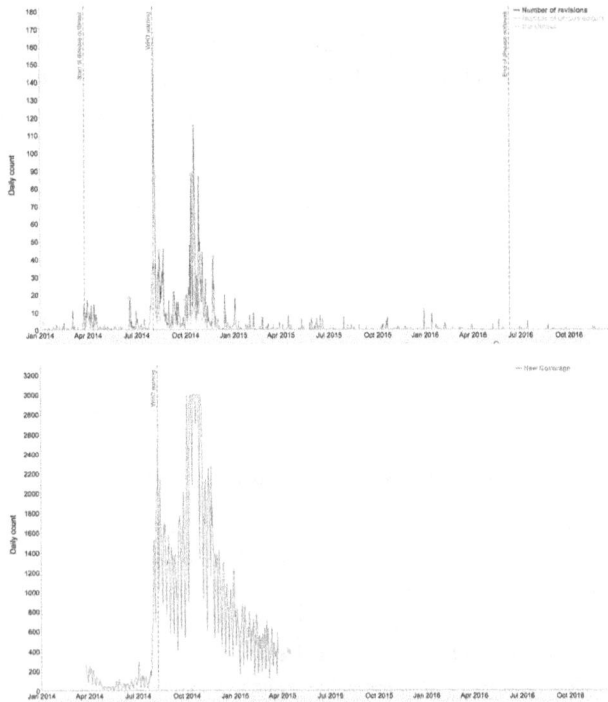

Figure 2:
Top plot, Ebola virus disease Wikipedia article;
Bottom plot, Corresponding news coverage.

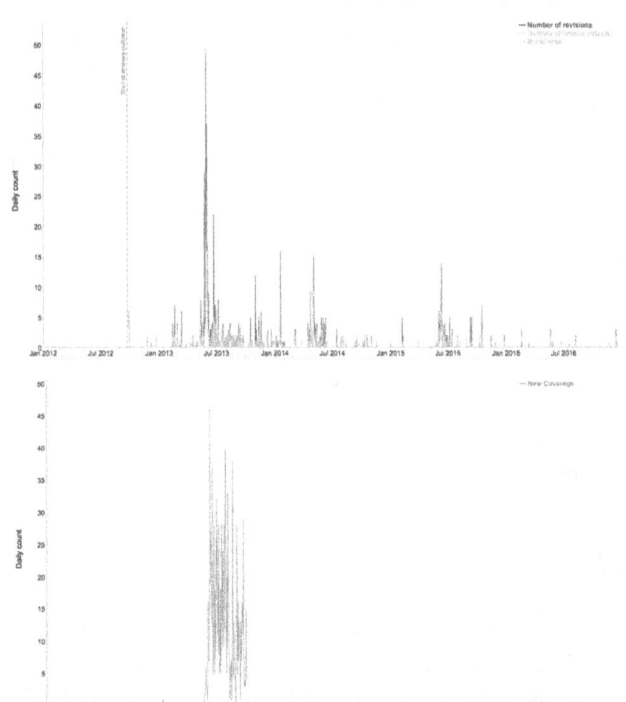

Figure 4:
Top plot, MERS Wikipedia article;
Bottom plot, Corresponding news coverage.

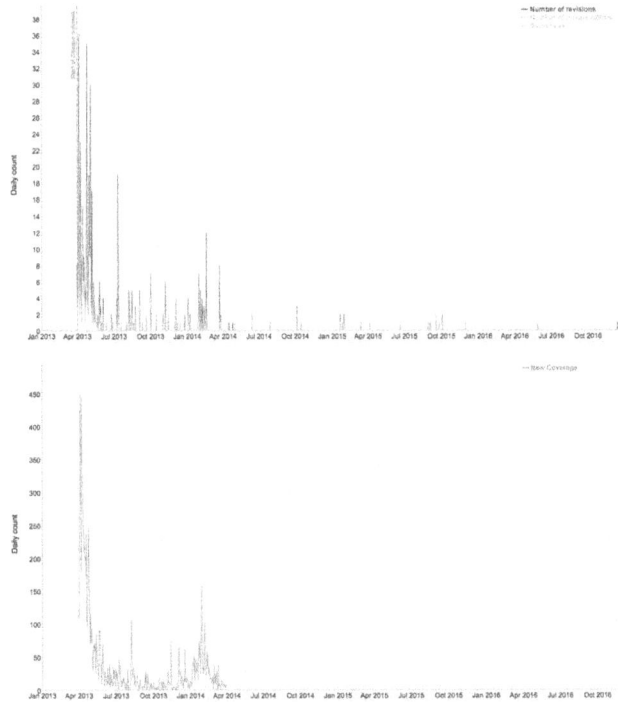

Figure 5:
Top Plot, H7N9 Wikipedia article;
Bottom plot, Corresponding news coverage.

Table 2: Pearson correlation test between the number of revisions and the number of news articles (α≦.05)

Disease	p-value	r
Zika	< 2.2e-16	0.6
Ebola	< 2.2e-16	0.5
Swine Flu	5.376e-16	0.4
MERS	< 2.2e-16	0.4
H7N9	< 2.2e-16	0.6

Table 3: Pearson correlation test between the number of unique editors and the number of news articles (α≦.05)

Disease	p-value	r
Zika	< 2.2e-16	0.6
Ebola	< 2.2e-16	0.5
Swine Flu	1.303e-13	0.4
MERS	< 2.2e-16	0.5
H7N9	< 2.2e-16	0.7

4 CLASSIFYING BURSTINESS

4.1 Determining the distribution of editing activities.

Here we categorize levels of burstiness as high, moderate, or low. The first step to analyze the distribution of the editing activities for all the 52 selected articles. Figures 6-7 show a distribution of the number of edits (revisions) and the daily number of unique editors for all the 52 selected articles. Additionally, Figures 8-9 show plots of the distributions in log-log axis.

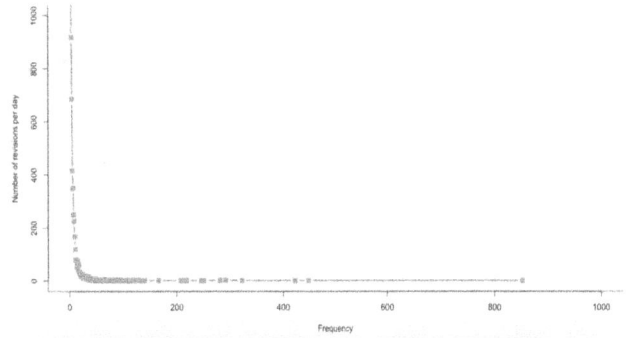

Figure 6: Distribution of the number of revisions

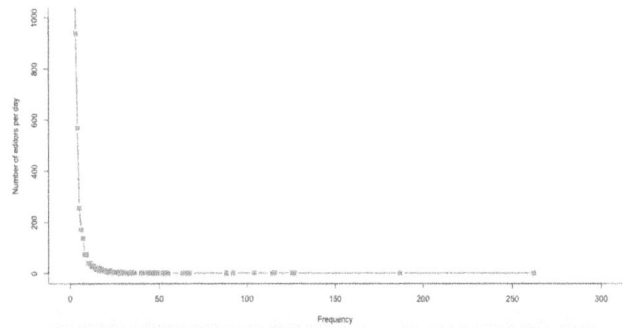

Figure 7: Distribution of the number of unique editors

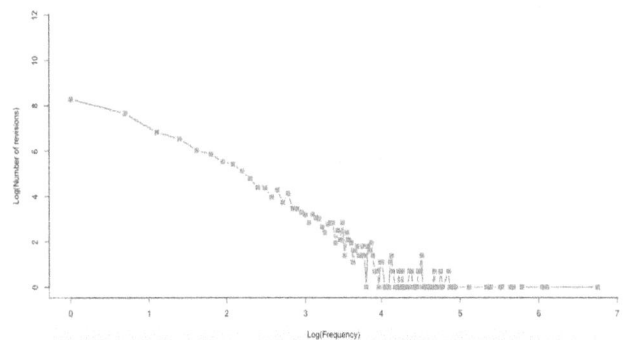

Figure 8: Distribution of the number of revisions (log scale)

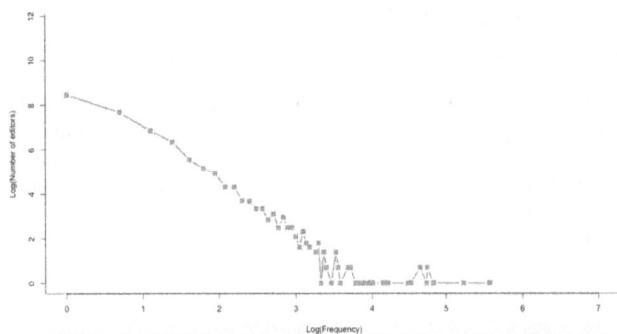

Figure 9: Distribution of the number of unique editors (log scale)

The average daily number of revisions is 5, while the average daily number of unique editors is 2. The range of daily number of revisions is 1-852; range of daily number of unique editors is 1-162. The distribution line is straight when graphed as a double-logarithm plot. This straight distribution line, which is the hallmark of a power law, is often used to detect the power law in double-logarithm plot [18].

The distribution of both the number of revisions and unique editors is skewed right because most of the articles have low daily number of revisions and daily number of unique editors (Revisions: β=1079, G_1=25; Unique editors: β=503, G_1=17). These statistics indicate that both distributions are highly skewed and leptokurtic. This suggests that small changes are less frequent than in a normal distribution, but extreme events are more likely to happen and are potentially much larger than in a normal distribution [47].

4.2 Determining head/tail breaks.

The second step is to use the results from the above distributions to categorize different types of burstiness. We adopted head/tail breaks, which is a classification scheme for data with a heavy-tailed distribution [18]. This classification scheme partitions all of the data values around the mean into two parts and continues the process iteratively for the values (above the mean) in the head until the head-part values are no longer heavy-tailed distributed. This approach is a clustering algorithm scheme typically used to classify geospatial data with a heavy-tail distribution such as power laws that, we have seen, characterize our data.

The head/tail breaks classification scheme demonstrates several advantages compared with the natural breaks and other classification schemes [18]. For example, the head/tail breaks is advantaged over natural breaks for its better representation of heavy-tailed distributions and better capturing the scaling or hierarchy of data [29]. Also, both the number of classes and class intervals are objectively determined, rather than subjectively imposed, such as with natural breaks. Finally, scaling is the essence of nature and society, in which there are far more small things than large ones [19].

The application of the head/tail breaks scheme resulted in our classifying burstiness into three categories based on the thresholds shown in Table 4. Accordingly, in order for an article in our dataset to be classified as *high burstiness*, the number of revisions should be greater than or equal 90 and the number of unique editors should be greater than or equal 33. Also, in order for an article to be classified as *moderate burstiness*, the number of revisions should be greater than or equal 39 and the number of

unique editors should be greater than or equal 15. Finally, to order for an article to be classified as *low burstiness*, the number of revisions should be greater than or equal 15 and the number of unique editors should be greater than or equal 6. Table 5 reports the classifications of the Wikipedia articles related to new disease outbreaks.

Table 4: Burstiness classification

Category	Number of revisions	Number of unique editors
High	≥ 90	≥ 33
Moderate	≥ 39	≥ 15
Low	≥ 15	≥ 6

The results indicate that the main articles that are related to Zika, Ebola and Swine Influenza have experienced high to moderate level of burstiness, while most of the articles related to MERS and H7N9 have experienced a low level of burstiness.

Table 5: Burstiness classifications of Wikipedia articles

Burstiness	Article title
High	Ebola virus disease
	Ebola virus cases in the United States
	2009 flu pandemic by country
	2009 flu pandemic
	Swine influenza
Moderate	Zika virus
	2015–16 Zika virus epidemic
	2009 flu pandemic in the UK
	2009 flu pandemic in Canada
Low	Zika virus outbreak timeline
	Zika fever
	Middle East respiratory syndrome
	2015 MERS outbreak in South Korea
	Influenza A virus subtype H7N9
	Avian influenza
	2009 flu pandemic in Spain
	2009 flu pandemic in Australia
	2009 flu pandemic in Asia

5 DISCUSSION

Our comparative analysis of edits on this set of Wikipedia articles on new disease outbreaks reveals that that there are common bursts of editorial activity—and these bursts can be classified as High, Moderate, or Low—followed a period of stasis. This reveals a potential model of burstiness that can be applied to other medical and health-related articles, or articles triggered by events for which there is relatively little pre-existing established knowledge, and where the triggering event is salient to a community.

5.1 A Model of Burstiness.

Our comparison of editorial bursts of Wikipedia articles on new disease outbreaks reveals the following high-level process:

(Pre-existingStasis)→Triggering Event→Mediation→Revisions→Stasis

This process suggests that articles are relatively static, but that a triggering event will result in a spike or burst of edits, and, over time, the articles will return to stasis with relatively low revision activity. In the case of the Wikipedia articles that we analyzed, the triggering event was the outbreak of a new disease. What each event had in common was that relatively little was known about the etiology of the disease, its spread, and the consequences for public health. The triggering event would be of great interest to specialists in respective fields, but most of all to the general public where anxiety may play a role in arousing interest.

When comparing the articles, we demonstrated that burstiness can be classified as high, moderate, or low. This difference in the intensity of the bursts can be explained by the *mediation* of the triggering event. In our case, the factors that mediate burstiness are: (1) The widespread and fast broadcast of the outbreak from a trusted source, such as the World Health Organization, which identified a public health risk that potentially requires a coordinated international response; (2) The relative lack of knowledge about the cause of the outbreaks and the precise mechanism of its spread—this is especially true of both Ebola and Zika; (3) The mortality and morbidity of the outbreaks, with Ebola resulting in mortality rates of 90%; and, we posit as a consequence of the first three factors, (4) The general public's perceived salience of the outbreak given the potential of disease spread and its consequences—and the public anxiety that attends the potential spread of a deadly disease. As we suggested earlier, one cannot underestimate the role of emotion in focusing attention to articles that, in turn, experienced high and moderate burstiness [13]. The public's perceived salience of the disease, and the concomitant press coverage, help to explain why MERS (which has a mortality rate of about 50%) had lower revisions than the Ebola virus, which has a mortality rate of 90%. Indeed, although there were only two contracted cases of Ebola in the United States, news coverage of the disease there was intense there, as was the news coverage of both Zika and Swine Flu. The popular press, for their part, tended to dramatize the effects [22].

5.2 Return to stasis.

We have explained why bursts occur, but how to explain the return to stasis? Our analysis of burstiness broadly aligns with the theory of punctuated equilibria in that an external event triggers a burst of revisions to an article, and the revisions subside to relative stasis. Niles and Gould [9], who coined the term, argued that

> The history of life is more adequately represented by a picture of 'punctuated equilibria' than by the notion of phyletic gradualism. The history of evolution is not one of stately unfolding, but a story of homeostatic equilibria, disturbed only "rarely" (i.e., rather often in the fullness of time) by rapid and episodic events of speciation. (p.84)

This theory grew out of paleontology, but has been subsequently applied in many domains since its introduction, including public policy [41], the diffusion of innovations [31], political science [10], and elsewhere. The theory has also been applied to online activities such as to how languished electronic petitions might suddenly, through an external trigger, encourage collective political action [7] [33].

Our theory also helps to explain the return to stasis: As Niles and Gould [9] argued,

> Evolutionary change is characterized by species and individuals as homeostatic systems—as amazingly well-buffered to resist change and maintain stability in the face of disturbing influences. (p. 114)

5.3 Context and provenance of Wikipedia articles.

This work has implications for readers and editors of Wikipedia articles to represent the context and provenance—that is, the history—of articles on Wikipedia. Our research shows that articles related to disease outbreaks are not constructed gradually and uniformly over time, but instead are constructed through a series of time-specific and context-specific bursts, the timing and magnitude of which are related to the trigger and specific mediation factors that affect the magnitude of bursts (such as press coverage). Such information provides the social and contextual provenance of a Wikipedia article such as when the major contributions to the article occurred, the relationship between exogenous factors and the article's content, and finally, as a consequence, the currency of the article. Such information for the reader can help to establish the level of trust that can be placed on the article, or inspire the reader to make updates to the article as new knowledge about the disease outbreak unfolds.

6 LIMITATIONS

One obvious limitation of this work is that it analyzed articles written only in English, which might explain the relatively low magnitude of editorial and news-report bursts regarding MERS. We examine only a subset of Wikipedia articles and, within that set, only a subset of health-related articles. We argue that the trigger for bursts were news reports, and that initially relatively little was known of the etiology or mechanism of contagion of these selected diseases. Further work may be needed to test that claim by comparing bursts between articles where there is a large body of accepted knowledge and those where there is not. However, one might find that stable medical knowledge is rare, especially when there are competing expert and public opinions (see, for example [23]) or when a conditions or courses of treatment are understood and interpreted in various ways [35]. Finally, we posit a positive correlation between the number of news articles on a disease and public anxiety. There is literature to support this claim, but further work is needed to test this empirically.

7 CONCLUSIONS

Our examination of the literature suggests that previous research examined *specific* Wikipedia articles to measure the spike of editing activities. Our research builds on Tinati's definition [28] that burstiness in Wikipedia is a period of high activity in a stream by applying a comparative approach that not only measures, but also compares burstiness across a set of Wikipedia articles. This approach reveals relative burstiness instead of absolute burstiness. This distinction is useful when considering a topic that involves a group of different articles, and when studying burstiness as a surge in two variables—the number of revisions per day and unique editors of articles per day.

This paper sought to apply new techniques to measure the editing activities burstiness across health-related articles in Wikipedia, and to categorize burstiness. We fit our data to the ARIMA model to measure burstiness, and we used the head/tail classification scheme to classify burstiness as high, moderate, or low. Our findings suggest that these techniques show promise in measuring and comparing burstiness across Wikipedia articles.

Our findings also reveal a model of burstiness: A period of stasis, followed by a trigger event that, in turn, is mediated. This mediating process influences the magnitude of the burst, and there is a return to stasis. We explain the burst and return to stasis by appealing to the theory of punctuated equilibria. Finally, our research suggests that articles on disease outbreaks are constructed through a series of time-specific and context-specific bursts, the timing and magnitude of which are related to the trigger and specific mediation factors. Such information provides the social and contextual provenance of a Wikipedia article that can help a reader establish the level of trust that can be placed on the article or inspire updates to the article as new knowledge unfolds.

ACKNOWLEDGMENTS

This work was supported by Qatar Foundation and the EPSRC Centre for Doctoral Training in Web Science Innovation under grant number EP/L016117/1.

REFERENCES

1. George Box and Gwilym Jenkins. 1970. *Time Series Analysis: Forecasting and Control.* San Francisco: Holden-Day.

2. Lawrence K. Altman. 1976. Legion Disease Tests Increase Mystery. *The New York Times.* Retrieved February 14, 2018 from https://www.nytimes.com/1976/09/05/archives/legion-disease-tests-increase-mystery-legion-disease-tests-increase.html

3. Albert-László Barabási. 2005. The origin of bursts and heavy tails in human dynamics. *Nature* 435, 7039: 207–211. https://doi.org/10.1038/nature03459

4. R. Crane and D. Sornette. 2008. Robust dynamic classes revealed by measuring the response function of a social system. https://doi.org/10.1073/pnas.0803685105

5. Sara Davies and Jeremy Youde. *The Politics of Surveillance and Response to Disease Outbreaks: The New Frontier for States and Non-state Actors (Hardback) - Routledge.* Routledge Taylor & Francis Group, NY, USA. Retrieved February 14, 2018 from https://www.routledge.com/The-Politics-of-Surveillance-and-Response-to-Disease-Outbreaks-The-New/Davies-Youde/p/book/9781409467182

6. Cambridge Dictionary. burst Meaning in the Cambridge English Dictionary. Retrieved February 14, 2018 from https://dictionary.cambridge.org/dictionary/english/burst

7. Catherine L. Dumas, Daniel LaManna, Teresa M. Harrison, S. S. Ravi, Loni Hagen, Christopher Kotfila, and Feng Chen. 2015. E-petitioning as Collective Political Action in We the People. *Scholar Commons*: 1.

8. Milad Eftekhar, Nick Koudas, and Yashar Ganjali. 2013. Bursty Subgraphs in Social Networks. In *Proceedings of the Sixth ACM International Conference on Web Search and Data Mining* (WSDM '13), 213–222. https://doi.org/10.1145/2433396.2433423

9. Niles Eldredge and Stephen Gould. 1972. Punctuated equilibria: an alternative to phyletic gradualism. In *Models in paleobiology*. 82–115. Retrieved February 14, 2018 from https://archive.org/details/B-001-004-118

10. David F. Prindle. 2012. Importing Concepts from Biology into Political Science: The Case of Punctuated Equilibrium. *Policy Studies Journal* 40: 21–44.

11. Gabriel Pui Cheong Fung, Jeffrey Xu Yu, Philip S. Yu, and Hongjun Lu. 2005. Parameter Free Bursty Events Detection in Text Streams. In *Proceedings of the 31st International Conference on Very Large Data Bases* (VLDB '05), 181–192. Retrieved February 14, 2018 from http://dl.acm.org/citation.cfm?id=1083592.1083616

12. Nicholas Generous, Geoffrey Fairchild, Alina Deshpande, Sara Y. Del Valle, and Reid Priedhorsky. 2014. Global disease monitoring and forecasting with Wikipedia. *PLoS computational biology* 10, 11: e1003892. https://doi.org/10.1371/journal.pcbi.1003892

13. Connie J. G. Gersick. 1991. Revolutionary Change Theories: A Multilevel Exploration of the Punctuated Equilibrium Paradigm. *The Academy of Management Review* 16, 1: 10–36. https://doi.org/10.2307/258605

14. A. Grabowski, N. Kruszewska, and R. A. Kosiński. 2008. Dynamic phenomena and human activity in an artificial society. *Physical Review. E, Statistical, Nonlinear, and Soft Matter Physics* 78, 6 Pt 2: 066110. https://doi.org/10.1103/PhysRevE.78.066110

15. A. A. Grace and B. S. Bunney. 1984. The control of firing pattern in nigral dopamine neurons: burst firing. *The Journal of Neuroscience: The Official Journal of the Society for Neuroscience* 4, 11: 2877–2890.

16. Jheser Guzman and Barbara Poblete. 2013. On-line Relevant Anomaly Detection in the Twitter Stream: An Efficient Bursty Keyword Detection Model. In *Proceedings of the ACM SIGKDD Workshop on Outlier Detection and Description* (ODD '13), 31–39. https://doi.org/10.1145/2500853.2500860

17. Hai-Bo Hu and Ding-Yi Han. 2008. Empirical analysis of individual popularity and activity on an online music service system. *Physica A: Statistical Mechanics and its Applications* 387, 23: 5916–5921. https://doi.org/10.1016/j.physa.2008.06.018

18. Bin Jiang. 2013. Head/Tail Breaks: A New Classification Scheme for Data with a Heavy-Tailed Distribution. *The Professional Geographer* 65, 3: 482–494. https://doi.org/10.1080/00330124.2012.700499

19. Bin Jiang and Daniel Z. Sui. 2014. A New Kind of Beauty Out of the Underlying Scaling of Geographic Space. *The Professional Geographer* 66, 4: 676–686. https://doi.org/10.1080/00330124.2013.852037

20. Brian Keegan, Darren Gergle, and Noshir Contractor. 2011. Hot off the Wiki: Dynamics, Practices, and Structures in Wikipedia's Coverage of the TŌHoku Catastrophes. In

Proceedings of the 7th International Symposium on Wikis and Open Collaboration (WikiSym '11), 105–113. https://doi.org/10.1145/2038558.2038577

21. Jon Kleinberg. 2003. Bursty and Hierarchical Structure in Streams. *Data Mining and Knowledge Discovery* 7, 4: 373–397. https://doi.org/10.1023/A:1024940629314

22. Celine Klemm, Enny Das, and Tilo Hartmann. 2016. Swine flu and hype: A systematic review of media dramatization of the H1N1 influenza pandemic. *Journal of Risk Research* 19, 1: 1–20. https://doi.org/10.1080/13669877.2014.923029

23. Daniel Krewski, Michelle C. Turner, Louise Lemyre, and Jennifer E. C. Lee. 2012. Expert vs. public perception of population health risks in Canada. *Journal of Risk Research* 15, 6: 601–625. https://doi.org/10.1080/13669877.2011.649297

24. Ravi Kumar, Jasmine Novak, Prabhakar Raghavan, and Andrew Tomkins. 2005. On the Bursty Evolution of Blogspace. *World Wide Web* 8, 2: 159–178. https://doi.org/10.1007/s11280-004-4872-4

25. Theodoros Lappas, Benjamin Arai, Manolis Platakis, Dimitrios Kotsakos, and Dimitrios Gunopulos. 2009. On Burstiness-aware Search for Document Sequences. In *Proceedings of the 15th ACM SIGKDD International Conference on Knowledge Discovery and Data Mining* (KDD '09), 477–486. https://doi.org/10.1145/1557019.1557075

26. Theodoros Lappas, Marcos R. Vieira, Dimitrios Gunopulos, and Vassilis J. Tsotras. 2013. STEM: A Spatio-temporal Miner for Bursty Activity. In *Proceedings of the 2013 ACM SIGMOD International Conference on Management of Data* (SIGMOD '13), 1021–1024. https://doi.org/10.1145/2463676.2463688

27. Michaël R. Laurent and Tim J. Vickers. 2009. Seeking Health Information Online: Does Wikipedia Matter? *Journal of the American Medical Informatics Association : JAMIA* 16, 4: 471–479. https://doi.org/10.1197/jamia.M3059

28. Sungjun Lee, Sangjin Lee, Kwanho Kim, and Jonghun Park. 2012. Bursty Event Detection from Text Streams for Disaster Management. In *Proceedings of the 21st International Conference on World Wide Web* (WWW '12 Companion), 679–682. https://doi.org/10.1145/2187980.2188179

29. Yue Lin. 2013. *A Comparison Study on Natural and Head/tail Breaks Involving Digital Elevation Models*. Retrieved February 15, 2018 from http://urn.kb.se/resolve?urn=urn:nbn:se:hig:diva-15609

30. Miles Lincoln. 2012. Death and Change Tracking: Wikipedia Edit Bursts. Retrieved from https://www.ocf.berkeley.edu/~milesl/content/deathedits.pdf

31. Christoph H. Loch and Bernardo A. Huberman. 1999. A Punctuated-Equilibrium Model of Technology Diffusion. *Management Science* 45, 2: 160–177. https://doi.org/10.1287/mnsc.45.2.160

32. Xinjiang Lu, Zhiwen Yu, Bin Guo, Jiafan Zhang, Alvin Chin, Jilei Tian, and Yang Cao. 2014. Trending Words Based Event Detection in Sina Weibo. In *Proceedings of the 2014 International Conference on Big Data Science and Computing* (BigDataScience '14), 4:1–4:6. https://doi.org/10.1145/2640087.2644156

33. Helen Margetts, Peter John, Scott Hale, and Taha Yasseri. 2015. *Political Turbulence: How Social Media Shape Collective Action*. Princeton University Press, Princeton, NJ, USA.

34. Ningfang Mi, Giuliano Casale, Ludmila Cherkasova, and Evgenia Smirni. 2008. Burstiness in Multi-tier Applications: Symptoms, Causes, and New Models. In *Middleware 2008* (Lecture Notes in Computer Science), 265–286. https://doi.org/10.1007/978-3-540-89856-6_14

35. Patricia Niland and Antonia C. Lyons. 2011. Uncertainty in medicine: meanings of menopause and hormone replacement therapy in medical textbooks. *Social Science & Medicine (1982)* 73, 8: 1238–1245. https://doi.org/10.1016/j.socscimed.2011.07.024

36. World Health Organization. World Health Organization, Disease outbreaks. *SEARO*. Retrieved February 14, 2018 from http://www.searo.who.int/topics/disease_outbreaks/en/

37. Mauro Politi and Enrico Scalas. 2008. Fitting the empirical distribution of intertrade durations. *Physica A: Statistical Mechanics and its Applications* 387, 8: 2025–2034. https://doi.org/10.1016/j.physa.2007.11.018

38. Yla Tausczik, Kate Faasse, James W. Pennebaker, and Keith J. Petrie. 2012. Public anxiety and information seeking following the H1N1 outbreak: blogs, newspaper articles, and Wikipedia visits. *Health Communication* 27, 2: 179–185. https://doi.org/10.1080/10410236.2011.571759

39. Ramine Tinati, Markus Luczak-Roesch, and Wendy Hall. 2016. Finding Structure in Wikipedia Edit Activity: An Information Cascade Approach. In *Proceedings of the 25th International Conference Companion on World Wide Web* (WWW '16 Companion), 1007–1012. https://doi.org/10.1145/2872518.2891110

40. Ramine Tinati, Thanassis Tiropanis, and Lesie Carr. 2013. An Approach for Using Wikipedia to Measure the Flow of Trends Across Countries. In *Proceedings of the 22Nd International Conference on World Wide Web* (WWW '13 Companion), 1373–1378. https://doi.org/10.1145/2487788.2488177

41. J.L. True, B.D. Jones, and F.R. Baumgartner. 2007. Punctuated Equilibrium Theory: Explaining stability and change in public policymaking. *Em Paul A. Sabatier (Org.) (2007)*: 155–187.

42. Michail Vlachos, Christopher Meek, Zografoula Vagena, and Dimitrios Gunopulos. 2004. Identifying Similarities, Periodicities and Bursts for Online Search Queries. In *Proceedings of the 2004 ACM SIGMOD International Conference on Management of Data* (SIGMOD '04), 131–142. https://doi.org/10.1145/1007568.1007586

43. Morten Warncke-Wang, Vivek Ranjan, Loren Terveen, and Brent Hecht. 2015. Misalignment between supply and demand of quality content in peer production communities. In *Proceedings of the 9th International Conference on Web and Social Media, ICWSM 2015*. Retrieved February 14, 2018 from https://experts.umn.edu/en/publications/misalignment-between-supply-and-demand-of-quality-content-in-peer

44. Xiaoxue Zhao, Takahiro Omi, Nanae Matsuno, and Shigeru Shinomoto. 2010. A non-universal aspect in the temporal occurrence of earthquakes. *New Journal of Physics* 12, 6: 063010. https://doi.org/10.1088/1367-2630/12/6/063010

45. Xin Zhao, Jing Jiang, Jing He, Xiaoming Li, Hongfei Yan, and Dongdong Shan. 2010. Context Modeling for Ranking and Tagging Bursty Features in Text Streams. 1769. https://doi.org/10.1145/1871437.1871725

46. Tao Zhou, Hoang Anh Tuan Kiet, Beom Jun Kim, Bing-Hong Wang, and Petter Holme. 2007. Role of Activity in Human Dynamics. https://doi.org/10.1209/0295-5075/82/28002

47. Leptokurtosis Definition from Financial Times Lexicon. Retrieved February 14, 2018 from http://lexicon.ft.com/Term?term=leptokurtosis

Early Public Responses to the Zika-Virus on YouTube: Prevalence of and Differences Between Conspiracy Theory and Informational Videos

Adina Nerghes
KNAW Humanities Cluster
Amsterdam, The Netherlands
adina.nerghes@dh.huc.knaw.nl

Peter Kerkhof
Vrije Universiteit Amsterdam
Amsterdam, The Netherlands
p.kerkhof@vu.nl

Iina Hellsten
University of Amsterdam
Amsterdam, The Netherlands
i.r.hellsten@uva.nl

ABSTRACT

In this paper, we analyze the content of the most popular videos posted on YouTube in the first phase of the Zika-virus outbreak in 2016, and the user responses to those videos. More specifically, we examine the extent to which informational and conspiracy theory videos differ in terms of user activity (number of comments, shares, likes and dislikes), and the sentiment and content of the user responses. Our results show that 12 out of the 35 videos in our data set focused on conspiracy theories, but no statistical differences were found in the number of user activity and sentiment between the two types of videos. The content of the user responses shows that users respond differently to sub-topics related to Zika-virus. The implications of the results for future online health promotion campaigns are discussed.

KEYWORDS

Zika-virus; YouTube; Informational and Conspiracy Theory Videos; Topic Modeling; Semantic Networks

ACM Reference format:
Adina Nerghes, Peter Kerkhof, and Iina Hellsten. 2018. Early Public Responses to the Zika-Virus on YouTube: Prevalence of and Differences Between Conspiracy Theory and Informational Videos. In *Proceedings of 10th ACM Conference on Web Science, Amsterdam, Netherlands, May 27–30, 2018 (WebSci '18),* 8 pages.
https://doi.org/10.1145/3201064.3201086

1 INTRODUCTION

During the onset of a possible epidemic, the information available to the public is typically incomplete, unclear and often contested. Limited as it may be, information at hand may still install fear among the public and impact people's behavior, which in turn may affect the course of the epidemic [e.g., 11]. Media play an important role in spreading information about possible epidemics. Increasingly, this information is spread not only by media institutions but also by media users through their social media channels, which have become an important forum for disseminating health information.

As the largest video-sharing network, YouTube is a popular social media forum for sharing videos on health related topics [e.g.,

4, 7, for recent examples], and searching for health information [17]. According to recent estimates, YouTube has over 1 billion monthly users, watching a total of 6 billion hours of video per month [26]. Much of the content on YouTube is health related and recent studies have investigated content related to a wide range of health issues, such as vaccines [7, 15], anorexia [27], Ebola [4], rheumatoid arthritis [25], and tanning bed use [14]. As both a mass communication tool allowing one-to-many communications [13], and a discussion forum enabling commenting on the videos and replying to comments provided by others, YouTube adds new dimensions to health communication. Mapping the prevalence and the content of health-related videos and user responses to those videos on YouTube provides information for designing and targeting health interventions and campaigns in online settings.

The quality of health related information found on YouTube varies. Although many videos contain information that can be qualified as correct and helpful, YouTube is also known as a source of misleading and incorrect information, information that is easily accessible to YouTube users [17]. YouTube videos have been discussed as a source of misinformation on various health related issues such as vaccines [7], obesity [36], skin cancer [3], anorexia [27] and Ebola[19]. For example, in an analysis of videos related to rheumatoid arthritis, 30% was qualified as misleading, yet the audience responses (popularity, number of viewers, number of likes) did not differ between useful and misleading videos [25].

1.1 Conspiracy Theories

In addition to misinformation, YouTube videos and public responses to these videos have been linked to conspiracy theories [22]. Douglas, Sutton, and Cichocka [8, p.537] define conspiracy theories as "explanations for important events that involve secret plots by powerful and malevolent groups". Conspiracy theories have emerged online during different crises and events on a regular basis –including the moon landing, 9/11, chemtrails, and climate change science. Conspiracy theories about medical issues appear to be widespread. For example, Oliver and Wood [20] show that 63% of the American public has heard of the rumor that the US Food and Drug Administration deliberately prevents the public from getting natural cures for cancer because of pressure from drug companies. Over a third of Americans believes this to be true. The existence of conspiracy theories regarding the spread of viruses has been shown in the case of AIDS [e.g., 16], H1N1 [2] and Ebola [1].

Recently, misinformation and the presence of conspiracy theories in social media has been linked to public health. In the United

States, lower vaccination rates were found in states where misinformation and conspiracies were more prevalent on Twitter [10]. Also, agreeing with conspiracy theories is related to a lower willingness to follow medical advice (e.g., using sunscreens or vaccines [20]).

During the early stages of an epidemic, misinformation and conspiracy theories may be especially pertinent since ill-informed behavioral responses (e.g., with regard to vaccination decisions or travel plans) may contribute to spreading the disease. Media portrayals of and attention to epidemics do not always reflect the most recent science based knowledge about how, to what extent, and with which consequences epidemic spreads. "Media logic does not equate to epidemiological logic" [23, p.10], and may as such contribute to how the public understands a health crisis. Indeed, recent evidence suggests that differences in public responses to the 2009 influenza A H1N1 outbreak were partly shaped by differences in information presented by the media [23]. The gap between information about epidemics in media and information from official sources is likely to be larger in the case of social media. Contributors to social media content are less closely linked to official sources and the process of posting, commenting, and sharing lacks the scrutiny and journalistic gatekeeping of traditional media.

Indeed, several studies link social media information to the spread of conspiracy theories. In a large-scale analysis of Twitter data, Vousoughi, Roym and Aral [33] show that false news, among which conspiracy theories, spread faster, farther and deeper than true news. False news, according to their analysis, is more novel than true news, and is met more often with fear, disgust and surprise. Yet, the question is whether the results of the analysis of Vousoughi et al. [33] apply to conspiracy theories in general: as the authors note themselves, conspiracy theories can be both true or false. Del Vicario et al. [32] directly compared how conspiracy theories vs. scientific information spread on Facebook and found that both conspiracy theories and scientific information are mainly spread among people with the same information preferences. Yet, the cascade dynamics differ between the two types of information: scientific information is assimilated more quickly and has a longer lifetime, yet lifetime is not related to size. Conspiracy theories assimilate more slowly and the size of cascades related to conspiracy theories is positively related to their lifetime. Bessi et al. (2015)[5] inspected how mainstream science news and conspiracy news were consumed by over 1,2 million individuals on Facebook, and concluded that the two types of information were related to polarized communities. Zollo et al., (2015)[37] observed that sentiment of comments to conspiracy news tended to be more negative than comments to science news, as is the average sentiment of comments by users of conspiracy pages.

1.2 Social Media and the Zika-virus

In the current study, we investigate the nature of the most popular videos (informational and conspiracy theory) providing health-information on the Zika-virus in YouTube videos, and the user responses (comments and replies to the comments) to these videos. The Zika-virus was first discovered in Uganda in 1947 but remained largely unknown to the general population. This changed when an outbreak of the virus in Brazil and neighboring countries, in early 2016, coincided with an increase in occurrences of microcephaly, a malformation of the brain which causes babies to be born with an abnormally small head. A link between the Zika-virus and microcephaly was only recently confirmed [18].

In social media, the spread of the Zika-virus was the center of much attention, especially after Zika was labelled an international health emergency by the World Health Organization on 1 February 2016 (see [12]). In an analysis of Zika related tweets, Dredze, Broniatowski, and Hilyard [9] find many references to conspiracy theories, in which microcephaly is explained as a side effects of larvicides allegedly produced by chemical company Monsanto, or as a side effect of existing vaccines.

The current paper aims to map the prevalence and popularity of videos containing Zika related conspiracy theories on YouTube during the onset of the Zika-virus crisis. We compare YouTube metrics that indicate or may affect the popularity of video?s (e.g., views, likes, comments, shares). Since Zollo et al. [37] observed that sentiment of comments to conspiracy news tended to be more negative than comments to science news, as is the average sentiment of comments by users of conspiracy pages, we also compared the content and sentiment of the comments.

We analyzed the 35 most popular videos referring to the Zika-virus during the recent outbreak (December 2015 - July 2016). These 35 videos were by far most popular according to the number of views, metric that places them at the top of searches on the Zika-virus. We mapped and compared user responses to videos containing informational and conspiracy theory content and analyzed the relation between the sentiment in the comments and video popularity. Our empirical research questions are:

(1) What type of Zika-related videos (informational vs. conspiracy) were most often viewed on YouTube?
(2) How did the number of comments, replies, likes and shares differ across the two video types?
(3) How did the sentiment of the user responses differ between the two video types?
(4) How did the content of the user responses differ between the video types?

2 DATA & METHODS

Using the number of views as an indicator of popularity and the search string "Zika-virus", we collected all the English language videos with at least 40,000 views on July 11, 2016, which resulted in a data set containing 35 videos. YouTube considers the number of views as the fundamental parameter of video popularity. Hence, collecting videos with the highest number of views, for our given search string, allows us to capture those videos that would be listed first by search engines (or the search function within YouTube). The upload dates for the 35 videos in our set range between December 30, 2015 and March 30, 2016.

For each of the 35 videos in our data set user responses were collected using the Netvizz YouTube Data Tool [24]. In total, 28795 user responses were collected, representing both comments (12584) and replies to comments (16211). Once collected, the user responses were cleaned prior to analysis. More specifically, noise-words, punctuation, and numbers were removed, and all words were lower-cased and stemmed (i.e., reducing inflected words to their word stem, such as plurals converted to singular forms).

We use a mixed methods approach to analyze both the videos and the user responses to these videos. In the following sub-sections we provide details on the different types of analysis used in this paper.

2.1 Categorization of video content

First, we employed content analysis to determine the main topic and type of information source used in each video. This analysis was based on close watching the sample of videos, and coding the video as either disseminating informational or conspiracy theory content. Furthermore, to explore relationships between the different popularity metrics for our data set, we use correlation and regression analysis based on the number of shares, comments, replies, likes, and dislikes between the two types of videos (i.e., information vs. conspiracy theories videos).

2.2 Analysis of comments and replies

We compared the content of the user responses to the two video types (informational and conspiracy theory) using topic modeling and semantic network analysis. For topic modeling, latent Dirichlet allocation (LDA), as implemented in the MALLET, was applied to the user responses content [6]. Topic models identify, extract, and characterize the various (latent) topics contained by collections of texts, such as YouTube user comments. More specifically, topics are automatically identified based on word co-occurrence patterns across a corpus of text documents, where a cluster of words that co-occur frequently across a number of documents constitute a topic. Based on the assumption that text documents are collections of multiple topics, where a topic represents a probability distribution over words, topic models connect words that are often used together. In this study each user response (i.e., comment and/or reply) was considered a distinct text document.

We compared the results of the LDA topic model with semantic network visualizations. Automated semantic network methods were used to visualize the co-occurrence patterns across the user responses as our cases, and the words as the variables. These semantic networks visualize clusters of concepts that co-occur across comments and replies to the videos [21]. The more often these concepts co-occur, the stronger the link between them in the resulting network [35]. A semantic network has been generated for all the user responses to the two types of videos (informational and conspiracy theory videos) using VOSviewer [29].

In order to examine sentiment in the user responses for the videos in our dataset, we used SentiStrength [28]. The SentiStrength opinion-mining algorithm is designed to extract positive and negative emotion from sentences, and was specifically developed to account for the grammar and spelling style often used in social media. The software uses a dual positive/negative sentiment strength scoring system to output a positive sentiment score from 1 to 5 and a negative score from -1 to -5 for each comment. A comment with a score of 5/-1 is to be interpreted as strongly marked by positive

Table 1: Descriptive statistics of video metrics

	Informational (n=23)		Conspiracy (n=12)	
	M	SD	M	SD
Views	205.097	211.859	159.224	163.452
Top Level Comments	404	367	274	293
Replies	517	473	361	359
Likes	3340	4417	1627	1981
Dislikes	122	109	102	151
Shares	109	833	689	630

sentiment, and one yielding 1/-5 is primarily negative in regards to sentiment content.

3 RESULTS

3.1 Informational vs. conspiracy theory videos

Most of the videos (23 out of 35) were categorized as informational videos, of which nine were delivering science-based information and fourteen circulating news media broadcasts on the topic. Informational videos provided, in general, facts about the origin, spreading, and consequences of the Zika-virus, or updates about the outbreak. Twelve of the videos collected presented conspiracy theory videos, either listing different alternative explanations for the epidemics of the Zika-virus (2 videos), or naming particular organizations and actors responsible for the Zika-virus. These videos attributed the virus to Bill Gates (4 videos), the Rockefeller foundation (2 videos) or Monsanto (2 videos), often linked to, for example argumentation that genetically modified (GMO) mosquitos cause the Zika-virus (5 videos), and that the virus is used as a bio-weapon (3 videos) for world depopulation. In addition, one video argued that the ban on DDT has caused a rise in the number of mosquitos, leading to the spread of the Zika-virus. In two videos the link between the Zika-virus and microcephaly was contested.

3.1.1 User activity. Table 1 presents the means and standard deviations of the main YouTube metrics for both types of videos. The means of all metrics appear higher for informational videos, but there are substantial differences between the videos, as is indicated by the high standard deviations. In order to test for differences between the metrics of informational and conspiracy theory videos, we applied negative binomial regression analysis, using the MASS package that is available in R [30]. Negative binomial regression analysis is suited for analyzing count data with high dispersion, i.e. variances that exceed the mean [31], which is the case in the YouTube metrics we report. The analyses revealed no significant differences ($p < .05$). Since the different metrics are strongly correlated (see Table 2 for the Spearman correlations), we repeated the analyses but this time added the number of views as a covariate. Again, no significant differences in terms of likes, dislikes, shares, number of top level comments, and replies were found.

In terms of the activity levels of unique users, the number of unique users (11498) generating a total of 20745 user responses to the 23 informational videos was almost three times larger than the number of unique users (4356) generating 8050 responses to the 12 conspiracy videos. To assess the levels of user activity in terms of responses (i.e., comments and replies) per video type, we conduct a

Table 2: Spearman Correlations between the video metrics

	Views	All Comments	Top Level Comments	Replies	Likes	Dislikes	Shares
Views	–						
All Comments	0.692***	–					
Top Level Comments	0.721***	0.967***	–				
Replies	0.669***	0.981***	0.926 ***	–			
Likes	0.696***	0.874***	0.915 ***	0.854***	–		
Dislikes	0.670***	0.914***	0.903 ***	0.884***	0.784***	–	
Shares	0.396*	0.455**	0.522 **	0.380*	0.549**	0.453**	–

$^*p < .05$, $^{**}p < .01$, $^{***}p < .001$ (two-tailed)

$t - test$ comparing the ratio of number of responses per video to the number of video views. While there are fewer responses (per view) in the informational videos ($M_{informational}$ = 0.0048; $M_{conspiracy}$ = 0.0056), the difference in means is insignificant (t(29.1) = 0.70; p > .05). Similarly, while there are fewer unique commenters per view in the informational videos ($M_{informational}$ = 0.0027; $M_{conspiracy}$ = 0.0033), the ratio does not vary significantly across video types ($t(27.4) = 1.05$; $p > .05$).

We also conducted a Negative Binomial Regression subtracting 1 from the dependent variable of the number of responses per unique user, thus testing the extent to which video type influences users to issue more than one response, controlling for the total number of responses per video. The effect of the informational videos is insignificant ($b = 0.07$; $p > .05$). Interestingly, though, the total number of responses for each of the video types predicts against additional responding per unique user ($b = -1.0x10-4$; $p < .001$).

Thus, we find no significant differences between informational and conspiracy theory videos when assessing user activity in terms of responses per view and unique users per view. We also find that the video type does not influence whether users issue more than one response. However, we do find that neither type of videos promotes additional responding per unique user, showing low engagement of YouTube users viewing Zika-virus related content.

3.2 Content of user responses

3.2.1 Sentiment analysis. All user responses were coded for sentiment in order to establish whether the sentiment differs between informational and conspiracy theory videos. In the sentiment analysis, most responses, fall within the zone of 1/-1 (31.78%), which indicates that such comments are not very affective in the case of Zika on YouTube. In the comments to the informational videos, only 0.05% of comments were maximum positive (score 5/-1), and only 0.50% of comments were maximum negative (score -5/1). As examples of highly positive (5/-1) and highly negative (-5/1) by the SentiStrength opinion mining algorithm:

Highly positive: "I fucking love Canada... Just cold enough to keep the bugs out"

Highly negative: "I fucking hate mosquitos so much. Make these fucking cancers on the earth extinct. Put all funding to making these little fucks a sentence in a history book."

Table 3: Mean sentiment scores of informational vs. conspiracy theory YouTube videos.

	Informational (n = 23)		Conspiracy (n = 12)	
	M	SD	M	SD
Positive sentiment	1.61	0.148	1.70	0.170
Negative sentiment	1.91	0.271	2.03	0.165

In order to establish whether the means of the sentiment scores differ between informational and conspiracy theory videos, the mean aggregate positive and negative sentiment scores were compared using a Mann-Whitney U t-test, which is fit for handling non-normal data (Table 3). None of the means were significantly different from each other (at $p < .05$), although the difference in positive sentiment scores almost reached conventional levels of significance ($p = .079$), suggesting that positive sentiment is lower among conspiracy theory video?s. Since the sentiment scores are nested in videos, we calculated the intraclass correlation coefficient (ICC), a measure of how much of the total variance can be attributed to differences between videos. The ICCs for negative and positive sentiment are between .02 and .03, indicating that differences between videos do not account for much of the variance in the sentiment of the comments. Also, for both negative and positive sentiment, the estimated variance that can be attributed to differences between videos ($\tau 00$) is lower than its corresponding standard deviation (positive sentiment: $\tau 00 = .0168$, $SD = .1295$; negative sentiment: $\tau 00 = .0314$, $SD = .1773$), another indication that the variance attributed to difference between videos is negligible.

3.2.2 LDA Topic Models. When fitting the LDA topic model to a collection of text documents, the analyst needs to specify the number of topics to be identified. This selection generally implies exploration of different solutions to achieving the best fit. Based on the weight values presented in the tables below, we choose four topics to be detected, running the algorithm for 3000 iterations with the $\sum \alpha = 5$. In Tables 4 and 5 we present the four topics identified for each of the video types and the top ten words belonging to each topic. The weight value for each topic represents the prominence of each topic across the collection of document. We also provide a label for each topic summarizing their content.

The results of the topic modeling show that the user responses to the two types of videos contain similarities as well as differences (see Tables 4 and 5). While both types of videos elicit topics related to the causes of the Zika-virus and affected stakeholders, we also note unique topics for each type of videos. Informational videos user responses discuss the consequences of the virus, while the conspiracy theory videos user responses also focus on the stakeholders responsible for the outbreak.

To further visualize the differences in content between the 20745 user responses to the 23 informational videos, and the 8050 responses to the 12 conspiracy videos, we visualized semantic maps of the co-occurring concepts (i.e., words and phrases) for each video type. In Figures 1a and 1b, concepts are the nodes (i.e., N) and co-occurrences of these concepts are represented by links (i.e., E).

In informational videos, the user responses focus on discussions surrounding man, woman, government, God, world, and Africa (red cluster), rights, abort, fetuses (yellow cluster), the causes of the outbreak; water, and virus mutation (green cluster), and to a lesser extent research, university (blue cluster) (Figure 1a). In the conspiracy video responses, Monsanto, government, Brazil and GMOs are mentioned (red cluster), while the problem is discussed in terms of pesticide, larvae and chemicals (green cluster). We also note an additional cluster in which the purpose of the Zika-virus is discussed in terms of control, life, and truth (blue cluster) as well as religion-linked words on man, woman, God and Bible (yellow cluster) (Figure 1b).

Taken together, the topic modeling and the semantic network analysis show that whereas the responses to informational videos discuss clusters around the causes and consequences of the Zika-virus, responses to conspiracy theory videos revolve around the Zika-virus as a means to population control and allocating responsibility for the spread of the virus to various organizations and actors.

4 DISCUSSION AND CONCLUSION

In conclusion, most of the videos that were analyzed in this article, provided informational content on the Zika-virus, whereas twelve out of the sample of 35 videos contained conspiracy theory content. Surprisingly, our results on user activity showed no statistically significant differences across the video types. However, the difference between mean shares to informational and to conspiracy videos, albeit not significant, is in line with the results by Vosoughi, Roya and Aral [33] on fake news spreading faster, and gaining more emotional responses than true news. These results are also in line with earlier research into misinformation in social media, in particular on that audience responses (popularity, number of viewers, number of likes) do not differ between useful and misleading videos, as also found by Singh et al., (2012)[25] in their study on videos on rheumatoid arthritis. This shows that YouTube users respond in similar ways, in terms of views, shares and likes, to videos containing informational and conspiracy theory content. For health care organizations, this result is striking as it indicates that both informational and conspiracy theory content spread online in similar ways. To counter the spread of misinformation, the monitoring of the content posted on YouTube deserves more attention by health organizations. In addition, we found no differences in the sentiment of the user responses to the two video types. Responses to both

informational and conspiracy theory videos were slightly negative, on average. This result contradicts Vousoughi, Roy and Aral [33] who found false news to trigger more negative sentiments than true news.

In terms of user (posting) activity, the only significant result we find is that neither of the two types of video content promotes additional responding per unique user. Hence, regardless of the type of video users watch, they are not likely to engage in conversations. The low engagement of YouTube users viewing Zika-virus related content is an important finding, showing that these users express their opinion in their responses without further participating in conversations. For health organizations, this finding indicates a need for careful consideration of the type of content they make available through social media platforms in order to engage users in conversations, both as a way of disseminating accurate information and as a way of addressing or debunking conspiracy theories.

Finally, our results on the content of the user responses show that comments to the two different types of videos (*informational, conspiracy theory*) discuss the Zika-virus using different framings: (1) Comments to *informational videos* discuss the Zika-virus as a problem for babies and pregnant women in Brazil; (2) Comments to *conspiracy theory videos*, in turn, frame the Zika-virus as a targeted means to population control and as a consequence of a larvicide produced by the chemical company Monsanto, similar to the findings on Zika-related tweets by Dredze, Broniatowski and Hilyard [9] . Two videos contest the link that Zika-virus is causing microcephaly in newborns. The extent to which the responses to both types of video overlapped requires further research into the content of the responses, for example, via a quantitative content analysis of both the videos and the related responses.

In conclusion, our findings have implications for health organizations designing online campaigns. As studies have confirmed, the influence of viewer comments on other audience members? perceptions of health-related YouTube content [34], understanding the various types of contestation present in YouTube video user responses on the Zika-virus is important for future online health promotion campaigns. Online health interventions can be targeted on the most active social media users, who can be identified using user activity information, and in particular the most active users promoting misleading information. Also, careful consideration of the type of information online health promotion campaigns make available to users is needed, to ensure participation and involvement in conversations. In addition, understanding the differences in the content of user responses to different video types can help in uncovering the most frequent topics related to conspiracy theories for intervention purposes. Such practices would help prevent an increase in deep-rooted conspiracy beliefs, which in turn may affect health choices and behavior.

REFERENCES

[1] Sharon Alane Abramowitz, Sarah Lindley McKune, Mosoka Fallah, Josepine Monger Kodjo Tehoungue, and Patricia A Omidian. 2017. The opposite of denial: Social learning at the onset of the Ebola emergency in Liberia. *Journal of Health Communication* 22, sup1 (2017), 59–65. https://doi.org/10.1080/10810730.2016. 1209599

[2] Laetitia Atlani-Duault, Arnaud Mercier, Cecile Rousseau, Paul Guyot, and John-Paul Moatti. 2015. Blood libel rebooted: traditional scapegoats, online media, and the H1N1 epidemic. *Culture, Medicine, and Psychiatry* 39, 1 (2015), 43–61.

Table 4: Topics of informational videos user responses

Topic	Weight	Words representing the topic
Affected stakeholders	0.731	virus, Zika, people, baby, pregnant, brazil, Ebola, year, spread, mosquito
Consequences of Zika	0.474	people, fuck, life, kill, abortion, country, comment, baby, world, stupid
Geographic and politics of Zika	0.376	live, mosquito, fuck, Canada, plague, zika, virus, video, Florida, Trump
Causes of Zika	0.339	mosquito, human, population, world, kill, people, control, virus, nature, food

Table 5: Topics of conspiracy videos user responses

Topic	Weight	Topic Members
Causes of Zika	0.876	people, world, population, control, kill, live, human, year, country, government
Everyday considerations	0.579	video, fuck, time, love, people, good, dark, truth, watch, word
Affected stakeholders	0.473	zika, virus, mosquito, brazil, microcephaly, case, vaccine, baby, woman, spread
Responsible stakeholders	0.465	Monsanto, fact, video, people, company, chemical, science, claim, prove, evidence

[3] Corey H Basch, Charles E Basch, Grace Clarke Hillyer, and Rachel Reeves. 2015. YouTube videos related to skin cancer: A missed opportunity for cancer prevention and control. *Journal of Medical Internet Research Cancer* 1, 1 (2015).

[4] Corey H Basch, Charles E Basch, Kelly V Ruggles, and Rodney Hammond. 2015. Coverage of the Ebola virus disease epidemic on YouTube. *Disaster medicine and public health preparedness* 9, 5 (2015), 531–535.

[5] Alessandro Bessi, Mauro Coletto, George Alexandru Davidescu, Antonio Scala, Guido Caldarelli, and Walter Quattrociocchi. 2015. Science vs Conspiracy: Collective narratives in the age of misinformation. *PloS one* 10, 2 (2015), e0118093.

[6] David M. Blei, Andrew Y Ng, and Michael I Jordan. 2003. Latent dirichlet allocation. *Journal of Machine Learning Research* 3 (2003), 993–1022.

[7] Rowena Briones, Xiaoli Nan, Kelly Madden, and Leah Waks. 2012. When vaccines go viral: an analysis of HPV vaccine coverage on YouTube. *Health communication* 27, 5 (2012), 478–85. https://doi.org/10.1080/10410236.2011.610258

[8] Karen M Douglas, Robbie M Sutton, and Aleksandra Cichocka. 2017. The psychology of conspiracy theories. *Current Directions in Psychological Science* 26, 6 (2017), 538–542. https://doi.org/10.1177/0963721417718261

[9] Mark Dredze, David A Broniatowski, and Karen M Hilyarde. 2016. Zika vaccine misconceptions: A social media analysis. *Vaccine* 34, 30 (2016), 3441. https://doi.org/10.1016/j.vaccine.2016.05.008

[10] Adam G Dunn, Didi Surian, Julie Leask, Aditi Dey, Kenneth D Mandl, and Enrico Coiera. 2017. Mapping information exposure on social media to explain differences in HPV vaccine coverage in the United States. *Vaccine* 35, 23 (2017), 3033–3040.

[11] Maria Espinola, James M. Shultz, Zelde Espinel, Benjamin M. Althouse, Janice L. Cooper, Florence Baingana, Louis Herns Marcelin, Toni Cela, Sherry Towers, Laurie Mazurik, M. Claire Greene, Alyssa Beck, Michelle Fredrickson, Andrew McLean, and Andreas Rechkemmer. 2016. Fear-related behaviors in situations of mass threat. *Disaster Health* 3, 4 (2016), 102–111. https://doi.org/10.1080/21665044.2016.1263141

[12] King-Wa Fu, Hai Liang, Nitin Saroha, Zion Tsz Ho Tse, Patrick Ip, and Isaac Chun-Hai Fung. 2016. How people react to Zika virus outbreaks on Twitter? A computational content analysis. *American Journal of Infection Control* 44, 12 (2016), 1700–1702.

[13] Daniel Gruhl, Ramanathan Guha, David Liben-Nowell, and Andrew Tomkins. 2004. Information Diffusion Through Blogspace. In *Proceedings of the 13th International Conference on World Wide Web (WWW '04)*. ACM, New York, NY, USA, 491–501. https://doi.org/10.1145/988672.988739

[14] Eric W Hossler and Michael P Conroy. 2008. YouTube as a source of information on tanning bed use. *Archives of Dermatology* 144, 10 (2008), 1395–1396.

[15] Jennifer Keelan, Vera Pavri-Garcia, George Tomlinson, and Kumanan Wilson. 2007. YouTube as a source of information on immunization: a content analysis. *JAMA* 298, 21 (2007), 2482–2484.

[16] Elizabeth A Klonoff and Hope Landrine. 1999. Do blacks believe that HIV/AIDS is a government conspiracy against them? *Preventive Medicine* 28, 5 (1999), 451–457.

[17] Kapil Chalil Madathil, A Joy Rivera-Rodriguez, Joel S Greenstein, and Anand K Gramopadhye. 2015. Healthcare Information on YouTube: A systematic review. *Health Informatics Journal* 21, 3 (2015), 173–194.

[18] Jernej Mlakar, Misa Korva, Nataša Tul, Mara Popović, Mateja Poljšak-Prijatelj, Jerica Mraz, Marko Kolenc, Katarina Resman Rus, Tina Vesnaver Vipotnik, Vesna Fabjan Vodušek, Alenka Vizjak, and Jože Pižem. 2016. Zika virus associated with microcephaly. *New England Journal of Medicine* 2016, 374 (2016), 951–958.

[19] Sajan Jiv Singh Nagpal, Ahmadreza Karimianpour, Dhruvika Mukhija, Diwakar Mohan, and Andrei Brateanu. 2015. YouTube videos as a source of medical information during the Ebola hemorrhagic fever epidemic. *Springer Plus* 4, 1 (2015), 457.

[20] Eric J Oliver and Thomas Wood. 2014. Medical conspiracy theories and health behaviors in the United States. *JAMA internal medicine* 174, 5 (2014), 817–818.

[21] Roel Popping. 2003. Knowledge Graphs and Network Text Analysis. *Social Science Information* 42, 1 (2003), 91–106. doi:10.1177/0539018403042001798. http://ssi.sagepub.com/cgi/doi/10.1177/0539018403042001798

[22] Amanda J Porter and Iina Hellsten. 2014. Investigating participatory dynamics through social media using a multideterminant âĂŽ"frameâĂŹâĂŽ approach: the case of Climategate on YouTube. *Journal of Computer-Mediated Communication* 19, 4 (2014), 1024–1041.

[23] Ralf Reintjes, Enny Das, Celine Klemm, Jan Hendrik Richardus, Verena Keßler, and Amena Ahmad. 2016. "Pandemic Public Health Paradox": time series analysis of the 2009/10 Influenza A/H1N1 epidemiology, media attention, risk perception and public reactions in 5 European countries. *PloS one* 11, 3 (2016), e0151258.

[24] Bernhard Rieder. 2015. YouTube Data Tools. (2015). https://tools.digitalmethods.net/netvizz/youtube/

[25] Abha G Singh, Siddharth Singh, and Preet Paul Singh. 2012. YouTube for information on rheumatoid arthritis – A wakeup call? *The Journal of Rheumatology* 39, 5 (2012), 899–903.

[26] Socialbakers.com. 2017. (2017). https://www.socialbakers.com/statistics/youtube/

[27] Shabbir Syed-Abdul, Luis Fernandez-Luque, Wen-Shan Jian, Yu-Chuan Li, Steven Crain, Min-Huei Hsu, Yao-Chin Wang, Dorjsuren Khandregzen, Enkhzaya Chuluunbaatar, Phung Anh Nguyen, and Der-Ming Liou. 2013. Misleading health-related information promoted through video-based social media: anorexia on YouTube. *Journal of Medical Internet Research* 15, 2 (2013).

[28] Mike Thelwall. 2013. Heart and soul: Sentiment strength detection in the social web with SentiStrength. *Proceedings of the CyberEmotions* (2013), 1–14.

[29] Nees Jan van Eck and Ludo Waltman. 2013. VOSviewer manual. (2013). http://www.vosviewer.com/documentation/Manual_VOSviewer_1.5.4.pdf

[30] William N Venables and Brian D Ripley. 2002. *Modern applied statistics with S.* Springer. http://www.stats.ox.ac.uk/pub/MASS2/VR2stat.pdf

[31] Jay M Ver Hoef and Peter L Boveng. 2007. Quasi-Poisson vs. Negative Binomial Regression: How should we model overdispersed count data? *Ecology* 88, 11 (2007), 2766–2772.

[32] Michela Del Vicario, Alessandro Bessi, Fabiana Zollo, Fabio Petroni, Antonio Scala, Guido Caldarelli, H Eugene Stanley, and Walter Quattrociocchi. 2016. The spreading of misinformation online. *Proceedings of the National Academy of Sciences* 113, 3 (2016), 554–559. https://doi.org/10.1073/pnas.1517441113

[33] Soroush Vosoughi, Deb Roy, and Sinan Aral. 2018. The spread of true and false news online. *Science* 359, 6380 (2018), 1146–1151. https://doi.org/10.1126/science.aap9559

[34] Joseph B Walther, David DeAndrea, Jinsuk Kim, and James C Anthony. 2010. The influence of online comments on perceptions of antimarijuana public service announcements on YouTube. *Human Communication Research* 36, 4 (2010), 469–492.

[35] Stanley Wasserman and Katherine Faust. 1994. *Social Network Analysis: Methods and Applications*. Vol. 24. Cambridge University Press, Cambridge.

[36] Jina H Yoo and Junghyun Kim. 2012. Obesity in the new media: A content analysis of obesity videos on YouTube. *Health Communication* 27, 1 (2012), 86–97.

[37] Fabiana Zollo, Petra Kralj Novak, Michela Del Vicario, Alessandro Bessi, Igor Mozetič, Antonio Scala, Guido Caldarelli, and Walter Quattrociocchi. 2015. Emotional dynamics in the age of misinformation. *PloS one* 10, 9 (2015), e0138740.

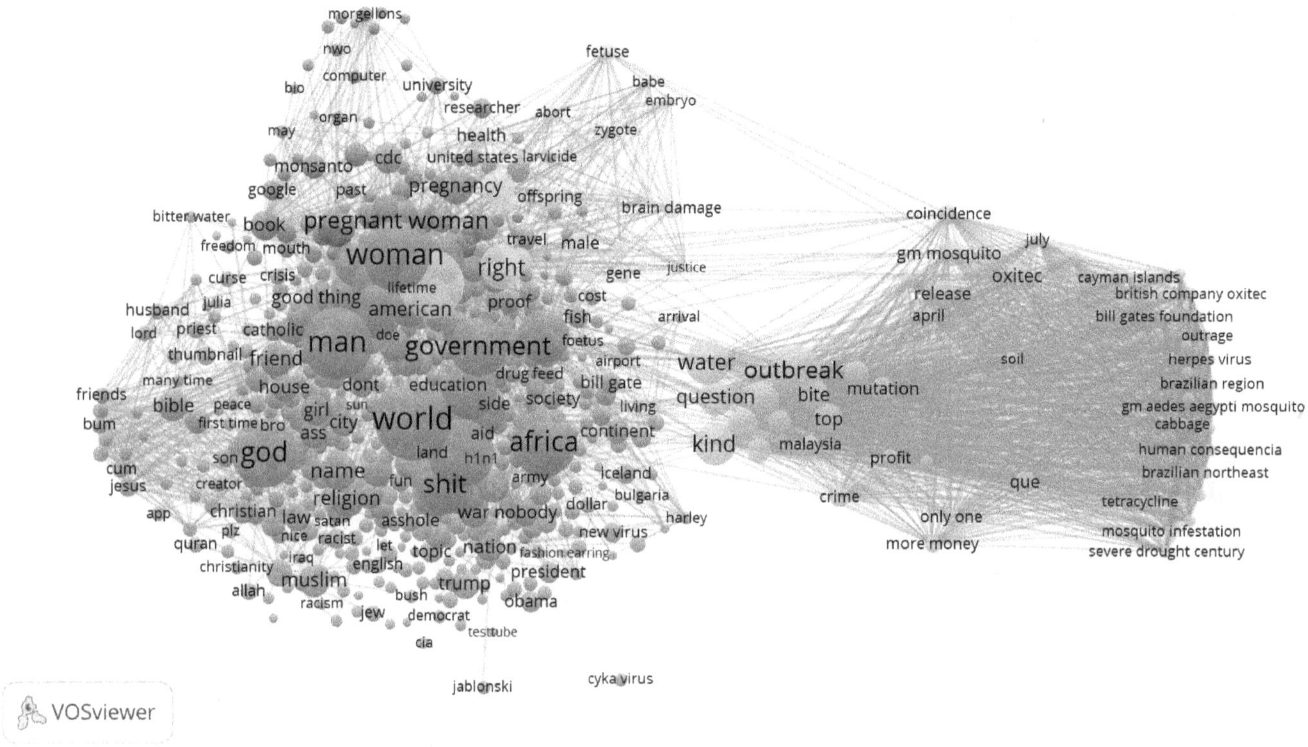

(a) Informational videos: $N = 421$, $E = 8854$

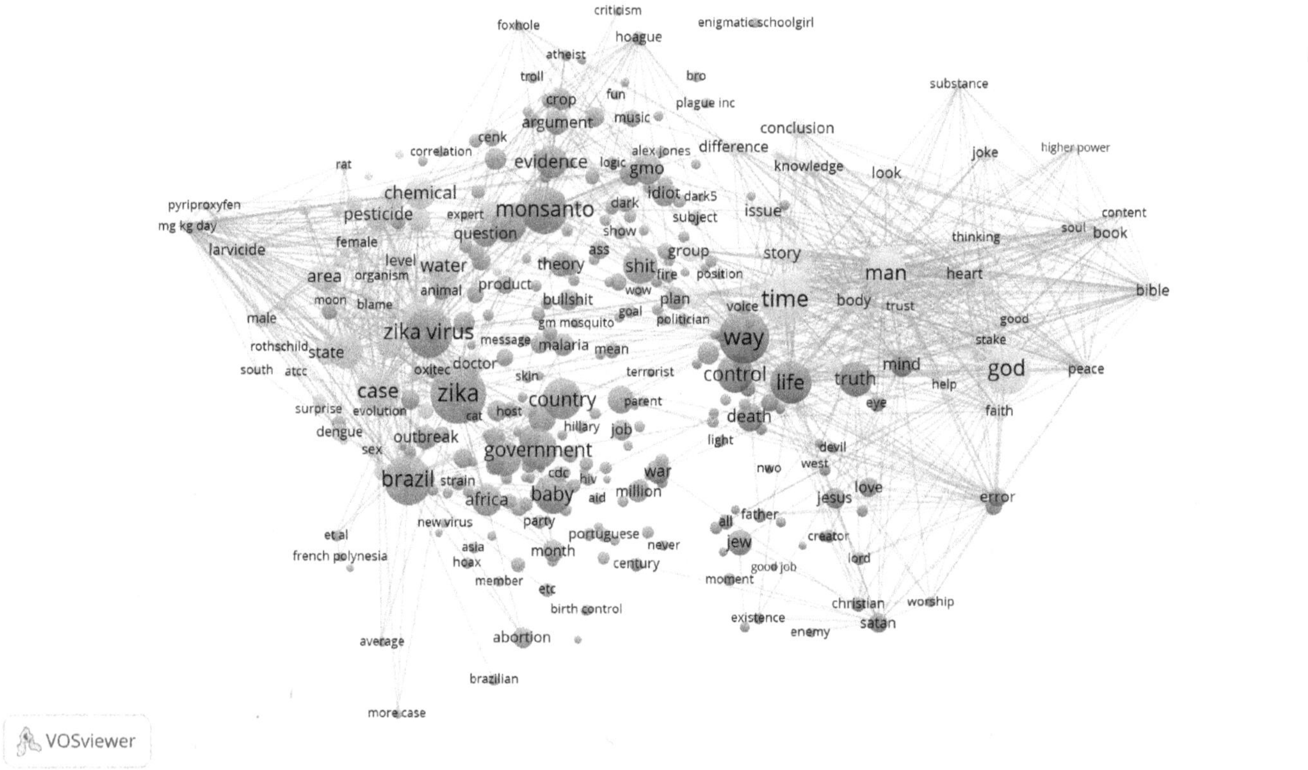

(b) Conspiracy theory videos: $N = 218$, $E = 6144$

Figure 1: Semantic maps of words and phrases co-occurring <10 times.

Social Gamification in Enterprise Crowdsourcing

Gregory Afentoulidis
Delft University of Technology
Delft, The Netherlands
gregafent@gmail.com

Zoltán Szlávik
IBM Netherlands
Amsterdam, The Netherlands
zoltan.szlavik@nl.ibm.com

Jie Yang
University of Fribourg
Fribourg, Switzerland
jie@exascale.info

Alessandro Bozzon
Delft University of Technology
Delft, The Netherlands
a.bozzon@tudelft.nl

ABSTRACT

Enterprise crowdsourcing capitalises on the availability of employees for in-house data processing. Gamification techniques can help aligning employees' motivation to the crowdsourcing endeavour. Although hitherto, research efforts were able to unravel the wide arsenal of gamification techniques to construct engagement loops, little research has shed light into the social game dynamics that those foster and how those impact crowdsourcing activities. This work reports on a study that involved 101 employees from two multinational enterprises. We adopt a user-centric approach to apply and experiment with gamification for enterprise crowdsourcing purposes. Through a qualitative study, we highlight the importance of the competitive and collaborative social dynamics within the enterprise. By engaging the employees with a mobile crowdsourcing application, we showcase the effectiveness of competitiveness towards higher levels of engagement and quality of contributions. Moreover, we underline the contradictory nature of those dynamics, which combined might lead to detrimental effects towards the engagement to crowdsourcing activities.

KEYWORDS

Enterprise Crowdsourcing; Gamification; Social Incentives

ACM Reference Format:
Gregory Afentoulidis, Zoltán Szlávik, Jie Yang, and Alessandro Bozzon. 2018. Social Gamification in Enterprise Crowdsourcing. In *WebSci '18: 10th ACM Conference on Web Science, May 27–30, 2018, Amsterdam, Netherlands*. ACM, New York, NY, USA, 10 pages. https://doi.org/10.1145/3201064.3201094

1 INTRODUCTION

Crowdsourcing is a computational paradigm that builds upon the idea of harnessing the collective intelligence of the crowd to overcome limitations of current technologies, which unavoidably require human intervention and intellect. Enterprises have been

adopting the paradigm to bolster their business needs and processes, transferring the practices of crowdsourcing from the online environment to the internal crowd of the enterprise: the *employees*.

Enterprise crowdsourcing allows the deployment of tasks of confidential nature, and it benefits from the utilisation of employees' working capacity and knowledge for quality task contributions [19]. However, it also suffers from traditional challenges of participation, retention to the crowdsourcing endeavour, and quality of the produced work [35]. Gamification[1] is often seen as a suitable tool for engagement and retention purposes. However, it is widely accepted that introduction of gamification involves several non-trivial steps that require strong consideration and scrutiny in order to achieve its goals [18, 24, 25]. In this respect, crowdsourcing is no exception.

Problem Statement. Previous work shows that gamification can incentivise the crowd and drive its behavioural outcome towards augmented and prolonging participation and task contribution, as well as quality output [9, 33, 34]. However, it is still unclear which game mechanics are more suitable for enabling crowdsourcing within an enterprise. This is mainly because gamification techniques are not always necessarily tied to the motivations of the employees. More importantly, limited research has been focusing on evaluating the interplay between *game elements* and *social incentives*, especially in an enterprise context in which synergy and competition are concepts that play an important role.

In this work, we aim at achieving a better understanding of the motives of employees behind participation in a gamified enterprise crowdsourcing application, so as to clarify the main requirements for selection of suitable tasks within an enterprise, and to adequately inform gamification design. We seek to answer the following research question:

> **RQ: How can gamification techniques enhance reliability and foster engagement in enterprise crowdsourcing?**

Original Contribution. We instrumented a study that involved 101 employees from two large multinational enterprises, for an observational interval that lasted two months. First, we performed a qualitative exploratory analysis of the dominant player types existent within the targeted enterprises, and highlight the importance of the social characteristics of the workforce that inform the design of enterprise gamification. We then set-up a quantitative study of gamified enterprise crowdsourcing by extending a mobile enterprise crowdsourcing application (ECrowd [30]) with pluggable

---

[1]The "process of enhancing a service with affordances" (e.g. game mechanics) "for gameful experiences to support user' value creation" (e.g. engagement) [24].

gamification elements. We implement *competitive* and *collaborative* game mechanics by designing a scoring function based on the number and quality of contributions, and task sharing capabilities within the enterprise to foster community collaboration.

We apply those two aspects of social gamification on top of traditionally employed game mechanics, to study the effects of synergistic and competitive dynamics in engagement and data quality in enterprise crowdsourcing. Finally, we compare the results obtained in the two enterprises, to gain a better understanding of the contextual effects that might exist between the relationship of gamification and crowdsourcing and how they mediate it.

Results suggest a preference of competitive game mechanics over the collaborative ones, and show the detrimental effects that their combination might yield to users engagement. As far as quality is concerned, the experiments showed that depending on the task type, we can expect higher quality contributions when competitive and collaborative game mechanics are used. Despite variations in the perception of gamification were noticed between employees of the two companies, we were not able to report significant differences.

Paper Organisation. The remainder of the paper is organised as follows. Section 2 presents related work. Section 3 describes the applied research methodology. Section 4 introduces the ECrowd enterprise crowdsourcing platform, and its extensions. Section 5 presents and discusses the experimental results. Section 6 concludes.

2 BACKGROUND AND RELATED WORK

Incentives in Enterprise Crowdsourcing. Enterprise crowdsourcing differs from traditional online crowdsourcing in terms of both the crowd it involves (i.e., employees) and the problem it targets (i.e., business problems) [35]. These two differentiating characteristics bring potential benefits for enterprises along with big challenges: it provides an effective way to exploit the internal knowledge profiles of employees and to leverage on their non-utilised working capacity to solve business critical and confidential tasks [15, 19], but it also faces challenges such as adherence to intellectual property legislation for the re-purposed work of employees, and minimising the risk of information leakage related to the business problems under consideration [35]. More importantly, as the main focus of the employees in a corporate environment is on accomplishing their daily duties and tasks, a strong consideration of the motivation of the crowd and fine engineered incentive mechanisms are required.

As opposed to money-based rewards in public crowdsourcing, in enterprise crowdsourcing, intrinsic motivations are mainly exploited. This is due to the conflict between money-based rewards and the already established compensation arrangements with the employees [35]. It is suggested that identifying what is the main interest of the employees in terms of personal values, causes and actions is pivotal for successful enterprise crowdsourcing [31]. Employees tend to be motivated by learning something new, improving the output of the company, contributing to their work community, improving appraisal for their work, but also by having fun [3]. Incentive mechanisms that account for these motivations are critical to worker engagement [21], which significantly affects the quantity and the quality of the performed tasks [16, 22].

Gamification in Crowdsourcing. Gamification has been widely recognised as an effective way to increase motivation towards better

user engagement and participation [7, 24, 27], also in crowdsourcing. Early works mainly study Games With A Purpose (GWAP) which denote the notion of disseminating tasks in a game that incites enjoyment. Notable examples include the ESP game [33], and Peekaboom [34]. While GWAP s start by defining games and afterward introducing crowdsourcing tasks, gamified crowdsourcing processes deal with existing tasks with gamification working as an added engagement layer. Tasks falling into this type include data collection [5, 23], entity and relation extraction [8], and relevance assessment [9]. The potential of gamification in enterprises has been increasingly noticed [18, 25], as it is flexible in addressing a variety of business processes and needs in an efficient manner [25]. To the best of our knowledge, little work has studied gamification in the context of enterprise crowdsourcing, which comes in contrast to the significant need for careful treatment of worker incentives required by the distinct characteristics of enterprise crowdsourcing.

Social & Contextual Factors in Gamification. Next to game mechanics, the success of gamification also depends on a set of contextual factors such as application type, task type, and user type [24]. At the application-level, Hamari [13] noted a discrepancy in the behavioural outcomes in traditional games and in a utilitarian service when badges are applied as game mechanics. Similar results were found in a gamified citizen science application [5]. At the task-level, Geiger and Schader [11] stress the need for different game mechanics used for tasks of different types. In processing and rating applications simpler game mechanics are preferred such as points, badges, and leaderboards. In tasks that require more creativity (e.g., content creation), more involved game mechanics are recommended to promote collaborative game dynamics and social influence, such as rewards, progress, social status, curiosity, and altruism. The user type relates to how the end users perceive gamification and how they react in its presence.

Bartle [2] identifies four main reasons why players typically enjoy a game, namely achievements within the game context, exploration of the game, socialising with others and imposition upon others. The categorization leads to the classical four player types: achievers, explorers, socialisers, and killers. Players might incorporate characteristics by all four types depending on the current state, but Bartle also suggests that a predominant preference to one of those four is existent in every player. The distinct incentives for different player types call for a better understanding of the effects of different game mechanics in gamified enterprise crowdsourcing. Using Bartle's taxonomy, game mechanics and dynamics for each player types have been suggested [26]. Such a necessity is confirmed in the context of online education [17] and task execution [14].

These works further suggest the importance of the social influence [14] in gamification, which motivates individuals to act in accordance with the social norms of the group. Similarly, Shi et al. [28] mention that social relatedness in a gamified context can be achieved, among others, through tagging, rating and commenting, which can be understood as social feedback. These works link to Thiebes [32], where a separate cluster called social influences was created in the taxonomy of game mechanics and dynamics, and two manifestations of social gamification were further identified, namely competition and collaboration.

Despite the literature, it remains an open question how social gamification implemented through different game mechanics, together with different contextual factors, i.e., user, task, and application types, affect worker engagement in enterprise crowdsourcing.

3 RESEARCH METHODOLOGY

Our research methodology starts with interviews with employees and experts to respectively understand employee player types and relevant tasks for enterprise crowdsourcing. Informed by their results, we design experimental conditions where specific gamification mechanics are applied, so as to understand the effects of different social gamification elements in enterprise crowdsourcing. To quantitatively analyze effects, we introduce the metrics for employee engagement and the reliability of their contribution.

To account for potential effects of enterprise environments, the research has been conducted within the Dutch headquarters of two multinational companies, which are referred to as **ET1** (a major Dutch bank) and **ET2** (one of the largest technology companies in the world). Their names are omitted due to legal requirements.

3.1 Interviews with Employees and Experts

Employee Player Types. To understand the player types of employees, we conducted 7 semi-structured interviews [10], a commonly used class of interviews to collect subjective opinions of people about their personal characteristics and also those of their peers. Interviews were structured into 5 parts: the first 4 parts contain questions related to discovering characteristics of the employees that pertain to one of the four player types suggested by Bartle's theory; the final part is designed to discover the predominant player type of the employee. Employees were also asked to provide their opinions on the player type of the general employee population that best suits the company. The employees were selected with a prior determination of the sample structure [10] based on gender, department, role and field of expertise, and considering availability.

In the following, we first describe qualitative findings obtained from the interviews, then we present the distribution of employee player types within the companies under consideration.

Socialiser Type. Respondents unanimously expressed that the ability to draw inspiration from coworkers and to develop a network within the company is of paramount importance for their ability to perform their work duties. Almost all employees expressed their personal desire to work in an environment where their feeling of relatedness is satisfied and opportunities are provided to create social connections. We were also interested to find out under which prism is social interaction expressed and preferred. All answers focused on collaborative characteristics rather than competitive, signifying that the former is much more valued in a working environment.

Achiever Type. In order to check how many of the characteristics of the achiever player type are incorporated to the employees, we set to find out how much reward oriented they are in their work. We were also interested to find out the types of rewards that are usually expected and how those are tied to their intrinsic or extrinsic motivation for doing their work. The employees' main preference resides on rewards that adhere to their intrinsic motivations. In addition, the majority of the employees recognised rewards as a

	Socialiser	Achiever	Killer	Explorer	Employee
S1	7-8	6-7	6	8	Socialiser
S2	-	-	-	-	-
S3	8	6	7-8	6	Killer
S4	6	8	9	7-8	Achiever
S5	8	7	7-8	6	Socialiser
S6	6	9	6	8	-
S7	8	7	9	8	Socialiser

Table 1: Employees' ratings on the level to which they match their personal characteristics to the 4 player types (from 1 to 10); and selection for the general population of the company.

main motivator for their work and also something that should be tied to their performance.

Killer Type. To unravel characteristics of the employees that might be related to the killer player category, we asked them to comment to what extent they are finding themselves challenging their standard way of working. Most employees suggested that following a standardised way of working is in general preferred. However, they also suggested that there is a compromise between blindly accepting a specific way of operating and also being aware of opportunities where they can intervene and break the conventional order. It is also interesting to note that most employees who expressed willingness to deviate from a standard way of working would only opt for this solution when they can critically assess that this is for the benefit of their work's end result, rather than an innate personal characteristic that incentivises them to act in this specific way.

Explorer Type. To determine how much of an explorer player type are the employees, we focused on gaining an understanding on whether they like to work independently and have their own path within their working environment. The responses were balanced between employees who prefer to work in an isolated fashion and are often given the opportunity to work on new things not closely related to their main work, and those who are more focused on it.

Most of the employees in our analysis responded positively in questions that were probing whether characteristics from the 4 types can be found in them. Such a result matches the hypothesis of Bartle's theory, that the player categories are not mutually exclusive and that multiple characteristics of them can be found in a person. In the concluding part of our discussions with the employees, we asked participants to select which of player types best suits their personality. We allowed them to rate in a scale from 1 to 10 how congruent they find themselves with this type. The responses are listed in Table 1 (subject 2 did not provide rates).

We can observe that there is a preference in the *Socialiser Killer* player type. Interestingly, when the employees were asked to provide their opinion on which of those categories best suits the general company population, most of the answers indicated the *Socialiser* type. It is also interesting to denote that the responses for the categories of *Socialiser* and *Achiever* had greater consensus compared to that of the *Killer* and the *Explorer*. Almost all respondents recognised qualities found in the first two categories in them while there was some dispersion in the answers we collected for the latter two. Those observations are in accordance with previous studies regarding gamification conducted at another Dutch company [30].

Gamification Elements	Contr.	Comp.	Collab.	Mixed
Score + Progress Bar	✔	✔	✔	✔
Leaderboard	–	✔	–	✔
Task Sharing	–	–	✔	✔

Table 2: The four experimental groups.

Enterprise Crowdsourcing Tasks. We conducted expert interviews to identify relevant tasks for enterprise crowdsourcing. For each company, we identified a use case in the domain of news analysis and summarisation.

Enterprise crowdsourcing would provide human-generated data used to train a machine learning model. Following the interview guide for expert interviewing [10], our interview addresses the following questions: 1) How do the experts conduct their research and produce their reports for which they need AI support? 2) Which are the data sources they use in their work? 3) What are some possible aspects of their work which could be automated by a machine learning model?

As a result of the interviews, several possible tasks were identified, out of which one was chosen as a focal point for experimentation: extraction of market information, i.e. the identification of key companies and corresponding relevant information in a specific domain. The objective of the machine learning algorithm utilising the crowdsourced data is to extract possible relations found between entities in unstructured online text data. The selection was promoted as a result of the easily accessible data sources which are mainly online articles and news as compared to the other options who involved proprietary data sources. We focused on 2 relations: identifying a CEO of a company, and extracting affiliation relation between companies (e.g. subsidiary company or acquisitions).

3.2 Experimental Conditions

Based on our interviews, we selected gamification elements which mostly adhere to the Achievers and Socialisers player types, namely: points, progression, leaderboard and community collaboration. Four experimental groups are created (Table 2):

Control, offering essential feedback gamification mechanics such as score and a progress bar. The scoring mechanism (described in Section 4) is based on the contributions and the quality of the work while the progress bar provides a visual representation of the amount of tasks completed from the total available.

Competitive, which promotes competitive dynamics by offering a leaderboard (based on the scoring mechanism), in addition to the progress bar.

Collaborative, which provides collaborative social gamification by means of two options for task submissions: 1) individually submit the task for one's own benefit (i.e. increase score and progress) or collaboratively (i.e. solve the task with a peer of choice). For the latter, the employee is able to submit a task and also assign it to another participant to annotate it (this takes place asynchronously).

Mixed, which provides all the previously mentioned game mechanics. This allows us to study the interaction effect of competitive and collaborative social gamification.

Legal and Privacy Aspects. The presence or real personal information about the employees participating in it is of paramount

importance: the ability of an employee to relate an account to one of his peers strengthens feelings of relatedness, community acknowledgment, synergy and competitiveness.

However, the enterprise environment might pose stricter requirements in terms of privacy: employees' personal information is sensitive and confidential; also, the logging functionalities that are necessary to obtain usage metrics, and the storage and use of personal and application usage information might not in accordance with enterprise privacy policies. This condition occurred with our experiments, as we were limited to the usage of anonymous users participating in each experimental group. This constraint unavoidably introduces limitations to our experiments, which is evident in *Competitive* and *Mixed* groups – where we are restricted to use leaderboards with not realistic user names – and in *Collaborative* and *Mixed* groups, where the task sharing functionality has to be based, again, on the same user names.

3.3 Measuring Engagement and Reliability

We operationalise employee engagement and reliability of the outcomes in enterprise crowdsourcing to quantitative metrics collected and logged through the interaction of the employees with the mobile crowdsourcing application.

Employee Engagement Metrics. Engagement metrics are used to evaluate the level of interaction of the employees with the application. We measure: 1) *Number of task executions*, i.e. the average number of tasks contributed by an employee, normalised by the observation interval during the experiment duration. 2) *Number of sessions*, i.e. the amount of times an employee opened and interacted with the app during the observation period. A session start is determined when the application starts or resumes. 3) *Session time*, i.e. the time each employee spends in interacting with the application. This is signified by an application start or resume event in their mobile device until an application paused or closed event. We average the total session time by the number of sessions an employee has had within a normalised time span. 4) *Task dwell time*, i.e. the amount of time elapsed since an employee selects a task until she submits or selects to collaborate a task. We average the dwell time across all task executions contributed by the employee. Since collaboration is implemented as a task sharing function, which might affect metric across different experimental conditions, we denote the end of task execution at the time an employee presses the submit or collaboration button.

Work Reliability Metrics. Due to the absence of golden standard labels for the tasks used in our experiments, we rely on agreement metrics. Depending on the input requested per task category we use different quality metrics elaborated as follows. 1) *Plurality answer agreement*: for tasks with numerical input the following formula is used to calculate plurality answer agreement:

$$S_p(e) = \frac{f}{F} \qquad (1)$$

where e represents an employee, F is the total amount of tasks the employee has provided annotations and f is the number of the tasks for which the employee's annotations are in accordance with those produced from the majority vote. This metric assumes majority vote as the golden standard on which the employee's annotations are directly assessed. 2) *Average worker-worker agreement*: for tasks where the employee is requested to annotate relations found in text, we use the average worker-worker agreement [1]:

$$avg\_wwa(e_i) = \frac{\sum_{i \neq j} |S_{i,j}| * wwa(e_i, e_j)}{\sum_{i \neq j} |S_{i,j}|} \quad (2)$$

where e_k denotes the employee k and $S_{i,j}$ is the set of common task annotated by both employees. $wwa(e_i, e_j)$ is the pairwise worker-worker agreement for all the tasks s annotated in common:

$$wwa(e_i, e_j) = \frac{\sum_{s \in S_{i,j}} RelationsInCommon(e_i, e_j, s)}{\sum_{s \in S_{i,j}} NumAnnotations(e_i, s)} \quad (3)$$

in which $RelationsInCommon(e_i, e_j, s)$ is the number of annotated relations that are in common between two employees in a specific task s and $NumAnnotations(e_i, s)$ is the total annotations produced by employee e_i for the same task.

4 THE ECROWD PLATFORM

The experiments have been enabled by ECrowd, an enterprise crowdsourcing platform [3]. This section discusses the design choices related to its extension with the functionalities required by the experimental setting. Figure 1 shows screenshots from the deployed application. Users can navigate the functionalities of the application via the main menu list (Figure 1a), accessible after authentication.

Task Types. The study includes three tasks, selected according to 1) their relation to the domain of enterprise crowdsourcing, 2) the incentives of the crowd, and 3) our research requirements. We introduced variability across those dimensions to isolate as much as possible the effect of gamification in worker engagement.

The *Information Extraction* task (Figure 2a) have been selected and designed according to the outcome of the qualitative research study (Section 3.1). Users are required to annotate the relations (i.e. being the CEO of a company, being a subsidiary of another company) and the participating entities. The task addresses incentives of the crowd related to their participation in innovative projects that also the improvement of the output of the company.

The *Moral Machine* task (Figure 2b) is a survey tasks, based on a research on the morality of future Artificial Intelligence [4].[2] The task mainly addresses learning incentives – as it helps to raise awareness about the importance of programming moral decisions in AI – and fun. It has low complexity, as it involves only the selection of one of the scenarios depicted in an image.

Finally, the *Cell Count* task (Figure 2c) involves the annotation of the number of human cells that are visible in a medical image. The input of the employees is used for the development of machine learning application in the medical domain, thus addressing incentives regarding participation in interesting and useful projects. They are also tasks of intermediate complexity, as it requires some basic knowledge in identifying cells in images.

Task Sharing. The task sharing capabilities underpin the requirements for the collaborative social gamification experimental condition. Users can choose between submitting the task individually and claiming their score (described below) when submitting it and *also* choosing a colleague in their group to share the task. If a user

---

[2]Authors deploy crowdsourcing to collect opinions regarding moral decisions for autonomous vehicles.

selects to collaborate then an action sheet slides up (Figure 1e) with all the available names of the colleagues in his group.

Upon selection of a peer from the list, the task execution is concluded as normal. After a task has been shared it is stored and forwarded to the receiver which can then choose to complete it asynchronously. To complement the social incentives of collaboration we also used a feedback mechanism, to allow the user who completes a shared task to get a brief notification of the answer of the sender, to check whether his/her annotation is the same or not with that of the sender (Figure 1f).

Scoring. Scoring is used as a feedback mechanism to inform participants about their progress while contributing tasks, and to rank them in leaderboards. The score should reflect the quality of the work; and should be fair, so to foster interest to the user. In the context of crowdsourcing, it might not be possible to reward users for their answers on the basis of a ground truth or a gold standard. We address this by means of a scoring function that rewards both the amount of contribution and the quality of their answers [24]. The quality of the contributions is measured according to the level of agreement to the annotations of other users [8, 12]: the more annotations from previous contributors are in accord with that of the user, the greater the rewarded score. The scoring function is defined as in Equation 4:

$$f(x, C) = \begin{cases} [log(x+3) * g(C)] - 50, & \text{if } C \neq 0 \text{ and } x > 0 \\ [log(x+3) * g(6)] - 50, & \text{if } C \neq 0 \text{ and } x = 0 \\ 50, & \text{if } C = 0 \end{cases} \quad (4)$$

where x is the number of answers equal to the user's, C is variable that represents the level of majority (i.e. majority answers get $C = 1$, the next group $C = 2$, etc.) and the function $g(C)$ is a selection of constants, that parameterise the scoring mechanism on C with different scoring functions (i.e. $g(1) = 65$, $g(2) = 60$, $g(3) = 55$, etc.). Intuitively, each user's annotation is rewarded a higher score depending on whether it belongs to higher levels of majority and also dependent on the number of annotations which form this specific majority. A score is rewarded for each annotation regardless of whether it is in agreement with previous ones, so that we can reward continuous contributions irrespective of their quality. 50 points are rewarded when there are no previous annotations.

A bonus of 30% of what would be normally awarded is given when two users are in agreement for a specific shared task. We penalise disagreement by awarding them 0 points for a collaboration that ended up with disagreement. In this way sharing a task with a peer introduces, from a scoring point of view, a risk of either being awarded bonus points or not being rewarded any points at all. This collaborative scoring strategy is also in accordance with popular gamified crowdsourcing application used in previous studies [20].

5 EXPERIMENTAL RESULTS

To answer the main research question, we structured the analysis into three research sub-questions: **RQ1)** What is the effect of competitive and collaborative game mechanics to employee engagement in enterprise crowdsourcing? **RQ2)** What is the effect of competitive and collaborative game mechanics to the quality of employee contributions in enterprise crowdsourcing? And, **RQ3)** What is the effect of competitive and collaborative game mechanics across different enterprise environments?

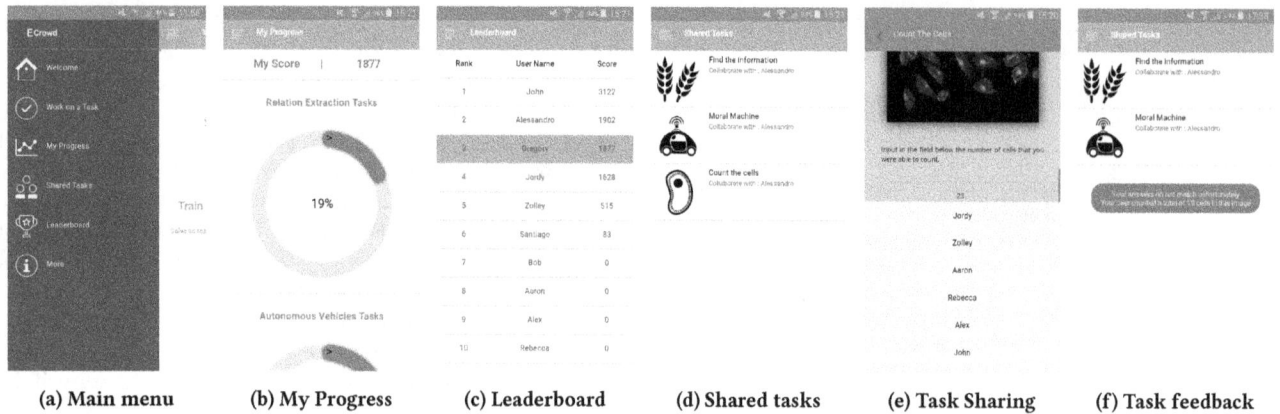

| (a) Main menu | (b) My Progress | (c) Leaderboard | (d) Shared tasks | (e) Task Sharing | (f) Task feedback |

Figure 1: Screenshots from the ECrowd application deployed in both companies.

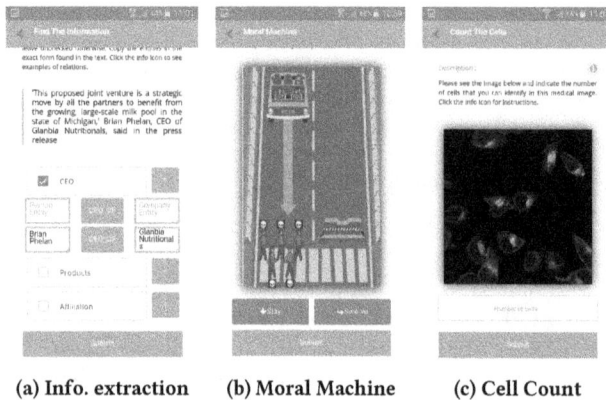

| (a) Info. extraction | (b) Moral Machine | (c) Cell Count |

Figure 2: Implemented Crowdsourcing Tasks.

5.1 Recruitment and Participation

The experiment consisted of 2 phases, and was performed in parallel in Company 1 (**ET1**) and Company 2 (**ET2**). The first phase, lasting 10 days, involved a dozen of selected employees, and helped bootstrap gamification elements, so as to prevent later participants being demotivated by the lack of previous activities. Recruitment for the second phase has been performed on a voluntary basis, through advertisement (flyers, posters in key locations, corporate mailing lists, corporate blogs). The second phase lasted from mid-May until mid-July, 2017. Participants could join the experiment at any time. To account for the variations of participation duration across different employees, we normalise our observation interval to a maximum of 1 month.

Table 3 summarised the tasks executed and employees demographics in the two companies. Despite the adoption of similar advertisement procedures, participation and attrition levels are notably different. 84 employees from **ET1** volunteered, and 75 logged in to the application.in **ET2** had an higher attrition rate in which 26 employees were active from 34 in total. We account those differences to two factors: 1) the number of employees (**ET1** has more); and 2) the popularity of the companies' app stores, which in **ET2** was lower. The distribution of employees across different experimental conditions is acceptable.

	Task Type				Employees Demographic				
	Info.	Moral	Cell	Tot.	F	M	Man.	N/Man.	Tot.
ET1	343	601	329	1237	27%	73%	28%	72%	75
ET2	88	313	101	502	19%	81%	4%	96%	26

Table 3: Executed tasks and worker demographics.

5.2 RQ1: Impacts of Social Gamification on Employee Engagement

The analysis of employee engagement includes number of task executions, session time, number of sessions, and task dwell time.

Number of task executions. Table 4 summarises the descriptive statistics for the number of tasks executions. We omit the contributions of one employee in the control group, who contributed 68.5% of the total task, and therefore regarded as an outlier.

Previous research [29] states that both competitive and collaborative game mechanics in isolation can have positive effects on engagement, while their combination can have detrimental effects.

		ET1			ET2		
	Type	μ	σ	Tot.	μ	σ	Tot.
Contr.	*Info.*	3.2	2	51 (32%)	2	2.2	14 (15%)
	Moral	3.7	3.4	70 (43%)	10.28	12.5	72 (75%)
	Cell	2.4	2.2	41 (25%)	1.42	1.3	10 (10%)
	All	**3.1**	**3.6**	**162**	**4.8**	**8.1**	**96**
Comp.	*Info.*	5.6	7.4	90 (21%)	4.3	4.6	26 (17%)
	Moral	13.2	12.2	224 (52%)	11.8	11.8	83 (55%)
	Cell	7.1	8.5	120 (27%)	6.1	4.7	43 (28%)
	All	**8.7**	**10**	**434**	**7.6**	**8.22**	**152**
Collab.	*Info.*	2.1	1.9	25 (14%)	6	9.6	30 (30%)
	Moral	8.1	10.5	121 (69%)	7.6	12.1	38 (39%)
	Cell	2	2.3	30 (17%)	6.2	9.0	31 (31%)
	All	**4.2**	**7**	**176**	**6.6**	**9.5**	**99**
Mixed	*Info.*	1.7	1.6	29 (19%)	2.8	1.9	14 (18%)
	Moral	4.9	8.4	74 (50%)	9.5	17.6	57 (75%)
	Cell	2.9	5.1	46 (31%)	1.7	1.5	5 (7%)
	All	**3.1**	**5.7**	**149**	**5.42**	**11.56**	**76**

Table 4: Descriptive statistics of number of task executions.

We therefore test the alternative hypothesis that, compared to the control group, *Competitive* and *Collaborative* mechanics increase the amount of tasks contributed by the users, while their combination will lessen the effect. We fit a Negative Binomial regression model.[3] The coefficients of this model and their significance are summarised in Table 6, omitting the intercept. There is a significant increase in task executions when competitive gamification elements were used in isolation. In **ET2**, leaderboards have a significant positive effect ($p < 0.05$), resulting in an increase of 282% ($e^{1.03}$) compared to the control group. The *Collaborative* mechanic also proved beneficial, with a slight positive effect on tasks sharing. There is also an indication that their combination (*Mixed* might be detrimental for crowdsourcing activities. We cannot however confirm the alternative hypothesis for these gamification elements since their effects were not found to be significant. Those results were consistent for both experiments.

Table 5 shows the number of tasks shared in the *Collaborative* and *Mixed* groups. 5.7% of the total tasks contributed by the *Collaborative* group in **ET1** were due to task sharing, while for *Mixed* group the percentage climbs to 35.6%. For **ET1** those percentages are respectively 13.13% and 13.15%.

	RT1		RT2	
	Collab.	Mixed	Collab.	Mixed
Shared Tasks	10	49	13	10
Responses	0	4	0	0

Table 5: Number of shared tasks and responses.

The results, in terms of number of shared tasks, are promising. But the collaboration effect was severely hindered by the very low response rate, which was essential in completing the engagement loop of this mechanic. We believe that this was mainly due to 1) the anonymity constraints imposed by the two companies; and 2) by the absence of a notification mechanism that could inform employees about tasks shared with them. Instead, we relied on the curiosity of employees, to navigate in the application and check for shared tasks. We deliberately omitted notifications to avoid bias against the control and *Competitive* groups.

Session time. The diminished effect of combining collaboration and competitiveness is also visible in the session time, especially with **ET1**. A Kruskal-Wallis test showed that differences between the experimental groups were statistically significant ($p = .001$) in **ET1**, but not in **ET2** ($p = .951$). This is a first indication that gamification was perceived differently between the two enterprises. We perform a post-hoc analysis only for the experiment in **ET1**. A pairwise Mann-Whitney U tests with Holm-Bonferroni correction found a significant difference between the *Control* and the *Collaborative* groups ($p = .005$), and between the *Competitive* and the *Collaborative* groups ($p = .006$). This signifies that employees with both a leaderboard and task sharing spent significantly less time per session in the application compared to only having basic gamification or only the leaderboards. The difference between *Competitive* and *Collaborative* groups coincides with the results in the previous section. No significant difference was observed between the *Mixed*

and any of the other groups. To further prove this assumption we looked into the net time spent by the employees interacting with the gamification elements; we found that employees in the *Mixed* group did not show higher levels of interaction.

Number of sessions. Table 8 compares the number of times employees opened the application across the different treatment groups. We observe results similar to the analysis of session time. We therefore test the hypothesis that when leaderboards or task sharing are present, employees would be motived to open the application more times, while when combined this might result in fewer times using the application. We use a Kruskal-Wallis test, and found insufficient evidence to reject the null hypothesis (**ET1**: $p = .926$; **ET2** $p = .101$). Another way of analyzing engagement of the employees is by counting the time interval between contiguous sessions, as defined in [22]. The results of the empirical cumulative distributions of inter-session times are depicted in Figure 3.

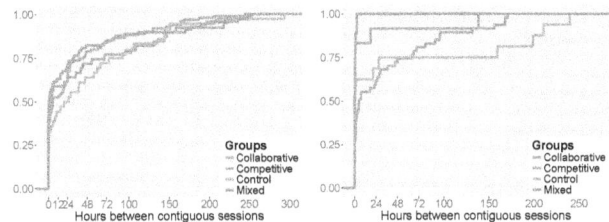

Figure 3: Empirical Cumulative Distribution of inter-session times (hours) for the application across the experimental groups and the two companies (ET1 left, ET2 right)

We notice higher probability of employees re-engaging with the application within 1 or 2 days for the conditions in which leaderboards were present. Also, small differences exist between the participants with task sharing functionality and the *Control* group. This is also an indication that employees who had leaderboards were more inclined to revisit the application.

Task dwell time. Dwell time is defined as the net time spent in task execution. The three task categories feature different levels of complexity, which influence the time spent executing them. We expect the *Information Extraction* tasks to require more time to be completed. compared to the others. Tasks also adhere to different incentives of the employees.

The descriptive statistics are illustrated in Table 9. In **ET1**, employees in the *Competitive* group spent less time executing simpler tasks; and employees in *Collaborative* and *Mixed* groups spent less time on average than the one in the *Control* group. With the *Information Extraction* tasks the differences are less profound, a result that we believe is due to the direct relevance of the task to the company's goal. In **ET2**, there is a general fluctuation of the observed values depending on the task type and experimental group.

We test the statistical significance of the observed differences. Being the dependent variable continuous, and given the positive skewness of our samples, we perform our analysis using a generalized gamma linear model.[4] First, we test the hypothesis that participants in the *Competitive* group would spend less time while

---

[3]The Negative Binomial regression model has been preferred to a Poisson model due to over-dispersion [6] – $p < 0.001$ – of the data

[4]Fitness to gamma distribution has been verified with a Kolmogorov-Smirnov test.

#Execs	ET1		ET2	
	Coeff.	Sig.	Coeff.	Sig.
Comp.	1.04	**0.013** *	.46	0.46
Collab.	0.25	0.56	.77	0.23
Mixed	-0.18	0.65	-0.08	0.90

Table 6: Negative Binomial regression models describing the effect of game mechanics to # task executions (*: .05 significance).

	ET1			ET2		
	μ	σ	m	μ	σ	m
Contr.	178	197	115	217	291	129
Comp.	180	194	119	226	288	96
Collab.	128	161	73	192	193	133
Mixed	109	202	42	205	286	100

Table 7: Descriptive statistics for session time (in seconds, rounded). μ: mean; σ: standard deviation; m: median.

	ET1				ET2			
	μ	σ	m	Tot.	μ	σ	m	Tot.
Contr.	4.25	3.04	4.5	51	4.4	3.2	3	22
Comp.	7.43	9.81	4	119	2.85	2.11	2	20
Collab.	4.5	3.42	3	54	16.66	17.78	9	50
Mixed	5.27	6.05	2	95	3.5	3	2	14

Table 8: Descriptive statistics for number of sessions. μ: mean; σ: standard deviation; m: median; Tot.: total.

		ET1				ET2			
	Type	μ	σ	m	Tot.	μ	σ	m	Tot.
Contr.	Info.	85	80	53	4320	101	81	100	1414
	Moral	38	36	24	2665	19	22	11	1340
	Cell	31	29	19	1255	36	20	37	359
	All	51	58	32	8240	32	46	15	3113
Comp.	Info.	101	77	81	9117	55	42	47	1427
	Moral	27	70	12	5987	20	17	13	1630
	Cell	20	20	14	2432	17	12	12	736
	All	40	70	16	17535	25	26	14	3792
Collab.	Info.	93	70	77	2329	99	55	78	2982
	Moral	20	20	13	2438	21	11	17	801
	Cell	32	22	26	958	27	21	19	823
	All	32	41	16	5726	46	48	29	4607
Mixed	Info.	90	62	79	2607	184	124	131	2580
	Moral	35	37	20	2561	28	38	14	1582
	Cell	24	21	15	1119	35	17	27	177
	All	42	46	22	6287	57	86	19	4340

Table 9: Descriptive statistics for task dwell time (in seconds, rounded). μ: mean; σ: std. deviation; m: median; Tot.: total.

executing tasks compared to the *Control* group – mainly focusing on gathering points and improving their position in the leaderboard faster. The hypothesis can be accepted for the *Cell count* task, where we observe a statistically significant decreasing effect for the task execution time, when only leaderboards are present, in both experiments (**ET1**: Coeff = −.74, Sig = .004; **ET2**: Coeff = −.41, Sig = .013). A similar negative effect is observable in **ET2** with the *Information Extraction* task (Coeff = −.61, Sig = .009). No significant effect could be observed for other configurations.

In **ET1**, the moral decision tasks shows a significant negative effect when task sharing functionality was present (Coeff = −.636, Sig = .029), while in **ET2** the effect is positive but significant only in the *Mixed* group (Coeff = .399, Sig = .034). In a similar way, the *Information Extraction* task features a significant positive correlation for *Mixed* in **ET2** (Coeff = .601, Sig = .023). In **ET1** the effect is positive but mild and not statistically significant.

We believe that those results are only partially explained by the use of game mechanics, as confounding factors such as employees incentives for specific tasks are also playing an important role. When such incentives were loosened, as for example for the moral decision tasks and the *Cell count*, then the role of gamification is more evident.

5.3 RQ2: Impacts of Social Gamification on Work Quality

We focus on the *Cell count* and *Information Extraction*, having more objective outcomes than the moral machine. Due to the lack of a golden standard, the quality of the contributions is calculated based on agreement metrics. To improve the robustness of agreement calculation, we also incorporate the labels obtained for the tasks from the participants in the pilot phase of both experiments in the two companies. In this way we were able to have more labels per task unit and stronger majorities which in turn leads to more robust results. Figure 4 depicts the distribution of agreement scores that we obtained for two tasks across the two experiments. Recall that different agreement metrics are used for the different tasks (Section 3.3). Results of significance tests using the Kruskal- Wallis non-parametric test indicate that there is no statistically significant evidence for a difference between the distribution of quality scores across the experimental conditions, for both task types. The following observations are therefore of interest in the context of the experiment, but not conclusive.

For the *Cell count* task, *Competitive* and *Collaborative* groups provide contributions of higher quality than the control group, indicating that social gamification can contribute to work quality. *Mixed* group in **ET1** yielded better results on average than in **ET2**, a result that we explain in terms of the difference in the total shared tasks. Revisiting Table 5 (number of shared tasks for each group that had collaborative game mechanics) the significant difference between **ET1** and **ET2**'s *Mixed* groups in terms of the total shared tasks might explain the difference in the quality of the contributions we observe between the two companies. Interestingly, quicker task execution times observed for *Competitive* and *Collaborative* groups, as we have seen in our results for task dwell time, comes without sacrifice of work quality.

Results for the *Information Extraction* task vary, as shown Figure 4. In both **ET1** and **ET2**, we observe an average lower agreement for the *Competitive* and *Mixed* groups, and a similar level of agreement for the *Collaborative*, compared to the *Control* one. The different results obtained for the different tasks suggest the potential benefits of such gamification elements are dependent on specific task types.

5.4 RQ3: Gamification and Enterprise Environments

In this section, the focus is on the analysis of the effect of gamification mechanics for different enterprise contexts, so to gain an understanding of how those might affect crowdsourcing activities.

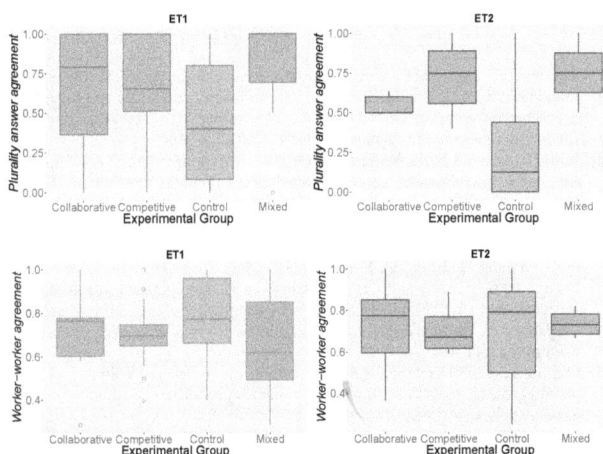

Figure 4: (Upper figures) Distribution of plurality answer agreement scores for the *Cell count* tasks. (Lower figures) Distribution of average worker-worker agreement scores for the *Information Extraction* tasks.

We hypothesise that enterprise environment plays a role in how gamification is perceived, which results in different patterns of crowdsourcing activities.

By juxtaposing the results found in the previous sections we were able to identify some similarities and some differences between **ET1** and **ET2**. Similarities are in terms of the number of task executions and the session time for the different experimental groups, where we noticed higher preference of the employees to the *Competitive* mechanics compared to the *Control*, a small increase when *Competitive* incentives were used, and a diminished effect when those were combined. On the other hand, we observe a slight increase in the number of executions for **ET1** compared to **ET2** when *Competitive* mechanics were used, while the opposite was observed when *Collaborative* mechanics where introduced and when they were combined. We were also able to notice differences in the session times calculated, where in **ET2** we had higher session times on average for all treatments used in our experiments. Furthermore, for the times that the application was opened by the employees, we noticed higher when leaderboards (*Competitive*) were introduced in **ET1** compared to **ET2**; while when only task sharing was used, **ET2**'s employees were more eager to open the application. Regarding the quality of contributions for the *Cell count* task type and the *Information Extraction* task type, by revisiting our results in Section 5.3, we see slight differences between the agreement scores calculated for the same experimental conditions across the different companies. The most profound one is noticed for the *Control* group in for the annotations collected for the *Cell count* tasks.

5.5 Discussion

Experimental results suggest a preference of *Competitive* game mechanics over the *Collaborative* ones. As far as quality is concerned, our experiments showed that depending on the task type, we can expect higher quality contributions when *Competitive* and *Collaborative* game mechanics are used. We attribute the result to the contradicting nature of combining these game dynamics which

does not provide a clear goal to the employees while undertaking tasks, from a gamification point of view. Finally, although differences in the perception of gamification were noticed by comparing our two experiments, in a more in-depth analysis we were not able to suggest significant differences between the two companies.

Post-experiment interviews. The use of gamification for enterprise crowdsourcing was viewed positively by the employees who engaged with the application. Informal interviews performed at the end of the experiments revealed that the experimental tool was intuitive and easy to use. One employee stated: *"The use of the application itself and what we needed to do, so fill in a couple of things or make a choice, that was definitely clear"*. Moreover, the gamification elements were perceived as motivating and retained their interest in contributing tasks. An employee revealed: *"At first I was just like, I needed to do the tasks as many times as possible and just contribute to the project. At a certain point I came across the leaderboard and as I am quite competitive that made it a game for me. I wanted to go as high as possible to the ranking"*. Another employee said that progress bars were giving him clear goals and kept him motivated by saying: *"I started with the one with the cars and I wanted to finish this to 100% and then I tried to finish the Information Extraction to 75%"*. Surprisingly, even gamification elements that we assumed would not incite great interest, such as the points in the control group and the social gamification group, where leaderboards were not present, proved motivating for the employees. Specifically, an employee from the control group stated: *"it kept me motivated, I tried to reach 500 points at first and then aimed for 1000 points"*.

Validity threats. We consider validity threats related to the history effect, selection and also diffusion of treatment. The history effect is addressed by starting the experimentation almost simultaneously in the two enterprises, so such effects are the same in each participant. We also opted for an observational period which does not contain major public holidays. Flexible sign up times for the participants, however, prevented us to completely control for effects that might arise. A possible history effect could have affected the results in **ET2**, where previous experiments in enterprise crowdsourcing have been conducted in the past. Although new tasks and a new application with gamification incorporated was used in our study, we recognize that the similarity to past studies might have affected the participation and engagement levels towards our experimental tool. We addressed the selection effect by assigning participants randomly to experimental conditions. Signing up for the application was permitted by requesting credentials, and employees were assigned to experimental groups in a round robin fashion. Looking back at the demographics of our experiments, we showed that this strategy yielded acceptable results considering the number of our samples. Diffusion of treatment refers to the potential threat to internal validity in which participants from different conditions communicate with each other. Although we recognize that in an enterprise environment we cannot completely control for this threat, we took care to promote the experiment in an as wide audience as possible inside the two companies, with the intention of recruiting participants from diverse departments. We also believe that the vast amount of departments existent as well as employees working in both enterprises minimize the potential effect of a diffusion of treatment significantly.

6 CONCLUSIONS

With this work, we aimed at furthering the understanding of how gamification can effectively support enterprise crowdsourcing activities, in terms of employee engagement and also the quality of their contributions. Based on Bartle's theory, the exploratory analysis has shown a non mutually exclusive player type characteristics of employees. By combining qualitative research results with those of previous studies on gamification in the enterprise, we were able to show the preference of employees in competitive and collaborative game dynamics. These results informed our explanatory research, for which we deployed a gamified mobile crowdsourcing application that combines competitive and collaborative game mechanics. We used our experimental tool into two large multinational enterprises for an observational interval that lasted two months and involved 101 employees. Results show that competitive game mechanics can better foster engagement than collaborative ones, and that their combination can have a detrimental effect.

As part of future work, we plan to investigate how personalisation can strengthen the competitive as well as the collaborative incentives of the employees especially when task sharing functionality is concerned. It would also be beneficial to study more intricate schemes of gamification such as competitiveness between collaborative groups of employees for crowdsourcing campaigns in the enterprise; and which task parameters mediate the effect of gamification in enterprise crowdsourcing and whether there are some which possibly negate its merits.

ACKNOWLEDGEMENT

The authors would like to thank Robert-Jan Sips for the helpful discussions in the early stage of the project.

REFERENCES

[1] Lora Aroyo and Chris Welty. 2013. Measuring crowd truth for medical relation extraction. In *2013 AAAI Fall Symposium Series*.
[2] Richard Bartle. 1996. Hearts, clubs, diamonds, spades: Players who suit MUDs. *Journal of MUD research* 1, 1 (1996), 19.
[3] Sarah Bashirieh, Sepideh Mesbah, Judith Redi, Alessandro Bozzon, Zoltán Szlávik, and Robert-Jan Sips. 2017. Nudge Your Workforce: A Study on the Effectiveness of Task Notification Strategies in Enterprise Mobile Crowdsourcing. In *Proceedings of the 25th Conference on User Modeling, Adaptation and Personalization*. ACM, 4-12.
[4] Jean-François Bonnefon, Azim Shariff, and Iyad Rahwan. 2016. The social dilemma of autonomous vehicles. *Science* 352, 6293 (2016), 1573-1576.
[5] Anne Bowser, Derek Hansen, Yurong He, Carol Boston, Matthew Reid, Logan Gunnell, and Jennifer Preece. 2013. Using gamification to inspire new citizen science volunteers. In *Proceedings of the First International Conference on Gameful Design, Research, and Applications*. ACM, 18-25.
[6] A Colin Cameron and Pravin K Trivedi. 1990. Regression-based tests for overdispersion in the Poisson model. *Journal of Econometrics* 46, 3 (1990), 347-364.
[7] Sebastian Deterding, Dan Dixon, Rilla Khaled, and Lennart Nacke. 2011. From game design elements to gamefulness: defining gamification. In *Proceedings of the 15th International Academic MindTrek Conference*. ACM, 9-15.
[8] Anca Dumitrache, Lora Aroyo, Chris Welty, Robert-Jan Sips, and Anthony Levas. 2013. Dr. Detective: combining gamication techniques and crowdsourcing to create a gold standard in medical text. In *Proceedings of the 1st International Conference on Crowdsourcing the Semantic Web-Volume 1030*. 16-31.
[9] Carsten Eickhoff, Christopher G Harris, Arjen P de Vries, and Padmini Srinivasan. 2012. Quality through flow and immersion: gamifying crowdsourced relevance assessments. In *Proceedings of the 35th international ACM SIGIR Conference on Research and Development in Information Retrieval*. ACM, 871-880.
[10] Uwe Flick. 2009. *An introduction to qualitative research*. Sage.
[11] David Geiger and Martin Schader. 2014. Personalized task recommendation in crowdsourcing information systems—Current state of the art. *Decision Support Systems* 65 (2014), 3-16.
[12] Ido Guy, Anat Hashavit, and Yaniv Corem. 2015. Games for crowds: A crowdsourcing game platform for the enterprise. In *Proceedings of the 18th ACM Conference on Computer Supported Cooperative Work & Social Computing*. ACM, 1860-1871.
[13] Juho Hamari. 2013. Transforming homo economicus into homo ludens: A field experiment on gamification in a utilitarian peer-to-peer trading service. *Electronic Commerce Research and Applications* 12, 4 (2013), 236-245.
[14] Juho Hamari and Jonna Koivisto. 2015. "Working out for likes": An empirical study on social influence in exercise gamification. *Computers in Human Behavior* 50 (2015), 333-347.
[15] Matthias Hirth, Tobias Hoßfeld, and Phuoc Tran-Gia. 2013. Analyzing costs and accuracy of validation mechanisms for crowdsourcing platforms. *Mathematical and Computer Modelling* 57, 11 (2013), 2918-2932.
[16] Panagiotis G Ipeirotis and Evgeniy Gabrilovich. 2014. Quizz: targeted crowdsourcing with a billion (potential) users. In *Proceedings of the 23rd International Conference on World Wide Web*. The International World Wide Web Conference Committee, 143-154.
[17] Markus Krause, Marc Mogalle, Henning Pohl, and Joseph Jay Williams. 2015. A playful game changer: Fostering student retention in online education with social gamification. In *Proceedings of the Second (2015) ACM Conference on Learning@ Scale*. ACM, 95-102.
[18] Janaki Kumar. 2013. Gamification at work: Designing engaging business software. In *Proceedings of the 2nd International Conference of Design, User Experience, and Usability*. Springer, 528-537.
[19] Gioacchino La Vecchia and Antonio Cisternino. 2010. Collaborative workforce, business process crowdsourcing as an alternative of BPO. In *Proceedings of the 10th International Conference on Web Engineering*. Springer, 425-430.
[20] Edith Law and Luis Von Ahn. 2009. Input-agreement: a new mechanism for collecting data using human computation games. In *Proceedings of the SIGCHI Conference on Human Factors in Computing Systems*. ACM, 1197-1206.
[21] Janette Lehmann, Mounia Lalmas, Elad Yom-Tov, and Georges Dupret. 2012. Models of user engagement. In *Proceedings of the 20th International Conference on User Modeling, Adaptation, and Personalization*. Springer, 164-175.
[22] Andrew Mao, Ece Kamar, and Eric Horvitz. 2013. Why stop now? predicting worker engagement in online crowdsourcing. In *First AAAI Conference on Human Computation and Crowdsourcing*.
[23] Elaine Massung, David Coyle, Kirsten F Cater, Marc Jay, and Chris Preist. 2013. Using crowdsourcing to support pro-environmental community activism. In *Proceedings of the SIGCHI Conference on Human Factors in Computing Systems*. ACM, 371-380.
[24] Benedikt Morschheuser, Juho Hamari, and Jonna Koivisto. 2016. Gamification in crowdsourcing: a review. In *Proceedings of the 49th Hawaii International Conference on System Sciences*. IEEE, 4375-4384.
[25] Marta Rauch. 2013. Best practices for using enterprise gamification to engage employees and customers. In *Proceedings of the 2013 International Conference on Human-Computer Interaction*. Springer, 276-283.
[26] Maik Schacht and Silvia Schacht. 2012. Start the game: Increasing user experience of enterprise systems following a gamification mechanism. In *Software for People*. Springer, 181-199.
[27] Katie Seaborn and Deborah I Fels. 2015. Gamification in theory and action: A survey. *International Journal of Human-Computer Studies* 74 (2015), 14-31.
[28] Lei Shi, Alexandra I Cristea, Suncica Hadzidedic, and Naida Dervishalidovic. 2014. Contextual gamification of social interaction–towards increasing motivation in social e-learning. In *Proceedings of the 13th International Conference on Web-Based Learning*. Springer, 116-122.
[29] Kristin Siu, Alexander Zook, and Mark O Riedl. 2014. Collaboration versus competition: Design and evaluation of mechanics for games with a purpose.. In *Proceedings of the 9th International Conference on the Foundations of Digital Games*.
[30] Laurentiu Catalin Stanculescu, Alessandro Bozzon, Robert-Jan Sips, and Geert-Jan Houben. 2016. Work and play: An experiment in enterprise gamification. In *Proceedings of the 19th ACM Conference on Computer-Supported Cooperative Work & Social Computing*. ACM, 346-358.
[31] Osamuyimen Stewart, Juan M Huerta, and Melissa Sader. 2009. Designing crowdsourcing community for the enterprise. In *Proceedings of the ACM SIGKDD Workshop on Human Computation*. ACM, 50-53.
[32] Scott Thiebes, Sebastian Lins, and Dirk Basten. 2014. Gamifying information systems-a synthesis of gamification mechanics and dynamics. In *Proceedings of the 22nd European Conference on Information Systems*.
[33] Luis Von Ahn and Laura Dabbish. 2004. Labeling images with a computer game. In *Proceedings of the SIGCHI Conference on Human Factors in Computing Systems*. ACM, 319-326.
[34] Luis Von Ahn, Ruoran Liu, and Manuel Blum. 2006. Peekaboom: a game for locating objects in images. In *Proceedings of the SIGCHI Conference on Human Factors in Computing Systems*. ACM, 55-64.
[35] Maja Vukovic and Claudio Bartolini. 2010. Towards a research agenda for enterprise crowdsourcing. In *Proceedings of the 3rd International Symposium On Leveraging Applications of Formal Methods, Verification and Validation*. Springer, 425-434.

A Fair Share of the Work?
The Evolving Ecosystem of Crowd Workers

Kinda El Maarry
Institute for Information Systems
Technische Universität Braunschweig
Braunschweig, Germany
elmaarry@ifis.cs.tu-bs.de

Kristy Milland
TurkerNation.com and
McMaster University,
Toronto, Canada
millandk@mcmaster.ca

Wolf-Tilo Balke
Institute for Information Systems
Technische Universität Braunschweig
Braunschweig, Germany
balke@ifis.cs.tu-bs.de

ABSTRACT

Crowdsourcing's ability to forge new digital, and thus not location-bound, job opportunities spurred many visions of crowdsourcing's social impact as an answer to failing economies and recessions, especially in developing countries. Yet, did the digital solution take the business world by storm and redefine the classical business process? Did it indeed mature into a stable source of income for a vast agile workforce, and did it fulfill the visions of social impact? While exploring whether the market place's visions were fulfilled or not, we uncover a whole ecosystem the workers have built to leverage their productivity and earnings in the market place. In this paper, we shed light upon this system and all of its components, thus providing insights into the inner workings of the crowdsourcing platforms from the crowd's side and raises attention to the need for engaging in research and creating tools.

ACM Reference Format:
Kinda El Maarry, Kristy Milland and Wolf-Tilo Balke. 2018. Not Every Remix is an Innovation: A Fair Share of the Work? The Evolving Ecosystem of Crowd Workers. In WebSci '18:WebSci '18 10th ACM Conference on Web Science, May 27–30, 2018, Amsterdam, Neterlands. ACM, New York, NY, USA, 8 pages. http://dx.doi.org/10.1145/3201064.3201074

KEYWORDS

Crowdsourcing; ecosystem; market place symmetry; social factors

1. INTRODUCTION

Crowdsourcing was coined as a term a decade ago by Jeff Howe [1], yet the essence of this internet-based manifestation has actually been around since the early 1700s. Namely, when the British government offered a prize to whoever came up with the best way to measure a ship's longitudinal position [2]. Adopting the same idea and mapping it to our current technologies led to the rise of what we know today as crowdsourcing. The core idea revolves around the creation of an open call on an online crowdsourcing platform for the hiring of workers, to finish a particular task that a requester posts. Re-questers could be companies, organizations, individuals, researchers, government, or anyone else who has work to complete. The crowd choose between tasks that require human intelligence steering, since they are still too difficult to solve even by state-of-the-art algorithms. Thus, such platforms are sometimes referred to as artificial artificial intelligence, although at the ire of the workers, who would rather be viewed as real human intelligence.

With these platforms continually growing in popularity and number, crowdsourcing has rightly also been more frequently under scrutiny. A rich body of research has been roughly dedicated to cover three broad topics of interest:

1. Aiding requesters by: finding the best practices for designing tasks [3], developing typical design patterns to be adopted by requesters [4], predicting optimal task parameters: number of labels per task, pay per HIT, size of HIT [5], investigating active learning strategies [6], creating hybrid solutions, which combines human intelligence with state-of-the-art yet still limited algorithms [7], developing crowd-capital [8], helping requesters to create workflows to manage complex work processes [9], etc.

2. Resolving quality issues by: designing effective quality counter measures to fight off spammers [10], [11] and strategic spammers [12], identifying and shielding honest yet low-skilled workers from exclusion [10], etc.

3. Analyzing the underlying workforce by: conducting surveys about the workers' demographics [11], [13], identify the workers' motivations [14], [15], survey data and user studies [16], [17], researching the community networks they build between each other [18], etc.

In this work, we aim to observe and understand crowdsourcing through a new lens. During our research, we uncovered a whole ecosystem that the workers have built in order to leverage the money-work balance, their productivity and earnings. All of the support mechanisms within this hidden ecosystem were mainly developed by the workers themselves due to the unsupportive infrastructure of the crowdsourcing market, which is apparent in how requesters and workers are differently handled and supported by the platforms.

While shedding light on this hidden crowd-web, we will also address questions like: How do the workers find and choose tasks? How do the workers maximize their productivity on the platform? How do they support each other and newcomers? How many newcomers actually stay and for how long? What and who are the Super Turkers [19] and how do they become Super Turkers?

It's important to note that in this work we give only a fleeting glimpse of a mostly hidden system upon which the crowd rely to leverage and optimize their work. This system is very agile however, and is continuously changing and evolving to fit the new needs of the workers. Our work provides an analysis of the foundational infrastructure being built to support them.

WebSci'18, May 27-30, 2018, Amsterdam, Netherlands.
© 2018 Association of Computing Machinery.
ACM ISBN 978-1-4503-5563-6/18/05...$15.00.
DOI: http://dx.doi.org/10.1145/3201064.3201074

We start off in chapter 2 by investigate the market place through online surveys and pin point our initial observations about the working conditions, which allows us to draw conclusions about why Super Turkers are quite scarce. In Chapter 3, we delve into the ecosystem and illustrate in details its different components. Although the ecosystem is mainly there to enable to workers to operate in a more efficient form, in Chapter 4 we showcase that it has its dark side, which enables the workers to take shortcuts and illegally cheat the system. Next in Chapter 5, we highlight the academic efforts and contributions to this ecosystem, and finally we conclude in Chapter 6.

2. OBSERVING THE MARKET PLACE

To investigate the working conditions and understand why the existence of Super Turkers is scarce, we ran surveys on MTurk[1] and Turker Nation[2]. In the following we report some first observations.

Observation 1 - *Crowdsourcing appears to be an asymmetric market place.* This can be observed in both the 1) information asymmetry [20], [21], [22] and 2) imbalance of power [23].

Information asymmetry. Materializes in the lack of reputation rating and general information provided by the platform about the requesters [14]. In contrast, workers are rated and filtered by their reputation, which is based on their previous work and made accessible to requesters. Whereas workers are scrutinized as early as at sign-up and are exposed to continuous monitoring that is apparent in computed reputation scores, requesters are allowed to choose any name they want, including: duplicate names, or anonymous names such as Survey Requester. Such information asymmetry hampers the market's transparency and aids in the violation of the workers' privacy [22]. We conducted a survey on Turker Nation, in which 86 workers participated. In this survey, we asked the workers about their satisfaction in regards to multiple factors on MTurk. Answers were given on a scale from 1 to 5 (1= not satisfied at all and 5=completely satisfied). We refer to this dataset as the workers' satisfaction data. When workers were asked how satisfied they were with the amount of information provided by MTurk about the requestors and their reputation

scores (see Figure 1A), more than half of them (~ 53%) expressed their dissatisfaction.

Imbalance of power. Materializes in the requester's power to irrefutably decline the workers' output and accordingly refuse to pay the promised money while retaining the submitted work. On the other hand, workers can only try to communicate over the platform's channels to challenge a requester's decision, resolve a conflict or unfair treatment. This communication may very well end up being one-sided, with the requesters not being obliged to answer. As MTurk plays only the role of a facilitator, it refuses to step in and mediate disputes (see MTurk participation agreement[3]). In short, workers are vulnerably exposed to exploitation.

In our workers' satisfaction data, workers were asked how satisfied they were with MTurk's overall effort in hindering wage theft and unscrupulous requestors (see Figure 1B). Again, many complaints were raised, with ~ 58% of the participants expressing their disappointment in MTurk's wage theft measures.

Observation 2 – *The daily task of finding HITs and making an informed decision about HIT selection is widely unsupported.* This task proves quite challenging; where on one hand good HITs do not last long before they are taken up (e.g. a good 10,000 HIT batch typically lasts for only 10 minutes[4] ór less[5]). On the other hand, the search functionality on the platform is far from able to cope with the fast dynamics of HIT offerings.

Yet, finding lucrative HITs is critical for workers, because the search itself is unpaid work. Theoretically, there are three built-in ways to search for a HIT on MTurk:

1. *Requester's search page*, where each requester has a page upon which all their posted HITs are listed. This can be accessed by clicking on a requester's name. Some Turkers bookmark particular requester's pages with whom they have had a good past experience, and use a script that continuously monitors that page and alerts them when new work is posted. Another trick is to bookmark the page of the HITs themselves as a HIT group keeps its URL as long as the requester does not change its name. The beauty of this method is that when HITs are posted they first appear on the site in

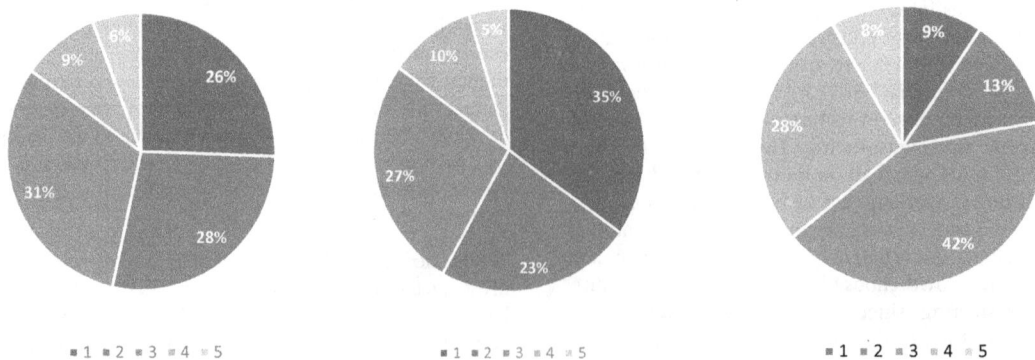

Figure 1. Workers' satisfaction with: A – general information provided by MTurk about Requesters (i.e. information asymmetry), B – MTurk's effort in hindering wage theft (i.e. power asymmetry), C – MTurk's HIT search functionality. Scale runs from 1 (not satisfied at all) to 5 (totally satisfied)

---

[1] The most prominent crowdsourcing platform.

[2] The oldest community for MTurk founded in 2005.

[3] http://requester.mturk.com/policies/conditionsofuse

[4] http://turkernation.com/showthread.php?13806-disappearing-HITs

[5] http://www.reddit.com/r/mturk/comments/2dkt8a/i_dont_know_how_you_guys_do_it/cjqi41n/

these HIT group URLs, but show up significantly later to the requesters' search page, so a worker who has this URL gets access to the work first without having to search at all.

2. *HIT-listing page* is a sorting facility provided by the platform, where available HITs are sorted by best-paid, etc. This page includes all HITs available on the platform at that time, but like the requester's search page, the HITs appear here long after they are actually uploaded to the platform. Most workers search for the most recently posted HITs first, keeping track of what has just been added to the platform. Second, they search for batches with a high number of HITs so they can be occupied with work for long stretches at a time, which is a lucrative method of working [24].

3. *Keyword search page* allows for a keyword search, as the name suggests. However, it is only as good as the keywords or tags that requesters attach to their tasks. In reality, these tags tend to be misleading and not very descriptive. For example, the Turkers once rallied against a requester who continually included "survey" in their keywords despite the work being transcription[6].

Generally speaking, all three options are too slow to deal with the fast posting dynamics of the platform and thus fail to present the available HITs in a timely fashion. The fastest search option is the generic list of HITs provided by the HIT-listing page, followed by the requester's search page, and lastly the keyword search page is the slowest. At this point, it becomes clear how Super Turkers do 80% of the work [25], since they can leverage the search function with automated scripts (see Section 3 for a comprehensive list of scripts and supporting software tools), bank of monitors and computer stations[7], and their social contacts. Indeed, in our workers' satisfaction dataset, when workers were asked to rate their satisfaction with the MTurk's search functionality (see Figure 1C), again an overall sense of dissatisfaction resonated.

But even if some matching HIT has been found, it spawns the next challenge of making an informed decision of whether to take on this work or not. This becomes extremely difficult given the information asymmetry [11]. Furthermore, MTurk fails to provide information about the hourly pay rate [25]. Only the monetary gain per assignment is given, without any mention of how long an assignment would take or the disclosure of the tasks' effective hourly rate [14].

Observation 3 – *There is a 70% attrition rate in the first six months of a worker's time on MTurk [26].* While observing the worker's longevity on the market place, we roughly identified four categories:

1. *Rejected applicants:* Clearly, many applicants are rejected upon signup since July of 2012. A post discussing the reasons for the apparent ban on international workers includes comments from around the world by those who were rejected[8]. Therefore, those who do not even make it to the point of being able to do a HIT and get paid for it may account for a large percentage of those who attempt to work on the system.

2. *One-day-workers:* applicants withstanding the approval process and receiving login credentials are instantly dealt a harsh dose of reality. Not having yet any qualifications or a high "HITs approved"-statistic leave them only with access to HITs having a payment of one or two pennies. In fact, 80% of the available HITs pay less than a dime, see e.g., the task given out in [27]. This quickly leads to a rapid and massive drop-off rate.

3. *Newbies:* workers who do not get discouraged by the shockingly low pay rates and make it through day one are already exceptional. Yet, the 70% attrition rate reported in [26] stems from these set of workers. About 10-30% of these workers will start to look for a forum to support their daily Turking activities.

4. *Super Turkers:* are in essence successful workers, who tap into the crowd's knowledge and leverage this knowledge to their advantage. As a Super Turker having social connections and being multifactorial is key. From a quantitative point of view, these workers do the bulk of work on all platforms. Some studies that have managed to actually interact with super Turkers [28] illustrate the 80/20 ratio, where only 20% of the crowd are doing 80% of the work. Some studies even claim a 90/10 ratio [13].

Observation 4 – *Crowdsourcing has not matured into a primary steady source of income for the majority of workers.* We conducted a survey early in 2015 on MTurk by posting a HIT with no restrictions (i.e. open to all workers). A total of 334 workers participated.

As illustrated in figure 2, based on the income figures we collected, about 4.49% of the workers earn more than $501 per month, with only 0.3% earning $5,001 or more. This leaves the majority of workers earning $100 or less per month, an amount that cannot be considered a household's main income.

The first two observations: the asymmetry in the market place and the lack of support in finding suitable HITs poses difficulties, which ultimately lead to high attrition rates and prevents

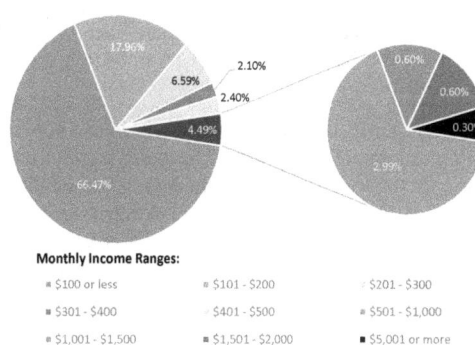

Figure 2. The workers' monthly income on MTurk

---

6   http://turkernation.com/showthread.php?22543-Petition-P9R-please-remove-the-keyword-quot-survey-quot-from-your-mTurk-transcription-hits

7   http://turkernation.com/showthread.php?9775-Workstation-Show-and-Tell

8   http://turkrequesters.blogspot.de/2013/01/the-reasons-why-amazon-mechanical-turk.html

crowdsourcing from maturing into a primary source of income. With these shortcomings hindering crowdsourcing from maturing into a steady widespread business solution, next we shed light as to how the workers and the academic community has intervened to overcome these difficulties.

3. UNCOVERING THE CROWD ECOSYSTEM

Indeed, for Super Turkers crowdsourcing has (to some extent) reached its full potential. That is, it has become a steady primary source of income and has transformed their work life from the typical classical business process. Yet, Super Turkers are the exception. So how and why are Super Turkers successful?

Observing the Super Turkers on Turker Nation, it seems that being part of the Ecosystem is key for being successful on the market place. This means actively participating in forums, Facebook groups, using scripts and extensions to optimize work, etc.

Next, we give a comprehensive insight into the inner workings of this ecosystem and explain how it overcomes the market's shortcomings listed in the previous section.

3.1 Online Forums and Facebook Groups

An online forum is a web-based site facilitating discussions among a group of subscribed users through posted messages. On such platforms, workers voluntarily share vital information like: 1) the best hardware technical setups, whether it is the computer, monitor, or keyboard, or even bank of computers[9], 2) how to organize and manage the work[10], 3) how to find good HITs in an efficient manner[11], 4) who are the good and bad requesters[12], 5) acceptable pay rates[13] etc. The major downside of forums as a supporting tool for crowd workers is that they take unpaid time to monitor.

MTurk has many external forums e.g. Turker Nation, mTurk Crowd, subreddit, etc. On Turker Nation, MTurk users can discuss requesters and work habits. Central to the forum are the Daily HIT Threads, where workers share news about good HITs and the Hall of Fame/Shame, which hosts ratings for requesters. Such information helps the worker get over the information asymmetry in the market place.

Upon analyzing the login data we got from Turker Nation for 2016, the attrition rates reported in the market place by [26] were also exhibited on the Forum. In total Turker Nation comprises 17,084 forum members.

Within a single month there will be between 200 to 400 unique individuals signing up. Every two to three months, the forum rejuvenates and the bulk of workers on the forum will be different. Focusing only on the first week of membership (see Figure 3), gives us a better overview on the longevity of active forum members, with active signifying logging onto the forum. Around 40.6% of the members who sign up are never active. Apart from those, the number of active members per day exponentially drops and many seem to give up. Those who stick around eventually become super posters (having more than 1,000 posts), which comprises only 0.2% of all members (see Figure 4).

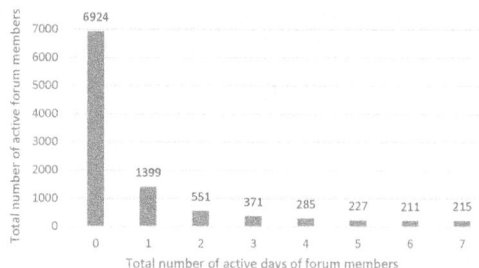

Figure 3. Forum member's first week longevity on the platform

A survey we ran in June 2017, targeting the top 50 super posters on Turker Nation (47 posters participated) attested to a clear correlation with the higher number of Hits completed: the Super poster with the highest forum posts at 34,371 entries completed 185,553 Hits within a period of 810 days, while the super poster with the least number of posts at 1,049 entries completed only 46,489 Hits within a period of 777 days. This correlation between high forum posts and high number of completed Hits leads us to the conclusion that the 0.2 % super posters corresponds more or

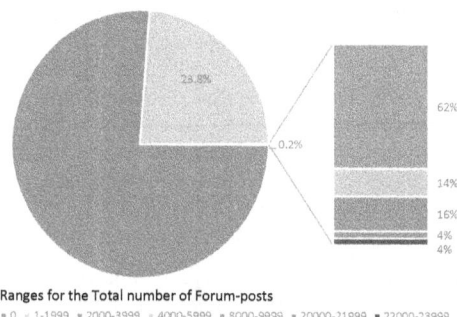

Figure 4. Number of workers' posts on Turker Nation

less to the 0.3% of workers earning more than $5,001 per month in Figure 2, that is, the Super Turkers.

Similar to the forums in their role, Facebook acts as a neutral playing field, where members of different forums get together. Super Turkers have private Facebook groups on which they share experiences, HITs, information, etc. (e.g. Turkers United, MTurk Alerts, Mturk Members). Such information helps them overcome the poor HIT search functionality's shortcoming on MTurk.

3.2 Scripts and Extensions

Scripts and extensions are basically computer software developed to automate cumbersome tasks. In order to support the workers in completing crowdsourcing work in a more optimized fashion, many scripts were developed and made open source. These scripts can be found in central repositories, which comprise aggregated lists of useful scripts, such as greasyfork[14]. Other repositories

---

[9] http://Turkernation.com/archive/index.php/f-78.html

[10] http://Turkernation.com/forumdisplay.php?167-mTurk-Scripts-Programs-amp-Tools

[11] http://Turkernation.com/forumdisplay.php?69-Make-Money-Fast-More-Efficiently-Questions

[12] http://Turkernation.com/forumdisplay.php?13-Requesters-Hall-of-Fame-Shame

[13] http://turkernation.com/forumdisplay.php?22-payment-questions

[14] https://greasyfork.org/en/scripts/by-site/mturk.com

comprising manually curated lists of links to scripts can be found on forum threads.

It is interesting to note that these scripts were mainly created by Super Turkers with programming skills. Next, we introduce and roughly categorize some of these scripts based on their functionality.

Filtering Requesters Scripts:

This type of scripts were developed by the workers to filter the available HITs based on favorite or unwanted requesters. Using color codes is common to display a requestor's reputation score. A few example scripts include:

- *Block Requesters* script, which filters out HITs from unwanted requesters. Other similar script extensions are available for Firefox[15] and Google Chrome[16].
- *HIT Scraper[17]*, which colors each HIT based on the Requester's TurkOpticon score (see section 3.3) or can filter out HITs based on various parameters e.g. Masters qualification, minimum pay threshold, worker's corresponding qualifications, etc.
- *Mmmturkeybacon Color Coded Search with Checkpoints[18]*, which not only colors HITs based on the Requester's TurkOpticon score (see section 3.3), but also allows workers to mark a HIT as completed or viewed so they will not attempt the same HIT twice

Search Optimizing Scripts:

These scripts are intended to speed up the search process by automatically loading the next search page upon scrolling down, or through push alerts when a worker's favorite requestor posts a HIT. For example:

- *Auto Pager[19]*, which automatically loads the next search page as the worker scrolls down.
- *Turk Master[20]*, which pushes alerts through a worker's Dashboard when their favorite requesters post HITs. Again, plugins for both Firefox and Chrome are available.
- *mmmturkeybacon Enhanced HIT Information Capsule[21]*, which converts a worker's favorite requester's name into a link, with which the worker can search with to find other HITs posted by the same requester.

Earnings Monitoring Scripts:

Many scripts are available to manage the earnings a worker is making. Some of the more useful scripts calculate the accumulated amount of pending earnings for the worker on a given day. For example:

- *Pending Earnings* script, which calculates the accumulated amount of pending earning for a particular worker.
- *Today's Project Earnings* script, which calculates the accumulated amount of earnings for the current day.

- *Amazon Payments mTurk Details*, which keeps track of the worker's transactions on MTurk and adds them to the worker's account activity page for easy monitoring.

HIT Organizer Scripts:

These scripts enable the user to organize HITs within their different stages: active, pending, rejected, accepted. A few representative examples of such scripts include:

- *Mturk Dashboard HIT status links*, which provides the workers with direct links to both rejected and pending HITs.
- *Requester ID & Auto Approval Time*, which keeps track of the requesters ID, since requesters can freely change their account names. Moreover, it also displays the requester's corresponding HIT autoapproval time (how long it will be before the HIT automatically approves) to help the workers in making a more informed decision about working with that particular requester.
- *mmmturkeybacon Queue Order Fix[22]*, which automatically detects when a worker finishes a HIT and then opens the next HIT with the shortest time left before it expires from their queue for the worker to instantly start working on it.

Reputation scripts:

These scripts help the workers to keep track of their approval percentage rate as well as the requesters' reputation. Examples for these scripts include:

- *Mturk Worst Case Scenario Calculator*, which computes for the worker how many rejections they can receive before their approval rating drops below a significant level.
- *Turkopticon*, which allows the user to see the community ratings of requesters on the MTurk search page or quickly rate a requester. See section 3.3 for a more detailed description.

Warning scripts:

Workers need alerts when something has gone wrong. These scripts provide such warnings.

- *Mturk Hit Not Accepted[23]*, which warns the worker that the HIT they are viewing has not been accepted by turning the background pink. Workers may find them-selves completing an exceptionally long HIT, but when they attempt to submit it they realize there is no submit button, only an accept button, as they never accepted it in the first place.
- *mmmturkeybacon Logged Out Alert[24]*, which alerts the worker that they have been logged out. Recently, MTurk began logging out workers every 12 hours, so this notice alerts a worker in case they are running a Search Optimizing script in an effort to find new work.
- *MTurk Captcha Alert[25]*, which displays an alert when a CAPTCHA, an image the worker has to transcribe to prove they are human, appears on a HIT. If a worker is engaging in "HIT hoarding", a term that describes the behavior of grabbing 25

---

[15] http://userscripts-mirror.org/scripts/show/69128

[16] http://userscripts-mirror.org/scripts/show/130929

[17] https://greasyfork.org/en/scripts/10615-hit-scraper-with-export

[18] https://greasyfork.org/en/scripts/3118-mmmturkeybacon-color-coded-search-with-check-points

[19] https://addons.mozilla.org/en-US/firefox/addon/autopager/

[20] https://greasyfork.org/en/scripts/4771-turkmaster-mturk

[21] https://greasyfork.org/en/scripts/3114-mmmturkeybacon-enhanced-hit-information-cap-sule-shows-automatic-approval-time

[22] https://greasyfork.org/en/scripts/3103-mmmturkeybacon-queue-order-fix

[23] https://greasyfork.org/en/scripts/2939-mturk-hit-not-accepted

[24] https://greasyfork.org/en/scripts/3098-mmmturkeybacon-logged-out-alert

[25] https://greasyfork.org/en/scripts/2586-mturk-captcha-alert

HITs to maximally fill their work queue before they begin working on the HITs one by one, they may reach a CAPTCHA as MTurk displays one after every 35th HIT the worker accepts. If they do not complete it and the page refreshes, or they have multiple tabs open each with the CAPTCHA displaying, their account will be temporarily suspended from the site for five minutes. This script allows the worker to be alerted that a CAPTCHA has appeared so they can stop their other activities and complete it, saving them from a five minute halt.

Refreshing and Page Monitoring extensions:

In order to get work, one must find their favorite requesters and HIT groups and refresh the pages that list that work continually. In fact, MTurk has a built in "preview and accept" mode that allows the worker to constantly refresh a HIT group URL and grab a new HIT each time they do. Without automated refreshing tools, a worker would have to manually refresh multiple pages to find new work. If the specific URL of new work is not known, a worker can instead use a page monitoring extension to alert them when the requester's HIT listing page is updated.

- Some refreshing extensions require you to keep the page open in a tab, such as *Easy Auto Refresh, ChromeReload, AutoRefresh*, and *ReloadEvery*. These are good to use when you are reloading "preview and accept" URLs as they will continue refreshing even if you accept a HIT, meaning you can quickly fill your queue.
- Other extensions monitor the page in the background, sending you a visual or audio alert when some content on the page changes. For the requester's HIT list page this is more appropriate as refreshing the page will not accept HITs for you. Instead, an extension such as *Page Monitor Plus, Distill Web Monitor, Update Scanner*, or *Check4Change* alert to changes on the page in general, which the worker can then visit to see if the new work is of interest to them.

Layout scripts:

Workers have created manuscripts that alter the layout in ways that help them to work more efficiently. Some examples include

- *mmmturkeybacon Butt-In Buttons[26]*, which adds many features to the site, including a "preview and accept" button that allows the worker to accept a HIT from the search page, a "return and accept" button so the worker can return this HIT and automatically accept the next one available, and moves all buttons closer to the workspace so the page is more efficiently laid out
- *MTurk Max Job Window Height[27]*, which makes the work iFrame a more acceptable size in the browser window, giving workers the ability to see all of the HITs at one time.
- *MTurk Queue Count[28]*, which displays how many HITs the worker has in their personal work queue at the top of the HIT, allowing them to keep tabs on their progress.

3.3 Activist Platforms

Multiple platforms were developed with the aim of supporting the workers and bridge the information asymmetry within the crowdsourcing platforms. Next, we present two prime examples of such platforms.

TurkOpticon:

TurkOpticon[29] is a website that was created and maintained by Lilly Irani (University of California San Diego) and Six Silberman (University of California, Irvine). TurkOpticon is a platform that enables the dissemination of requesters' subjective star ratings [29]. Basically, workers can evaluate requesters and make this information available directly on the MTurk website through plugins. The qualitative attributes upon which TurkOpticon ranks the requesters are: 1) Generosity, in terms of the amount of money paid relative the amount of time needed to finish the task, 2) Promptness of a requester in terms of accepting the work and paying, 3) Fairness of a requester in his/her decision to accept or reject the work provided, and 4) Communicativity in terms of the availability of a requester to respond to concerns.

Dynamo:

The community platform *Dynamo[30]*,is the product of the combined efforts of Turkers and academic researchers from Stanford University and the University of California, San Diego. The forum paves the way for collective action, thus empowering the crowd to push for needed change [30]. On the platform, ideas and issues can be proposed and supported pseudonymously by Turkers. When an idea receives more than 25 up votes, where at least 50% of the votes in total are in favor, an action is mobilized.

3.4 Communal Sharing

Very similar to the spirit in the forums, communal sharing can be strongly exhibited in particular with Indian Turkers, where a true sense of sharing is displayed through the dissipations of recommendations and information about HITs through cellphone calls and texts, emails, and even yelling across houses [30].

4. THE DARK SIDE OF THE ECOSYSTEM

Although our focus is geared towards the ecosystem the honest workers rely on in order to have the best time-money return, we still found it interesting to briefly report about other used tools, as listed in [31], unfortunately in ways which both provide low quality data to the requester and violate MTurk's Conditions of Use[31], thus endangering the workers' accounts.

Generic and task-tailored bots:

Due to low pay, scammers use "bots" (automated answering systems) and generic malicious algorithms that can sign up for tasks and submit answers, either through random output generation or by utilizing minimal artificial reasoning [31]. *AutoHotKey*, as mentioned above, enables scripters to create automated bots that complete HITs with no human intervention.

Shared Question Answering Dictionary (SQAD):

SQAD is an online repository, where answers to questions can be stored. When the same question is encountered, the same answer

---

[26]   https://greasyfork.org/en/scripts/9088-mmmturkeybacon-butt-in-buttons

[27]   https://greasyfork.org/en/scripts/6137-mturk-max-job-window-height

[28]   https://greasyfork.org/en/scripts/6150-mturk-queue-count

[29]   https://Turkopticon.ucsd.edu/

[30]   http://www.wearedynamo.org/

[31]   https://www.mturk.com/mturk/conditionsofuse

is given. Thus, quality safe guards such as majority voting will always be in favor of the workers. This is more like an organized group attack where workers can system submit entries through an automated request to a SQAD. Similarly, they can automatically retrieve an answer that was given to a particular question before.

Artificial Clones:

Unlike the coordinated effort with SQAD, with artificial clones a worker needs only to rely on himself. The strategy here is to have a clone program that duplicates the behavior of the worker. Thus for a given task, the spammer answers truthfully a set of questions and stores them. The clone program would then give the same answers to already seen questions. For unseen questions, either a skip strategy is followed, a random answer generation is deployed, or another worker is asked.

5. ATTENTION IN THE ACADEMIC COMMUNITY

Of course some of these problem have already raised awareness in the academic community. In the following we present some of the academic contributions that were developed to aid the workers in leveraging their productivity.

Turkmotion:

Turkmotion[32] is a website and a new browser extension developed at Technical University of Berlin. In addition to being able to rate requesters, workers can also rate HIT groups. The system comprises two parts: 1) a browser extension that enables workers to rate the tasks based on fair payment and enjoyable factor, which then automatically appear beside the respective HITs on MTurk, 2) a website that lists the top rated tasks and provides a filtering service, which the workers can use to choose the HITs based on their preferences.

TurkBench:

TurkBench is a tool that was developed at Xerox Research center [29]. TurkBench aims at eliminating unpaid search work by providing workers with a list of HITs to complete. It consists of three main components: 1) a personalized market visualization that presents the workers a current personalized state of the market, 2) a session manager that manages automatically created work sessions, and 3) a scheduler that crawls MTurk and creates individual schedules for the workers.

6. CONCLUSION AND OUTLOOK

It is clear to see that crowdsourcing has not yet reached the envisioned potential. We have observed two major factors: *the market place's asymmetry* and the *HIT search functionality's inadequacy*, which have hindered crowdsourcing from becoming a primary steady source of income as well as discouraged many new workers explaining the very high attrition rates (70%).

Still, a very small number of workers have indeed secured a comfortable living out of crowdsourcing: Super Turkers. By observing both MTurk and Turker Nation, we investigated how and why Super Turkers actually are successful. In essence, Super Turkers have created an ecosystem within which they can leverage the crowd's knowledge to their advantage. In this ecosystem, a set of diverse tools were created to tackle the two major shortcomings mentioned above at least to some degree.

In terms of the market's asymmetry, activist platforms have been created, e.g. Dynamo or TurkOpticon, with promptness and fairness scores recorded per requestor to relieve the power asymmetry problem. On the other hand filtering request scripts and reputation scripts as well as Forums e.g. Turker Nation and its 'Hall of Fame and Shame' fight off the information asymmetry. Moreover, communal sharing and search optimizing scripts aid the workers in their daily HIT search, which is unfortunately inadequately supported. Similarly, the academic community also developed some tools to tackle both shortcomings e.g. Turk-Bench, Turkmotion and Crowd Workers.

Yet despite of this ecosystem, the percentage of Super Turkers unfortunately remains small. This may be because many workers are simply unaware of this ecosystem. But even if workers are aware of this ecosystem, being an effective part of it solely remains on the individual effort and requires much perseverance due to its distributed nature.

In summary, there is a definite need for the providers of crowdsourcing platforms to invest in designing technologies that would support workers in leveraging their productivity and in easily finding suitable HITs. Moreover, transparency is needed, since workers are given way less information about the requesters than the other way around.

If crowdsourcing is truly a serious aspect for the future of work, we must take action in engaging in research and creating tools that are seamlessly integrated within the platforms, and which will allow workers to exert their rights in a fair fashion and thus, pave the way to a sustainable career by work models based on crowdsourcing.

7. REFERENCES

[1] J. Howe, "The Rise of Crowdsourcing," in Journal: North, Wired Magazine, 2006, vol. 14, no. 6, pp. 1–4.

[2] L. A. Plummer, "Longitude: The True Story of a Lone Genius Who Solved the Greatest Scientific Problem of His Time.,"Book., vol. 3, no. 2, pp. 220–222, 2004.

[3] H. A. Sampath, R. Rajeshuni, and B. Indurkhya, "Cognitively Inspired Task Design to Improve User Performance on Crowdsourcing Platforms," in Proc. of the 32th Int. Conf. on Humans Factors Computer System (CHI'14), Toronto, Canada, pp. 3665–3674, 2014.

[4] C. Lofi and K. El-maarry, "Design Patterns for Hybrid Algorithmic-crowdsourcing Workflows," in proc.of the 16th IEEE Conf. on Business Informatics (CBI'14), Geneva, Switzerland, vol. 1, pp 1–8, 2014.

[5] E. Huang, H. Zhang, D. C. Parkes, K. Z. Gajos, and Y. Chen, "Toward Automatic Task Design: A Progress Report," in Proc. of the ACM SIGKDD Workshop on Human Computation (HCOMP'10), pp. 77-85, 2010.

[6] V. V. Ambati, S. Vogel, and J. Carbonell, "Active Learning and Crowd-Sourcing for Machine Translation," in proc. of the 7th Int. conf. on Language Resources and Evaluation (LREC'10), Malta, pp. 2169–2174, 2010.

[7] C. Lofi, K. El Maarry, and W.-T. Balke, "Skyline Queries in Crowd-Enabled Databases," in proc. of the 16th Int. Conf. on Extending Database Technology (EDBT'13), Genoa, Italy, pp. 465–476, 2013.

---

[32] http://turkmotion.com/index.html

[8] J. Prpic, P. P. Shukla, J. H. Kietzmann, and I. P. McCarthy, "How to work a crowd: Developing crowd capital through crowdsourcing," in Journal of Business Horizons, vol. 58, no. 1, pp. 77–85, 2015.

[9] A. Kittur, S. Khamkar, P. André, and R. E. Kraut, "CrowdWeaver : Visually Managing Complex Crowd Work," in Proc. of Conf. on Computer Cooperative Work (CSCW'12), Seattle, USA, pp. 1033–1036, 2012.

[10] K. El Maarry, and W.-T. Balke, "Retaining Rough Diamonds: Towards a Fairer Elimination of Low-skilled Workers," in proc. of the 20th Int. Conf. on Database Systems for Advanced Applications (DASFAA'15), Hanoi, Vietnam, pp. 169–185, 2015.

[11] J. Ross, A. Zaldivar, L. Irani, and B. Tomlinson, "Who are the Turkers? Worker Demographics in Amazon Mechanical Turk," Technical report, Department of Informatics, University of California, Irvine, USA, Technical report SocialCode-2009-01, 2009.

[12] K. El Maarry, U. Güntzer, and W.-T. Balke, "A Majority of Wrongs Doesn't Make it Right," in proc.of the 16th Int.Conf. on Web Information Systems Engineering (WISE'15), Miami, Florida, vol. 9418, pp. 293–308, 2015.

[13] P. Ipeirotis, "Demographics of Mechanical Turk," New York University, Working Paper, CEDER-10-01, 2010.

[14] D. Martin, B. V Hanrahan, J. O'Neill, and N. Gupta, "Being a turker," in Proc.of the 17th ACM Conf. on Computer Supported Cooperative Work & Social Computing (CSCW'14), Baltimore, Maryland, USA, pp. 224–235, 2014.

[15] N. Kaufmann, T. Schulze, and D. Veit, "More than fun and money. Worker Motivation in Crowdsourcing – A Study on Mechanical Turk,"in Proc. of the 17th Americas Conf. on Information Systems (AMCIS'11), Detroit, Michigan, pp. 1–11, 2011.

[16] A. Kittur, E. H. Chi, and B. Suh, "Crowdsourcing user studies with Mechanical Turk," in Proc. of the 26th annual SIGCHI conf. on Human factors in computing systems (CHI'08), Florence, Italy, pp. 453–456, 2008.

[17] B. Zhan, D. N. Monekosso, P. Remagnino, S. a. Velastin, and L. Q. Xu, "Crowd analysis: A survey," published in Journal of Machine Vision and Applications, vol. 19, no. 5–6, pp. 345–357, 2008.

[18] M. Yin, S. Suri, M. L. Gray, and J. W. Vaughan, "The Communication Network Within the Crowd," in proc. of the 25th Int. World wide web Conference (WWW '16), Montreal, Canada, pp. 1293-1303, 2016.

[19] J. Bohannon, "Social Science for Pennies," in Journal Science, vol. 334, no. 6054, pp. 307–307, 2011.

[20] B. B. Bederson and A. J. Quinn, "Web Workers Unite ! Addressing Challenges of Online Laborers," in Proc. of Extended Abstracts on Human Factors in Computing Systems, Vancouver, Canada, pp. 97–105, 2011.

[21] M. S. Silberman, L. Irani, and J. Ross, "Ethics and tactics of professional crowdwork," in magazine: XRDS Crossroads, vol. 17, no. 2, pp. 39–43, 2010.

[22] A. Felstinerf, "Working the Crowd : Employment and Labor Law in the Crowdsourcing Industry," in Berkeley Journal of Employment Labor Law, vol. 32, no. 1, pp. 143–204, 2011.

[23] A. Felstiner, "The Weakness of Crowds," in Limn, no. 2: Crowds and Clouds, 2013.

[24] L. B. Chilton, J. J. Horton, and R. C. Miller, "Task search in a human computation market," Proc. of the ACM SIGKDD Workshop on Human Computation (HCOMP'10), Washington, DC, USA, pp. 1–9, 2010.

[25] A Kittur, J. Nickerson, and M. Bernstein, "The Future of Crowd Work," in Conf. on Computer supported cooperative work, Portland, Oregon, USA, pp.1–17, 2013.

[26] P. Hitlin, "Research in the Crowdsourcing Age, a Case Study," article in the Pew Reaserch Center, Internet & Tech, July, 2016.

[27] D. Harwath and J. Glass, "Deep multimodal semantic embeddings for speech and images," in IEEE Workshop on Automatic Speech Recognition and Understanding (ASRU'15), Scottsdale, Arizona, USA, pp. 237–244, 2015.

[28] J. Zhang, S. Ma, M. Sameki, S. Sclaroff, M. Betke, Z. Lin, X. Shen, B. Price, and R. Mech, "Salient Object Subitizing," in Proc. of the Conf. on Computer Vision and Pattern Recognition (CVPR'15), vol. 07, Boston, Massachusetts,USA, pp. 4045–4054, 2015.

[29] N. Salehi, L. C. Irani, M. S. Bernstein, A. Alkhatib, E. Ogbe, K. Milland, and Clickhappier, "We Are Dynamo: Overcoming Stalling and Friction in Collective Action for Crowd Workers," in Proc. of the ACM Conf. on Human Factors Computing Systems (CHI'15), Seoul, Korea, vol. 1, pp. 1621–1630, 2015.

[30] N. Gupta, D. Martin, B. V Hanrahan, J. O'Neill, and J. O. Neill, "Turk-Life in India," in Proc. of the 18th Int. Conf. on Supporting Group Work (GROUP'14), Sanibel Island, Florida, USA, pp. 1–11, 2014.

[31] D. E. Difallah, G. Demartini, and P. Cudre-Mauroux, "Mechanical cheat: Spamming schemes and adversarial techniques on crowdsourcing platforms," in CrowdSearch Workshop in conj. with World Wide Web Conf. (WWW'12), Lyon, France, vol. 842, pp. 20–25, 2012.

Not Every Remix is an Innovation: A Network Perspective on the 3D-Printing Community

Christian Voigt

Centre for Social Innovation (ZSI)

Vienna, Austria

voigt@zsi.at

ABSTRACT

A better understanding of how information in networks is reused or mixed, has the potential to significantly contribute to the way value is exchanged under a market- or commons-based paradigm. Data as collaborative commons, distributed under creative commons licenses, can generate novel business models and significantly spur the continuing development of the knowledge society. However, looking at data reuse in a large 3d-printing community, we show that the remixing of existing 3d models is substantially influenced by bots, customizers and self-referential designs. Linking these phenomena to a more fine-grained understanding of the process and product dimensions of innovations, we conclude that remixing patterns cannot be taken as direct indicators of innovative behavior on sharing platforms. A further exploration of remixing networks in terms of their topological characteristics is suggested as a way forward. For the empirical underpinning of our arguments, we analyzed 893,383 three-dimensional designs shared by 193,254 members.

CCS CONCEPTS

• **Information systems** → **Collaborative and social computing systems and tools**; • **Applied computing** → *Education*; • **Hardware** → *Emerging tools and methodologies*;

KEYWORDS

networks, 3d printing, online community, innovation, remixing

ACM Reference Format:

Christian Voigt. 2018. Not Every Remix is an Innovation: A Network Perspective on the 3D-Printing Community. In *WebSci '18: WebSci '18 10th ACM Conference on Web Science, May 27–30, 2018, Amsterdam, Netherlands*. ACM, New York, NY, USA, 9 pages. https://doi.org/10.1145/3201064.3201070

1 INTRODUCTION

Reusing information is key to the continuing development of the knowledge society and the emergence of the Zero Marginal Cost Society, that is the paradigm shift from market capitalism to the collaborative commons [32]. Rifkin envisioned an era, where competition leads to ever leaner production mechanisms and sharing platforms turn consumers into prosumers as they create, adapt and remix existing designs into personalized designs [32] . Hence, data is not only the new oil but also the basis for a new understanding of how value is exchanged, within a market- or commons-based framework. Data as collaborative commons can thereby make established business models obsolete.

An example of platform collaboration are 3d-printing communities, sharing and remixing their 3d models. Remixing as a form of peer production is also referred to as a shift towards a more collaborative culture, increasing the quality of collaboration outcomes, since members of the 3D printing community can iterate and refine each others' designs [8]. More generally, remixing describes the practice of "taking ideas and modifying or recombining them " [27].

One of the stated goals of Web science is to track and reflect upon large-scale platform activities and explore, for example, the extent and nature of sharing that can be found [20] . Developing a richer understanding of platform activities is not only critical for economic reasons, when knowledge production and use is often shared among thousands of users, but it is also hugely relevant if we search for design principles that might facilitate or limit specific forms of collaboration [9].

The specific sharing platform we analyse in this paper is Thingiverse.com, a platform providing reusable designs at an entry-level, as well as meta-models or complete design files using 3D modelling applications such as OpenSCAD, Blender or Fusion360. Whereas the first two file formats are generated by free software, the latter requires a commercial digital prototyping tool, where free licences are granted, but only for educational purposes. By the end of 2017 Thingiverse featured more than 993,850 3D Models or Things and states on its Website to represent the world's largest 3D printing community [37].

3D printing is a hugely dynamic area, becoming ever more accessible to a growing number of tech-affine tinkerers [41]. 3D printing is also a corner stone of the Maker movement, which lowers the entry barriers to innovation by enabling fast prototyping and experimenting with ideas [39]. While declining in price, printing materials are constantly improving, printers become more reliable and the opportunities seem limitless, as indicated in an early cover story from the Economist in February, 2011, which said "Print me a Stradivarius" [14].

The specific background to our paper is the question whether Thingiverse content can support educators, either by identifying models useful to their specific subject matters (e.g. geometric shapes, miniature models of cells or a Pythagorean cup, showing the transmission of fluid-pressure) or by providing models students could adapt and print themselves.

2 RELATED WORK: REMIXING 3D-MODELS AND INNOVATION

Innovation, collaboration and knowledge reuse are research topics, that have gained in interest among researchers of maker communities[27–30]. Platform usage data have been used to explore

- the differences between collaboratively and individually authored projects in Scratch, a programming platform for youth [21];
- the accessibility of maker knowledge based on discourse styles [40]or
- the participation patterns of female and male makers, on Instructables.com [35].

2.1 Remixing 3d-models

Thingiverse data, as well, have been analysed previously, e.g. testing whether meta-models - parametric models easily adaptable through slides or web forms - are reused more frequently than other types of 3D models which would require the use of a text editor or a specific CAD program to make the desired adaptations [24]. This hypothesis could be confirmed, moderated by the community experience of the meta-model's designer, i.e. their duration of membership or the number of designs they had already provided to the community. Another stream of research is looking into remixing patterns, i.e. exploring the originality of adapted designs, whether remixes transgress design categories or the structural diversity of remixes (e.g. number of sources or derivatives) [17]. Related to users' remixing behaviour, is the provision of non-physical knowledge, that helps novice users in the process of fabrication, e.g. step-by-step descriptions, indication of parameters for different 3D printers and filaments, successfully used with a specific design [28].

Another, equally relevant, stream of research takes reuse of design knowledge as a means to explore other, higher level concepts such as open innovation and co-creation. For example, co-creation can concern different stages of the making process as in users downloading a 3D model and printing it themselves instead of sending it to an on-line printing service [31]. Whether or not 3D models can be considered open innovations, according to the authors, depends then on whether they are used by a community in response to an actual need [38]. The latter can be supported by commercial or non-profit organisations, but could also be the result of a more informal bottom up movement. Research has shown, that there is also a strong component of craftsmanship behind the process of 3d printing. This takes often the form of tacit knowledge, since it is not hard-coded within the actual 3d model. An important source for clarifications is the built-in discussion platform here, where some design have drawn hundreds of comments. The most common questions included: (a) knowing how to actually use the 3d object correctly, (b) how to customize or remix a design, (c) print quality on a given printer and (d) how a design was created[1].

Using the comments section, authors can reply to users' questions and novice practitioners can learn from previous experiences and questions already posted [40]. Comments were also the place

where modifications were requested. In a study done by Alcock et al. [1], comments were related to adapting existing designs in about 24%, with a split of 86 % related to changing a design's functionality and 14 % aiming to improving printability.

2.2 Varying degrees of innovativeness

As stated by the authors of a recent study of innovation on Thingiverse.com [17], reusing existing knowledge is indispensable for the creation of novel designs. Although there is no lack of definitions for innovations, there is a consensus that innovations imply a discontinuity or disruption:

- either in the way a novel product addresses an existing problem or user need or
- because a new, parallel market place is developing, e.g. electronic typewriters, smartphones and currently e-cars can be seen as products disrupting existing markets[18].

This view is very much in line with Schumpeter's classical definition of innovation as 'new combinations of production factors' leading to the creative destruction of incumbent products or production methods. Replacing the incumbent is then less a matter of price - minimizing costs - but it is a capability driven process, i.e. offering new features or better performance [36].

For our current discussion of remixing behaviour specific to a sharing platform of 3D-models the question is whether remixed models include 'new features' or show 'better performances'. For that to answer, it is helpful to have a more fine-grained typology of innovations. A common categorization includes 2 dimensions [18]:

- micro versus macro level innovations (referring to the scale of impact, i.e. is it an innovation to a single firm or an entire market) innovations and
- the innovation's power to disrupt technology and market directions.

According to the authors in [18], radical innovations include macro level discontinuities, affecting markets and technologies, and incremental innovations are micro level discontinuities, where it is sufficient if either technology or markets are affected. Hence, the questions we need to add to our research agenda are: 'What added value do users have of remixed designs?' and 'Does this value originate from a model's features or is it more the associated production process of the model that creates the value?'. For example, a 3d model with additional functionalities might exhibit better use qualities, whereas a customizable 3d model drastically simplifies the remixing process (*production process*).

3 RESEARCH OBJECTIVES

Being an open platform, Thingiverse.com encourages sharing of 3D models under a Creative Commons license, meaning that all designs can be altered and reused. The ease with which a design can be adapted or remixed is critical in driving the maker movement, where you do not invent from scratch but reuse existing, partly proven solutions[4]. Other features determining sharing and collaboration patterns include the possibility to easily credit original sources, a positive community spirit which supports newcomers and the general usability of the sharing platform, including design categories, detailed search functions or the featuring of high quality designs. Of course, remixing can take different shapes, such as merging two designs, extracting a specific part from a design or simply slicing a design so that it fits a smaller printer chamber or leads to a less error prone printing process. And there are questions that go beyond dyadic relationships between 3d models, such as how often a remix has been remixed, leading to chains or networks of models forming increasingly complex prints.

While there is consensus on the importance of sharing designs in the maker movement, this is less the case for other aspects such as licensing models, e.g. creative commons with or without commercial derivatives, or the way remixing is supported best, e.g. by creating a customizable model or by referring to the original CAD files. Customizable models are parametric designs where some characteristics can be changed without any knowledge of the underlying programming language. Typically, users change the dimensions of an object or the writing on things like key chains. The creation of customizable models is supported by Thingiverse though its Customizer App. The introduction of the Customizer App had a huge impact on the number of designs hosted on Thingiverse. The year after the introduction, content on Thingiverse almost tripled [28]. However, Blikstein [10] argues that the 'key-chain syndrome' should be of no surprise, since a relatively high 'product value' is achieved with a relatively low 'investment in learning'. Our interest in remixing activities on Thingiverse is primarily motivated by our interest in exploring the platform's potential to provide content in a way that supports educators. The underlying hypothesis is that a model, which has been remixed, has already shown its printability. However, screening the first remixes we quickly realized that this assumption would be incomplete. Thingiverse featured very different types of remixing behaviours, some of which would lead to very innovative, novel outcomes whereas others would mimic the original design with only minimal changes.

Hence, we established three research directions to obtain a more differentiated understanding of remixing:

(1) What is the extent to which remixing is already happening? Exploring different statistics, are there any attention-grabbing characteristics of remixes? In what ways is the number of sources being remixed related to the innovativeness of the remixed product?

(2) What role do other network activities play? Here we are interested in users' liking or downloading behaviour, or the way remixing stays within or transgresses nominal design categories.

(3) Finally, can we go beyond the analysis of dyadic remixing relationships, identifying chains of remixes in the quest for more complex innovations.

Similar questions have been studied bevor, hence the following section will clarify some underlying concepts and assumptions guiding our interpretations.

4 METHOD AND DATA

This paper explores data which have been collected through the official Thingiverse API [22] during the first 2 weeks of November 2017. The data set comprises 893,383 designs (hereafter also referred to as things or 3d models), which have been provided by 193,254

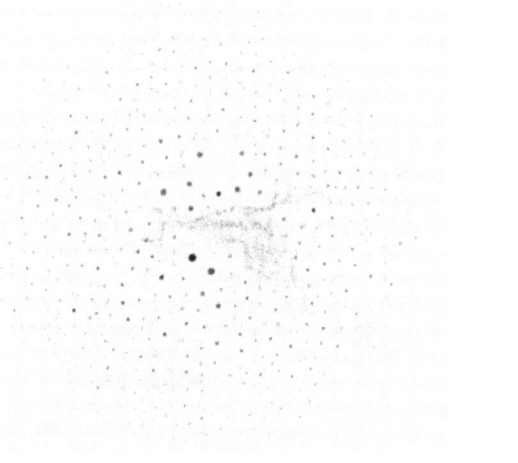

Figure 1: Remixing relationships between designs (n=893,529)

authors. This reflects an almost complete set of designs as far as designs have been published and were accessible through the API.

In network terms designs are nodes which are connected if design R-(emix) uses information coming from design O-(riginal), or put differently R is a derivative or remix of O. It is important to clearly state the technicalities, i.e. on what grounds such a relationship can be established. For example, if the original model is a customizer, then a remix connection with O is automatically established, clearly indicated under the platform's 'remixed from' section. However, if a user decides to download the SCAD (Solid 3D CAD) file of a design, modifies it and uploads it again, then he or she is strongly encouraged to list the original, but there is no technically enforced mechanism for tracking the remixing of existing models. Similar issues with attribution have been explored within the Scratch programming community, showing that even automated crediting is not sufficient if users feel that a remix is more an act of plagiarism than of remixing, especially if the 'remix' consisted of a minor change of colour [25]. This implies that the connections between designs need to be seen as an approximation, either because remixers did not credit the original author (false negative) or because a claimed remix is in essence a copy (false positive)[27].

Figure 1 shows the complete graph of Thingiverse designs, using Gephi's force-directed layout[7]. The high number of nodes shown only allows for a low resolution of network relationships. The figure shows 893.529 nodes, which are clustered in 403.096 components (i.e. groups of linked nodes). Within those components the connectivity is largely low as indicated by a mean clustering coefficient of 0.0057. A cluster coefficient of zero indicates a star graph and a coefficient of 1 refers to a complete graph.

A more meaningful way of looking the structure of the network is presented in Figure 2. Here we can look for a network's uniformity or assortativity (e.g. the correlation between the degree of a node and the average degree of its neighbours). The Thingiverse network is dissortative for nodes with less than 10 connections, i.e. designs with few connections are linked to designs with many connections. A reflection in line with the low clustering coefficient.

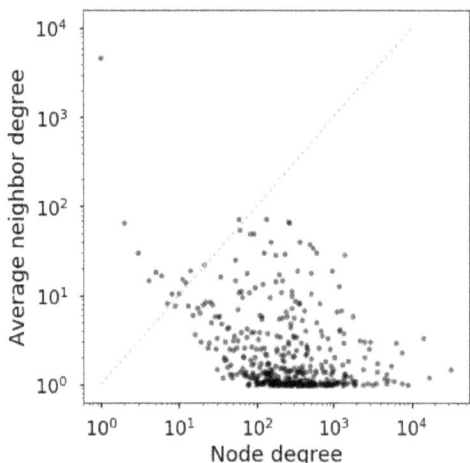

Figure 2: Nodes' degrees and average degrees of neighbours

Table 1: Remixing on a user level (u=193,254)

Remixing Variable	Mean	SD	50%	95%	Max
Users remixing activities	2.5	14.0	1	10	4,485
Users own designs being remixed	2.5	137.0	0	2	37,092
Number of designs per user	4.6	13.1	2	16	2,199

Table 2: Remixing on a design level (n=893,383)

Remixing Variable	Mean	SD	50%	95%	Max
A design has been reused	0.56	0.59	1	1	29
Number of designs being integrated	0.55	49.55	0	1	32,923

The reverse situation, called homophily and referring to a node's propensity to connect with similar nodes, is only given along the dotted line, on which the original nodes have as many connections as their neighbours. In social networks for examples, we see more homogeneous groupings which counteracts the diversity of the maker community [42].

As of November 2017, there were 499,750 connections between designs, showing a 'heavy-tailed' distribution of remixes, resembling a log-normal distribution (Figure 3).

The figure shows three probability density functions, with the continuous line indicating the degree distribution of the Thingiverse network, the dotted line shows a powerlaw distribution and the dashed line shows a log-normal distribution. The approximation to a powerlaw or log-normal distribution is in so far interesting, as it implies a number of assumptions as to how networks evolve, e.g. well connected nodes attract even more connections [6]. This way attractive designs turn into hubs, getting most of the attention of peers, who can decide to contribute to or further elaborate a design.

The power law fit of the degree distribution has been tested as described in [11] using the power law python package [3]. The practical implication of 'heavy-tailed' distributions can be circumscribed with the 'rich get richer model' of growing networks, i.e. nodes which already show a certain popularity are more likely to attract remixes than nodes which have only a few connections yet, a mechanism also called 'preferential attachment'[5] .

For a more in-depth analysis, each node of the Thingiverse network has a number of attributes including 'author', 'design category', 'views', 'likes', 'collected', 'downloads', 'license' and 'self-citation'. Most of these attributes are self-explanatory: 'author' refers to nicknames, not real names; 'collected' indicates the number of times a design has been included in another user's collection and 'self-citation' indicates the number of times a design was remixed by its own author.

For analysing the dataset, we use a mix of descriptive statistics and graph analytics (for indirect effects). The fitting of the distribution of node degrees is an example of the former and analysing the topology of remixing behaviours, e.g. chains of remixes, an example of the latter. Throughout the paper we make an effort to avoid potential misunderstandings by clearly stating the intent and scope of the underlying research question, how that intent matches the nature of the empirical evidence captured in the graph and what that means for the resulting network patterns or network parameters.

5 A NETWORK VIEW ON THINGIVERSE

The first parameter we were interested in, was the number of remixes happening and whether people whose designs got remixed a lot were also remixers themselves. As shown in Figure 4, there is a substantial difference between the users who remixed most (e.g. 'shivinteger' with 4,485 remixes) versus a user such as 'wstein' who engage in very little remixing but whose designs got remixed about 37,092 times.

Looking at the distribution of remixes on a design level (Table 2), we see a distinctive difference between the number of designs that

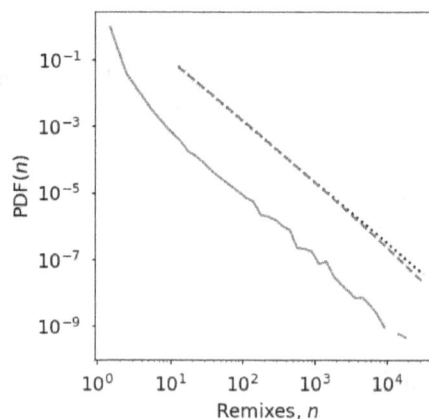

Figure 3: Probability density function of remixes and fitted log-normal distribution.

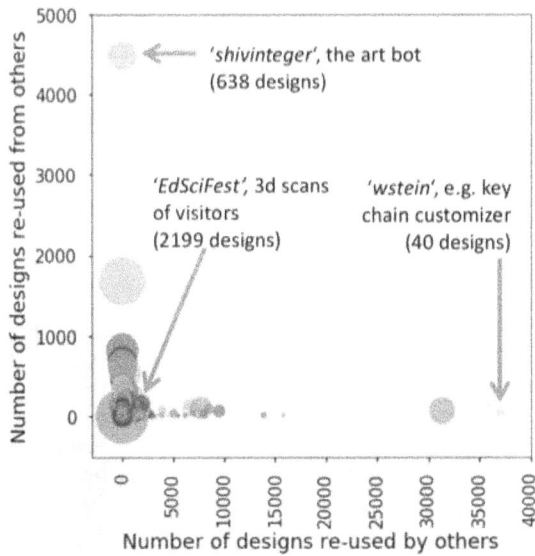

Figure 4: Remixing relationships between designs (n=893,529).

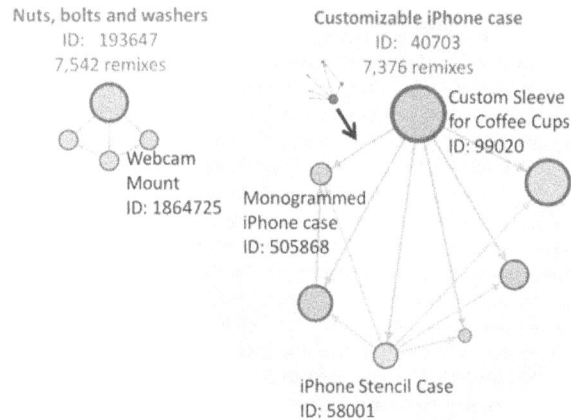

Figure 5: Remixes of two of the most remixed designs with more than one connections.

get remixed (29) and the remixes a design can attract (32,923). In fact, the design including 29 others is a typeface composed of objects from Thingiverse itself, so it is more like a collection of several designs. Whereas the second highest import of designs (26) results in an artistic Buddha figure integrating stylistic elements of movie characters, such as Yoda and Batman. Designs which could attract huge numbers of remixes are largely customizers for key chains (thing ID: 739573) or lithopanes (thing ID: 739573), which are photos transformed into a 3d print, which, if backlit reveal the image. For example, the second most frequently remixed design is a lithopane customizer provided by MakerBot, the company that owns and runs the Thingiverse platform. For this particular case, also the downside of a customizers becomes apparent, the customizer version of this design was repeatedly broken, causing docents of complaints in Thingiverse's discussion forums. The issues could be circumvented by using the off-line application of openSCAD, which is open source [29], but without the ease of remixing within an on-line application many users felt lost.

Both tables and Figure 4 fit findings, which state that there are two distinct groups on Thingiverse, one that almost never uses customizers and one that almost exclusively relies on customizers for remixing[17].

5.1 Customizers, Bots and self-referential designs

A second question we are interested in, was whether remixing is an indicator for a design's innovativeness. Referring back to section 3.2, where we distinguished between product and process innovation, we would classify remixes of highly popular customizers as process innovation.

Key benefit is the intuitive adaptation of an existing design in a prescribed way. Even though it would be possible to remix a remix

into a novel, improved product, this has rarely happened among the top 6 most remixed designs (representing 9.8% of the total Thingiverse network captured), Figure 5 shows two customizers and their remixed remixes, i.e. nodes with more than one connection. The size of the nodes emphasizes the number of connections and the colour indicates different design categories. The 'nuts and bolts' design has been uploaded under the design category 'parts' and was remixed in the '3d printer accessories' category. Just like the iPhone case has been also remixed in the 'kitchen & dinning' and the 'accessories' category. Behind the iPhone graph the amount of 7,376 nodes, to provide a visual impression of the proportions between the number of times the iPhone case was integrated into a novel design versus the number of times the design was replicated.

As stated in section 2, design ideas coming from outside the Thingiverse ecosystem could enriched the design of an iPhone case as well, but these ideational imports are rarely explicitly documented. Another source of 'noise' within the network's remixing topology are bots. Although not yet as endemic as in the Twitter community, where the followership of prominent figures consists to 20-30% of social bots[13]. In today's highly interconnected world, Bots tampering with the social web can influence public debate by manipulating the perception of reality among users unaware of how much social media are infiltrated by bots [16].

Thingiverse's most prominent bot is 'shivinteger', with 4,485 remixes (some 0.9% of all network connections), leading the list of the most prolific remixers. Unlike some of his Twitter counterparts, shivinteger's purpose is not to manipulate the 3d printing community, but to produce media art. Randomly selected designs are cobbled together, generating bizarre mash-ups which are then uploaded again. The bot's creations have since been presented at art events and generated a discussion about whether bots can create art or whether their art is in fact spam, as it interferes with search results[26].

A third phenomenon we discovered were 'self-citations', i.e. if the authors of the remix and the remixed designs were the same users, then this was counted as self-citation. This could often be seen if users iterated over their own designs, reacting to user comments,

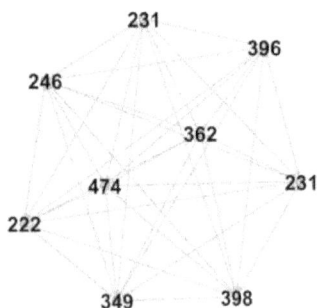

Figure 6: The complete graph of a nine pieces marble race track (Thing ID: 61049 by user 'cassandra').

Table 3: Views, downloads, likes and collections (n=893,383)

Thing Variable	Mean	SD	50%	95%	Max
Views	927	5,883	128	3,619	912,276
Downloads	255	1,542	52	915	342,708
Likes	18	145	1	62	18,248
Being collected	23	289	1	83	220,309
Being remixed	0.55	49.55	0	1	32,923

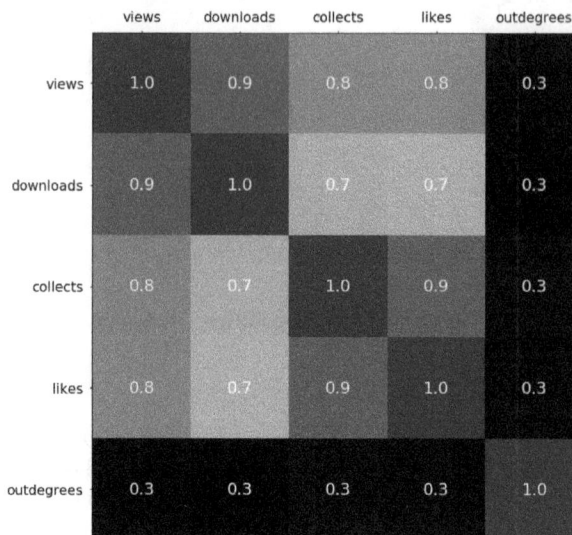

Figure 7: Spearman - Correlation matrix (n=873,875).

e.g. providing a model with higher resolution or functional changes. Self-citations were also used to indicate a collection of models that belong together, like a nine pieces marble race track (Thing ID: 61049 by user 'cassandra'). Figure 5 shows the complete graph of the track's nine building blocks, where each element references every other element (numbers indicate downloads).

All in all, self-citing was not a very widespread practice. Only 0.013% of all models (12,389) got remixed by their own authors. The two designs that had the highest number of self-citations (12) were a collection of polyhedral wireframes (ID: 282868) and a printed book of bas-reliefs from the Art Institute of Chicago (ID: 463657). The first example presented a collection of similar things, their author wanted to provide as a single download. Overall, we could see multiple cases where the remix was not primarily about changing or adding actual design elements, but it rather was about increasing the convenience of the reusing process, i.e. having related designs in one place or providing STL files when only SCAD files were available. From a novice user's perspective, SCAD is not as straight forward to print then STL, since it still needs to compile and generate the STL (accepted by most additive manufacturing tools) [19].

5.2 A fragmented view: Views, downloads, likes and collections

Part of our research objectives was to explore the interplay between different activities (viewing, downloading, liking, categorizing etc.) and their impact on remixing. By that we want to revisit the boundaries of our interpretations drawn from a network perspective. As stated earlier, networks are based on decisions about what to in- or exclude, and hence they present an incomplete view of the real world. For example, we use the explicit credits given on a design's Thingiverse page as a proxy for real world remixing behaviour.

Table 3, however, shows remixing in comparison to other platform activities. Where we can see that, like remixing, all variables are heavy-tailed.

Hence, given the lack of normal distribution, we used Spearman's correlation coefficient (Figure 6). Due to the extreme values (outliers) of some designs (cf. Figure 3), we discarded the first and last percentile (resulting in 19,508 designs discarded) before calculating the correlation coefficient. First, we can see high correlation coefficients between 'views' and 'downloads' as well as between

'likes' and 'collects'. But what is also apparent, is the very small correlation between out-degrees (i.e. out-degrees are remixes in network analytical terms) and all other variables. We suspect that an influential variable, i.e. a design being a customizer or not, is missing - as it was not available through the API. But as previous research has shown, customizers are much more likely to be remixed than other designs, regardless of their visibility ('views') and appeal ('likes') [17].

A similar discrepancy between views, downloads and remixes can be seen, if we look at the case of a specific design category in Thingiverse. To obtain a network of a reasonable size, that could also be visualized and interpreted qualitatively, we chose a subsection of the 'Chess' design category, with 242 designs (Figure 7). The color of nodes varies with the number of 'remixes' a design got, the darker a node the more 'remixes' it has (see Table 4 for some concrete values). The size of nodes is used to demonstrate a node's relative change in importance when (a) we look at a node's size indicating 'views' - right side of Figure 7 - and (b) when looking at size indicating 'downloads' on the left side of Figure 7.

Again, independently of 'remixes' indicted by colour, we see:

- Design b has relatively few 'views', but then it shows proportionally more 'downloads'. For design c, the reverse situation is shown. For both designs, however, the number of remixes is low (1 remix in total).

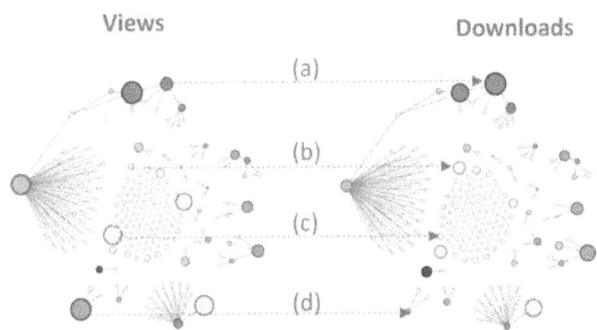

Figure 8: Views, downloads and remixes within a network of chess related designs (n = 242).

Table 4: Views, downloads, likes, collections and remixes for selected nodes

ID / Views	Downloads	Likes	Collections	Remixes
ID: 1732292				
62,199	8,804	2,717	2,665	55
ID: 224664				
22,663	3,193	505	558	21
(a) ID: 1482617				
66,882	15,584	2,320	2,212	6
(b) ID: 18070				
11,820	9,615	107	141	1
(c) ID: 578700				
58,053	3,432	237	221	0
(d) ID: 143991				
66,016	21,366	1,534	1,772	5

- Designs a and d, however, show the same proportional changes in downloads and views, showing relatively more remixes (11 remixes in total).

All 4 designs (a-c) represent sets of chess figures, based on either classic motives or designs inspired by Pokèmon or Minecraft.

Below an overview of each node's attributes as discussed in Figure 7. The red nodes, are 'customizers', and we can already see that they have two or four times as many remixes than non-customizers in the table.

Putting this discussion in perspective with previous studies, a similar average of 14.8 likes [1] was found previously, compared to 18 likes (Table 3). Also, [17] did not consider dynamic variables such as 'views' and 'downloads', but rather derived a regression model including variables such as 'customizer status', 'self-citations', 'days since publication' and 'number of tags'.

5.3 Innovation chains

Understanding not only the dyadic relationships between designs, but also pathways and chains of innovations (e.g. the topology of sub-networks) can benefit our understanding about category spanning innovations, iterative design processes and the integration of multiple ideas.

- Remixing ideas across design categories: This pattern is related to the non-disciplinary nature of user communities as described in Hippel's 'Democratizing innovation' [43]. The underlying rational is that users' innovation behaviour is not restricted by pondering about the commercialization potential of an innovation. Moreover, users, including companies, tend to represent a wide diversity of background knowledge they can bring to the innovation process if needed. Additionally, cross-category innovations tend to explore different contexts and can thereby overcome the limitations of contextually localized search, tapping into spatially confined knowledge [2, 15].
- Iterations over the same design: Iterations are typical for prototyping processes. The interaction with the actual prototype opens up the design space and directs users to possible areas for improvement. The actual experience of using a physical prototype or going through an actual prototypical service arrangement, goes often beyond the original product or service specification [12]. Schön [33], referring to the role of reflection in designing, explains how materials 'talk back to the designer' and that the materiality of a design is a critical in determining whether a design is accepted or not.
- Remixing of more than one original idea: Although we do not assume that remixes of 4 designs are necessarily more innovative than remixes of 2 designs, the nature of innovation (disruptive versus incremental) relates to the breadth and depth of remixing existing knowledge from diverse sources[15, 17]. Enkel and Gassmann discuss cases, where the ropes of mountain climbers help to innovate elevator cables or where 70% of a car engine are reused to design a less fuel demanding engine for small business air-crafts [15].

In Figure 8 we use the example of 'stereographic projection' to illustrate how a mathematically inspired design (1), can spur novel designs across multiple categories, including a projector (2) and a lamp (3). First, 'stereographic projection' is a process for mapping a spherical model to a straight-line grid on a plane, a 3d-model exemplifying this mechanism is the seed for the activities we see below.

At the center is node 202774 (green), whose author provides a collection of designs, visualizing mathematical concepts such as pattern formation, four-dimensional spaces or stereographic projection [34]. All red nodes (e.g. 2094215) are remixes of a mathematical principle, integrated with a projector design and a LED lamp, so that photos transformed into 3d surfaces could be projected against a wall. Whereas the centre node has a moderate amount of remixes (36), the project design has more than 200 remixes for one version alone. This is the effect of providing a customizable projector where each user can upload a photo and generate his or her personalized picture projector. Finally, the design of the picture projector is remixed with a skull (from the 'biology' design category).

6 CONCLUSION

The present analysis has shown the variety of remixing behaviours in a network as large as Thingiverse. Introducing varying degrees of innovativeness, we distinguished between feature-driven innovations and production-driven innovations, whereas customizers are

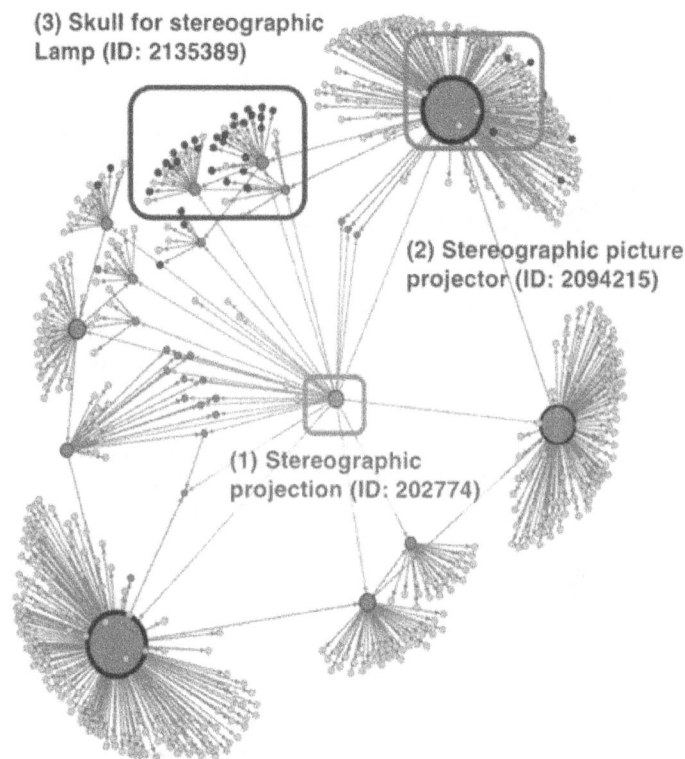

Figure 9: Innovation chains around stereographic projection

an example for the latter. Some of the dominant patterns, such as the huge number of remixes attracted by customizers are technologically induced, i.e. through the provision of a customizer app, which dramatically simplifies the remixing process. Other patterns, such as bots and self-referential designs are less frequent, buts still show the limits of interpreting re-combinations of designs as innovations in the sense of increasing the usefulness of a product or improving a tangible feature of a product.

However, for educational purposes, more complex chains of innovation as describe in the previous section support constructionist and experiential learning more directly, through the need to reiterate, adapt and ensure that the physical product actually fulfils the promises of the conceptual design. In that sense, platform users generating more complex remixes learn to respond to the constraints imposed by the use of specific materials and tools. In the end, complex designs not only promote technical competencies but also personal traits such as self-efficacy (being confident in one's abilities) or creativity (being resourceful in the face of adverse circumstances)[23]. Hence, knowing how to identify topologically more complex chains of innovation will help to avoid the trivialization of 'making', also known as the 'keychain syndrome', which refers to the fact that keychains are among the most remixed designs [10]. Yet, going a step further, from the platform owner's perspective, introducing the customizer was a huge success, as it almost tripled the number of designs hosted. Whether or not, future Thingiverse features will allow for distinguishing between trivial and complex innovation chains remains to be seen.

ACKNOWLEDGMENTS

This research was supported by the eCraft2Learn project (H2020) funded under Grant Agreement No 731345.

REFERENCES

[1] Celena Alcock, Nathaniel Hudson, and Parmit K. Chilana. 2016. Barriers to Using, Customizing, and Printing 3D Designs on Thingiverse. In *Proceedings of the 19th International Conference on Supporting Group Work.* ACM, 195–199.
[2] Paul Almeida and Bruce Kogut. 1999. Localization of knowledge and the mobility of engineers in regional networks. *Management science* 45, 7 (1999), 905–917.
[3] Jeff Alstott, Ed Bullmore, and Dietmar Plenz. 2014. powerlaw: a Python package for analysis of heavy-tailed distributions. *PloS one* 9, 1 (2014), e85777.
[4] Chris Anderson. 2012. *Makers: the new industrial revolution.* Crown Business, NY.
[5] Albert-Laszlo Barabasi. 2002. *Linked: the new science of networks.* Perseus Pub, Cambridge, Mass.
[6] Albert-László Barabási. 2012. Network science: Luck or reason. *Nature* 489, 7417 (2012), 507.
[7] Mathieu Bastian, Sebastien Heymann, and Mathieu Jacomy. 2009. Gephi: an open source software for exploring and manipulating networks. *Icwsm* 8 (2009), 361–362.
[8] Yochai Benkler. 2006. *The wealth of networks: How social production transforms markets and freedom.* Yale University Press.
[9] Tim Berners-Lee, Wendy Hall, James Hendler, Nigel Shadbolt, and Daniel J. Weitzner. 2006. Creating a Science of the Web. *Science* 313, 5788 (2006), 769–771.
[10] Paulo Blikstein. 2013. Digital fabrication and 'making'in education: The democratization of invention. *FabLabs: Of machines, makers and inventors* 4 (2013), 1–21.
[11] Anna D. Broido and Aaron Clauset. 2018. Scale-free networks are rare. *arXiv preprint arXiv:1801.03400* (2018).
[12] Fritz Böhle, Markus Bürgermeister, and Stephanie Porschen. 2012. *Innovation management by promoting the informal: Artistic, experience-based, playful.* Springer Science & Business Media.

[13] John P. Dickerson, Vadim Kagan, and V. S. Subrahmanian. 2014. Using sentiment to detect bots on twitter: Are humans more opinionated than bots?. In *Advances in Social Networks Analysis and Mining (ASONAM), 2014 IEEE/ACM International Conference on.* IEEE, 620–627.

[14] Economist. 2011. *Technology: Print me a Stradivarius.* Technical Report. http://www.economist.com/node/18114327

[15] Ellen Enkel and Oliver Gassmann. 2010. Creative imitation: exploring the case of cross-industry innovation. *R&d Management* 40, 3 (2010), 256–270.

[16] Emilio Ferrara, Onur Varol, Clayton Davis, Filippo Menczer, and Alessandro Flammini. 2016. The rise of social bots. *Commun. ACM* 59, 7 (2016), 96–104.

[17] Christoph M. Flath, Sascha Friesike, Marco Wirth, and Frederic Thiesse. 2017. Copy, transform, combine: Exploring the remix as a form of innovation. *Journal of Information Technology* 32, 4 (2017), 306–325.

[18] Rosanna Garcia and Roger Calantone. 2002. A critical look at technological innovation typology and innovativeness terminology: a literature review. *Journal of product innovation management* 19, 2 (2002), 110–132.

[19] Ian Gibson, David Rosen, and Brent Stucker. 2014. *Additive manufacturing technologies: 3D printing, rapid prototyping, and direct digital manufacturing.* Springer.

[20] Wendy Hall, Jim Hendler, and Steffen Staab. 2017. A Manifesto for Web Science@ 10. *CoRR* abs/1702.08291 (2017).

[21] Benjamin Mako Hill and Andrés Monroy-Hernández. 2013. The cost of collaboration for code and art: evidence from a remixing community. In *Proceedings of the 2013 conference on Computer supported cooperative work.* ACM, 1035–1046.

[22] MakerBot Industries. 2018. Thingiverse REST API Reference. (Jan. 2018). https://www.thingiverse.com/developers/rest-api-reference

[23] Eva-Sophie Katterfeldt, Nadine Dittert, and Heidi Schelhowe. 2015. Designing digital fabrication learning environments for Bildung: Implications from ten years of physical computing workshops. *International Journal of Child-Computer Interaction* 5 (2015), 3–10.

[24] Harris Kyriakou, Jeffrey V. Nickerson, and Gaurav Sabnis. 2017. Knowledge Reuse for Customization: Metamodels in an Open Design Community for 3d Printing. *MIS Quarterly* 41, 1 (2017), 315–332.

[25] Andrés Monroy-Hernández, Benjamin Mako Hill, and Jazmin Gonzalez-Rivero. 2011. Computers can't give credit: How automatic attribution falls short in an online remixing community. In *Proceedings of the SIGCHI Conference on Human Factors in Computing Systems.* ACM, 3421–3430.

[26] Annalee Newitz. 2018. That time a bot invaded Thingiverse and created weird new 3D objects. (2018). https://arstechnica.com/gadgets/2016/05/that-time-a-bot-invaded-thingiverse-and-created-weird-new-3d-objects/

[27] Jeffrey V. Nickerson. 2015. Collective design: remixing and visibility. In *Design Computing and Cognition'14.* Springer, 263–276.

[28] Lora Oehlberg, Wesley Willett, and Wendy E. Mackay. 2015. Patterns of physical design remixing in online maker communities. In *Proceedings of the 33rd Annual ACM Conference on Human Factors in Computing Systems.* ACM, 639–648.

[29] OpenSCAD. 2018. *OpenSCAD The Programmers Solid 3D CAD Modeller.* Technical Report. http://www.openscad.org/

[30] Spiros Papadimitriou, Evangelos Papalexakis, Bin Liu, and Hui Xiong. 2015. Remix in 3D Printing: What your Sources say About You. In *Proceedings of the 24th International Conference on World Wide Web.* ACM, 367–368.

[31] Thierry Rayna, Ludmila Striukova, and John Darlington. 2014. Open innovation, co-creation and mass customisation: what role for 3D printing platforms?. In *Proceedings of the 7th World Conference on Mass Customization, Personalization, and Co-Creation (MCPC 2014), Aalborg, Denmark, February 4th-7th, 2014.* Springer, 425–435.

[32] Jeremy Rifkin. 2014. *The zero marginal cost society: The internet of things, the collaborative commons, and the eclipse of capitalism.* Macmillan.

[33] Donald A. Schön. 1995. *The reflective practitioner : how professionals think in action.* Arena, Aldershot, England.

[34] Henry Segerman. 2016. *Visualizing Mathematics with 3D Printing.* JHU Press.

[35] John T. Sherrill. 2017. Gender, technology, and narratives in DIY instructions. In *Proceedings of the 35th ACM International Conference on the Design of Communication.* ACM, 9.

[36] Aron S. Spencer and Bruce A. Kirchhoff. 2006. Schumpeter and new technology based firms: Towards a framework for how NTBFs cause creative destruction. *International Entrepreneurship and Management Journal* 2, 2 (2006), 145–156.

[37] Thingiverse. 2018. Thingiverse.com. (2018). https://www.thingiverse.com/about/

[38] Elisabeth Unterfrauner and Christian Voigt. 2017. Makers' ambitions to do socially valuable things. Rome, Italy.

[39] Elisabeth Unterfrauner, Christian Voigt, Maria Schrammel, and Massimo Menichinelli. 2017. The Maker Movement and the Disruption of the Producer-Consumer Relation. In *Internet Science Workshops.* Thessaloniki, GR.

[40] Derek Van Ittersum. 2014. Craft and narrative in DIY instructions. *Technical Communication Quarterly* 23, 3 (2014), 227–246.

[41] Christian Voigt, Calkin Suero Montero, and Massimo Menichinelli. 2016. An empirically informed taxonomy for the Maker Movement. In *International Conference on Internet Science.* Springer, Florence. IT, 189–204.

[42] Christian Voigt, Elisabeth Unterfrauner, and Roland Stelzer. 2017. Diversity in FabLabs: Culture, Role Models and the Gendering of Making. In *International Conference on Internet Science.* Springer, Thessaloniki, GR.

[43] Eric Von Hippel. 2005. Democratizing innovation: The evolving phenomenon of user innovation. *Journal für Betriebswirtschaft* 55, 1 (2005), 63–78.

And Now for Something Completely Different: Visual Novelty in an Online Network of Designers

Johannes Wachs
Central European University
Budapest, Hungary
wachs_johannes@phd.ceu.edu

Bálint Daróczy
Institute for Computer Science and
Control, Hungarian Academy of
Sciences (MTA SZTAKI)
Budapest, Hungary
daroczyb@ilab.sztaki.hu

Anikó Hannák
Central European University
Budapest, Hungary
hannaka@ceu.edu

Katinka Páll
Institute for Computer Science and
Control, Hungarian Academy of
Sciences (MTA SZTAKI)
Budapest, Hungary
pall.katinka@sztaki.mta.hu

Christoph Riedl
Northeastern University
Boston, MA
Harvard University
Cambridge, MA
c.riedl@neu.edu

ABSTRACT

Novelty is a key ingredient of innovation but quantifying it is difficult. This is especially true for visual work like graphic design. Using designs shared on an online social network of professional digital designers, we measure visual novelty using statistical learning methods to compare an image's features with those of images that have been created before. We then relate social network position to the novelty of the designer's images. We find that on this professional platform, users with dense local networks tend to produce more novel but generally less successful images, with important exceptions. Namely, users making novel images while embedded in cohesive local networks are more successful.

KEYWORDS

Novelty; image analysis; neural networks; Fisher information; social networks

ACM Reference Format:
Johannes Wachs, Bálint Daróczy, Anikó Hannák, Katinka Páll, and Christoph Riedl. 2018. And Now for Something Completely Different: Visual Novelty in an Online Network of Designers. In *WebSci '18: 10th ACM Conference on Web Science, May 27–30, 2018, Amsterdam, Netherlands*. ACM, New York, NY, USA, 10 pages. https://doi.org/10.1145/3201064.3201088

1 INTRODUCTION

High-quality creative design work can create tremendous value for organizations. It helps technical products gain acceptance [26] and it often serves as the basis for competition in cultural markets [59].

Consequently, there has been mounting interest in the use of designers by organizations as a source of value creation [43, 46, 47]. One important ingredient to successful designs is novelty: the degree to which a design is new, original, or unusual relative to what has come before. One reason for this is that derivative work is frowned up in creative fields [6]. Indeed novelty is the prime ingredient of innovation and the production of new things [19]. Economists have long known that innovation is the driving influence behind economic growth and development [50], and recent studies suggest that successful companies make 80% of their revenue with products younger than five years [34].

Despite its importance novelty is difficult to measure, especially in the context of creative design. In this paper we investigate three research questions related to novelty in design: (1) how can we measure novelty in digital design? (2) who produces novel work? and (3) what is the relationship between novelty and success? We develop and compare different mathematically-grounded measures of novelty or distinctiveness of digital images to better understand its antecedents and subsequent effect on success in a community of professional designers.

To investigate these questions we collect roughly 40,000 images posted by over four thousand professional designers on an online community over a period of about four years. We propose and evaluate a measure of novelty for digital design at the image level using two feature sets: one capturing content and structure defined using an Inception neural network, the other capturing visual aesthetics using classical compositional features. We visualize the distributions of images in low dimensional projections of these feature spaces to better understand what these features capture and how they may capture novelty of an image.

We calculate novelty by comparing an image with prior images in terms of these derived features using information theoretic methods. This focus on temporal order distinguishes novelty from more "timeless" notions like beauty or appeal [18]. Calculating novelty using the compositional features yields a measure of aesthetic or style novelty based on colors, spatial arrangement, and symmetry, while using Inception features results in a measure of content novelty. We validate our measures by showing that the earliest images annotated with emerging labels or "tags" for new kinds of designs are indeed more content-novel.

With these measures of novelty for digital design in hand, we ask two questions: who produces novel images? How does novelty relate to success? The social networks literature makes two suggestions. Individuals with open, diverse social networks have access to diverse sources of information, which they may synthesize in novel ways [10, 24]. But individuals in cohesive, closed networks have greater access to trust and social support, allowing them to more easily take the risk inherent in the creation of novelties [12, 35]. The literature suggests that when the domain is quickly changing and when the space of possible novelties is large, it is rather cohesive networks that facilitate novelty [3]. We argue that our topic of study is such a domain: design evolves quickly and new trends can be drastically different, and so we hypothesize that cohesive local networks do more to facilitate novelty in this domain than diverse ones.

Using a regression framework to analyze our panel data, we find a positive relationship between the local cohesion of a user's network on the site and the novelty of her images. Users in the global center of the network make less novel images. We suggest one possible explanation: that standing out is a form of risk-taking and that local network density facilitates this behavior. Furthermore, we find that novel images are on average less successful, but can be successful when originating from the right network position. Finally, we demonstrate that our novelty measures add explanatory power to a machine learning model predicting success, above and beyond a user's network position. This suggests that network position does not entirely mediate the relationship between novelty and success.

Our paper makes three contributions to the literature. First, we qualitatively compare the data encoded in different feature sets that can be derived from images. Second, we define a statistically-sound measure of the novelty of images, applicable to either set of features. Third, we provide empirical evidence for relationships between novelty, network position, and success, showing that novelty and network position together can predict success.

2 RELATED WORK

In this section we first survey research on the quantification of novelty. Next, we overview literature on the relationship between novelty, social network position, and success, and finally, introduce studies that have looked at design in an online setting.

2.1 Quantifying Novelty

As novelty is a complex construct with various dimensions, many different measures of it have been proposed [9, 21, 44]. One key notion underlying the measurement of novelty is the concept of recombination: that novelty is the result of reconfiguration of old ideas [58]. Novelty is distinguished from aesthetic quality or beauty because it carries an intrinsic temporal property. For example, it is difficult to judge in retrospect how novel a product was at the time of its release. Previous studies on the beauty of images utilize the

fact that crowdsourced judgments of beauty are relatively stable over time [49].

Recent models of novelty frame it in terms of the "actual" and the "possible". Models consider what it means for something to be new in terms of a path of discovery in an evolving complex space [37]. When something new is done for the first time, the space of the "adjacent possible" grows, making new things possible. In this framework, novelties are discrete, binary events.

Previous work from the data mining community on novelty of images has mostly been concerned with the detection of outliers or anomalies within images, rather than across images [8, 52]. Most applications concern the detection of verifiable facts about an image: the presence of specific objects in satellite images, detecting biological abnormalities like cancer, etc. One commonality across these efforts, and indeed our own, is that features need to be extracted from an image to make computational analysis tractable.

Several recent data-driven studies quantify novelty in creative fields. In a study of popular music, Askin and Mauskapf compare songs with their predecessors using cosine similarity of a set of derived features like danceability and tempo [4]. Past work has quantified the creativity of visual art as a combination of both novelty and influence using visual features [18]. Redi et al. quantify the novelty of short video clips using a similar approach to ours [44], while Khosla et al. use image features to predict engagement on social media [32]. Natural language processing has also been applied to measure the novelty of textual content including scientific article abstracts [9, 20] and equity crowdfunding campaigns [29]. We do not define novelty of a thing in terms of success [51] or surprise [5]. Novelty of a thing as we consider it says nothing intrinsically about its impact, influence, or outcomes. At the same time, we acknowledge that any attempt to measure novelty or distinctiveness can only capture a small facet of the phenomenon.

2.2 Network Position, Novelty, Success

Psychological research emphasizes that creativity is a demanding enterprise, requiring focus and concentration [13]. Given the apparent difficulty of creative endeavors, it is perhaps no surprise that social network structure plays a significant role in both facilitating novelty and shaping its reception. In fact, recent studies of creativity emphasize that novel products, even nominally created by a single author, can sometimes be understood as "products of a momentary collective process" [27]. How the networks that synthesize creative products fit together have strong predictive power of their eventual success [16].

So what kind of network position facilitates novelty? Creators embedded in a cohesive social network can hope to benefit from high amounts of social capital and support [12]. Strong ties represent avenues of trust, which greatly facilitates the kind of risk-taking inherent in making a novel product in a professional, creative environment [35]. One study indicates that central actors in a network of research scientists produce more creative outputs, indicating that established actors can feel the freedom to experiment more broadly [42].

It is also true that diversity of social connections has been shown to foster creativity. Weak ties in social networks tend to bridge groups and provide an actor with access to novel information [24].

Indeed the same study of research scientists cited above shows that creativity increases with the number of weak ties [42]. This line of thought is built on the idea that bridging actors occupying "structural holes" can create their own social capital by leveraging their unique access to diverse information [10]. Whether open or closed networks better support novelty creation in our context is therefore an empirical question.

Besides the relationship of network position and novelty, the perception of novelty is also of interest to the research community. What ratio of traditional and novel maximizes success? Work across many disciplines find an inverse-U shaped relationship between novelty and success [4, 9]. One prolific strand of the literature models novelty as the recombination of known ideas in new ways, and that the key to successful novelty is the combination of many conventional ingredients with relatively few new ones [56].

2.3 Online Design Communities

Closest to our work empirically are studies on online design communities, like Dribbble, Behance, or Threadless. These studies generally focus on the question of how users or products become successful, and how different groups of users fare [17, 45]. For instance several studies find significant differences in the behavior and success of men and women on these sites [33, 57].

Dribbble has received attention from researchers because of its importance to the professional design community and its exclusive, invitation-only nature. In an interview-based study researchers found that users leverage the site and its social network to gather inspiration, learn skills by reverse engineering examples, anticipate trends in the marketplace, and to gather feedback [40]. The study also found that users invested significant effort in developing a professional identity through the site. As in many other online communities, users reported the status importance of having many followers and collecting likes.

More recently, machine vision researchers have taken an interest in learning from image data taken from online design communities, as they offer substantively different opportunities to develop machine vision than, say, photographs [60]. Similarly, the dual functions of online digital communities as places to post and places to be inspired offer interesting opportunities for bespoke recommendation systems [48].

3 DATA

In this section we describe the Dribbble platform, our data collection method, and outline the extracted features at the image, user, and network levels.

3.1 Dribbble

Dribbble, founded in 2009, is an online community where designers share their work by posting images. It is a highly-visited site, with an Alexa rank of 1104, the second most popular website for design sharing after Behance. Unlike most content-sharing platforms, the site operates on an invitation-only basis: though the site can be viewed by anyone, only invited users can post images. Active users are occasionally given invitations which they can use to invite other designers. Moreover, the number of images a user can post in a given time frame is capped. All together, this leads to high-quality

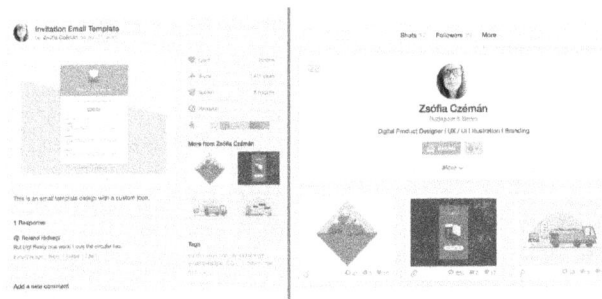

Figure 1: Shot (Image) and User Pages on Dribbble.

content and the feeling of belonging to an "elite" community among users.

The stakes on Dribbble are high. Interviews with users on the site reveal that individuals use the site to develop their professional identities [40]. Indeed most users use their real names, post photographs of themselves for their account image, and link to their accounts on other online platforms including Linkedin and Twitter. Users build their portfolio of designs over many years. They accumulate reputation by gathering views and likes (engagement) on their images, called shots on the site, and followers on their account. The social network aspect of the site facilitates continued interactions as users see more and more of each others' work. Success on Dribbble has impact outside the site itself, as it can bring significant employment opportunities and influence. The platform has recently added a job board and special recruiter accounts.

3.2 Data Collection

Our data sample consists of all Dribbble users who were members of a team at the time of the data collection. Typically companies form teams on Dribbble as paid umbrella accounts that users can join. We select this sample in order to gather a comparable set of users who are both active and committed members of the site. We then crawled the profiles of 6,215 users identified as team members. Next, we crawled all 60,406 images made by these users. In subsequent analysis, we discard users making fewer than five images[1]. We also discard images posted by the team account with identifiable individual author. We share examples of an image and a user page in Figure 1. Data collection took place between September and November 2016 and observed listed rate-limits on the Dribbble API.

3.3 Extracted User features

At the shot level we first record the image itself, the date it was made, and the identity of the author. We also note the tags the author annotated the shot with. Tags are free-form key words that say something about the image. Others can search for images listing specific tags. Tags therefore serve a dual purpose: to describe what the author is doing, and to help others find the image. Each shot has a count of the likes that it received, which can be thought of as the main success measure in the community.

At the user level we collect the name of the author, whether the author has a "pro-badge", and the author's tenure on the platform

---

[1]Our results are robust to including these users.

(in days). A pro-badge is a sign that the user has paid for a premium account, which facilitates job search features on the site and lifts the cap on the number of shots a user can make in a given amount of time. We consider pro-badges as a proxy for buy-in on the platform. At the shot level we calculate how many shots a user has made before to quantify their experience. Finally, we also estimate the gender of each user. Since the profiles do not directly list gender, we infer them from the users' first names using the US baby name data set [1]. For any user with a name not in the database or an ambiguous gender score (i.e. greater than 10% and less than 90%) we manually check their self-portrait on Dribbble and on linked social media accounts.

3.4 Network Features

Like many other online communities, Dribbble is built on top of a social network. When a user follows another user, the second user's future shots are included in the default newsfeed of the first user and so following a user has bandwidth costs. We collect a list of all following relationships amongst our users and when they were created. These timestamped edges allow us to recreate the social network of our users at the time when an image was submitted . For each image we calculate several network measures quantifying the position of the user at the time of creation.

- *In-degree:* How many followers the user has.
- *Out-degree:* How many other users the user follows.
- *Closeness centrality:* One over the average distance of the user from all other nodes [7]. This measures how close the user is to the center of network.
- *Constraint:* Burt's measure of the extent to which a user's outgoing connections are redundant [10].
- *Density:* The ratio of observed ties to possible ties among the users the user follows.

In- and out-degree quantify the simple connectivity of a user. Closeness centrality is a global network measure which increases as the user is closer to the center of the network. Constraint and density of the user measure the cohesiveness of his local social network.

4 EXTRACTING IMAGE FEATURES

In this section we describe two sets of images features upon which we calculate an image's novelty. First we calculate *compositional features*. Then we use a neural network framework to extract a set of unsupervised features. We compare the two feature spaces by projecting them to a low-dimensional space in which similar images are placed closer to one another. We examine what kind of images are similar according to the two feature sets, finding that the compositional features capture color and style while the neural network features capture content.

4.1 Compositional Features

Imitating precisely previous work on the qualitative features of images [49], we define 47 compositional features for each image. These features are derived from aesthetic considerations and have proven to have significant predictive power of the beauty or attractiveness of images. Previous work groups the features into the following categories: colors, spatial arrangements, and texture.

Color features include contrast (defined in terms of luminance) and the averages of hue, saturation, and brightness across both the whole image and a subset in its center [15]. We also include three "emotional" features which are linear combinations of saturation and brightness: pleasure, arousal, and dominance [39]. Binning hue, saturation, and brightness yield *Itten Color Histograms* and taking their standard deviations yields *Itten Color Contrasts* after a careful segmentation. Spatial features include symmetry and salience [30], the distribution of which describes how attention-grabbing different regions of the image are. Finally, Haralick's texture features quantify image complexity: entropy, energy, homogeneity, and contrast [25].

4.2 Neural Network Features

Feedforward-based neural networks have made tremendous strides in object-in-image classification tasks in recent years. Many such networks have penultimate layers which reduce images input for classification into a feature space for the classification layer. It is possible to extract these features from pre-trained neural networks. We harness one such network: the Inception v3 [54], originally constructed to optimally classify a large dataset of images into 1000 categories. We acknowledge here that there are many alternative specifications to generate similar sets of features. Passing our images through the network we generate 2048 features that encode highly discriminating facets of the data.

4.3 Visualizing Image Features

Before proceeding, we pause to visualize and inspect our data in the two visual feature spaces. We reduce the 47 and 2048 dimensional spaces to two-dimensions using t-SNE, a popular dimensionality reduction method that uses information theoretic methods to minimize distances between data points in the projection as a function of their similarity [38]. In Figure 2, we visualize the 2-D t-SNE projections of a random sample of 200 images a year from 2012 to 2016 using the Inception and compositional features, respectively.

In both projections we observe the clustering of images into groups. The qualitative attributes that define the clustering, however, are quite different. As highlighted in Figure 2, clustering on compositional features is based on color and aesthetic style, as expected. In the projection based on Inception features, however, we observe that images cluster based on their content. In other words, images with highly similar Inception features are likely to represent similar concepts, be they logos, mobile phone interfaces, icons, wireframes, etc. This is perhaps not surprising given Inception's origin as an object-in-image classification tool. This characterization of the two features sets as describing style and content is important for understanding their novelty.

5 NOVELTY MEASURES

In this section we define a reference novelty based on user annotations or tags of an image by defining the relative surprise of seeing a set of tags on image, compared with the tags that came before. We then define a measure of novelty for our visual feature spaces using Gaussian mixtures and Fisher information.

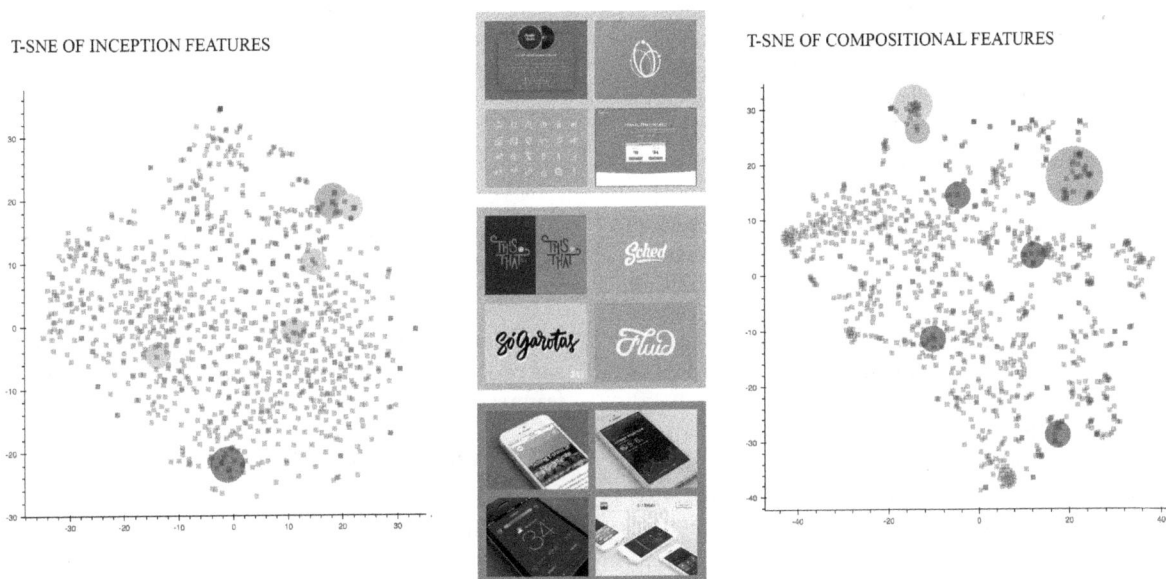

Figure 2: Visualizing sample images using t-SNE dimensionality reduction of Inception and compositional features. We highlight three example groups of images. Images from the gold group are close together in the compositional feature space but spread out in the Inception feature space. The teal group is close in both feature spaces, with one exception in the compositional space. Images from the purple group are close in Inception space but scattered in compositional space. The gold group consists of a logo, a collection of icons, a web page design, and an email flier: they are likely clustered in compositional space because of their color. The members of the purple group are all mobile phone screens. Members of the teal group are likely clustered in both spaces because they share both structural and compositional qualities.

5.1 Tag Novelty

Before calculating novelty using visual features, we create a novelty measure using the tags an author gives an image. Following [53], we calculate the "surprise" of each tag of an image. That is, given all the images and their tags posted before the image, we define the probability of observing a tag t as $P(t)$, the proportion of previous images listing that tag. The log of $P(t)$ is our measure of the surprise of a tag. As we are especially interested in completely new tags, we also include the focal image and its tag when we calculate $P(t)$, to avoid taking the log of 0. We then define tag novelty N_i of an image i with tags $t_1, t_2, \ldots t_n \in T_i$ as the aggregate the surprise of an image's tags:

$$N_i = -\frac{1}{|T_i|} \sum_{t \in T_i} \log P(t)$$

In order to make our measure robust to the order of the images, we scale each image's tag novelty by the maximum possible novelty. Namely, if I is the number of images made before image i, we normalize the equation above by $-\log(|I|)$.

5.2 Visual Novelty via Fisher Information

To study the visual novelty of images, we define a parametric model for images in terms of their position in a given feature space. Given a new image, we consider the distribution of previous images in a feature space and approximate them using Gaussian mixture models. We calculate the likelihood of the focal image relative to these

distributions using its Fisher information, an information theoretic measure which we prefer to alternatives such as the Akaike information criterion because of its reparametrization-invariance. Specifically we define novelty as one minus the norm of the Fisher vector of an image over the Gaussian mixture models. This approach is similar in style to a recent method to calculate novelty using a data point's distance to the centroids of a k-means clustering [44].

Formally, let be $x \in \mathbb{R}^d$ a finite d-dimensional real representation of an image and a parametric model $p(x|\theta)$ where θ is the parameter of the density function. If the model is a Gaussian mixture model (GMM) with N Gaussians, the pdf is $p(x|\theta) = \sum_i^N \omega_i g_i(x)$ where the $g_i(x)$ is the density function of the i-th Gaussian. The continuously evolving model changes the parameters of the probabilistic model with the emergence of new images in time. We consider two different likelihood measures to apply to the probabilistic model:

- Akaike's information criterion (AIC) [2]: we measure the AIC per image according the actual state of our generative model.
- Fisher information: after calculating the Fisher score [31] of for each image according to the shape of the model we can measure the similarity of images x and y with the Fisher kernel, as

$$K_\theta(x, y) = \nabla_\theta \log p(x|\theta)^T F_\theta^{-1} \nabla_\theta \log p(y|\theta) \quad (1)$$

where F_θ is the Fisher information matrix. The gradient of the likelihood indicates how the model may change to fit the actual point, in our case an image. Our choice was driven by the unique invariance properties (e.g. reparametrization invariance) of the Fisher information matrix and the Fisher kernel [11, 36, 55]. Applying Cholesky decomposition, the kernel can be defined as a simple scalar product, as $K_\theta(x, y) = \mathcal{G}_\theta(x)^T \mathcal{G}_\theta(y)$ where $\mathcal{G}_\theta(x) = \nabla_\theta \log p(x|\theta) F_\theta^{-1/2}$ is the normalized Fisher score or the Fisher vector of image x. We note that the Fisher vector has dimension $O(d|\theta|)$.

On account of its reparametrization invariance we choose to continue with the Fisher information as our measure of likelihood. Although estimation of the Fisher information matrix is difficult, there are known closed form approximations for both Gaussian mixture models [41] and special classes of Markov random fields [14]. We suggest two potential definitions of novelty measures based on the Fisher information:

- Norm of the Fisher Vector over Gaussian Mixture (FVGMM): as the Fisher score highlights how the model parameters should change to best fit the focal image, our first novelty measures the norm of the Fisher vector for each image as

$$N_{FV}(x) = ||\mathcal{G}_\theta(x)|| = ||\nabla_\theta \log p(x|\theta) F_\theta^{-1/2}||. \quad (2)$$

In case of Gaussian Mixtures the pdf is $p(x|\theta) = \sum_i^N \omega_i g_i(x)$ where θ consists of the mixture weights, mean, and covariance parameters of the Gaussian mixture. In practice we observe that the Fisher score for both compositional and Inception features is very sparse because of the "peakness" property of the *membership probability*, defined as the probability that a point is generated from one of the Gaussians. In comparison with [4] this method puts the most weight on the most similar images that came before the focal image.

- Similarity graph over the Gaussian Mixture (FVMRF): one approach to overcoming the "peakness" property while still capturing the temporal distribution is to define a Markov random field following [14] with the mean of the Gaussian mixture as the sample set. The main idea is to define an undirected random field, which is a graph with N nodes consisting of random variables and sample points, connected to our image as a separate random variable in a star. The probability density function of the new distribution can be factorized over the maximal cliques in the resulting graph. In our case the edges and therefore the pdf are:

$$p(x|\alpha, \theta) = \frac{e^{-\sum_i \alpha_i ||x-\mu_i||}}{\int_{x \in \mathcal{X}} e^{-\sum_i \alpha_i ||x-\mu_i||} dx} \quad (3)$$

where μ_i is the mean vector of the i-th Gaussian, α is the relative importance of the cliques. The Fisher vector can be approximated in this context with a simple formula [14]:

$$N_{FVMRF}(x) = \{\frac{d_i(x) - \mathbf{E}[d_i(x)]}{Var^{-\frac{1}{2}}(d_i(x))}\}$$

where $d_i(x) = ||x - \mu_i||$ and $i \in 1, ..., N$.

Given the relatively high complexity of the random field approach, we define novelty using the norm of the Fisher vector[2]. As the method returns a similarity score, we subtract one to define visual novelty. For the rest of the paper we refer to this novelty score

[2]In applications where the aforementioned peakness issue is more pronounced, we recommend using the random field approach

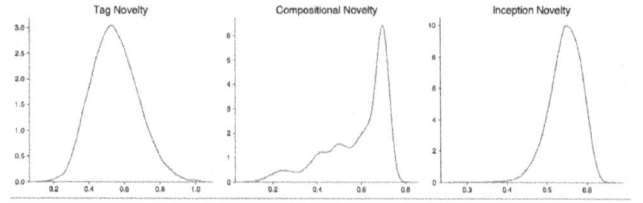

Figure 3: Kernel density estimated distributions of tag, compositional, and Inception novelty.

as *Inception novelty* when it is calculated using Inception features, and *compositional novelty* when it is calculated using compositional features.

5.3 Comparison of Novelty Scores and Validation

We visualize the distribution of tag, Inception, and compositional novelty scores in Figure 3. We correlate the two novelties with tag novelty and several user-level features in Table 1. We find that both visual novelties are weakly correlated with tag novelty. The correlation is roughly twice as strong for Inception novelty than compositional novelty. This suggests that tags are used to describe images in a conceptional rather than stylistic manner. The two visual novelties are significantly correlated, and, together with tag novelty, are negatively correlated with engagement. We note that the platform's design may explain the trade-off between engagement and tag novelty: users can search for images by tags.

5.3.1 Validation of Visual Novelty. As discussed, novelty is an ephemeral quality of a cultural product and its measurement implicitly requires comparison, more so than, for example, its beauty. We cannot, for instance, ask someone to evaluate the novelty of a four-year-old mobile phone application layout. In this case success and perceptions of novelty are likely anti-correlated: success breeds familiarity.

One approach to validate our measures of visual novelty, besides the correlations with tag novelty noted above, is to identify a population of images which are likely to be covering a new kind of product that emerges in the middle of our dataset. We identify emerging product types by finding tags which are used only after 2013, yet still are among the 200 most used tags. We find two such tags[3] which we can verify as representing truly emerging novelties: "material" and "principle".

[3]Other examples of tag fitting our quantitative criteria are tags used by groups of designers to indicate group membership. Though these tags certainly merit further study, they do not capture the emergence of a new design approach or method

	(1)	(2)	(3)	(4)
Tag Novelty (1)				
Inception Novelty (2)	0.123			
Compositional Novelty (3)	0.067	0.274		
Likes (Log) (4)	-0.138	-0.082	-0.014	
Views (Log) (5)	-0.138	-0.114	-0.058	0.927

Table 1: Correlation matrix of novelty and success features.

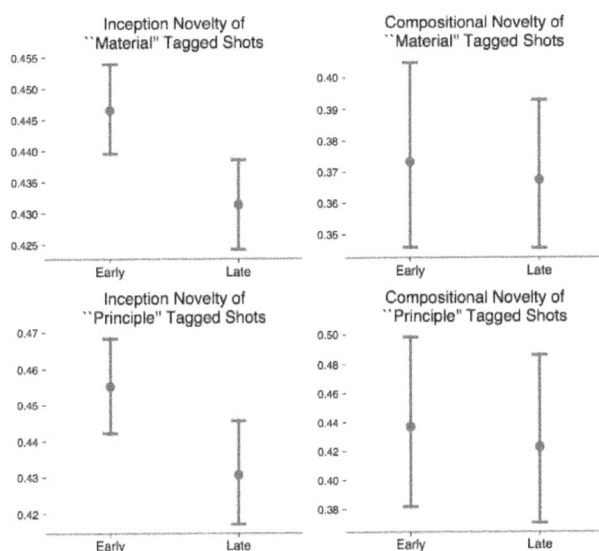

Figure 4: Comparison of visual novelty scores of images with the tags "material" and "principle". We consider those images in the first 10% and most recent 10% of all images created using the tags. We find that Inception novelty is significantly higher for images listing these "emerging" tags.

Material design[4] is a design language or vocabulary created by Google, announced to the public in June 2014. Like other design languages, it has guidelines and principles that shape the design process, resulting in a consistent look with certain qualities. Material design was created especially for use in digital and technological areas. It emphasizes the use of print design best practices together with motion. Material or "material design" appears as a tag in 748 images in our dataset.

Principle[5] is a new software design tool for creating interactive and dynamic user interfaces. Released in August 2015, it is a popular tool for designers to prototype UIs. 243 images in our dataset include a "principle" tag.

For both tags we compare the distributions of novelty for the first 10% of images using the tag, with the most recent 10% of images using the tag. In figure 4 we plot the resulting distributions. We find that Inception novelty is significantly higher for the earliest images tagged with "material" (Mann-Whitney U = 1897, p<.01) and "princple" (Mann-Whitney U = 190, p<.01) compared with the most recent ones. Though the average compositional novelty is higher for the earliest images in both cases, the differences are not statistically significant (resp. U = 2465, p .26; U = 288, p .32).

6 NOVELTY, NETWORKS, AND SUCCESS

In this section we investigate which users are more likely to create novel images and whether novel images are more or less likely to be successful. We consider both Inception and compositional novelty.

----
[4]https://material.io/
[5]http://principleformac.com/

First we use hierarchical linear regression [23] on data at the image level with user random-effectsand controls to predict novelty. Our aim is understand who makes novel images. Then we predict success using novelty and network position. In both cases we control for gender, the (log) number of shots made previously, the (log) number of days the user has been active on the site at the time of the shot, and whether the user has a paid account. In other words we control for gender, productivity/experience, tenure, and investment into the site.

6.1 Who makes novel shots?

We find several significant predictors of Inception novelty, both among our control variables and network variables. Interestingly, the network features we consider do not impact compositional novelty. We summarize these findings in Table 2.

For both compositional and Inception-based measures we find that pro-users are less likely to make novel images. One interpretation is that users who take the site more seriously are more risk-averse and less likely to experiment. Users making more shots in the past make slightly more novel shots. There is mixed evidence that users active for a longer period of time make less novel shots. We detect no gender disparity.

The two novelty measures diverge when we consider the impact of network features. The Inception-based measure of novelty is significantly lower for users closer to the core of the network, and higher for users with cohesive local networks defined by density and constraint. This supports our hypothesis that cohesion facilitates novelty. We find no significant relationship between network position and compositional novelty.

6.2 When are novel shots successful?

We now turn to the question of predicting engagement, measured by likes, using novelty. We find that novel shots are generally less successful. We summarize our findings in Table 3. Pro users are more successful, as are those who have many followers. We find that constrained users are less successful. Finally, novel images are in general less successful.

We find an interesting interaction between constraint and Inception novelty. Namely, users embedded in highly constrained networks making novel images do better than those in unconstrained networks making novel images. To better interpret this finding we visualize this relationship in Figure 5. In other words, the least constrained users have a penalty for novelty while the most constrained users have a bonus for novelty. We also find a significant interaction between inception novelty and closeness centrality: novelty has an increasingly negative relationship with success as a user is more central in the network, but no relationship between local density and either novelty measure.

Finally, using a machine learning framework, we check how well our features can predict success binned into three separate class labels: less than ten likes, between ten and one hundred likes, and more than one hundred likes. As an initialization we used the first year as the first training period and for every consecutive quarter thereafter we consider the previous year. We found that the random field approach to calculating the Fisher vector (FVMRF) was most effective in predicting engagement. Using the area under

	Dependent variable:					
	Inception Novelty			Composition Novelty		
	(1)	(2)	(3)	(4)	(5)	(6)
Days Active (log)	−0.015*** (0.002)	−0.016*** (0.002)	−0.017*** (0.002)	−0.000 (0.002)	0.000 (0.002)	−0.000 (0.002)
nShots Previous	0.020*** (0.007)	0.022*** (0.007)	0.022*** (0.007)	0.013* (0.007)	0.013* (0.007)	0.013* (0.007)
Male	−0.002 (0.013)	0.001 (0.013)	0.001 (0.013)	−0.000 (0.013)	−0.000 (0.013)	−0.000 (0.013)
Pro	−0.036*** (0.010)	−0.034*** (0.010)	−0.034*** (0.011)	−0.034*** (0.011)	−0.034*** (0.011)	−0.034*** (0.011)
In-Degree (log)	0.004 (0.004)	0.002 (0.004)	0.001 (0.004)	0.004 (0.004)	0.004 (0.004)	0.004 (0.004)
Closeness	−0.042*** (0.008)			0.001 (0.008)		
Constraint		0.060** (0.025)			0.018 (0.026)	
Density			0.046** (0.023)			−0.005 (0.024)
Constant	0.002 (0.025)	−0.009 (0.026)	−0.002 (0.026)	−0.048* (0.026)	−0.053** (0.026)	−0.047* (0.026)
Observations	37,799	37,799	37,799	37,799	37,799	37,799
Log Likelihood	−25,740.880	−25,749.400	−25,750.350	−25,731.900	−25,730.540	−25,730.860
Bayesian Inf. Crit.	51,576.620	51,593.660	51,595.570	51,558.660	51,555.950	51,556.580

User random effects   *p<0.1; **p<0.05; ***p<0.01

Table 2: Predicting novelty with network position.

	Dependent variable:	
	Log Likes	
	(1)	(2)
Days Active (log)	−0.006** (0.003)	−0.004* (0.003)
nShots Previous	0.086*** (0.023)	0.090*** (0.023)
Male	−0.046 (0.044)	−0.047 (0.045)
Pro	0.196*** (0.037)	0.196*** (0.037)
In-Degree (log)	0.371*** (0.009)	0.373*** (0.009)
Out-Degree (log)	−0.046*** (0.013)	−0.046*** (0.013)
Constraint	−0.234*** (0.059)	−0.233*** (0.059)
Incep. Nov.	−0.108*** (0.009)	
Incep. Nov. × Constraint	0.084** (0.039)	
Comp. Nov.		−0.025*** (0.010)
Comp. Nov. × Constraint		0.017 (0.040)
Constant	2.930*** (0.088)	2.908*** (0.089)
Observations	37,799	37,799
Log Likelihood	−36,353.290	−36,450.650
Bayesian Inf. Crit.	72,833.060	73,027.780

User random effects   *p<0.1; **p<0.05; ***p<0.01

Table 3: Predicting success with novelty and network position.

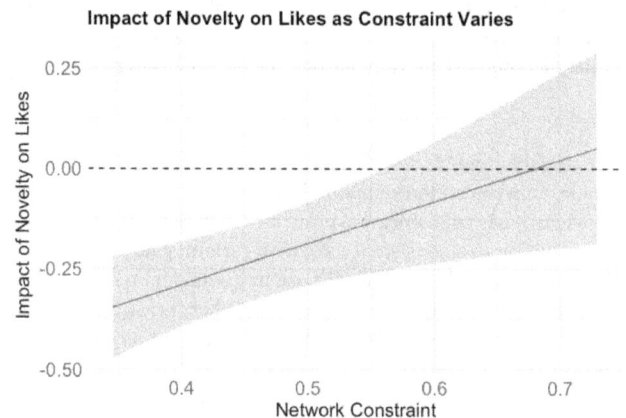

Figure 5: Relationship between success and novelty as constraint varies. Low constraint users have less success when making novel shots. High constraint users have more success with novel shots.

the receiver operating characteristic curve (AUC), we find that a gradient boosted trees model [22] on network and content features has significant predictive power. As we can see in Figure 6, even though the network features are the best indicators of success, the content and novelty of the images, encoded using the Inception-based Fisher vectors offer additional predictive power. This suggests that it is possible to use image features to predict success on the site. It is likely possible to do better if features are extracted with the aim of predicting success.

7 CONCLUSIONS

In this paper we developed, evaluated, and compared measures of novelty of images using data from an online community of digital designers. We first compared different feature sets of images, noting that compositional features like entropy, contrast, and brightness capture qualitatively different facets of an image and features derived from an Inception neural network learning framework capture qualitatively different facets of an image. Specifically, compositional features seem to capture stylistic aspects and while Inception features capture content, in line with their origins.

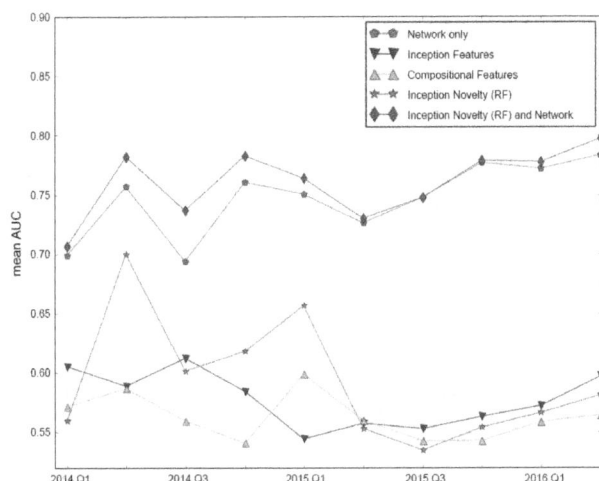

Figure 6: Average AUC of quarter to quarter success prediction. We predict success of the images using gradient boosted trees on the visual image features, novelty scores, and network position of the users. We find that novelty scores extracted image features increase the predictive power of the model including the network features, This suggests that network position does not entirely mediate the relationship between novelty and success.

Next, we created a mathematical framework to compare images with all images that came before in terms of either set of image features. To calculate the novelty of an image, we estimate the distribution of previous shots in the given feature space using a Gaussian mixture model. We then calculate the likelihood of the the image - in other words we quantify how statistically similar the image is to those that came before. We define novelty of an image as one minus this similarity score.

We find that both novelties calculated from the Inception features and compositional features are significantly correlated with a measure of novelty based on author text annotations or "tags" of their images. We also found that Inception novelty was significantly higher for images created in the early stages of an emerging tag compared with images using the same tag later.

Attempting to understand the profile of a user who makes more novel shots, we turned to the site's social network. Using temporal following data, we related social network position at the time of the creation of an image to its novelty. We found that users with cohesive local networks (quantified by density or Burt's constraint measure) tend to post images with higher Inception novelty.

We also find that users close to the center of the network, in a global sense, make less novel shots. Users with a "pro-badge" (paid account) likewise make less novel images. Given the professional atmosphere of the site, including for example its invitation-only participation, the presence of significant players and companies in the field, and the potential for economic opportunities, it seems reasonable that established designers may have reason to make more conventional images. That Dribbble is an online community

only compounds the potential costs of creating unsuccessful novelty: though a designer's support system and network of strong ties cannot vastly grow, her audience can scale drastically. The underestimated permanence of online identities makes this asymmetry all the more important when we consider what it means for a designer to take a risk with a distinctive image.

Indeed professional online communities present a dilemma for users in general. Though the feelings of anonymity and distance may facilitate bold experimentation, members of online communities who wish to leverage their investment of time and effort into professional advancement must credibly link their online identities to their real ones. Even users who want to stay anonymous often have a hard time doing so [28]. Once this identification has occurred, the individual must consider that anything they share online is widely broadcast and more consistently recorded and preserved than what they may say or share offline. We claim that as the labor market becomes increasingly digital, online social networks merit closer study.

Turning to the relationship between novelty and success, we find that novelty is related to worse outcomes. We also find that users in highly constrained positions are less successful. On the other hand, the interaction between constraint and novelty is positive: users with cohesive local networks of strong ties making novel images find more success. We argue that these relationships merit further study. Are these embedded designers better positioned to take risks? Can we interpret images with high novelty score, according to our definition, as being risky? The negative relationship between novelty and network centrality raises even more questions.

Our study has several limitations. Given the transient nature of novelty, we have only limited tests of validity for our measures. Given the ubiquity of digital technology, a highly novel digital design from five years ago likely looks highly outdated now. Moreover, the networking behavior of designers on this platform is highly tailored to the situation. For example, users adopting a strategy of aggressive following anticipating reciprocity, may end up in highly dense networks. All at once, Dribbble serves as a social network, professional portfolio, information network, and status hierarchy for the field. Any attempt to infer causal relations between social network structure and the creation of new ideas on this platform must disentangle the complicated layers driving interactions. We also concede that novelty is multi-faceted: no single measure can totally capture such a broad concept. In future work we aim to better understand influence and spreading of novelty.

8 ACKNOWLEDGEMENTS

The authors wish to thank Zsófia Czémán, Anna May, and anonymous referees for their helpful suggestions. This research has been funded in part by NSF grant IIS-1514283. D.B was supported by the Momentum Grant of the Hungarian Academy of Sciences (LP2012-19/2012).

REFERENCES

[1] 2016. Baby Names from Social Security Card Applications-National Level Data. data.gov. (2016). https://catalog.data.gov/dataset/baby-names-from-social-security-card-applications-national-level-data.
[2] Hirotugu Akaike. 1981. Likelihood of a model and information criteria. *Journal of econometrics* 16, 1 (1981), 3–14.

[3] Sinan Aral and Marshall Van Alstyne. 2011. The diversity-bandwidth trade-off. *Amer. J. Sociology* 117, 1 (2011), 90–171.

[4] Noah Askin and Michael Mauskapf. 2017. What Makes Popular Culture Popular? Product Features and Optimal Differentiation in Music. *American Sociological Review* 82, 5 (2017), 910–944.

[5] Andrew Barto, Marco Mirolli, and Gianluca Baldassarre. 2013. Novelty or surprise? *Frontiers in psychology* 4 (2013).

[6] Julia Bauer, Nikolaus Franke, and Philipp Tuertscher. 2016. Intellectual property norms in online communities: How user-organized intellectual property regulation supports innovation. *Information Systems Research* 27, 4 (2016), 724–750.

[7] Alex Bavelas. 1950. Communication patterns in task-oriented groups. *The Journal of the Acoustical Society of America* 22, 6 (1950), 725–730.

[8] Giacomo Boracchi, Diego Carrera, and Brendt Wohlberg. 2014. Novelty detection in images by sparse representations. In *Intelligent Embedded Systems (IES), 2014 IEEE Symposium on*. IEEE, 47–54.

[9] Kevin J Boudreau, Eva C Guinan, Karim R Lakhani, and Christoph Riedl. 2016. Looking across and looking beyond the knowledge frontier: Intellectual distance, novelty, and resource allocation in science. *Management Science* 62, 10 (2016), 2765–2783.

[10] Ronald S Burt. 2004. Structural holes and good ideas. *American journal of sociology* 110, 2 (2004), 349–399.

[11] LL Campbell. 1986. An extended Čencov characterization of the information metric. *Proc. Amer. Math. Soc.* 98, 1 (1986), 135–141.

[12] James S Coleman. 1988. Social capital in the creation of human capital. *American journal of sociology* 94 (1988), S95–S120.

[13] Mihaly Csikszentmihalyi. 1996. *Flow and the psychology of discovery and invention.* New York: Harper Collins.

[14] Balint Daroczy, David Siklois, Robert Palovics, and Andras A Benczur. 2015. Text Classification Kernels for Quality Prediction over the C3 Data Set. In *Proceedings of the 24th International Conference on World Wide Web*. ACM, 1441–1446.

[15] Ritendra Datta, Dhiraj Joshi, Jia Li, and James Z Wang. 2006. Studying aesthetics in photographic images using a computational approach. In *European Conference on Computer Vision*. Springer, 288–301.

[16] Mathijs De Vaan, David Stark, and Balazs Vedres. 2015. Game changer: The topology of creativity. *Amer. J. Sociology* 120, 4 (2015), 1144–1194.

[17] Biplab Deka, Haizi Yu, Devin Ho, Zifeng Huang, Jerry O Talton, and Ranjitha Kumar. 2015. Ranking designs and users in online social networks. In *Proceedings of the 33rd Annual ACM Conference Extended Abstracts on Human Factors in Computing Systems*. ACM, 1887–1892.

[18] Ahmed Elgammal and Babak Saleh. 2015. Quantifying Creativity in Art Networks. In *Proceedings of the Sixth International Conference on Computational Creativity June. 39*.

[19] Maria-Isabel Encinar and Felix-Fernando Munoz. 2006. On novelty and economics: Schumpeter's paradox. *Journal of Evolutionary Economics* 16, 3 (2006), 255–277.

[20] James A Evans and Jacob G Foster. 2011. Metaknowledge. *Science* 331, 6018 (2011), 721–725.

[21] L. Fleming. 2001. Recombinant uncertainty in technological search. *Management Science* 47, 1 (2001), 117–132.

[22] Jerome H Friedman. 2001. Greedy function approximation: a gradient boosting machine. *Annals of statistics* (2001), 1189–1232.

[23] Andrew Gelman and Jennifer Hill. 2006. *Data analysis using regression and multilevel/hierarchical models.* Cambridge university press.

[24] Mark S Granovetter. 1973. The strength of weak ties. *American journal of sociology* 78, 6 (1973), 1360–1380.

[25] Robert M Haralick. 1979. Statistical and structural approaches to texture. *Proc. IEEE* 67, 5 (1979), 786–804.

[26] A. Hargadon and R.I. Sutton. 1997. Technology brokering and innovation in a product development firm. *Administration Science Quarterly* 42, 4 (1997), 716–749.

[27] Andrew B Hargadon and Beth A Bechky. 2006. When collections of creatives become creative collectives: A field study of problem solving at work. *Organization Science* 17, 4 (2006), 484–500.

[28] Emöke-Ágnes Horvát, Michael Hanselmann, Fred A Hamprecht, and Katharina A Zweig. 2012. One plus one makes three (for social networks). *PloS one* 7, 4 (2012), e34740.

[29] Emöke-Ágnes Horvát, Johannes Wachs, Aniko Hannak, and Rong Wang. 2018. The Role of Novelty in Securing Investors for Equity Crowdfunding Campaigns. In *The 6th AAAI Conference on Human Computation and Crowdsourcing (HCOMP)*. AAAI.

[30] Xiaodi Hou and Liqing Zhang. 2007. Saliency detection: A spectral residual approach. In *Computer Vision and Pattern Recognition, 2007. CVPR'07. IEEE Conference on*. IEEE, 1–8.

[31] Tommi S Jaakkola, David Haussler, et al. 1999. Exploiting generative models in discriminative classifiers. *Advances in neural information processing systems* (1999), 487–493.

[32] Aditya Khosla, Atish Das Sarma, and Raffay Hamid. 2014. What makes an image popular?. In *Proceedings of the 23rd international conference on World wide web*. ACM, 867–876.

[33] Nam Wook Kim. 2017. Creative Community Demystified: A Statistical Overview of Behance. *arXiv preprint arXiv:1703.00800* (2017).

[34] W Chan Kim and Renée Mauborgne. 1997. *Value innovation: The strategic logic of high growth.* Harvard Business School Pub.

[35] David Krackhardt. 2003. The strength of strong ties. *Networks in the knowledge economy* (2003), 82.

[36] Guy Lebanon. 2004. An extended Čencov-Campbell characterization of conditional information geometry. In *Proceedings of the 20th conference on Uncertainty in artificial intelligence*. AUAI Press, 341–348.

[37] Vittorio Loreto, Vito DP Servedio, Steven H Strogatz, and Francesca Tria. 2016. Dynamics on expanding spaces: modeling the emergence of novelties. In *Creativity and Universality in Language*. Springer, 59–83.

[38] Laurens van der Maaten and Geoffrey Hinton. 2008. Visualizing data using t-SNE. *Journal of Machine Learning Research* 9, Nov (2008), 2579–2605.

[39] Jana Machajdik and Allan Hanbury. 2010. Affective image classification using features inspired by psychology and art theory. In *Proceedings of the 18th ACM international conference on Multimedia*. ACM, 83–92.

[40] Jennifer Marlow and Laura Dabbish. 2014. From rookie to all-star: professional development in a graphic design social networking site. In *Proceedings of the 17th ACM conference on Computer supported cooperative work & social computing*. ACM, 922–933.

[41] Florent Perronnin and Christopher Dance. 2007. Fisher kernels on visual vocabularies for image categorization. In *Computer Vision and Pattern Recognition, 2007. CVPR'07. IEEE Conference on*. IEEE, 1–8.

[42] Jill E Perry-Smith. 2006. Social yet creative: The role of social relationships in facilitating individual creativity. *Academy of Management journal* 49, 1 (2006), 85–101.

[43] D. Ravasi and G. Lojacono. 2005. Managing design and designers for strategic renewal. *Long Range Planning* 38 (2005), 51–77.

[44] Miriam Redi, Neil OHare, Rossano Schifanella, Michele Trevisiol, and Alejandro Jaimes. 2014. 6 seconds of sound and vision: Creativity in micro-videos. In *Computer Vision and Pattern Recognition (CVPR), 2014 IEEE Conference on*. IEEE, 4272–4279.

[45] Christoph Riedl and V Seidel. 2018. Learning from Mixed Signals: Evidence from a Contest-based Online Innovation Community. *Organization Science* (2018).

[46] V. Rindova, E. Dalpiaz, and D. Ravasi. 2011. A cultural quest: A study of organizational use of new cultural resources in strategy formation. *Organization Science* 22, 2 (2011), 413–431.

[47] V.P. Rindova and A.P. Petkova. 2007. When is a new thing a good thing? Technological change, product form design, and perceptions of value for product innovations. *Organization Science* 18, 2 (2007), 217–232.

[48] Maja R Rudolph, Matthew Hoffman, and Aaron Hertzmann. 2016. A joint model for who-to-follow and what-to-view recommendations on behance. In *Proceedings of the 25th International Conference Companion on World Wide Web*. International World Wide Web Conferences Steering Committee, 581–584.

[49] Rossano Schifanella, Miriam Redi, and Luca Maria Aiello. 2015. An Image Is Worth More than a Thousand Favorites: Surfacing the Hidden Beauty of Flickr Pictures. In *Ninth International AAAI Conference on Web and Social Media*.

[50] Joseph Schumpeter and Ursula Backhaus. 2003. The theory of economic development. *Joseph Alois Schumpeter* (2003), 61–116.

[51] Roberta Sinatra, Dashun Wang, Pierre Deville, Chaoming Song, and Albert-László Barabási. 2016. Quantifying the evolution of individual scientific impact. *Science* 354, 6312 (2016), aaf5239.

[52] Alex Smola, Le Song, and Choon Hui Teo. 2009. Relative novelty detection. In *Artificial Intelligence and Statistics*. 536–543.

[53] Sameet Sreenivasan. 2013. Quantitative analysis of the evolution of novelty in cinema through crowdsourced keywords. *Scientific reports* 3 (2013).

[54] Christian Szegedy, Wei Liu, Yangqing Jia, Pierre Sermanet, Scott Reed, Dragomir Anguelov, Dumitru Erhan, Vincent Vanhoucke, and Andrew Rabinovich. 2015. Going deeper with convolutions. In *Proceedings of the IEEE conference on computer vision and pattern recognition*. 1–9.

[55] N. N. Čencov. 1982. Statistical decision rules and optimal inference. *American Mathematical Society* 53 (1982).

[56] Brian Uzzi, Satyam Mukherjee, Michael Stringer, and Ben Jones. 2013. Atypical combinations and scientific impact. *Science* 342, 6157 (2013), 468–472.

[57] Johannes Wachs, Anikó Hannák, András Vörös, and Bálint Daróczy. 2017. Why Do Men Get More Attention? Exploring Factors Behind Success in an Online Design Community. In *Eleventh International AAAI Conference on Web and Social Media*.

[58] M.L. Weitzman. 1998. Recombinant growth. *Quarterly Journal of Economics* 113, 2 (1998), 331–360.

[59] N.M. Wijnberg and G. Gemser. 2000. Adding Value to Innovation: Impressionism and the Transformation of the Selection System in Visual Arts. *Organization Science* 11, 3 (2000), 323–329.

[60] Michael J Wilber, Chen Fang, Hailin Jin, Aaron Hertzmann, John Collomosse, and Serge Belongie. 2017. BAM! The Behance Artistic Media Dataset for Recognition Beyond Photography. *arXiv preprint arXiv:1704.08614* (2017).

Perspectives on Data and Practices

Heidrun Allert
Christian-Albrechts-Universität zu Kiel
Kiel, Germany
allert@paedagogik.uni-kiel.de

Christoph Richter
Christian-Albrechts-Universität zu Kiel
Kiel, Germany
richter@paedagogik.uni-kiel.de

ABSTRACT

There is not something like *big data research*, but a variety of diverse *big data research practices* in different fields. They are based on different logics, rationalities, epistemological beliefs, types of data, and even different forms of objectivity as well as concepts of theory. Practices are specific regarding their temporalities and materialities. Furthermore, big data practices are not necessarily about doing research, but also about governance. To make these differences explicit is a step towards better collaboration in the many fields of the web sciences.

CCS CONCEPTS

• **General and reference** → *General literature*;

KEYWORDS

big data research, research practices, social science, objectivity, epistemology, epistemic beliefs, data

ACM Reference Format:
Heidrun Allert and Christoph Richter. 2018. Perspectives on Data and Practices. In *WebSci'18: 10th ACM Conference on Web Science, May 27–30, 2018, Amsterdam, Netherlands.* ACM, New York, NY, USA, 4 pages.
https://doi.org/10.1145/3201064.3201109

1 INTRODUCTION

The notions of *web science* and *big data research* might suggest a set of unique and coherent approaches. In this paper we argue that in the web science community there is not a unique approach on data, objectivity and research rationality, but a plurality of scientific practices and epistemic believes. Researching and understanding them would allow for better interdisciplinary work. The proliferation of big data and computer-based procedures for the collection and analysis of large datasets not only gave rise to new methods and technologies in the humanities and social sciences but also introduced new players and epistemic beliefs. This already becomes evident in the rival conceptions of data as something that is either to be generated or collected. This paper will: 1. Shed light on different research practices and their enactments of theories (theories in data collection and analysis vs. programmed theories in data

generation). 2. Tell apart different perspectives on data and forms of objectivity.

2 THEORIES ENACTED

In this section we argue that data practices inevitably involve theories, but theories are enacted at various times and in different forms. The temporality of practices and the enactment of theory in big data practices differs from several social science research practices.

Some proponents of big data analytics have repeatedly proclaimed the end of theory in recent years. But how could this thesis catch ground in light of the extensive critique on any positivistic take on data in the social sciences and the humanities? Referring to the notion of "data-behaviorism" [18] it has for example been claimed that such approaches "would be mechanistic, reductionistic and authoritarian as they privilege the scientist in relation to the researched subject" ([20], p. 200, own translation). Big Data conveys the impression that the observer would have access to more extensive and more accurate information of a person and his/her behavior than s/he has access to her/himself (ibid.). The above quote however already insinuates, that processes of algorithmic data analysis should be understood as a form of scientific observation and hence would fit into the established debates in the theory of science. But we question this, as big data comprises not only research but also governance practices.

Qualitative research in the social sciences, in contrast to quantitative approaches, is not a coherent approach but refers to a huge variety of approaches [4]. As there are diverse approaches in the qualitative field, their use and development is accompanied by respective methodological discourses (ibid.), discussions on methods and techniques of data collection, analysis and interpretation. A major question is, whether the data gathered actually represents the phenomena observed or whether methods and research practices become performative regarding the phenomena, i.e. having an effect on the reality observed. [19] has a close look at qualitative research practices regarding their temporality. He states that research practices in social science are organized in a way that allows for separating data analysis from data collection. Transcribing interviews, arranging field notes, sharing material among inter-raters and so forth separates data collection from analysis and takes reasonable time. It is these practices and discourses, shared among researchers, which make it sound unreasonable that big data practices are claimed to be theory-free. From this perspective (performing research practices in the social sciences), big data practices seem to take a short-cut between data collection and data analysis (as in big data practices *actions* are taken immediately after *data generation*), and thus to cause a short circuit which is unjustifiable. Algorithms are designed to perform action (e.g. a search machine presenting search results). Considering temporality, big data practices allocate no time to actually bring in theory between data collection and analysis (or better: between data generation and performing action). Social media applications and search machines directly translate data generation into action (e.g. displaying search results). In contrast to this, the social scientists aim to perform methodologically controlled steps to go from *collecting data* to *analyzing data*. Furthermore, moving from *data analysis* to *taking action* requires for *creative design/synthesis* (this step is most often referred to as *intervention*, not as *research*). But does that mean that big data practices are theory-free? Here we state that the theory is implemented in the instrument. We call this: *programmed theories*. Be it a theory on what a good shopping experience looks like, a theory on the user, and so on. This theory is materialized (programmed) in an online shop, a social media platform, an application, a research instrument, a search machine, and so on. Big data practices are not theory-free, but theory comes in at a different stage (at the design phase). [21] demonstrate this for *big data in the physical sciences* where theory is in the Large Hadron Collider. According to [4], programmed theory is also known in social science: He states that theories are in instruments used in qualitative data analysis, i.e. research software. Thus, theory becomes performative in big data practices as well as in social science practices.

3 DIGITALE DATA AND DIFFERENT FORMS OF OBJECTIVITY

Closely related to the idea of analytic procedures that operate independent of theoretical commitments is the question of our understanding of the "nature" of digital data and their "objectivity". Again, we are facing a peculiar coexistence of two contradictory positions in the current discourse on digital data. While on the one hand digital data is conceived as a "natural resource", that can be mined, exploited and processed (e.g. [15]), scholars in the social sciences and the humanities on the other hand have stressed the inevitable subjectivity and social constitution of data and its interpretation (e.g. [3],[16]). But how can the persistence of these disparate conceptions of (digital) data be explained? How can it be that not only software engineers and vendors of respective technologies but also decision makers and managers assume the objectivity of data to be given while the discourse in the social sciences and humanities points into the exact opposite direction? A way to overcome this (apparent) contradiction is not to ask whether one of these positions is right and the other wrong but to have a closer look at the way data is actually used and the functions that data fulfill in different contexts. This change in perspective is in line with the observation that there is hardly any agreement on what data actually is, neither in science nor in applied disciplines (cf. [7]). If we shift the focus towards the practical usage of data we also have to reconsider the question of when and under which conditions data qualifies as "objective". Instead of asking whether "objectivity" can principally be achieved or ensured, the primary focus is on how different *forms objectivity* are produced and established within different contexts of practical action (cf. [7]). In the following we aim to roughly outline three basic perspectives on (digital) data and the related *processes of objectification* we spot in the current discussion on big data and the algorithmic processing of data. Tracing these three perspectives, we aim to trigger a more differentiated discussion on data in the web sciences and provide a framework for critical data studies.

3.1 Objectivity as a Representational Function – the Observers' Perspective

The first perspective, that can also be understood as the *observers' perspective*, is closely related to the methodological traditions and discourses grounded in empirical (social) research. From this perspective (digital) data is primarily conceived of as a means for the description of empirical matters. Data in this view is first and foremost something that depicts or represents something else. The use of digital data, from this perspective, is conceived of in reference to the usage of measurement or observational data. Data, hence, are not given, but have to be collected, elicited or extracted by means of dedicated procedures. For example, from an observer' perspective data are collected from Twitter in order to explore the linguistic conventions applied. The matters, things or phenomena to be represented and analysed thereby are conceived, at least ideally, as independent of the data collection procedures [1]. Due to their role as depictions and recordings of an empirical matter, the collected data allows for a systematic, repeated and collective analysis, an analysis functionally decoupled from the matter itself. Towards this end it does not matter whether the actor adopt a quantitative approach, trying to ensure objectivity by means of experimental control, sampling and standardized data collection techniques or whether they opt for the collective and methodologically reflected interpretation of qualitative data. As data in this perspective is relevant only to the extent that it refers to something else, objectivity is a representational function. Objectivity, in both cases, is established by disciplinary legitimized forms of signification, backed up by the respective procedures and standards of data-collection, -analysis and - interpretation. As a consequence, objectification from the observer' perspective is primarily a concern for a common understanding of some empirical matter in a situation where the actors are relieved from any direct action on this very subject matter. The materiality of data and of the instruments used for data-elicitation and processing plays a marginal role at best (cf. [7]). To put it brief: data, in this perspective, stands in for something else.

3.2 Objectivity as a Product of Articulation – the Users' Perspective

In the case of social matters, however, data are often not just means of representation but also of transformation. Data cannot only be depictions or recordings of something but also for something. The transformation of the world by the production and usage of data is the central motive of the second perspective, that can also be read as the *users' perspective*. From the users' perspective data is an integral element of (social) interaction. Data are not just means for the description of certain matters but, an especially in digital contexts, constitutively entangled with the matters itself. The creation of a Tweet is coextensive with the production of data, data that can be processed, stored, reused and (re-)interpreted by computers in very different contexts. As this is a fact the users are principally aware of, it consequently (directly or indirectly) shapes the way the respective technologies are used. The data and the subject matter are therefore

---

[1] Concerns for the reactivity of data collection procedures or the occurrence of measurement artifacts can be understood as practical problems to achieve the ideal of purely representational data.

reflexively entangled from the users' perspective. As [14] has argued, these kinds of circular effects shape the instrumental, social, and aesthetic qualities of social media usage. For example, Twitter's 140-characters limit has not simply been a technical restriction but was a co-constitutive moment for the emergence of specific linguistic conventions, memes, genres and collaborative practices unfolding on Twitter. From the users' perspective, the production of qualitative and quantitative data is embedded in processes of articulation and social positionings (cf. [9]). Data here are not just carriers of meaning but enter into practice as material entities that come along with specific forms of resistance. It is only by means of data that the respective forms of sociotechnical interaction become possible while at the same time they produce a surplus of meaning, which is neither intended or controlled by those evoking the data [10]. The medium leaves its marks: it co-constitutively shapes what we are doing. The production of data, from this perspective, is not so much focused on description and retrospection but geared towards the initiation and opening of options for future interactions. The objectification of data does not depend on its (retrospective) interpretation but is achieved in the process of articulation itself. The actors, in this perspective, are "reflexive fellow players" [8] that cannot escape their active involvement in the production of data but are constitutively entangled with the data they are producing. The observers' perspective and the corresponding forms of distant critique is no option for them. Critical engagement, form the users' perspective, instead requires an experimental take on the established practices geared towards the exploration of new forms of socio-technical intercourse.

3.3 Objectivity as Operationalization – the Processors' Perspective

The third perspective, that we deem relevant in the current discussion on big data and algorithmic data processing, is focused on the utilization and usage of data from a technical and information processing point of view. This *processors' perspective* does not approach data as representations of or for something but conceives data as objects that are amenable to algorithmic processing in the first place. Data is defined here as "reinterpretable representation of information in a formalized manner suitable for communication, interpretation, or processing", which is organized in discrete "data objects" [1] . Data, from this perspective, is the primary *material* on which digital and computer-based technologies operate. The materiality and objectness of data is central to this position, as it are the data objects that are processed and operated on. The data of an email is the thing itself - the email only exists as a data object. As objects they are also objectively given, there is hardly any doubt whether a data object exists or not. From an informatics point of view, data can be understood as signs that are reduced to their material dimension, as signs that are stripped of their relationality, as Nake (quoted in [13]) put it. Accordingly, data and sets of data are a resource that exits independent of their interpretability. The read- and interpretability of data is not given but has to be explicitly produced and therefore can also get lost so that data might become "rotten" (see [2]). The read- and interpretability of data, this is another important specific of this perspective, has to be ensured both for the algorithmic processor as well as the human

user. The development of digital technologies hence takes place at the interface of two systems, the computational system on the one and a socio-material reference system on the other hand and shapes the relation between these two. The interpretation of data however is fundamentally different among humans and computers [12]. While human users inevitably make sense of digital data in relation to the situation and context they find themselves in as well as their motives and interest, computers can interpret and operate on data only on the basis of the formalized procedures available to them. In this sense computers are determined by the data they are provided with. In this sense, a piece of software such as Google Translate does not need to *understand* a natural language utterance in order to generate a translation but can do so by the algorithmic processing of a respective dataset. The core challenges from the processors' perspective is to device "auto-operational forms" [5] that allow to abstract from the specifics of a particular situation in a way that algorithmic data processing becomes possible while ensuring a meaningful interpretation of the data in relation to some sociomaterial practice. Digital technologies, therefore are not just closely related to the development of respective algorithms but also to the establishment of formalized systems of description, models and ontologies. From the processor' perspective objectivity is essentially achieved to the extent data is made accessible to operational processing, both on the semantic as well as the ontological layer. Data have an instrumental function and are means in order to do something. To achieve this, respective technologies effectively *short-circuit* the processes of data elicitation (production), analysis and intervention.

3.4 Options for Practical Data Critique

In the contrasting juxtaposition of the three perspectives on digital data it should have become obvious that the understanding of data, the way objectivity is established but also the ways in which data can be criticized, is dependent on the way data is used in different social arenas. Depending on whether the observers', the users' or the processors' perspective is adopted different conceptions of data come to the fore. At the same time these different perspectives do not exist in isolation but are closely interwoven in practical encounter, even though the cannot be reduced to one another. As a consequence, empirical scientists cannot simply take a person's posting on a social media site as an authentic articulation of this person's opinion but have to account for the reflexivity of data-production on these platforms (cf. [11]). Similarly, the scientific critique of digital research methods also has to reflect on the material qualities of the technologies used in the research process (e.g. [6]). By the same token users of digital technologies are not just producers but also recipients of data and therefore also entangled in processes of observation, reflection and collective meaning making. In addition, they are also forced to deal with the resistance of digital technologies and to position themselves in relation to these technologies and the regimes of governance they are implicating. Finally, those engaged in the development of the technologies, to some extent have to draw on or rely on observational data in order to device model, ontologies and auto-operational form, while at the same time they articulate themselves in the development process and position themselves in relation to other social actors, be it vendors, users or some other public entity. To foster the multidisciplinary discourse on digital data and technologies it seems important to overcome a reductionist understanding of how data is *produced, made sense of* â and *objectified*. Instead it appears important to have a closer look at the practices and the rationalities in and through which data are made up and used. This also requires theoretical perspectives and methodological approaches, that account for symbolic and material nature of digital data. Towards this end we concur with [6] and [16], that timely forms of critical data studies have to have a close look on the actual practices through which data is generated, interacted with and used. It also implies that we have to analyze the historical, cultural and societal processes that gave rise to but are also implicated by todays digital data practices.

4 FURTHER WORK

This paper shows that there are different logics and epistemic beliefs concerning research, data, objectivity and theory-based data analysis. A consequence is, that in the web science community we should not talk about big data research as a unique approach and epistemological stance but refer to big data research as various big data practices. Based on this, further work in the science and technology studies may be on investigating a variety of big data practices. Ethnographic methods and practice-based accounts are appropriate to take into account the doings and sayings, the materiality and temporality of specific practices. A respective approach on different rationalities of creative design is taken in [17]. We would like to present examples where the perspectives come together as well as examples that address each perspective only. Addressing a reviewer comment: How do these three perspectives, alone or together, shed light on different issues? How do these perspectives become useful for conceptualizing and articulating research problems in action?

REFERENCES

[1] ISO/IEC 2382:2015. 2015. *Information technology – Vocabulary*. Technical Report. https://www.iso.org/standard/63598.html
[2] Tim Boellstorff. 2014. Die Konstruktion von Big Data in der Theorie. In *Big Data – Analysen zum digitalen Wandel von Wissen, Macht und Ökonomie*, Ramon Reichert (Ed.). transcript, 105–131.
[3] danah boyd and Kate Crawford. 2011. Six provocations for big data. In *A decade in internet time: Symposium on the dynamics of the internet and society*. Oxford

[4] Rainer Diaz-Bone. 2011. Die Performativität der qualitativen Sozialforschung. *Forum Qualitative Sozialforschung/Forum Qualitative Social Research* 12, 3 (2011). http://www.qualitativeresearch.net/index.php/fqs/article/view/1750/3254
[5] Christiane Floyd. 2002. Developing and Embedding Auto-Operational Form. In *Social Thinking - Software Practice*, Yvonne Dittrich, Christiane Floyd, and Rolf Klischewski (Eds.). MIT Press, Cambridge, 5–28.
[6] Sebastian Gießmann and Markus Burkhardt. 2014. Was ist Datenkritik? Zur Einführung. *Mediale Kontrolle unter Beobachtung* 3, 1 (2014), 0–13. http://www.medialekontrolle.de/wp-content/uploads/2014/09/Giessmann-Sebastian-Burkhardt-Marcus-2014-03-01.pdf
[7] Lisa Gitelman and Virginia Jackson. 2013. Introduction. In „*Raw Data*" *Is an Oxymoron*, Lisa Gitelman (Ed.). MIT Press, Cambridge, 1–14.
[8] Karl-Heinz Hörning. 2004. Soziale Praxis zwischen Beharrung und Neuschöpfung. Ein Erkenntnis- und Theorieproblem. In *Doing Culture – Neue Positionen zum Verhältnis von Kultur und sozialer Praxis*, Karl-Heinz Hörning and Julia Reuter (Eds.). transcript, Bielefeld, 19–39.
[9] Benjamin Jörissen. 2014. Artikulationen - Bildung in und von medialen Architekturen. In *Schriften zur Medienpädagogik: School's out? - informelle und formelle Medienbildung*, Sandra Aßmann, Dorothee M. Meister, and Anja Pielsticker (Eds.). Kopaed, München, 13–27.
[10] Sybille Krämer. 1998. Das Medium als Spur und als Apparat. In *Medien Computer Realität – Wirklichkeitsvorstellungen und Neue Medien*, Sybille Krämer (Ed.). Suhrkamp, Frankfurt a.M., 73–94.
[11] Lev Manovich. 2011. Trending: The promises and the challenges of big social data. *Debates in the digital humanities* 2 (2011), 460–475. http://www.manovich.net/DOCS/Manovich_trending_paper.pdf
[12] Frieder Nake. 2001. Das algorithmische Zeichen. *GI Jahrestagung* 2 (2001), 736–742.
[13] Erhard Nullmeier. 2007. Wissensbasierte Systeme. In *Wissensmanagement in der Wissenschaft: Wissenschaftsforschung Jahrbuch 2004*, Klaus Fuchs-Fittkowski, Walther Umstätter, and Roland Wagner-Döbler (Eds.). GeWiF, Berlin, 43–61.
[14] Johannes Paßmann. 2014. From Mind to Document and Back Again. In *Big Data – Analysen zum digitalen Wandel von Wissen, Macht und Ökonomie*, Ramon Reichert (Ed.). transcript, Bielefeld, 259–285.
[15] Bob Picciano. 2014. Why Big Data is the New Natural Resource. *Forbes Brand Voice* (2014). https://www.forbes.com/sites/ibm/2014/06/30/why-big-data-isthe-new-natural-resource/#55a8b3656628
[16] Florian Püschel. 2014. Big Data und die Rückkehr des Positivismus: Zum gesellschaftlichen Umgang mit Daten. *Mediale Kontrolle unter Beobachtung* 3, 1 (2014), 0–23. http://www.medialekontrolle.de/wpcontent/uploads/2014/09/Pueschel-Florian-2014-03-01.pdf
[17] Christoph Richter and Heidrun Allert. 2017. Different Rationalities of Creative Design – A Comparative Case Study. In *Research into Design for Communities*, Vol. 1. Springer Nature, Singapore, 3–13.
[18] Antoinette Rouvroy. 2013. The end(s) of critique: data-behaviorism vs. due process. In *Privacy, Due Process and the Computational Turn: The Philosophy of Law Meets the Philosophy*, Katja de Vries and Mireille Hildebrand (Eds.). Routledge, Abingdon, 143–165.
[19] Tim Seitz. 2017. *Design Thinking und der neue Geist des Kapitalismus: Soziologische Betrachtungen einer Innovationskultur*. transcript, Bielefeld.
[20] Felix Stalder. 2016. *Kultur der Digitalität*. Suhrkamp, Berlin.
[21] Anna Wilson, Terrie-Lynn Thompson, and Cate Watson. 2017. Big Data and Learning Analytics: Singular or Plural? *Firstmonday* 22, 4 (2017). http://firstmonday.org/ojs/index.php/fm/article/view/6872/6089#author

Internet Institute, 0–17. https://ssrn.com/abstract=1926431orhttp://dx.doi.org/10.2139/ssrn.1926431

Predicting Email and Article Clickthroughs with Domain-adaptive Language Models

Kokil Jaidka
University of Pennsylvania
Philadelphia, Pennsylvania
jaidka@sas.upenn.edu

Tanya Goyal
University of Texas
Austin, Texas
tanyagoyal.93@gmail.com

Niyati Chhaya
Adobe Research
Bangalore, India
nchhaya@adobe.com

ABSTRACT

Marketing practices have adopted the use of computational approaches in order to optimize the performance of their promotional emails and site advertisements. In the case of promotional emails, subject lines have been found to offer a reliable signal of whether the recipient will open an email or not. Clickbait headlines are also known to drive reader engagement. In this study, we explore the differences in recipients' preferences for subject lines of marketing emails from different industries, in terms of their clickthrough rates on marketing emails sent by different businesses in Finance, Cosmetics and Television industries. Different stylistic strategies of subject lines characterize high clickthroughs in different commercial verticals. For instance, words providing insight and signaling cognitive processing lead to more clickthroughs for the Finance industry; on the other hand, social words yield more clickthroughs for the Movies and Television industry. Domain adaptation can further improve predictive performance for unseen businesses by an average of 16.52% over generic industry-specific predictive models. We conclude with a discussion on the implications of our findings and suggestions for future work.

KEYWORDS

email marketing, subject lines, linguistic analysis, copy-writing strategies, machine learning, domain adaptation, open rate prediction, clickthroughs, online ads, advertisements

ACM Reference Format:
Kokil Jaidka, Tanya Goyal, and Niyati Chhaya. 2018. Predicting Email and Article Clickthroughs with Domain-adaptive Language Models. In *Proceedings of 10th ACM Conference on Web Science (WebSci'18)*. ACM, New York, NY, USA, 8 pages. https://doi.org/10.1145/3201064.3201071

1 INTRODUCTION

The language used in a subject line plays an important role as a determinant of relevance. For example, it can lead to recipients choosing to open an email sooner rather than later, or to delete the email without opening it at all; it could lead to them marking the email as spam or even unsubscribing from the mailing list. Email servers also use language models to predict whether or not an email

is spam. In the case of news websites, copywriters tailor sponsored articles to get the reader's attention with interesting or provocative headlines that are relevant to their personal interests.

We propose to use click information to predict the performance of future promotional emails. The findings can be used to formulate copy–writing cues for different industries, and for captioning news articles (see, for instance, the subject line performance predictors developed by Persado[1] and Adobe Campaign[2]). Modeling the language of email subject lines is also increasingly relevant for tasks such as inbox management, email stacking, and information retrieval, in order to understand the relevance of an email to its recipient. Intelligent inbox management techniques, such as the stacking of emails under tabs [1] use features based on the subject lines, content and sender information.

Since language-based models do not generalize well to out-of-domain samples, we implement domain–adaptive approaches to tailor a generic predictive model towards making better predictions for different businesses, where the distribution of clicks may differ widely from the industry norm.

In summary, our contributions include: 1) a new NLP task for clickthrough prediction on email subject lines from a variety of businesses and industries (Table 1); 2) an exploration of the effectiveness of language modeling for predicting email clickthroughs and identifying clickbait articles. Our models show promise in predicting email open rates (hereafter referred to as clickthrough rates or *CTR*), with an average mean absolute error (MAE) of 4.5% (Table 2). On the clickbait detection task, the proposed approach provides a performance gain of 7.7% in recall and a 4.8% gain in F1-score over the state of the art (Table 3); and 3) the implementation of domain adaptation approaches to make these language models generalizable to out-of-domain samples, leading to a 16.5% improvement over prior results (Table 6).

2 RELATED WORK

The literature exploring the relationship between the language of emails and recipient behavior has drawn on mixed methods to offer linguistic and predictive insights into the best strategies for garnering email responses. The paper by Miller and Charles [21] provides a qualitative analysis of 150 personal emails from the Enron email dataset[3] and 150 spam emails from the Spamdex dataset[4], to propose 40 rules for improving the impact of marketing emails. However, these qualitative analyses are necessarily small in scope,

---

[1] https://persado.com/wp-content/uploads/2015/06/PersadoGoDatasheet.pdf
[2] https://blogs.adobe.com/digitalmarketing/email/amplifying-email-insights-predictive-subject-lines/
[3] http://cs.cmu.edu/ enron/
[4] http://www.spamdex.co.uk

and do not compare between the best strategies for different types of businesses.

Studies have predicted email clickthroughs [2, 18, 28] using simplistic keywords, syntactic features, and time–based features [9, 19]. The study by Shish et. al has used email subject lines among other features for the detection of email spam [31], while Ferriera et. al have used subject lines to identify phishing emails [10]. Most studies profiling user behavior on emails have been conducted in a relative small scope on a small set of monitored users [14, 18, 26]. The study by Di et al. [9] analyzed a corpus of conversations between known contacts. The problem takes on a different set of challenges when the focus is on targeting marketing emails, sent by a corporate entity. Studies have measured user preferences in terms of ad clickthroughs [12] and consumers' motivations in passing along emails in viral marketing campaigns [23], as well as the cognitive predictions which may lead them to forward or click the links in marketing emails [15, 34]. The authors observed recipients evaluate marketing emails on a number of cognitive factors such as the benefit goals related to the message, trusting beliefs in the message sender, involvement with the message and the cost of future efforts required to follow through with the message.

We have compared our method against the work of Sahni et. al [28]. The authors test the contribution of email subject line personalization in boosting the rate of email clickthroughs. They conducted randomized control trials on 68000 recipients and concluded that adding the name of the message recipient to the email's subject-line increases the probability of the recipient opening it by 20%. Although we have used personalization as one of our features, unexpectedly we did not observe it to play a role in determining email clickthroughs, once linguistic features were also included.

Some studies on ad clickthroughs have modeled the problem using website content features [27], advertising-based features such as hotness, promotion, events and sentiment [5], similarity to surrounding ads [8], user demographics [6, 13] and attractiveness features or attractive words [16]. However, the case of predicting email clickthroughs is quite different because the relevant cues are limited to information about the sender and the email subject line. There are a few online tools and plug-ins such as 'Downworthy' which detects clickbait headlines by following a rule–based approach [11]. The qualitative analysis by Blom and Hansen[3] used a dictionary of forward-references at the discourse level ("This news will blow your mind") and at the phrase level ("This name is hilarious.") to identify that clickbait articles occur mostly in commercial, ad-funded, and tabloid news websites. However, they did not propose an approach for clickbait detection. Evidently, these approaches are not scalable because they operate on a manually curated list of phrases or links. Potthast et al. [24] developing a clickbait classifier for Twitter based on a small annotated dataset.

We compare our approach against the clickbait classifier developed by Chakraborty et. al [4] on a corpus of 15000 article headlines scraped from WikiNews and various tabloid news websites. Their best-performing classifier used sentence structure, topical similarity, lexical patterns and n-grams in a support vector machine (SVM) set-up to achieve an accuracy of 0.93.

3 METHOD

There are three parts to this study:

- **Predictive modeling**: We compare the performance of these features in predicting email opens and clickbait articles. We demonstrate that the best predictive models are data-driven and significantly outperform the state-of-the-art.
- **Language insights**: We highlight the successful copy–writing strategies in different contexts by conducting univariate regressions of these features with email clickthroughs.
- **Domain adaptation**: We demonstrate how domain adaptation improves out-of-sample predictions on unseen domains and businesses and further for diagnosing the differences through insights.

4 DATA AND FEATURE EXTRACTION

The Email dataset: The email dataset was collected from Edatasource[5], an email inbox monitoring organization which tracks over 25 million emails for 90000 distinct businesses per day. The data is categorized into 98 industries. Using their licensed API, we were able to download the email meta-data and aggregate recipient response information for up to 20000 promotional emails each, sent over a one–year period (April 2015 to March 2016) for three categories of businesses: Finance, Cosmetics, and Movies & Television. Statistics about the data sets are provided in Table 1. The distribu-

Table 1: Dataset description: email subject lines

	Finance	Cosmetics	Movies & TV
Emails	18941	3394	3165
Businesses	47	57	69
Users	24m	5.7m	3.5m
Training Set	15168	2731	2555
Test Set	3773	663	610
μ Clickthrough Rate (%)	26.0	13.0	12.0
σ S.D.	13.0	9.0	9.0
γ Skewness	0.29	2.1	2.2

tion of clickthrough rates for Cosmetics ($\mu = 0.13$) and Movies & Television ($\mu = 0.12$) are fairly Gaussian, and much like each other, while Finance ($\mu = 0.26$) has a few outliers and a mean twice that of that the former industries. The final plot demonstrates that there is a wide variance in the clickthrough rates across businesses within the same industry. This highlights the need for intra-industry domain adaptation in predictive models for email clickthrough rates, especially when the prediction is for unseen businesses.

The Clickbait dataset: The Clickbait dataset comprises a total of 15000 randomly sampled articles, half of which are labeled positive (clickbait present) or negative (non–clickbait), and were collected from Buzzfeed, Scroll and several news websites. Detailed about data collection and sampling are provided in the original paper by Chakraborty et. al [4].

---

[5]see http://www.edatasource.com. Edatasource monitors the email inboxes of millions of email users, after obtaining their consent, and saves email contents and user responses in a de–identified form for the purposes of marketing research.

4.1 Pre-processing the Email dataset

We discarded those emails which were received by less than 100 users. This is because the clickthrough rates (as provided by eData-source) are extrapolated for a larger population, based on the actual responses of a smaller sample of users. Our expectation is that if the actual no. of observations is more, then there is more confidence that the observed clickthrough rate is closer to the actual click-through rate. The law of large numbers states that the observed response rate for m recipients converges to the actual response rate as the value of m increases. We conducted a preliminary weighted regression analysis, by assigning a weight to each sample subject line, which dictates its contribution to the regression loss function. Let S denote the n subject lines in the data set. For each sample s_i, the weight is defined as,

$$w_i = log(m_i/m_o) \qquad (1)$$

where m_i is the number of recipients of email campaign with subject line s_i, whose responses were recorded.

Thus, in the loss function, we give more weight to subject line samples whose response rates have been calculated based on the reaction of larger number of recipients.

We identified that the best performance was obtained by aggressively down-weighting those subject lines which had an actual recorded volume of under 100 emails, which always had a click-through rate of 0%. They also appeared to be mis-categorized as industry-specific emails. After filtering out emails with less than 100 users, we were left with 18941, 3364, and 3165 subject lines respectively for Finance, Cosmetics, and Movies & Television.

4.2 Feature Extraction

This section provides an overview of the feature extraction process used to construct sets of meta-features (lengths and other counts), syntactic features (Parts-of-speech) and linguistic features (lexicon-based and data-driven) from the email and the clickbait datasets.

N-grams(3000 features): We use the bag-of-words representation to reduce the line of text in either dataset (either subject line or article headline) to a normalized frequency distribution over a vocabulary. Due to our sample size, we reduced the dimensionality of our n-gram feature space by retaining only the most frequent 1000 1-, 2-, and 3-grams each, used in at least 10% of the emails.

$$freq_{rel}(line, ng) = \frac{freq(line, ng)}{\sum_{ng' \in ngs} freq_{abs}(line, ng')} \qquad (2)$$

(GI) General Inquirer categorization (184 features): The General Inquirer lexicon [32] comprises over 15000 words arranged in 184 thematic categories[6], such as Social, Motion, Food, Power and Money. Each line in either dataset was thus represented in terms of the percentage proportions of the 184 lexicon categories within the General Inquirer.

Word2Vec embeddings(100 features): Data-driven topics are expected to be more representative of the short text in our datasets as compared to the General Inquirer dictionary. We represent subject lines through topic clusters of their neural embeddings trained on the skip-gram Word2Vec Twitter corpus [20], factorized using a word-context PMI matrix [17]. We use the Gensim implementation

[6]http://www.wjh.harvard.edu/ inquirer/homecat.htm

provided by [25] to generate 100 'topics' of closely related words.

Topic modeling (2000 features): A total 2000 social-media specific topics provided as an open-sourced resource by Schwartz et al. [29] are used for topic modeling. These topics were created from approximately 18 million Facebook updates, by using the Mallet package in Python to implement Latent Dirichlet Allocation (LDA) with the alpha set to 0.30 for the LDA computation in order to favor fewer topics per document. Each line in either dataset is transformed into 2000 features, derived from **a.** its probability of mentioning words, $p(word|line)$ and **b.** the probability of the words being in the given topics, $(p(topic|word))$. The distribution of topics for each line is thus calculated as:

$$p(topic|line) =$$
$$\sum_{word' \in topic} p(topic|word) \times p(word, line) \qquad (3)$$

where $p(topic|line)$ is the normalized word use in a line and $p(topic|word)$, the probability of the topic given the word, is provided by LDA. Furthermore, we use the joint probability, $p(word, topic)$, in order to determine a word's prevalence in a topic.

(POS) Part of Speech tagging (36 features): We extracted part of speech tags for each line using the TweetNLP tagger, which is trained on social media text [22].

Meta-feature extraction (13 features): We also mined the raw counts for character length and word count, number of punctuation marks, number of symbols and the presence or absence of personalization elements in the subject line (for example, the mention of the recipients' names).

5 PREDICTIVE PERFORMANCE

5.1 Clickthrough rate prediction

We used DLATK's implementation of Python's scikitlearn package [30] to model email clickthroughs in terms of the language of the subject lines. We conducted a five-fold cross-validated weighted linear regression on the dataset with Ridge, Elastic-net, and Lasso regularization. The performance is measured on the held-out sample by using the Mean Absolute Error (MAE) and the goodness-of-fit (R^2). To avoid overfitting, we use randomized principal component analysis (PCA) after filtering out any features which were not significantly correlated with the outcome in univariate regressions. We also set a feature occurrence threshold of 10% to discard sparse features. We have reported the results from Elastic Net regularization in the following section.

State-of-the-art model: We use the approach proposed by Balakrishnan and Parekh [2] and the average clickthrough rate over the entire dataset as our baseline models.

All our models improve upon the baselines – the mean click-through rate for the industry as well as the state-of-the-art model. Parts-of-speech were not useful for predicting email clickthroughs, which suggests that general structure of a subject line is somewhat similar across all emails. The General Inquirer model had an average goodness-of-fit of 0.31. A remarkable improvement is observed when data-driven features i.e. the topics and the top 1000 n-grams are used with an average goodness-of-fit of 0.45 and 0.58 respectively. Finally, we combined individual feature sets and obtained the best performances using models built on General Inquirer + n-grams, and topics + n-grams, with average goodness-of-fit of 0.52

Table 2: RMSE, MAE and R^2 results from Elastic Net regression on the held-out sample on different meta-, syntactic and linguistic feature sets. The best-performing predictor is built on topics + n-grams, with an MAE of 0.04.

	Feature Set	Baseline (Mean)	Balakrishnan & Parekh 2014	Meta-features	POS	GI	Word2Vec	Topics	N-grams	GI + N-grams	Topics + N-grams
Finance	RMSE	13.0	13.1	10.3	12.2	11.4	15.1	10.4	7.3	9.2	**7.1**
	MAE	11.1	11.0	10.3	10.5	9.1	12.1	7.0	5.3	6.0	**5.0**
	R^2	–	.09	.09	.15	.33	0.15	.45	.67	.56	**.69**
Cosmetics	RMSE	9.3	9.0	8.1	9.2	8.0	12.4	6.3	6.0	7.1	**6.0**
	MAE	6.4	7.2	6.1	6.0	6.3	9.1	5.5	4.0	5.3	**4.0**
	R^2	–	.06	.06	.11	.30	0.19	.50	.51	.47	**.56**
Movies	RMSE	8.1	9.2	8.4	9.3	7.0	9.4	5.0	5.1	6.2	**5.0**
&	MAE	6.0	7.1	6.2	6.4	5.3	7.1	4.3	4.4	4.1	**4.0**
Television	R^2	–	.06	.06	.14	.32	.17	.58	.63	.57	**.64**

and 0.64 respectively. Our Word2Vec topics did not yield promising results, perhaps because of the mismatch between training and test corpora.

5.2 Clickbait Detection

We compare the performance of an SVM classifier trained on topics + n-grams (our best performing feature set from Table 2) on the clickbait detection task, against the results reported by Chakraborty et. al [4] in Table 3. We report a 7.7% gain in recall, and a 4.8% gain in F1-score over their best performing SVM classifier. This exercise helps establish the validity of our approach across another similar task and a different, standardized dataset.

Table 3: Results on the Clickbait classification task, against the best–performing SVM classifier by Chakraborty et. al.

	Accuracy	Precision	Recall	F1 Score
[4]	0.93	0.95	0.90	0.93
N-grams	0.89	0.85	0.92	0.89
Topics + N-grams	**0.97**	**0.98**	**0.97**	**0.98**

6 LANGUAGE INSIGHTS

We conduct a regression analysis between all features sets, and the percentage user responses per subject line. We use least squares linear regression over standardized independent variables (linguistic and meta–features extracted from subject lines), which produces a standardized coefficient equivalent to Pearson's R correlation coefficients. All results are significant after Benjamini-Hochberg corrections for multiple comparisons.

Table 4 illustrates the textual features among meta-features and parts of speech, General Inquirer categories, n-grams and topics. The effect sizes for individual features ranged from −0.15 to 0.29 across the industries.

6.1.1. N-Grams: Figure 1 depicts the 1-to-3 grams with a) positive and b) negative Pearson correlation with clickthrough rate, represented as a word cloud. All the correlations were Bonferroni-corrected, and are significant at $p < 0.01$. The size of the word reflects a higher Pearson correlation with clickthrough rate, while a darker shade reflects a higher frequency in the dataset. In Cosmetics, words such as 'please' and phrases such as 'surprises!' led

to more clickthroughs; on the other hand, phrases mentioning discounts as '% off' were negatively correlated with clickthroughs. In Movies & Television, phrases such as 'might like' in the subject line were more likely to be clicked open, and subject lines mentioning news coverage or livestreaming footage ('is live!') were less likely to be clicked open. Likewise, for Finance we observed that subject lines with words such as 'statement' and 'card' were more likely while 'reward' was less likely to be clicked open.

6.1.2. General Inquirer: Power Gain (words about increasing power, or being powerful such as *emerge, ascend, appoint*) is positively correlated with clickthrough rates in Finance; on the other hand it is negatively correlated with clickthrough rates in Movies & Television. Food (*bacon, breakfast, cereal*) is correlated with higher clickthrough rates in Cosmetics; on the other hand, it is negatively correlated with clickthrough rates in the Movies & Television. Both Cosmetics and Movies & Television demonstrate a negative correlation of clickthrough rates with words depicting body parts (*arms, belly*).

6.1.3. Topics: Data-driven topics are helpful to contextualize the results from the n-gram analysis, as they provide an intermediate level of granularity between the two. Subject lines about saving on grocery shopping (*money, earn, pocket, savings*) are less likely to be clicked open for Finance, and subject lines about specific bathing products (*shampoo, make-up, soap*) are less likely to be clicked open in Cosmetics.

6.1.4. Parts of Speech and meta–features: Short and crisp subject lines devoid of punctuation are evidently preferred in the Finance industry, and are more likely to be clicked open; on the other hand, proper nouns perform well in Cosmetics, and possessive pronouns do well in Movies & Television.

7 DOMAIN ADAPTATION

In the previous section, we showed that the topics + n-grams model has the best in-domain prediction. The challenge arises for predictions for a different industry or a new business. Table 5 shows that predictive performance can drop by 85% on predictions on other domains and by up to 28% on unseen businesses. We diagnose these differences based on the very different regression coefficients for the same General Inquirer categories, in Table 4 and Figure 2. We address this problem by implementing an unsupervised and a supervised domain adaptation method and comparing the performance to the pre-domain adaptation step.

Table 4: Different copy-writing strategies succeed in different industries. Standardized regression coefficients (βs) between different features of subject lines, and email clickthroughs. All correlations are Bonferroni-corrected and significant at p < .000, two tailed t-test.

Finance		Cosmetics		Movies	
Feature Set	R^{**}	Feature Set	R^{**}	Feature Set	R^{**}
Topics					
false, rumors, statement etc.	.25	*wife, sweetheart, hubby* etc.	.28	*flick, horror, scary* etc.	.18
card, credit, sim, visa etc.	.21	*smile, compliment, stares* etc.	.08	*pause, button, snooze* etc.	.18
spree, grocery, shopping etc.	-.11	*sell, discount, item* etc.	-.05	*livestream, lifestyle* etc.	-.12
money, pocket, savings etc.	-.11	*shampoo, make-up, soap* etc.	-.05	*news, report, flash* etc.	-.18
General Inquirer					
Power Gain (*emerge, ascend etc.*)	.06	Food (*bacon, breakfast*)	.12	Commn Object (*content, check*)	.18
Social Relations (*accept, act*)	.05	Causal (*because, chance*)	.10	Communication (*account, address*)	.17
Positive (*create, achieve*)	-.10	Body Parts (*arms, belly*)	-.08	Food (*bacon, breakfast*)	-.09
Understatement (*few, hard*)	-.06	Virtue (*cute, desire*)	-.08	Power Gain (*emerge, ascend etc.*)	-.11
Parts of Speech & Meta-Features					
Word Count	-.11	Brackets	.17	Possessive Pronoun	.20
Verb	-.10	Proper Noun	.09	Verb, third person singular	.16
Currency	-.08	Present Tense	-.08	Numbers	-.12

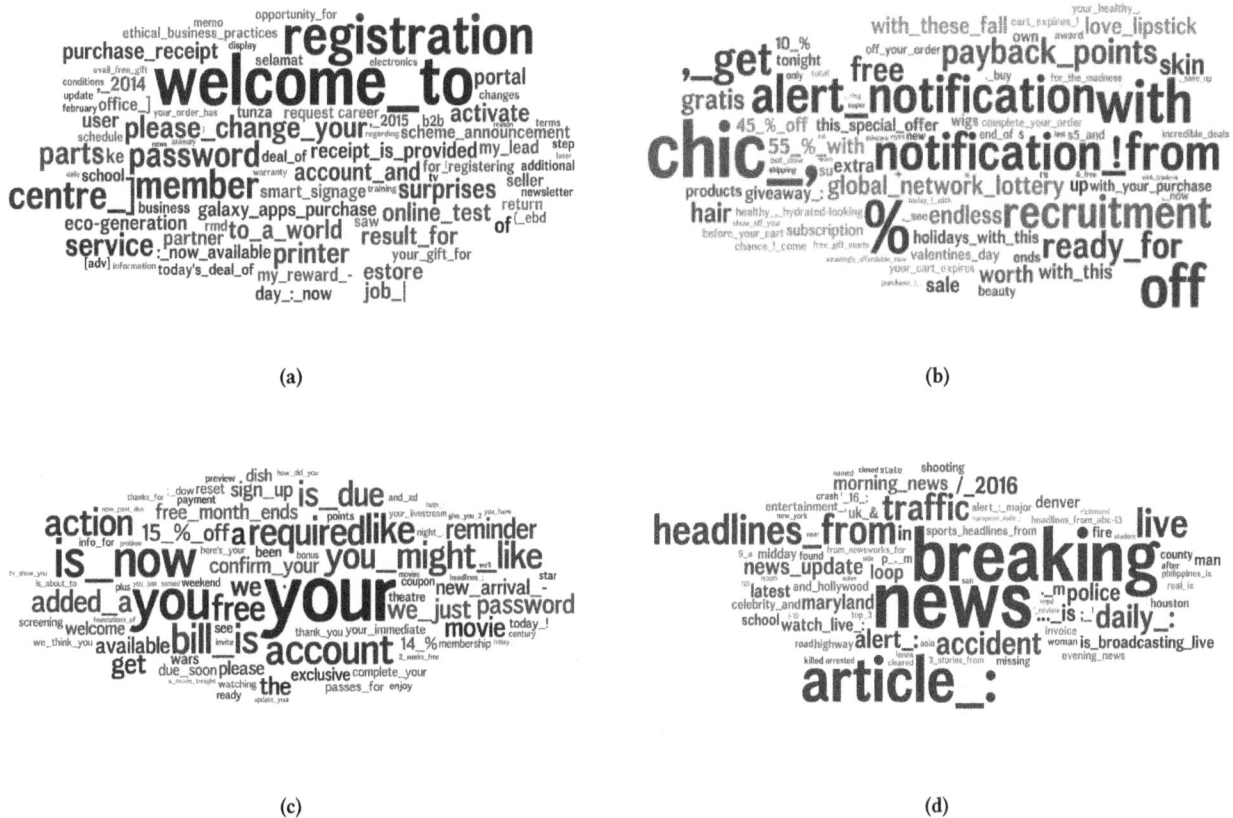

(a)

(b)

(c)

(d)

Figure 1: The word clouds show the ngrams that are significantly correlated with the clickthrough rate in the Cosmetics (a,b) and Movies (c,d) industry. The word clouds in blue and red represent the positively and negatively correlated words respectively. All the correlations were Bonferroni-corrected, and are significant at $p < 0.01$. The size of the word reflects a higher Pearson correlation with clickthrough rate, while a darker shade reflects a higher frequency in the dataset.

Table 5: Average out-of-domain prediction performance (RMSE) by the Topics + ngrams model from Table 2 over a five-fold cross-validation. Performance drops by up to 85% on out-of-domain predictions.

Training Set	In-domain RMSE	Out-of-domain RMSE		
I. Prediction on unseen domains				
		Finance	Cosmetics	Movies & TV
Finance	7.0	-	7.0	6.0
Cosmetics	6.0	13.0	-	6.0
Movies & TV	5.0	11.0	7.0	-
II. Prediction on unseen businesses				
Training Set	RMSE on Test Set			
		Business 1	Business 2	Business 3
Finance	7.0	9.0	9.0	10.0
Cosmetics	6.0	9.0	5.0	7.0
Movies & TV	5.0	5.0	5.0	6.0

7.1 Prediction on new businesses

Predictive performance also suffers when a model is used for prediction for unseen businesses within the same industry. Any model trained on an industry-wide dataset normalizes the effect of individual features across individual businesses. In Figure 2, we show the Hinton diagram of β values of a few significantly correlated General Inquirer features for specific businesses within the Finance industry as well as the industry overall. The area occupied by a square is proportional to the magnitude of the coefficient, and the color (green/red) indicates its sign (positive/negative). The variation in the values demonstrates the difference in the influence of features between businesses. For instance, the *Overstate* category has a large positive influence on the clickthrough rate for Business B, however, employing an industry-wide model would predict a decrease in clickthrough rate due to the normalization enforced in generic models. While a business specific model will nearly always perform better than an industry wide model, it is often not possible to train a separate model for every business due to unavailability of sufficient business specific data. Domain adaptive approaches would allow a generic industry-level predictive model to make better predictions for a business.

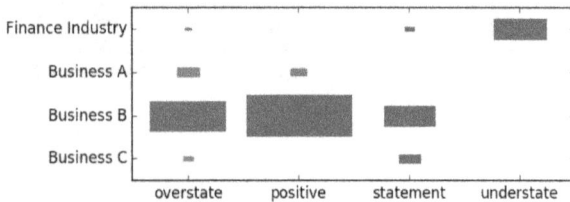

Figure 2: Different businesses in the same industry also pursue different copy-writing strategies. This Hinton diagram illustrates the β values for three different businesses within Finance for a few of the significant General Inquirer categories. The area occupied by a square is proportional to a value's magnitude, and the color (green/red) indicates its sign (positive/negative).

7.2 Domain–adaptation Methods

In the rest of this paper, we test two standard domain adaptation techniques for clickthrough rate prediction for unseen businesses within a particular industry domain. The first approach, Correlation Alignment (CORAL) [33], is an unsupervised approach which was developed for visual domain adaptation. The second approach, Easy Adapt [7], is a supervised approach that uses labeled data from both the source and the target to retrain a model.

7.2.1 CORAL. CORAL minimizes the distance (using the Frobenius norm) between the covariance matrices of the source and target features after the source domain is transformed [33].

$$\min_A ||C_{\hat{S}} - C_T||_F^2$$
$$= \min_A ||A^T C_S A - C_T||_F^2 \quad (4)$$

where $C_{\hat{S}}$ is covariance of the transformed source features $X_S A$, C_T is covariance of the target features, $X_T A$, and $||.||_F^2$ denotes the squared matrix Frobenius norm. The transformed feature matrices are computed in the following manner:

$$C_S = cov(X_S) + diag(size(X_S; 2))$$
$$C_T = cov(X_T) + diag(size(X_T; 2)) \quad (5)$$
$$A = X_S \times C_S^{\frac{-1}{2}} \times C_T^{\frac{1}{2}}$$

7.2.2 EasyAdapt. EasyAdapt is a supervised approach [7] to transform the source feature space. Let X denote the original feature space, $X = \mathbb{R}^F$. We construct an augmented feature space $\widetilde{X} = \mathbb{R}^{3F}$, by creating an industry-generic, industry\{business} and business-specific version of each feature in X. For this, we define $\Phi_{ind}, \Phi_{bus} : X \longrightarrow \widetilde{X}$ to transform feature vectors corresponding to the industry-wide and business-specific subject lines respectively. The mappings are defined by the following equation:

$$\Phi_{ind}(x) = \langle x, x, \mathbf{0} \rangle, \Phi_{bus}(x) = \langle x, \mathbf{0}, x \rangle \quad (6)$$

Here, $\mathbf{0} = \langle 0, 0, ..., 0 \rangle \in \mathbb{R}^F$ is the zero vector. Intuitively, the above transformation ensures that the model acknowledges that the same feature can have different effect on the clickthrough rate (characterized by the β values in linear regression) for different businesses.

7.3 Predictive Performance after Domain Adaptation

We train a regression model between the augmented feature space described above and the clickthrough rates per subject line. We use a corpora of 9 businesses across the three industries as the target domain set and report results from a 5–fold cross validation, comparing the MAEs and Root Mean Square Errors (RMSEs) obtained after domain adaptation, against the pre-domain adaptation condition: the best-performing predictive model (trained on the General Inquirer + n-grams features). Table 6 provides a summary of the domain adaptation results. CORAL models, being unsupervised, offers modest improvements over the pre-domain adapted models; on the other hand, supervised EasyAdapt models markedly outperform either of the previous models, with an average decrease of 16.52% in the RMSE and 19.2% in the MAE and offer significant improvements over the pre-domain adaptation condition for Finance and Cosmetics businesses. It should be kept in mind that the clickthrough rates of 95% of all emails lie within a 10% margin of error from the mean. This implies that even a 1% drop in MAE after Domain Adaptation is actually an appreciable improvement.

Table 6: Domain Adaptation results per industry, using three businesses each as unseen data. ** indicate that the model significantly improved over the pre-domain adaptation conditions in a two-tailed t-test, p < 0.01.

Finance								
Training Set		Test Set	Pre-Domain Adaptation		CORAL		EasyAdapt	
N_1 #(ind)	N_2 #(bus)	M	RMSE	MAE	RMSE	MAE	RMSE	MAE
5313	432	1728	9.7	6.6	8.0**	4.8	7.6**	4.6**
6059	707	707	9.8	7.4	8.9**	6.8**	8.3**	6.2**
6881	296	296	10.7	9.2	9.0**	7.0	8.3**	6.7**
Cosmetics								
Training Set		Test Set	Pre-Domain Adaptation		CORAL		EasyAdapt	
N_1 #(ind)	N_2 #(bus)	M	RMSE	MAE	RMSE	MAE	RMSE	MAE
991	360	360	9.7	7.4	9.2	7.0	8.9**	6.7**
1514	98	99	5.0	3.7	4.5	3.5	3.3**	2.7**
1644	33	34	6.7	5.3	6.5	5.2	6.2**	4.7**
Movies and Television								
Training Set		Test Set	Pre-Domain Adaptation		CORAL		EasyAdapt	
N_1 #(ind)	N_2 #(bus)	M	RMSE	MAE	RMSE	MAE	RMSE	MAE
2057	227	228	5.6	4.8	5.5	4.5	4.8**	3.9**
2412	40	160	3.6	2.9	3.5	2.9	3.1**	2.4**
2057	166	389	6.1	5.1	6.0	5.0	5.4**	4.3**

We can visualize the implications of these changes in terms of the differences in feature coefficients (β values) before and after the better performing domain adaptation approach – EasyAdapt – is implemented. The Figure 3 demonstrates the change in the β values of a few features for the business-specific model after implementing EasyAdapt, compared to the original industry-specific model for Finance. As before, the area occupied by a square is proportional to a value's magnitude, and the color (green/red) indicates its sign (positive/negative). Consider the feature *Individuals* that has no effect on the clickthrough rate according to the industry specific model, but a large positive impact according to the business-specific model.

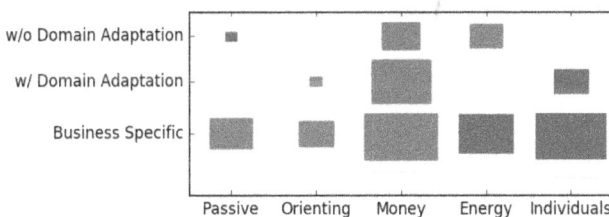

Figure 3: After domain adaptation: Hinton diagram for the β coefficients of business specific model, domain adaptation model and the industry model for a particular business in the Finance industry. Some features have no effect on the clickthrough rate according to the industry-specific model, but a large positive impact according to the business-specific model.

8 DISCUSSION AND CONCLUSION

Our paper presents the first multi-domain study treating language use in subject lines as a factor for inferring the clickthrough rate of promotional emails. We have framed prediction as a linear regression problem. Our results highlight the advantages of data-driven topic modeling in short text corpora. We also use language insights to distinguish the successful copywriting strategies in different domains and highlight the need for domain adaptation in language modeling for this problem. We implement a supervised and an unsupervised domain adaptation approach involving feature space transformations for incorporating out-of-domain data points. Not surprisingly, the supervised domain adaptation approach performs better than the unsupervised approach and considerably improves clickthrough rate prediction for unseen businesses by an average of 19%. The domain adaptation techniques ensure that the model learns a positive β value for the *Individuals* feature, by using the same industry-wide dataset. This explains how a domain adaptive approach allows a predictive model to better emulate a business' data, thereby improving its prediction accuracy for subject line clickthroughs.

In future work, we plan to apply our findings in generative models for email subject line and news headline recommendations. Our results also suggest that language modeling is useful in other downstream applications in the area of marketing.

REFERENCES

[1] Douglas Aberdeen, Ondrej Pacovsky, and Andrew Slater. 2010. The learning behind gmail priority inbox. In *LCCC: NIPS 2010 Workshop on Learning on Cores, Clusters and Clouds.*
[2] Raju Balakrishnan and Rajesh Parekh. 2014. Learning to predict subject-line opens for large-scale email marketing. In *Big Data (Big Data), 2014 IEEE International Conference on.* IEEE, 579–584.
[3] Jonas Nygaard Blom and Kenneth Reinecke Hansen. 2015. Click bait: Forward-reference as lure in online news headlines. *Journal of Pragmatics* 76 (2015), 87–100.
[4] Abhijnan Chakraborty, Bhargavi Paranjape, Sourya Kakarla, and Niloy Ganguly. 2016. Stop Clickbait: Detecting and preventing clickbaits in online news media. In *Advances in Social Networks Analysis and Mining (ASONAM), 2016 IEEE/ACM International Conference on.* IEEE, 9–16.
[5] Yi-Ting Chen and Hung-Yu Kao. 2013. Constructing Social Intentional Corpora to Predict Click-Through Rate for Search Advertising.. In *ROCLING.*
[6] Haibin Cheng and Erick Cantu-Paz. 2010. Personalized click prediction in sponsored search. In *Proceedings of the third ACM international conference on Web search and data mining.* ACM, 351–360.
[7] Hal Daumé III. 2009. Frustratingly easy domain adaptation. *arXiv preprint arXiv:0907.1815* (2009).
[8] Kushal S Dave and Vasudeva Varma. 2010. Learning the click-through rate for rare/new ads from similar ads. In *Proceedings of the 33rd international ACM SIGIR conference on Research and development in information retrieval.* ACM, 897–898.
[9] Dotan Di Castro, Zohar Karnin, Liane Lewin-Eytan, and Yoelle Maarek. 2016. You've got mail, and here is what you could do with it!: Analyzing and predicting actions on email messages. In *Proceedings of the Ninth ACM International Conference on Web Search and Data Mining.* ACM, 307–316.
[10] Ana Ferreira and Rui Chilro. 2017. What to Phish in a Subject?. In *International Conference on Financial Cryptography and Data Security.* Springer, 597–609.
[11] Alison Gianotto. 2014. Downworthy: A browser plugin to turn hyperbolic viral headlines into what they really mean. *downworthy. snipe. net* (2014).
[12] Qi Guo, Eugene Agichtein, Charles LA Clarke, and Azin Ashkan. 2008. Understanding abandoned ads: towards personalized commercial intent inference via mouse movement analysis. *Information Retrieval in Advertising* (2008).
[13] Qi Guo, Eugene Agichtein, Charles LA Clarke, and Azin Ashkan. 2009. In the mood to click? Towards inferring receptiveness to search advertising. In *Proceedings of the IEEE/WIC/ACM International Joint Conferences on Web Intelligence and Intelligent Agent Technologies*, Vol. 1. IEEE, 319–324.
[14] Simon Jones, Stephen Payne, Ben Hicks, James Gopsill, and Christopher Snider. 2015. Subject lines as sensors: co-word analysis of email to support the management of collaborative engineering work. In *International Conference on Engineering Design 2015 (ICED 2015).* University of Bath.

[15] Rebeca San José-Cabezudo and Carmen Camarero-Izquierdo. 2012. Determinants of opening-forwarding e-mail messages. *Journal of Advertising* 41, 2 (2012), 97–112.

[16] Sungchul Kim, Tao Qin, Tie-Yan Liu, and Hwanjo Yu. 2014. Advertiser-centric approach to understand user click behavior in sponsored search. *Information Sciences* 276 (2014), 242–254.

[17] Omer Levy and Yoav Goldberg. 2014. Dependency-Based Word Embeddings.. In *ACL (2).* 302–308.

[18] Kwan Hui Lim, Ee-Peng Lim, Binyan Jiang, and Palakorn Achananuparp. 2016. Using online controlled experiments to examine authority effects on user behavior in email campaigns. In *Proceedings of the 27th ACM Conference on Hypertext and Social Media.* ACM, 255–260.

[19] Xiao Luo, Revanth Nadanasabapathy, A Nur Zincir-Heywood, Keith Gallant, and Janith Peduruge. 2015. Predictive Analysis on Tracking Emails for Targeted Marketing. In *International Conference on Discovery Science.* Springer, 116–130.

[20] Tomas Mikolov, Ilya Sutskever, Kai Chen, Greg S Corrado, and Jeff Dean. 2013. Distributed representations of words and phrases and their compositionality. In *Advances in neural information processing systems.* 3111–3119.

[21] R Miller and EYA Charles. 2016. A psychological based analysis of marketing email subject lines. In *Advances in ICT for Emerging Regions (ICTer), 2016 Sixteenth International Conference on.* IEEE, 58–65.

[22] Olutobi Owoputi, Brendan O'Connor, Chris Dyer, Kevin Gimpel, Nathan Schneider, and Noah A Smith. 2013. Improved part-of-speech tagging for online conversational text with word clusters. Association for Computational Linguistics.

[23] Joseph E Phelps, Regina Lewis, Lynne Mobilio, David Perry, and Niranjan Raman. 2004. Viral marketing or electronic word-of-mouth advertising: Examining consumer responses and motivations to pass along email. *Journal of advertising research* 44, 4 (2004), 333–348.

[24] Martin Potthast, Sebastian Köpsel, Benno Stein, and Matthias Hagen. 2016. Clickbait detection. In *European Conference on Information Retrieval.* Springer, 810–817.

[25] Daniel Preoţiuc-Pietro, Vasileios Lampos, and Nikolaos Aletras. 2015. An analysis of the user occupational class through Twitter content. The Association for Computational Linguistics.

[26] Rui Filipe Cerqueira Quaresma, Sílvia Paula Rosa da Silva, and Cristina Galamba Marreiros. 2013. E-mail usage practices in an organizational context: a study with Portuguese workers. *JISTEM-Journal of Information Systems and Technology Management* 10, 1 (2013), 5–20.

[27] Matthew Richardson, Ewa Dominowska, and Robert Ragno. 2007. Predicting clicks: estimating the click-through rate for new ads. In *Proceedings of the 16th international conference on World Wide Web.* ACM, 521–530.

[28] Navdeep S Sahni, S Christian Wheeler, and Pradeep K Chintagunta. 2016. Personalization in Email Marketing: The Role of Non-Informative Advertising Content. (2016).

[29] H Andrew Schwartz, Johannes C Eichstaedt, Margaret L Kern, Lukasz Dziurzynski, Stephanie M Ramones, Megha Agrawal, Achal Shah, Michal Kosinski, David Stillwell, Martin EP Seligman, et al. 2013. Personality, gender, and age in the language of social media: The open-vocabulary approach. *PloS one* 8, 9 (2013), e73791.

[30] H Andrew Schwartz, Salvatore Giorgi, Maarten Sap, Patrick Crutchley, Lyle Ungar, and Johannes Eichstaedt. 2017. DLATK: Differential Language Analysis ToolKit. In *Proceedings of the 2017 Conference on Empirical Methods in Natural Language Processing: System Demonstrations.* 55–60.

[31] Dong-Her Shih, Hsiu-Sen Chiang, and C David Yen. 2005. Classification methods in the detection of new malicious emails. *Information Sciences* 172, 1-2 (2005), 241–261.

[32] Philip J Stone, Dexter C Dunphy, and Marshall S Smith. 1966. The General Inquirer: A Computer Approach to Content Analysis. (1966).

[33] Baochen Sun, Jiashi Feng, and Kate Saenko. 2015. Return of frustratingly easy domain adaptation. *arXiv preprint arXiv:1511.05547* (2015).

[34] E Vance Wilson, Adrienne Hall-Phillips, and Soussan Djamasbi. 2015. Cognitive predictors of consumers' intention to comply with social marketing email appeals. 52 (2015), 307–314.

Quest for the Gold Par: Minimizing the Number of Gold Questions to distinguish between the Good and the Bad

Kinda El Maarry
Institute for Information Systems
Technische Universität Braunschweig
Braunschweig, Germany
elmaarry@ifis.cs.tu-bs.de

Wolf-Tilo Balke
Institute for Information Systems
Technische Universität Braunschweig
Braunschweig, Germany
balke@ifis.cs.tu-bs.de

ABSTRACT

The benefits of crowdsourcing for data science have furthered its widespread use over the past decade. Yet fraudulent workers undermine the emerging crowdsourcing economy: requestors face the choice of either risking low quality results or having to pay extra money for quality safeguards like e.g., gold questions or majority voting. Obviously, the more safeguards injected into the workload, the lower the risks imposed by fraudulent workers, yet the higher the costs are. So, how many of them are really needed? Is there such a 'one size fits all' number? The aim of this paper is to identify *custom-tailored numbers of gold questions per worker* for managing the cost/quality balance. Our new method follows real life experiences: the more we know about workers before assigning a task, the clearer our belief or disbelief in this worker's reliability gets. Employing probabilistic models, namely Bayesian belief networks and certainty factor models, our method creates worker profiles reflecting different a-priori belief values, and we prove that the actual number of gold questions per worker can indeed be assessed. Our evaluation on real-world crowdsourcing datasets demonstrates our method's efficiency in saving money while maintaining high quality results. Moreover, our methods performs well despite the quite limited information known about workers in today's platforms.

ACM Reference Format:
Kinda El Maarry and Wolf-Tilo Balke 2018. Quest for the Gold Par: Minimizing the Number of Gold Questions to distinguish between the Good and the Bad. In WebSci '18: 10th ACM Conference on Web Science, May 27–30, 2018, Amsterdam, Netherlands. ACM, New York, NY, USA, 10 pages. http://dx.doi.org/10.1145/3201064.3201073

KEYWORDS

Crowdsourcing; quality control; worker-awareness; gold questions

1. INTRODUCTION

In recent years, several hybrid solutions for augmenting and extending traditional database capabilities with intelligent human steering have been developed. For example: 1) processing queries that can't be adequately answered by database systems [5], such as skyline queries [11], top-k and group-by queries [3], [27], and 2) dealing with missing information [17]. The benefits for data science come as no surprise, since crowdsourcing is relatively cheap, agile, and offers an intelligent and global 24/7 online labor pool.

Yet the anonymity of workers on the platforms and the short-term nature of the work contracts also invite *fraudulent misuse* threatening to cancel the benefits. In contrast to traditional work places, crowdsourcing requestors don't know much about the workers they're hiring: there is no interview process, no CVs, no personal impressions. In the best case for crowdsourcing, platforms offer *reputation scores* from previous work. Unfortunately, it has been shown that reputation systems only work for *long standing* relationships. As an analogy, remember peer-to-peer networks: also here reputation systems have been proposed to combat malicious peer behavior, see e.g., [1], [8]. But meaningful scores were difficult to construct, since reputations suffered from the cold start problem [2] and were easy to fake [26]. These problems become even more pronounced in crowdsourcing due to the high attrition rates of workers ([22] reports about 70%), i.e. relationships tend to be *even more short-termed* than in peer-to-peer systems. Hence, crowdsourcing requestors usually favor on-the-run methods to instantly judge workers leveraging the limited amount of information provided.

For the rest of this paper and without loss of generality we will focus only on *gold questions* as a quality mechanism, i.e. questions whose correct answers are actually known to the requestor and where failing to answer a preset number of them indicates fraud. Until now the problem of "how many gold questions to use?" has no definitive answer [15]. Obviously, there is a cost/quality trade-off: the more gold questions are used, the better the output's quality will be, yet the higher the costs are. If too many gold questions are posed, after a certain number of questions the returned benefit becomes minimal and the costs become unjustifiably high. On the other hand, if too little gold questions are posed, the returned result remains inconclusive in determining the worker's reliability or fraudulence. Moreover, what might be considered excessively many gold questions for one worker, might still be too little for some other worker. In real life interviewers may for instance dig deeper whenever an applicant only has qualifications from non-prestigious institutions. Similarly, more gold questions should be asked to workers who come at a higher risk and vice versa.

In this paper, we develop a *worker-aware ad hoc method that exploits the limited information known about the short-term hired workers*. We transform this information into a digital personal impression indicating whether a worker matches the profiles of fraudulent or reliable workers. Profiles of fraudulent workers come at a higher risk, and should then be tested more rigorously, where areas profiles of reliable workers come at a lower risk, and need only be loosely tested. This reasoning of whether a worker matches a fraudulent high risk profile or that of an honest low risk profile is done under uncertainty, i.e. it is uncertain how such digital impressions of workers in fact relate to their reliability or fraudulence, which simultaneously leads to an uncertain representation.

Accordingly, for our method's technical implementation we turn to well established approaches for uncertainty management. Namely, we investigate the usage of both: 1) probabilistic certainty factor models [24] pioneered for uncertain deduction of diagnoses by medical expert systems. Basically, the model reflects the *relative change of belief and/or disbelief* in some hypothesis given new observations, i.e. in our case the relative change in the high/low risk associated with a worker. 2) Bayesian Belief Networks, which express uncertainty through probabilities. Using either of these models allows to build a system of decision rules, which create digital impressions of each worker and what we refer to as *enhanced worker profiles*. These worker profiles do not only encode what is known about a worker, but also assess the risks involved with a worker by either 1) relative a-priori belief or disbelief measures as given by the certainty factor model or 2) probabilities as given by the Bayesian belief network.

The underlying idea is that the higher the belief value or the probability in a worker's reliability, the lower the risk, and the less gold questions may be used. The higher the disbelief value or the lower the probability in a worker's reliability, the higher the risk, and the more gold questions should be used. By personalizing the number of questions to be asked based on these enhanced profiles, we can then save some money, while maintaining a high level of result quality. To realize this underlying idea, we identify the exact number of gold questions to be asked (the '*gold par*'), by fitting an exponential distribution of number of questions to be asked on top of the values of belief/disbelief and probabilities. We demonstrate the applicability of our method on real world crowdsourcing test data of 200 workers and compare how well it performs in terms of overall result quality, effectiveness of the algorithm, fraud detection's failure rates, and discrimination rates against reliable workers. Our contributions can be summarized as follows:

1. To the best of our knowledge, this is the first *anonymized, yet worker-aware safeguard method* that dynamically adapts the number of questions needed to assess the reliability of current workers. We compare our work against the *rule of thumb* for the optimal number of gold questions provided in [15].
2. We provide requestors with a personalized database of *enhanced worker profiles* associated with probabilities and belief/disbelief values, where these profiles change depending on the individual requirements of the different requestors.
3. We define a method for determining *each worker's gold par*, that is, a sufficient number of gold questions such that costs are controlled, while maintaining high quality results.
4. We show enhanced worker profiles to be effective even facing the *limited amount* of information about workers available. We use only four common attributes: country, crowdsourcing channel workers are signed up to, time they initiated the task, and a trust value based on the last task as given by platforms.

2. SAFE GUARDS IN PRACTICE

Many safeguards for quality issues in crowdsourcing systems have been investigated. We identify four families of safeguards:

Pessimistic safeguards ensure high quality by directly identifying fraudulent workers and excluding them. The most common approach in this family are *gold questions* randomly injected into the workload. Failing to answer a preset number of these questions (whose correct answers are known by the system),

declares the corresponding worker as fraudulent, in turn leading to exclusion. These safeguards are typically *worker-oblivious*, i.e. no distinction in the underlying testing mechanism is made for different workers. A notable exception are skill-adapted gold questions [13] and adaptive gold questions [12], which aim at adapting gold questions to the underlying skills of workers for a fairer judgement of workers in alignment with the vision of impact sourcing.

Optimistic safeguards ensure high quality by aggregating the results of multiple workers on a given task. The best known aggregation method here is *majority voting*. Other weighted aggregation methods in the literature include the expectation maximization (EM) algorithm [4], a Bayesian version of the EM algorithm [19], and a probabilistic approach in [25]. This family is more *worker-aware*, as it tries to identify the workers' reliability and may distinguish different levels of skills, which can then be incorporated as weights in the final step of aggregation.

Feedback-based safeguards ensure high quality by monitoring the history of workers and their outputs' feedback [7], thus making it also a *worker-aware* family of safeguards. A typical example of this family is *reputation-based systems*, whether based on a reputation model [10-11], or on deterministic approaches [18].

Incentive-based safeguards ensure high quality by motivating the workers either intrinsically or extrinsically [6]. Intrinsic refers to motivations inherent to the task itself, e.g. Zooniverse[1]. Extrinsic refers to external motivations that offer some kind of reward, e.g. monetary rewards [9].

Our proposed method falls under the *pessimistic safeguard* family, but is a *worker-aware* method. Moreover, in contrast to the pessimistic safeguards, our method is designed to adapt to each new worker, by re-computing the sufficient number of gold questions needed to distinguish between reliable and fraudulent workers.

The most relevant work on adaptive quality control is [15] who investigate the universal number of gold questions needed. Although they concluded that the problem is unlikely to reach a definitive answer, their work provides a *rule of thumb* for the optimal number of gold questions to be used: either *linearly with* or following the *order of the square root* of the total size of the task given to a worker. The choice of either rule of thumb depends on the corresponding level of aggregation used: two-stage or joint inference. Since this is closest to our work, we designated it as baseline and compared our results against the order of the square root scaling rule for the optimal number of questions to be used. We compare among others the overall number of gold questions needed, overall accuracy rate of the gold questions as a safeguard for distinguishing between reliable and fraudulent workers (see Section 5).

3. CREATING WORKER PROFILES

We can formally define the problem in a concise manner as follows

Problem Definition – Given a crowdsourcing task T comprising n questions, we want to find the minimal number of gold questions m, such that $0 < m < n$ needed to determine the reliability of a given worker w. A reliable worker is defined as a worker, whose accuracy rate on a crowdsourcing task > 0.75

---

[1] https://www.zooniverse.org/

Our method can be divided into three basic steps:

1. Creating a system of *decision rules*: the enhanced worker profiles. For building these profiles and their corresponding encoding of involved risks, we experiment with two approaches: a) Bayesian belief networks, which encode risks with probabilities and b) certainty factor models, which encode risks with relative a-priori measures of belief and disbelief. We turned to both of these models, as they are well-established approaches for uncertainty management. The uncertainty in our problem materializes in our attempt to reason whether a new incoming worker is reliable or not based on uncertain knowledge.
2. Identifying the minimum required number of gold questions for each enhanced worker profile, the *gold par*.
3. Mapping the workers to their corresponding enhanced profile.

In this section, we focus on the first step of creating enhanced worker profiles; Section 4 covers the second and third step. Starting with certainty factor models and Bayesian belief networks, we map and redefine both models' parameters to our crowdsourcing setup.

3.1 The Certainty Factor Model – (CF)

The probabilistic certainty factor model (*CFM*) was first developed by [23] for MYCIN, a medical expert system employing certainty factors (*CF*) for uncertain deduction within heuristic systems.

In essence, *CF*s do not correspond to probabilities, but rather depict the relative change of belief and/or disbelief in some hypothesis H given a certain observation E. The combinations of these **Measures of Belief** $MB(H|E)$ and **Disbelief** $MD(H|E)$ constitutes the *CF*s. These measures are relatives and are not to be confused with probabilities. Nevertheless, their values are normalized to span between [0,1], with 1 representing the highest belief or disbelief with respect to a certain hypothesis H, and 0 representing the lowest belief or disbelief, again with respect to a certain hypothesis H. Moreover, these measures are individually observed, i.e. for $MB(H|E) = x$ and $MD(H|E) = y \nRightarrow x + y = 1$

Definition 1- MB, MD and CF
Given an observation E and a Hypothesis H, we can compute the $MB(H|E)$, $MD(H|E)$, and the $CF(H|E)$

$$MB(H|E) = \begin{cases} \dfrac{max[P(H|E),P(H)] - P(H)}{1 - P(H)} &, if \ P(H) \neq 1 \\ 1 &, otherwise \end{cases}$$

$$MD(H|E) = \begin{cases} \dfrac{P(H) - min[P(H|E),P(H)]}{P(H)} &, if \ P(H) \neq 0 \\ 1 &, otherwise \end{cases}$$

$$CF(H|E) = MB(H|E) - MD(H|E)$$

In other words, $CF(H|E)$ can also be formulated as follows:

$$CF(H|E) = \begin{cases} \dfrac{P(H|E) - P(H)}{1 - P(H)} &, if \ P(H|E) \geq P(H), P(H) \neq 1 \\ \dfrac{P(H|E) - P(H)}{P(H)} &, if \ P(H) \geq P(H|E), P(H) \neq 0 \end{cases}$$

The *CF* rules' value span between [-1.0, 1.0]. Subsequently we distinguish two types of rules: 1) Confirming *CF* rules: are those having a high measure of belief, i.e. positive certainty factor

value $CF(H|E) \geq 0$, 2) Disconfirming CF rules: are those having a high measure of disbelief, i.e. negative certainty factor value $CF(H|E) < 0$.

Given a set of CF rules, new rules/deductions can be automatically drawn: 1) chaining and 2) parallel combination. The latter is of particular interest: it consolidates different observations leading to the same hypothesis. This allow us to create more complex *CF* rules, which combine several independent observations. Parallel combination can be efficiently computed from the rules directly, that is, there is no need to go back to the data for computations.

Definition 2- Deduction by Parallel Combination:
Given two CF rules: $CF_{E_1}(H)$ and $CF_{E_2}(H)$, where two observations E_1 and E_2 lead to the same Hypothesis H.

A new $CF_{E_1 E_2}(H)$ can be deduced by parallel combination as follows:

$$CF_{E_1 E_2}(H) = \begin{cases} x + y - x * y, & for \ x \geq 0, y \geq 0 \\ x + y + x * y, & for \ x \leq 0, y \leq 0 \\ \dfrac{x + y}{1 - min(|x|, |y|)}, & for \ -1 < x * y < 0 \end{cases}$$
$, where \ x = CF_{E_1}(H) \ and \ y = CF_{E_2}(H)$.

In case of combining more than two *CF* rules with different observations, the above definition applies by taking the result of the first two combined *CF* rules and designating it as x when combining it with the next *CF* rule and so on [16].

3.2 Bayesian Belief Network – (BN)
Bayes nets belong to the family of probabilities graphic models and are used to represent/infer knowledge about an uncertain domain [19-20]. Rather similar to our crowdsourcing problem, Bayes nets have been applied to the target recognition problems, where transponders should be identified as Friend or Foe [10].

Bayes nets encode a directed acyclic graph G. The directed property of the graph complies with our problem, since our underlying idea is that observing certain attributes of the workers lead to a certain belief value in the reliability of a worker. Accordingly, this directed relationship from the observations to the hypothesis can be represented in Bayes Nets with a directed graph .

Formally, Bayes nets B is given by the pair $B = \langle G, \theta \rangle$. The graph G is made up of set of random Variables V , depicted by n nodes $x_1, x_2, ..., x_n$, and directed edges $E: x_i \rightarrow x_j$. The underlying semantics of Bayes nets, namely, the *local markov property* defines an ordering of the nodes such that only the nodes indexed lower than i can have a directed path to x_i. The nodes are the worker's observations and the hypothesis to be inferred, i.e. the reliability of the worker. There are different types of nodes: Root, Parent and Child nodes. The edges E represent the probabilistic dependency between the nodes. For discrete variables, the relationship between them is given by the conditional probability distribution. The second parameter θ depicts the full joint distribution as follows:

Definition 3- Full Joint distribution of BN:
The full joint distribution for a Bayes nets B having n nodes $x_1, x_2, ..., x_n$, can defined by the product of the local conditional distributions

$$P(x_1, x_2, ..., x_n) = \prod_{1 \leq i \leq n} P(x_i | Parents(x_i))$$

There are two types of reasoning: *Predictive support* and *diagnostic support*. Predictive support is a top-down reasoning starting from the parents' node to the child node, while diagnostic reasoning is a bottom-up reasoning starting from the child node. Since our aim is to infer whether a worker is reliable, i.e. inferring the child node/hypothesis, we follow the predictive support inference (see Definition 4). In our crowdsourcing setup, the random variables V are the workers' observations and are depicted by the parent nodes. The parent nodes in our case also happen to be the root nodes, since they have no predecessor nodes, while the hypothesis is the child node. Each root node has a prior probability distribution.

Definition 4- Inferencing in BN:

We can infer the strength of our hypothesis H having seen a worker's observation E using the Bayes nets conditional probability formula

$$P(child|parent) = \frac{P(child, parent)}{P(parent)}$$

i.e.

$$P(H|E) = \frac{P(H, E)}{P(E)}$$

3.3 Formulating the Hypothesis: *H*

For our crowdsourcing setup, the hypothesis is always the same. Namely, given a pool of workers W, a worker $w \in W$ is a reliable worker. It follows then that workers fitting low risk profiles (i.e. profiles with a positive CF value, where $MB(H|E) > MD(H|E)$ or profiles with P (H|E) >= 0.5) come at lower risk, while those fitting high risk profiles (i.e. profiles with a negative CF value, where $MB(H|E) < MD(H|E)$ or profiles with P (H|E) < 0.5) come at higher risk (more on how to map a worker to a worker profile is explained in Section 4.2). But the question of how to define such a reliable worker instantly arises. The difficulty of this question lies within the scarcity of the data the requestor has on a particular worker, who is more often than not, a new worker. Currently, the only ad hoc quantitative metric available to the requestors is the accuracy rate of a worker on the gold questions.

In general, we seek workers whose overall accuracy rate is higher than 75%. An initial correlation investigation between the accuracy rate on the gold questions and the overall accuracy rate on the whole task shows, as expected, a high positive correlation of 0.7 (see Figure 1). Outliers can also be observed, which is attributed to: 1) strategic spammer schemes, where they always submit the frequent answer label, 2) inherently small crowdsourcing tasks, e.g. 5 tasks and 1 gold question. We ran this experiment on real crowdsourcing datasets comprised of 1006 workers, with 40% gold questions (see Section 5.1).

Accordingly, we generally define the hypothesis that a worker is reliable, if he/she attains at least 75% accuracy rate on the gold questions. Eventually however, workers fitting low risk profiles are assigned lesser gold questions, while workers fitting high risk profiles are assigned more gold questions. Consequently, we vary the expected quality thresholds such that workers fitting the disconfirming profile with the lowest value i.e. $CF(H|E) \rightarrow -1.0$ or P (H|E) = 0, should attain at least 75% quality rate, while workers fitting profiles with higher values should attain higher quality

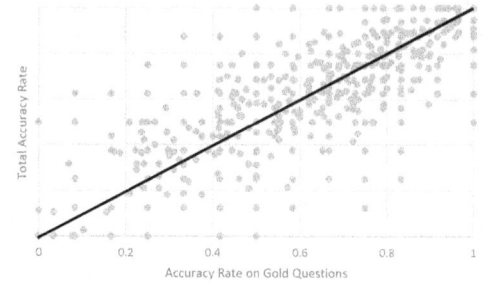

Figure 1. Correlation between workers' gold question's accuracy and overall accuracy rate

rates. The idea is to decrease the discrimination rate against workers fitting high risk profiles, while still maintaining the threshold quality. On the other hand, workers fitting low risk profiles should prove their reliability even more so by scoring higher quality thresholds. Thus, we uniformly fit the quality thresholds to be attained on the belief/disbelief values and probabilities, such that the thresholds range between 75% - 100%, where the high risk worker profile: $CF(H|E) \rightarrow -1.0$ or P (H|E) = 0 should attain at least 75% accuracy rate on gold questions to be considered reliable, while the low risk worker profile: $CF(H|E) \rightarrow 1.0$ or P (H|E) = 1 should attain a perfect 100% accuracy rate to be considered reliable. In practice, such a perfect profile doesn't exist.

3.4 Formulating the Observations: *E*

Observations capture the limited information we know about workers. Of course, all attributes available in crowdsourcing platforms can and should be exploited for best discrimination accuracy. As all crowdsourcing tasks were run on the CrowdFlower[2] platform (see Section 5.2), below we list the publicly available attributes offered by CrowdFlower. For each attribute we also investigated its domain to find out which of its instances should be considered as an observation. An attribute's instance is a valid observation if it is *frequent*, since both CF rules and the Bayesian conditional probabilities becomes unreliable if based on sparse observations.

1. *Channel:* There are 30 different crowdsourcing channels, from which workers are hired. Only 8 channels, however, are dominating our labor quota, leaving 22 channels providing only around 4.3% of the total workforce (see Figure 2). Accordingly, we only use the top 8 channels as observations, which constitute 95.6% of the data.

2. *Country:* In total, we have workers from 75 different countries. Figure 3 shows a clear Zipfian distribution, with 85% of workers coming from only 24 countries. We limit our observation to these 24 countries ignoring the distribution's tail.

3. *Started_at:* this attribute marks the time (GMT) at which a worker started working. On its own, this attribute wouldn't make much sense, but rather in combination with the country, since it would indicate whether working in the morning, evening or night is more reliable. As seen in Figure 4, about 88.7% of the workers worked between 08 am -18pm. We used these hours for our observations.

---

[2] https://www.crowdflower.com/

4. *City:* the city attribute proved too sparse, as it is only available for 71% of the workers (i.e. 716 workers). Moreover, it exhibited an extremely long-tailed distribution of 462 cities. The head of the distribution on the other hand had two cities: Caracas and Belgrade, comprising 7% of the workers. Accordingly, we chose to disregard the city attribute all together as a discriminating observation.

5. *Trust:* the trust attribute ranges between 0.0 and 1.0 and is computed by the platform based on the last task a worker performed. For this attribute, all values proved sensible to be taken as observations. We aggregated the values by grouping them into intervals of 0.1, thus yielding 10 values of trust.

Over all, our models' observations comprise 8 channels, 8 different hours to work within, 24 countries and 10 levels of trust.

4. TOWARDS THE GOLD PAR
After computing the enhanced worker profiles, the next step is to determine how many gold questions are sufficient per profile, depending on the profiles' encoded risk.

4.1 Mapping Profiles to the Gold Par
Following our notion that low risk workers should be asked lesser gold questions than high risk workers, both the uniform and the exponential distribution could mimic this notion when fitted on top of the enhanced worker profiles, such that at the worst case scenario, e.g. $CF(H|E) \rightarrow -1.0$, 50% gold questions should be asked, and at the best case scenario, e.g. $CF(H|E) \rightarrow 1.0$, only 1 gold question needs to be asked. Note that such a perfect profile doesn't exist in practice. The exponential distribution however has a lower discrimination rate than the uniform distribution, since low risk workers are given more gold questions, thus more chances, to break away from their high risk profile. Moreover, the exponential distribution also takes into account, that gold questions could be imbalanced and that some of them might be more difficult .i.e. honest workers fitting high risk profiles might end up getting the short end of the stick. Whereas, workers fitting low risk profiles get exponentially lesser questions, which also decreases the overall costs of utilizing safeguards.

Experimenting with various exponential distributions having different rate parameters yielded the best results with the exponential distribution $\mathcal{F}(x, \lambda) = \lambda e^{-x\lambda}$, where $\lambda = 2$ (see Figure 5). As discussed in Section in 3.3, although workers fitting low risk profiles get lesser number of gold questions, they are expected to score higher accuracy rates. This is similar to real world situations, where workers compete with front runners in their field.

4.2 Mapping Workers to their Profile
After computing the enhanced worker profiles for all the different observations and for all the different combination of observations, these profiles could be stored in a database, against which new incoming workers can be mapped to. The mapping of a new worker to a profile is based on the matching of observations. Since we combine observations to create more complex profiles, a worker may fit multiple profiles which could be low risk or high risk. There are multiple strategies here to choose which profile to use:

- **Optimistic mapping,** where the worker is mapped to the enhanced worker profile with the highest belief value or probability. Here, workers are given the benefit of the doubt, and they are assigned lesser gold questions.

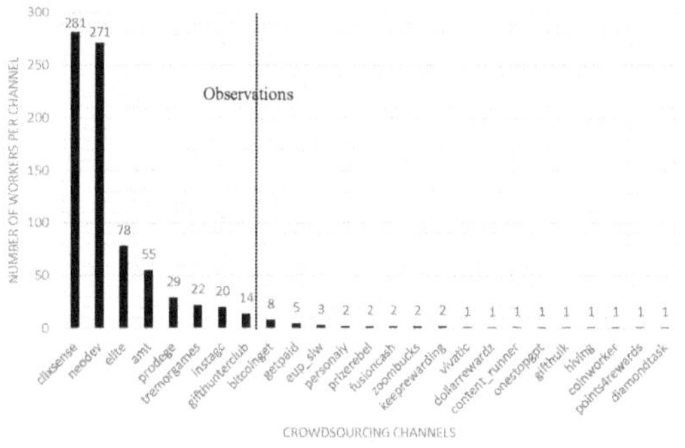

Figure 2. Channel attribute domain analysis

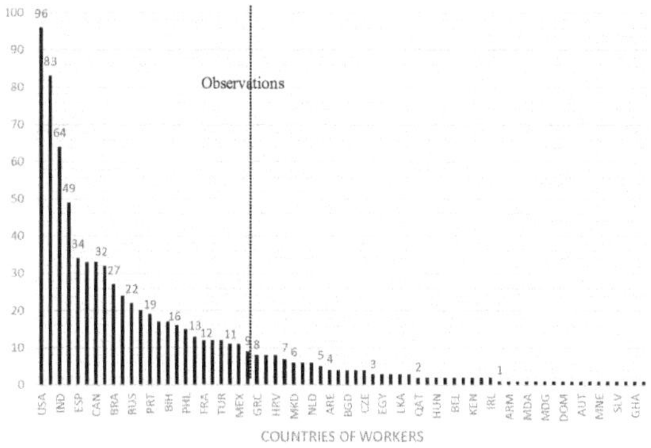

Figure 3. Country attribute domain analysis

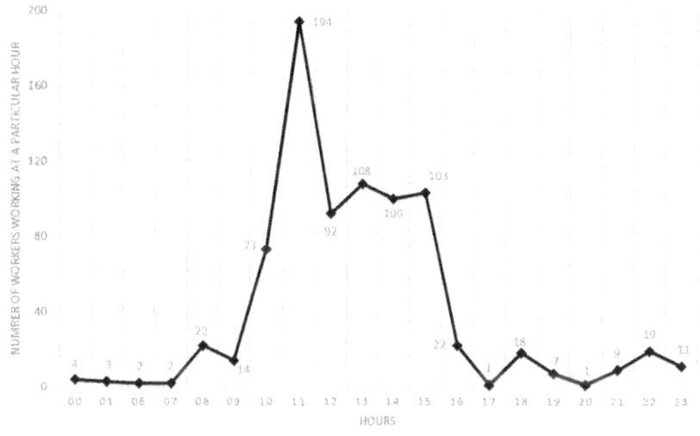

Figure 4. Started_at attribute domain analysis

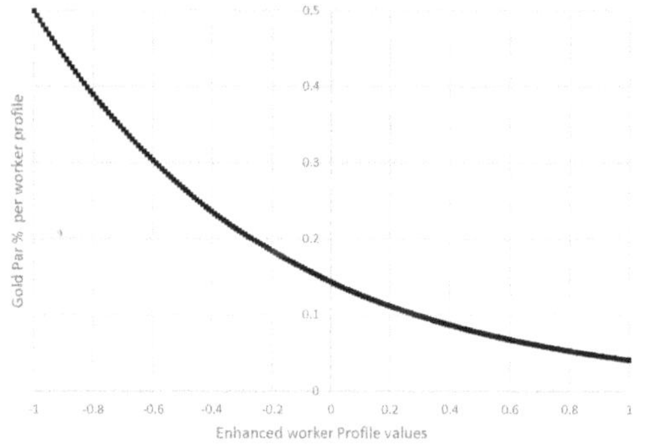

Figure 5. Exponentially Fitting the Gold Par to the enhanced worker profiles

- **Pessimistic mapping,** where the worker is mapped to the enhanced worker profile with the highest disbelief value or lowest probability. Here, a more skeptical approach is taken and the workers are subject to more gold questions.

In our evaluation section, we tested both the optimistic and pessimistic mapping. As to be expected, the pessimistic mapping is more expensive, since more safeguards are used.

5. EVALUATION

We now demonstrate the applicability/efficiency of our method in saving costly safeguards while maintaining high quality in real crowdsourcing tasks. We compare our method against the baseline in [15], to which we refer henceforth as the *'Optimal K'* method.

5.1 Data and Crowdsourcing tasks' Overview

For six different datasets we designed a crowdsourcing task and posted a total of 25 jobs on the CrowdFlower crowdsourcing platform. We chose quite a *heterogeneous set* of crowdsourcing tasks to generate a more universal set of enhanced worker profiles:

1. *Sharpness Image dataset*, comprising 192 in-house high quality images. In total 6 jobs were submitted to the crowd, each job had 48 questions. The crowd was given 5 versions of the same picture and were asked to order them according to their level of sharpness. A total of 184 workers were hired.

2. *Definition dataset*, crawled from the verbal practice questions section of the Graduate Record Examination (GRE) dataset[3] 2015. 176 questions were assigned to 70 workers over 5 jobs. The crowd was given multiple-choice questions, where correct corresponding definitions of words had to be chosen.

3. *Cars dataset*, crawled from Heise.de[4] in 2011. 125 questions were assigned to 87 workers over 7 jobs. The crowd was asked to look up missing data for a particular car model.

4. The open source *"Image descriptions" dataset[5]*, comprising 225,000 tuples. 1,320 questions were assigned to 482 workers over 3 jobs. The workers were shown a large variety of images with a corresponding word. Their task was to identify whether the word matched and described the image.

5. The open *"Semantic relationships between two concepts" dataset[4]*, comprising 3,536 tuples. 50 questions were assigned to 39 workers over 1 job. Workers were asked to judge whether the semantic equivalence in sentences was correct or not.

6. The open source "Decide whether two English sentences are related" dataset[4], comprising 555 tuples. A total of 730 questions were assigned to 404 workers over 3 jobs. Given two sentences: a fact and a deduction sentence, the workers had to judge if the deduction sentence were true.

Throughout the 25 jobs we ran, a total of 1,266 workers were hired. Yet while processing the workers' data, we found that about 35% (i.e. 445) of workers had worked in more than one job. After

removing duplicate workers by merging their data, we ended up with 1,006 workers. For evaluation, we split our database of workers into two datasets: A training dataset was used to create the enhanced worker profiles (806 workers), and a test dataset of 200 workers was used for evaluation. For the test dataset, we created 5 datasets with different percentages of spammers and reliable workers in order to observe their impact on the overall accuracy of our method:

- **Spammers75 (*S75*):** 75:25 ratio of spammers/rel. workers.
- **Spammers66 (*S66*):** 66:34 ratio of spammers/rel. workers.
- **Balanced (*B*),** 50:50 ratio of spammers/reliable workers.
- **Reliable66 (*R66*):** 34:66 ratio of spammers/reliable workers.
- **Reliable75 (*R75*):** 25:75 ratio of spammers/reliable workers.

5.2 Populating the worker profiles database

To generate the set of enhanced worker profiles, we used the training dataset comprising 806 workers and used the following attributes as observations: Channel, Country, Started_at, and Trust.

5.2.1 CFM-generated enhanced worker profiles

In total, 16,199 enhanced worker profiles of different granularities were generated. Namely, 47 single observation profiles (in total we had 50 different observations, but for three trust values, no profiles were generated since the values never occurred given the hypothesis). Moreover, parallel combinations generated the following combined-observation profiles: 728 2-Set Observation profiles, 4,672 3-Set observation profiles, and 10,752 4-Set observation profiles.

Single-Observation Profiles: Figures 6–9 plot CF values for single observation profiles. In figure 6, highest quality work tends to be done around 12 GMT, i.e. $CF(reliable\ worker|12) \rightarrow 0.35$. Further analysis uncovered that this work was mostly done by German workers, probably during lunch breaks. In Figure 7, workers hired from Amazon Mechanical Turk seem more reliable than those from gifthunterclub: $CF(reliable\ worker|gifthunterclub) \rightarrow -0.27$ vs. $CF(reliable\ worker|AMT) \rightarrow 0.6$. German workers show a high confirming profile: $CF(reliable\ worker|GER) \rightarrow 0.58$, where workers from Pakistan have the lowest disconfirming profile: $CF(reliable\ worker|PAK) \rightarrow -0.77$ (Figure 8). Lastly, in figure 9 it comes as no surprise that workers with highest trust value 1.0 show confirming profiles: $CF(reliable\ worker|1.0) \rightarrow 0.5$, while those having the lowest trust value of 0.4 have highest disconfirming profiles: $CF(reliable\ worker|0.4) \rightarrow -0.65$.

Combined-Observation Profiles: Below we show the top generated confirming/disconfirming 3-Set and 4-set observation profiles. The hours encoded in the rules for the Started_at attribute have been converted from GMT to the local time of the corresponding country within the same profile. For profiles without a corresponding country, the time is indicated in GMT format. The decimal numbers are trust values, the whole numbers refer to Started_at observations.

---

[3] http://www.graduateshotline.com/

[4] http://www.heise.de/autos/neuwagenkatalog

[5] http://dbgroup.cs.tsinghua.edu.cn/ligl/crowddata/

Top Ten Confirming 3-SET Observation Profiles:

1. $CF(reliable\ worker|amt, DEU, 1.0) \rightarrow 0.921$
2. $CF(reliable\ worker|instagc, DEU, 1.0) \rightarrow 0.899$
3. $CF(reliable\ worker|amt, DEU, 16) \rightarrow 0.896$
4. $CF\big(reliable\ worker|amt, 14, 1.0\big) \rightarrow 0.876$
5. $CF(reliable\ worker|amt, DEU, 0.9) \rightarrow 0.873$
6. $CF(reliable\ worker|DEU, 16, 1.0) \rightarrow 0.869$
7. $CF\big(reliable\ worker|instagc, DEU, 16\big) \rightarrow 0.868$
8. $CF\big(reliable\ worker|amt, GBR, 1.0\big) \rightarrow 0.864$
9. $CF\big(reliable\ worker|amt, DEU, 0.8\big) \rightarrow 0.858$
10. $CF(reliable\ worker|amt, ITA, 1.0) \rightarrow 0.856$

Top Ten Disconfirming 3-SET Observation Profiles:

1. $CF\big(reliable\ worker|PAK, 16, 0.4\big) \rightarrow -0.943$
2. $CF(reliable\ worker|PAK, 19, 0.4) \rightarrow -0.942$
3. $CF\big(reliable\ worker|gifthunter, PAK, 0.4\big) \rightarrow -0.941$
4. $CF(reliable\ worker|neodev, PAK, 0.4) \rightarrow -0.935$
5. $CF(reliable\ worker|PAK, 15, 0.4) \rightarrow -0.935$
6. $CF(reliable\ worker|clixsense, PAK, 0.4) \rightarrow -0.928$
7. $CF(reliable\ worker|elite, PAK, 0.4) \rightarrow -0.928$
8. $CF(reliable\ worker|PAK, 13, 0.4) \rightarrow -0.925$
9. $CF(reliable\ worker|PAK, 18, 0.4) \rightarrow -0.92$
10. $CF(reliable\ worker|PAK, 21, 0.4) \rightarrow -0.892$

Top Ten Confirming 4-SET Observation Profiles:

1. $CF(reliable\ worker|amt, DEU, 14, 1.0) \rightarrow 0.949$
2. $CF(reliable\ worker|instagc, DEU, 14, 1.0) \rightarrow 0.935$
3. $CF(reliable\ worker|amt, DEU, 15, 1.0) \rightarrow 0.929$
4. $CF(reliable\ worker|amt, DEU, 16, 1.0) \rightarrow 0.923$
5. $CF\big(reliable\ worker|amt, DEU, 12, 0.9\big) \rightarrow 0.918$
6. $CF\big(reliable\ worker|Prodege, DEU, 12, 1.0\big) \rightarrow 0.918$
7. $CF(reliable\ worker|amt, GBR, 12, 1.0) \rightarrow 0.9123$
8. $CF(reliable\ worker|instagc, DEU, 15, 1.0) \rightarrow 0.910$
9. $CF\big(reliable\ worker|amt, DEU, 12, 0.8\big) \rightarrow 0.908$
10. $CF(reliable\ worker|amt, ITA, 12, 1.0) \rightarrow 0.907$

Top Ten Disconfirming 4-SET Observation Profiles:

1. $CF(reliable\ worker|gifthunter, PAK, 16, 0.4) \rightarrow -0.959$
2. $CF(reliable\ worker|gifthunter, PAK, 19, 0.4) \rightarrow -0.958$
3. $CF(reliable\ worker|neodev, PAK, 16, 0.4) \rightarrow -0.955$
4. $CF\big(reliable\ worker|neodev, PAK, 19, 0.4\big) \rightarrow -0.954$
5. $CF(reliable\ worker|gifthunter, PAK, 15, 0.4) \rightarrow -0.953$
6. $CF(reliable\ worker|clixsense, PAK, 16, 0.4) \rightarrow -0.95$
7. $CF(reliable\ worker|elite, PAK, 16, 0.4) \rightarrow -0.95$
8. $CF(reliable\ worker|clixsense, PAK, 19, 0.4) \rightarrow -0.949$
9. $CF(reliable\ worker|elite, PAK, 19, 0.4) \rightarrow -0.949$
10. $CF(reliable\ worker|neodev, PAK, 15, 0.4) \rightarrow -0.948$

The combined-observation profiles show similar insights to the single-observation profiles: Work done at 12 GMT by German workers showing trust values higher than 0.8 and hired from the *AMT* channel, have high belief values in the hypothesis: a low risk profile. In contrast, work done at 11 GMT by Pakistani workers

Figure 6. Single *Started_at* CF Rules

Figure 7. Single *Channel* CF Rules

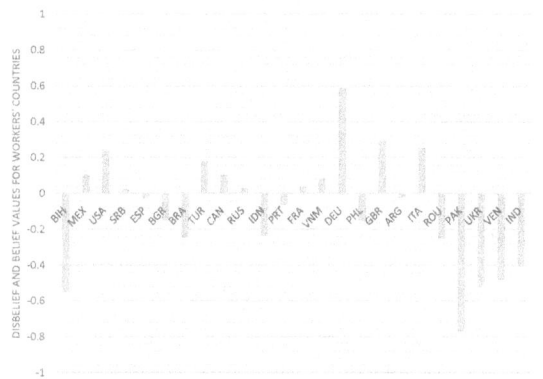

Figure 8. Single *Country* CF Rules

Figure 9. Single *Trust* CF Rules

showing trust values lower than 0.7 and hired from the *gifthunter-club* channel, tend to have high disbelief values, a high-risk profile.

5.2.2 BN-generated enhanced worker profiles

In total, 1,454 enhanced worker profiles of different granularities were generated, in particular 47 single observation profiles. For the Bayesian belief network, these single observation profiles are nothing but *prior* distributions, i.e. world probabilities that need to be estimated. For the country attribute, we turned to the population statistics of the world[6] to estimate the countries' prior estimations. The other priors proved difficult to estimate from the data we had. This is one of BN's drawbacks: biases in estimations may easily be introduced. Moreover, unlike CFM's computation of more complicated profiles by parallel combination, BN repeatedly needs to scan the data for generating these profiles. The following combined-observation profiles were deduced: 1169 2-Set Observation profiles, 213 3-Set observation profiles, and 25 4-Set observation profiles. Compared to the CF database of profiles, the BN database is significantly smaller. This comes as no surprise, since BN computes conditional probabilities based on actual occurrences of combined-observation: unseen combined-observations are not generated.

In Figure 10, we show an actual snippet of our constructed belief network. Single-observation profiles for the BN are basically prior probabilities. For the country observation, we easily computed it based on real world data, with P (DEU) = 0.011. Other priors were difficult to get and were accordingly estimated from the underlying dataset. The combined-observation profiles for the BN are on the other hand simple conditional probabilities (see Definition 4).

5.3 Evaluating the Gold Par

Using our test dataset of 200 workers for evaluation, the relatively small database of enhanced worker profiles on average profiled 96.5% of new incoming workers (i.e. 193 workers fit at least one of the enhanced worker profiles) when using the CF database, and 94% of new incoming workers (i.e. 188 workers) when using BN.

Next, we evaluate our method with both types of profile mapping (*optimistic* and *pessimistic*) and compare it against *optimal k* (see Section 2), in terms of overall quality, effectiveness of the algorithm, number of gold questions used, i.e. incurred costs, fraud detection failure rates, and discrimination against reliable workers.

5.3.1 Method's Effectiveness & the Gold Par

We evaluate two trading-off parameters: 1) the method's effectiveness, that is, how effective the method is in including reliable workers, while simultaneously removing spammers. 2) The gold par percentage, that is the overall percentage of gold questions posed in the crowdsourcing task. The more questions are posed, the more information the method gets, which directs it to the correct decision. Nevertheless, more gold questions, incur higher costs .e.g. *BN- pessimistic* method is overall the most effective (90.04%), yet comes at the highest cost of gold questions usage (19.31%).

In general, all methods seem to be more effective on datasets with higher spammers' percentage, with effectiveness values decreasing as more reliable workers are present (see Figure 11(a)) i.e. the discrimination rate against reliable workers is high, as can be seen in Figure 11(d). However, our *CF-based* and *BN-based* methods, whether utilizing the *pessimistic* or *optimistic* mapping, are more

effective with datasets having higher spammers' percentage: *S75* and *S66*, while *optimal k* seems more effective with datasets including more reliable workers: *R66* and *R75* (see Figure 11(a)). This implies that our method can reliably detect spammers, while *optimal k* is better at detecting reliable workers. Whereas the *pessimistic* methods have the highest percentage of gold par cost, and thus the highest cost. The *CF-based optimistic* method seem to score the trade-off balance by having the lowest percentage of gold par, and thus the lowest cost (see Figure 11 (a)), while still being as effective as *Optimal K* for *S75*, *S66* and *B* datasets. For our test dataset, we have a total of 6631 tasks. If we for instance compute 5 cents per question, then on average for the *CF-based optimistic* method, 10.8% gold par costs around 36$, while *optimal k* costs 42.5$ at 12.8% gold questions. *This means a cost reduction of about 18%.*

More gold questions should be asked in datasets having higher levels of spammers, since more workers will be mapped to high-risk profiles, which consequently leads to a higher percentage of gold par usage. Surprisingly, we experienced a relatively similar percentage of gold par regardless of the composition of the dataset. Looking into the data, we attribute that to the inherent size of our tasks, i.e. most are relatively small (~20 questions per job).

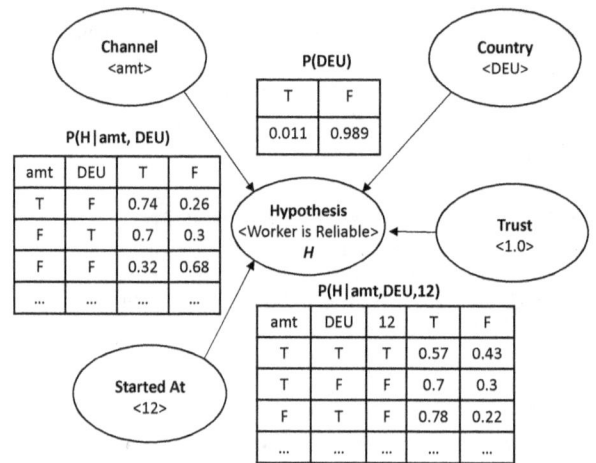

Figure 10. A snippet of the Constructed Belief Network

5.3.2 Failure Rate

Next, we evaluated the failure rate of the methods in overseeing spammers and letting them through to work on the tasks (i.e. the False Positives). The lower the failure rate the better. Figure 11(c), supports the previous results, where *optimal k* has the worst failure rate. Naturally, the failure rate is more pronounced in *S75* and *S66* and becomes less noticeable in *R66* and *R75* due to their inherent nature of having lesser spammers. On the other hand our methods have lower failure rates, which again adheres to their effectivity when handling datasets with high percentages of spammers e.g. for dataset *S66*, the following failure rates were experienced: *Optimal K* had 24.69%, *CF-based methods* had on average 16.3%, and *BN-based methods* had on average 5% failure rate. Here the *BN-based methods* have lower failure rates than the *CF-based methods*, since they utilize more gold questions and are thus more informed.

---

6 http://www.worldometers.info/world-population/population-by-country/

5.3.3 Reliable Worker Pool and Discrimination Rate

After looking at failure rates, we test the second parameter impacting the methods' effectiveness: discrimination rates against reliable workers (i.e. the False Negatives). The lower the discrimination rate, the better. *Optimal k* shows lowest discrimination rates. Naturally, this becomes more pronounced for the R66 and R75 datasets and is alike for all the other methods. The *CF-based* and *BN-based optimistic* methods are slightly more discriminating than their *pessimistic* counterparts, which would indicate, that perhaps the small number of gold questions that were given to the reliable workers might have been inherently difficult. This is also attributed to the inherent design of our methods, which enforces a higher quality threshold on workers with low-risk profiles. Looking at the overall actual number of reliable workers hired from the available pool (see Figure 11 (e)), backs up the discrimination rates in Figure 11(d).

5.3.4 Overall Resulting Quality

Regardless of the discrimination rates, or the effectiveness of the method, for a requestor or a data scientist, the ultimate quality measure for any safeguard is the resulting quality plus the costs it incurs. We can see that throughout our experiments that indeed all the methods achieved about the same quality level as illustrated in Figure 11(f); although it came as a pleasant surprise that despite needing less gold questions the *CF-based optimistic* method in fact achieves even slightly better quality levels. For example for dataset: *B*, the *CF-based pessimistic* method achieves 90%, the *CF-based optimistic* method achieved 89%, while *optimal k* achieves only 87% quality rate. Measuring the standard error for the overall resulting quality yielded a very small rate of 0.0007. Posing crowdsourcing tasks of bigger size might reflect savings in gold questions even better, yet most of our crowdsourcing tasks had only 20 questions (thus 5% gold questions vs. 10% gold questions amounts to only 1 more gold question to be used).

6. CONCLUSION AND OUTLOOK

Data science has a lot to gain from crowdsourcing applications like exploration, data completion, or complex analysis, if the result quality is high. However, designing effective safeguards to combat fraudulent misuse remains an open problem on crowdsourcing platforms. Of course, in return for investing money data scientists rightfully expect high quality. Thus, managing the quality/cost-tradeoff needs to find the minimal, yet sufficient number of safeguards.

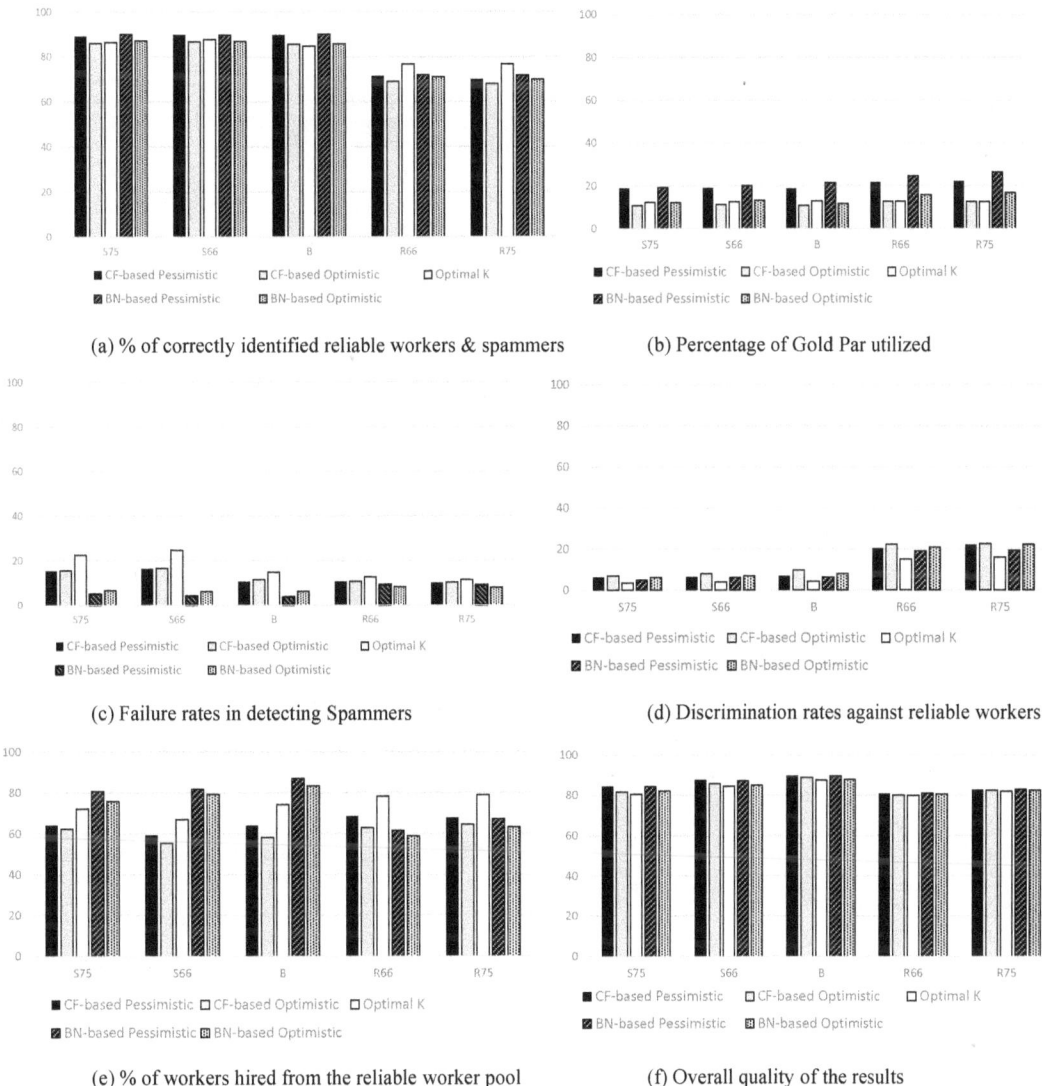

(a) % of correctly identified reliable workers & spammers

(b) Percentage of Gold Par utilized

(c) Failure rates in detecting Spammers

(d) Discrimination rates against reliable workers

(e) % of workers hired from the reliable worker pool

(f) Overall quality of the results

Figure 11. Evaluating Optimal k vs. CF-based/ BN-based (Pessimistic and Optimistic) methods on S75, S66, B, R66, and R75

We designed a method for using individualized numbers of gold questions that leverages the limited amount of information known about short-term hired anonymous workers. Surprisingly, with as little as 4 publicly available attributes, we were already able to create meaningful enhanced worker profiles. The generated enhanced profiles encode the risk associated with each worker regarding a certain task by exposing relative a-priori belief/disbelief measures or probabilities. In a nutshell, the higher the belief value or probability of a worker's reliability, the lower the risk, and the lesser the number of gold questions to be used. And the higher the disbelief value or the lower the probability of a worker's reliability, the higher the risk, and the more gold questions need to be used. We fitted an exponential distribution of number of gold questions to use on top of these belief/disbelief values and probabilities, such that new workers fitting some high-risk profile should be asked more gold questions than new workers fitting a low-risk profile.

For generating this profile database we experimented with certainty factor models and Bayesian belief networks. Interestingly, the Bayesian belief network did not outperform simple certainty factors. This might be caused by the inherently small amount of training data, in addition to biases introduced while estimating priors.

In our evaluation, we illustrated the applicability of our method on practical crowdsourcing tasks and demonstrated its potential in saving money while maintaining high quality results. We tested our method against 5 different datasets with different compositions of spammers and reliable workers. Our method works best when there are more spammers, and always achieved at least comparable quality results to the 'optimal k' baseline. Moreover, our CF-based optimistic method achieved higher quality rates at a lower number of gold questions: only 12.8% gold questions were used in contrast to 14.8% with optimal k (i.e. about 18% cost reduction). We anticipate that further analysis on different attributes would augment our enhanced worker profiles and that bigger underlying crowdsourcing tasks would reflect even more profound savings in gold questions.

In summary, in this paper our profiles database was derived from a heterogeneous set of crowdsourcing tasks, which however yielded a meaningful and rather universal set of enhanced worker profiles. In contrast, data scientists with more homogenous tasks (i.e. similar, often repeated tasks) might benefit from a profile database designed for their specific type of task. Such task-personalization is actually easy with the certainty factor model, and dynamically adapts to different scientists' needs. Thus, data scientists may start with universal profiles and continuously refine them as they post more and more tasks. And what is more, different specialized databases of profiles serving different commonly used types of tasks could already be made available by the crowdsourcing platforms as a service to their various requestors. In future work we plan to investigate this effect and its potential benefits in more detail.

7. REFERENCES

[1] Aberer, K., Despotovic, Z., "Managing trust in a peer-2-peer information system," *Procs. of Int. Conf. on Information and Knowledge Management (CIKM)*, Atlanta, GA, USA, 2001.

[2] Daltayanni, M. de Alfaro, L and Papadimitriou, P., "WorkerRank: Using Employer Implicit Judgements to Infer Worker Reputation," *Procs. of ACM Int. Conf. on Web Search and Data Mining (WSDM)*, Shanghai, China, 2015.

[3] Davidson, S.B., Khanna, S., Milo, T. and Roy, S., "Using the Crowd for Top-k and Group-by Queries," *Procs. of the Int. Conf. on Database Theory (ICDT)*, Genoa, Italy, 2013.

[4] Dawid, A.P., Skene, A.M., "Maximum likelihood estimation of observer error-rates using the EM algorithm," *Jour. of the Royal Statistical Society (JSTOR)*, vol. 28, no. 1, 1979.

[5] Franklin, M., Kossmann, D., Kraska, T., Ramesh, S., Xin, R., "CrowdDB: Answering queries with crowdsourcing," *Proceedings of the 2011 ACM SIGMOD Int. Conf. on Management of Data (SIGMOD)*, Athens, Greece, 2011.

[6] Hossain, M., "Users' motivation to participate in online crowdsourcing platforms," *Procs. of Int. Conf. on Innovation, Management and Technology Research (ICIMTR)*, Malacca, Malaysia, 2012.

[7] Ignjatovic, A., Foo, N., Lee, C.T., "An Analytic Approach to Reputation Ranking of Participants in Online Transactions," *Procs. of Int. Conf. on Web Intelligence and Intelligent Agent Technology (WI-IAT)*, Sydney, Australia, 2008.

[8] Kamvar, S.D., Schlosser, M.T., Garcia-Molina, H., "The Eigentrust algorithm for reputation management in P2P networks," *Procs. of Int. Conf. on World Wide Web (WWW)*, Budapest, Hungary, 2003.

[9] Kazai, G., "In Search of Quality in Crowdsourcing for Search Engine Evaluation," *Proc. of European Conf. on Advances in Information Retrieval (ECIR)*, Dublin, Ireland, 2011.

[10] Krieg, M.L.,"A tutorial on Bayesian belief networks," *Technical report in the Defense Science and Technology Organization publications (DSTO)*, 2001.

[11] Lofi, C., El Maarry, K., Balke, W.-T., "Skyline Queries in Crowd-Enabled Databases," *Procs. of Int. Conf. on Extending Database Technology (EDBT)*, Genoa, Italy, 2013.

[12] El Maarry, K., Güntzer, U., Balke, W.-T., "Realizing Impact Sourcing by Adaptive Gold Questions: A Socially Responsible Measure for Workers' Trustworthiness," *Procs. of Int. Conf. on Web-Age Inf. Mgmt (WAIM)*, Qingdao, China, 2015.

[13] El Maarry, K., Balke, W.-T., "Retaining Rough Diamonds: Towards a Fairer Elimination of Low-skilled Workers," *Procs. of Int. Conf. on Database Systems for Advanced Applications (DASFAA)*, Hanoi, Vietnam, 2015.

[14] El Maarry, K., Balke, W.-T., Cho, H., Hwang, S., Baba, Y., "Skill ontology-based model for Quality Assurance in Crowdsourcing," *in Procs. of UnCrowd Workshop (at DASFAA'14)*, Bali, Indonesia, 2014

[15] Liu, A.I.Q., Steyvers, M., "Scoring Workers in Crowdsourcing: How Many Control Questions are enough?" *Procs. of Adv. in Neural Inf. Proc. Systems (NIPS)*, volume 26, Stateline, NV, USA, 2013.

[16] Mellouli, T. "Complex Certainty Factors for Rule Based Systems – Detecting Inconsistent Argumentations," *Procs. of Int. Workshop on Functional and (Constraint) Logic Programming*, Wittenberg, Germany, 2014.

[17] Nieke, C., Güntzer, U., Balke, W.-T, "TopCrowd: Efficient Crowd-enabled Top-k Retrieval on Incomplete Data", *Procs. of Int. Conf. on Conceptual Modeling (ER)*, Atlanta, GA, USA, 2014.

[18] Noorian, Z., Ulieru, M., "The State of the Art in Trust and Reputation Systems: A Framework for Comparison," *Jour. of Theor. and Appl. Electr. Commerce Research*, vol. 5(2), 2010.

[19] Pearl, J., "Bayesian Networks: A model of self-activated memory for evidential reasoning," *Procs. of Conf. of the Cognitive Science Society*, Irvine, CA, USA, 1985.

[20] Pearl, J., "Probabilistic Reasoning in Intelligent Systems: Networks of Plausible Inference", *Morgan Kaufmann Publishers Inc.*, San Francisco, CA, USA, 1988.

[21] Raykar, V.C., Yu, S., Zhao. L.H., Valadez, G.H., Florin, C., Bogoni, L., Moy,L., "Learning From Crowds," *Jour. of Machine Learning Research (JMLR)*, vol. 11, 2010.

[22] Ross, J., Zaldivar, A., Irani, L., Tomlinson, B., "Who are the Turkers? Worker Demographics in Amazon Mechanical Turk," *Tech. Report, Dept. of Information*, UC Irvine, USA, 2009.

[23] Shortliffe, E.H., Buchanan, B.G., "A model of inexact reasoning in medicine," *Jour. of Mathematical Biosciences*, vol. 23(3-4), 1975.

[24] Stadler, F., "Induction and Deduction in the Sciences," *Springer Netherlands*, 2011.

[25] Whitehill, J., Ruvolo, P., Wu, T., Bergsma, J., Movellan, J., "Whose Vote Should Count More: Optimal Integration of Labels from Labelers of Unknown Expertise," *Procs. of Adv. in Neural Inf. Proc. Systems (NIPS)*, Vancouver, Canada, 2009.

[26] Yu, B., Singh, M., "Detecting Deception in Reputation Management," *Procs. of Int. Joint Conf. on Autonomous Agents and Multiagent Systems*, Melbourne, Australia, 2003.

[27] Zheng, Y., Wang, J., Li, G., Cheng, R., Feng, J., "QASCA: A Quality-Aware Task Assignment System for Crowdsourcing Applications," *Procs. of ACM Int. Conf. on Management of Data (SIGMOD)*, Melbourne, Australia, 2015.

Automated Discovery of Internet Censorship by Web Crawling

Alexander Darer
Dept. Computer Science
University of Oxford
Oxford, UK

Oliver Farnan
Dept. Computer Science
University of Oxford
Oxford, UK

Joss Wright
Oxford Internet Institute
University of Oxford
Oxford, UK

ABSTRACT

Censorship of the Internet is widespread around the world. As access to the web becomes increasingly ubiquitous, filtering of this resource becomes more pervasive. Transparency about specific content and information that citizens are denied access to is atypical. To counter this, numerous techniques for maintaining URL filter lists have been proposed by various individuals, organisations and researchers. These aim to improve empirical data on censorship for benefit of the public and wider censorship research community, while also increasing the transparency of filtering activity by oppressive regimes.

We present a new approach for discovering filtered domains in different target countries. This method is fully automated and requires no human interaction. The system uses web crawling techniques to traverse between filtered sites and implements a robust method for determining if a domain is filtered. We demonstrate the effectiveness of the approach by running experiments to search for filtered content in four different censorship regimes. Our results show that we perform better than the current state of the art and have built domain filter lists an order of magnitude larger than the most widely available public lists as of April 2018. Further, we build a dataset mapping the interlinking nature of blocked content between domains and exhibit the tightly networked nature of censored web resources.

CCS CONCEPTS

• **Social and professional topics** → **Censorship**; • **Security and privacy** → *Social aspects of security and privacy*; • **Networks** → *Naming and addressing*;

KEYWORDS

censorship; DNS; filtering; transparency; monitoring

ACM Reference Format:
Alexander Darer, Oliver Farnan, and Joss Wright. 2018. Automated Discovery of Internet Censorship by Web Crawling. In *WebSci '18: 10th ACM Conference on Web Science, May 27–30, 2018, Amsterdam, Netherlands.* ACM, New York, NY, USA, 10 pages. https://doi.org/10.1145/3201064.3201091

1 INTRODUCTION

The effort expended by censorship regimes around the world attempting to filter Internet resources they deem to be too sensitive or against the morality of their own interests is on-going. As Internet access has become more ubiquitous, the scale of deployed filtering systems is increasing. A recent study has shown that blocking the reachability of popular sites at national levels is widespread and disruptive [24][29]. Advocates for free-speech and a free Internet push for transparency and openness, while censors attempt to repress the flow of certain information within their networks. Key to this is the blocking of specific webpages and the URLs that point to them.

In response to large scale filtering of web resources, there have been numerous studies over recent years aimed at determining the type of content being blocked in different countries. Of particular interest are periods of time when blocking has occurred and the development of techniques to monitor filtered URLs and keywords [12][13][18][23][33][41].

We introduce an approach for discovering filtered domains in different countries at scale and reasonable cost. The system is fully automated and does not require per-country expertise or cooperation - meaning that the safety of individuals within censored regimes won't be compromised. Our method applies web crawling techniques to find blocked content and uses a seed list of known filtered URLs to initiate the search. We make use of DNS servers within a target country as measurable devices. This allows us to monitor the filter status of individual domains and sub-domains without human intervention. The system is recursive so newly discovered filtered URLs are fed back into the search to allow on-going measurement. Results from our experiments using four different test countries have shown that our approach can be used to find filtered URLs that are not present in the original seed lists. Furthermore, we collect data about the linked nature of various filtered domains to gain further insight into how different pieces of filtered content are associated.

1.1 Related Work

Over the last decade there have been many approaches for detecting censorship of the Internet around the world. Of these, many are country specific and have focused on China [10][18][22][25][40], Indonesia [21][36], Iran [7][8], Pakistan [2][27] and Thailand [19] among others.

The most widely adopted and current URL filter lists are maintained by the *CitizenLab* [9]. They are constructed using local knowledge and reports of filtering in different countries and collate data from different sources such as *OONI* [16].

Developing new techniques for discovering filtered URLs is a challenging problem. Yet, this is a rich research field with numerous techniques published over recent years [4]. The use of DNS as a means of testing censorship of web content is not new, but can be advantageous due to its scalability and remote nature [35]. These attributes make DNS a common tool for other censorship monitoring architectures such as *UBICA* [3], *FilteredWeb* [13] and *CensMon* [33].

Building in-depth and accurate URL filter lists is an important aspect for censorship research. These collections are in widespread use among the research community for various different measurements and tests for internet reachability, web content blocking and circumvention techniques [30][38]. Furthermore, the subsequent and on-going maintenance of these lists provides opportunities for insight into the condition of internet filtering around the world. The data collected by the aforementioned monitoring architectures is vital if we are to construct a model of censorship as it develops.

1.2 Contributions

This paper introduces a new approach for discovering filtered domains within target censorship regimes. We have created an implementation of the technique and, through experimentation, shown it to be an effective tool for building URL filter lists. Furthermore, our results reveal that the approach has found significantly more filtered URLs for the test countries than were currently available in the largest public filter lists. Our formalised contributions are:

- A new approach for discovering previously unknown filtered domains
- Experimental analysis of the technique through measurement of filtering activity within four know censorship regimes
- Category breakdown of the types of content being blocked within these regimes
- Analysis of forward filtered links and filtered backlinks of webpages on filtered domains

A substantial research output from this body of work is a test list containing a large number of currently filtered domains within China, Indonesia, Iran and Turkey that have previously been unpublished. We aim to make this list available as soon as possible to the wider censorship research community.

2 TRAVERSAL OF FILTERED WEBPAGES

Traversal between webpages using embedded hyperlinks is the most widely used method for content discovery on the Web. Our aim is to exploit the connections between different filtered webpages to efficiently crawl sites in search for more blocked content. An important assumption for this approach is that different filtered webpages do indeed link to others. We demonstrate this through experimental analysis of four different countries that are known to filter websites via DNS manipulation. The method we describe is not dissimilar to conventional web crawling techniques widely used by large search engines. Given this, we aim to build a new dataset that contains information pertaining to backlinks[1] of filtered webpages.

This technique works on a simple premise - filtered webpages contain links to other filtered webpages. We begin the discovery

---

[1]Backlinks are hyperlinks that point to a certain page from other pages.

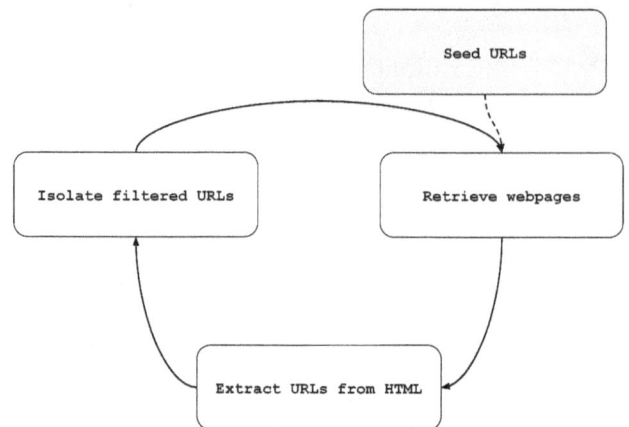

Figure 1: High-level overview of filtered webpage traversal

by seeding the system with a number of known filtered URLs with the presupposition that these will contain hyperlinks to further blocked content. A high-level overview of the technique is shown in Figure 1 and works as follows:

(1) Start with a list of known filtered URLs for country c
(2) Retrieve webpages for all known filtered URLs in our list
(3) Extract any URLs from the downloaded webpages
(4) Isolate the URLs that are filtered in country c from the extracted URLs
(5) Add the newly identified filtered URLs to the list, then goto step 2

A number of hyperlinks in any webpage will point to resources that do not provide utility for our discovery. We ignore any URLs that point to static HTML assets - such as javascript, css or image files and also remove any self-referencing URLs - hyperlinks to the same domain for the webpage. We aim to reduce the possibility of having the crawler becoming stuck in cliques such as affiliate or adult site networks this way. For purposes of analysis of the approach we visit each unique URL only once.

2.1 Methods for Checking Webpage Availability

A key part of this system is the capability to determine if a domain is filtered in a certain country or not. This is important as crawling unnecessarily large portions of the Web will make the discovery inefficient. Furthermore, an inaccurate checking procedure could produce large numbers of false positives - detracting from the usefulness of the results. We must also be prudent in regards to ethical issues when taking internet measurements using such a system. Since, we will be probing for blocked content, we want to ensure that the safety of individuals is not compromised as described by [14].

Given these requirements, we employ a checking system that uses DNS infrastructure to determine if domains are being filtered within a given country. The exploitation of DNS as a means for blocking access to certain web resources is in widespread use around the globe [15][24][25][30]; and because resolvers operated by large Internet Service Providers (ISPs) are often open, we can use these as a basis for our measurements.

To determine the filter status of a domain, we require a globally non-censored DNS server as a control and a measurement DNS server located within a target country. Using these, we run through a process to comprehensively check if a domain is filtered by the measurement server. We examine responses to DNS queries made for the test domain to determine if the server is poisoned [15] or acting rogue. This procedure is described in Algorithm 1.

The following six checks are used to ascertain the filter status of domains:

(1) A DNS query is intercepted in the target country when sent to a non-existent DNS server
(2) The measurement server times out but the control server does not
(3) The measurement server responds with a private IP address but the control does not
(4) The measurement server resolves an IP that times out on an HTTP GET request, whereas the resolved IP from the control server does not
(5) The control server resolves an IP that times out on an HTTP GET request, whereas the resolved IP from the measurement server does not
(6) The content length of the webpages from each resolved IP differs by more than a defined percentage amount

If the results from any of the above are found to be positive, we consider the domain to be filtered by the measurement DNS server.

This procedure has a number of useful features. Firstly, it does not require cooperation of any person or individual within a censored country, it solely makes measurements on infrastructure. Second, it is an efficient mechanism that is scalable and yields fast results. Third, we can perform measurements from outside target countries giving us the capability to analyse filtering within a wide array of censorship regimes.

The limitation with this approach is that we lose fine grain information about individual URLs that may be blocked. This is due to the sole use of DNS servers as a checking mechanism - since one can only query about entire domains or sub-domains. Further, we require that measurement DNS servers respond to queries from remote countries in the same manner they do for queries made domestically. Yet, as we need to make a trade-off between effectiveness, efficiency and ethical considerations, this method is sufficient for use to generate good results to show the usefulness of this technique for discovering filtered domains as a whole.

2.2 Ethical Considerations

Implications of censorship measurements open us up to a number of ethical issues that we must give thought to. First and foremost, it is imperative that we do not cause harm to any persons or organisations that are unaware of our actions, intent or motivation. This can be a causal problem in numerous ways, not least because testing of internet filtering often requires sending network traffic to and from—in and out—of countries controlled by censorship regimes [11]. Certain studies within the field have required the use of aware

---

Algorithm 1 Pseudocode for Domain Filtering Check

$MAXDIFF \Leftarrow p$ {content length % difference that indicates filtered domain}
dom {domain to check}
$mDNS$ {measurement DNS server in target country}
$mDNSFake$ {fake DNS server in target country}
$cDNS$ {control DNS server}

    {the following variables are $NULL$ on timeout}
1: $mFakeIP \Leftarrow resolveDNS(dom, mDNSFake)$
2: $mIP \Leftarrow resolveDNS(dom, mDNS)$
3: $cIP \Leftarrow resolveDNS(dom, cDNS)$
4: $mIPContent \Leftarrow httpGETRequest(mIP)$
5: $cIPContent \Leftarrow httpGETRequest(cIP)$

6: **if** $mFakeIP \neq NULL$ **then**
7:     **return** $TRUE$ {DNS query was intercepted in target country}
8: **end if**

9: **if** $mIP == NULL$ **and** $cIP \neq NULL$ **then**
10:     **return** $TRUE$ {$mDNS$ is rogue server}
11: **end if**

12: **if** $mIP \neq cIP$ **then**
13:     **if** $isPrivateIP(mIP) == TRUE$ **and** $isPrivateIP(cIP) == FALSE$ **then**
14:         **return** $TRUE$ {mIP is private address}
15:     **end if**
16:     **if** $mIPContent == NULL$ **and** $cIPContent \neq NULL$ **then**
17:         **return** $TRUE$ {$mDNS$ is rogue server}
18:     **end if**
19:     **if** $mIPContent \neq NULL$ **and** $cIPContent == NULL$ **then**
20:         **return** $TRUE$ {$mDNS$ is rogue server}
21:     **end if**
22:     **if** $length(mIPContent)/length(cIPContent) > MAXDIFF$ **then**
23:         **return** $TRUE$ {mIP points to incorrect content}
24:     **end if**
25: **end if**
26: **return** $FALSE$ {dom not filtered}

---

volunteers who are located within countries of interest. While these individuals are generally knowledgeable of the motivation of the study and potential ramifications of their actions if implicated, this is not something we as researches should take lightly. In many cases, it is simply not appropriate to use human participants for this type of work. Furthermore, there are a number of legal issues with measurements of censorship based on the techniques used - especially if inference is made using direct observations within a target country [42].

We must also consider the use and deployment of these kinds of discovery techniques by antagonists. Since we aim to build a system that can automatically find alternative content that is blocked based on *known* blocked content, such a framework could be utilised in an adverse way to filter further web resources. Unfortunately, we cannot guarantee that this use-case will never occur given the fact that censors generally do not publish technological details about their infrastructure and systems.

These concerns should not however reduce our willingness to practice this kind of research. If considerable effort is made to ensure our measurements will not affect individuals, we are able to provide empirical data concerning censorship around the world. This can give us as researchers a substantial insight into complex socio-political issues that are of benefit to the community and are of wider public interest given the state fragile of international relations. Moreover, our proposed approach does not pose a risk to individuals or rely human volunteers and vulnerable subjects. We take measurements directly from infrastructure in a manner that the services were originally designed for.

3 EXPERIMENTAL ANALYSIS

We conduct experiments on four different countries with an aim to build domain filter lists that are longer and more in-depth than are currently available. This was achieved using an implementation of the approach written in *Python* with the following parameters:

- Control DNS server: 8.8.8.8
- *MAXDIFF* (content-length difference that indicates filtering): 50%
- Filter check timeout: 10 seconds
- Maximum recursion depth[2]: 100
- Seed URLs obtained from the CitizenLab filter lists [9]

The *MAXDIFF* value is used based on a study that found the content-length of censorship block pages are 95% likely to differ by more than 50% compared to the genuine page [1]. Further, we ensure that the system does not follow links that self-reference the parent site - this is to say we attempt to stop looping behaviour with pages that link to others on the same domain. Also, we never revisit a URL that has previously been seen - it will be counted in the statistics we gather, but not checked again.

The target countries tested were: China, Indonesia, Iran and Turkey. Each experiment ran for seven days, or until no more filtered domains were found. The DNS servers used for each test country are shown in Table 1. The real DNS servers were selected from large ISPs in the target countries and the fake from the pool of unallocated IP addresses also owned by the same ISPs. We do this because we aim to take measurements on mass infrastructure within the target countries rather than smaller organisations or individuals. It is also extremely important to keep testing within the bounds of how the network was designed to operate. We *only* make DNS queries and do not send any other crafted (or benign) packets to the target servers. While we acknowledge that our requests will likely contain queries for censored sites, the infrastructure we measure has been developed to process these kinds of transactions.

3.1 Results

Table 2 depicts the number of unique URLs extracted over the course of each experiment and how many of those were filtered in the given country. We also perform a count on the number of unique filtered domains within the list of filtered URLs. As a measure for the breadth of each run, the Alexa Top 1000 domains were removed

---

[2]This is the maximum depth of recursion from the seed URLs

so we can analyise how deep the system is able to penetrate to lesser known sites with lower numbers of visitors and backlinks.

In total, we extracted over 80 million URLs from filtered web pages, of which 5.7 million were themselves from a filtered domain. The number of blocked domains identified for Turkey and Indonesia are an order of magnitude larger than those found for China and Iran. This is due to the widespread censorship of adult related sites within these particular censorship regimes. Turkey passed a law in 2007 prompting the explicit blocking of over 80,000 sites, of which many contained adult content [6], and Indonesia, a similar ban in 2010 [20] & 2017 [31].

We perform a comparison with the most widely available public URL filter lists, maintained by the CitizenLab. To ensure a fair comparison, we run these lists through our filtering check and report those numbers. The figures are shown in Table 3. From this we can show that we have performed efficiently and identified more filtered domains than were present in the original seed lists. To gain further insight into the types of content filtered in Turkey and Indonesia, we remove the adult domains to create separate counts for better comparison.

Our results demonstrate that this approach is effective at finding previously unknown filtered domains. A major advantage of this technique is that *only* URLs from filtered domains are visited, meaning that we can achieve efficient web crawling.

4 FURTHER ANALYSIS

The experiments we performed have yielded an interesting dataset that lends itself to further investigation. We are able to track the paths that lead to filtered content by analysing routes taken by the crawler. This gives us a useful base for examining how deeply connected collections of blocked sites are. Further, we can identify the backlinks of filtered pages and the outbound (forward) links to other filtered sites, we can discover networks of filtered sites.

We find that the results found in Turkey and Indonesia contain large numbers of adult sites - which as explained, are known to be banned. This observed behaviour of our tool may be due to the way that adult websites and businesses associate their domains together with the use of vast networks of traffic brokers, domain redirectors and link collections [39]. Based on this networking effect the web crawler may traverse content within this subject matter given the tightly linking nature of the sites - site A references site B and site B references site A, etc. However, this is important behaviour for this approach because different pages within each site may contain distinct filtered URLs. The limitation is that the crawler may get stuck in a loop within a closed network. Even so, our results contain over 1292 filtered non-adult domains for Indonesia and 528 filtered non-adult domains for Turkey.

The results for China and Iran show significant improvement over the original seed lists of filtered domains, with our number for China over 10 times greater than the input to the system and Iran over 60% higher.

4.1 Top-Level-Domain Enumeration

We perform an enumeration of all publicly available top-level-domains (TLDs) that can be attributed to different domains - and

Table 1: DNS servers used for experiments

	Real Servers	Fake Servers	ISP
China	202.46.32.29 180.76.76.76	220.181.57.217 223.96.100.100	Shenzhen Sunrise Technology Co. Ltd.
Indonesia	202.134.0.155 202.134.1.10	202.134.2.10 180.131.144.44	PT Telkom Divisi Multimedia
Iran	94.183.43.170 2.179.167.100	94.183.92.90 5.161.128.10	Aria Shatel Company Ltd
Turkey	195.175.39.39 195.175.39.40	195.175.30.39 195.175.30.100	Turk Telekomunikasyon Anonim Sirketi

Table 2: Results from experimental analysis

	Extracted URLs *(HTML assets and self-linking URLs removed)*	Filtered URLs	Filtered Domains	Filtered Domains *(Alexa Top 1000 removed)*
China	33,082,217	2,098,264	1576	1454
Indonesia	12,580,357	835,395	47,143	47,065
Iran	15,381,873	1,868,852	651	576
Turkey	19,250,931	913,213	39,725	39,614
Totals:	80,295,378	5,715,724	89,095	88,709

Table 3: Comparison of results to CitizenLab filter lists
CitizenLab figures accurate as of 1st Sept 2017

	Filtered Domains *(Alexa Top 1000 removed)*	
	CitizenLab	Darer et al.
China	127	1454
Indonesia *(Adult domains removed)*	124	1280
Iran	351	576
Turkey *(Adult domains removed)*	131	513

Table 4: Filtered domain counts after TLD enumeration

	Filtered Domains	Of which, hosts exist
China	97,167	5408
Indonesia	1479	1543
Iran	5970	4527
Turkey	789	584

therefore different DNS records. We use the Public Suffix List maintained by the Mozilla Foundation [17]. This list of TLDs contains all known public suffixes, common examples such as *.com* and *.org*, and less well-known instances such as *pvt.k12.ma.us*. For each filtered domain discovered in a target country, we remove the TLD and check the domain, along with any subdomains, with all suffixes in the list for filtering in that country. For Indonesia and Turkey, we run the test on the non-adult domains only for better comparison. Results of the enumeration are shown in Table 4.

Having completed this process, we find a large number of alternative TLDs for the filtered domains discovered through the traversal are also themselves filtered. During this process, we find that many of the enumerated domains found to be blocked by DNS in the target countries do not have records associated with them held by

the control server. In particular, 94% of the enumerated domains found to be filtered in China received NXDOMAIN responses from the control which could therefore not resolve them. A reason for this could be that censored websites may be "retired" or move onto new domains and hosting infrastructure to evade the block. While this is a case for completely removing them from the set of results presented here, they are still explicitly filtered within the country - showing that the authorities continue to block access to them. This could be due to the stance of the censorship regime or the fact that once a site is filtered, the process for removing them from blacklists is less than trivial.

4.2 Categories of Filtered Domains

To gain insight into the types of content being blocked, we run a category analysis on our list of filtered domains using the WebShrinker Categories API [37]. This returns a list of categories attributed to each domain and allows us to isolate from a high level different genres of websites that are being blocked in each target country.

Figure 2 shows the breakdown of categories for each country. From this we can see that certain types of site are overwhelmingly being blocked over others. Of particular interest is the filtering of news and media, search engines and translators by China, personals and shopping by Indonesia and games and streaming media by Turkey. We also note that the proportion of proxy and filter avoidance sites blocked by China and Iran to be comparatively high too. This is in line with recent statements from the Chinese government concerning mandatory blocking of VPNs by network providers in the country [28] and a similar circumstance around the Iranian presidential election in 2013 [34].

Figure 3 shows a comparison of categories of the filtered domains between the four test countries. This is the proportion of filtered domains per category per country. From this we can infer the different types of content that are under attention by the different regimes. For example, filtering of content within the topic of weapons is even between China, Indonesia and Iran, however censorship of religious sites is more prevalent in Iran.

4.3   Geographical location of blocked hosts

In addition to inferring the types of content being blocked, we identify the locations of the servers hosting filtered domains in each test country. This is achieved by making a DNS query for each domain to the control server and using MaxMind GeoIP2 country database [26] to locate the resulting IP addresses by country of origin. The breakdown of the origin of hosts of filtered domains to test country is shown in Figure 4.

Unsurprisingly, we find that the largest number of servers are hosted within the United States. This is expected due to the way many content-delivery-networks maintain peers in North America and the fact that over 50% of all Internet hosts are located on this continent [5].

During the course of this investigation we observe that a disproportionate percentage of blocked domains for Turkey were hosts in the Republic of Ireland. On further analysis of the domains and IP address records we find that the country appears to block any subdomain of *evennode.com* which is a hosting provider for NodeJS and Python web applications. The IP addresses of the blocked domains are owned by Amazon Technologies Inc. as part of their datacentres supporting Amazon Web Services. Further examination of this peculiarity was not performed, but it opens the questions as to whether certain censorship regimes will filter entire blocks of IP addresses and domains based on their hosted locations.

Other cases of interest are the irregular blocking of Dutch sites by Indonesia and Russian sites by China.

4.4   Backlink Analysis

For a more in-depth look into the networking effect between blocked websites, we find the number of filtered backlinks to and filtered forward links from each blocked webpage[3]. This allows us to see how deeply integrated each censored site is within the network of filtered content. We can look at the number of sites referencing *a given* blocked domain and also which filtered sites reference the most *other* blocked domains.

---

[3]Note that the backlinks and forward links are also themselves filtered in the given target country

To calculate these, we log every backlink we find to a filtered domain along with the filtered domains found to be linked *from* each filtered domain (forward filtered links). This results in a large graph of interconnected nodes (where each node is a filtered domain) and edges representing hyperlinks between them. From this, we can gain an insight into which domains are highly referenced within the network and which domains contain the most references to other filtered domains. Figures 5, 6, 7 and 8 show the backlinks of filtered domains for each target country.

Notable observations in Figures 6a and 8a are that the top sites that link to other filtered domains appear to be adult link collections which supports the findings in [39]. We can also see in Figures 5b and 7b that many of the linkers to filtered content are freedom of expression and independent news sites, both of which often contain political criticism.

4.5   Limitations

As mentioned previously, the filter check is limited by the sole use of DNS. While this reduces cause for ethical concerns, it does mean that content filtered by other means - such as IP filtering, keyword filtering or Deep Packet Inspection - will not be marked as blocked. Improvements to this check could increase the performance of the tool. Despite this, we still achieve good results.

A second limitation of this approach is the way that localised loops can form between networks of filtered content. This is a key issue with any web crawling system and often requires human interaction to break the loops - large search engines offer the ability for webmasters to provide links to new sites to improve reach. The looping behaviour we encounter can reduce the effectiveness of the system since the crawler does not have a means to connect other networks of filtered sites. Currently, this can only be altered by manipulating the seed URLs, but is not a fundamental issue with the approach. For purposes of testing and evaluation, limits were not imposed on the traversal between different domains and webpages, but a future implementation could handle looping behaviours in a similar way that search engines avoid spider traps [32].

5   CONCLUSIONS

This work has presented a new approach for building domain filter lists. We demonstrate the method is effective and capable at discovering censored web content in multiple different countries. Given the recursive nature of this method, we envisage that it will be a useful tool for organisations who maintain lists of blocked URLs. Furthermore, the system does not require large amounts of infrastructure to operate or special access to third-party systems or APIs. The use of DNS as a means of checking for filtering has scope to be improved, however, it allows us to test the effectiveness of these kinds of techniques, without incurring ethical issues in regards to the safety of individuals.

Through experimentation on four censorship regimes, we have discovered a large number of filtered domains that have not been previously published. This information will be of significant benefit to future studies concerning research within this field and for organisations that build circumvention tools. We aim to release this data as soon as possible.

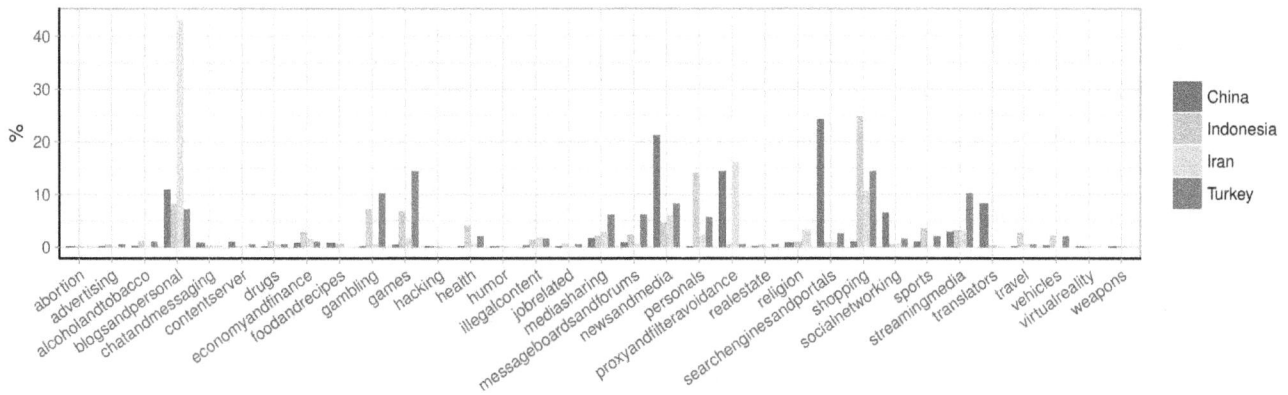

Figure 2: Category breakdown of filtered domains for each target country

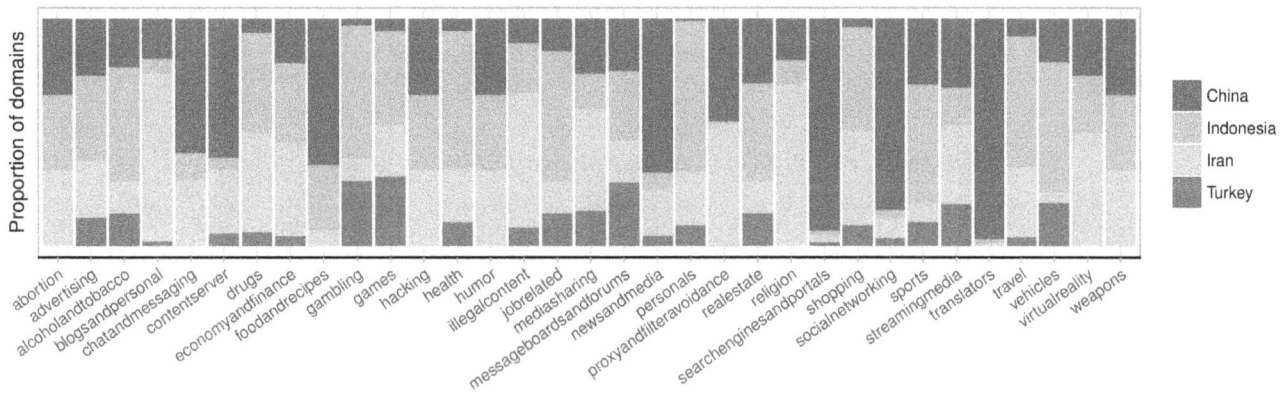

Figure 3: Category comparison of filtered domains between target countries

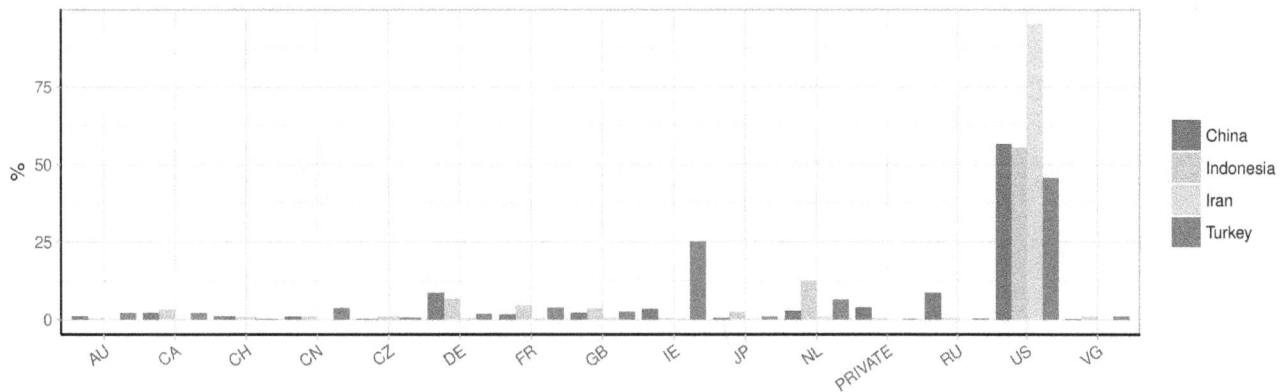

Figure 4: Location breakdown of hosts serving filtered domains for each target country

Our analysis of the collected data shows the relationship between backlinks of filtered webpages and hyperlinks to other filtered pages. This shows there is indeed a networking effect between different pieces of filtered content and provides a basis for future investigation. Furthermore, our analysis of the types and locations of content being blocked gives insight into the current state of Internet censorship within these regimes.

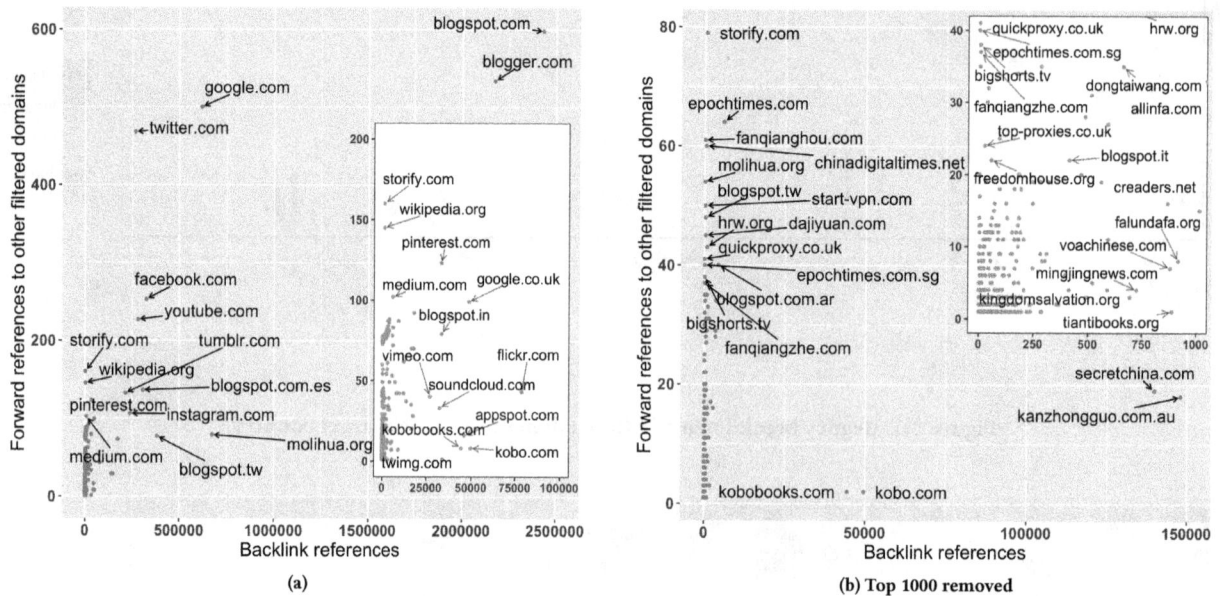

Figure 5: Backlinks of discovered filtered domains - China

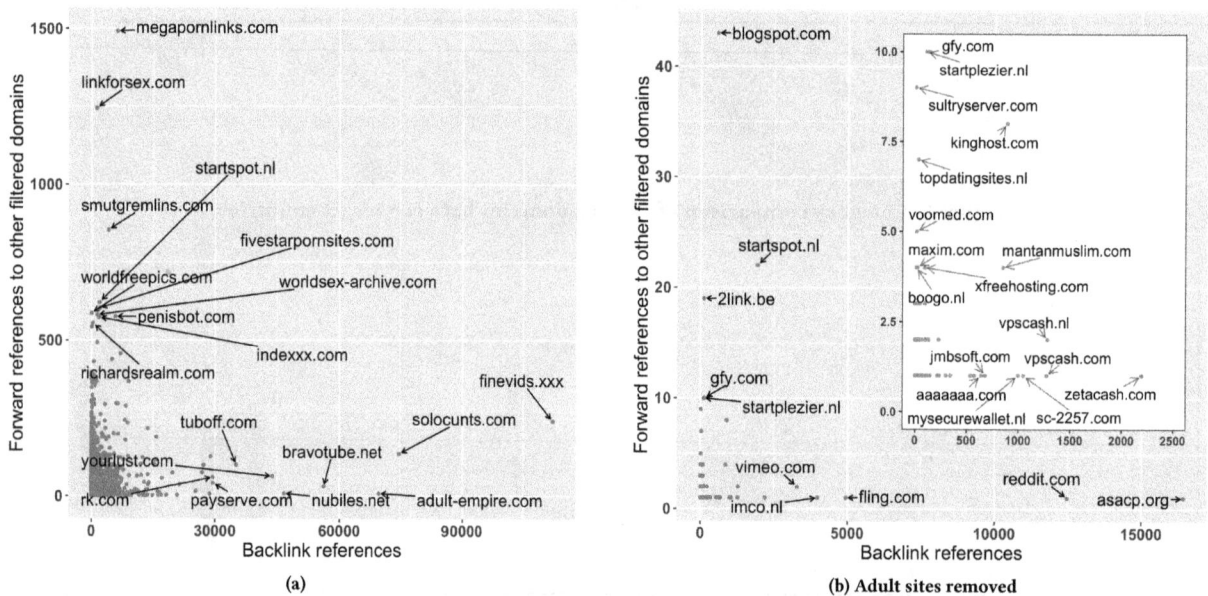

Figure 6: Backlinks of discovered filtered domains - Indonesia

6 FUTURE WORK

The approach described in this paper lends itself to refinement and extension. Firstly, the method of checking the filter status of URLs could be improved so it takes into account more factors than only DNS, although care will need to be taken to limit potential harm to people inside censored regions of the world. This could improve the accuracy of the system and potentially increase the scope within which it can operate.

Secondly, the technique could be integrated with others to form a hybrid system. This may improve performance and reduce the reliance on individual networks of filtered URLs. For example, the search engine based method used by [13] would integrate well with this approach. A combined system of this type could improve both

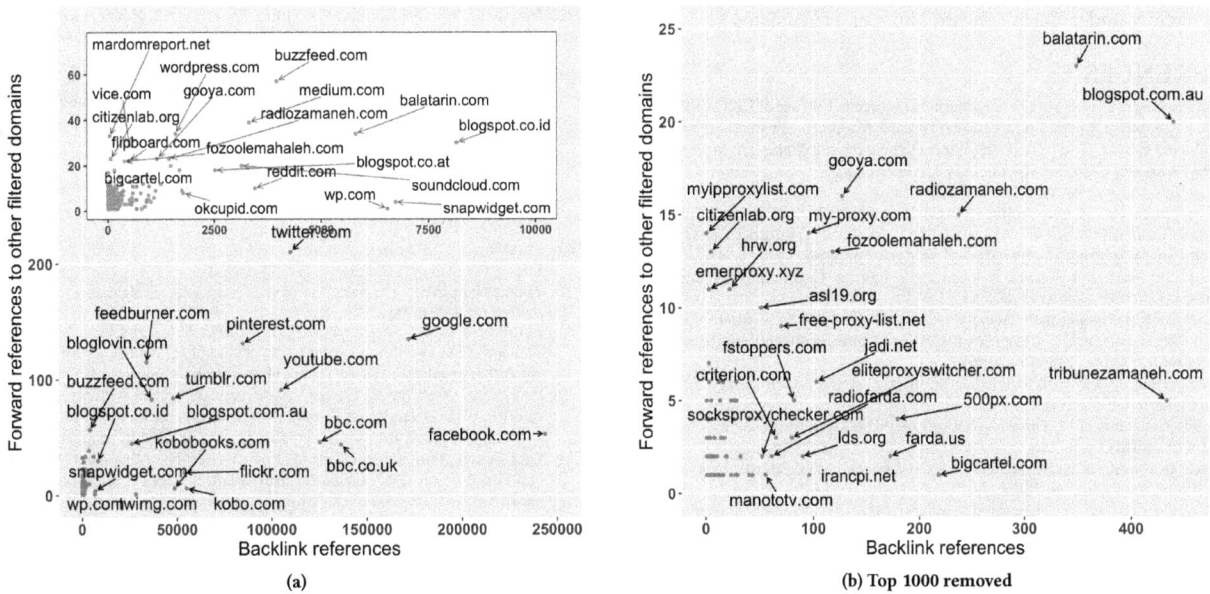

Figure 7: Backlinks of discovered filtered domains - Iran

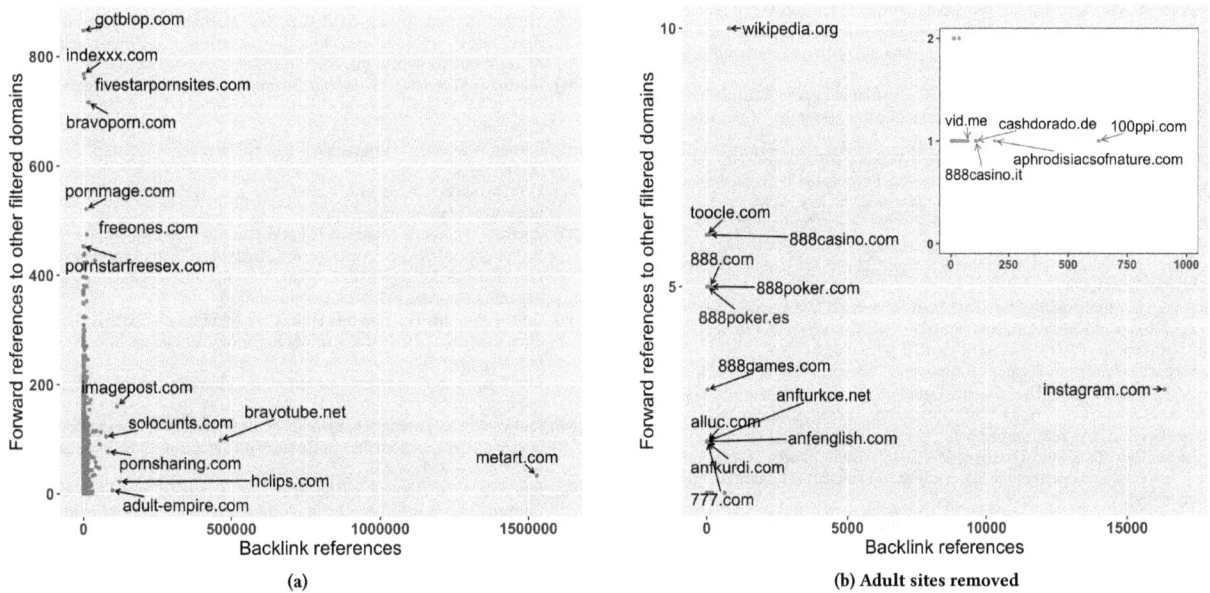

Figure 8: Backlinks of discovered filtered domains - Turkey

the breadth and depth of discovery for filtered URLs by traversing hyperlinks as well as making web searches. Furthermore, this may reduce the closed looping behaviour of solely web crawling.

Thirdly, the data collected by traversing between filtered URLs has potential for further analysis and experimentation. We have touched upon the connectivity between filtered URLs, but there is opportunity for deeper investigation into this concept.

ACKNOWLEDGMENTS

This work was supported by EPSRC through the Centre for Doctoral Training in Cyber Security, University of Oxford and The Alan Turing Institute under the EPSRC grant EP/N51012.

Alexander Darer & Oliver Farnan are funded by the Centre for Doctoral Training in Cyber Security.

Joss Wright is partially funded by the Alan Turing Institute as a Turing Fellow under Turing Award Number TU/B/000044.

REFERENCES

[1] Giuseppe Aceto. 2014. Monitoring Internet censorship: the case of UBICA. (2014).

[2] Giuseppe Aceto, Alessio Botta, Antonio Pescapé, M Faheem Awan, Tahir Ahmad, and Saad Qaisar. 2016. Analyzing internet censorship in Pakistan. In *Research and Technologies for Society and Industry Leveraging a better tomorrow (RTSI), 2016 IEEE 2nd International Forum on*. IEEE, 1–6.

[3] Giuseppe Aceto, Alessio Botta, Antonio Pescapè, Nick Feamster, M. Faheem Awan, Tahir Ahmad, and Saad Qaisar. 2015. Monitoring Internet Censorship with UBICA. In *Traffic Monitoring and Analysis*. Springer.

[4] Giuseppe Aceto and Antonio Pescapè. 2015. Internet Censorship detection: A survey. *Computer Networks* (2015).

[5] U.S. Central Intelligence Agency. Accessed Oct 2017. *Internet hosts, CIA World Factbook*. https://www.cia.gov/library/publications/the-world-factbook/rankorder/2184rank.html.

[6] Mustafa Akgul and Melih Kirlidog. 2015. Internet censorship in Turkey. *Internet Policy Review* 4, 2 (2015), 1–22.

[7] Collin Anderson. 2013. Dimming the Internet: Detecting throttling as a mechanism of censorship in Iran. *arXiv preprint arXiv:1306.4361* (2013).

[8] Simurgh Aryan, Homa Aryan, and J Alex Halderman. 2013. Internet Censorship in Iran: A First Look.. In *FOCI*.

[9] citizenlab.org. 2017 (accessed May, 2017). *citizenlab/test-lists*. https://github.com/citizenlab/test-lists.

[10] Richard Clayton, Steven J Murdoch, and Robert NM Watson. 2006. Ignoring the great firewall of china. In *Privacy Enhancing Technologies*. Springer, 20–35.

[11] Jedidiah R. Crandall, Masashi Crete-Nishihata, and Jeffrey Knockel. 2015. Forgive Us our SYNs: Technical and Ethical Considerations for Measuring Internet Filtering. In *Ethics in Networked Systems Research*. ACM.

[12] Jedidiah R Crandall, Daniel Zinn, Michael Byrd, Earl T Barr, and Rich East. 2007. ConceptDoppler: a weather tracker for internet censorship.. In *ACM Conference on Computer and Communications Security*. 352–365.

[13] Alexander Darer, Oliver Farnan, and Joss Wright. 2017. FilteredWeb: A Framework for the Automated Search-Based Discovery of Blocked URLs. In *Network Traffic Measurement and Analysis*. IFIP. http://tma.ifip.org/wordpress/wp-content/uploads/2017/06/tma2017_paper32.pdf

[14] David Dittrich, Erin Kenneally, et al. 2011. The Menlo Report: Ethical principles guiding information and communication technology research. *US Department of Homeland Security* (2011).

[15] Oliver Farnan, Alexander Darer, and Joss Wright. 2016. Poisoning the Well: Exploring the Great Firewall's Poisoned DNS Responses. In *Proceedings of the 2016 ACM on Workshop on Privacy in the Electronic Society*. ACM, 95–98.

[16] Arturo Filasto and Jacob Appelbaum. 2012. OONI: Open Observatory of Network Interference.. In *FOCI*.

[17] Mozilla Foundation. 2017 (accessed Sept, 2017). *Public Suffix List*. https://publicsuffix.org/.

[18] King-wa Fu, Chung-hong Chan, and Marie Chau. 2013. Assessing censorship on microblogs in China: Discriminatory keyword analysis and the real-name registration policy. *Internet Computing, IEEE* 17, 3 (2013), 42–50.

[19] Genevieve Gebhart, Anonymous Author, and Tadayoshi Kohno. 2017. Internet Censorship in Thailand: User Practices and Potential Threats. In *European Symposium on Security & Privacy*. IEEE. http://homes.cs.washington.edu/~yoshi/papers/GebhartEtAl-IEEEEuroSP.pdf

[20] Open Net Initiative. 2011 (accessed Jan, 2018). *ONI Country Profile - Indonesia*. http://access.opennet.net/wp-content/uploads/2011/12/accesscontested-indonesia.pdf.

[21] Arturo FilastÃš Khairil Yusof Tan Sze Ming Kay Yen Wong, Maria Xynou. 2017 (accessed May, 2017). *The State of Internet Censorship in Indonesia*. https://ooni.torproject.org/post/indonesia-internet-censorship/.

[22] Gary King, Jennifer Pan, and Margaret E Roberts. 2013. How censorship in China allows government criticism but silences collective expression. *American Political Science Review* 107, 02 (2013), 326–343.

[23] Jeffrey Knockel, Jedidiah R Crandall, and Jared Saia. 2011. Three Researchers, Five Conjectures: An Empirical Analysis of TOM-Skype Censorship and Surveillance.. In *FOCI*.

[24] Marc Kührer, Thomas Hupperich, Jonas Bushart, Christian Rossow, and Thorsten Holz. 2015. Going wild: Large-scale classification of open DNS resolvers. In *Proceedings of the 2015 Internet Measurement Conference*. ACM, 355–368.

[25] Graham Lowe, Patrick Winters, and Michael L Marcus. 2007. The great DNS wall of China. *MS, New York University* 21 (2007).

[26] MaxMind. Accessed Oct 2017. *GeoIP2 Databases*. https://www.maxmind.com/en/geoip2-databases.

[27] Zubair Nabi. 2013. The anatomy of web censorship in Pakistan. *arXiv preprint arXiv:1307.1144* (2013).

[28] Bloomberg News. Accessed Oct 2017. *China Tells Carriers to Block Access to Personal VPNs by February*. https://www.bloomberg.com/news/articles/2017-07-10/china-is-said-to-order-carriers-to-bar-personal-vpns-by-february.

[29] Paul Pearce, Roya Ensafi, Frank Li, Nick Feamster, and Vern Paxson. 2017. Augur: Internet-Wide Detection of Connectivity Disruptions. In *Symposium on Security & Privacy*. IEEE. http://www.ieee-security.org/TC/SP2017/papers/586.pdf

[30] Paul Pearce, Ben Jones, Frank Li, Roya Ensafi, Nick Feamster, Nick Weaver, and Vern Paxson. 2017. Global Measurement of DNS Manipulation. In *USENIX Security Symposium*. USENIX. https://www.usenix.org/system/files/conference/usenixsecurity17/sec17-pearce.pdf

[31] The Jakarta Post. 2017 (accessed May, 2017). *Indonesia blocks 800,000 websites*. http://www.thejakartapost.com/news/2017/01/07/indonesia-blocks-800000-websites.html.

[32] Maria Praetzellis. Accessed Oct 2017. *Identify and avoid crawler traps*. https://support.archive-it.org/hc/en-us/articles/208332943-Identify-and-avoid-crawler-traps-.

[33] Andreas Sfakianakis, Elias Athanasopoulos, and Sotiris Ioannidis. 2011. CensMon: A Web Censorship Monitor. In *Free and Open Communications on the Internet*. USENIX.

[34] Yeganeh Torbati. Accessed Oct 2017. *Iran blocks use of tool to get around Internet filter*. https://www.reuters.com/article/us-iran-internet/iran-blocks-use-of-tool-to-get-around-internet-filter-idUSBRE9290CV20130310.

[35] Matthäus Wander, Christopher Boelmann, Lorenz Schwittmann, and Torben Weis. 2014. Measurement of globally visible DNS injection. *IEEE Access* 2 (2014), 526–536.

[36] Barney Warf. 2011. Geographies of global Internet censorship. *GeoJournal* 76, 1 (2011), 1–23.

[37] WebShrinker. Accessed 2017. *WebShrinker Categories API*. https://www.webshrinker.com/.

[38] Zachary Weinberg, Mahmood Sharif, Janos Szurdi, and Nicolas Christin. 2017. Topics of Controversy: An Empirical Analysis of Web Censorship Lists. *Privacy Enhancing Technologies* 2017, 1 (2017), 42–61. https://petsymposium.org/2017/papers/issue1/paper06-2017-1-source.pdf

[39] Gilbert Wondracek, Thorsten Holz, Christian Platzer, Engin Kirda, and Christopher Kruegel. 2010. Is the Internet for Porn? An Insight Into the Online Adult Industry.. In *WEIS*.

[40] Joss Wright. 2014. Regional variation in Chinese internet filtering. *Information, Communication & Society* 17, 1 (2014), 121–141.

[41] Joss Wright, Alexander Darer, and Oliver Farnan. 2015. Filterprints: Identifying Localised Usage Anomalies in Censorship Circumvention Tools. *arXiv preprint arXiv:1507.05819* (2015).

[42] Joss Wright, Tulio Souza, and Ian Brown. 2011. Fine-Grained Censorship Mapping: Information Sources, Legality and Ethics. In *Free and Open Communications on the Internet*. USENIX.

Worth its Weight in Likes: Towards Detecting Fake Likes on Instagram

Indira Sen[*]
IIIT-Delhi
indira15021@iiitd.ac.in

Anupama Aggarwal
IIIT-Delhi
anupamaa@iiitd.ac.in

Shiven Mian
IIIT-Delhi
shiven15094@iiitd.ac.in

Siddharth Singh
IIIT-Delhi
siddharth14105@iiitd.ac.in

Ponnurangam Kumaraguru
IIIT-Delhi
pk@iiitd.ac.in

Anwitaman Datta
NTU, Singapore
Anwitaman@ntu.edu.sg

ABSTRACT

Instagram is a significant platform for users to share media; reflecting their interests. It is used by marketers and brands to reach their potential audience for advertisement. The number of likes on posts serves as a proxy for social reputation of the users, and in some cases, social media influencers with an extensive reach are compensated by marketers to promote products. This emerging market has led to users artificially bolstering the likes they get to project an inflated social worth. In this study, we enumerate the potential factors which contribute towards a genuine like on Instagram. Based on our analysis of liking behaviour, we build an automated mechanism to detect fake likes on Instagram which achieves a high precision of 83.5%. Our work serves an important first step in reducing the effect of fake likes on Instagram influencer market.

CCS CONCEPTS

• **Networks** → **Online social networks**; • **Information systems** → Social networks;

KEYWORDS

Fake Social Engagement, Online Social Networks, Instagram

ACM Reference Format:
Indira Sen, Anupama Aggarwal, Shiven Mian, Siddharth Singh, Ponnurangam Kumaraguru, and Anwitaman Datta. 2018. Worth its Weight in Likes: Towards Detecting Fake Likes on Instagram. In *WebSci '18: 10th ACM Conference on Web Science, May 27–30, 2018, Amsterdam, Netherlands*. ACM, New York, NY, USA, 5 pages. https://doi.org/10.1145/3201064.3201105

1 INTRODUCTION

Apart from being used as a medium of communication, Online Social Networks (OSNs) are also used to gain popularity, increase social self-worth and promote businesses. Even brands, advertisers

and the background recommender algorithms of OSNs rely on the popularity metrics of users and content shared on these services. To get more benefits, users often artificially increase the popularity and engagement on their content in several ways. Some of the prevalent ways are – to leverage bots, purchase social metrics such as – likes, followers, and shares from black market services, and become part of collusion networks which can be used to trade inorganic engagement. Such artificial bolstering of popularity can cause brands to lose money [1], advertisers to not reach the relevant audience, and recommender algorithms to give poor suggestions [13].

There have been several prior efforts to identify fraud [6], spam [4] and fake users [6] on OSNs. In this study, we instead focus on inorganic engagement received by a user. Previous studies aiming to detect fake liking behaviour, assume that if a user has given one or two fake likes, all her likes are fake [2, 8]. However, we believe this is a limited understanding of fake engagement since a single user can generate organic, as well as inorganic engagement. For instance, an Instagram user can *like* content which she is genuinely interested in, and in addition, the same user can also be a part of a colluding 'like-back' network, where she likes unrelated and random content only to receive back some likes and increase her own popularity. Therefore, we propose that the true reach / social-worth of the user should be determined by canceling out the effect of fake engagement which she receives, and should largely depend only on the organic engagement (we use the terms organic and genuine interchangeably). We define organic liking engagement on Instagram as a *like*-action which a user gives to a post when she has genuine interest in the content, or in the user posting the content (poster). In this study, our goal is to identify the ingenuity of likes by determining user's intention of liking a post. In particular, we define the goal as — *Given* a liker $\mathcal{L}$, who likes a specific post p of a poster $\mathcal{S}$ – *Find out* the features of $\mathcal{L}$, p and $\mathcal{S}$, *to determine* the probability of liker $\mathcal{L}$ *genuinely* liking a post p.

Here, we find attributes of fake liking which can help us distinguish such behavior from organic liking activity. Unlike previous studies on spam detection which assume that a single spam post translates into the user being a spammer [2, 8], we infer the reach of an Instagram user as a function of the organic and fake likes, reducing the effect of fake likes (to some extent - subject to the efficacy of our approach) in the process. Our contributions are –
Characterizing Fake and Organic Likes. We discern fake and organic likes by determining the factors which can lead to a user genuinely liking a post on Instagram. While previous studies have looked at meta-features of profiles, content, and structure, we focus

---

[*]the work was done partly while the author was visiting NTU Singapore as part of the NTU-India Connect Research Internship Programme.

our efforts in identifying the probability of a user liking particular content based on various factors like topical interest and proximity with the source user. We study an extensive list of features indicating genuineness of a like instance. Our findings show that topical interest of liker with the post, and profile quality are most helpful. **Automatic Detection of Fake Likes.** As next step, based on the understanding we gain in the previous step, we build a machine learning based model to automatically distinguish a fake like from an organic like. We are able to detect fake liking instances with a precision of 83.5% using a neural network model.

2 RELATED WORK

User Behaviour. While not as widely researched as other OSNs, such as Facebook and Twitter, studies on Instagram explore user behaviour [11, 20]. Especially close to our work is Jang et al.'s analysis of Instagram but without a focus on fraud [12] where they note the lack of reciprocity when it comes to liking behaviour. **Malicious Engagement on OSNs.** Malicious entities on OSNs have been widely studied with a particular focus on Facebook [9, 15], Twitter [4, 21], and to a lesser extent, on Instagram [6]. Our work differs from these since we aim to spot suspicious *behaviour*, specifically, fake liking. While fake liking and other fraudulent activities may co-occur, the former can exist without the latter.

While not explored as widely as detection of fake entities, fake engagement on OSNs has been previously studied on Facebook [2, 5, 8], Twitter [10] and Youtube [16]. Beutel et al. presents an understanding of the 'lock-step' behaviour in coordinated fake likers on Facebook, using temporal snapshots [5]. Giatsogolou et al. study fraudulent retweeting behaviour on Twitter by analyzing network and temporal patterns [10] while Li et al. detect fake engagement on Youtube using spectral clustering [16]. While network and temporal features are effective, they are often difficult to obtain. In such cases, content-based analysis can yield fruitful results. Badri et al. aims to weed out fake liking on Facebook pages using profile and post features of likers using a supervised classification model [2].

This present work adds to the use of content-based features in two ways - *first*, by also taking into account the relationship between a poster and a liker. *Second*, we account for Instagram's visual nature by taking the properties of the image into consideration.

3 DATA

Fake Like Instances (FakeLike_data): There are multiple sources of fake likes such as paid web-services or apps, trading platforms where a user participates in a giving likes in exchange for likes, and bots which are triggered based on hashtags. Instagram also allows users to post videos and maintains its view count and like count [1]. We assume that if a video has received likes, but has zero views, then the like instances are fake, because they were generated without properly seeing the content. We capture 16,448 such *like instances* (information about the liker, post, and source user), and add it to FakeLike_data. Such fake likes instances could have been generated from any of the aforementioned sources. We acknowledge that our fake like instances dataset can be much more comprehensive; we leave it for future work.

Random Like Instances (RandLike_data): It is hard to obtain a true positive dataset of genuine likes. Therefore, instead we collect a much larger random set of like instances to draw comparison with fake likes, and to use as negative class to build a machine learning model to identify fake likes. Since Instagram does not provide a direct way to sample random users/posts, we obtain a seed set of Instagram users, [2] and extract their follower and followee connections in a breadth-first-search manner. This gives us a sample of 1 million Instagram users, from which we take a smaller subset of users and extract their posts, and likes on each of those posts. In this manner, we obtain a dataset of 134,669 like instances in RandLike_data. Note that this sample is much larger (more than 8 times) than the fake like instance dataset. Therefore, despite the noise, we assume that predominantly, the like instances in RandLike_data would be genuine. Though a noisy dataset is one of our current limitations, but with a clean negative dataset, our results showing differences between fake and other likes, and supervised learning based identification of fake likes would only improve. We summarize the data collected in Table 1.

Table 1: Dataset of Instagram like instances. We also collect meta-information of likers, posts and posters.

	#likes	#posts (p)	#Likers ($\mathcal{L}$)	#Posters ($\mathcal{S}$)
FakeLike_data	16,448	9,932	9,301	7,822
RandLike_data	134,669	1,717	47,233	738

4 ANALYSIS

In this section, we present and validate hypotheses that explain liking behaviour on Instagram. While it is virtually impossible to know why a user might like a post, it is possible to understand how the user could have come across the post, which is a non-trivial prerequisite for liking. Based on this intuition, we enumerate the plausible reasons behind a user genuinely liking another user's post. We begin by giving our definition of a *like instance* — *Given a poster $\mathcal{S}$ whose post p has been liked by liker $\mathcal{L}$, we define a like instance as the tuple $(\mathcal{L}, p, \mathcal{S})$.* A like instance is designed to contain post properties to ensure that a liker is evaluated on the basis of individual posts she likes. We do not assume that if a single like generated by a liker is fake, then all her other likes are also fake. Next, we define the following set of hypothesis which shed light on genuinely garnering likes on Instagram.

4.1 Network Effects

Instagram enables the user to view posts by her followees in her feed, and also *explore* the content liked by the followees. Previous studies have noted the role of social ties in reinforcing engagement on OSNs [3]. We take cues from this to propose the following – **H1.1: A liker $\mathcal{L}$ is more likely to genuinely like $\mathcal{S}$'s post if $\mathcal{L}$ is a follower of $\mathcal{S}$.** In this case, $\mathcal{L}$ will receive the content posted by $\mathcal{S}$ in her home feed, and hence there is a higher chance of $\mathcal{L}$ genuinely liking that post. In addition, if $\mathcal{L}$ is following $\mathcal{S}$, we can assume that $\mathcal{L}$ is interested in $\mathcal{S}$'s content. **H1.2: A liker $\mathcal{L}$ is more likely to genuinely like $\mathcal{S}$'s post if $\mathcal{L}$ is a follower of $\mathcal{S}$'s followers.** Instagram also lets the users

---

[1]View count increases by one when a user watched the content for more than 3 seconds. Like count increases by one on an explicit like action by the user.

[2]Seed set contains users whose content was featured on Instagram's official account.

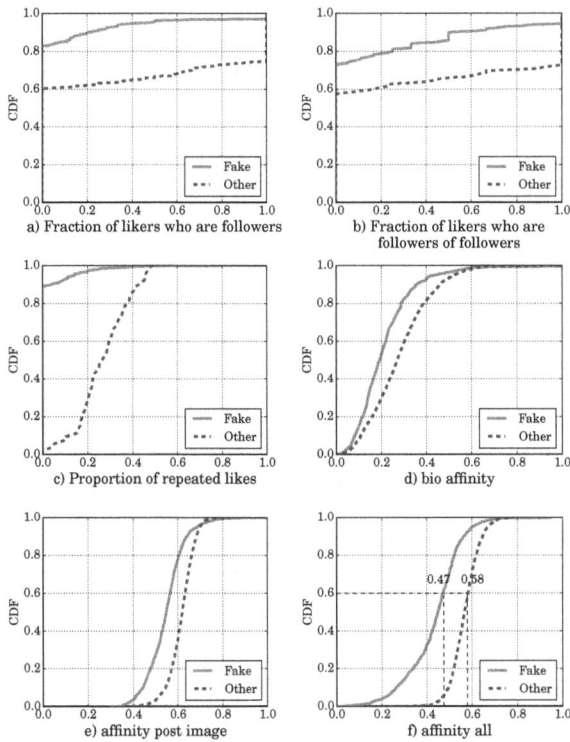

Figure 1: Cumulative distribution function of the like properties for fake likes and other likes.

follow the activities of the users being followed. Therefore, a liker $\mathcal{L}$ can also come across the liked post p if it is liked by one of the users which $\mathcal{L}$ follows. We also consider such an instance to indicate a higher level of confidence in the genuineness of the like instance.

To test H1.1 and H1.2, we study the *follower*, and *follower-of-follower* connections of the posters in our dataset of fake and random likes, and found that genuine likers do indeed like their followees post more than fake likers do (KS-test =0.303, p < 0.001). For fake like engagements, there are significantly less proportion of likers which are followers of the poster. In case of fake engagements, only 16.8% of likers of a post are followers of the poster, as compared to a much higher fraction of 39.1% likers being followers in case of random like engagements (Figure 1(a)). We see similar observation in a two-hop network in Figure 1(b). Only 2.8% of likers of a post in case of fake likes are follower-of-follower of the poster, as compared to 42.4% in case of random like engagement [3].

4.2 Interest Overlap

H2: A user $\mathcal{L}$ will have a higher chance of genuinely liking S's post if $\mathcal{L}$ and S share interests. To capture interest overlap between two Instagram users, we first define their *Interest Profile* and the extent of overlap as *Affinity*.

Interest Profile: . *Given a user u we define u's interest profile as a set of topics $(t_u^1, t_u^2, ..., t_u^n)$, where these topics are inferred from u's bio b_u and posts $(p_u^1, p_u^2 ..., p_u^k)$.*

Topic Extraction. Inspired by previous studies, which have used Instagram bios to detect user interests [19], we infer topics from textual sources such as bio and post captions using Wikification [17]. Instagram is an image-based OSN and the post images may also have latent topical information, which we leverage using Densecap captioning [14] to obtain meaningful captions. Wikification is applied on these captions to extract fine-grained topics.

Topic Matching. To match topics we utilize word2vec similarities [18] between two tuples of interests [4]. We define a post's attributes t_i as the wikified topics of the post, and define the topical similarity between users as follows –

Affinity. *Given user a and b's interest profile as $I_a = (t_a^1, ..., t_a^n)$ and $I_b = (t_b^1, ..., t_b^m)$, we define*

$$Affinity(T_a, T_b) = \frac{1}{n} \sum_{i=1}^{n} \max_{1 \leq j \leq m} w2vec(t_a^i, t_b^j)$$

We extract a user's interest profile from her bio, and by converting the post image into relevant text using Densecap. Note that this metric is not commutative and therefore penalizes likers with a very wide variety of interests, which is an indicator of suspicious behavior. It has been seen previously that genuine likers tend to like things related to a limited set of topics and are more discerning [2]. Therefore, we consider topical affinity as one of the distinguishing features to identify fake liking engagement. Note that the value of affinity is between [0, 1], with higher affinity value indicating high topical matching. We found that 60% of fake likers have an affinity value of 0.475, as compared to 0.58 affinity for same proportion of random set of likers (as seen in Figure 1(f) We have similar observations for affinity calculated over only bio (Figure 1(d)), and only text extracted from post image (Figure 1(e)). However, we combine both of these to enhance the discriminative effect.

4.3 Liking Frequency

H3: A liker $\mathcal{L}$ will genuinely like more than one post of the poster S. We observe that legitimate likers keep coming back to the same poster. Figure 1(c) shows that 90% posters with fake likes get 7% repeated likers on their posts, as compared to the same fraction of posters with other likes getting 42% repeated likes.

4.4 Influential Poster

H4: A user $\mathcal{L}$ will have a higher chance of genuinely liking S's photo if S is an 'influential' user or a celebrity. It has been observed that celebrities garner a higher number of likes on their content [7]. We use the Instagram verification badge as a proxy for celebrity users. We observe that in our dataset, only 1.9% users were celebrities who got fake likes, as compared to 7.5% celebrities who got genuine likes, indicating that celebrities are more likely to attract a higher number of likes. Therefore, we consider a poster being a celebrity as a feature to gauge the genuineness of a like.

4.5 Link Farming Hashtags to get Fake Likes

Hashtags have been shown to play an important role in Instagram in spreading the reach of posts and attracting more likes [20], therefore we examine their role in fake liking behaviour.

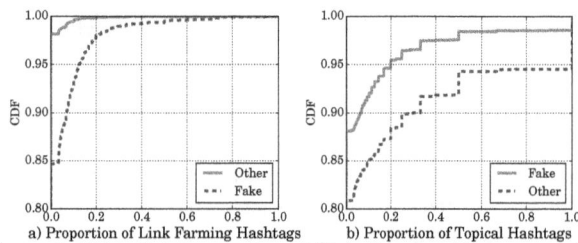

a) Proportion of Link Farming Hashtags

b) Proportion of Topical Hashtags

Figure 2: CDF of a) Proportion of Link Farming Hashtags and b) Proportion of Topical Hashtags used by posters. Fake like instances show a high proportion of link farming hashtags which can be used to solicit likes, but show a relatively lower proportion of topical hashtags.

H5.1: A user S is more likely to attract fake likes if she uses link farming hashtags in her posts. *Link farming* hashtags, such as 'like4like', 'like2follow', can be used to elicit fake likes. Such hashtags are often used by a community of users who collude to inflate each other's likes and followers. We curate a list of 112 such hashtags [5] and find that 20.8% posts with fake likes have at least one link farming hashtag as compared to 1.8% posts with random likes. Figure 2(a) shows that fake like instances tend to have a higher proportion of link farming hashtags.

4.6 Topical Hashtags

H5.2: A user S with genuine likes will have topical hashtags in their posts. Another aspect of posting behaviour is related to topical hashtags used in a post, instead of occasional (#throwbackthursday, #ootd), trending (#mayweather) or link farming hashtags (#like4like). We adopt a two-step process to detect topical hashtags. We first filter out all link farming hashtags as well as popular non-topical hashtags [6]. Next, we segment these hashtags and use Wikifier to see what proportion of hashtags pertain to a topic. Figure 2(b) shows that fake like instances tend to have a lower proportion of topical hashtags (KS test = 0.342, p < 0.001).

5 DETECTING FAKE LIKES

In addition to the features based on the hypotheses previously described, we also consider user-based attributes, viz, volume of posts generated, average number of posts per day [2] and profile completeness (presence of profile picture, name and bio) [8]. Finally, we compute the Chi-square values to rank features in the order of their efficacy in distinguishing between fake and other likes. Topical affinity scores high (16%) as do user based features, particularly profile completeness (11%), and fraction of topical hashtags (9%). [7]

5.1 Building a Classification Model

While the actual ratio of fake to genuine likes in Instagram is unknown, based on previous literature on spam detection [4], we maintain a ratio of roughly 1:8. This proportion ensures that any

machine learning model trained on such a dataset can perform well 'in-the-wild' where the ratio of likes would be highly imbalanced. Therefore, we obtain the aforementioned features from `FakeLike_data` and `RandLike_data`, and train a supervised model on these features with fake likes as the positive class. We experiment with different classification algorithms viz. Logistic Regression, Random Forest, SVM (RBF kernel), AdaBoost (with Random Forest as base initiator), and XGBoost. We also use a simple feed-forward neural network – Multi-Layer Perceptron (MLP) which gives us the best performance. In all our experiments we perform 10-fold cross-validation, using 80% of the dataset as training data and 20% for validation. For the MLP based model, we use 2 hidden layers with 200 neurons each. Both layers use sigmoid activation function, and the output layer has a dropout of 0.2 to prevent overfitting.

Baseline. As a baseline, we use Badri et al.'s method to detect fake likers on Facebook [2]. Their work focuses on the properties of the liker, without considering the relationship between a liker and a poster. As the source code was unavailable, we implemented this method on our own based on the features detailed in the paper. The authors propose a supervised method for the detection of fake likes based on profile (length of biography, lifespan of account, number of bidirectional connections), posting activity (average number and maximum posts per day, total posts and skewness of posting), page liking (category entropy of pages liked, proportion of verified pages) and social attention (average number of likes and comments received) of the liker. We discard two features: (1) proportion of shared photos and (2) average number of shares received, since there is no concept of sharing posts on Instagram, unlike Facebook. The authors experiment with multiple classifiers and find XGBoost to perform best. We use Precision, Recall and Area under the ROC curve (AUC) to measure the performance of all models in detecting fake likes, with the latter being especially important in understanding the performance of a classifier trained on imbalanced data.

5.2 Experimental Results

We observe that boosted trees, Adaboost and XGBoost (also used in the baseline), perform well due to robustness against outliers. However, we achieve highest performance using the MLP with an average precision of 83% and recall of 81% (AUC of 89%) in detecting fake likes. Our results are inline with previous studies on fraud detection where neural networks have shown competitive performance [21]. We compare validation loss and training loss across training epochs and observe that they are close to each other, almost converging with increasing epochs. We, therefore, conclude that our fake like detection system does not overfit and generalizes well to unseen likes. Table 2 summarizes our results.

The baseline model gives a precision of 61%, a recall of 69%. Compared to the baseline model, our model obtains an 83% precision and 81% recall to detect fake like instances. The strength of our method lies in effectively capturing the parameters which affect genuine liking behavior on Instagram. We perform a manual investigation of 200 randomly sampled fake likes labeled genuine (false negatives) by the baseline. We find that these likes are given by users with well-formed profiles who superficially appear to be benign users. On the other hand, our method classifies 78% of these

---

[5]This list was shortlisted from a list of popular hashtags by two active Instagram users and we make it publicly available here: goo.gl/UshiXk

[6]Like the link farming hashtags, popular hashtags were curated by the same annotators and are available in the same URL.

[7]We exclude the follower-of-follower from the feature list since the 2-hop network of the entire dataset could not be collected due to API restrictions.

Table 2: Results of various classifiers in differentiating between fake and random like instances across different feature types. We report precision and recall in detection of fake likes. The MLP model performs best.

Classifier	LogReg			Random Forest			SVM(RBF)			Adaboost			XGBoost			MLP		
Feature Type	Prec	Rec	AUC	Prec	Rec	AUC	Prec	Rec	AUC	Prec	Rec	AUC	Prec	Rec	AUC	Prec	Rec	AUC
H1: Network Effect	0.1	0.71	0.32	0.12	0.67	0.35	0.16	0.72	0.66	0.15	0.75	0.59	0.17	0.70	0.64	0.24	0.73	0.67
H2: Interest Overlap	0.36	0.5	0.49	0.38	0.54	0.56	0.54	0.59	0.73	0.56	0.54	0.72	0.60	0.59	0.79	0.68	0.68	0.80
H3: Liking Frequency	0.11	0.62	0.38	0.12	0.53	0.36	0.18	0.6	0.65	0.13	0.35	0.61	0.15	0.43	0.68	0.22	0.51	0.71
H4: Influential Poster	0.11	0.62	0.33	0.11	0.5	0.35	0.12	0.71	0.6	0.16	0.6	0.68	0.22	0.59	0.69	0.31	0.70	0.72
H5: Hashtag features	0.21	0.56	0.54	0.21	0.55	0.51	0.28	0.6	0.69	0.49	0.26	0.72	0.44	0.34	0.71	0.60	0.51	0.76
User based features	0.32	0.16	0.57	0.3	0.21	0.57	0.4	0.22	0.70	0.53	0.61	0.74	0.54	0.67	0.73	0.61	0.74	0.79
All Features	0.39	0.67	0.67	0.39	0.64	0.62	0.58	0.65	0.77	0.65	0.60	0.78	0.69	0.65	0.81	**0.83**	**0.81**	**0.89**

likes as fake likes. We find that the affinity between the likers and posters in these like instances are lower than average. We also note the presence of link farming hashtags in the posts of these like instances. Therefore, we believe our system can detect fake likes given by genuine looking entities, as well, unlike current methods which entirely rely on the user properties to determine fake liking.

Error Analysis. To understand why our model is not able to detect 19% of the fake likes, we randomly sample 100 undetected fake likes and manually inspect them. We find that in 27 fake like instances, the likers were followers of the poster, potentially leading our model to misclassify such like instances as genuine. It suggests that some posters have fake followers and the fake likes are from such followers, something our current methodology is unable to capture. However, our approach can be modularly applied in a cascade, after detecting fake followers using previous techniques [6]. Furthermore, we found that 61 likers had a high topical interest overlap with the posts they had liked. A more thorough analysis showed that this was happening due to small set of interests (just one or two) of the liker, which results in high affinity value.

6 CONCLUSION

To complement previous studies on fake liking in other OSNs, we perform the first exploration of fake liking behaviour on Instagram. We build on existing content-based techniques of fraud detection on OSNs by incorporating factors that motivate liking on Instagram, such as liker-poster interest overlap. Additionally, we also account for Instagram's visual aspect by examining the contents of images. Our automated method is able to detect fake likes with 83% precision (22% increase on the baseline).

Limitations and Future Work. For collecting our ground truth data, we restrict ourselves to videos with likes but no views. In future, we plan to explore other sources such as trading web services and mobile apps. Our preliminary investigations show that there is a thriving underground ecosystem for fake liking on Instagram, including paid services and trading platforms, which we can analyze using our existing model. Another limitation and area of improvement is our affinity metric which has unpredictable behaviour when user interest tuples are small. Finally, other than these improvements, we plan to leverage our detection model to nullify or penalize the effect of fake likes and provide the actual reach of an Instagram user in terms of the genuine likes they get.

REFERENCES

[1] 2017. Social Media Experiment reveals how easy it is to create fake Instagram accounts and make money from them. http://www.independent.co.uk/life-style/gadgets-and-tech/social-media-experiment-fake-instagram-accounts-make-money-influencer-star-blogger-mediakix-a7887836.html. (2017).

[2] Prudhvi Ratna Badri Satya, Kyumin Lee, Dongwon Lee, Thanh Tran, and Jason Jiasheng Zhang. 2016. Uncovering fake likers in online social networks. In *ACM International Conference on Information and Knowledge Management*.

[3] Saeideh Bakhshi, David A Shamma, and Eric Gilbert. 2014. Faces engage us: Photos with faces attract more likes and comments on instagram. In *ACM Conference on Human factors in Computing Systems*.

[4] Fabricio Benevenuto, Gabriel Magno, Tiago Rodrigues, and Virgilio Almeida. 2010. Detecting spammers on twitter. In *Annual Collaboration, Electronic Messaging, Anti-Abuse and Spam Conference*.

[5] Alex Beutel, Wanhong Xu, Venkatesan Guruswami, Christopher Palow, and Christos Faloutsos. 2013. Copycatch: stopping group attacks by spotting lockstep behavior in social networks. In *International Conference on World Wide Web*.

[6] Qiang Cao, Xiaowei Yang, Jieqi Yu, and Christopher Palow. 2014. Uncovering large groups of active malicious accounts in online social networks. In *ACM SIGSAC Conference on Computer and Communications Security*.

[7] Meeyoung Cha, Hamed Haddadi, Fabricio Benevenuto, and P Krishna Gummadi. 2010. Measuring user influence in twitter: The million follower fallacy. In *International AAAI Conference on Web and Social Media*.

[8] Emiliano De Cristofaro, Arik Friedman, Guillaume Jourjon, Mohamed Ali Kaafar, and M Zubair Shafiq. 2014. Paying for likes?: Understanding facebook like fraud using honeypots. In *ACM SIGCOMM conference on Internet Measurement*.

[9] Hongyu Gao, Jun Hu, Christo Wilson, Zhichun Li, Yan Chen, and Ben Y Zhao. 2010. Detecting and characterizing social spam campaigns. In *ACM SIGCOMM Conference on Internet Measurement*.

[10] Maria Giatsoglou, Despoina Chatzakou, Neil Shah, Christos Faloutsos, and Athena Vakali. 2015. Retweeting Activity on Twitter: Signs of Deception. In *Pacific-Asia Conference on Knowledge Discovery and Data Mining*.

[11] Yuheng Hu, Lydia Manikonda, and Subbarao Kambhampati. 2014. What We Instagram: A First Analysis of Instagram Photo Content and User Types. In *International AAAI Conference on Web and Social Media*.

[12] Jin Yea Jang, Kyungsik Han, and Dongwon Lee. 2015. No reciprocity in liking photos: Analyzing like activities in Instagram. In *ACM Conference on Hypertext & Social Media*.

[13] Nitin Jindal and Bing Liu. 2008. Opinion spam and analysis. In *International Conference on Web Search and Data Mining*.

[14] Justin Johnson, Andrej Karpathy, and Li Fei-Fei. 2016. Densecap: Fully convolutional localization networks for dense captioning. In *IEEE Conference on Computer Vision and Pattern Recognition*.

[15] Kyumin Lee, James Caverlee, and Steve Webb. 2010. Uncovering social spammers: social honeypots+ machine learning. In *International ACM SIGIR Conference on Research and Development in Information Retrieval*.

[16] Yixuan Li, Oscar Martinez, Xing Chen, Yi Li, and John E Hopcroft. 2016. In a world that counts: Clustering and detecting fake social engagement at scale. In *International Conference on World Wide Web*.

[17] Rada Mihalcea and Andras Csomai. 2007. Wikify!: linking documents to encyclopedic knowledge. In *ACM International Conference on Information and Knowledge Management*.

[18] Tomas Mikolov, Wen-tau Yih, and Geoffrey Zweig. 2013. Linguistic regularities in continuous space word representations. In *North American Chapter of the Association for Computational Linguistics: Human Language Technologies*.

[19] Aditya Pal, Amaç Herdagdelen, Sourav Chatterji, Sumit Taank, and Deepayan Chakrabarti. 2016. Discovery of topical authorities in instagram. In *International Conference on World Wide Web*.

[20] Ramine Tinati, Aastha Madaan, and Wendy Hall. 2017. InstaCan: Examining Deleted Content on Instagram. In *ACM Conference on Web Science*.

[21] Svitlana Volkova and Eric Bell. 2017. Identifying Effective Signals to Predict Deleted and Suspended Accounts on Twitter Across Languages. In *AAAI International Conference on Weblogs and Social Media*.

Public Opinion Spamming:
A Model for Content and Users on Sina Weibo

Ziyu Guo
Shandong University
Jinan, China

Liqiang Wang*
Shandong University
Jinan, China

Yafang Wang[†]
Shandong University
Jinan, China

Guohua Zeng
Chinese Academy of Social Sciences
Beijing, China

Shijun Liu
Shandong University
Jinan, China

Gerard de Melo
Rutgers University – New Brunswick
USA

ABSTRACT

Microblogs serve hundreds of millions of active users, but have also attracted large numbers of spammers. While traditional spam often seeks to endorse specific products or services, nowadays there are increasingly also paid posters intent on promoting particular views on hot topics and influencing public opinion. In this work, we fill an important research gap by studying how to detect such opinion spammers and their micro-manipulation of public opinion. Our model is unsupervised and adopts a Bayesian framework to distinguish spammers from other classes of users. Experiments on a Sina Weibo hot topic dataset demonstrate the effectiveness of the proposed approach. A further diachronic analysis of the collected data demonstrates that public opinion spammers have developed sophisticated techniques and have seen success in subtly manipulating the public sentiment.

CCS CONCEPTS

• **Information systems** → **Spam detection;** • **Human-centered computing** → **Social media;** • **Applied computing** → **Sociology;**

KEYWORDS

Opinion Spam, Public Opinion, User Classification

ACM Reference Format:
Ziyu Guo, Liqiang Wang, Yafang Wang, Guohua Zeng, Shijun Liu, and Gerard de Melo. 2018. Public Opinion Spamming: A Model for Content and Users on Sina Weibo. In *WebSci '18: WebSci '18 10th ACM Conference on Web Science, May 27–30, 2018, Amsterdam, Netherlands.* ACM, New York, NY, USA, 5 pages. https://doi.org/10.1145/3201064.3201104

*The first two authors contributed equally.
[†]Corresponding author: yafang.wang@sdu.edu.cn

1 INTRODUCTION

Social network services provide platforms for massive information dissemination and sharing between hundreds of millions of users. Unfortunately, they also have led to new opportunities for malicious users. This is particularly true of the most well-known Chinese microblogging platform Sina Weibo, which reportedly has a larger base of daily active users than Twitter. Hot, trending topics on this platform attract remarkable public interest and have substantial significance for business and society. As a result, it has attracted spammers with malicious intent. Widespread spamming threatens the quality and credibility of the user-generated content on social media platforms, and erodes the publicness of these platforms. Thus, it is important to develop techniques to detect such spammers and to examine their impact on the formation of public opinion.

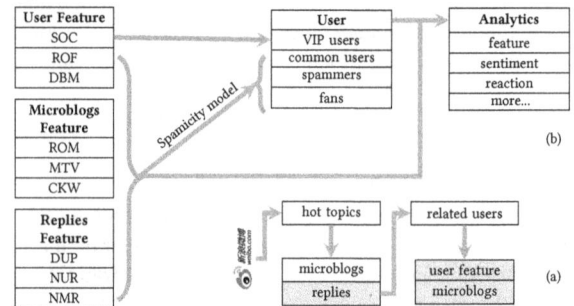

Figure 1: Data capture and model.

The publicness of social media platforms has long been a major concern in academia. Early research highlights the political and social polarization [13, 18], and the impact of the underlying algorithms [14]. More recent research focuses on the mechanisms and impact of "fake news" created and circulated on social media [1, 17]. However, how opinion spammers subtly steer and manipulate the public opinion on such platforms and what impact these micro-techniques may exert on society remains underexplored.

There has been ample research on detecting spammers, including specifically for Sina Weibo [2, 3, 9, 15], as well as several supervised learning methods [5, 12, 16] to detect instances of opinion spam. However, such models are largely based on a dichotomy of fake vs. non-fake labels. Unsupervised methods have as well been proposed [4, 6, 8, 10, 11, 20]. Despite this progress, such previous work has focused on identifying spammers seeking to place ads for products or services, as well as detecting imposters, extremists and the like.

This paper instead focuses on the unique problem of *public opinion spamming*, i.e. identifying spammers that seek to influence public opinion on hot topics. As we will explain in further detail, such actors operate quite differently both from traditional ad-like product promotion spammers [7, 19] as well as from the kind of opinion spammers that post fake product reviews. We propose a novel and principled model to detect public opinion spamming. The model is an unsupervised one that does not require labeled training data and overcomes the limitations of existing work discussed above. We adopt a fully Bayesian modeling approach. This setting allows us to model the *spamicity* of users as latent, while treating other observed behavioral features as known. The *spamicity* here refers to the degree to which the exhibited behavior can be regarded as public opinion spamming. Our key ideas hinge on the hypothesis that opinion spammers differ from others on behavioral dimensions. This creates a separation margin between the population distributions of three naturally occurring groups: spammers, fans, and regular users. The inference procedure enables us to learn the distributions of these groups by means of the behavioral features.

Figure 1(b) illustrates our approach. Based on pertinent social media data, we extract features from user profiles, postings, and replies under hot topics. For user classification, we identify VIP users based on the official certification on the platform, while other features are used to train our model to assess a user's degree of spamicity and categorize them with respect to the three remaining clusters. Subsequently, we proceed to explore how and to what extent spammers shape the public opinion on specific topics.

In summary, this paper makes the following contributions:

(1) It proposes a novel and principled method to exploit observed behavioral footprints to classify users and detect public opinion spammers in an unsupervised Bayesian framework, without the need for laborious manual labeling, which is both time-consuming and error-prone. Unlike existing work, this allows both detection and analysis to occur in a single framework, providing deeper insights into the data.

(2) We conduct a comprehensive set of experiments to evaluate the proposed model based on human expert judgments.

(3) On the basis of the spammer behavior detection, we conduct a diachronic analysis of a specific case, "Wang Baoqiang's divorce", to examine the effectiveness of the spammers' behavior in shaping public opinion. The results showcase that the spammers have developed rather sophisticated tactics in reshaping the public opinion, which calls for more attention in academia and industry to be paid to this underexplored, yet extremely important issue.

2 DATA

In the following, we consider an instructive example as a case study. On August 14, 2016, popular Chinese actor Wang Baoqiang issued a public statement accusing his wife Rong Ma, an actress, of having an extramarital relationship with Wang's agent Zhe Song and collusively transferring their mutual assets to Song. He went on to denounce their wedlock with a lawsuit against Rong Ma. This statement stirred up enormous, long-lasting attention in both digital and traditional media outlets. Sina Weibo was one of the major involved online platforms – The hashtag "#Wang Baoqiang

divorced#" (in Mandarin) and related ones frequently emerged in the Top Topics lists.

Thus, we collected pertinent data from Sina Weibo from 14 August to 15 December 2016, a period when this event attracted massive public attention. Sina Weibo contains **Voting posts**, as well as **Topic posts**, in which certain keywords are marked with ##. We first crawled the 440 most popular microblog postings about the hot topic #*Wang Baoqiang divorced#* as seeds, as well as replies to them. We then retrieved all relevant users for these comments and replies. From their home pages, we then crawled their postings in the same time window. After data cleaning, we chose 2,000 users for our experiment, with data from December 2016. The posting features are computed for a user's postings posted from August to December 2016. In May 2017, we re-crawled the data again to check if these users were banned or the topic-related postings were deleted. Finally, in August 2017, we re-crawled the data once again to determine whether any such ban had been lifted.

3 MODEL

3.1 Observed Features

Users participating in a hot topic are categorized into four different subsets: *regular users*, *fans* (i.e., enthusiastic devotees or admirers of one of the parties), *spammers* (i.e., paid posters specifically seeking to sway public opinion), and *VIP users* (i.e., those verified by Sina Weibo). In the following, we propose some characteristics of abnormal behavior that may prove useful as observed features in our model to learn to distinguish these clusters of users.

User Reply Features: Replies here refer to a user's responses to hot topic postings. Spammers often post multiple replies that are duplicate or near-duplicate versions of previous replies or replies of others on the same topic (**DUP**). The number of user replies (**NUR**) and number of postings that a user responded to (**NMR**) are two important features to detect spammers, due to the more limited time and effort spent online by regular users.

Posting Features: Posting features are based on all postings that a user has made within a given time period, beyond just those pertaining to the hot topic under consideration. Regular users tend to express their personal opinion in original postings, while spammers tend to copy template postings for efficiency. To highlight their arguments, spammers also post or repost more topic postings and voting postings. They also tend to post more postings containing certain specific keywords to make the topic more hot. Correspondingly, for each user, we compute the ratio of original mircroblog postings (**ROM**), the ratio of that user participating in the postings about topics or with voting polls (**MTV**), and the ratio of postings containing keywords (**CKW**).

User Features: We select three features, taken from the user profile data, as features: whether the user deletes all of their postings or the user is banned a few months later (**DBM**), the ratio of followers to followees (**ROF**), and the Sina official certification (**SOC**). The SOC feature is not considered in the model, but instead serves as a marker to identify VIP users.

3.2 The Graphical Model

A number of factors may aid in spam detection, including replies on a particular hot topic, a user's postings on their microblog, and user features. Normalized continuous features in [0, 1] are modeled as following a Dirichlet distribution. This enables the model to capture more fine-grained dependencies between user behavior and spamming. θ_k^f for each feature $f_1, \ldots, f_8$ denote the per class/cluster (spam vs. non-spam) probability of emitting feature f. Latent variables π_U denote the spamicity of a user U. The objective of the model is to learn the latent behavior distributions for *spammer*, *fan*, and *common user* clusters along with spamicity scores of users as π_U. We detail the generative process in Algorithm 1. For model inference, we rely on Gibbs sampling with the following equations:

$$p(\pi_U = i \mid \pi_U = -i) \propto (n^{\pi_{Ui}} + \gamma) \prod_f \frac{n_f^{\pi_{Ui}} + \alpha^f}{n^{\pi_{Ui}} + U^f \alpha^f} \quad (1)$$

$$f \in \{DUP, NUR, NMR, ROM, MTV, CKW, DBM, ROF\}$$

Notations	Description
u; U	User u; set of all users U
π_U	Spam/Non-spam class label for users based on homepage
α^f	Dirichlet shape parameters (priors) for θ^f for each feature f
β	Dirichlet shape parameters (priors) for π_U of users
θ^f	Per class prob. of exhibiting the user behavior, for $f_1, \ldots, f_8$
π^f	The class each of a user's features belongs to, for $f_1, \ldots, f_8$
$n^{\pi_{ui}}$	Counts of user u being assigned to i
$n_f^{\pi_{ui}}$	Counts of feature f of user u being assigned to i
U^f	Total number of features f

Table 1: List of notational conventions.

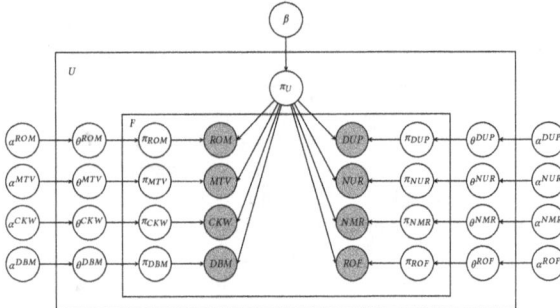

Figure 2: Plate notation

Algorithm 1 The generation process for users.

1: **for** each cluster π_U **do**
2:     Draw a user type mixture distribution $\pi_U \sim \text{Dirichlet}(\beta)$.
3: **for** each user $u \in U$ **do**
4:     **for** each feature $f \in \{1, \ldots, 8\}$ **do**
5:         Draw a multinomial distribution $\theta^f \sim \text{Dirichlet}(\alpha^f)$
6:         Draw user type assignment $\pi_f \sim \text{Multinomial}(\theta^f)$
7:         Draw spamicity for feature f from distribution π_U with π_f

---

4 EXPERIMENT 1 – USER CLASSIFICATION

Our first experiment focuses on distinguishing between common users, fans, spammers, and VIP users for a given hot topic. For this, we are not aware of any gold-standard labeled data identifying public opinion spammers. Hence, we hired 15 students to label users manually. The judges are first briefed with many typical characteristics of public opinion spam: The content is not practical and full of praise or belittling words. The content is purely praise

without counterarguments for one party or purely negative without counterarguments for the other party. The postings posted earlier and later do not match. Given a user, their postings, and their replies, the judges were asked to independently examine the entire profile and to provide a label so as to classify the user.

From these users, we selected 2,000 users, including 500 spammers, 500 fans, 500 common users, 70 VIP users, and some random users for our experiments. In our supervised experiments, among the spammers, fans, and common users, we use 300 for training and reserve 200 for testing. Among the VIP users, we use 50 for training and 20 for testing. In our unsupervised experiments, we considered the users with the top 150 spamicities as spammers, the ones with the lowest 150 spamicities as regular users, and the 150 users with spamicities closest to 0.5 as fans, as well as 60 VIP users.

Model with Estimated Priors (MEP). This setting estimates the hyperparameters α^f, $f_1, \ldots, f_8$, and β by a Monte Carlo EM algorithm, which learns hyperparameters α and β that maximize the model's complete log-likelihood L. Posterior estimates are drawn after 3,000 iterations with an initial burn-in of 250 iterations.

SVM. As we have manually annotated some users, we can use supervised support vector machines (SVM) as a baseline.

	MEP (unsupervised)			SVM (supervised)		
	B_1	B_2	B_3	B_1	B_2	B_3
P	0.87	0.87	0.85	0.65	0.65	0.64
R	0.83	0.77	0.99	0.8	0.42	0.68
F_1	0.85	0.81	0.91	0.72	0.51	0.66
kappa coefficient	0.7931			0.4542		

Table 2: P: Precision, R: Recall, and F_1: F_1-Score of using the average human evaluation results, B_1: spammers, B_2: fans, B_3: regular users.

Discussion. From the results in Table 2, we observe that the proposed MEP is remarkably effective at discriminating between the groups of users, despite being an unsupervised algorithm. Only the predictive accuracy for fans is comparably lower. On one hand, some fans behave much like spammers, especially when they continue expressing their views and arguing with others to defend the interests of one party. On the other hand, when some fans just present their opinions without continuously paying attention to the topic-related discussions, their behavior is quite similar to that of regular users. Furthermore we notice that the kappa coefficient of MEP is much higher, which indicates not only the reliability of the MEP results, but also that the SVM results are more difficult for the judges to estimate. Section 5 will explain the differences in behavior between fans, spammers, and regular users in more detail.

5 EXPERIMENT 2 – FEATURE ANALYSIS

Apart from generating a spamicity scores π_U for users, the model also estimates θ^f, the latent distributions of users' spamicity scores corresponding to each observed feature dimension f, as reflected in the spamicity. It is interesting to analyze the posterior on the learned distributions θ^f for each feature dimension f. We report the posterior on the latent spamicity distributions under each feature $f(\theta^f)$ estimated by MEP.

Duplicate/Near Duplicate Comments (π^{DUP}). From Figure 3(a), where 0 means *non-duplicate reply users* and 1 means *duplicate or*

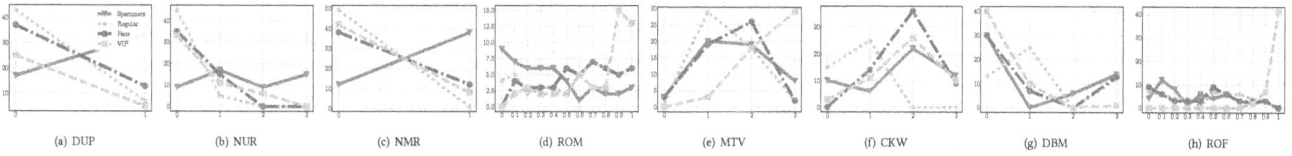

Figure 3: The frequency distribution of arranged events. Spammers (solid red), regular users (dotted blue), fans (dash-dotted green), and VIP users (dashed orange)

near-duplicate reply users, we note that many spammers post numerous duplicate or near-duplicate replies, while fans and regular users as well as VIP ones post very few such duplicates. However, compared with common users and VIP users, the number of duplicates for fans is somewhat higher. This feature is in line with expectations and contributes quite notably to the model.

The number of user replies (π^{NUR}). In Figure 3(b), there are four kinds of users with different amount of replies (N_r): 0 ($N_r = 0$), 1 ($0 < N_r \leqslant 5$), 2 ($5 < N_r \leqslant 10$), and 3 ($10 < N_r$). The density curve for non-spammers reaches its peak towards the left, evincing that non-spammers attain much lower values for NUR. Spammers yield an ascending curve, showing that they attain much higher values for NUR. In addition, the average number of replies is 9.5 for spammers, 1.1 for common users, 1.4 for fans, and 1.5 for VIP users.

The number of microblog postings that the user responded to (π^{NMR}). In Figure 3(c), 0 implies that the user responded to one, while 1 means that the user responded to more than one posting. This feature is very similar to DUP, with the difference that most regular users only reply to one posting and VIP users include some replying to more than one posting. Further analysis reveals some VIP users exhibiting spammer-like behavior for a given hot topic.

Ratio of Original Microblogs (π^{ROM}). In Figure 3(d), the scale of $0 \ldots 1$ refers to the ratio of original postings. Unlike for the aforementioned behaviors, the density curve for spammers has its peak towards the left, showing that spammers attain much lower values. Fans and regular users are very similar in their behavior. VIP users show a very high ratio of original postings, averaging about 0.95, which means that almost all of their postings are original.

Ratio of User participating in Topic and Voting Microblog Postings (π^{MTV}). In Figure 3(e), for spammers, the peak value is smaller and the extreme value is larger than for regular users or fans. This shows that the spammer's MTV values are not concentrated. Apart from VIP users, it is more difficult to distinguish between the remaining three categories of users. Relative to other characteristics, this feature's contribution to the model is rather low.

Ratio of Containing Keywords (π^{CKW}). In Figure 3(f), there are four kinds of users with different amounts of postings containing relevant keywords (N_p), 0 ($N_p = 0$), 1 ($0 < N_p \leqslant 5$), 2 ($5 < N_p \leqslant 100$) and 3 ($10 < N_p$). For this feature, regular users reach their peak on the left, whereas spammers, VIP users, and fans reach theirs on the right. This implies that except for regular users, most of the considered users post hot topic-relevant posts.

Whether the user deletes all their postings or is banned later (π^{DBM}). In Figure 3(g), there are four kinds of users, 0 (users who have never been banned or deleted all of their postings), 1 (who have been banned a few months later and the ban was not lifted), 2 (users who delete the postings on their home page), 3 (user who

have been banned but the ban was soon thereafter lifted). Banned users for whom the ban was soon lifted are usually spammers rather than fans. Users deleting all their postings tend to be spammers. Yet, users who have been banned without the ban being lifted, interestingly, tend *not* to be spammers for particular topics.

Ratio of Followers (π^{ROF}). In Figure 3(h), values in $0 \ldots 1$ refer to the ratio of followers, as defined earlier. The curves for this feature are similar to those for ROM, in that the density curve for spammers attains it peak towards the left of the plot, while others attain their peak towards the right of the plot. That is to say, most spammers have fewer followers, and vice versa. In addition, VIP users have a very high ratio of followers.

6 EXPERIMENT 3 – SENTIMENT ANALYSIS

Sentiment Evaluation. Our final experiment assesses the sentiment, i.e. positive/negative attitude. This is computed based on a sentiment lexicon labeling words as "negative" (negative dictionary D_{neg}) or "positive" (D_{pos}). We also consider any boosting words appearing before a sentiment-bearing term to enhance the weight of that term, e.g. "very", "extremely", etc. The default for the boost score b_t is 1, while if a boosting word is encountered for a term t, it is set to 2. For each post, we first split it into words or phrases as a term set P. Then, we compute the sentiment as follows.

$$S_p = \frac{\sum_{t \in P \cap D_{pos}} b_t - \sum_{t \in P \cap D_{neg}} b_t}{|P|} \tag{2}$$

Figure 4 plots the diachronic trends of the sentiment towards this event, and considers the volume of spamming posts over time.[1] Spamming activities emerged right at the onset of this event and appears to have exerted a strong influence on the public attitude. Initially, spammers in favor of Wang aided in mobilizing a positive sentiment towards Wang. However, after reposting unverified claims alleging that Wang had as well had extramarital affairs and had exhibited domestic violence behavior, spammers supporting Rong Ma swayed back the public attitude, and wrestled with the opposing side for about a month. From September 10 through October 3, including the September 20–23 spamming surge, there was extensive publicity for Wang's new film *Buddies in India*, which indirectly contributed to steering the sentiment in a positive direction.

Two more indicative spamming periods emerged afterwards. The first one, from October 20 through November 15, was in favor of Wang. Having witnessed a negative trend lasting for several days, spammers supporting Wang initiated a strong fightback campaign

---

[1]Note that on some dates, e.g., October 17 and November 28, 2016, the number of posts genuinely relevant to the topic was lower than indicated in Fig. 4 (top), because on these dates, there were many other spamming posts lacking any identifiable stance towards this event, most of which were promoting other businesses, e.g., finance management, divorce consultancy, and private detective services

(including employing or coincidentally attracting spammers with an unidentifiable stand), which largely deterred the negative trend, until around October 28, when spammers in favor of Ma reversed the trend. Although Wang's spammers still effected a resurge on November 4, the second more decisive period was from November 5. Spammers supportive of Ma exhibited sophisticated manipulating skills and successfully remained in control for more than 20 days, despite several minor efforts from the opposing side.

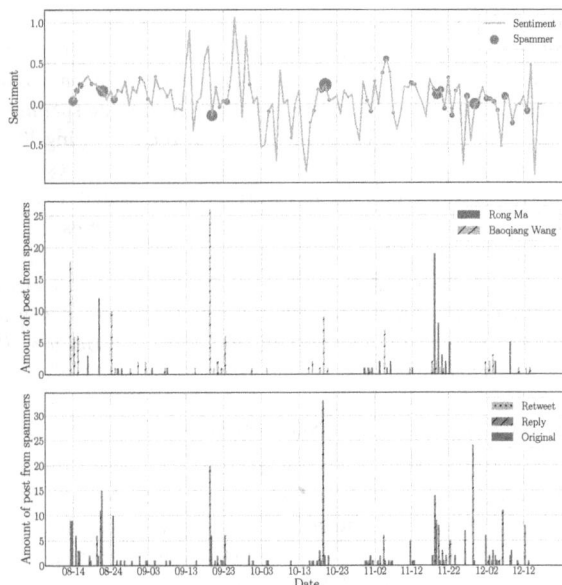

Figure 4: Sentiment, posting amount, and post type of spammers for the two main protagonists involved in the event.

Another noteworthy result drawn from our diachronic analysis is that opinion spammers on Sina Weibo displayed a deliberate micro-tactic of hiding. Given that it is not possible anymore to analyze the impact of spamming "liking" behavior (Sina Weibo no longer displays the users who "liked" a posting), this work focuses on reposting of existing articles, posting of original articles, and replies to posts. The result reveals a different finding from Allcott & Gentzkow [1], and further works, which posit that posting thematic articles serves a vital role in mobilizing endorsement to a specific political opinion. The opinion spammers on Sina Weibo, in contrast, deliberately avoid posting or reposting articles. Instead, they preferred to reply to existing posts to avoid mention (@) of their client's names, trying to alter the general attitude towards a post (tweet) with overwhelmingly sentimental replies. Since Sina Weibo typically displays replies to a posting one by one under that tweet, this practice can often create an exclusive "bubble filter" [13] that repels users on the opposite side. The replies may evoke the feeling in other readers that the opinion reflected in the article is false (if replies denounce it) or true (if replies support it). Original writing is also an option less frequently used. This specific combination of spamming tactics, while being effective in shifting the public sentiment towards an event as analyzed, makes the spamming activity more challenging to detect (Sina Weibo deletes tweets or posts that are deemed spam or for which they receive heavy complaints of it being such), and therefore, more subtle and effective.

7 CONCLUSIONS

This paper proposes a novel and principled method to exploit observed microblog posting behavior to detect spammers in the special setting of public opinion spamming on Sina Weibo, and examine the impact it exerts on the public opinion. The precision of model affirmed the estimated characterization of spamming behavior. Based on the precise detection of public opinion spamming, a diachronic analysis about the impact of opinion spammers on a widely noted case in China demonstrates that such spammers subtly manipulated the public sentiment on Sina Weibo, one of the top social media platforms in China. This work, therefore, sets the path towards new research on public opinion spamming, and calls for a more detailed and nuanced analysis of the spammers' impact on public opinion, and potentially, on the social justice and well-being of the society.

8 ACKNOWLEDGEMENTS

The authors wish to acknowledge the support provided by the National Natural Science Foundation of China (61503217, 91546203), the Key Research and Development Program of Shandong Province of China (2017CXGC0605) and China Scholarship Council (201606220187). Gerard de Melo's research is funded in part by ARO grant W911NF-17-C-0098 (DARPA SocialSim).

REFERENCES

[1] Hunt Allcott and Matthew Gentzkow. 2017. *Social Media and Fake News in the 2016 Election*. Working Paper 23089. National Bureau of Economic Research.
[2] Hao Chen, Jun Liu, Yanzhang Lv, Max Haifei Li, Mengyue Liu, and Qinghua Zheng. 2017. Semi-supervised Clue Fusion for Spammer Detection in Sina Weibo. *Information Fusion* (2017).
[3] Hao Chen, Jun Liu, and Jianhong Mi. 2016. SpamDia: Spammer Diagnosis in Sina Weibo Microblog. In *MobiMedia 2016*. 116–120.
[4] G. Fei, A. Mukherjee, B. Liu, M. Hsu, M. Castellanos, and R. Ghosh. 2013. Exploiting burstiness in reviews for review spammer detection. In *ICWSM*.
[5] Song Feng, Ritwik Banerjee, and Yejin Choi. 2012. Syntactic stylometry for deception detection. In *ACL short*. 171–175.
[6] Song Feng, Longfei Xing, Anupam Gogar, and Yejin Choi. 2012. Distributional Footprints of Deceptive Product Reviews. In *ICWSM*.
[7] Kunal Goswami, Younghee Park, and Chungsik Song. 2017. Impact of reviewer social interaction on online consumer review fraud detection. *Journal of Big Data* 4, 1 (15 May 2017), 15.
[8] Ee-Peng Lim, Viet An Nguyen, Nitin Jindal, Bing Liu, and Hady Wirawan Lauw. 2010. Detecting product review spammers using rating behaviors. In *CIKM*.
[9] Yingcai Ma, Niu Yan, Ren Yan, and Yibo Xue. 2013. Detecting Spam on Sina Weibo. *CCIS-13* (2013).
[10] Arjun Mukherjee, Bing Liu, and Natalie Glance. 2012. Spotting fake reviewer groups in consumer reviews. In *WWW*. 191–200.
[11] Arjun Mukherjee, Bing Liu, Junhui Wang, Natalie Glance, and Nitin Jindal. 2011. Detecting group review spam. In *WWW Companion*. 93–94.
[12] Myle Ott, Yejin Choi, Claire Cardie, and Jeffrey T. Hancock. 2011. Finding Deceptive Opinion Spam by Any Stretch of the Imagination. (2011), 309–319.
[13] Eli Pariser. 2011. *The Filter Bubble: What the Internet Is Hiding from You*. The Penguin Group.
[14] Cornelius Puschmann and Jean Burgess. 2014. *The Politics of Twitter Data*. Peter Lang Publishing Inc.
[15] Yang Qiao, Huaping Zhang, Min Yu, and Yu Zhang. 2016. Sina-Weibo Spammer Detection with GBDT. In *Chinese National Conference on Social Media Processing*.
[16] Shebuti Rayana and Leman Akoglu. 2015. Collective Opinion Spam Detection: Bridging Review Networks and Metadata. In *SIGKDD*. 985–994.
[17] Laura Spinney. 2017. The Shared Past that Wasn't: Facebook, fake news and friends are warping your memory. 543 (2017), 168–170.
[18] Cass R Sunstein. 2009. *Going to extremes: How like minds unite and divide*. Oxford University Press.
[19] Zhuo Wang, Tingting Hou, Dawei Song, Zhun Li, and Tianqi Kong. 2016. Detecting Review Spammer Groups via Bipartite Graph Projection. *Comput. J.* 59, 6 (2016), 861–874.
[20] Sihong Xie, Guan Wang, Shuyang Lin, and Philip S. Yu. 2012. Review spam detection via temporal pattern discovery. In *SIGKDD*. 823–831.

Can We Count on Social Media Metrics?
First Insights into the Active Scholarly Use of Social Media

Maryam Mehrazar
ZBW Leibniz Information Centre
for Economics, Kiel, Germany
m.mehrazar@zbw.eu

Christoph Carl Kling
www.c-kling.de
Cologne, Germany
datascience@c-kling.de

Steffen Lemke
ZBW Leibniz Information Centre
for Economics, Kiel, Germany
s.lemke@zbw.eu

Athanasios Mazarakis
Kiel University
Kiel, Germany
a.mazarakis@zbw.eu

Isabella Peters
ZBW Leibniz Information Centre
for Economics, Kiel, Germany
i.peters@zbw.eu

ABSTRACT

Measuring research impact is important for ranking publications in academic search engines and for research evaluation. *Social media metrics*, or *altmetrics*, measure the impact of scientific work based on social media activity. Altmetrics are complementary to traditional, citation-based metrics, e.g. allowing the assessment of new publications for which citations are not yet available.

Despite the increasing importance of altmetrics, their characteristics are not well understood: Until now it has not been researched what kind of scholars are *actively* using which social media services and why – important questions for scientific impact prediction. Based on a survey of 3,430 scientists, we uncover previously unknown and significant differences between social media services: We identify services which attract young and experienced researchers, respectively, and detect differences in usage motivations. Our findings have direct implications for designing future altmetrics for scientific impact prediction.

KEYWORDS

social media, digital scholarship, altmetrics, motivations

ACM Reference Format:
Maryam Mehrazar, Christoph Carl Kling, Steffen Lemke, Athanasios Mazarakis, and Isabella Peters. 2018. Can We Count on Social Media Metrics? First Insights into the Active Scholarly Use of Social Media . In *WebSci '18: 10th ACM Conference on Web Science, May 27–30, 2018, Amsterdam, Netherlands.* ACM, New York, NY, USA, Article 4, 5 pages. https://doi.org/10.1145/3201064.3201101

1 INTRODUCTION

The use of the web is an integral part of scientific work. On social media, researchers discover new research, discuss research ideas with fellows and disseminate research results to the public and to

the scientific community [7, 9, 21]. Additionally, academic search engines support scientists in finding scholarly literature.

In order to improve their performance, academic search engines employ *scholarly metrics*: citation-based measures for the scientific impact of authors and scientific works [1]. In fact, scholarly metrics are also important for other applications such as hiring decisions and project and application evaluation [23, 26].

One drawback of traditional, citation-based metrics is that citations are not available for new publications – the first citation of a paper may take years. Additionally, scholarly metrics do not cover the impact of scientific publications on the web. Therefore, *social media metrics* or *altmetrics* were introduced as a complement to traditional metrics: By analysing usage patterns on social media, altmetrics evaluate the quality of scholarly products through their impact on the web [21]. Altmetrics which predict the *scientific* impact of scholarly work [32] will likely play a central role in many future applications such as scientific literature retrieval.

Current altmetrics data providers such as *altmetric.com* or *PlumX* use sums [6] or simplistic weightings [27] for aggregating altmetrics from different social media services. For instance, view counts are aggregated across services using (arbitrarily weighted) sums. It has not yet been investigated whether this practice reflects the diversity of users on social media. In order to improve altmetrics for scientific impact prediction, it is essential to understand the demographics and motives of scholarly social media users. If social media services differ significantly in the demographics or motives of their users, the mechanisms of altmetrics would have to be improved: One example could be a service-specific correction for the share of postdocs, who are known to have a high productivity [5] and thus create more citations, which are to be predicted.

This paper analyses the results of a survey among 3,430 scientists, providing first insights into the scholarly use of social media by detecting and describing **(i) demographic differences of active scholarly users of social media** and **(ii) variations in the motivation for scholarly use of social media** between services.

It is well-known that a small share of active users in social media contributes the majority of observed activities, the so-called "90:9:1 rule" [17]. As a result, active users are responsible for most of the activities measured by altmetrics. Unlike previous analyses of the scholarly use of social media [9, 32], **we therefore only consider *active* users** who use social media at least weekly for scientific purposes.

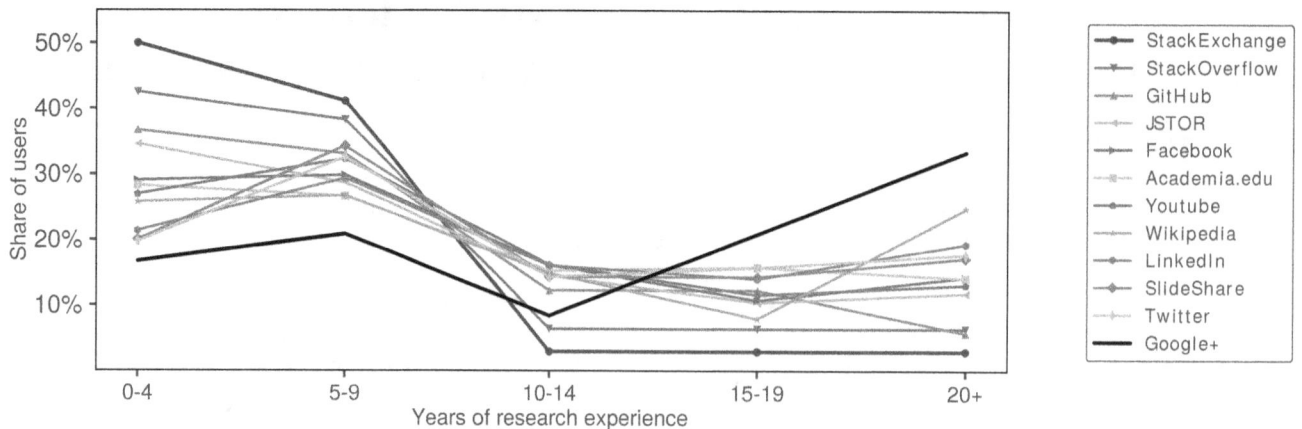

Figure 1: Academic experience of active users per service. Q&A and programming-related services (StackExchange, StackOverflow, GitHub) are more popular with young scientists, while networking services (Google+, Twitter, LinkedIn), SlideShare and Wikipedia have the highest percentage of experienced scientists. The legend shows services ordered by their share of young scientists (0-4 years of experience). The services with the highest share of young researchers (StackExchange) and the highest share of experienced academics (Google+) are highlighted. Social media services show substantial differences in the experience level of active scholarly users.

2 RELATED WORK

Social media have become increasingly popular for scholarly communication [19, 28]. Several metrics based on scholarly social media activities have been shown to correlate with traditional, citation metrics [14, 32], though previous studies have pointed out that there is wide variability in the social media use of researchers. Differences have been observed in age, academic role, discipline and country, among others [4, 7, 13, 16, 22].

Using metrics based on social media activities comes with various challenges such as the assurance of data quality, the variety of users and their motivations in social media, and the prevention of bias [3, 8]. One key problem of scholarly social media data is the systematic bias towards scholars with certain demographic characteristics such as bias towards younger users [20] and towards users with a professional interest in research [15]. Several studies state that the lack of accurate user statistics or sample descriptions for social media sites complicates the quantification of these biases [3, 26].

Scholars use social media for various reasons. Van Noorden [30] identified multiple categories of motivations for scholarly social media use: *contacting peers, posting content, sharing links to authored content, actively discussing research, commenting on research, following discussions, tracking metrics, discovering jobs, discovering peers, discovering recommended papers, offering a contact possibility* and *curiosity*. Jordan [9] identified motivation categories by manually coding questions asked by researchers on Academia.edu.

It is well known that a small minority of active social media users is responsible for a large share of activities [10, 31]. Russo et al. [24] give an overview of multiple studies on various social media sites and Kunegis [11] shows statistics for dozens of social networks, all confirming the effect. To the best of our knowledge, there is no study on the demographics and motivations of *active* scholarly users on social media.

3 DATA AND METHODS

We analyse data from an exploratory online survey on the professional scholarly use of social media, which we conducted as part of a larger research project on metrics. Our survey provides detailed insights into user activities by including questions on the intensity and the extent to which social media services and their interactions (e.g. like, share or post) are used. Analysing the stated frequency of interactions enables us to identify active users.

In total, the survey contains 20 questions; among others, we asked participants for their research experience, their academic role, the social media services they use, and how often and why they are using social media services. The full questionnaire is available online[1].

3.1 Survey data

Our survey on social media usage was distributed via multiple channels: Authors who had at least one publication after 2015 with an email listed in the Web of Science[2] or RePEc[3] and multiple mailing lists related to Economics, Social Sciences or its subfields were contacted. As the survey was conducted as part of an interdisciplinary project involving partners from economics and social sciences, our main target group was economists and social scientists.

More than 3,430 international researchers participated in our survey from March to May 2017 with a response rate of about 6%. Most of the researchers are from the fields of economics (60%) and social sciences (22%). Researchers from 84 countries participated, the majority of them from Germany (51%), followed by the US (10%), the UK (5%) and Italy(5%). Participants were 19 to 89 years of age (median age 38). The distribution of academic roles is as follows: About 44% of the participants are professors, followed by PhD students / research assistants (31%) and postdocs (19%).

---

[1]https://github.com/marymm/-metrics/raw/master/questionnaire.pdf
[2]http://apps.webofknowledge.com
[3]http://repec.org

This is in line with studies showing that professors together with PhD students have the highest share of profiles on academic social media [13, 18].

More than half of the participants – 1,731 researchers – use at least one interaction (e.g. like, share or post) of a social media service per week. We call these researchers *active users*.[4]

Though our sample is not representative, the high share of active users in our survey allows us to analyse differences between social media services. If we find significant differences between services in our survey, we also expect to find differences in the parent population.

3.2 Experience differences and motivations

In our survey, we asked participants to state their research experience since graduation using predefined ordinal categories (0-4 years etc.). For detecting significant differences in the distribution of research experience, we look at all possible pairs between the twelve most-mentioned services and use pairwise χ^2 tests on category counts of the answers of participants. We apply the Benjamini-Hochberg procedure with a false discovery rate of 0.05 and only pairs with strong effect sizes (> 0.25) were considered. Using answers on a question on participants role in academia (options include professor, postdoc, PhD student / research assistant), we applied the same statistical test to detect significant differences in the distribution of academic roles between pairs of services.

Our survey contains a question on reasons for using social media. In order to detect latent motivations for using social media, we ran Latent Dirichlet Allocation (LDA) [2], the most common topic model, on the free text answers. Topic models detect sets of semantically related words using the co-occurrence of words in documents. We chose to set the topic parameter to 10 topics (the lowest number yielding meaningful topics), and used sparse, symmetric document-topic and topic-word Dirichlet priors with $\alpha = \beta = 0.1$. Changing the Dirichlet parameters to other common sparse values did not change the topics significantly. Negative answers (e.g. "none") were manually deleted and stopwords (from NLTK [12]) were removed from the remaining answers, resulting in 997 answer texts.

4 RESULTS

In this section, we look at differences between social media services in terms of demographics and motivations of active users.

4.1 Research experience

To check for demographic differences between the active users of services, we plot the distribution of research experience among active users for the twelve most-frequently named services, shown in Figure 1. We find that services for software development and question and answering – StackExchange, StackOverflow and GitHub – have the highest share of young researchers. On the other hand, services for networking like Google+, Twitter and LinkedIn as well as services for spreading research and information to the general public, like SlideShare and Wikipedia, have a far higher share of

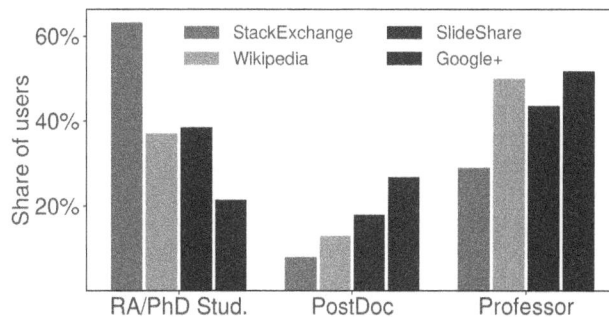

Figure 2: Role distribution of active scholarly users for selected services. We found strong differences between services: StackExchange is mostly used by research assistants and PhD students, while in our survey Google+, SlideShare and Wikipedia are mainly used by Professors. While the share of professors is roughly the same for Wikipedia and Google+, the share of post docs is twice-as-high for Google+, indicating a relationship between role and service use.

experienced researchers. We identified multiple pairs of services with significant differences and large effect sizes (> 0.25): The difference between StackExchange and Google+ is significant (p-value 0.00005), as well as the difference to LinkedIn. Additionally, Google+ is significantly different from StackOverflow and GitHub. Another pair with significant differences is GitHub-Wikipedia. This is the first evidence that research experience influences the active scholarly use of social media. Altmetrics based on social media with a focus on software development will be biased towards young researchers, metrics on services mainly used for networking will be biased towards the actions of experienced researchers.

To take a closer look at this finding, we compare the distribution of academic roles between services with significant differences in user experience in Figure 2. Google+ and Wikipedia have the highest share of experienced users. Looking at their distribution of academic roles, we see that Wikipedia has twice as many PhD students as Google+, while the latter has about twice as many postdocs compared to Wikipedia. The distributions of Google+ and StackExchange are significantly different (p-value: 0.0001).

Both findings indicate that different social media services fulfill different demands and thus both role and experience distributions of their users vary.

4.2 User motivations

The motivations for using social media are known to vary among scholars [9, 30]. In our survey, we asked researchers to name reasons for using social media. We ran LDA [2] on their answers to detect these latent motivations.

Table 1 shows the detected topics. By looking at the top words of the topics and at answers with high topic probabilities in the corpus, we found that the topics can be interpreted as follows: *Topic 0*: sharing and accessing papers of peers/other people, *Topic 1*: users who think that their research is relevant to others, *Topic 2*: finding and sharing interesting works, *Topic 3*: getting information on new

---

[4]We found active users to show different characteristics compared to other participants. For instance, the share of inexperienced researchers (0-4 years of academic experience after graduation) is slightly higher for active users (33%) compared to others (29%).

topics, *Topic 4*: spreading interesting results, *Topic 5*: showing interesting topics to the community, *Topic 6*: downloading articles, *Topic 7*: sharing relevant research with friends, *Topic 9*: promoting important work of colleagues. *Topic 8* repeats the words from the question, indicating an influence of the question on the answers. We therefore ignore this topic in our analysis.

In order to check whether there are differences between user motivations between the different services, we compare the topic distributions of the active users for different services. A user can be active in multiple services. The global topic distribution is shown in Figure 3a. To find services with strong differences, we show the difference from the global topic distribution for services with a significant difference in user experience in Figure 3b.

We see that different social media services meet different needs: StackExchange has less users who want to find interesting academic works (Topic 2) and more active users who want to share research with friends (Topic 7) and to get new information (Topic 3). In contrast, Wikipedia has a below-average share of users who want to share relevant research with friends or their community (Topic 5 and 7), but they like to share relevant research and interesting findings with a general audience (Topic 1 and 2). Similarly, SlideShare has an above-average share of users who use social media because they think that their research is relevant for others (Topic 1) and they like to spread interesting results (Topic 4) but have a lower probability for sharing content in their community (Topic 5 and 7). Finally, Google+ has a higher share of users who want to share relevant research with friends but a lower probability for promoting work of colleagues (Topic 9).

These findings contribute to the understanding of the patterns found in Figure 1: Google+ attracts relatively more scholars who want to share their research – and this could explain why we see a higher share of professors / experienced users. StackExchange attracts more users who search for information – and we can assume that this causes a high share of research assistants and PhD students, who have more practical duties and a higher need for question answering services.

Table 1: Top-5 words for topics detected in the answers on "What are other common reasons for you to like/retweet/share/... academic research on [...] services?". The topics are interpretable and expose latent motives of researchers active on social media.

Topic 0	Topic 1	Topic 2	Topic 3	Topic 4
share	relevant	find	get	interest
peers	others	interesting	information	interesting
access	research	work	new	results
read	think	share	topic	spread
people	work	knowledge	findings	content

Topic 5	Topic 6	Topic 7	Topic 8	Topic 9
interesting	articles	research	research	make
topics	download	work	share	researchers
show	public	relevance	like	important
article	news	good	academic	work
find	available	friends	retweet	colleagues

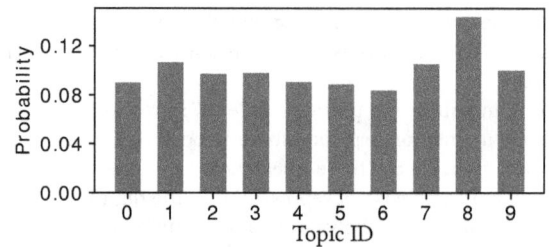

(a) Average topic probabilities for active users

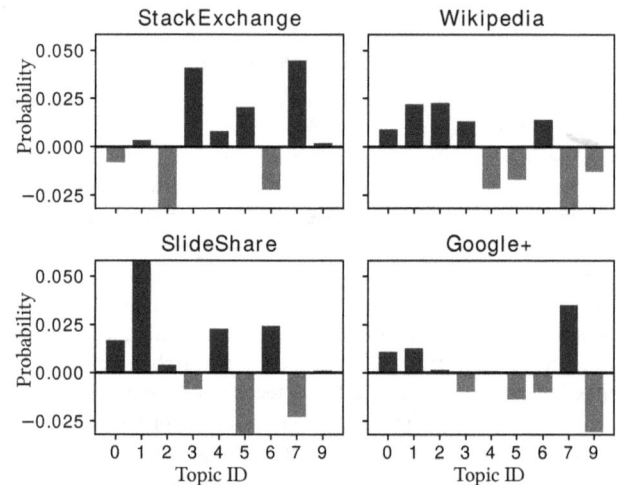

(b) Deviation from average topic probabilities for selected services

Figure 3: Analysis of topics found in user responses on the question on reasons for using social media. These topics can be interpreted as latent motives and they vary for different services. The differences in motives could explain observed variations in research experience and academic roles.

5 DISCUSSION AND CONCLUSION

In order to assess differences in demographics and usage motives between social media services, we studied survey responses of 1,731 active scholarly social media users. Our first analysis shows that **(i) the distribution of research experience and professional roles per social service varies greatly for active users**: Experienced users use social networks and services which make research results available to the general public, young researchers are more dominant in question answering services and platforms for publishing code; and **(ii) the motivation of researchers for using social media services varies per service**: While services with a higher share of inexperienced researchers may attract users who search for information, services with a high share of professors / experienced researchers attract users who want to share their research results with friends or the general public.

These findings have implications for the future development of altmetrics for scientific impact prediction: The observed variety of experience and of motivations for social media use is likely to influence the meaning of actions per service. While a post mentioning a paper on StackExchange is likely a question of a young researcher (satisfying a need for information), a post mentioning a paper on Google+ is more likely explained by an experienced researcher sharing a relevant publication with friends. This variety should be accounted for when measuring the activities of scholars in social media for scientific impact prediction, e.g. for improving literature search engines or the evaluation of research.

Altmetrics have been shown to be positively correlated with future citation counts [25, 29]. Researchers with different roles and research experience have different levels of productivity in terms of citation counts. For example, postdocs are known to have a high productivity and create more citations on average [5]. The distributions of the citation rate of users per year (which depends on their research experience and role) could be extracted from citation databases. Knowing the distribution of research experience and roles per service allows us to link these distributions with the distribution of the citation rate of users. This enables the prediction of citation counts in a probabilistic fashion using basic altmetrics (direct observations from social media) and thus for improved aggregated altmetrics scores.

Our study is mainly limited to participants from the fields of Economics and Social Sciences, most of them from Germany. In future work, we will conduct surveys to better approximate a more general distribution of research experience per service, in order to create and evaluate novel altmetrics for scientific impact prediction.

6 ACKNOWLEDGEMENT

This work is part of the DFG-funded *metrics project (project number: 314727790). Further information on the project can be found on metrics-project.net.

REFERENCES

[1] Jöran Beel and Bela Gipp. 2009. Google Scholar's ranking algorithm: an introductory overview. In *Proceedings of the 12th International Conference on Scientometrics and Informetrics (ISSI'09)*, Vol. 1. Rio de Janeiro (Brazil), 230–241.
[2] David M. Blei, Andrew Y. Ng, Michael I. Jordan, and John Lafferty. 2003. Latent Dirichlet allocation. *Journal of Machine Learning Research* 3 (2003), 2003.
[3] Lutz Bornmann. 2014. Do altmetrics point to the broader impact of research? An overview of benefits and disadvantages of altmetrics. *Journal of informetrics* 8, 4 (2014), 895–903.
[4] Timothy David Bowman. 2015. *Investigating the use of affordances and framing techniques by scholars to manage personal and professional impressions on Twitter.* Ph.D. Dissertation. Indiana University.
[5] Nicolas Carayol and Mireille Matt. 2006. Individual and collective determinants of academic scientists' productivity. *Information Economics and Policy* 18, 1 (2006), 55–72.
[6] Robin Champieux. 2015. PlumX. *Journal of the Medical Library Association: JMLA* 103, 1 (2015), 63.
[7] Asmelash Teka Hadgu and Robert Jäschke. 2014. Identifying and analyzing researchers on twitter. In *Proceedings of the 2014 ACM conference on Web science.* ACM, 23–32.
[8] Stefanie Haustein. 2016. Grand challenges in altmetrics: heterogeneity, data quality and dependencies. *Scientometrics* 108, 1 (2016), 413–423.
[9] Katy Jordan. 2015. What do academics ask their online networks?: An analysis of questions posed via Academia.edu. In *WebSci*, David De Roure, Pete Burnap, and Susan Halford (Eds.). ACM, 42:1–42:2. http://dblp.uni-trier.de/db/conf/websci/websci2015.html#Jordan15
[10] Aniket Kittur, Ed Chi, Bryan A Pendleton, Bongwon Suh, and Todd Mytkowicz. 2007. Power of the few vs. wisdom of the crowd: Wikipedia and the rise of the bourgeoisie. *World wide web* 1, 2 (2007), 19.
[11] Jérôme Kunegis, Steffen Staab, and Daniel Dünker. 2012. KONECT – The Koblenz Network Collection. In *Proc. Int. Sch. and Conf. on Netw. Sci.*
[12] Edward Loper and Steven Bird. 2002. NLTK: The Natural Language Toolkit. In *In Proceedings of the ACL Workshop on Effective Tools and Methodologies for Teaching Natural Language Processing and Computational Linguistics. Philadelphia: Association for Computational Linguistics.*

[13] Susanne Mikki, Marta Zygmuntowska, Øyvind Liland Gjesdal, and Hemed Ali Al Ruwehy. 2015. Digital presence of Norwegian scholars on academic network sites – where and who are they? *PloS one* 10, 11 (2015), e0142709.
[14] Ehsan Mohammadi, Mike Thelwall, Stefanie Haustein, and Vincent Larivière. 2015. Who reads research articles? An altmetrics analysis of Mendeley user categories. *Journal of the Association for Information Science and Technology* 66, 9 (2015), 1832–1846.
[15] Cameron Neylon and Shirley Wu. 2009. level metrics and the evolution of scientific impact. *PLoS biology* 7, 11 (2009), e1000242.
[16] David Nicholas and Ian Rowlands. 2011. Social media use in the research workflow. *Information Services & Use* 31, 1-2 (2011), 61–83.
[17] J Nielson. 2006. Alertbox participation inequality: encouraging more users to contribute. *useit. com* (2006).
[18] José Luis Ortega. 2015. How is an academic social site populated? A demographic study of Google Scholar Citations population. *Scientometrics* 104, 1 (2015), 1–18.
[19] Diego Ponte and Judith Simon. 2011. Scholarly communication 2.0: Exploring researchers' opinions on Web 2.0 for scientific knowledge creation, evaluation and dissemination. *Serials review* 37, 3 (2011), 149–156.
[20] Jason Priem. 2015. Altmetrics (Chapter from Beyond Bibliometrics: Harnessing Multidimensional Indicators of Scholarly Impact). *CoRR* abs/1507.01328 (2015). arXiv:1507.01328 http://arxiv.org/abs/1507.01328
[21] Jason Priem, Dario Taraborelli, Paul Groth, and Cameron Neylon. 2011. Altmetrics: a Manifesto. (2011). http://altmetrics.org/manifesto/
[22] Rob Procter, Robin Williams, James Stewart, Meik Poschen, Helene Snee, Alex Voss, and Marzieh Asgari-Targhi. 2010. Adoption and use of Web 2.0 in scholarly communications. *Philosophical Transactions of the Royal Society of London A: Mathematical, Physical and Engineering Sciences* 368, 1926 (2010), 4039–4056.
[23] NISO Alternative Assessment Metrics Project. 2014. NISO Altmetrics Standards Project White Paper. https://groups.niso.org/apps/group_public/download.php/16268/NISO%20RP-25-201x-1,%20Altmetrics%20Definitions%20and%20Use%20Cases%20-%20draft%20for%20public%20comment.pdf
[24] Angelina Russo and Darren Peacock. 2009. Great expectations: Sustaining participation in social media spaces. In *Museums and the Web 2009.* Archives & Museum Informatics, 23–36.
[25] Hadas Shema, Judit Bar-Ilan, and Mike Thelwall. 2014. Do blog citations correlate with a higher number of future citations? Research blogs as a potential source for alternative metrics. *Journal of the Association for Information Science and Technology* 65, 5 (2014), 1018–1027.
[26] Cassidy R. Sugimoto, Sam Work, Vincent Larivière, and Stefanie Haustein. 2017. Scholarly use of social media and altmetrics: A review of the literature. *Journal of the Association for Information Science and Technology* 68, 9 (2017), 2037–2062. https://doi.org/10.1002/asi.23833
[27] Altmetric Support. 2017. How is the Altmetric Attention Score calculated? (2017). https://help.altmetric.com/support/solutions/articles/6000060969-how-is-the-altmetric-attention-score-calculated-
[28] Carol Tenopir, Rachel Volentine, and Donald W King. 2013. Social media and scholarly reading. *Online Information Review* 37, 2 (2013), 193–216.
[29] Mike Thelwall. 2018. Early Mendeley readers correlate with later citation counts. *Scientometrics* (26 Mar 2018). https://doi.org/10.1007/s11192-018-2715-9
[30] Richard Van Noorden. 2014. Online collaboration: Scientists and the social network. *Nature* 512, 7513 (2014), 126–129.
[31] Steve Whittaker, Loen Terveen, Will Hill, and Lynn Cherny. 2003. The dynamics of mass interaction. In *From Usenet to CoWebs.* Springer, 79–91.
[32] Daniel Zoller, Stephan Doerfel, Robert Jäschke, Gerd Stumme, and Andreas Hotho. 2015. On Publication Usage in a Social Bookmarking System. In *Proceedings of the 2015 ACM Conference on Web Science.*

DistrustRank: Spotting False News Domains.

Vinicius Woloszyn
Federal University of Rio Grande do Sul / L3S Research
Center
Porto Alegre, Brazil
vwoloszyn@inf.ufrgs.br

Wolfgang Nejdl
L3S Research Center
Hannover, Germany
nejdl@L3S.de

ABSTRACT

In this paper we propose a semi-supervised learning strategy to automatically separate fake News from reliable News sources: DistrustRank. We first select a small set of unreliable News, manually evaluated and classified by experts on fact checking portals. Once this set is created, DistrustRank constructs a weighted graph where nodes represent websites, connected by edges based on a minimum similarity between a pair of websites. Next it computes the centrality using a biased PageRank, where a bias is applied to the selected set of seeds. As an output of the proposed model we obtain a trust (or distrust) rank that can be used in two ways: a) as a counter-bias to be applied when News about a specific subject is ranked, in order to discount possible boosts achieved by false claims; and b) to assist humans to identify sources that are likely to be source of fake News (or that are likely to be reputable), suggesting websites that should be examined more closely or to be avoided. In our experiments, DistrustRank outperforms the supervised approaches in either ranking and classification task.

CCS CONCEPTS

• **Information systems** → *World Wide Web*; *Content ranking*;

KEYWORDS

Credibility Analysis, Rumor Detection, Text Mining

ACM Reference Format:
Vinicius Woloszyn and Wolfgang Nejdl. 2018. DistrustRank: Spotting False News Domains.. In *WebSci '18: 10th ACM Conference on Web Science, May 27–30, 2018, Amsterdam, Netherlands*, Jennifer B. Sartor, Theo D'Hondt, and Wolfgang De Meuter (Eds.). ACM, New York, NY, USA, 8 pages. https://doi.org/10.1145/3201064.3201083

1 INTRODUCTION

Many people have access to News through different online information sources, ranging from search engines, digital forms of mainstream News channels to social network platforms. Compared with traditional media, information on the Web can be published quickly,

but with few guarantees on the trustworthiness and quality. This issue can be found in different domains, such as fake reviews on collaborative review websites, manipulative statements about companies, celebrities, and politicians, among others [5, 9].

The task of assessing the believability of a claim is a thorny issue. Kumar's work [8] reports that even humans sometimes are not able to distinguish hoax from authentic ones, and that quite a few people could not differentiate satirical articles from the true News (e.g. www.nypost.com/2018/02/01/mom-teams-up-with-daughter-to-fight-girl-on-school-bus/). With the increasing number of hoaxes and rumors, fact-checking websites like *snopes.com, politifact.com, fullfact.org*, have become popular. These websites compile articles written by experts who manually investigate controversial claims to determine their veracity, providing shreds of evidence to for the verdict (e.g. true or false).

Many works have addressed the problem of false claims detection. Most of them rely on supervised algorithms such as classification and regression models [2, 7, 8, 13–15, 17]. However, the quality of results produced by supervised algorithms is dependent on the existence of a large, domain-dependent training data set. The task of creating a data set of News claims, besides being a manual process dependent on motivated annotators, fails to consider the most recent News. Despite the typical inferior performance, semi-supervised methods are an attractive alternative to avoid the labor-intense and error-prone task of manual annotation of training data sets.

In this paper, we propose DistrustRank, a novel semi-supervised algorithm that identifies unreliable News websites based only on the headline extracted from the News article's link. In the News Websites, the News article is generally shared using a long link which contains the News headline and acts as a good summary of the News article content. This choice is motivated by performance issues, since for a fast and scalable method the extraction of features for comparison cannot be time-consuming. Additionally, using only links instead of entire News article content is a good strategy to help the integration of DistrustRank with search engines since it does not need additional features. The use of links as the main feature is also a common strategy in other areas, such as Query Re-Ranking [1, 16].

DistrustRank constructs a weighted graph where nodes represent websites, connected by edges based on a minimum similarity between a pair of websites, and then compute the centrality using a biased PageRank, where a bias is applied to the selected set of seeds. In addition, DistrustRank takes into account fake websites similarities, as a minimum similarity threshold is dynamically defined based on the characteristics of the set of false websites. The resulting graph is composed of several components, where each component represents websites with similar characteristics. Next, a search that begins at some particular node v will find the entire connected component containing v. Finally, the centrality index of the neighbors of v are used to compose the final distrust rank.

The output of the method presented in this paper is a trust (or distrust) rank that can be used in two ways:

(1) as a counter-bias to be applied when News about a specific subject is ranked, in order to discount possible boosts achieved by false websites;

(2) to assist people to identify sources that are likely to be fake (or reputable), suggesting which websites should be examined more closely or to be avoided.

Our experiments on websites indexed by Internet Archive[1] reveal that DistrustRank outperforms the chosen supervised baseline (Support Vector Machine) in terms of imitating the human experts judging about the credibility of the websites.

The remaining of this paper is organized as follows. Section 2 discusses previous works on fake News detection. Section 3 presents details of the DistrustRank algorithm. Section 4 describes the design of our experiments, and Section 5 discusses the results. Section 6 summarizes our conclusions and presents future research directions.

2 RELATED WORK

Several studies have addressed the task of assessing the credibility of a claim. For instance Popat et al. [13] proposed a new approach to identify the **credibility** of a claim in a text. For a certain claim, it retrieves the corresponding articles from News and/or social media and feeds those into a distantly supervised classifier for assessing their credibility. Experiments with claims from the website *snopes.com* and from popular cases of Wikipedia hoaxes demonstrate the viability of Popat et al proposed methods. Another example is TrustRank [6]. This work presents a semi-supervised approach to separate reputable good pages from spam. To discover good pages it relies on an observation that good pages seldom point to bad ones, i.e. people creating good pages have little reason to point to bad pages. Finally, it employs a biased PageRank using this empirical observation to discover other pages that are likely to be good.

Controversial subjects can also be indicative of dispute or debate involving different opinions about the same subject. Detect and alert users when they are reading a controversial web page is one way to make users aware of the information quality they are consuming. One example of **controversy** detection is [2] which relies on supervised k-nearest-neighbor classification that maps a webpage into a set of neighboring controversial articles extracted from Wikipedia. In this approach, a page adjacent to controversial pages is likely to be controversial itself. Another work in this

sense is [12] which aims to generate contrastive summaries of different viewpoints in opinionated texts. It proposes a Comparative LexRank, that relies on random walk formulation to give a score to a sentence based on their difference to others sentences.

Factuality Assessment is another way to asses the information quality. Yu et al.'s work [20] aims to separate opinions from facts, at both the document and sentence level. It uses a Bayesian classifier for discriminating between documents with a preponderance of opinions, such as editorials from regular News stories. The main goal of this approach is to classify a document/sentence in factual or opinionated text from the perspective of the author. The evaluation of the proposed system reported promising results in both document and sentence levels. Other work on the same line is [14], which proposes a two-stage framework to extract opinionated sentences from News articles. In the first stage, a supervised learning model gives a score to each sentence based on the probability of the sentence to be opinionated. In the second stage, it uses these probabilities within the HITS schema to treat the opinionated sentences as Hubs, and the facts around these opinions are treated as the Authorities. The proposed method extracts opinions, grouping them with supporting facts as well as other supporting opinions.

There also some works that analyze how a piece of information flows over the internet. For instance, [3] presents an interesting analysis about how Twitter bots can send spam tweets, manipulate public opinion and use them for online fraud. It reports the discovery of the 'Star Wars' botnet on Twitter, which consists of more than 350,000 bots tweeting random quotations exclusively from Star Wars novels. It analyzes and reveals rich details on how the botnet is designed and gives insights on how to detect **virality** in Tweeter.

Other works analyze the writing style in order to detect a false claim. [7] reports that Fake News in most cases are more similar to satire than to real News, leading us to conclude that persuasion in the fake News is achieved through heuristics rather than the strength of arguments. It shows that the overall title structure and the use of proper nouns in titles are very significant in differentiating fake from real. It gives an idea that fake News is targeted for audiences who are not likely to read beyond titles and that they aim at creating mental associations between entities and claims. Decrease the **readability** of texts is also another way to overshadow false claims on the internet. Many automatic methods to evaluate the readability of texts have been proposed. For instance, CohMetrix [4], which is a computational tool that measures cohesion, discourse, and text difficulty.

Most of the works just cited rely on supervised learning strategies addressed to assess News articles using few different aspects, such as credibility, controversy, factuality and virality of information. Nonetheless, a common drawback of supervised learning approaches is that the quality of the results is heavily influenced by the availability of a large, domain-dependent annotated corpus to train the model. Unsupervised and semi-supervised learning techniques on the other hand, are attractive because they do not imply the cost of corpus annotation. In short, our method uses a semi-supervised strategy where only a small set of unreliable News

---

[1]https://web.archive.org/

websites is used to spot another bad News websites using a biased PageRank.

3 DISTRUSTRANK ALGORITHM

To spot unreliable News websites, without a large annotated corpus, we rely on an important empirical observation: fake News pages are similar to each other. This notion is fairly intuitive, while News websites approach a broad scope of subjects, unreliable pages are built to mislead people in specific areas, such as fake News about companies, politicians and celebrities. Additionally, some of the News websites analyzed share copies of the same unreliable News. Figure 1 shows the distribution of the similarity between fake and true News websites. Using a Wilcoxon statistical test [18] with a significance level of 0.05, we verified that the similarity between false News websites is statistically higher to true News websites.

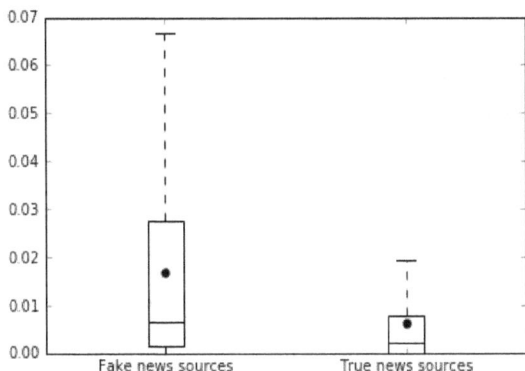

Figure 1: The distribution of the URL similarity between false and true News domains, where * represent the mean.

The intuition behind DistrustRank is that the credibility score of a website can be regarded as the problem of encountering websites which headlines do not differ much from fake websites headlines. To solve this problem, our approach relies on the concept of graph centrality to rank websites according to their estimated centrality.

We propose to represent the relationship between websites as a graph, in which the vertices represent the website, and the edges are defined in terms of the similarity between pairs of vertices. We define similarity as a function that measures the textual similarity of the headlines present in the URLs shared by News websites. Our hypothesis is that fake News websites have a high centrality index since they are similar to many other fake News websites. The biased centrality index produces a ranking of vertices' importance, which in our approach indicates the distrust of websites.

Let L be a set of websites, and $r \in L$ a tuple $\langle d, u \rangle$, where $r.d$ represents the domain of a website and $r.u$ a set of links for their News. DistrustRank builds a graph representation $G = (V, E)$, where $V = R$ and E is a set of edges that connects pairs $\langle u, v \rangle$ where $v, u \in V$, and uses biased PageRank to calculate centrality scores for each vertex. The main steps of the DistrustRank algorithm: (a) it builds a similarity graph G between pairs of News websites; (b)

the graph is pruned (G') by removing all edges that do not meet a minimum similarity threshold, dynamically calculated based on the average similarity between URLs of fake domains; (c) a search that begins at some particular node v will find the entire connected component containing v; (d) using biased PageRank, the centrality scores are calculated and used to construct a ranking. The pseudo-code of DistrustRank is displayed in Algorithm (1), where G and G' are represented as adjacency matrices W and W'. In the remaining of this section, we detail the similarity function, and the process to obtain the centrality index ranking.

Algorithm 1 - DistrustRank Algorithm (L, S, β): S

- Input: a set of websites L, a set of unreliable websites S and β is the base threshold.
- Output: ordered list O containing the their distrust score.

1: %building a similarity graph
2: **for** each $u, v \in L$ **do**
3: $\quad W[u, v] \leftarrow sim\_txt(u.u, v.u)$
4: **end for**
5: %pruning the graph based on mean similarity of S
6: $\bar{E} \leftarrow mean\_similarity(S)$
7: **for** each $u, v \in L$ **do**
8: $\quad$ **if** $W[u, v] \geq \bar{E} * \beta$ **then**
9: $\quad\quad W'[u, v] \leftarrow 1$
10: $\quad$ **else**
11: $\quad\quad W'[u, v] \leftarrow 0$
12: $\quad$ **end if**
13: **end for**
14: %computing a biased centrality
15: $B \leftarrow BiasedPageRank(W', b)$
16: $N \leftarrow \{\}$
17: %finding components that contain S
18: **for** each $s \in S$ **do**
19: $\quad Q \leftarrow \{s\}$
20: $\quad$ **while** there is an edge (u, v) where $u \in Q$ and $v \notin Q$ **do**
21: $\quad\quad Q \leftarrow Q \cup \{v\}$
22: $\quad$ **end while**
23: $\quad N \leftarrow N \cup Q \cap s$
24: **end for**
25: %reordering N according to their centrality
26: $O \leftarrow sort\_by\_centrality(N, B)$
27: Return O

3.1 Similarity between websites

News websites usually provide a long link to their News articles which contains the headline of the News, and this link is a good summary of the News article content. For instance, Table 1 gives two examples of long links to News articles and their headlines. DistrustRank only takes into consideration the terms (i.e. words) extracted from the long links, represented as unigrams weighted by Term *Frequency-Inverse Document Frequency* (TF-IDF) in order to compute the similarity of pairs of websites. This choice is motivated by performance issues, since for a fast and scalable method, we must be able to handle big graphs and the extraction of features for comparison cannot be time-consuming. Crucially, to use only the links instead of the full articles content is a good strategy. In this way, DistrustRank can easily be integrated to search engines, as it does not need additional features.

Therefore, we define the similarity between websites as the cosine similarity of News headlines, represented by their respective TF-IDF vectors, as detailed in Equation 1.

$$f(u, v) = sim\_txt(u, v) \tag{1}$$

where $sim\_txt \in [0, 1]$ represents the cosine similarity between the *TF-IDF* vectors of two websites u and v.

Table 1: Reliable News' URLs, their headlines and Extracted Terms

URL	News Headline	Terms extracted from URL
www.nydailyNews.com/new-york/education/bronx-teacher-sparks-outrage-cruel-slavery-lesson-article-1.3793930	Bronx teacher sparks outrage for using black students in cruel slavery lesson	[new-york, education, bronx, teacher, sparks, outrage, cruel, slavery, lesson]
www.nypost.com/2018/02/01/mom-teams-up-with-daughter-to-fight-girl-on-school-bus/	Mom teams up with daughter to fight girl on school bus	[mom, teams, up, with, daughter, to, fight, girl, on, school, bus]

3.2 Similarity Threshold (β)

Since centrality in our approach is highly dependent on significant similarity, we can disregard websites links which the similarity scores are below a minimum threshold. However, setting an appropriate threshold is a tricky problem [19]. While a high threshold may mistakenly consider as similar websites that have very little in common, conversely, a low threshold may disregard important links between websites.

Using Equation 2, we prune the graph based on a minimum similarity between websites. The result is a weighted graph represented by the adjacency matrix W', where $W'(u, v)$ assumes 1 if an edge that connects u and v exists, and 0 otherwise. To tune our results, we employ a base threshold β that varies according to the mean similarity of false News websites.

$$W'(u, v) = \begin{cases} 1, & f(u, v) \geq \overline{E} * \beta \\ 0, & otherwise \end{cases} \tag{2}$$

In Equation 2, $f(u, v)$ is the similarity score according to Equation 1; $\overline{E}$ is the mean similarity of the News website dataset, and β is the base threshold.

3.3 Biased Centrality

While a regular version of PageRank algorithm computes a static score to each website, a biased version of PageRank [6] can increase artificially the score of some specific websites. A vector of scores is employed to assign a non-zero static bias to a special set of websites. Then the biased PageRank spreads the bias during the iterations to the pages they point to. The matrix equation of Biased PageRank is:

$$r = \alpha * T * r + (1 - \alpha) * b \tag{3}$$

where b is the bias vector of non-negative entries summing up to one, r is the final centrality score, T is the transaction matrix and α a decay factor for bias.

DistrustRank employs a bias to the selected set of seeds (false News websites) which will be spread to their neighborhoods (similar websites). The intuition behind this approach is that we can reduce the 'distrust' score as we move further and further away from the bad seed websites.

Once the centrality scores are computed, we perform the breadth-first search (BFS) on a network graph, starting at some particular node $v \in Seeds$, and explore the neighbor nodes first, before moving to the next level neighbors. The centrality index of the neighbors of v is used to compose the final rank.

4 EXPERIMENT DESIGN

In this section, we detail the experimental setting used to evaluate DistrustRank. We describe the dataset used, the methods employed for comparison and the metric applied for evaluation, as well as details about DistrustRank parameterization.

4.1 Datasets

In order to evaluate our approach, we created two different data sets containing reliable and unreliable News extracted from true News websites and prominent fake News websites, as follows:

- **Reliable**: we extracted the most popular News websites from 10 different categories indexed by SimilarWeb[2]. SimilarWeb provides a ranking of the top world News websites in different categories. The categories used in this set are *Automotive, Celebrities and Entertainment, Sports, News and Media, Newspapers, Business, College and University, Weather, Technology, Magazines and E-Zines*. From each of these categories of News we used the 100 first most popular websites.
- **Unreliable**: The unreliable News websites were extracted from the Wikipedia's list of prominent fake News[3]. The total of websites in this list is 47, which represents nearly 5% of the total of reliable News sources used in this experiment.

For all websites in both data sets previously listed, we used Internet Archive in order to extract the links to their News articles. Figure 2 depicts the distribution of the URLs collected in this task. However, not all of these websites were employed in the evaluation process, since we are just interested in reliable News that could

---

[2]https://www.similarweb.com/top-websites/category/News-and-media
[3]https://en.wikipedia.org/wiki/List_of_fake_News_websites

provide a fair evaluation. For that, we performed a pre-selection of the Reliable News according to the following aspects:

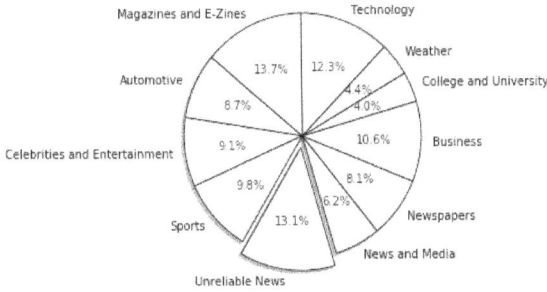

Figure 2: Distribution of collected URLs per category of News, where the categories were extracted from similar-web.com

(1) We only used reliable News articles that are similar to our unreliable News data set. This choice is motivated to make sure that our approach is able to identify fake News in a set of similar News, since it increases the difficulty of the task and makes it comparable to a real-world problem. Therefore, we compared the intersection of the two sets using the Jaccard similarity coefficient[11]. Some News categories, namely *Weather, College and University* and *Automotive*, did not achieve a minimum similarity (> 0.4) and therefore were not used in our final data set. Figure 5 shows the similarity between Reliable News categories and our Unreliable News data set.

(2) We only used URLs where the extracted headline contains more than 3 words recognized by an English Dictionary [4]. We only considered headlines extracted from the long links, because less than 3 words links do not provide enough information to provide a right classification. Figure 4, shows the distribution of URLs per website.

(3) we only used News Articles that were published after 2010. This ensures an evaluation that uses a broad scope of News, increasing the diversity of the vocabulary, therefore making the problem harder. Figure 3 shows the distribution of the News over the years used in this work.

Table 5 provides some statistics about the final data set employed in this work. From the initial 1000 Reliable News websites collected, we ended-up with 502 in accordance with our requirements previously described.

4.2 Validation

We adopted k-fold cross-validation, where the unreliable sample is randomly partitioned into k equal size subsamples. For each fold, a single subsample is retained as the validation data for testing the model, and the remaining k-1 subsamples are used as training data. The cross-validation process is then repeated k times, where

---
[4]https://www.abisource.com/projects/enchant/

Table 2: Summary of the reliable and Unreliable News websites used in this work.

	Domains	URLs (News)	Terms	URL/Terms
Unreliable	47	37320	158501	4.24
Reliable	502	396422	1281794	3.23

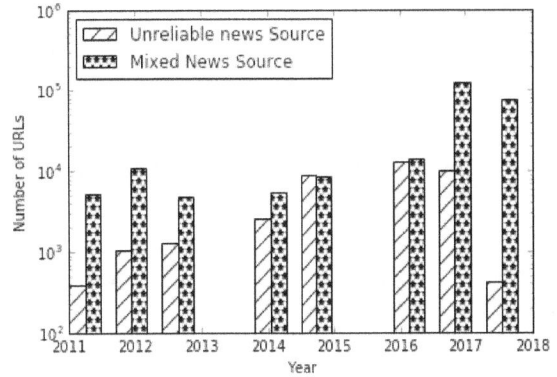

Figure 3: Year's distribution of collected News, ranging from 2010 to 2018.

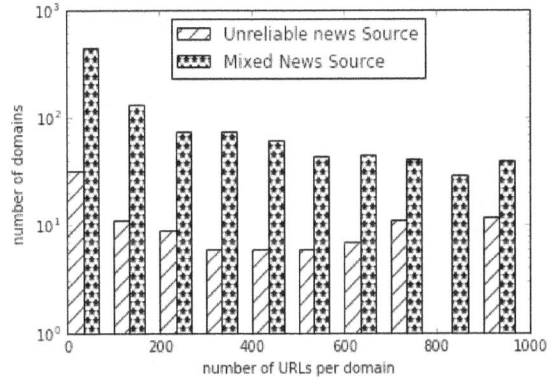

Figure 4: Distribution of URL's number collected per domain.

at the end of the process all instances in the unreliable set are used for both training and validation, and each observation is used for validation exactly once. The full reliable data set, which contains unlabeled websites, is used to construct the Graph in all the folds. Finally, the mean precision is computed by using the precision of the k results from each fold, producing a single estimation.

4.3 Defining a Similarity Threshold (β)

The parameter β has influenced the results obtained. In order to get more accurate rank, we estimated the best parameter using

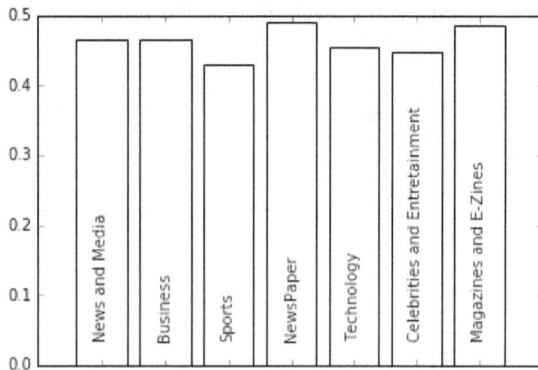

Figure 5: Jaccard Similarity between News categories and fake News that achieve the minimum similarity (>0.4).

a numerical optimization method. We used Newton-Conjugate-Gradient, which is employed to minimize functions of multiple variables, where the best β found that minimizes the Mean Squared Error in our dataset is $\beta = 0.849$.

4.4 Metrics

In order to evaluate our proposed work in a classification task we adopted the standard information metrics, such as precision, recall and f1. For the assessment of the ranking task, we used precision@k. The metrics employed ca be briefly described as follows:

- *Precision:* the fraction of the websites classified as fake that are really fake News. $Precision = \frac{tp}{tp+fp}$
- *Recall* is the fraction of the fake websites that were successfully identified. $Recall = \frac{tp}{tp+fn}$
- *F-1* corresponds to the harmonic mean between precision and recall. $f1 = 2 * \frac{precision*recall}{precision+recall}$
- *Precision@k* corresponds to the precision using the k-firsts elements of the rank.

where tp is the number of positive instances correctly classified as positive, tn number of negative instances correctly classified as negative, fp negative instances wrongly classified as positive, and fn is the number of positive instances wrongly classified as negative. We defined positive instances as fake News websites and negative instance as reliable News websites.

4.5 Baseline

To measure the gap between our method and a supervised one, we compared our results with the ones using Support Vector Machine, referred to as *SVM*. We employed a linear kernel, recommended for text classification, and which generally uses TF-IDF vectors with a lot of features.

5 RESULTS AND DISCUSSION

In this section, we present the results and discuss the evaluation of our proposed approach in two different tasks: Ranking of websites and Binary classification.

5.1 Ranking Task Assessment

To perform a comparison between the ranking of websites generated by DistrustRank and SVM, we used Precision@10, i.e. we evaluate the precision of the models using the top-10 firsts elements of the rank. We adopted Precision@10 because it usually corresponds to the number of relevant results on the first page on a search engine (e.g. google.com). Additionally, in order to better understand the behavior of the models in a small training data set, we vary from 0 to 10 the quantity of websites. It is important to note that for the training step, each model received exactly the same seed set (that was randomly selected from the training set).

Figure 6 shows that Distrustrank yields better results for all quantity of seeds analyzed, which are excellent results for a semi-supervised model. While DistrustRank needs only 7 seeds to achieve a precision of 100% (i.e. all the top 10 websites ranked are truly fake), SVM needs 9 seeds to obtain the same precision. Additionally, all the results obtained by our approach using different quantities of seeds showed to be superior to the baseline, where the difference ranges from 10 to 40 percentage points (pp). Using a Wilcoxon statistical test [18] with a significance level of 0.05, we verified that DistrustRank results are statistically superior in this task.

As a matter of fact, the good performance of Distrustrank in this task is expected. Supervised learning strategies generally need a large training data set to yield models with higher predictive power that can generalize well to a new data set. DistrustRank however, is designed considering the empirical observation, that fake News websites are similar to each other. The use of this domain knowledge in our model, trough a biased graph centrality, allows a better performance in small data sets.

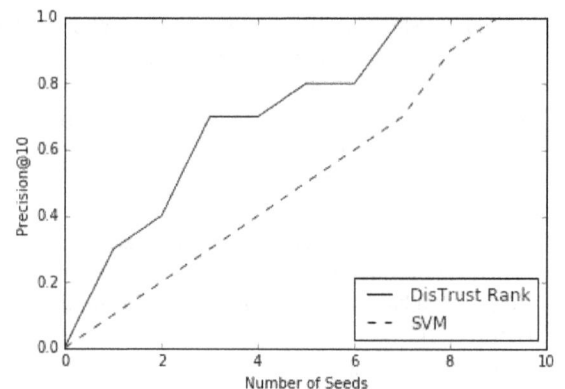

Figure 6: Number of seeds used to train the model.

5.2 Classification Task Assessment

This task consists in predicting the class of a website (e.g. Reliable or Unreliable News website). In this experiment, the positive class represents the Unreliable News websites and, the Negative class represents Reliable News websites. We used 2-fold cross-validation, where we randomly shuffle the data set into two sets d_0 and d_1 with equal size. We then train on d_0 and validate on d_1, followed by training on d_1 and validating on d_0. This choice is motivated by the lack of positives instances of fake News websites.

DistrustRank was originally designed to rank websites, however, in order to provide a proper evaluation against SVM, we adapted the ranking to act as a classifier. In a classification task, we are able to compare our approach using complex metrics, such as ratios of false positive and negatives, true positives and negative, as well as precision, recall, and f-1. To transform a ranking into a classification, we used the first k-top websites of DistrustRank's rank as positive class and the rest of the rank as negative. Obviously, setting an optimal value of k without a priori knowledge of the distribution of fake news websites is a tricky problem. Nonetheless, for evaluation purposes, we use k=47, since we know a priori that this is the number of fake websites in our data set.

Table 3 and 4 show that DistrustRank presented a lower error rate in both positive and negative classes, where the differences range from 38 to 47 pp. Additionally, we also analyzed the performance of the models using standard Information Retrieval metrics. Table 5 shows that DistrustRank outperformed the SVM model in Precision, Recall and f1, where differences are 16.96, 14.89 and 15.89 pp, respectively.

Table 3: Confusion Matrix of DistrustRank.

	Predicted Positive	Predicted Negative
Actual Positive	**36**	11
Actual Negative	9	**493**

Table 4: Confusion Matrix of SVM.

	Predicted Positive	Predicted Negative
Actual Positive	**29**	18
Actual Negative	17	**485**

Table 5: Summary of Results

	Precision	Recall	F1
DistrustRank	**0.8**	**0.7659**	**0.7825**
SVM	0.6304	0.6170	0.6236

The SVM model presented a similar error distribution among positive and negative. This was expected, since for the learning step we used an equal quantity of positive and negative instances, and that it generally leverages in a learning of an equal distribution of the classes. However, even using a larger amount of data for the training, it still presents lower precision and recalls when compared to our approach. In our experiments, we observed that the vocabulary employed by fake News is similar to the one used in reliable News. This textual similarity explains the worst results of the supervised learning model. On the other hand, DistrustRank presented better results using the same amount of data to the training step, due to its semi-supervised strategy.

6 CONCLUSION AND FUTURE WORK

In this paper we have put forward a novel semi-supervised approach to spot fake News website: DistrustRank. From a small set of fake News website, it creates a graph where vertices correspond to websites and edges to the similarity between the News that they share. Next it applies a biased Pagerank to identify other fake websites. The similarity is defined in therms of cosine difference of the TF-IDF vectors of words extracted from the News links, which usually contains the headline.

Our evaluation showed that DistrustRank can effectively identify a significant number of unreliable News (fake News) websites with less data to the training step. In a search engine, DistrustRank can be used either to filter the pages retrieved to the user, or in combination with other metrics to rank search results. The main contributions of this work are the following:

(1) a new semi-supervised method to identify Unreliable News Websites, i.e. it does not depend on a large annotated training set;
(2) formulation of a similarity function that is computational inexpensive since it only relies on links to represent the similarity between websites;
(3) a better performance in the tasks of ranking and classification, using only a small set of unreliable News websites;
(4) creation of pre-selected data set, containing the News category, date and similarity content; this final data set contains News websites, long links to the News and their headlines.

As future work, we would like to consider different ways to measure the similarity between websites. One possible way is using Word Embedding [10]. It provides a vector representation that allows words with similar meaning to have a similar representation. For instance, this representation could be applied to News links that contain different terms but the same semantic meaning: e.g. *killer* and *murderer*. Another research direction would be to employ different features, such as the time of each News as a decay parameter to measure the similarity between nodes.

ACKNOWLEDGMENTS

This work was partially funded by the European Research Council under ALEXANDRIA (ERC 339233) and CAPES, a Brazilian government institution for scientific development.

REFERENCES

[1] Eda Baykan, Monika Henzinger, and Ingmar Weber. 2013. A comprehensive study of techniques for URL-based web page language classification. *ACM Transactions on the Web (TWEB)* 7, 1 (2013), 3.
[2] Shiri Dori-Hacohen and James Allan. 2013. Detecting controversy on the web. In *Proceedings of the 22nd ACM international conference on Conference on information & knowledge management.* ACM, 1845–1848.

[3] Juan Echeverria and Shi Zhou. 2017. Discovery, Retrieval, and Analysis of the 'Star Wars' Botnet in Twitter. In *Proceedings of the 2017 IEEE/ACM International Conference on Advances in Social Networks Analysis and Mining 2017*. ACM, 1–8.

[4] Arthur C Graesser, Danielle S McNamara, and Jonna M Kulikowich. 2011. Coh-Metrix: Providing multilevel analyses of text characteristics. *Educational researcher* 40, 5 (2011), 223–234.

[5] Aditi Gupta, Hemank Lamba, Ponnurangam Kumaraguru, and Anupam Joshi. 2013. Faking sandy: characterizing and identifying fake images on twitter during hurricane sandy. In *Proceedings of the 22nd international conference on World Wide Web*. ACM, 729–736.

[6] Zoltán Gyöngyi, Hector Garcia-Molina, and Jan Pedersen. 2004. Combating web spam with trustrank. In *Proceedings of the Thirtieth international conference on Very large data bases-Volume 30*. VLDB Endowment, 576–587.

[7] Benjamin D Horne and Sibel Adali. 2017. This just in: fake news packs a lot in title, uses simpler, repetitive content in text body, more similar to satire than real news. *arXiv preprint arXiv:1703.09398* (2017).

[8] Srijan Kumar, Robert West, and Jure Leskovec. 2016. Disinformation on the web: Impact, characteristics, and detection of wikipedia hoaxes. In *Proceedings of the 25th International Conference on World Wide Web*. International World Wide Web Conferences Steering Committee, 591–602.

[9] Xian Li, Xin Luna Dong, Kenneth Lyons, Weiyi Meng, and Divesh Srivastava. 2012. Truth finding on the deep web: Is the problem solved?. In *Proceedings of the VLDB Endowment*, Vol. 6. VLDB Endowment, 97–108.

[10] Tomas Mikolov, Ilya Sutskever, Kai Chen, Greg S Corrado, and Jeff Dean. 2013. Distributed representations of words and phrases and their compositionality. In *Advances in neural information processing systems*. 3111–3119.

[11] Suphakit Niwattanakul, Jatsada Singthongchai, Ekkachai Naenudorn, and Supachanun Wanapu. 2013. Using of Jaccard coefficient for keywords similarity. In *Proceedings of the International MultiConference of Engineers and Computer Scientists*, Vol. 1.

[12] Michael J Paul, ChengXiang Zhai, and Roxana Girju. 2010. Summarizing contrastive viewpoints in opinionated text. In *Proceedings of the 2010 Conference on Empirical Methods in Natural Language Processing*. Association for Computational Linguistics, 66–76.

[13] Kashyap Popat, Subhabrata Mukherjee, Jannik Strötgen, and Gerhard Weikum. 2016. Credibility assessment of textual claims on the web. In *Proceedings of the 25th ACM International on Conference on Information and Knowledge Management*. ACM, 2173–2178.

[14] Pujari Rajkumar, Swara Desai, Niloy Ganguly, and Pawan Goyal. 2014. A novel two-stage framework for extracting opinionated sentences from news articles. In *Proceedings of TextGraphs-9: the workshop on Graph-based Methods for Natural Language Processing*. 25–33.

[15] Shafiza Mohd Shariff, Xiuzhen Zhang, and Mark Sanderson. 2017. On the credibility perception of news on Twitter: Readers, topics and features. *Computers in Human Behavior* 75 (2017), 785–796.

[16] Tarcisio Souza, Elena Demidova, Thomas Risse, Helge Holzmann, Gerhard Gossen, and Julian Szymanski. 2015. Semantic URL Analytics to support efficient annotation of large scale web archives. In *Semanitic Keyword-based Search on Structured Data Sources*. Springer, 153–166.

[17] Gabriel Stanovsky, Judith Eckle-Kohler, Yevgeniy Puzikov, Ido Dagan, and Iryna Gurevych. 2017. Integrating Deep Linguistic Features in Factuality Prediction over Unified Datasets. In *Proceedings of the 55th Annual Meeting of the Association for Computational Linguistics (Volume 2: Short Papers)*, Vol. 2. 352–357.

[18] Frank Wilcoxon, SK Katti, and Roberta A Wilcox. 1970. Critical values and probability levels for the Wilcoxon rank sum test and the Wilcoxon signed rank test. *Selected tables in mathematical statistics* 1 (1970), 171–259.

[19] Vinicius Woloszyn, Henrique DP dos Santos, Leandro Krug Wives, and Karin Becker. 2017. Mrr: an unsupervised algorithm to rank reviews by relevance. In *Proceedings of the International Conference on Web Intelligence*. ACM, 877–883.

[20] Hong Yu and Vasileios Hatzivassiloglou. 2003. Towards answering opinion questions: Separating facts from opinions and identifying the polarity of opinion sentences. In *Proceedings of the 2003 conference on Empirical methods in natural language processing*. Association for Computational Linguistics, 129–136.

Where in the World Is Carmen Sandiego?
Detecting Person Locations via Social Media Discussions

Konstantina Lazaridou
Hasso-Plattner-Institut, Potsdam,
Germany
konstantina.lazaridou@hpi.de

Toni Gruetze
Hasso-Plattner-Institut, Potsdam,
Germany
toni.gruetze@hpi.de

Felix Naumann
Hasso-Plattner-Institut, Potsdam,
Germany
felix.naumann@hpi.de

ABSTRACT

In today's social media, news often spread faster than in mainstream media, along with additional context and aspects about the current affairs. Consequently, users in social networks are up-to-date with the details of real-world events and the involved individuals. Examples include crime scenes and potential perpetrator descriptions, public gatherings with rumors about celebrities among the guests, rallies by prominent politicians, concerts by musicians, etc. We are interested in the problem of tracking persons mentioned in social media, namely detecting the locations of individuals by leveraging the online discussions about them.

Existing literature focuses on the well-known and more convenient problem of user location detection in social media, mainly as the location discovery of the user profiles and their messages. In contrast, we track individuals with text mining techniques, regardless whether they hold a social network account or not. We observe what the community shares about them and estimate their locations. Our approach consists of two steps: firstly, we introduce a noise filter that prunes irrelevant posts using a recursive partitioning technique. Secondly, we build a model that reasons over the set of messages about an individual and determines his/her locations. In our experiments, we successfully trace the last U.S. presidential candidates through millions of tweets published from November 2015 until January 2017. Our results outperform previously introduced techniques and various baselines.

CCS CONCEPTS

• **Information systems** → **Web searching and information discovery**; **Social networks**; **Document filtering**; **Information extraction**; • **Computing methodologies** → **Supervised learning by classification**;

KEYWORDS

person tracking, event detection, text classification, social network analysis

ACM Reference Format:
Konstantina Lazaridou, Toni Gruetze, and Felix Naumann. 2018. Where in the World Is Carmen Sandiego? Detecting Person Locations via Social

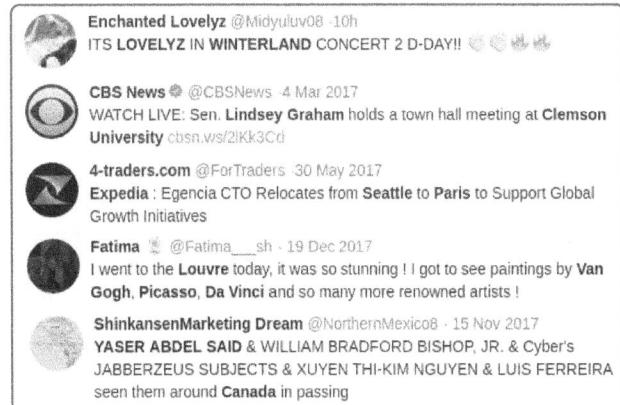

Figure 1: Tweets that indicate the locations of different entities: Lovelyz, Lindsey Graham, Expedia, Van Gogh, Picasso, Da Vinci and Yaser Abdel Said.

Media Discussions. In *WebSci '18: 10th ACM Conference on Web Science, May 27–30, 2018, Amsterdam, Netherlands.* ACM, New York, NY, USA, 10 pages. https://doi.org/10.1145/3201064.3201068

1 NEWS SPEED AND COVERAGE IN SOCIAL MEDIA

Millions of people publish their thoughts and experiences on various social networks and microblogs, such as Facebook, Twitter, etc. Users share real-time information via text messages, geo-located images, live videos etc. An example of the speed and brevity specifically of Twitter is the shooting outside the Texas Irving mall in 2011. The incident was reported by a very short tweet immediately after the shooting, in contrast to newspapers that reacted with a 3-hour delay [11]. Similarly, one is also likely to inform their peers about a natural disaster outbreak, even before the first news story is published [7]. Hence, Twitter can be seen as a fast and decentralized news media.

Furthermore, users keep their peers up-to-date, by retweeting, quoting and engaging in discussions about the current affairs. When considering that most of the posts on Twitter have no visibility restrictions, it is reasonable to claim that this platform "breaks down the communication barriers" [20]. According to Kwak et al., regardless the popularity of the original account, any random retweet spreads over the network almost instantly [9]. This means that every retweet is expected to reach 1,000 users on average, imposing its impact to the rest of the network. Thus, Twitter users can be extremely influential by sharing real-time ongoing news, including civil unrest, entertainment activities, earthquakes and floods, etc. This vast amount of information has attracted various Twitter analyses, particularly related to the problem of event [5] and location [17] detection in social media, with the latter being essential due to the very low amount of geo-tagged tweets.

In this work, we are interested in a location detection problem that leverages the up-to-dateness of social media (e.g. microblogs), that is: the task of "person tracking". Unlike related work on user location detection, we consider the individuals to be mentioned in discussions in the Twittersphere, rather than assuming that they hold a user profile. We prefer to rely on the wisdom of the crowd that discusses about a given person p, because we hypothesize that it brings many more tweets as evidence on p's locations than p might potentially share him/herself. We also do not assume that a location mentioned in a user post is identical to this user's current position. Thus, we allow users who discuss event locations asynchronously.

As shown in Figure 1, by detecting where a music band (**Lovelyz**) is or plans to be, a user can decide to join their concert and browse people's comments and anticipation about this specific event. Similarly for politicians (**Lindsey Graham**), we can leverage tweets discussing about them to discover the town hall meeting they hold. Additionally, target entities might also be companies that relocate (**Expedia**), or objects, such as famous art pieces that are moving to different countries over time (**Van Gogh, Picasso, Da Vinci**). Tracking vulnerability in software products over time could also be tackled by analyzing the mentions of exploit kits on the Web[1].

Moreover, an important use case covered by our approach is the ability to track people that are national risks, such as wanted criminals and warlords. An example of a well-known fugitive is **Yaser Abdel Said**, who is still missing and for whom FBI offers a high reward in exchange of valuable leads on his arrest. To demonstrate the benefits of a person tracking approach in social media, we performed a simple query in the Twitter Search API, namely, "Yaser Abel Said seen in". Only one tweet is returned by *NorthernMexico8* posted on November 2017 and as shown in Figure 1, it places him in Canada.

As we can observe, this basic test shows the challenge of analyzing a limited amount of valuable data, yet the potential of tackling the (person) entity tracking problem via social network discussions. Note that, even when the available data are more, i.e., individuals are very popular and draw a lot of attention in the media, there are still important challenges to face. Particularly, the high amount of spam and fake messages makes it crucial to filter the data, in order to detect correct person locations and avoid any misinformation or chatter, e.g. false positives and farces.

Hence, our goal is to harvest the wisdom of the crowd that can potentially provide us with ongoing events, but at the same time we must make sure to avoid noisy tweets. In addition, even though tracking people that do not want to be found is useful in the case of criminals, it might raise ethical concerns and have negative implications on the target individuals, such as when locating protesters and activists[2].

Unlike most prior work that mainly deals with location identification of social network users themselves [13], their home [16] or messages [24], we consider the tweets as a means to derive the

---

[1]https://www.recordedfuture.com/tracking-exploit-kits/
[2]http://www.complex.com/life/2016/11/police-surveillance-activists-people-of-color

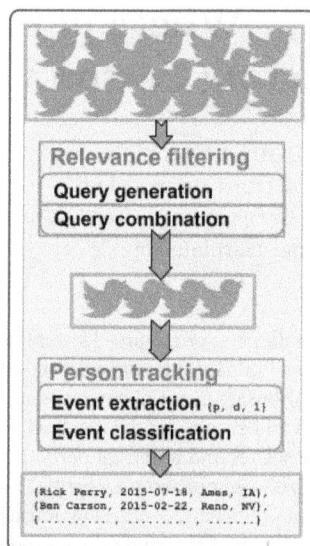

Figure 2: Our overall approach: Given a tweet stream, we apply a relevance filter that prunes the noise and supply the remaining tweets to a person tracker that outputs person locations.

physical position of mentioned individuals. We seek to answer the following question: Given a target person entity p, can we identify the locations of p over time only by observing what people say about p in social media? To address this problem, we analyze tweets that mention p to determine all p's physical locations and gain insights from a big tweet dataset spanning one year. Our approach uses millions of tweets relevant to the U.S. general elections in 2016 with the goal to track the presidential candidates and it considerably outperforms existing techniques and baselines. As demonstrated in Figure 2, our contributions include:

- A greedy two-phase algorithm that filters relevant tweets for person tracking
- A novel approach for predicting the locations of individuals by leveraging their third-person references in social media posts
- Evaluation results on tracing U.S. politicians' locations

The rest of the paper is organized as follows: Section 2 presents related work, Section 3 describes how we discover relevant tweets and Section 4 discusses how we determine the individuals' locations. Section 5 shows our results and Section 6 concludes this work with ideas for future work.

2 RELATED WORK

An extensive body of literature focuses on novel information discovery in user-generated content, such as news pieces, trending topics, popular events, etc. Related research includes *TwitterStand* [20], a framework that provides a geographic overview of breaking news on Twitter and *TwitterMonitor* [14], which performs real-time trending topic tracking. Since we are interested in detecting localized events and their timestamps, which we consider as the places a target individual visits, we find our work relating better to the task of event detection, rather than trend detection. An event usually appears as a bursty occurrence of novel information in a certain time period [1] and a sudden increase of the occurrence of certain words [5]. The attention that events attract typically fades over time as other significant incidents arise, e.g., in our case, the target entity moving to another location.

Event detection has been studied extensively for various application areas, e.g., predicting earthquakes [18], real-time discovery of sports competitions [1] and detection of event-related information [12]. However, prior work is mainly motivated by the need to keep the users up-to-date in emergency situations and few works identify and analyze events independently of their type [5]. The majority focuses on the cases of incidents of public interest [25] , e.g., natural disasters, instances of civil unrest, or disease outbreaks.

In contrast, we do not address the problem of event detection aiming at public awareness, but we solve the task of person tracking in social media. Given an individual as a user query, we show that social media can help us create a timeline of his/her locations. Each event in the timeline is independent from the others regarding its kind and duration, and the frequency of these events depends entirely on the individual's profile. Hence, we are limiting our search to locations that these persons visit, yet at the same time we consider all possible types of events.

Another line of research that is closely connected to our work is the identification of locations in social media. Its emergence can be justified by the lack of geolocated user posts, especially on Twitter, since only 1% of the messages includes geotags [21]. Related works include *PETAR* [10], a time-aware point of interest (POI) extraction system and *TWILOC*, which determines the location of a tweet based on various content and network features [6]. Backstrom et al. study the relationship of social and spatial proximity and use the network properties to predict the location of users [2]. It is shown that social data, such as the location of a user's friends, can enhance prediction performance.

Unlike the above-mentioned works, we take into account tweets by various users that are published in a certain time frame, instead of performing a user-focused analysis [22]. Thus, we are not interested in geo-locating neither a tweet nor its user. Instead, we analyze the location and person mentions that are contained in tweets, in order to track the mentioned individuals.

Our goal is to gain insights about a discussed entity p and hence, we treat any potential tweet posted by p as all other tweets that share information about p in the third person. A representative example of a tweet we wish to discover is: "'History is made by the dreamers, not the doubters'. **Donald Trump** just now in **Des Moines**. #Politics @POTUS @realDonaldTrump @IvankaTrump @FLOTUS". This is an appropriate post for our task regardless the account that it originates from. By mining the textual content of such messages, we cope with the lack of geotags on Twitter, as well as with location inconsistencies. For instance, users might also share their thoughts about an event they attended earlier this day, which means that their current location is not identical with the event's location anymore. Thus, we choose to find locations in the content of the tweets instead, by applying a named entity linking approach [3].

The most relevant study to our current work is our previously introduced basic approach that discovers *located-in* patterns in the tweets [4] . We applied the Apriori algorithm on a very small set of tweets to discover frequent terms that can be used as queries for the Twitter API to retrieve relevant posts to politicians' locations. Consequently, it was naively assumed that each event that yields a minimum support of ten or more tweets in the result set corresponds to an actual event. Limited results were reported about the locations of Donald Trump, Hillary Clinton, Bernie Sanders, and Ted Cruz on the day prior to Super Tuesday.[3]

Drawing inspiration by these preliminary findings, we now perform a large-scale analysis on almost a billion of tweets and various events and individuals. We introduce a novel approach for noise detection in the context of person tracking, which is based on recursive partitioning and carefully generates higher quality queries than our previously proposed method. Instead of solely relying on the popularity of the mentioned events, we use a supervised constraint-based approach to detect which of the event locations are valid.

3 FINDING THE NEEDLE IN A HAYSTACK OF TWEETS

The first part of our person tracking approach is responsible for excluding noisy messages, which provide misleading information about the target entities and their associated events. We define an *event* as a triplet $e = (p, l, d)$, where an individual p appears in a specific location l on a particular date d. We model our noise detection task as an Information Retrieval task: given the tweets published in a certain time period, we wish to retrieve the ones that are relevant to person tracking. That is why we design a query for the Twitter API that will return suitable messages for our goal. Given the clean result set, we detail how we classify the discussed events into correct and incorrect in Section 4.

One can easily grasp that the terms {*rally*} or {*rally, today*} might be promising choices if one is searching for political campaigns in social media. However, given the almost infinite amount of words and hashtags that one can search with, choosing the right query is a cumbersome and complex task. The appropriate query terms depend on how users like to describe the locations of others, such as "live in", "don't miss the", or "just saw". Since the phenomenon of misinformation in media has risen in the past years [15], a naive query might return tweets that are fake or spam regarding the target entities.

Figure 3 depicts the number of tweets we found for four popular entities on four randomly selected dates: the U.S. politicians Donald Trump and Hillary Clinton, and the bands U2 and Red Hot Chili Peppers. The number of tweets that simply refer to an entity p is shown in *blue*, while the portion of them that contains a reference to an actual event location of p is depicted in *red*. The events are public speeches and concerts respectively. Although we depict a limited data sample[4] that is often biased by the medium's sampling process [19], we can already observe that irrelevant tweets are orders of magnitude more common than relevant ones are. Therefore, noise detection becomes an important, often domain dependent problem and a person tracking method is expected to distinguish which context provides correct person information and which not.

---

[3]https://en.wikipedia.org/wiki/SuperTuesday
[4]The Public Streaming API is limited to a maximum of 1% of the overall traffic on Twitter (i.e., around 5 million tweets per day).

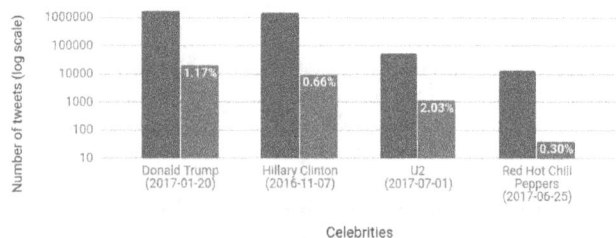

Figure 3: For four public figures and four respective dates, we depict the number of tweets referring to a) this entity (left) and b) the entity and a correct location (right).

3.1 Problem Statement

Given a set of entities we wish to detect, let us assume that the set of Twitter statuses mentioning at least one entity is denoted as T. Each tweet $t \in T$ represents a document that consists of a set of words, s.t., $t = \{w_1, w_2, ..., w_i\}$. All unique words in T form the existing vocabulary V. We aim to discover the tweets $T^+ \subset T$ that contain relevant information for our task. We refer to the rest of the tweets as $T^- \subset T$, where $T = T^+ \cup T^-$ and $T^+ \cap T^- = \emptyset$ hold.

A relevant tweet $t \in T^+$ is a message that refers only to correct event information, that is, contains an actual event triplet, $e = (p, l, d)$. For instance, during the U.S. election campaigns, the current U.S. president Donald Trump conducted a rally in Georgia on 29/2/2016. Thus, the tweet "LIVE Stream: **Donald Trump** Rally at Valdosta St. University in **Valdosta, GA**" belongs to T^+, whereas "It's Leap Day 2016. February has 29 days. And **Washington** is in an uproar. **Donald Trump** is trying to have the extra day deported" belongs to T^-. The second example is a tweet that refers to a false location of Donald Trump for that date and our approach makes it feasible to detect it, since it learns the context that individuals' locations are likely to be discussed on Twitter.

The Twitter API provides an interface for *Boolean queries*, where a query Q is a combination of terms $w \in V$ and boolean operators $\neg$, $\wedge$, and $\vee$. Our goal is to create a filtered tweet set T_Q, s.t., $T_Q \cap T^+$ is maximized and $T_Q \cap T^-$ is minimized. This optimization task can be reduced to the knapsack problem, which is known to be NP-hard. Given the fixed-size rucksack (queries allowed by the Twitter API), we aim to fill it with the most valuable items (most promising queries). Because the number of possible queries is exponential to $|V|$, it is not possible to enumerate them and select the best one. Therefore, it is not feasible to find an optimal solution in reasonable time.

To design a good query, we propose a greedy approach that is based on recursive partitioning. We generate Q in a disjunctive normal form. That is, Q is defined as an $\vee$-combination of queries, i.e. $Q = q_1 \vee q_2 \vee ... \vee q_i$, where each q_x is an conjunction of words or their negations, e.g., $q_x = w_1 \wedge \neg w_2 \wedge ... \wedge w_j$. For instance, we discovered that promising queries to trace politicians in the context of U.S. elections are "night $\wedge$ primary", "holds $\wedge in$" and "rally $\wedge\neg monday$". Our noise filtering algorithm consists of two phases: first, we discover promising conjuction queries q_x that maximize the positive examples in T_{q_x} and second, we combine candidate conjunctions in a query Q. The retrieved tweets are further examined by our event classifier in Section 4.

```
1:  function FIND_CANDIDATES(T, V, P)
2:      Ω = ∅
3:      for p in P do
4:          for i in 1..⌊√|V|⌋ do
5:              V_i = fold(i, V \ p)
6:              Ω = Ω ∪ PARTITION(T, V_i, {p})
7:      return Ω
8:  function PARTITION(T, V_i, q)
9:      Ω = {q}
10:     if |q| < θ_len then
11:         w = arg max IG(q, w)
                 w∈V_i
12:         if χ²(T_q, w) then
13:             if |T⁺_{q∧w}|/|T_{q∧w}| > |T⁺_{q∧¬w}|/|T_{q∧¬w}| and |T⁺_{q∧w}| ≥ θ_supp then
14:                 Ω = Ω ∪ PARTITION(q ∧ w, V_i \ w)
15:             else if |T⁺_{q∧¬w}| ≥ θ_supp then
16:                 Ω = Ω ∪ PARTITION(q ∧ ¬w, V_i \ w)
17:     return Ω
```

Figure 4: Candidate query discovery: recursive partitioning algorithm that creates queries that prune irrelevant tweets.

3.2 Candidate Query Discovery

Inspired by the principle of boosting in machine learning, we construct a variety of term-conjunctions that are built on independent data portions. Figure 4 demonstrates our approach for generating candidate queries, motivated by the principles of decision tree learners. Consider a set of pivot terms P (queries containing only one word) with a high coverage in T^+ (Line 3). Each seed term provides us with a high quality start, which propagates to the conjunctions that will be generated in the next recursive partitioning step (Line 6). For instance, let us assume the football player Luis Suarez and as pivot term the word *seen*. If *seen* is found in a high number of correct tweets (T^+) about Luis Suarez, e.g., "Just seen #**LuisSuarez** in Park Guell #**Barcelona**", this also increases the chances that the combination of *seen* and *in* would retrieve correct locations of the player.

Furthermore, for every pivot term, we split the vocabulary into $k = \sqrt{|V|}$ random and equally sized folds V_i (Line 4 and 5). In each iteration we expand the candidate query (that initially consists of p) with new terms from V_i. Note that every fold has the same size: $\forall i \in \{1, 2, ..., k\} : |V_i| \approx \sqrt{|V|}$, while $\bigcup_{V_i} = V$ and $\bigcap_{V_i} = \emptyset$ hold. The partitioning process (Lines 8- 17) works as follows: Assuming that the current q does not exceed the permitted length θ_{len} (Line 10), the algorithm expands it further. Although the length threshold is rarely hit, we adopt this constraint to prevent very long conjunctions that might lead to overfitting or conflict the restrictions of the Twitter API. Moreover, we perform a query expansion and select the term w (Line 11) that results in the highest information gain regarding the separation of the sets T^+ and T^-. We measure information gain as:

$$IG(q, w) = H(q) - \frac{\left|T_{q \wedge w}\right| * H(q \wedge w) + \left|T_{q \wedge \neg w}\right| * H(q \wedge \neg w)}{\left|T_q\right|}$$

where the *Shannon* entropy $H(q)$ is defined as:

$$H(q) = - \sum_r \left(\frac{\left|T_q^r\right|}{\left|T_q\right|}\right) \log\left(\frac{\left|T_q^r\right|}{\left|T_q\right|}\right), r \in \{-, +\}$$

and the set T_x refers to the tweets that x satisfies. The expansion based on the information gain is inspired by the greedy feature selection of the $C.45$ decision tree learner. It fits well to our task, because we leverage that the term conjunctions fulfill the monotonicity property.

Our overall goal is to distinguish between the vocabulary that users choose to discuss about actual events (of the target entities) and the vocabulary in any other topic that is irrelevant to our task. Thus, in order to capture and successfully avoid words that typically appear in incorrect context, we allow either w or $\neg w$ to expand q (Lines 13 to 16).

For the purpose of avoiding overly specific queries that overfit the data associated to the current fold, we stop expanding when the improvement of w (or $\neg w$) over q is not statistically significant (Line 12). To quantify the significance, we consider the null hypothesis that q's application will not affect the distribution of T^+ and T^-. We perform a χ^2 test to test the hypothesis and reject it if it cannot be supported with the typical significance level of at least $\alpha = 0.05$. We also prevent the query expansions $q \wedge w$ (or $q \wedge \neg w$) to be too specific, by ensuring that the new partition yields sufficient support over T^+, denoted as θ_{supp}.

3.3 Candidate Query Combination

Armed with a valuable set of promising queries Ω, we now combine them to generate our final query Q in a disjunctive normal form that provides us with fewer noisy tweets for person tracking. Given Ω and our document collection T, Figure 5 demonstrates our approach to greedily derive a good disjunction by maximizing the expected query quality *score*:

$$score(q, T) = \frac{\left|T_q^+\right|}{|T^+| + \left|T_q\right|}$$

It is evident that our *score* definition is proportional to the F_1 metric, given that T^+ is the set of relevant and T_q the set of retrieved documents. Therefore, Combine_Candidates finds a local optimum for our problem.

Note that the number of possible combinations is exponential to the size of Ω and hence, enumerating all solutions is not feasible. If the maximum length of Q is reached or Q cannot be improved by adding further conjunctions $q \in \Omega$ (Line 6), the combination phase terminates. The monotonicity property of the disjunctions combined with the repeated improvement of the *score*, results in an extended query that covers a high number relevant tweets.

```
1: function COMBINE_CANDIDATES(Ω, T)
2:     Q = ∅
3:     repeat
4:         Q' = Q
5:         Q = Q ∨ arg max score(Q ∨ q', T)
                    q'∈Ω
6:     until score(Q, T) > score(Q', T) or |Q| > θ_len
7:     return Q
```

Figure 5: Candidate query combination: combining different conjunctions to form a final disjunction query that minimizes the irrelevant and maximizes the relevant tweets.

4 CONSTRAINT-BASED PERSON TRACKING

Given the relevant data we discovered in Section 3, we can now address the question: How can one accurately extract people's locations by examining their references in social media posts? Inferring the places that individuals attend from social network discussions is a very challenging task. Realistic constraints should be taken into account, such as, any person cannot visit more than a reasonable number of locations per day, e.g., music artists usually schedule only one big gig per day, even during a tour. Additionally, many tweets are expected to talk about real-world events in contrast to incorrectly discovered events that won't dominate the online discussions. For instance, users share their experiences about various situations, ranging from popular global events (a concert by a famous band) to local community fairs that will most likely gain more attention in social than mainstream media.

We model this reasoning problem as a binary classification task and decide for each mentioned event on Twitter whether it is true or not. In order to ensure a good tracking performance, our constraint-based person tracking method leverages both the characteristics of the discussed events as well as the tweets themselves.

4.1 Event extraction

Each discussed event $e = (p, l, d)$ in our tweet set T is associated with a person p, a location l and a date d. It is denoted as $e \in E^T$, while the messages about e are denoted as T_e ($T_e \subset T$). To infer the date of e_i from a tweet t that discusses e_i, we use t's publication date, inspired by the up-to-dateness of microblogs as Twitter [9]. Thus, we leverage the daily reactions on e_i, by considering asynchronous discussions about it within the course of a day. We leave more flexible temporal tagging for our future work.

We allow that a person can visit the same location on different dates and can appear in multiple locations on the same date. To identify l and p, we use a named entity linking approach based on *CohEEL* [3] and apply it on the tweet text. Given a knowledge base, e.g. YAGO [23], CohEEL discovers potential mentions that are likely to be linked to a certain entity in the knowledge base. As a second step, the algorithm explores the entity graph derived from the knowledge base with a random walk approach and it extracts the final and coherent entity mentions.

We apply CohEEL with WIKIPEDIA and WIKIDATA (an open knowledge base) and extract from the tweets two different types of entities: persons (the target individuals) and locations (cities). We perform our analysis on a city level, that is, if an entity is found in n different city venues in n different tweets (various streets, buildings

Table 1: Twitter data extracted from November 2015 until January 2017.

All tweets	Tweets with entities	Correct tweets
903,239,572	29,208,457	321,530

etc.), we map the venues to the appropriate city name and consider each of them as a visit to this particular city. Taking into account that CohEEL can also be used for other kinds of target entities (e.g., companies and organizations) and locations in different granularities can be allowed (e.g., states, countries), our approach is easily adapted to other tracking use cases.

4.2 Event classification

After identifying the events mentioned in the tweets, we classify them using a number of features, inspired by the previously mentioned realistic constraints:

Popularity. The *popularity* or *prevalence* of an event on Twitter can be estimated based on the number of unique original tweets discussing about it (disregarding retweets). We refer to the popularity as $prev(e) = |T_e|$. This feature has already been proven as a good indicator for actual events in previous work [4]. For instance, on 31/8/2017 we found that the football player Cristiano Ronaldo was tweeted to be on a trip in the UK. There are more than 3 different tweets on that date all placing him in Manchester, as well as three others, about Tottenham, Longsight and Wolverhampton respectively. Thus, from a statistics point of view, Manchester seems more likely to be a true location.

Another interesting example is shown in Figure 6, which presents the city locations of the politician Jeb Bush during his South Carolina (SC) rally. The color indicates the number of tweets in a specific region. Despite the fact that many locations outside South Carolina are mentioned, the dominance of SC venues on Twitter gives a strong indication towards events in this particular region.

Distance. In the previously described example about Christiano Ronaldo, we observed that all tweets are published in a timeframe of only two hours, which raises the question of how far these three mentioned locations are from each other. Therefore, given all location mentions on a date, an event classifier should be able to understand how far an entity can travel within a certain time period.

We introduce the feature *distance*, i.e., the average pairwise distance of a certain location to the rest on a specific date. Similarly to the *popularity*, in a real-time experiment, this distance is updated as more locations are mentioned in newly published tweets. Moreover, each city is considered as a point on the earth and given its longitude and latitude, we calculate its Haversine distance from the other cities. Namely, given the locations of a person p on a date d, the associated tweets are denoted as $T_{p,d}$. The events found in $T_{p,d}$ are defined as follows:

$$E_{p,d}^T = \left\{ e_i \in E^T \mid p_i = p, d_i = d \right\}$$

and the distance feature of an event e is:

$$dist(e) = \frac{1}{|T_{p,d}|} \sum_{e_i \in E_{p,d}} |T_{e_i}| \cdot \text{Haversine}(geo(l), geo(l_i))$$

Figure 6: Heatmap of Jeb Bush's locations identified in tweets on 11/02/2016 during his South Carolina rally.

By using this feature, we aim to preserve the events that are held reasonably close to each other and eliminate locations that are very far from each other. We extract the geolocations of the cities from WIKIDATA: $geo(l) = \text{wd:P625}(l)^5$.

Population. We hypothesize that the size of a location, such as the *population* of an event's city, can be indicative of whether this event is true or not. We test this hypothesis by including the city's population as a feature of our event classifier and expect that the popularity of a target individual might be correlated to the size of the locations he or she visits. The city populations are retrieved from WIKIDATA with the query: $pop(e) = \text{wd:P1082}(l)^6$.

4.3 Datasets

We evaluate our approach for person tracking on a set of messages extracted via the Public Twitter API during a period of approximately one year.

Tweets. Our dataset consists of millions of messages published by more than 33 million users. The posts mention various individuals related to the last U.S. presidential election (2016). In order to ensure a high coverage on political discussions, we used 241 queries with politicians' names and usernames, as well as popular hashtags related to the election. Since the language found in the Twittersphere can be eccentric, the queries we posed contain not only the individuals' names and Twitter user accounts, but also potential aliases (such as *Hillary Rodham Clinton*, *Secretary of State*, *@HillaryClinton* and *#HRC*), extracted from WIKIPEDIA.

As shown in Table 1, the overall amount of tweets we gathered from the Twitter API is approximately one billion. This results in an amount of 2 million tweets per day. Among these data, there are 29 million posts that discuss our target entities (contain mentions to presidential candidates and locations discovered by *CohEEL* [3]). Furthermore, there are only 321,530 tweets revealing the actual locations of our target entities, which makes our task particularly challenging. The list of tweet ids for every discussed location and politician can be found in our homepage[7].

Events. To evaluate our approach for person tracking in social media, we collected a series of publicly available event records regarding the U.S. presidential candidates in 2016. Our ground truth is a set of events that presidential candidates hosted or participated

---

[5]https://www.wikidata.org/wiki/Property:P625
[6]https://www.wikidata.org/wiki/Property:P1082
[7]https://hpi.de/naumann/projects/web-science/social-media-analysis/politics-on-twitter.html

prior and after the general elections extracted from the 4President blog [8]. This website contains information about events related to the past four elections in the U.S.A. We automatically extract the reported events related to the presidential candidates of the last general election in 2016. Many entries on the website are usually a single event, e.g., the title of the entry page explicitly refers to an event triplet, person-location-date (e.g., Donald Trump, Youngstown, Ohio, 25/7/17).

In the cases where the title contains a broader location, i.e. a state, we apply *CohEEL* on the page's body text to determine the different cities within the state that a presidential candidate has visited. For the purpose of ensuring the validity of each event in our gold standard collection, any other blog entry whose title does not describe an event triplet, namely politician-city-date, is disregarded by our extractor. The resulting gold standard consists of almost three thousand events for various candidates, such as Ben Carson, Lincoln Chafee, Chris Christie, Hillary Clinton, Lindsey Graham, Rick Santorum, Jim Webb etc.

5 RESULTS

In this section, we evaluate our noise detector based on **Rec**ursive **Par**titioning (RECPAR) and our **Co**nstraint-based **P**erson **T**racker (CoPT). RECPAR leverages the wisdom of the crowd to discover relevant tweets and CoPT categorizes them into true or false person locations. First, we show the optimal setup of RECPAR and compare it with our previously introduced approach that is based on **Freq**uent **Item**sets (FREQITEM) [4]. Second, we demonstrate results on person tracking and compare CoPT with other approaches and baselines. In general, we conduct our experiments in consecutive monthly time intervals, namely we use the earliest months of our dataset to learn RECPAR's query, afterwards we train CoPT, and in the last part of the dataset we test the performance of the overall approach.

5.1 Relevance filtering

RECPAR consists of two consecutive phases: candidate query discovery and candidate query combination. The set of candidates, denoted as Ω, is generated by the first component and is also referred to as conjunctions or subqueries of the final query combination Q. In the current evaluation task, we show how RECPAR behaves with different parameter settings. There are four parameters that we must consider in our approach:

- the maximum length of the final combined query Q (maxQLen)
- the maximum length of each subquery in Ω (maxSubQLen)
- the minimum support –number of tweets– that a subquery should exhibit to be included in Ω (θ_{supp})
- the minimum pivot support (θ_{supp}^p) that determines which terms will be the pivots

An example combination of the first two parameters could be a setting where maxQLen = 100 and maxSubQLen = 10. Herewith, RECPAR would create a query Q with at most 10 subqueries, whose length will be 100/10=10 at maximum. For instance, a query combination that tracks art exhibitions of Picasso could be (*must* $\wedge$ *see* $\wedge$ *art* $\wedge$ *exhibition* $\wedge$ *Picasso*) $\vee$ (*don't* $\wedge$ *miss* $\wedge$ *art* $\wedge$ *work* $\wedge$ *Picasso*) $\vee$

[8]http://blog.4president.org/

Table 2: Given different values of θ_{supp}^p and θ_{supp}, the precision (PREC) and true negative rate (TNR) are shown, computed after the candidate query generation phase (Ω) and the candidate query combination phase (Q) respectively.

θ_{supp}^p (%)	θ_{supp} (%)	PREC		TNR	
		Ω	Q	Ω	Q
10	0.25	0.133	**0.523**	0.019	**0.928**
5	0.25	0.133	0.515	0.012	0.926
1	0.25	0.132	0.516	0.002	0.924
0.50	0.25	0.132	0.513	0.002	0.923
0.25	0.25	0.132	0.510	0.001	0.921
10	10	0.133	0.519	0.019	0.931
10	5	0.133	**0.530**	0.019	**0.937**
10	1	0.133	0.500	0.019	0.927
10	0.50	0.133	0.512	0.019	0.927
10	0.25	0.133	0.514	0.019	0.926

(*interesting* $\wedge$ *exhibition* $\wedge$ *inspired* $\wedge$ *by* $\wedge$ *Picasso*). Both parameters are influenced by the restrictions of the Twitter API, yet affect RECPAR's performance as well. In a real-time setting, our system would query the Twitter Streaming API with the target's name and meaningful keywords, and as the tweets arrive, it would categorize each mentioned event as true or false. Thus, we take into account that as of today, the Twitter API allows searches with at most 400 terms. This means that at least one of the query terms needs to be the name of the target person and the rest will be generated by our model.

Our intuition is that the more queries we allow our model to generate, the better the chances to capture more helpful tweets. In contrast, experimenting with different maxQLen values (i.e., 100, 200, 300 and 400) showed that this aspect influences our final event classification results only up to approximately 1%! We conclude that selecting promising and relevant queries is more essential than their number. Hence, in all our experiments maxQLen is set to its potential maximum, i.e. 395, leaving five terms to contain the person's name or alias (e.g., nickname) we aim to discover.

We also examined different values for maxSubQLen (between 2 and 20). Similarly to maxQLen, the results were not significantly affected for values higher than 5. Assigning a small number to maxSubQLen seems logical if we consider that tweets are limited to 140 characters, among which the name of the target person and a location have to appear. Therefore, we chose to set maxSubQLen to 5 for the rest of our experiments.

5.1.1 Support thresholds. As shown earlier in Figure 3, the number of tweets mentioning real-world events is extremely low, i.e., below 2% of all tweets. Thus, we experiment with low values for θ_{supp}^p and θ_{supp} and define these two thresholds as a percentage of the correct tweets in our training set. We train RECPAR's query with the first 3 months of our dataset (2015-11-01 – 2016-01-31) and use the next month (2016-02-01 – 2016-02-29) as a validation set to optimize the parameters. The results are shown in Table 2. The maximum depicted values for θ_{supp}^p and θ_{supp} are 3,686 tweets (i.e., 10%), given that there exist 36,868 positive examples (out of 2,011,085) in our training set. Note that we exclude the messages

Table 3: RECPAR is compared to FREQITEM in terms of precision (PREC), recall (REC), f1 score (F1) and accuracy (ACC).

Model	PREC	REC	F1	ACC
RECPAR	0.48	0.47	0.47	0.83
FREQITEM	0.25	0.60	0.35	0.64

that refer to multiple persons and locations as it is not clear how to assign one of the locations to one of the persons. Examining the word order in the text with the help of a syntax parser is a challenging problem and we leave this task for future work.

Initially, θ_{supp} is set constant and θ^p_{supp} is decreased, and then vice versa. By setting the pivot support higher than the overall support, we aim to be strict with our seed set so that limited ensemble models are created. The first conclusion we draw is that both thresholds affect RECPAR's performance, but not drastically. For instance, in a strict setting where a pivot term has to appear in least 3,687 tweets (θ^p_{supp}=10%), the precision and the TNR are improved only by approximately 1% in comparison to the softest constraint (θ^p_{supp}=0.25%). Similarly for the θ_{supp}, its second highest value achieves the most successful result.

Another interesting finding is the crucial contribution of the candidate combination phase to RECPAR's performance. It is evident that the naive usage of all subqueries would achieve poor precision results (first column under PREC). The reason behind this is that RECPAR's first phase is recall-oriented and the candidates of this phase accomplish 95-99% True Positive Rate (TPR) and False Positive Rate (FPR). However, the combination phase improves the precision by a factor of 4 and the TNR by more than an order of magnitude. Additionally, our experiments show that the second phase diminishes the FPR and boosts the TNR significantly, leading to fewer noisy and irrelevant tweets in our dataset. To conclude, for the rest of our study, we use RECPAR's best query combination, which is learned in 2015-11-01 – 2016-01-31 with θ^p_{supp} = 10% and θ_{supp} = 5%.

5.1.2 Comparison between filtering approaches. This tweet-based experiment is an intermediate evaluation of our overall approach, before the evaluation of the event discovery. We measure how many of the remaining tweets after the filter are correct (i.e., refer to real events). We compare against the previously introduced approach for person tracking [4]. Similarly to RECPAR, we apply FREQITEM's query to every tweet t in the test set and if t satisfies it, then we classify t to the correct class. We expect FREQITEM to perform poorer than RECPAR, due to the fact that it is trained with a very small set of correct tweets and because it does not support negative predicates ($\neg w$).

Furthermore, the recursive nature of RECPAR and the higher diversity of its query candidates, originating from independent data partitions in the generation phase, should lead to better queries. In contrast, in this work, we leverage millions more tweets and anticipate that the recursive nature of RECPAR will dominate the naively constructed queries of FREQITEM. The test set for both approaches is March 2016 (subsequent to RECPAR's validation set).

As depicted in Table 3, RECPAR prevails in terms of precision, f1-measure, and accuracy, since it generates more sophisticated and

Table 4: The results of our proposed solution (RECPAR+CoPT), compared to alternative variations (RECPAR+PoPT, CoPT, PoPT), the existing person tracking technique (FREQITEM+Po), a naive baseline (Po) and the event detection algorithm MABED [5].

Approach	PREC	REC	F1
RECPAR+CoPT	**0.68**	0.43	**0.53**
RECPAR+PoPT	0.64	0.37	0.47
CoPT	0.32	0.24	0.28
PoPT	0.17	0.23	0.19
FREQITEM+Po	0.15	0.67	0.25
Po	0.01	**0.87**	0.02
MABED	0.14	0.00	0.00

carefully designed queries, which guarantee that the result set will contain more relevant than irrelevant tweets. However, FREQITEM achieves a higher recall, because it generates a very high amount of naive queries and hence many relevant (and irrelevant) tweets are covered by it.

5.2 Person tracking

We now evaluate our constraint-based approach (CoPT) on the promising filtered tweets. We initially show the necessity of our realistic constraints (*population*, *popularity* and *distance*) by comparing our proposed solution RECPAR+CoPT to RECPAR+PoPT (**Po**pularity-based **P**erson **T**racking), which considers only the *popularity* of an event on Twitter. We use a Random Forest classifier for both approaches. Our goal is to see whether this obvious and simple constraint is adequate to retrieve the locations of the target individuals.

In addition, not only does RECPAR enhance our overall efficiency in terms of time and memory consumption, but it also improves the tracking performance. Thus, in order to show the filter's necessity, we compare against CoPT and PoPT without filtering the tweets. As discussed earlier, our previous technique [4] applies FREQITEM at first and then it assumes that each event that yields a *popularity* score higher than 10 corresponds to an actual event. We refer to this person tracking approach as FREQITEM+Po (**Po**pularity) and we also compare simply against Po, as a naive baseline.

We train the above-mentioned models with events from April and May 2016 and test them monthly in a six-month period prior to the general elections in the US (from June till November). Various evaluation metrics are shown in Table 4, computed as an average of all test sets. RECPAR+CoPT outperforms almost all techniques and competes closely to its variation, RECPAR+PoPT, especially in terms of precision. That is, the *popularity* of a discussed event in social media is a very strong indicator about its validity, but not enough on its own. The importance of the RECPAR phase is also evident, since CoPT and PoPT cannot outperform our overall proposed approach. Moreover, FREQITEM+Po and Po achieve higher probability of detection (REC) than RECPAR, due to their simplistic nature.

5.2.1 As time goes by. Multiple events related to our target persons happened prior to the US general elections[9], e.g., primaries/caucuses in June, e-mail leakage in July and October, the Green National Convention in August, the first presidential debate in September, etc. In order to explore how the models work on each occasion, we show the monthly precision values in Table 5. We see that our person tracker outperforms all competitors, while having similar results to RECPAR+PoPT for certain tests sets. For instance, in August 2016, the two techniques perform the same and in October 2016, RECPAR+PoPT outstrips RECPAR+CoPT.

As expected, the number of published tweets enhances significantly the performance of RECPAR+PoPT, which can be observed in October 2016, the month with the highest amount of published tweets. However, our proposed combination RECPAR+CoPT appears to be more consistent and robust, by always achieving a minimum precision of 60% and maintaining satisfying recall levels, as depicted in Table 4 as well.

5.2.2 Person tracking as event detection. One can argue that tracking the locations of mentioned entities in social media is a problem that can be tackled by an event detection algorithm. We hypothesize that existing literature on event discovery will not be as successful for our task, since the works are not focused on the involved individuals and thus, they will discover other events in our dataset that the target entities did not attend. To verify our intuition, we consider another competitor, namely MABED, a mention-anomaly-based event detection algorithm [5]. MABED leverages the creation frequency of dynamic mentions to discover events. Noise is avoided by allowing fine-tuned and dynamic events, which do not have to fit to a predefined time duration. This setting serves as a helpful noise "filter", given our highly imbalanced dataset.

An event is defined in MABED by a starting and ending date, a main keyword, and a set of related terms. We are looking for person and location mentions in these keywords by applying *CohEEL* and we use the event timeframe to create event triplets. As long as the detected event exists in our ground truth, we consider it a true positive.

In addition, the system is user-parametrizable and we tune it appropriately for our task. Namely, after experimenting with different parameter settings, we set the time window to 120 minutes to allow medium time precision and the number of words describing an event to 10. Increasing this number did not improve our results, because the longer the event summary is, the more are the chances that multiple politicians and locations are included in it and our evaluation setting does not allow such cases (as discussed in Section 5.1). The threshold for selecting relevant words is the default one (0.6). Since we perform monthly experiments and the most popular month in our dataset contains 400 events, we set k (the maximum number of returned events in MABED) to 400.

Unsurprisingly, we can see in Table 4 that MABED is not performing well, specifically it is unable to capture almost any event in our ground truth and it achieves similar precision to PoPT and FREQITEM+Po. We observed that MABED can generally capture the political discussions and oftentimes, there exist mentions of presidential candidates and U.S. cities in the event descriptions. However, at

[9]https://en.wikipedia.org/wiki/United_States_presidential_election,_2016_timeline

Table 5: Monthly precision results in 2016 for each technique.

Approach	June	July	Aug.	Sept.	Oct.	Nov.
RECPAR+CoPT	**0.62**	**0.66**	**0.66**	**0.67**	0.72	**0.80**
RECPAR+PoPT	0.56	0.64	**0.66**	0.60	**0.80**	0.74
CoPT	0.14	0.26	0.45	0.34	0.31	0.47
PoPT	0.16	0.13	0.21	0.17	0.19	0.17
FREQITEM+Po	0.13	0.13	0.16	0.14	0.21	0.15
Po	0.01	0.01	0.01	0.01	0.01	0.01
MABED	0.10	0.00	0.06	0.14	0.20	0.33

least one item in the discovered event triplets (person-location-date) is usually incorrect and thus the triplet does not refer to an actual location that a person visited on a certain date. This confirms our hypothesis that event detection models are not designed for predicting the precise locations of people mentioned in social media. The results are also not as consistent as of other models, e.g., there are no true positives discovered by MABED in July 2016, as shown in Table 5.

6 CONCLUSIONS AND FUTURE WORK

In this work, we tackled the problem of person tracking via online discussions in social networks. It is shown that social media posts reveal more than the obvious and they make it feasible to discover which places the discussed individuals visit and when. Our proposed approach extracts facts from tweet text and it could be applied to any domain whose entities move over time. The problem we study has several applications, such as detecting singers' concerts, politicians' speeches, companies' relocations, sport teams' games etc., but also in emergency situations, one can identify mentions of missing persons or any kind of threat, such as, fugitives, criminals etc.

We introduced RECPAR, a recursive partitioning algorithm, which carefully generates queries for the Twitter API that return relevant information to the target entities and their locations. An extensive experimental analysis was conducted to examine RECPAR's behavior and optimize its input parameters. We also proposed a constraint-based person tracking approach (CoPT), which reasons over the filtered tweets and categorizes the mentioned events as true or false. Social media as well as location characteristics were used to classify the events. Our overall person tracking method (RECPAR + CoPT) outperformed the previously introduced tracking technique [4], the event detection algorithm MABED [5] and multiple baselines.

The more tweets are used for tracing the target entities, the more correct events can be discovered. Namely, one can use more sophisticated methods for assigning a time to an event, i.e., temporal labeling of the tweets instead of considering the publication time of the message. In this way, more tweets would contribute to the detection of the events and our intuition says that the person tracking results can be further enhanced. We currently perform daily analysis, i.e., we use the tweets of a certain day d to discover the events happened on d. Thus, we allow users who discuss events asynchronously, but only within 24 hours. One can use temporal expressions [8], e.g., yesterday, 2night, tomorrow and also dates mentioned in the text. Given a more flexible temporal tagging approach, we can update our confidence not only about today's events, but also about other future and past events.

Moreover, in order to report the crowd's impression about an individual's event and also the anticipation for an upcoming event (e.g., how inspiring a TED talk was by an entrepreneur and how long-awaited the next event is), our system could additionally provide the average sentiment of the past and newly published tweets respectively. Another interesting improvement would be to consider various granularities of locations. For instance, considering fine-grained locations, such as towns and villages, can be useful when the individual of interest is a national risk and the accuracy of the reported information about him/her is essential. More abstract locations, such as on a country-level, might also be adequate for entertainment or business related activities, such as concerts and conferences.

REFERENCES

[1] Hamed Abdelhaq, Christian Sengstock, and Michael Gertz. 2013. EventTweet: online localized event detection from twitter. *VLDB Endowment* 6 (2013), 1326–1329.

[2] Lars Backstrom, Eric Sun, and Cameron Marlow. 2010. Find me if you can:Improving Geographical Prediction with Social and Spatial Proximity. In *WWW*. North Carolina, USA, 61 – 70.

[3] Toni Gruetze, Gjergji Kasneci, Zhe Zuo, and Felix Naumann. 2016. CohEEL: Coherent and Efficient Named Entity Linking through Random Walks. *Web Semantics: Science, Services and Agents on the World Wide Web* 37 (2016), 75–89.

[4] Toni Gruetze, Ralf Krestel, Konstantina Lazaridou, and Felix Naumann. 2017. What Was Hillary Clinton Doing in Katy, Texas?. In *WWW*. Perth, Australia, 783–784.

[5] Adrien Guille and Cécile Favre. 2014. Mention-anomaly-based event detection and tracking in twitter. In *ASONAM*. Beijing, China, 375–382.

[6] Bahareh Rahmanzadeh Heravi and Ihab Salawdeh. 2015. Tweet Location Detection. *Computation Journalism Symposium* (2015).

[7] Mengdie Hu, Shixia Liu, Furu Wei, Yingcai Wu, John Stasko, and Kwan-Liu Ma. 2012. Breaking News on Twitter. In *SIGCHI*. Texas, USA, 2751–2754.

[8] Ali Hürriyetoglu, Nelleke Oostdijk, and Antal van den Bosch. 2014. Estimating Time to Event from Tweets Using Temporal Expressions. In *EACL*. Gothenburg, Sweden, 8–16.

[9] Haewoon Kwak, Changhyun Lee, Hosung Park, and Sue Moon. 2010. What is Twitter, a social network or a news media?. In *WWW*. North Carolina, USA, 591.

[10] Chenliang Li and Aixin Sun. 2014. Fine-grained location extraction from tweets with temporal awareness. In *SIGIR*. 43–52.

[11] Rui Li, Kin Hou Lei, Ravi Khadiwala, and Kevin Chen-Chuan Chang. 2012. Tedas: A twitter-based event detection and analysis system. In *ICDE*. VA, USA, 1273–1276.

[12] Debanjan Mahata, John R. Talburt, and Vivek Kumar Singh. 2015. From Chirps to Whistles: Discovering Event-specific Informative Content from Twitter. In *WebSci*. Oxford, United Kingdom, 1–110.

[13] Jalal Mahmud, Jeffrey Nichols, and Clemens Drews. 2014. Home Location Identification of Twitter Users. *ACM Transactions on Intelligent Systems and Technology* 5 (2014), 1–21.

[14] Michael Mathioudakis and Nick Koudas. 2010. TwitterMonitor: trend detection over the twitter stream. In *SIGMOD*. Indiana, USA, 1155–1158.

[15] Eni Mustafaraj and Panagiotis Takis Metaxas. 2017. The Fake News Spreading Plague: Was It Preventable?. In *WebSci*. Troy, New York, USA, 235–239.

[16] Adam Poulston, Mark Stevenson, and Kalina Bontcheva. 2017. Hyperlocal Home Location Identification of Twitter Profiles. In *HT*. Prague, Czech Republic, 45–54.

[17] Søren B. Ranneries, Mads E. Kalør, Sofie Aa. Nielsen, Lukas N. Dalgaard, Lasse D. Christensen, and Nattiya Kanhabua. 2016. Wisdom of the Local Crowd: Detecting Local Events Using Social Media Data. In *WebSci*. Hannover, Germany, 352–354.

[18] Takeshi Sakaki, Makoto Okazaki, and Yutaka Matsuo. 2010. Earthquake shakes Twitter users. In *WWW*. North Carolina, USA, 851.

[19] Justin Sampson, Fred Morstatter, Ross Maciejewski, and Huan Liu. 2015. Surpassing the Limit: Keyword Clustering to Improve Twitter Sample Coverage. In *HT*. Guzelyurt, Northern Cyprus, 237–245.

[20] Jagan Sankaranarayanan, Hanan Samet, Benjamin E. Teitler, Michael D. Lieberman, and Jon Sperling. 2009. TwitterStand: news in tweets. In *SIGSPATIAL*. Seattle, Washington, 42.

[21] Axel Schulz, Aristotelis Hadjakos, Heiko Paulheim, Johannes Nachtwey, and Max Mühlhäuser. 2013. A Multi-Indicator Approach for Geolocalization of Tweets.. In *ICWSM*. Boston, USA, 573–582.

[22] Yangqiu Song, Zhengdong Lu, Cane Wing-ki Leung, and Qiang Yang. 2013. Collaborative Boosting for Activity Classification in Microblogs. In *SIGKDD*. Chicago, IL, USA, 482–490.

[23] Fabian M Suchanek, Gjergji Kasneci, and Gerhard Weikum. 2007. Yago: a core of semantic knowledge. In *WWW*. Alberta, Canada, 697–706.

[24] Dennis Thom, Harald Bosch, Robert Krueger, and Thomas Ertl. 2014. Using large scale aggregated knowledge for social media location discovery. In *HICSS*. HI, USA, 1464–1473.

[25] Shiguang Wang, Prasanna Giridhar, Hongwei Wang, Lance Kaplan, Tien Pham, Aylin Yener, and Tarek Abdelzaher. 2017. StoryLine: Unsupervised Geo-event Demultiplexing in Social Spaces without Location Information. In *IoTDI*. Orlando, Florida, 83–94.

Assessing Twitter Geocoding Resolution

Short Paper

Nicholas C. Bennett
University of Southampton
Southampton, SO17 1BJ, UK
n.bennett@soton.ac.uk

David E. Millard
University of Southampton
Southampton, SO17 1BJ, UK
dem@ecs.soton.ac.uk

David Martin
University of Southampton
Southampton, SO17 1BJ, UK
d.j.martin@soton.ac.uk

ABSTRACT

User-defined location privacy settings on Twitter cause geolocated tweets to be placed at four different resolutions: precise, point of interest (POI), neighbourhood and city levels. The latter two levels are not described by Twitter or the API, resulting in a risk that clustered tweets are unintentionally treated as real clusters in spatial analyses. This paper outlines a framework to address these differing spatial resolutions and highlight the impact they can have on cartographic representations. As part of this framework this paper also outlines a method of discovering sources (third-party applications) that produce geolocated tweets but do not reflect genuine human activity. We found that including tweets at all spatial resolutions created an artificially inflated importance of certain locations within a city. Discovering device-level geocoded tweets was straight forward, but querying Foursquare's API was required to differentiate between neighbourhood level clusters and POIs.

CCS CONCEPTS

• **Human-centered computing** → **Social media**;

KEYWORDS

Twitter, census, POI, mapping, framework

ACM Reference Format:
Nicholas C. Bennett, David E. Millard, and David Martin. 2018. Assessing Twitter Geocoding Resolution: Short Paper. In *WebSci '18: 10th ACM Conference on Web Science, May 27–30, 2018, Amsterdam, Netherlands.* ACM, New York, NY, USA, 5 pages. https://doi.org/10.1145/3201064.3201098

1 INTRODUCTION

Online user-generated data within social networks provide an insight into individual and societal behaviour at scale. Twitter, a micro-blogging platform established in 2006 allows users to post 140 character[1] blogs, called "tweets". These tweets can contain text, image or video data and cover any topic the user desires. The user is also able to include location metadata to geolocate the tweet to a specific or general area. The tweets thus contribute to a rich dataset of location-based content that researchers with a registered application can access through the Twitter API. Location-based tweet analysis is the focus of several different areas such as disaster management, with researchers analysing geolocated tweets and their content for the spread of diseases [16], as a method for detecting and predicting the progression of natural disasters [13] and in responding to such events [2, 9], as well as in determining city centre and residential locations [15] and retail centre locations [10].

Due to Twitter's privacy settings, users can either geolocate a tweet to their precise location, a point of interest (e.g. a monument or café), a generalised nearby area (neighbourhood) or to the city[2]. This creates a noisy database as there is no metadata field to indicate whether the tweet's accuracy is precise or generalised[3]. This creates the risk within location-based analyses that the results reflect a wider area than expected, creating an impression of a precise location that in reality represents a neighbourhood or city. This paper creates a framework for distinguishing between local, neighbourhood and city level location resolution and integrates this tiered data with census data to understand how adjusting for coordinate spaces impacts the signal generated by the tweets.

2 RELATED WORK

Existing work does not openly recognise the different user-defined spatial resolutions and thus does not recognise the impact of low resolutions affecting their results. Existing literature for analysing location resolution is sparse and only covers administrative levels of geography rather than acknowledging how a user's privacy settings can affect the accuracy of their location data. Unankard et al. [17] propose an event detection methodology on a large scale, differentiating between city and state levels in the US. Their method used Named Entity Extraction (NER) to match proper nouns within sentences to locations from a GeoNames gazetteer as well as location data from geolocated tweets, but did not acknowledge the effect of clustering on the resolution of the data. Further work by Zhao et al. [18] to discover events in real-time also refer to spatial resolution as administrative rather than user-defined. As tweets can be encoded with a user's precise location, work that aggregates this data removes the benefit of high resolution location information.

Tweet imprecision is enhanced by automated accounts (bots) or semi-automated (cyborg) users who contribute static or otherwise irrelevant data, thus existing research focuses on developing methodologies to detect these accounts.

---

[1] Recently increased to 280 but at the time of writing the data reflects tweets with 140 characters.

---

[2] http://help.twitter.com/en/safety-and-security/tweet-location-settings
[3] There is the "place_type" field which contains either 'poi', 'admin' or 'city' but these are assigned even when the user has precise coordinates. Tweets originating from third party applications do not pass on the 'poi' field.

In their 2010 work, Chu et al. [3] created a methodology for detecting the different types of users on social media. Their methodology relied on a machine learning algorithm that compared human-labelled spam accounts to new tweets and found those that were classified as spam more often originated from automated users. On top of text analysis, their methodology included account characteristics such as tweet frequency, source device (application), follower-to-following ratio and time since account creation. While their work did not focus on location, their methodological approach to removing spam accounts is useful with any Twitter analysis. However, identifiying bots based on their account profile is not always beneficial; Clemence et al. [5] were unsuccessful in using follower statistics to identify bots. An alternative methodology proposed by Adams and Remiro-AzÃşcar [1] removed all sources that originated from a website, claiming that this removed almost all bots. While bots do often use third-party websites, this approach does not allow for new mobile sources to be analysed nor does it address mobile-based third-party applications.

It has not been until recently that researchers have focused on 'Source' as key metadata. This can often differentiate between the user types; bots will more frequently use third party software than Twitter's native products [8]. Building upon the work of Chu et al. [3] in 2010, Gilani et al. [7] describe which sources are used by humans and bots with their results forming a useful summary of how this has changed since 2010, highlighting the increase of bots using Web and mobile devices rather than third party applications. They describe how bots tend to use more sources than humans, but aside from account classification do not expand upon the usefulness of source analysis for other research purposes.

This paper will build upon previous work by creating a comprehensive framework to differentiate between the levels of user-specified geolocation resolution and bring clarity to noisy location data obtained through Twitter. It will assess the impact of distinguishing between precise, neighbourhood and city granularities for spatial representation and build upon previous work on source analysis as a key part in location-based experiments. It will evaluate the framework by applying it to tweets from Southampton, UK.

3 DEVELOPING THE FRAMEWORK

From previous literature, it is clear a robust framework is needed to understand location resolution that takes into account user-defined privacy settings. While a 'place_type' field does exist within the metadata that could have offered insight into the precision level, it is user-defined and can be filled even if the user is not within the area[4], thus will not be included as part of the analysis.

3.1 Tweet Source

The literature has confirmed the source metadata field can be a strong indicator of irrelevant accounts [3, 4]; however, previous work on location data does not include a focus on the source field despite its usefulness. The 'source' field relates to the device or software that created the tweet, thus often reflects bots and spam accounts creating noisy data via third party software.

Sources that programatically add tweet content are not useful in understanding genuine human activities or representation, thus

should be removed. While accounts that use third-party sources are not necessarily automated [7], some sources can be identified as predominantly irrelevant due to the behaviours of accounts that use them. For example, a popular source called "dlvr.it" is used to manage different accounts across social media and generates automated tweets about various news topics with links to the source, often including a latitude and longitude coordinate. While this data is useful to understand general stories within areas, the content is broad and not location-specific despite it being geocoded, therefore should be removed.

3.2 Understanding Tweet Spatial Resolution

To understand the impact of user-defined privacy settings on location accuracy it is necessary to stratify the coordinate data.

As it is currently unknown which gazetteer Twitter uses to define a focal point for neighbourhood or city levels[5], it would seem likely that if a user has enabled location aggregation the API would return tweets with identical coordinate data. Therefore, identical coordinates should be clustered and removed from the primary dataset. The extracted coordinates will form a secondary dataset that may with validity be related to a wider area.

While clustering coordinates is a relatively straightforward task, difficulty arises in distinguishing between city and neighbourhood level resolution. A simple count could suffice, but this can be skewed by popular neighbourhoods such as those including sports or music venues. Therefore, more advanced analyses are required. As Foursquare is used by Twitter to obtain POI coordinates, it is an appropriate source for querying the clustered coordinates to discover POIs.

3.3 Census Data

The subject of Twitter's representivity of both population and location has been a research topic for some time [12, 14]. While an estimated 10.6% of Southampton's population uses Twitter[6], this number is great enough to be used as a proxy for social activity. Therefore, to determine the extent to which this tweet data can be used as a proxy for city, neighbourhood and local activity, census data will be used to inform us about population composition of the area.

To compare tweet activity to population, Output Areas (OAs) are used. OAs are the smallest available areas specifically created for the publication of census data and are generally aggregations of the smallest postal codes[7].

4 CASE STUDY: SOUTHAMPTON, UK

To test the ability of the framework to recognise the impact of stratifying the different tweet spatial resolutions found in tweet datasets, a case study using local tweet and spatial data was carried out.

---

[4]http://developer.twitter.com/en/docs/tweets/data-dictionary/overview/geo-objects

[5]Twitter uses Foursquare's gazetteer for POIs but do not specify other location types.
[6]Estimated Southampton population from the 2011 census is 236,900. Unique users in our dataset whose profile location contains 'Southampton' is 25,110.
[7]http://www.ons.gov.uk/methodology/geography/ukgeographies/censusgeography

Table 1: Breakdown of tweet dataset

Tweet Type	Tweet Number	Users	Coordinates
Total	5,000,098	640,044	36,471
Unique	3,085,426	54,589	36,468
Retweets	1,914,672	601,388	3

4.1 Data Collection

Tweets were collected from the Twitter API from November 2016 to April 2017 covering a 26 mile radius around Southampton's central geocode of 50.9097, -1.4044. This large radius encompassed the city of Southampton as well as collecting tweets from other neighbouring settlements for future comparison as part of a PhD project. In total, 5,000,098 tweets were collected from 640,044 users. Table 1 shows a breakdown of this dataset in terms of retweets, unique sources and location data.

4.2 Pre-Processing

To test the geolocation resolution, only tweets that were hard coded with a coordinate field were used. Methods exist to derive location data from text fields such as Named Entity Extraction (NER) [11]; however, as this experiment relies on already noisy location data, increasing this amount was not desired. From a total tweet count of 5,000,098 there were 36,471 geolocated tweets, representing 0.73%. To further refine the dataset, only those geolocated tweets that fell within Southampton's boundary were considered. This further reduced the applicable tweets to 28,393, or 0.57% of the main dataset. These tweets are mapped in figure 1.

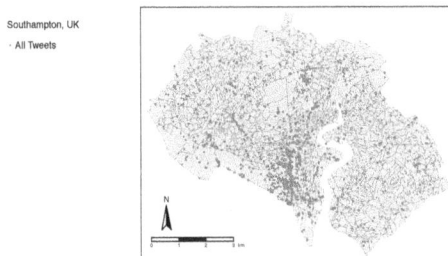

Figure 1: Map of Southampton showing all geocoded tweets.

4.3 Source Analysis

In total, 833 unique sources were identified within the dataset with 67 sources including at least one geolocated tweet. The 67 sources were ranked according to frequency and matched against the users of the source. As there were a small number of location-based sources remaining, these were analysed manually to identify which sources should be removed. The sources that generated a high volume of tweets but with a low volume of unique users were removed as these originated from automated accounts. Sources with 5 or fewer users or fewer than 10 tweets also tended to belong to automated accounts and thus were removed - table 4 summarises the content of these sources. This included 39 sources that had only one user. Sources with "job" in the name were removed as these

Table 2: Breakdown of top 10 Sources

Source	Tweet Number	Users
Twitter for iPhone	1,245,506	28,765
Twitter for Android	487,752	11,252
Twitter Web Client	394,828	14,189
IFTTT	108,318	251
Twitter for iPad	74,394	3,362
Facebook	69,418	1,443
Hootsuite	67,186	800
TweetDeck	58,733	843
Instagram	58,223	7,649
Southampton FC chat zone	58,054	1

Table 3: Breakdown of top 10 Geo Sources

Source	Tweet Number	Users
Instagram	21,065	5,340
dlvr.it	4,313	4
Blue Rhinos Web Services	3,142	2
Foursquare	1,719	214
Twitter for Android	806	104
Untapped	625	62
TweetMyJOBS	533	18
Tweetbot for iS	512	42
Twitter for Windows Phone	299	16
Twitter for iPhone	251	52

have been shown to primarily belong to spam accounts [6]. This resulted in 54 sources, 9,179 tweets and 103 users being removed with 13 sources, 25,871 tweets and 5,935 users remaining.

4.4 Stratifying Coordinate Spaces

To understand the level of aggregation within the tweet dataset, the tweets were clustered by the coordinate field. In total, 1,888 clusters comprised of at least two identical coordinates with 3,290 remaining unique coordinates. The mean cluster size was 12 and the median was 4. As the coordinate field extends to 8 decimal places, i.e. millimetre-level resolution, it is unlikely that more than 4 human-made tweets would organically share the same coordinate field unless they are using a static device such as a desktop computer, in which case they are not as informative of a smaller area as those using mobile devices. Therefore, the median was used as the threshold for stratifying the tweets; tweet clusters below 4 formed the primary dataset and those above 4 formed the secondary dataset. These datasets are mapped in figures 2 and 3.

To discover clusters at the neighbourhood and city levels, as opposed to clusters generated by static users, clusters within the secondary dataset were ranked according to number of unique users within them. In total there were 301 clusters, with 228 comprising at least two unique users. The top cluster had 631 unique users and 1,759 tweets while the second had 194 unique users and 295 tweets. The city level cluster is likely to have the most users and tweets with a steep drop in numbers to the first neighbourhood

Table 4: Example of geo sources with 5 or fewer users (text from human users anonymised)

Source	Users	Tweet Count	Example tweet
Crowdfire - Go Big	5	8	'I use Product A to get myself going or delegate jobs!'
dlvr.it	4	4313	'#Boats: Youth Regionals, Everything smooth? http://...'
Fenix for Android	3	5	'Chrome keeps crashing'
Talon (Plus)	2	19	'Got tickets to the Game'
TweetLogix	2	12	'Happy birthday Jane'
Blue Rhinos Web Services	2	3142	'Boat has just set sail for Flensburg'
WordPress.com	2	5	'Blogging is tough http://...'
auotmicv12demo	1	198	'enjoy 30% off all products all day today with Promotion Code: 0013397014'
Ratlake Transponder	1	109	'ping Vespa has entered geofence Ratlake http://...'
mtvan.com news feed	1	13	'Courier available Southampton to Basingstoke by car.'

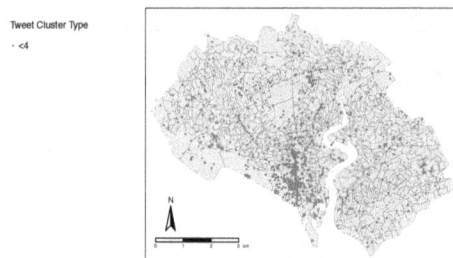

Figure 2: Map of Southampton showing the tweet clusters comprising of fewer than 4 tweets.

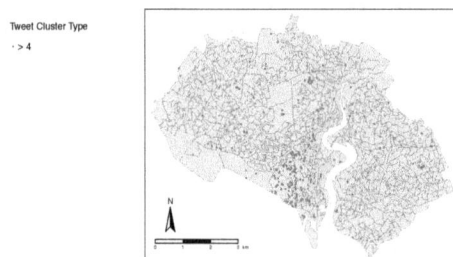

Figure 3: Map of Southampton showing the clusters comprising greater than 4 tweets.

level cluster. The differences between users in a cluster is plotted in figure 4. The differences are converted to a log scale to more easily see them. There is a steep drop from the first cluster to subsequent ones, thus we can be confident in concluding that the first cluster is at city level. To understand which of the remaining clusters are neighbourhood foci rather than popular venues, the Foursquare API was queried with the coordinates from the clusters as the query parameters. As Foursquare is used by Twitter to generate POI coordinates, it seemed an appropriate source to compare against tweet cluster locations. The API returned results based on an exact match for the coordinate clusters within a radius of 25 metres[8], resulting in 129 POI matches and 99 without any matches, which

[8]As GPS can be several metres off the true coordinate due to the angles of satellites relative to the device or a building obstructing the signal, a 25m value allowed for leeway and returned parent venues such as shopping centres rather than component shops while still returning regular POIs. This also accounted for different gazetteers having slightly different coordinate data for the same venue.

indicated a neighbourhood cluster. This method circumvented the lack of POI metadata in tweets not originating from Twitter's native applications.

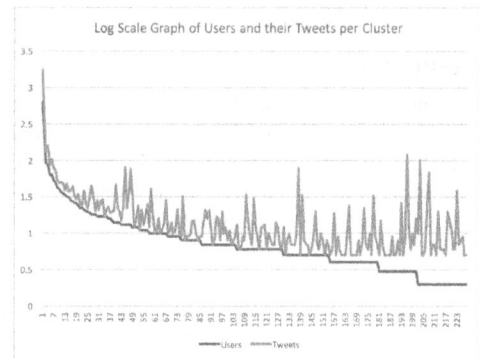

Figure 4: Graph showing the log differences in users and tweets.

4.5 Applying Census Data

The 2011 census data was obtained from Nomis[9]. This dataset is comprised of counts of people living within each Output Area (OAs). To emphasise the impact of cleaning the tweets using the framework outlined in this paper, two census maps are plotted. The first, figure 5, shows the clusters classified as neighbourhoods. They are typically spread out across Southampton with a few close together in popular areas. The second, figure 6, shows only the points of interest, highlighting how many there are in the dataset that would have otherwise been overlooked without applying this framework. This highlights the impact of stratifying the coordinates, these types of clusters would otherwise be contributing noise to an assumed high resolution analysis.

5 CONCLUSION & FUTURE WORK

This paper aimed to understand user-defined tweet spatial resolution and how it can be stratified and combined with source analysis and census data to better represent human activity at different spatial resolutions. Irrelevant sources were identified and removed from the dataset and coordinate clusters separated to discover the extent of neighbourhood and city level resolution. The resulting

[9]http://nomisweb.co.uk/census/2011

Figure 5: Map showing the clusters classified as neighbourhoods.

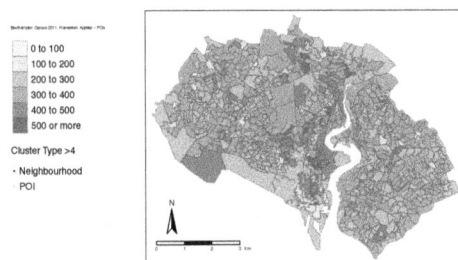

Figure 6: Map showing the clusters of POIs, emphasising how many there are in the dataset.

maps demonstrate the importance of identifying and stratifying different tweet location resolutions for representing the underlying population.

The Foursquare API can return several results per query. This is especially important for identifying shops within shopping centres or sports grounds. Future work would focus on extracting these POIs for an improved representation.

Issues arose with some coordinate clusters whose latitude and longitude values had fewer than 5 decimal places. For example, a cluster over a fast food outlet next to St Mary's Stadium contained many tweets about the stadium rather than the outlet, despite these POIs being 30-40 metres apart. Improving the results by matching the tweet textual content to the venue will improve the reliability of these outliers.

A key area for future work would be understanding the impact of tweets for different denominator populations. A useful future experiment would be to map the neighbourhood clusters on to different population resolutions to assess tweet patterns at these levels.

REFERENCES

[1] Philip Adams and Antonio Remiro-Azócar. 2016. *City-wide Mobility Mapping Using Social Media Communications*. Ph.D. Dissertation. Unversity of Bath. https://doi.org/10.13140/RG.2.1.3499.4161

[2] Junghoon Chae, Dennis Thom, Harald Bosch, Yun Jang, Ross Maciejewski, David S. Ebert, and Thomas Ertl. 2012. Spatiotemporal social media analytics for abnormal event detection and examination using seasonal-trend decomposition. In *IEEE Conference on Visual Analytics Science and Technology 2012, VAST 2012 - Proceedings*. IEEE, 143–152. https://doi.org/10.1109/VAST.2012.6400557

[3] Zi Chu, Steven Gianvecchio, Haining Wang, and Sushil Jajodia. 2010. Who is Tweeting on Twitter: Human, Bot, or Cyborg? *Acsac 2010* (2010), 21. https://doi.org/10.1145/1920261.1920265

[4] Eric M. Clark, Jake Ryland Williams, Chris A. Jones, Richard A. Galbraith, Christopher M. Danforth, and Peter Sheridan Dodds. 2016. Sifting robotic from organic text: A natural language approach for detecting automation on Twitter. *Journal of Computational Science* 16 (2016), 1–7. https://doi.org/10.1016/j.jocs.2015.11.002 arXiv:1505.04342

[5] Michael Clemence, Carl Miller, Steve Ginnis, Rowena Stobart, and Alex Krasodomski-Jones. 2015. *The Road to Representivity*. Technical Report. Ipsos MORI, London. http://www.demos.co.uk/wp-content/uploads/2015/09/Road

[6] Xiaowen Dong, Dimitrios Mavroeidis, Francesco Calabrese, and Pascal Frossard. 2015. Multiscale event detection in social media. *Data Mining and Knowledge Discovery* 29, 5 (2015), 1374–1405. https://doi.org/10.1007/s10618-015-0421-2 arXiv:arXiv:1404.7048v1

[7] Zafar Gilani, Reza Farahbakhsh, Gareth Tyson, Liang Wang, and Jon Crowcroft. 2017. An in-depth characterisation of Bots and Humans on Twitter. *arXiv preprint arXiv:1704.01508* (2017). arXiv:1704.01508 https://arxiv.org/pdf/1704.01508.pdfhttp://arxiv.org/abs/1704.01508

[8] Zafar Gilani, Ekaterina Kochmar, and Jon Crowcroft. 2017. Classification of Twitter Accounts into Automated Agents and Human Users. In *Proceedings of ASONAM 2017, the 2017 International Conference on Advances in Social Networks Analysis and Mining*. https://doi.org/10.1145/3110025.3110091

[9] Muhammad Imran, Shady Elbassuoni, Carlos Castillo, Fernando Diaz, and Patrick Meier. 2013. Extracting information nuggets from disaster-related messages in social media. *ISCRAM, Baden-...* May (nov 2013), 791–800. https://doi.org/10.1145/2534732.2534741

[10] Alyson Lloyd and James Cheshire. 2017. Deriving retail centre locations and catchments from geo-tagged Twitter data. *Computers, Environment and Urban Systems* 61 (2017), 108–118. https://doi.org/10.1016/j.compenvurbsys.2016.09.006

[11] Diana Maynard, Kalina Bontcheva, and Dominic Rout. 2012. Challenges in developing opinion mining tools for social media. In *LREC 2012*. 15–22. http://www.lrec-conf.org/proceedings/lrec2012/workshops/21.LREC2012NLP4UGCProceedings.pdf

[12] Alan Mislove, Sune Lehmann, Yong-yeol Ahn, Jukka-pekka Onnela, and J Niels Rosenquist. 2011. Understanding the Demographics of Twitter Users. *Artificial Intelligence* (2011), 554–557. http://www.aaai.org/ocs/index.php/ICWSM/ICWSM11/paper/viewFile/2816/3234

[13] Takeshi Sakaki, Makoto Okazaki, and Yutaka Matsuo. 2010. Earthquake shakes Twitter users: real-time event detection by social sensors. *WWW '10: Proceedings of the 19th international conference on World wide web* (2010), 851. https://doi.org/10.1145/1772690.1772777 arXiv:0808.0743v3

[14] L. Smith, Q. Liang, P. James, and W. Lin. 2015. Assessing the utility of social media as a data source for flood risk management using a real-time modelling framework. *Journal of Flood Risk Management* (apr 2015). https://doi.org/10.1111/jfr3.12154

[15] Enrico Steiger, René Westerholt, Bernd Resch, and Alexander Zipf. 2015. Twitter as an indicator for whereabouts of people? Correlating Twitter with UK census data. *Computers, Environment and Urban Systems* 54 (2015), 255–265. https://doi.org/10.1016/j.compenvurbsys.2015.09.007

[16] Avaré Stewart, Sara Romano, Nattiya Kanhabua, Sergio Di Martino, Wolf Siberski, Antonino Mazzeo, Wolfgang Nejdl, and Ernesto Diaz-Aviles. 2016. Why is it Difficult to Detect Sudden and Unexpected Epidemic Outbreaks in Twitter? *arXiv preprint arXiv:1611.03426* (2016). arXiv:1611.03426 https://arxiv.org/pdf/1611.03426.pdfhttp://arxiv.org/abs/1611.03426

[17] Sayan Unankard, Xue Li, and Mohamed A. Sharaf. 2015. Emerging event detection in social networks with location sensitivity. *World Wide Web* 18, 5 (2015), 1393–1417. https://doi.org/10.1007/s11280-014-0291-3

[18] Liang Zhao, Junxiang Wang, Feng Chen, Chang Tien Lu, and Naren Ramakrishnan. 2017. Spatial Event Forecasting in Social Media with Geographically Hierarchical Regularization. *Proc. IEEE* 105, 10 (2017), 1953–1970. https://doi.org/10.1109/JPROC.2017.2719039

Domain-Independent Detection of Emergency Situations Based on Social Activity Related to Geolocations

Hernan Sarmiento
Department of Computer Science
University of Chile
Santiago, Chile
hsarmien@dcc.uchile.cl

Barbara Poblete
Department of Computer Science
University of Chile
Santiago, Chile
bpoblete@dcc.uchile.cl

Jaime Campos
Department of Geophysics
University of Chile
Santiago, Chile
jaime@dgf.uchile.cl

ABSTRACT

In general, existing methods for automatically detecting emergency situations using Twitter rely on features based on domain-specific keywords found in messages. This type of keyword-based methods usually require training on domain-specific labeled data, using multiple languages, and for different types of events (e.g., earthquakes, floods, wildfires, etc.). In addition to being costly, these approaches may fail to detect previously unexpected situations, such as uncommon catastrophes or terrorist attacks. However, collective mentions of certain keywords are not the only type of self-organizing phenomena that may arise in social media when a real-world extreme situation occurs. Just as nearby physical sensors become activated when stimulated, localized citizen sensors (i.e., users) will also react in a similar manner. To leverage this information, we propose to use self-organized activity related to geolocations to identify emergency situations. We propose to detect such events by tracking the frequencies, and probability distributions of the interarrival time of the messages related to specific locations. Using an off-the-shelf classifier that is independent of domain-specific features, we study and describe emergency situations based solely on location-based features in messages. Our findings indicate that anomalies in location-related social media user activity indeed provide information for automatically detecting emergency situations independent of their domain.

CCS CONCEPTS

• **Information systems** → **Data stream mining**; *Spatial-temporal systems*;

KEYWORDS

Emergency Situations; Citizen Sensors; Social Media

ACM Reference Format:
Hernan Sarmiento, Barbara Poblete, and Jaime Campos. 2018. Domain-Independent Detection of Emergency Situations Based on Social Activity

Related to Geolocations. In *WebSci'18: 10th ACM Conference on Web Science, May 27–30, 2018, Amsterdam, Netherlands*. ACM, New York, NY, USA, 10 pages. https://doi.org/10.1145/3201064.3201077

1 INTRODUCTION

Social media has become a major communication channel during high-impact real-world events, such as elections, sports events, emergency situations, among others. In each case, users act as "citizen sensors" sharing and posting their mood, opinion, photos, videos and geographical points of interest.

According to United Nations Department of Humanitarian Affairs [8], an emergency situation can be defined as "a sudden and usually unforeseen event that calls for immediate measures to minimize its adverse consequences". During these events, traditional media may suffer infrastructure issues and real-time communications could be disrupted. Instead, microblogging has played a critical role over the last fifteen years allowing users to share real-time information from people local to the incident, such as status updates, casualties, damages and alerts [15, 19, 29, 30]. For this reason, researchers have studied user behavior during these events to detect, summarize and classify messages with the goal of helping authorities, and the general public, with situational awareness to provide fast and conscientious responses during crisis situations.

Twitter is a microblogging platform that allows users to share short messages (called *tweets*) and is currently used worldwide by over 300 million people.[1] About 80% of Twitter users access from mobile devices, which contributes to the immediacy of diffusion of information, especially during crisis situations [7]. One of the most important tasks during these situations, is to timely detect incoming real-world events. This is because, as with most social media conversations, messages are often overridden with irrelevant and redundant noise. In current works [5, 14, 19, 23], these tasks are solved with methods that rely on keyword based filters on the *Twitter Public Streaming API*.[2] However, a drawback of keyword-based methods is that they require to train for each specific domain, and for different type of events. For instance, Olteanu et al. [26] generated a set of keywords for event detection based on different datasets. However, these keywords are not sufficient for cases in which specific, and previously unseen, terms arise for particular events (e.g., the hashtags: #eqnz, used for Earthquakes in New Zealand, and #pabloph, used for Typhoon Pablo in Philippines) [3, 17, 28]. Furthermore, domain-specific keywords are commonly extracted using a particular language and do not apply to others.

---

[1]http://www.statista.com/statistics/282087/number-of-monthly-active-twitter-users/
[2]https://developer.twitter.com/en/docs/tweets/filter-realtime/overview

In addition, prior work related to crisis situations in social media, show a strong relationship between the type of event (the *what*) and spatio-temporal dimensions (the *when* and *where*). For example, the top-trends during earthquakes are usually related to location mentions [25], and that there is a strong relationship between the proximity to a hurricane path and hurricane-related social media activity [18]. Other works have addressed the extraction of locations and points of interest during floods [21], as well as mixing geographic information system (GIS) information with geo-tagged messages to improve disaster mapping and real-time event tracking [12].

In order to complement prior findings, we propose to address the following research question: *Can we detect automatically emergency situations, based solely on location-related information found in user messages?.*

We propose a method based on recurring references to country-level locations in message metadata. For this task, we create a gazetteer tree based on the hierarchy of the specific country, divide the messages into fixed time-windows and compute the frequency and the probability distributions of the interarrival time of the messages for each geographical hierarchy. To detect an emergency situation, we train a SVM classifier for each hierarchy and apply a geographic spread to filter false positive detections considering that an emergency situation can be either *focalized* (i.e., that affects a reduced area) or *diffused* (i.e., that affects a large area).

Our main contribution is to create a methodology for on-line detection of emergency situations, which uses only information related to the amount of activity detected in locations of a specific country. Since an emergency situation is a high-impact real-world event, we study locations at different geographical hierarchies. This allows us to detect simultaneously bursty activity at the lowest hierarchical levels (such as cities and states) and at the highest levels (such as countries). Since our approach uses only activity related to locations, it does not use any textual features of the messages, which allows our method perform detections in a domain and language independent manner. In addition, we also contribute by providing a characterization of case studies of focalized and diffused crisis situations.

The paper is organized as follows: we first introduce an overview of relevant literature related to emergency situations and event detection using social media. Next, we present a description of our proposal. Then, we describe our dataset and summarize our experimental validation. Finally, we deliver our discussion, conclusions and future work.

2 RELATED WORK

We discuss relevant work for our proposal, primary from two areas: (1) crisis-related social media monitoring and (2) event detection based on locations.

2.1 Crisis-Related Social Media Monitoring

Twitter has been used extensively during emergency situations to extract and identify relevant information. However, social media exchanges during emergency situations are so intense that it can be necessary to sift through millions of data points to find useful information [13].

One of the main tasks related to emergency management is to timely detect emerging real-world crisis situations using social media. Currently, most of the existing methods for this task, described in the literature, are based on domain-specific keywords. For instance, *TweetTracker* [19] presented a case study using tweets that discuss a cholera outbreak in Haiti. The primary mechanism for monitoring tweets is through specific keywords and hashtags filters related to Haiti. To detect a new event, emerging trends are identified based on the analysis of older tweets. In the same way, *EMERSE* [5] used a set of keywords related to the Haiti earthquake and applies a random forests algorithm for classifying messages. Likewise, the *Twicalli* system [23] introduced an unsupervised approach to detect earthquakes that only requires a general list of keywords that are specific to earthquakes.

Researchers at CSIRO Australia proposed *ESA* [4, 35], a system to detect disasters in Australia and New Zealand. This system is based on a probabilistic method to identify bursty keywords and historical data to build a language model of word occurrences. Alerts are identified if a term has a probability distribution that significantly deviates from the language model. Similarly, *Twitcident* [1] system was developed for detecting incidents which relies on emergency broadcasting services, such as the police, the fire department and other public emergency services. The *Twitcident* framework translates the broadcasted message into an initial incident profile that is applied as query to collect messages from Twitter, where an incident profile is a set of weighted attribute-value pairs that describe the characteristics related to the incident.

CrisisLex [26] is introduced to extract different crisis-related terms to filter messages in Twitter. In this work, authors collected six disasters which affected several millions of people. Data was collected from Twitter using two samples: a keyword-based sample and location-based sample. Based on datasets, they created a lexicon of the most frequent terms that appear in relevant messages posted during different types of crisis situations.

Our work differs from prior methods, in the sense that we focus on the social media activity that is related to different locations. This allows our approach to perform detections in a language independent manner, that is not specific to a particular domain of emergency situations.

2.2 Event Detection Based on Locations

In addition to crisis-related social media monitoring, there are also some unsupervised event detection approaches based on location information. *Jasmine* [33] detected local real-world events using geolocation information from microblog documents. To detect such events, they identify a group of tweets that describe a particular theme, which are generated within a short time frame and a same geographic area. Similarly, Unankard, Li, and Sharaf [31] proposed an approach for early detection of emerging hotspot events in social networks with location sensitivity. In this work, the authors identified strong correlations between user locations and event locations when detecting emerging events using content similarity between clusters. In the work of Walther and Kaisser [32] real-world events were detected in a small scale with messages from the New York metropolitan area. There, clusters were created for each candidate event and evaluated using cluster score based on textual features (sentiment analysis, common theme, duplicate, etc) and other features (tweet count, unique coordinates, etc.).

Supervised approaches have also been proposed. *TEDAS* [20] detected, analyzed and identified events using refined rules (e.g., keywords, hashtags) and classify messages based on content as well Twitter specific features as URLs, hashtags and mentions. Besides, location information is extracted using both explicit geographical coordinates and implicit geographical references in the content. In the same way, Becker et al. [2] proposed an on-line clustering technique, which continuously clusters similar tweets and then classifies the clusters using Support Vector Machine algorithm. Finally, events (clusters) are classified into real-world events or nonevents.

Summary. Most of the existing work for detecting emergency situations, rely on keywords using probabilistic temporal models for specific domains (e.g., using keywords or locations). In general, these approaches require background knowledge about the event, and therefore, they will not identify new types of emerging crisis situations. In the case of existing approaches for event detection based on locations, these have been designed for small areas and are based on historical data. Regardless of the type of approach used (supervised or unsupervised), events are always characterized based on textual features, and on-line clustering is the most common technique used to create candidate events.

Based on the works presented by Guzman and Poblete [10] and Maldonado et al. [23], we extend the ideas of bursty keywords and *z-score* variation between fixed time-windows and we apply these proposals over locations to identify anomalies in social media activity. Furthermore, we do not use a set of keywords to detect specific types of events. In contrast, our proposal is focused on detecting bursty activity related to such events by tracking frequencies, and probability distributions of the interarrival time of the messages in specific locations.

3 PROPOSED APPROACH

Our focus in this proposal is to detect an emergency situation based on identifying anomalies in social media activity related to locations. In this way, the main task is to extract locations from messages by reducing the noise and irrelevant information. For this reason, data is pre-processed to allow for better analysis.

For the location extraction task, we use a geographical dictionary (also known as gazetteer) to create a geographic hierarchy for a specific country. To understand the effect of an emergency situation inside to the country, we create signals at different levels of the geographic hierarchy and of the social media metadata. Next, we discretize these time-signals in fixed time-windows and compute non-textual features for each. Then, with the goal of filtering false positives, we create a geographic spread based on location proximities by using an adjacency matrix.

In order to provide a complete coverage of location-based detection of emergency situations, we divide our approach into four stages (depicted in the "data processing" module in Figure 1). Next, we describe each stage:

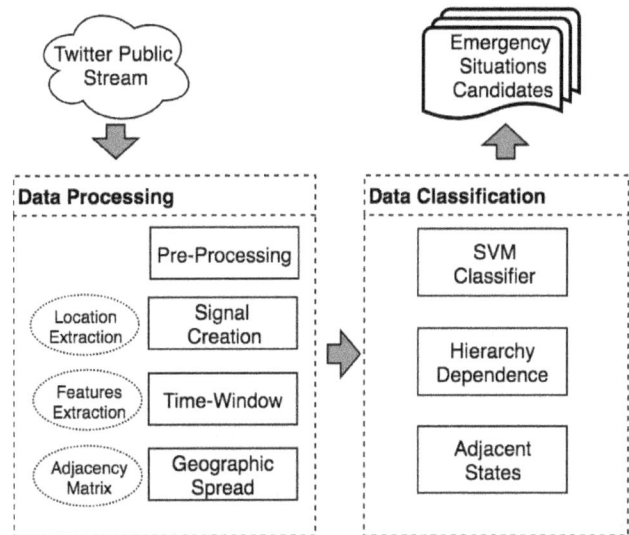

Figure 1: Key components of the proposed approach.

3.1 Data Pre-Processing

Our focus is on localized bursty user activity. Therefore, initially, we filter messages according to the most common language used in each country (using the attribute *lang* in tweet metadata[3]). For example, when analyzing Italy, we only take into account messages written in Italian. This helps to filter noise of unrelated messages. We also remove user mentions, URLs, special characters, and apply text tokenization. We do not remove hashtags nor stopwords, because some locations can be included as hashtags, and some location names contain stopwords, which differentiate them from other locations or other terms.

3.2 Signal Creation

We create a set of discrete-time signals for each location, which indicates the time that each message related to a specific location was posted. In order to explain the effect of an emergency situation in a local and national scope, we use the lowest possible geographical hierarchy level available with the aim of comparing the impact in the highest level. Furthermore, we study the anomalies at different metadata levels to understand how locations are shared in Twitter. For instance, either based in the locations set by users in their profile or in the locations shared in their messages.

3.2.1 Geographical Hierarchy. We use the idea of *gazetteer as a tree* presented in [34] in which each place is associated with a canonical taxonomy node. We create our gazetteer tree based on Geonames[4] and Wikipedia[5]. However, in [34] the gazetteer hierarchy presents four levels where the lowest level represents a specific point of interest. In our approach, we use a subset of the gazetteer hierarchy with only three levels: *city*, *state* and *country*. We do so because a large amount of users specify their location

---

[3]https://developer.twitter.com/en/docs/tweets/data-dictionary/overview/tweet-object
[4]http://download.geonames.org/export/dump/
[5]http://www.wikipedia.org/

Figure 2: Example of gazetteer tree for Italy.

down to city level [11]. For example, if we have the *city:Manchester*, we associate this location with *region-state:North West* and also with *country:England*. As indicated in our data pre-processing stage, we consider only locations in the native language of the country. For instance, in the case of Italy locations, we consider *Roma* and not *Rome* (Figure 2).

3.2.2 Location Extraction. The structure of the tweet metadata contains information about the message and the user. Given a small portion of users sharing their current location using GPS coordinates [9], we do not consider this level of the tweet metadata in this work.

Considering the aforementioned geographical hierarchy, we extract locations from different parts of the metadata, creating 3 signals for each location:

- *tweet text:* the location is mentioned in the attribute `text` of the tweet, that is, on the body of the message.
- *user location:* the location is mentioned in the attribute `location` inside the `user object`, that is, the location set by the user in their profile.
- *tweet text - user location:* the location is mentioned in the attribute `text` of tweet object and also location is mentioned in the attribute `location` inside the `user object`. This means that the location is mentioned in the body of the message and the user who shares message has the same location in his profile. In this case, tweet text and user location can be different in the smallest hierarchy, but in the highest level can be equal.

In this way, by combining geographical hierarchy and locations in microblog metadata, we create *NxM* signals where *N* is the number of locations obtained by the gazetteer tree and *M* is the number of metadata-levels extracted from the tweet object. For instance, we create a signal for *city:Manchester* and we find this hierarchy in *metadata:Tweet text* and also in *metadata:User location*. That means that we track the mention of *city:Manchester* at the level of the body of message and at the level of the location of the user profile individually.

3.3 Time-Window

In this stage we address the problem of how to divide and determine the time-window size to detect a new emergency situation and what features by the time-window allow it.

3.3.1 Determining Optimal Window Size. According to Guzman and Poblete [10]: "If the window size is too small, the occurrence of empty windows for a term increases, making the noise rate increase and frequency rate tend towards zero. On the other hand, if the window size is too large, the stability of the signal becomes constant and bursty keyword detection is delayed". Using this definition, we divide our signals into windows of six minutes because it divides a 24-hour day exactly, making the analysis easier to understand and to compare from different days.

3.3.2 Normalized Frequency. We compute the number of the messages of each time-window by signal. To normalize frequency, we compute *z-score* as following:

$$zscore = \frac{x_i - \mu_k}{\sigma_k} \qquad (1)$$

where x_i is the frequency of the current i time-window, μ_k and σ_k are mean and standard deviation of the previous k time-windows respectively.

3.3.3 Interarrival Time. To characterize the urgency of the messages during a time-window, we compute the *interarrival time* which is defined as $d_i = t_{i+1} - t_i$, where d_i denotes the difference between two consecutive social media messages i and $i + 1$ that arrived in moments t_i and t_{i+1} respectively. Using this definition, which follows the work of Kalyanam et al. [16], high-activity events have a high-frequency in the first bins represented by values $d_i \approx 0$.

To quantify a high-frequency in very small values of d_i, we compute the measures *skewness* and *kurtosis*, which represent the asymmetry and the tailedness of the shape of probability distribution respectively [24]. Finally, we apply the equation 1 over *skewness* and *kurtosis* to calculate variation based on previous values.

3.4 Geographic Spread

An emergency situation that affects and mobilizes a response in a small area is defined as *focalized*, while a disaster with a large geographic impact is defined as *diffused* [27]. Using this definition, we extend this concept to represent neighborhoods between locations obtained from section 3.2.1. For that purpose, we create an *adjacency matrix M*, where $M_{i,j} = 1$ represents if two locations are geographically connected and $M_{i,j} = 0$ if they are not connected. For instance, if an event is diffused (e.g., earthquake), the detection should be in adjacent-locations independently of metadata-level. On the other hand, if an event is focalized (e.g., terrorist attack), just one location should be detected but in different metadata-levels simultaneously.

4 EXPERIMENTAL ANALYSIS

Our experiments aim to find empirical evidence that location-related activity allows to detect emergency situations. Thereby, we used the locations for a specific country in different levels of the geographic hierarchy and the tweet metadata. We constructed our ground truth based on two publicly available earthquake catalogs and applied the proposal presented in the above section. Thereafter, we studied the performance of our methodology mainly based on the concept of affected adjacent locations during an emergency situation.

Table 1: List of earthquakes studied as ground truth, sorted by date.

Country	Datetime (UTC)	Magnitude (Mw)	Language
Italy	2016-10-26 17:10:36	5.5	Italian
Italy	2016-10-30 06:40:17	6.6	Italian
Chile	2016-12-25 14:22:26	7.6	Spanish
Chile	2017-04-23 02:36:06	5.9	Spanish
Chile	2017-04-24 21:38:28	6.9	Spanish

4.1 Dataset Description

We collected data from Twitter Public Streaming API, which allows access to subsets equal to 1% of public status descriptions in real-time. With this tool, we can retrieve either messages using a set of keywords or messages from specific locations setting a bounding box. In our approach, we got entire subsets of messages without use of keywords or specific locations. Then, we retrieved random messages about any topic and any place in the world.

4.2 Ground Truth

We selected earthquakes as crisis situations for our ground truth evaluation. According to Carr [6], earthquakes are a type of event that are also known as *instantaneous-diffused* events. These types of events are characterized in that they cannot be avoided and they affect the life of people in the community. This definition is relevant because an unexpected (or instantaneous) event generates an anomaly in the frequency of the social media activity, because it disrupts the users' daily activities. Furthermore, diffused events that affect a large portion of users produce a collective reaction in nearby locations as well.

We analyzed five earthquakes with magnitudes between $5.5Mw$ and $7.6Mw$[6], occurring in Italian-speaking and Spanish-speaking countries between October 2016 and April 2017 (Table 1). For that purpose, we collected 20 million messages 12 hours before and after the emergency situation events.

According to our proposal we created both the gazetteer hierarchies[7] for each country and created signals based on each hierarchical and metadata-level. In the end we discarded all signals related to city hierarchy since a great amount of small cities have zero frequency in a normal situation unlike to capital or metropolitan cities (Table 2).

4.2.1 Labeled Emergency Situations. The exact event date and time was obtained from the National Seismology Agency in Chile[8] and the National Institute of Geophysics and Volcanology in Italy[9]. With the purpose of labeling a time-window as positive class (detection), we set as detection those time-windows with positive variation in frequency, skewness and kurtosis with respect to the normalization of the previous values. Moreover and according to (Figure 3), we included the three next time-windows after the event

---
[6]Mw: the moment magnitude scale
[7]http://users.dcc.uchile.cl/~hsarmien/gazetteer.html
[8]http://www.sismologia.cl/
[9]http://www.ingv.it/it/

Table 2: Number of messages by signal.

Hierarchy	Metadata-level	Messages
All	All	87,291
Country	Tweet Text	11,584
	User Location	25,313
	Tweet Text - User Location	1,417
State	Tweet Text	4,110
	User Location	13,352
	Tweet Text - User Location	86
City	Tweet Text	1,415
	User Location	8,971
	Tweet Text - User Location	20

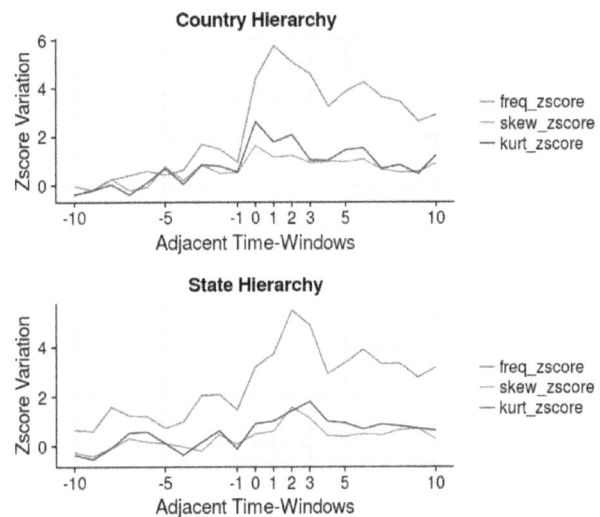

Figure 3: Average variation in emergency situations between time-windows. Positive and negatives values in x-axis represent the following and previous time-windows from the beginning of the event respectively.

to compensate the imbalance between classes given that after these number of time-windows, the variation in the features decrease.

4.3 Methodology

According to the "data classification" module (Figure 1), we first trained a classifier to identify emergency events. Also, we introduced the hierarchy dependence to understand the local and national impact when an high-impact real-world event occurs. Besides, diffused and focalized events are identified with the goal of filtering false positives detections.

Our filtering task can be seen as binary classification task. The positive class (*detection label*) corresponds to messages related to instantaneous emergency situations, while the negative class (*nothing label*) corresponds to the remaining or non-related to crisis situations.

Country Hierarchy

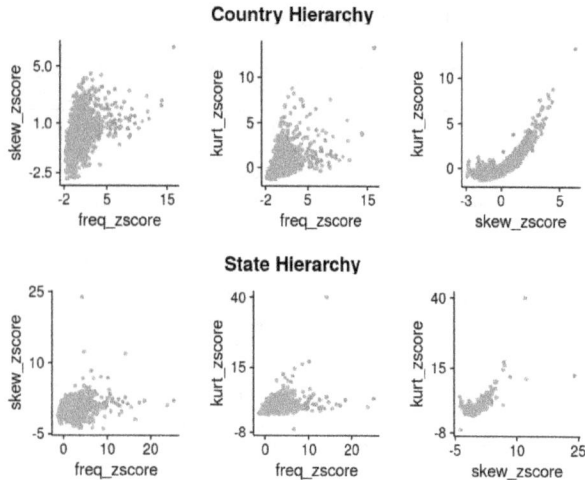

State Hierarchy

Figure 4: Relationship between features in country and state hierarchy. Red circles represent positive class (*detection*) and blue circles represent negative class (*nothing*).

To classify messages we employed traditional binary classifier Support Vector Machine *(SVM)*. As a result of the analyzed data scattering (Figure 4), we separated country and state in different datasets and set both kernels and classification parameters independently. On the one hand, *country* classifier uses a polynomial kernel and strict-parameters for gamma, cost and weights since a great amount of messages are included in country hierarchy as an effect of the minor hierarchies. On the other hand, *state/region* classifier uses a linear kernel with soft-weights and cost.

Given that an emergency situation is not a usual event, we had an highly unbalanced data respect to the classes after labeled ($1 \approx 2\%$ of positive class corresponding to *detection*). Therefore, we used *under-sampling* [22] over country and state datasets increasing our positive class to $15 \approx 18\%$. Additionally, to validate our model, we used *5-fold cross-validation* where one earthquake dataset is used as testing and the remaining earthquakes dataset as training.

Table 3 shows the average results of our model applying 5-fold cross validation. In order provide a extended analysis about incorrect labels and time-windows, we include the metric *False Positive Rate (FPR)*.

4.3.1 Independent Analysis of Hierarchies. Our first analysis is just considering the hierarchies as isolated detections. The top of the Table 3 shows the results considers only the prediction over each label in our datasets. As noted above, the assignation from the lowest level (*city*) to the highest (*country*) in the gazetteer hierarchy generated high frequency of messages which cause multiple *bursts* in our country signal for non emergency situations. This concept can explain the values of Precision (*P*) and *FPR*.

In addition to the analysis of number of detections by labels, we also studied the number of detections by time-windows. For this analysis, we searched the time-windows for each hierarchy where the all metadata-levels are well classified with correct class. According to the results shown on the middle of the Table 3, when we

Table 3: Average performance of 5-fold cross-validation by hierarchy and geographic spread (G.S.)

	Hierarchy	P	R	F1	FPR
label	Country	0.3	0.83	0.45	0.14
	State	0.35	0.83	0.5	0.08
time-window	Country	0.15	0.77	0.25	0.15
	State	0.17	0.88	0.29	0.12
	Country-State	0.35	0.7	0.47	0.03
	Country(2)-State with G.S.	1	0.64	0.78	0
	Country(3)-State with G.S.	1	0.47	0.64	0

analyzed country and state independently the values of Precision, F1 and FPR had worst values than the analysis by label .

4.3.2 Dependent Analysis of Hierarchies. Our second analysis considered the hierarchies as non-isolated detections. In the results explained above, we considered country and state hierarchy independently, which is not a correct analysis because an emergency situation affects states and country at the same time. For this reason, we inspected the time-windows where all metadata-level for country and state hierarchy have a correct detection simultaneously. The results are shown in the row *Country-State* in the Table 3. In contrast to the independent analysis of country and state, we improve the Precision, F1 and FPR values as a consequence of a smaller amount of the time-windows related to non emergency situations are assigned as detection. However, when we see the value obtained for FPR (*FPR* = 0.03), this rate represents an incorrect number of time-windows assigned as detection equal to 23. This means that we have 23 new emergency situations detected by our classifier.

4.3.3 Geopraphic Spread Analysis. Our third analysis considered the hierarchies as non-isolated detections and applies the Geographic Spread (G.S.). Using the *Adjacency Matrix* to represent neighborhoods between regions/states, we considered as a correct detection those time-windows where the state/s classified as detection are defined as *Focalized* or *Diffused* and exist dependency between hierarchies.

In addition to the results of the dependency analysis explained above, we saw that a large amount of time-windows for country hierarchy ($\approx 82\%$) have more than one metadata-level when exist a correct detection. This can be explained since an emergency situation produce a collective reaction on the level of body of the message (*tweet text*), users sharing any messages with profile location in a specific country (*user location*) or mixing both concepts (*tweet text - user location*).

Considering the geographic spread by states and the number of metadata-levels by country hierarchy, we analyzed the results shown on the bottom of the Table 3. On the one hand, the row with value equal to *Country(2)-State with G.S.* represents the detection when we considered at least two metadata-levels for the country hierarchy and the geographic spread for states. In contrast to the the previous analyses, we improve the values of the Precision, F1 and FPR. The last metric is very important because there are no time-windows incorrectly assigned as emergency situations.

Table 4: On-line evaluation of events occurred in England by time-windows (T-W) using Country(2)-State with G.S. method. The table shows the total number of detected time-windows, the number of detected time-windows before to the beginning and after to the end of the event. Last two columns show the detection delay time respect to the beginning of the event and the top 3 bigrams when the detection occurs.

Event	Detected T-W	T-W Before Event	T-W After Event	Delay (min)	Top 3 Bigrams
Premier League Soccer Matches	2	-	-	-	(man, utd), (new, year), (happy, new)
Westminster Terrorist Attack	13	0	13	32	(stay, safe), (terror, attack), (safe, everyone)
Manchester Terrorist Attack	12	1	11	23	(ariana, grande), (incident, arena), (grande, concert)
London Terrorist Attack	14	7	7	36	(stay, safe), (incident, bridge), (borough, market)
U.K. Elections	5	-	-	-	(theresa, may), (vote, labour), (van, dijk)
Adele Live in Wembley	9	7	2	-	(elland, road), (new, times), (phil, jackson)
England vs Slovenia Soccer Match	4	4	0	-	(simon, brodkin), (join, us), (theresa, may)
Metallica Live in London	4	4	0	-	(always, said), (chance, win), (carabao, cup)

Table 5: On-line evaluation of events occurred in England by time-windows (T-W) using Country(3)-State with G.S. method. The table shows the total number of detected time-windows, the number of detected time-windows before to the beginning and after to the end of the event. Last two columns show the detection delay time respect to the beginning of the event and the top 3 bigrams when the detection occurs.

Event	Detected T-W	T-W Before Event	T-W After Event	Delay (min)	Top 3 Bigrams
Premier League Soccer Matches	0	-	-	-	
Westminster Terrorist Attack	4	0	4	32	(terror, attack), (stay, safe), (terrorist, attack)
Manchester Terrorist Attack	2	0	2	23	(ariana, grande), (praying, everyone), (everyone, affected)
London Terrorist Attack	1	1	0	-	(ariana, grande), (around, world), (lady, gaga)
U.K. Elections	0	-	-	-	
Adele Live in Wembley	0	0	0	-	
England vs Slovenia Soccer Match	1	1	0	-	(per, day), (menswear, sample), (closed, roads)
Metallica Live in London	2	2	0	-	(happy, birthday), (chance, win), (always, said)

Consequently, the Recall values decrease which means that our method remove some time-windows classified as detection. Beside the percent of emergency situations detected is equal to 100% with an average delay equal to 10.4 minutes ($min = 6$, $max = 14$) from the impact of the event to the first detection.

On the other hand, *Country(3)-State with G.S.* represent the detection when we considered three metadata-levels for country hierarchy and the geographic spread for states. Similar to *Country(2)-State with G.S.*, we improve the values of Precision, F1 and FPR but our

recall decrease from $R = 0.64$ to $R = 0.47$, detecting 80% of the emergency situations with an average delay equal to 11.5 minutes ($min = 8$, $max = 14$) from the impact of the event to the first detection.

5 RESULTS

In this section, we present an on-line evaluation of our methodology for emergency situation detection. We identify several events occurred in England that includes emergency situations and non-emergency situations. In this way, our main goal is to detect emergency events in non labeled data and using a different language with respect to the languages used in our classifier. To reduce (as much as possible) the false positive detections, we use the analysis with the best performance presented in the Section 4.3.

5.1 On-line Evaluation

For our evaluation in the Twitter Public Stream, we trained a classifier with five earthquakes identified in our ground truth. Furthermore, our on-line evaluation dataset is formed by eight different events that occurred in England between December 2016 and October 2017. For each event we considered the full-day in which they occurred. The main goals of this evaluation is to know the capacity of our method to detect emergency situations and discard those non-related to emergency events that involve location references. Geographic spread analysis is used to evaluate our method because decrease the number of false positives detection. In the same way of the experiments in Section 4.3.3, we compare the results using the two presented methods respect to the number of metadata-levels by country hierarchy.

As can be noted on Table 4 and Table 5, we studied three terrorist attacks and five high-impact real-world events related to soccer matches, music concerts and political elections. In the case of the terrorist attacks, we studied this type of events since that according to Carr [6], these crisis are identified as *instantaneous-focalized* events, where an unexpected event affects to the community but in a reduced area. Unlike to earthquakes (identified as *instantaneous-diffused* events), we studied the capacity of our classifier to detect another type of event where the number of affected people are smaller than earthquakes, tsunami, and others *instantaneous-focalized* events.

For *Premier League Soccer Matches* and *U.K Elections*, we can not identify the beginning of the event, since in the first one there are many soccer matches during the analyzed day and in the second one there is no a specific start time. In order to know the topics when our method detects an event, we computed the Top 3 Bigrams in the detected time-windows. Also, we calculated the delay time for emergency events since the beginning of the event until the first detection.

On the one hand, the first evaluation *Country(2)-State with G.S.* had full detection of the terrorist attacks with average delay time equal to 30.3 minutes. These detections are related to the event given that the bigrams represent terms associated with crisis situations. However, the *London Terrorist Attack* has 50% of the detected time-windows after the event, which means that there are seven time-windows non-related to emergency situations. Besides the crisis situations analysis, we also studied the number of detected time-windows in non-related to emergency situation events. In the same way, we had a large amount of misclassified time-windows that do not represent crisis situations as we can see in the Top 3 Bigrams for each non-related to event.

On the other hand, the second evaluation *Country(3)-State with G.S.* decreases the number non-related to emergency situations events detected as crisis situations. We can see three time-windows in two events detected as emergency situations (*England vs Slovenia,*

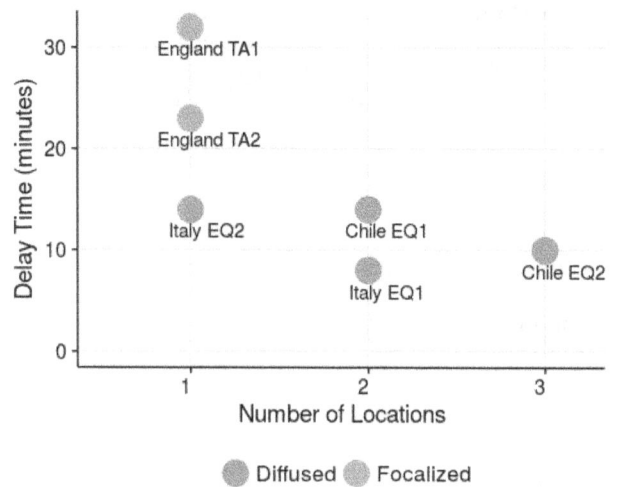

Figure 5: Relationship between delay time and number of locations in the first detection for diffused and focalized emergency situations.

and *Metallica Live in London*). In these cases, the time-windows are detected before the event and corresponding a non emergency situations according to the bigrams. Furthermore, when we analyzed the number of the detected emergency situations, two-thirds (66%) of the events are detected correctly with average delay time equal to 30.3 minutes. In the case of *London Terrorist Attack*, our method detects one time-window before the event but the bigrams describe that the detections do not correspond to crisis situations.

6 DISCUSSION

Our findings suggest that there is evidence to detect an emergency situation based on anomaly frequency of messages that contain locations for a specific country. Indeed, our method based on the number of metadata-levels by country hierarchy and geographic spread by state, detects a 80% of the events related to emergency situations as we could demonstrate in our ground truth. Also, our method is independent of the textual features because we apply the model over different languages as Spanish, Italian and English. Furthermore, we test our model in different types of crisis events such as earthquakes (EQ) and terrorist attacks (TA), where these are identified in the literature as *instantaneous-diffused* and *instantaneous-focalized* events respectively. Also, we apply our methodology on different magnitudes (in the case of earthquakes) and number of affected people (e.g., *Manchester Terrorist Attack* vs *Westminster Terrorist Attack*).

However, when we apply our method in the on-line evaluation, we detect 66% of the emergency situations that affected England. This explains that the signals, and for various reasons: the number of active users in United Kingdom[10] which can affect the anomaly frequency of the messages since there exists a high daily average activity of the messages; similar locations in other countries (York

---

[10]http://www.statista.com/statistics/242606/number-of-active-twitter-users-in-selected-countries/ visited on January 2018

≈ New York); and soccer teams with names of cities (Manchester United, Liverpool). These issues also can affect the number of false positive detection in which in the case of England was 30% of the non-related to emergency events.

Regarding the geographic spread where we define an emergency situation as diffused or focalized, we find some evidence that differentiates them. In the case of diffused events, the delay time of the our first detection was less than 12 minutes and in focalized events was greater than 30 minutes (Figure 5). This explains that, in diffused events such as earthquakes, a high number of people are affected (thousands or millions) at the same time by an event which generates a collective reaction in social media in the locations where the event impacted. In Figure 5, we can see that earthquakes have at least two detected locations in the first detection (except Italy EQ2). In contrast, focalized events have less amount of eyewitness (hundreds or thousands) then when the users share messages in social media, the frequency does not affect the average daily message of the country in the first minutes. This can be explained in Figure 5 where the terrorist attacks have just 1 detected location in the first detection.

Additionally, the delay time can be different for many reasons: datetime of the event (for example, during the early hours), few differences with the end of the current time-window, type of the affected locations (rural, urban cities) and the number of active users by locations.

7 CONCLUSION

In this paper we have presented a methodology for detecting an emergency situation based on location for a specific country. This approach is independent of the textual features and can be used in different types of events and languages. We show that the users act as self-organized in the affected locations like citizen sensors when an emergency situation occurs. We furthermore have presented an analysis of geographic spread for different types of events that can be categorized. However, our experiment considers just a small portion of emergency situations, which is not representative for all types of crisis situations according to either the hazard type (natural or human-induced), temporal development (instantaneous or progressive) or geographic spread (diffused or focalized).

There are many things that can improve our results. We will add Point of Interest to our gazetteer tree to increase the frequency by time-windows in each hierarchy. Furthermore, we will add more non-textual features as number of retweets and tweets, unique locations detected and special locations. We also plan to study the relevance of the different metadata-levels and assign weights for each. Finally, we will create a web application to visualize events in real-time.

ACKNOWLEDGMENTS

This work has been partially funded by the Millennium Institute for Foundational Research on Data and FONDECYT 1170218.

REFERENCES

[1] Fabian Abel, Claudia Hauff, Geert-Jan Houben, Richard Stronkman, and Ke Tao. 2012. Twitcident: fighting fire with information from social web streams. In *Proceedings of the 21st International Conference on World Wide Web*. ACM, 305–308.

[2] Hila Becker, Mor Naaman, and Luis Gravano. 2011. Beyond Trending Topics: Real-World Event Identification on Twitter. *ICWSM* 11, 2011 (2011), 438–441.

[3] Axel Bruns and Jean E Burgess. 2012. Local and global responses to disaster:# eqnz and the Christchurch earthquake. In *Disaster and emergency management conference, conference proceedings*, Vol. 2012. AST Management Pty Ltd, 86–103.

[4] Mark A Cameron, Robert Power, Bella Robinson, and Jie Yin. 2012. Emergency situation awareness from twitter for crisis management. In *Proceedings of the 21st International Conference on World Wide Web*. ACM, 695–698.

[5] Cornelia Caragea, Nathan McNeese, Anuj Jaiswal, Greg Traylor, Hyun-Woo Kim, Prasenjit Mitra, Dinghao Wu, Andrea H Tapia, Lee Giles, Bernard J Jansen, et al. 2011. Classifying text messages for the Haiti earthquake. In *Proceedings of the 8th international conference on information systems for crisis response and management (ISCRAM2011)*. Citeseer.

[6] Lowell Juilliard Carr. 1932. Disaster and the sequence-pattern concept of social change. *Amer. J. Sociology* 38, 2 (1932), 207–218.

[7] Carlos Castillo. 2016. *Big crisis data: social media in disasters and time-critical situations*. Cambridge University Press.

[8] UN DHA. 1992. Internationally agreed glossary of basic terms related to disaster management. *UN DHA (United Nations Department of Humanitarian Affairs)*, Geneva (1992).

[9] Mark Graham, Scott A Hale, and Devin Gaffney. 2014. Where in the world are you? Geolocation and language identification in Twitter. *The Professional Geographer* 66, 4 (2014), 568–578.

[10] Jheser Guzman and Barbara Poblete. 2013. On-line relevant anomaly detection in the Twitter stream: an efficient bursty keyword detection model. In *Proceedings of the acm sigkdd workshop on outlier detection and description*. ACM, 31–39.

[11] Brent Hecht, Lichan Hong, Bongwon Suh, and Ed H Chi. 2011. Tweets from Justin Bieber's heart: the dynamics of the location field in user profiles. In *Proceedings of the SIGCHI conference on human factors in computing systems*. ACM, 237–246.

[12] Qunying Huang, Guido Cervone, Duangyang Jing, and Chaoyi Chang. 2015. DisasterMapper: A CyberGIS framework for disaster management using social media data. In *Proceedings of the 4th International ACM SIGSPATIAL Workshop on Analytics for Big Geospatial Data*. ACM, 1–6.

[13] Muhammad Imran, Carlos Castillo, Fernando Diaz, and Sarah Vieweg. 2015. Processing social media messages in mass emergency: A survey. *ACM Computing Surveys (CSUR)* 47, 4 (2015), 67.

[14] Muhammad Imran, Carlos Castillo, Ji Lucas, Patrick Meier, and Sarah Vieweg. 2014. Aidr: Artificial intelligence for disaster response. In *Proceedings of the companion publication of the 23rd international conference on World wide web companion*. International World Wide Web Conferences Steering Committee, 159–162.

[15] Muhammad Imran, Shady Elbassuoni, Carlos Castillo, Fernando Diaz, and Patrick Meier. 2013. Extracting information nuggets from disaster-Related messages in social media.. In *ISCRAM*.

[16] Janani Kalyanam, Mauricio Quezada, Barbara Poblete, and Gert Lanckriet. 2016. Prediction and Characterization of High-Activity Events in Social Media Triggered by Real-World News. *PloS one* 11, 12 (2016), e0166694.

[17] Sarvnaz Karimi, Jie Yin, and Cecile Paris. 2013. Classifying microblogs for disasters. In *Proceedings of the 18th Australasian Document Computing Symposium*. ACM, 26–33.

[18] Yury Kryvasheyeu, Haohui Chen, Nick Obradovich, Esteban Moro, Pascal Van Hentenryck, James Fowler, and Manuel Cebrian. 2016. Rapid assessment of disaster damage using social media activity. *Science advances* 2, 3 (2016), e1500779.

[19] Shamanth Kumar, Geoffrey Barbier, Mohammad Ali Abbasi, and Huan Liu. 2011. TweetTracker: An Analysis Tool for Humanitarian and Disaster Relief.. In *ICWSM*.

[20] Rui Li, Kin Hou Lei, Ravi Khadiwala, and Kevin Chen-Chuan Chang. 2012. Tedas: A twitter-based event detection and analysis system. In *Data engineering (icde), 2012 ieee 28th international conference on*. IEEE, 1273–1276.

[21] John Lingad, Sarvnaz Karimi, and Jie Yin. 2013. Location extraction from disaster-related microblogs. In *Proceedings of the 22nd international conference on world wide web*. ACM, 1017–1020.

[22] Nicola Lunardon, Giovanna Menardi, and Nicola Torelli. 2014. ROSE: A Package for Binary Imbalanced Learning. *R Journal* 6, 1 (2014).

[23] Jazmine Maldonado, Jheser Guzman, and Barbara Poblete. 2017. A Lightweight and Real-Time Worldwide Earthquake Detection and Monitoring System Based on Citizen Sensors. In *Proceedings of the Fifth Conference of Human Computation and Crowdsourcing*. AAAI, 137–146.

[24] Kanti V Mardia. 1970. Measures of multivariate skewness and kurtosis with applications. *Biometrika* 57, 3 (1970), 519–530.

[25] Marcelo Mendoza, Barbara Poblete, and Carlos Castillo. 2010. Twitter Under Crisis: Can we trust what we RT?. In *Proceedings of the first workshop on social media analytics*. ACM, 71–79.

[26] Alexandra Olteanu, Carlos Castillo, Fernando Diaz, and Sarah Vieweg. 2014. CrisisLex: A Lexicon for Collecting and Filtering Microblogged Communications in Crises.. In *ICWSM*.

[27] Alexandra Olteanu, Sarah Vieweg, and Carlos Castillo. 2015. What to expect when the unexpected happens: Social media communications across crises. In

Proceedings of the 18th ACM Conference on Computer Supported Cooperative Work & Social Computing. ACM, 994–1009.

[28] Liza Potts, Joyce Seitzinger, Dave Jones, and Angela Harrison. 2011. Tweeting disaster: hashtag constructions and collisions. In *Proceedings of the 29th ACM international conference on Design of communication*. ACM, 235–240.

[29] Christian Reuter and Marc-André Kaufhold. [n. d.]. Fifteen years of social media in emergencies: a retrospective review and future directions for crisis informatics. *Journal of Contingencies and Crisis Management* ([n. d.]).

[30] Kevin Stowe, Michael J Paul, Martha Palmer, Leysia Palen, and Kenneth Anderson. 2016. Identifying and categorizing disaster-related tweets. In *Proceedings of The Fourth International Workshop on Natural Language Processing for Social Media*. 1–6.

[31] Sayan Unankard, Xue Li, and Mohamed A Sharaf. 2015. Emerging event detection in social networks with location sensitivity. *World Wide Web* 18, 5 (2015), 1393–1417.

[32] Maximilian Walther and Michael Kaisser. 2013. Geo-spatial Event Detection in the Twitter Stream.. In *ECIR*. Springer, 356–367.

[33] Kazufumi Watanabe, Masanao Ochi, Makoto Okabe, and Rikio Onai. 2011. Jasmine: a real-time local-event detection system based on geolocation information propagated to microblogs. In *Proceedings of the 20th ACM international conference on Information and knowledge management*. ACM, 2541–2544.

[34] Jie Yin, Sarvnaz Karimi, and John Lingad. 2014. Pinpointing locational focus in microblogs. In *Proceedings of the 2014 Australasian Document Computing Symposium*. ACM, 66.

[35] Jie Yin, Sarvnaz Karimi, Bella Robinson, and Mark Cameron. 2012. ESA: emergency situation awareness via microbloggers. In *Proceedings of the 21st ACM international conference on Information and knowledge management*. ACM, 2701–2703.

Pathways to Fragmentation
User Flows and Web Distribution Infrastructures*

Harsh Taneja
University of Illinois Urbana-Champaign
Urbana, IL, USA
harsh.taneja@gmail.com

Angela Xiao Wu
New York University
New York, NY, USA
angelaxwu@nyu.edu

ABSTRACT

This study analyzes how web audiences flow across online digital features. We construct a directed network of user flows based on sequential user clickstreams for all popular websites *(n=1761)*, using traffic data obtained from a panel of a million web users in the United States. We analyze these data to identify constellations of websites that are frequently browsed together in temporal sequences, both by similar user groups in different browsing sessions as well as by disparate users. Our analyses thus render visible previously hidden online collectives and generate insight into the varied roles that curatorial infrastructures may play in shaping audience fragmentation on the web.

CCS CONCEPTS

• **Information systems → Traffic analysis**; • **Social and professional topics → Socio-technical systems**;

KEYWORDS

Clickstream, fragmentation, network analysis, infrastructure, curation, web usage

ACM Reference Format:
Harsh Taneja and Angela Xiao Wu. 2018. Pathways to Fragmentation: User Flows and Web Distribution Infrastructures. In *WebSci '18: 10th ACM Conference on Web Science, May 27–30, 2018, Amsterdam, Netherlands*. ACM, New York, NY, USA, 5 pages. https://doi.org/10.1145/3201064.3201107

1 INTRODUCTION

Constellations of websites competing for user attention result in patterns of online audience fragmentation, which has garnered enormous interest. Yet we know little about broader patterns in people's browsing pathways and how these pathways contribute to macro patterns of web use. Hence, in this study, we analyze how users flow across online digital features with a focus on the role of digital infrastructures in shaping online consumption patterns. Studying user flows enriches our understanding of audience behavior in today's digital environment by teasing out various patterns

---

*Both authors contributed equally to this work.

of user trajectories as building blocks of macro fragmentation. It also helps investigate into the roles played by digital platforms with distinct mechanisms of traffic curation, such as those of social media, search engines, and web portals [3].

2 USER FRAGMENTATION

Although there's general agreement that web audiences are fragmented in their patterns of exposure, opinions are divided on its underlying mechanisms and consequences. Given that people have a lot of choice, one school of thought believes that people are now free to exercise their preferences and media actors have less control over what people get exposed to [5, 6]. In this vein, we would expect web users to retract into their own echo chambers, or their online "filter bubbles" [4]. Studies at the user level, which focus on people's engagements with specific online content and digital platforms, typically advance such findings.

Others argue people's online behavior often does not reflect their self-reported preferences [10]. This is because, most people, despite their divergent preferences tend to gravitate towards a handful of popular items due to media producers promoting these aggressively as well as under social influence. This view emanates from studies that analyze macro patterns of web use and are based on snapshots of shared consumption between outlets [12]. The focal unit in latter studies is audience duplication which, simply put, is the extent to which two media outlets (e.g., websites) are consumed by the same set of people in a given time period. In a hypothetical universe of 100 people, if on a given day 20 people accessed both CNN.com and Google.com, the audience duplication between these two outlets would be 20 or 20%. Examining pairwise duplication simultaneously for all possible pairs of media outlet, these provide insights into outlets commonly consumed together in the aggregate. For instance a study found that in the US in 2009 most outlets across the 200 most used TV channels and websites had high audience overlaps, contrarian to the popular worry about online polarization [11].

We argue that in addition to the efforts by media actors and user preferences, technological infrastructures are foundational to shaping online user behavior. On the web, both media actors and users simultaneously utilize multifarious ensembles of curatorial practices. For instance, a user active on online social networks may access news articles by a particular publisher who more regularly promote their news through its pages on social networks. Another user who has a portal as a homepage may tend to access news from publishers that make their news available on that portal. In other words, there are just myriad such curated flows that influence people's exposure to content [8]. To unravel these requires a novel empirical strategy, which we develop in this study.

3 ANALYZING CLICKSTREAMS

Analysis of audience duplication does provide a holistic snapshot of media consumption patterns in a high choice environment. However, it is a static snapshot unable to capture the dynamics of audience flows leading to such patterns. We elaborate on this with an example. Consider two partisan news outlets Fox News and CNN. Audience duplication data have consistently shown greater than expected audience overlaps between their TV channels [9] as well as their websites [2]. However, this high duplication between these two ideologically opposing outlets may result from different pathways. Over the time period of analysis, people may be directly visiting these outlets (in succession) to "check out the other side," or they may be directed to both these outlets from search engines or social networks. But discerning these differences in pathways is beyond the radar of audience duplication analysis.

To overcome this limitation, we demonstrate a "sequential" audience centric approach to audience fragmentation that uses clickstream data to unravel audience flows. Clickstreams are traces of user activity as they move from browsing one webpage to the other [13]. Analyzing these clickstreams alongside audience duplication, our sequential approach unpacks the aggregated shared traffic between websites by teasing out the constituent browsing sequences users undertake across the web. This approach has two major merits: (1) By examining groups of websites that are associated with one another in terms of recurring traffic flows, we render visible previously hidden online populations. These collectives are distinct not (merely) by demographic profiles or commonly used online outlets, but by sequential movements on the Web. (2) Linking the patterns of sequential browsing sessions we observe to existing debates about the "curatorial mechanisms" of sites such as search engines and social media, we are able to further discern the nature of these sequential sessions. This generates insight into the varied roles that curatorial infrastructures may play in shaping audience fragmentation online.

3.1 Data

In clickstream data, when a user on outlet i switches to outlet j and then to outlet k, outlet i is a source of traffic for j, which in turn is a source of traffic for k. Aggregating all these clickstreams in a media ecosystem, one can deduce how audiences "flow" at a macro-scale.

We obtained US national level web usage (traffic) data from comScore. Our sample includes all the 1761 web outlets visited by at least 1 % (2.6 million) of all US web users in October 2015. For each web outlet, we extracted its clickstream data, which reflects the number of total unique users during the said month that landed on it immediately after visiting other outlets. Owing to the large and expansive sample size, for most sites, we had the complete extent of their sources of incoming traffic. We aggregated these data for all websites to create a User Flow Matrix, which is a directed network with web outlets as nodes and the user volumes from one outlet to another as the edges. We also obtained the pairwise audience duplication between all 1761 outlets, which for any outlet pair is the percentage of users that visited both.

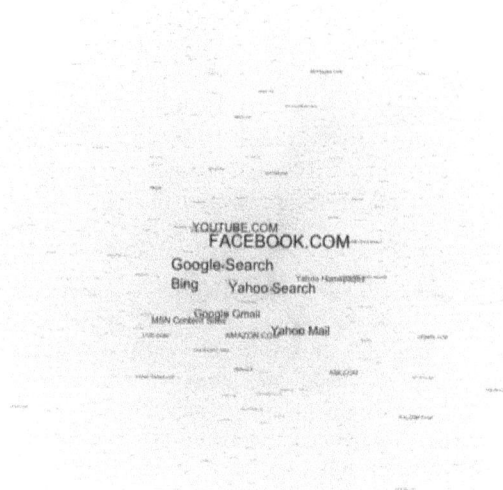

Figure 1: Clickstream network (1761 nodes, 89453 edges)

3.2 Analysis and Results

3.2.1 Clickstream Volumes. First, we calculated the weighted in-degrees and out-degrees of each node. In this network, a node's weighted out-degree represents the total volume of user traffic that flows out of this site to all other sites in the network. Although both distributions are quite skewed leading to a highly centralized network, the latter are highly concentrated (Gini Coefficient = 0.64). Thus, in the aggregate, we find that most web traffic flows outwards from an extremely small number of web outlets. We visualize this graph using force atlas algorithm, which also takes into account tie weights (see Figure 1). The nodes are sized according to their out degree weights and we can see the largest sized nodes which are also at the center of the graph are the most popular search engines, email providers, social networks and portals. Their large out-degrees suggest that these handful sites precede whichever other sites users visit on the web.

3.2.2 Clickstream Constellations. We conducted a cluster analysis using a modularity based community detection algorithm [1]. Modularity based clustering isolates groups of websites with dense interconnections within groups relative to edges between groups. A cluster in this network contains pairs of websites that users tend to access in succession, which may be seen as an aggregation of socially shared browsing sequence, which we refer to as "constellations." Consistent with our research objective, we accepted a cluster solution where we could identify for each constellation either content similarity or some underlying digital infrastructures (including customized curation embodied by search engines and social network sites, as well as top-down embedded architectures such as web portals). Our solution, shown in Figure 2, revealed 14 clusters or constellations, which represent distinct patterns of web browsing trajectories. Owing to the small number of websites and

Constellation	Size
Google Complex	557
Social Media Complex	505
Yahoo Homepages	215
Yahoo Search	150
Porn	77
Bing / Microsoft	67
User Data Solicitors	56
Job Search	41
AOL Homepages	34
Travel	30
CitiBank-Retailers	21
E-College	4
Elsevier	2
Scribol	2

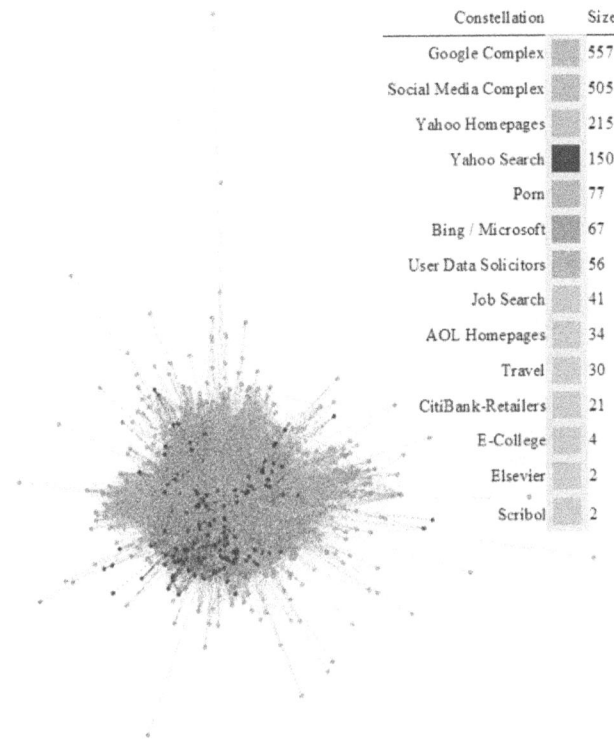

Figure 2: 14 Clickstream constellations

highly specialized nature of their content we did not consider the three smallest clusters for further analysis.

To determine the extent to which a handful of sites "anchored" these browsing sequences, by serving as starting and returning points during browsing sessions, for each cluster we calculated a Gini coefficient (reported in Table 1) based on the distribution of the weighted out-degrees of its constituent sites. A high Gini coefficient indicates that a handful of sites anchor the browsing sequence among constituent sites–that is, within the browsing sequence, whichever websites the users land on, their preceding visits tend to be on these anchor sites. Given how people usually browse the web, it is more likely that they move from anchor sites to the subsequent site through clicking embedded links instead of deliberately entering the subsequent site's URL. To further discern the likely mechanisms, we examine the nature of the anchors (those with the highest weighted outdegrees in each constellation, also listed in Table 1). It turns out that most of these anchors embody certain infrastructural designs. As discussed, anchors in high-Gini constellations are more influential in shaping the browsing sequences within each constellation.

Google Complex: With the largest number of sites, this cluster mainly contains utilitarian websites such as those of retailers (including Amazon and eBay) along with those of service providers in domains such as government, finance, travel, telecom and shipping. One common feature about all these sites is that users visit them to accomplish a particular purpose and are unlikely to encounter them as part of random browsing. Its highest outdegree suggests that users rely on Google Search to visit most constituent websites.

Table 1: Analyses of clickstream distributions

Constellation	Gini (Out-degrees)	Anchor(s)
Bing/Microsoft	0.89	Bing, MSN Content Sites
Google Complex	0.85	Google Search, Youtube, GMail
Social Media Complex	0.83	Facebook
Yahoo Homepages	0.82	Yahoo Homepages, Yahoo Mail
Yahoo Search	0.81	Yahoo Search
AOL Homepages	0.72	AOL Homepages, AOL Email
User Data Solicitors	0.62	Swagbucks
Citibank-Retailers	0.62	Citibank, Macy
Porn	0.61	Pornhub
Job Search	0.56	Indeed
Travel	0.43	Tripadvisor, Expedia, Priceline

Notably, YouTube and Gmail are also main anchors, suggesting they receive intermittent visits during typical browsing sessions.

Social Network Complex: This cluster has the most popular online social networks such as Facebook (also the anchor with impregnable dominance), Instagram, Twitter, and LinkedIn, among others. Also included are a bulk of symbolic content spanning news, sport and entertainment sites both by legacy media organizations (e.g., CNN and New York Times) as well as digital native providers (e.g., Buzzfeed and DrugeReport). Further, there are "socially-driven" outlets such as GoFundMe, Spotify, Fitbit, and Legacy.com, and sites of various banks and mobile/ISPs that long-term customers most likely access directly amidst their social media browsing through bookmarks or typing the URL, without turning to search engines.

Yahoo Homepages: A third somewhat smaller cluster contains a variety of Yahoo's biggest online properties (e.g., Yahoo Homepage, Yahoo News, Yahoo Sports, and Yahoo Mail). It also has many sites specialized in elaborate political news commentaries (e.g., Vox.com, Slate, Atlantic, Politico, Dailybeast, TheHill), general "soft" news (e.g., Huffpost and USAToday), business news (Bloomberg and Business Insider), online services for investments and mortgages, as well as Classmates.com that helps search for past high school friends.

Yahoo Search: Other than Yahoo Search, this cluster has many other utilitarian websites most of which serve a specific purpose and originated in the 1990s including as Ask.com, Ehow, MapQuest and WedMD. This cluster probably represents a segment of web users that still use Yahoo Search as their gateway to the web and are presumably older than the average web user.

Porn Constellation: This is a cluster comprised of adult sites. Owing to its high outdegree, our analysis suggests that for most users Pornhub.com serves as a gateway to other adult websites, many of which (e.g., Youporn and Xtube) are linked to by Pornhub.com's homepage and are part of the "Pornhub Network." Many of the other adult sites that feature in this cluster appear to regularly advertise their content through adult advertising networks on the Pornhub network sites.

Bing / Microsoft: We also observe a cluster (with the highest Gini) anchored by Microsoft's search engine Bing. It consists of many other web services and content portals owned or aligned with Microsoft, such as Office, Windows or AccuWeather (Bing's default weather widget).

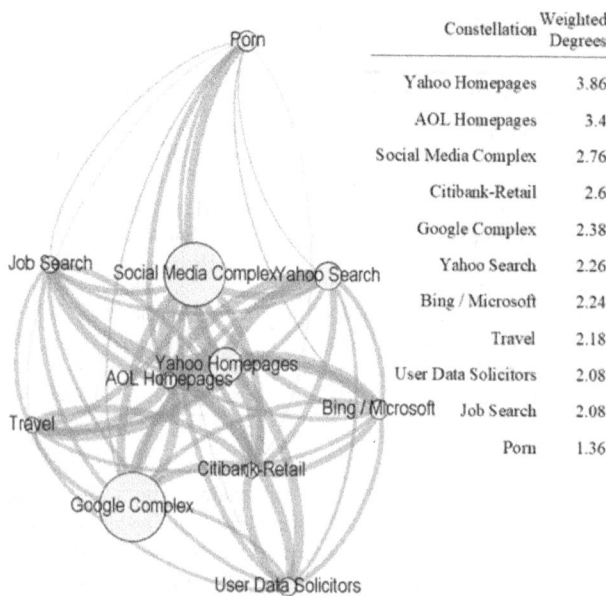

Constellation	Weighted Degrees
Yahoo Homepages	3.86
AOL Homepages	3.4
Social Media Complex	2.76
Citibank-Retail	2.6
Google Complex	2.38
Yahoo Search	2.26
Bing / Microsoft	2.24
Travel	2.18
User Data Solicitors	2.08
Job Search	2.08
Porn	1.36

Figure 3: Audience duplication between constellations

User Data Solicitors: This cluster contains content that solicits user inputs for commercial data extraction through ads or popups on other websites. Constituent sites include online survey interfaces, rewards and discount solicitations as well as some of the market research companies' websites that design these surveys and analyze the collected user responses.

Job Search: A group of popular job search and application portals such as Indeed.com and Monster.com, as well as websites of companies that job portals use for database management.

AOL Homepages: This is a relatively small cluster anchored by "AOL Homepages," which contains a few AOL websites (e.g., AOL Email). It also has sites such as USMagazine, EverydayHealth, and ZergNet, all part of the AOL brand.

Travel: With TripAdvisor as the biggest anchor, this cluster contains sites specialized in booking flights, hotels, and travel packages along with hotel and airline websites.

Citibank-Retailers: This cluster consists of Citibank and many online retailers such as Macy, K-Mart, OldNavy, and Sears, all of which have credit card programs managed by Citibank.

3.2.3 Audience Duplication between Constellations. To discern the degree to which each clickstream constellation shares users with other constellations, we computed the greater than expected (random) audience duplication between each website pair. Then we averaged these pairwise duplication figures for each constellation pair. For example, for two constellations with a site count of "m" and "n" respectively, we averaged the greater than expected duplication for each of the constituent "m*n" website pairs. This resulted in an 11*11 symmetric matrix, where each cell indicates the average greater than expected duplication between websites at the level of constellation pairs. Figure 3 plots this matrix as a force directed network map using the Force Atlas 2 layout in Gephi, which also considers the edge weight.

In Figure 3, each node is a constellation, sized according to its number of websites. The weighted degrees on each node indicated the extent to which a constellation's constituent websites share users with websites in other constellations. The edges with the highest edge weights in this network are those between the three constellations with highest weighted degrees. The top edges are, respectively, those between Yahoo Homepages and AOL Homepages, Social Media Complex and Yahoo Homepages, and AOL Homepages and Social Media Complex.

4 A SEQUENTIAL EXPLANATION

4.1 In-constellation Fragmentation

Within each constellation, we examined the curatorial characteristics of major anchoring sites in relation to other constituent websites in light of the constellation's general distribution of traffic flows. This revealed how the different mechanisms of the anchors' digital curation shape online user fragmentation and online browsing routines at large.

First, our analysis suggests that social media and search engines, which embody two distinct mechanisms in curating traffic, impact different parts of the web. A social media site directs users as it runs its curatorial algorithms on content updates generated by user's personal network. A search engine, in contrast, directly responds to requests submitted by individual users. We found that websites in search engine-anchored clickstream constellations tend to differ in nature from those anchored by social networks. The former are largely websites for retail, banking, everyday services such as map and health consultation. In contrast, the latter tend to be websites providing news, commentaries, and entertainment content, basically information as an end in itself. This differentiation is one between utilitarian, functional goods and symbolic, experiential goods. Our results thus suggest that people tend to land on news information sites largely through social networks (the Facebook Constellation include multiple other popular social media sites). Driven by social media use, the nature of such encounter is most likely incidental. In contrast, people tend to fulfill their everyday tasks by deliberately seeking services via search engines.

Second, the composition of clickstream constellations anchored by web portals suggests strong evidence of infrastructural bundling, by which we mean conglomerates using architectural design to foster people already on one of their sites to visit other sites owned by the same companies. For example, both the AOL and the Yahoo Constellations include not only bundles of the whole spectrum of the brand's online services and content offerings, but also discrete websites with underlying capital connections to the brands. The Porn Constellation is another striking example, where by design niche adult sites owned by the MindGeek conglomerate form a closed maze that confines sequential users' flows.

Less visible to users, a third type of traffic curation is more of a function of back-end infrastructural bundling due to interorganizational arrangements. For example, Citibank-Retailer comes into being because all the retailer sites have Citibank as their payment gateway. Likewise, the Job Search Constellation is stitched together due to the various job portals managing their data through common vendors such as Salesforce or Oracle. In summary, while search engine usage entails some user initiation, other anchoring sites ranging from social media, web portals, and contracted technical platforms on the backend seem to direct traffic in ways that require decreasing levels of conscious planning and participation on the part of the user.

4.2 Across-constellation Fragmentation

We used audience duplication between website pairs in different constellations to discern the extent to which they are used by similar or dissimilar user groups. Viewed in light of the nature of anchors, this result illuminates broad contours of fragmentation across the user bases of distinct constellations.

To begin, we indeed observed evidence of content preferences of what seem specific user niches. The relatively isolated constellations, Porn, Job Search, and User Data Solicitors point to particular populations by gender, age, and class. The Solicitors Constellation, for example, with its notable connections to Citibank-Retailers, and Yahoo and AOL Homepages, suggests browsing activities of a middle-aged homemaker user group. That said, bulk of the reported evidence shows that various infrastructural factors, on which we elaborate next, can explain across-constellation fragmentation.

First, routines of everyday web use, usually neglected in extant research, come to the fore. Specifically, "anchor" websites are incorporated into people's browsing routines based on the sites' distinct functionalities along the infrastructural dimension. "Infrastructural functionality" explains the lower mutual user overlaps between sites in the three constellations driven by search engines (i.e., Google Search, Yahoo Search, and Bing), as users typically rely on one search engine, the algorithm of which comes to be increasingly responsive to their individual behavior. This result further suggests that people tend to fragment into using different clusters of websites respectively anchored by different engines. Infrastructural functionality also explains the fact that, relative to sites in search engines-anchored constellations, sites in the Social Media Complex has higher tendency to share users with sites in constellations anchored by general interest portals such as Yahoo Homepages and AOL Homepages. This is because for typical web users, it is habitual to linger on and around social network sites and share content to which portals also link.

We also observe effects of infrastructural bundling across constellations, further highlighting the striking influences of commercial packaging by design. Notably, sites in the AOL Homepages and Yahoo Homepages constellations have the highest user overlaps, most likely driven by their content partnerships. The sports section on AOL is populated by "Yahoo Sports" and HuffPost (an AOL company) provides business and lifestyle news on the Yahoo.com home page. More recently, Yahoo and AOL have both been incorporated into one company, Oath Media.

Finally, we found significant portions of users browsing sites in the Bing/Microsoft Constellation also browse those in AOL and Yahoo Homepages. This suggests the influence of "infrastructural residuals," or effects of enduring infrastructural features in shaping media habits [7]. This simultaneous engagement with sites across these constellations points to the collective habitat of a senior user population that has been habituated into the reliance on AOL and Yahoo sites (both long-standing web brands); a substantial portion of this population also uses Bing due to technical prompts as Bing

is set as the default landing website for the age-old IE browsers. Infrastructural residuals thus lead to fragmentation by generation as a result of temporally variant habituation with new media.

5 CONCLUSION

Our results show that there seems to exist one relatively expansive user population whose online life is anchored by Google Search, one (presumably relatively older) population who relies on portals such as Yahoo and AOL homepages and a third user group that defaults to Microsoft and uses Bing. Importantly, this fragmentation results from an interaction between users intentions and structural conditions including infrastructural functionality, infrastructural bundling, and infrastructural residuals. After users embark on major anchoring sites, different curatorial architectures that foster specific browsing sequences further user fragmentation.

In sum, viewed in the aggregate, rather than subjective preferences, the infrastructural dimension explains a great extent of online fragmentation. In fact, it owes much of its power to its invisibility to the user. Furthermore, infrastructural factors that have arisen from the established political economy configuring the internet industry and media industries at large appear to shape online fragmentation more resolutely than the much-debated "customizing technologies" such as social networks and search engines.

REFERENCES

[1] Vincent D Blondel, Jean-Loup Guillaume, Renaud Lambiotte, and Etienne Lefebvre. 2008. Fast unfolding of communities in large networks. *Journal of Statistical Mechanics: Theory and Experiment* 2008, 10 (2008), P10008. http://dx.doi.org/10.1088/1742-5468/2008/10/P10008

[2] Matthew Gentzkow and Jesse M. Shapiro. 2011. Ideological Segregation Online and Offline. *The Quarterly Journal of Economics* 126, 4 (2011), 1799–1839. https://doi.org/10.1093/qje/qjr044

[3] Philip M. Napoli. 2014. Automated Media: An Institutional Theory Perspective on Algorithmic Media Production and Consumption. *Communication Theory* 24, 3 (2014), 340–360. https://doi.org/10.1111/comt.12039

[4] Eli Pariser and Dr Ellen Helsper. 2011. *The filter bubble: what the internet is hiding from you.* Penguin, New York, NY.

[5] Markus Prior. 2007. *Post-broadcast democracy: how media choice increases inequality in political involvement and polarizes elections.* Cambridge University Press, New York, NY.

[6] Natalie Jomini Stroud. 2010. Polarization and Partisan Selective Exposure. *Journal of Communication* 60, 3 (2010), 556–576. https://doi.org/10.1111/j.1460-2466.2010.01497.x

[7] Harsh Taneja, Angela Xiao Wu, and Stephanie Edgerly. 2017. Rethinking the generational gap in online news use: An infrastructural perspective. *New Media & Society* 0, 0 (2017), 1–39. https://doi.org/10.1177/1461444817707348

[8] Kjerstin Thorson and Chris Wells. 2016. Curated Flows: A Framework for Mapping Media Exposure in the Digital Age. *Communication Theory* 26, 3 (2016), 309–328. https://doi.org/10.1111/comt.12087

[9] James G. Webster. 2012. Beneath the veneer of fragmentation: Television audience polarization in a multichannel world. *Journal of Communication* 55, 2 (2012), 366–382. https://doi.org/10.1093/joc/55.2.366

[10] James G Webster. 2014. *The Marketplace of Attention: How Audiences Take Shape in an Age of Digital Media.* MIT Press, Cambridge, MA; London, England.

[11] James G. Webster and Thomas B. Ksiazek. 2012. The Dynamics of Audience Fragmentation: Public Attention in an Age of Digital Media. *Journal of Communication* 62, 1 (2012), 39–56. https://doi.org/10.1111/j.1460-2466.2011.01616.x

[12] Angela Xiao Wu and Harsh Taneja. 2016. Reimagining Internet Geographies: A User-Centric Ethnological Mapping of the World Wide Web. *Journal of Computer-Mediated Communication* 21, 3 (2016), 230–246. https://doi.org/10.1111/jcc4.12157

[13] Lingfei Wu and Robert Ackland. 2014. How Web 1.0 fails: the mismatch between hyperlinks and clickstreams. *Social Network Analysis and Mining* 4, 1 (2014), 1–7. https://doi.org/10.1007/s13278-014-0202-8

Locations & Languages: Towards Multilingual User Movement Analysis in Social Media

Yuanyuan Wang
Yamaguchi University
Ube, Yamaguchi, 755-8611 Japan
y.wang@yamaguchi-u.ac.jp

Muhammad Syafiq Mohd Pozi
Universiti Tenaga Nasional
Kajang, Selangor, 43000 Malaysia
syafiq.pozi@uniten.edu.my

Panote Siriaraya
Kyoto Sangyo University
Kyoto, 603-8555 Japan
spanote@gmail.com

Yukiko Kawai
Kyoto Sangyo University
Kyoto, 603-8555 Japan
kawai@cc.kyoto-su.ac.jp

Adam Jatowt
Kyoto University
Kyoto, 606-8501 Japan
adam@dl.kuis.kyoto-u.ac.jp

ABSTRACT

Social microblogging platforms such as Twitter have been used by many users to express their sentiments and opinions resulting in exponentially growing amounts of heterogeneous data. This opens new research proposals to map with such data many natural phenomena. In this paper, we visualize various patterns related to multilingualism on social microblogging platforms. In particular, we analyze characteristics of Twitter users based on their choice of languages and the change in locations from which they tweet. The analysis we undertake assumes language and location of tweets as key factors. The results show that locations and languages are correlated with mobility patterns of multilingual Twitter users.

CCS CONCEPTS

• **Information systems** → **Social networks**; Data mining; • **Networks** → *Location based services*;

KEYWORDS

Multilingual; Mobility; Twitter

ACM Reference Format:
Yuanyuan Wang, Muhammad Syafiq Mohd Pozi, Panote Siriaraya, Yukiko Kawai, and Adam Jatowt. 2018. Locations & Languages: Towards Multilingual User Movement Analysis in Social Media. In *WebSci' 18: 10th ACM Conference on Web Science, May 27–30, 2018, Amsterdam, Netherlands*. ACM, New York, NY, USA, 10 pages. https://doi.org/10.1145/3201064.3201096

1 INTRODUCTION

Social media services and especially microblogging services such as Twitter are increasingly being adopted by users to access and distribute information on a large variety of topics. Twitter can be then used as a database gathering data from many distributed sensors, in which the sensors are the Twitter users themselves describing

current events, expressing opinions, carrying conversations and reporting their lives in nearly any location [23]. Nearly one-in-five tweets are geo-tagged according to recent studies [24], making it possible to infer an exact location where the tweet message originated from. As the average number of tweets per day has reached over 500 millions[1], it is possible to investigate specific real world behavior simply by inspecting geo-tagged tweets alone.

Twitter can be for example used to model human mobility behavior by making use of tweet geo-coordinates. Recent studies addressed the task of extracting and identifying mobility patterns from Twitter data considering the spatial and temporal aspects of individual records [2, 11, 25] from local to global (across countries) mobility scales. This line of research includes using tweet sentiment to recommend safest routes for travelers [12] or trajectory model to predict next user location based on named entity recognition in user tweets [27]. In addition, some researches use user social profiles to predict users' next location such as ones where their friends or followers live [13, 14]. All those studies aim at revealing global mobility patterns related to each individual message.

However, the connection between linguistic aspects and the geographical position of Twitter users including their mobility has not been sufficiently covered in prior literature. This work is motivated by the study in [10], in which the authors show that language plays an important role in shaping the human mobility behavior. Since, languages and countries are highly correlated we believe that language can be used to support modeling human travel behavior at the country level. Also, economic, cultural, social, and demographic factors can be associated with the decision-making process of travelers. In this paper, we connect the user mobility analysis with the language use and with the scope of users' multilingualism. In particular, we have performed the user mobility analysis of multilingual users based on Twitter data, and we have investigated mobility patterns, locations, and countries of multilingual Twitter users. The results of our study could be useful in Point of Interest (POI) recommendation, route suggestion or prediction, and travel planning systems.

Two main questions guide our research in this work:

(1) What are the connecting factors between multilingual Twitter users and geographical locations they tweet from?

---

[1]http://www.businessinsider.com/twitter-tweets-per-day-appears-to-have-stalled-2015-6

(2) What are the language-oriented characteristics of multilingual Twitter users who travel between different countries?

The remainder of this paper is structured as follows. Section 2 reviews related work. Section 3 describes our methodology for data collection and data preprocessing. Section 4 explains the multilingualism-focused analysis based on location, and further discusses the obtained experimental results of the proposed multilingual analysis. We conclude the paper in the last section and outline our plans for future work.

2 RELATED WORK

Recently, location-aware smart devices have allowed users to conveniently publish information on their locations by attaching it to microblogs. Novel and innovative real time applications have started to appear by capitalizing on such data, which, to large degree, are publicly available. For example, in scientific and geographic research, the location-based social media (LBSM) allow researchers to study natural phenomena such as mapping auroral [3] and earthquake activity [4] as well as characterizing geographic places [16, 17]. Specifically, Case et al. [3] have shown that Twitter can provide real time indication about a single aurora event of when, and even from where, an aurora is visible. These research works make use of location stamp, time stamp, and location mention of each tweet.

In human mobility research, Twitter has been used to correlate and simulate human mobility in real world. Hasan et al. [9] found that the regularities among users visiting different places follow Zipf's law [7]. Luini et al. [15] proposed that Twitter can be used to discriminate cognitive factors that may explain criminal spatial behavior. As a matter of fact, there is a study on mapping neighborhood happiness, diet and physical activity using Twitter data [18], where the authors find that there is a strong correlation between tweet messages and the overall population happiness level in the region of study. These research works make use of location stamp, location mention, time mention and time stamp.

As previously mentioned, Twitter users are the mixture of locals, migrants, expatriates, minorities, and language learners. As the Internet adoption rate rapidly increased due to wider coverage, the numbers of non-native speakers have also increased. Multilingual study among Twitter users can be considered as a niche research topic as evidenced in the previously mentioned research works which do not explicitly consider the multilingualism's aspect. This is however quite an important research, as, in microblogging sites such as Twitter, information spread across languages and countries.

Eleta and Golbeck [5] performed a study on how multilingual Twitter users mediate between language groups in their particular social networks. They proposed a model to determine the language of choice given a group of social network multilingual users. However, in this particular scenario, sometime a tweet can contain more than one language. Hence, several language classification models have been proposed to determine how many languages are used inside a particular single tweet [1, 20, 21].

Multilingual activities can be observed not only in Twitter. For example, a framework to include multilingual aspect into E-Government has been designed in [8, 22] to improve government efficiency in dealing with non-native speakers such as to design a social network based mechanism in facilitating non-native speaker needs.

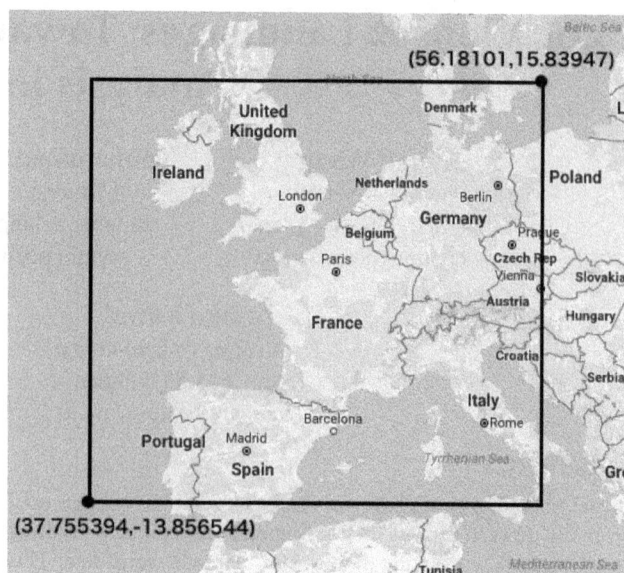

Figure 1: Spatial region used for crawling Twitter.

Multilingualism also plays an important role that needs to be considered when designing an analytic framework which can determine useful reviews, comments or any critical response from various multilingual sources about a particular subject [19, 26].

Nevertheless, the previously mentioned multilingual research works are not specific toward the study of multilingual Twitter users, especially, regarding their spatial locations. Hence, with a view on future research about the roles of multilingual users and their demographic characteristics based on spatial-temporal aspects, we conducted an analysis, at broader level, on their language usage in relation to their spatio-temporal locations in large area of Europe.

3 METHODOLOGY

3.1 Data Collection

Approximately 1 year of geo-tagged Twitter data were gathered from 30th April 2016 to 18th May 2017 for this analysis using Twitter Streaming API[2], accumulating to around 7 gigabytes in memory size. The dataset includes 2.74×10^7 tweets produced by 1.39×10^6 unique Twitter's users from Western Europe, which is represented by an area bounded by the rectangle as illustrated in Figure 1. Table 1 lists the countries involved in the region of our study. The reason we decided to focus on the subarea of Europe is because this continent is characterized by the large density of diverse languages, and, thanks to EU and to the Schengen agreements, by free, unrestricted travel between the EU member countries. 24 languages spoken in Europe are official languages. In addition, Europe has one of the highest ratios of immigrants in the world. Based on these, European countries can be considered as an excellent target area for multilingual studies.

---

[2]https://dev.twitter.com/streaming/overview

Table 1: Country code description.

Country Code							
AD	Andorra	BE	Belgium	CH	Switzerland	CZ	Czech Repulic
DE	Germany	DK	Denmark	ES	Spain	FR	France
GB	United Kingdom	GG	Guernsey	HR	Crotia	IE	Ireland
IM	Isle of Man	IT	Italy	JE	Jersey	LI	Liechtenstein
LU	Luxembourg	MC	Monaco	NL	Netherlands	PL	Poland
PT	Portugal	SE	Sweeden	SM	San Marino	VA	Vatican
AT	Austria						

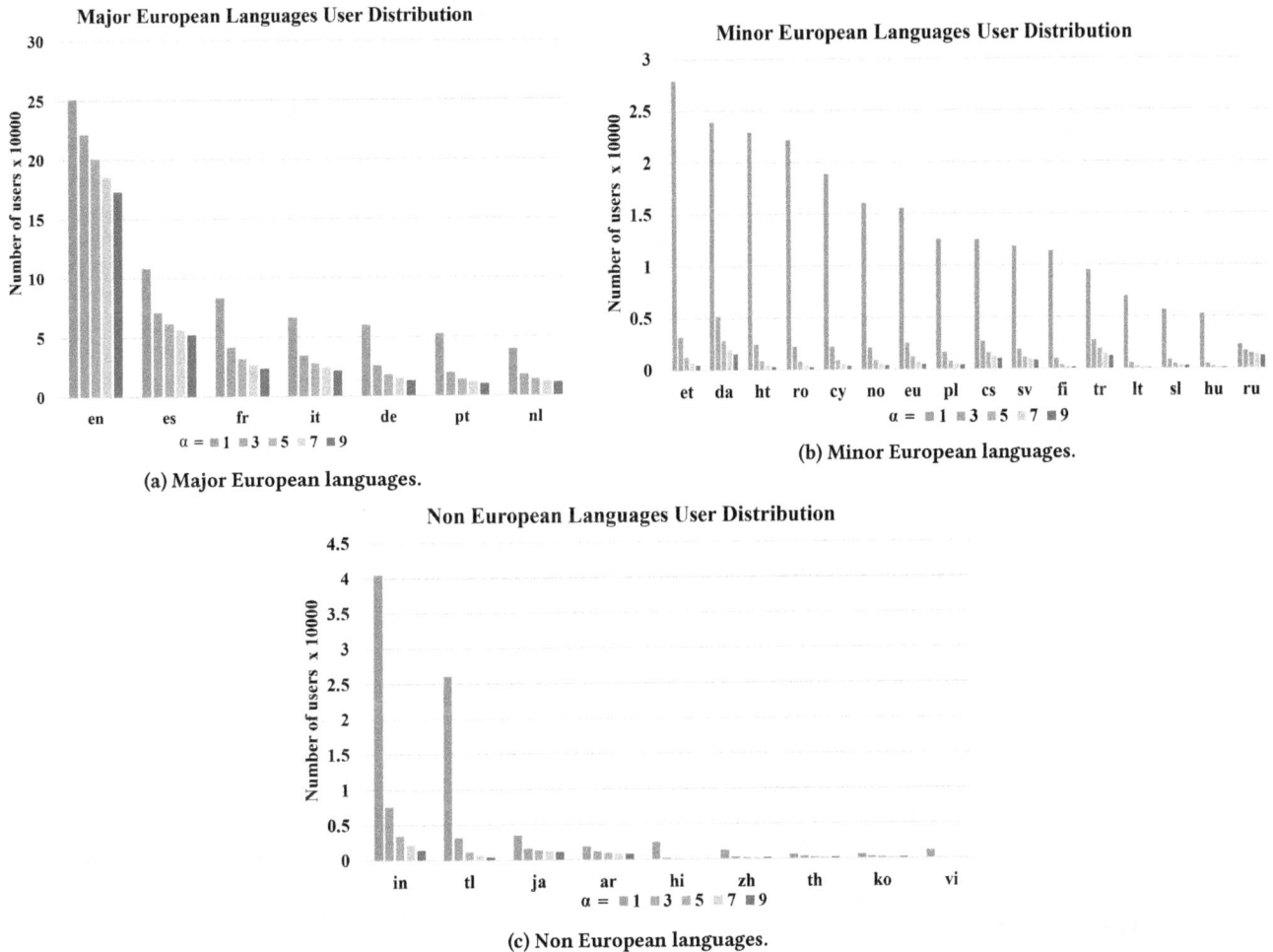

Major European Languages User Distribution

(a) Major European languages.

Minor European Languages User Distribution

(b) Minor European languages.

Non European Languages User Distribution

(c) Non European languages.

Figure 2: Number of users based on major, minor and non European languages used in Twitter.

Table 2: Dataset before and after being cleaned.

	Total Tweets	Total Users
Before	27,431,733	1,396,414
After	14,442,541	272,759

3.2 Data Preprocessing

A certain portion of Twitter data is generated by bots such as weather or advertisement bots. We then removed all users who issued over 1,200 tweets in the entire period and users with less than 12 tweets. The latter number is to reflect that each valid user should have at least more than 1 tweet per month. Finally, retweets were also removed from the dataset.

Table 3: Language code description.

Major European Languages	en	English	es	Spanish	fr	French
	it	Italian	de	German	pt	Portuguese
	nl	Dutch				
Minor European Languages	da	Danish	et	Estonian	ht	Haitian
	ro	Roman	cy	Welsh	eu	Basque
	no	Norwegian	cs	Czech	tr	Turkish
	sv	Swedish	pl	Polish	fi	Finnish
	lt	Lithuanian	ru	Russian	sl	Slovene
	hu	Hungarian				
Non-European Languages	in	Indonesian	tl	Tagalog	ja	Japanese
	ar	Arabic	hi	Hindi	zh	Chinese
	th	Thai	ko	Korean	vi	Vietnamese

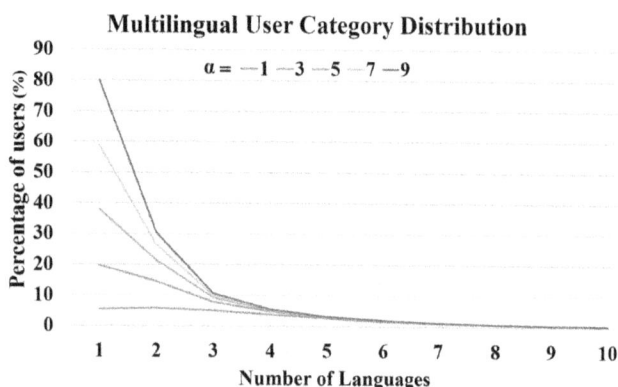

Multilingual User Category Distribution

$\alpha = $ —1 —3 —5 —7 —9

Figure 3: Percentage of users based on the number of used languages as determined by different thresholds of α tweets.

Table 2 gives the description of the data before and after the cleaning process. From the cleaned data after the removal of over one million users, we obtained the total number of Twitter users that tweet in the number of commonly used languages in Europe, and we manually grouped the languages into three categories, major, minor and non European languages based on α values ($\alpha > 1$) (to be described later), illustrated in Figures 2a, 2b, 2c, respectively (Table 3 resolves language acronyms). We relied on Twitter API to identify each tweet's language.

In addition, Figure 3 shows the rate of monolingual and multilingual users that can use certain number of languages under given value of threshold. The figure is also based on α values, such that, a user that issues more than α tweets in a particular language is considered as being able to use that language. Figure 3 is computed such as follows:

(1) Select every user that has tweeted at least α tweets in n language(s).
(2) Count users selected in step (1).
(3) Divide the user count computed in step (2) by the count of all users tweeting in n language(s), regardless of alpha value.

We need to use the threshold in order to mitigate situations when users occasionally copy some text in a particular language[3].

As mentioned before, we classify European languages into three groups: *major European languages, minor European languages,* and *non-European languages.* The major European language is defined as language that is used by at least 10,000 Twitter users in our dataset, the minor European language is defined as language that is used by at least 50 Twitter users and less than 10,000 users, and, lastly, the non-European language is defined as language that originates from non European countries and it is not official language in any European country.

Figure 2a shows that English (en) is the most popular major European language in Europe. Estonian (et) is the most popular minor European language as shown in Figure 2b, and Indonesian (in)[4] as the most popular non European language as shown in Figure 2c. It is interesting to see that there are some non-European languages that are actually more popular than some European languages such as Indonesian (in) - the official language of Indonesia, Tagalog (tl) - the native language of Philippines and Haitian (ht), a French-based creole language and the native language of Haiti.

Figure 3 also shows that for $\alpha > 1$, most users tweet in no more than 4 languages. It can be seen that as α is approaching 9 tweets, most of the Twitter users are considered as monolingual users, perhaps tweeting in their respective native languages.

4 MULTILINGUAL ANALYSIS

In this section, we perform multilingualism-focused analysis based on location and time. From the observations made in the graph in Figure 3, we assume that majority of Twitter users are only capable of tweeting in less than or equal to 4 languages, we then use $\alpha = 5$ tweets as a threshold for deciding if a user has the ability to tweet in a given language.

---

[3]Note that there is no perfect guarantee that a user can speak a given language when he or she has tweeted in that language. Similarly, there may be a case such that a user has not tweeted in a given language despite he or she knows that language. Nevertheless, we expect positive correlation between tweeting in a given language and knowing that language. We further discuss this issue in Section 4.4.
[4]Note that based on country populations, Mandarin would be the expected most popular foreign language; however, this is not the case, mainly, because Twitter is blocked in China.

Table 4: Monolingual vs multilingual users mobility and average visited countries.

	#Mono	#Multi	Avg. visited countries (Mono, Multi)
Non-Travelers	98,020	30,790	(1, 1)
Travelers	84,966	58,983	(2.93, 3.25)

4.1 Location

We first explore the popularity of major languages tweeted from different countries listed in Table 1[5].

Figure 4 shows 21 languages tweeted by Twitter users from each of 25 European countries.

English (en) is the popular language in all countries. However, countries like Spain (ES), France (FR), and Poland (PL)[6] (denoted by pink color font in Figure 4) have a low adoption rate of English while the United Kingdom (GB) obviously has the highest rate of English tweets, followed by Isle of Man (IM), Jersey (JE), and Guernsey (GG).

In cases of Czech Republic (CZ) and Austria (AT), the Twitter users use English over 40% time, and so, it can be considered that English is not their primary language.

We next determine the rates of monolingual and multilingual users for each country. We analyze each country based on the total number of monolingual and multilingual users as shown in Figure 5. The country (actually territory) with the highest density of monolingual users is Guernsey (GG) followed by Jersey (JE), and United Kingdom (GB), all of them having English as the first official language. The country with the highest rate of multilingual users is Belgium (BE) followed by Portugal (PT). This is because these countries have sizeable multilingual population, due to their sizes, economy activities and job opportunities attracting immigration.

From Figure 5, we can see that countries that made English as their official languages are mostly populated by monolingual users. However, Ireland (IE) is an exception. Most of users were tweeting in English in Ireland, but at least 20% of them are multilingual users. The same pattern can be observed in Isle of Man (IM) where almost 40% are multilingual users.

4.2 Mobility

In this section, we analyze the mobility aspect of monolingual and multilingual users. Mobility is based on the number of countries that the users visited. The minimum number of visited countries necessary to consider a user as a traveler is set here to 2.

4.2.1 Languages used by Travelers. Table 4 compares user type based on her or his mobility status showing that majority of monolingual users are non-travelers and the majority of multilingual users are travelers. This is intuitive since travelers, which are here defined as Twitter users who move from one country to another one, have higher chance to be exposed to different languages or to actually need other languages than own ones for their work or life.

With a large variety of different languages used in Europe, as shown in Figure 6, it might be interesting to know how many countries monolingual users visit on average in Europe. Based on the average values computed and shown in Table 4 (see the last column), we see that both monolingual and multilingual travelers visited nearly 3 countries on average. Interestingly, the value for monolinguals is lower by about 10% than the one for multilinguals, which indicates that the latter tend to travel more on average.

We can next observe which language in which country is popular among monolingual and multilingual travelers, as shown in Figure 7 and Figure 8, respectively. The red line gives the total number of tweets of monolingual and multilingual travelers in Figure 7 and Figure 8, respectively. We can find that the most popular countries visited by monolingual travelers are the United Kingdom (GB) followed by Spain (ES), France (FR), and Italy (IT). Figure 7 also shows that English (en) is the most popular language for monolingual travelers. They are largely attracted to English-dominant countries such as the United Kingdom (GB), Ireland (IE), Jersey (JE), Isle of Man (IM), and Guernsey (GG). Hence, it can be said that there are few non-English monolingual travelers.

Figure 8 shows popular countries visited by multilingual travelers. English is still the most used language by multilingual travelers, used in English based countries such as Isle of Man (IM), United Kingdom (GB), Jersey (JE) and Guernsey (GG). Spanish language is the second most popular language that being used in the study, which is frequently being used in Spain (ES), and Andorra (AD). Italian language is the third frequently used language in this study which is being used in Italy (IT), Vatican City (VA), and San Marino (SM).

4.2.2 Pairwise Analysis of Languages used by Travelers. To gain more insight into mobility patterns of monolingual travelers that have limited or no English skills, we aggregate the entire sequence of user tweets to a static weighted contact graph, $G_c = (V, E_l)$ such that $c = \{mono, multi\}$ for monolingual and multilingual users category, respectively, excluding English. Each node represents a given country (country codes are defined in Table 1) and V is the set of most popular countries. $E_l = \{v_i, v_j\}$, represents tweets that originated from users traveling from country v_i to country v_j or otherwise. Edge thickness is bound to the number of users who travel between any two countries. The most common language that users use during their travels between a given pair of countries is used to annotate the edge. The font size of the language annotating each edge represents the number of users who travel between two countries and who use that particular language. For example, in Figure 9, when people from the United Kingdom (GB) are visiting Germany (DE), most of them use German (de).

The following description will use A ↔ B to indicate the flow of the set of users moving from country A to country B and users moving from country B to country A. Each edge is labeled by the most common languages they are using in the visited country. Usually there are two languages displayed for each edge unless one of the languages is too insignificant to be shown. For example, for A ↔ B with l_m on the left side of the edge and l_n on the right side of the edge, it means that most of the users who visit country B from country A tend to speak the language l_n when visiting country B,

---

[5]For efficiency and simplicity we consider only major and some minor languages out of all 32 languages found in our datasets by setting threshold of 12,000 tweets in a given language.
[6]While we only covered small area in Poland, the number of tweets originated from Poland was sufficiently large.

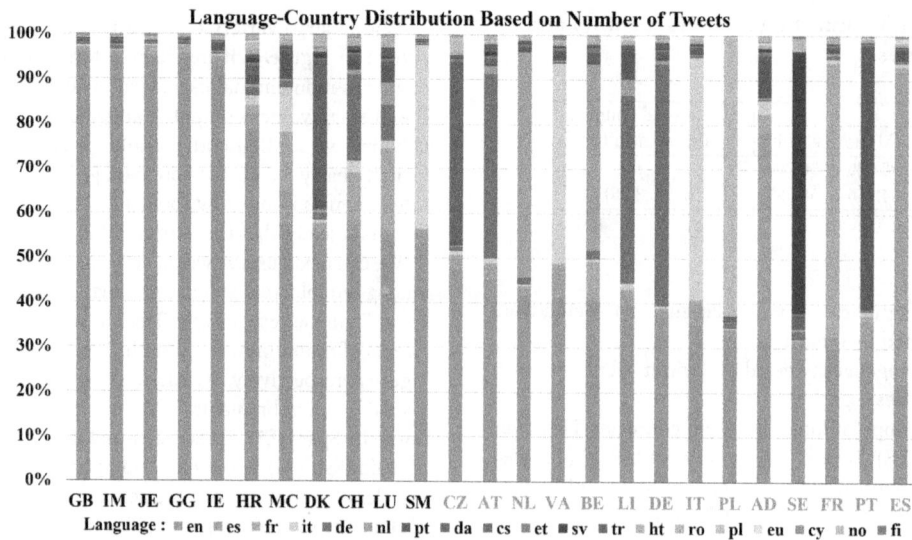

Figure 4: Language distribution of each country.

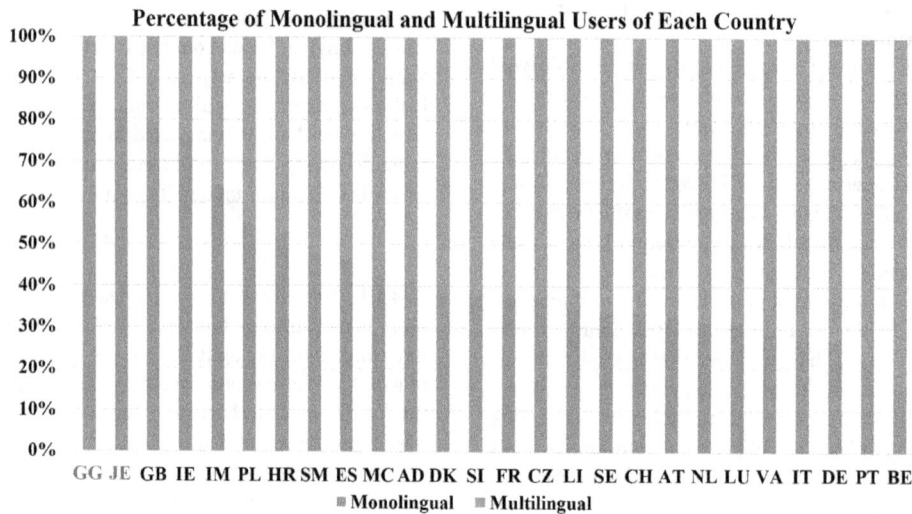

Figure 5: Categories of Twitter users in countries of study.

while users who travel in the opposite direction tend to speak the language l_m in country A.

Figure 9 shows the most popular countries visited by non-English speaking monolingual users (recall that we have excluded English from this study) as nodes, which are United Kingdom (GB), Spain (ES), German (DE), France (FR), Italy (IT), Netherlands (NL), Portugal (PT), Switzerland (SE), Belgium (BE), Ireland (IE), Vatican (VA), and Denmark (DK). Spanish (es) is the most commonly used in many countries, and it is more spoken in Spain ↔ France than French (fr). This pattern is also observed at Spain ↔ Portugal, Spain ↔ Italy, Spain ↔ Netherlands, Spain ↔ Belgium, and Spain ↔ United Kingdom. Following the same pattern but different language can be seen in Italy ↔ Vatican and Italy ↔ Switzerland, where Italian

(it) is the common language, and in Italy ↔ France, France ↔ Belgium, United Kingdom ↔ France where French (fr) is the common language, United Kingdom ↔ German where Germany (de) is the common language and Belgium ↔ Netherlands where Dutch (nl) is commonly used.

Besides, there are countries that have two different languages associated with the edge. For example, Portuguese (pt) and French (fr) for Portugal ↔ France, French (fr) and German (de) for France ↔ Germany, and German (de) and Dutch (nl) for Germany ↔ Netherlands. There are also edges that have only one language associated. This is because the other language is too insignificant to be shown on the graph. Such connections are observed for the

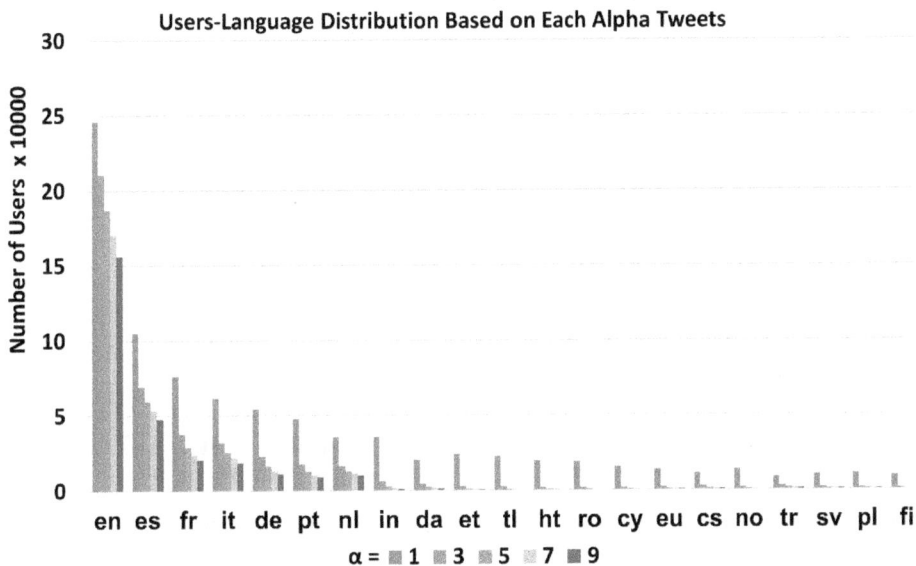

Figure 6: Number of users based on each language used.

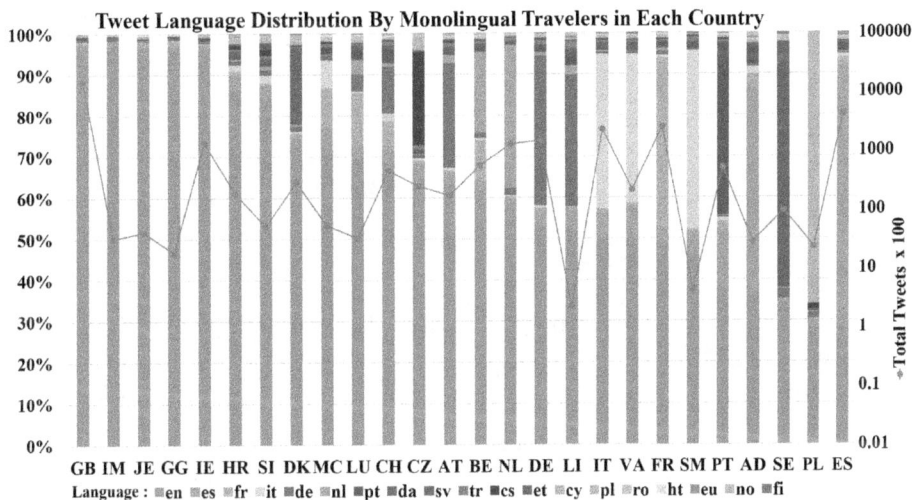

Figure 7: Language distribution based on monolingual travelers and their visited countries.

United Kingdom → Denmark where Danish (da) is used and Belgium → United Kingdom where Dutch (nl) is commonly used for monolingual travelers.

Again, in order to gain more insight about multilingual travelers excluding English language, Figure 10 is given similar to Figure 9. By excluding English, we obtained the list of popular countries that are visited by multilingual travelers which are France (FR), Spain (ES), Italy (IT), Belgium (BE), United Kingdom (GB), Switzerland (CH), Netherlands (NL), Portugal (PT), Germany (DE), Austria (AT) and Czech Republic (CZ). An edge is usually associated with two different languages, except for several edges that are annotated with Italian (it) for Italy ↔ Switzerland, with German for Denmark ↔ Germany, with French (fr) for United Kingdom ↔ France, with

Dutch (nl) for Netherlands ↔ United Kingdom and with Spanish (es) for United Kingdom ↔ Spain.

It can been seen that in Figure 9, the most popular language for monolingual travelers to use seems to be French followed by Spanish, regardless of where they are coming from (note that English was excluded from this study). While, in Figure 10, multilingual travelers tend to use the first language of any country they are visiting, such as French language for France when they coming from other countries. This can be observed when multilingual travelers visited France from Belgium, Spain and Germany. While in France they tweet in French, yet they tend to tweet in Dutch, Spanish and German language when they are in those countries, respectively.

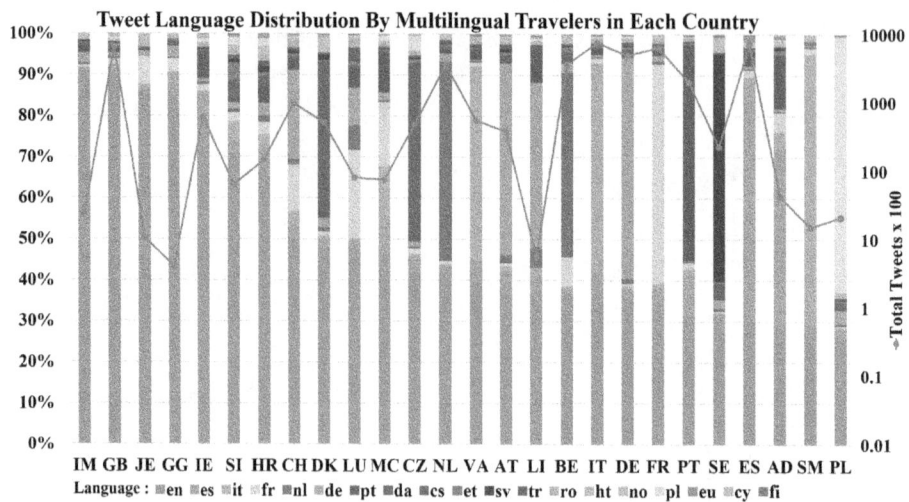

Figure 8: Language distribution based on multilingual travelers and their visited countries.

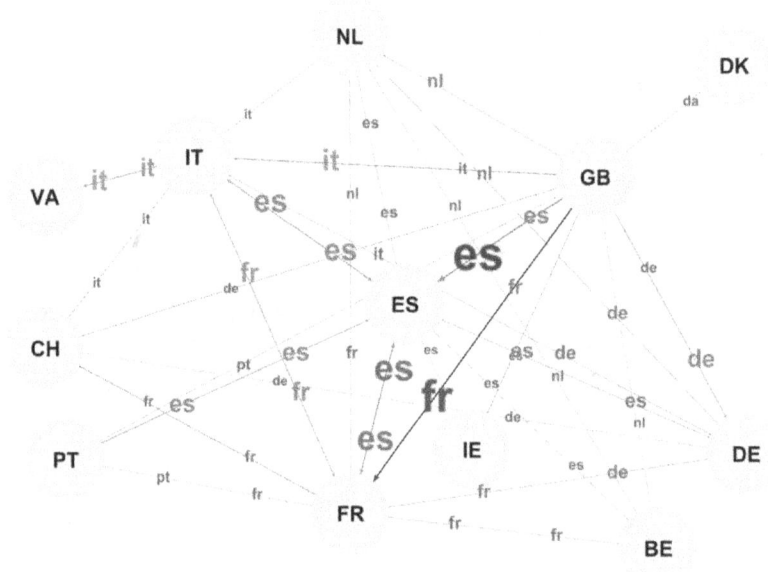

Figure 9: Common languages used by European monolingual users when traveling between countries. For example, when users from France visit United Kingdom, they tend to tweet in French language.

4.3 Map-based Visualization of Multilingual and Monolingual User counts

Finally, for the sake of completeness, we show the correlation between monolingual and multilingual users based on geographic locations, regardless of country borders. Figure 11 shows the heatmap depicting density of monolingual and multilingual users. The heatmap is a direct visualization from results obtained after applying DB-SCAN clustering algorithm [6]. In order to determine the relation between multilingual users and their locations with monolingual users, we performed two separate clustering processes: one of multilinguals and one of monolinguals based on the location of both the types of users. Contrasting the results from these two clusterings can provide novel information on the co-occurrence patterns of the two user groups.

From the figure it can be observed that there is positive correlation between monolingual and multilingual users, such that, for any location with high density of monolingual users, the total number of multilingual users also increases. This is especially true for Madrid, Barcelona, Paris, London, Lisbon, Florence, Milano and Balearic Islands - places that belong to the main touristic attractions in Europe.

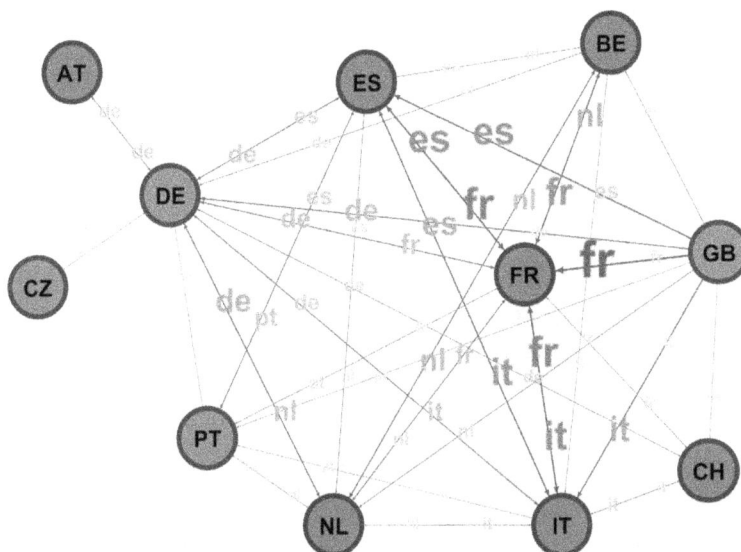

Figure 10: Common languages used by European multilingual users when traveling between countries. For example, when a user from France visits Spain, he or she tends to tweet in Spanish language.

4.4 Discussion

The multilingual analysis is an interesting topic in linguistic studies. In this research, we have shown that languages and locations are correlated with mobility patterns and their study can lead to novel observations. Those aspects can be used for understanding the behavior of people in particular locations. For example, in Figure 9, whenever people are coming from Spain (ES) visiting Italy (IT), Spanish is the common language used by these travelers. This seems to suggest that Italian people may not travel very much to Spain. This is also suggested by Figure 8, where the most popular country for multilingual travelers to go is Italy (IT). However, from the data it appears that not many Italian people went outside and visit other countries.

Note that our assumption is limited to only users that are using Twitter. Essentially, this work is under the closed world assumption with regards to the used data. The assumption applied here such as the user being able to speak other languages is then based solely from Twitter data. There is, however, no easy way to make sure that a user actually speaks given language even if he or she tweets in that language sufficient number of times. Similarly, for determining travelers, if a user does not tweet from two different countries there is no easy way to detect that he or she has actually visited them[7].

One important thing left out is time-focused analysis. Obviously, travel takes time. To some extent we did involve time in Section 4.2, as we record the countries visited by users sequentially according to time order of their corresponding tweets. However, in the future, the time aspect will be thoroughly evaluated together with the exploration of other geographical areas (e.g., Asia and America).

5 CONCLUSIONS

In this paper we describe and visualize how languages and locations can be correlated with Twitter users. Through several statistical analyses, we find that locations and languages are correlated with mobility patterns of multilingual Twitter users. It also can be observed that the number of visited countries and number of languages used by a single Twitter user are proportionally related.

In the future we will deeply analyze mobility patterns of multilingual travelers, e.g., if they often travel back and forth between two countries which might suggest that a business-related travel, or a one-time event travel. Furthermore, we plan to expand the current analysis method to recommend Points of Interest (POIs), to predict routes, and to make travel plans.

6 ACKNOWLEDGMENTS

This work was partially supported by SCOPE of the Ministry of Internal Affairs and Communications of Japan (#171507010), JSPS KAKENHI Grant Numbers 16H01722, 17K12686, 17H01822, and TNB Seed Fund U-TD-RD-17-02.

REFERENCES

[1] S. Bergsma, P. McNamee, M. Bagdouri, C. Fink, and T. Wilson. 2012. Language identification for creating language-specific twitter collections. In *Proceedings of the second workshop on language in social media*. Association for Computational Linguistics, 65–74.

[2] M. Birkin, K. Harland, N. Malleson, P. Cross, and M. Clarke. 2014. An Examination of Personal Mobility Patterns in Space and Time using Twitter. *International Journal of Agricultural and Environmental Information Systems (IJAEIS)* 5, 3 (2014), 55–72.

[3] N. A. Case, E. A. MacDonald, M. Heavner, A. H. Tapia, and N. Lalone. 2015. Mapping Auroral Activity with Twitter. *Geophysical Research Letters* 42, 10 (2015), 3668–3676.

[4] A. Dingli, L. Mercieca, R. Spina, and M. Galea. 2015. Event detection using social sensors. In *Proc. of ICT-DM 2015*. 35–41. https://doi.org/10.1109/ICT-DM.2015. 7402054

[5] I. Eleta and J. Golbeck. 2014. Multilingual use of Twitter: Social networks at the language frontier. *Computers in Human Behavior* 41 (2014), 424–432.

---

[7]In future we plan to apply text mining techniques for detecting the fact of traveling abroad based on the analysis of the content of user tweets.

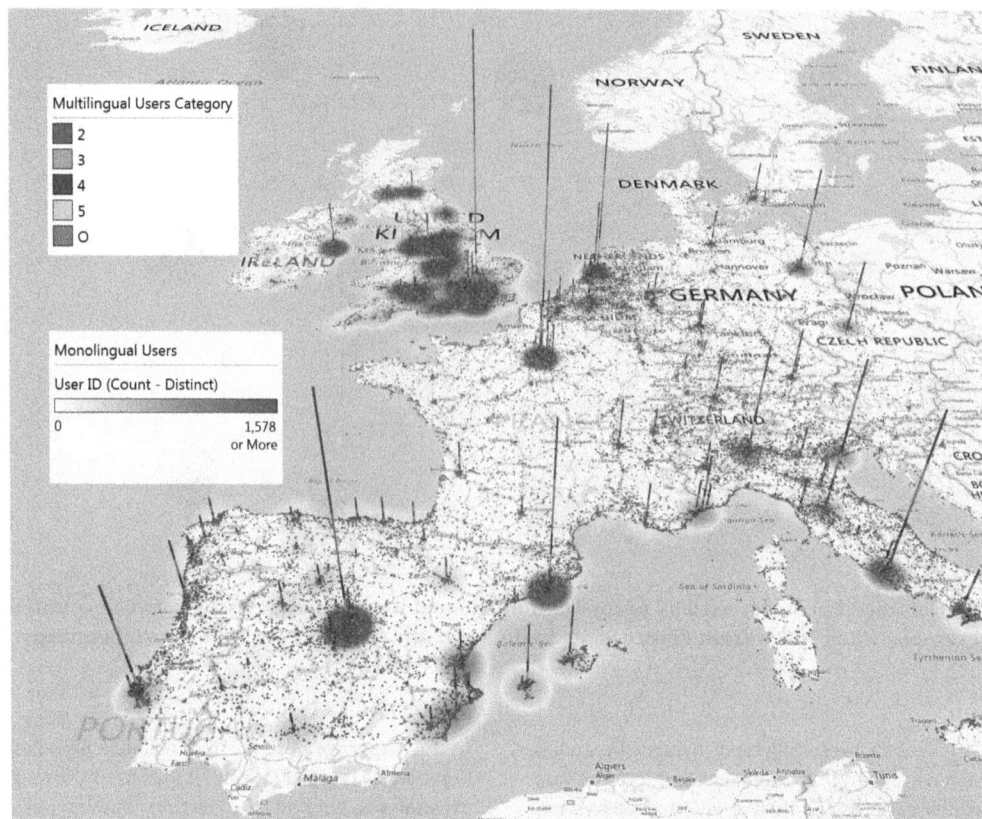

Figure 11: Multilingual Twitter users with respect to monolingual coverage (the counts of multilingual users for each multilingual category, from 2, 3, 4, 5 and more than 5, are shown as stacked vertical bars, while the ones of monolingual users are displayed as colored horizontal circles with color intensity bound to the user count).

[6] M. Ester, H.-P. Kriegel, J. Sander, X. Xu, et al. 1996. A density-based algorithm for discovering clusters in large spatial databases with noise.. In *Proc. of KDD 1996*, Vol. 96. 226–231.

[7] G. Eysenbach. 2011. Can tweets predict citations? Metrics of social impact based on Twitter and correlation with traditional metrics of scientific impact. *Journal of medical Internet research* 13, 4 (2011), e123.

[8] Julia Gremm, Julia Barth, Kaja J Fietkiewicz, and Wolfgang G Stock. 2018. E-Government. In *Transitioning Towards a Knowledge Society*. Springer, 131–158.

[9] S. Hasan, X. Zhan, and S. V. Ukkusuri. 2013. Understanding Urban Human Activity and Mobility Patterns using Large-Scale Location-based Data from Online Social Media. In *Proceedings of the 2nd ACM SIGKDD International Workshop on Urban Computing*. ACM, 6.

[10] Gabrielle Hogan-Brun. 2017. *Linguanomics: What is the Market Potential of Multilingualism?* Bloomsbury Publishing.

[11] R. Jurdak, K. Zhao, J. Liu, M. AbouJaoude, M. Cameron, and D. Newth. 2015. Understanding human mobility from Twitter. *PloS one* 10, 7 (2015), e0131469.

[12] J. Kim, M. Cha, and T. Sandholm. 2014. SocRoutes: safe routes based on tweet sentiments. In *Proceedings of the 23rd International Conference on World Wide Web*. ACM, 179–182.

[13] D. Kotzias, T. Lappas, and D. Gunopulos. 2016. Home is where your friends are: Utilizing the social graph to locate twitter users in a city. *Information Systems* 57 (2016), 77–87.

[14] Z. Liu and Y. Huang. 2016. Closeness and structure of friends help to estimate user locations. In *International Conference on Database Systems for Advanced Applications*. Springer, 33–48.

[15] L. P. Luini, D. Cardellicchio, F. Felletti, and F. S. Marucci. 2015. Socio-Spatial Intelligence: Social Media and Spatial Cognition for Territorial Behavioral Analysis. *Cognitive Processing* 16, 1 (2015), 299–303. https://doi.org/10.1007/s10339-015-0711-z

[16] F. Luo, G. Cao, K. Mulligan, and X. Li. 2016. Explore spatiotemporal and demographic characteristics of human mobility via Twitter: A case study of Chicago. *Applied Geography* 70 (2016), 11–25.

[17] G. McKenzie, K. Janowicz, S. Gao, and L. Gong. 2015. How where is when? On the regional variability and resolution of geosocial temporal signatures for points of interest. *Computers, Environment and Urban Systems* 54 (2015), 336–346.

[18] Q. C Nguyen, S. Kath, H.-W. Meng, D. Li, K. R Smith, J. A VanDerslice, M. Wen, and F. Li. 2016. Leveraging geotagged Twitter data to examine neighborhood happiness, diet, and physical activity. *Applied Geography* 73 (2016), 77–88.

[19] Barbara Pernici, Chiara Francalanci, Gabriele Scalia, Marco Corsi, Domenico Grandoni, and Mariano Alfonso Biscardi. 2018. Geolocating social media posts for emergency mapping. *arXiv preprint arXiv:1801.06861* (2018).

[20] F. Pla and L.-F. Hurtado. 2016. Language identification of multilingual posts from Twitter: a case study. *Knowledge and Information Systems* (2016), 1–25. https://doi.org/10.1007/s10115-016-0997-x

[21] K. C. Raghavi, M. K. Chinnakotla, and M. Shrivastava. 2015. "Answer Ka Type Kya He?": Learning to Classify Questions in Code-Mixed Language. In *Proc. of WWW 2015*. ACM, New York, NY, USA, 853–858. https://doi.org/10.1145/2740908.2743006

[22] Diana Sutton. 2017. Multilingual Britain–Towards a coherent policy framework for children with EAL. (2017).

[23] S. Wakamiya, A. Jatowt, Y. Kawai, and T. Akiyama. 2016. Analyzing Global and Pairwise Collective Spatial Attention for Geo-social Event Detection in Microblogs. In *Proc. of WWW 2016*. 263–266.

[24] C. Weidemann and J. Swift. 2013. Social Media Location Intelligence: The Next Privacy Battle-An ArcGIS add-in and Analysis of Geospatial Data Collected from Twitter. com. *International Journal of Geoinformatics* 9, 2 (2013).

[25] Q. Yuan, G. Cong, Z. Ma, A. Sun, and N. M. Thalmann. 2013. Who, Where, when and What: Discover Spatio-temporal Topics for Twitter Users. In *Proc. of KDD 2013*. 605–613.

[26] Ying Zhang and Zhijie Lin. 2018. Predicting the helpfulness of online product reviews: A multilingual approach. *Electronic Commerce Research and Applications* 27 (2018), 1–10.

[27] X. Zheng, J. Han, and A. Sun. 2017. A Survey of Location Prediction on Twitter. *arXiv preprint arXiv:1705.03172* (2017).

The Refugee/Migrant Crisis Dichotomy on Twitter:
A Network and Sentiment Perspective

Adina Nerghes
KNAW Humanities Cluster
Amsterdam, The Netherlands
adina.nerghes@dh.huc.knaw.nl

Ju-Sung Lee
Erasmus University Rotterdam
Rotterdam, The Netherlands
lee@eshcc.eur.nl

ABSTRACT

Media reports, political statements, and social media debates on the refugee/migrant crisis shape the ways in which people and societies respond to those displaced people arriving at their borders world wide. These current events are framed and experienced as a crisis, entering the media, capturing worldwide political attention, and producing diverse and contradictory discourses and responses. The labels "migrant" and "refugee" are frequently distinguished and conflated in traditional as well as social media when describing the same groups of people. In this paper, we focus on the simultaneous struggle over meaning, legitimization, and power in representations of the refugee crisis, through the specific lens of Twitter. The 369,485 tweets analyzed in this paper cover two days after a picture of Alan Kurdi – a three-year-old Syrian boy who drowned in the Mediterranean Sea while trying to reach Europe with his family – made global headlines and sparked wide media engagement. More specifically, we investigate the existence of the dichotomy between the "deserving" refugee versus the "undeserving" migrant, as well as the relationship between sentiment expressed in tweets, their influence, and the popularity of Twitter users involved in this dichotomous characterization of the crisis. Our results show that the Twitter debate was predominantly focused on refugee related hashtags and that those tweets containing such hashtags were more positive in tone. Furthermore, we find that popular Twitter users as well as popular tweets are characterized by less emotional intensity and slightly less positivity in the debate, contrary to prior expectations. Co-occurrence networks expose the structure underlying hashtag usage and reveal a refugee-centric core of meaning, yet divergent goals of some prominent users. As social media become increasingly prominent venues for debate over a crisis, how and why people express their opinions offer valuable insights into the nature and direction of these debates.

KEYWORDS

Refugee Crisis; Twitter; Network Analysis; Sentiment Analysis

ACM Reference format:
Adina Nerghes and Ju-Sung Lee. 2018. The Refugee/Migrant Crisis Dichotomy on Twitter: A Network and Sentiment Perspective. In *Proceedings*

of 10th ACM Conference on Web Science, Amsterdam, Netherlands, May 27–30, 2018 (WebSci '18), 10 pages.
https://doi.org/10.1145/3201064.3201087

1 INTRODUCTION

Media reports, political statements, and popular discourse on the refugee crisis shape the ways in which people and societies respond to those arriving at their borders. These current events are framed and experienced as a crisis, entering the media, capturing worldwide political attention, and producing diverse and contradictory discourses and responses.

The labels "migrant" and "refugee" are frequently distinguished and conflated in media, political, and popular discourse when describing the same groups of people. Such labelings do not only create a demarcation between the refugee versus the migrant, but also point towards the causes of displacement – specifically those related to the overlapping dichotomies of voluntary/forced, (im)migrant or refugee, and economic/political. These types of dichotomies have shaped how states and other actors have responded to displaced people [15, 19, 43].

International conventions establish refugees as involuntarily displaced by political circumstances, including war and violence, and natural disasters; refugees are thus framed as "deserving". On the other hand, immigrants or migrants are portrayed as economic opportunists, voluntarily leaving their home communities in search of a better life, and hence become viewed as "undeserving" of understanding or sympathy. The use of such dichotomies has the potential to shape the story on migration, and the ways in which we perceive migrants and refugees. Labeling these displaced people as either refugees or migrants in communication contexts may affect receivers by emphasizing different frames for the evaluation of the same issue or event [e.g., 7, 10, 11, 14, 33].

Through framing, certain features of an event are selected while others are excluded [23], and frames may shape one's interpretation of that story by making certain perspectives more salient [16, 23, 29]. Drawing from the work of Goffman [14], we understand that frames elicit, as well as constrain, the interpretative activities of audiences [29]. Entman [11] defines framing as a way "...to select some aspects of a perceived reality and make them more salient in a communicating text, in such a way as to promote a particular problem definition, causal interpretation, moral evaluation, and/or treatment recommendation." By highlighting certain characteristics of an issue and concealing others, framing reflects the emphasis of the author.

Without trying to reduce the crisis to mere text or discourse, we seek to analyze representations of displaced people in popular discourse as well as the increasingly evident demarcation between the "deserving" *refugee* versus the "undeserving" *migrant*. As previous research has shown, such dichotomized characterizations strongly relate to sentiment towards the refugees and the crisis itself [20, 25], while framing both groups as outsiders threatening the well-being of the host societies. This discourse of deservingness shifts blame and responsibility away from political and economic actors, placing it instead onto the displaced people themselves. Furthermore, such dichotomized categorizations together with media representations of Syrian refugees – as connected to the violent November 2015 attacks in Paris [1], refugee centers being set on fire in several European countries (e.g., Germany, Sweden etc.), politicians being violently attacked for supporting refugees [21], and boats of refugees being turned back to sea [24] – build what [Feitlowitz] refers to as a "lexicon of terror."

In this paper, we focus on the simultaneous struggle over meaning, legitimization, and power in representations of the refugee crisis, through the lens of social media, through which the refugee crisis has received much attention. In particular, Twitter users have been increasingly vocal in their opinions of the crisis ever since the reporting of the death of Alan Kurdi on September 4, 2015.

Twitter debates expose public-opinion-based characterizations of global events [31], such as the refugee/migrant crisis, while also revealing opinion communities and their interactions (i.e., through mentions of other users and following/follower relationships) [17]. To uncover patterns of opinion and influence, meaning structures as well as social interactions related to the refugee crisis debates on Twitter, we employ a suite of analysis methods, including the increasingly popular socio-semantic framework [3, 9, 17, 35–37].

2 AIMS AND HYPOTHESES

The main aims of this paper are to investigate the existence of the dichotomy between the "deserving" refugee versus the "undeserving" migrant (discussed above) in the refugee crisis debates on Twitter, as well as to explore the relationship between sentiment expressed in tweets, their influence, and the popularity of Twitter users. Based on these aims we formulate a number of hypotheses:

> **H1:** Tweets employing hashtags containing the word refugee will be more positive in sentiment, while those employing hashtags containing the word migrant will be more negative in sentiment.

The sentiments of tweets themselves have influential impacts, that may be heightened by the popularity of the tweet poster (i.e. 'tweeter' or user) or the tweet itself. For example, the top one percent of social media authors have been found to significantly influence the whole sentiment of a topic [34]. Popularity confers not only readership but influence as well. That is, the sentiments expressed by popular users in their tweets have been found to influence the sentiment of their audience [2]. The outcomes of such influential forces can be broad reaching. For example, many studies have linked sentiments on Twitter as predictors of elections [8, 27, 41]. Along those lines, we first consider the sentiment quality of popular Twitter users and hypothesize that intense expression is likely to garner more attention, and those Twitter users who are the center of attention may express themselves with more intense rhetoric:

> **H2:** The popularity of Twitter users is strongly related to the average sentiment intensity of their tweets.

Retweeting, an indicator of the influence of a tweet, can be driven, in part, by a tweet's sentiment. For example, sentiment occurring in politically relevant tweets has been found to have an effect on their re-tweetability (i.e., how often these tweets will be retweeted) [38]. In fact, it has been observed that tweets with positive sentiment polarity spread 15-20 percent more than tweets containing negative sentiment polarity [6]. Here, we hypothesize that incendiary or otherwise sentiment-laden tweets will be more influential:

> **H3** The influence of a tweet is directly related to the sentiment intensity of the tweet.
> **H4** Positive tweets are retweeted more often than negative tweets.

3 DATA AND METHODS

We analyze a total of 369,485 historical tweets collected using the ten most popular and relevant Twitter hashtags surrounding the refugee/migrant crisis.[1] This data set was obtained from historical Twitter data providers Gnip/Sifter and constitute 100% of the available tweets within our search criteria and searched dates (similar to the Twitter Firehouse). The data spans two full days, between September 4, 2015 – when the death of Alan Kurdi sparked wide social media engagement to the crisis – and September 5, 2015.

In analyzing this data set, we employ sentiment analysis, regression analysis, and network analysis. In the following sub-sections, we elaborate on each of these methods.

3.1 Network analysis

In recent decades, network analysis has gained popularity across the social sciences, yielding explanations for a wide variety of social phenomena [5]. Network analysis methods investigate social phenomena through the use of network structures and graph theory, and they characterize networked structures in terms of nodes (e.g., individual actors) and the links (relationships or interactions) that connect them [42].

In this paper, we make use of network analysis methods to uncover interconnections between users and tweet contents, and thus co-addressing both meanings and actors surrounding the refugee crisis debate on Twitter. To this end, we investigate two types of networks: 1) the network of hashtags and 2) the socio-semantic network of users and their used hashtags. While the first type of network comprises nodes of a single type (i.e., hashtags) and hence is unimodal, the second type of network is called bimodal.

Bimodal networks (also known as affiliation, bipartite, or two-mode networks) contain two different sets of nodes, distinguished by qualitative, nominal categories. These networks link nodes belonging to different sets [4, 26, 28]. In the specific case of our user-to-hashtag network, the two types of nodes represent Twitter users and the hashtags they employed. This specific network helps us explore the relationships between users through the shared usage of relevant hashtags, which serve as proxies for larger topics.

Furthermore, both types of networks analyzed in this paper are co-occurrence networks and hence the value of strength for each link in these networks is determined by the frequency of

---

[1]The following hashtags have been used when collecting our data: #migrantcrisis, #migrants, #migrant, #refugee, #refugees, #refugeecrisis, #syrianrefugees, #syrianrefugeesgr, #refugeeswelcome, and #muslimrefugees.

co-occurrence [42]. In other words, we do not only account for the existence of the the connection between co-occurring hashtags within each tweet or co-occurring users and hashtags, but also for the frequencies of these co-occurrences. For example, if #RefugeesWelcome and #Syria are observed together in exactly 100 tweets, then the link weight between these two hashtags would be the weight of 100.

For the purpose of this paper, we explore single snap-shots of these two types of networks via visualizations and also by measuring and reporting the weighted degree centrality of the network nodes. Degree centrality is one of the most commonly used centrality measures in social network analysis [18]. The degree centrality of a node in a network reflects the number of other nodes incident to the focal node [13] (or, in the case of weighted networks, the sum of the weights of all the incident links), and thus measures the involvement of a node in its local network. Nodes with low (weighted) degree centrality are potentially more peripheral to the network [22] unless they are connected to popular others. Thus, by calculating the weighted degree centrality of the nodes in our networks, we identify the most popular hashtags and the most central Twitter users, respectively. While some could argue that hashtag frequency, or the number of tweets a users has generated, are arguably more parsimonious metrics than popularity (i.e.,degree centrality), the network linkages (such structures surrounding connective hashtags and users) would remain obscured, resulting in a less accurate depiction of hashtag use.

In sum, through these two types of networks, we investigate several critical issues regarding the discussion of the refugee crisis on Twitter. Furthermore, we identify opinion leaders by their hashtag usage and structural positions, since networks, more than demographics, can characterize Twitter opinion leaders [30].

3.2 Sentiment Analysis

In order to explore the relationships between sentiment expressed in tweets, their influence, and the popularity of Twitter users, we use Thelwall's SentiStrength [40], which provides scores on two dimensions of sentiment (positivity and negativity) per emotional term and phrases within the tweet. In addition to the lexicon-based sentiment identification, SentiStrength also assigns sentiment to emoticons based on a list with human-assigned sentiment scores. SentiStrength employs a lexicon similar to LIWC (Linguistic Inquiry and Word Count) [32]. Sentiment scores from SentiStrength range from 0 to 4 for capturing the extent of the Positive and Negative sentiment dimensions in a segment of text (i.e., tweet). The initial SentiStrength scores of -1 to -5 for negativity and $+1$ to $+5$ for positivity were recoded into the 0-4 range, in which higher numbers indicate more intense sentiment, since -1 and $+1$ represent neutrality in the software. Thus, a tweet with a 0/0 score would be considered neutral, a tweet scored 4/0 would be considered extremely positive, while a tweet scored 0/-4 would be considered extremely negative.

Adding the two sentiment dimensions yields a sum score (we call 'Sentiment') capturing the overall sentiment of each tweet. Thus, a Sentiment score of +1 would indicate that the net sentiment of a tweet is slightly positive. Finally, an Intensity score — operationalized as the Euclidean distance of the sentiment score

to (0,0), $\sqrt{\mathrm{Pos.}^2 + \mathrm{Neg.}^2}$ – captures the overall intensity of both sentiment valences together. As the term 'refugee' and its variants are detected as carrying negative sentiment (rescaled score of -1 in SentiStrength), they are omitted from the analysis, given our focus of analysis on the sentiment surrounding (and not including) the use of the terms refugee and migrant in hashtags. Incidentally, the term 'migrant' bears no such sentiment bias.

As the hypotheses relate Twitter user and tweet characteristics (metadata) to sentiment, we operationalize user popularity, influence of the user, and influence of the tweet. Popularity is expressed as the number of followers for each tweet's user. Influence, a score provided by Texifter [39], is the ratio of 'followers' to 'friends' (i.e., count of those whom the user follows). When the number of friends is 0, the Influence score is undefined; hence, we introduce a slight bias by adding 1 to the friends count, thereby capturing the influence of those without any friends (i.e. do not follow others).

However, given that the Influence score does not capture the impact of a tweet, we also include Retweets, the number of times each unique tweet has been retweeted. Retweets may appear multiple times in the data set, so we only account for highest retweet count of each retweeted tweet. Each of these metadata-based dependent variables has been transformed by $\log(x + 1)$ so that their distributions are less skewed and more Gaussian (i.e. normal).

3.3 Regression Analysis

Additionally, ordered logit (i.e., ordinal logistic) and OLS (ordinary least squares) regressions are used to predict key measures. For the integer sentiment measures (Positivity, Negativity, and Sentiment), the ordered logit is employed, while OLS is more appropriate for the sentiment Intensity measure. These sentiment measures are predicted by hashtag usage in order to test H1.

OLS regressions are also used to regress popularity, influence of the user, and influence of the tweet on sentiment measures, while controlling for the hashtags employed in order to test H2 and H3.[2] Popularity refers to the number of followers of the users, Influence refers to the influential position of the tweeter, while Retweets is simply the maximum number of times a unique tweet was retweeted by other users. The covariates of these regressions can be used to characterize the popularity, influence of user, and influence of the tweet.

4 RESULTS

4.1 Network Analysis

4.1.1 Hashtag Usage. In Figure 1, we show a hashtag co-occurrence network with the top 10 most central hashtags highlighted by revealing their labels. All hashtags in this network are colored by frequency of overall occurrence, ranging from blue for low frequency (minimum of 1) to red for high frequency (maximum of 18232). This frequency of occurrence refers to total usage of the hashtag, not dependent on co-occurring use with other hashtags. The nodes are sized by the total number of co-occurrence links to other hashtags (i.e., their weighted degree centrality). The links in the network are scaled by their weight (hashtags occurring together in tweets will have a stronger, and thus thicker, link).

---

[2]Specifically, we predict the logarithms of the dependent variable plus 1 to render their distributions and the residuals more normal while accounting for 0 values.

Table 1: Frequency counts for hashtag co-occurrence

Hashtag	Hashtag	Freq. of co-occurrence
hungary	refugee	18232
austria	refugee	9488
austria	hungary	8899
refugeeswelcome	refugeecrisis	8553
syria	refugee	7408
refugee	refugeeswelcome	6466
refugee	refugeecrisis	6116
refugeeswelcome	aylan	5403
refugee	budapest	5269
hungary	refugeecrisis	3922

Based on this portrayal, in Figure 1, we note that #refugee is by far the most frequent hashtag as well as the hashtag that is most frequently used in combination with other hashtags. Also, we note that migrant-related hashtags are very low in both frequency and centrality in our data set, indicating that they were not used as frequently as the refugee relate hashtags. In fact, only two migrant hashtags appear in the network.

Table 1 displays the top ten pairs of hashtags based on co-occurrence in tweets (link weights). These pairs of hashtag clearly contain those countries directly involved in the crisis back in September 2015. Many of the refugees fled conflict in Syria and entered Hungary, in large numbers, posing logistical and political difficulties. Austria, bordering Hungary, was similarly affected and demarcated refugees' transition further into Europe. Interestingly, the more positive hashtag #RefugeesWelcome is not associated with any of the country hashtags.

By all appearances, these findings seem to point towards the fact that the Twitter debate on the refugee crisis captured by our data sample has been predominantly focused on the refugee label, and not so much on the migrant labels. Based on the dichotomy we referred to earlier between the "deserving" refugee versus the "undeserving" migrant, a debate mostly focused on the refugee label may indicate a highly sympathetic tone towards those at the center of the debate – the displaced people fleeing zones of conflict. To further investigate whether the sentiments associated with refugee hashtags are indeed more positively laden, in Section 4.2 we perform sentiment analysis on tweets containing the two different types of hashtags, and on those tweets containing both types of hashtags.

4.1.2 Socio-Semantic Networks. For our socio-semantic network analysis, through which we explore both meanings and users within the Twitter refugee crisis debate, we present a snapshot of a bimodal user-to-hashtag network in Figure 2. In this network, Twitter users are linked to the hashtags they used in their tweets.

In Figure 2a, only nodes having a weighted degree centrality greater than or equal to 50 are displayed, in order to identify the more prolific actors and the most used hashtags. The center of the network is occupied by hashtags, the visible ones being the refugee-related ones appearing in Table 1, the most prominent of which is '#refugee' (frequency = 8474). The next two are #refugeeswelcome (5059) and refugeecrisis (4288). Surrounding this core are

the users who employed those hashtags, while the periphery contains less prominently used hashtags. The most prominent user also lies in the periphery. However, this users' hashtag use, while sharing #refugee, appears to also employ lesser used hashtags that focus on women's issues in relation to the crisis: #refugee, #women, #womenshealthday, #girls, #displaced, #health.

In Figure 2b, we focus in on the top three most central users. The most central Twitter user in our data set is connected to the other two next most central users only through the common use of the #refugee hashtag.[3] By central, we refer to high weighted degree centrality (i.e., high hashtag usage) rather than a visually central position. Furthermore, by noting the width of the link connecting this highly central user to #refugee, we can easily note the frequent usage of this hashtag (more precisely 413 times).[4]

The central user is further distinguished by the visual distance between the user and its hashtags, indicating its hashtags are either not co-used by others, or used by others that employ very different hashtags. This heterogeneity of hashtag use by this user (with high level of use of each of those distinct hashtags) may indicate a singular focus not readily shared by other users. Hence, this lack of shared meaning with others renders this active user to be peripheral. Future analysis on tweets occurring after September 2015 will reveal whether or not this focus on women becomes shared by others or remains isolated.

While this central user focuses on topics unrelated to the other two central users, the latter two do share several common hashtags. Furthermore, these users exhibit greater variety of hashtag use, meaning their Twitter expression is more qualitatively central to the larger refugee/migrant discussion.

The bimodal socio-semantic depiction is particularly useful in this case, as it exposes the distinct position of the most central user, as being structurally and topically peripheral and, at that stage of the crisis, uninfluential and less embedded in the broader discussion. A unimodal network of users connected by co-use of hashtags (i.e., shared meanings) is more typical in network analysis; however, this depiction may be misleading by revealing this "central" user to be even further embedded than he or she actually is.

4.2 Sentiment Analysis

In Figure 3, we explore the sentiment distribution across tweets by partitioning them based on use of 'migrant'-related hashtags only (e.g., #migrantcrisis or #migrant), use of 'refugee'-related hashtags only (e.g., #refugeeswelcome or #refugeecrisis), and those containing both types of hashtags (see number of tweets for each type in Table 2). Each cell's percentage refers to the proportion of tweets for each type of hashtag use that are scored with a particular pair of positive and negative sentiment scores. The colors denote the balance of sentiment (sentiment sum): green for net positivity and red for net negativity.

While a good proportion of all three types of tweets are scored as purely neutral (upper left cell of Figure 3), their differences point to general sentiment variations. Migrant tweets (i.e., those tweets having only migrant-related hashtags) show the least neutrality,

---

[3]The #refugee and #refugees hashtags are merged to a singular #refugees node.
[4]For anonymity reasons, we choose not to reveal the usernames of the actors in our networks.

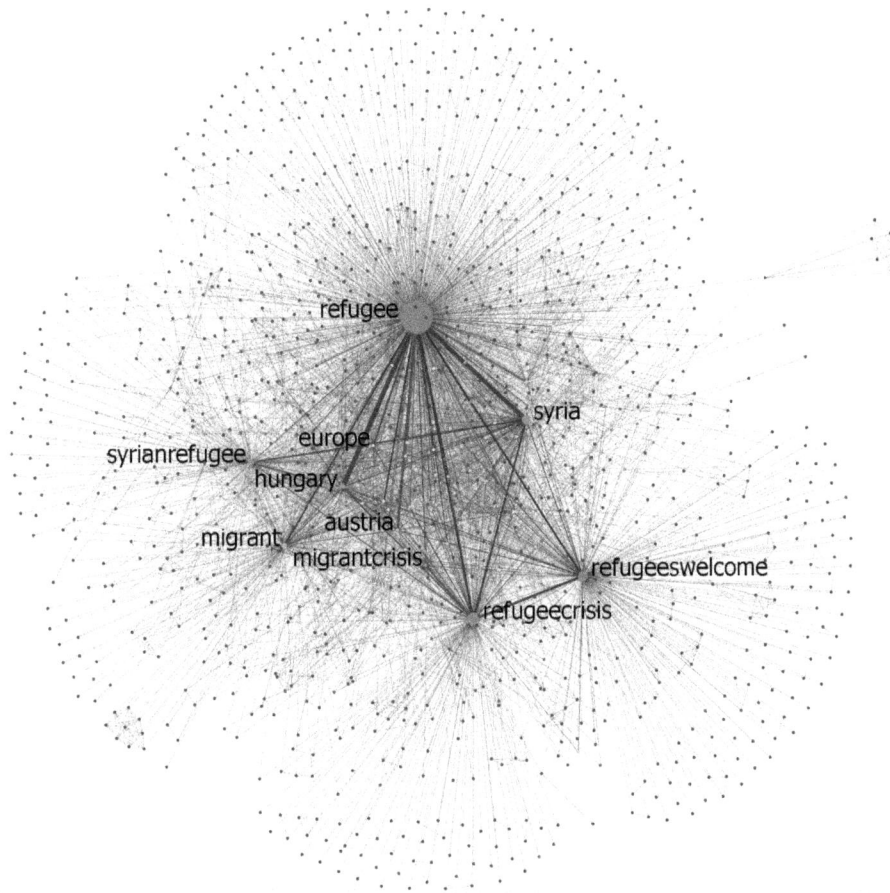

Figure 1: Hashtag co-occurence network ($N = 1335$, $E = 9508$); Nodes are sized by total degree centrality and colored by frequency; Link widths scaled by weight.

Table 2: Number of tweets using migrant, refugee or both hashtags

Type of tweet	Number of tweets
Migrant hashtags only	16,657
Refugee hashtags only	339,476
Both hashtags only	13,350

meaning higher levels of sentiment of some degree and valence. Refugee tweets bear the most neutrality, which is largely due to its incurring less negativity; the percentages in the distribution along the 1st column, where positive sentiment is 0, show overall less negativity for the non-neutral cells in Figure 3b. As argued earlier, the concept of refugee is likely to draw less controversy (i.e., negativity), which is evidenced in its sentiment distribution.

The distribution of tweets for joint hashtag use reflects the mixture of sentiment incurred by the more negative migrant discussion and the more positive refugee discussion. Interestingly, the $(+2, 0)$ cell deviates noticeably from this pattern. A greater proportion of mixed refugee-migrant hashtag tweets harbor moderate positivity,

potentially attesting to some level of recognition and sympathy to the refugee-migrant dichotomy.

In regression models of Table 3, the extent of hashtag usage impacting Positivity, Negativity, overall Sentiment, and sentiment Intensity are reported. Negativity has been rescaled to 0–4, with higher values indicating more negativity in a tweet. The Constant here refers to when both types of hashtags are used in the same tweet.

We find that tweets employing only refugee hashtags are significantly more positive and less negative than those tweets using both refugee and migrant hashtags. Naturally, the overall Sentiment of the refugee-only tweets are more significantly positive than the other two types of hashtag use. Further, those using only migrant hashtags are also significantly more negative than either types of hashtag use, although it is only slightly more negative than those tweets with both types of hashtags. These observations confer less Intensity in refugee-only related tweets and slightly more (due to higher negativity) in migrant-only related tweets. Thus, we confirm higher antipathy towards the "undeserving" migrants and/or greater sympathy towards the "deserving" refugee, as proposed in the introduction to this study and in H1.

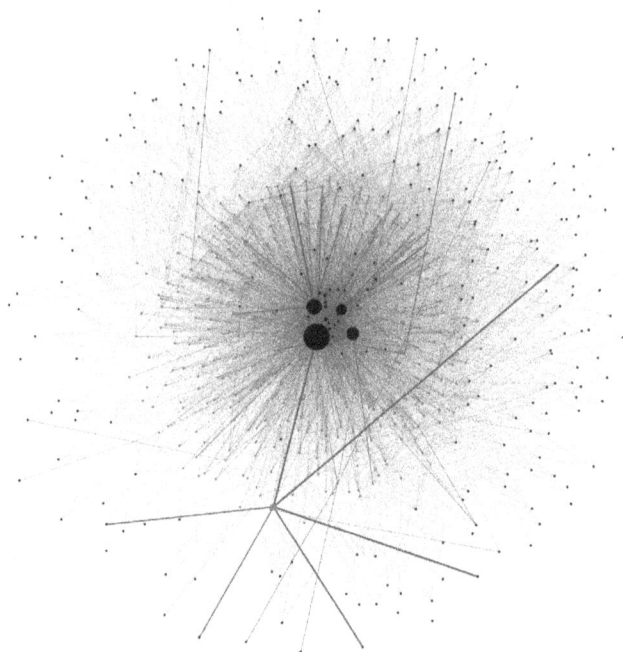

(a) Larger subnetwork (n = 568, $|E|$ = 7731)

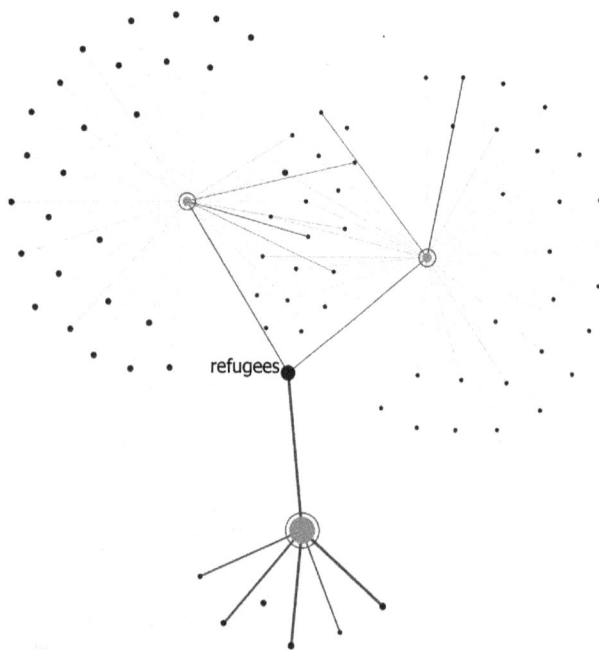

refugees

(b) Top three users (n = 82, $|E|$ = 100)

Figure 2: User-to-hashtag co-occurrence networks. Nodes are sized by total degree centrality; colors denote the type of node (users and hashtags); link widths are scaled by weight.

Negative ⌐	Positive 0	1	2	3	4
0	75.61%	6.15%	4.29%	0.17%	0.01%
-1	23.33%	4.16%	0.88%	0.05%	0.01%
-2	16.54%	2.39%	0.67%	0.08%	
-3	3.61%	1.29%	0.49%	0.01%	
-4	0.28%	0.08%			

(a) Tweets containing Migrant hashtags

Negative ⌐	Positive 0	1	2	3	4
0	46.49%	7.81%	5.27%	0.25%	0.01%
-1	17.42%	4.87%	1.69%	0.12%	0.01%
-2	8.16%	2.88%	0.72%	0.05%	
-3	2.86%	0.85%	0.28%	0.02%	
-4	0.19%	0.05%	0.02%		

(b) Tweets containing Refugee hashtags

Negative ⌐	Positive 0	1	2	3	4
0	43.32%	6.28%	9.24%	0.10%	0.01%
-1	16.86%	5.30%	0.93%		
-2	12.76%	1.08%	0.25%		
-3	1.99%	0.34%	0.15%	0.01%	
-4	0.77%	0.01%			

(c) Tweets containing both Migrant and Refugee hashtags

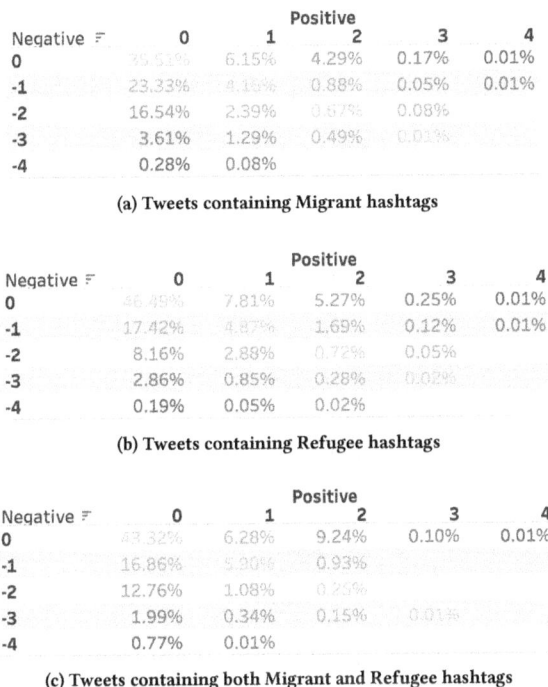

Figure 3: Sentiment percentages in tweets containing specific hashtags.

Table 3: Regression of sentiments

	Dependent variable:			
	ordered logit regression			*OLS*
	Positivity	Negativity	Sentiment	Intensity
Constant (i.e. refugee & migrant hashtags)				0.996***
				(0.011)
Migrant hashtags only	−0.0003	0.040*	−0.022	0.058***
	(0.020)	(0.017)	(0.017)	(0.008)
Refugee hashtags only	0.237***	−0.508***	0.562***	−0.136***
	(0.028)	(0.022)	(0.022)	(0.011)
Observations	369,483	369,483	369,483	369,483
R^2				0.002
Adjusted R^2				0.002
Log Likelihood	-271,640	-389,817	-518,520	
F Statistic				349*** (df = 2; 369480)

Note: $^\wedge p<0.1$; $^*p<0.05$; $^{**}p<0.01$; $^{***}p<0.001$
Constants for the ordered logit models not reported

Next in Table 4, as mentioned in the methods section, we regress popularity, influence of the user, and influence of the tweet (i.e., retweets) on sentiment measures, while controlling for the hashtag usage, in order to characterize these dependent variables and test H2 and H3. Sentiment Intensity of a tweet does not appear to have a main effect in characterizing the popularity of the tweeter. However, this is largely due to the interaction of the intensity and

the tweet type, based on hashtag use. Those that tweeted with just one kind of hashtag and with muted sentiment tended to be more popular, given the negative and significant unstandardized coefficients of −0.066 for use of refugee hashtags and −0.086 for use of migrant hashtags. This points towards less Intensity employed by popular users, particularly those focusing their discussion on either refugee or migrant. Thus, H2 is unsupported, and in fact the

Table 4: Regression of popularity and influence

	Dependent variable:		
	Popularity	Influence	Retweets
Constant	6.032***	0.921***	0.253***
	(0.041)	(0.018)	(0.036)
Intensity	0.005	−0.023^	−0.063**
	(0.028)	(0.012)	(0.024)
#Refugee hashtags only	0.126***	−0.123***	0.124***
	(0.030)	(0.013)	(0.026)
#Migrant hashtags only	0.069**	0.057***	0.010
	(0.022)	(0.010)	(0.021)
Positivity	0.007	−0.010^	0.040**
	(0.014)	(0.006)	(0.012)
Negativity	−0.006	0.004	0.060***
	(0.015)	(0.006)	(0.013)
Intensity and #Refugee	−0.066**	0.020*	−0.010
	(0.022)	(0.009)	(0.019)
Intensity and #Migrant	−0.085***	−0.038***	−0.008
	(0.017)	(0.007)	(0.016)
Observations	369,483	369,483	102,773
R^2	0.001	0.002	0.001
Adjusted R^2	0.001	0.002	0.001
F Statistic	58*** (df = 7; 369475)	85*** (df = 7; 369475)	20*** (df = 7; 102765)

Note: ^$p<0.1$; *$p<0.05$; **$p<0.01$; ***$p<0.001$

opposite effect is detected. We also observe a significant positive effect of each hashtag use, indicating that use of both hashtags is associated with less popular users. Those that are more popular tend to be more focused and slightly more polarized (as inferred through Table 3) than those who jointly employ the refugee and migrant hashtags. Meanwhile, popularity does not seem at all characterized by positivity or negativity separately in tweets.

Further, Intensity alone and interacting with the exclusive use of refugee and migrant hashtags does significantly characterize the influential quality of a user; however, the effects are mixed. The use of refugee hashtags alone appears characteristic of less influential users, but this effect is tempered by those tweeting with more emotional intensity (via the positive interaction). Conversely, the use of the migrant hashtag is characteristic of more influential users, the positive effect of which is also tempered by emotional intensity (via the negative interaction). Overall, more influential users are characterized by less emboldened statements, which also mute the extent to which the refugee and migrant hashtags distinguish the influential quality of a user. These observations provides indirect evidence for disconfirming H3, that influential tweets are associated with higher sentiment intensity. Here, we see that the influential quality of the user is associated with less sentiment intensity.

However, the influential quality of a tweet itself also lies in its spread, via retweeting. Here, we more clearly observe that the intensity of a tweet does indeed detract from its spread. Thus, we can claim that H3 is disconfirmed when considering both the influential quality of the tweet and the user.

Controlling for the negative influential effect of intensity, both positivity and negativity contribute significantly to retweeting, indicating singularly positive or negative tweets (i.e., not harboring

mixed sentiment) mitigate the reduction of influence incurred by more emotional tweets. The effects of positivity and negativity differ, with negativity's contribution being higher (0.060 > 0.040); their difference being significant ($Z = −63.90, p < .001$). Thus, we find that negativity for tweets carrying hashtags related to refugee, migrant, or both contributes more to retweeting than positivity, thereby disconfirming H4.

5 CONCLUSION

Social media platforms only exist through the continual and growing participation of millions of users, and depend on individual and collective participation and creation of content. Thus, social media responses to societal events can lead to empowered, uninhibited, and impactful opinion expression. Consequently, social media discussions can undermine public support, steer public opinion, and influence reactions to the refugee crisis or even the refugees themselves.

The debate of the refugee/migrant crisis on social media, and on Twitter in particular, has been heated since the news reports and subsequent viral sharing of an image of the death of the toddler Alan Kurdi on Sept. 4, 2015. Since then, sentiments in social media discussion have been associated with differential use of relevant labels surrounding the crisis, including 'refugee' and 'migrant' (e.g., on YouTube [25]). The biases inherent in terms such as 'refugee' and 'migrant' have led to our investigation on the impacts of these biases on important characteristics of Twitter content.

The network analysis methods employed in this paper have revealed important aspects of hashtag usage, as well as interconnections between users and hashtags they employed. Here, one of our main findings are that the Twitter debate on this crisis –

captured by our data set – has been predominantly focused on refugee-related hashtags. Also, by employing bimodal network analysis, we were able to uncover the distinct position of the most active and seemingly central user, whom upon close inspection is rendered structurally and topically marginal to the refugee crisis debate, and perhaps uninfluential.

In order to further investigate whether the sentiment of this debate was a more sympathetic — as suggested by our proposed demarcation between the "deserving" refugee versus the "undeserving" migrant, we employed sentiment and regression analysis. The assumption that tweets containing the refugee-related hashtags would carry more positivity and less negativity than migrant-related hashtags (H1) was confirmed. Additionally, the sympathetic bias for the refugee is qualified by its lesser intensity, while the controversial nature of the migrant is slightly emphasized by more intense sentiment in the corresponding tweets.

Users and their tweets have the power to influence others, as evidenced by multiple studies. However, the expectations of positivity and sentiment intensity characterizing popular and influential users and tweets were not met (H2, H3, and H4). In fact, the results showed largely opposite effects. Popular users and influential tweets are characterized by less emotional intensity and slightly less positivity when it comes to the debate on the refugee/migrant crisis. These findings may be more characteristic of controversial topics (such as the refugee/migrant crisis), whereby the public nature of tweets in conjunction with the concept of the deserving refugee mutes outrageous or hyperbolic claims and opinions.

The popularity of a user and influence of a tweet (via retweeting) appear to be more characterized by the use of refugee-only hashtags. That is, users (both popular and retweeters) have been paying more attention to the refugee-labeled perspective of the crisis and not migrant perspective. However, this observation alone does not necessarily confirm the sympathetic bias towards the refugee; that bias can be observed through the findings supporting H1, above.

The results presented in this paper prompt us to further explore the relationship between the network typology, the types of information shared by Twitter users, and the role sentiment intensity in the refugee crisis debate. Our work aims to bring a contribution towards a better understanding of how displaced people are framed and how various actors respond to them. Future directions for this research will include larger data samples with wider time horizons, allowing for comparisons across time. Also, the sentiment and socio-semantic perspectives will be merged and focused on influential Twitter users, and how they are central to the crisis debate.

The dataset analyzed in this study pertains to English language Tweets posted in the span of only two days, and thus it limits the extent to which we can generalize our findings in several ways. Firstly, many of the countries affected by the refugee/migrant crisis are not anglophone and thus the framing of the crisis in these countries may differ. As such, a more comprehensive understanding of the overall perception of this crisis would require the inclusion of tweets that employ the languages of all the countries affected by the influx of displaced people. Secondly, the relatively short time span covered by our data set (only 2 days), although yielding a considerable number of tweets, can be considered limiting in terms

of the wider social media debate on the refugee/migrant crisis. This is way future plans for our work involve the inclusion of multiple data samples, spanning longer time periods, to delve into patterns of opinion and influence and their evolution across time.

The sentiment analysis method employed in this article comes from Thelwall [40] and uses a human-coded lexicon of words and phrases specifically built to work with online social (media) data. The proposed algorithm, SentiStrength, utilizes this human-coded lexicon to identify the sentiment strength of informal text (e.g., tweets, status updates, YouTube comments). Although SentiStrength has proven relatively accurate and consistent in analyzing social media data, its results remain confined to the fixed set of words that appear in its lexicon. This may pose problems when dealing with online textual data, where new expressions and jargon constantly emerge.

As social media become more prevalent communication tools in times of crisis, studies jointly investigating discussions as well as social structures – such as this one – become increasingly valuable by offering insights into the nature and direction of these discussions, public actors, and their sentiments surrounding the crisis.

REFERENCES

[1] Christiane Amanpour and Thom Patterson. 2015. Passport linked to terrorist complicates Syrian refugee crisis. (nov 2015). http://edition.cnn.com/2015/11/15/europe/paris-attacks-passports/index.html

[2] Younggue Bae and Hongchul Lee. 2012. Sentiment analysis of twitter audiences: Measuring the positive or negative influence of popular twitterers. *Journal of the Association for Information Science and Technology* 63, 12 (2012), 2521–2535.

[3] Nikita Basov, Ju-Sung Lee, and Artem Antoniuk. 2016. Social Networks and Construction of Culture: A Socio-Semantic Analysis of Art Groups. In *Proceedings of the International Workshop on Complex Networks and their Applications*. Springer, 785–796.

[4] Stephen P Borgatti and Martin G Everett. 1997. Network analysis of 2-mode data. *Social networks* 19, 3 (1997), 243–269.

[5] Stephen P. Borgatti, Ajay Mehra, Daniel J. Brass, and Giuseppe Labianca. 2009. Network Analysis in the Social Sciences. *Science* 323, 5916 (2009), 892–895. https://doi.org/10.1126/science.1165821

[6] Benny Bornfeld, Sheizaf Rafaeli, and Daphne Ruth Raban. 2014. Electronic Word-of-mouth Spread in Twitter as a Function of the Message Sentiment. In *Proceedings of The Fourth International Conference on Social Eco-Informatics*. IARIA.

[7] Dennis Chong and J James N. Druckman. 2007. Framing theory. *Annual Review of Political Science* 10 (2007), 103–126.

[8] Nicholas A. Diakopoulos and David A. Shamma. 2010. Characterizing debate performance via aggregated twitter sentiment. In *Proceedings of the SIGCHI Conference on Human Factors in Computing Systems*. ACM, 1195–1198.

[9] Jana Diesner, Amirhossein Aleyasen, Jinseok Kim, Shubhanshu Mishra, and Kiumars Soltani. 2013. Using socio-semantic network analysis for assessing the impact of documentaries. In *Proceedings of theWorkshop of Information in Networks*. New York, 1–5.

[10] James N Druckman. 2011. What's it all about? Framing in political science. In *Perspectives on framing*, G Keren (Ed.). Psychology Press, New York, 279–302.

[11] Robert M Entman. 1993. Framing: Toward clarification of a fractured paradigm. *Journal of Communication* 43, 4 (1993), 50–58. doi:10.1111/j.1460-2466.1993.tb01304.x.

[12] Marguerite Feitlowitz. 2011. *A lexicon of terror: Argentina and the legacies of torture, revised and updated with a new epilogue*. Oxford University Press, New York.

[13] Linton C Freeman. 1979. Centrality in social networks conceptual clarification. *Social Networks* 1, 3 (1979), 215–239.

[14] Erving Goffman. 1974. *Frame analysis: An essay on the organization of experience*. Harvard University Press, New York.

[15] Alfonso Gonzales. 2013. *Reform without justice: Latino migrant politics and the homeland security state*. Oxford University Press, New York.

[16] Kirk Hallahan. 1999. Seven Models of Framing: Implications for Public Relations. *Journal of Public Relations Research* 11, 3 (1999), 205–242. https://doi.org/doi:10.1207/s1532754xjprr1103_02

[17] Iina Hellsten and Loet Leydesdorff. 2017. Automated Analysis of Topic-Actor Networks on Twitter: New approach to the analysis of socio-semantic networks. (2017), 1–31. arXiv:1711.08387 http://arxiv.org/abs/1711.08387

[18] Geraldine Henderson, Dawn Iacobucci, and Bobby J Calder. 1998. Brand diagnostics: mapping branding effects using consumer associative networks. *European Journal of Operational Research* 111, 1998 (1998), 306–327.

[19] Seth M Holmes. 2011. Structural vulnerability and hierarchies of ethnicity and citizenship on the farm. *Medical Anthropology* 30, 4 (2011), 425–449.

[20] Seth M. Holmes and Heide Castañeda. 2016. Representing the "European refugee crisis" in Germany and beyond: Deservingness and difference, life and death. *American Ethnologist* 43, 1 (2016), 12–24. https://doi.org/10.1111/amet.12259

[21] Justin Huggler. 2016. German mayor beaten up by mob after expressing support for asylum seekers. (sep 2016). http://www.telegraph.co.uk/news/2016/09/30/german-mayor-beaten-up-by-mob-after-expressing-support-for-asylu/

[22] Dawn Iacobucci, Geraldine Henderson, Alberto Marcati, and Jennifer Chang. 1996. Network analyses of brand switching behavior. *International Journal of Research in Marketing* 13 (1996), 415–429.

[23] S Iyengar. 1987. Television News and Citizens' Explanations of National Affairs. *American Political Science Review* 81 (1987), 815–831. doi:10.2307/1962678. Issue 3.

[24] Silia Klepp. 2013. Europeanisation Spot. An Ethnography of the Frontex Nautilus II Mission. *Journal of Peace and Conflict Research* 2, 1 (2013), 36–69.

[25] Ju-Sung Lee and Adina Nerghes. 2017. Labels and sentiment in social media: On the role of perceived agency in online discussions of the refugee crisis. In *Proceedings of the 8th International Conference on Social Media & Society.* ACM, New York, 1–10. https://doi.org/10.1145/3097286.3097300

[26] Joel H Levine. 1979. Joint-space analysis of "pick-any" data: analysis of choices from an unconstrained set of alternatives. *Psychometrika* 44, 1 (1979), 85–92.

[27] Brendan O'Connor, Ramnath Balasubramanyan, Bryan R Routledge, and Noah A Smith. 2010. From tweets to polls: Linking text sentiment to public opinion time series.. In *Proceedings of the Fourth International AAAI Conference on Weblogs and Social Media.* AAAI, 122–129.

[28] Tore Opsahl. 2013. Triadic closure in two-mode networks: Redefining the global and local clustering coefficients. *Social Networks* 35, 2 (2013), 159–167.

[29] Zhongdang Pan and Gerald M Kosicki. 1993. Framing analysis: An approach to news discourse. *Political Communication* 10, 1 (1993), 55–75. https://doi.org/10.1080/10584609.1993.9962963

[30] Chang Sup Park and Barbara K Kaye. 2017. The tweet goes on: Interconnection of Twitter opinion leadership, network size, and civic engagement. *Computers in Human Behavior* 69 (2017), 174–180.

[31] Vanessa Peña-Araya, Mauricio Quezada, Barbara Poblete, and Denis Parra. 2017. Gaining historical and international relations insights from social media: spatiotemporal real-world news analysis using Twitter. *EPJ Data Science* (2017), 25. https://doi.org/10.1140/epjds/s13688-017-0122-8

[32] James W Pennebaker, Martha E Francis, and Roger J Booth. 2001. *Linguistic inquiry and word count: LIWC 2001.* Technical Report 2001. Austin, TX. http://www.LIWC.net

[33] Meg J Rohan. 2000. A rose by any name? The values construct. *Personality and Social Psychology Review* 4, 3 (2000), 255–277.

[34] Vala Ali Rohani, Shahid Shayaa, and Ghazaleh Babanejaddehaki. 2017. How Social Media Influencers Govern Sentiment Territory. *International Journal of Applied Evolutionary Computation (IJAEC)* 8, 1 (2017), 49–60.

[35] Camille Roth. 2013. Socio-semantic frameworks. *Advances in Complex Systems* 16, 04n05 (2013), 1350013. https://doi.org/10.1142/S0219525913500136

[36] Camille Roth and Jean-Philippe Cointet. 2010. Social and semantic coevolution in knowledge networks. *Social Networks* 32, 1 (2010), 16–29.

[37] Johanne Saint-Charles and Pierre Mongeau. 2018. Social influence and discourse similarity networks in workgroups. *Social Networks* 52 (2018), 228–237. https://doi.org/10.1016/j.socnet.2017.09.001

[38] Stefan Stieglitz and Linh Dang-Xuan. 2011. The Role of Sentiment in Information Propagation on Twitter–An Empirical Analysis of Affective Dimensions in Political Tweets. In *Proceedings of the 22nd Australasian Conference on Information Systems (ACIS), Sydney (Australia). Retrieved from: http://aisel. aisnet. org/acis,* Vol. 38.

[39] Texifier. 2018. (2018). https://texifter.com

[40] Mike Thelwall. 2013. Heart and soul: Sentiment strength detection in the social web with SentiStrength. *Proceedings of the CyberEmotions* (2013), 1–14.

[41] Andranik Tumasjan, Timm Oliver Sprenger, Philipp G Sandner, and Isabell M Welpe. 2010. Predicting elections with twitter: What 140 characters reveal about political sentiment. In *Proceedings of the Fourth International AAAI Conference on Weblogs and Social Media,* Vol. 10. AAAI, 178–185.

[42] Stanley Wasserman and Katherine Faust. 1994. *Social network analysis: Methods and applications.* Vol. 24. Cambridge University Press, Cambridge.

[43] Kristin Yarris and Heide Castaneda. 2014. Ethnographic insights on displacement, migration, and deservingness in contemporary global contexts. *International Migration* 53 (2014), 644–69. Issue 3.

Ego-Centric Analysis of Supportive Networks

André Costa, Roberto Nalon, Wagner Meira Jr. and Adriano Veloso

Computer Science Department
Universidade Federal de Minas Gerais
{ahsilva,nalon,meira,adrianov}@dcc.ufmg.br

ABSTRACT

The way we think about ourselves has a direct influence on our emotional state and our mood. Consequently by changing the way we think we can positively influence our mood and how we respond to situations. Many studies have shown a robust relationship in which emotional support from others positively affects how we think about ourselves. Emotional support can come from many sources, such as family, friends, neighbors, and more recently we have seen the emergence of emotional support networks. In such networks users share their moods and receive emotional support from others, and the objective is to nurture supportive relationships and build a social support network. In this paper we present an ego-centric study of supportive networks to show how user mood evolves as the user ego-network is expanded. We considered different types of ego-networks induced by gender and psychological disorders. We found that the way user mood evolves strongly depends on the type of connections that are created. The behavior of users that show mood improvement is very distinct from the behavior of users that do not show mood improvement.

CCS CONCEPTS

• **Computing methodologies** → **Machine learning**;

KEYWORDS

Social Networks; Mood; Ego-Centric Analysis

ACM Reference Format:
André Costa, Roberto Nalon, Wagner Meira Jr. and Adriano Veloso. 2018. Ego-Centric Analysis of Supportive Networks. In *WebSci '18: 10th ACM Conference on Web Science, May 27–30, 2018, Amsterdam, Netherlands*. ACM, New York, NY, USA, 5 pages. https://doi.org/10.1145/3201064.3201099

1 INTRODUCTION

Emotional support is an important factor for dealing with life's difficulties. Loneliness has been associated with a wide variety of health problems including high blood pressure, diminished immunity, cardiovascular disease and cognitive decline [27]. In fact, low levels of social support have even been linked to increased risk of death from cardiovascular disease, infectious diseases and cancer [33]. Other studies have demonstrated that having a network of supportive relationships contributes to psychological and mental well-being [28, 30].

ACM acknowledges that this contribution was authored or co-authored by an employee, contractor or affiliate of a national government. As such, the Government retains a nonexclusive, royalty-free right to publish or reproduce this article, or to allow others to do so, for Government purposes only.
WebSci '18, May 27–30, 2018, Amsterdam, Netherlands
© 2018 Association for Computing Machinery.
ACM ISBN 978-1-4503-5563-6/18/05...$15.00
https://doi.org/10.1145/3201064.3201099

Supportive networks – groups comprising an individual's family, friends and peers who are able to support her or him psychologically and emotionally – have evolved steadily over the last decades. One evolution direction is the development and maturation of sites such as Mood247,[1] MoodScope,[2] and MoodPanda,[3] in which people share their moods on a daily-basis, and "hear" the stories of other people who have gone through similar experiences.

In this paper we aim to understand the mechanisms by which the mood of an individual evolves as she expands her supportive network. Specific questions we want to answer include:

- How does mood change over time as a function of the amount of emotional support received?
- How does mood change over time as a function of the connections acquired by the individual?
- What are the main characteristics of supporters that make them more effective for the sake of mood improvement?

We propose an approach to answer these questions, apply our approach to a large dataset, and present significant results showing clear trends with real implications. Our analysis is centered on individuals, and, thus, instead of focusing on understanding the statistical properties of the network [2, 8, 9, 23, 26], we consider the network as an overlapping community of "egocentric networks" (or ego-networks for short). Our rationale is to focus on individuals as ego-networks, so that we can capture how they manage their supportive networks formed by their immediate neighbors (a.k.a., alters) and associated interconnections.

An ego who is connected to alters that are not directly connected to each other has opportunities to mediate between them. Intuitively, the absence of a connection between two alters enables the ego to act as a broker among the alters [16]. We examine how individuals construct and tune their ego-networks in order to consciously or unconsciously acquire new connections. We consider affiliations such as gender and psychological disorder (e.g., Attention Deficit Hyperactivity Disorder, Borderline Personality, Obsessive-Compulsive Disorder, and Post-traumatic Stress Disorder) in order to build the ego-networks.

Contributions: Our main contributions are as follows:

- We designed approaches based on ego-centric networks to evaluate how the mood of an individual changes over time as she acquires new connections into her supportive network.
- We collected and analyzed the MoodPanda online supportive network. We study fourteen-month data from this network: 10,045 users contributed with more than 96,000 mood posts and more than 350,000 supportive replies.

---

[1] www.mood247.com
[2] www.moodscope.com
[3] www.moodpanda.com

- We performed a set of empirical analyses, and the results show interesting trends such as: mood is usually improved when emotional support is provided by the opposite gender, and people with borderline personality disorder should not receive emotional support from other people with borderline personality disorder.

2 RELATED WORK

Many studies have shown how emotional and social support from others affect how we think about ourselves and how our mood and emotions can influence other people in a social network.

Emotional Contagion. The tendency for two individuals to emotionally converge is usually named Emotional Contagion [17]. Such expression conveys the notion that people tend to synchronize their emotions with those who are close. This convergence depends on many factors such as mood-regulation norms and social interdependence [3]. For instance, Fowler and Christakis [15] monitored about 4,800 individuals during a period of 20 years, from 1983 to 2003. They showed that happiness can be spread from person to person (friends, friends' friends and so on, up to 3 degrees of separation). They also observed that groups of happy people formed over time depend not only on the tendency for people to associate with similar individuals (homophily) but also on the spread of happiness. On the other hand, Neumann and Strack [28] showed that such emotional convergence does not require people to be close (e.g. friends). They recruited 30 students and randomly asked them to listen to a philosophical text recited in a happy, neutral or sad voice, and concluded that the exposure to emotional expression led to a congruent mood in the respective listeners.

In a more comprehensive approach, DeLongis et al. [14] found correlations between daily stress, health problems, and mood changes, analyzing questionnaires and interviews, applied to 75 married couple in a study conducted over a period of six months. They observed that people with low self-esteem and low social support (e.g., who does not have support from family and friends) were more susceptible to have psychological problems and stress than those with high self-esteem and high social support. In a similar fashion, Hill et al. [18] investigated the mood spread in a adolescent social network and found that having sufficient friends with healthy mood can double the chances of recovering from depression. More recently, Araújo et al. [1] studied another kind of contagion in social networks. They showed that the level of physical activity of a person can be influenced by other people activities in her social network. Finally, [24, 31] found that users stress state is closely related to that of his/her friends in social media. The authors performed a systematically study of the correlation between users' stress states and their social interactions. They defined a set of stress-related attributes, and then propose a model to leverage tweet content and social interaction information for stress detection.

Social Sharing of Emotions. People living emotional events tend to recall and discuss the event with other people in order to share their experiences. This process of reactivating the emotion is named Social Sharing of Emotions [30]. With the emergence of social media channels (e.g., Twitter, Facebook) it becomes increasingly easier

for people to share their emotions with others. In this scenario, the social sharing of emotions has a even broader aspect. People can more than just recount a emotional experience they have gone through, they can share a emotional event in real time impacting other people. Many studies have investigated the relationship between sharing of emotions in social platforms and individual's social network structure [7, 19, 20, 25]. They observed that emotional content expressed in such platforms can explain the mood variance of users and their interaction between has a strong influence on it. On the other hand, Kramer et al. [22] presented evidence that emotions like happiness, sadness, depression, shared in massive social networks can be transferred from person to person, even if they are not connected. In other words, a given message, posted by a certain author, with sad content may cause commotion in several people, not only in the author's friends.

Other studies observed the emotional contagion through the social sharing of emotions in social media. For instance, Kramer [21] investigated large-scale emotional contagion on Facebook. In his work, he showed that emotional contagion may happen through emotion content written by users and the spreading of this content via interactions across the social network. In a similar approach, Coviello et al. [10] measured the effect of exogenous variables (e.g. rainfall) on individuals expression and the respective influence on their friends. More recently, Bazarova et al. [4] analyzed how social media properties affect how people share emotions in Facebook. They considered two different channels: public and private. They found that in the public channel (e.g. timeline), users tend to share more messages with positive emotions whilst in the private channel (e.g. private messages), users usually share text with negative emotions. Finally, Park et al. [29] report that a user's behavior and her activities on Facebook are related with her depressive state.

3 DATASET

In this section, we describe key features of the MoodPanda service and the way we gathered data. Then, we present a characterization study in order to better understand the data.

3.1 Platform Description

MoodPanda is an interactive mood diary where users can update and track their moods on a daily-basis. User's self-reported moods are given as free-text accompanied by a numerical value of how they feel on a scale from 1 to 10 (best possible mood). Moreover, users are allowed to view their mood history over the time and use this information in therapy sessions. On MoodPanda users manage their ego-networks through *hugs* and supportive replies. That is, a user who *hugs* another user is interested in following her mood diary in order to help her with supportive messages.

3.2 Data Collection Process

MoodPanda provides an Application Programming Interface (API)[4] to collect and gather data. There were 10,045 active MoodPanda users on September 2014, and these users will be the subject of our analysis. Thus, we only collected data regarding these users (i.e., users that entered the system after September 2014 were not included as egos in the dataset). We focused on these 10,045 users

---

[4]http://www.moodpanda.com/api/

because the dataset will be used to analyze how the mood of these users evolved from September 2014 to October 2015. Also, from September 2014 to October 2015, we collected 84,843 edges between the 10,045 user profiles, 96,022 mood messages (with ratings), and 352,421 *hugs*/supportive replies.

3.3 Data Characterization

We were able to collect a varied level of details about each user, depending on the kind of information they provide in their profiles and diaries. In our dataset, almost all users (99.97%) provided name and gender, and 85.39% of all users provided their age. Female users (75.79%) and people aging from 20 to 29 years (33.52%) constitute the majority of the users, and 41.50% of all users were involved in therapy sessions and reported a specific psychological disorder. The four most frequently reported disorders are Attention Deficit Hyperactivity Disorder (17.35%), Port-Traumatic Stress Disorder (15.28%), Borderline Personality Disorder (12.02%), and Obsessive-Compulsive Disorder (10.88%). Mentions to these disorders were obtained using entity extraction approaches [11, 12].

Considering the number of posts, the dataset contains 96,022 mood messages and 352,421 supportive messages. Of these, 2,916 users wrote at least one mood message, while 887 users wrote at least one supportive message. Table 1 presents some descriptive statistics about the number of messages.

Table 1: Descriptive statistics of the MoodPanda dataset.

Valid profiles	10,045
Mood Messages	96,022
Supportive messages	352,421
Messages per day	214.81 (±87.89)
Messages per user	9.56 (±43.89)
Words per message	16.17 (±11.78)
Supportive messages per message	6.53 (±5.52)
Words per supportive messages	2.97 (±6.41)
Supportive messages per user	2.18 (±31.52)

4 METHODOLOGY

Ego-networks consist of a focal node (i.e., "ego"), the nodes to whom ego is directly connected to (i.e., "alters" or friends), and the social ties, if any, that exist among the alters. This is a realistic representation of how a user typically views the network, because a user can hardly perceive the structure of the entire network. However, a user can easily identify her supportive links as well as (most of the) connections that exist among alters. Alter-alter ties are also included in the structure, making it possible to judge the role of ego in the network. We built the ego-networks of MoodPanda users considering the following affiliation attributes:

- **Gender** – Users' genders are fixed as male and female.
- **Psychological disorder**: Users may provide this information in their diaries, and we focused on the four most frequently reported disorders: Attention Deficit Hyperactivity Disorder (ADHD), Borderline Personality Disorder (BPD), Obsessive-Compulsive Disorder (OCD), and Posttraumatic Stress Disorder (PTSD).

Roles in the Network. Most social structures are characterized by the existence of dense clusters and structural holes (i.e., a gap between two individuals with complementary resources or characteristics) [5]. In this case, "brokerage" is defined as the activity performed by individuals located at the intersection of distinct clusters, acting as brokers who can control the flow between disconnected clusters [6]. When two otherwise disconnected clusters are connected through a broker, a structural hole is filled. We will investigate such brokerage opportunities from the perspective of ego-networks (i.e., when the broker is the ego node).

Specifically, in order to determine the brokerage roles played by a given ego, we examine every open triad in which the ego lies on the directed path between two alters. Therefore, the ego may have many opportunities to act as a broker. For each of the triads where the ego is a broker, we examine the group affiliation of each of the three individuals involved. We considered four possible roles:

- **Coordinator** – All individuals are member of the same affiliation group.
- **Consultant** – The two alters are members of the same group, but the ego is not a member of that group. Hence, ego "consults" the group.
- **Gatekeeper** – The ego and the outgoing alter are members of the same group, but the incoming alter is not a member of that group. Hence, ego controls access of outsiders to the group.
- **Representative** – The ego and the incoming alter are members of the same group, but the outgoing alter is not a member of that group. Hence, ego acts as the contact point.

In order to estimate the brokerage intensity associated with each ego, we count the number of open triads corresponding to each role (i.e., coordinator, consultant, gatekeeper, and representative), and normalize this number based on the same number of open triads obtained by chance [13, 32]. Thus, the Brokerage Intensity (*BI*) for an arbitrary ego is defined as:

$$BI(x) = \frac{|T_x|}{|T|},$$

where T_x is the set containing just open triads of role x, x is one of the four brokerage roles, and T is a set of the same size of T_x containing open triads obtained by chance. The group membership is defined based on characteristics (or affiliation) associated with its participants. Hence, in case of gender, nodes of the same gender type belong to the same group.

5 EGO-CENTRIC ANALYSIS

We now apply the ego-centric analysis to identify which roles are frequently played by ego nodes in the MoodPanda network. Further, we calculate the mood change for each user based on the slope obtained through a simple linear regression applied to the mood time series. Then, we mapped the coefficients to groups with the same range in order to categorize those who present decline, constant behavior, and progress in their moods.

5.1 Analysis by Gender

Figure 1 shows brokerage intensities, taking into account egos' gender (female, and male). It shows that *coordinator* and *consultant*

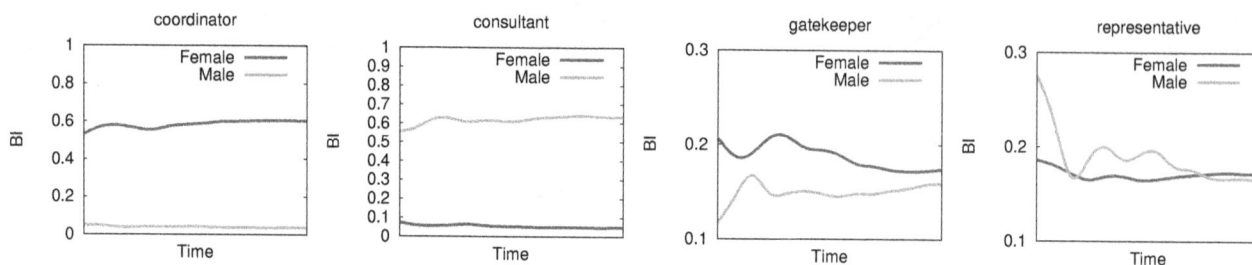

Figure 1: Brokerage intensities of the ego nodes: Gender.

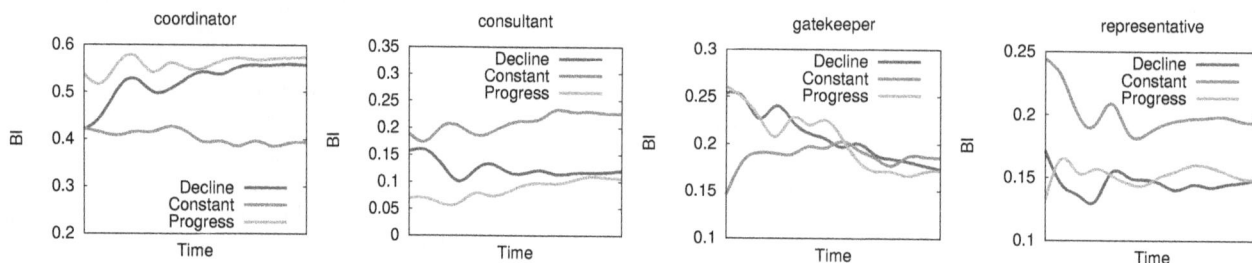

Figure 2: Mood change as a function of brokerage intensities: Gender.

roles are the most intensively performed activities. Considering *coordinator* role, we can see that *female egos* often seek to interact with *female* alters (who belong to the same gender group), while *male* egos seldom interact with each other. On the other hand, *male* egos frequently act as a *consultant*: in this case, a given *male* ego is mediating a relation between two *female* alters.

Mood Change. Figure 2 shows brokerage intensities for ego nodes with *large decline*, *constant* behavior, and *large progress* in mood, taking into account egos' gender. We find that *coordinator* is the most intensively performed activity. Moreover, from September, 2014 to October, 2015, *coordinator* role often increased for ego nodes with *large decline* and *large progress* – the egos seek to interact, over the months, with alters of the same gender –, while decreased for ego nodes with *constant* mood – the egos seek to interact with alters of different gender. In other words, people who have *large decline/progress* in mood tend to interact with people of the same gender, while those who have *constant* mood tend to interact with people of different gender. *Consultant* and *representative* roles are activities usually performed by ego nodes with *constant* mood, while *gatekeeper* role is performed by all ego nodes (*large decline*, *constant* behavior, and *large progress* in mood).

By inspecting our data, we found that male users present a slightly better mood than female users. On the other hand, female users show a slightly better mood improvement over time.

5.2 Analysis by Psychological Disorder

The last experiment is concerned with evaluating the behavior of the users based on personality disorder. As it can be seen in Figure 3, most of the egos and alters with the same psychological disorder rarely interact with each other. Nevertheless, the activity of *coordination* is more common to observe in users with OCD. Moreover, OCD egos also act as *representative*.

The *coordination* role (interactions and connections between ego and alters from the same disorder group) is performed with little intensity by PTSD egos, rarely by ADHD egos, and never by BPD egos. A similar network behavior happens with *representative* role.

Mood Change. Figure 4 shows that egos who act as *coordinator* or *representative* tend to have *large progress* in their mood. As described above, such brokerage roles are frequently performed by users with OCD, followed by PTSD. By inspecting our data, we found that users with OCD and PTSD present an improvement in their average mood over time, while ADHD shows a decline and BPD a large oscillation in mood (typical behavior of people with such disorder).

6 CONCLUDING REMARKS

In supportive networks, users share their moods and feelings, writing their diaries and receiving emotional support from others. The focus of this paper was to design approaches, based on ego-centric networks, to observe and evaluate the behavior of such networks over time by applying ego-centric analysis. Before making this analysis, we considered three user attributes – age, gender, and personality disorder – for the construction of the ego-networks. We were able to evaluate how the mood of an individual changes with the acquisition of new network connections over time. We collected and analyzed data from an online supportive network, and we performed an extensive set of experiments. We found that elderly individuals act as *consultant*, giving support and help for young and adult individuals. Moreover, we shown that individuals with borderline personality disorder (BPD) have a large oscillation in mood, what influences their behavior on the network. We have also shown that individuals with OCD commonly interact with each other, as opposed to what happens with other personality disorders (ADHD, BPD, and PTSD).

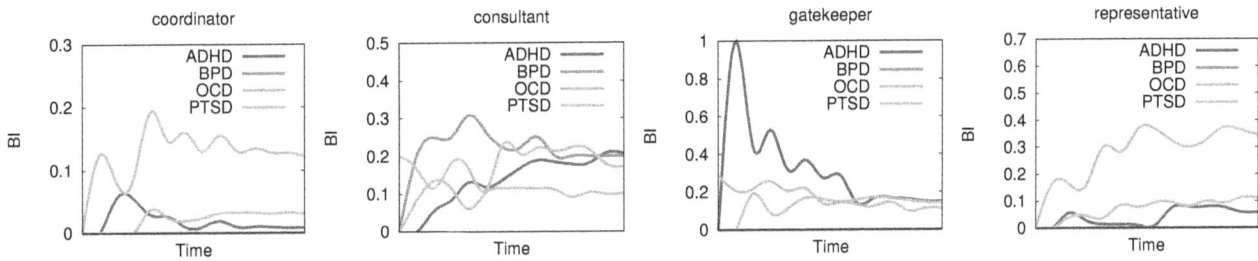

Figure 3: Brokerage intensities of the ego nodes: Disorder.

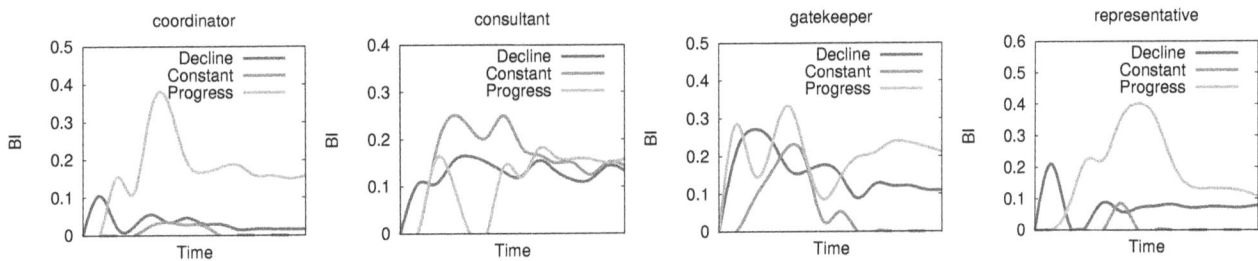

Figure 4: Mood change as a function of brokerage intensities: Disorder.

ACKNOWLEDGMENTS

This work was partially funded by projects InWeb (grant MCT/CNPq 573871/2008-6) and MASWeb (grant FAPEMIG/PRONEX APQ-01400-14), and by the authors individual grants from CNPq and FAPEMIG. AV thanks the support received from Kunumi.

REFERENCES

[1] E. Araújo, A. Tran, J. Mollee, and M. Klein. 2015. Analysis and Evaluation of Social Contagion of Physical Activity in a Group of Young Adults. In *ASE BigData & SocialInformatics 2015*. Article 31, 6 pages.

[2] L. Backstrom, P. Boldi, M. Rosa, J. Ugander, and S. Vigna. 2011. Four Degrees of Separation. *CoRR* abs/1111.4570 (2011).

[3] Caroline A. Bartel and Richard Saavedra. 2000. The Collective Construction of Work Group Moods. *Administrative Science Quarterly* 45 (2000), 197–231.

[4] N. Bazarova, Y. Choi, V. Sosik, D. Cosley, and J. Whitlock. 2015. Social Sharing of Emotions on Facebook: Channel Differences, Satisfaction, and Replies. In *CSCW*. 154–164.

[5] R. Burt. 1995. *Structural holes: The social structure of competition*. Russel Sage Foundation.

[6] Ronald Burt. 2005. *Brokerage and Closure: An Introduction to Social Capital*. Oxford University Press.

[7] D. Centola. 2010. The Spread of Behavior in an Online Social Network Experiment. *Science* 329 (2010), 1194–1197.

[8] Meeyoung Cha, Hamed Haddadi, Fabricio Benevenuto, and Krishna P. Gummadi. 2010. Measuring User Influence in Twitter: The Million Follower Fallacy. In *ICWSM*.

[9] G. Comarela, M. Crovella, V. Almeida, and F. Benevenuto. 2012. Understanding factors that affect response rates in twitter. In *HT*. 123–132.

[10] L. Coviello, Y. Sohn, A. Kramer, C. Marlow, M. Franceschetti, N. Christakis, and J. Fowler. 2014. Detecting Emotional Contagion in Massive Social Networks. *PLoS ONE* 9, 3 (2014), e90315.

[11] A. Davis, A. Veloso, A. da Silva, A. Laender, and W. Meira Jr. 2012. Named Entity Disambiguation in Streaming Data. In *ACL*. 815–824.

[12] D. Marinho de Oliveira, A. Laender, A. Veloso, and A. da Silva. 2013. FS-NER: a lightweight filter-stream approach to named entity recognition on twitter data. In *WWW*. 597–604.

[13] R. de Oliveira Jr., A. Veloso, A. Pereira, W. Meira Jr., R. Ferreira, and S. Parthasarathy. 2014. Economically-efficient sentiment stream analysis. In *ACM SIGIR*. 637–646.

[14] A. DeLongis, S. Folkman, and R. Lazarus. 1988. The impact of daily stress on health and mood: psychological and social resources as mediators. *Journal of personality and social psychology* 54, 3 (1988), 486.

[15] J. Fowler and N. Christakis. 2008. Dynamic spread of happiness in a large social network: longitudinal analysis over 20 years in the Framingham Heart Study. *Bmj* 337 (2008), a2338.

[16] R. Gould and R. Fernandez. 1989. tructures of Mediation: A Formal Approach to Brokerage in Transaction Networks. *Sociological Methodology* 19 (1989), 89–126.

[17] E. Hatfield, J. Cacioppo, and R. Rapson. 1993. Emotional Contagion. *Current Directions in Psychological Science* 2 (1993), 96–100.

[18] E. M. Hill, F. E. Griffiths, and T. House. 2015. Spreading of healthy mood in adolescent social networks. *Proc. Royal Society B* 282 (2015).

[19] F. Kivran-Swaine, S. Brody, N. Diakopoulos, and M. Naaman. 2012. Of Joy and Gender: Emotional Expression in Online Social Networks. In *CSCW*. 139–142.

[20] F. Kivran-Swaine and M. Naaman. 2011. Network Properties and Social Sharing of Emotions in Social Awareness Streams. In *CSCW*. 379–382.

[21] A. Kramer. 2012. The Spread of Emotion via Facebook. In *ACM SIGCHI*. 767–770.

[22] A. Kramer, J. Guillory, and J. Hancock. 2014. Experimental evidence of massive-scale emotional contagion through social networks. *Proceedings of the National Academy of Sciences* 111, 24 (2014), 8788–8790.

[23] J. Leskovec, L. Backstrom, R. Kumar, and A. Tomkins. 2008. Microscopic evolution of social networks. In *KDD*. 462–470.

[24] H. Lin, J. Jia, L. Nie, G. Shen, and T. Chua. 2016. What Does Social Media Say about Your Stress?. In *IJCAI*. 3775–3781.

[25] H. Lin and L. Qiu. 2012. Sharing Emotion on Facebook: Network Size, Density, and Individual Motivation. In *ACM SIGCHI*. 2573–2578.

[26] G. Magno, G. Comarela, D. Saez-Trumper, M. Cha, and V. Almeida. 2012. New Kid on the Block: Exploring the Google+ Social Graph. In *IMC*. 159–170.

[27] C. Masi, H. Chen, L. Hawkley, and J. Cacioppo. 2011. A meta-analysis of interventions to reduce loneliness. *Personality and Social Psychology Review* 15, 3 (2011), 219–266.

[28] R. Neumann and F. Strack. 2000. Mood Contagion: The Automatic Transfer of Mood Between Persons. *Journal of Personality and Social Psychology* 79 (2000), 211–223.

[29] S. Park, I. Kim, S. Won Lee, J. Yoo, B. Jeong, and M. Cha. 2015. Manifestation of Depression and Loneliness on Social Networks: A Case Study of Young Adults on Facebook. In *CSCW*. 557–570.

[30] B. Rimé, B. Mesquita, S. Boca, and P. Philippot. 1991. Beyond the emotional event: Six studies on the social sharing of emotion. *Cognition and Emotion* 5 (1991), 435–465.

[31] G. Shen, J. Jia, L. Nie, F. Feng, C. Zhang, T. Hu, T. Chua, and W. Zhu. 2017. Depression Detection via Harvesting Social Media: A Multimodal Dictionary Learning Solution. In *IJCAI*. 3838–3844.

[32] R. Silva, M. Gonçalves, and A. Veloso. 2011. Rule-Based Active Sampling for Learning to Rank. In *ECML/PKDD*. 240–255.

[33] B. Uchino. 2009. Understanding the links between social support and physical health. *Perspectives on Psychological Science* 4, 3 (2009), 236–255.

Everybody Thinks Online Participation is Great – for Somebody Else

A Qualitative and Quantitative Analysis of Perceptions and Expectations of Online Participation in the Green Party Germany

Gefion Thuermer[1]   Silke Roth[1]   Kieron O'Hara[2]   Steffen Staab[2]

[1] Social Sciences   [2] Electronics and Computer Science
University of Southampton, UK
{gefion.thuermer, silke.roth, K.M.O'Hara, S.R.Staab} @soton.ac.uk

ABSTRACT

Based on a case study from the Green Party Germany, we discuss the expectations and potential effects of the introduction of new online participation opportunities. These methods are often used in hopes of drawing in a wider group of participants, but existing literature on digital inequality suggests that this is unlikely to happen. Applying a mixed methods approach, we investigate how likely the expectations related to these new opportunities are to be met. We used semi-structure interviews to draw out what effects party members think online participation will have. We then conducted a survey asking members about their plans to change their behaviour. Comparing expectations to prospective behavioural changes, we find that the high hopes of both party members and leaders – to draw in those members who currently do not engage – are likely to be disappointed. Members who are better off, better educated, and already more active, will likely benefit more than those the party hopes to engage. We argue that this is linked to the prevailing digital divide, and that those who are targeted for more participation need to be more actively addressed to achieve broader participation.

ACM Reference Format:
Gefion Thuermer, Silke Roth, Kieron O'Hara and Steffen Staab 2018. Everybody Thinks Online Participation is Great – for Somebody Else. In WebSci'18: 10th ACM Conference on Web Science, May 27–30, 2018, Amsterdam, Netherlands. ACM, New York, NY, USA, 10 pages. https://doi.org/10.1145/3201064.3201069

KEYWORDS

Digital divide; inclusion; mobilisation; non-use; participation; political parties; reinforcement

1 INTRODUCTION

Online Participation in politics is a widely researched field, but most of that research focuses on citizen participation at various levels, from local to regional to states or nation states

[1]–[4]. We are interested in how members of political parties participate in party-internal decision-making processes. The processes that parties employ to develop positions and manifestos are important, because – given sufficient success in elections – these positions may eventually lead to new legislation that governs society. Engagement in political parties is one important route for citizens to not only influence the politics of their country or place of residence, but also to learn about the democratic process, take part in public discourse [5], and improve their own efficacy [6].

Using digital technology like the internet in participation processes has raised high hopes for a broadening of democratic engagement, particularly to groups that are historically not engaged [7], [8]. Although some positive effects have been identified, particularly for young people and soft forms of engagement [4], [9], [10], there is plenty of evidence against a broadening of participation, and for continued influence of social and socio-economic inequalities on the internet [11]–[13].

This paper investigates how likely it is that the expectations related to the introduction of new online participation tools within a political party will be met. After an overview of the digital divide literature and the theory discussed in this paper (Section 2), we introduce the organisation we are studying (Section 3), and explain the reasons for and details of our mixed methods approach (Section 4). Based on interview and survey data, we discuss whether the expectations of individuals for online participation are likely to be met (Section 5). We find that they are not, and that the expectations held by party members and leaders – that online participation will benefit others – are in practice still overshadowed by the digital divide (Section 6).

2 RELATED WORK

In this section we discuss the theoretical foundations of the digital divide (Section 2.1), and give an overview of mobilisation and reinforcement theory, which will be used to discuss the effect of online participation methods on practical participation levels (Section 2.2).

2.1 Digital Divide

Access to the internet today is largely treated as a matter of course in most post-industrial societies, including Germany. Although there are some structurally weak areas, for example in Eastern Germany or Lower Bavaria, where access is limited, 92% of the population of Germany are now connected to broadband [14], and access is no longer the key division. However, while access seems to become less important, other aspects have become more important. Even if people are online, the benefits they derive from using the internet differ with socio-demographic factors such as gender, age, income and education [15]. A further consideration is the skills necessary to use the technology and derive benefit from it [16]. Inequalities that exist offline have been shown to be perpetuated in the use of the internet [17]. Thus, those who are already disadvantaged offline may stay disadvantaged when they use the internet.

With regards to political participation online in Germany, the strongest explanatory factor for differences in online use is habit [12]: Only those who are already used to using the internet for a variety of activities will also adopt it for political participation. Age is important in this context, as habits form with age, and those who were older when the internet was widely adopted will be less likely to change already existing habits – though they do adopt it for some activities [18]. Benefits for those who use the internet for political participation are mostly in the area of political information and discussion, and the group that benefits most, dubbed 'digital citizens', are males in their mid-twenties, with university education, no children and low income [12]. In terms of gender as well as education, this is not surprising, as it reflects the typical party member in Germany [19], as well as the overall lower participation and representation of women in politics [20]. Age however is distinctly different: Among party members, people under 35 are underrepresented [19].

These differences are highly problematic for democratic processes: Democratic ideals generally assume some form of equal opportunity to participate. Dahl describes democracy as the "process of making collective and binding decisions" [21, p. 5], which are based on equality: If all members of a group are equal, then they all ought to have the same influence on decisions that affect them. This applies to democratic republics as well as to democratic parties and their internal processes. As it stands, participation is not equal regardless of whether it is conducted offline or online, and the question is not whether democratic participation can be achieved online or offline, but whether adding online elements to existing offline processes can *improve* democratic participation.

2.2 Mobilisation & Reinforcement

Mobilization and reinforcement theories can be used to describe potential effects of online participation. On the one hand, mobilization theory [7] argues that with new online participation methods, more people can be drawn in, leading to broader participation. Reinforcement theory [22], [23] on the other hand states that new online participation methods will be picked up by those who are already active, thus increasing – or reinforcing – the influence they already have. We would like to add two further dimensions to this discussion: Replacement [24], [25] and Non-Use [26].

Online participation may simply replace existing offline methods, without effect on who participates, or with which intensity: Things that were previously done offline are now done online, by the same people. This effect has been described in some variations and with different terms (such as 'normalisation' [11]), but we consider 'replacement' to be the

most accurate description, as we refer specifically to one type of media *replacing* another, without other side-effects.

Lastly, there is a risk, especially for large organisations, that online participation methods are introduced, and not used at all. Non-use has been considered with regards to internet access [26], [27], but with regards to political participation it is a new and still underdeveloped topic [11], [28]. We did find in literature as well as our own preliminary results that non-use – members not using tools that have been implemented – can be a problem because these tools cost considerable amounts of resources to implement. Whether new tools are adopted by party members appears to be related to the way new platforms are introduced. This was demonstrated during the introduction of the Green Parties' internal knowledge management platform 'Wurzelwerk' in 2009, which was perceived as so unintuitive by users [29], [30], that even an eventual relaunch could not save its reputation – an experience the party is not keen to repeat.

3 CASE STUDY: GREEN PARTY GERMANY

Parties in Germany are governed by legislation, such as the Basic Law, which stipulates that they 'shall participate in the formation of the political will of the people' [31, Para. 21.1] and must follow democratic procedures; and the Political Parties Act [32], which stipulates that they must have a certain structure, with a general or delegate assembly at national level as the highest decision-making body, and equal voting rights for all members. This requirement to make decisions democratically and with equal rights is implemented differently in different parties [33].

In this section we will introduce the Green Party Germany as the case study we are focussing on, argue why they are a particularly good example of an organisation that attempts to introduce online participation, and give an outline of the problem the party is trying to address.

3.1 History

The Green Party Germany was founded in 1980, and has roots in the women's, peace, and environmental social movements [34]. It has been represented in the German Bundestag since 1981. The party has had a strong grass-roots orientation from the very beginning, with processes designed to limit the power of spokespeople and MPs. After the German reunification, the Western Green Party merged with the Eastern 'Bündnis 90', an alliance with similar roots and intentions, which already formed a parliamentary group with the Eastern German Green Party. After the party failed to be elected into the national parliament in 1990, they softened some of the old rules that were supposed to maintain strong grass-roots [34], and formally developed wings for different ideologies. These are the 'Realos' (now *Reformer*), who favour pragmatism and government responsibility, and the 'Fundis', (now *Linke*), who favour close adherence to the parties ideals [35]. The party re-entered the German Bundestag in 1994, and formed part of the government coalition between 1998 and 2005.

Despite all of these developments, the party remains focussed on grass-roots participation. There are still regulations that prevent members from holding mandates and executive board positions at the same time, and a ban on members of government simultaneously holding positions in the party above the local level [36]. Members of the Green Party continue to have a stronger position in the parties' decision-making processes than in other major German parties [37]. They are typically highly educated, with 58% holding university degrees, and 37% working as public servants – both the highest proportion in all major German parties, and well above average in the population [38].

In contrast to other parties, decisions in the Green Party are largely made bottom-up, with quotas to ensure equal participation of women, as this is a founding ideal. The party leadership has a strong interest in allowing and encouraging participation in decision-making processes by the whole member base. This ideal includes allowing members to participate online, and consequently, tackling the digital divide for their internal processes. If as many members as possible should participate, they need to be enabled to do this, and none should be excluded based on gender, skills, or resources [39].

For all this, the Green Party is a 'most likely case' [40]: Given their commitment to participation and equality, if online participation can work in any political party, it should work here. If it fails here, this can give important indications to challenges that need to be addressed, wherever online participation is introduced.

3.2 Problem Description

Given the persistent digital divide in Germany, using the internet in party-internal processes poses a challenge: If these processes are not perceived to be as inclusive and accessible as all the other (offline) processes the party uses, that might reduce the legitimacy of their outcomes.

The party leadership wants to actively use the internet in order to draw more members into participation. A special task force [41] has developed a set of new online participation processes that the party voted to introduce at the national delegate assembly in November 2016: The 'Mitgliederbefragung' (*Befragung*), an online survey, which is sent to all members at least annually, and aims to bring their opinions into discussion processes in the parties bodies and task forces; and a 'Mitgliederbegehren' (*Begehren*), a new process similar to a petition, by which 250 members can collectively 'demand' something from the executive board. This could be a specific action, or the discussion of a topic. The *Befragung* has been used since 2016, and the *Begehren* is due to launch in 2018. Both processes are web-based, with alternative offline routes. For example, members can request a paper copy to fill in the *Befragung*, or send a signed fax to the parties' headquarters to support a *Begehren*.

The Green Party wants to achieve mobilisation and prevent reinforcement; they want to include the excluded. As discussed above, the literature on the digital divide suggests that mobilisation is unlikely to happen without specific measures to motivate currently inactive members. The inherent inequalities both in political participation, and use of the internet, as well as in benefits derived from that use, are at odds with the democratic ideal of equality in the Green Party. However, the potential

benefits of internet use – speed, ease of use, low cost, and the potential to reach members that were previously not involved – make its use worthwhile. The party wants to actively tackle the deterministic 'it cannot work', and find a way to overcome these inherent inequalities, so they can use the internet in a way that does not contravene their ideals.

4 METHODOLOGY[1]

To identify how members perceive online participation, and what potential it has to mobilize more members to participate, a mixed methods approach is taken, consisting of interviews, observations, and a survey. We will show, based on qualitative, semi-structured interviews and participant observations, what effects party members *think* online participation will have, and who they believe will benefit. We will then compare these assumptions to a dataset of survey responses among the whole member base, which gives an indication as to how members *plan* to change their own behaviour with these new online participation methods.

4.1 Observations & Interviews

Observations were conducted during the general delegate assembly of the Green Party in Münster in November 2016, where the above described key decisions about the future of online participation were made. We focused on the debates about these decisions at the assembly, as well as following the discussion on the parties' online platform for proposals, where members exchanged arguments for and against them.

Table 1: **Interview Participants**

Age	Gender	Position	Place of Residence	Wing
18-25	m	1	City	R
26-35	f	2	City	R
26-35	f	2	Suburb	-
26-35	m	2	City	-
36-45	f	3	City	-
36-45	m	3	Rural	L
46-55	m	2	Suburb	L
46-55	f	1	City	L
56-65	m	2	Rural	-
56-65	m	1	City	L
56-65	f	3	City	-

N = 11; Position: 1=Local Level, 2= State Level 3=Above State Level; Wing: R=Reformer, L=Left

Semi-structured interviews were conducted with participants of these debates, both online and during the assembly. Questions revolved around how they perceived democracy and participation within the party, they current participation, and whether, how and why the party should or should not use online participation methods. A total of 11 interviews were conducted. A brief overview of participants is shown in Table 1.

---

[1] All data collection and analysis was done by the first author

The observations and interviews were recorded, transcribed, and used in a qualitative content analysis [42], [43]. The data was coded inductively, to generate a set of criteria that were relevant to the participants.

4.2 Survey

The Green Party regularly conducts online surveys among their member base – the *Befragung* they introduced at the assembly in Münster formalised this practice. We were given the opportunity to add some questions about participation to one of these surveys in April 2017. All party members were invited to participate in the survey. Emails were sent to everyone who had an email address registered in the party's members' database (about 84%), and letters to those who did not. The latter were invited to respond to the survey online, rather than the survey being posted directly. All members could request a paper copy of the survey – an option which was not used at all in this instance. The survey returned just under 3500 responses, which equals a response rate of about 6%.

The parties' survey focussed on the upcoming election campaign, with our questions, based on findings from the interviews and observations, circling around the current and potential future use of online participation methods. While the qualitative data focussed on general expectations and assumptions around online participation, the survey asked explicitly how members plan to change their own behaviour through these tools.

The majority of questions focussed on how members already participate (*Channel*), what type of activity they engage in (*Activity*), and how they plan to use the newly introduced online methods. We further asked them to order a set of statements about their democratic preferences, which consisted of two pairs of statements:

- All members can participate in votes
  All members can participate in discussions
- All members can participate equally
  All members can participate as much as possible

These were turned into binary variables for the preferred participation *Type* (votes/discussions) and *Intensity* (equally/as much as). Alongside demographic information, we also asked about their position in the party, as well as their position on the political spectrum.[2]

The survey data was analysed in two stages: First an exploratory factor analysis was conducted, then binary logistic regression models were generated.

4.2.1 Factor Analysis

Factor Analysis is used to reduce the amount of variables in the analysis, and to identify underlying factors that the data did not include explicitly [44]. The factor analysis was conducted in SPSS using principal axis factoring. Only one factor was generated (Cronbach Alpha: 0.861). It included both *Activities* and *Channels* for participation that members use, as well as their *Position* within the party. We use this factor as an indicator for participants' level of 'Institutional Activity'. The higher the factor score, the more members are engaged in institutional activities within the party. The individual factor loadings are shown in Table 2.

Table 2: **Factor Loadings for Institutional Activity**

Variable	Loading
Activity: Discussed proposals	0.791
Activity: Supported proposals	0.745
Activity: Attended assembly as delegate	0.724
Activity: Worked in party bodies	0.692
Channel: Supra-local Meetings	0.673
Position	0.651
Activity: Discussed relevant topics	0.624
Activity: Wrote proposals	0.566
Channel: Local Meetings	0.455
Channel: Non-localised Meetings	0.411
Channel: Social Media	0.356

A second factor, indicating the 'Propensity to Participate Online', based mainly on *Age* and *Internet Use*, was discarded as too unreliable for use, with a Cronbach's Alpha value of just 0.381.

Due to the purpose of factor analysis – generating a new variable that summarises existing data – we consider this analysis to be part of the method, and do not provide detailed analysis of the results. More detail is given in the interpretation of the logistic regression models which use the factor (Section 5.2.2).

4.2.2 Logistic Regression Models

Binary logistic regression is the a suitable analysis for our survey data, since it allows prediction of non-linear dependent variables [44].

Two models were generated to identify what variables best predict members' behaviour. The dependent variables are based on participants' response "I will participate more" to the survey question "How do you think [the new participation methods] will affect your own participation?" We turned these into binary responses: 'I will participate more through *Befragung*': *Yes/No* and 'I will participate more through *Begehren*': *Yes/No*. The models, summarised in Table 3: identify which variables are significant for predictions of an anticipated increase in participation through either tool.

5 FINDINGS & DISCUSSION

Based on the above described data, we found that what members expect to happen and how they expect to act personally is very different, and that the expected benefits of online participation do not appear to be likely to materialise. We will now in turn discuss the results of the qualitative data – what members expect – and the survey data – what members expect to do.

5.1 What members expect to happen

Participants of the assembly and interviews generally had a very positive attitude towards online participation, having experienced it as enabling themselves as well as others. They

---

[2] The full survey questions and response options can be found online at https://zenodo.org/record/1171109

generally assume that online participation methods are currently both enabling and inhibiting for different groups. The plans that members were aware of were perceived as improvements, and the expectations were that the new processes would be more enabling than constraining. However, most participants did neither consider these processes as particularly useful for themselves, nor did they see them as hindering their own participation - although all of them were already actively using online platforms, such as mailing lists or social media, to participate. *They were enthusiastic on behalf of others, but indifferent for themselves.*

We found many assumptions about what online participation already does within the party, with regards to tools or processes that are already in use, such as email or *Wurzelwerk*. These were neither perceived as enabling nor inhibiting the participants themselves, though they assumed considerable effects in both directions for other members. For example, a member living in the suburb of a large industrial metropolis believed that online participation would help those in rural areas:

> *"With emails, it is a lot easier to find fifty or sixty people to support a proposal, than it was to find twenty in the past. And that is also the case for rural areas, as most of them should have internet by now."*

However, a member who lived in a rural area made the experience that processes are more of a barrier in the countryside, regardless of whether they are online or offline, simply because there are fewer members, and with a smaller network, support is harder to find. Even if it were easier to recruit supporters online, because their local network is limited, so is their opportunity to reach out to others. This shows how offline inequalities are perpetuated online [17].

Experience of members sometimes confirmed (or led to) expectations for other members. For example, a member of the parties' youth organisation 'Young Greens' described how the *Befragung* was accessible, and thus user friendly for older members:

> *I think the surveys were very accessible, so that everyone, including old people, could participate. It stated clearly to ,now click this link in the next line.'"*

This is also reflected in the view of a state executive board member, who described how online participation can make it easier for older members to participate:

> *"Online participation is one way to improve inclusion. For example, we have older people who are less mobile who could participate through this route."*

It is important to note that none of these persons considered themselves 'old', 'digitally illiterate' or 'immobile' – they described what they thought members who were in these categories would experience. This is a theme that is visible through all interviews and observations: There are many expectations of what online participation will do to enable or inhibit 'others'' participation – groups that the members who made these comments do not belong to themselves. Some of these groups are likely to not have strong online habits, such as the elderly, women, parents, or persons with disabilities [12],

[18]. It seems unlikely that their habits would change simply because new tools are available.

This effect is particularly interesting where it happens in opposing directions. This is the case for example between the party leadership and grass-roots: A grass-roots member was convinced that online methods would be beneficial for the party leadership:

> *"There are networks where you can communicate in line with the statutes, where the executive board can network with the state boards, where only selectively, people have access based on their roles within the party."*

On the other hand, the executive board is very interested in introducing new and more online participation methods because of the conviction that it will make it easier for grass-roots members to participate:

> *"We want to develop more tools so that everyone can discuss online and offline, all members can participate who currently cannot get involved through the classic party structure." [Comment of an executive board member at the assembly in Münster]*

The same effect applies to factors like age, where older members think that online participation methods are particularly relevant to the next generation:

> *"I am not a person with a deficit in participation. (...) There's others, in the local branches, for example teenagers, or especially teenagers (...) There's a requirement. I don't have that requirement."*

Participants without care responsibilities also expect that online participation will help those who have these responsibilities:

> *„Our assemblies always happen at children's' bedtime. It sounds trivial, but highly specifically excludes parents. For polls, discussions and so on, online participation would be really great."*

And lastly, participants with plenty of time expect that online methods will help others who have limited availability due to their jobs:

> *"[Online Participation] is really good because it allows easy access independent of people's life and circumstances. For example, shift workers who work at night and can then go online and participate when they have the time."*

These differences are particularly important, because they show how *everyone thinks that online participation will be great – for somebody else.* Although all participants were already actively using online platforms, these were taken for granted and not considered in any detail, while the expectations for future benefits for those who are not in this situation were very high indeed. While participants also saw the risk of potential exclusion through online processes, the expected benefits outweighed the possible constraint, which was also considered to be dealt with by offering alternative routes (such as sending letters instead of emails).

Table 3: Binary logistic regression models of increased participation through new online participation methods

	N	Model 1: Befragung						Model 2: Begehren					
		Odds Ratio	S.E.	CI-LB	CI-UB	p	sig	Odds Ratio	S.E.	CI-LB	CI-UB	p	sig
Constant		1.782	0.267			0.031	*	0.037	0.460			0.000	**
Preferred Participation Type (Vote)	1411	1.446	0.086	1.221	1.712	0.000	**	1.428	0.094	1.187	1.718	0.000	**
Preferred Participation Intensity (Equal)	1751	0.762	0.093	0.635	0.915	0.004	**	0.794	0.099	0.654	0.965	0.020	*
Institutional Activity	2584	0.569	0.050	0.515	0.627	0.000	**	0.760	0.066	0.668	0.866	0.000	**
Participation through Online Channels	1196	1.354	0.095	1.123	1.632	0.001	**	1.275	0.101	1.045	1.555	0.017	*
Gender (Female)	733	0.805	0.095	0.667	0.969	0.022	*	0.845	0.105	0.688	1.039	0.110	
Difference between Party and own Position	2584	1.081	0.031	1.017	1.149	0.013	*	0.889	0.024	0.484	0.933	0.000	**
Participant Rating of own Position	2584	0.913	0.036	0.851	0.979	0.011	*						
Age Group (70+)	130					0.000	**						
Below 18	15	1.096	1.007	0.152	7.888	0.927							
18-29	373	3.198	0.226	2.052	4.981	0.000	**						
30-39	446	2.781	0.216	1.819	4.247	0.000	**						
40-49	459	1.757	0.210	1.163	2.652	0.007	**						
50-59	662	1.638	0.202	1.103	2.434	0.014	*						
60-69	499	1.172	0.204	0.785	1.748	0.437							
Highest Education Qualification (PhD)	257					0.027	*						
Still at school	19	1.790	0.959	0.273	11.731	0.544							
Secondary School (Volks-/Hauptschule)	42	0.427	0.357	0.212	0.861	0.017	*						
GCSE (Realschule)	185	0.587	0.212	0.387	0.890	0.012	*						
A-Levels (Fach-/Hochschulreife)	460	0.747	0.180	0.525	1.062	0.104							
University degree or national diploma	1621	0.654	0.152	0.485	0.881	0.005	**						
Internet Use (Every week)	37											0.052	
Every Day	1666							2.384	0.441	1.005	5.654	0.049	*
All the Time	881							2.720	0.447	1.134	6.527	0.025	*
Interaction: Institutional Activity & Gender	2584							1.256	0.113	1.006	1.570	0.044	*
Increased participation through Befragung	1598							11.322	0.122	8.921	14.368	0.000	**

Data from all members survey, N = 2584. Nagelkerke's R Square (Befragung) = 0.139, (Begehren) = 0.321.

* Significant at 0.05; ** Significant at 0.

5.2 What members expect to do

The statistical analysis of our survey data suggests that the likelihood for members to increase their own participation through the new online methods varies, following at least some of the expected lines of the digital divide – age, education, gender [15], [45] – and not the expectations of the 'others' discussed above. Both models share a set of significant predictors, with some other predictors being significant for only one of the models.

5.2.1 Demographics.

Participants *Age* and *Education* were only significant predictors for anticipated increased participation through the *Befragung*. The younger members are, the more likely they are to state that they will increase their participation, with members between 18 and 29 being more than three times as likely to state this than members above 70. Members between 40 and 59 years are still twice as likely to say they will participate more. This is in line with the digital divide literature, which suggests that online participation methods are primarily used by the younger generations [45].

This age difference also shows in education, where members who are still at school are 1.8 times as likely to say they will participate more than members with PhDs. There is a clear direction in the type of degree members have: the higher the degree, the more likely they are to state that they will participate more online, with (among members who have completed school) those with PhDs being the most likely to say they will increase their participation. Members with lower qualifications (Secondary School / GCSE / lower university degrees) are between 0.4 and 0.7 times as likely to say they will participate more as those with PhDs. This is again in line with the digital divide, as higher education indicates both more activity and benefit online, as well as more political engagement [15], [16].

Members who use the internet every day are more than twice as likely to say they will increase their participation through the *Begehren* as those who only use it on a weekly basis. However, there are very few participants who use the internet that rarely. While this is in line with current internet usage rates in broader society [46], the sample might be biased towards members who are already active online, e.g. those who use the internet less are also less likely to have participated in the survey. In addition to members already using the internet to participate in party processes, this can nevertheless be seen as further evidence that those who are already familiar with the internet are more likely to use it to their own advantage, and as such supports the reinforcement theory [12], [23].

Women are only 0.8 times as likely to say they will participate more with the *Befragung* as men. This corresponds to the digital divide literature, where women are still less likely to use the internet and engage in political activity online [45], as well as women's overall lower participation and representation in politics [20]. Moreover, it also corresponds to participation in the actual survey – which was part of a *Befragung* – where only 30% of respondents were women.

While there are certainly other factors that would justify distinction (e.g. race, class), gender is particularly important in the Green Party, as gender equality is one of their founding principles. Given these roots, and members' high expectations for gender equality, this result is both surprising and disturbing. The party has solid processes to ensure equal participation offline – such as quotas for all elections, or speaker lists that prioritise women – but no such process for online participation methods. Women are not specifically encouraged to engage online, which makes it little surprising that the gender divide that still prevails in society at large [45] is reflected in their internal participation. However, literature suggests that their participation might increase over time [13] – this will again be monitored in future surveys.

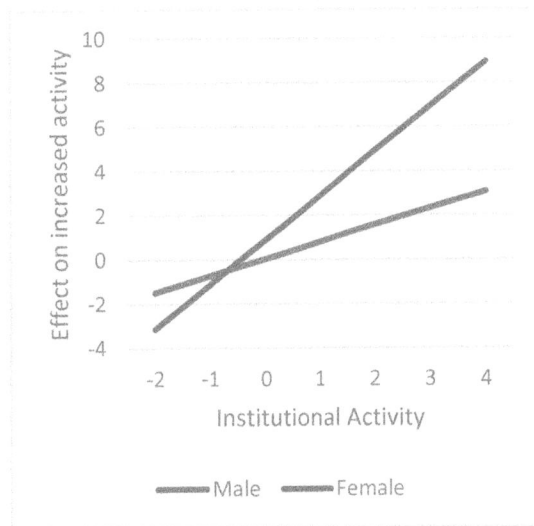

Figure 1: Interaction between Institutional Activity and Gender

There is however an interaction effect between institutional activity and gender on anticipated increased activity through the *Begehren*: Less active women are less likely to say they will increase their participation than comparably active men, while more active women are more likely to say they will increase their participation than comparably active men. Potentially being active increases women's confidence to participate more in other areas as well; or those who are already more confident become more active, to the same effect. Which of these is the cause does not matter as much as the effect in itself: Once women are active, they do participate, and they intend to do more.

The place of residence, whether members live in West or East Germany, and particularly whether they live in cities or the countryside, had no significant influence on their participation intention with either of the tools. This points to either a bias in the sample (those who would not participate more might not have participated in the survey), or there simply is no difference between residence areas, which would be unexpected given the digital divide literature [12]. Whether one or the other is the case might be explored in a future survey which includes a group of members who are not communicating with the party online. For now we can say that among this sample, where members live does not make a difference to whether they are planning to participate more online or not.

5.2.2   Current Participation

Whether members already participate through online channels is a positive predictor for anticipated increased participation through both tools, with members who are already using online tools being 1.4 times as likely to anticipate an increase in participation through the *Befragung* as those who do not, and 1.3 times through the *Begehren*. This is little surprising in itself. After all, why would members who are already online *not* participate? However, this does point to the risk the party is taking by assuming that online participation will mobilise currently inactive members: If those who are already engaging with the party online are more likely to increase their participation than those who are not, then these groups' opinions will likely be reinforced [23].

Institutional Activity – the factor score described above – is a negative predictor for both the *Befragung* and *Begehren*: Members who are more active in the parties' established institutions are 0.6 times as likely to say they will increase their participation through the *Befragung* and 0.8 times as likely to do so through the *Begehren* as less active members. This is likely due to the fact that with them already being very active, there simply is not much room for them for an *increase* in activity, while for less active members, the new methods allow them to do more with a low threshold. The results for the *Begehren* in particular are consistent with the interviews: Those who already have positions have more direct connections with the executive board and thus have less need for the *Begehren* – they can simply ask the board directly, and expect a response. This points to a likely mobilisation effect, with new members being drawn into active participation [7].

5.2.3   Political Orientation

Political orientation measured on a 1-11 scale of political orientation (Left (1) to Right (11)) is commonly used by German political research institute Infratest dimap. This is loosely associated with the party wings [35], with the *Linke* positioning left of the *Reformer*, but neither being expected on the right (>6) of the spectrum [47]. We used members' own position, and the difference between where members positioned themselves and the party on the same spectrum.

Members who position themselves further right on the political spectrum are 0.9 times as likely to say they will increase their own participation through the *Befragung* as those further to the left. However, if they position themselves right of where they see the party, this effect reverses, and they are instead 1.1 times as likely to say they will participate more. This is different for the *Begehren*: Members who position themselves further right than the party are 0.9 times as likely to say they will increase their participation through as those who position themselves the other way around. This change of direction is the only distinct difference between the two models, and there does not appear to be a substantial reason for that. The link between political orientation and online activity will be a focus in future analysis.

5.2.4   Participation Preferences

The preferred participation 'Type' and 'Intensity' are about equally strong predictors for both models, with members preferring participation through votes being 1.4 times as likely to say they would increase their participation through either tool as members who prefer discussions.

This is also a theme that arose during the interviews: The *Befragung* is seen as a good way for the party leadership to gather large scale feedback from the grass-roots, but some members see a danger that there will not be sufficient discussion before these surveys take place. Members who prefer votes plan to add their voice to the type of engagement that bears most similarity to a vote, while those preferring discussions do not.

Members who favour equal over most possible participation on the other hand are only 0.8 times as likely to say they will increase their participation through the new online tools as those with the opposite preference. Members who think everyone should participate as much as possible are more likely to say they will increase their participation through both methods. This is also consistent with the qualitative data: Where members were sceptical about online systems, this largely referred to the systems' performance against the parties' ideal of equality.

5.2.5   Anticipated participation through Befragung

The strongest predictor for an anticipated increase in participation through the *Begehren* is whether members intend to participate more through the *Befragung*. Those who do are 11.3 times as likely to say they will participate more through the *Begehren*, too. This can likely be ascribed to a general willingness to engage with online participation methods. Since both tools are new and have no equivalent (offline) processes, it seems sensible that members assume they will either use both or none.

This might however point to a lack of understanding of the purpose of the tools: The *Befragung* will be conducted by the executive board, and as such the process (though not the result) very much functions top-down: the board decides about the topic, the questions, the timeline, and all members need to do is respond when they get an email invitation. The federal executive board has an obligation, embedded in the initial decision to introduce the *Befragung*, to hold them regularly. This looks very different for the *Begehren*, which is very much a bottom-up process. It will not become active unless the grass-roots make it happen. *Begehren* can be started or supported by all members, with the expectation that it will be a tool for the grass-roots to bring topics onto the agenda of the executive board. However, if there are no members willing to start the process and collect supporters, there is no automatism by which members *can* engage in this way.

5.2.6   Differences between Befragung and Begehren

The model for increased participation through the *Begehren* looks very different compared to the one for the *Befragung*. The digital divide does *not* show here: Neither age nor gender or education were significant predictors for an anticipated increase in participation. Instead, those who are online more regularly, and already participate through online channels, are more likely to say they will participate more in the *Begehren*. These results are likely due to the fact that members – neither at grass roots nor at leadership level – know how the *Begehren* can or will be used. It does not relate to any process they are familiar with, and therefore they are unsure what to expect.

6   CONCLUSIONS

The new online participation tools that the Green Party introduces raise hopes of including more members in participation processes. Party members of all ranks believe that with the introduction of new online participation methods there should be more people willing to engage, more things to do, a broader group of members involved, and those who are currently not engaging will have another opportunity to become involved. At the same time, existing participation online appears to be so seamless that current advantages are hardly recognised.

Both hopes and expectations are that the new online tools will have a mobilising effects. Our results indicate that this is unlikely. Even though members expect all kinds of benefits, especially for their less-privileged peers, the *Befragung* appears to be unable to overcome the social and digital divide: Members who are better off, better educated, and already more active, will benefit more than those the party hopes to engage. Reinforcement is a more likely result of the introduction of the *Befragung* than mobilisation.

This is different for the *Begehren*, which does not reflect the digital or participation divide – neither gender nor age or education are significant predictors for an anticipated increase in participation. This offers cause for hope, as the *Begehren* might indeed be a tool that *overcomes* existing divides, both digital and participation, and even between the party 'elite' and grass-roots. The fact that active women intend to become even more active online with the *Begehren* is particularly promising, because this also means that if the party can manage to encourage women to participate *either online or offline*, they are likely to be mobilised further.

The literature on participation and the digital divide tells us that there are still clear distinctions in terms of who participates, and to which effect: Social class, available resources and time, gender and education all play a role in determining how likely a person is to be active, both politically and on the internet. All of this is likely to occur with the *Befragung* in the Green Party. This is problematic for the party, as – though the goal of increasing participation may be met – the goal of holding participation *equal* will likely not be. Even if more participation happens, it will be 'more of the same*.

In practical terms, there might be room to re-think some of the processes in order to change this, for example by introducing quotas or such for a balance in gender, or by specifically addressing and supporting those members that are currently underrepresented. For example, the party could develop methods to increase women's participation online that correspond to the processes they use offline. They could also offer explicit training across their member base, to increase their skills and thus confidence to participate.

7 FUTURE WORK

The major limitation of this paper is that the data, and the predicted variables – an anticipated increase in participation through different new online participation methods – is only based on what members *say* they *will do*. This will not necessarily happen. The next step will therefore be to actually measure the change in participation across the introduction of these new online participation tools, and see whether what members say they will do will actually come to pass.

ACKNOWLEDGEMENTS

This research was funded by the EPSRC Centre for Doctoral Training in Web Science Innovation, EP/L016117/1. Funding for fieldwork was supplemented by the Green Party Germany.

We are grateful to our interview partners, and to all those who responded to our survey, for their participation in this study. We would like to thank the Green Party Germany, especially general secretary Michael Kellner, and head of members' participation Thomas Künstler, for their extensive and continued support of this project.

None of the authors are members of the party, and the party had no influence on the analysis and conclusions drawn.

REFERENCES

[1] G. C. N. Smith, *Democratic innovations: designing institutions for citizen participation*. Cambridge University Press, 2009.

[2] P. Aragón *et al.*, "When a Movement becomes a party," 2013.

[3] A. Kolleck, "Kommunale Online-Beteiligung: Stand und Herausforderungen kommunaler Bürgerbeteiligung.," *Der Bürger im Staat*, vol. 64, no. 4, pp. 238–245, 2014.

[4] M. Cantijoch, D. Cutts, and R. Gibson, "Moving Slowly up the Ladder of Political Engagement: A 'Spill-over' Model of Internet Participation," *Br. J. Polit. Int. Relations*, vol. 18, no. 1, pp. 26–48, Feb. 2015.

[5] A. Michels and L. De Graaf, "Examining Citizen Participation: Local Participatory Policy Making and Democracy," *Local Gov. Stud.*, vol. 36, no. 4, pp. 477–491, 2010.

[6] M. E. Morrell, "Deliberation, democratic decision-making and internal political efficacy," *Polit. Behav.*, vol. 27, no. 1, pp. 49–69, 2005.

[7] P. Norris, *Digital Divide: Civic Engagement, Information Poverty, and the Internet Worldwide*. Cambridge: Cambridge Universiy Press, 2001.

[8] R. Gibson, W. Lusoli, A. Römmele, and S. J. Ward, "Introduction: representative democracy and the Internet," *Electron. Democr. mobilisation, Organ. Particip. via new ICTs*, vol. 33, pp. 1–16, 2004.

[9] S. Boulianne, "Does Internet Use Affect Engagement? A Meta-Analysis of Research," *Polit. Commun.*, vol. 26, no. 2, pp. 193–211, 2009.

[10] S. Vissers, M. Hooghe, D. Stolle, and V.-A. Maheo, "The Impact of Mobilization Media on Off-Line and Online Participation: Are Mobilization Effects Medium-Specific?," *Soc. Sci. Comput. Rev.*, vol. 30, no. 2, pp. 152–169, 2012.

[11] K. Gerl, S. Marschall, and N. Wilker, "Does the Internet Encourage Political Participation? Use of an Online Platform by Members of a German Political Party," *Policy and Internet*, vol. 10, no. 1, pp. 87–118, 2018.

[12] G. Vowe, "Digital Citizens und Schweigende Mehrheit: Wie verändert sich die politische Beteiligung der Bürger durch das Internet? Ergebnisse einer kommunikationswissenschaftlichen Langzeitstudie," in *Internet und Partizipation*, no. Mpfv 2011, Wiesbaden: Springer Fachmedien Wiesbaden, 2014, pp. 25–52.

[13] A. Kerr and J. Waddington, "E-Communications: An Aspect of Union Renewal or Merely Doing Things Electronically?," *Br. J. Ind. Relations*, vol. 52, no. 4, pp. 658–681, Dec. 2014.

[14] Eurostat, "Privathaushalte, die einen Breitbandzugang haben," 2017. [Online]. Available: http://ec.europa.eu/eurostat/tgm/table.do?tab=table&init=1&language=de&pcode=tin00073&plugin=1&tableSelection=1. [Accessed: 24-Jan-2018].

[15] E. Hargittai, "The Digital Reproduction of Inequality," in *Social Stratification*, D. Grusky, Ed. Boulder, CO: Westview Press, 2008, pp. 936–944.

[16] E. Ferro, J. R. Gil-Garcia, and N. Helbig, "The digital divide metaphor: understanding paths to IT literacy," in *Electronic Government*, Springer, 2007, pp. 265–280.

[17] S. Halford and M. Savage, "Reconceptualizing Digital Social Inequality," *Information, Commun. Soc.*, vol. 13, no. 7, pp. 937–955, Oct. 2010.

[18] A. Quan-Haase, K. Martin, and K. Schreurs, "Interviews with digital seniors: ICT use in the context of everyday life," *Information, Commun. Soc.*, vol. 4, no. 5, 2016.

[19] T. Spier, M. Klein, U. Von Alemann, H. Hoffmann, A. Laux, and A. Nonnenmacher, *Parteimitglieder in Deutschland*. Wiesbaden: VS Verkag für Sozialwissenschaften.

[20] B. Busse, A. Hashem-Wangler, and J. Tholen, "Two worlds of participation: young people and politics in Germany," *Sociol. Rev.*, vol. 63, no. 1958, pp. 118–140, 2015.

[21] R. Dahl, *Democracy and its Critics.* Yale University Press, 1989.

[22] M. Margolis, D. Resnick, and C.-C. Tu, "Campaigning on the Internet - Parties and candidates on the World Wide Web in the 1996 primary season," *Harvard Int. J. Press.*, vol. 2, no. 1, pp. 59–78, 1997.

[23] W. Lusoli, S. Ward, and R. Gibson, "Political organisations and online mobilisation: Different media - same outcomes?," *New Rev. Inf. Netw.*, vol. 8, no. 1, pp. 89–107, Jan. 2002.

[24] S. Ward, R. Gibson, and W. Lusoli, "Online Participation and Mobilisation in Britain: Hype, Hope and Reality," *Parliam. Aff.*, vol. 56, no. 4, pp. 652–668, Oct. 2003.

[25] J. L. Jensen, "Political Participation Online: The Replacement and the Mobilisation Hypotheses Revisited," *Scan. Polit. Stud.*, vol. 36, no. 4, pp. 347–364, Dec. 2013.

[26] B. C. Reisdorf and D. Groselj, "Internet (non-)use types and motivational access: Implications for digital inequalities research," *New Media Soc.*, vol. 19, no. 8, pp. 1157–1176, 2017.

[27] S. Wyatt, "Non-users also matter. The construction of users and non-users of the internet," in *How users matter. The co-construction of users and technologies*, no. January 2003, 2003, pp. 67–80.

[28] C. Lutz and C. P. Hoffmann, "The dark side of online participation: exploring non-, passive and negative participation," *Information, Commun. Soc.*, vol. 20, no. 6, pp. 876–897, 2017.

[29] L. Heimrich, "Parteien digital: Mitgliederkommunikation im Zeitalter des Internets," Technische Universität Ilmenau, 2013.

[30] R. Heinrich and M. Spitz, "Relevanz gewinnt - Online-Partizipation im Wahlkampf bei den Grünen!," in *Internet und Partizipation*, Wiesbaden: Springer Fachmedien Wiesbaden, 2014, pp. 223–236.

[31] Germany, *Basic Law for the Federal Republic of Germany (Grundgesetz für die Bundesrepublik Deutschland).* 2010.

[32] Germany, *Political Parties Act. Translation as of 15 March 2009.* Germany, 2004.

[33] K.-R. Korte, "So entscheiden Parteien: Umfeld-Bedingungen innerparteilicher Partizipation," *Wie Entscheid. Parteien? Prozesse Inn. Willensbildung Deutschl. (ZPol Sonderband 2012)*, pp. 267–286, 2012.

[34] E. G. Frankland, "The Evolution of the Greens in Germany: From Amateurism

to Professionalism," in *Green Parties in Transition: The End of Grass-Roots Democracy?*, E. G. Frankland, P. Lucardie, and B. Rihoux, Eds. Farnham, Surrey: Ashgate, 2008, pp. 19–42.

[35] N. Switek, "Bündnis 90/ Die Grünen: zur Entscheidungsmacht grüner Bundesparteitage," in *Wie entscheiden Parteien? Prozesse innerparteilicher Willensbildung in Deutschland (ZPol Sonderband 2012)*, K.-R. Korte and J. Treibel, Eds. Baden-Baden: Nomos, 2012, pp. 121–154.

[36] Bündnis 90 / Die Grünen, "Grüne Regeln (Satzung)." p. 91, 2015.

[37] U. von Alemann and A. Laux, "Die Mitglieder als Faktor innerparteilicher Willensbildung und Entscheidungsfindung," in *Wie entscheiden Parteien – Prozesse innerparteilicher Willensbildung in Deutschland, ZPol Zeitschrift für Politikwissenschaft, Sonderband 2012*, K.-R. Korte and J. Treibel, Eds. Baden-Baden: Nomos, 2012, pp. 249–266.

[38] R. Heinrich, M. Lübker, and H. Biehl, "Parteimitglieder im Vergleich: Partizipation und Repräsentation," Potsdam, 2002.

[39] M. Kellner, "Beteiligungspartei 2019," 2015.

[40] B. Flyvbjerg, "Five Misunderstandings About Case-Study Research," *Qual. Inq.*, vol. 12, no. 2, pp. 219–245, 2006.

[41] M. Kellner, "Task Force Beteiligung." 2014.

[42] M. Q. Patton, "Enhancing the quality and credibility of qualitative analysis.," *Health Serv. Res.*, vol. 34, no. Patton 1990, pp. 1189–1208, 1999.

[43] V. A. Anfara, K. M. Brown, and T. L. Mangione, "Qualitative Analysis on Stage: Making the Research Process More Public," *Educ. Res.*, vol. 31, no. 7, pp. 28–38, 2002.

[44] A. Field, *Discovering Statistics Using IBM SPSS Statistics*, 4th Editio. SAGE Publications, 2013.

[45] M. Emmer, G. Vowe, and J. Wolling, *Bürger online: die Entwicklung der politischen Online-Kommunikation in Deutschland.* Konstanz: UVK Verlagsgesellschaft, 2011.

[46] Statistisches Bundesamt (Destatis), "Häufigkeit der Internetnutzung 2017," 2017. [Online]. Available: https://www.destatis.de/DE/ZahlenFakten/GesellschaftStaat/EinkommenKonsumLebensbedingungen/_Grafik/ITNutzung_Haeufigkeit.png?__blob=poster. [Accessed: 28-Mar-2018].

[47] W. Rudzio, *Das politische System der Bundesrepublik Deutschland.* Wiesbaden: Springer Fachmedien Wiesbaden, 2015.

Tweets, Death, and Rock 'n' Roll

Social Media Mourning on Twitter and Sina Weibo

Xinyuan Xu
Australian National University
xinyuan.xu@anu.edu.au

Terhi Nurmikko-Fuller
Australian National University
terhi.nurmikko-fuller@anu.edu.au

Bernardo Pereira Nunes
UNIRIO and PUC-Rio
bnunes@inf.puc-rio.br

ABSTRACT

This paper introduces a new line of investigation into Social Media Mourning (SMM), the act of individual and collective grieving on social media. Previous research has analysed this behaviour as a response to a death within a family unit or amongst a group of friends. We report on SMM in the context of the death of a celebrity.

We present a comparative analysis of two social media platforms, Twitter and Sina Weibo (henceforth 'Weibo'). Uniquely, we have also sought to understand the feelings and attitudes of social media users who do not engage in SMM, but inevitably encounter the posts of others. This was accomplished through online surveys in both English and Chinese, representing the majority language groups of each platform.

We have critically evaluated the theoretical frameworks of *slacktivism*, *information cascades*, and *herd behaviour*, and found herd behaviour to be the most applicable lens for understanding our specific case study: SMM centred on the death of Chester Bennington, an American singer-songwriter best known as the lead vocalist for the group Linkin Park.

Through a mixed method approach combining qualitative and quantitative analyses, we discovered that Twitter users, who are more likely than Weibo users to actively mourn the death of a celebrity by posting on social media, are also more likely to be emotionally affected by it. Weibo users, on the other hand, are more willing to see the content of mourning the death of a celebrity, but being more emotionally distanced, viewing SMM postings simply as news. Finally, although SMM is a manifestation of herd behaviour in our case study, we also point to an example where the power of the masses was successfully harnessed for real world effect.

CCS CONCEPTS

• **Information systems** → **Web searching and information discovery**; **Social networks**; • **Human-centered computing** → **Social media**;

KEYWORDS

Social Media Mourning, Slacktivism, Information Cascade, Herd Behaviour

ACM Reference Format:
Xinyuan Xu, Terhi Nurmikko-Fuller, and Bernardo Pereira Nunes. 2018. Tweets, Death, and Rock 'n' Roll: Social Media Mourning on Twitter and Sina Weibo. In *Proceedings of 10th ACM Conference on Web Science (WebSci'18)*. ACM, New York, NY, USA, 10 pages. https://doi.org/10.1145/3201064.3201079

1 INTRODUCTION

Why do we publicly mourn the passing of someone we never knew? Collective grieving is not a new phenomenon, but the technological advances that have revolutionized our daily lives have also affected the way we grieve, individually and collectively. Social media platforms have given us new ways to interact with our friends, relatives, peers and colleagues, but they have also (at least seemingly) reduced the schism that separates the public from the select few who enjoy the privileged status of *celebrity*.

We define "celebrity" as a person who is known (or is the offspring of someone who is known) for their "outstanding achievements in sports, music and suchlike...[distinguished] from the man in the street and [in] a special position in society" [26]. Celebrity status – closely connected to mass visibility and purposefully helped and promoted by the media – has enabled a small number of individuals to exert a great deal of *influence* (c.f. political, religious or military *power*) over the general populace [22, 23, 27]. Those who identify with a particular celebrity are prone to mimic them, adopting their attitudes, behaviors, and even beliefs [19]. A poignant example of this is how, in 1991, the basketball star "Magic" Johnson publicly announced that he had contracted HIV. Since then, he has successfully called on young people to change their attitudes towards the disease, and to reduce high-risk sexual behavior [4]. In short, celebrities have the power to affect the (social) behavior of other people.

The death of a celebrity can trigger a wave of grief online. This pattern of behavior could be observed in 2016, when a seemingly disproportionately high number of very well-known celebrities (such as Alan Rickman, David Bowie, Prince, and George Michael) passed away. The vast numbers of posts on social media platforms such as Twitter (an act of social media mourning, henceforth SMM) was highlighted throughout the spectrum of mass media from tabloids[1] to broadsheet newspapers[2][3]. To our knowledge, only few academic papers have examined SMM patterns of behavior specifically in the context of the death of a celebrity.

---

[1]"From Elton John and Mick Jagger to the Vatican: Tributes pour into David Bowie with 4.3 million tweets dedicated to the unforgettable icon" http://www.dailymail.co.uk/tvshowbiz/article-3393666/Madonna-Kayne-West-David-Beckham-lead-Twitter-tributes-David-Bowie.html.

[2]"Celebrities flood social media with tributes to Alan Rickman" http://www.cbc.ca/news/trending/alan-rickman-dies-twitter-reaction-1.3403399

[3]"Roger Moore dead: Tributes to the James Bond actor flood social media" http://www.independent.co.uk/arts-entertainment/films/news/roger-moore-dead-tributes-james-bond-age-89-a7751706.html

Rather than examine the phenomenon of SMM in general, we have chosen to base our analysis on a case study example. In this paper, we will focus exclusively on Chester Bennington, the lead singer of Linkin Park. Chester died on July 20 2017 at the age of 41.

Our study examines Twitter and Sina Weibo (henceforth "Weibo"), two micro-blogging platforms with a combined active user-base of 670 million people.[4] Twitter is known for its flexible user interface and semi-anonymousness: it has been suggested that Twitter users are more likely than Facebook users to follow people they do not know personally [13]. The publicness of Twitter facilitates open discussion regarding a celebrity's passing. This blend of public and private may invite new developments in collective mourning [10].

Weibo shares many similarities with Twitter, and has become the most popular microblogging platform for the Chinese speaking community. Since almost all the users on Weibo are Chinese, data harvested from this platform can offer a complementary contrast to Twitter data, which in turn, is blocked in China.

The paper is organized as follows: Section 2 outlines prior research into SMM. Section 3 presents the two aspects of the methodological considerations of this work, data collection and the theoretical framework. Results of the data collection are presented in Section 4. The interpretative frameworks outlined in Section 3 are critically evaluated in Section 5. Section 6 concludes the paper.

2 RELATED WORK

The study of SMM has increased alongside the numbers of users who actively utilize social media to express their grief [6, 10, 24]. Prior research has focused on examining the practices of publicly mourning the death of a family member or close friends in the context of identifying the reason behind the decision to use social media to express their grief, and how these public platforms affect the mourning process itself [24]. Analyses have also been carried out on the content of SMM posts [5, 12, 25], or to examine the language used [6]. Other studies have focused on the ways people use SMM to create new connections and extend their community [16]; to find social support [28]; to maintain relationships with the deceased [10]; and to better cope with the loss and ease grieving [2, 29]. SMM has also been found to be used as an alternative method for expressing condolences when mourners are unable to attend the funeral and memorial service in person [8].

Our investigation differs from these prior papers as we focus on celebrity - and thus the act of publicly grieving for the loss of someone with whom the mourner is unlikely to have had extensive (or indeed any) personal contact. Other researchers who focused on celebrity include Holiman [15], who discussed the motivations for SMM over the death of Steve Jobs. Holiman found that people utilized Facebook to express their condolences not only because it enabled them to feel that they could forge a strong connection with the deceased, but also that in doing so they are able to share their grief instinctively in a way that reflected traditional forms of mourning. He also pointed out that SMM behaviors contributed to a collective memory of Jobs. Courbet & Fourquet-Courbet [11] examined SMM behaviors around the death of Michael Jackson.

They found that SMM enabled users to express their sorrow, engage in the mourning process, leave behind a lasting and personal trace, provide support, and interact with others via social media.

Uniquely, we have considered the thoughts, feelings, and attitudes of the *receivers* of these posts (users in the social networks who do not engage in SMM themselves, but are likely to witness postings by their friends), in the context of a specific case study.

3 METHODOLOGY

Our methodology consists of two parts: data collection, and three possible interpretative frameworks.

3.1 Data Collection

Data was collected using Twitter hashtags and Weibo keywords (Table 1). We collected posts using Twitter's public APIs for the period between July and November 2017: a total of 25,604 tweets. An additional 6,662 tweets were collected manually. For Weibo, data was harvested using keywords: 14,006 posts in all.

Twitter asserts an 11 day limit to data recovery. The data was collected in three different periods: the *Mourning period* (20/07 - 31/07/2017) captured by 11,873 Weibo posts and 6,662 tweets; the *Post-mourning period* (30/10 - 09/11/2017) of 1,284 Weibo posts and 11,748 tweets; and the *Forgetting period* (30/1 - 9/2/2018) in which 849 Weibo posts and 7,194 tweets had been published.

We randomly selected 100 Twitter users and 100 Weibo users who had posted online to mourn the death of Chester Bennington during the Mourning period to check whether they has mentioned Chester Bennington or Linkin Park in previous posts.

We also reviewed the numbers of Google searches for "Chester" and "Linkin Park" to verify whether we would see a peak in searches soon after the news of his death was released to the public.

3.2 Interpretive frameworks

We hypothesized that one or more of the following could be used to understand SMM: *slacktivism, information cascades*, or *herd behaviour*.

Slacktivism is a term that refers to participation in meaningless activities as an expedient alternative to time-consuming effort to solve a problem [7]. It is "the desire people have to do something good without getting out of their chair" [21]. Slacktivists are "happy to click a 'like' button about a cause and may make other nominal and supportive gestures. But, they are hardly inspired by the kind of emotional fire that forces a shift in public perception" [20]. Could the phenomenon of SMM be explained through similar motives?

Information cascades occur when a piece of information or decision being cascaded among a set of infinite sequence individuals causes them to ignore their private information when making a decision [3, 9]. It begins with a *cascade initiator*, with others joining in by linking to the initiator or other members of the cascade [18]. Farajtabar et al.[14] found that social media platforms serve as the large information networks where individuals search for, share, and discuss information. Users often forward information they are exposed to through their followers, causing the emergence of information cascades that spread throughout the network. To quote Machiavelli (from 1514): "Men nearly always follow the tracks made

---

[4]Statistics for Twitter and Weibo user numbers in May 2017 from BBC news "Twitter user numbers overtaken by China's Sina Weibo" http://www.bbc.com/news/technology-39947442.

Table 1: Data Summary

	Weibo Keywords				Twitter Hashtags			
Mourning period 20/7/2017 - 31/7/2017	查斯特贝宁顿 Chester Bennington	870	林肯公园主唱自杀 Linkin Park lead singer commit suicide	3,373	#ChesterBe	487	#iMissYouChester	20
	林肯公园主唱 Linkin Park lead singer	3,599	Chester Bennington	1,967	#wemissyouchester	36	#ripchesterbennington	2,441
	林肯公园查斯特 Linkin Park Chester	2,064			#RIPChester	3,678		
Post-mourning period 30/10/2017 - 09/11/2017	查斯特贝宁顿 Chester Bennington	23	林肯公园主唱自杀 Linkin Park lead singer commit suicide	125	#ChesterBe	62	#iMissYouChester	8
	林肯公园主唱 Linkin Park lead singer	389	Chester Bennington	330	#wemissyouchester	157	#ripchesterbennington	1,267
	林肯公园查斯特 Linkin Park Chester	417			#MakeChesterProud	10,000	#RIPChester	254
Forgetting period 30/1/2018 - 9/2/2018	查斯特贝宁顿 Chester Bennington	8	林肯公园主唱自杀 Linkin Park lead singer commit suicide	185	#ChesterBe	23	#iMissYouChester	7
	林肯公园主唱 Linkin Park lead singer	485	Chester Bennington	65	#wemissyouchester	9	#ripchesterbennington	134
	林肯公园查斯特 Linkin Park Chester	106			#MakeChesterProud	6,658	#RIPChester	363
Total	14,006				25,604			

by others and proceed in their affairs by imitation" [3]. In social media, information cascades occur when the information propagates through immediate neighbors (friends) [30].

Herd behaviour arises in situations where individuals act by observing the behaviour of others. It occurs "when an infinite sequence of individuals make an identical decision, not necessarily ignoring their private information" [1]. To summarise, "an informational cascade implies a herd, but a herd is not necessarily the result of an informational cascade" [9].

4 SMM ON WEIBO & TWITTER

We analysed SMM behaviours centred on Chester Bennington's death. We collected Twitter tweets and Weibo posts, and assessed the feelings and opinions of other users who do not engage in SMM through an online survey.

Activity was measured based on a given user's participation in Twitter and Weibo in a square root to reduce possible right skewness of the data following the *activity formula* [17]:

$$activity = \sqrt{\frac{total\ number\ of\ posts\ acquired}{covered\ period\ (days)}}$$

As shown in Figure 1, the activity indexes for Twitter users are – in the Post-mourning period – much higher (32.68) than that for Weibo users (10.83). In the Forgetting period, however, the activity index of the Weibo user dropped much slower (and to a lesser extent) than that of the Twitter users. The activity index suggests

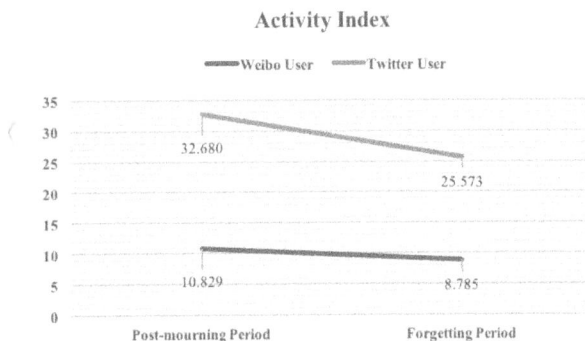

Figure 1: Activity index for Twitter and Weibo users

that the interest in Chester Bennington's death was shorter-lived but more intense on Twitter than on Weibo.

4.1 Mourning period

We analyzed high-frequency words in SMM content (Figure 2). During the Mourning period on Twitter, these include "love" (in 374 tweets), "mikeshinoda"[5] (in 329 tweets), "music" (in 275 tweets), "lpmemorial" (in 184 tweets), and "rip" (in 176 tweets). SMM on

---

[5]Mike Shinoda is co-founder and rhythm guitarist of Linkin Park, and it is he who confirmed the news of Chester Bennington's death

Twitter high-frequency words (Mourning)		
High frequency word	Number of instances	%
love	388	0.440
mikeshinoda	332	0.376
music	294	0.333
lpmemorial	277	0.314
rip	228	0.258

Weibo high-frequency words (Mourning)		
High frequency word	Number of instances	%
自杀(commit suicide)	7,599	1.531
身亡(died)	2,331	0.470
上吊(hung himself)	1,885	0.380
音乐(music)	1,606	0.324
视频(video)	1,476	0.297

Mourning Period (20/07/2017 - 31/07/2017)

Twitter high-frequency words (Post-Mourning)		
High frequency word	Number of instances	%
AMAs	6,248	2.023
voting	5,899	1.910
artist	5,875	1.902
alternative	5,762	1.866
rock	5,750	1.862

Weibo high-frequency words (Post-Mourning)		
High frequency word	Number of instances	%
视频(video)	895	1.138
演唱(singing)	766	0.974
纪念(commemorate)	704	0.895
自杀(commit suicide)	574	0.730
现场(live)	492	0.626

High-frequency words in SMM content regarding the death of Chester Bennington

Post-mourning Period (30/10/2017 - 09/11/2017)

Twitter high-frequency words (Forgetting)		
High frequency word	Number of instances	%
fuckdepression	3,150	2.096
talindab	2,960	1.969
miss	1,702	1.132
best	1,428	0.950

Weibo high-frequency words (Forgetting)		
High frequency word	Number of instances	%
自杀(commit suicide)	502	1.455
视频(video)	480	1.391
节目(program)	334	0.968
笑容(smile)	331	0.959
录制(record)	330	0.956

Forgetting Period (30/1/2018 - 9/2/2018)

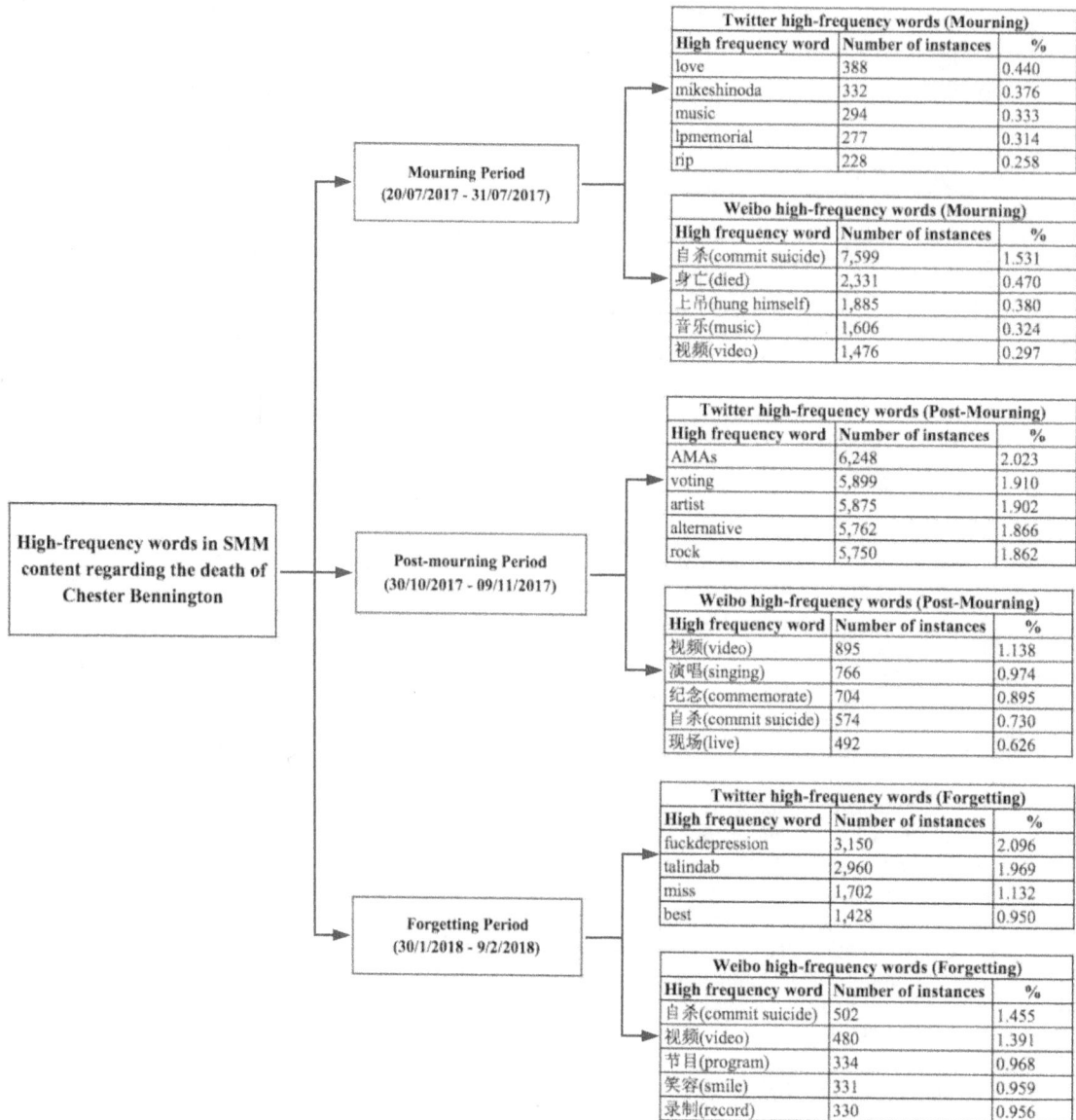

Figure 2: High-frequency words in collected tweets and Weibo posts

Twitter appears to mainly focus on expressing concern about this event and mourning on the death of Chester Bennington.

High-frequency words in the collected Weibo (Figure 2) posts include "自杀(commit suicide)", mentioned in 7,599 posts; "身亡(died)", from 2,331 posts; "上吊(hung himself)", in 1,885 posts; "音乐(music)", in 1,478 posts; and "视频(video)", in 1,287 posts. It appears then that the focus of Weibo users is predominantly on the *news* rather than Chester Bennington personally. The high-frequency content on Weibo during this period included various descriptions, such as:

【摇滚天团"林肯公园"主唱查斯特·贝宁顿自杀，年仅41岁】据英国广播公司（BBC）报道，20日晚上10时许，美国摇滚天团"林肯公园"主唱查斯特·贝宁顿在美国加州洛杉矶的住宅内上吊自尽，年仅41岁。生前也曾有药物及酒精成瘾的问题。过去查斯特·贝宁顿也透露，幼时曾遭成年男子性侵，让他一直有轻生念头。

"The lead singer of rock band 'Linkin Park' Chester Bennington has committed suicide at the age of 41. According to the BBC, at 10 pm on 20th, the lead singer of the American rock band 'Linkin Park' Chester Bennington hanged himself at his private residence in Los Angeles, California, the United States. He was only 41 years old. Before his death, he had struggled with drug and alcohol addiction. He had also previously revealed that he had been sexually assaulted at a young age, and had always had suicidal thoughts."

4.2 Post-mourning period

High-frequency words in tweets published in the Post-mourning period (Figure 2) include "AMAs" (in 5,851 tweets), "voting" (in 5,721 tweets), "artist" (in 5,724 tweets), "alternative" (in 5,727 tweets), and "rock" (in 5,728 tweets). This period has a unique feature: it coincided with the American Music Awards (AMAs). The public were encouraged to vote for their favorites, and SMM on Twitter was harnessed to appeal to voters (for Linkin Park). This appears to have resulted in flurry of SMM related activity.

SMM on Weibo manifested primarily as postings or repostings of videos of Linkin Park in concert. The high-frequency words from this period include "视频 (video)", in 407 posts; "纪念 (commemorate)", in 400 posts; "演唱 (singing)", in 445 posts); "自杀 (commit suicide)", in 362 posts; and "现场 (live)", in 268 posts.

4.3 Forgetting period

During the Forgetting period, the high-frequency words in collected tweets (Figure 2) included "fuckdepression" (in 3150 tweets), "talindab" (in 2,943 tweets), "miss" (in 1,702 tweets), and "best" (in 1,428 tweets). These words can be largely traced back to a single, actively retweeted posting. The original was by Talinda Bennington:

"Miss you more & more everyday. I'm lost without my best friend #fuckdepression #makechesterproud".

Twitter users would engage in SMM by either replying to Talinda in an effort to mourn Chester Bennington together with her, or through retweeting her post – effectively sharing and promoting an activity of shared grief online.

By comparison, Weibo users during this period were more likely to post or repost an episode of the TV comedy Carpool Karaoke.[6] The high-frequency word in collected Weibo posts during this time include "自杀 (commit suicide)", in 501 posts; "视频 (video)", in 472 posts; "节目 (program)", in 334 posts; "笑容 (smile)", in 331 posts, and "录制 (record)", in 330 posts.

The most popular content on Weibo during this period was:

林肯公园主唱查斯特自杀前6天曾录制《开车唱歌秀》... 这集节目刚刚被放出。当时的他还是满脸笑...没想到...

"Six days before Linkin Park lead singer Chester Bennington committed suicide, he had recorded 'Carpool Karaoke'... This episode has just been released. At that time, he was still smiling... Never thought...)"

---

[6]This is a segment of The Late Late Show with James Corden, featuring Chester Bennington.

The content of SMM posts on Twitter was thus more focused on Chester Bennington himself. Twitter users connected (or attempted to connect) with his widow through comments and retweets, as well as actively voting for Linkin Park to win at the AMAs. In contrast, Weibo users focused on the news itself. Those who mourned the death of Chester Bennington did so through disseminating Linkin Park's videos and music.

4.4 Prior posts

Given the vast numbers of users on both Twitter and Weibo, we randomly selected 100 users of each platform as a representative sample.

Of the 100 randomly selected Twitter users (who posted about Chester Bennington and Linkin Park during the Mourning period), 31% had previously published tweets about Chester Bennington or Linkin Park (Figure 3). Subsequent tweets were posted by 7% users. We hypothesize that this decline in the number of users posting about Chester and Linkin Park after the Forgetting period is indicative of users' attention shifting to other celebrities.

Of the 100 Weibo users, only 2% had published posts about Chester Bennington or Linkin Park prior to the Mourning period (Figure 4). Subsequent posts were also written by 2% users, showing no change to the original number of users posting. This consistency in the user numbers suggests that they represent the genuine fanbase of Linkin Park, with all other users engaging in SMM around this event for alternative reasons.

4.5 Google searches

Google Analytics display clear peaks (Figure 5) in queries related to Chester and Linkin Park. The highest by far – perhaps unsurprisingly – on the day of his death. Based on these statistics it would seem that Chester Bennington received more attention than usual on the day of his death. Is it thus possible to suggest that a large part of the people who posted on social media to mourn the death of Chester Bennington may not have done so motivated by their appreciation of this celebrity or their sincere sorrow for his death, but for some alternative reason? We hypothesize that such reasons may include being swept along with herd behavior, or be a deliberate attempt by a user to draw attention to themselves.

4.6 Online Survey

In an effort to understand both the motivations of for SMM postings, and the feelings, thoughts, and attitudes of those users who do not engage in SMM but encounter it on their social media platforms, we conducted an online survey.

4.6.1 Attitudes to SMM. Almost all of both Twitter (92%) and Weibo users (94%) reported that they felt that it is appropriate to post content about mourning deceased celebrity on the social media (Figure 8). Users of both platforms (69% on Twitter and 83% on Weibo) reported that SMM content posted by others was acceptable.

A small minority disagreed:

我认为名人逝世这个沉重而严肃的话题不便于在社交平台上谈论登出

Twitter User

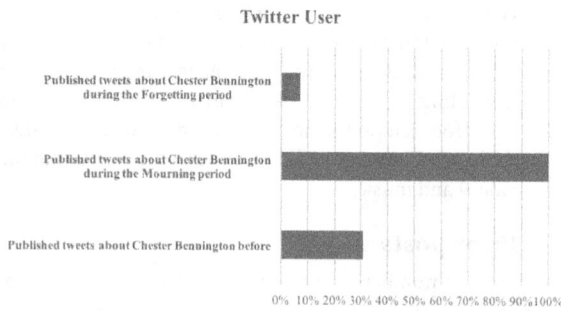

Figure 3: Behaviour of 100 randomly selected Twitter users

Weibo User

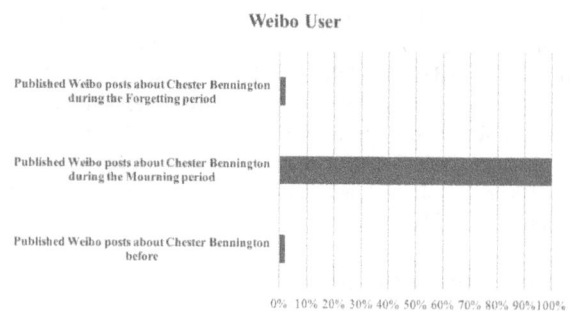

Figure 4: Behaviour of 100 randomly selected Weibo users

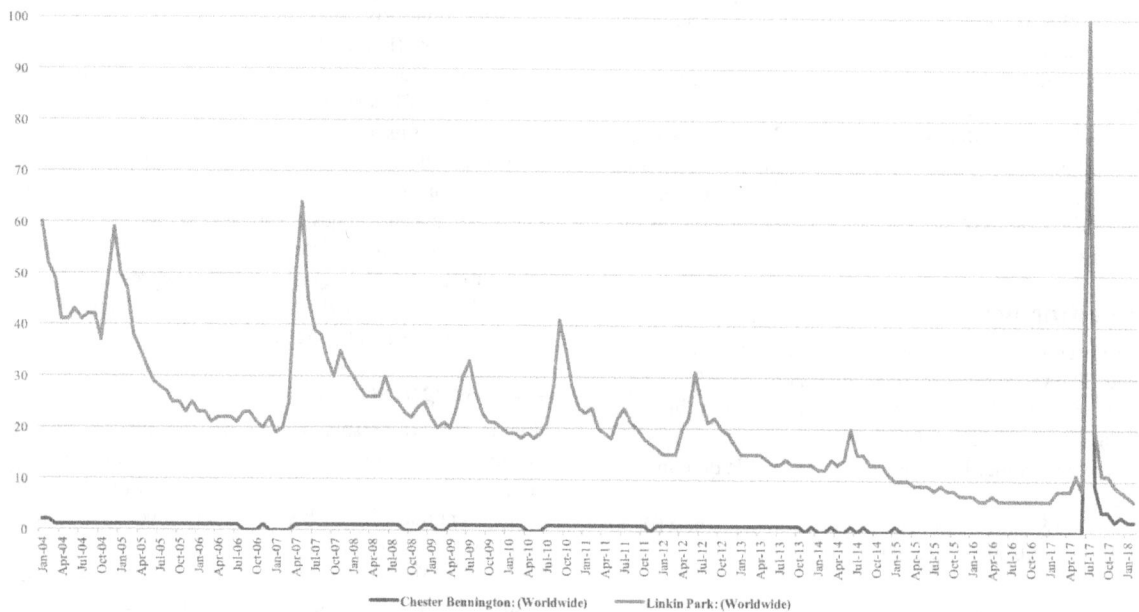

Figure 5: Google queries for "Chester Bennington" and "Linkin Park" since January 2004

"I think it is inappropriate to discuss topics as heavy and serious as the death of a celebrity on social networking platforms."

Twitter users appear to be more active producers of SMM content (original and retweeted), and more likely to engage in SMM than Weibo users. They also report a more emotional response (and are seemingly more affected by) SMM.

Weibo users in general were more willing to see the content of mourning the death of a celebrity, but report to be engaging with it less emotionally. Those who answered the survey likened these posts to news, capturing current events:"当作了解实事 (Such posts are a way to know about current events)", with astute observations "可能有不实报道 (They may be fake news)". Weibo users also listed SMM simply as "种悼念/纪念方式 (A way of mourning/ commemorating)".

4.6.2 Reasons for SMM posting - Self-declared. 63% of Twitter users reported that their reason for posting about the death of a celebrity was their desire to show their sympathy to other social media users. 50% of Weibo users reported different motivations, stating that they mourn the deceased celebrity by posting on social media because:

- "我个人崇拜这个名人并且希望我的朋友看到 ("I personally worship that particular celebrity, and I want my friends to see.")"

- "缅怀名人作出的贡献，并为他们所做出的贡献进行传播 ("To commemorate the contributions made by the deceased celebrity and to disseminate their contributions")"

- "缅怀 ("To commemorate the deceased celebrity")"

- "真心的哀悼 ("Sincerely mourn the death of a celebrity")"

- "敬仰 ("Show respect to the deceased celebrity")"

4.6.3 Assumed reasons for SMM posting by others. Both user groups reported their belief that most SMM content centered on celebrities was produced by users who were just following a trend.

Twitter users who had seen others post SMM content relating to the death of a celebrity but do not engage in SMM themselves described those tweets as "understandable", but also "weird" and "unnecessary". They also accused others of simply in engaging in SMM as a sign of herd behaviour: "I find most of them annoying. Only some people were honest. Most of posts were part of hype."

Similar views were reported from Weibo users:

> 我觉得第一反应会觉得都是跟风，除非曾经就知道朋友可能真的喜欢那个人

"I think your first reaction would be to assume that the people who published these posts are just following the crowd, unless you already knew that they really liked the deceased celebrity".

4.6.4 Weibo backlash. Weibo users who recently posted on the platform mentioning the death of Chester Bennington have done so in the context of SMM around the death of another singer, Dolores O'Riordan.[7] They noted that others who posted SMM content regarding Chester may have just been following a trend:

> 林肯公园主唱自杀的时候朋友圈一溜儿的悼念，现在小红莓主唱去世了朋友圈又是一片忧伤，到底有几个人是真正听过并喜欢他们的歌的啊，要搁平时他们准不知道这两人是谁，都瞎凑热闹

"There were a bunch of people who posted tributes on Friend Circle when the lead singer of Linkin Park committed suicide. Now, the lead singer of The Cranberries has passed away, and there are a lot of people on Friend Circle who say they are sad. How many people have really listened to their songs and love them? If you had asked them who these people were [before], they definitely would not have known. All of them are just following the crowd."

> 没有不尊重的意思，我只是很不明白，平常也没见别人多关注，怎么人一死了就满屏的朋友圈微博地发？！这次的韩国明星是这样，上次的林肯公园也是这样。这也是一种潮流？

"No disrespect, I just do not understand since [previously] I did not see very many people paying attention to these celebrities. Why is it, that when a celebrity dies, then the Friend Circle and Weibo are just full of people's tributes? The case of the Korean star is an example of this, and so was Linkin Park. Is this a trend, too?"

> 真受不了悼念林肯公园已逝歌手的一些人啊！林肯公园的歌你听过几首啊！能说出他们叫啥名字吗，能说出他们各自成长历程吗！不知道别跟风发朋友圈发微博好嘛，你不尴尬我都替你尴尬

"I can't stand some of the people who were mourning the deceased singer of Linkin Park. How many songs of Linkin Park have

you heard? Can you name them and talk about their story? If you don't know that, do not just follow the crowd to post on Weibo. You don't feel embarrassed, but I feel embarrassed for you."

5 ANALYSIS

We hypothesized that SMM mourning could be understood within the context of at least one of the following theoretical frameworks: *slacktivism*, *information cascades*, or *herd behaviour*.

5.1 Slacktivism

A small percentage (14%) of Weibo users answered open-ended questions such as "What will you do to mourn the death of a celebrity in an offline context?" with replies such as "默默哀悼 ("Mourn the deceased celebrity silently")", and "Read his work, study his success, because these things are the continuation of his spirit" – both passive activities with little social interaction or visibility, and ones that are unlikely to result in any measurable change at a greater, societal level – suggesting slacktivism might be the most suitable interpretative framework for understanding SMM.

However, a closer examination of the most popular tweets and hashtags in a historical context unequivocally eliminates slacktivism as a possible interpretative framework: 37% of those Twitter users who answered the questionnaire self-identified as individuals who join (or are likely to join) *offline* memorial services or mourn the celebrity in other ways. Furthermore, the highest frequency tweets were calls to action:

- "I'm voting for linkinpark for Favorite Artist Alternative Rock at the #AMAs #fuckdepression #MakeChesterProud #wemissyouchester"

- "And yes, I say it again I'm voting for linkinpark for Favorite Artist Alternative Rock at the #AMAs #fuckdepression #MakeChesterProud #ChesterBe #wemissyouchester"

- "RT JoyDasRock: Let's win this 4 #Chesterbe 1 RT = 1 Vote I'm voting for linkinpark for Favorite Artist Alternative Rock at the #AMAs #ForeverChester"

The most popular hashtag was #makechesterproud.[8][9] It played a significant role in the campaign for encouraging voting for Linkin Park in the American Music Awards (#AMAs): 1 RT (retweet) = 1 Vote. This successful online campaign led to Linkin Park winning "Best Alternative Rock Band Winner (AMAs 2017)". The band also used Twitter to thank their fans for voting for them:

"Thank you to all the fans who voted. We love you so much. Take a moment to appreciate the people you love and #MakeChesterProud #AMAs @AMAs."

Talinda Bennington, Chester's widow, has also continued to raise awareness for depression and suicide prevention by communicating

---

[7]Dolores O'Riordan was the lead singer of the group the Cranberries. She passed away 15.01.2018.

[8]This hashtag was created by Linkin Park band member Mike Shinoda to help fans remember Chester Bennington. He asked his Twitter followers to remember Bennington as being kind and generous to others.
[9]The words "street" and "India" also occur among the most frequent words. "Recently a street has been renamed as Chester Bennington Street at Newtown in Kolkata India." @arkahueman https://twitter.com/arkahueman/status/928119737761988608?lang=en

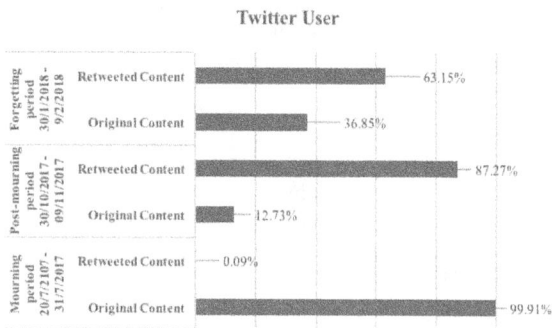

Figure 6: Extent of retweeted SMM content on Twitter

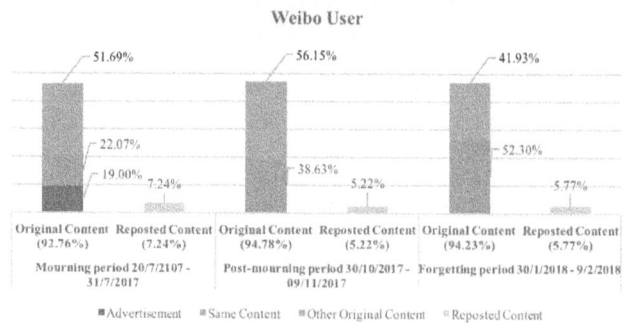

Figure 7: Extent of reposted SMM content on Weibo

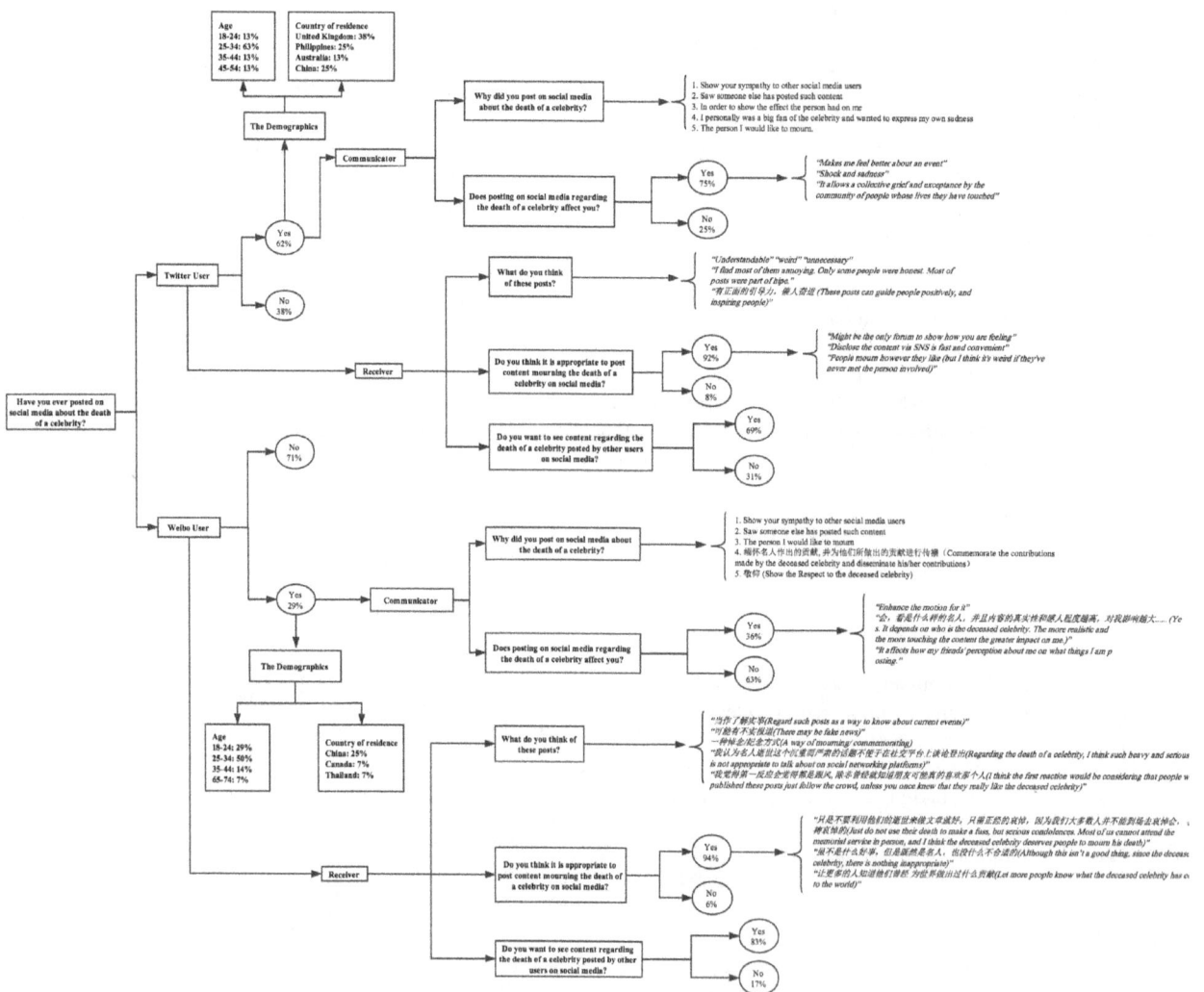

Figure 8: The pattern of SMM regarding the death of a celebrity

with fans using the #FuckDepression hashtag. This type of engagement with the public through social media, as well as successfully harnessing the power of the masses for real world effect (the result of the vote) mean that this particular case study into SMM cannot be analyzed from the perspective of slacktivism.

5.2 Information cascades

SMM manifests as a particular kind of collective activity. Interpreting this behavior in the context of an information cascade could be misleading, as the focus of the analysis may be challenging to determine. What *information* is cascading through the network?

If the focus of the analysis of the spread of news regarding the death of Chester Bennington had been at the center of our investigation, we could have used information cascades as a theoretical framework. However, in this examination of SMM, the information is not that of the news of the death of the celebrity, but rather, the announcement that a particular user makes to notify their network that they are engaging in SMM. The user does this by producing a SMM post. If the network was then to reiterate that post as a source of information, it could be analyzed in this context - for example, through reposted content. However, focusing exclusively on such content would provide an incomplete picture, as many users also generate their own, new posts. As a result, information cascades do not provide a suitable framework for our case study.

5.3 Herd behavior

A quarter of the Twitter users (25%) but only 14% of the Weibo users who answered the questionnaire reported that they engaged in SMM because they had seen someone else posting such content. Figures 6 and 7 illustrate that in each period, the majority of users on both Twitter and Weibo have a tendency to retweet and repost rather than create new content themselves. The processes of retweeting and reposting are interesting particularly since they can be seen to be simultaneously symptomatic of herd behavior, but also potentially promotive of information cascades as each user in turn disseminates the content through their own social networks.

The high quantity of reposted material on both platforms, the self-identification of herd behavior by questionnaire participants, and the judgment of other users about the motives behind the SMM behavior all suggest that SMM on Twitter and Weibo regarding the death of a celebrity in the context of our case study example is best to be understood in the context of herd behavior.

6 CONCLUSIONS

This paper has reported on an investigation into the patterns of SMM centered on the death of a celebrity through a comparison of user behavior on Twitter and Weibo. The vast majority of both Twitter users (92%) and Weibo users (94%) reported that they feel posting content about mourning a deceased celebrity on social media is acceptable, and most (69% of Twitter users and 83% of Weibo users) were willing to see SMM content relating to a celebrity posted by others. Users of both platforms (especially those who did not engage in SMM themselves) did however report a belief that SMM content was predominantly produced as a result of herd behavior (other users who were simply following a trend), rather than a genuine expression of grief rippling though a vast fan base.

Our comparative analysis highlighted four key findings: Firstly, that Twitter users are more likely to actively mourn the death of a celebrity by posting on social media. Secondly, that they (Twitter users) are more likely to be (emotionally) affected by such content. Our third finding was that Weibo users are more willing to see the content of mourning the death of a celebrity, possibly as a result of being more emotionally distanced, and viewing SMM postings as news rather than expressions of sorrow. Finally, although SMM was shown to be a manifestation of herd behavior in our case study example, the power of the masses could also be harnessed for positive real world effect when a social media campaign was successfully used to influence the winners of the American Music Awards in 2017.

For future analyses, we intend to collect more data regarding this SMM event to enrich the results from the research presented in this paper. Our aim is to provide a practical basis for a deepening study of various factors which we will consider in order to determine whether such aspects as age and gender affect SMM behavior. We will examine the sentiments expressed in the content of SMM posts, the receivers' attitudes, and the other posts published by users who used specific hashtags. A further investigation of data sources such as Google Trends also form part of our plans for future expansions and additions to this work.

REFERENCES

[1] Abhijit V Banerjee. 1992. A simple model of herd behavior. *The quarterly journal of economics* 107, 3 (1992), 797–817.
[2] Jo Bell, Louis Bailey, and David Kennedy. 2015. 'We do it to keep him alive': bereaved individuals' experiences of online suicide memorials and continuing bonds. *Mortality* 20, 4 (2015), 375–389.
[3] Sushil Bikhchandani, David Hirshleifer, Ivo Welch, and others. 2005. *Information Cascades and Observational Learning*. Charles A. Dice Center for Research in Financial Economics, Fisher College of Business, Ohio State University.
[4] William J Brown and Michael D Basil. 1995. Media celebrities and public health: Responses to'Magic'Johnson's HIV disclosure and its impact on AIDS risk and high-risk behaviors. *Health Communication* 7, 4 (1995), 345–370.
[5] Jed R. Brubaker and Gillian R. Hayes. 2011. "We Will Never Forget You [Online]": An Empirical Investigation of Post-mortem Myspace Comments. In *Proceedings of the ACM 2011 Conference on Computer Supported Cooperative Work (CSCW '11)*. ACM, New York, NY, USA, 123–132. DOI:http://dx.doi.org/10.1145/1958824.1958843
[6] Jed R. Brubaker, Gillian R. Hayes, and Paul Dourish. 2013. Beyond the Grave: Facebook as a Site for the Expansion of Death and Mourning. *The Information Society* 29, 3 (2013), 152–163. DOI:http://dx.doi.org/10.1080/01972243.2013.777300
[7] Mary Butler. 2011. *Clicktivism, slacktivism, or "real" activism cultural codes of American activism in the internet era*. University of Colorado at Boulder.
[8] Brian Carroll and Katie Landry. 2010. Logging on and letting out: Using online social networks to grieve and to mourn. *Bulletin of Science, Technology & Society* 30, 5 (2010), 341–349.
[9] Boğaçhan Çelen and Shachar Kariv. 2004. Distinguishing informational cascades from herd behavior in the laboratory. *American Economic Review* 94, 3 (2004), 484–498.
[10] Nina Cesare and Jennifer Branstad. 2018. Mourning and memory in the twittersphere. *Mortality* 23, 1 (2018), 82–97.
[11] Didier Courbet and Marie-Pierre Fourquet-Courbet. 2014. When a celebrity dies... Social identity, uses of social media, and the mourning process among fans: the case of Michael Jackson. *Celebrity studies* 5, 3 (2014), 275–290.
[12] Brian De Vries and Judy Rutherford. 2004. Memorializing loved ones on the World Wide Web. *OMEGA-Journal of Death and Dying* 49, 1 (2004), 5–26.
[13] Maeve Duggan and Aaron Smith. 2016. The Political Environment on Social Media. (2016). http://www.pewinternet.org/2016/10/25/political-content-on-social-media/.
[14] Mehrdad Farajtabar, Yichen Wang, Manuel Gomez Rodriguez, Shuang Li, Hongyuan Zha, and Le Song. 2015. Coevolve: A joint point process model for information diffusion and network co-evolution. In *Advances in Neural Information Processing Systems*. 1954–1962.
[15] J. M. Holiman. 2013. *iGrieve: Social Media, Parasocial Mourning and the Death of Steve Jobs*. Ph.D. Dissertation. Southern Utah University.

[16] Stacy Kowalczyk and Andrew Mancuso. 2014. Mourning Online: Social Media, Community, and Grief. (2014).

[17] Paraskevi Lazaridou, Athanasia Ntalla, and Jasminko Novak. 2016. Behavioural Role Analysis for Multi-faceted Communication Campaigns in Twitter. In *Proceedings of the 8th ACM Conference on Web Science (WebSci '16)*. ACM, New York, NY, USA, 344–345. DOI : http://dx.doi.org/10.1145/2908131.2908202

[18] Kristina Lerman and Rumi Ghosh. 2010. Information contagion: An empirical study of the spread of news on Digg and Twitter social networks. *Icwsm* 10 (2010), 90–97.

[19] Siegwart Lindenberg, Janneke F Joly, and Diederik A Stapel. 2011. The norm-activating power of celebrity: The dynamics of success and influence. (2011).

[20] Dennis McCafferty. 2011. Activism vs. slacktivism. *Commun. ACM* 54, 12 (2011), 17–19.

[21] Zoe Zhao Mengyang. 2013. Gauging slacktivism in China: Taking micro-blog users as an example. *Unpublished manuscript, The Chinese University of Hong Kong, Shatin, NT, Hong Kong* (2013).

[22] David S Meyer. 1995. The challenge of cultural elites: Celebrities and social movements. *Sociological Inquiry* 65, 2 (1995), 181–206.

[23] Brian Moeran. 2003. Celebrities and the name economy. In *Anthropological perspectives on economic development and integration*. Emerald Group Publishing Limited, 299–321.

[24] Jensen Moore, Sara Magee, Ellada Gamreklidze, and Jennifer Kowalewski. 2017. Social Media Mourning: Using Grounded Theory to Explore How People Grieve on Social Networking Sites. *OMEGA-Journal of Death and Dying* (2017), 0030222817709691.

[25] Pamela Roberts and Lourdes A Vidal. 2000. Perpetual care in cyberspace: A portrait of memorials on the web. *OMEGA-Journal of Death and Dying* 40, 4 (2000), 521–545.

[26] Hajo Rupp. 2014. Who Owns Celebrity-Law and the Formation of Fame. *ESLJ* 12 (2014), xx.

[27] Richard Schickel. 2000. *Intimate strangers: The culture of celebrity in America*. Ivan R Dee.

[28] Ylva Hård Af Segerstad and Dick Kasperowski. 2015. A community for grieving: affordances of social media for support of bereaved parents. *New Review of Hypermedia and Multimedia* 21, 1-2 (2015), 25–41. DOI : http://dx.doi.org/10.1080/13614568.2014.983557

[29] Amanda L. Williams and Michael J. Merten. 2009. Adolescents' Online Social Networking Following the Death of a Peer. *Journal of Adolescent Research* 24, 1 (2009), 67–90. DOI : http://dx.doi.org/10.1177/0743558408328440

[30] Reza Zafarani, Mohammad Ali Abbasi, and Huan Liu. 2014. *Social media mining: an introduction*. Cambridge University Press.

The Shape of Arab Feminism on Facebook

Nada AL BUNNI
University of Southampton
Southampton, UK
na11g10@soton.ac.uk

David E. Millard
University of Southampton
Southampton, UK
dem@soton.ac.uk

Jeff Vass
University of Southampton
Southampton, UK
jmv@soton.ac.uk

ABSTRACT

Much has been said about the influence of Western culture on social movements worldwide, and this claimed influence has caused some to accuse Arabic feminism of being merely an alien import to the Arab world. New waves of feminism have arisen as a reaction to the claimed prevalent western culture. Global Feminism argues that women worldwide experience similar subjugation in many social constructs because many cultures are based on a patriarchal past, but other waves reject the concept of a universal women's experience and stresses the significance of diversity in women's experiences and see their activities as transnational rather than global. Others expect that the confrontation of secular and Islamist paradigms will dominate. Social Media has global reach, and there are signs that Facebook pages are used by feminists worldwide to boost their social and political activism. Facebook gives public pages' owners the ability to associate their pages with pages with similar ideologies. This provides a global space where feminist pages are clustered and exposes clues about their patterns of influence. By crawling Arabic feminist pages over Facebook, this paper builds a dataset that can be analysed using social network analysis tools and reveals the map of influence between Arabic feminist network and the western, transnational, and Global feminist networks. The map shows that Arabic womens pages are clustered in two segments: Arab feminism, and Sect feminism. The later consists of pages which distance themselves from associating with 'secular' feminism pages whether they are Arabic or not, and in contrary to the former, they are less likely to restrict themselves with national Identity.

CCS CONCEPTS

• Social and professional topics → Cultural characteristics; *Women*;

KEYWORDS

Globalization, Facebook, Feminism, Web Science, SNA, Social Network Analysis, Post-colonialism, Arabic Feminism, Women Empowering Projects, Nationalism, Islamic Feminism, Muslim women, Arab women Activists, Identity politics, Salafism, Salafist movement, Islamist ideology, Salafist movement.

WebSci '18, May 27–30, 2018, Amsterdam, Netherlands
© 2018 Association for Computing Machinery.
ACM ISBN 978-1-4503-5563-6/18/05...$15.00
https://doi.org/10.1145/3201064.3201090

ACM Reference Format:
Nada AL BUNNI, David E. Millard, and Jeff Vass. 2018. The Shape of Arab Feminism on Facebook. In *WebSci '18: 10th ACM Conference on Web Science, May 27–30, 2018, Amsterdam, Netherlands*. ACM, New York, NY, USA, 9 pages. https://doi.org/10.1145/3201064.3201090

1 INTRODUCTION

The processes of globalization suggests the emergence of a "global space" within which rational debates, and collective action take place[52]. The rapidly advancing technologies that have fostered the expansion of a global economy have aided the rise of transnational social movements. Relatively cheap airline tickets, more widely available telephone and Internet access, expanding use of English as a global working language, and a globalized mass media enable people from more diverse classes and geographic origins to share information and cultivate cooperative relationships across huge distances[59]. Therefore, a new literature is dedicated to explore this emergent global space: "transnational public sphere"[29], "transnational social movements"[60][3][10] as well as "transnational feminist networks"[51][25][63].

Feminism is a range of political and social movements. Each has its own ideology and strives for its own goals. However, these goals and ideology might intersect in various degrees. Hawkesworth [34] argues that globalization is a feminist issue, and argues that women have forged international networks and alliances to address specific gender issues beyond the borders of the nation-state. McLaughlin[47] asserts that thinking through transnational feminism goes beyond locating Anglo-American feminists' complicity in colonial and neo-colonial discursive formations, instead offering an opening into collective feminist praxis within global contexts and revealing new possibilities for collaboration. Cooke [16] marked women's participation in the Arab Spring as a transnational feminist revolution "because it involved not just one people exceptionally up in arms against its colonizers or unjust rulers; several societies simultaneously rose up against cruel men. Even if not all those dictators are gone, the people now realize that they too have power. They are listening to each others' music, admiring each others' art, reading each others' stories, and building their own activism out of those resonances."

Web Science offers the potential to investigate these questions with new methods and sources of data. This paper therefore aims to investigate the claimed influence of Western feminism on Arab feminism by exploring the ideological clustering of online communities, and in particular by analyzing the online spaces of activism provided by Facebook Pages. Facebook allows page owners to associate their pages with other pages. This functionality enables activists to situate their pages in the context of other like-minded pages. Analysing the network established by these clustered pages using social network analysis enables us to get some indicators about the extent of connection and influence between Western and Arab feminism.

The paper is structured as follows. Section 2 describes the literature around globalisation and feminism, and explores the potential identity of an Arab feminism. Section 3 then presents the methodology used to create our sample of the Facebook pages network, and our approach to the analysis. Section 4 then describes the network and gives the details of that analysis, in particular investigating the existence of different clusters that can be mapped to the different types of feminism. Section 5 presents a discussion of the findings, and applies them to the question of the relationship between Western feminism and different forms of Arab feminism. Finally, Section 6 concludes the paper, discusses the advantages and limitations of our approach, and outlines our plans for future work.

2 BACKGROUND

Egyptian women first used the term feminism in public in 1923 [5], but the rise of modern Arab feminism is widely attributed to the groundbreaking book of Qasim Amin, "The Liberation of Women". published in 1899. Amin[2] claims that the education and liberation of women was essential to strengthen and emancipate the Egyptian nation from British colonial rule. He argues that men oppressed and silenced women, which caused society in general to suffer. However, attribution of the rise of Arab feminism to Amin's work has received criticism by recent feminist scholars. Badran and Cooke [9] argue that Amin is not the movement's founder in any sense of the word and call the feminism attributed to him men's feminism, associating its development with contact with Europe, whereas in comparison women's feminism arose out of women's reflections on their own lives and problems. Leila Ahmed [19] builds on this critique, arguing that Amin's ideas are built on a comparison with the West, in which the West is refined, cultured, and advanced, and the East is not.

2.1 The hegemony of Western Feminism

Amin's work was not alone in receiving such critics. Homogeneous perspectives and presuppositions in some of the Western feminist texts that focus on women in the third world was criticized too in many works[26][65][13].

Scholars argue that the feminist movement in the West has been taken as "the" feminist movement[53].

Using her account on Central and Eastern European Feminism, Cerwonka [15] confirms the hegemony of Western feminist experience "In the East-West divide discourse, people remark on the challenge of trying to identify and theorize gender issues important to post-state socialist societies in the shadow of an already well-established feminist legacy fromNorth America and Western Europe". Hana Havelkova[36] explains "the tensions in the dialogue between Western and East European women are rooted in the direct application of Western feminist theory to post-communist reality, which leads to the false assumption that East European women are second-class citizens and that they are conservative".

Women's and gender studies have become more international in scope in response to pressure from university administrations and governments and the increased border crossing of faculty and students, and as a consequence of widespread use of the Internet[15].

However, there is some dispute around the degree of influence that western feminism has placed on other feminist movements in non-Western countries. This dispute is documented in the emerged literature of global or post-Colonial feminism[40][24][54], global south feminism[25][23][21] and transnational feminism[14][48][30][62].

Arab feminism is an example of a feminist movement that has been accused as being part of a cultural invasion that accompanied colonialism [50][64].

Arab feminism is also frequently overlooked in Western discourse. "The textured image of exoticism which has been woven in the West over the centuries still dominates the way in which the Arab world is perceived. Orientalist discourses have influenced the way that Arab feminism, in particular, has been received and understood in the West. According to such discourses, the movement for women's liberation is, again, not indigenous to Arab countries. When such movement is recognised, it is described as mere imitation of similar movements in Europe and the USA"[27].

To some the cultural gulf is significant. "It is even argued that Western feminists have described Arab women's lives as being so different from theirs that they cannot possibly develop any kind of feminism. Even when Arab women speak for themselves, Elly Bulkin argues, they are accused of being pawns of Arab men"[27].

It is also the case that images of Muslim women were decontextualized and circulated in the American mass media to depict the veil as an icon of Islamic fundamentalism, and thus Islam as an enemy of both Muslim women and Western democracy[66].

2.2 The Influence of Islamism

The relationship between Islamism and Feminism is complex. "Beyond the enduring anxiety of Islamism versus secularism, there are women in the Arab and Muslim world who are deeply concerned about the forceful imposition of sharia law. There are other women for whom the sharia is not an imposition but a blessing"[18].

The term Islamic feminism has emerged Since the 1990s and brought a widely discussed phenomenon. "On one hand, this debate is due to the ways in which it is embedded in the wider discourses concerning women's rights and Islam, and the position of women in Muslim-majority societies as well as of Muslim women in societies. On the other hand, the debate entangles to the controversies between the labeling practices and the positionalities of those who seek to resist the given labels: who is entitled to speak as and/or name someone else as an 'Islamic feminist'?"[43].

Part of the issue is that as part of their polarising political project, Islamists reinvigorate not only the secular/religious binary but also East/West, public/private and male/female oppositions. Their consistent promotion of the notion that the secular is alien, foreign, non-native and hence inauthentic and that the religious constitutes the indigenous, native and authentic, affected feminisms negatively and has brought divisive implications. This is in contrast to earlier practice in Muslim majority societies when feminist movements were locally grounded and organised within a national context [7].

""Islamic Feminism", which is defined as a cross-border movement that brings together all Muslim women seeking to redefine their identity in a more genuinely modern manner that befits their religion and culture"[31] should be distinguished from the

Table 1: Thematic Coding of the pages

Feminism Theme	Markers
Arabic	Location, national names or symbols, Arabic Language
Western	Location, Sexual rights,Abortion, national western names or symbols
Sect	using Political-Islam names or symbols
Non western	Stating it is international,Location, nationality, race or multi-races, custom-dresses
Transnational Project	Stating it is national chapter of international project for empowering women

Islamist's project regarding imposing what is so called 'sharia law' over everyone including women.

2.3 The Influence of Nationalism

National consciousness is considered as a reaction to Western colonialism. Most research on Arab feminism denotes the interconnection between feminism and nationalism in the Arab world[42][9][4]. "Feminism is not autonomous, but bound to the signfying network of the national context which produces it"[41]. In the case of Arab states, Feminist and national consciousness emerged at the same time and as a reaction to Western imperialism since the early 19th century. However, those who oppose the emancipation of women argue that feminism irrelevant to Arab culture[27]. Nevertheless, the extent to which feminists' views are grounded in their own culture has been overlooked in the discourse of feminism[22]. In a discussion linking Western colonialism and feminism, Leila Ahmed [1] distinguishes two strands of feminism propounded by Egypt's "First Feminists". The first stand is the Westward looking feminism advocated by Huda Sha'rawi (1879 – 1947) and the other one, espoused by Malak Hifni Nasif (1886 – 1918) that did not affiliate itself with Westernization. "Nationbased feminist movements, such as the pioneering Egyptian feminist movement, accessed the world of international feminism and did so on its own terms. These national feminist movements were organised and directed by women as citizens of different religions. Organising activism along communal lines and exporting social movement activism from the global arena to national space is new to our time"[7].

National liberation movements,in general, brought changes that vary in the pace and extent according to the intervention of Western imperialism. One of these changes is the situation of Arab women [27].

2.4 Transnational Projects for Empowering Women

"The concept of patriarchy probably must be seriously addressed in any theoretical work that claims to be feminist" [11]. "A patriarchy may be thought of as having two basic components: A structure, in which men have more power and privilege than women, and an ideology that legitimizes this arrangement"[61]. This system, which MacKinnon [45] calls "perhaps the most pervasive and tenacious system of power in history," characterizes most societies, past and present, albeit with significant variations in particular historical epochs, under different modes of production, and across cultures, classes, and other social structures[11][12][20]. Change in patriarchy and patriarchal structures has been conceived either as a top-down or bottom-up process, depending upon which

approach to women's position within the patriarchy has been adopted. Some see that women are powerless; these are likely to promote the idea of "empowering" women, implying a top-down approach. Whereas, some argue that despite patriarchal subordination, women have power; these perceive empowerment as inherently a bottom-up process[39]. Arab states embody various patriarchal structures and Arab society clings to a patriarchal system[67]. However, Nation-states, international organizations and other actors are legitimized to empower Arab citizens, women among them[67][49]. In recent years, development agencies have substantially increased funding for ICT projects that specially aim to empower women[46]. Information and communication technologies (ICTs) have been increasingly promoted as a key solution for the empowerment of historically disadvantaged groups, such as women and minorities in the Global South[33][38][32].

3 METHODOLOGY

Crossley [17] argues that Facebook and feminist blogs enlarge and nourish feminist networks, create online feminist communities, expand recruitment bases for online and offline mobilization, and increase opportunities for online interaction with adversaries. Arabic female activism is a clear example. There are signs that female activists used Facebook in the Arab world during the recent political movements[57]. Facebook pages are used by Arab women to group themselves and boost their social and political activism[56][28][55]. They also associate these pages with other pages that strive for similar goals or that hold to the same ideology. Some of these associated pages represent activism in wider geographic areas or that work as international hubs.

It is clear that these Facebook pages are potentially a valuable source of data in understanding the different feminisms described in Section 2. Therefore in order to obtain some empirical evidence, and to explore these relationships in more detail, we undertook a network analysis of Arabic Facebook Pages relating to women with a topic that was predominantly political or related to activism, with the aim of analyzing the network formed by these pages and studying how they are situated among similar Arab and global pages.

3.1 Sampling: Collecting Data from Facebook

We created the network we intended to analyse using a snowball sample approach. To create an initial starting set a search was made using Facebook's own search engine for pages with titles using the words usually used in Arabic to refer to women.

While there are two main words(المرأة: woman - single,النساء: women - plural), the Arabic language gives more options by adding suffix

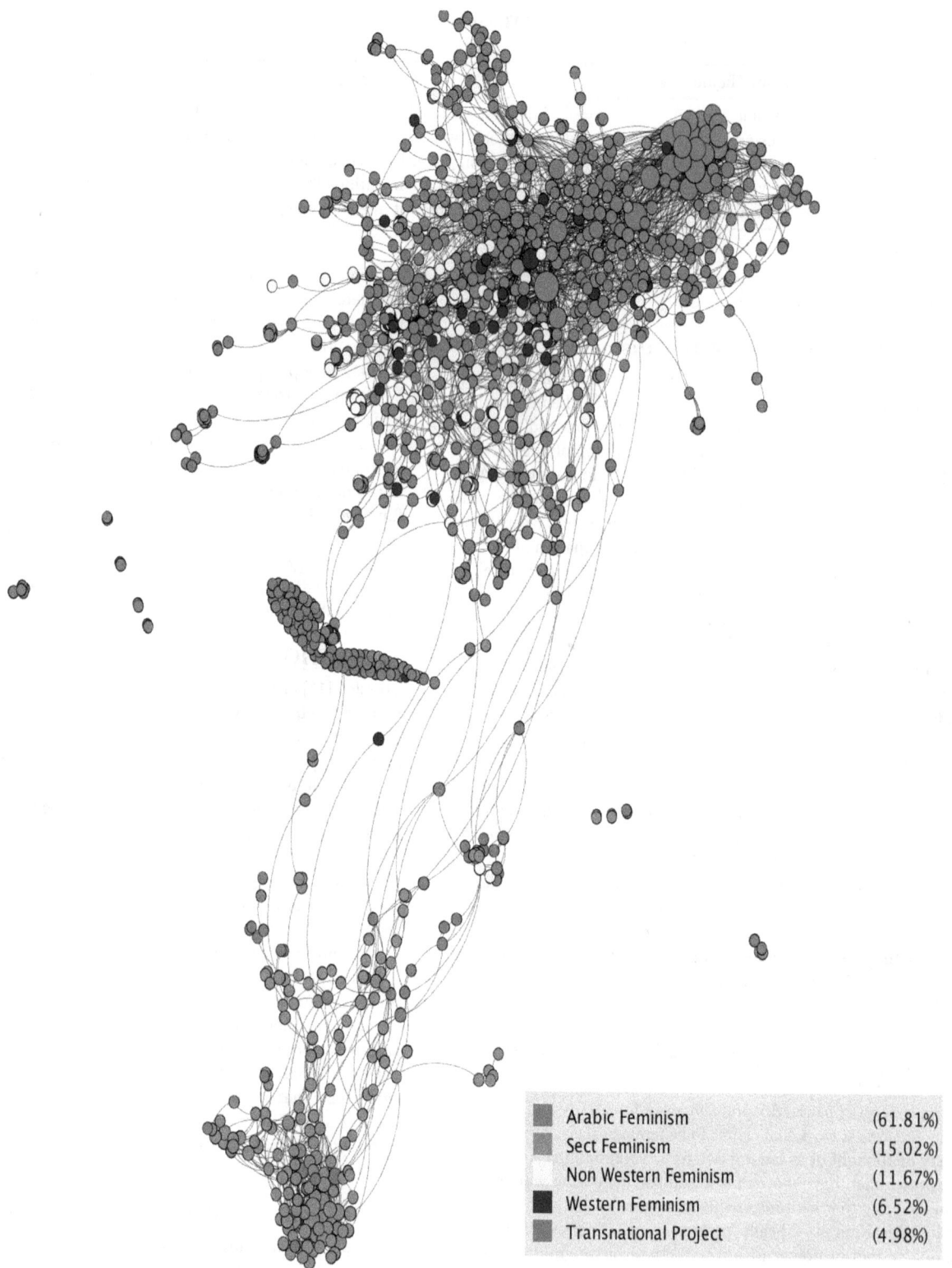

	Arabic Feminism	(61.81%)
	Sect Feminism	(15.02%)
	Non Western Feminism	(11.67%)
	Western Feminism	(6.52%)
	Transnational Project	(4.98%)

Figure 1: The graph of Facebook pages, connected by like relations, colour coded according to theme.

(تاء : aat) to any adjective to make it a name of women with that adjective (i.e.ثائرات : female rebels, مناضلات , ناشطات : Female activists).

Our search took these words (woman, women, female rebels, two words for female activists) to get lists of pages that will be used as a starting set for the snowball process.

We then manually filtered the search results according to two criteria. Firstly, the pages were genuinely related to women (the Female suffix makes it relatively straightforward to do this), and secondly that they related to activism in some way (for example, they were centered on a female activist, politician or blogger).

Starting from the remaining pages in the search set, a manual crawl of each pages' list of liked pages took place. Liked pages that met our two criteria and which were not already in the search set were added to it and edges that represent the like relationship were added to a table of directed edges. In this way we exhaustively expanded the network, until all of the pages in the search set had been crawled.

We did not use a criteria that pages must be in Arabic to be included in our sample network. However, we halted the crawl whenever a non-Arabic page was found and went no deeper. This means that the resulting network includes a rich set of Arabic pages and their interconnections, as well as the relationships they have to non-Arabic pages - however the relationships between these non-Arabic pages was not captured, and they therefore represent the border of our Arabic feminist network.

3.2 Coding the Sample

We applied a deductive approach to coding the pages in the sample according to how well they matched with the different types of feminism. Table 1 shows the five codes that we used, and an example of common markers that enabled us to classify each page. As discussed in Section 2, the literature suggests there might be two strands of Arabic feminism with different attitude to Western feminism, we therefore used two seperate codes for Arab women pages. We marked those pages who display political-Islam identities (for example, holding Islamists' flags or symbols with a special code) calling them "Sect Feminism", while leaving the other pages that don't have these distinctive features with the original name " Arabic Feminism".

The expected attitude of Non-western feminisms towards the western and the post-colonial influences made us choose two codes to distinguish the Western feminism from Global feminism (or feminisms of other nations).

This five codes enable us to distinguish the two Arabic feminisms (explicitly-Islamist or not) from those of non- Arabic ones (Western Feminism and the non-western feminism).

The fifth code is used to show the pages of transnational projects implemented in Arabic states such as UN Women projects, or IEEE national chapters.

4 RESULTS AND ANALYSIS

The network constructed by our sampling process is formed by 1105 nodes and 3331 directed edges and is shown in Figure 1 using a Force Atlas layout algorithm, the size of the node is representing the in-degree (in the range of 0-204). Each node represents a single page, and they are colour-coded according to the themes that we

identified in Table 1. To give some idea of the size and characteristics of each sub-network we filtered the network by each theme in turn, and the results are shown in Table 2. Note that there are no edges in the 'Western' sub-network as a result of our crawl halting when we reached non-Arabic pages.

98 nodes have a degree of 0 and these represent 8.87 % of all pages in our sample. These are pages that were in the initial search set, but which do not like any other pages that fulfill our criteria, and are not liked by any other pages in our sample.

Figure 2 shows the distribution of degree, from lowest to highest. As might be expected this follows a power law, with very few high degree nodes.

The network structure reveals a stark difference between the two types of Arab feminism, and both types also seem to use very different terms to identify themselves and name their pages. There are also significant differences the scope (or intended area of concern) between them. All three observations are explored further in the next subsections.

4.1 Connectedness between feminisms of Middle East with feminism of other nations

The network structure shows a significant difference between the way that pages we identifies as Arab feminism, and those as Sect feminism, connect to other types of pages in our sample.

There are only 86 edges connecting Arab feminism and Sect feminism, while Arab feminism are linked with non-Western feminism pages with 225 edges and with Western feminism pages with 136 edges. Arab feminism pages have 161 edges linking them with Transnational pages.

This shows that Arabic feminism pages are more connected to the other nations feminism pages than to pages of Arabic feminism that use religious ideologies to identify themselves.

Not only are Sect feminist pages less linked to Arab pages, they are linked with only 4 edges with Non-western pages, one edge with Western pages, and no edges at all with Transnational project pages.

This shows that in terms of their network connections Sect feminism pages are more isolated from the outside world than Arab feminism pages, and that objectively we can see that they have very few connections at all (5 edges, across 166 pages).

4.2 Naming Paradigms

We also looked at the terms used in the pages for each category of feminism, although a somewhat coarse measure, these do reveal the different concerns of the different types of feminism as expressed on Facebook.

We counted the common words used and made a comparison between "Arab feminism" and "Sect feminism" in the Table 3. The table is in three sections, where the first section shows the word used to indicate a feminist slant to the page, the second section shows the words which were used to describe goals, and the third section shows words associated with identity.

The word "Feminism" (or its directives, such as "Feminist") is used very sparsely within the sample. It is used in English (10 occurrences) and French (6 occurrences) and even Arabic spelled in Latin letters (2 occurrences), but only used only 4 times in

Degree Distribution

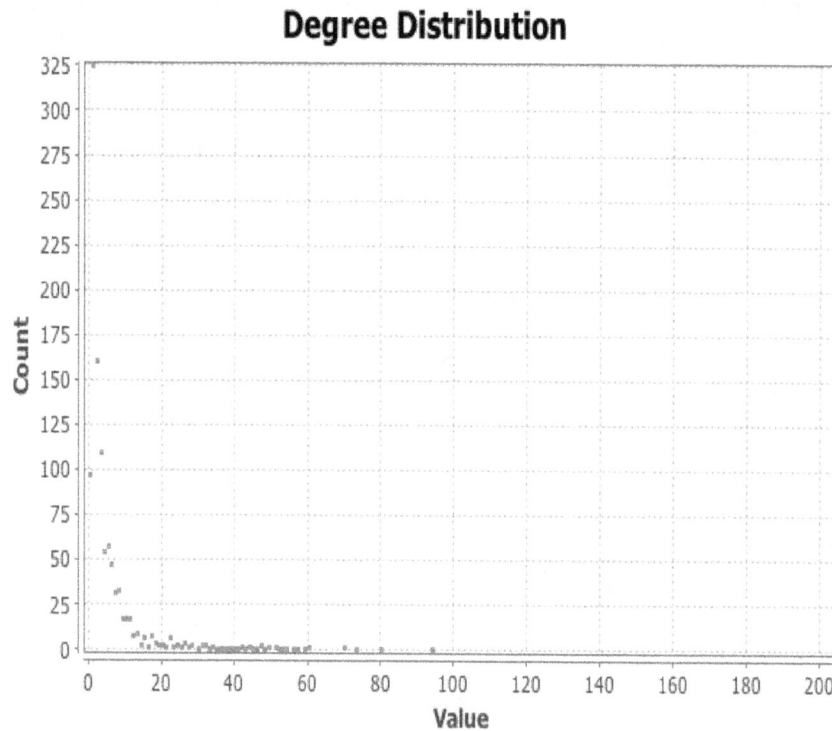

Figure 2: The degree distribution of the overall sample

Table 2: Results

Feminism Theme	Nodes	Edges	Diameter	Avrg.Degree	Density
All Pages	1106	3332	22	6.029	0.003
Arabic	683	2096	13	6.138	0.004
Sect	166	495	9	6.037	0.019
Non Western	129	8	1	0.128	0.001
Western	72	0	1	0	0.001
Transnational	55	48	4	1.811	0.017

Arabic (making a total of 22 occurrences in the sample, less than 2.6%) . Pages coded with "Sect feminism" did not use it at all. This scarcity across the sample could be because it is assumed within these particular spaces, but it may also indicate that the word itself is explicitly avoided - perhaps because of its associations with colonialist interpretations of feminism [64]. We consider this further in the discussion below.

Issues normally associated with Western feminism do appear in the the Arab feminism pages (words such as "violence" or "harrass-ment"), appearing 83 times in the sample. But there is not a single use in the Sect pages.

In the third section we see a variety of identities in the Arab feminism pages, ranging from the debate around veiling, to aspirations of freedom and liberation, to stronger terms associated with direct action ("activist" or "rebels"). In the Sect feminism section the identities are much narrower. There is a shared concern with the issue

of whether of not to wear a veil - although the Arab feminism pages identified with unveiling (11 occurrences) and the Set feminism with veiling (10 occurrences), however the most significant group identifies as Salafi (a religious-political ideology associated with a strict interpretation of Islam), these 48 pages represent 28.9% of the total Sect sample.

Intended Scope. The intended scope of pages (in most of the cases) is declared in the title of the page or in the "about" section of the page. We manually inspected each of these in order to classify the page as either personal (relating to the activities of a specific individual), city (focused on a major metropolitan area), country (mainly focused on a particular nation state), or pan-arabic (the widest focus, covering the Arab world).

While transnational project pages are obviously defined by the nature of their projects. The intended scope of Arabic and Sect

Table 3: Words Used in The titles

Word	count in AraFem	count in SectFem
نسوية (Nasawyia)	4	0
Feminist	10	0
Femes	6	0
Nasawyia	2	0
عنف (Violence)	15	0
تحرش (Harassment)	18	0
حجاب (headscarf)	8	3
حرية (Freedom)	17	0
ثورة (Revolution)	25	0
منتقبة ات (Face-veiled)	0	10
سافرات (Not veiled)	11	0
سلفيات (Female Salafi [44])	0	48
مناضلات (female Activists)	20	0
متحررات (liberated women)	12	0
حرائر (Free women)	12	1
متمردة ات (female rebels)	13	0
لا قديسات ولا عاهرات (Not saints nor whores)	9	0

Arabic

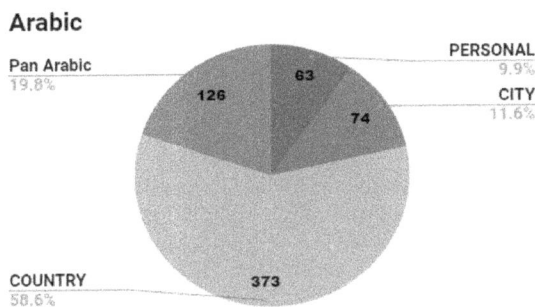

Figure 3: The Scope of Pages in the Arab Feminism Sample

Sect

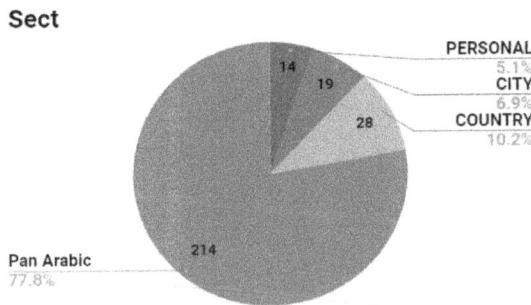

Figure 4: The Scope of Pages in the Sect Feminism Sample

pages varies considerably. Pages marked as Sect feminism in our thematic coding are most likely do not restrict their intended scope or its target publics by state or city names, 77.8% of our sample where classified as Pan-Arabic. The detail of all percentages are

shown in Figure 4. While the Arab feminism pages are more likely to define their intended scope by stating the country or the city name where their activity is based (58.6% were classidied as focused on country), this is shown in Figure 3 .

5 DISCUSSION

5.1 Two major feminist paradigms

Badran [6] reports two major feminist paradigms. She denotes that these two feminisms evolved in historical contexts in which new subjects and identities were being re/fashioned out of shifting combinations of religious and national affiliation. Our network clearly exposed this expected polarization around the identity of women activism. The two Arab segments of the network (Arab and Sect feminsim) show multiple distinct characteristics, including openness to other nation's feminisms, and openness to transnational women empowering projects.

At the outset of her book, Badran differentiates between Western feminisms and Muslim women's feminisms, which have been termed "secular feminism" and "Islamic feminism" respectively. She then examines how in the Muslim world "secular feminism" has been "action-oriented" and emerged as a social movement "in the context of a secular territorial nation-state composed of equal citizens regardless of religious affiliation, whereas "Islamic feminism emerged as a new discourse grounded in independent investigation and interpretation of the Quran and religious texts (ijtihad). Badran's main argument, however, is that the emergence of "Islamic feminism" in Muslim countries did not indicate the nonexistence of "secular feminism" even as gender equality has been approached differently there." [64]

As shown above the words that refer to feminism are used in the title of only 22 pages. All of them are coded as Arabic Feminism in our dataset. Drawing on Badran, best known for her writing on Islamic feminism, we can assert that Arab women activist are avoiding calling themselves feminists. In 1994 she identified "a kind of feminism or public activist mode without a name. It is represented by Muslim women who decide for themselves how to conduct their lives in society. Because the women who do this work resist the term feminism, which has largely "Western association". She shows that pro-feminist women avoid the feminist label for pragmatic reasons, the term is confining and potentially misleading. Further, Islamist women reject feminism as "superfluous or heretical", and therefore also preclude the possibility of an "Islamic feminism." Despite these proscriptions upon feminism, Badran explains that this gender activism is a new and "unencumbered, analytic construct," and its protagonists (amongst them feminists, pro-feminists and Islamists) represent a convergence that "transcends ideological boundaries of politically articulated feminism and Islamism."[58] Our data certainly supports this view.

5.2 Identity politics

The words used in the title of pages reveal the ideology behind the two strands of feminist pages. While words such as right, violence, harassment are used widely in the pages of Arabic feminism, you find them rarely used and words that reveal identity are used instead (veiled women). This brings more evidences to what Marieme Helie-Lucas[35] is arguing about in an article titled "What is your tribe?"Women's struggles and the construction of Muslimness". She accuses "many well-meaning people, outside as well as inside Muslim contexts, in good faith, play into the game of fundamentalists and their identity politics. There are many forms and varieties of fundamentalism. However, they have common characteristics. In particular, one key element of their politics is the control of women".

The titles of most Sect pages show identities expressed by veiling and other customs, they ignore the common causes of women struggle such as the struggle to stop all sort of violence. This struggle form " a new strand of feminism triggered by the physical and sexual violence perpetrated against women. It is felt and recognized but often unnamed. Anti-sexual-violence activists not only works to stop violence through direct action, but it investigates the root causes and contexts of sexual violence and works to turn around the thinking of offenders whom they detain. The activists develop and share with offenders a feminist analysis of aggression against women that is contextualized in the sociology and culture of their environment."[8]

Htun and Weldon [37] show that, over four decades, the autonomous mobilization of feminists in domestic and transnational contexts (and not leftist parties, women in government, or national wealth) is the critical factor accounting for policy changes on violence against women. Their analysis suggests that the impact of global norms on domestic policy making is conditional on the presence of feminist movements in domestic contexts, pointing to the importance of ongoing activism and a vibrant civil society. Therefore it could be argued that absence of such common causes in the Sect pages means that we should not interpret them as feminist at all, but rather women's part in a separate religious and ideological debate,

5.3 The claimed holistic feminism

Observing the feminist trajectory during the last century, Badran [7] reported the transition from secular feminism to Islamic feminism to "the emerging Muslim holistic feminism". From the feminism which created in the twentieth century by Muslim and non-Muslims in contexts of anti-colonial struggle and early nation-state building to the emergence of a new feminism in the time when religious identity is fore-fronted and there is an international preoccupation with Muslim women's rights. "communalism is being fed from within the world of feminism and more specifically through progressive Muslim women's global organising. I look at Musawah (equality in Arabic), which is a transnational organisation created and run by and for Muslims. Musawah announced itself as 'A global movement for equality and justice in the Muslim Family at its launch in the spring of 2009 at a large conference in Kuala Lumpur. The event was hosted by Sisters in Islam, the veteran Islamic feminist organisation now two decades old, which has played a central role in the creation of Musawah." [7]

Although the Sect pages show more emphasis on pan-arabic issues, it is the Arab feminism pages that best display the links described by Badran, clearly manifest in the connections with transnational and Western feminist movements.

6 CONCLUSIONS

In this paper we have applied Web Science methods to help understand the shape of on-line Arab feminism. Much has been written about how globalization, and on-line communication platforms, have created a global political space. This has caused some to accuse Arabic feminism of being an alien import to the Arab world, and problematic because of its association with Western colonialism and secular values. We set out to investigate these links, and in particular to explore the structure of Arabic Facebook pages associated with women - examining their connections to global and transnational networks, the language with which they identified themselves, and the scope of their concerns.

Based on a snowball sample, we built a network of 1106 pages and 3332 edges (representing Facebook likes between pages). In this network we discovered two distinct sets of Arabic pages, linked by only 86 edges.

The first, which we labeled Arab feminism, is larger (683 nodes), has a more significant link to western, national, and transnational pages (522 edges), is concerned more strongly with common global feminist issues (e.g. violence, or harrassment), identifies with freedom and activism, and tends to have a national (58.6%) or city (11.6%) scope.

The second, which we labeled Sect feminism, is smaller (166 nodes), has almost no links to western, national, and transnational pages (5 edges), is not concerned with global feminist issues, identifies with Salafi (a strict and political interpretation of Islam), and tends to have a pan-arabic scope (77.8%) perhaps because ideology has no borders.

We could differentiate these as between activism that is effectively the women sections of Islamist movements (Sect) and Muslim women's struggle for their rights (Arab). The intricacy of the history and politics makes the naming of these two approaches a complex issue as using Islam as a name might not only be mistaken with Islamist activism but also by implication suggests that other female activisms are secular - which is not (usually) the case.

Our work supports the argument that Arabic feminism includes both Western-style values of women's equality and liberation, and a more Islamist interpretation of feminism focused on women's role in Islam. But it also shows that rather than being a continuum of values, there is rather more of a division between these two groups. In the first the influence of other feminisms is limited, but in the second there is a more radical reinterpretation of those values in an Islamic and Pan-Arabic context.

REFERENCES

[1] Leila Ahmed. 1992. *Women and gender in Islam: Historical roots of a modern debate.* Yale University Press.
[2] Qāsim Amīn. 2000. *The liberation of women: And, the new woman: Two documents in the history of Egyptian feminism.* American Univ in Cairo Press.
[3] Jeffrey M Ayres, Beth Schaefer Caniglia, Sean Chabot, Marco G Giugni, Michael Hanagan, Tammy L Lewis, Gregory M Maney, Sharon Erickson Nepstad, Pamela E Oliver, Kim D Reimann, et al. 2002. *Globalization and resistance: Transnational dimensions of social movements.* Rowman & Littlefield Publishers.
[4] Margot Badran. [n. d.]. HAPTER 4 'Dual Liberation: Feminism and Nationalism in Egypt, 1870s-1925'. ([n. d.]).
[5] Margot Badran. 1988. Dual liberation: Feminism and nationalism in Egypt, 1870s - 1925. *Gender Issues* 8, 1 (1988), 15-34.
[6] Margot Badran. 2005. Between secular and Islamic feminism/s reflections on the Middle East and Beyond. *Journal of Middle East women's studies* 1, 1 (2005), 6-28.

[7] Margot Badran. 2011. From Islamic feminism to a Muslim holistic feminism. *IDS Bulletin* 42, 1 (2011), 78–87.

[8] Margot Badran. 2016. Creative Disobedience: Feminism, Islam, and Revolution in Egypt. In *Women's Movements in Post-'Arab Spring' North Africa*. Springer, 45–60.

[9] Margot Badran and Miriam Cooke. 1994. *Opening the Gates*. Random House.

[10] Joe Bandy and Jackie Smith. 2005. *Coalitions across borders: Transnational protest and the neoliberal order*. Rowman & Littlefield.

[11] Michelle Barrett. 1983. Women's oppression today: Problems in Marxist feminist analysis. In *Women's Oppression Today: Problems in Marxist Feminist Analysis*. JSTOR, 338–340.

[12] Veronica Beechey. 1979. On patriarchy. *Feminist Review* 3, 1 (1979), 66–82.

[13] Susan Bordo. 2004. *Unbearable weight: Feminism, Western culture, and the body*. Univ of California Press.

[14] Johanna Brenner. 2003. Transnational feminism and the struggle for global justice. *New Politics* 9, 2 (2003), 78.

[15] Allaine Cerwonka. 2008. Traveling feminist thought: Difference and transculturation in Central and Eastern European feminism. *Signs: Journal of Women in Culture and Society* 33, 4 (2008), 809–832.

[16] miriam cooke. 2016. Women and the Arab Spring : A Transnational, Feminist Revolution. *Women's Movements in Post-'Arab Spring' North Africa* (2016), 31–44.

[17] Alison Dahl Crossley. 2015. Facebook feminism: Social media, blogs, and new technologies of contemporary US Feminism. *Mobilization: An International Quarterly* 20, 2 (2015), 253–268.

[18] Hamid Dabashi. 2012. *The Arab Spring: the end of postcolonialism*. Zed Books Ltd.

[19] Susan Muaddi Darraj. 2002. Understanding the other sister: the case of Arab feminism. *Monthly Review* 53, 10 (2002), 15.

[20] R Emerson Dobash and Russell Dobash. 1979. *Violence against wives: A case against the patriarchy*. Free Press New York.

[21] Hester Eisenstein. 2015. *Feminism seduced: How global elites use women's labor and ideas to exploit the world*. Routledge.

[22] Fadwa El Guindi. 1999. Veiling resistance. *Fashion Theory* 3, 1 (1999), 59.

[23] Leona M English. 2005. Third-space practitioners: Women educating for justice in the global south. *Adult Education Quarterly* 55, 2 (2005), 85–100.

[24] Myra Marx Ferree and Carol McClurg Mueller. 2004. Feminism and the women's movement: A global perspective. *The Blackwell companion to social movements* (2004), 576–607.

[25] Myra Marx Ferree and Aili Mari Tripp. 2006. *Global feminism: Transnational women's activism, organizing, and human rights*. NYU Press.

[26] Susan Stanford Friedman. 1998. *Mappings: Feminism and the cultural geographies of encounter*. Princeton University Press.

[27] Nawar Al-Hassan Golley. 2004. Is feminism relevant to Arab women? *Third World Quarterly* 25, 3 (2004), 521–536.

[28] Amal Grami. 2013. Islamic Feminism: a new feminist movement or a strategy by women for acquiring rights? *Contemporary Arab Affairs* 6, 1 (2013), 102–113.

[29] John A Guidry, Michael D Kennedy, and Mayer N Zald. 2000. *Globalizations and social movements: Culture, power, and the transnational public sphere*. University of Michigan Press.

[30] Jyotsna Agnihotri Gupta. 2006. Towards transnational feminisms: Some reflections and concerns in relation to the globalization of reproductive technologies. *European Journal of Women's Studies* 13, 1 (2006), 23–38.

[31] Yvonne Yazbeck Haddad and John L Esposito. 1997. *Islam, gender, and social change*. Oxford University Press.

[32] Nancy Hafkin, Nancy Taggart, et al. 2001. *Gender, information technology, and developing countries: An analytic study*. Office of Women in Development, Bureau for Global Programs, Field Support and Research, United States Agency for International Development.

[33] Nancy J Hafkin and Sophia Huyer. 2006. *Cinderella or cyberella?: Empowering women in the knowledge society*. Kumarian Press, Incorporated.

[34] Mary E Hawkesworth. 2006. *Globalization and feminist activism*. Rowman & Littlefield Publishers.

[35] Marie-Aimèe Hèlie-Lucas. 1999. What is your tribe?: WomenâǍżs struggles and the construction of Muslimness. In *Religious fundamentalisms and the human rights of women*. Springer, 21–32.

[36] Barbara Hobson. 2000. *Gender and citizenship in transition*. Psychology Press. 118–238 pages.

[37] Mala Htun and S Laurel Weldon. 2012. The civic origins of progressive policy change: Combating violence against women in global perspective, 1975–2005. *American Political Science Review* 106, 3 (2012), 548–569.

[38] Sophia Huyer and Swasti Mitter. 2003. ICTs, globalisation and poverty reduction: Gender dimensions of the knowledge society. *Kampala (Uganda): Comisión de Ciencia y Tecnología para el Desarrollo (Naciones Unidas), Junta Consultiva sobre Cuestiones de Género. Puede consultarse en http://gab. wigsat. org/policy. htm* (2003).

[39] Sophia Huyer and Tatjana Sikoska. 2003. *Overcoming the gender digital divide: understanding ICTs and their potential for the empowerment of women*. INSTRAW.

[40] Alison M Jaggar. 1998. Globalizing feminist ethics. *Hypatia* 13, 2 (1998), 7–31.

[41] Deniz Kandiyoti. 1991. Identity and its Discontents: Women and the Nation. *Millennium* 20, 3 (1991), 429–443.

[42] Jayawardena Kumari. 1986. of the Book: Feminism and Nationalism in the Third World. (1986).

[43] Anitta Kynsilehto. 2008. Islamic feminism: current perspectives. *Islamic feminism* (2008), 9.

[44] Henri Lauzière. 2010. The construction of Salafiyya: Reconsidering Salafism from the perspective of conceptual history. *International Journal of Middle East Studies* 42, 3 (2010), 369–389.

[45] Catharine A MacKinnon. 1983. Feminism, Marxism, method, and the state: Toward feminist jurisprudence. *Signs: Journal of women in culture and society* 8, 4 (1983), 635–658.

[46] Sylvia Maier and Usha Nair-Reichert. 2007. Empowering women through ICT-based business initiatives: An overview of best practices in e-commerce/e-retailing projects. *Information Technologies & International Development* 4, 2 (2007), pp–43.

[47] Lisa McLaughlin. 2004. Feminism and the political economy of transnational public space. *The Sociological Review* 52, 1_suppl (2004), 156–175.

[48] Breny Mendoza. 2002. Transnational feminisms in question. *Feminist Theory* 3, 3 (2002), 295–314.

[49] Beverly Dawn Metcalfe. 2011. Women, empowerment and development in Arab Gulf States: a critical appraisal of governance, culture and national human resource development (HRD) frameworks. *Human Resource Development International* 14, 2 (2011), 131–148.

[50] Valentine M Moghadam. 1991. Islamist Movements and Women's Responses in the Middle East. *Gender & History* 3, 3 (1991), 268–286.

[51] Valentine M Moghadam. 2005. *Globalizing women: Transnational feminist networks*. JHU Press.

[52] Valentine M Moghadam and Fatima Sadiqi. 2006. Women's Activism and the Public Sphere: Introduction and Overview. *Journal of Middle East Women's Studies* 2, 2 (2006), 1–7.

[53] Chandra Talpade Mohanty. 1984. Under Western eyes: Feminist scholarship and colonial discourses. *Boundary 2* (1984), 333–358.

[54] Uma Narayan. 2000. *Decentering the center: Philosophy for a multicultural, postcolonial, and feminist world*. Indiana University Press.

[55] Victoria A Newsom and Lara Lengel. 2012. Arab Women, Social Media, and the Arab Spring: Applying the framework of digital reflexivity to analyze gender and online activism. *Journal of International Women's Studies* 13, 5 (2012), 31.

[56] Maurice Odine. 2013. Role of social media in the empowerment of Arab women. *Global Media Journal* 2013 (2015).

[57] Courtney C Radsch and Sahar Khamis. 2013. In their own voice: Technologically mediated empowerment and transformation among young Arab women. *Feminist Media Studies* 13, 5 (2013), 881–890.

[58] Fatima Seedat. 2013. When Islam and feminism converge. *The Muslim World* 103, 3 (2013), 404–420.

[59] Jackie Smith. 2008. *Social movements for global democracy*. JHU Press.

[60] Jackie Smith, Charles Chatfield, and Ron Pagnucco. 1997. *Transnational social movements and global politics: Solidarity beyond the state*. Syracuse University Press.

[61] Michael D Smith. 1990. Patriarchal ideology and wife beating: A test of a feminist hypothesis. *Violence and victims* 5, 4 (1990), 257.

[62] Aili Mari Tripp. 2006. The evolution of transnational feminisms. *Global Feminism: Transnational Women's Activisms* (2006), 51–75.

[63] Jacqui True and Michael Mintrom. 2001. Transnational networks and policy diffusion: The case of gender mainstreaming. *International studies quarterly* 45, 1 (2001), 27–57.

[64] Claudia Yaghoobi and Margot Badran. 2011. Feminism in Islam: Secular and Religious Convergences. *International Journal of Middle East Studies* 43, 4 (2011), 754.

[65] Meyda Yegenoglu. 1998. *Colonial fantasies: Towards a feminist reading of Orientalism*. Cambridge University Press.

[66] Lamia Ben Youssef Zayzafoon. 2004. Review of Saliba, Therese; Allen, Carolyn; Howard, Judith A., eds., Gender, Politics, and Islam. *H-Gender-MidEast, H-Net Reviews* (2004).

[67] Sherifa Zuhur. 2003. Women and empowerment in the Arab world. *Arab Studies Quarterly* (2003), 17–38.

Hater are not Always Psychopaths - Understanding the Origin of Cyber-Hatraterism - the Psycho-Sociological Facets of Users

Srinivas P Y K L
Indian Institute of Information
Technology, Sri City
srinivas.p@iiits.in

Amitava Das
Indian Institute of Information
Technology, Sri City
amitava.das@iiits.in

Björn Gambäck
Norwegian University of Science and
Technology,Norway
gamback@ntnu.no

ABSTRACT

The paper investigates the connections between hate speech propagators and some psychopathic personality traits. First, a deep learning-based hate-speech classifier is introduced to separate text into non-hate speech, sexist, and racist types. Previous research has suggested that trolling enjoyment and troll identities are strongly correlated with psychopathy. To understand the nature of psychopathy, we borrow the well-defined Dark Triad of personality model [*Narcissism, Machiavellianism, and Psychopathy*] and as a second step build a classifier which can assess social media users' orientation towards these Dark Triad traits by analyzing their texts and online activities. Then, the correlation between users and Dark Triad orientations is analyzed empirically, showing that there is a strong (67% of of the total haters) connection between hate speech propagation and psychopathic disorder. But, the essential question we ask here is what about the rest 33% haters. To understand their psycho-sociological orientations we borrow the well-established Big5 personality model [*Openness, Conscientiousness, Extroversion, Agreeableness, Neuroticism*], could be further described as person-level sentiment model and to analyze users' societal orientation we bring in Schwartz' Values model consists of ten [*Achievement, Benevolence, Conformity, Hedonism, Power, Security, Self-Direction. Stimulation, Traditional and Universalism*] human value types. Our analysis unleash - i) gender-insensitive people are mostly extroverts and socially power and achievement seeking. ii) racist are indeed socially conform, outgoing extroverts, and socially traditional.

CCS CONCEPTS

• **Networks** → **Social media networks**;

KEYWORDS

Social Media, Dark Triad, Hate Speech

ACM Reference Format:
Srinivas P Y K L, Amitava Das, and Björn Gambäck. 2018. Hater are not Always Psychopaths - Understanding the Origin of Cyber-Hatraterism - the Psycho-Sociological Facets of Users. In *WebSci '18: 10th ACM Conference on Web Science, May 27–30, 2018, Amsterdam, Netherlands.* ACM, New York, NY, USA, 6 pages. https://doi.org/10.1145/3201064.3201106

1 INTRODUCTION

Many types of antisocial behaviour can be observed in social media and promotors of hateful activities are to an increasing extent exploiting social media, raising concern in the society. In social networks, antisocial actions are committed by those users who are trolling, harassing and dominating others—often persons they have no personal relationship to, such as a celebrity or a politician, but also individuals in their vicinity, companies, products, etc. People who are trolled or harassed are put under emotional stress [2] and hate speech is commonly used when performing these antisocial activities, to put further stress on the victims, this can include racist or sexist comments, attacks on minority groups, promotion of violence, or other types of cyber-bullying that go far beyond offensive language, as discussed by Davidson et al. [4]. In previous work, it has been claimed that people writing hateful comments are influenced by their own unique personality traits [3]. In order to understand the origins and mechanisms behind hate speech and trolling, their connections to human behaviour and psychology need to be studied further. The proliferation of large amounts of social media data has made this possible.

Hate speech detection and classification has become topical within language processing research in recent years, after social media sites such as Facebook, Twitter and Youtube having been strongly criticised for failing to take sufficient and quick enough action against hate speech [5]. The 1st Workshop on Abusive Language Online was organised in 2017[1] and included an "unshared task" on hate speech detection (i.e., the organisers provided datasets, but there was no common evaluation).

However, classification of hate speech is still an under-researched problem, and the motivation behind the work in this paper is to study the origins of hate speech in terms of human behaviour. To this end, a set of tweets annotated for hate speech (sexism or racism) was taken as a starting point to train a deep learning-based hate speech classifier. To charter user personalities, another set of tweets was utilized, with the users who posted them being classified into the Dark Triad of personalities (Narcissism, Machiavellianism, and Psychopathy). Based on these two datasets and classifiers, it is possible to empirically study the correlation between hate speech propagators and Dark Triad orientations, and specifically address two questions: i) *Do people having Dark Triad orientations post hate speech content more often than the regular users?* ii) *If so, do some Dark Triad traits associate closer with some hate speech types?* iii) *What if non Dark Triad orientation post hate speech content?* iv) *if non Dark Triad orientation post hate speech in social network what personality and social behaviour acting them do so?*

---

[1]sites.google.com/site/abusivelanguageworkshop2017/

Our analysis unleash on and around 67% (at least in our dataset) of of the total haters are positively dark triad oriented. Now it is essential to ask what about the rest of the 33% - who are they? If they are not psychopaths then what are their personal (psychological) and societal (sociological) motivations while spreading cyber-haterism. To understand their psychological orientations we borrow the well-established Big5 [6] personality model [*Openness, Conscientiousness, Extroversion, Agreeableness, Neuroticism*], could be further described as person-level sentiment model and to analyze users' societal orientation we bring in Schwartz' Values [11] model consists of ten [*Achievement, Benevolence, Conformity, Hedonism, Power, Security, Self-Direction. Stimulation, Traditional and Universalism*] human value types. Then we ask similar questions here.i) *What kinds of Personality spread more haterism than the regular users? what kinds of social upbringings they have? ii) Which kinds of Personality and Values are closely associated with specific hate speech types?*

This paper presents an empirical study to answer above cited questions - related to the psycho-sociological behaviors of individual and their influences on cyber-haterism.

2 DATASETS

As described in the next section, four different classifiers were built, i) to identify and classify hate speech, ii) for classifying Dark Triad personalities, iii) for Big5 Personality classification, and iv) for Social values behaviour classification. The output of these classifiers were then merged to gain empirical insight into the research questions.

2.1 Hate Speech - Data

Waseem and Hovy [15] first published a collection of tweets (Twitter posts) annotated for various types of hate speech. The dataset was then extended by Waseem [14] and is publicly available online,[2] having 6,909 tweet ids together with annotation of the tweet content with four class labels: *sexism, racism, both, and neither (non-hate speech)*, with each tweet being annotated by one expert in the field and three amateurs. Only a handful of tweets were classified as belonging to both sexism and racism, so the present study concentrated on the major categories, i.e., sexism, racism, and neither. Some of the annotated tweets have been deleted since 2016, so only 6,534 tweets were available for the present work and used to build a hate speech classifier, after having assigned one class only to each tweet. This was done by extracting the maximum number of votes given by the four annotators, using the expert's vote as tie-breaker in case there were equal number of votes for several classes. The distribution of the annotated tweets is shown in Table 1.

Table 1: Distributions of Hate Speech Tweets

Class	Tweets
Sexism	1745
Racism	433
Neither	4356
Total	6534

[2]github.com/zeerakw/hatespeech

2.2 Dark Triad of Personality - Data

The dark orientation of personalities and its manifestation in human behaviour has been an interesting topic for psychologists for centuries. Be it either the serial killer Jack the Ripper or the fictional character Prof. Moriarty, it has always also aroused the interest of the general population. Today, the wide spread of social media platforms offers a medium for expressing darker traits of human personality such as self-promotion, vanity, anti-social behaviour, alteration of the truth, and self-interest. Some of these characteristics have been addressed in psychology research and leadership studies under the heading of the Dark Triad of personality [7], which consists of three traits that are linked to negative personal and societal outcomes, but that can also be advantageous for the individual under some circumstances (e.g., for certain types of leaders):

- **Narcissism:** grandiose, inflated self-views; sense of entitlement; craving for admiration; lack of guilt and shame.
- **Machiavellian:** self-interest, cynicism, power and dominance; tendency to manipulate, charm and exploit others.
- **Psychopathy:** lack of empathy; enduring antisocial behaviour; impulsively.

The questions that modern researchers are facing are whether, and in what way, psychopaths reflect their personalities in their actual behaviour in social media. The first data driven research endeavour to examine that for the Dark Triad was carried out by Preoţiuc-Pietro et al. [10] who used a questionnaire to obtain user personality information. This dataset was made available by the authors and consists of tweet id for 864 users together with the users' log scores for the Dark Triad personality traits. This data has been used to create the dark triad classifier.

2.3 Big5 Personality - Data

To understand nature of the user why s/he is posting hate speech on the social network we analyze user personality - using the Big5 [6] personality model [*Openness, Conscientiousness, Extroversion, Agreeableness, Neuroticism*] also called the Five Factor Model (FFM) or the OCEAN model from Psychology -

- **Opennes [O]:** Imaginative, insightful, and have wide interest
- **Neuroticism [N]:** Anxious, timid, immature, and unstable in their actions.
- **Conscientiousness [C]:** Organized, thorough, planned, and punctual.
- **Agreeableness [A]:** Amiable, generous, co-operative, and alturistic.
- **Extroversion [E]:** Articulative, boastful, and energetic.

The personality labeled gold corpus (10K Facebook status updates of 250 users and their Facebook network properties), released in WCPR'13[3] workshop ,is used to build the personality model.

2.4 Schwartz Values - Data

Social upbringings are indeed a salient exposure towards cyber-haterism. To understand the social behavior of a user we make use of the Schwartz values[11] comprises of ten value traits [*Achievement, Benevolence, Conformity, Hedonism, Power, Security, Self-Direction. Stimulation, Traditional and Universalism*]. However, we further describe it as societal sentiment model

- **Self-direction [SD]:** wants to be independent and free.

[3]http://mypersonality.org/wiki/doku.php?id=wcpr13

Table 2: Performance of Dark Triad Classifier

Dark Triad Trait	Accuracy
Narcissism	73.3%
Machiavellianism	71.7%
Psychopathy	73.4%

- **Stimulation [ST]:** seeks exhilaration and adventurers.
- **Hedonism [HE]:** seeks pleasure and enjoyment.
- **Universalism [UN]:** seeks peace, social justice and tolerance for all.
- **Conformity [CO]:** obeys clear rules, laws and structure.
- **Security [SE]:** seeks health and safety.
- **Benevolence [BE]:** lot of helping nature towards others and provide general welfare.
- **Tradition [TR]:** does things blindly because they are customary.
- **Power [PO]:** controls and dominates others, control resources.
- **Achievement [AC]:** sets goals and aims at achieving them.

For building Values&classifier we have used a Twitter data-set which consists of users who are self-assessed using Portrait Value Questionnaire (PVQ) on Amazon Mechanical Turk (AMT) a crowdsourcing method. In this data set about 367 unique users is present with the average of 1,608 tweets. Users who took part in this crowdsourcing they are distributed across the world a few East-Asians (Singaporeans, Malaysian, Japanese, Chinese), South Asia (India, Pakistan, Bangladesh) and Americans (USA, Canada, Mexico, Brazil) . Based on the datasets described in the previous section, four classifiers were trained to respectively - i) to identify tweets as hate speech, ii) to investigate online users' tendencies towards the Dark Triad traits, iii) to identify the users' personality in terms five factor model, and iv) to classify users into Schwartz values classes.

2.5 Hate Speech Classifier

To classify tweets into three categories (sexism, racism, and neither), a 3-layered Convolutional Neural Network was designed. The first two convolutional layers use an exponential linear unit (ELU) activation function . The output of the second layer is flattened to generate a 1-dimensional vector, which is given to a dense output layer of size 3 with a softmax activation function, providing the scores for the three categories.

The network was trained on the hate speech annotated dataset, containing tweet ids and the annotation score Waseem [14]. The words were first tokenized and two tensors were created: data tensors of size $T * L$ and label tensors of dimension $T * C$, where T is the number of tweets, L the maximum sequence length, and C the number of hate speech classes. Each word was then converted into its respective word vector of dimension 128*100, creating an embedding matrix of size $W * D$, where W is the number of unique tokens and D the embedding dimension. Global Vectors for Word Representations (GloVe) of 100 dimensions [9] were used to create the word vectors for each word in a tweet, and then to build an embedding layer that generates an embedding sequence which is fed to the network.

2.6 Dark Triad Personality Classifier

The data set provided by Preoţiuc-Pietro et al. [10] was used for building the Dark Triad classifier. In the dataset, the twitter ids are given with log score for each personality trait (Narcissism, Machiavellianism, and Psychopathy). We have used Twitter API.[4] to crawl tweets for given tweet id in dataset and collected (652,324 tweets altogether, with around 700–800 tweets per user) to annotate collected tweets median value was calculated for each personality trait, and each Twitter user was labelled as having that personality trait if their score for the trait was above the median. Feature vectors were then created for the tweets based on Linguistic Inquiry and Word Count (LIWC) by Pennebaker et al. [8], the Harvard General Inquirer [12], the MRC Psycholinguistic Database [16], Sensicon,[5] and speech act classes [1]. The resulting feature vector was given to a Random Forests for training and testing. The results are shown in Table 2.

2.7 Big5 Personality Classifier

We use a SVM-based model that outperforms the state-of-the-art[13] by 10%, achieving average F-Score of 79.35%. Features used in this model are same as disscued in Dark Triad Personality Classification sub-section.

2.8 Schwartz Values Classifier

A SVM-based values classifiers achieves an average F-Score of 80%. Features used in this model are same as disscued in Dark Triad Personality Classification sub-section.

3 SEXISTS ARE MACHIAVELLIAN, RACISTS ARE NARCISSISTIC

To understand the correlations between the Dark Triad of personalities and hate speech types, experiments were performed in three steps, first identifying the users' personalities, then classifying their tweets, and finally exploring the correlation between user personality types and hate speech.

3.1 Step 1:

For each user $u \in U$ (where U is the set of all users; here size 864), the dominating personality type of the user, $P(u)$, was identified by taking the maximum score among the Dark Triad traits for that user. To perform this step, an input matrix was given with dimension $U \times P$ where P holds the Dark Triad categories (Narcissism, Machiavellianism, and Psychopathy). Hence:

$$\forall u : P(u) = \max_{1 \leq i \leq 3} P_i(u) \qquad (1)$$

where $P_i(u)$ are the Dark Triad scores of user u.

3.2 Step 2:

In this step, we are finding the hate speech score for the twitter id which is used for building dark triad classifiers ??.To get the hate speech scores a matrix is generated which has $U \times T$ dimension, where U are the users and T the maximum number of tweets for any user (each user has 700–800 tweets). This matrix was given to the CNN-based hate speech classifier and the result of an individual tweet of each user was stored in a matrix with dimension $U \times T \times C$, where C stores the score of each of the three hate speech classes (racism, sexism, and neither). To get the hate speech scores for each user, the steps shown in Equation 2 are performed on this matrix— normalizing the scores for each hate speech class with the total

---

[4]twitter4j.org/en/
[5]hlt-nlp.fbk.eu/technologies/sensicon

number of tweets—and the results are stored in a $U \times C$ dimensional matrix, $H_{u,c}$.

$$\begin{cases} R = \sum_{u=1}^{U} \sum_{t=1}^{T} r & : \quad r = M_{u,t,1} \\ H_{u,1} = R/T \\ S = \sum_{u=1}^{U} \sum_{t=1}^{T} s & : \quad s = M_{u,t,2} \\ H_{u,2} = S/T \\ N = \sum_{u=1}^{U} \sum_{t=1}^{T} n & : \quad n = M_{u,t,3} \\ H_{u,3} = N/T \end{cases} \quad (2)$$

3.3 Step 3:

To get the correlations between Dark Triad and Hate Speech, the output of step 1, i.e., $D_{u,p}$, and output of step 2, i.e., $H_{u,c}$ are used. $D_{u,p}$ provides the Dark Triad personality information of each user and $H_{u,c}$ provides the hate speech class scores for each user (i.e., the scores for racism, sexism, and neither). To get the correlations ($\forall u \forall p$):

$$\begin{cases} Cr(p) = \sum_{u=1}^{U} r & : \quad r = H_{u,1} \\ R(p) = Cr(p)/U \\ Cs(p) = \sum_{u=1}^{U} s & : \quad s = H_{u,2} \\ S(p) = Cs(p)/U \\ Cn(p) = \sum_{u=1}^{U} n & : \quad n = H_{u,3} \\ N(p) = Cn(p)/U \end{cases} \quad (3)$$

where P gives personality scores (for Narcissism, Machiavellianism, and Psychopathy) and U is the number of users.

4 TAKE-AWAY POINTS - DARK TRIAD VS. HATE SPEECH

Several interesting correlations can be deduced from Figure 2, which plots the results obtained after the calculations in Equation 3.

(i) In general, it is clear that all users who are posting sexist and racist content on Twitter have some type of Dark Triad personalities.

(ii) Specifically, the Machiavellian personality appears often among the users who tweet sexist content and Narcissism is common among the users who post racist tweets.

(iii) Another interesting result can be seen in the difference between the users who tweet non-hate speech and the people who post racist tweets: the non-hate speech users have clearly lower Narcissism personality values compared to the users who tweet more racist content.

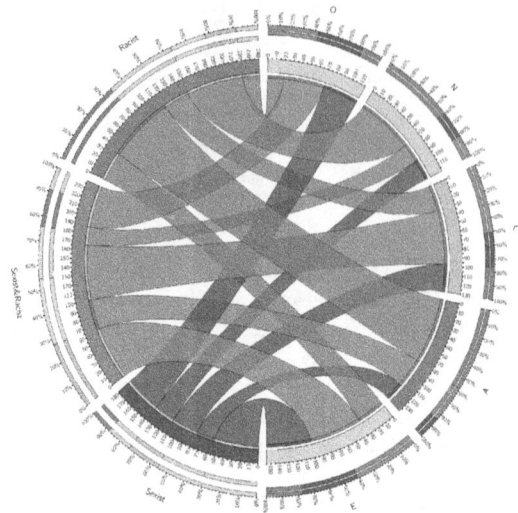

Figure 1: Fuzziness between Big5 model and Hate speech types

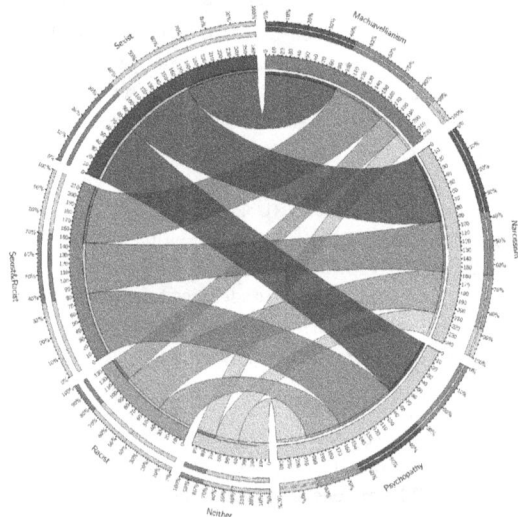

Figure 2: Sexists are Machiavellian, Racists are Narcissistic:Correlations Between the Dark Triad of Personalities and Hate Speech

5 NON-PSYCHOPATHS - POWER AND ACHIEVEMENT SEEKERS ARE GENDER-INSENSITIVE AND RACIST ARE SOCIALLY CONFORM, AND TRADITIONAL

To understand the relationship between non-dark triad users and hate speech type's an experiment was performed in three steps, in the first step we identified all the non-dark triad users then we counted the total number of hate speeches propagated by those non-dark triad users. Finally, we are reporting the empirically obtained relationship between hate speech types vs. Big5 Personality and Schwartz Values types.

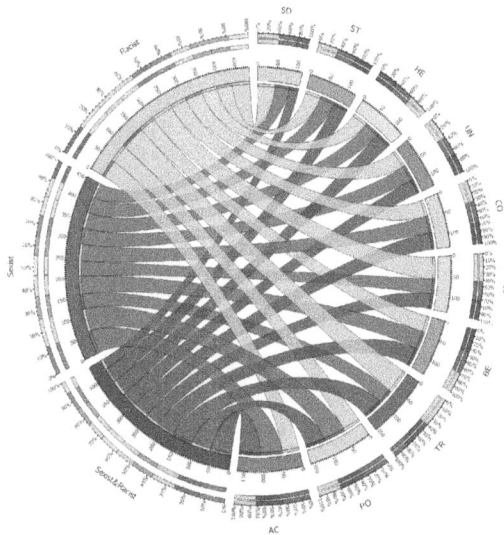

Figure 3: Sexist are Power and Achievement Seekers,Racist are Tradition: Relation between Social behavior and Hate speech types

5.1 Step 1:

In this step, unique 941 users (33%) were identified from Waseem and Hovy [15] dataset, users who posted hate speeches but non-psychopaths - according to our Dark Triad classifier. For these 941 users, we have collected altogether 35,30,100 tweets.

5.2 Step 2:

To understand the personal level exposure towards cyber-haterism we have analyzed Big5 Personality of all the non-dark traid people and then counted how many number of sexist tweets, racist tweets and neither tweets are posted by which kind of personality. Results presented in the Figure: 1.

5.3 Step 3:

Finally, to get the relationships among social exposures and hate speech types - we counted number of sexist tweets, racist tweets and neither tweets posted by different values types users as reported in the Figure: 3.

6 TAKE AWAY POINTS - NON-PSYCHOPATHS VS. HATE SPEECH

The interesting relation has been interrupted from Figure: 1 with respect to personalities and Non-Dark Triad users who are posting hate speech on the social network. From the analysis, we interrupted that user who is posting sexist tweets are high in Extroverts personality and the user posting racist tweets are high in Neurotic and Agreeable personality. Finally, the user who is posting both sexist and racist tweets have high Extroverts and Conformity personality

To understand more clearly what relation exists between hate speech and non-dark triads with respect to society, for that analysis has made with respect to social behavior which is shown in Figure: 3 from that interesting results were observed which is showing users who are posting racist tweets on social network are highly traditional oriented were as users who are posting sexist tweets are

highly achievement and power oriented and users who post both the tweets can be tradition, power, and achievement oriented

7 CONCLUSIONS & FUTURE AVENUES

We report an empirical study to investigate whether Dark Triad personality traits are linked to certain types of hate speech postings in social media. Indeed, our empirical analysis unleash -

(i) In general (for 67% cases), it is clear that all users who are posting sexist and racist content on Twitter have some type of Dark Triad personalities.
(ii) Specifically, the Machiavellian personality appears often among the users who tweet sexist content and Narcissism is common among the users who post racist tweets.
(iii) Another interesting result can be seen in the difference between the users who tweet non-hate speech and the people who post racist tweets: the non-hate speech users have clearly lower Narcissism personality values compared to the users who tweet more racist content.

But, the essential question we ask here is what about the rest 33% haters. To understand their psycho-sociological orientations we borrow the well-established Big5 personality model and Schwartz Values models. Our analysis reveals -

(i) gender-insensitive people are mostly extroverts and socially power and achievement seeking.
(ii) racist are indeed socially conform, outgoing extroverts, and socially traditional.

We are not studying the how can trolling spread from person to person in a community - the hate speech diffusion pattern. between

REFERENCES

[1] D. Scott Appling, Erica J. Briscoe, , Heather Hayes, and Rudolph L. Mappus. 2013. Towards Automated Personality Identification Using Speech Acts. In *Proceedings of the 7th International Conference on Weblogs and Social Media*. AAAI, Boston, Massachusetts, 10–13.
[2] Tanya Beran and Qing Li. 2005. Cyber-Harassment: A Study of a New Method for an Old Behavior. *Journal of Educational Computating Research* 32, 3 (2005), 265–277.
[3] Erin E. Buckels, Paul D. Trapnell, and Delroy L. Paulhus. 2014. Trolls just want to have fun. *Personality and Individual Differences* 67, Supplement C (Sept. 2014), 97–102.
[4] Thomas Davidson, Dana Warmsley, Michael Macy, and Ingmar Weber. 2017. Automated Hate Speech Detection and the Problem of Offensive Language. In *Proceedings of the 11th International Conference on Weblogs and Social Media*. AAAI, Ann Arbor, Michigan, 512–515.
[5] Björn Gambäck and Utpal Kumar Sikdar. 2017. Using Convolutional Neural Networks to Classify Hate-Speech. In *Proceedings of the 55th Annual Meeting of the Association for Computational Linguistics*. ACL, Vancouver, Canada, 85–90. 1st Workshop on Abusive Language Online.
[6] Lewis R Goldberg. 1990. An alternative" description of personality": the big-five factor structure. *Journal of personality and social psychology* 59, 6 (1990), 1216.
[7] D.L. Paulhus and K.M. Williams. 2002. The Dark Triad of Personality: Narcissism, Machiavellianism, and Psychopathy. *Journal of Research in Personality* 36, 6 (2002), 556–563.
[8] James W. Pennebaker, Roger J. Booth, Ryan L. Boyd, and Martha E. Francis. 2015. *Linguistic Inquiry and Word Count: LIWC2015*. Pennebaker Conglomerates, Austin, Texas.
[9] Jeffrey Pennington, Richard Socher, and Christopher D. Manning. 2014. GloVe: Global Vectors for Word Representation. In *Proceedings of the 2014 Conference on Empirical Methods in Natural Language Processing*. ACL, Doha, Qatar, 1532–1543.
[10] Daniel Preoţiuc-Pietro, Jordan Carpenter, Salvatore Giorgi, and Lyle Ungar. 2016. Studying the Dark Triad of Personality Through Twitter Behavior. In *Proceedings of the 25th International Conference on Information and Knowledge Management*. ACM, Indianapolis, Indiana, 761–770. https://doi.org/10.1145/2983323.2983822
[11] Shalom H Schwartz. 2012. An overview of the Schwartz theory of basic values. *Online Readings in Psychology and Culture* 2, 1 (2012), 11.

[12] Philip J. Stone, Dexter C. Dunphy, Marshall S. Smith, and Daniel M. Ogilvie. 1966. *The General Inquirer: A Computer Approach to Content Analysis.* MIT Press.

[13] Ben Verhoeven, Walter Daelemans, and Tom De Smedt. 2013. Ensemble methods for personality recognition. *Proceedings of WCPR13, in conjunction with ICWSM-13* (2013).

[14] Zeerak Waseem. 2016. Are You a Racist or Am I Seeing Things? Annotator Influence on Hate Speech Detection on Twitter. In *Proceedings of the 2016 Conference on Empirical Methods in Natural Language Processing.* ACL, Austin, Texas, 138–142.

[15] Zeerak Waseem and Dirk Hovy. 2016. Hateful Symbols or Hateful People? Predictive Features for Hate Speech Detection on Twitter. In *Proceedings of the 15th Annual Conference of the North American Chapter of the Association for Computational Linguistics: Human Language Technologies.* 88–93.

[16] Michael Wilson. 1988. MRC Psycholinguistic Database: Machine-usable dictionary, version 2.00. *Behavior Research Methods, Instruments and Computers* 20, 1 (1988), 6–10.

Analyzing Right-wing YouTube Channels:
Hate, Violence and Discrimination

Raphael Ottoni
DCC/UFMG, Brazil
rapha@dcc.ufmg.br

Evandro Cunha
DCC/UFMG, Brazil
LUCL/Univ. Leiden, The Netherlands
evandrocunha@dcc.ufmg.br

Gabriel Magno
DCC/UFMG, Brazil
magno@dcc.ufmg.br

Pedro Bernardina
DCC/UFMG, Brazil
pedronascimento@dcc.ufmg.br

Wagner Meira Jr.
DCC/UFMG, Brazil
meira@dcc.ufmg.br

Virgilio Almeida
DCC/UFMG, Brazil
Berkman Klein Center/Harvard, USA
virgilio@dcc.ufmg.br

ABSTRACT

As of 2018, YouTube, the major online video sharing website, hosts multiple channels promoting right-wing content. In this paper, we observe issues related to hate, violence and discriminatory bias in a dataset containing more than 7,000 videos and 17 million comments. We investigate similarities and differences between users' comments and video content in a selection of right-wing channels and compare it to a baseline set using a three-layered approach, in which we analyze (a) lexicon, (b) topics and (c) implicit biases present in the texts. Among other results, our analyses show that right-wing channels tend to (a) contain a higher degree of words from "negative" semantic fields, (b) raise more topics related to war and terrorism, and (c) demonstrate more discriminatory bias against Muslims (in videos) and towards LGBT people (in comments). Our findings shed light not only into the collective conduct of the YouTube community promoting and consuming right-wing content, but also into the general behavior of YouTube users.

CCS CONCEPTS

• **Human-centered computing** → **Empirical studies in collaborative and social computing**; • **Information systems** → *Social networks*; • **Applied computing** → Law, social and behavioral sciences;

KEYWORDS

YouTube; comments; hate speech; discriminatory bias

ACM Reference Format:
Raphael Ottoni, Evandro Cunha, Gabriel Magno, Pedro Bernardina, Wagner Meira Jr., and Virgilio Almeida. 2018. Analyzing Right-wing YouTube Channels: Hate, Violence and Discrimination. In *Proceedings of the 10th ACM Conference on Web Science*. ACM, New York, NY, USA, 10 pages. https://doi.org/10.1145/3201064.3201081

1 INTRODUCTION

A recent wave of right-wing activity, including far-right and alt-right extremism, seems to be in course of progress in developed countries (especially in the United States of America [3] and in Western Europe [15, 33]), but also in developing countries, including Brazil [32]. According to the Jewish non-governmental organization Anti-Defamation League (ADL), "Internet has provided the far-right fringe with formerly inconceivable opportunities", making it possible for extremists to reach a much larger audience than ever before and easily portray themselves as legitimate [2]. Analyzing how this kind of content is related to the reactions that it produces is of utmost importance to understand its peculiarities and tendencies.

YouTube, the major online video sharing website, is one of the virtual services that host a high variety of right-wing voices [17, 46]. Since YouTube makes it possible for users to not only watch videos, but also to react to them through comments, it is interesting to observe how these comments are related to the content of the videos published in the platform. It is also valuable to investigate whether behaviors connected to hate, violence and discriminatory bias come into sight in right-wing videos. This becomes even more relevant if we consider the findings of a 2018 newspaper investigation [30] which shows that YouTube's recommendations often lead users to channels that feature highly partisan viewpoints – even for users that have not shown interest in such content.

In this study, we analyze the content of videos published in a set of right-wing YouTube channels and observe the relationship between them and the comments that they receive from their audience using a three-layered approach in which we analyze (a) lexicon, (b) topics and (c) implicit biases present in the texts. We also use the same approach to compare right-wing channels with a set of baseline channels in order to identify characteristics that differentiate or associate these two groups.

Research questions. Our main goal is to investigate the presence of hateful content and discriminatory bias in a set of right-wing channels through the analysis of the captions of their videos and the comments posted in response to them, and to compare these captions and comments with those of a group of baseline channels. Our initial research questions are the following:

RQ-1: is the presence of hateful vocabulary, violent content and discriminatory biases more, less or equally accentuated in right-wing channels?

RQ-2: are, in general, commentators more, less or equally exacerbated than video hosts in an effort to express hate and discrimination?

One of the side contributions of this paper is the proposal of a three-layered method that can be used to evaluate the presence of hate speech and discriminatory bias not only on YouTube videos and comments, but in any kind of text instead. Our method, which uses only open source tools, is an aggregation of three already established procedures that, in our view, complement each other and favor a multi-directional analysis when combined together.

This article is structured as follows: in the next section, we describe the process of acquisition and preparation of the dataset used in our investigations; then, in Section 3, we detail our three analyses and present the results found; later, in Section 4, we present previous works related to the analysis of hate, violence and bias in YouTube and in online social networks in general; finally, we conclude this paper in Section 5 by summarizing its outcomes and by pointing out some possible future works.

2 DATA ACQUISITION AND PREPARATION

2.1 Dataset

To select the YouTube channels to be analyzed, we used the website InfoWars[1] as a seed. InfoWars is known as a right-wing news website founded by Alex Jones, a radio host based in the United States of America. The InfoWars website links to Alex Jones' YouTube channel, which had more than 2 million subscribers as of October 2017. As stated in a The Guardian's article [24], "The Alex Jones Channel, the broadcasting arm of the far-right conspiracy website InfoWars, was one of the most recommended channels in the database of videos" used in a study which showed that YouTube's recommendation algorithm was not neutral during the presidential election of 2016 in the United States of America [23, 25]. At the moment of our data collection, Alex Jones expressed support to 12 other channels in his public YouTube profile. We visited these channels and confirmed that, according to our understanding, all of them published mainly right-wing content.

Alex Jones' channel and these other 12 channels supported by him were then collected using the YouTube Data API[2] from September 28 to October 12 2017. From all videos posted in these channels (limited to around 500 videos per channel due to API limits), we collected (a) the *video captions* (written versions of the speech in the videos, manually created by the video hosts or automatically generated by YouTube's speech-to-text engine), representing the content of the videos themselves; and (b) the *comments* (including replies to comments) posted to the videos. The total number of videos collected from these channels is 3,731 and the total number of comments collected from them is 5,071,728.

In order to build a baseline set of channels to compare the results of the analyses performed in these right-wing channels with a more general behavior in YouTube videos, we collected the same information (captions and comments) from videos posted in the ten most popular channels (in terms of number of subscribers in November 7 2017) of the category "news and politics" according to

the analytics tracking site Social Blade[3]. To be part of our baseline dataset, the content of these channels needed to be mainly in English language and non hard-coded captions needed to be available for the most part of the videos. The total number of videos collected from the baseline channels is 3,942 and the total number of comments collected from them is 12,519,590. It is important to notice that this selection of baseline channels does not intend to represent, by any means, a "neutral" users' behavior (if it even exists at all). Table 1 shows statistics regarding all collected channels.

Table 1: Statistics regarding all collected channels.

Right-wing channels	Subscribers	Videos collected	Comments collected
The Alex Jones Channel	2,157,464	564	955,705
Mark Dice	1,125,052	204	2,025,513
Paul Joseph Watson	1,043,236	230	1,747,497
THElNFOWARRlOR	177,736	467	112,060
Millennial Millie	79,818	359	167,569
Resistance News	36,820	112	40,829
Owen Shroyer	36,125	157	8,000
David Knight InfoWars	30,940	508	1,786
PlanetInfoWarsHD	22,674	206	4,903
Real News with David Knight	12,042	208	3,902
Infowars Live	9,974	8	216
War Room	7,387	188	2,036
Jon Bowne Reports	5,684	520	1,712
Total	**4,744,925**	**3,731**	**5,071,728**

Baseline channels	Subscribers	Videos collected	Comments collected
YouTube Spotlight	25,594,238	262	734,591
The Young Turks	3,479,018	540	1,652,818
Barcroft TV	3,459,016	427	1,279,400
Vox	3,103,138	448	1,389,170
DramaAlert	3,081,568	470	4,904,941
VICE News	2,476,558	451	897,056
YouTube Spotlight UK	2,307,818	75	23,280
TomoNews US	1,928,700	543	338,501
SourceFed	1,713,646	501	838,431
Anonymous Official	1,700,812	225	461,402
Total	**23,275,686**	**3,942**	**12,519,590**

2.2 Textual preprocessing

First, HTML tags and URLs were removed from both video captions and users' comments. Also, we used `langid.py`[4] [27], a language identification tool, to filter only video captions and comments with a probability ≥ 0.8 of being in English. This filtering resulted in the 3,278 videos and 4,348,986 comments from right-wing channels and in the 3,581 videos and 9,522,597 comments from baseline channels used in our investigations. Then, for each video we created two documents, each one originating from one of the two sources (*caption* and *comments*).

---

[1] https://www.infowars.com/
[2] https://developers.google.com/youtube/v3/
[3] https://socialblade.com/
[4] https://github.com/saffsd/langid.py

When additional preprocessing stages were required for an analysis, we mention them in the subsection corresponding to the specific methodology of that analysis, in Section 3.

3 ANALYSES AND RESULTS

We use a three-layered approach to investigate the problem of hate, violence and discriminatory bias in our set of right-wing videos and to address the research questions formulated in Section 1. Our three analyses, through which we evaluate (a) lexicon, (b) topics and (c) implicit biases, are the following:

- **lexical analysis**: we compared the semantic fields of the words in the captions with the semantic fields of the words in the comments, focusing on semantic fields related to hate, violence and discrimination. We did the same to compare right-wing channels to baseline channels;
- **topic analysis**: we contrasted the topics addressed in the captions with the ones addressed in the comments. Again, we did the same to contrast right-wing channels to baseline channels;
- **implicit bias analysis**: we analyzed implicit biases based on vector spaces in which words that share common contexts are located in close proximity to one another. Through this method, we compared biases between captions and comments, and once again between right-wing and baseline channels.

3.1 Lexical analysis

Lexical analysis, that is, the investigation of the vocabulary, reveals how society perceives reality and indicates the main concerns and interests of particular communities of speakers [11]. According to lexicological theories, vocabulary is the translation of social realities and thus it is natural to study it as a means to comprehend characteristics of groups that employ certain words in their discourse [8, 28]. Several different ways of analyzing vocabulary are possible. In this study, we model each channel based on the semantic fields (i.e. groups of semantically related items) of the words used in its videos and in the comments that it received.

3.1.1 Methodology. In addition to the preprocessing tasks mentioned in Section 2.2, lemmatization was applied by employing the WordNet Lemmatizer function provided by the Natural Language Toolkit [4] and using *verb* as the part-of-speech argument for the lemmatization method. For this analysis, lemmatization was necessary in order to group together the inflected forms of the words, so they could be analyzed as single items based on their dictionary forms (*lemmas*). In this way, words like *cat* and *cats* were grouped together under the same lemma (in this case, *cat*).

Then, each word was classified according to categories that represent different semantic fields, such as diverse topics and emotions, provided by Empath [12], "a tool for analyzing text across lexical categories" [5]. From the 194 total Empath categories, we selected the following (a) 15 categories related to hate, violence, discrimination and negative feelings, and (b) 5 categories related to positive matters in general:

---

[5] https://github.com/Ejhfast/empath-client

- **negative**: *aggression, anger, disgust, dominant personality, hate, kill, negative emotion, nervousness, pain, rage, sadness, suffering, swearing terms, terrorism, violence*
- **positive**: *joy, love, optimist, politeness, positive emotion*

For a given video video v, we calculated the word count for each one of these selected categories as

$$\vec{E}_{v,\text{source}} = (e_1, e_2, \ldots, e_{19}, e_{20}), \tag{1}$$

where e_i is the number of words from category i, and *source* is either *caption* or *comments*, resulting in two vectors for each video. Since the videos vary in terms of size and number of comments, we also created normalized vectors, defined for a video v as

$$\vec{EN}_{v,\text{source}} = \frac{\vec{E}_{v,\text{source}}}{\sum_{i=1}^{20} e_i} = \left(\frac{e_1}{\sum e_i}, \frac{e_2}{\sum e_i}, \ldots, \frac{e_{19}}{\sum e_i}, \frac{e_{20}}{\sum e_i} \right), \tag{2}$$

which contain the normalized fraction of words presented in each Empath category. Again, for each video we have two normalized vectors: one for its captions and another one for its comments.

In order to have an unique vector representing an entire channel (instead of a single video only), we defined an average vector that aggregates all videos of that particular channel. For a given channel c, we define

$$\vec{EC}_{c,\text{source}} = (ec_1, ec_2, \ldots, ec_{19}, ec_{20})$$

$$ec_i = \frac{\sum_{v \in V_c} \left(\vec{EN}_{v,\text{source}}[i] \right)}{|V_c|}, \tag{3}$$

where V_c is the set of all videos of a channel c. In words, the vector $\vec{EC}_c$ contains the average fraction of each Empath category present in the caption or in the comments of the videos in channel c.

Finally, we defined a metric that measures the similarity between content and comments of a video. This metric measures the cosine similarity [39] between the two vectors of a particular video v and is defined as

$$S_v = \cos \left(\vec{EN}_{v,caption}, \vec{EN}_{v,comments} \right). \tag{4}$$

Since our vectors do not hold negative values, the cosine similarity between them varies from 0 (totally different) to 1 (identical).

3.1.2 Results.

Comparing semantic fields between channel types and between sources. First, we analyze the semantic fields present in each channel type (right-wing vs. baseline) and those arising from each source (caption vs. comments). As explained above, we computed two normalized vectors of percentage for each video, and then calculated the average value for each channel ($\vec{EC}_{caption}, \vec{EC}_{comments}$).

Figure 1 depicts the normalized percentage of words in each semantic field represented by an Empath category. We observe a clear and consistent dominance of some negative categories, including *nervousness*, *rage* and *violence*, among captions (if compared to comments). On the other hand, comments contain predominantly more *swearing terms*. Interestingly, for the category *hate*, while there is no significant difference for right-wing channels, for the baseline channels there is a considerable difference between captions and comments: median of 3.5% vs. 6.8%, respectively, thus reporting a percentage of *hate* for baseline comments even greater than for right-wing comments.

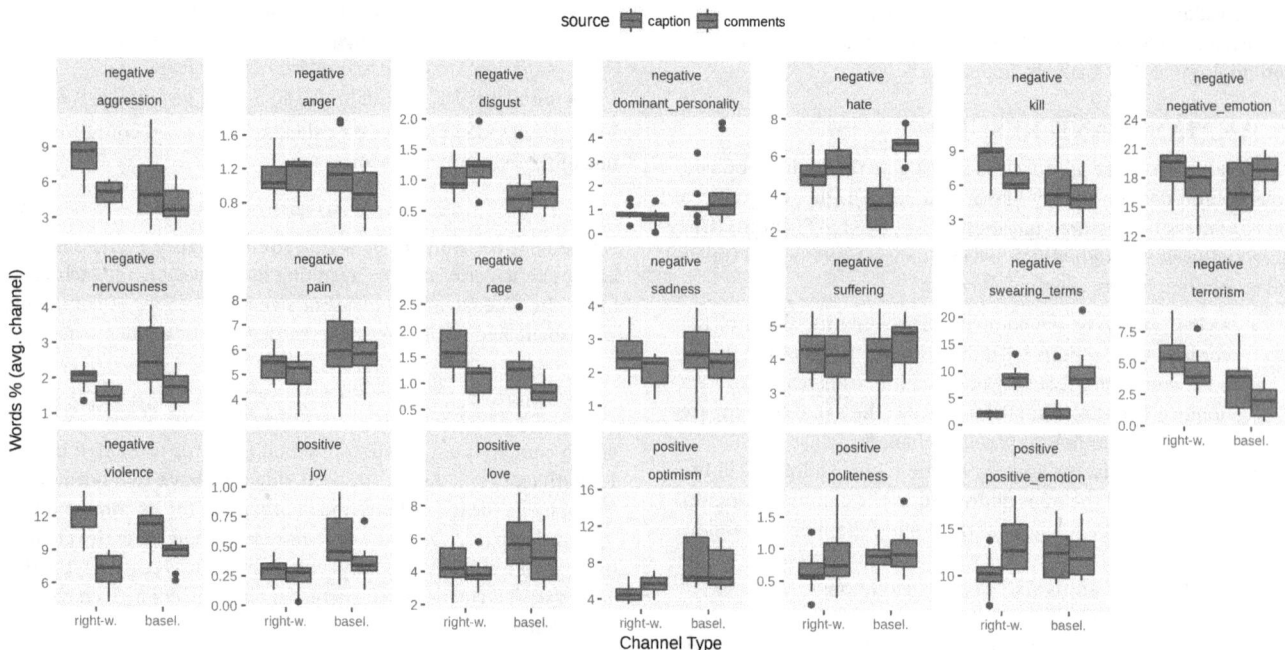

Figure 1: Normalized percentage of words in each semantic field represented by an Empath category. The bottom and top of the box are always the first and third quartiles, the band inside the box is the median, the whiskers represents the minimum and maximum values, and the dots are outliers.

Comparing channel types, we observe that right-wing channels have higher fractions of words from other negative categories, such as *disgust, kill* and *terrorism*, while baseline channels present higher fractions of positive categories such as *joy* and *optimism* (although also presenting higher fraction for the category *pain*). It is also worth noting categories that show no statistical difference between channel types, like *disgust* and *swearing terms*. Another interesting result regards the category *positive emotion*: although there is no statistical difference between baseline's captions and comments, the same is not true for right-wing channels, for which there are more words of this category in comments than in captions.

Similarity between caption and comments. Now, we compare the similarity between the semantic fields present in the caption and in the comments of a given video v by calculating the previously defined metric S_v. Figure 2 depicts the boxplot distribution of this similarity in each channel's videos.

We notice a high variation among the similarity values in videos of a same channel: while in some videos the occurring semantic fields in the host's discourse (represented by the caption) and in the audience's speech (represented by the comments) are very similar, in others the similarity can be close to zero.

This similarity also varies among channels. For instance, while "The Alex Jones Channel" holds a median similarity of 0.9, the median similarity in videos at "Jon Bowne Reports" is as low as 0.5. Interestingly, the variance of the distributions for the baseline channels is lower than the one for right-wing channels, meaning that the former generally have more consistent levels of similarity between caption and comments. It is important to notice that it

seems to exist a correlation between a channel's popularity and the similarity between the semantic fields occurring in the captions of its videos and the ones occurring in the comments of its videos: more popular channels (according to Table 1) generally present higher values of similarity. This could be an explanation for the higher and more consistent values of similarity among baseline channels, since all of them had at least 1,700,000 subscribers at the moment of our data collection.

Correlation between channel's similarity and semantic fields. Finally, we focus on identifying characteristics that could explain the levels of lexical similarity between the host and the commentators. To do that, we measured the correlation between the average similarity and the average fractions of Empath categories (that is, the dimensions of $\vec{EC}$) using the Pearson correlation coefficient. We measured the average fraction of both captions and comments, also aggregating the channels by type (right-wing and baseline). We present the correlation values in Figure 3, highlighting the significant correlation values (with p-value<0.05).

Regarding the captions, we observe no significant correlation for the right-wing channels, and a significant positive correlation for the categories *hate* and *negative emotion* for the baseline channels. These results imply that baseline channels with higher fraction of words related to hate and negative emotions also have a higher degree of similarity between caption and comments.

Now considering the comments, we observe a significant positive correlation for several categories in the right-wing channels, such as *agression, hate* and *violence*. There is also a negative correlation

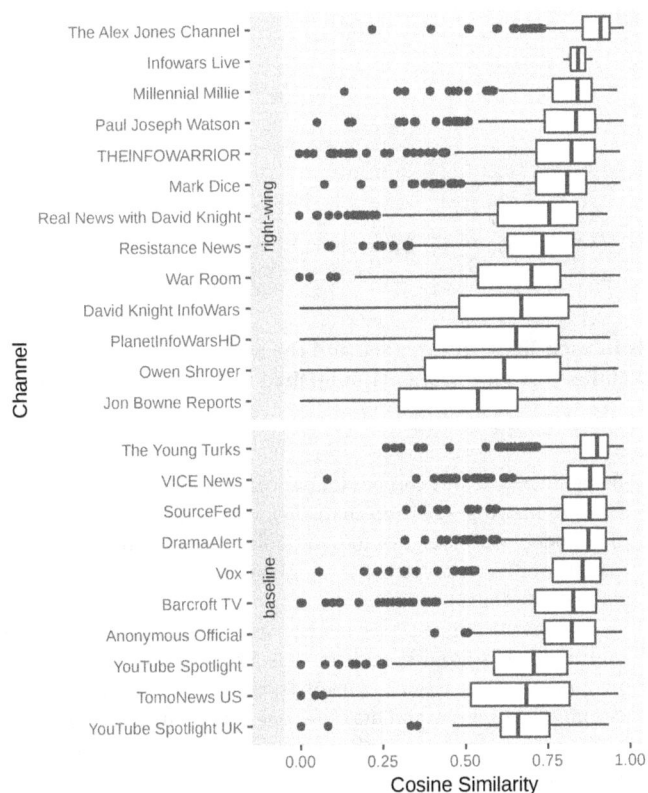

Figure 2: Distribution of the similarities between caption and comments in each channel's videos, according to our lexical analysis. Values close to 0 indicate no correlation and values close to 1 report maximum correlation.

for the *positive emotion* category, meaning that channels with less words related to positive emotions in their comments hold a higher similarity. By looking at the baseline channels, we only detect a significant positive correlation for *violence*, resembling right-wing channels, but with lower intensity. There is, though, a significant negative correlation for *politeness*, implying that channels with a lower fraction of these words in their comments hold a higher similarity.

3.2 Topic analysis

In subsection 3.1, we address a lexical analysis of our textual corpora by studying the semantic fields of the words employed in the captions and in the comments of the videos posted in right-wing and baseline channels. Now, we employ latent Dirichlet allocation (LDA) [5], a way of automatically discovering topics contained in textual datasets, to investigate latent topics present in these videos' captions and comments.

3.2.1 Methodology. For this analysis, beyond the preprocessing steps mentioned in Section 2.2, we also removed punctuation, multiple white spaces and stop words[6]. We lowercased and tokenized the whole corpus as well.

We ran the LDA algorithm using the implementation provided by gensim [34], "a Python library for topic modeling, document indexing and similarity retrieval with large corpora" [7]. Due to limitations of gensim's parallel LDA implementation, we randomly selected a maximum of 2,000 tokens for each document. We chose the parameters $\alpha = \beta = 1.0/num\_topics\ prior$ and $k = 300$. The parameter k indicates the number of topics to be returned by the algorithm, so our LDA model returned 300 topics, each one containing words ordered by importance in that topic. With a trained LDA model, we then assigned a topic to each document by generating a topic distribution for both the video's caption and comments, and then selected the most likely topic as the representative of this document.

3.2.2 Results. Table 2 shows a partial output of our LDA model by displaying the top 2 topics for each document and the top ranked 20 words produced by the LDA. As frequently, the words concerning each topic inferred by LDA are not strongly cohesive among each other, and are not very conclusive. Another problem is that a topic word can have multiple connotations, so that its interpretation is ambiguous. In any case, we discuss possible interpretations of the topics through a qualitative observation of the word lists.

Among the top ranked topics for the right-wing captions, we observe a relevant frequency of words related to war and terrorism, including *nato*, *torture* and *bombing*, and a relevant frequency of words related to espionage and information war, like *assange*, *wikileaks*, possibly *document* and *morgan* (due to the actor Morgan Freeman's popular video in which he accuses Russia of attacking United States' democracy during its 2016 elections[8]).

Regarding the top ranked topics for the right-wing comments, it is possible to recognize many words probably related to biological and chemical warfare, such as *rays*, *ebola*, *gamma*, *radiation* and *virus*. It is also interesting to observe the presence of the word *palestinian* in the highest ranked topic: it might indicate that commentators are responding to the word *israeli*, present in the top ranked topic of the captions.

As expected, the words in the top ranked topics of the baseline channels seem to cover a wider range of subjects. The terms in the top ranked topics of the baseline captions include words regarding celebrities, TV shows and general news, while the ones in the baseline comments are very much related to Internet celebrities such as *RiceGum* and *PewDiePie*, and computer games, like *Minecraft*. In the second highest ranked topic, however, we also observe a small political interest through the presence of the words *antifa* and *feminists*.

We observe that, in general, topics in the captions and comments of right-wing channels are more specific than those of our baseline channels. This was somewhat expected, since our baseline dataset is composed of channels about varied topics and general interests.

3.3 Implicit bias analysis

After investigating vocabulary and topics, we now move up one more level of analysis and observe implicit discriminatory biases that can be retrieved from our dataset of video captions and comments.

---

[6]Using the list of stop words suggested by the Python library gensim in https://github.com/RaRe-Technologies/gensim/blob/develop/gensim/parsing/preprocessing.py

[7]https://radimrehurek.com/gensim/
[8]http://bbc.in/2BQljyP

Lexical Category

Channel Type		aggression	anger	disgust	dominant_personality	hate	kill	negative_emotion	nervousness	pain	rage	sadness	suffering	swearing_terms	terrorism	violence	joy	love	optimism	politeness	positive_emotion
		negative															positive				
caption	right-w.	-0.00	-0.11	-0.04	0.22	0.49	-0.00	0.24	0.01	0.29	-0.03	-0.32	0.40	0.53	-0.55	0.52	-0.36	-0.24	-0.00	-0.13	-0.18
caption	basel.	0.15	-0.00	0.45	-0.40	0.82	0.05	0.71	0.26	0.20	0.05	0.05	0.32	0.42	0.08	0.48	-0.34	-0.13	-0.60	-0.24	-0.30
comments	right-w.	0.63	0.68	-0.07	0.52	0.76	0.39	0.83	0.39	0.83	0.45	0.54	0.86	0.34	0.12	0.96	0.88	-0.01	-0.47	-0.31	-0.83
comments	basel.	0.45	0.45	0.41	-0.59	0.14	0.38	0.37	0.47	0.42	0.58	0.29	0.47	-0.16	0.27	0.67	-0.40	-0.08	-0.51	-0.76	-0.35

correlation
1.0
0.5
0.0
-0.5
-1.0

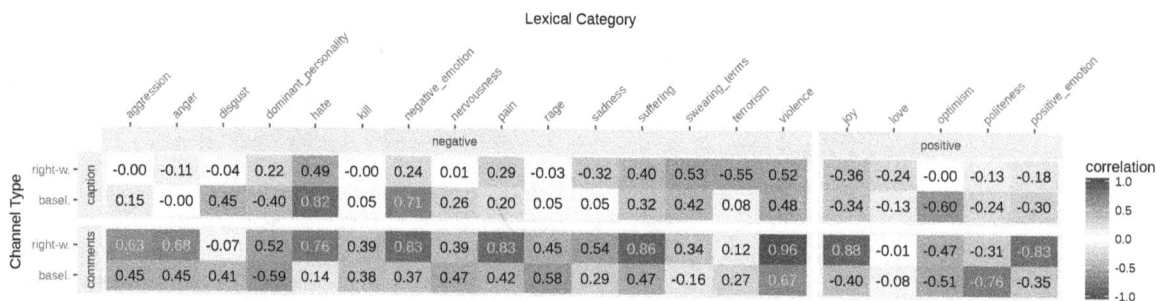

Figure 3: Correlations between normalized frequencies of words in each Empath category and the average cosine similarity between the vocabulary of all captions of a channel and the vocabulary of all comments published in this channel's videos. Highlighted values indicate correlations with p-value<0.05 .

The *Implicit Association Test* (IAT) was introduced by Greenwald et al. [16] to study unconscious, subtle and often unintended biases in individuals. Its core idea is to measure the strength of associations between two target concepts (e.g. *flowers* and *insects*) and two attributes (e.g. *pleasant* and *unpleasant*) based on the reaction time needed to match (a) items that correspond to the target concepts to (b) items that correspond to the attributes (in this case, *flowers + pleasant, insects + pleasant, flowers + unpleasant, insects + unpleasant*). The authors found that individuals' performance was more satisfactory when they needed to match implicit associated categories, such as *flowers + pleasant* and *insects + unpleasant*.

Caliskan et al. [7] propose applying the IAT method to analyze implicit biases based on vector spaces in which words that share common contexts are located in close proximity to one another, generated by a technique called *word embedding*. By replicating a wide spectrum of biases previously assessed by implicit association tests, they show that cosine similarity between words in a vector space generated by word embeddings is also able to capture implicit biases. The authors named this technique *Word Embedding Association Test* (WEAT).

3.3.1 Methodology. We created three WEATs focused on harmful biases towards the following minorities and/or groups likely to suffer discrimination in North America and Western Europe: immigrants, LGBT people and Muslims. The words that compose each class and attribute in our tests are shown in Table 3. According to Caliskan et al. [7], the two classes to be evaluated must contain the same number of words, but the sizes of the sets of attributes can be different. Words from "Class 1" are related to discriminated groups, while words from "Class 2" concern dominant groups; attributes from "Attributes 1" are negative elements and attributes from "Attributes 2" are positive elements.

Then, we used a collection containing all the articles of Wikipedia's English-language edition[9] to pre-train a base model with 600 dimensions employing word2vec[10][44, 45]. We chose to use data from Wikipedia due to its popularity as a base model for language modeling applications using word embeddings, since it is a large dataset often considered to be a good representation of contemporary English [22, 29]. Also, due to limited access to

domain-specific text corpora (in our case, captions and comments from right-wing YouTube channels), it is beneficial to initialize the models with weights and vocabulary trained in a large text corpus and then re-train the weights with the domain-specific dataset [10, 20, 38].

Once the Wikipedia base model was created, we used it as the starting point for our specific models. For each YouTube channel in our dataset, we trained two word2vec models: one of them concerning the captions and the other one concerning the comments in the videos. Then, we implemented our WEATs according to the method proposed by Caliskan et al. [7], that is, measuring (a) the association between a given word w and the attributes A_1 and A_2 (Equation 5), and (b) the association between the two sets of target words belonging to the classes C_1 and C_2 and the two sets of attributes A_1 and A_2 (Equation 6), as in

$$s(w, A_1, A_2) = Mean_{a \epsilon A_1}(\cos(\vec{w}, \vec{a})) - Mean_{b \epsilon A_2}(\cos(\vec{w}, \vec{b})) \quad (5)$$

and

$$s(C_1, C_2, A_1, A_2) = \sum_{x \epsilon C_1} s(x, A_1, A_2) - \sum_{y \epsilon C_2} s(y, A_1, A_2), \quad (6)$$

where $\cos(\vec{x}, \vec{y})$ indicates the cosine of the angle between the vectors $\vec{x}$ and $\vec{y}$. The effect sizes of these associations are the normalized measures of how separated the two distributions of associations between classes and attributes are, and are calculated through Cohen's d, which, in this case, is defined as

$$d = \frac{Mean_{x \epsilon C_1}(s(x, A_1, A_2)) - Mean_{y \epsilon C_2}(s(y, A_1, A_2))}{\sigma_{w \epsilon C_1 \bigcup C_2} s(w, A_1, A_2)}, \quad (7)$$

where σ stands for the standard deviation. The significance of the effect sizes are represented by p-values calculated asserting the one-sided permutation test using all the possible partitions of the two classes into two sets of equal size (X_i, Y_i). In this case, the p-value is defined as the probability that one of these possible permutations yields a test statistic value greater than the one observed by our WEAT definitions in Table 3:

$$P_{value} = Pr(s(X_i, Y_i, A_1, A_2) > s(C_1, C_2, A_1, A_2)). \quad (8)$$

---

[9]Downloaded in March 5 2017 and available at https://dumps.wikimedia.org/
[10]https://code.google.com/archive/p/word2vec/

Table 2: Top 2 topics for each document. Inside each topic, 20 words are presented in order of importance according to the LDA output.

Document	Topic rank	Topic words
Right-wing captions	1	vaccine, vaccines, vox, cenk, ukraine, millie, flight, nato, bike, morgan, infrastructure, fluoride, keem, ukrainian, labour, israeli, torture, jeremy, awards, bombing
	2	abortion, solar, assange, kelly, wikileaks, petition, vox, beck, sheriff, jinx, react, petitions, owen, syrian, nfl, arpaio, rushmore, document, pregnancy, oath
Right-wing comments	1	quot, rays, speaker, ebola, gamma, palestinians, cruz, ksi, radiation, virus, ray, maher, candace, ted, palestinian, memes, ukraine, keem, irish, dnc
	2	millie, quot, owen, korean, gangs, ricegum, manifesto, rice, drone, rainbow, depression, discrimination, flu, speaker, feminists, jay, radiation, professor, dodger, cook'
Baseline captions	1	gt, quot, whale, n, pluto, puerto, horizons, loopholes, irish, rico, playlist, nasa, sheriff, axis, maryanne, megyn, swamp, faze, vox, surface
	2	gt, commentary, hurricane, papa, sarry, kevin, quot, ali, fifa, n, hammer, cenk, wolf, donors, symbols, shark, keem, trudeau, starbucks, warren
Baseline comments	1	keem, rice, ricegum, leafy, dramaalert, scarce, faze, squad, lizard, pewdiepie, rap, rain, idubbbz, keems, michelle, diss, bleach, subbed, quantum, ty
	2	dan, cenk, phil, ana, bees, keem, millie, bee, leafy, quot, minecraft, mars, generic, turks, roger, antifa, ava, todd, flight, feminists

Table 3: Words that compose each class and set of attributes in our Word Embedding Association Tests (WEATs).

	Immigrants	Muslims	LGBT people
Class 1 (discriminated)	immigrant, migrant	islamism, muhammed, muslim, quran	bisexual, gay, homosexual, lesbian
Class 2 (dominant)	citizen, native	bible, christian, christianity, jesus	het, hetero, heterosexual, straight
Attributes 1 (negative)	bad, burden, pirate, plague, taker, thief	assassin, attack, bomb, death, murder, radical, terrorist	immoral, outrageous, promiscuous, revolting, sinner
Attributes 2 (positive)	good, honest, maker, rightful	compassionate, gentle, humane, kind, tolerant	moral, natural, normal

3.3.2 Results. We present in Figure 4 the values of biases of the three topics in terms of effect size (Cohen's *d*) for all the right-wing and baseline channels, both for captions and comments. In the plot, we only show the biases with *p*-value<0.1, being the ones in the range [0.05, 0.1] in orange and the ones <0.05 in green. The dashed line is a reference value indicating the bias present in the Wikipedia corpus alone. The signed numbers indicate the difference of bias between comments and captions, where a positive value represents a higher bias for comments and a negative value indicates a higher bias for caption. We also depict, in Figure 5, the boxplot of these values, aggregating for channel type and source, and considering only the biases with p-value<0.05.

Comparing channels' implicit biases with Wikipedia corpus. First, we highlight that, according to our WEATs, the baseline Wikipedia corpus holds a relatively high bias by itself. This is consistent with previous studies [6, 7, 42], indicating that cultural biases are transmitted through written language.

When contrasting the reference Wikipedia bias with the YouTube biases, we observe different trends depending on the topic. For instance, the bias against Muslims was almost always amplified when compared to the reference, especially for captions. On the other hand, bias against LGBT people was weakened in most of the observed channels, even in the right-wing ones. Concerning the bias against immigrants, the values appear close to the reference.

Comparing biases in captions with biases in comments. It is interesting to notice that, for immigrants and Muslims, captions hold higher biases than comments in 75% of the right-wing channels, considering the statistically significant cases (Figure 4). The fact that, in right-wing channels, comments hold lower bias against immigrants and Muslins when compared to captions can also be stated by looking at Figure 5. For LGBT people, however, comments hold higher discriminatory bias in right-wing channels.

Comparing right-wing and baseline biases. We observe that, concerning Muslims, the captions of right-wing channels present higher biases (median = 1.7) than baseline channels (median = 1.5). For the other topics, the differences were not very pronounced. It is also worth to mention that, as shown in Table 3, the fraction of channels with statistically significant biases is much higher for right-wing channels, regardless of source (captions or comments). For this reason, for many baseline cases, we cannot conclude that a significant difference exists, nor conclude that it does not exist.

3.4 Multi-layered analysis

Now, we summarize the findings of each of the three previous analyses and combine their results in order to answer the research questions proposed in Section 1.

RQ-1: is the presence of hateful vocabulary, violent content and discriminatory biases more, less or equally accentuated in right-wing channels? Our lexical analysis shows that right-wing channels,

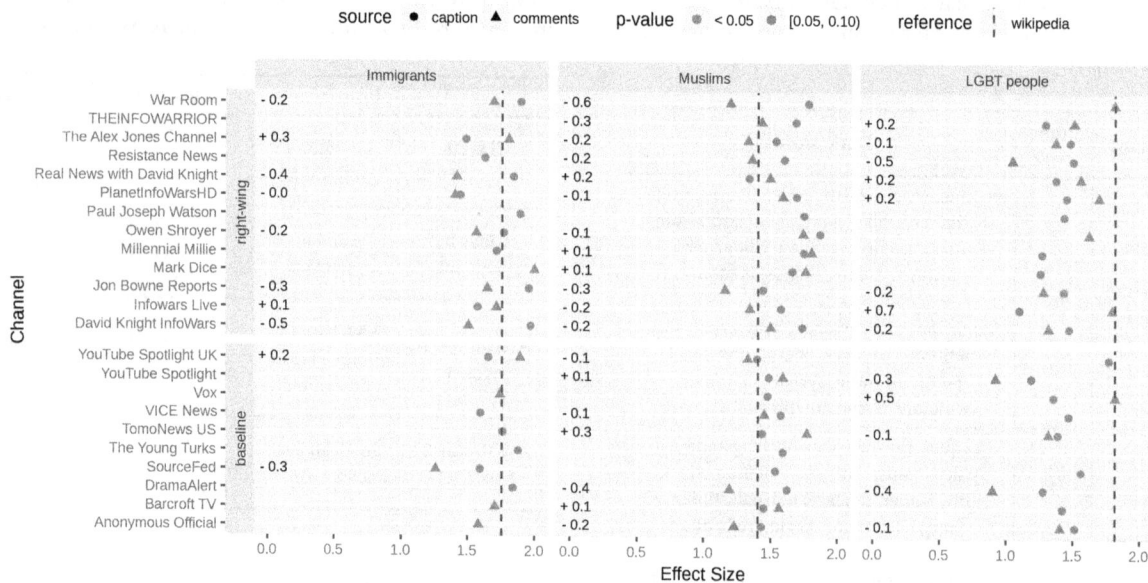

Figure 4: Value of WEAT biases for the three topics analyzed. Dashed lines indicate the reference value calculated from the Wikipedia corpus. The numbers indicate the difference between biases calculated for comments and captions.

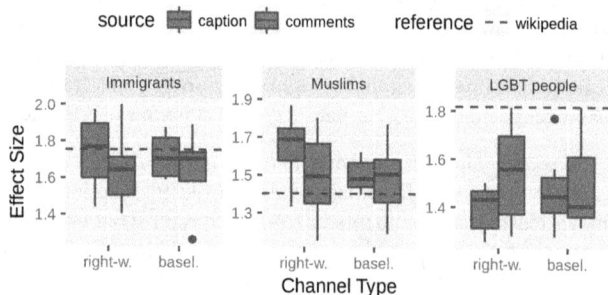

Figure 5: Distribution of WEAT biases for the three topics analyzed. Dashed lines indicate the reference value calculated from the Wikipedia corpus.

when compared with baseline channels, incorporate higher percentages of words conveying semantic fields like *aggression, kill, rage* and *violence*, while baseline channels hold a higher percentage of positive semantic fields such as *joy* and *optimism*. Even though the most frequent LDA topics do not show high evidences of hate, they did report that right-wing channels debates are more related to subjects like war and terrorism, which might corroborate the lexical analysis. Also, the implicit bias analysis shows that, independently of channel type (right-wing or baseline), the YouTube community seems to amplify a discriminatory bias against Muslims, depicted as assassins, radicals and terrorists, and weaken the association of LGBT people as immoral, promiscuous and sinners when compared to the Wikipedia reference.

Although the lexical and topic analysis show evidences of negative feelings, they are unable to indicate towards whom these feelings are addressed. The implicit bias analysis shows no differences between right-wing and baseline captions regarding immigrants and LGBT people, but it does show against Muslims. We might conclude, then, that hateful vocabulary and violent content seems to be more accentuated in right-wing channels than in our set of baseline channels, and also that a discriminatory bias against Muslims is more present in right-wing videos.

RQ-2: are, in general, commentators more, less or equally exacerbated than video hosts in an effort to express hate and discrimination? The lexical analysis reports that comments generally have more words from the semantic fields *disgust, hate* and *swearing terms*, and captions express more *aggression, rage* and *violence*. Regarding biases against immigrants and Muslims, in 75% of the right-wing channels the comments show less bias than the captions. On the other hand, although the implicit bias against LGBT people in YouTube is generally lower than in the Wikipedia reference, it is greater on right-wing comments than in right-wing captions.

Our conclusion is that, in general, YouTube commentators are more exacerbated than video hosts in the context of hate and discrimination, even though several exceptions may apply.

4 RELATED WORK

On hate, violence and bias on the Web. The analysis of hate, violence and discriminatory bias in online social networks is gaining a lot of attention in the field of social computing as platforms such as Facebook, Instagram and Twitter, to name a few, connect more and more users at a global level – being one of the topics covered by what has been called *computational social science* [21].

The identification of hateful messages in online services is still an open question. Schmidt and Wiegand [37] show that the manual inspection of hateful content in a social media service is not feasible, and present a survey describing key areas on natural language processing that have been explored to automatically recognize hateful content. Ribeiro et al. [35] propose a different approach, focusing on a user-centric view of hate speech and characterizing hateful Twitter users instead of hateful messages. The authors show that these users tend to be more negative, more profane and, counter-intuitively, use less words associated with topics such as hate, terrorism, violence and anger.

Hate and violence in the video sharing website YouTube is also increasingly receiving scholarly attention. Sureka et al. [43] propose a solution based on data mining and social network analysis to discover hate videos, users and virtual hidden communities on YouTube, while Agarwal and Sureka [1] present a focused-crawler based approach for mining hate and extremism in this social platform.

Case studies are also useful for the purpose of elucidating the dynamics and the strength of online activity related to hate, violence and discriminatory bias. For instance, Chatzakou et al. [9] investigate the behavior of users involved in the *Gamergate controversy*, a harassment campaign against women in the video game industry that lead to many incidents of cyberbullying and cyberaggression. The authors compare the behavior of Twitter users considered *gamergaters* with the behavior of baseline users, finding that gamergaters "post tweets with negative sentiment, less joy, and more hate than random users". On another vein, Savage and Monroy-Hernández [36] analyze a militia uprising unfolded on social media in the context of the Mexican War on Drugs, illustrating its "online mobilization strategies, and how its audience takes part in defining the narrative of this armed conflict".

On comment behavior on the Web. The behavior of commentators in websites and in online social media services is also a growing research topic in social computing. Through the analysis of interviews with frequent Internet commentators, French [14] shows that the reasons for users to comment on websites are many and varied. Stroud, Van Duyn and Peacock [41] indicate that social media is the most prevalent place for Internet users to comment and read comments. They add that most commentators and comment readers "agree that allowing anonymity in comment sections allows participants to express ideas they might be afraid to express otherwise", while nearly half of them believe that "allowing commenters to remain anonymous raises the level of disrespect". Nevertheless, Stroud et al. [40], through a survey with more than 12,000 Internet users, argue that anonymity might actually not play much of a role in uncivil discourse from commentators on the Web. On this, Li et al. [26] propose a methodology to identify malicious users on commenting platforms, with an overall classification accuracy of almost 81%.

Kalogeropoulos et al. [18] show that political partisans are more likely than non-partisans to engage in commenting on news stories in social media, while Park et al. [31] reveal that it is possible to automatically predict the political orientation of news stories through the analysis of the behavior of individual commentators. Specifically regarding comment behavior in YouTube, Ksiazek, Peer and Lessard [19] explore the relationship between popularity and interaction in news videos published to this service, concluding that "users engage with content in various ways and at differing levels, ranging from exposure to recommendation to interactivity".

5 CONCLUSIONS AND FUTURE WORK

In this paper, we present an investigation regarding comments and video content in a set of right-wing YouTube channels and compare it to a set of baseline channels. We perform a three-layered analysis through which we examine lexicon, topics and discriminatory bias in videos and comments from the collected channels.

Findings. The two research questions proposed in Section 1 are partially answered by our analyses. Our main findings suggest that right-wing channels are more specific in their content, discussing topics such as terrorism and war, and also present a higher percentage of negative word categories, such as *agression* and *violence*, while the baseline channels are more general in their topics and use more positive words. Although not capturing a difference of bias against immigrants and LGBT people, we were able to capture a negative bias against the Muslim community. When comparing comments and video hosts, we observe that, while there is a difference on the actual semantic fields, both commentators and hosts use negative words. By analyzing the implicit bias, the differences for baseline channels are not very strong, while for right-wing channels we notice a higher bias against immigrants and Muslims among captions, and a higher bias against LGBT people among comments. These findings contribute to a better understanding of the behavior of general and right-wing YouTube users.

The method presented in this study, which uses only open source tools, combines together three already established analytical procedures. By performing these different but complementary analyses in our dataset, we are able to tackle the examined issues by distinct angles and to observe aspects that would have been ignored in one-layered investigations. For example, lexical and topic analysis measure the presence of words that semantically convey feelings, but they are not good estimators about towards whom or what those feelings are about. Related works often use part-of-speech tagging and named entity recognition [13] to tackle this problem. However, the Word Embedding Association Test (WEAT) takes advantage of word embeddings in which words that share common contexts are located in close proximity to one another. Through this method, it is possible to measure implicit associations and then complement the lexical and topic analyses.

Future work. Here, we do not handle with negation, i.e. we do not consider whether a hateful word is accompanied by a negation that reverses its meaning. This is especially important for our lexical analysis, that simply counts the occurrence of words in given semantic fields. The use of our multi-layered approach mitigates this problem, but, in future work, we plan to improve our analyses in this regard. Also, we analyze our data from a synchronic point of view – that is, we observe it as one single point in time. In the following steps, we plan to incorporate a temporal aspect to our investigations, since we believe that diachronic information will make it possible to elucidate to what extent do violent and discriminatory behavior in videos stimulate violent and discriminatory behavior in comments and vice versa. The incorporation of time analysis may also improve our LDA results, since it would be possible to create the notion of conversation sessions and to split the large documents that aggregate all videos' comments into smaller document sessions.

ACKNOWLEDGMENTS

This work was partially supported by CNPq, CAPES, FAPEMIG and the projects InWeb, MASWEB, Atmosphere and INCT-Cyber.

We would like to thank Nikki Bourassa, Ryan Budish, Amar Ashar and Robert Faris, from the Berkman Klein Center for Internet & Society at Harvard University, for their insightful discussions and suggestions.

REFERENCES

[1] Swati Agarwal and Ashish Sureka. 2014. A focused crawler for mining hate and extremism promoting videos on YouTube. In *Proceedings of the 25th ACM Conference on Hypertext and Social Media*. ACM.
[2] Anti-Defamation League. 2013. The consequences of right-wing extremism on the Internet. Available online at http://bit.ly/2yUatCZ. (2013).
[3] BBC. 2017. White supremacy: Are US right-wing groups on the rise? BBC, http://bbc.in/2wGBvNZ. (August 2017).
[4] Steven Bird, Edward Loper, and Ewan Klein. 2009. *Natural language processing with Python*. O'Reilly Media Inc.
[5] David M Blei, Andrew Y Ng, and Michael I Jordan. 2003. Latent Dirichlet allocation. *Journal of Machine Learning Research* 3, Jan (2003), 993–1022.
[6] John A Bullinaria and Joseph P Levy. 2007. Extracting semantic representations from word co-occurrence statistics: A computational study. *Behavior research methods* 39, 3 (2007), 510–526.
[7] Aylin Caliskan, Joanna J Bryson, and Arvind Narayanan. 2017. Semantics derived automatically from language corpora contain human-like biases. *Science* 356, 6334 (2017), 183–186.
[8] César N Cambraia. 2013. Da lexicologia social a uma lexicologia sócio-histórica: caminhos possíveis. *Revista de Estudos da Linguagem* 21, 1 (2013), 157–188.
[9] Despoina Chatzakou, Nicolas Kourtellis, Jeremy Blackburn, Emiliano De Cristofaro, Gianluca Stringhini, and Athena Vakali. 2017. Measuring #GamerGate: A Tale of Hate, Sexism, and Bullying. *CoRR* abs/1702.07784 (2017). arXiv:1702.07784 http://arxiv.org/abs/1702.07784
[10] Ronan Collobert, Jason Weston, Léon Bottou, Michael Karlen, Koray Kavukcuoglu, and Pavel Kuksa. 2011. Natural language processing (almost) from scratch. *Journal of Machine Learning Research* 12, Aug (2011), 2493–2537.
[11] Evandro Cunha, Gabriel Magno, Marcos André Gonçalves, César Cambraia, and Virgilio Almeida. 2014. How you post is who you are: Characterizing Google+ status updates across social groups. In *Proceedings of the 25th ACM Conference on Hypertext and Social Media (HT'14)*. Association for Computing Machinery (ACM), New York, NY, USA, 212–217. https://doi.org/10.1145/2631775.2631822
[12] Ethan Fast, Binbin Chen, and Michael S Bernstein. 2016. Empath: Understanding topic signals in large-scale text. In *Proceedings of the 2016 CHI Conference on Human Factors in Computing Systems*. ACM, 4647–4657.
[13] Ethan Fast, Tina Vachovsky, and Michael S Bernstein. 2016. Shirtless and Dangerous: Quantifying Linguistic Signals of Gender Bias in an Online Fiction Writing Community. In *ICWSM*.
[14] Eric French. 2016. What Do Frequent Commenters Want? The Coral Project, https://blog.coralproject.net/interviews-with-frequent-commenters/. (October 2016).
[15] Angela Giuffrida. 2018. Italy used to be a tolerant country, but now racism is rising. The Guardian, http://bit.ly/2Hr6qDk. (February 2018).
[16] Anthony G Greenwald, Debbie E McGhee, and Jordan LK Schwartz. 1998. Measuring individual differences in implicit cognition: the Implicit Association Test. *Journal of Personality and Social Psychology* 74, 6 (1998), 1464.
[17] John Herrman. 2017. For the New Far Right, YouTube Has Become the New Talk Radio. The New York Times, http://nyti.ms/2hrec7c. (August 2017).
[18] Antonis Kalogeropoulos, Samuel Negredo, Ike Picone, and Rasmus Kleis Nielsen. 2017. Who Shares and Comments on News?: A Cross-National Comparative Analysis of Online and Social Media Participation. *Social Media + Society* 3, 4 (2017).
[19] Thomas B Ksiazek, Limor Peer, and Kevin Lessard. 2016. User engagement with online news: Conceptualizing interactivity and exploring the relationship between online news videos and user comments. *New Media & Society* 18, 3 (2016), 502–520.

[20] Matt Kusner, Yu Sun, Nicholas Kolkin, and Kilian Weinberger. 2015. From word embeddings to document distances. In *International Conference on Machine Learning*. 957–966.
[21] David Lazer, Alex Sandy Pentland, Lada Adamic, Sinan Aral, Albert László Barabási, Devon Brewer, Nicholas Christakis, Noshir Contractor, James Fowler, Myron Gutmann, et al. 2009. Computational Social Science. *Science (New York, NY)* 323, 5915 (2009), 721.
[22] Omer Levy and Yoav Goldberg. 2014. Neural word embedding as implicit matrix factorization. In *Advances in Neural Information Processing Systems*. 2177–2185.
[23] Paul Lewis. 2018. 'Fiction is outperforming reality': how YouTube's algorithm distorts truth. The Guardian, http://bit.ly/2EqBq8p. (February 2018).
[24] Paul Lewis. 2018. Senator warns YouTube algorithm may be open to manipulation by 'bad actors'. The Guardian, http://bit.ly/2EtlimT. (February 2018).
[25] Paul Lewis and Erin McCormick. 2018. How an ex-YouTube insider investigated its secret algorithm. The Guardian, http://bit.ly/2DWX8AQ. (February 2018).
[26] Tai Ching Li, Joobin Gharibshah, Evangelos E Papalexakis, and Michalis Faloutsos. 2017. TrollSpot: Detecting misbehavior in commenting platforms. In *Proceedings of the 2017 IEEE/ACM International Conference on Advances in Social Networks Analysis and Mining 2017*. ACM.
[27] Marco Lui and Timothy Baldwin. 2012. langid. py: An off-the-shelf language identification tool. In *Proceedings of the ACL 2012 System Demonstrations*. Association for Computational Linguistics, 25–30.
[28] Georges Matoré. 1953. *La méthode en lexicologie: domaine français*. Didier, Paris.
[29] Grégoire Mesnil, Xiaodong He, Li Deng, and Yoshua Bengio. 2013. Investigation of recurrent-neural-network architectures and learning methods for spoken language understanding. In *Interspeech*. 3771–3775.
[30] Jack Nicas. 2018. How YouTube Drives People to the Internet's Darkest Corners. The Wall Street Journal, http://on.wsj.com/2BMKvHa. (February 2018).
[31] Souneil Park, Minsam Ko, Jungwoo Kim, Ying Liu, and Junehwa Song. 2011. The politics of comments: predicting political orientation of news stories with commenters' sentiment patterns. In *Proceedings of the ACM 2011 Conference on Computer Supported Cooperative Work*. ACM, 113–122.
[32] Dom Phillips. 2017. Brazil's right on the rise as anger grows over scandal and corruption. The Guardian, http://bit.ly/2uYrRaX. (July 2017).
[33] Alan Posener. 2017. Like it or not, the far right is heading for Germany's Bundestag. The Guardian, http://bit.ly/2y5y985. (September 2017).
[34] Radim Řehůřek and Petr Sojka. 2010. Software Framework for Topic Modelling with Large Corpora. In *Proceedings of the LREC 2010 Workshop on New Challenges for NLP Frameworks*. ELRA, Valletta, Malta, 45–50. http://is.muni.cz/publication/884893/en.
[35] Manoel Horta Ribeiro, Pedro H Calais, Yuri A Santos, Virgilio AF Almeida, and Wagner Meira Jr. 2017. "Like Sheep Among Wolves": Characterizing Hateful Users on Twitter. In *Proceedings of WSDM Workshop on Misinformation and Misbehavior Mining on the Web (MIS2)*. ACM.
[36] Saiph Savage and Andrés Monroy-Hernández. 2015. Participatory Militias: An Analysis of an Armed Movement's Online Audience. In *Proceedings of the 18th ACM Conference on Computer Supported Cooperative Work & Social Computing*. ACM, 724–733.
[37] Anna Schmidt and Michael Wiegand. 2017. A survey on hate speech detection using natural language processing. In *Proceedings of the Fifth International Workshop on Natural Language Processing for Social Media*.
[38] Scharolta Katharina Sienčnik. 2015. Adapting word2vec to named entity recognition. In *Proceedings of the 20th Nordic Conference of Computational Linguistics*. Linköping University Electronic Press, 239–243.
[39] Amit Singhal. 2001. Modern information retrieval: a brief overview. *Bulletin of the IEEE Computer Society Technical Committee on Data Engineering* 24 (2001), 2001.
[40] Natalie Jomini Stroud, Emily Van Duyn, Alexis Alizor, Alishan Alibhai, and Cameron Lang. 2017. 12,000 people have something to say. Engaging News Project. (January 2017).
[41] Natalie Jomini Stroud, Emily Van Duyn, and Cynthia Peacock. 2016. News Commenters and News Comment Readers. Engaging News Project. (March 2016).
[42] Michael Stubbs. 1996. *Text and corpus analysis: Computer-assisted studies of language and culture*. Blackwell Oxford.
[43] Ashish Sureka, Ponnurangam Kumaraguru, Atul Goyal, and Sidharth Chhabra. 2010. Mining YouTube to discover extremist videos, users and hidden communities. *Information Retrieval Technology* (2010), 13–24.
[44] Greg Corrado Tomas Mikolov, Kai Chen and Jeffrey Dean. 2013. Efficient Estimation of Word Representations in Vector Space. In *Proceedings of Workshop at ICLR*.
[45] Kai Chen Greg Corrado Tomas Mikolov, Ilya Sutskever and Jeffrey Dean. 2013. Distributed Representations of Words and Phrases and their Compositionality. In *Proceedings of the Conference on Neural Information Processing Systems (NIPS)*.
[46] Tom Whyman. 2017. Why the Right Is Dominating YouTube. Vice, http://bit.ly/2sS5Aw6. (March 2017).

Focused Crawl of Web Archives to Build Event Collections

Martin Klein
Los Alamos National Laboratory
Research Library
Los Alamos, NM, USA
http://orcid.org/0000-0003-0130-2097
mklein@lanl.gov

Lyudmila Balakireva
Los Alamos National Laboratory
Research Library
Los Alamos, NM, USA
http://orcid.org/0000-0002-3919-3634
ludab@lanl.gov

Herbert Van de Sompel
Los Alamos National Laboratory
Research Library
Los Alamos, NM, USA
http://orcid.org/0000-0002-0715-6126
herbertv@lanl.gov

ABSTRACT

Event collections are frequently built by crawling the live web on the basis of seed URIs nominated by human experts. Focused web crawling is a technique where the crawler is guided by reference content pertaining to the event. Given the dynamic nature of the web and the pace with which topics evolve, the timing of the crawl is a concern for both approaches. We investigate the feasibility of performing focused crawls on the archived web. By utilizing the Memento infrastructure, we obtain resources from 22 web archives that contribute to building event collections. We create collections on four events and compare the relevance of their resources to collections built from crawling the live web as well as from a manually curated collection. Our results show that focused crawling on the archived web can be done and indeed results in highly relevant collections, especially for events that happened further in the past.

CCS CONCEPTS

• **Information systems → Digital libraries and archives;**

KEYWORDS

Collection Building, Web Archiving, Focused Crawling, Memento

ACM Reference Format:
Martin Klein, Lyudmila Balakireva, and Herbert Van de Sompel. 2018. Focused Crawl of Web Archives to Build Event Collections. In *WebSci '18: 10th ACM Conference on Web Science, May 27–30, 2018, Amsterdam, Netherlands.* ACM, New York, NY, USA, 10 pages. https://doi.org/10.1145/3201064.3201085

1 INTRODUCTION

The pace at which real-world events happen paired with the level of event coverage on the web has by far outgrown the human capacity for information consumption. Therefore, archivists and librarians are interested in building special event-centric web collections that humans can consult post-factum. Web crawling on the basis of seed URIs is a common approach to collect such event-specific web resources. For example, the Archive-It service[1] is frequently used to crawl the web to build archival collections on the basis of seeds

URIs[2][3][4] that were manually collected by librarians, archivists, and volunteers. This approach has drawbacks since the notion of relevance is solely based on the nomination of seed URIs by humans. Focused web crawling guided by a set of reference documents that are exemplary of the web resources that should be collected is an approach that is commonly used to build special-purpose collections. It entails an algorithmic assessment of the relevance of the content of a crawled resource rather than a manual selection of URIs to crawl. For both web crawling and focused web crawling, the time between the occurrence of the event and the start of the crawling process is a concern since stories quickly disappear from the top search engine result pages [15], links rot [12], and content drifts [10]. Web archives around the world routinely collect snapshots of web pages (which we refer to as Mementos) and hence potentially are repositories from which event-specific collections could be gathered some time after the event. However, the various web archives have different scopes e.g., national vs. international resources, cover different time spans, and vary in size of their index[5]. This makes collection building on the basis of distributed web archives difficult when compared to doing so on the live web. Moreover, to the best of our knowledge, focused crawling across web archives has never been attempted. Inspired by previous work by Gossen et al. [9], in this paper, we present a framework to build event-specific collections by focused crawling of web archives. We utilize the Memento protocol [20] and the associated cross-web-archive infrastructure [3] to crawl Mementos in 22 web archives. We build collections by evaluating the content-wise and temporal relevance of crawled resources and we compare the resulting collections with collections created on the basis of live web crawls and a manually curated Archive-It crawl. As such, we take the previous work to the next level and ask the following questions:

- Can we create event collections by focused crawling web archives?
- How do event collections created from the archived web compare to those created from the live web?
- How does the amount of time passed since the event affect the collections built from the live and the archived web?
- How do event collections built from the archived web compare to manually curated collections?

We consider the main contribution of our work to be the exploration of the feasibility of performing focused crawls on the archived web. To the best of our knowledge, we are the first to do so.

---

[1]https://archive-it.org/

[2]https://twitter.com/archiveitorg/status/960564121577181184
[3]https://twitter.com/internetarchive/status/806228431474028544
[4]https://twitter.com/internetarchive/status/797263535994613761
[5]https://twitter.com/brewster_kahle/status/954889200083509248

Event Page

Event Data Extraction

Wikipedia Page Version
Event Datetime
Crawl Seed URIs
Event Vector
Aggregate Relevance Threshold

Crawled Resources

Focused Crawler	
Live Web Crawl	Web Archive Crawl

Resource Datetime
Candidate Vector
Content Relevance
Temporal Relevance
Aggregate Relevance

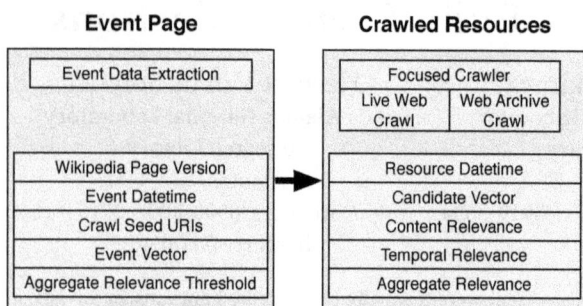

Figure 1: Focused crawling framework

2 RELATED WORK

Previous work by Gossen et al. [9] inspired this work. They developed a focused extraction (not web crawling) system to create event-centric collections from a large static archival collection stored on a server under their control. The content of the Wikipedia page for an event is used to guide the focused extraction. The event datetime is derived from HTML elements in the Wikipedia page and external references in that page are used as seed URIs. They found that their approach outperforms a naive extraction process that is not guided by content and that an approach that combines content-wise and temporal relevance scores mostly performs best. Our approach builds on this work. We deploy a focused crawler that operates on the real web and is not bound to a static, locally stored archival collection. We actually utilize 22 web archives for our crawls and compare the results to comparable focused crawls on the live web. A significant amount of work has been done on focused crawling in general [1, 4, 16]. Some work has additionally explored time-aware focused crawling, such as Pereira et al. [17]. In that work, the authors incorporated temporal data extracted from web pages to satisfy a particular temporal focus of the crawl. They used temporal segmentation of text in a page to determine temporal focus. We follow common practice for our focused crawling approach, for example, by implementing a priority queue. The temporal segmentation of text could have been of interest for our temporal relevance assessment, but, for this experiment we use extraction methods as seen in [6]. Relevant with regard to event-centric collection building is the work by Farag et al. [6] and Littman et al. [14]. Farag et al. introduced an intelligent focused crawling system that works on the basis of an event model. This model captures key data about the event and the focused crawler leverages the event model to predict web page relevance. As a result, the system can successfully filter unrelated content and perform at a high level of precision and recall. The work by Littmann et al. pertains to deriving event collections from social media. The authors focused on increasing the alignment between web archiving tools and processes, and social media data collection practice, for the overall goal of event-centric collection building. Both efforts relate to our work in that the common goal is to build specific collections of web resources. However, both Farag et al. and Littmann et al. are concerned with live web resources only.

3 ESTABLISHING A CRAWLING FRAMEWORK

Our intent is to compare focused crawling of the live web and of web archives for the creation of collections pertaining to unpredictable events such as natural disasters and mass shootings. Inspired by [9], we use the Wikipedia page that describes an event as a starting point. However, we do not use the current version of that page but rather a prior version that is expected to describe the actual event and does not yet include post-event auxiliary content such as references to future related events or analysis of a range of similar events. We select external references of the Wikipedia version page as seeds for crawling and the page's text to assess content relevance of crawled resources. We additionally use a temporal interval starting with the datetime of the event to assess the temporal relevance of crawled resources. For both the live web and web archive crawls, crawled pages that are relevant, both content-wise and temporally, are added to the respective event collection. We describe the details in the remainder of this section and provide a conceptual overview of the framework in Figure 1.

3.1 Wikipedia Page Version

All data required to guide the crawling process is generated from the canonical Wikipedia page of the event. However, our events of interest have happened at some point in the past and their Wikipedia pages, very likely created shortly after the event, have with high probability evolved significantly since then. This raises the question of which version of a Wikipedia page to use as the starting point for our crawls. Since Wikipedia maintains all page versions along with the datetime they were created, we can, in theory, choose any version between the very first and the current one. We know from related work [18] that the majority of edits to a Wikipedia page happen early on in its lifetime. However, event coverage often evolves beyond that point and hence consecutive page edits may still lead to significant changes. For example, other, related events may happen at some later point and may result in the inclusion of new links and references into the event's Wikipedia page. We therefore conjecture that using the current live version of an event's Wikipedia page could introduce too much content and references that do not directly pertain to a description of the event.

We approach the selection of a Wikipedia page version from the perspective of edit frequency. Our goal is to determine the date on which the vast majority of edits over the entire history of the page were completed. We select the page with that version date and consider that page to comprehensively capture the essence of the event. For this purpose we plot all edits of a Wikipedia page and their datetimes. Figure 2 shows an example of such a plot where the edit datetimes are on the x-axis and the percentage of edits on the y-axis. We then use the standard R changepoint library [11] to determine the change point in this graph. The change point is the point after which the graph assumes a significantly different shape. In our case, this point is the datetime after which the edit frequency drastically decreases. Hence, we can consider the page version that corresponds with that datetime as capturing the essence of the event. We refer to the change point datetime as DT_{CP}. Figure 2 shows the edits of the San Bernadino Attack Wikipedia page[6] and

---

[6] https://en.wikipedia.org/wiki/2015_San_Bernardino_attack

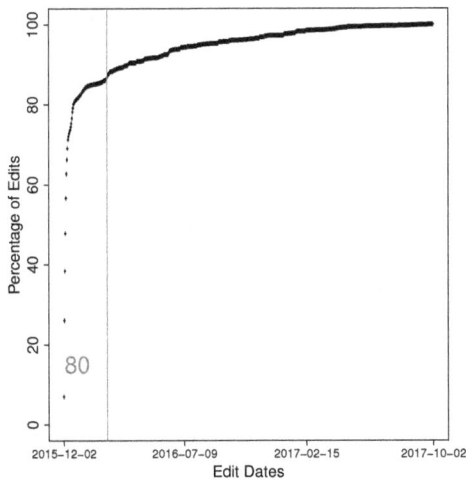

Figure 2: Change point in Wikipedia article edit frequency

the detected change point at 80 days after the creation of the page. In this example, we select the version of the Wikipedia page that was live 80 days after the event[7] for our experiment and refer to this version as the DT_{CP} version of the Wikipedia page.

3.2 Event Datetime

The first data point that we extract from the DT_{CP} version of the Wikipedia page is the event datetime. The format and granularity of the provided datetime can vary across Wikipedia pages. For uniformity, we express the event datetime in date, month, year, hour, minute, and seconds. In case no exact time is available from the DT_{CP} version of the Wikipedia page, we set the time to 00:00:01 of the day of the event. We refer to the event datetime as DT_E.

3.3 Crawl Seed URIs

Similar to [9], we extract all external references contained in the DT_{CP} version of the Wikipedia page and consider their URIs as seeds for the focused crawl. For simplicity, we filter out references that do not point to English language content or that point to resources in a representation other than HTML. All remaining references are used as seeds for both the web archive and live web crawls as well as for the content relevance computation outlined below.

3.4 Content Relevance

This section describes the process aimed at determining the extent to which a crawled resource is content-wise relevant for inclusion in the event collection.

3.4.1 Event Vector. We use the textual content of the DT_{CP} version of the Wikipedia page to create an event vector that will serve as our baseline to assess the content relevance of crawled pages. In an effort to stabilize the event vector, we further incorporate the textual content of a random 60% of outgoing references from

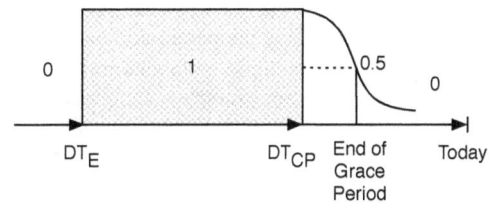

Figure 3: Temporal Relevance Interval

the DT_{CP} version of the Wikipedia page. In order to reduce noise, such as advertisements, we apply the common boilerpipe library[8], introduced in Kohlschütter et al. [13], to the Wikipedia page as well as to its outgoing references. From the remaining text of the page, we extract 1-grams and 2-grams, store their term frequency (TF), and extract their inverse document frequency (IDF) from the Google NGram dataset [7]. These 1-grams and 2-grams, along with their combined TF-IDF score, make up the event vector.

3.4.2 Candidate Vector and Content Relevance of a Crawled Resource. The textual content of a crawled page is used to generate a candidate vector. We create this candidate vector in a manner very similar to the event vector. After crawling a candidate page, we apply the boilerpipe library and extract the remaining textual content. We determine TF-IDF values from extracted 1-grams and 2-grams to build the candidate vector. We then compute the cosine similarity between the candidate vector and the event vector to obtain a content relevance score R_{cont}. The resulting cosine value is between 0 and 1 where a higher score indicates a greater level of similarity and hence content relevance of the crawled page. The way in which the content relevance is determined is identical for resources in live web and web archive crawls.

3.4.3 Content Relevance Threshold. We compute a content relevance threshold for an event on the assumption that resources referenced in the DT_{CP} version of the Wikipedia page are relevant themselves. We therefore run the same vector computation process for the content of the 40% of references that remain after the process of generating the event vector and compute the cosine similarity between both vectors. We repeat this process 10 times, each time with a different random set of 60% of references for the event vector and hence different remaining 40% of references for comparison. The computed average of the 10 obtained cosine similarity scores serves as our content relevance threshold TH_{cont} for the event.

3.5 Temporal Relevance

This section describes the process aimed at determining the extent to which a crawled resource is temporally relevant for inclusion in the event collection.

3.5.1 Temporal Interval and Temporal Relevance of a Crawled Resource. Inspired by [9], [8], and [5], we introduce a temporal interval to support assessing whether a crawled resource is temporally relevant. The interval, illustrated by Figure 3, serves the purpose of assigning low temporal relevance score to web resources that

[7]https://en.wikipedia.org/w/index.php?title=2015_San_Bernardino_attack&oldid=706012350

[8]https://github.com/kohlschutter/boilerpipe

were published prior to the event or a long time after it. Equation 1 outlines the computation of the temporal relevance score, which we refer to as R_{temp}. For example, a crawled resource that has an associated datetime DT_R, for example its publication date (see 3.5.2), prior to DT_E gets a temporal relevance score of $R_{temp} = 0$. A resource with DT_R that falls between DT_E and DT_{CP}, on the other hand, is assigned $R_{temp} = 1$. Additionally, a grace period beyond DT_{CP} is considered. The grace period is not unlike the cool-down period introduced in [9] and is additionally motivated by the fact that web archives may take a while to archive a resource after it was published. For web archive crawls, the grace period provides a fair chance for resources that were published some time before DT_{CP} but archived beyond it to still be considered relevant. As can be seen in Equation 1, during the grace period, a resource can obtain a R_{temp} score of less than 1 and greater or equal to 0.5. In this equation, $\Delta t\prime$ represents the difference between DT_{CP} and DT_R and Δt is equal to 1/4 of the period between DT_E and DT_{CP}. Different arguments can be made regarding the choice of the length of the grace period. Rather than setting a duration arbitrarily, we determine it using the time it took for references in the DT_{CP} version of the Wikipedia page to be archived. More specifically, we use the average time between the datetimes associated with all references of the DT_{CP} version of the Wikipedia page (as indicated in the article) and their corresponding archival datetime as the length of the grace period. For resources captured in the live crawl, we apply a grace period to give certain resources published past DT_{CP} a fair chance to be considered relevant. In this case, we determine its duration as the average distance between the associated datetimes of all references from the DT_{CP} version of the Wikipedia page (as indicated in the article).

$$R_{temp} = \begin{cases} 1 & \text{if } DT_E \leq DT_R \leq DT_{CP} \\ 0 & \text{if } DT_E > DT_R \\ e^{-\left(\left(\frac{ln(2)}{\Delta t}\right) * \Delta t\prime\right)} & \text{if } DT_R > DT_{CP} \end{cases} \qquad (1)$$

3.5.2 Resource Datetime. As described in the previous section, the datetime DT_R associated with a crawled resource plays a core role in determining its temporal relevance score. The manner in which this datetime is obtained is different for live web resources and Mementos. To determine the DT_R for a resource from the live web crawl, we use various approaches, some of which have also been used in Farag et al. [6]. The first approach is to extract a datetime from the URI of a page, as many news publishers use URI patterns that contain a datetime, for example: http://www.cnn.com/2017/12/09/us/wildfire-fighting-tactics/. Second, we consider the page's HTML, as news publishers and content management systems frequently embed datetimes. For example, the following HTML excerpt is from a New York Times article:

```
<meta property="article:published"
    itemprop="datePublished"
    content="2017-12-09T10:14:50-05:00"/>
```

Third, we utilize the CarbonDate tool[9], first introduced by Sala-hEldeen and Nelson [19]. The tool looks for first mentions of the URI on Twitter and Bitly. If these methods return more than one extracted datetime, we choose the earliest one as the page's DT_R.

[9]http://carbondate.cs.odu.edu/

If all methods fail and no datetime is extracted, we dismiss the crawled resource.

To determine the DT_R for a resource from the archived web crawl, a feature of the Memento protocol [20] that is supported by all archives included in the experiment, is leveraged because it yields a datetime with minimal effort involved. A web archive that returns a Memento also returns the datetime it was archived in the Memento-Datetime HTTP response header. If this datetime falls within the temporal interval between DT_E and DT_{CP} as shown in Figure 3, we use it as our DT_R. This kind of Memento will obtain a temporal relevance score of 1. Understanding that web archives commonly archive pages quite some time after they were published, this approach can lead to pages that were published prior to DT_E (but archived past it) receiving a score of 1. However, given the temporal threshold will be combined with a content-based threshold, this risk is outweighed by the benefit of a straightforward means to determine a DT_R. In cases where the archival datetime is beyond DT_{CP}, we can not merely dismiss the Memento because it could have been archived a long time after it was initially published. Hence, in these cases we attempt to determine the publication date of the page on the basis of the Memento. To that end, we use the CarbonDate tool again. If the tool can assign a date to the Memento, we use it as DT_R. If the tool is unsuccessful, we leverage archived HTTP headers, which some web archives convey as custom X-headers in the HTTP response of a Memento. For example, if a Memento provides an X-Last-Modified header, we use its datetime as DT_R. If all methods fail, the crawled resource is dismissed.

3.5.3 Temporal Relevance Threshold. We compute a temporal relevance threshold for an event on the assumption that resources referenced in the DT_{CP} version of the Wikipedia page are temporally relevant themselves. We therefore compute the temporal relevance of each URI in the same random set of 60% of references that we use for the computation of TH_{cont}. We repeat this process 10 times, each time with a different set of random 60% and use the computed average of all obtained scores as our temporal relevance threshold TH_{temp}.

3.6 Aggregate Relevance and Aggregate Relevance Threshold

Following the same reasoning as in [9], we use an aggregate relevance score R_{aggr} based on the sum of the content and temporal relevance scores, respectively R_{cont} and R_{temp}. In order to aggregate both scores into one, we introduce two weighting factors α and β, as shown in Equation 2. These factors can be used to weigh the significance of either relevance score. For our experiments we balance the weight equally and assign the value of 0.5 to both α and β, as also seen in [9].

$$R_{aggr} = \alpha * R_{cont} + \beta * R_{temp} \qquad (2)$$

$$TH_{aggr} = \alpha * TH_{cont} + \beta * TH_{temp} \qquad (3)$$

Similarly, as shown in Equation 3, we define an aggregate threshold. We use the same weighting factors as seen in Equation 2 to balance the significance of both parts.

Based on the R_{aggr} score of a page and the computed TH_{aggr} of the corresponding event, we determine whether the crawled page will be selected for the event collection or not. We classify

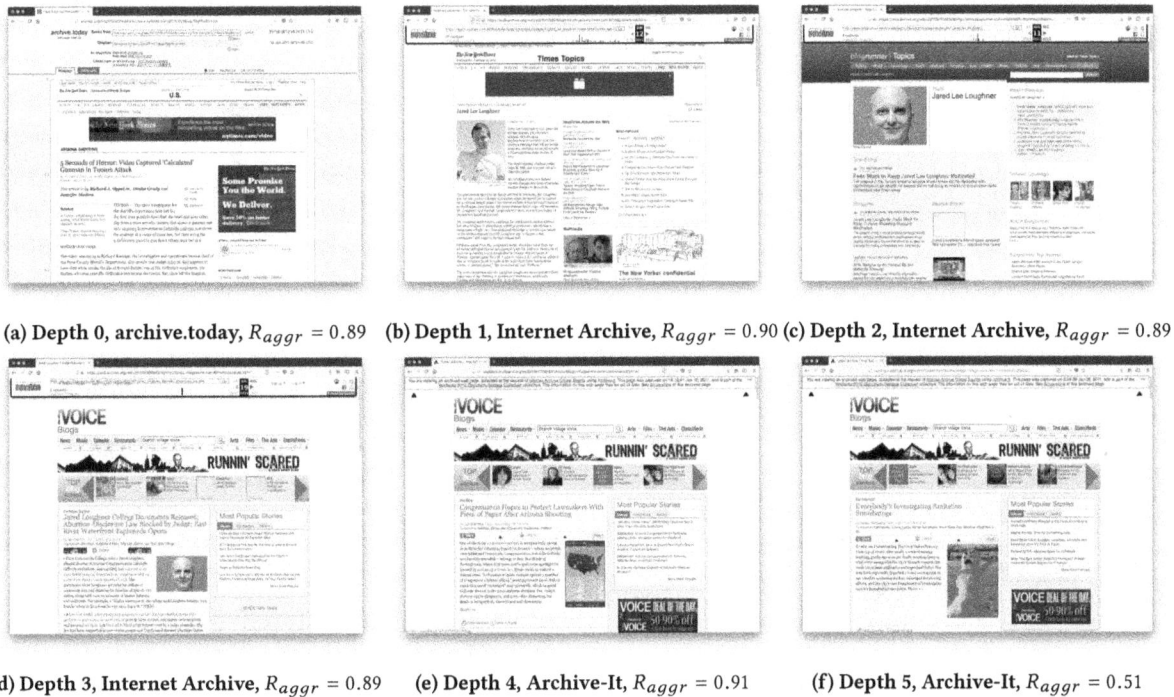

(a) Depth 0, archive.today, $R_{aggr} = 0.89$ (b) Depth 1, Internet Archive, $R_{aggr} = 0.90$ (c) Depth 2, Internet Archive, $R_{aggr} = 0.89$

(d) Depth 3, Internet Archive, $R_{aggr} = 0.89$ (e) Depth 4, Archive-It, $R_{aggr} = 0.91$ (f) Depth 5, Archive-It, $R_{aggr} = 0.51$

Figure 4: Mementos resulting from the TUC web archive crawl at depth 0 (seed) through depth 5 obtained from various web archives using the Memento infrastructure

a page with an aggregate relevance score equal to or above the threshold ($R_{aggr} \geq TH_{aggr}$) as relevant and hence select it into the collection. On the other hand, we consider a page with a score below the threshold ($R_{aggr} < TH_{aggr}$) as not relevant and reject it.

4 CRAWLING THE LIVE AND ARCHIVED WEB

Our crawling process, just like other implementations of focused crawlers, is deployed with a priority queue that informs the crawler which URIs to crawl next. In our case, resources linked from pages with a higher aggregate relevance score will be ranked higher in the priority queue. Our crawling process also needs to stop at some point. The simplest stop condition for a focused crawler is when the queue is empty and there are no documents left to crawl. However, under this condition, depending on the event and the length of the list of seed URIs, the crawl can run for a long time. Other typical stop conditions for crawlers are a maximum number of documents crawled, a maximum size of the crawled dataset, a maximum runtime, or a maximum crawl depth. We chose to implement the latter condition and run our focused crawler for a maximum depth of six. A seed URI is considered depth 0 and as long as the outlinks remain relevant, our crawler follows outlinks up until crawl depth 5. Arguably, the chosen crawl depth is somewhat arbitrary but our preliminary tests indicated that smaller depths tended to result in too few documents and larger depths took too long to complete. Clearly, this stop condition is configurable and we leave a thorough investigation of an optimal stop condition

for future work. We modify the code base of the crawler4j[10] tool for our focused crawler and run all crawls on an Amazon virtual machine.

The remainder of this section provides further details about the crawling process with a focus on web archive crawling because, to the best of our understanding, the work described here is the first to use focused crawling across web archives.

4.1 Live Web Crawls

The crawl of the live web follows established focused crawl practice, starting by fetching a seed URI page from the live web and determining and evaluating its aggregate relevance R_{aggr}. If the page is deemed relevant, it is added to the event collection, its outlinks are extracted and added to the priority queue. Each URI in the priority queue is handled in the same manner until the crawler's stop condition is met.

4.2 Web Archive Crawls

Crawling the archived web is done by utilizing the Memento protocol [20] and associated infrastructure. Unlike previous work [9], in order to generate the richest possible event collections, we are interested in obtaining Mementos from as many publicly available web archives around the world as possible. The Memento infrastructure, and in particular the Memento Aggregator [3], makes this possible. For each URI that needs to be crawled (seed URIs and URIs in the priority queue) until the crawler's stop condition is met, the crawler

---

[10]https://github.com/yasserg/crawler4j

Table 1: Crawled events

Event	DT_E	DT_{CP}	Wikipedia page version
NYC	10/31/2017	NA	https://en.wikipedia.org/wiki/2017_New_York_City_truck_attack
SB	12/02/2015	02/20/2016	https://en.wikipedia.org/w/index.php?title=2015_San_Bernardino_attack&oldid=706012350
TUC	01/08/2011	01/12/2012	https://en.wikipedia.org/w/index.php?title=2011_Tucson_shooting&oldid=471037980
BIN	04/03/2009	11/11/2009	https://en.wikipedia.org/w/index.php?title=Binghamton_shootings&oldid=325176468

obtains a Memento of that URI that was archived temporally closest but after DT_E. Closest to that datetime, in order to avoid using a version of the resource for which the content may have drifted [10] since it was originally linked to. And after that datetime because, clearly, pages that were archived prior to DT_E were also published before it and hence are not relevant when unplanned events are concerned.

The Memento protocol and the Memento Aggregator provide two ways to discover a Memento with an archival date closest to a desired date. The TimeMap approach consists of requesting a list of URIs of all available Mementos (URI-Ms in Memento protocol lingo) for a certain original URI (URI-R in Memento protocol lingo). From that list, the Memento closest to and after DT_E can be selected. The TimeGate approach entails performing datetime negotiation by providing an original URI as well as a preferred archival datetime, and receiving the URI of the Memento with an archival datetime temporally closest to the preferred datetime in return. However, this approach can yield a Memento that is either prior to or after the preferred datetime. Both the TimeMap and TimeGate approaches require the Memento Aggregator to issue a request to multiple web archives for each URI. As such, in both cases, extra HTTP requests are involved when compared to live web crawling where a URI is accessed directly. Therefore, a web archive crawl will necessarily be slower than a live web crawl. However, the TimeMap approach can involve significantly more HTTP requests than the TimeGate approach because obtaining a complete TimeMap from a single archive itself may entail multiple requests. As such, in order to reduce the overall web archive crawling time, we use the TimeGate approach for our experiments and use DT_E as the preferred datetime. In case the returned Memento has an archival datetime prior to our DT_E, we simply follow the next memento HTTP link header, which is provided in the TimeGate HTTP response. This header points to the temporally "next" Memento that, as per the Memento protocol's datetime negotiation, has a datetime greater or equal to DT_E.

For each URI that needs to be crawled, this process yields the URI of a Memento. The crawler fetches that Memento from the web archive that holds it, computes its R_{aggr} score and evaluates it vis-a-vis the TH_{aggr}. If the Memento is deemed relevant, it is added to the event collection, its outlinks are extracted and added to the priority queue. We note that most web archives rewrite outlinks in their Mementos to point back into the same archive rather than to the live web, even when the archive does not hold a Memento for the linked resource or only holds Mementos that are temporally distant from the desired time, which in our case is DT_E [2]. We therefore add the original URI (URI-R) of the outlink, which can be obtained using features of the Memento protocol, to the priority queue rather than the rewritten URI-M of the outlink. This allows

us to discover the Memento for outlinks that is temporally closest and past the event datetime DT_E across all web archives covered by the Aggregator.

Figure 4 shows six screenshots of consecutively crawled Mementos. Figure 4a shows the Memento of the seed URI, Figure 4b the Memento of one of the seed's outlinks (crawl depth 1), Figure 4c the Memento of an outlink of the prior Memento of crawl depth 1 (crawl depth 2), and so on. These screenshots show the diversity of contributing web archives: the Memento for the seed URI was found in archive.today, the Mementos for crawl depths 1..3 were provided by the Internet Archive, and depths 4..5 by Archive-It. The figure also shows the R_{aggr} scores for each Memento. The threshold TH_{aggr} for this crawl was 0.75 and hence the first five Mementos are classified as relevant but the last one is not. Since our crawl depth was set to five, the outlinks of the Memento shown in Figure 4f were not added to the priority queue. If, however, it had been set to a number larger than five, the Memento's outlinks would also not have been added to the queue as the Memento's $R_{aggr} < TH_{aggr}$.

5 WEB CRAWL COMPARISON

We present the results of crawls for four different events: the 2017 New York City attack (NYC), the 2015 San Bernadino attack (SB), the 2011 Tucson shooting (TUC), and the 2009 Binghampton shootings (BIN). We chose these events because they are fairly similar in nature, they all happened in the U.S., and their coverage on the web is predominantly in English. We assumed that this uniformity would better support detecting patterns in our results. We ran our crawls in November of 2017, a few days after the New York City attack, and more than eight years after the Binghampton shootings. Table 1 summarizes the four events for which we created an event collection with our focused crawling framework. The table also shows the event dates DT_E, the change points DT_{CP}, and the URIs of the DT_{CP} versions of the Wikipedia event page. Note that we did not compute a change point for the NYC event because we crawled resources very soon after the attack happened, at which point the number of Wikipedia page edits had not yet reached the change point. As such, for the NYC event, we used the live version of the Wikipedia event page as it was at the time of crawling.

5.1 Relevant URIs

Our first results are visualized in Figure 5, distinguished by event. For example, the crawl data for the New York City attack is shown in Figure 5a, for the San Bernadino attack in Figure 5b, and so on. The left-hand plot for each event shows the results from the web archive crawl, and the right plot displays our results from the live web crawl. All subfigures of Figure 5 show the number of URIs

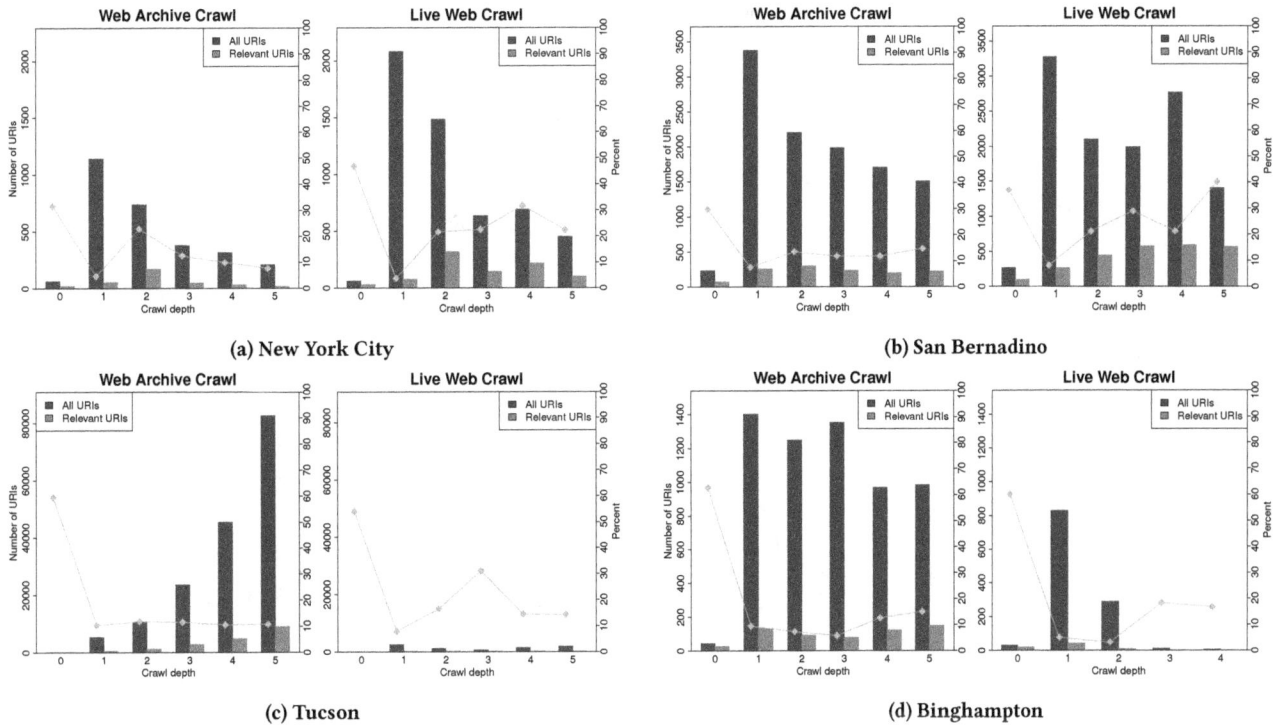

(a) New York City

(b) San Bernadino

(c) Tucson

(d) Binghampton

Figure 5: Relevant URIs

crawled at each crawl depth (0..5). The blue bars indicate the total number of URIs crawled and the red bars represent the number of URIs that were classified as relevant, per corresponding crawl depth. The bars refer to the left y-axis. The lines, representing the fraction of relevant URIs, refer to the right y-axis. For the NYC event, the live web crawl is the clear winner as it returns significantly more URIs as well as relevant URIs. The fraction of relevant URIs on depth 0 (the seeds) is almost 50% for the live web vs. 30% for the web archive crawl. On crawl depth 1, the first outlinks from the seeds, and on depth 2, the fractions are fairly similar. But for the further depths 3, 4, and 5 the live crawl shows ratios above 20% of relevant URIs whereas the web archive crawl only shows ratios around 10%. This result makes intuitive sense as we conducted the crawl merely days after the event happened. It is highly likely that web archives did not have a chance to archive a significant amount of the relevant resources and hence our web archive crawl did not surface many (relevant) URIs. The results for the SB crawls, shown in Figure 5b, are similar in that the live crawl returns a higher ratio of relevant URIs at all crawl depths. While the number of total URIs crawled is comparable between both crawls, the number of relevant URIs is consistently higher for the live web crawl. Our interpretation of these results is that, since the event datetime is two years in the past, web archives have had enough time to create Mementos of many relevant web pages. However the web archive crawl does not outperform the live web crawl. Figures 5c and 5d show a very different pattern. In both cases the live web crawl results in fewer total URIs and fewer relevant URIs crawled than the web archive crawl. The BIN live crawl does not even return

any URIs on depth 5. Our interpretation of this pattern is based on the fact that the TUC and BIN events happened in 2011 and 2009, respectively. Hence, a lot of time has passed for pages on the live web to either completely disappear or to have their content drift to something less relevant compared to the event vector. This is a phenomenon that we have previously investigated in the realm of scholarly communication [10, 12] and that seems to also happen for web coverage of unplanned events. In essence, our finding suggests that live web resources pertaining to an event that were available at the time of the event are by now more likely available in web archives than on the live web.

5.2 Accumulated Relevance

Inspired by the evaluation shown in [9], we also analyze the accumulated relevance of all crawled resources, understanding that even resources that do not meet the aggregate relevance threshold still have an aggregate relevance score. Just like in this related work, we simply add individual R_{aggr} scores of all crawled resources to obtain the accumulated relevance. Since our crawl stop condition is defined by crawl depth, we are able to show two different analyses of the accumulated relevance. First, we present the accumulated relevance over elapsed crawl time. We expect the web archive crawl to take longer than the live crawl as we query the Memento Aggregator for each candidate URI. As described earlier, this results in polling several of the 22 compliant web archives, which adds to crawling time.

Figure 6 displays the accumulated relevance (on the y-axis) over time (on the x-axis) for all four events. The green lines represent

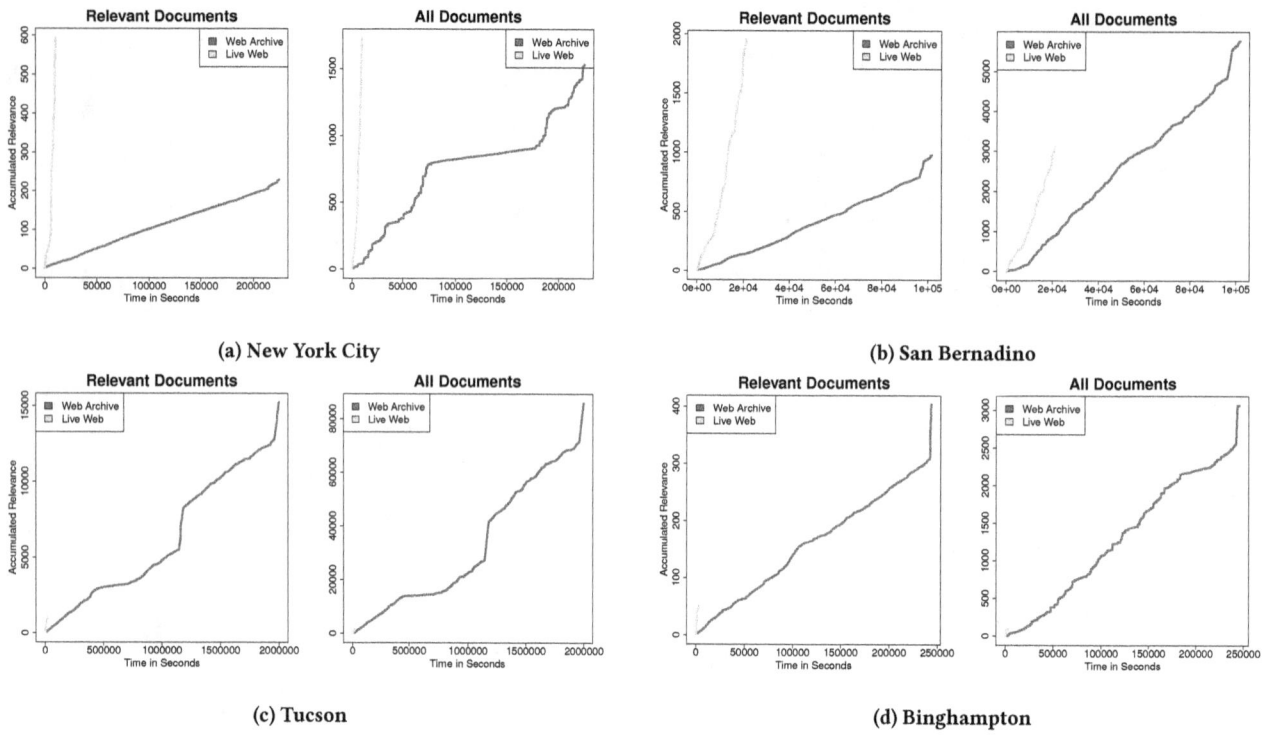

(a) New York City

(b) San Bernadino

(c) Tucson

(d) Binghampton

Figure 6: Accumulated relevance over time

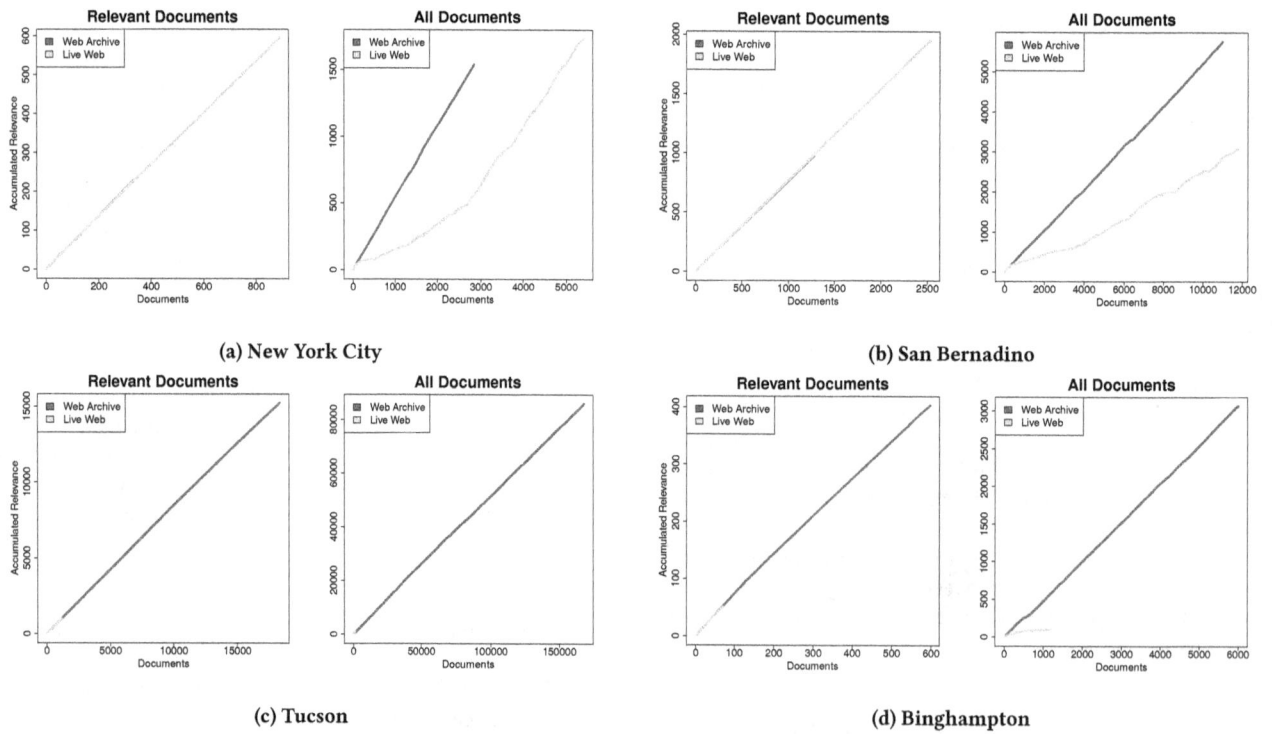

(a) New York City

(b) San Bernadino

(c) Tucson

(d) Binghampton

Figure 7: Accumulated relevance over documents

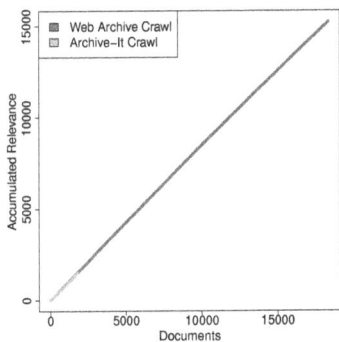

Figure 8: TUC web archive crawl vs Archive-It crawl

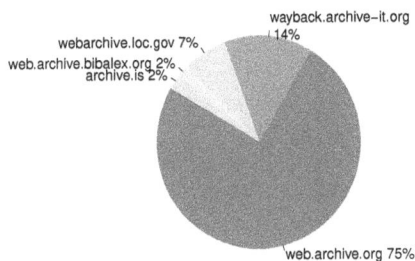

Figure 9: Contributions to the TUC web archive crawl

the live web crawl and the purple line the web archive crawl. Each subfigure shows two distinct plots. The plot on the left-hand side shows the data for all resources that were classified as relevant. The plot on the right shows the data for all crawled resources, including the ones that were crawled because their parent was categorized as relevant but they themselves had a relevance score below the threshold. These resources, while "failing" our threshold test, may still have value for an event-centric collection and hence they are considered here. Unlike the previous figures, subfigures of Figure 6 do not distinguish between crawl depths.

Figure 6a shows the accumulated relevance over time for the NYC crawl. Considering all relevant documents (plot on the left), we can observe that the accumulated relevance of the live crawl increases very rapidly and that the web archive crawl takes much longer, as expected, and never reaches the same relevance. The accumulated relevance for all crawled documents (plot on the right) for the web archive crawl gets closer but still does not reach the accumulated relevance level of the live crawl. Given the results from the previous section, these observations are not surprising.

Figure 6b shows a similar picture for relevant documents in the SB crawl. However, the data for all crawled documents is surprising. The web archive crawl takes much longer but eventually surpasses the accumulated relevance level of the live web crawl. Figures 6c and 6d show an even more dramatic picture. The accumulated relevance of the live web crawls is quickly surpassed by the web archive crawls. Given relatively few URIs were obtained in the live crawls (as seen in Figures 5c and 5d), it is not surprising to see these crawls finish rather quickly. The web archive crawls, again, take significantly longer to complete.

The second analysis of the accumulated relevance is over the number of documents crawled. Figure 7 visualizes this data in a similar fashion as seen in the previous figures. The data for the NYC crawl is displayed in Figure 7a where we see twice as many relevant documents for the live web than for the web archive crawl. The accumulated relevance therefore is much higher. When we consider all crawled documents, we also find roughly twice as many resources in the live crawl and, while the relevance of the web archive crawl is closer, it does not catch up. These data points confirm our previous findings.

The picture for the live crawl of the SB event (Figure 7b) is similar to the NYC event. The plot for all documents, however, shows an interesting fact: the total number of documents crawled is very similar ($11,806$ for the live web vs. $11,007$ for the web archive crawl) while the accumulated relevance of the web archive crawl ends up to be almost twice that of the live web crawl. As previously indicated in Figures 6c and 6d, Figures 7c and 7d confirm that web archive crawls perform considerably better than live crawls for the TUC and BIN events, respectively.

6 COMPARISON TO A MANUALLY CREATED COLLECTION

We utilized Wikipedia event pages, specifically the URIs of external references as seeds for our crawls. However, a common approach for building event-centric collections from web pages is based on manual suggestion of seed URIs. We are therefore motivated to compare our approach with an event collection that was created using manually selected seed URIs. The Archive-It service provided by the Internet Archive is frequently used to build such collections. At the time we conducted our experiments, the only Archive-It collection that matched one of our events was the Tucson shooting collection, originally created by scholars at Virginia Tech. We were able to obtain a copy of the crawled data and compared it to our TUC web archive crawl.

To build this collection, the Archive-It crawler was configured to merely crawl all $1,997$ seed URIs and not go beyond this crawl depth. In terms of our experiment, this equals to crawl depth 0 and hence a comparison of relevant URIs per crawl depth $0..5$ is not applicable. Instead, we compute the accumulated relevance of all crawled resources and compare it to the data from our web archive crawl. Figure 8 shows the results. It is apparent that the Archive-It crawl has significantly fewer documents crawled compared to our web archive crawl, an obvious result of the crawl depth constraint. However, what is interesting is that the slope of the line is equally steep for both crawls i.e., the orange line (Archive-It crawl) and the purple line (our web archive crawl). It would not have been unreasonable to assume that the manually curated seed list would result in more relevant URIs crawled than the automatically generated seed list stemming from the references of the DT_{CP} version of the Wikipedia page.

This comparison raises the question of the level of overlap between the manually curated URIs from the Archive-It collection and the automatically crawled URIs of our TUC web archive crawl.

We classified 1,795 out of all 1,997 URIs in the Archive-It collection as relevant. On the other hand, we deemed 18,353 out of 167,641 crawled URIs in the TUC archived crawl relevant. We found that only 92 URIs overlap in both collections, which indicates that both collections are rather disjoint.

Another distinguishing element between these two crawls is the variety of web archives that contribute to the crawl. Given our framework for crawling the archived web, we are able to crawl archived resources from a total of 22 web archives. Naturally, the Archive-It crawl only stems from one archive. Figure 9 shows the distribution of web archives that have contributed to our TUC archived crawl. The figure shows the top five contributing archives only, with the Internet Archive providing 75% of all Mementos. We note, however, the diversity of other contributing archives. Besides resources provided from the Library of Congress and the Library of Alexandria, as shown in Figure 9, our crawl further includes resources crawled from the Portuguese, the Icelandic, the UK, and the Northern Ireland Web Archives, not labeled in Figure 9.

7 CONCLUSION AND FUTURE WORK

Inspired by previous work, we were motivated to investigate a focused crawling approach to build event-centric collections. In this paper we outline our focused crawling framework, detail its methodology, describe its crawling process of the live and archived web, and present the results on four unpredictable events. Our results prove that focused crawling on the archived web is feasible. The Memento protocol and infrastructure play a vital role in this process.

Comparing web archive crawls and live web crawls for events, we observe the following patterns:

(1) For rather recent events, such as the NYC event in our experiments, a crawl of the live web results in more total URIs, more relevant URIs, and a higher level of accumulated relevance over all documents. A web archive crawl is not competitive and takes much longer to complete.

(2) For events that are less recent but took place in the not too distant past, such as the SAN event in our experiments, our results show a mixed pattern. If we consider relevant documents only, the live web crawl outperforms the web archive crawl and, as expected, finishes much quicker. However, if time is not a main concern and we can consider all crawled resources, the web archive crawl provides more documents that, in aggregate, are more relevant.

(3) For events that happened in the more distant past, such as the TUC and BIN events in our experiments, the web archive crawl, while taking much longer to complete, returns many more relevant results. A live web crawl does not provide compelling results.

The comparison of our web archive crawl on the TUC event with the manually curated Archive-It crawl shows that both collections, while distinct in terms of their crawled URIs, are highly relevant to the event. In addition, we find that the inclusion of an array of web archives clearly provides merit to the collection building. We therefore suggest that, especially for collections of events that took place in the more distant past, augmenting manually curated collections that are based on human-evaluated seed URIs with a focused crawl that is based on the extraction of references from Wikipedia pages can be very beneficial.

Our chosen events are constrained in dimensions such as event type, language, location and hence more experimentation is required to draw general conclusions from our findings. In addition, various aspects of our crawling framework (event vector, threshold computation, weighting factors) deserve further evaluation in the future.

8 ACKNOWLEDGMENTS

We would like to express our thanks to Liuqing Li, Edward Fox, and Zhiwu Xie from Virginia Tech for making their Archive-It collection on the Tucson shooting available for this experiment.

REFERENCES

[1] Charu C Aggarwal, Fatima Al-Garawi, and Philip S Yu. 2001. Intelligent crawling on the World Wide Web with arbitrary predicates. In *Proceedings of WWW'01*. 96–105.

[2] Scott G Ainsworth and Michael L Nelson. 2015. Evaluating sliding and sticky target policies by measuring temporal drift in acyclic walks through a web archive. *International Journal on Digital Libraries* 16, 2 (2015), 129–144.

[3] Nicolas J. Bornand, Lyudmila Balakireva, and Herbert Van de Sompel. 2016. Routing Memento Requests Using Binary Classifiers. *CoRR* abs/1606.09136 (2016).

[4] Soumen Chakrabarti, Martin van den Berg, and Byron Dom. 1999. Focused crawling: a new approach to topic-specific Web resource discovery. *Computer Networks* 31, 11 (1999), 1623 – 1640.

[5] Miguel Costa, Francisco Couto, and Mário Silva. 2014. Learning Temporal-dependent Ranking Models. In *Proceedings of SIGIR '14*. 757–766.

[6] Mohamed M. G. Farag, Sunshin Lee, and Edward A. Fox. 2018. Focused crawler for events. *International Journal on Digital Libraries* 19, 1 (2018), 3–19.

[7] Yoav Goldberg and Jon Orwant. 2013. A dataset of syntactic-ngrams over time from a very large corpus of english books. In *Proceedings of *SEM' 13*, Vol. 1. 241–247.

[8] Gerhard Gossen, Elena Demidova, and Thomas Risse. 2015. iCrawl: Improving the Freshness of Web Collections by Integrating Social Web and Focused Web Crawling. In *Proceedings of JCDL '15*. 75–84.

[9] Gerhard Gossen, Elena Demidova, and Thomas Risse. 2017. Extracting Event-Centric Document Collections from Large-Scale Web Archives. In *Proceedings of TPDL' 17*. 116–127.

[10] Shawn M. Jones, Herbert Van de Sompel, Harihar Shankar, Martin Klein, Richard Tobin, and Claire Grover. 2016. Scholarly Context Adrift: Three out of Four URI References Lead to Changed Content. *PLoS ONE* 11, 12 (2016).

[11] Rebecca Killick and Idris A. Eckley. 2014. changepoint: An R Package for Change-point Analysis. *Journal of Statistical Software* 58, 3 (2014), 1–19.

[12] Martin Klein, Herbert Van de Sompel, Robert Sanderson, Harihar Shankar, Lyudmila Balakireva, Ke Zhou, and Richard Tobin. 2014. Scholarly Context Not Found: One in Five Articles Suffers from Reference Rot. *PLoS ONE* 9, 12 (2014).

[13] Christian Kohlschütter, Peter Fankhauser, and Wolfgang Nejdl. 2010. Boilerplate Detection Using Shallow Text Features. In *Proceedings of WSDM '10*. 441–450.

[14] Justin Littman, Daniel Chudnov, Daniel Kerchner, Christie Peterson, Yecheng Tan, Rachel Trent, Rajat Vij, and Laura Wrubel. 2018. API-based social media collecting as a form of web archiving. *International Journal on Digital Libraries* 19, 1 (2018), 21–38.

[15] Alexander C. Nwala, Michele C. Weigle, and Michael L. Nelson. 2018. Scraping SERPs for archival seeds: it matters when you start. In *Proceedings of JCDL'18*.

[16] Gautam Pant and Padmini Srinivasan. 2005. Learning to crawl: Comparing classification schemes. *ACM Transactions on Information Systems (TOIS)* 23, 4 (2005), 430–462.

[17] Pedro Pereira, Joaquim Macedo, Olga Craveiro, and Henrique Madeira. 2014. Time-aware focused web crawling. In *European Conference on Information Retrieval*. 534–539.

[18] Jacob Ratkiewicz, Santo Fortunato, Alessandro Flammini, Filippo Menczer, and Alessandro Vespignani. 2010. Characterizing and Modeling the Dynamics of Online Popularity. *Phys. Rev. Lett.* 105 (2010), 158701. Issue 15.

[19] Hany SalahEldeen and Michael L. Nelson. 2013. Carbon Dating The Web: Estimating the Age of Web Resources. *CoRR* abs/1304.5213 (2013).

[20] Herbert Van de Sompel, Michael L. Nelson, and Robert Sanderson. 2013. HTTP Framework for Time-Based Access to Resource States – Memento. (2013). https://tools.ietf.org/html/rfc7089.

Decay of Relevance in Exponentially Growing Networks

Jun Sun
Institute WeST, Universität
Koblenz–Landau
Koblenz, Germany
junsun@uni-koblenz.de

Steffen Staab*
Institute WeST, Universität
Koblenz–Landau
Koblenz, Germany
staab@uni-koblenz.de

Fariba Karimi
GESIS — Leibniz-Institut für
Sozialwissenschaften
Cologne, Germany
fariba.karimi@gesis.org

ABSTRACT

We propose a new preferential attachment–based network growth model in order to explain two properties of growing networks: (1) the power-law growth of node degrees and (2) the decay of node relevance. In preferential attachment models, the ability of a node to acquire links is affected by its degree, its fitness, as well as its *relevance* which typically decays over time. After a review of existing models, we argue that they cannot explain the above-mentioned two properties (1) and (2) at the same time. We have found that apart from being empirically observed in many systems, the exponential growth of the network size over time is the key to sustain the power-law growth of node degrees when node relevance decays. We therefore make a clear distinction between the *event time* and the *physical time* in our model, and show that under the assumption that the relevance of a node decays with its age τ, there exists an analytical solution of the decay function f_R with the form $f_R(\tau) = \tau^{-1}$. Other properties of real networks such as power-law alike degree distributions can still be preserved, as supported by our experiments. This makes our model useful in explaining and analysing many real systems such as citation networks.

CCS CONCEPTS

• **Networks** → *Network architectures*; • **Human-centered computing** → Social network analysis;

KEYWORDS

network growth model, preferential attachment, decay of relevance

ACM Reference Format:
Jun Sun, Steffen Staab, and Fariba Karimi. 2018. Decay of Relevance in Exponentially Growing Networks. In *WebSci '18: 10th ACM Conference on Web Science, May 27–30, 2018, Amsterdam, Netherlands.* ACM, New York, NY, USA, 9 pages. https://doi.org/10.1145/3201064.3201084

1 INTRODUCTION

Network growth models try to explain the evolution of numerous types of networks, such as social networks, citation networks and

---

*Also with Institute WAIS, University of Southampton.

the World Wide Web. These networks — despite of their heterogeneity in terms of their purposes, their origins and the natures of their nodes and links — tend to have certain phenomena in common. At the macro level, most real networks appear to be a scale-free structure indicated by the presence of power-law like node degree distributions [6, 13]. Many networks grow exponentially, especially as long as each node is able to attract yet another, similar sized group of nodes as the ones before it [7]. Such growth might eventually slow down due to the limited number of potential nodes [15], for example when a social network already covers most of the population. At the micro level, nodes in the networks have varying abilities to attract new nodes, thus having different degree growth curves. Besides, new nodes "prefer" to "attach" to existing nodes with higher degrees [1]. A node's ability to attract new nodes is also affected by its intrinsic *fitness* [3] and its *relevance* which typically decays over time [12].

Preferential attachment models including the Barabási-Albert model [1] or the Bianconi-Barabási model [3] have been proposed and have successfully enlighted one important connection between the two levels of phenomena: The *rich-get-richer* effect resulting from preferential attachment at the micro level leads to the scale-free nature of the network at the macro level. Other preferential attachment models have been proposed to deal with individual aspects of phenomena such as the accelerated growth of the network [7] and the decay of node relevance [11, 12].

In our study, we try to reveal another connection among the growth of network sizes, the growth of node degrees and the decay of node relevance. More specifically, we argue that existing preferential attachment models cannot well explain the micro level phenomenon: power-law growth of node degrees under the decay of node relevance. We therefore propose a new preferential attachment–based network growth model that shows the exponential growth of the network size at the macro level — apart from being empirically observed — is the key to sustain the power-law growth of node degrees when node relevance decays. We show analytically that the node's age τ and the node relevance decay function $f_R(\tau) = \tau^{-1}$ may connect the micro and macro levels of phenomena. To make our model work with a wider range of networks, we also discuss situations where the exponential growth slows down.

First, we review basic notations of networks and some existing network growth models in Section 2. We then look into real world examples of networks in Section 3, and show various empirical observations which existing models cannot explain well at the same time. In Section 4, we propose our model on the basis of these observations, and analytically show its self-consistency. In order to evaluate our model, in Section 5 we generate synthetic networks using our model with different parameters, and compare

Table 1: List of Notations

Sym.	Meaning
s	the event time, whose advance is driven by events in the network. When written as s_i with a subscript i, it represents the event time that node i joins the network;
t	the physical time. t_i represents the physical time that node i joins the network;
τ	the age of a node in physical time. For mathematical simplicity we let τ start at 1 when the node joins the network. τ_i represents the age of node i;
η	the fitness of a node that remains constant over time (see Section 2.3). η_i represents the fitness of node i;
$\rho(\eta)$	the probability density function characterizing the fitness distribution of nodes in the network;
Π	the preferential attachment probability of a node (see Section 2.2). Π_i represents the preferential attachment probability of a new node to attach to node i;
T	the age of the whole network in physical time;
k	the (in)degree[1] of a node. When written as k_i with a subscript i, it represents the degree of node i. k_i is a function of s, s_i and η_i: $k_i(s, s_i, \eta_i)$, or a function of τ_i and η_i: $k_i(\tau_i, \eta_i)$;
$f_R(\tau)$	the relevance decay function which is a monotonically decreasing function with regard to the node age τ that characterises the decay of node relevance (see Section 2.4);
$p(k)$	the probability density function characterizing the degree distribution of the network.

the generated networks with real world networks. In Section 6, we conclude with some discussions and point to potential future work.

2 RELATED WORK

In this section, we review some existing preferential attachment models, namely the Barabási-Albert model [1], the Bianconi-Barabási model [3] and the relevance model [12].

2.1 Notations in Preferential Attachment Models

In order to compare preferential attachment models with each other and with our model, we have come up with a common notation displayed in Table 1 that we will use consistently in the remainder of this paper.

Note that conventionally t has been used to represent timesteps in the three existing models that we discuss in this section, and indeed there is no need to distinguish s and t if a uniform growth of the network size is assumed. In this paper we lift this assumption and explicitly distinguish s and t.

---

[1]Since in our model the outdegree of a node is trivially constant, without explicitly mentioning, the term *degree* always stands for indegree.

2.2 Barabási-Albert Model

Albert and Barabási have proposed the well known Barabási-Albert model for network growth [1]. The model starts with one node with a self loops at timestep $s = 1$. At each later timestep $s > 1$, a new node joins the network and creates a constant number of m links to existing nodes, each with the *preferential attachment probability* Π_i proportional to the degree k_i of the existing node i [5]:

$$\Pi_i = \frac{k_i}{\sum_j k_j}. \tag{1}$$

When the network is large enough to apply the continuum approximation, the model analytically leads to two properties of the network.

(1) At the micro level, the power-law growth of node degrees:

$$k_i(s, s_i) \sim (\frac{s}{s_i})^{1/2}, \tag{2}$$

where s_i is the timestep when node i joins the network.
(2) At the macro level, the power-law degree distribution:

$$p(k) \sim k^{-3}. \tag{3}$$

2.3 Bianconi-Barabási Model

The Barabási-Albert model successfully explains the scale-free property of networks. However, it predicts that the degrees of all nodes grow with a power function with the same exponent $\frac{1}{2}$, therefore old nodes tend to remain more popular than late comers. However in reality degrees of nodes grow with different rates, and often we see new nodes get more popular than old ones. Bianconi and Barabási have proposed to use the *fitness* value η to quantify the ability of a node to acquire new links in the network [3]. When a node joins the network, it is assigned a fitness value η which does not change over time. Being an extension of the Barabási-Albert model, the fitness model modifies the preferential attachment probability Π_i that a newly arriving node links to an existing node i to be proportional to the product of the degree k_i and fitness η_i of node i:

$$\Pi_i = \frac{\eta_i k_i}{\sum_j \eta_j k_j}. \tag{4}$$

The degree growth of a node still follows a power-law:

$$k_i(s, s_i, \eta_i) \sim (\frac{s}{s_i})^{\beta(\eta_i)}, \tag{5}$$

but with an exponent $\beta(\eta_i)$ that is proportional to its fitness. The degree distribution of the network is however determined by the fitness distribution $\rho(\eta)$. For most fitness distributions, the resulting degree distribution still reflects the scale-free property of real world networks, although not being a perfect power-law.

2.4 Relevance Model

The Bianconi-Barabási model does not consider the decay of interest or *relevance* of nodes (e.g., scientific papers) that is often observed in reality. In the relevance model [12], the temporal decay of node relevance is modelled by a monotonically decreasing function $f_R(\tau)$ where τ is the age of a node (here in event time). The preferential

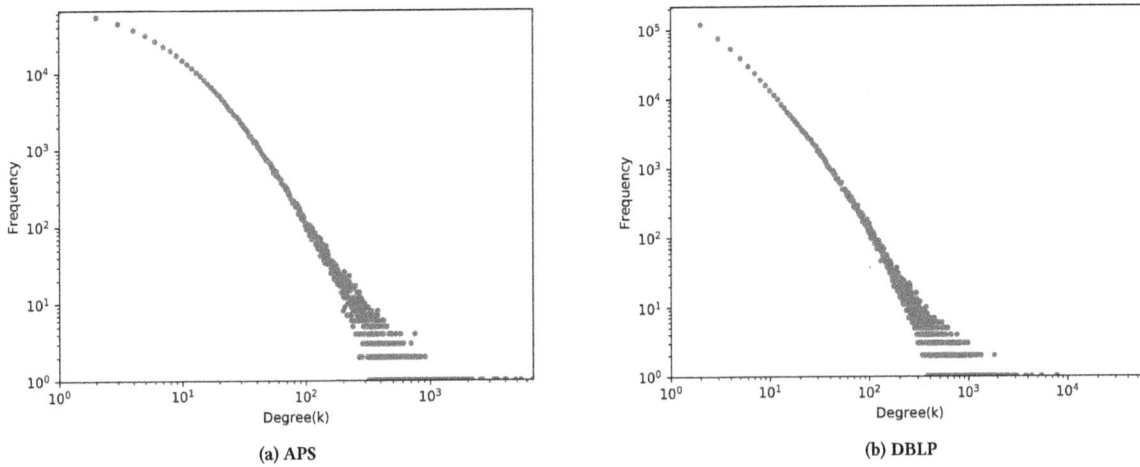

(a) APS   (b) DBLP

Figure 1: The degree distributions of the (a) APS and (b) DBLP citation networks. Estimated power-law exponents (for $k > 5$): 1.906 for APS and 1.947 for DBLP.

attachment probability is thus:

$$\Pi_i = \frac{\eta_i k_i f_R(\tau_i)}{\sum_j \eta_j k_j f_R(\tau_j)}. \quad (6)$$

Medo et al. have reported that the relevance model can result in realistic degree distributions, such as exponential, log-normal and power-law distributions, depending on the input parameters [12].

3 EMPIRICAL OBSERVATIONS

In this section, we first introduce the two datasets that we use report the empirical findings on them. We then argue that existing models cannot well explain some observations.

3.1 Datasets

We use two datasets in this paper, each consisting of a citation network of research papers in two different diciplines.

The APS dataset is provided by the American Physical Society (APS)[2]. It contains a citation network consisting of 564,517 papers published in APS journals from 1893 to 2015, and 6,715,562 citations to other papers within the network.

The DBLP dataset is extracted by Tang et al. in the ArnetMiner project [16]. It contains 3,272,991 papers which were published from 1936 to 2016 and indexed in the DBLP Computer Science Bibliography [9], and 8,466,859 citations to other papers within the network. Since the original DBLP index is incomplete, there exist missing links in DBLP.

Both datasets contain the publication dates of papers. APS has a monthly granularity of dates, and DBLP has a yearly granularity.

3.2 Scale-free Degree Distribution

Figure 1 shows the degree distribution of the two networks. Several observations can be made from the plots. The two distributions display power-law like behaviour, although not for very small degrees (under about 10) in APS. Additionally, the curve of APS has a well-defined long tail. The curve of DBLP displays an exponential cut-off when the degree is large (above around 200), which is also observed in many other networks [4]. We use the method by Clauset et al. [6] to estimate the power-law exponents of the two distributions and have found that they have comparable values (1.906 for APS and 1.947 for DBLP).

3.3 Exponential Growth of the Network Size

The growth of real systems is rarely linear. In the two datasets that we use, the network size s (defined as the total number of publications) exhibits exponential growth with regard to the time t (see Figure 2), as is observed in many systems [8] especially in their early stages. This exponential relationship $s = e^{\alpha t}$ can be explained by the Malthusian growth model, where α is the growth rate.

Being non-linear to the *physical time t*, the network size s can be seen as the *event time* whose addition is driven by the arrival of new nodes. The non-linear relationship between s and t is however not considered in the models discussed in Section 2. In this paper we make a clear distinction between them.

3.4 Power-law Growth of Node Degrees

In the Bianconi-Barabási model, the growth of a node degree follows a power-law, with an exponent monotonic to the node's fitness.

We also observe power-law growths of node degrees in our datasets. Since the growth of individual nodes can be highly influenced by randomness, instead, we first group the papers in our

---

[2]https://journals.aps.org/datasets

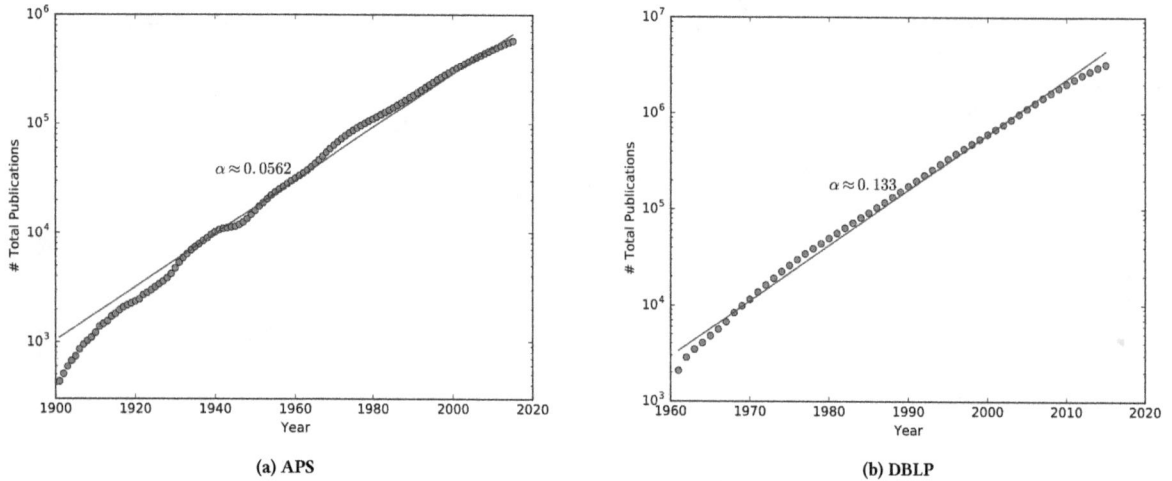

(a) APS

(b) DBLP

Figure 2: Total number of publications till each year in (a) APS and (b) DBLP. In each plot, the X-axis shows the physical timeline t in years; while the Y-axis shows the total number of publications s until the end of the corrsponding year in a logarithmic scale. The two approximately straight lines suggest the exponential growth of network sizes, i.e. $s \simeq e^{\alpha t}$.

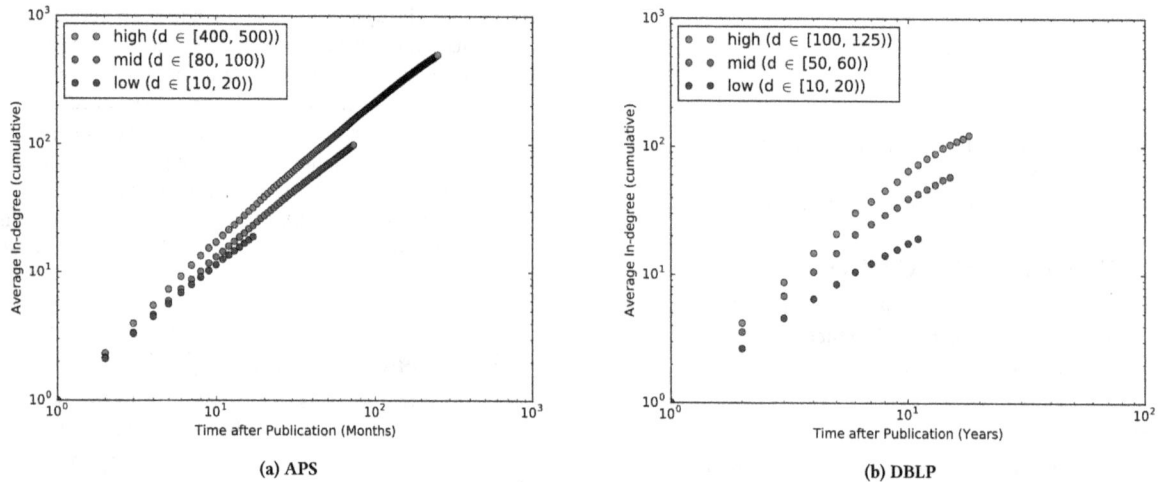

(a) APS

(b) DBLP

Figure 3: The average growth curve of number of citations of papers in (a) APS and (b) DBLP, grouped by their final indegrees.

datasets by their final citations received[3], and then plot the average growth of their degree in Figure 3. We observe linear curves in the log-log plot, but with different slopes. This indicates the power-law growth of node degrees with a fitness dependent exponent, as in the Bianconi-Barabási model.

3.5 Problems in Existing Models

In the Bianconi-Barabási model, the degree k_i of a node i with fitness η_i at timestep s can be written as Equation 5: $k_i \sim (s/s_i)^{\beta(\eta_i)}$. This indicates that the degree of a newer node u will grow slower than an

older one v, even if they have the same fitness, because $s/s_u < s/s_v$. However when we observe the degree growths of nodes grouped by their publication time in Figure 4, we see similar average growth curves of papers published in different time periods, which indicates that the growth depends on the age of the node τ_i but not s/s_i as in the Bianconi-Barabási model, i.e. we have empirically:

$$k_i(\tau_i, \eta_i) \sim \tau_i^{\beta(\eta_i)}. \tag{7}$$

In Section 5.2 we discuss the difference between the two kinds of power-law growths (Equation 5 and 7) in detail.

Moreover, the initial derivation resulting in Equation 5 is based on linear network growth and no decay of relevance. If we solely

---

[3]Finding the actual fitness values is tricky. Mariani et al. have shown that the indegree is a good measurement to rank nodes by their fitness in such temporal networks [10].

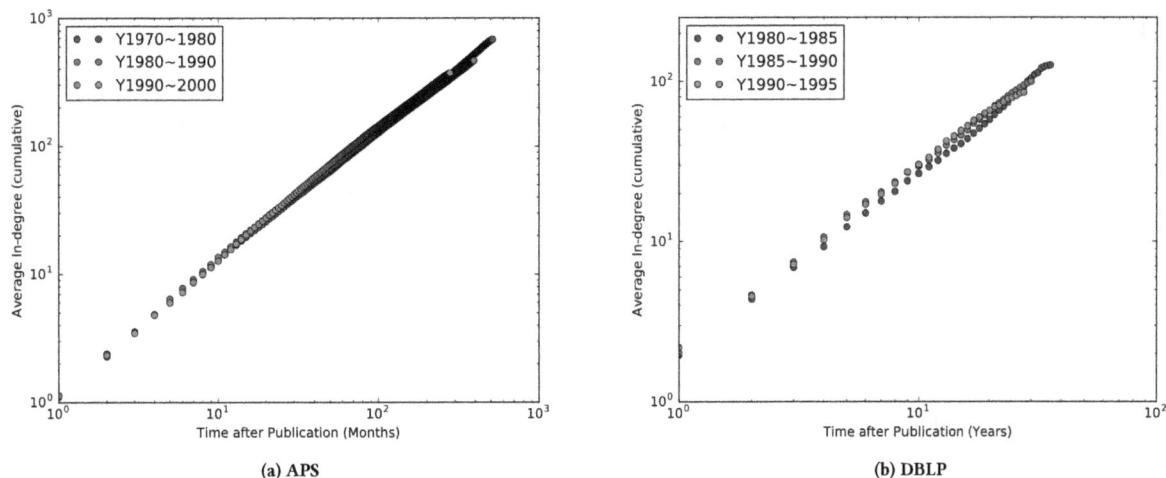

(a) APS

(b) DBLP

Figure 4: The average growth curve of number of citations of papers published in different time periods in (a) APS and (b) DBLP. Papers in the two datasets are grouped according to their publish year (papers with citation fewer than 20 are excluded).

consider (1) the decay of node relevance as in the relevance model, or solely consider (2) the exponential growth of the network size, the power-law growth of node degrees will be lost. In our model we propose to combine the two.

4 MODEL

In this section, we propose our model as an extension of the Bianconi-Barabási model and the relevance model (see Section 2.4). Based on the above described empirical observations on real-world data, we specify the following three assumptions of our model at an abstract level.

- Preferential attachment with decay of relevance;
- Exponential growth of the network size;
- Power-law degree growth of nodes with regard to their ages.

4.1 Network Generation

We now demonstrate the process of network generation using our model. The generative model takes three parameters:

- α: the exponential growth rate of the network size;
- m: the number of links a node creates at its arrival;
- $\rho(\eta)$: the fitness distribution.

4.1.1 Preferential Attachment with Decay of Relevance. Similar to the models in Section 2, our model starts with one node with a self loop (thus having indegree $k_1 = 1$) at the initial event time $s = 1$. The first node is assigned a fitness value η sampled from the fitness distribution $\rho(\eta)$.

At each later step, a new node joins the network with a self loop and is also assigned a fitness value η sampled from $\rho(\eta)$. The new node creates a constant number of m links to existing nodes. The probability Π_i that a new link connects to an existing node i, is proportional to the product of its degree k_i, its fitness η_i and a decay function value $f_R(\tau_i)$ that depends on its age τ_i.

Since the new node creates m links, for an existing node i the growth of its degree $\frac{\partial k_i}{\partial s}$ with respect to the event time s is thus m times its preferential attachment probability Π_i:

$$\frac{\partial k_i}{\partial s} = m\Pi_i = m\frac{k_i\eta_i f_R(\tau_i)}{\sum_j k_j\eta_j f_R(\tau_j)} \quad (8)$$

4.1.2 Exponential Growth of the Network Size. We follow observations about network growth made in Section 3.3 and model network growth to be exponential over physical time t. We realize this by defining event time s to proceed by one unit every time a new node joins in. This leads to the following exponential relationship between t and s:

$$s = e^{\alpha t} \quad (9)$$

4.2 Analytical Solution of the Decay Function $f_R(\tau)$

The last assumption in our model, the power-law growth of node degrees:

$$k_i(\tau_i, \eta_i) = \tau_i^{\beta(\eta_i)} \quad (10)$$

does not appear in the generative process. Instead, it is used to derive the decay function $f_R(\tau)$. Later we evaluate the degree growth in Section 5.2.

We first calculate the denominator $\sum_j k_j\eta_j f_R(\tau_j)$ in Equation 8. When the age of the network T is large enough, applying the continuum approximation we get:

$$\sum_j k_j\eta_j f_R(t_j) = \int d\eta\rho(\eta)\eta \int_1^T d\tau k(\tau,\eta)f_R(\tau) \cdot \alpha e^{\alpha(T-\tau)} \quad (11)$$

Intuitively, the tern $e^{\alpha(T-\tau)}$ says there are more nodes with smaller ages in the system. Now let us assume that the decay function has a form of $f_R(\tau) = \tau^{-1}$. Plugging in Equation 10, for a certain fitness η we have:

$$\int_1^T d\tau k(\tau, \eta) f_R(\tau) \cdot \alpha e^{\alpha(T-\tau)} = \alpha e^{\alpha T} \int_1^T d\tau \frac{\tau^{\beta(\eta)-1}}{e^{\alpha \tau}} \quad (12)$$

$$= \alpha e^{\alpha T} \cdot \frac{\Gamma(\beta(\eta), \alpha)}{\alpha^{\beta(\eta)}} \quad (13)$$

where $\Gamma(a, b) = \int_b^{+\infty} x^{a-1} e^{-x} \, dx$ is the upper incomplete gamma function. Thus, the denominator of Equation 8 when $T \to +\infty$ is proportional to the network size $e^{\alpha T}$:

$$\lim_{T \to +\infty} \sum_j k_j \eta_j f_R(\tau_j) = C e^{\alpha T}, \quad (14)$$

with the constant

$$C = \alpha \int d\eta \rho(\eta) \eta \cdot \frac{\Gamma(\beta(\eta), \alpha)}{\alpha^{\beta(\eta)}}. \quad (15)$$

Recalling Equation 8 we get

$$\frac{\partial k_i}{\partial s} = m\Pi_i = m \frac{k_i \eta_i f_R(\tau_i)}{\sum_j k_j \eta_j f_R(\tau_j)} = m \frac{k_i \eta_i}{C e^{\alpha T} \tau} = \frac{\partial k_i}{\partial t} \cdot \frac{dt}{ds} \quad (16)$$

We therefore have

$$\frac{\partial k_i}{\partial t} = \frac{\alpha m \eta_i k_i}{C\tau}, \quad (17)$$

which has an analytical solution that recovers Equation 10:

$$k_i(\tau_i, \eta_i) = \tau_i^{\beta(\eta_i)} \quad (18)$$

given $\beta(\eta_i) \sim \eta_i$ (as in the Bianconi-Barabási model):

$$\beta(\eta_i) = \frac{\alpha m \eta_i}{C}, \quad (19)$$

and the initial value of k_i being 1:

$$k_i(1, \eta_i) = 1. \quad (20)$$

To summarise, the decay function $f_R(\tau) = \tau^{-1}$ is a function that let the model be self consistent.

4.2.1 Other Forms of Decay Functions. Other forms of decay functions that differ from our solution such as the exponential decay have been suggested [12]. We now explain why an exponential decay function having the form $f_{R(\exp)} = e^{-\gamma \tau}$ will not let Equations 8, 9 and 10 be self consistent.

Rewriting the denominator of Equation 8 with $f_{R(\exp)}$ we find that when $T \to +\infty$ the denominator is still proportional to the network size $e^{\alpha T}$:

$$\lim_{T \to +\infty} \sum_j k_j \eta_j f_R(\tau_j) = C_{\exp} \cdot e^{\alpha T}, \quad (21)$$

with the constant

$$C_{\exp} = \alpha \int d\eta \rho(\eta) \eta \cdot \frac{\Gamma(\beta(\eta) + 1, \alpha + \gamma)}{(\alpha + \gamma)^{\beta(\eta)+1}}. \quad (22)$$

Thus, the counterpart of Equation 17:

$$\frac{\partial k_i}{\partial t} = \frac{\alpha m \eta_i k_i \cdot e^{-\gamma \tau}}{C_{\exp}} \quad (23)$$

leads to:

$$k_i = \exp\left(-\frac{\alpha m \eta_i e^{-\gamma \tau}}{\gamma C_{\exp}} + c\right) \quad (24)$$

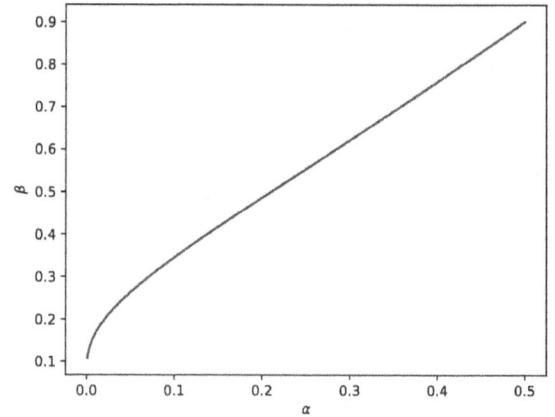

Figure 5: The relationship between α and the power-law exponent β of the degree growth when we take $m = 1$.

which is a double exponential function and does not recover Equation 10. Whether the exponential relevance decay recovers other forms of degree growth functions is however an open question.

4.3 Theoretical Degree Distribution

We now give the theoretical stationary degree distribution of our model. When we have a constant fitness η for all nodes, the theoretical degree distribution when $T \to +\infty$ will converge to:

$$p(k) = \frac{\alpha}{\beta} \cdot k^{-1} \cdot e^{-\alpha k^{1/\beta}} \cdot k^{1/\beta} \quad (25)$$

which is a product of a power function and a stretched exponential function.

When we have a distribution of fitness the degree distribution will be a superposition of Equation 25 with different β values corresponding to different η values:

$$p(k) = \alpha k^{-1} \int d\eta \rho(\eta) \cdot \beta(\eta)^{-1} e^{-\alpha k^{1/\beta(\eta)}} \cdot k^{1/\beta(\eta)} \quad (26)$$

Particularly if the fitness distribution follows a Zipf's law i.e., $\rho(\eta) \sim \eta^{-1}$, Equation 26 reduces to:

$$p(k) \sim \frac{e^{-\alpha k}}{k \cdot \ln k} \quad (27)$$

Note that for our model we do not get a perfect power-law distribution as in the Barabási-Albert model. However one should keep in mind that in empirical data, it is often hard if not possible to discern whether the observed data is closer to a power-law or a similar distribution with a heavy tail [6], thus we cannot presuppose every distribution with a heavy tail to be power-law.

4.4 Slowing-down Growth of the Network Size

Now we discuss the situation where the exponential growth of the network size slows down. In our model, such slowdown can be realised by varying the parameter α. Suppose we have a constant fitness η, the relationship between α and the power-law exponent

(a) $\eta = \eta_c$

(b) $\rho_{\mathrm{unif}}(\eta) = 1$

(c) $\rho_{\mathrm{norm}}(\eta) \sim \mathcal{N}(0.5, 0.1^2)$

(d) $\rho_{\mathrm{zipf}}(\eta) \sim \eta^{-1}$

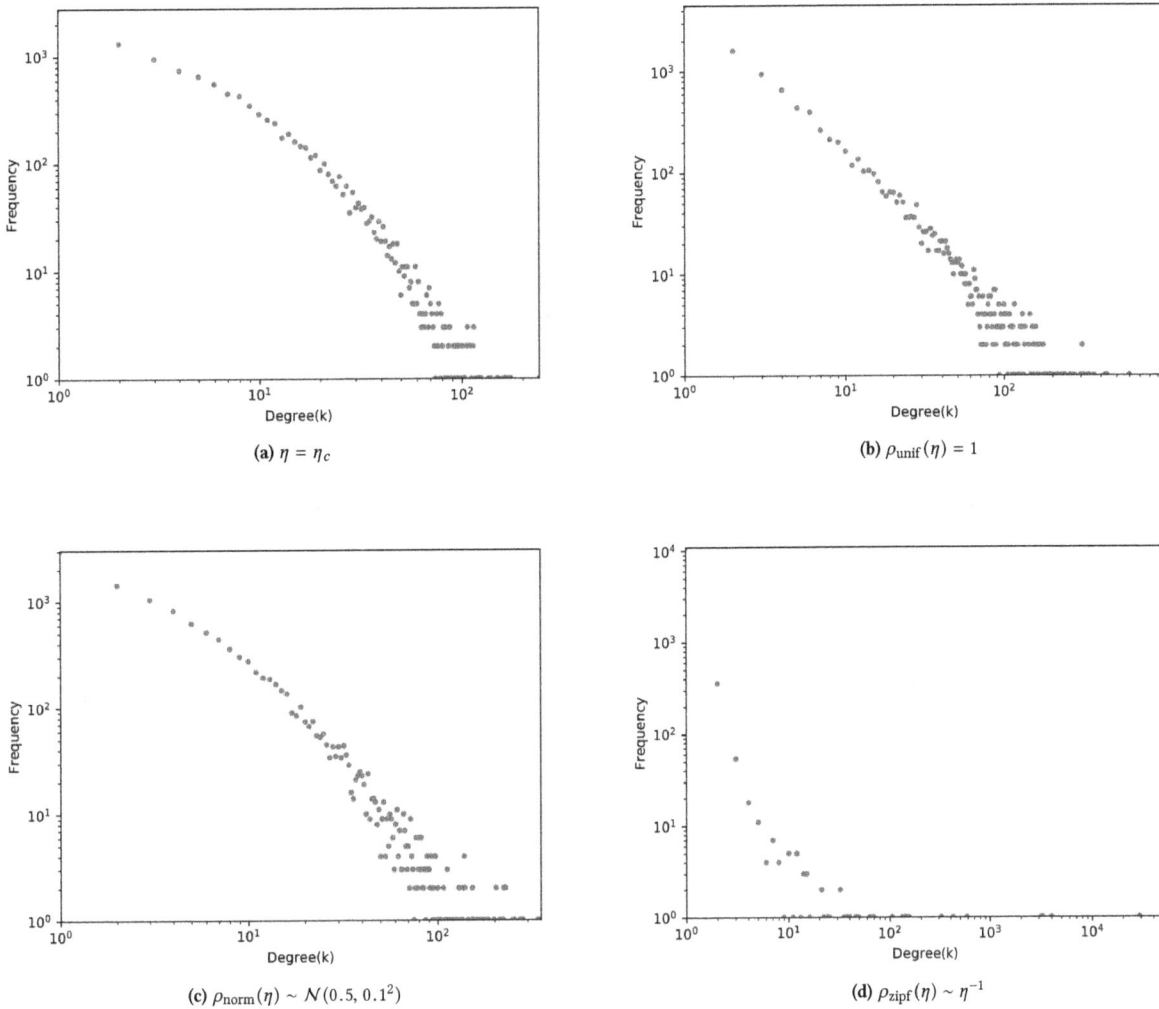

Figure 6: The degree distributions of the synthetic networks generated with different fitness distributions.

of degree growth β can be obtained from Equation 15 and 19:

$$\beta = \frac{\alpha m \eta}{C} = \frac{m \alpha^\beta}{\Gamma(\beta, \alpha)} = \frac{m}{E_{1-\beta}(\alpha)}, \tag{28}$$

where $E_{1-\beta}(\alpha)$ is the generalised exponential integral function [14]. Numerically we show the relationship between α and β in Figure 5. As we can see, β is monotonically decreasing as α decreases. This indicates the slowdown of the growth of the network size causes the slowdown of the degree growth of individual nodes. In the extreme case when α falls down to zero, the network size stops growthing completely, and there is no degree growth of individual nodes as well.

5 EVALUATION

In this section, we use our model to generate synthetic networks with different parameters in order to evaluate its plausibility. At the

macro level, we evaluate the degree distributions of the generated networks. At the micro level, we evaluate the assumption we have made but not directly reflected in the generative model: the power-law growth of node degrees.

5.1 Degree Distribution

Now we generate synthetic networks with our model using different fitness distributions $\rho(\eta)$ and observe the resulting degree distributions of the network. The four fitness distributions we look at are:

- constant fitness

$$\eta = \eta_c \tag{29}$$

- uniform distribution

$$\rho_{\mathrm{unif}}(\eta) = 1, \qquad \eta \in (0, 1) \tag{30}$$

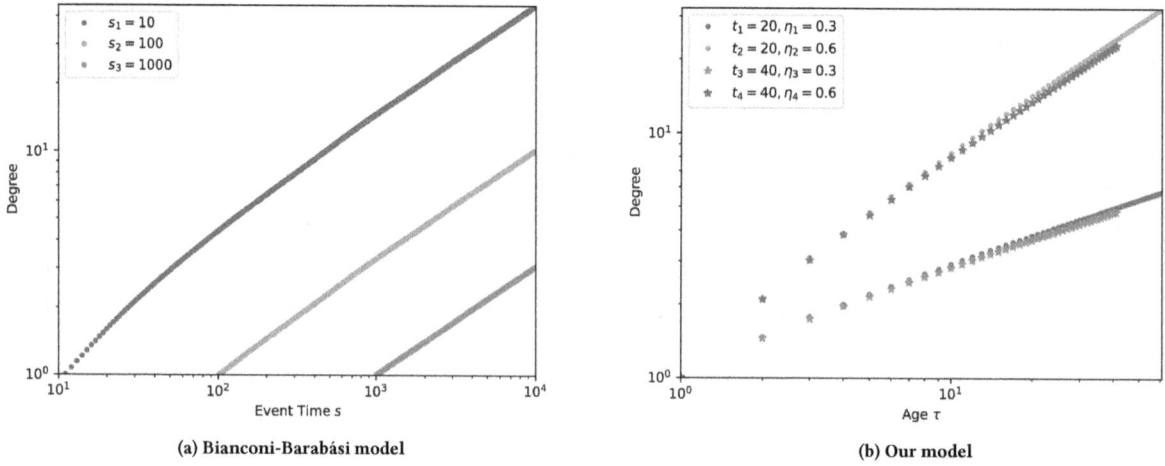

(a) Bianconi-Barabási model   (b) Our model

Figure 7: The degree growth curves of nodes with different parameters in the synthetic network generated by (a) the Bianconi-Barabási model, and (b) our model. Note the difference in the X-axes: In (a) it represents the event time s, while in (b) it represents the node age τ in physical time.

- normal distribution

$$\rho_{\text{norm}}(\eta) \sim \mathcal{N}(0.5, 0.1^2), \qquad \eta \in (0, 1) \qquad (31)$$

- Zipf's law distribution

$$\rho_{\text{zipf}}(\eta) \sim \eta^{-1}, \qquad \eta \in (0, 1) \qquad (32)$$

Other parameters of our model are set to $\alpha = 0.1$ and $m = 8$. We plot the degree distributions of the generated networks at $T = 70$ in Figure 6.

The curves in all four subfigures decay slower than exponentially as the degree k grows. In Figure 6a an obvious cut-off can be observed. In Figures 6b and 6c the degree distribution curves well reflect what we have observed empirically in Figure 1. In Figure 6d we observe a strong imbalance in the degree distribution: Few nodes are so well connected ($k > 10^3$) while the majority of nodes have degrees less than 10. This is due to the fact that in the case where we have a Zipf's law distribution of fitness, the "rich-get-richer" effect has become so dominant that it turns into "winner-takes-all", akin to the Bose-Einstein condensation [2] in the Bianconi-Barabási model.

5.2 Power-law Degree Growth

The degree growth of a node is power-law in both our model and the Bianconi-Barabási model [3], but with different bases. The latter predicts Equation 7: $k_i \sim (s/s_i)^{\beta(\eta_i)}$, which means that the degree growth of a node i does not only depend on its age, but also the time it joins the network s_i itself. Therefore, nodes who join the network earlier have faster degree growth rates than those who join later, as known as the first-mover advantage. This is due to the fact that the Bianconi-Barabási model does not consider the decay of node relevance over time. In our model however, the degree growth of a node i solely depends on its fitness η_i and its age τ_i, but not the time it joins the network, i.e., $k_i \sim \tau_i^{\beta(\eta_i)}$, as in Equation 10.

To illustrate the difference numerically, we generate synthetic networks[4] using both models, and plot the degree growth curves of different nodes in Figure 7. We choose a uniform fitness distribution as in Equation 30.

Figure 7a shows exactly what the Bianconi-Barabási model predicts. We see the degree growth curves of three nodes which joined at timestep $s_1 = 10$, $s_2 = 100$ and $s_3 = 1000$ respectively, and have the same fitness $\eta = 0.5$. The three parallel straight lines suggest that their degree growths follow power-law with the same exponent. However, node 2 needs ten times longer time to get the same degree of node 1, and node 3 needs 100 times longer, matching Equation 7 in the Bianconi-Barabási model.

We see in Figure 7b that in our model, nodes with the same fitness ($\eta_1 = \eta_3 = 0.3$, while $\eta_2 = \eta_4 = 0.6$) have comparable exponents of the power-law degree growth, regardless of the time when they joined the network ($t_1 = t_2 = 20$, while $t_3 = t_4 = 40$). Besides, nodes with higher fitness have faster degree growth, and the exponents are proportional to the fitness values. These observations match Equation 10 in our model.

Comparing with the empirical observations in real datasets (Figures 3 and 4), we find that our model has a more realistic power-law degree growth function.

6 CONCLUSION

We have proposed a new preferential attachment–based network growth model. Our model connects the macro and micro levels of phenomena in evolving networks: the growth of network sizes, the growth of node degrees and the decay of node relevance, leading to deeper thoughts about the co-existence of the two mechanisms in networks: decay and growth.

---

[4]To avoid the nondeterminism in micro actions caused by discreteness, here we allow degrees to have continuous values.

We have been focusing on citation networks where link creation is only allowed at the arrival of new nodes. The problem posed in our model can be generalised to other networks on the Web which allow the creation or even the removal of links between existing nodes, and lead to more interesting yet more challenging studies.

ACKNOWLEDGMENTS

The authors would like to thank the APS for providing the dataset. The research leading to these results has received funding from the European Community's Horizon 2020 - Research and Innovation Framework Programme under grant agreement n° 770469, CUTLER.

REFERENCES

[1] Réka Albert and Albert-László Barabási. 2002. Statistical mechanics of complex networks. *Reviews of modern physics* 74, 1 (2002), 47.
[2] Ginestra Bianconi and Albert-László Barabási. 2001. Bose-Einstein condensation in complex networks. *Physical review letters* 86, 24 (2001), 5632.
[3] Ginestra Bianconi and Albert-László Barabási. 2001. Competition and multiscaling in evolving networks. *EPL (Europhysics Letters)* 54, 4 (2001), 436.
[4] Marián Boguná, Romualdo Pastor-Satorras, and Alessandro Vespignani. 2004. Cut-offs and finite size effects in scale-free networks. *The European Physical Journal B* 38, 2 (2004), 205–209.
[5] Béla Bollobás, Oliver Riordan, Joel Spencer, Gábor Tusnády, et al. 2001. The degree sequence of a scale-free random graph process. *Random Structures & Algorithms* 18, 3 (2001), 279–290.
[6] Aaron Clauset, Cosma Rohilla Shalizi, and Mark EJ Newman. 2009. Power-law distributions in empirical data. *SIAM review* 51, 4 (2009), 661–703.
[7] Sergey N Dorogovtsev and José Fernando F Mendes. 2001. Effect of the accelerating growth of communications networks on their structure. *Physical Review E* 63, 2 (2001), 025101.
[8] Bernardo A Huberman and Lada A Adamic. 1999. Internet: growth dynamics of the world-wide web. *Nature* 401, 6749 (1999), 131–131.
[9] Michael Ley. 2002. *The DBLP Computer Science Bibliography: Evolution, Research Issues, Perspectives*. Springer Berlin Heidelberg, Berlin, Heidelberg, 1–10. https://doi.org/10.1007/3-540-45735-6_1
[10] Manuel Sebastian Mariani, Matúš Medo, and Yi-Cheng Zhang. 2015. Ranking nodes in growing networks: When PageRank fails. *Scientific reports* 5 (2015).
[11] Matúš Medo. 2014. Statistical validation of high-dimensional models of growing networks. *Physical Review E* 89, 3 (2014), 032801.
[12] Matúš Medo, Giulio Cimini, and Stanislao Gualdi. 2011. Temporal effects in the growth of networks. *Physical review letters* 107, 23 (2011), 238701.
[13] Mark EJ Newman. 2001. Clustering and preferential attachment in growing networks. *Physical Review E* 64, 2 (2001), 025102.
[14] FWJ Olver. 1994. The generalized exponential integral. In *Approximation and Computation: A Festschrift in Honor of Walter Gautschi*. Springer, 497–510.
[15] Bongwon Suh, Gregorio Convertino, Ed H Chi, and Peter Pirolli. 2009. The singularity is not near: slowing growth of Wikipedia. In *Proceedings of the 5th International Symposium on Wikis and Open Collaboration*. ACM, 8.
[16] Jie Tang, Jing Zhang, Limin Yao, Juanzi Li, Li Zhang, and Zhong Su. 2008. ArnetMiner: Extraction and Mining of Academic Social Networks. In *KDD'08*. 990–998.

Micro Archives as Rich Digital Object Representations*

Helge Holzmann
L3S Research Center
30167 Hannover, Germany
holzmann@L3S.de

Mila Runnwerth
German National Library
of Science and Technology (TIB)
30167 Hannover, Germany
Mila.Runnwerth@tib.eu

ABSTRACT

Digital objects as well as real-world entities are commonly referred to in literature or on the Web by mentioning their name, linking to their website or citing unique identifiers, such as DOI and OR-CID, which are backed by a set of meta information. All of these methods have severe disadvantages and are not always suitable though: They are not very precise, not guaranteed to be persistent or mean a big additional effort for the author, who needs to collect the metadata to describe the reference accurately. Especially for complex, evolving entities and objects like software, pre-defined metadata schemas are often not expressive enough to capture its temporal state comprehensively. We found in previous work that a lot of meaningful information about software, such as a description, rich metadata, its documentation and source code, is usually available online. However, all of this needs to be preserved coherently in order to constitute a rich digital representation of the entity. We show that this is currently not the case, as only 10% of the studied blog posts and roughly 30% of the analyzed software websites are archived completely, i.e., all linked resources are captured as well. Therefore, we propose Micro Archives as rich digital object representations, which semantically and logically connect archived resources and ensure a coherent state. With Micrawler we present a modular solution to create, cite and analyze such Micro Archives. In this paper, we show the need for this approach as well as discuss opportunities and implications for various applications also beyond scholarly writing.

KEYWORDS

Web Archives; Crawling; Data Representation; Scientific Workflow

ACM Reference Format:
Helge Holzmann and Mila Runnwerth. 2018. Micro Archives as Rich Digital Object Representations. In *Proceedings of 10th ACM Conference on Web Science (WebSci '18)*. ACM, New York, NY, USA, 5 pages. https://doi.org/10.1145/3201064.3201110

*This work is partly funded by the European Research Council under ALEXANDRIA (ERC 339233)

1 INTRODUCTION

In the area of digital libraries and in the scholarly domain in general exist many digital identifiers used to reference objects and entities in literature, most prominently, the *Digital Object Identifier* (DOI)[13]. These identifiers are commonly backed by a set of metadata that describe the referenced object. While meta information are easy to create and maintain for fixed objects, such as scientific publications, which do not change anymore after they have been published and assigned their DOI, this approach does not scale well for more dynamic entities.

As one such subject, we consider software, an omnipresent good in science that is often referenced in literature. Software is constantly being developed and can have a different state in every moment, especially if it is open source and being developed by a large community. In such cases, it is difficult to permanently keep corresponding metadata up to date. Even more challenging, a software that is developed by thousands of developers, with every developer working on a small piece of it, is nearly impossible to be precisely expressed by a fixed set of metadata values. Further is such a representation in many cases not what a reader requires to fully understand the referenced asset. Way more useful would be a description, documentation, or even the source code in case of software. We found in previous work that most of these information already exist on the Web [12].

From an author's perspective who wants to reference some entity or object that is not explicitly prepared for this, the collection of all required meta information to comprehensively describe the referenced asset means a big additional effort. Instead, we often see very vague references in literature, e.g., only a name, sometimes with the version or date. Similarly, references to Web resources, such as blog articles, are made as a footnote containing the URL. However, even if the date of visit is specified, this is not very helpful as the referenced blog post or linked resources may already have changed by the time it is read.

Many of these problems could be solved if we had richer presentations of the cited objects. If the reader does not only see the name, version and author of a referenced software, but can actually read the documentation at the time when the author accessed it. For that reason, we propose *Micro Archives*: microscopic collections of archived resources on the Web that describe a single entity or object, cohesively preserved for future reference. While existing Web archives already provide the necessary infrastructures to preserve all required resources individually, Micro Archives can be considered a logical and semantic connection of such resources to provide a holistic view onto a cited object. Furthermore, metadata that may be available in unstructured or semi-structured form as part of such a Micro Archive can be dynamically extracted and presented as needed whenever required.

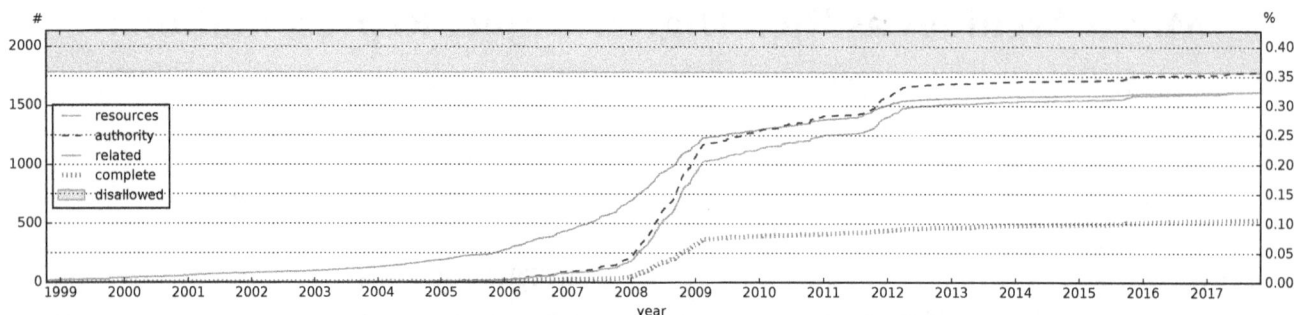

Figure 1: Web Archive Timeline: Blogs.

In the following, we present Micrawler, a modular proof-of-concept prototype that implements the entire pipeline of creating, archiving, analyzing, presenting and citing Micro Archives, along with a practical example of how our approach can be used within the scientific publication workflow. Further, we showcase two use case scenarios, i.e., 1) blog articles, 2) software, which we have investigated in terms of inconsistencies that could be fixed with Micrawler in the future. Finally, we will highlight the opportunities created by Micro Archives in various areas and stress why we think the presented concepts are an inevitable step in our digital world.

2 RELATED WORK

Piwowar et al. [21] provided evidence that enhanced access to research data lead to an increased number of citations. Although there has been quite some work on research data and its use in literature [17, 18, 22] as well as on Web archives as containers for cultural, personal or scientific entities [15, 19, 20], there is not much on combining both aspects as we intent with our work. Dynamic research data, such as software, has been neglected for a long time because of its volatility and its development process that cannot be suitably mapped by traditional metadata. Only recently, several initiatives have emerged to foster the use of software in a scientifically sound manner, such as the *Software Sustainability Institute*, *Software Heritage* or *FORCE11*[1] [4, 7, 8, 23]. However, we are the first to propose the incorporation of Web archives for this purpose.

Web archives have been of growing interest as they allow to explore the Web with regard to a dimension that is often neglected in common tasks, like search and entity linking, but also the use of the Web in science: time. These valuable collections allow to study the Web and its development over time [2, 10]. Further, it has become a dire need to preserve scientific information before it vanishes from the Web [3, 16, 24]. However, access capabilities are still limited [6]. Works that attempt to improve this, deal with the efficient processing of Web archive data at scale [9] as well as temporal search and ranking [5, 11]. While these approaches can be used to retrieve temporally relevant and related resources for a given entity in an automatic manner, Micro Archives aim at making such semantic, temporal connections more explicit and sustainable.

3 CASE STUDIES

We have investigated two use case scenarios for which Micro Archives would immediately create a major benefit in their scientific use, i.e., blog articles and software. The question we raise is: How complete and coherent is the archived Web with respect to related resources linked on the corresponding webpages? Micrawler can improve the coherence of Web archives by making sure for an object or entity cited today, all related resources are archived today as well, resulting in a Micro Archive.

3.1 Datasets and Methodology

The retrospective analysis of blog articles was done using the *TREC Blogs'08*[2] collection. This corpus consists of 28,488,766 blog posts, collected between 2007 and 2008 for the *TREC 2008 Blog Track*. Hence, we can assume the blog articles to be published during that time period. Although some older ones are included as well, there are definitely no posts composed later than Feb 2009.

As it is more difficult to relate software to a specific point in time, we study its state as of today. For this analysis, we collected all 22,022 URLs[3], each corresponding to a single software, as listed on *swMATH*[4], a catalog and information service for mathematical software.

All webpages linked from any of the processed URLs are considered related. Although maybe not complete, we found that many software websites link to corresponding documentation, artifacts, source code and other related artifacts from their homepage [12]. These resources were gathered from the archived snapshot of the corresponding software or blog page. In case of software, we picked the latest captures, and for the retrospective study of blog articles, we picked the earliest snapshot that was available in the Internet Archive's Wayback Machine[5].

As the process of retrieving an archived snapshot for an URL with all its linked resources is quite time consuming, we limited our analysis to a random sample of 5,000 objects from each dataset. A single unit of 1 represents a completely archived object with all related resources, the percentage is relative to these. Partially archived objects would be represented by a corresponding floating

---

[1]https://www.force11.org/about/manifesto
[2]http://ir.dcs.gla.ac.uk/test_collections/blogs08info.html
[3]state at Dec 7, 2017
[4]http://www.swmath.org
[5]http://web.archive.org

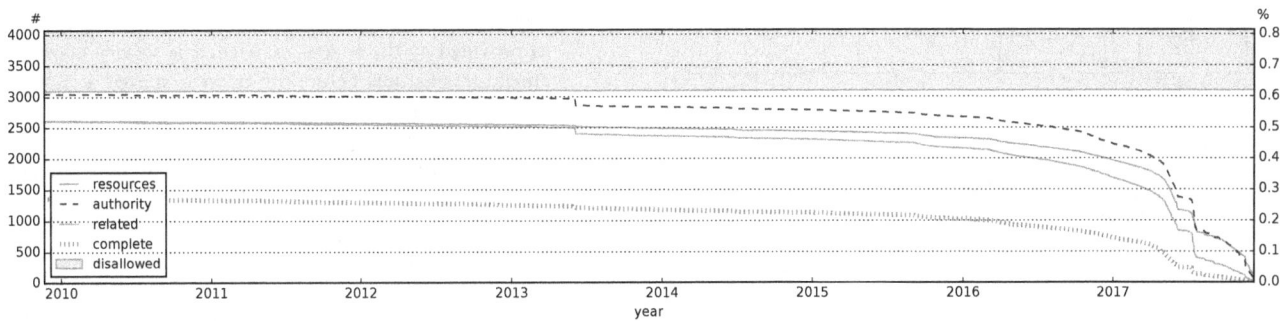

Figure 2: Web Archive Timeline: Software.

point unit. For better readability, the plots have been limited to the 2,134 blog posts and 4,074 software websites for which at least the authority page available, i.e., the actual blog post or representative webpage of a software. Together with the related sources we ended up with a total of 243,336 URLs that we had to fetch for blogs and 123,060 URLs for software, resulting in 48 related resources per blog article and 24 related resources per software on average.

Another fraction was covered by the Web archive, but disallowed themselves from being archived through a policy specified in their robots.txt. For these, the corresponding objects could not be studied, neither can they be captured with our proposed approach. There are depicted in our plots by the gray bar at the top. For an authority that is archived, but that links to pages that are disallowed, these related resources were ignored.

Each plot contains four lines to show the coverage of the studied objects in the Web archive over time: **resources** represents an object as fraction of its archived resources, **authority** considers the authority pages only, **related** denotes the fraction of *resources* for an object only if the *authority* is archived, and **complete** shows the completely archived ones.

3.2 Results: Blogs

The timeline in Figure 1 shows the results of our study of blog articles. Due to the time of the dataset, which was collected around year 2008, we can observe a major growth in the archive around this time as expected. However, as shown by the resources line, some of the related resources were already preserved long before the blog posts were published, e.g., in 2006 around 5% of the links in an article on average. This makes sense as they have to be online before they are referenced by a blog.

The steep increase of the archived resources to 25% together with the growth of the actual articles (authority pages) indicates that the blogs reference rather recent resources, assuming that they were captured by the archive not too long after publication. This is encouraged by the fact that they were archived slightly before the blog posts, hence, the archive discovered them not through the articles but independently of them.

Once the authority URLs are archived as shown by the dashed line, the related resources go up as well, suggesting these were already archived before that point. However, although this is a positive finding, it only goes from around 20% at the beginning of 2009 to slightly over 30% today on average for the resources related

to the archived authorities, a unfortunately small fraction. The gap to the completely archived articles stays rather large and only reaches about 10% today. This makes us wonder whether actually a coherent and useful impression of the archived blog articles with their hyperlinked references can be obtained from the studied Web archive.

3.3 Results: Software

Software on the other hand was studied from its current state, going back until the latest snapshot of a resource had been archived. Positive is the steep growth on the very right of the timeline, resulting in almost 50% of all software authority websites archived already only about one year back from now, at the beginning of 2017. Unfortunately, there is not much gain by going back in time and even in 2010 and before not more than slightly over 60% are archived overall. Similar to blogs, the line of complete snapshots is rather low. A noticeable difference to the timeline of blogs is that the lines of overall resources and related resources are much closer at any time. That means only a few related resources are recaptured more recently than the corresponding authority page. In contrast to blogs, it is quite likely that these are only discovered by the archive crawler through the software websites.

4 USE CASE SCENARIO

As our case studies have shown, the coherence among related resources in Web archives is not sufficient to reference a consistent state of the represented object. This is what we intent to improve with the introduction of Micro Archives. The following steps outline a common workflow to create and cite a Micro Archive.

Specifying Micro Archives. In order to use a Micro Archive as digital representation of any object, it first needs to be defined. Anyone can specify a Micro Archive with the required set of resources: their URL along with labels and possibly comments. A Micro Archive specification should include the name of the represented object as well as additional properties, such as the type, e.g., blog, software, person, company, etc.. Such crawl specifications can be shared, refined as well as reused. Predefined specifications can be provided or extracted from suitable services, such as repositories or directories, accessible through a dedicated link to cite included items. In case of software, this could be any service that is aware of the relevant URLs, such as a software catalogs like *swMath* (s. Section 3.1). A click on this cite link could immediately trigger the

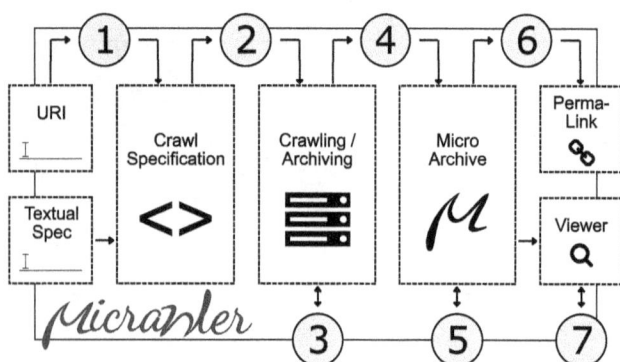

Figure 3: Micrawler Architecture and Extension Points / Related Services.

archiving process (using a software like Micrawler, s. Section 5). To create a Micro Archive of a blog post, the specification can be automatically derived from the links in the post itself.

Crawling / Archiving. Based on the given crawl specification all related resources should be crawled and archived at the same time or with as little delay as possible. Whether only the given URLs are captured or used as seeds for a broader crawl depends on the type of application. The archiving process can be performed by any Web archive, treating each resource as an independent item. Depending on the type of resource, even different archives may be used, like Web archives for webpages, but more software-specific archive for the raw source code. The resulting Micro Archive now serves as an additional layer that connects these captured resources and takes care of a coherent state among them.

Presentation / Citing. Once created, the Micro Archive is anchored to the time when it was crawled and represents the corresponding object or entity through the resources that were part of the specification. For future reference, a unique handle that is assigned to the Micro Archive, would now be sufficient to cite the preserved state of the represented object. This may be a short URL or more specific identifiers, such as a DOI or others.

5 MICRAWLER

Micrawler (*Micro Crawler*) is a reference implementation and proof-of-concept prototype to perform the aforementioned steps of creating and citing Micro Archives. It runs the entire pipeline from specifying over crawling to citing and analyzing Micro Archives. Figure 3 gives an overview of the steps performed by Micrawler and how these connect to the modules as explained in the following. The codebase of Micrawler is open source and published under https://github.com/helgeho/Micrawler. The running prototype has been deployed to http://tempas.l3s.de/Micrawler.

(1) **Spec Proxy:** A specification (spec) of what to crawl/preserve can be provided to Micrawler textually or a URI to load/extract a spec from. The *spec proxy* is in charge of deriving the textual spec from the given resource. Our current prototype implements a few special cases, such as software listed on *swMATH* (s. Section 3.1), for which a corresponding spec is generated from the included software website and linked resources.

(2) **Crawl Queue:** While in many cases the exact list of URLs as provided by the spec is crawled, this service allows to amend this list just before the crawl is started, e.g., to include deep links into certain websites. For software with a GitHub page in the spec, our demo adds the corresponding URL to GitHub's metadata API to preserve these valuable information.

(3) **Archiving/Crawl Service:** Each URL in the queue is now sent to an archive to be preserved. Such a service may be the *Save Page Now* feature of the Internet Archive's Wayback Machine, which we use in the current implementation. Alternatively, each URL could be send to a different service, e.g., source code might be stored at a more specialized service, like *Software Heritage*[6].

(4) **Archive Meta Service:** After all resources in the queue have been preserved, the created Micro Archive is documented by enriching the original spec with corresponding metadata for each capture in the archive. The *archive meta service* retrieves this information, such as the exact timestamp from the used archive.

(5) **Analyzers:** For different types of archives, Micrawler can be configured with different analyzers, to dynamically identify and derive additional information of the archived entity from the archived resources, such as a version number in case a software or information about the author in case of blog articles.

(6) **Persistence Provider:** To be shared and cited, the created spec that describes a Micro Archive and points to the archived resources has to be stored persistently. In this step, the *persistence provider* should assign a persistent identifier to the Micro Archive and guarantee permanent access. Therefore, our current prototype should not be used in production. With the assigned identifier, Micrawler generates BibTeXand BibLaTeXto be used scientific publications as follows [1]:

```
@misc{SageMath,
    title = {{SageMath}},
    type = {software},
    howpublished = {\url{http://tempas.l3s.de/micrawler/permalink/8bcbcec}},
    note ={Archived using Micrawler: 2018-01-10T09:03:35.000Z}
}
```

(7) **Viewer:** Depending on which archiving services are used, suitable viewers need to be configured accordingly. Web archives commonly provide an instance of the Wayback Machine to replay archived resources in its original state. Viewers are called and opened by Micrawler when a resource of a Micro Archive is clicked.

6 OUTLOOK AND OPPORTUNITIES

Our case study has shown that only 10% of the studied blog posts and roughly 30% of the analyzed software websites are archived completely, i.e., all linked resources are captured as well. With Micrawler and Micro Archives we presented novel concepts to increase these numbers in the future to enable coherent citations. While this is the primary use case, we see a lot of potential in such microscopic collections by establishing the missing semantic and logical link among the resources on the Web combined with a temporal embedding:

---

[6]https://www.softwareheritage.org

Supporting Web Archives. An infrastructure around Micrawler that allows for sharing and maintaining crawl specifications as well as existing Micro Archives in combination with a headless implementation that can be triggered programmatically may support Web archives by ensuring coherent snapshots at relevant times. For instance, such a database that is aware of the resources related to an entity would enable publishers or libraries to trigger a snapshot whenever a mention of the entity is detected in a new publication, e.g., all websites and social media accounts of a person can be captured whenever he or she is mentioned in the news. Web archives itself can incorporate this information to prioritize related resources of a page at crawl time as well as use it to improve their access capabilities.

Temporally Relevant Collections. A huge issue in the research field of *Temporal Information Retrieval* [14] and temporal Web archive search [11] is the lack of a ground truth dataset for temporally relevant search results of a query. Micro Archives as a first step towards structuring the Web as well as Web archives in a semantical way constitute exactly such collections for the corresponding entities as queries across time. Hence, a central, curated database as described above, which allows for the retrieval of existing Micro Archives along with the snapshots of related resources would be of importance for these applications and finally enable proper evaluation of temporal retrieval systems. In addition to this, these collection can also be of direct use for the users of Web archives to discover lost webpages from the past.

Structuring the Web. Micro Archives add a semantical as well as a logical structure to Web archives, which represent single entities or objects at different points in time. The identification of such structures along with the existence of archived snapshots for corresponding resources opens up new opportunities in studying the Web. For instance, Web graphs that are typically constructed based on single URLs, hosts or domains, may now be formed according to objects and entities based on their related resources. Scientists would be able to study relations among entities not just based on textual information, which are hard to extract, but based on related resources across time. The coherent snapshots ensure a temporal coverage and realistic topologies in the sub-graphs, which are currently widely broken due to the present incompleteness of Web archives.

Rich Information. A very ambitious and visionary aspect of Micro Archives, is the complete reconstruction of represented entities. Wikipedia is a great example of how entities can be represented on the Web. It is not only used for reading and learning about facts, but even to link and disambiguate entity mentions on the Web or in machine learning tasks. However, Wikipedia articles are not written from scratch, they are rather compiled of information found all around the Web, indicated by the many references in these articles. Thus, collections and temporal snapshots of related resources that are representative for an entity may allow for automatic generation of such articles or semantic representations like in knowledge bases. Furthermore, these representation are temporal and thus, can reflect the evolution of corresponding entities.

REFERENCES

[1] 2018. SageMath. http://tempas.l3s.de/micrawler/permalink/8bcbcec. (2018). Archived using Micrawler: 2018-01-10T09:03:35.000Z.

[2] Teru Agata, Yosuke Miyata, Emi Ishita, Atsushi Ikeuchi, and Shuichi Ueda. 2014. Life span of web pages: A survey of 10 million pages collected in 2001. In *JCDL*.

[3] Scott Ainsworth, Ahmed Alsum, Hany SalahEldeen, Michele C. Weigle, and Michael L. Nelson. 2011. How much of the web is archived?. In *JCDL*.

[4] Roberto Di Cosmo and Stefano Zacchiroli. 2017. Software Heritage: Why and How to Preserve Software Source Code. In *iPRES*.

[5] Miguel Costa, Francisco Couto, and Mário Silva. 2014. Learning Temporal-dependent Ranking Models. In *SIGIR*.

[6] Miguel Costa, Daniel Gomes, Francisco Couto, and Mário Silva. 2013. A Survey of Web Archive Search Architectures. In *WWW Companion*.

[7] Stephen Crouch, Neil Chue Hong, Simon Hettrick, Mike Jackson, Aleksandra Pawlik, Shoaib Sufi, Les Carr, David De Roure, Carole A. Goble, and Mark Parsons. 2013. The Software Sustainability Institute: Changing Research Software Attitudes and Practices. *Computing in Science and Engineering* 15 (2013).

[8] Simon Hettrick, Mario Antonioletti, Les Carr, Neil Chue Hong, Stephen Crouch, David De Roure, Iain Emsley, Carole Goble, Alexander Hay, Devasena Inupakutika, Mike Jackson, Aleksandra Nenadic, Tim Parkinson, Mark I Parsons, Aleksandra Pawlik, Giacomo Peru, Arno Proeme, John Robinson, and Shoaib Sufi. 2014. UK Research Software Survey 2014. (Dec. 2014).

[9] Helge Holzmann, Vinay Goel, and Avishek Anand. 2016. ArchiveSpark: Efficient Web Archive Access, Extraction and Derivation. In *Proceedings of the 16th ACM/IEEE-CS on Joint Conference on Digital Libraries (JCDL '16)*. ACM, New York, NY, USA, 83–92. DOI: https://doi.org/10.1145/2910896.2910902

[10] Helge Holzmann, Wolfgang Nejdl, and Avishek Anand. 2016. The Dawn of Today's Popular Domains: A Study of the Archived German Web over 18 Years. In *Proceedings of the 16th ACM/IEEE-CS on Joint Conference on Digital Libraries, JCDL 2016, Newark, NJ, USA, June 19 - 23, 2016*. 73–82. DOI: https://doi.org/10.1145/2910896.2910901

[11] Helge Holzmann, Wolfgang Nejdl, and Avishek Anand. 2017. Exploring Web Archives Through Temporal Anchor Texts. In *Proceedings of the 2017 ACM on Web Science Conference - WebSci '17*. ACM Press. DOI: https://doi.org/10.1145/3091478.3091500

[12] Helge Holzmann, Wolfram Sperber, and Mila Runnwerth. 2016. Archiving Software Surrogates on the Web for Future Reference. In *TPDL*.

[13] ISO. 2012. 26324: 2012 Information and Documentation-Digital Object Identifier System. (2012).

[14] Nattiya Kanhabua, Roi Blanco, Kjetil Nørvåg, and others. 2015. Temporal information retrieval. *Foundations and Trends® in Information Retrieval* 9, 2 (2015), 91–208.

[15] Nikos Kasioumis, Vangelis Banos, and Hendrik Kalb. 2014. Towards building a blog preservation platform. *World Wide Web* 17, 4 (2014), 799–825. DOI: https://doi.org/10.1007/s11280-013-0234-4

[16] Martin Klein, Herbert Van de Sompel, Robert Sanderson, Harihar Shankar, Lyudmila Balakireva, Ke Zhou, and Richard Tobin. 2014. Scholarly Context Not Found: One in Five Articles Suffers from Reference Rot. *PLOS ONE* 9, 12 (12 2014), 1–39. DOI: https://doi.org/10.1371/journal.pone.0115253

[17] Angelina Kraft, Jan Potthoff, and Matthias Razum. 2016. Establishing a generic Research Data Repository. In *iPRES*.

[18] Angelina Kraft, Matthias Razum, Jan Potthoff, Andrea Porzel, Thomas Engel, Frank Lange, Karina van den Broek, and Filipe Furtado. 2016. The RADAR Project - A Service for Research Data Archival and Publication. *ISPRS Int. J. Geo-Information* 5, 3 (2016), 28. DOI: https://doi.org/10.3390/ijgi5030028

[19] Siân E. Lindley, Catherine C. Marshall, Richard Banks, Abigail Sellen, and Tim Regan. 2013. Rethinking the Web As a Personal Archive. In *WWW*.

[20] Catherine C. Marshall and Frank M. Shipman. 2012. On the Institutional Archiving of Social Media. In *JCDL*.

[21] Heather A. Piwowar, Roger S. Day, and Douglas B. Fridsma. 2007. Sharing Detailed Research Data Is Associated with Increased Citation Rate. *PLOS ONE* 2 (2007).

[22] Andrew Treloar. 2014. The Research Data Alliance: globally co-ordinated action against barriers to data publishing and sharing. *Learned Publishing* 27 (2014).

[23] Greg Wilson, D. A. Aruliah, C. Titus Brown, Neil P. Chue Hong, Matt Davis, Richard T. Guy, Steven H. D. Haddock, Kathryn D. Huff, Ian M. Mitchell, Mark D. Plumbley, Ben Waugh, Ethan P. White, and Paul Wilson. 2014. Best Practices for Scientific Computing. *PLoS Biology* 12 (2014).

[24] Ke Zhou, Claire Grover, Martin Klein, and Richard Tobin. 2015. No More 404s: Predicting Referenced Link Rot in Scholarly Articles for Pro-Active Archiving. In *JCDL*.

Internet Regulation Media Coverage in Russia: Topics and Countries

Anna Shirokanova*

National Research University Higher School of Economics

Moscow, Russia

a.shirokanova@hse.ru

Olga Silyutina

National Research University Higher School of Economics

St.Petersburg, Russia

oyasilyutina@gmail.com

ABSTRACT

Russia first introduced Internet regulation in 2012 with site blockings and then progressed to personal data retention and ban on VPNs. This makes an interesting case because online media had spread and established a parallel political agenda in Russia in the 2000s, before the onset of regulations. The focus of this study is the contents and dynamics of media coverage of Internet regulation in Russia over years, particularly the topics covered and the countries involved. It uses topic modeling and social network analysis to analyze 6,140 texts from Russia's largest mass media collection. The automatic modeling approach helps obtain reproducible evidence on the structure and actors of the otherwise highly politicized discourse. The study demonstrated, first, the growing interest of Russian media to Internet regulation, with comparable shares of state-controlled and private media in this discourse. Second, it revealed the structure of 50 topics arranging into nine clusters, from gambling to international relations, with one dominant network segment spanning over five clusters. Third, it identified groups of countries by their appearance in the texts and co-appearance in one text as 'communities' of countries that can 'put on the map' the discourse on certain topics of Internet regulation in Russia.

CCS CONCEPTS

• **Social and professional topics** → **Governmental regulations**; • **Computing methodologies** → *Topic modeling*; • **Human- centered computing** → *Social network analysis*;

KEYWORDS

Internet regulation, Russia, social network analysis, topic modeling

ACM Reference Format:

Anna Shirokanova and Olga Silyutina. 2018. Internet Regulation Media Coverage in Russia: Topics and Countries. In *Proceedings of 10th ACM Conference on Web Science (WebSci'18)*. ACM, New York, NY, USA, 5 pages. https://doi.org/10.1145/3201064.3201102

---

*Laboratory for Comparative Social Research & Department of Sociology

---

1 INTRODUCTION

It was not until recently that the Internet appeared as free from national laws, or at least from following them closely. While this posed challenges of criminal nature, online communication and, later, online media were a breakthrough, the 'liberation technology' [8] that allowed for the free exchange of opinions in heavily regulated media regimes. In such contexts, social media, blogs and microblogs in particular, inform a 'parallel public sphere, not spacious in terms of audience and specific in character' [11]. Growth of the Internet and social networks in Russia has been credited with decreasing the control of the political elite over the information flow and cultivating the 'public counter-sphere' online [12].

About a decade ago, though, governments went online massively. Part of this were the first big leaps in technical Internet regulation ranging in scope from physical infrastructure to online behavior. As a result, online communication has become subject to national legal regulation, even though it is still more flexible than traditional media. Russia is an interesting case for analysis as, despite introducing strict Internet regulation that puts it ahead of many other countries, it also boasts a wide landscape of traditional media with many voices and large audiences.

This paper presents the findings of an ongoing project on media coverage of Internet regulation in Russia in its remarkable trajectory from 2009 to 2017. Our purpose was to identify who talked about what regarding both newly introduced and existent regulation of the Internet communication. We collected all the texts on Internet regulation from the largest digital mass media library in Russia and classified them with automatic topic modeling algorithms. We identified 50 topics and their groupings into clusters. Moreover, we investigated which countries were mentioned (e.g. China with its 'great firewall', or Estonia, a digitally advanced neighboring country). Then we ran a community detection algorithm and obtained clusters of countries based on co-occurrences, in order to draw a more precise conclusion on counties' mutual connections. As a result, we obtained clusters of topics and clusters of countries mentioned together in the Russian Internet regulation media coverage.

1.1 No Internet for Authoritarian States?

There is an ongoing debate between the technological optimists viewing the Internet as a set of liberating and democratizing technologies (e.g., [21]), and the skeptics emphasizing the instrumental character of any media, eventually capable of supporting both democratization and repression (e.g., [17]).

The Internet has created a great potential for civic engagement and democratization [8]. Higher Internet use increases citizens' demand for democratic governance [18]. The most prominent and well documented example of this has been the Arab Spring movement of 2011, where the masses mobilized via social media.

However, the key to Arab Spring outcomes was not the technology itself but 'how the technology resonated in the various local contexts' [23]. Moreover, social media mobilization might be equally helpful to autocratic consolidation, e.g. in China [9]. In the 2000s, scholars used the concept of 'dictator's dilemma' when picturing an autocrat who was not willing to face the democratization but readily embraced the economic benefits of the Internet [9] [14].

Nowadays, political regimes cannot be clearly divided by their use, or non-use, of the Internet. Economic globalization works as a strong driver for authoritarian countries to excel in e-participation above and beyond democracies [1]. The term 'networked authoritarianism' is used to denote the use of the Internet to consolidate autocratic regimes [14]. There is a variety of strategies for this. In the 2010 global report on Internet policy, Russia was directly contrasted to China as 'instead of utilizing Chinese-style filtering to control Internet access, the Russian government prefers to employ second- and third-generation techniques such as legal and technical instruments and national information campaigns' [7] which it has vigorously developed since then. In today's Russia, Internet policy can be seen as part of the larger information security strategy [15]. Thus, even authoritarian states have now become major actors in online communication. Irrelevant of their ideology, governments across the world engage into Internet communication to pursue their goals and regulate it accordingly.

2 HYPOTHESES, DATA AND METHOD

We put forward three research questions: 1. Who speaks about Internet regulation in Russia? 2. What do they say? and 3. Which countries are they speaking about?

The largest Russian digital media library, *Integrum*, provides access to the content of major Russian news agencies, national and regional media (mostly offline and some online media), in contrast to separate online resources which require a personalized approach to data collection. Therefore, at this stage we focus on the digital archive of Integrum.

Our hypotheses were that (1) the media coverage of Internet regulation would be rather scarce but growing steadily and that it would rather come from private than state-controlled media because of the critical social media culture developed in Russia in the 2000s; (2) that such news would largely focus on legal and economic aspects rather than on polemics; and (3) that the countries mentioned together with Russia would be known for systematic Internet control, but otherwise would group geographically.

First, we placed the following inquiry: (regulat* OR govern*) AND (Internet NOT (Internet-site OR Internet-project*)). The search spanning from 2009 till July 2017 returned 7,240 documents. We preprocessed the data by lemmatizing words, taking out numbers and Latin letters. After deleting stop-words, the final sample included 6,140 documents which were used for analysis. Both pre-processing and analysis were carried out in R.

Second, we conducted topic modeling to identify and, later, group all the topics within these texts. Topic models, including the latent Dirichlet allocation algorithm, LDA [3], and structural topic modeling, STM [5], are unsupervised techniques, which means that 'they

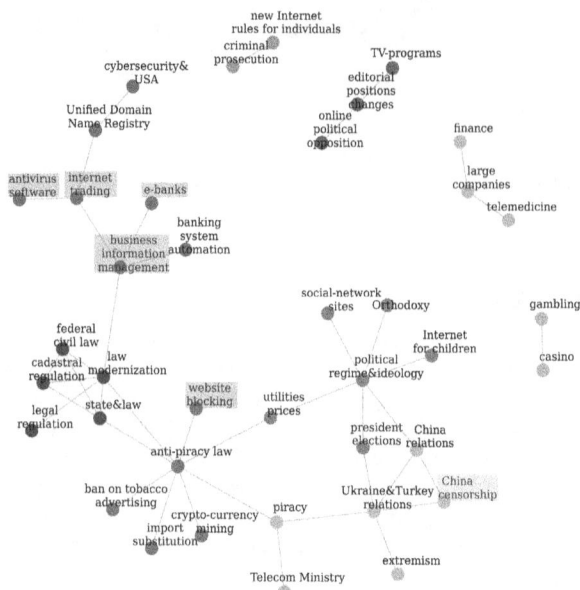

Figure 1: The correlation network of topics

infer rather than assume' the content of texts, in contrast to the supervised methods where the analyst defines the topics ex ante, usually by hand-coding a set of documents into pre-established categories [20]. In manual topic coding, scholar's perspective and preexisting concepts may affect the framing of the results of media analysis [10]. The advantage of the automated approach adopted in this paper is that it can provide hard evidence even for politicized topics' coverage. At the same time, the usefulness of unsupervised topic modeling algorithms depends on the correspondence between topics and the constructs of theoretical interest [10]. In STM, each document is seen as a mixture of k-number topics, like in LDA. However, the edge over LDA is that STM allows for topical prevalence to vary with any user-specified covariates. In addition, in STM topics can correlate; each document has its own prior distribution over topics, and the word use within a topic can change depending on the values of covariates [19] [20]. STM without covariates is equivalent to correlated topic modeling, which also has an improved predictive power and more realistic correlation structure than LDA [4]. In addition, STM provides more consistent patterns of topic modeling and allows us to observe and analyze the link between topics and covariates [22]. We tried extracting 30, 50, and 70 topics. The performance of 50-topic model we used for analysis was superior to the 30-topic solution in semantic coherence [16] and exclusivity [2], while, comparing to the 70-topic model, it delivered a more interpretable solution.

Third, we created a network of countries' co-occurrences in one text and left the top 48 countries with a degree of 100 and over for analysis because they are more likely to be involved in the discourse on Internet regulation. Then we ran the fast greedy hierarchical clusterization algorithm [13]. This community detection algorithm is based on the modularity measure which riches maximum in each cluster, so that detected groups of countries are most likely to appear together in the given texts. The resulting communities informed 3 distinct levels of covariates. We also created groups of texts mentioning low-degree countries and texts without countries mentioned at all; those were added as additional levels of covariate. Such an approach of considering country clusters as covariates makes our model more likely to converge.

Finally, phi-coefficients were calculated as a measure of co-appearance of countries in one text. We then created a network of countries with correlations equal to or higher than +0.2, which is the mean correlation for the third quartile of all the data, where all correlation links are significant. Then we obtained clusters using the same fast greedy algorithm. The resulting network is based both on co-appearance of countries and modularity and represents the overall discussion on Internet regulation grouped around more specific clusters of countries.

3 RESULTS

3.1 Who speaks about Internet regulation in Russia?

The ten media sources with maximum number of publications on Internet regulation in the Russian media are the RBK agency (1,670 items, private), CNews.ru (1,389 items, part of RBK, private), and major national newspapers, Kommersant (647 items, private), Rossiyskaya Gazeta (575 items, government), Izvestia (440 items, government-controlled), Komsomolskaya Pravda (409, government-controlled), the MK (304, government-controlled), Nezavisimaya Gazeta (262, private), Novye Izvestia (224, ceased in 2016, private), the Profil weekly (132, private), and Novaya Gazeta (128, private). This makes about 2.5 times more publications from private media. For newspapers and weeklies, there were more publications in government-controlled media.

In 2009-2017, the number of publications rose steeply starting from the end of 2011, when December parliamentary elections opened a wave of protest rallies which were to last until presidential elections in March 2012 but extended to several subsequent occasions. The protests gathered more than 100,000 people in big cities attracting the middle-class and white collars [6]. More than 5,000 were detained, some of them convicted and sentenced. One of the results of this social movement was the citizens' observation campaign during the mayoral elections in Moscow in 2013. The first peak of publications falls between July 2012 and June 2013, from the introduction of blacklist pages till the adoption of the anti-piracy bill that fights against counterfeit by blocking the IP address of resources on which illegal content is placed.

First blockings of whole social media sites followed in March 2014. Starting from September 2015, a new law came into force demanding all personal data of Russian citizens to be stored on the territory of Russia, only to be followed in July 2016 by the 'Yarovaya laws' prescribing the retention of all the contents of electronic communications of Russians and its on-demand use. In June 2017, a new federal law is passed that bans the use of software for blockage bypass i.e., online anonymizers, VPNs, and anonymous messengers. Thus, the introduction of Internet regulation in Russia has been really dynamic and has involved new, direct methods of Internet regulation as compared with earlier practices [7]. This process has also been full of media-related events, leaving rich media coverage in its aftermath for analysis.

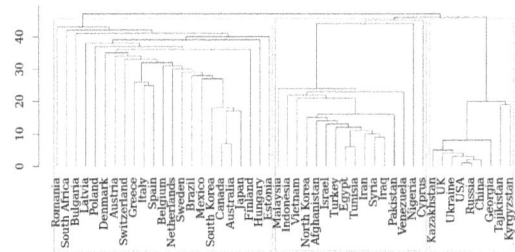

Figure 2: Communities of countries in Internet regulation texts by fast greedy algorithm

3.2 What do they say?

To answer the second question, we used structural topic modeling (STM). We extracted 50 topics, i.e. latent patterns of vocabulary use, among all the 6,140 texts of various size and contents. The advantage of STM is that it allows the topics to correlate, which is why we structured the topics in a correlation network (see Fig. 1).

Figure 1 shows the topics with significant positive correlations. There are nine groups in which the fifty topics fall. Five out of nine groups are linked in one segment; four others are small fragments. The most popular topics, marked by shadowing, are website-blocking, censorship in China, business information management, Internet trading, antiviruses, and banking automation. As expected, a substantial number of popular topics are related to economic and legal aspects of Internet regulation. However, this expectation is only partly true as another popular topic is censorship in China, which is politics.

The nine groups of topics share the following subjects (from the top dyad clockwise): (1) taxes and criminal prosecution; (2) political opposition; (3) corporations/finance; (4) gambling; (5, a star-like network) internal policies; (6, bottom) foreign policy; (7, a star-like network) legislation; (8, containing a clique) federal agency checks; and (9) business. One can see that the latter five community clusters are parts of the same network spanning from business to internal policies. They constitute, therefore, the major part of the Russian media narrative about Internet regulation.

After identifying and interpreting the clusters, four of them can be further united into two larger metatopics, two clusters each: these are state politics (5+6) and law enforcement (7+8) connected by the topics of Internet prices and piracy. Therefore, politics is by no means out of the agenda of the Internet regulation discourse in Russia, but the online opposition politics cluster is an isolated fragment cut off from the major themes on internal and foreign policies.

3.3 Which countries are they speaking about?

Figure 2 shows the result of community detection that delivered three distinct clusters for countries mentioned in the texts with other countries at least 100 times. The smallest cluster surrounding Russia consists of the USA, China, Ukraine, the UK, Kazakhstan,

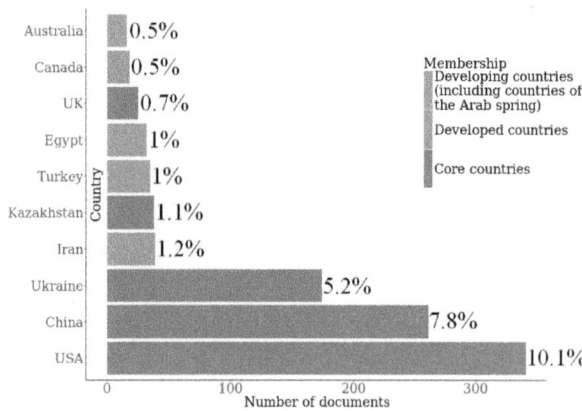

Figure 3: Top countries by the number of mentionings in documents and country their clusters, with a percentage from the number of texts about Russia

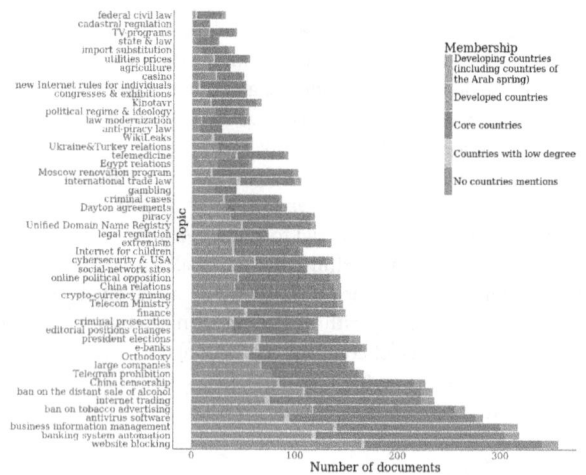

Figure 4: Distribution of documents of particular topic according to the country cluster of documents

Georgia, Tadzhikistan, and Kyrgyzstan. These countries have the largest probability of occurring in the same text as Russia and highest absolute frequency, which is why we interpret these countries as the 'core' in the discourse on Internet regulation in Russia. The second cluster contains a group of Middle Eastern and Central Asian countries, as well as separate developing countries from all over the world. The third cluster is the largest, and it contains developed countries from Europe and across the world.

Detection of these country communities allows for several further maneuvers with the data. Thus, we can structure the most popular countries in the texts by their cluster to find out that the core cluster includes the most popular countries (Russia, the US, China, Ukraine, etc.), while next popular are Middle East countries, while developed countries other than the US are following only after. Unsurprisingly, Russia was mentioned most frequently (3,300 documents; about 23,370 times overall). Second was the USA, with 341 document (which is about 10 per cent of the mentions of Russia), then China, with 262 documents (7.8 per cent of mentions of Russia), and Ukraine, with 172 documents (see Fig. 3). This demonstrates the prevalence of the Russia-specific 'core' countries in the documents but also the presence of all three clusters among the top countries most often mentioned in the documents. Not having analyzed the texts themselves, we are not claiming that US and China set the standards for Russian Internet regulation, but their presence is much more pronounced than that of any country with 'Internet freedom'.

Moreover, this dominance is visible along all the 50 topics we derived (see Fig. 4). The nine countries from the first cluster including Russia cover up a good half of all the texts, while second largest are the texts without any countries mentioned. It means that the scope, or the discursive space, of Internet regulation for Russia is largely limited to these 'core' societies. It is mostly they that make the headings and play a substantial role in framing the Internet policy in Russia. In addition, the estimated effect of the five derived country clusters is significant for the international relations topics, e.g. Egypt relations, China censorship, or cybersecurity and the USA.

The clusters in Fig. 2 are based on simple co-occurrence of countries in the articles, which can tell us only about the overall distribution of countries in the given texts. To find out more about the discourse of Internet regulation considering those top 48 countries, we took a closer look at correlations between those countries and identified communities with the fast greedy algorithm (see Fig. 5). In comparison with clusters in Fig. 2, we get not all of the 48 countries because we do not consider those with low correlation. Moreover, we obtain twice as many clusters now, which can really help in understanding what the given articles speak about. Thus, from the top of the network to the right we have a cluster of Asian countries, then the CIS countries and post-socialist European countries, then Western European countries, 'core' countries such as the USA, China, Japan, and, lastly, Middle Eastern countries. The most interesting countries in this network are those with high betweenness, such as the USA and the UK, which connect several communities. The Middle Eastern community also clearly denotes politically salient countries in the region. Russia is not on this map as it has low correlations due to its overall very high frequency.

4 CONCLUSIONS

In this paper, we shed some light on the media coverage of Internet regulation and, wider, Internet governance in Russia. We analyzed 6,140 texts and explored the scale of the discussion over years, its key country players and topics. We found out that there are more texts on Internet regulation coming from private media and news agencies; however, among the daily and weekly print media the balance between private and state-controlled media is close to 50:50.

We also found out that several topics among those 50 we derived with STM are part of seven large groups, and five of them belong to one network segment spanning from foreign policy, to law enforcement, to e-banking. The most popular topics across texts are on business, but also on site blockings and censorship in China.

Last, we focused on the groups of countries appearing in the texts and on 'country communities'. We discovered that there is a core group of countries such as the US, China, Ukraine, the UK, or

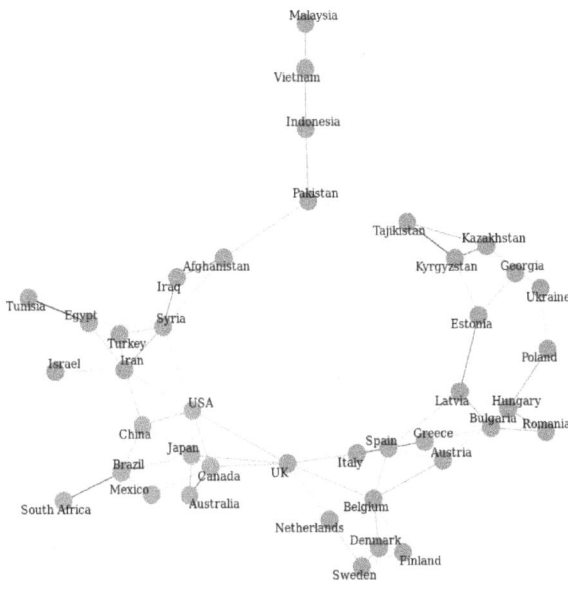

Figure 5: The correlation network of communities of countries in Internet regulation texts by fast greedy algorithm

Kazakhstan, with which Russia is most likely to appear systematically and that this core group dominates in half of all the texts in the collection, while other countries appear only sporadically in the Russian media reporting on Internet governance. In the last part, we demonstrated six country communities based on correlations and modularity that represent the groups of countries from the perspective of Russian media publishing on Internet regulation.

Our next steps are to look into the covariance of topics with external variables such as media ownership, and carry out sentiment analysis which would help distinguish the internal structure of the identified country groups and metatopics on Internet regulation in Russia. The obtained topics are unique for Russia, but the proposed methodology can serve as a foundation of comparative research of media coverage of Internet regulation in other countries.

ACKNOWLEDGMENTS

The authors would like to thank Ilya Musabirov and Stanislav Pozdniakov for their friendly critique and help with obtaining texts.

The authors would also like to thank the anonymous referees for their valuable comments and helpful suggestions. The work is supported by the Basic Research Program at the National Research University Higher School of Economics (HSE) and a subsidy by the Russian Academic Excellence Project '5-100'.

REFERENCES

[1] Joachim Åström, Martin Karlsson, Jonas Linde, and Ali Pirannejad. 2012. Understanding the rise of e-participation in non-democracies: Domestic and international factors. *Government Information Quarterly* 29, 2 (2012), 142–150.
[2] Jonathan Bischof and Edoardo M Airoldi. 2012. Summarizing topical content with word frequency and exclusivity. In *Proceedings of the 29th International Conference on Machine Learning (ICML-12)*. 201–208.
[3] David M Blei. 2012. Probabilistic topic models. *Commun. ACM* 55, 4 (2012), 77–84.
[4] David M Blei and John D Lafferty. 2007. A correlated topic model of science. *The Annals of Applied Statistics* (2007), 17–35.
[5] David M Blei, Andrew Y Ng, and Michael I Jordan. 2003. Latent dirichlet allocation. *Journal of machine Learning research* 3, Jan (2003), 993–1022.
[6] Svetlana S Bodrunova and Anna A Litvinenko. 2015. Four Russias in communication: fragmentation of the Russian public sphere in the 2010s. In *Democracy and Media in Central and Eastern Europe 25 Years On*. Peter Lang GmbH Europaeischer Verlag der Wissenschaften, 63–79.
[7] Ronald Deibert, John Palfrey, Rafal Rohozinski, Jonathan Zittrain, and Miklos Haraszti. 2010. *Access controlled: The shaping of power, rights, and rule in cyberspace*. Mit Press.
[8] Larry Diamond. 2010. Liberation technology. *Journal of Democracy* 21, 3 (2010), 69–83.
[9] Christian Göbel. 2013. The information dilemma: How ICT strengthen or weaken authoritarian rule. (2013).
[10] Carina Jacobi, Wouter van Atteveldt, and Kasper Welbers. 2016. Quantitative analysis of large amounts of journalistic texts using topic modelling. *Digital Journalism* 4, 1 (2016), 89–106.
[11] Ilya Kiriya. 2012. Piracy cultures| the culture of subversion and Russian media landscape. *International journal of communication* 6 (2012), 21.
[12] Olessia Koltsova and Andrey Shcherbak. 2015. "LiveJournal Libra!": The political blogosphere and voting preferences in Russia in 2011–2012. *New Media & Society* 17, 10 (2015), 1715–1732.
[13] Andrea Lancichinetti and Santo Fortunato. 2009. Community detection algorithms: a comparative analysis. *Physical review E* 80, 5 (2009), 056117.
[14] Rebecca MacKinnon. 2011. China's "networked authoritarianism". *Journal of Democracy* 22, 2 (2011), 32–46.
[15] Nathalie Maréchal. 2017. Networked authoritarianism and the geopolitics of information: Understanding Russian Internet policy. *Media and Communication* 5, 1 (2017).
[16] David Mimno, Hanna M Wallach, Edmund Talley, Miriam Leenders, and Andrew McCallum. 2011. Optimizing semantic coherence in topic models. In *Proceedings of the conference on empirical methods in natural language processing*. Association for Computational Linguistics, 262–272.
[17] Evgeny Morozov. 2011. *The net delusion: How not to liberate the world*. Penguin UK.
[18] Erik C Nisbet, Elizabeth Stoycheff, and Katy E Pearce. 2012. Internet use and democratic demands: A multinational, multilevel model of Internet use and citizen attitudes about democracy. *Journal of Communication* 62, 2 (2012), 249–265.
[19] Margaret E Roberts, Brandon M Stewart, and Edoardo M Airoldi. 2016. A model of text for experimentation in the social sciences. *J. Amer. Statist. Assoc.* 111, 515 (2016), 988–1003.
[20] Margaret E Roberts, Brandon M Stewart, Dustin Tingley, Christopher Lucas, Jetson Leder-Luis, Shana Kushner Gadarian, Bethany Albertson, and David G Rand. 2014. Structural Topic Models for Open-Ended Survey Responses. *American Journal of Political Science* 58, 4 (2014), 1064–1082.
[21] Clay Shirky. 2011. The Political Power of Social Media: Technology, the Public Sphere, and Political Change. *Foreign Affairs* 90, 1 (2011), 28.
[22] Ryan Wesslen. 2018. Computer-Assisted Text Analysis for Social Science: Topic Models and Beyond. *Unpublished manuscript, University of North Carolina at Charlotte* (2018). arXiv:"cs-CL"/1803.11045
[23] Gadi Wolfsfeld, Elad Segev, and Tamir Sheafer. 2013. Social media and the Arab Spring: Politics comes first. *The International Journal of Press/Politics* 18, 2 (2013), 115–137.

EPICURE - Aspect-based Multimodal Review Summarization

Abhinav Ramesh Kashyap   Christian von der Weth   Zhiyong Cheng   Mohan Kankanhalli

SeSaMe Centre, Smart Systems Insitute, National University of Singapore

abhinav@comp.nus.edu.sg,vonderweth@nus.edu.sg,chengzy@comp.nus.edu.sg,mohan@comp.nus.edu.sg

ABSTRACT

Restaurant reviews are popular and a valuable source of information. Often, large number of reviews are written for restaurants which warrants the need for automated summarization systems. In this paper we present EPICURE, a novel text and image summarization platform. For the summarization of opinionated content like reviews, considering different aspects have largely been ignored, and we address this by creating balanced reviews for different aspects like food and service. We argue that traditional criteria for extractive review summarization such as coverage and diversity have limited applicability. We draw on the power and usefulness of submodular functions for extractive summarization and introduce novel submodular functions such as importance, freshness, purity, trustworthiness and balanced opinion. We are also one of the first to provide an image summary for different aspects of a restaurant by mapping text to images using a multimodal neural network, for which we provide initial experiments. We show the effectiveness of our platform by evaluating it against strong baselines and also use crowdsourcing experiments for a subjective comparison of our approach with existing works.

KEYWORDS

Multimodal Summarization, Online Reviews, Sentiment Analysis, Sentence-to-Image Mapping, Text Classification, User Study

ACM Reference Format:

Abhinav Ramesh Kashyap   Christian von der Weth   Zhiyong Cheng Mohan Kankanhalli. 2018. EPICURE - Aspect-based Multimodal Review Summarization. In *WebSci '18: 10th ACM Conference on Web Science, May 27–30, 2018, Amsterdam, Netherlands.* ACM, New York, NY, USA, 5 pages. https://doi.org/10.1145/3201064.3202917

1 INTRODUCTION

User-generated reviews on the Web have become an invaluable source of information to decide which product to buy, which restaurant to visit etc.Nowadays, however, the abundance of reviews makes reading each individual review impractical, which makes summarization necessary.

Summarizing a large collection of documents involves novel challenges. Reviews are opinionated documents where redundant opinions provide more information, unlike summarization of factual documents where redundancy is unfavorable. Thus objectives

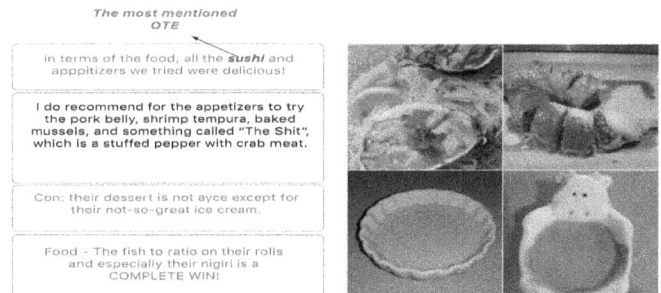

Figure 1: An example of a EPICURE food summary. The summary includes positive and negative sentences. Sushi is the most frequently mentioned Opinion Term Expression in all reviews. The summary aptly contains sentences that talk about food alone and are written by credible users.

like coverage and diversity are not enough for opinionated document summarization. A balanced summary should contain diverse opinions, prefer content from more trustworthy users, and emphasize more recent information without completely disregarding older reviews, and give a concise overview of different aspects of the restaurant. However these facets of a comprehensive summary have been ignored by previous summarization methods [4, 12, 21]. Also existing efforts focus solely on textual content, but online reviews also contain images which have not been considered for summarization; We present EPICURE, our platform that forms multimodal summaries for restaurant reviews with the following contributions.

Submodular Summarization. We identify importance, freshness, purity, balance, and trustworthiness as five important characteristics of a good summary. We model these characteristics as submodular functions that provide theoretical guarantees for optimal subset selection given a set of objectives.

Sentence-to-image mapping. We use the images that users upload together with their captions to train a deep autoencoder neural network. This allows us to find the most relevant images for a textual summary, and we provide first experimental results.

Evaluation. We use ROUGE to evaluate our summaries against established baselines and a state-of-the-art submodular extractive summarization method. We also perform crowdsourced experiments where users compare and rate different summaries.

An example of a text and corresponding image summary for food formed by EPICURE is shown in Figure 1.

2 APPROACH

Basic notations. In the rest of the paper, we use the following basic notations: Let $V = \{v_1, v_2, ...\}$ denote the set of restaurant venues, $U = \{u_1, u_2, ...\}$ the set of users, $R = \{r_1, r_2, ...\}$ the set of reviews, and $T = \{t_1, t_2, ...\}$ the set of sentences. We write $V(\cdot)$, $U(\cdot)$, $R(\cdot)$, $T(\cdot)$ to specify subsets of restaurants, users, reviews, and sentences,

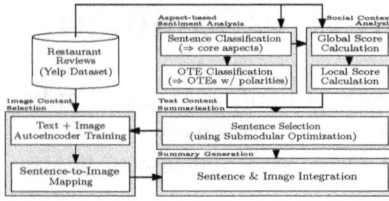

Figure 2: System Architecture of EPICURE

respectively. For example, $R(u)$ refers to the set of reviews written by user u, and $R(u, v)$ to the set of u's reviews about restaurant v. Since a user u can write a single review for a restaurant r, we represent $R(u, v)$ as $r_{u,v}$. The system architecture is shown in Fig 2

2.1 Aspect-Based Sentiment Analysis

Review sentences can talk about multiple coarse aspects. For example, *"Although the pizza was great, the service was poor"* talks about the coarse aspects *food* and *service* with a positive opinion towards *pizza* and a negative opinion towards *service*. We call *pizza* an OTE (Opinion Term Expression), an expression towards which a sentiment is expressed. We have trained and evaluated the classification of coarse aspects as well as the extraction and classification of OTEs using the annotated datasets provided by the SemEval '14 and '16 workshops. For more information on the dataset we refer the reader to [22]. We employ a 70-30 train-test split for all experiments.

Coarse aspect classification. We adopt FASTTEXT [14] for multilabel classification. We replace the normally used Softmax Cross-Entropy Loss with a Sigmoid Cross-Entropy (CE) loss that is more suitable for multilabel classification. The output of FASTTEXT is a probability distribution over different coarse aspects. However, learning a threshold on the probability distribution to decide the relevance of labels is a non-trivial task. We adopt a linear regression-based thresholding method [20] to address this. We achieve a F1 measure of 0.6966 on the test dataset for multilabel classification.

OTE extraction & sentiment analysis. Identifying different OTEs can be regarded as a Named Entity Recognition task. We have adopted a bi-directional Long Short-Term Memory (LSTM) network with a Conditional Random Field (CRF) on top for the extraction of OTEs from [16] and target-dependent LSTMs for sentiment classification towards these OTEs [25]. We achieve a F1 measure of 0.602 on the test dataset for the OTE extraction phase and for our sentiment analysis model, we achieve a test accuracy of 0.72.

2.2 Social Context Analysis

In the context of reviews, favoring content from more reputable users arguably yields more credible summaries. We calculate credibility score for a user considering the upvotes/likes denoted by $up(r)$ that a user review received. We also say that if a user mostly writes about food, his/her reputation is mostly contributed from the food aspect. We use $w(r, ca)$ to denote the relative frequency of coarse aspect ca in review r

$$w(r, ca) = freq(ca, r) / \sum_{ca \in CA} freq(ca, r), \quad (1)$$

where $freq(ca, r)$ represents the frequency of ca in review r.

Global user score. The global reputation score of a user is independent from restaurant v for which we create a summary. It avoids the case that user u's review about v is ignored if $up(r_{u,v}) = 0$

(or very low), even though u is in general considered a very good reviewer (note that $s_g(u, ca) = 0$ if $|V(u)| = 0$):

$$s_g(u, ca) = \sum_{v \in V(u)} \left[up(r_{u,v}) \cdot w(r_{u,v}, ca) \right] / |V(u)| \quad (2)$$

Local user score. The local score emphasizes a user u's reputation with respect to restaurant v. This reflects the case where u might have an overall low reputation but received a lot of upvotes for the review about v. Let $sim(v_i, v_j) \in [0, 1]$ with $sim(v, v) = 1$ be a function measuring the similarity between two restaurants. Let $V^*(v)$ be the set of restaurants k restaurants that are most similar to v with respect to $sim(v_i, v_j)$. The local score is then calculated as

$$s_l(u, v, ca) = \sum_{v_i \in V^*(v)} \left[sim(v, v_i) \cdot up(r_{u,v_i}) \cdot w(r_{u,v_i}, ca) \right] / |V^*(v)| \quad (3)$$

Similarity $sim(v_i, v_j)$ between two restaurant i and j can be calculated based on similar cuisine, price range etc. In this work we use a simple cosine similarity to measure how similar two restaurants are w.r.t. their ratings and it works well. We normalize the global and the local user score such that $\hat{s}_g(u, ca) \in [0, 1]$ and $\hat{s}_l(u, ca) \in [0, 1]$ before linearly combining them to provide an overall user score

$$\hat{s}_g(u, ca) = s_g(u, ca) / \max_{u \in U}(s_g(u, ca)) \quad (4)$$

$$\hat{s}_l(u, v, ca) = s_v(u, v, ca) / \max_{u \in U}(s_l(u, v, ca)) \quad (5)$$

$$score(u, v, ca) = \alpha \cdot \hat{s}_g(u, ca) + (1 - \alpha) \cdot \hat{s}_l(u, v, ca), \quad (6)$$

where parameter α balances the global and location reputation scores. In our experiments, we set $\alpha = 0.5$ which gives good results.

3 TEXT CONTENT SUMMARIZATION

In EPICURE, we create an *extractive summary* about a restaurant v as a set of sentences selected from the set of all reviews about v. Let $T_{ca}(R(v))$ be the set of sentences of all reviews about restaurant v labeled with coarse aspect ca. $S_{ca}(v)$ is a set of all possible summaries for v derived from the power set of $T_{ca}(R(v))$, i.e., $S_{ca}(v) = 2^{T_{ca}(R(v))}$. With N as the maximum number of sentences to be included for ca, we can define summary $S_{ca}(v)$ as

$$S_{ca}(v) = \underset{S \in S_{ca}(v)}{argmax} f(S), \quad \text{with } |s| \le N. \quad (7)$$

Summary $S_{ca}(v)$ maximizes objective function $f(S)$ which is a linear combination of objectives capturing different facets of a summary. Since finding the optimal subset of sentences is NP-hard, most existing works either greedily solve this task with no guarantees for the optimum [1], or formulate objectives just based on heuristics such as number of likes etc. [19]. In contrast, we model the selection of sentences as a submodular optimization problem. They have many properties that are suitable for summarization. A linear combination of submodular functions is a submodular function and optimizing a normalized monotone submodular function greedily is not worse than 63% of the optimal solution.

Submodular functions. In our context, a single submodular function represents an objective when creating a summary. In the following, we motivate and present our set of objectives and define their respective submodular functions.

Since we create a summary about a restaurant v for each coarse aspect ca, we write simply S, instead of $S_{ca}(v)$, to ease presentation.

(1) Importance: Restaurants are famous for a few important dishes or noteworthy characteristics such as live music, ambience, etc. A good summary needs to cover the OTEs that are more frequently mentioned and our notion of importance is based on the intuition that frequently mentioned OTEs are more important.

$$f_{imp}(S) = \sum_{ote \in S} freq_{R(v)}(ote) \,, \tag{8}$$

where $freq_{R(v)}(ote)$ returns the number of mentions of an opinion term expression *ote* among all reviews about restaurant v.

(2) Freshness: The quality of a restaurant in terms of food, drinks, service or ambience can change over time. Review summarization should therefore favor more recent information without completely ignoring the old information. We define this freshness of a sentence t using a decay function

$$freshness(t) = e^{-\lambda \Delta^{mth}(r_t, r^*)}, t \in T(R(v)) \,, \tag{9}$$

where $\Delta^{mth}(r_t, r_{t^*})$ denotes the difference in months between the review containing sentence t and the most recent review r^*. Note that we decay the freshness of reviews on a simple month-by-month basis to reflect the average time between new reviews being submitted. Parameter λ specifies the strength of the decay. In our evaluation, we currently set λ empirically to 0.1.

We can then define the corresponding submodular function. The intuition is that for a sentence that is not included in the summary, if there is a sentence in the summary that is fresher than the sentence considered, then the freshness value of the summary is larger.

$$f_{time}(S) = \sum_{t_i \in T(R(v)) \setminus S} \sum_{t_j \in S} 1(freshness(t_i) \le freshness(t_j)) \,. \tag{10}$$

(3) Purity: Reviews may contain references to different coarse aspects, e.g., *"I liked the pizza and the service was very good"*. In EPICURE, since we create a summary for each coarse aspect, we try to avoid sentences talking about different aspects. We define the purity of a sentence t as

$$purity(t) = \frac{1}{|ca(t)|}, t \in T(R(v)) \,. \tag{11}$$

With this, we can define a submodular optimization function that maximizes the value for a summary S, if S contains only sentences that mention only one or very few coarse aspects:

$$f_{purity}(S) = \sum_{t_i \in T(R(v)) \setminus S} \sum_{t_j \in S} |purity(t_i) - purity(t_j)| \,. \tag{12}$$

(4) Trustworthiness: We argue that sentences stemming from more helpful reviews are more likely to yield a good summary. We define the trustworthiness of a summary S using the user score that we described earlier.

$$f_{trust}(S) = \frac{1}{|S|} \sum_{t \in S} score(u_t, v, ca) \,, \tag{13}$$

where u_t is the user who wrote the review that contains sentence t.

(5) Balanced Opinion: A summary should contain diverse opinions that are expressed in the reviews. A function that depends on the inter-sentence pairwise dissimilarities within the summary is called as *dispersion* which needs to be maximized [5]. Although *dispersion* is not submodular, when it is optimized with other submodular functions – provides good guarantees. For two candidate sentences u, v, let P_u and P_v represent the probability distribution of the opinions (positive, negative and neutral) expressed in a sentence. The dissimilarity between two sentences can then be measured using the well known Jensen Shannon Divergence (JSD).Now we define the balance of a summary S as the aggregated divergences between the sentences in the summary as presented in [5].

$$f_{balance}(S) = \sum_{u, v \in S} JSD(P_u, P_v) \tag{14}$$

Final submodular optimization function. Utilizing the properties of submodular functions, we can define the final submodular optimization function $f_{submodular}(S)$ as a linear combination of the individual submodular functions with non-negative weights w_i:

$$f_{submodular}(S) = \sum_{i \in F} w_i \cdot f_i(S) \,, \tag{15}$$

where $F = \{imp, trust, time, purity, balance\}$ and $\sum_{i \in F} w_i = 1$. We set each $w_i = 1/5$ and also normalize the submodular functions so that the range of each objective function is $[0, 1]$. The optimal values for the weights w_i can be learned, but it requires a large collection of gold-standard summaries which is unavailable.

4 SENTENCE-TO-IMAGE MAPPING

An image summary would enable users to get a quick view of the restaurant for aspects like ambience. We enrich the textual summary with images matching the textual content. We formulate image summarization as a cross-modal retrieval of images given the textual query, where the query in our context is a sentence in the summary and detail our first experiments below. We consider the coarse aspects *food* and *ambience* for image summarization. For training we use all images in the Yelp dataset that have captions.

We use a cross modal autoencoder (Fig 3) which has found success in cross-modal retrieval [8, 27]. The overall goal of the network is not only to minimize the reconstruction error of the two individual networks (convolutional autoencoder and sequence-to-sequence autoencoder) but also to reduce the distance between the latent representations of the two networks such that semantically related images and texts are closer to each other in the latent representation space. Let $I = \{m_1, m_2, ..., m_n\}$ be the set of images and $C = \{c_1, c_2, ..., c_n\}$ be the corresponding set of captions.

For the convolutional autoencoder we use convolutions of size 3×3 followed by ReLU activation and Max-pooling with a window size of 2×2. For the sequence-to-sequence autoencoder we use an LSTM network that captures long-term dependencies better. With $CNN_{\theta_I}^{enc}(m_i)$ and $RNN_{\theta_I}^{enc}(c_i)$ being the latent representations learned by the two networks, the two reconstruction losses L_1 and L_2, the latent representation loss L_3 are:

$$L_1(m_i, \hat{m}_i) = -\{m_i * log(\hat{m}_i) + (1 - m_i)log(1 - \hat{m}_i)\} \tag{16}$$

$$L_2(c_i, \hat{c}_i) = \sum_{t=1}^{T} \|c_i - \hat{c}_i\|^2 \,, \tag{17}$$

$$L_3(m_i, c_i) = \left\| CNN_{\theta_I}^{enc}(m_i) - RNN_{\theta_T}^{enc}(c_i) \right\|^2 \tag{18}$$

The final loss L is the sum of all losses: $L = L_1 + L_2 + L_3$.

5 EVALUATION

5.1 Text Content Summarization.

Comparing and evaluating different summarization methods is traditionally very challenging since it requires the availability of

SUMMARY TYPE	FOOD			SERVICE			PRICE			AMBIENCE			ALL		
	R-1	R-2	R-4	R-1	R-2	R-4	R-1	R-2	R-4	R-1	R-2	R-4	R-1	R-2	R-4
RANDOM	0.250	0.051	0.082	0.303	0.059	0.091	0.353	0.095	0.133	0.371	0.086	0.153	0.320	0.073	0.115
MAX-UPVOTES	0.354	0.097	0.148	0.292	0.03	0.084	0.381	0.111	0.145	0.437	0.152	0.198	0.366	0.098	0.145
LEXRANK	0.413	0.107	0.171	0.341	0.062	0.0114	0.470	0.137	0.217	0.463	0.141	0.199	0.422	0.112	0.176
MEAD	0.395	0.089	0.135	0.361	0.024	0.110	0.375	0.061	0.118	0.375	0.071	0.122	0.376	0.061	0.121
KLSUM	0.400	0.134	0.176	0.397	**0.133**	**0.194**	0.398	0.167	0.196	0.473	0.257	0.302	0.417	0.172	0.217
LIN/BILMES	**0.469**	0.109	0.174	0.403	0.085	0.153	0.403	0.060	0.131	0.406	0.112	0.161	0.419	0.092	0.155
EPICURE	**0.461**	**0.140**	**0.195**	**0.444**	0.114	0.180	**0.475**	**0.198**	**0.240**	**0.525**	**0.306**	**0.324**	**0.476**	**0.190**	**0.235**

Table 1: ROUGE-1 ROUGE-2 & ROUGE-4 scores for different competing systems for different aspects of the restaurant and the average across different aspects.

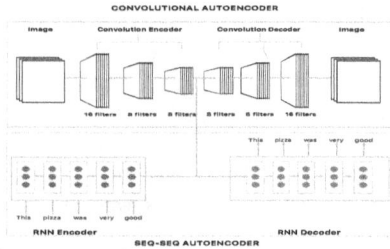

Figure 3: Autoencoder for sentence-to-image mapping

manually created gold-standard summaries as references. We use the Yelp dataset in this work.[1] For our evaluation, we selected the 100 most recent reviews of 5 popular restaurants in the dataset. We then asked two experts to create a gold-standard summary for each restaurant by selecting 25 sentences – 5 for each coarse aspect – from all the reviews, such that each summary is not more than 50 words. This task took about 2 hours for a single restaurant. We evaluated EPICURE against the following baselines: RANDOM randomly picks sentences from all reviews, MAX-UPVOTES (favors sentences from reviews with the highest number of upvotes), LEXRANK [7], MEAD [24],KLSUM [9], and LIN/BILMES [18].

ROUGE scores. The de facto standard to evaluate the quality of automatically generated summaries compared to a reference summary is ROUGE [17]. Hong et al. [10] argue that settings of ROUGE has been inconsistent in the literature and they provide a common ground for evaluation of extractive summarization. Based on that we use ROUGE-1, ROUGE-2 and ROUGE-4 recall measures and the same ROUGE settings as described in [10] has been used.

Table 1 shows the results for all methods across different aspects. Note that we applied the text classification step for the all the competing methods before extractive summarization for fair comparison. For example RANDOM only considers sentences labeled with coarse aspect ca when picking a sentence for the summarization of ca. Overall EPICURE outperforms the other methods and has the best ROUGE-1, ROUGE-2 AND ROUGE-4 scores. For *food*, it has similar ROUGE-1 scores when compared to LIN/BILMES method and has the best ROUGE-2 and ROUGE-4 scores. Similarly for *price* and *ambience*, EPICURE has the best ROUGE scores. For the *service*, EPICURE has the best ROUGE-1 scores and performs competently with the KLSUM method on the ROUGE-2 and ROUGE-4 scores. To highlight the benefits of the text classification step, we additionally applied all baseline methods over the full set of reviews for each restaurant. When different aspects in the sentences are not considered, the sentences in the summaries might contain mixed

[1]https://www.yelp.com/dataset/challenge

aspects. We observed that it results in very low ROUGE scores when compared to the gold-standard summaries.

Qualitative Analysis. To obtain deeper insights we compared summaries with similar scores from different methods . In general, summaries provided by EPICURE contain sentences with both positive and negative sentiments, thus exhibiting diversity w.r.t. users' opinions. EPICURE also prefers sentences from more reputable users. These facets of reviews are not taken into account by the other baseline methods. However, ROUGE, which is based on the syntactical similarities between summaries, fails to properly quantify this. We argue that facets like opinion diversity and reputation are important when generating summaries for opinionated content such as reviews. This also highlights the need for better summarization metrics that go beyond syntactical similarities.

5.2 Image Content Selection

Lastly, we evaluated the sentence-to-image mapping component. To quantitatively evaluate the cross modal retrieval, we compare our method with the method (CROSS-MODAL-AE) presented in [8]. We extract the same features and evaluate our methods using MAP@50 as used in [8]. Our method performs better with a MAP of 0.667 when compared to a best MAP of 0.630 of CROSS-MODAL-AE on the test dataset. We also perform a subjective evaluation with the following methods as baselines.

- **Text similarity matching (NAIVE).**: Given a summary sentence s, we calculate for each caption c_i a text-based similarity score $sim(s, c_i) = |s \cap c|/|s \cup c|$ and rank the captions (and corresponding images). We then select the top-k images to be added to the summary containing s
- **Random**: Images for the summary are picked at random.

For the experiment, we asked Crowdflower workers to assess the quality of the selected images. We generated a collage based on the set of selected images for each method. Given a textual summary for a restaurant and coarse aspects *food* or *ambience* as reference, we show two image collages and asked the workers to choose the image summary they deemed more appropriate for the textual summary. Five different workers validated each question.

We counted the number of times a method won each pair-wise comparison of two collages to get the score of the method. Figure 4 shows the results. For *ambience*, EPICURE performs the best when compared to the other two methods and for *food* EPICURE performs similar to the NAIVE method. On the one hand, this means that there is generally a good overlap between the selected sentences and the image captions. Note that, unlike the autoencoder, the NAIVE method can only pick images that have captions. On the

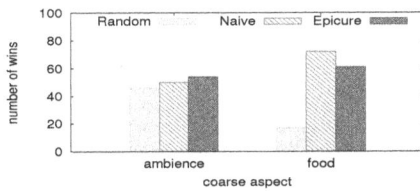

Figure 4: Sentence-to-Image mapping results (Crowdflower)

other hand, we argue that the deep autoencoder currently performs only suboptimal due to the rather small dataset of ~32k images. Another interesting observation is that, for *ambience*, RANDOM is almost comparable to the other two methods. We observed that in many cases the workers always favored food images even for *ambience* summaries. Compared to food, ambience is a more vague aspect which might include the appearance of the food for many workers. More experiments are needed to gain deeper insights.

6 RELATED WORK

Image summarization. The most popular methods for image summarization include clustering [28, 29], graph-based methods [3, 13] and hybrid methods [23]. In contrast, [26] uses a combination of submodular functions and learns a large-margin structured prediction model. Traditional image summarization itself is not enough for image summarization of reviews, but should reflect the counterpart textual summaries of reviews for a holistic summarization. The closest approach to ours is presented in [15], where the authors aim to obtain a set of images for multiple paragraph queries. However, this work aims at visualizing travel-related blog posts.

Review summarization. Summarizing content which expresses opinions towards an entity has to express the overall opinion of the users [11]. Hu et al. [11] and Blair et al [2] perform product feature extraction and sentiment analysis to produce a summary. Nishikawa et al. [21] propose to improve the informativeness and readability of a summary. Carenini et al. [4] form extractive summaries based on the most frequent terms extracted from the text. Jayanth et al. [12] formulate five submodular functions to capture the coverage of subjectivity to form movie review summaries. The authors of [6] use KL divergence to preserve the overall opinion distribution when forming summaries. Reviews encompass not only sentiments and opinions, but also a submission date and user reputation. Furthermore, existing works focus on textual content only and do not provide any theoretical guarantees in selecting the optimal subset of sentences. With EPICURE, we present a platform that generates well-balanced multimodal summaries using submodular optimization which provides good theoretical bounds.

7 CONCLUSIONS

The large number of restaurant reviews and images makes browsing all the reviews and images to get a comprehensive picture impractical. With EPICURE, we have addressed this issue by generating multimodal summaries for restaurant reviews. Each summary features a balanced textual summary and corresponding image summary. We have shown that including submodular functions like importance, freshness etc. produces strong results against other baselines and also, our image summarization method performs well against other methods.

ACKNOWLEDGEMENT

This research is supported by the National Research Foundation, Prime Minister's Office, Singapore under its International Research Centre in Singapore Funding Initiative.

REFERENCES

[1] Jingwen Bian, Yang Yang, and Tat-Seng Chua. 2013. Multimedia summarization for trending topics in microblogs. In *CIKM '13*. ACM.
[2] Sasha Blair-Goldensohn, Kerry Hannan, Ryan McDonald, Tyler Neylon, George A Reis, and Jeff Reynar. 2008. Building a sentiment summarizer for local service reviews. In *WWW workshop on NLP in the information explosion era*, Vol. 14.
[3] Liangliang Cao, Andrey Del Pozo, Xin Jin, Jiebo Luo, Jiawei Han, and Thomas S Huang. 2010. RankCompete: simultaneous ranking and clustering of web photos. In *WWW '10*. ACM.
[4] Giuseppe Carenini, Jackie Chi Kit Cheung, and Adam Pauls. 2013. Multi-Document Summarization of Evaluative Text. *Computational Intelligence* 29, 4 (2013).
[5] Anirban Dasgupta, Ravi Kumar, and Sujith Ravi. [n. d.]. Summarization Through Submodularity and Dispersion.
[6] Giuseppe Di Fabbrizio, Ahmet Aker, and Robert Gaizauskas. 2011. Starlet: multi-document summarization of service and product reviews with balanced rating distributions. In *ICDMW '11*. IEEE.
[7] Günes Erkan and Dragomir R Radev. 2004. Lexrank: Graph-based lexical centrality as salience in text summarization. *JAIR* 22 (2004).
[8] Fangxiang Feng, Xiaojie Wang, and Ruifan Li. 2014. Cross-modal retrieval with correspondence autoencoder. In *MM*. ACM.
[9] Aria Haghighi and Lucy Vanderwende. 2009. Exploring content models for multi-document summarization. In *Proceedings of Human Language Technologies: The 2009 Annual Conference of the North American Chapter of the Association for Computational Linguistics*. ACL, 362–370.
[10] Kai Hong, John M Conroy, Benoit Favre, Alex Kulesza, Hui Lin, and Ani Nenkova. [n. d.]. A Repository of State of the Art and Competitive Baseline Summaries for Generic News Summarization.
[11] Minqing Hu and Bing Liu. 2004. Mining and summarizing customer reviews. In *ACM SIGKDD '04*. ACM.
[12] Jayanth Jayanth, Jayaprakash Sundararaj, and Pushpak Bhattacharyya. 2015. Monotone Submodularity in Opinion Summaries.. In *EMNLP '15*.
[13] Yushi Jing and Shumeet Baluja. 2008. Visualrank: Applying pagerank to large-scale image search. *IEEE Transactions on Pattern Analysis and Machine Intelligence* 30, 11 (2008).
[14] Armand Joulin, Edouard Grave, Piotr Bojanowski, and Tomas Mikolov. 2016. Bag of tricks for efficient text classification. *arXiv preprint arXiv:1607.01759* (2016).
[15] Gunhee Kim, Seungwhan Moon, and Leonid Sigal. 2015. Ranking and retrieval of image sequences from multiple paragraph queries. In *CVPR '15*.
[16] Guillaume Lample, Miguel Ballesteros, Sandeep Subramanian, Kazuya Kawakami, and Chris Dyer. 2016. Neural architectures for named entity recognition. *arXiv preprint arXiv:1603.01360* (2016).
[17] Chin-Yew Lin. 2004. ROUGE: A Package for Automatic Evaluation of summaries. In *Proc. ACL workshop on Text Summarization Branches Out*. 10.
[18] Hui Lin and Jeff Bilmes. 2010. Multi-document summarization via budgeted maximization of submodular functions. In *HLT-NAACL '10*. ACL.
[19] Philip J McParlane, Andrew James McMinn, and Joemon M Jose. 2014. Picture the scene...;: Visually Summarising Social Media Events. In *CIKM '14*. ACM.
[20] Jinseok Nam, Jungi Kim, Eneldo Loza Mencía, Iryna Gurevych, and Johannes Fürnkranz. 2014. Large-scale multi-label text classification–revisiting neural networks. In *ECML PKDD '14*. Springer.
[21] Hitoshi Nishikawa, Takaaki Hasegawa, Yoshihiro Matsuo, and Genichiro Kikui. 2010. Optimizing informativeness and readability for sentiment summarization. In *ACL '10*. Association for Computational Linguistics.
[22] Maria Pontiki and Dimitris Galanis. 2014. Semeval-2014 task 4: Aspect based sentiment analysis. *Proceedings of SemEval* (2014), 27–35.
[23] Guoping Qiu. 2004. Image and feature co-clustering. In *ICPR '04*, Vol. 4. IEEE.
[24] Dragomir R Radev, Hongyan Jing, and Malgorzata Budzikowska. 2000. Centroid-based summarization of multiple documents: sentence extraction, utility-based evaluation, and user studies. In *Proceedings of the 2000 NAACL-ANLP Workshop on Automatic summarization*. ACL, 21–30.
[25] Duyu Tang, Bing Qin, Xiaocheng Feng, and Ting Liu. 2015. Effective LSTMs for Target-Dependent Sentiment Classification. *arXiv preprint arXiv:1512.01100* (2015).
[26] Sebastian Tschiatschek, Rishabh K Iyer, Haochen Wei, and Jeff A Bilmes. 2014. Learning mixtures of submodular functions for image collection summarization. In *Advances in neural information processing systems*.
[27] Wei Wang, Beng Chin Ooi, Xiaoyan Yang, Dongxiang Zhang, and Yueting Zhuang. 2014. Effective multi-modal retrieval based on stacked auto-encoders. *Proceedings of the VLDB Endowment* 7, 8 (2014).
[28] Hao Xu, Jingdong Wang, Xian-Sheng Hua, and Shipeng Li. 2011. Hybrid image summarization. In *ACM Multimedia '11*. ACM.
[29] Xin Zheng, Deng Cai, Xiaofei He, Wei-Ying Ma, and Xueyin Lin. 2004. Locality preserving clustering for image database. In *ACM Multimedia '04*. ACM.

Query for Architecture, Click through Military:
Comparing the Roles of Search and Navigation on Wikipedia

Dimitar Dimitrov
GESIS – Leibniz Institute for the Social Sciences
& University of Koblenz-Landau
dimitar.dimitrov@gesis.org

Florian Lemmerich
RWTH Aachen University &
GESIS – Leibniz Institute for the Social Sciences
florian.lemmerich@gesis.org

Fabian Flöck
GESIS – Leibniz Institute for the Social Sciences
fabian.floeck@gesis.org

Markus Strohmaier
RWTH Aachen University &
GESIS – Leibniz Institute for the Social Sciences
markus.strohmaier@humtec.rwth-aachen.de

ABSTRACT

As one of the richest sources of encyclopedic information on the Web, Wikipedia generates an enormous amount of traffic. In this paper, we study large-scale article access data of the English Wikipedia in order to compare articles with respect to the two main paradigms of information seeking, *i.e.*, search by formulating a query, and navigation by following hyperlinks. To this end, we propose and employ two main metrics, namely (i) searchshare – the relative amount of views an article received by search –, and (ii) resistance – the ability of an article to relay traffic to other Wikipedia articles – to characterize articles. We demonstrate how articles in distinct topical categories differ substantially in terms of these properties. For example, architecture-related articles are often accessed through search and are simultaneously a "dead end" for traffic, whereas historical articles about military events are mainly navigated. We further link traffic differences to varying network, content, and editing activity features. Lastly, we measure the impact of the article properties by modeling access behavior on articles with a gradient boosting approach. The results of this paper constitute a step towards understanding human information seeking behavior on the Web.

CCS CONCEPTS

• **Information systems** → **Web log analysis**; **Traffic analysis**;

KEYWORDS

Search Behavior; Navigation Behavior; Log Analysis; Wikipedia

ACM Reference Format:
Dimitar Dimitrov, Florian Lemmerich, Fabian Flöck, and Markus Strohmaier. 2018. Query for Architecture, Click through Military: Comparing the Roles of Search and Navigation on Wikipedia. In *WebSci '18: 10th ACM Conference on Web Science, May 27–30, 2018, Amsterdam, Netherlands.* ACM, New York, NY, USA, 10 pages. https://doi.org/10.1145/3201064.3201092

1 INTRODUCTION

Before the age of the World Wide Web [1], information was predominantly consumed in a linear way, *e.g.*, starting at the first page of a book and following the laid out narrative until the end. With the introduction of hypertext [22] in digital environments, the way people consume information changed dramatically [4, 18–20]. While on early websites, users still predominantly visited a main page through a fixed address and were sometimes even bounded by a more directory-like navigation structure, the rise of search engines and tighter interlinking of websites have corroded the linear consumption paradigm even further. Today, users access a single website through a multitude of webpages as entry points and can usually choose from numerous paths through the available linked content at any time. In such a setting, understanding at which (kind of) pages users typically begin and end their journey on a given website, vs. which pages relay traffic internally from and to these points, provides several useful insights. On one hand, it has high practical importance since it provides the first and last contact opportunity; pages could be shaped to leverage their function as an entry point (*e.g.*, by prioritizing improvements of navigational guidance for these pages to retain visitors), or as an exit point (*e.g.*, by surveying visitors for their user experience before leaving, or by providing increased incentives to continue navigation). On the other hand, knowledge about entry, relay and exit points is also closely tied to the relation of the major information seeking strategies, *i.e.*, search and navigation: the first page visited in a session on a website is frequently reached via search engine results, after a query formulation, while navigation has been often used when the exact information need cannot be easily expressed in words [9, 10]. Understanding under which circumstances search or navigation dominate the users' information seeking behavior can help in developing an agenda for improving the web content in order to optimize visitor rates and retention.

Scope and research questions. Information consumption on the Web has been of special interest to researchers since the Web's earliest days [13, 14]. While both search [21, 32, 34] and navigation [7, 11, 15–17] have been investigated thoroughly in related work, they were mostly looked at separately. Consequently, so far little is known about which parts and content types of a specific website (inter)act in which structural roles, begetting different information access patterns.

In this work, we analyze how these patterns manifest on the online encyclopedia Wikipedia. With more than 5 million articles, Wikipedia is one of the primary information sources for many Web users and through its openly available pageview data provides an essential use case for studying information seeking behavior, as made apparent by numerous studies [6, 16, 24]. Yet, there is a lack of understanding how search and navigation as the two major information access forms *in combination* shape the traffic of large-scale hypertext environments, such as the world's largest online encyclopedia. To this end, we are interested in answering the following research questions: (i) How do search and navigation interplay to shape the article traffic on Wikipedia? Given an article, we want to know how its acting as a search entry point is related to (not) relaying navigation traffic into Wikipedia, and vice versa. This also addresses the issue of how search and navigation contribute to the article's popularity. Beyond these characteristics of the system in general, we also examine which specific properties of articles influence their roles in the search-vs-navigation ecosystem. We hence ask: (ii) Which article features (*i.e.*, topic, network, content and edit features) are indicative for specific information access behavior?

Materials, approach and methods. Building our analysis on large-scale, openly available log data for the English edition of Wikipedia, we propose two metrics capturing individual traffic behavior on articles, *i.e.*, (i) searchshare – the amount of views an article received by search –, and (ii) resistance – the ability of an article to channel traffic into and through Wikipedia (*cf.* Section 2).

We use searchshare and resistance to first explore the relation between search and navigation and their effect on the popularity of articles independent of their content (*cf.* Section 3). Depending on these two measures, we assign articles to four groups describing the role they assume for attracting and retaining visitors. Subsequently, we characterize the influence of several article attributes, including the general topical domain, edit activity and content structure on the preferred information access form (*cf.* Section 4). Finally, we fit a gradient boosting model to determine the impact of these article features on the preferred user access behavior (*cf.* Section 5).

Contributions and findings. Our contributions are the following: (i) Regarding the general (collective) access behavior on Wikipedia, we provide empirical evidence that for the most viewed articles search dominates navigation in the number of articles accessed and received views. For the tail of the view distributions, navigation appears to become more and more important. (ii) We link article properties, *i.e.*, position in the Wikipedia network, number of article revisions, and topic to preferred access behavior, *i.e.*, search or navigation. Finally, (iii) we quantify the strength of the relationship between article properties and preferred access behavior.

Our analysis suggests that (i) while search and navigation are used to access and explore different articles, both types of information access are crucial for Wikipedia, and (ii) that exit points of navigation sessions are located at the periphery of the link network, whereas entry points are located at the core. (iii) Edit activity is strongly related with the ability of an article to relay traffic, and thus with the preferred access behavior.

Our results may have a variety of applications, *e.g.*, improving and maintaining the visual appearance and hyperlink structure of articles, identifying articles exhibiting changes in access behavior patterns due to vandalism or other online misbehavior. We consider our analysis as an initial step to better understand how search and navigation interplay to shape the user access behavior on platforms like Wikipedia and on websites in general.

2 TRANSITION DATA AND DEFINITIONS

Below, we give an overview of the used dataset capturing the traffic on Wikipedia articles and define *searchshare* and *resistance* as our main metrics for describing the individual article traffic behavior.

2.1 Transition Data

For studying the access behavior on Wikipedia articles, we use the clickstream dataset published by the Wikimedia Foundation [38]. The used dataset contains the transition counts between webpages and Wikipedia articles in form of (*referrer, resource*) pairs extracted from the server logs for August, 2016, and is limited to pairs that occur at least 10 times. The referrer pages are either external (*e.g.*, search engines, social media), internal (other Wikipedia pages), or missing (*e.g.*, if the article is accessed directly using the browser address bar). The navigation targets are purely internal pages.[1] Since we are interested in contrasting Wikipedia article access from search engines and navigation (see also our discussion in Section 7), we focus our analyses only on those articles in the clickstream dataset that have received views through search or internal navigation, setting aside remaining view sources (mostly "no referrer"). Accordingly, we define *total views* of an article as the sum of all page accesses by either search or navigation.

The resulting dataset consists of 2,830,709 articles accessed through search 2,805,238,298 times and 14,405,839 transitions originating from 1,370,456 articles and accounting for 1,251,341,103 views of 2,149,104 target articles. In total, the dataset consists of 3,104,702 articles viewed 4,056,579,401 times, with a ratio of 69% stemming from search and 31% from internal navigation – in line with previous reports on the clickstream data [7, 15].

2.2 Definitions

To achieve a fundamental understanding of the parts that search and navigation each play for the distribution of views in Wikipedia, we take a look at the functional roles articles can assume for the overall traffic flow in respect to their *searchshare* and *resistance*.

Searchshare. A high *searchshare* value indicates that search is the predominant paradigm of accessing an article, and thus that the article acts as an *entry point* for a site visit. In contrast, articles with a low value receive most of their views from users visiting them by means of navigation. The *searchshare* metric is defined as

$$searchshare(a) = \frac{in_{se}(a)}{in_{se}(a) + in_{nav}(a)} \tag{1}$$

where $in_{se}(a)$ is the number of pageviews an article a received directly from search engine referrers, and $in_{nav}(a)$ is the number of views from navigation as recorded in the Wikipedia clickstream.

Resistance. A low *resistance* value signals that an article forwards most of its received traffic to other articles within Wikipedia, hence

---

[1]Leaving a Wikipedia page is treated as the end of the visit in the logs, whether by clicking on an external link or closing the page.

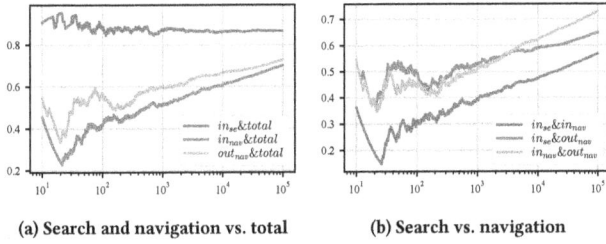

(a) Search and navigation vs. total

(b) Search vs. navigation

Figure 1: Ranking overlap. Four rankings are shown, according to the total number of pageviews (*total*), the number of pageviews coming from search (in_{se}) as well as in- (in_{nav}) and out-navigation (out_{nav}). The y-axis indicates overlaps between pairs of rankings, considering the top-k articles of each ranking as marked on the x-axis (log-scaled, top articles on the left). As a result, the overall ranking of total pageviews shows a very high overlap with the incoming search ranking. The top pages by search and navigation differ substantially. Notably, being a distribution point of traffic (high out_{nav}, *cf.* (b)) is correlated most to receiving search, but only for top out_{nav} articles, with lower ranks being supplied with traffic predominantly through in_{nav}.

does not block the flow of incoming traffic onward. A high value in turn indicates that an article acts as an *exit point*. Thus, it rarely relays users to other Wikipedia articles. These articles are traffic sinks in the Wikipedia information network. We define the resistance metric as

$$resistance(a) = 1 - \frac{out_{nav}(a)}{in_{se}(a) + in_{nav}(a)} \qquad (2)$$

where $out_{nav}(a)$ is the number of pageviews that had article a as a referrer. Additionally, we restrict the values to be in the interval [0,1]. This is necessary since a small number of articles generates more out-going traffic than they receive pageviews, *e.g.*, due to a user opening several links in a new tab each.

3 GENERAL ACCESS BEHAVIOR

In this section, we investigate how exogenous and endogenous traffic contribute to article popularity on Wikipedia, and we study the distribution of traffic features. We provide a first overview of the general access behavior on Wikipedia regarding search and navigation, aided by a division of articles into four groups with respect to searchshare and resistance; in Section 4, we will subsequently take a deeper look at dissimilarities between different types of articles.

Search and navigation in relation to total views. As can be expected from related research on Wikipedia and similar online platforms, the distribution of pageviews over articles is long-tailed with a heavy skew towards the head (80% views generated by the top-visited 5.2% of all articles). To better investigate the relationship between search and (incoming and outgoing) navigation on the articles popularity, we calculate the cumulative overlap (intersection)

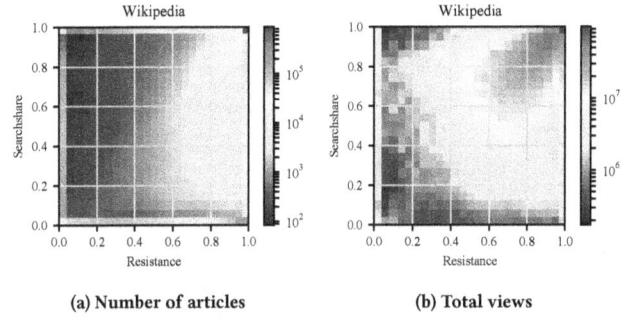

(a) Number of articles

(b) Total views

Figure 2: Articles and article views by access behavior. For a given searchshare (y-axis) and resistance (x-axis), the figure shows (a) the number of articles and (b) the sum of their views in each heatmap square bin. Warm colors denote high values, using a logarithmic scale. We observe that search dominates navigation in terms of number of accessed articles (note the single top data bin in (a)) and that a substantial amount of articles exhibits high resistance values. When focusing on views, we see a more spread-out pattern, evidencing that a relatively small amount of articles attracts a substantial amount of search views and channels them onward to other articles (upper left side of (b)), corresponding to the *search-relay* group (*cf.* Table 1).

of the descendingly ranked articles at each rank k, divided by k; this is an adaptation of the Rank Biased Overlap[2] measure.

Figure 1(a) shows that the top k articles ordered by search traffic (top-k-search) are highly overlapping with the top articles by total views (top-k-total) at any k, underscoring the general importance of search as a driver of incoming views. In-navigation, in contrast, is not a deciding factor to belong to the top most visited pages, but sees an extreme increase in the influence on overall views for articles up to top-k-total around 8000, at which point the increase continues, but levels off. Apparently, while search is the overall main driver for traffic, in-navigation rapidly becomes a more central source of traffic beyond the extremely popular articles. Turning to navigation passed on *from* articles to other articles, we can glean from Figure 1(a) that (i) while the very top of viewed articles contribute little in relation to their accumulated views to the internal traffic flow of Wikipedia (low overlap for out_{nav}&$total$), we (ii) see a rapid and constant drop in the amount of traffic "dying" at a given page with increasing top-k-total.

Further, while it is not surprising that the outgoing traffic accumulates generally in line with the overall received views, up until around top-k-total 1,500,000 it is generated at a rate *surpassing* the relative increase of total views, with the highest ranks of top-k-total contributing comparably little to it, just as to in-navigation. These observations are in line with Figure 1(b), where we see that a higher rank in receiving navigation - rather than from search - is more strongly correlated with distributing views to other articles for the

---

[2]Rank Biased Overlap [35] is a common metric for similarity between rankings using cumulative set overlap in cases where the two lists do not necessarily share the same elements (as is the case here). Top-weighting as can be specified for RBO is neither suited nor necessary for the distinction of different k that we aim for here.

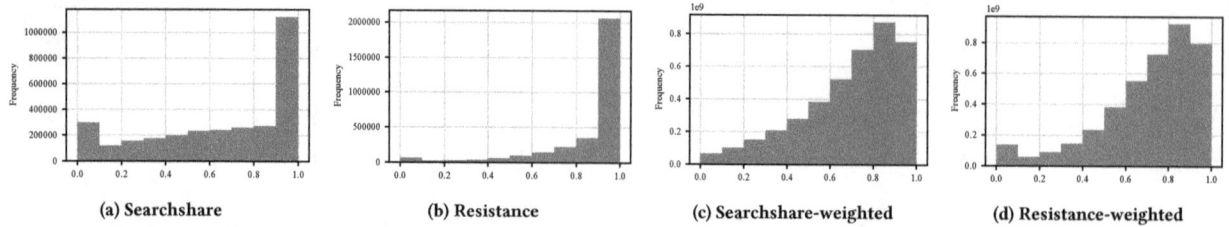

| (a) Searchshare | (b) Resistance | (c) Searchshare-weighted | (d) Resistance-weighted |

Figure 3: Traffic feature distributions. Figures (a) and (b) show an unweighted histogram of searchshare and resistance, while (c) and (d) respectively weight articles by their pageview counts. Most articles have a very high value for searchshare and resistance. However, extreme values close to 1.0 in (a), (b) stem mostly from rarely visited pages.

largest portion of pages, after top-k-total 3000; up until that point, the largest share of channeled traffic stems from search views. As bottom line, we see a pattern that points to a small number of pages at the extreme top of the pageview counts that are mostly searched, but *in relation to their popularity* rather isolated in terms of navigation; with in- and out-navigation similarly gaining notably in correlation with overall views for lower top-k-total ranks.

Traffic feature distributions. Figure 3 depicts the system-wide distribution of searchshare and resistance. Pages are generally much more searched than navigated to (searchshare median = 0.74, mean = 0.66) as seen in Figure 3(a). It is also apparent from Figure 3(b) that most articles do not tend to forward much of their received traffic internally, with the median for resistance for all articles lying at 1.0 and the mean at 0.88. This general tendency prevails when these scores are weighted by their received views (Figures 3(c) and 3(d)), but a notably less skewed distribution emerges, implying that – even when accounting for regression-to-the-mean effects – a majority of views is acquired via search and that a majority of views hits rather high-resistance targets.

Relation between searchshare and resistance. We observe a light positive correlation (pearson = 0.26, spearman = 0.33) indicating that the more likely an article is used to start a session, the more likely it is also to be the last article accessed in a session. Figure 2 depicts this association for all articles in our dataset.

To explore this relation further, we assign each article to one of four groups, determined by the *mean* of both searchshare and resistance as the thresholds.[3] We label each group according to its traffic behavior, i.e., (i) *search-relay* articles that are often searched while simultaneously contributing to further navigation (above-mean searchshare, below-mean resistance); (ii) *search-exit* articles with above-average searchshare that are often accessed from search but do not lead to users navigating further (above-mean searchshare,

---
[3]A delimitation by median yields groups with the sole resistance value 1.0 and was therefore not used. Cut-offs at 0.5 would have created extremely unbalanced groups.

Table 1: Article group sizes and views. For each group, the table shows the percentage of articles and their received views. The majority of the articles are less visited and act as exit points of user session, whereas only popular articles are able to further relay traffic.

above-mean resistance); (iii) *navigation-exit* articles that receive their traffic mostly from navigation but cannot channel traffic to other pages (below-mean searchshare, above-mean resistance); (iv) *navigation-relay* articles that are mainly accessed from within Wikipedia and able to pass traffic on internally (below-mean searchshare, below-mean resistance). Table 1 reports the share of articles and views pertaining to each group. We observe that a small group of highly visited articles is able to inject considerable amounts of traffic (search-relay) into Wikipedia while about a fifth of the articles' role is mainly to channel traffic internally (nav.-relay). On the other hand, exit points receive less views while covering a much bigger portion of Wikipedia articles. Overall, these observations are in line with Figure 3.

Summary. Our analysis shows that search dominates navigation with respect to the number of articles accessed and visit frequency. However, the less viewed an article is, the more significant navigation becomes as an information access form. Further, only popular articles are able to relay traffic while the majority of the articles acts as exit points for user search and navigation sessions.

4 CHARACTERIZING ACCESS BEHAVIOR

In the previous section, we analyzed the general Wikipedia information access behavior, setting aside individual page attributes. However, Wikipedia articles have different properties that may influence the way they are retrieved (*cf.* Section 4.1). To this end, we analyze the general Wikipedia access behavior dependent on the article network (*cf.* Section 4.2), and content and edit properties (*cf.* Section 4.3). Subsequently, we highlight differences between general access behavior on Wikipedia and on Wikipedia topics dominated by search and navigation, respectively (*cf.* Section 4.4).

4.1 Wikipedia Article Data and Features

To study the influence of the content on the preferred access behavior, we focus on a snapshot of all Wikipedia articles contained in the main namespace of the English language version from August, 2016[4]. We obtained the articles using the Wikipedia API[5]. The collected article data represent the HTML version of each article on which the transitions data used to study the Wikipedia traffic has been generated (*cf.* Section 2.1). By parsing and rendering the HTML version of the articles, we are able to extract article features

---
[4]https://archive.org/details/enwiki-20160801
[5]https://www.mediawiki.org/wiki/API:Main_page

	search-exit	search-relay	nav.-relay	nav.-exit	total
articles	43%	9%	21%	27%	100%
views	17%	37%	39%	7%	100%

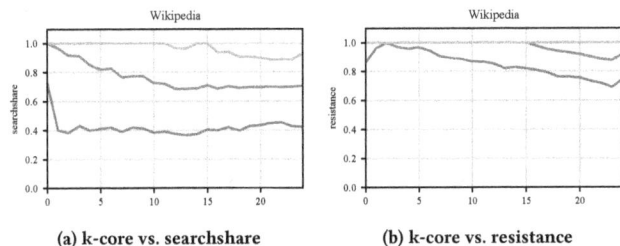

(a) k-core vs. searchshare

(b) k-core vs. resistance

Figure 4: Network position. The figure shows the first (blue), second (red), and third (green) quartile of searchshare (a) and resistance (b) as function of the article position in the network indicated by its k-core. K-core values are divided into 25 bins. The access behavior on articles is influenced by their position in the network. The more central an article, the lower its searchshare and resistance – i.e., the more traffic it relays through the network.

capturing aspects related to the content of the articles. The dataset contains roughly 5 million articles connected by 391 million links.

For these Wikipedia articles, we determine a wide variety of features describing their characteristics. We categorize these features into three different groups, i.e., (i) network properties, (ii) content and edit properties and (iii) article topics. The network features consist of in-, out- and *total degree* of the article in the Wikipedia link network as well as the k-core value for this network as a typical centrality measure. Regarding the content and edit properties, we calculated for each article the *number of sections*, the *number of figures* and the *number of lists* contained in the article. These features capture visual appearance of the article, whereas the *number of revisions and editors* represent content production process. We also consider the article *age* measured in years to account for differences between mature and young articles. To account for the amount of information provided in an article, we calculate its *size in kilobytes*. The features capturing the content production process are extracted from the TokTrack dataset [8] and consider the period between article creation and the end of August 2016. As the Wikipedia article categories are often too specific[6], we fit a Latent Dirichlet Allocation (LDA) [2] model on article texts using Gensim [27] bag of words article vectors with removed stop words. To allow for manual interpretation of the topics, we fit a model for 20 topics. Subsequently, we asked five independent researchers to provide topic labels based on the top words and Wikipedia articles for each topic and summarized their labels. Section 4.4 describes the extracted topics. The following analyses are based on a random sample of 50000 articles.

4.2 Network Features

To understand the role of the network features, we compute the median of the features for each of the four article groups *search-exit*, *search-relay*, *nav.-relay*, and *nav.-exit* (*cf.* Section 3). The results are shown in Table 2. We can observe that articles with below-average

searchshare and resistance (article group *nav.-relay*) have higher median values across all network features, *i.e.*, they are located more in the center of the network and consistently have more incoming and outgoing links. Although search-relay articles are not as well connected as nav.-relay, their relatively central position in the network and high number of outgoing connections is important in order to inject traffic into Wikipedia. By contrast, articles that are often used as exit points (*search-exit* and *nav.-exit*) are located more in the periphery of the network (low k-core value), are less often linked to, and contain less out-links themselves, which eventually results in higher resistance values, signifying the termination of user sessions.

For further analysis, we sort the articles according to their k-core value and discretize them into 25 equally-sized bins. For each bin, we compute the quartiles for searchshare and resistance, as seen in Figure 4. Looking at the median (center red line), we find that for articles with increasing k-core values the searchshare indeed decreases (*cf.* Figure 4(a)). However, this effect stops at around 50% of the dataset, *i.e.*, for half of the articles, which are located in high k-core network layers, the searchshare is mostly independent from the exact centrality. Regarding the resistance, there exists a substantial amount of nodes with a resistance of 1.0 for all k-core values, *cf.* the green line indicating the upper quartile. However, for the more central nodes, an increased number of pages have a significantly lower resistance (*cf.* Figure 4(b)).

4.3 Content and Edit Features

Next, we characterize the article groups in terms of the article content and edit history which account for the content presentation and content production process. Table 3 reports the median values of these features in the four article groups. We can observe that the content features (number of tables, number of sections, size of the article) are modestly increased for relay articles, *i.e.*, articles that contain more content tend to be less often exit points of navigation sessions. By contrast, the revision history plays a more important role: we can see that articles in the *search-relay* group have (as a median) more than twice the number of editors and revisions compared to exit articles, and tend also to be somewhat older. Articles in the group *nav.-relay* show similar, but slightly lower values with the same tendency. The median feature values for both "exit" article

Table 2: Network features. For each network feature, the table shows the *median* feature values of the articles in the respective group. The article network properties influence the preferred access behavior. Nav.-relay articles act as intersections for the traffic as they occupy central network positions and provide lots of in- and outgoing links. Search-relay articles are similarly well-connected, which is important for injecting traffic into Wikipedia. Exit points (search-exit and nav.-exit articles) lack connectivity and are unable to channel external and internal traffic, respectively.

M	search-exit	search-relay	nav.-relay	nav.-exit	overall
in-degree	14	38	54	18	22
out-degree	33	56	71	35	41
degree	51	105	131	57	69
k-core	44	76	95	49	57

---

[6]I.e., very specific categories of articles are not linked to the relevant super-category; in other cases, two conflicting categories are linked or fitting categories are missing completely.

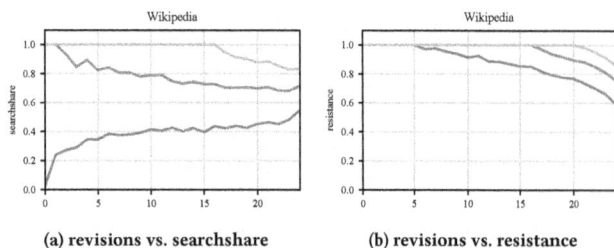

(a) revisions vs. searchshare　　　(b) revisions vs. resistance

Figure 5: Edit activity. The figure shows the first (blue), second (red), and third (green) quartile of searchshare (a) and resistance (b) as function of the article editors' activity indicated by the number of revisions. Revisions values are divided into 25 bins. Except for the most edited articles, high edit activity has a negative effect on the resistance, which on the other hand has a positive effect on navigation indicated by the lower searchshare.

groups are very similar and show slightly lower editor and revision numbers. Overall, content and edit features provide strong indicators for articles relaying traffic (as opposed to being exit points), but only weak indicators for being accessed by search or by navigation.

We will have a more detailed look at an exemplary edit feature, *i.e.*, the number of revisions. Analogously to above (network features), we assign the articles to one of 25 bins according to their revision count, compute the distribution of searchshare and resistance for each bin, and plot the quartiles. The results are shown in Figure 5. We can see that the median searchshare continuously decreases with increasing number of revisions. The effect is in particular significant for very low number of revisions (*cf.* Figure 5(a)). Additionally, the spread of the distribution – measured by the interquartile range (IQR) – also substantially decreases the more revisions an article has. This can likely be explained by *regression to the mean* since articles with less revisions receive overall less views, making more extreme searchshare values more likely. With regard to the resistance, we can observe that specifically high number of revisions correlate with a lower resistance scores (*cf.* Figure 5(b)). The number of editors, and the age of an article is highly correlated with the number of revisions and reveal a very similar behavior with respect to searchshare and resistance.

Table 3: Content and edit features. For each content and edit feature, the table shows the median feature values of the articles in the respective group. The content production process influences the access behavior as search- and nav.-exit points have low edit activity, and offer less content. On the other hand, relay articles are more frequently edited, and congruently, are generally more extensive.

M	search-exit	search-relay	nav.-relay	nav.-exit	overall
editors	21	52	46	21	25
revisions	38	97	86	37	46
sections	6	7	7	4	6
tables	3	3	4	3	4
age	9	11	10	8	9
size	41	50	54	41	44

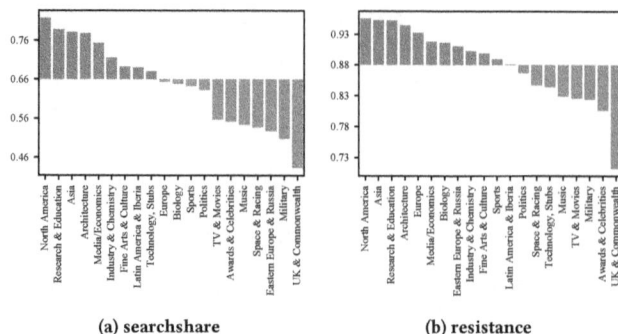

(a) searchshare　　　(b) resistance

Figure 6: Access behavior for all topics. Topics are ordered from highest (left) to lowest (right) for searchshare (a) and resistance (b). Values over (blue) and below (red) the respective mean value are colored respectively. There are pronounced differences in the dominant access behavior on different Wikipedia topics.

4.4　Topic Features

Search-related popularity, navigability as well as other characteristics related to traffic might be highly dependent on the topical domain of an article. We hence investigate the access behavior across Wikipedia's numerous article themes, represented by the 20 topics we have extracted. Table 4 provides descriptive statistics of these topics. With 32% "TV and Movies" is the topic with the most views while consisting of a mere 7.5% of all articles on Wikipedia. "Technology, Stubs" and "Architecture" show an opposing dynamic,

Table 4: Topic statistics. The table shows the percentage of articles and views for each topic. Additionally, it reports the median age in years, number of editors and revisions, and the size of the articles in kB. Not surprisingly, popular articles are generally longer in terms of text, edited more and by higher number of editors, and relatively old.

topic	% articles	% views	M age	M editors	M revisions	M size
Technology, Stubs	19.3	7	7	20	36	38
Architecture	12.4	5	8	31	61	56
Sports	12.0	8	7	37	86	68
Politics	8.1	8	8	47	103	60
TV&Movies	7.5	32	8	96	197	55
Fine Arts&Culture	7.2	6	8	49	100	49
Biology	7.0	6	7	29	57	46
Music	6.9	9	8	64	136	53
Research&Education	4.8	2	7	40	87	47
Media/Economics	3.3	4	8	54	115	49
Military	3.1	4	8	47	105	65
Industry&Chemistry	3.0	6	9	66	126	55
North America	1.2	0	9	23	39	52
Space&Racing	1.2	2	8	52	114	73
Europe	0.9	0.0	7	19	36	52
Asia	0.7	0.0	5	8	14	60
Latin America&Iberia	0.5	0.0	7	20	33	58
UK&Commonwealth	0.5	0.0	7	19	40	43
Eastern Europe&Russia	0.4	0.0	7	15	24	49
Awards&Celebrities	0.0	0.0	6	22	42	41

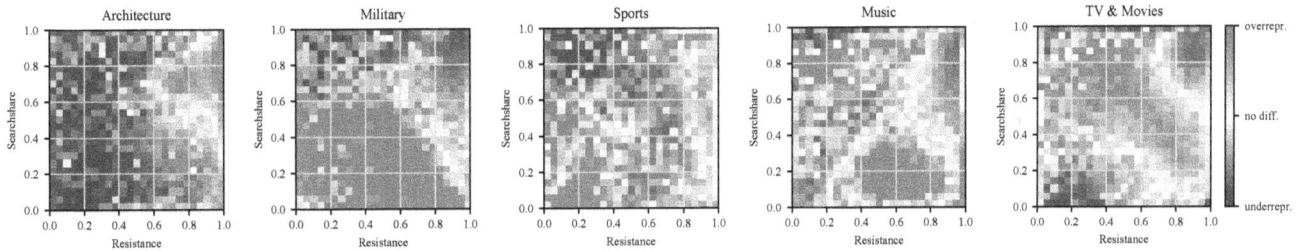

Figure 7: Relative difference of individual topics to the overall view distribution of searchshare vs. resistance (*cf.* Figure 2(b)). White denotes no relative difference, blue denotes underrepresentation (down to 0), while red denotes overrepresentation (max. over all topics at 2). The figure highlights the differences between search-heavy and navigation-heavy topics compared to the all-articles baseline. "Architecture", exhibiting above-mean searchshare and resistance (*cf.* Figure 6) stands representative for six similarly distributed topics and mainly attracts search hits that it cannot pass on. "Military" shows an almost inverted pattern, mostly receiving as well as producing internal navigation. The bi-focal distribution of "Sports" can be found in "Politics" and "Fine Arts & Culture" as well, while patterns for "Music" and "TV & Movies" are more unique.

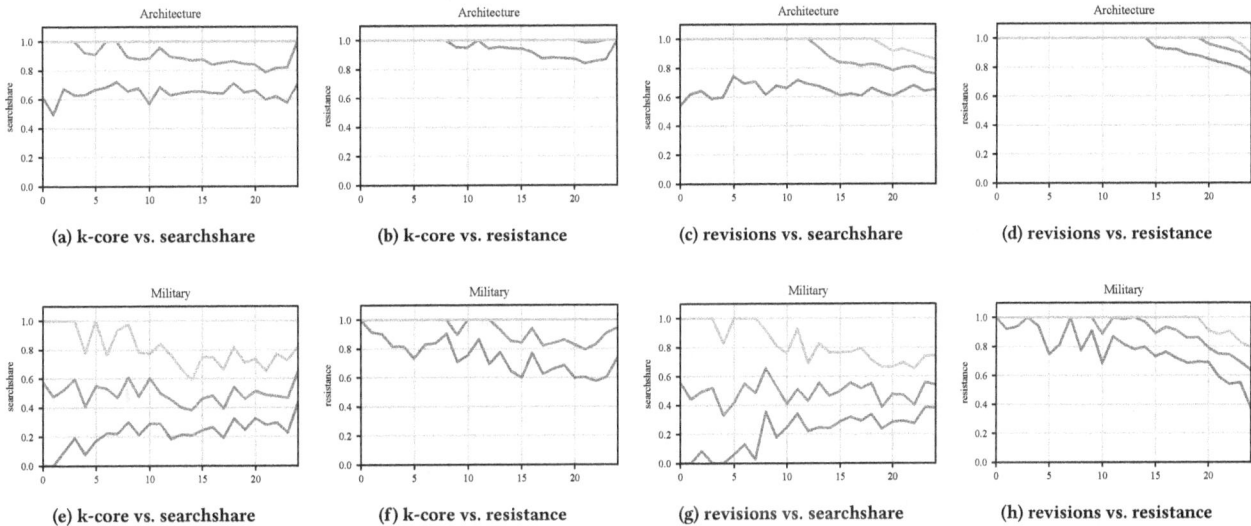

Figure 8: Relation of traffic features with network and content features. For a topic dominated by search ("Architecture") and one dominated by navigation ("Military"), the figure shows the first (blue), second (red), and third (green) quartile of the article searchshare and resistance as function of its position in the network indicated by its k-core and editors' activity indicated by the number of revisions. Articles are divided into 25 bins by k-core and revision values. Apart from base-level differences of searchshare and resistance, the topics exhibit comparable trends, with the exception of searchshare not being influenced as much by network position or edit activity features for "Military" articles.

providing a large amount of articles, but relatively few views.[7] Overall, the amounts of articles and view counts are not strongly correlated. Consistent with previous research, we also observe that the popular articles are in general longer, relative old, and revised more often by more editors [32].

A look at the distribution of searchshare and resistance in the overview provided by Figure 6 reveals the different access behaviors for Wikipedia topics. To examine these pronounced differences further, we set out to highlight the dissimilarities of the overall searchshare vs. resistance distribution for total views – as shown

in Figure 2(b) – with the same distribution for the individual topics. To do so, we create heatmaps pinpointing the *relative differences* of each topic to the baseline of the overall distribution. This is achieved by performing a bin-wise division of a topic's normalized view count for a given searchshare-resistance bin with the respective normalized bin for the general Wikipedia traffic behavior. The resulting heatmaps are shown in Figure 7 for selected topics. They draw a clear picture of the over- and under-representation of certain article types (in terms of views) in each topic against the whole-system baseline. "Architecture" in Figure 7 stands as one representative for a group of topics ("Biology", "Industry & Chemistry", "Research & Education", "Space & Racing") that all exhibit a very similar distribution with their article views occurring

---

[7] "Technology, Stubs" is a compound of general Wikipedia:Stub articles and often short technology articles that were not sufficiently distinguishable by LDA. We exclude it from discussion here due to its ambivalent nature.

at high searchshare and high resistance, *i.e.*, these topics are mostly searched and not used for further navigation. In stark contrast, views for "Military" topics occur to the largest part in comparably low-resistance articles, that are mostly navigated to (views for "UK & Commonwealth" are distributed almost analogously). "Sports" reveals a similar inclination for *nav-relay* types of articles attracting views, yet sports articles also frequently get accessed by search and abandoned immediately (closely related patterns: "Fine Arts & Culture" and "Politics"). Lastly, "Music" and "TV & Movies" exhibit remarkably idiosyncratic distribution patterns, not mirrored by another topic. "Music" attracts many views in a *search-relay* fashion, but on the other hand also explicitly acts as a "dead end" for internal navigation.

As "maximally different" topics in respect to these traffic patterns and with overall high view counts, we select "Architecture" for search-heavy topics, and "Military" for navigation-heavy topics to conduct a deeper analysis regarding article network, content and edit properties. While "Architecture" includes articles covering popular buildings, landmarks and municipalities, "Military" consists of articles covering significant historic events often associated with violence such as wars and notable battles, along with many articles dedicated to military units, personnel and equipment (*cf.* [28]). For the general access behavior concerning the network, content and edit features, we again assign the articles to one of 25 bins according to their k-core and revision counts, compute the distribution of searchshare and resistance for each bin, and plot the quartiles (*cf.* Figure 8). For "Architecture", searchshare (a) initially decreases for increasing k-core but sees an uptick for very central nodes, and a very similar behavior can be observed for resistance (b). "Military" is characterized by generally lower levels of both metrics, yet shares the trend of decreasing resistance with increasing k-core (e), meaning that for both topics, the more central articles in the network are able to channel visitors into Wikipedia, with the top-most central nodes excluded from this trend. Being edited more implies decreasing resistance for both topics ((d), (h)), although this trend reveals itself only for much higher revision counts for "Architecture", most likely to its generally higher resistance. Edit counts have no clearly distinguishable influence on "Military" articles' searchshare, for "Architecture" it, however, implies lower searchshare.

Summary. The results presented in this section suggest that the content heavily influences the access behavior on Wikipedia. Particularly, topical domains are accessed differently, *i.e.*, users prefer to access articles about architecture and landmarks mainly through search, whereas more historical articles about military actions are navigated. Moreover, mature articles with high revision numbers and article located in the core of the network are more likely to channel traffic through Wikipedia, whereas articles located at the network periphery act as exit points.

5 MODELING ACCESS BEHAVIOR

Our previous analysis characterized the user access behavior on Wikipedia articles with respect to their traffic from search and navigation dependent on the article features. However, this analysis does not reveal the impact of the feature groups on the access behavior. To this end, we set out to model the access behavior on articles in order to measure the influence of each feature group. The

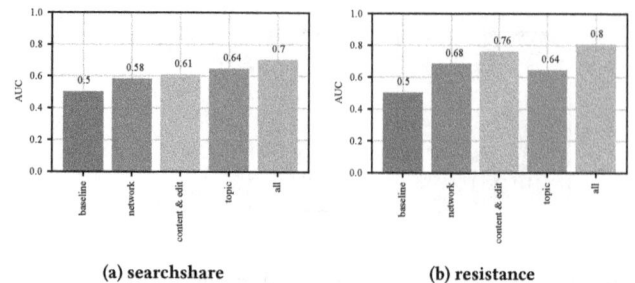

(a) searchshare   (b) resistance

Figure 9: Results. The figure shows the model performance (ROC AUC) for (a) searchshare and (b) resistance. Predicting searchshare is more challenging than predicting resistance. The article topic determines the preferred access behavior (search or navigation). However, position in the network, content maturity and presentation of the article are indicative for the resistance, and thus if an article will be an entry-exit point or a relay point for the traffic.

higher the predicative performance of a feature group, the higher the influence of the group is on the role articles play with respect to the traffic (entry-exit and relay articles), and thus on the preferred information access form (search and navigation).

Modeling searchshare. We ask, given a Wikipedia article, if it is possible to classify it as dominated by search, *i.e.*, *searchshare* > 0.66 or dominated by navigation, *i.e.*, *searchshare* ≤ 0.66. The threshold used for the separation is the searchshare mean (*cf.* Section 3). In our experiments, we consider four different sets of article features: (i) network features, *i.e.*, in-, out-degree, k-core, (ii) content & edit features, *i.e.*, number of revisions and editors, article size, number of tables, pictures, lists, and (iii) topic. For predicting the preferred access form, we fit a model using gradient boosting and evaluate the model's performance with ROC AUC. The model is trained using 10-fold cross validation at a balanced dataset. On this dataset random guessing results in 50% accuracy, which is also used as baseline. Figure 9(a) shows the individual performance for each feature group, as well as the performance for the combination of all features. We observe that modeling searchshare is difficult even with all features (AUC = 0.70). As expected, the network features are the least indicative (AUC = 0.58). Further, the topic feature predicts searchshare best (AUC = 0.64), which suggests strong user preferences for specific information access form, *i.e.*, search or navigation for different topics.

Modeling resistance. To model the resistance of Wikipedia articles, *i.e.*, they ability to relay traffic, we treat an article as a relay point if *resistance* ≤ 0.88 and an exit point if *resistance* > 0.88. Again, the separation of the articles is based on the resistance mean (*cf.* Section 3). We consider the same feature groups as for modeling searchshare and use random guessing as our baseline. For classifying the articles, we again utilize 10-fold cross validation to train a gradient boosting model on a balanced dataset. The performance is measured in terms of ROC AUC. Figure 9(b) shows the individual classification performance for that task for each feature group. The content and edit features are the most important (AUC = 0.76). This makes the case for an influence of the way content is presented to the user on lowering or increasing the resistance of a page. Unlike for searchshare, the network features are indicative for the resistance of an article (AUC = 0.68). This suggests that the network position of an article influences the extent to which it channels traffic. The topic plays only a small role, which again highlights the importance of the quality of the content presentation and production process.

Summary. In general, modeling article resistance is easier than modeling searchshare as suggested by the higher ROC AUC values. Modeling searchshare is challenging due to the influence of external events (*e.g.*, the transition data exhibits high view numbers on articles about the Summer Olympics 2016), and the content diversity. However, investing in diverse content from different topics seems to be the best way for Wikipedia to attract people as the article's topic is the most indicative feature regarding searchshare. On the other hand, the content presentation, and the article's position in the network are decisive for its ability to relay traffic.

6 RELATED WORK

Since the inception of the Web, researchers have been studying the user content consumption behavior. Initially, content has been accessed by traversing hyperlinks on the Web [14]. This navigational user behavior on the Web and on Wikipedia is often modeled using well-established methods such as Markov chains [3, 23, 25, 29, 30] and decentralized search models [5, 12]. Numerous navigational hypotheses on Wikipedia have also been presented based on, *e.g.*, click traces stemming from navigational games and on click data from server logs. For example, West and Leskovec observed a trade-off between similarity and popularity to the target article in the user sessions of Wikispeedia [37]. Lamprecht *et al.* studied the general navigability of several Wikipedia language editions and showed how the Wikipedia article structure influences the user click behavior [15, 16]. Dimitrov *et al.* conducted a large-scale study on the navigational behavior on Wikipedia. They found that users tend to select links located in the beginning of Wikipedia articles and links leading to articles located in the network periphery [6, 7]. By constructing a navigational phase space from transition data, Gilderslave and Yasseri studied internal navigation on Wikipedia and identified articles with extreme, atypical, and mimetic behavior [11]. Web content can be also discovered by formulating and executing a search query. Kumar and Tomkins performed an initial characterization of the user search behavior [13], while Weber and Jaimes studied the search engine usage with respect to the users demographics, topics, and session length [36]. Earlier Wikipedia reading behavior studies focused on explaining bursts, dynamics of topic popularity and search query analysis to Wikipedia [17, 26, 32–34]. A more recent study by Singer *et al.* investigated the Wikipedia readers motivations [31]. By complementing a reader survey with server log data, they discovered specific behavior patterns for different motivations, *i.e.*, bored readers tend to produce long article sequences spanning different topics. McMahon *et al.* focused on the interdependence between search engines, *i.e.*, Google and Wikipedia [21]. They showed that Google is responsible for generating high traffic to Wikipedia articles, although, in some cases traffic is reduced due to the direct inclusion of Wikipedia content in search results. Compared to our work, McMahon *et al.* concentrate on the

peer production site and not on the content consumption. While there is a long line of research with respect to search and – more so – navigation, they have rarely been studied together which is the focus of this work.

7 DISCUSSION

As a general observation, our results shed light on the different roles of articles with respect to traffic entering and leaving Wikipedia. On one hand, an overwhelming amount of pages attracts mostly direct search traffic and only little internal navigation, thanks to Wikipedia's strong symbiotic relationship with web search engines. Yet, notably, most of that traffic goes to articles that act mainly as exit points, *i.e.*, users to not continue visiting Wikipedia directly afterwards. This is congruent with, but not necessarily because of, a pure "look up" nature of search. Only a very small share of searched articles is responsible for relaying disproportionally large amounts of traffic into the rest of Wikipedia. We see that these articles are well-connected, more edited and more extensive than their exit counterparts, although we cannot yet conclude whether this is because of a "worn path" paradigm, wherein links and content are built because of the natural thematic positioning and suitability of an article to act as an entry point *and* as a bridge to more content, or because the a-priori structure of these article facilitates the observed navigational patterns. A longitudinal study, which we plan for future work, could obtain more detailed insights on this co-evolution of structural features and navigation. Furthermore, our data shows that articles, which are able to forward traffic, sit mostly at the very (k-)core of the link network. However, this is not necessarily the case for being a receiver of navigation traffic, with searchshare values stabilizing already at lower k-cores – and with inlinks not being more highly correlated with k-core than outlinks. This hints to the fact that – to some extent – users enter Wikipedia by search on more central articles, and then navigate outwards from more to less central nodes. This is consistent with previous findings studying navigation on Wikipedia [7].

Regarding articles with different topical alignments, we see certain evidence that the thematic domain of a user's information pursuit seems connected with the "mode" of how this information is attained. While the highly aggregate data used in this work does not allow for direct inferences as to the type of information retrieval in the continuum between a targeted and well-defined lookup and a completely serendipitous discovery process, we can nonetheless discern distinct patterns between article topics. Although "Architecutre" articles are not more devoid of in- or out-navigation opportunities than "Military" ones, they show far higher amounts of search views and exit points, while the latter one is navigated at a constantly high level, regardless of their connectedness. A possible explanation of the navigation-heavy behavior on "Military" articles is that people like follow paths through events in order to understand historical developments.

For our analysis, we utilize publicly available clickstream data about Wikipedia. However, due to privacy restrictions, the data contains only (referrer, resource) pairs that occurred at least ten times during the data collection period. This could lead to a skewed view on the access behavior when contrasting search and navigation. For example, if an article is navigated in total much more than ten times over different links, but each individual link is transitioned less than ten times, all of these transitions will not be included in the data. In this case, the searchshare for this article might get substantially overestimated. Since this might occur specifically for articles with overall few page views, it may be a potential explanation for some findings, *e.g.*, that article in the periphery of the link network show a stronger prevalence of search.

8　CONCLUSION AND FUTURE WORK

In this work, we studied the prevalence of user access preferences across articles on Wikipedia. For that purpose, we introduced *searchshare* and *resistance* as two key features to characterize article traffic. While we can identify search as the more dominant access paradigm compared to navigation on Wikipedia overall, we observe heterogeneous behavior at different types of articles. That is, depending on the article topic and other article properties, the share of navigation and search strongly varies, as well the amount of traffic an article relays to other Wikipedia pages. For example, articles on topics such as "Military" exhibit above average access by navigation, while topics such as "Architecture" show a strong prevalence of search. Furthermore, edit activity on a an article and its position in the network is strongly correlated with its ability to relay traffic on Wikipedia. Thus, we find overall that both, search and navigation play a crucial role for information seeking on Wikipedia.

In the future, we plan to extend our studies over time intervals and to other language editions in order to further explore cultural differences in the identified access patterns.

REFERENCES

[1] Tim Berners-Lee, Mark Fischetti, and Michael L Foreword By-Dertouzos. 2000. *Weaving the Web: The original design and ultimate destiny of the World Wide Web by its inventor.* HarperInformation.

[2] David M Blei, Andrew Y Ng, and Michael I Jordan. 2003. Latent Dirichlet Allocation. *Journal of Machine Learning Research* 3, Jan (2003), 993–1022.

[3] Flavio Chierichetti, Ravi Kumar, Prabhakar Raghavan, and Tamas Sarlos. 2012. Are web users really markovian?. In *Proceedings of the 21st international conference on World Wide Web.* ACM, 609–618.

[4] Julie Coiro and Elizabeth Dobler. 2007. Exploring the online reading comprehension strategies used by sixth-grade skilled readers to search for and locate information on the Internet. *Reading research quarterly* 42, 2 (2007), 214–257.

[5] Dimitar Dimitrov, Philipp Singer, Denis Helic, and Markus Strohmaier. 2015. The Role of Structural Information for Designing Navigational User Interfaces. In *Conference on Hypertext and Social Media.*

[6] Dimitar Dimitrov, Philipp Singer, Florian Lemmerich, and Markus Strohmaier. 2016. Visual Positions of Links and Clicks on Wikipedia. In *Int. Conference Companion on World Wide Web.*

[7] Dimitar Dimitrov, Philipp Singer, Florian Lemmerich, and Markus Strohmaier. 2017. What Makes a Link Successful on Wikipedia?. In *Proceedings of the 26th International Conference on World Wide Web.* International World Wide Web Conferences Steering Committee, 917–926.

[8] Fabian Flöck, Kenan Erdogan, and Maribel Acosta. 2017. TokTrack: A Complete Token Provenance and Change Tracking Dataset for the English Wikipedia. https://aaai.org/ocs/index.php/ICWSM/ICWSM17/paper/view/15689

[9] George W Furnas. 1997. Effective view navigation. In *Proceedings of the ACM SIGCHI Conference on Human factors in computing systems.* ACM, 367–374.

[10] George W. Furnas, Thomas K. Landauer, Louis M. Gomez, and Susan T. Dumais. 1987. The vocabulary problem in human-system communication. *Commun. ACM* 30, 11 (1987), 964–971.

[11] Patrick Gilderslave and Taha Yasseri. 2017. Inspiration, Captivation, and Misdirection: Emergent Properties in Networks of Online Navigation. *arXiv:1710.03326* (2017).

[12] Denis Helic, Markus Strohmaier, Michael Granitzer, and Reinhold Scherer. 2013. Models of human navigation in information networks based on decentralized search. In *Conference on Hypertext and Social Media.*

[13] R Kumar and A Tomkins. 2009. A Characterization of Online Search Behaviour. *Data Engineering Bullettin* 32, 2 (2009), 2009.

[14] Ravi Kumar and Andrew Tomkins. 2010. A characterization of online browsing behavior. In *Proceedings of the 19th international conference on World wide web.* ACM, 561–570.

[15] Daniel Lamprecht, Dimitar Dimitrov, Denis Helic, and Markus Strohmaier. 2016. Evaluating and improving navigability of Wikipedia: A comparative study of eight language editions. In *Proceedings of the 12th International Symposium on Open Collaboration.* ACM, 17.

[16] Daniel Lamprecht, Kristina Lerman, Denis Helic, and Markus Strohmaier. 2017. How the structure of wikipedia articles influences user navigation. *New Review of Hypermedia and Multimedia* 23, 1 (2017), 29–50.

[17] Janette Lehmann, Claudia Müller-Birn, David Laniado, Mounia Lalmas, and Andreas Kaltenbrunner. 2014. Reader preferences and behavior on wikipedia. In *Conference on Hypertext and Social Media.*

[18] Donald J Leu, Jill Castek, D Hartman, Julie Coiro, L Henry, J Kulikowich, and Stacy Lyver. 2005. Evaluating the development of scientific knowledge and new forms of reading comprehension during online learning. *Final report presented to the North Central Regional Educational Laboratory/Learning Point Associates. Retrieved May* 15 (2005), 2006.

[19] Donald J Leu, Heidi Everett-Cacopardo, Lisa Zawilinski, Greg McVerry, and W Ian O'Byrne. 2012. New Literacies of online reading comprehension. *The Encyclopedia of Applied Linguistics* (2012).

[20] Anne Mangen. 2008. Hypertext fiction reading: haptics and immersion. *Journal of research in reading* 31, 4 (2008), 404–419.

[21] Connor McMahon, Isaac Johnson, and Brent Hecht. 2017. The Substantial Interdependence of Wikipedia and Google: A Case Study on the Relationship Between Peer Production Communities and Information Technologies. (2017).

[22] Theodor H Nelson. 1965. Complex information processing: a file structure for the complex, the changing and the indeterminate. In *Proceedings of the 1965 20th national conference.* ACM, 84–100.

[23] Lawrence Page, Sergey Brin, Rajeev Motwani, and Terry Winograd. 1999. The PageRank citation ranking: bringing order to the web. Stanford InfoLab.

[24] Ashwin Paranjape, Robert West, Leila Zia, and Jure Leskovec. 2016. Improving Website Hyperlink Structure Using Server Logs. In *Int. Conference on Web Search and Data Mining.*

[25] Peter LT Pirolli and James E Pitkow. 1999. Distributions of Surfers' Paths through the World Wide Web: Empirical Characterizations. *World Wide Web* 2, 1-2 (1999), 29–45.

[26] Jacob Ratkiewicz, Santo Fortunato, Alessandro Flammini, Filippo Menczer, and Alessandro Vespignani. 2010. Characterizing and modeling the dynamics of online popularity. *Physical review letters* 105, 15 (2010), 158701.

[27] Radim Řehůřek and Petr Sojka. 2010. Software Framework for Topic Modelling with Large Corpora. In *Proceedings of the LREC 2010 Workshop on New Challenges for NLP Frameworks.* ELRA, 45–50.

[28] Anna Samoilenko, Florian Lemmerich, Katrin Weller, Maria Zens, and Markus Strohmaier. 2017. Analysing Timelines of National Histories across Wikipedia Editions: A Comparative Computational Approach. In *Proceedings of the Eleventh International AAAI Conference on Web an Social Media (ICWSM 2017).* 210–219.

[29] Philipp Singer, Denis Helic, Andreas Hotho, and Markus Strohmaier. 2015. Hyptrails: A bayesian approach for comparing hypotheses about human trails on the web. In *Int. Conference on World Wide Web.*

[30] Philipp Singer, Denis Helic, Behnam Taraghi, and Markus Strohmaier. 2014. Detecting memory and structure in human navigation patterns using markov chain models of varying order. *PloS One* 9, 7 (2014), e102070.

[31] Philipp Singer, Florian Lemmerich, Robert West, Leila Zia, Ellery Wulczyn, Markus Strohmaier, and Jure Leskovec. 2017. Why We Read Wikipedia. In *Proceedings of the 26th International Conference on World Wide Web.* International World Wide Web Conferences Steering Committee, 1591–1600.

[32] Anselm Spoerri. 2007. What is popular on Wikipedia and why? *First Monday* 12, 4 (2007).

[33] Marijn ten Thij, Yana Volkovich, David Laniado, and Andreas Kaltenbrunner. 2012. Modeling and predicting page-view dynamics on Wikipedia. *CoRR abs/1212.5943* (2012).

[34] Vivienne Waller. 2011. The search queries that took Australian Internet users to Wikipedia. *Information Research* 16, 2 (2011).

[35] William Webber, Alistair Moffat, and Justin Zobel. 2010. A similarity measure for indefinite rankings. *ACM Transactions on Information Systems (TOIS)* 28, 4 (2010), 20.

[36] Ingmar Weber and Alejandro Jaimes. 2011. Who uses web search for what: and how. In *International Conference on Web Search and Data Mining.*

[37] Robert West and Jure Leskovec. 2012. Human wayfinding in information networks. In *Int. Conference on World Wide Web.* .

[38] Ellery Wulczyn and Dario Taraborelli. 2016. Wikipedia Clickstream. figshare. doi:10.6084/m9.figshare.1305770. Accessed: 2017-5-3.

Using the Web of Data to Study Gender Differences in Online Knowledge Sources: the Case of the European Parliament

Laura Hollink
Centrum Wiskunde & Informatica
Amsterdam, The Netherlands
l.hollink@cwi.nl

Astrid van Aggelen
Centrum Wiskunde & Informatica
Amsterdam, The Netherlands
aggelen@cwi.nl

Jacco van Ossenbruggen
Centrum Wiskunde & Informatica
Amsterdam, The Netherlands
Jacco.van.Ossenbruggen@cwi.nl

ABSTRACT

Gender inequalities are known to exist in Wikipedia. However, objective measures of inequality are hard to obtain, especially when comparing across languages. We study gender differences in the various Wikipedia language editions with respect to coverage of the Members of the European Parliament. This topic allows a relatively fair comparison of coverage between the (European) language editions of Wikipedia. Moreover, the availability of open data about this group allows us to relate measures of Wikipedia coverage to objective measures of their notable actions in the offline world. In addition, we measure gender differences in the content of Wikidata entries, which aggregate content from across Wikipedia language editions.

CCS CONCEPTS

• **Human-centered computing** → **Wikis**; • **Social and professional topics** → **Gender**; • **Computing methodologies** → *Knowledge representation and reasoning*; • **Information systems** → *World Wide Web*;

KEYWORDS

Web of Data, Wikipedia, Wikidata, Gender Inequality, European Parliament

ACM Reference Format:
Laura Hollink, Astrid van Aggelen, and Jacco van Ossenbruggen. 2018. Using the Web of Data to Study Gender Differences in Online Knowledge Sources: the Case of the European Parliament. In *WebSci '18: 10th ACM Conference on Web Science, May 27–30, 2018, Amsterdam, Netherlands*. ACM, New York, NY, USA, 5 pages. https://doi.org/10.1145/3201064.3201108

1 INTRODUCTION

We study gender differences in Wikipedia language editions with respect to how members of the European Parliament are covered. Gender differences are known to exist in Wikipedia. Studies have uncovered gender inequalities with respect to the coverage of people [6, 10], the textual and structural content of the articles [9, 10], and the quality [4] of the articles. Given the scale at which Wikipedia

is accessed[1] and used as a source of knowledge, it is important to reliably assess to what extent and in what way the content of this collaboratively edited online encyclopedia might be biased.

Objective measures of inequality are hard to obtain. The difficulty stems from the fact that we don't know who (or what) has not been covered. Several studies have used reference corpora of notable people to measure what is missing from Wikipedia [6, 9]. The downside of this approach is that the reference corpus itself might be biased. In addition, the two groups of people that are to be compared (in this case men and women) might differ in ways that make them hard to compare. For example, people of different genders may have had different occupations or roles, and the quality of their historic records may be different. Wagner et al. [10] use two metrics to estimate how "notable" a person in a reference corpus is. They find that coverage bias with respect to gender is small among highly notable people but large among less-notable people. In other words, women need to be very notable to be included in Wikipedia, while little-notable men may be included relatively easily.

Cross-language comparisons of Wikipedia editions are even more complicated, since they involve a comparison of different (but overlapping) groups of people: a person who is relevant to one language community might not meet the criteria for inclusion for another community. As a result, most studies focus on one or a few languages.

In this study, we focus on Wikipedia coverage of a relatively small and homogeneous group of people that is of European-wide importance: the 3662 (past and current) Members of the European Parliament (MEPs). This group is relevant for all member states of the European Union, and thus allows a relatively fair comparison of coverage between the (European) language editions of Wikipedia. Moreover, the availability of open data about this group of people provides us with objective data of their notable actions in the European Parliament. Thus, we can relate the observed differences in how men and women are presented on Wikipedia to their characteristics and actions in the offline world. We use various sources of open data, collected and published as Linked Open Data in the Talk of Europe project[2]. We use Wikidata to connect all Wikipedia editions to each other and to the open data about the European Parliament, and to get reliable data about the gender of MEPs.

2 RELATED WORK AND MOTIVATION

Wagner et al. [9] distinguished four types of gender-bias on Wikipedia: visibility, structural, lexical and coverage bias. They analyzed bias in six Wikipedia language editions: English, German, French, Spanish, Italian and Russian. They found that men and women are equally

---

[1]See e.g. https://www.alexa.com/siteinfo/wikipedia.org for access rates.
[2]http://talkofeurope.eu/

visible; that a structural bias exists in that men are on average more central (in all language editions except Spanish); and that a lexical bias exists in the content of biographic articles, where woman's biographies contain more words related to family and relationships. The latter finding is a confirmation of Bamman and Smith [1], who also analyzed Wikipedia article texts and found that articles about women contain more information about marriage and divorce. Graells-Garrido et al. [3] studied differences in content between articles about men and women as well. Next to text analysis, they included structural properties from (English) DBpedia[3] entries, and found that the representation of women varies greatly between DBpedia categories with, for instance, an over-representation of women in the Artist and Model categories but an over-representation of men in the Athlete and Politician categories. Halfaker [4] studied article quality on Wikipedia. He shows that article quality for women scientists was initially below average, but that since the start of targeted efforts to increase the coverage of women on Wikipedia the opposite effect is now true: women scientists' articles have an above-average quality.

We complement the above work in a number of ways. First, we include 23 Wikipedia language editions where previous studies have focused on one or a few languages. Second, we include Wikidata [8] in our analysis. This online knowledge base contains structured knowledge that is, in many cases, aggregated from various Wikipedia language editions. Third, our focus on one specific category, namely members of the European Parliament, allows us to uncover biases which may remain invisible in general analyses over all categories, as [3] remarks. The choice for a European Union-wide topic allows a (relatively) fair comparison of coverage across (European) language editions. The fact that we have a complete reference corpus, including data on the notable actions of the men and women involved, solves many of the difficulties that other studies face with respect to measuring coverage bias.

On the other hand, the present study is several orders of magnitude smaller than the studies described above, and is limited to an investigation of coverage and content, where content is studied strictly in terms of Wikidata properties (in contrast to e.g. a textual analysis of Wikipedia article content).

3 DATA AND METHODS

Data about the European Parliament was taken from the Talk of Europe project [7]. In Talk of Europe, various Web sources about the European Parliament were combined and translated into the Web format RDF. This data includes, for example, information about the speeches that MEPs perform in the plenary debates of the parliament, crawled from the website of the EP[4], and information about professional affiliations of the members of the EP [5], including committee membership and the roles that people have (chair, vice-chair, substitute, member of the bureau, etc.). The Talk of Europe data includes links to Wikidata entries for MEPs, which were generated based on unique identification numbers used on both the EU website and Wikidata.

From Wikidata we retrieved all entries of Members of the European Parliament. This data consists of the property-value pairs

associated to each MEP, including the Gender property, as well as links to the Wikipedia language editions that cover them. We limit the analysis to language editions that correspond to 23 languages spoken at the European Parliament[5]. Wikidata includes several genders, but only the values "male" and "female" have enough occurrences among the MEPs to allow a valid comparison. We include one "transgender female" MEP in our analysis as "female".

We examine differences between male and female MEPs with respect to (1) the number of Wikipedia language editions that cover them, (2) which Wikipedia language editions cover them, and (3) the number of property-value pairs in their Wikidata entries. In addition (4), we examine the properties that are typical for either one of the two genders. Next to raw frequency counts, we use Pointwise Mutual Information (PMI) [2] as a measure for how typical a property is for a gender. The PMI value of a property Y for a gender X is defined as:

$$PMI(X, Y) = \log \frac{P(X, Y)}{P(X)P(Y)}$$

where the value of $P(X)$ is the proportion of gender X in the data and $P(X, Y)$ is the proportion MEPs who's Wikidata entry includes property Y.

We relate the observed gender differences in Wikipedia and Wikidata to characteristics and actions of the MEPs in the European Parliament. Specifically, we look at (a) the amount of male and female representatives of each country in the Parliament, (b) the number of speeches of each MEP in the Parliament, and (c) the number of chair-positions that the MEPs held within the European Parliament. The latter two can be seen as external measures of notability. We use them to test whether we can replicate the findings by [10] that women need a higher notability to be included in Wikipedia than men. Note that a one-to-one mapping between countries of the European Union and Wikipedia language editions is not always possible. Some languages are spoken in multiple countries (e.g. English and German) and some countries have multiple official languages (e.g. Luxembourg and Austria).

Throughout the paper we have used the nonparametric Wilcoxon rank sum test to compare men and women, and Spearman's rank correlation coefficient (ρ), which is robust to outliers, for correlations between variables.

4 ANALYSIS AND RESULTS

4.1 Number of Wikipedia Language editions

Female members of the European Parliament are covered by slightly more Wikipedia language editions than male members ($p < 0.01$, Figure 1). The 969 female MEPs have a median of 5 and mean of 5.9 Wikipedias; the 2693 male MEPs have a median of 4 and mean of 6.4. This is in line with earlier studies (e.g. [10]), who found that women on Wikipedia - at least those born since 1900 - had a higher Wikipedia language edition count then men.

There is a relation between Wikipedia presence and an MEP's effort as recorded in the European Parliament. We found a positive correlation between the amount of speeches that a person held in parliament and the number of Wikipedia language editions that

---

[3]http://dbpedia.org/
[4]http://www.europarl.europa.eu, with speech data available since 1999

[5]See   http://www.europarl.europa.eu/aboutparliament/en/20150201PVL00013/
Multilingualism. We don't have speech data in Gaelic.

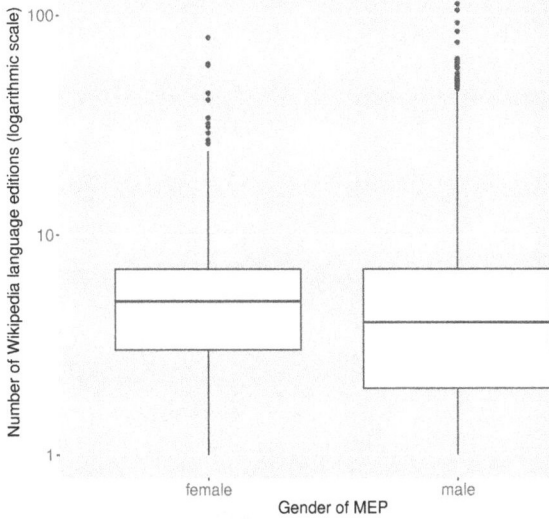

Figure 1: Boxplot of the number of Wikipedia language editions that cover female and male MEPs.

cover them (ρ =0.54, p < 0.01). When we split the MEPs into those that spoke a lot (>= 100 times) and those that spoke less (<100 times), we find that those who spoke a lot have more Wikipedia presence - a median of 6 Wikipedias vs. 4 for those who spoke less. The same effect is present for MEPs who have held chair-positions within the EP vs. those that were never chairs (5 and 4 Wikipedias, respectively). Table 1 lists the median number of Wikipedias for each group per gender.

The observed effect that women are covered by more Wikipedias is only present in the groups with low effort recorded: women have more Wikipedias than men in the groups that speak less or were never chairs (p < 0.01 for both), but there is no significant difference between the two genders in the groups of MEPs that speak a lot or held chair positions (p = 0.4 and 0.28, respectively),

These results are different from what was found in an earlier study over all Wikipedia biographies by Wagner et al. [10]. They use the number of Wikipedia language editions as an (internal) measure of notability and observe a larger negative bias against women in the group of less notable people. They conclude that women need a higher notability to be included in Wikipedia than men. If we treat the number of speeches and chair-positions as (external) measures of notability, we would expect a negative bias against women in the *spoke-less* group and in the *nonchairs* group. This is not the case in our data and, hence, we cannot confirm that female MEPs need a higher notability to be included in a Wikipedia edition than male MEPs. Further research on other measures of notability is needed to determine the solidity of this conclusion.

4.2 Variation in Wikipedia Language editions

We found large differences between Wikipedia language editions with respect to overall coverage of MEPs and gender balance. Some editions over-represent women, while others over-represent men. Figure 2 shows the percentage of female and male MEPs that are

Table 1: Median Wikipedia language editions of MEPs.

MEPs	All	female	male
All	4	5	4
Spoke-a-lot	6	6	6
Spoke-less	4	4	3
Chairs	5	6	5
Nonchairs	4	5	4

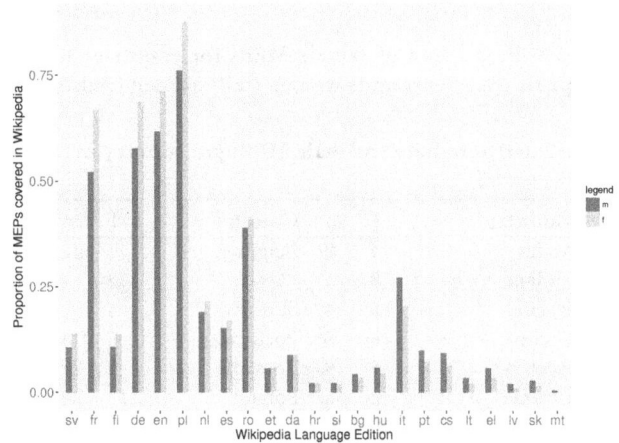

Figure 2: The proportion of female and male MEPs that are covered in 23 Wikipedia language editions.

covered in each edition. None of the editions cover 100% of the MEPs. Ten language editions include a higher percentage of women than men. Thirteen editions cover a lower percentage of female MEPs than male MEPs.

There is a strong correlation between completeness of the edition and the size of the imbalance[6] (ρ = 0.75, p < 0.01). This may suggest that biographies of males are prioritized by the Wikipedia editor communities, but further study on Wikipedia edit histories is needed to confirm this hypothesis.

The observed differences between Wikipedia language editions are in line with the gender-balances among representatives of the member states in the EP. Figure 3 plots the number of MEPs from 1999 to 2017 for the countries whose Wikipedia language edition[7] most strongly over-represents women (left) or men (right). While the numbers vary per country and over time, the data suggest that the countries with Wikipedias that over-represent women have a higher percentage of female MEPs than the countries whose Wikipedia over-represents men. For completeness, table 2 lists the

---

[6]completeness is operationalized as the percentage of MEPs covered, and the size of the imbalance as the percentage of female MEPs covered divided by the percentage of male MEPs covered

[7]As mentioned in section 3, a one-to-one mapping between countries and Wikipedia language editions is not always possible. For the ten countries in Figure 3, a mapping was created manually. We have left the UK out of this figure because we assume that the English Wikipedia is edited by a wider community.

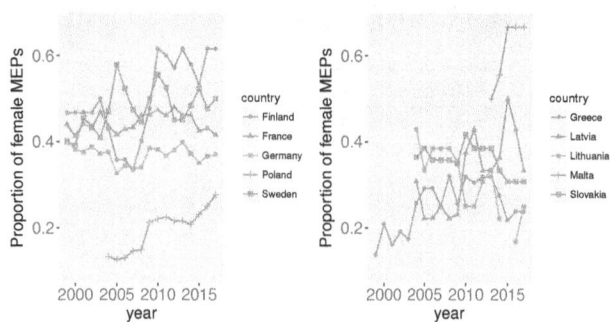

Figure 3: Proportion of female MEPs for countries whose Wikipedia over-represents women (left) or men (right).

Table 2: Nr. of female and male MEPs per country in 2017.

Country	f	m	Country	f	m
Malta	4	2	Belgium	7	12
Finland	8	5	Latvia	2	4
Ireland	5	4	Slovakia	4	9
Croatia	6	5	Portugal	6	14
Austria	9	9	Romania	9	22
Estonia	3	3	Poland	13	34
Sweden	10	10	Czech Republic	5	15
Spain	24	29	Denmark	3	9
France	27	38	Lithuania	2	6
Netherlands	11	16	Greece	5	16
United Kingdom	26	39	Bulgaria	4	13
Slovenia	3	5	Hungary	4	16
Germany	33	56	Luxembourg	1	4
Italy	24	41	Cyprus	1	5

number of female and male MEPs for all countries in 2017, ordered by decreasing proportion of female representatives[8].

4.3 Properties in Wikidata entries

We found no difference between the *number* of property-value pairs in Wikidata entries of male and female MEPs (p = 0.09, Figure 4). Both have a median of 20 properties (Table 3). Small gender-differences are visible within specific groups of MEPs but these are not significant (only the small difference of 19 vs. 20 properties observed within the spoke-less group is significant with p = 0.03).

We also inspected differences in the *content* of Wikidata entries of male and female MEPs. Raw counts of property occurrence do not reveal these differences. For example, the top 10 most frequent properties for female MEPs is identical to the top 10 for males except for slight differences in ranking. When inspecting properties with a high PMI value for male or female MEPs - in other words, those properties that are typical for either of the two genders - differences become visible. To characterize these differences, we manually identified properties that relate to relationships or family

<hr>

[8]The representatives change periodically with EP elections as well as incidentally throughout parliamentary years. We have included the 702 MEPs who spoke in parliament in the year 2017.

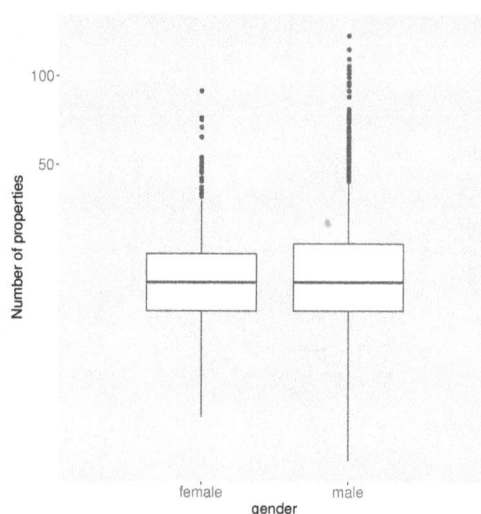

Figure 4: Number of properties per Wikidata entry for MEPs.

Table 3: Median Wikidata properties in entries of MEPs.

MEPs	All	female	male
All	20	20	20
Spoke-a-lot	21	21	21
Spoke-less	20	19	20
Chairs	24	22	24
Nonchairs	20	19	20

(cf. [10]). We only tagged the properties that occur at least once in a male entry and a female entry, aiming to exclude properties that are not applicable to one of the genders. This was the case for 224 of the 396 distinct properties that appear in our dataset.

Family/relationship-properties with a positive PMI value for female MEPs are (in order of PMI) "spouse", "father" and "number of children." The family/relationship-properties typical for men are "partner", "child", "sibling", "family", "relative", "sexual orientation" and "mother." Some of these properties have a frequency of occurrence that is too low to draw valid conclusions. For example, "sexual orientation" is recorded for only four MEPs. Table 4 lists the top 20 properties with highest PMI values for male or female MEPs that occur at least 30 times. Properties relating to classifications schemes in use in a particular country, which may be unfamiliar to the reader, are identified as such.

Based on these data, we see no evidence that Wikidata entries of female MEPs contain more relationship- or family-related content than entries of male MEPs. Rather, the differences in content seem to be related to nationality. Typical properties for men are used in countries that over-represent men in the EP (e.g. Czech Republic, Poland, Latvia) and/or in countries whose Wikipedia over-represents men (Latvia, Czech Republic, Italy). The properties most typical for women include identifiers from classifications schemes in Finland, Sweden, the U.K., Austria, France and Germany

Table 4: Properties with highest PMI values for men and women that occur in at least 30 Wikidata entries of MEPs.

Property	Freq.		National
	m	f	Class. scheme?
Highest PMI value for men:			
topic's main category	30	2	
described by source	39	3	
NLA (Australia) ID	37	3	Australia
signature	48	4	
National Library of Israel ID	32	3	Israel
SHARE Catalogue author ID	41	4	Italy
NDL Auth ID	51	5	Japan
Gran Enciclop. Catalana ID	81	8	Catalonia
Encyclop. Univers. Online ID	59	6	France
BAV ID	29	3	Italy (Vatican)
Perlentaucher ID	29	3	Germany
PM20 folder ID	48	5	Germany
Encyclop. Britannica Online ID	76	8	
NLP ID	45	5	Poland
child	154	18	
CANTIC-ID	84	10	Catalonia
NNDB people ID	41	5	
NKCR AUT ID	76	10	Czech rep.
LNB ID	30	4	Latvia
place of death	354	48	
Highest PMI value for women:			
Finnish MP ID	23	27	Finland
birth name	51	51	
Riksdagen person-id	36	31	Sweden
residence	36	30	
Google Knowledge Graph ID	22	16	
parliament.uk ID	25	18	U.K.
video	62	43	
spouse	90	55	
Twitter username	240	142	
Austrian Parliament ID	46	27	Austria
Facebook profile ID	140	73	
SELIBR Id	51	25	Sweden
Babelio author ID	25	12	France
biogr. at the Bundestag of DE	23	11	Germany
Who's Who in France biogr. ID	142	67	France
official website	387	178	
Commons category	1011	451	
image	1360	600	
participant of	185	81	
IPA transcription	30	13	

- countries with more women in the EP than average, and whose Wikipedias over-represents women MEPs.

Another possible cause of the observed differences is age. The fact that "child" is typical for entries of men could be due to the fact that in the past the proportion of male MEPs was larger than in recent years. Therefore, the average age of the male MEPs is higher, making it more likely that their children are notable enough to appear on Wikidata. This also explains why "place of death" is typical for men. The relatively young group of female MEPs is more likely to have records of their Twitter and Facebook IDs.

5 DISCUSSION AND CONCLUSION

We found a very small gender-difference in the number of Wikipedia language editions that cover an MEP, with women covered by slightly more editions. The variation among language editions is large, with some editions over-representing women and others over-representing men. The inequality in a Wikipedia edition seems to correspond to the gender (im)balance among the representatives of the nations in the EP. It may suggest a larger gender inequality in those countries, but further studies are necessary.

Male and female MEPs have a similar number of property-value pairs in the Wikidata entries, but we found differences in the content of the entries. We could not reproduce findings of previous studies regarding the content of male and female (Wikipedia) entries, namely that those of women over-emphasize family and relationship topics. Rather, in our data, the differences seem to relate to differences in the real world, namely gender imbalance among the EP representatives of the various member states, and birth year of the MEPs.

Several things could play a role here. First, it is possible that a subtle bias is noticeable in natural language text of Wikipedia articles but not in the structured data that we analyzed. Second, our study is limited to one profession and includes only fairly notable people. Previous studies showed large differences between professions and between notable and less-notable people, which may explain why we could not reproduce their findings. Finally, the fact that Wikidata aggregates information from many Wikipedias might help diversity and decrease inequality of the content. This would be a very positive effect of the efforts of Wikidata editors and developers.

ACKNOWLEDGMENTS

We thank Jan Wielemaker for providing help with data analysis on SWISH DataLab. This research was partially supported by the VRE4EIC project, funded from H2020 grant No 676247.

REFERENCES

[1] David Bamman and Noah A. Smith. 2014. Unsupervised Discovery of Biographical Structure from Text. *TACL* 2 (2014), 363–376. https://tacl2013.cs.columbia.edu/ojs/index.php/tacl/article/view/371
[2] Kenneth Ward Church and Patrick Hanks. 1990. Word Association Norms, Mutual Information, and Lexicography. *Computational Linguistics* 16, 1 (1990), 22–29.
[3] Eduardo Graells-Garrido, Mounia Lalmas, and Filippo Menczer. 2015. First women, second sex: gender bias in Wikipedia. In *Proceedings of the 26th ACM Conference on Hypertext & Social Media*. ACM, 165–174.
[4] Aaron Halfaker. 2017. Interpolating Quality Dynamics in Wikipedia and Demonstrating the Keilana Effect. In *Proceedings of the 13th International Symposium on Open Collaboration*. ACM, 19.
[5] Bjørn Høyland, Indraneel Sircar, and Simon Hix. 2009. Forum section: an automated database of the european parliament. *European Union Politics* 10, 1 (2009), 143–152.
[6] Joseph Reagle and Lauren Rhue. 2011. Gender bias in Wikipedia and Britannica. *International Journal of Communication* 5 (2011), 21.
[7] Astrid van Aggelen, Laura Hollink, Max Kemman, Martijn Kleppe, and Henri Beunders. 2017. The debates of the European Parliament as Linked Open Data. *Semantic Web* 8, 2 (2017), 271–281. DOI:http://dx.doi.org/10.3233/SW-160227
[8] Denny Vrandecic and Markus Krötzsch. 2014. Wikidata: a free collaborative knowledgebase. *Commun. ACM* 57, 10 (2014), 78–85. DOI:http://dx.doi.org/10.1145/2629489
[9] Claudia Wagner, David Garcia, Mohsen Jadidi, and Markus Strohmaier. 2015. It's a Man's Wikipedia? Assessing Gender Inequality in an Online Encyclopedia.. In *ICWSM*. 454–463.
[10] Claudia Wagner, Eduardo Graells-Garrido, David Garcia, and Filippo Menczer. 2016. Women through the glass ceiling: gender asymmetries in Wikipedia. *EPJ Data Science* 5, 1 (2016), 5.

Author Index

www.ingramcontent.com/pod-product-compliance
Lightning Source LLC
Chambersburg PA
CBHW080702220326
41598CB00033B/5278